"What they have to say is of such value that it will be thumbed over by historians for many years to come."

Professor Lewis Minkin, *European Labour Forum*

"I cannot remember when I enjoyed social (or socialist) history so much . . . These works are a must for any student of industrial relations."

Diana Warwick, *The Guardian*

"Method and commitment combine to produce a history that is not just an invaluable account of the making of a union, but is also a significant historical and political response to past limitations and current denials."

Professor David Howell

". . . a superb volume . . ."

Jim Mortimer (first Chairman of ACAS and former General Secretary of the Labour Party)

". . . breathlessly exciting from first to last; not one of its thousand pages is wasted . . ."

Professor Kenneth O. Morgan, *New Statesman and Society*

"This marvellous feast is the story about the sinews of the Labour movement; and I hope profoundly that it will be produced in cheaper editions so that those who have grown up in contemporary times will be able to buy the story of a heritage which belongs to us all."

Geoffrey Goodman, *Tribune*

". . . a very good read . . ."

Nina Fishman, *Financial Times*

"Should be read by all who wish to see a re̲_____ ∘ union and labour movement."

*Morning Star*

". . . the special merit o_____ ⌐ot merely about a union, but in the spirit _____ — at this stage there were no women — who co_____ ⌐ı."

Professor ı̲_____ ̲wm, *Industrial Relations Journal*

# The Making Of The Labour Movement

THE NEW WORLD UNITES WITH THE OLD WORLD TO HELP THE DOCK LABOURER

DOCK STRIKE 1889

JUSTICE — HUMANITY

AM I NOT A MAN — A BROTHER

BY UNION THE UNIVERSAL BROTHERHOOD OF LABOUR WE SECURE OUR RIGHTS

IN COMMEMORATION OF THE GREAT STRIKE SEPTR 1889

# THE MAKING OF THE LABOUR MOVEMENT

The Formation
of the Transport &
General Workers' Union
1870-1922

KEN COATES & TONY TOPHAM

SPOKESMAN

First paperback edition published in 1994 by
Spokesman
Bertrand Russell House
Gamble Street, Nottingham, NG7 4ET, UK
Tel: 0602 708318
Fax: 0602 420433
ISBN 0 85124 565 X

First published in 1991 by
Basil Blackwell Ltd, 108 Cowley Road, Oxford, OX4 1JF, UK

Copyright ©Ken Coates and Tony Topham, 1991, 1994

All rights reserved. Except for the quotation of short passages for the purposes of criticism
and review, no part of this publication may be reproduced, stored in a retrieval system, or
transmitted, in any form or by any means, electronic, mechanical, photocopying, recording
or otherwise, without the prior permission of the publishers.

*British Library Cataloguing in Publication Data*
A CIP catalogue record for this book is available from the British Library.
Printed in Finland by WSOY

*To the memory of the pioneers who dreamed of
One Big Union, and to the success of their
heirs, the members of the Transport and General
Workers' Union.*

# Foreword to the
# Paperback Edition

## by David Howell,
## Professor of Labour Studies,
## University of Manchester

Some trade union historians have been self-consciously official and ultra-discreet. Some have collapsed into antiquarianism or hagiography. There have been heroic odysseys and there have been triumphant celebrations of Labour's Forward March. Some historians have been mind-numbingly dull, and stocks have slumbered undisturbed in union offices. The focus has often been on formal institutions and the searchlight has typically been restricted to the activities of leaders.

Such limitations reflect, to some degree, a characteristically unavoidable reliance on official sources. Often these are thoroughly political documents and inevitably constrain the territory of feasible investigations. Yet the typical weaknesses extend beyond those encountered often in the study of formal organisations. An appropriate pride in solidarity can degenerate into an anxiety that embarrassing episodes should be marginalised or excluded. Alternatively, a trade union can be constructed within a factional perspective that generates only a partial vision. Perhaps most seriously such histories have often been straitjacketed by the imagery of the Forward March of Labour, a teleology which offers Labour's development as normal or inevitable. Recent difficulties have demonstrated the illusory politics of this outlook; it always was bad history.

There is a temptation, therefore, to claim that the writing of trade-union history is old-fashioned; that out-dated and flawed approaches are used in inadequate attempts to understand institutions that are increasingly anachronistic. In part this reflects the recent balance of political forces, and in part methodological debates amongst historians. It also, in the new entrepreneurial age, indicates the willingness of some academics to pursue lucrative research grants through the development of appropriate projects. Why bother with trade unions when "Business History" is available?

Coates and Topham's account of the formative years of the Transport and General Workers must be distinguished from those contexts of political conservatism, methodological uncertainty and academic fashion which can degenerate into intellectual corruption. One of the work's many merits is that such dismissals and doubts are effectively answered in a text that is lively and thorough, honest and sympathetic, provocative and authoritative. The authors have taken on perhaps the most demanding of trade union subjects — the construction over more than three decades of a general union from a myriad of occupations and a kaleidoscope of industrial traditions — and they have produced a coherent and riveting account. They have faced contemporary denigrations of trade unions as sectional and economistic; and insist that this story is ineluctably one element in the development of a labour movement that has fused — sometimes in aspiration and sometimes in practice — the political and the industrial. Against the condescending dismissals of trade union practices as myopically nationalist, they argue that an international dimension has always been crucial.

The text is constructed around two kinds of refusal. One is methodological — a refusal to accept the old certainties either of Labour's Forward March, or of the forthcoming proletarian revolution. Instead the dominant motifs express creative agency; the construction of organisations in often unpropitious circumstances as workers pit their resources against managerial hostility, and their imaginations against the pessimism engendered by the routinisation of inequalities. The second refusal is political — a denial of fashionable attempts to denigrate the industrial and political relevance of trade unions. Method and commitment combine to produce a history that is not just an invaluable account of the making of a union, but is also a significant historical and political response to past limitations and current denials.

The style of the work — its diverse coverage, its ambitious scope, its idiosyncrasies, even its size — mirror its subject. In a real sense the book is the Transport and General; but its significance extends beyond even this monument to the working class.

Manchester
February 1994

# Contents

xii

# List of Illustrations

1   The Dockers' Call-on, Liverpool.
2   Glendower Gosling and Hotspur Punch (by permission of *Punch* Publications).
3   James Larkin (by permission of Emmet Larkin).
4   James Connolly (by permission of Lawrence and Wishart).
5   An Appeal for Dublin, from the Federation, 1913.
6   James Sexton, Ben Tillett, Ernest Bevin and Joseph Houghton, 1920 (by permission of The Hulton Picture Library).
7   Soldiers camped in Kensington Gardens, in preparation for the 1921 Coal Strike (by permission of The Hulton Picture Library).
8   One Big Union, 1921.
9   Some of the founders of the amalgamation.
10  Internationalists: Robert Williams, Harry Gosling and Hermann Jochade at the ITWF (by permission of the International Transport Workers' Federation).
11  Regionalist: George Milligan of Merseyside.
12  The First Executive Officers: Stanley Hirst, John Cliff and Ernest Bevin.
13  The Amalgamation Conference, Leamington, 1921.
14  A new record begins: the first issue of the *TGWU Record*, August 1921.

# List of Figures

# List of Tables

# List of Acronyms

| | |
|---|---|
| AATVW | Amalgamated Association of Tramway and Vehicle Workers (shortened form: AAT) |
| ADM | Annual Delegate Meeting |
| AEU | Amalgamated Engineering Union |
| AFL | American Federation of Labour |
| AGC | Annual General Council (of the NTWF) |
| AMWU | Amalgamated Marine Workers' Union |
| APEX | Association of Professional, Executive, Clerical and Computer Staff |
| ASE | Amalgamated Society of Engineers |
| ASLEF | Amalgamated Society of Locomotive Engineers and Firemen |
| ASRS | Amalgamated Society of Railway Servants |
| AS of WL & B | Amalgamated Society of Watermen, Lightermen and Bargemen |
| AUCE | Amalgamated Union of Co-operative Employees |
| BSP | British Socialist Party |
| BSU | British Seafarers' Union |
| CAWU | Clerical and Administrative Workers' Union |
| CGT | Confédération Générale du Travail |
| CPGB | Communist Party of Great Britain |
| CRC | Cardiff Railway Company |
| CTU | Coal Trimmers' Union |
| DWRGLU | Dock, Wharf, Riverside and General Labourers' (later Workers') Union |
| DWRGWU | see above |
| EC | Executive Council/Committee |
| F & EC | Finance and Emergency Committee (of the TGWU) |
| GEC | General Executive Council (of the TGWU) |
| GFTU | General Federation of Trade Unions |

| | |
|---|---|
| GLNC | General Labourers' National Council |
| GMBATU | General, Municipal, Boilermakers' and Allied Trades Union |
| ILP | Independent Labour Party |
| ITF | International Transport Workers' Federation |
| ITGWU | Irish Transport and General Workers' Union |
| IWW | Industrial Workers of the World |
| LCC | London County Council |
| LDCMU | Liverpool and District Carters' and Motormen's Union |
| LMSA | London Master Stevedores' Association |
| LPL | Labour Protection League |
| LPULVW | London and Provincial Union of Licensed Vehicle Workers (shortened form: LPU) |
| LRC | Labour Representation Committee |
| MEA | Municipal Employees' Association |
| NAC | National Administrative Council (of the ILP) |
| NACWU | National Amalgamated Coal Workers' Union |
| NALU | National Amalgamated Labourers' Union |
| NAUL | National Amalgamated Union of Labour |
| NDL | National Democratic League |
| N of ET & TA | North of England Trimmers' and Teemers' Association |
| NFGW | National Federation of General Workers |
| NFLA | National Free Labour Association |
| NFWW | National Federation of Women Workers |
| NIC | National Industrial Council |
| NJIC | National Joint Industrial Council (shortened form: JIC) |
| NMB | National Maritime Board |
| NSFU | National Seamen's and Firemen's Union |
| NTWF | National Transport Workers' Federation (shortened form: TWF) |
| NUDAW | National Union of Distributive and Allied Workers |
| NUDL | National Union of Dock Labourers |
| NUDWSS | National Union of Docks, Wharves and Shipping Staffs |
| NUGMW | National Union of General and Municipal Workers |
| NUGW | National Union of General Workers |
| NUR | National Union of Railwaymen |
| NUVW | National Union of Vehicle Workers |
| PEC | Provisional Executive Committee (of the TGWU) |
| PLA | Port of London Authority |
| PLC | Port Labour Committee |
| PLP | Parliamentary Labour Party |
| RCA | Railway Clerks' Association |
| SDF | Social Democratic Federation |
| SSLPL | South Side Labour Protection League |
| SSTA | Short Sea Traders' Association |

| | |
|---|---|
| TA | Triple Alliance |
| TGWU | Transport and General Workers' Union |
| TUC | Trades Union Congress |
| UCS | Upper Clyde Shipbuilders |
| ULC | United Labour Council |
| UOGL | United Order of General Labourers |
| URTU | United Road Transport Union |
| USDAW | Union of Shop, Distributive and Allied Workers |
| UVW | United Vehicle Workers |
| WU | Workers' Union |

# Foreword

No one before has written a comprehensive history of the TGWU. There have been many special studies and some key biographies, making up many thousands of words, some in important works. But I believe that this double volume is the beginning of a major book because it starts out with a sort of pre-history, with the 1870s and the period running up to the great dock strike of 1889 – the 'Dockers' Tanner Strike', as we have come to know it from history passed down through dockers' families.

This background history had to be done, so that we can start to understand how the 'One Big Union' amalgamation of 1922 actually came into being. In looking back into our real origins, the authors have found a lot more, some of it controversial, some of it potentially of great value in helping the union chart its way through the final decade of the twentieth century, after bitter and difficult times in recent years for trade unionism right across the world. Their book shows how TGWU origins lie deep in Labour history and class development in our country. Indeed, part of the title of this work tries to capture the point that the emergence of the TGWU has been central to the whole character of the British Labour movement and its socialist aspirations.

The authors have tabled some clear challenges, in the best spirit of debate and searching for the truth. Our formal co-operation with their work has been 'warts and all', to coin a phrase that probably hasn't been put like that in the minutes. It was given in the spirit that our movement deserves candour, straightforward argument and analysis. Have no doubt, we have got these from the authors. I have every confidence that they will carry on in the same way as they approach more recent times in further volumes.

Their narrative includes the familiar heroes, some new ones, and some villains against whom our predecessors struggled hard. In a sense, the TGWU was never born – it was made by hard labour, by incessant struggle, a monumental achievement that was at risk time and again. The authors have argued strongly for the essential continuity of the movement for amalgamation from the 1870s, through the great dock strike and up until the Leamington Conference of 1921. They argue that the unskilled workers who built the general labourers' unions were people of invention and imagination, setting trends with new forms of organization and policy and strategy for the whole Labour movement. That is a different picture to the common one of the unskilled labourers somehow 'catching up' with the pre-existing craft-union traditions, and then taking their due place in an established Labour movement. What these workers did was revolutionize this very movement, not least in its political aspirations, seen in the creation of the ILP and the Labour Party and the turn away from dependence on the Liberals; and also in their willingness to join with pioneer socialist thinkers and agitators when others sought respectable incorporation.

The labourers fashioned the unique multi-industrial structure of the eventual TGWU, going beyond federation to organizational unity, but keeping the proper autonomy of trade-group interests against a divisive sectionalism. They consistently demanded recognition and institutional-ized bargaining machinery from employers and the state, long before they were achieved, amidst competing pressures for immediate gains in wages and conditions, the heady temptations of utopian independence, and moderation and subordination to the employers. The distinct strategy of securing independent trade unionism through joint regulation remains a strength to this day, a feature of mainstream trade unionism that politicians too often ignore in their attacks on trade-union power.

The authors portray leaders who were quick in the field of building international trade unionism, especially in the transport industries, as a power-base for spreading their influence. Their 'new unionism' gave birth to the movement for independent labour representation, with the two dockers' unions and the Amalgamated Society of Railway Servants jointly convening the first union conference for forming labour's own political party.

Above all, the authors show how the pioneers were people of vision, capable of setting big targets and sustaining them in bad times as well as good. So it is a story of big thinking, rooted in bread-and-butter organization, professional skills and political vision, in committed energy and incessant hard work.

It is a long time back, but it may be the case that some of the problems we face in the British trade-union movement today are not so far removed from those covered in this first part of our history, least of all in the battle between the new unionism of today's TGWU and the various types of new realism espoused by some other trade unions.

We have been looking to extend our base by organizing amongst the new army of part-time and temporary workers, the so called 'periphery' of the modern labour market, now totalling around a quarter of all workers. We have carried this and other important messages into the Labour Party at a time when there is a strong current of opinion in favour of a historic loosening of those very ties which came into being in the period which this history covers. We are seeking major mergers and looking to new kinds of links with European unions, below the formal levels already in existence, so that trade-union solidarity can be developed, and common demands can be formulated, as close as possible to the factories and offices, as our economies become more deeply integrated. We have kept our focus wide, helping South Africa's oppressed workers to form their unions, and championing opposition to obscene militarism, when others have counselled a narrower focus on the immediate interests of employees, whatever they may be, and assuming that it is actually possible to separate the industrial and the political so neatly.

For organizations like ours, it has always made sense to examine where we have been, before asking where it is best to go now. I sense the end of a period and the opening of a new one. Not the end of working-class struggle and organization; not the end of broad socialist aspiration; not the end of opposition to market forces and social domination by powerful classes who control and own the core capital of our societies; not the end of struggling against injustice and privileges secured through daily control of our societies, often by subtle, but sometimes brutal means; not the end of independent trade unionism, rooted in workplace democracy, and its replacement by a carefully controlled system run by anonymous backroom committees and murmuring manipulators. No, I sense a renewal of emphasis on public interest, commonwealth and community, and on human decency undertaken as a social obligation. A new and clear sense of what democracy is for ordinary people now that the Cold War competition about freedom is behind us.

I sense that a new era of international Labour movement organization is near, most obviously in Europe and in what is fast becoming greater Europe. If there is to be a meaningful socialist political party for the Europe of the future, then it must surely find its power and democracy in partnership with an extended trade unionism. And I sense that the terrible burden of military expenditure in advanced and less-developed countries alike will be overturned – if future generations play their politics correctly – by forces committed to overcoming the vast problem of world poverty and the ecological threat.

As usual, there is much to be done. That is in the essential spirit of the TGWU, as friends and foes alike know. But I make a direct appeal, again in our best traditions, for time to be found by even the most active of our members to study this story closely. For, have no doubt, as you follow this first part of our common history – a leading history for the whole of working-class organization in Britain and internationally – I am confident that you will draw energy and commitment from reading about the battles that were fought in the early days. In many respects things are overwhelmingly better today than then: that is what we have helped substantially to achieve. But in other respects we cannot relax our guard. Nor can we safely carry on fighting unless we know our place in history and look to take its lessons on board.

Someone else will write a Foreword to later sections of this history. For my part, I am pleased that the first full history of the whole of the TGWU was started during my period of office as General Secretary. I take comfort that the terms of reference have been wide and free, and that the first instalment has turned out as neither the authors nor the union originally expected. We looked forward to having our story told with the focus on the great amalgamation, but I think we already have a lot more than that in the challenges presented from this crucial foundation period in the history of our whole Labour movement. The implications for the subsequent periods could be large. But for the moment, let it suffice that our sort of history requires that we respond in future action, making new history as we read the old.

Ron Todd
General Secretary, TGWU
September 1990

# Acknowledgements

Since the Transport and General Workers' Union is the largest trade union in modern Britain, those adult-education tutors who teach trade-union students are prone to meet a large number of TGWU members in their classes. Both in extra-mural work and in courses organized by the union itself, we became very much aware of a gap in our reading lists: there was no history of our biggest union.

We began to nurture the idea that we might try to fill this gap, and for many years we mulled it over with officers and members of the union. Our first and most abiding debt of gratitude therefore lies with the members and officers of the union who have encouraged us and taught us far more than they realize. We must begin with Ron Todd, who saw the need for this study and gave us every possible support. His Executive and its national officers were encouraged to help us, and indeed they did so, unstintingly. Ron Todd very keenly followed our progress in the cellars of Transport House and all the other archives. He combined patience with understanding and sympathy, and his reactions were shared by very many of his staff. Our debt to him and his team is immense, and we shall not be able to repay it until we have carried this absorbing story forward into recent times.

We are very grateful indeed to the Leverhulme Trust, which made a research grant available to Nottingham University in order to sustain this work over three years.

Professor Michael Stephens, at the time director of Nottingham University's Adult Education Department, and Kenneth Lawson, his deputy director, gave every possible support to the project, and were an unfailing source of good advice and practical assistance.

Rita Maskery, secretary to the project, worked ceaselessly in typing and retyping the text as it grew, and in transcribing innumerable interviews. She was a model of patience and skill.

In Transport House, and beyond, Regan Scott, the Union's national secretary for education and research, a true collaborator and colleague, has been, and continues to be, our essential 'anchorman', guiding us through the accumulated records housed there, always prompting new thought and opening avenues of research and enquiry. He has given freely of his time in a busy schedule of union duties, and offered his own extensive knowledge and experience of the union at all times, as well as making us welcome and comfortable in our work in the union's archives and library. The central office staff, in the library and in Trade Group and other departments, have responded warmly to the lead given by Regan, and by Ray Collins, the union's administrative officer, in smoothing our way through the records and the cellars.

Academic and library staffs in Nottingham and Hull Universities have provided continuous support, facilities and advice. On our visits to the Modern Records Centre at Warwick University, which houses an important archive on the TGWU, and the Bevin Papers, we have benefited from the expert advice and service of Richard Storey and Alistair Tough. Similar services were afforded us in the John Rylands Library in Manchester, and at the National Museum of Labour History.

Gordon Phillips and Paul Smith very kindly loaned copies of their important theses, and Arthur Marsh allowed us access to his joint manuscript (with Victoria Ryan) of the now published history of the Seamen's Union. Bruce Spencer, lecturer in Trade Union Studies at Leeds University, undertook enquiries for us in Region 9 of the union, and we have had the benefit of John Saville's advice: he provided access to important sources and his expertise on labour history was always available to us. Ted Gillett, historian of Hull, culled his files of press reports in our aid.

Professor Tsuzuki went to great efforts to provide us with access to chapters of his important new work on the life of Tom Mann. Graham Stevenson, at the time a trade-group secretary in the union's Region 5, has written a comprehensive account of trade unionism in Derbyshire, and we are most grateful for the loan of his manuscript.

We wish also to thank all who read and commented on drafts of chapters and sections, including Ken Fleet, Michael Barratt Brown, John Hughes, the late Steve Bodington, Walt Greendale, Tom Watkinson, Michael Somerton, Daniel Vulliamy, Denis Mayhew, Geoff Brown and Brian Barker.

We must place David Howell, Professor of Politics at Manchester University, in a special category. He undertook a systematic reading of the whole text, when it had reached an advanced stage of preparation, following which we spent two fascinating days with him as he led us through his corrections, comments and appraisal. We learned so much, and we are very grateful.

Geoff Stuttard, now retired from a lifetime of teaching on trade-union day-release for London University's Extra-mural Department, and a colleague in many TGWU schools and in trade-union studies publication, invited us to give three 'progress reports' to his London seminar series on Industrial Relations. We derived much valuable advice, as well as enthusiastic encouragement, from him and his groups. Their selfless identification with our work became important to us. Rodney Mace supplied us with details of the career of Cardinal Manning's father.

Before his death, Frank Cousins gave us several extended interviews: his insights have been of great value. Jack Jones has given us a preliminary interview, has made texts and records available to us, and has been warmly supportive of our work. We shall have occasion to record an even greater debt to him, and to his generation of the union, when our projected study down to recent times is complete.

The same is true of a large number of retired and senior union leaders and officers, whose interviews, documentary loans and advice have already helped our understanding of the structure and traditions of the union, and pointed us on our way into Volume II. These include Moss Evans, Tim O'Leary, Bill Lindley, the late Bill Jones, Stan Pemberton, Walt Greendale, Sid Easton, Eddie Roberts, the late Bob Edwards, Alex Kitson, Sid Forty and Jack Ashwell.

A further source which overlaps this, and subsequent work, has been the archive of the Communist Party, where Francis King has been an expert and helpful guide. We also received valuable help from Noreen Branson of the Labour Research Department.

We wish to make collective acknowledgement of all those authors on whose published work and theses we have drawn so freely and so gratefully. Our debt to them will be evident in our text and footnotes.

At the outset of the project, we published appeals in the press and in the *Record* asking for memories and documents held by private individuals and retired members. Among union members and others who kindly wrote to us, often sending books and papers, some of which were of very great interest, are the following: Mrs W. J. Barnshaw, Mrs R. Bannister, Bertie Bassett, E. J. Brawn, J. K. Cochrane, Fred Cole, J. E. Constantine, F. G. Deacon, Douglas Dean, J. R. Foskett, Mike Gibbons, Bill Gillman, W. Howard, G. Johnson, Vic Kerviel, J. K. Leathwood, Les Nichols, Allan Parfitt, W. T. Parsons, D. Payne, Bill Punt, H. W. Pusey, Mrs A. Roots, Mrs G. Sinclair, Gavan Smith, R. H. Thomas, Sir Robert Thomas, Harry Tindell, Reg Weller, P. R. Whili, Albert Wyman.

Tony Topham wishes to add his personal thanks to Monica Hare and Tony Eyles of the Foundation for Communication for the Disabled, and to Mike Portus, Sally Hubbard, Brian Charles and Dave Tuck of the Disablement Advisory Service, for their invaluable technical and advisory services to him.

Finally, we thank René Olivieri, Tim Goodfellow and Jane Robertson of Basil Blackwell for their great labours in seeing the work through all stages of its publication, and Brenda Thomson for her thorough, sympathetic, and immensely helpful work on this very large text, as our copy-editor. Our grateful thanks are also due to Colin Hutchens and Valerie Mendes, who read the proofs, and to Sarah Ereira, who compiled the index.

Whatever errors remain after the helpful scrutiny of colleagues and friends will, we hope, be corrected by our critics, of whom we anticipate no shortage.

Ken Coates, Matlock
Tony Topham, Hull
November 1990

The authors and publishers are indebted to the following for permission to quote from copyright material:

Lord Askwith and John Murray (Publishers) Ltd (Lord Askwith, *Industrial Problems and Disputes*); the London School of Economics and Political Science (Beatrice Webb, *My Apprenticeship*, and Sidney and Beatrice Webb, *The History of Trade Unionism*); H. C. G. Mathew, R. I. McKibbin, J. A. Kay, J. M. Roberts, G. A. Holmes and the Longman Group (*The English Historical Review*, vol. XCI, 1976); Harvester Wheatsheaf (C. J. Wrigley, *A History of British Industrial Relations*, vol. II); Lawrence and Wishart (Yvonne Kapp, *Eleanor Marx*, vol. II: *The Crowded Years*); Oxford University Press, (H. A. Clegg, Alan Fox and A. F. Thompson, *A History of British Trade Unions since 1889*, vol. I: *1889–1910*; H. A. Clegg, *A History of British Trade Unions since 1889*, vol. II: *1911–1933*; Gordon Phillips and Noel Whiteside, *Casual Labour*; and C. H. Feinstein and S. Pollard, *Studies in Capital Formation in the United Kingdom, 1750–1920*); Cambridge University Press, (B. R. Mitchell, *Abstract of British Historical Statistics*); and the Trustees of the Yorkshire Bulletin of Economic and Social Research (Sydney Pollard, 'Trade Unions and the Labour Market, 1870–1914', vol. 17, no. 1, May 1965).

# Introduction

When he returned from climbing Mount Everest, Sir Edmund Hillary was asked why he had done it. 'Because it was there,' he is said to have answered. It was perhaps in something of the same frame of mind that we embarked upon the project of preparing a history of the Transport and General Workers' Union. Unkind people will tell us, as indeed they told Sir Edmund, that this involved no small degree of folly. However, no one can deny that it also reveals a certain commitment.

We began our trek when the union was nearing its centenary, by most conventional reckoning. Towering over the industrial scene, for years it had been Britain's largest trade union. As it reached its ninetieth birthday, in 1979, it produced a colourful poster to commemorate itself. It said:

> There is a TGWU member in almost every family in Britain. They are the people who make our cars, drive the lorries, load and unload ships, keep the buses and taxis running, work in the power stations, build the motorways, operate vital oil, food processing, chemical, rubber and engineering plants. They are the lighthouse keepers, coachbuilders, tugboatmen, trawlermen, civil aviation workers, office workers, supervisors and managers, laundry and canteen staffs. They are the men and women whose skill and expertise keeps Britain going.

At that time, there were 2 million of these people.

A truly vast effort of human organization had brought them together, joining their individual powers into a real collective strength, and enabling them, together, to dominate the industrial and political landscapes. But while lesser mountain ranges of big unions had all been scaled, often in histories of great complexity and detail, and, indeed, while dozens of smaller hillocks had been extensively mapped and chronicled, this one major peak had inspired no comprehensive history. Its presence had become unavoidable. It represented an enduring and yet innovative influence, and this fact was necessarily reflected in a vast literature. A library of monographs raked over this and that face of the great ascent, explored the screes of particular strikes and disputes, and charted their institutional effects. Here and there major biographies had left pitons to help us over formidable cliffs.

But although much good work existed when we began, we have no doubt that the hitherto neglected archives of the union will still provoke much more. There are many important lessons to be drawn from all the detail which remains in them. None the less, we think that the time was overripe for an effort to see the processes which created our union, as a whole, in their interrelationships. Even in the errors of such an attempt, others will learn things of value.

Neither of us has been a professional historian. Both of us regret this, for we have had to learn painfully what practised scholars could have achieved with much greater ease. Our experience was won as partisans of the trade-union movement, and although both of us have spent most of our working lives learning from trade unionists, as adult educationists, we come, initially, from different disciplines.

For this reason, when we began we thought that we should start our story in 1922, when the new Transport and General Workers' Union was finally born, and carry on through a series of phases which we thought we understood until we reached the recent past. Of course, we knew of a body of writings about what we saw as the 'prehistory' of the union, which we thought to subsume in a preliminary chapter. The more we discovered, however, the more questions we found to need exploration. Our focus moved inexorably further back. Soon we began to joke with one another about the fact that our book was going to resemble Laurence Sterne's immortal *Tristram Shandy*, whose hero takes a hundred pages to get himself born. In fact, Sterne was present at what we now know to have been a very easy parturition, because our own subject has involved us in one volume of two fat books of nearly a thousand pages before its umbilicus has at last been tied.

It is comforting to know that at least one very distinguished historian has acknowledged similar problems. John King Fairbank, the American authority on China, tells us candidly that

I had two years by the tail, and both were pulling me back to earlier times. In my observation this regression in time is typical . . . would-be modernists have wound up as medievalists. The rule seems to be, if you want to study the mid-period of a century, begin at the end of it and let the problems lead you back. *Never* try to begin at the beginning. Historical research progresses backward, not forward.[1]

Our reverse progression took us to the London docks in 1889, and then beyond that, to the rudimentary organizations of the 1870s. The reasoning behind this is not abstruse, and we think that it will be accepted when we come to unravel the events in the docks in the 1950s and 1970s. Books may start or finish wherever their authors take the whim, but the events which shape the choices which people feel it sensible to make, and which close those options into apparent inevitabilities, are subject to no such caprice.

Inevitably, this appreciation involves us in argument about the framework of periods into which we have been led. Starting back from the formation of the great general unions in the 1920s, we were led by a continuous thread directly to the impulses of 'new unionism', following the upheavals among allegedly unskilled workers in the late 1880s. Of course, this was not at all a new perception, although it has had distinguished challengers in recent years. We believe that our narrative will largely reinforce the case of an older generation of historians, although not without some important cavils. We also believe that the forgotten voices which have been reawoken in these pages will speak not only for a different past, but perhaps also for a different future.

The goals of trade-union democracy have never been simply external targets. Unions have always known that, for the dispossessed to change the world, they first must change themselves. Always their creative drive has involved the dynamism of self-reliance and, within whatever collective space they have been able to win, they have always asserted their commitment to self-development, self-realization and, quite literally, self-government. So, the idea of 'One Big Union', which was proclaimed with such fervour as all the potential constituents of the Transport and General Workers' Union began to ballot for amalgamation, may be traced back over all the setbacks and defeats not only to the high days of the great strikes of 1911, but on through to its germ of 'general' organization, back to 1889 and then further behind.

As a goal, One Big Union was a means of defence for those whose jobs were otherwise in jeopardy from the competition of unorganized labour. It was an agency for reform, in that it could bargain from strength. It was a school in which men and women could learn those skills and techniques which could offer them some rudiments of authority and control over their own toil. It was a university, in which they could generate new aspirations, political programmes, a new charter for the recovery of power over the machines and capital which were dominating their lives. Indeed, it was a way of life.

This way of life was once widely celebrated as the pursuit of industrial democracy. It was never confined to the ritual dimensions of Westminster. In the high years of Labour advance after the First World War, our narrative traces the developments of the transport workers' programme for a comprehensive Board of Communications, to administer publicly owned ports, road, rail, sea and air transport, postal and telephone services. But this conception was formed in the struggle for joint control, with employers and the state, of the crisis-torn war-transport industries. And behind this shaping movement, tracing back the influences which made it possible, we find ourselves eavesdropping on the Royal Commissioners of 1892, reacting in a state of shock, bemused, to the claims of Ben Tillett for municipal ownership of the Port of London, and the plans of Tom Mann for the reconstruction of the whole port area. Moreover, we hear there a succession of dock workers extolling the merits of trade-union control over all these processes.

One Big Union was never far removed from the ideals of workers' control and self-management. It was also never narrowly confined. Its tributaries lead us to the Knights of Labour in the United States, to the anarcho-syndicalists of France, to Australia and New Zealand.

But if we have been led backwards in time and outwards in space, our narrative has to follow the calendar, and to register firmly the spirit of the places on which it depends. A great man once told us that the universal *is* the particular, and it is in the particular lives of these, our people, that we have been moved to search for whatever universal meanings can be found.

Maybe we are too close to our subjects fully to appreciate some current ideas about what constitutes history, and maybe this makes us over-empirical. The feel of poverty and oppression tends to render its victims prone to a certain pragmatism, and even we, as mere observers, cannot claim immunity from this process. Certainly we have tried to create a narrative which actually relates what happened, and which seeks to explain why people reacted as they did. But while our people lived by bread, they never lived by bread alone. Many of them went without, not because they must, but because they were proud and honest enough to hope that the world could be different. Today this is an unfashionable belief, but tomorrow, we think, it might be more widely shared. Objectivity asks us to consider indices of earnings, inflation and productivity. But it also compels us to seek to discover what kinds of people the subjugated workers had it in themselves to be, and what thoughts and aspirations they could nurture in pursuit of their freedom.

Where the modern systems-theorists do engage us is in the attempt to comprehend how far the real choices of living people are determined by the social inheritance in which they are locked.

Imperial Britain gave birth to a socialist rebellion, which directly fostered the young trade-union activists who began to organize the poor – hitherto unorganizable – masses of uneducated and relatively 'unskilled' labourers. Had we been drafting a brief synopsis of the story we have tried to tell, we would have sought to identify a point of juncture where this happened.

The late nineteenth century found the metropolis in a condition which fell a long way short of democracy, and not only in industry. Many working people lacked votes. Women were all disenfranchised. Plural votes gave advantage to the business community and graduates. Access to the levers of power within most nation states was formally closed to many people who might be thinking of joining the new trade unions. At the same time, the world was rapidly shrinking, as innovations in shipping, together with the extension of railways, made communication between working people a much easier and more normal occurrence. Transport workers, in particular, might range freely across a very much wider world than that imagined by their grandparents. True, wherever they went, they would be liable to find some similarities in the conditions of life.

The battle for democracy has been widely represented as a unilinear process, because in one country after another Chartists and suffragettes demanded a widening of the franchise, popular upheavals insisted upon the vote, strikes and demonstrations mounted in great waves in protest against exclusion from the political process. But the aspiration for democracy during these turmoils might plausibly have been led in either of two directions. Yes, perhaps nation states might have been compelled to yield a general suffrage. But also, perhaps the growing identification of allegiances to class and occupation might have burst through national integuments, and created new institutions for democratic representation, on an international scale. Not only the socialists, but also the new unionists, including such conservative leaders as the seamen's Havelock Wilson, laboured with all their powers to achieve precisely this. Even in 1911 Wilson called the British seamen to strike under the banner of the Seamen's and Firemen's International Movement.[2] After the event, it is easy to efface from the mind the alternative choices, because it is quite evident that trade unionism, like socialism, was led into reconciliation with strictly national spaces. However, the notion of internationalist democracy died hard, if it ever died at all.

Today, the internationalization of capital has become so comprehensive that trade unions have been compelled to reassert priorities for transnational linkages. Nation states in Western Europe have been similarly compelled to seek new forms of association, culminating in a headlong rush towards a federal order. The extent of global problems, both economic and environmental, is encouraging a new globalism in radical thinking, including the thinking of trade unions. Accordingly, traditions which have been submerged over very many years of nationalist ascendancy suddenly seem to acquire a bright new relevance, even if they had previously been perceived as the rosy fingers of a false dawn.

Of course, the trade unionists of the late nineteenth century were reacting to a socialist message which had been spelt out almost half a century before. In the *Communist Manifesto*, Marx identified the modern bourgeoisie as the product of 'a series of revolutions in the modes of production and of exchange'. The bourgeoisie has 'put an end to all feudal, patriarchal, idyllic relations'. It has not severed feudal ties, but replaced them with 'callous "cash payment"' . . .

Yet this same bourgeoisie

cannot exist without constantly revolutionizing the instruments of production, and thereby the relations of production, and with them the whole
relations of society . . . all fixed, fast frozen relations . . . are swept away . . .
all that is privileged and established melts into air . . . the need of a
constantly expanding market for its products chases the bourgeoisie over
the whole surface of the globe. It must get a footing everywhere, settle
everywhere, establish connections everywhere.

To have seen the cosmopolitan force of capitalism in 1848 was no mean achievement. It might have been thought an audacious perception in 1889, and it is not at all an accident that workers in communication saw it first. But to fail to see it today, in the era of gigantic multinational corporations, is to fall over one's own feet. Unfortunately, in some Labour movements there is a propensity to do just that. The unexpected longevity of capitalism has left its revolutionary propensities undimin-ished, and the advent of the transnational corporation has radically impacted on the nation state itself. In the 1990s all but the most powerful states feel themselves to be mere contenders for influence in a world of major forces, in which great companies commonly outweigh govern-ments and united nations.

Addressing himself to the working class, Marx gave us the immortal phrase, 'The working men have no country. We cannot take from them what they have not got.' He followed this with a prescription which has often been seen as containing a contradiction: 'Since the proletariat must first of all acquire political supremacy, must rise to be the leading class of the nation, must constitute itself *the* nation, it is, so far, itself national though not in the bourgeois sense of the word.'

Had the workers refused the advice of Marx, it is conceivable that it might have remained true that 'national differences and antagonisms between peoples are daily more and more vanishing' because of the growth of commerce and the corrosive solvent of the world market. But in fact, the struggle of the proletariat to 'acquire political supremacy' was precisely, as Marx himself said, the struggle to win 'the battle for democracy'. When that battle confined its scope within the nation, then, to the extent that it succeeded, its partial victors gained a stake in the nation. They won representation in its Parliament, and even designated some of the ministers in its governments. More fundamentally, closer to their daily experience, they won important powers over local administra-tions. And, more important still, influencing all their perceptions of their rightful status in society, they won recognition and representation in institutional frameworks for collective bargaining.

Work-people in one country might run in front of their opposite numbers in another. The struggle for democracy, like economic growth, has always been uneven. Its gains have always been particular. By slow degrees, these gains led to a general presumption that social democracies might be established separately, in one country after another. The nation had become an aspiration for the subject class within it.

This book may be seen as a detailed study of how this happened. Other volumes will be needed to trace the story of this one trade union down to our own times, when the ideal of One Big Union is already beginning to reappear, with some urgency, as an international aspiration.

## Notes

1   J. K. Fairbank, *Trade and Diplomacy on the China Coast* (Stanford University Press, 1969), pp. vii–xii; cited in A. G. Frank, 'A Theoretical Introduction to Five Thousand Years of World System History', *Review*, vol. XIII, no. 2 (Fernand Braudel Center, Binghamton, New York, spring 1990), pp. 162–3.

2   In Hull, Southampton, the Bristol Channel and on the Mersey, the strike banners all carried the same inscription: 'War is Declared: Strike Hard for Home and Liberty!' (A. P. Lloyd, 'The Influence of Syndicalism on the Hull and Manchester Dock Strikes of 1911', unpublished MA thesis, Warwick University, 1973, pp. 25–6).

# PART I

## 1870–1911

### *From Forerunners to Federation*

# I

# The Earliest Forerunners

## I

### *Introduction*

Fourteen trade unions came together in the amalgamation of 1 January 1922 to form the Transport and General Workers' Union. Waterfront workers had taken the initiative and provided the drive to integration: to the new union's estimated total membership of 350,000, they contributed a core component.[1]

The 1889 London dock strike has commonly been regarded as the starting-point of the TGWU story, and no one can doubt its impact. The courage of those who took part, the sheer verve of their leaders, the widespread support that was aroused all insist that it is entirely proper to celebrate it. But recent historical research has documented substantial organization amongst dock workers long before that great event. Nearly two decades of struggle against overwhelming difficulties left permanent influences behind them to colour and influence the new unionism. The breakthrough of 1889 was real enough, but it was not a total break with what had gone before.

Although there are scattered records of spasmodic local stoppages by dockers in earlier times, historians have found little or no trace of stable trade-union organization amongst waterfront workers before the 1870s, with the notable exception of the guild-inspired Society of London Watermen and Lightermen, which had pre-industrial origins. In the conditions of that time 'stability' was difficult to achieve, but the idea of trade-union organization commonly took root and survived, even when particular organizations were unable to keep going. People remembered. Children listened to their parents. Once lit, the torch was passed from hand to hand, and from one generation to the next. It is therefore necessary to begin our account of the origins of the TGWU with the rise of waterfront unionism from the 1870s. What kind of world was it in which these long unorganized people began to try to join forces with one another?

## Boom and Slump

In the years after 1870, powerful though it remained, Britain was losing its dominant position in the world economy. German and American rivals pressed harder and harder, and Britain's industrial lead was coming to an end. The global economy of these decades was uneven, and the British economy was less buoyant than in the past. Growth continued, but at a slower pace. The Russian economist N. D. Kondratieff[2] later identified a series of 'long waves' in the world's capitalist economy going back to the French Revolution, in addition to the generally recognized ups and downs of the business cycle. From 1789 to 1814, he suggested, there was an upswing of twenty-five years, followed by a decline to 1849, a period of thirty-five years. The first cycle therefore lasted for sixty years. The second wave 'begins in 1848 and ends in 1873, lasting twenty-four years . . . the decline of the second wave begins in 1873 and ends in 1896, a period of twenty-three years. The length of the second wave is forty-seven years'.[3] The third wave (1896–1945) will occupy us throughout most of this volume and for a good part of the next. The down-wave of Kondratieff's second major period was widely recognized by British historians, and was frequently referred to as 'the Great Depression'. This term has recently been questioned, but in spite of innovations the period was certainly a difficult one, even in Britain with all its earlier advantages as the frontrunner. Productivity began to lag. Within the global long waves, the curve of activity bumped up and down in a succession of lesser cyclical slumps. These appear to differ, depending on how one looks at them: the movement of industrial output gives one picture, and that of foreign trade another. Michael Barratt Brown has tabulated the relevant figures for the period, using these two variables, and juxtaposing them against the pattern of innovation (see table 1.1).[4]

During the slump years, unemployment rose, output commonly fell, and times were hard. For the poorest people they brought not only relative distress, but real hunger. In between there were recurrent recoveries and upturns, which were periods of more optimistic activity. Throughout the nineteenth century unemployment relief was unknown, so that each of the downturns spelt privation for many and widespread social tumult.[5] But the upturns were times in which labour could often answer back.

Not very far into the downturn, in 1876, Queen Victoria assumed the title of Empress of India. Before her death, she was to add 5 million more

### Table 1.1  Boom and Slump, 1848–1921

| Boom or Slump | Years | Industrial Output Index (1880=100) | Foreign Trade Volume Index | Industrial Changes and Foreign-Trade Developments |
|---|---|---|---|---|
| Boom | 1848–53 | 39–52 | 25–37 | Electric telegraph and |
| Slump | 1854–5 | 52–51 | 36–34 | railway building in Europe |
| Boom | 1856–60 | 51–63 | 41–49 | and USA. New machine |
| Slump | 1861–2 | 60–58 | 48 | tools make the UK the 'workshop of the world'. |
| Boom | 1863–74 | 61–92 | 49–81 | US Civil War and European |
| Slump | 1875–9 | 91–85 | 84–91 | war. Iron and steel development and US railway boom. |
| Boom | 1880–3 | 100–110 | 100–111 | Shipbuilding boom, iron |
| Slump | 1884–6 | 104–101 | 108–109 | ships and agricultural |
| Boom | 1887–91 | 106–122 | 114–180 | machinery and markets in |
| Slump | 1892–3 | 116–113 | 128–125 | Canada, Australia and South America. |
| Boom | 1894–9 | 120–142 | 134–160 | UK development of electric |
| Slump | 1900–4 | 142–141 | 160–175 | power. Tramways and house-building boom. Russian, Japanese and African markets grow. |
| Boom | 1905–7 | 151–160 | 182–198 | Internal combustion engine. |
| Slump | 1908–9 | 152–154 | 187–193 | Naval and arms race. Oil and |
| Boom | 1910–13 | 159–184 | 203–232 | the Near East market. Rapid growth of US industry. |
| War | 1914–18 | 173–149 | 200–127 | US and Japanese arms |
| Boom | 1919–20 | 163–168 | 169–187 | booms – iron, steel, |
| Slump | 1921 | 105 | 153 | chemicals, motors – challenging UK trade. |

Note: In both indices the first figure gives the proportion of 1880 levels in the first year of boom or slump, the second figure the proportion for the last year.
Sources: B. R. Mitchell and P. Deane, Abstract of British Historical Statistics (Cambridge University Press, 1962), pp. 271–2 and 282–3; Ernest Mandel, Marxist Economic Theory (Merlin Press, 1968), pp. 359–60.

square miles and 90 million additional souls to her domains. Thus she died as sovereign of 13 million square miles and 370 million people, most of whom were Indians. Stamps bearing her portrait franked the mails in Shanghai and Vancouver, in Lagos and Calcutta, all across Africa and Asia. Missionaries flocked around the globe to spread Victorian morality, and where they were not prudently broiled or otherwise seen off by the indigenous populations, they were commonly followed by trade, the flag and the imperial armies. Rows and rows of streets in England's burgeoning towns took on the names of distant, exotic places, commemorating the victories of Birmingham technology over the courage of a hundred resistance movements. The riches of the new dominions were not spread about among the English poor, however, and London's East End, like many northern slums, festered and sweltered in squalor, vice and distress. Domestic poverty was widespread and growing, and civil turbulence was not far beneath the ordered surface. In Ireland trouble brewed and stewed.

Just as Britain was losing its industrial pre-eminence, so too the end of the age when Britannia ruled the waves was approaching. Europeans and North Americans entered into hot competition for territories in Africa and Asia. Excluding the unlimited Sahara, the French gathered 3.5 million African square miles and a population of 40 million to their own empire. Belgium and Germany grabbed 1 million square miles apiece, with 30 and 17 million Africans, respectively, resident in their new colonies. Portugal joined the plunder. The Americans seized a chain of former Spanish outposts across the Pacific and dominated the Caribbean. Everyone chipped away at China, in the last throes of the decline of her classic empire. The Russians joined in this process, spreading to the ocean boundary and pushing down to Manchuria. This was the age of imperialism, and it was to culminate in global collision, mayhem and catastrophe. Before that, it was savagely to distort the politics of Europe, and colour the attitudes of even the poorest wage-slaves in the great imperial centres.

## The Glamour of Trade . . .

British ports, which handled the trade of the largest empire and stowed and unloaded the new vessels which carried that trade, were the first point of contact with this rapidly changing world.

Henry Mayhew had published his *London Labour and the London Poor* two decades earlier, in 1851. It was crisp reading, and even today provides an inexhaustible mine for historians in search of a graphic vignette or sweeping phrase. Here is his description of the London docks, then spread across 90 acres of St George, Shadwell and Wapping.

As you enter the dock the sight of the forest of masts in the distance, and the tall chimneys vomiting clouds of black smoke, and the many coloured flags flying in the air, has a most peculiar effect . . . Along the quay you see, now men with their faces blue with indigo, and now gaugers, with their long brass-tipped rule dripping with spirit from the cask they have been probing. Then will come a group of flaxen-haired sailors chattering

German; and next a black sailor, with a cotton handkerchief twisted turban-like round his head. Presently a blue-smocked butcher, with fresh meat, and a bunch of cabbages in the tray on his shoulder; and shortly afterwards a mate, with green paroquets in a wooden cage. Here you will see sitting on a bench a sorrowful woman, with new bright cooking tins at her feet, telling you she is an emigrant preparing for her voyage. As you pass along this quay the air is pungent with tobacco; on that it overpowers you with the fumes of rum; then you are nearly sickened with the stench of hides, and huge bins of horns; and shortly afterwards the atmosphere is fragrant with coffee and spice. Nearly everywhere you meet stacks of cork, or else yellow bins of sulphur, or lead-coloured copper-ore. As you enter this warehouse, the flooring is sticky, as if it had been newly tarred, with the sugar that has leaked through the casks . . . Here you sniff the fumes of the wine, and there the peculiar fungus-smell of dry rot; then the jumble of sounds as you pass along the dock blends in anything but sweet concord.[6]

It is not surprising that Mayhew was so powerfully impressed by the sensuous images of the import trade. But, of course, it all had to balance with the outflow of manufactures, textiles, coal and machines. These export trades were more the business of the Mersey and the Humber than that of the capital. All this merchandise had to be carried to the quays, and from the time of Mayhew's description down to the years after the great London dock strike, all the long-haul work was done by railway. Once goods had arrived in depots, they would then enter the short-haul system: they would be put in carts and drawn through crowded thoroughfares by horses. Otherwise, railways and ships were the Victorian means of transport. But, needless to say, carterage was the most labour-intensive of these operations. At the same time, it was a greater problem for would-be labour organizers. For prospective trade unionists, the closer co-operative division of labour between railwaymen and seamen made it much easier for them to associate than it was for the carters, who were living in an older world, altogether more fragmented.

Speed of transit meant that all Mayhew's exotic products could be funnelled out to customers with little delay. Storage costs were cut, as ease of access to regular supplies meant that provincial traders could coast along on very meagre stocks. Money circulated faster as trade increased its tempo. The railways, with trade, promoted the growth of towns and the migration of peoples. The scale of expansion was phenomenal, but understandable in modern terms if we compare it with that of twentieth-century urbanization in South America. Between 1801 and 1901, London's population multiplied five times, from 957,000 to 4,536,000. Liverpool's increased ninefold, from 82,000 to 704,000. Hull's went up eight times, from 30,000 to 240,000. Scotland's largest port, Glasgow, exceeded all these: it registered a tenfold growth, from 77,000 to 776,000. The principal Welsh port, Cardiff, however, grew by eighty times, from 2,000 to 164,000. Concentration called and pushed the rural population to move. At the same time, ocean transport was stimulated and its technologies improved. By 1838 the first purely steam crossing of the Atlantic had been made in nineteen days. As engines developed, so new screw propulsions came to displace the paddle wheel. A gigantic growth of port capacity followed. In 1820, London handled 777,858 tons of imports. The figure rose to 4,089,366 in 1870, and to 10,000,000 in 1901. The Mersey took 4,500,000 tons of shipping in 1848; by 1908, it received 16,000,000 tons. Glasgow doubled its harbour area in the last quarter of the nineteenth century, and the dock area of Hull almost trebled between 1863 and 1885.[7]

While Mayhew wrote, 3 per cent of cargoes were mechanically propelled. By 1861 the figure had become 10 per cent. It was to pass the halfway mark in 1883, and before the First World War it reached 91 per cent. The growth of empire locked these advances into place. Sail could not pass the Suez Canal, so that after 1869 steam ruled the Eastern trade.

## . . . and the Reality of Toil

All these developments were the spectacular evidence of progress. But what of the people who earned their living in this upheaval and turmoil? Once again, let us start with Mayhew:

> He who wishes to behold one of the most extraordinary and least-known scenes of this metropolis, should wend his way to the London Dock gates at half-past seven in the morning. There he will see congregated within the principal entrance masses of men of all grades, looks and kinds . . .
> Presently you know, by the stream pouring through the gates and the rush towards particular spots, that the 'calling foremen' have made their appearance. Then begins the scuffling and scrambling forth of countless hands high in the air, to catch the eye of him whose voice may give them work. As the foreman calls from a book of names, some men jump up on the backs of the others, so as to lift themselves high above the rest, and attract the notice of him who hires them. All are shouting. Some cry aloud his surname, some his christian name, others call out their own names, to remind him that they are there. Now the appeal is made in Irish blarney – now in broken English. Indeed, it is a sight to sadden the most callous, to see thousands of men struggling for only one day's hire; the scuffle being made the fiercer by the knowledge that hundreds out of the number there assembled must be left to idle the day out in want. To look in the faces of that hungry crowd is to see a sight that must be ever remembered. Some are smiling to the foreman to coax him into remembrance of them; others, with their protruding eyes, eager to snatch at the hoped-for pass. For weeks many have gone there, and gone through the same struggle – the

same cries; and have gone away, after all, without the work they had screamed for.[8]

This description of the savage ritual of the call-on was to lose none of its force in succeeding years. The social scientists of the 1880s and 1890s registered the same shock. The press of casual labourers demanding work simply grew and grew, as the railways brought more and more people to the port cities, and successive immigrations either were added to the crowds or ousted existing workers from other trades to join the scramble for work in their place. It was a scene that would have been recognized by port workers right up to the 1960s.

For Mayhew, the scrimmage was made even more dreadful by an understanding of its object, which was employment in conditions of utter inhumanity:

The work may be divided into three classes.
1. Wheel-work, or that which is moved by the muscles of the legs and weight of the body; 2. jigger, or winch-work, or that which is moved by the muscles of the arm. In each of these the labourer is stationary; but in the truck work, which forms the third class, the labourer has to travel over a space of ground greater or less in proportion to the distance which the goods have to be removed.

The wheel-work is performed somewhat on the system of the treadwheel, with the exception that the force is applied inside instead of outside the wheel. From six to eight men enter a wooden cylinder or drum, upon which are nailed battens, and the men laying hold of the ropes commence treading the wheel round . . . The wheel is generally about sixteen feet in diameter and eight to nine feet broad; and the six or eight men treading within it, will lift from sixteen to eighteen hundred weight, and often a ton, forty times in an hour, an average of twenty-seven feet high. Other men will get out a cargo of from 800 to 900 casks of wine, each cask averaging about five hundred weight, and being lifted about eighteen feet, in a day and a half. At trucking each man is said to go on an average thirty miles a-day, and two-thirds of that time he is moving one and a half hundredweight at six miles and a-half per hour.[9]

The pay for such a day's work, Mayhew tells us, would be 2s. 6d.; and for those men not hired until the afternoon, the hourly rate would be 4d.

These conditions were a continuing affliction, impeding port workers in their efforts to organize, not only during the movements of the trade cycle in the 1870s but on through to the great strike of 1889 and beyond it well into the twentieth century.

As a young man, Ben Tillett, who figures very largely in the chapters which follow, felt real shame about working on the docks. 'So real was the stigma', he wrote 'that [we] concealed the nature of our occupation from our family as well as our friends.'[10] A contractor would describe his employees as 'dock rats'. In his memoirs, Tillett claimed to have originated the term 'docker'; if this be true, we can count it as the first of many steps he took towards affirming the human status and dignity of his members. The brutal indignity of the call-on goes far to explain these attitudes. 'Coats, flesh and even ears were torn off. The strong literally threw themselves over the heads of their fellows and battled . . . through the kicking, punching, cursing crowds to the rails of the "cage" which held them like rats – mad human rats who saw food in the ticket.'[11]

## An Observant Participant

Tillett saw the life of the dockers from inside. During the 1880s, more and more witnesses followed in Mayhew's footsteps to see it from outside.

In 1886 Beatrice Potter (the future Beatrice Webb) took up work as a researcher in Charles Booth's team at the Charity Organization Society, which had begun a sustained investigation of London poverty. Early the next year she was assigned to the study of the docks. Bare statistics were not enough for her: 'I want local colouring; a clear description of the various methods of employing men, of types of character of men employed, and where they live. Must realise the "waiting at the gates", and find out for myself'.[12]

This was a classic definition of the role of 'participant observer', to which Beatrice applied herself with great zeal. Morning after morning she reported at the dock gates and watched the often brutal struggle for work. She also observed 'the leisurely unloading of sailing vessels, compared to the swift discharge of steamers.'[13] Day after day the entries in her diary record an undiminished sense of shock. Her experiences were digested into an essay on dock life in East London, which was immediately published in *Nineteenth Century*. Beatrice was dissatisfied with this essay, but it was to prove more than capable of extending her own sense of outrage to a much wider circle. At the same time, her prescriptions for reform were also strongly canvassed.

Writing about the behaviour of 'the lowest class of casual labourers', she expressed a mixture of fascination and distress in her contribution to Booth's final research:

These men hang about for the 'odd hour' work, or one day in the seven. They live on stimulants and tobacco, varied with bread and tea and salt fish. Their passion is gambling. Sections of them are hereditary casuals; a larger portion drift from other trades. They have a constitutional hatred to regularity and forethought, and a need for paltry excitement. They are late risers, sharp-witted talkers, and, above all, they have that agreeable tolerance for their own and each other's vices which seems characteristic of a purely leisure class, whether it lies at the top or the bottom of society.

But if we compare them with their brothers and sisters in the London Club and West-end drawing-room we must admit that in one respect they are strikingly superior. The stern reality of ever-pressing starvation draws all together. Communism is a necessity of their life: they share all with one another, and as a class they are quixotically generous. It is this virtue and the courage with which they face privation that lend a charm to life among them.[14]

The shock of dockland, red in tooth and claw, of course registered more than a disapproval of poverty and deprivation. The conditions of the dockers went along with radically different attitudes. Dock work was different. Subject to irregular movements of trade, as well as to the other variables we have already discussed, it was strangely pre-industrial in the challenges it posed to normal notions of factory discipline, the rule of the clock and the ordered regularity of work which had become ingrained in Victorian social organization.

## Accidents Were Not an Accident

Dock life in London in the declining years of the nineteenth century was hell, and getting worse. In January 1888 the *East London Observer* carried a report of the death of a dock worker, who was discovered in his last minutes at the kerbside. James Butler, who was forty-five, was found by a carman who had seen him sitting by the road, 'apparently very ill'. He was wheeled on a barrow to the London Hospital, where he was found to have died of heart failure. 'At one time deceased was a very strong man, but lately he had become weak', testified his brother at the inquest.[15] True, the weather at the time was bad. That same January, during a fog, numbers of dockers were drowned. Had they 'belonged to a better class of society', reported the *East End News*, 'the clamour . . . would have changed the insouciance of the dock authorities into active measures for the prevention of a similar recurrence but –

> "rattle his bones over the stones
> He's only a docky whom nobody owns".[16]

Casualties, fatal and otherwise, were by no means confined to the Port of London. The man who was to lead Liverpool's dockers, James Sexton, recorded the story of the accident which disfigured him for life. He got the chance to work over Christmas, on 24 and 25 December, and he was overjoyed, because double-time payments would ensure that his family could celebrate, albeit a day late.

In the early hours of the morning an incompetent man at the winch and a defective hook on the end of the rope-fall caused me to be struck in the face with a whole sling of bags of grain which broke loose, and I was hurled into the hold of the barge to which the cargo was being transferred

. . . my face struck the keelson of the barge. My right cheekbone was smashed, my right eye forced out of the socket, and my skull was slightly fractured. But such happenings were too common to be allowed to interfere with work, especially when a rush job like this was being tackled, so I was just hoisted out of the hold and laid in the shed whilst my mates carried on.

I was left there for two hours whilst somebody hunted up a cab – no ambulances were stationed at the docks in those days – and this exposure on a bitter winter's night caused such serious complications that I was detained in hospital for nearly two months, with my head packed in ice for most of the time.

This happened in 1881, immediately after the passing of the Employers' Liability Act, of which I knew nothing – not even of its existence – until I heard about it from one of my workmates . . . who visited me in hospital seven weeks after my admission. He . . . imparted to me something of his belief that I was entitled to compensation under [the Act]. The resident surgeon, who happened to be near, asked my mate for particulars of what had happened. Two days later he told me he thought I was well enough to risk a visit to my employers. He played the part of the good Samaritan so far as to hire a cab and go with me for an interview which did not seem so alluring now.

The boss met the statement of my case with a blunt denial of any liability on his part and raised a second line of defence by pointing out that even if he were liable, I had no claim, as he ought to have had notice of the accident within six weeks of its occurrence. The best he could be induced to do was to say that when I was physically fit he would see what possibility there was of finding some light work for me.

The consequence was that when I got back I was offered a lad's job – driving a winch, with one and six-pence a day less than I had been accustomed to as a 'casual labourer' (when I could get any casual labouring to do!). However, total starvation was the only alternative, so, propelled by the devil of dire necessity, and with the thought of my wife before me, I took it on. I had a broken week, and at the end of it, on reckoning up my time, I found I had earned fifteen shillings. When I crawled round to the pay table to draw that magnificent sum, all that my wife and I would have to live on until another pay day came round, I was 'docked' half a crown for the fare for the cab that had taken me to hospital.[17]

## II

## *Trade Unions in the 1870s*

How could men endure such things without resistance? The answer is that they did resist, at every moment when the possibility presented itself. Between 1863 and 1874, industrial output grew by 50 per cent and export volume by 65 per cent (see table 1.1). Here was opportunity.

The three principal ports, London, Liverpool and Hull, all experienced strikes and attempts at trade-union organization on the docks in the

1870s. All of these were of local or at best regional dimensions, although all were influenced by national economic conditions and by national trade-union responses to them. That is why, in order to understand what was happening in our sector, we need also to understand the main features of trade unionism as a whole during these formative years of dockers' organization.

In 1871 the population of England and Wales was 22.7 million, and of Scotland and Ireland 3.4 and 5.4 million respectively. Of these people taken together, 8.2 million men and 3.2 million women were employed. The proportion of people in trade unions was very small, and figures are in any case inaccurate, since no attempt at official counts was made until 1886; but the Webbs calculated a total membership of under 143,000. By 1881 the population had grown to about 35 million for the entire British Isles, and employment had reached 12.7 million. During the decade, trade unionism had expanded to 266,000. What kinds of organizations were involved?

The great 'amalgamated' societies of craftsmen, categorized as the 'New Model' unions in the Webbs' classic *History of Trade Unionism*, had dominated the scene in the 1850s and 1860s: in 1868 they had, along with miners and cotton workers, made up the bulk of membership in the affiliates which formed the Trades Union Congress in 1868. Their leaders had also been the grouping with whom Karl Marx had built the International Working Men's Association, the First International, in 1864. This was the trade unionism which, through the agency of the TUC's Parliamentary Committee, was to campaign successfully for an acceptable legal status, which Parliament finally granted in the Acts of 1871 and 1875. In that year the TUC's secretary, George Howell, declared that 'the legislation with respect to Trade Unions was then so perfect that the natural time had run for the existence of Trade Union Congresses so far as Parliamentary action was concerned'.[18]

Yet the rather complacent craft societies began to lose their dominance over the movement as trade unionism experienced a substantial phase of growth in the early 1870s. Stable non-craft organization already existed in cotton, where, however, it remained localized; and in mining, where it took on national proportions in the 1860s. Two miners' unions could, after spectacular growth in 1873, claim 100,000 members each. Both of them organized all grades of workers. More akin to the cotton unions, where organization was not only local but mainly confined to the skilled operatives, were the unions in iron and steel.

New sections of the working population, however, participated in the sharp increase of union membership in the prosperous years of the early 1870s. They included gasworkers, who formed an East End Union in 1872; London's builders' labourers, who formed their General Amalgamated Labourers' Union in the same year; agricultural labourers, led

by Joseph Arch, whose National Union of 1872 reached a turbulent peak
with membership of 100,000 in only eighteen months; and railwaymen,
whose Amalgamated Society of Railway Servants dates from 1871. In
their efforts to engage hitherto unorganized occupations and industries,
all these bodies anticipated the 'new unionism' of the 1880s. In addition,
some, such as the agricultural and railway workers, aspired to *national*
organization. They were also frequently touched and inspired by the
national movement for the nine-hour day, which was accompanied by
large and successful strike actions.

In structure and general aspirations, however, they made no dramatic
break with the older unions of the skilled workers, and sometimes, as in
the case of the railway servants, they depended for encouragement,
strategies, and even finance, on middle-class sympathizers. Nevertheless,
the union upsurge of these years was substantial, even on the Webbs'
calculation quoted above. Others claim a much greater representation at
the beginning of the decade, and a sharp rise immediately afterwards,
from a total membership of 199,000 in 1866, to 735,000 in 1873.[19]
Some of the new organizations were destroyed and most were seriously
squeezed in the acute depression of the later 1870s; or again, after partial
recovery in 1881–3, by the severe slump of 1887. But vestigial
organizations often survived, to reach into and to qualify the 'newness' of
the new unionism of the 1880s. Perhaps more important, their members
survived, having learned from hurtful experience which only reinforced
their efforts when the time became ripe.

Activist farmworkers were victimized and driven for survival to seek
work in the towns, where many of them became carters, since their skill
with horses was the most saleable asset they could bring to the urban
labour market. How many of these displaced people were later involved
in the recruitment of carters, cab-drivers and other transport workers to
the experimental new organizations which began to develop?

None of the standard trade-union histories which describe this period
pays any sustained attention to dock workers' organization or strikes in
the 1870s.[20] It has been left to a later generation of labour historians to
remedy this omission, and to show that, in London, Liverpool and Hull,
at least, the dockers participated fully in the ferment of the 1870s.[21]

## Dock Unions: Sectionalism and Casualism

Out of a total employed population of 11.4 million in 1871, 600,000
worked in transport. Their numbers had risen to 900,000 by 1881.

For much of the nineteenth century the London docks were
characterized by the fragmented organization of cargo-handling. Small-
scale capital dominated many branches of the industry. Different firms
specialized in particular operations. Thus there were separate entities in

lighterage, in stevedoring (which was originally the separately organized function of loading ships, as distinct from unloading, but which later came to include all shipboard work, as distinct from work on the quayside and in warehousing). Separate trades, such as tea, timber, coal- and corn-handling, were also owned or operated by distinct enterprises. These subdivisions had to be reflected in the labour force engaged in them. Far from 'dockers' being an undifferentiated mass of interchange- able labour-atoms acting according to textbook notions of individualism, the regular core of port workers formed discrete, highly specialized groups. These developed strong bonds of loyalty and local pride, which in turn could lead to intimate relationships with individual specialist employers.

Nor was this the end of the complicated process, since the division of functions took different forms in the enclosed docks and on the riverside wharves, whilst still other traditions prevailed on the river in the lighterage and watermen's trades. This fragmentation was common to all the main ports of the country, although it was more marked in London than elsewhere. The distinction between shipboard and quayside work, giving rise to the sectionalism of the stevedores, was particularly marked in the capital. There, craft exclusiveness, reaching back to memories of the guild status of the Thames lightermen, and bolstered by the high proportion of 'over-side' transhipment to and from lighters and barges, was also most marked. This is not to say that sectionalism was confined to London: as we shall see, it created problems in the other ports too; but it was most deep-seated in London.

Moreover, the older view of Victorian dock work as an occupation dominated by its casual nature remains broadly true, even after recent historical research has emphasized the complex reality summarized here. There were two elements to the dockers' poverty and insecurity. One was that, even amongst the core of workers who pursued the work regularly, there was a permanent over-supply. This arose partly to suit the port employers' widely fluctuating demands for labour. Their operations were dependent upon tides, weather, seasons and the state of trade. The problem was reinforced by the specialisms we have described, which were rendered even more inflexible by the tendency of dockers, even when short of work, to look for employment only in their immediate neighbourhood. Geographical immobility was thus added to occupational specialization. In the 1870s, the waterfront workers overcame many of these divisions in their early drive for unionization, but as the upturn of trade receded, old sectionalism reasserted itself in the ensuing depression.

At the same time, what stability there had been in the division of labour became more liable to disruption by new types of employers and the growth of capital concentration in the ports. The shipping companies themselves, swollen in size by the need to finance larger steamships and transcontinental refrigeration[22] moved into handling their own cargoes, as did bulk-handling flour-milling and cement companies. The ship- and port-owners developed new docks to take the larger, deeper draft ships down the estuary at Tilbury, 26 miles from the port of London. These developments destabilized the sectional unions which emerged from the growth of the 1870s, and drove them either to attempt more open methods of association or, working against such adaptation, to turn in on themselves in self-defence.

The other element in the casual nature of port employment was the fact that non-regular workers surrounded the docks, and at certain seasons, or when a general depression closed other jobs and laid them off, would present themselves at the dock gates for hire. This happened, for example, with the gasworkers of the East End during the summer months, when employment in the gasworks was slack, and with agricultural labourers during the winter. Without the protection of all-inclusive unionism, and with casual hiring occurring several times a day, the dock workers' vulnerability from all these causes was of course extreme. This was a longstanding problem. We have evidence of its extent as far back as 1844, when Henry Mayhew estimated the London docks' maximum employment figures at 3,012, while its minimum need for labour was 1,189. At St Katharine's Dock, the jobs available varied between 1,713 and 515, while there was a fluctuation between 4,000 and 1,300 at the East and West India Docks.[23]

## London Forerunners

The first record of modern trade unionism in the Port of London is in 1871, a year in which the port employers chose to impose wage cuts. The dockers responded: clergymen conducted their first protest meetings and urged an appeal to public conscience. ('The poor cannot strike,' they advised.) But the dockers won the support of Patrick Hennessey, an Irish tailor and trade unionist, and of Charles Keen, an activist in the First International. Both men were involved in the Land and Labour League, which had been formed in 1869 following a decision of the Basle Congress of the First International in favour of land nationalization. George Eccarius, a friend of Karl Marx, and Martin Boon, a follower of the Chartist Bronterre O'Brien, were the first joint secretaries of this League, and the founding treasurer was John Weston, the Owenite.[24] If the Land and Labour League thus looked back to the Chartist preoccupation with access to the land, which was becoming less and less appropriate to a fully industrial society, it none the less offered a link to a developed organizational experience.[25]

In December 1871 Hennessey and Keen helped the dockers to form the Labour Protection League (LPL). At first, there was only poor support from the general dockers, the biggest stimulus being to the stevedores, who had set up five branches and recruited 3,000 members by 1872. Enrolment followed on the wharves, involving corn-porters and then general labourers. Building and engineering labourers, dustmen, slopmen and scavengers also joined its ranks, which added up to 30,000 by October 1872.

Sectional strikes in different parts of the port won wage increases – mostly to 5d. an hour. The objective of the 'tanner' was canvassed – seventeen years before its realization in the great strike. Mass unionism had arrived, and its day was celebrated in an East End demonstration of 20,000 people, complete with bands and banners.

But problems arose in the government of the LPL. Its leaders were not subject to membership control, for its growth had been too rapid to allow for the careful creation of any adequate central representative machinery; there was no co-ordination between the fifty branches. Later in the 1870s its leaders evolved into a rather conservative clique, and were ousted from office. Even in the upsurge, some groups preferred to form sectional unions of their own, such as the lightermen and the coal-whippers. Separatism was also evident within the LPL as corn-porters and others formed occupational, rather than local branches. Their aim was the preservation of job control; port-level solidarity was secondary to that purpose. The bulk of the union's funds remained in the branches, which were largely self-governing.[26] The Executive Committee had a very weak constitutional position. Efforts were made to overcome this by the appointment of district delegates with powers to visit and inspect branches, but with no powers to sanction strikes.

The recession of the later 1870s wore away the LPL. Such an experience was not uncommon for trade unions at that time. The leaders attempted an early form of federation, and at a conference of the LPL, the Carmen's Union, the Lightermen and Watermen, and the Railway Servants, a loose alliance with a joint Executive Committee was formed to co-ordinate industrial action. Entitled the Amalgamated Labour Union, there is no evidence of its having been effective.

A lock-out at the Millwall Docks in 1876 drained the LPL's funds and reduced its membership to about 2,000. By the 1880s it was further reduced to just six branches, five of which were of stevedores on the North Bank, the other of corn-porters on the South.

These two sectional survivals from the London dockers' struggles of the 1870s made significant contributions later on – the corn-porters in London, and the stevedores ultimately in three major ports. It is reasonable to say that 'mass unionism on the London waterfront began in 1872',[27] and that the LPL was more than ephemeral. But when the Labour Protection League changed its name to the Amalgamated Stevedores' Labour Protection League, the corn-porters' branch opted for secession and revived as the South Side Labour Protection League in the great movement of 1889. It was ultimately absorbed into the TGWU in 1922. The stevedores, on the other hand, kept up a sectional organization down to very recent times. This was strong enough to frustrate the objective of dockers' unity. Moreover, London dockers' unionism in the 1870s was local in its ambitions, and this distinguishes it sharply from the new unions which were to come at the end of the next decade. Many years later those local and sectional bodies were to try to recruit further afield. But we shall consider this change in their style, after the Second World War, in volume II.

## Stevedores: a Sectional Model

The stevedores' now separate organization was the most lasting result of the movement of the 1870s. As export shipboard workers, they had a measure of mobility throughout the docks of the north side. Most worked for small master-stevedoring companies, in whose ambit the very smallness of scale fostered a marked occupational identity. Such employers were relatively weak in any dispute, and wages of 6s. a day (of nine hours) were possible, with 1s. an hour overtime. More, the masters recognized the union, something which the big shipping companies resisted until the First World War. Union stevedores, whilst not enforcing a closed shop, obtained preference of employment, and calling-on rules were elaborated and accepted by the masters. Union cards were inspected at the call-on, providing a sanction against arrears and ensuring membership stability. In return, the employer derived real benefits, as the union promoted order and maintained a high quality of work. This is therefore an example of closed, craft-like unionism which consciously restricted entry – so much so that the death-rate amongst members regulated the rate of entry, with stevedores' sons having preference. No one under the age of eighteen was admitted unless he was a stevedore's son, in which case he would join at one-quarter of the standard entrance fee. Adult entrants had to have a background of shipwork, and many were ex-sailors. Even so, the union sometimes closed its book to all except sons of members. Ben Tillett, although a former seaman, was refused admission when he arrived in the Port of London from Bristol. The stevedores also had a large Irish membership, which helped to cement group solidarity at a time when the Irish question was becoming an urgent issue.

The stevedores' closed society suffered from inflexibility in the face of technical and structural change, a defect inherent in this kind of unionism. Coming into existence in the last days of the sailing ship, it failed to adapt as the new oceangoing steamers, owned and run by large-scale companies, took over. The change brought with it the building of new docks, including that at Tilbury, remote from the stevedores' established controls. The big shipping companies defied the union's rules and controls, hiring non-unionists in the docks which they operated with their own stevedoring businesses. The union faced the classic choice of closed unions in this situation: either to amend and dilute its restrictions on entry in order to recruit the workers in the new companies and locations, or to preserve its working rules by accepting a reduced sphere of influence confined to its existing territory. It chose the latter, more cautious, defensive option with consequences which were to mark port unionism deep into the twentieth century. These go a long way towards explaining the problematic management of dockers' unionism at key moments in the TGWU's history. But the immediate consequence was that non-unionism emerged during the 1880s in the new docks and in the employ of the big shipping companies, and a new, less rigid United Stevedores' Union was formed to cater for them. The original five-branch union stayed within its limited horizons, remaining isolated also from the labour movement on general questions of trade unionism and politics, preferring to foster a tight, status-conscious social life within its fraternity and community.

## The Workmen's Elite: Lightermen

The organization of lightermen in the Port of London dates back to Elizabethan times, when it took the form of a liveried company. (They were originally 'watermen', but usage of this term declined as passenger trade on the river dwindled.) They were the elite of all labour in the port, with a formal apprenticeship system. The guild system, in which journeymen could expect to make the transition to become masters in their turn, gave way to wage-earning capitalist employment relations with increased scales of operation, and the masters broke with the apprenticeship system in the mid-nineteenth century. The result was that the wage-workers formed the Amalgamated Society of Watermen and Lightermen in 1872, thus joining the general wave of unionization of the period. Although its formation was stimulated by a wage dispute, for a long time it remained heavily preoccupied with the defence of the apprenticeship system in order to perpetuate the elite status of its members.

Some picture of the ancient traditions of the watermen is recorded in the memoirs of Harry Gosling, who was to become the founding president of the TGWU. Gosling was the great-grandson of a Thames waterman who owned several barges, in addition to his 'dumb craft', the chief of which was a clipper called the *Effort*, moored in the Surrey docks to receive merchandise which was bound for Ramsgate, Margate, Herne Bay, 'and sometimes to Chatham and Sheerness'.[28]

At the age of fourteen, Gosling himself was bound apprentice for seven years at a ceremony in the hall of the Watermen's Company, St Mary-at-Hill, in a room 'practically unaltered since 1785'.

> My father and I arrived at the court on the day I was to be bound, and were ushered in by a uniformed beadle who used to act as a kind of river policeman, a modernised type of those who in earlier days impressed men for service in the Navy . . . Under the flags of the Watermen's Company, in a high-backed state chair, sat the Master of the court, wearing a heavy chain of office . . . on the wall hung a great oil painting of the Judgement of Solomon . . .[29]

The beadle solemnly proclaimed that William Gosling wished to bind his son apprentice for seven years. Then the master of the court asked the boy whether he was willing to be bound, and after he and his father had made the appropriate avowals, indentures were signed, 'and copies handed to us both'. The terms were tough. Each apprentice swore

> to learn his Art, and with him (after the manner of an Apprentice) to dwell and serve upon the river of Thames from the Day of the Date hereof until the full End and Term of seven years from thence next following, to be fully complete and ended; during which Term the said Apprentice his said Master faithfully shall serve as aforesaid, his Secrets keep, his lawful Commandments everywhere gladly do; He shall not waste the Goods of the said Master, nor lend them unlawfully to any; He shall not commit Fornication, nor contract Matrimony within the said Term; He shall not play at Cards, Dice, Tables nor any other unlawful games whereby his said Master may have any loss. With his own Goods or others during the said Term, without License of his said Master he shall not buy nor sell; He shall not haunt Taverns nor Play Houses, nor absent himself from his Master's service Day nor Night, unlawfully, but in all things as a faithful Apprentice he shall behave himself towards his said Master and all his during the said Term.[30]

In return for all this the master also undertook certain responsibilities: 'He his said Apprentice in the Same Art, which he useth, by the best means that he can, shall teach and instruct, or cause to be taught and instructed, feeding unto the said Apprentice Meat, Drink, Apparel, Lodging, and all other necessaries according to the custom of the City of London.[31]

The whole induction ceremony was dauntingly conducted and, at the end, young Gosling was issued with a tract entitled *The Honest Waterman*, an inspirational account of the life of Thomas Mann, a saint among Thames watermen. The virtues of Thomas Mann were abundant, but deferent to a fault:

> He (the Honest Waterman) was a very early riser, and would often do nearly a day's work before the other people were up in the morning; and then he was so very honest in never asking more than his fare, and so very

civil, and his boat and his person always so clean and neat and comfortable, that I suppose he had generally more fares than other watermen . . . His constitution being excellent, his attention unceasing, and his deportment invariably correct, business of course increased, and he never by intemperance abused the good health by which he had been blessed . . . Not only in his youth, but when far advanced in years, it was commonly his custom to row as if matched against time, and after rowing twenty or thirty miles he would row in to the Irongate Stairs by the Tower in the lively spirited manner in which he set out. He made a point, however of never rowing for a wager, and was never known to lay a bet of any kind . . . When discussions on the subject of parliamentary reform were so generally held as often to come under the notice of our watermen, he would calmly endeavour to inculcate just and moderate sentiments or change the discourse, by showing the much greater importance of self-reformation . . . His charity was so universal, so constantly and daily practised that the detail of it would be as monotonous as it was unceasing, and he died worth something under three thousand pounds.[32]

'It was', wrote the future leader of the transport workers, somewhat wryly, 'with this bright beacon shining ahead that I emerged into the everyday life of the river on June 13th, 1875'.[33]

As evidence of the attitudes of Gosling's workmates, we should note that they excluded from membership of their organization a new labour force, the bargemen, which arose as the enclosed docks and the canal system were developed. These workers did not have a licence to work on the Thames tidal waters and were, for this reason, ostracized by the Lightermen's Union.

The lightermen's clannishness [and] isolation . . . were common to all waterside groupings, although perhaps not to the same exaggerated extent. Waterside unionism was essentially defensive and restrictive in character. This was so whatever the trade, the port or even the country. In a casual, overstocked labour market such a form of organisation followed inevitably from the uncertainty of employment. The 'new unionists' of 1889 were to find that this was the framework within which they had to work. Expansive gospels of general unionism carried little weight on the waterfront.[34]

This thesis is overstated: the new unionism strove against sectionalism for good pragmatic reasons. But it was a long, hard struggle, in which sectional unions often played a retarding role but sometimes provided checks and balances against over-powerful bureaucracy in the more inclusive organization.

## Liverpool Dockers

The history of trade unionism on the Liverpool docks has been overshadowed by the focus upon London and the great strike of 1889.

Since the 1970s, however, Liverpool has found its historian, Eric Taplin, who has provided accounts to parallel the local studies of London produced by John Lovell.[35] Taplin is able to demonstrate that important activity, including unionism and major strikes, were features of Liverpool's history as they were of London's. These reached climactic proportions in the 1870s.

The economics and labour relations of the Liverpool docks had much in common with those of London. The same picture emerges of a core workforce of experienced, specialized and relatively immobile dockers, employed by a variety of bosses: master-stevedores, master-porters, some owned by shipowners and some engaged under contracts, the shipowners themselves who did their own stevedoring and porterage, and the Mersey Docks and Harbour Board, owner of the port, which had its own (smaller) labour force. As in all the ports of the major trading nations, an upheaval in scale and modes of operation was surging through the last quarter of the nineteenth century, as steam replaced sail and big capitalist shipping companies in consequence began displacing the small capital of the 'master' cargo-handling firm.

Taplin is as concerned as Lovell to dispel the legend of the dockworker as uncouth and unskilled. He also rejects the idea that port employment was wholly casual.

> most dock workers looked to the docks as their sole source of employment, frequently within a narrow range of docks. Thus the majority were known by their employers and would receive preference in employment over those less well known . . . The genuine floating labourer who drifted into the docks in search of work would be taken on only if the supply of experienced, known dockers was fully employed . . . the inexperienced worker was slow, inefficient, and a danger, for the job required considerable physical stamina allied to a knack of handling and moving heavy weights. Such expertise could not be picked up in a matter of days but was the result of many years' experience.[36]

Strikes in the port have been traced back to the 1850s, and occurred also in 1866. In the early 1870s Liverpool shared in both the general trade boom and in the wave of unionization. A minor strike in one dock in 1870 led to the brief appearance of a 'rudimentary' trade union, the Steamboat Labourers' Friendly Burial Society. In 1872 the nine-hours' movement swept through the city, involving carters, omnibus workers, shop assistants, rag-pickers and many others. Two middle-class sympathizers, William Simpson and James Samuelson, businessmen active in Liverpool's Liberal politics, emerged as spokesmen for the unskilled, one advocating 'moral force' and mediation, the other encouraging 'New Model' unionism, friendly-society methods, conciliation and arbitration.[37]

On the docks, pay claims, strikes and deputations from the men led by

Simpson and Samuelson rained down on the employers throughout 1872. Many of them were successful. Another ephemeral union was formed – the Liverpool North End Steamship Dock Labourers' Friendly Burial Society. Its innocuous name misled, for in addition to friendly benefits it submitted claims to the employers that only society members be engaged as foremen and that society men would not work with non-members. These views were wholly unacceptable to the employers and remained so for forty years. A strike called in support of the claims failed and the society is not heard of again. Within a year the wave of disputes petered out, as the boom was succeeded by a trade recession in 1873–4. Defensive strikes on a local scale did occur in 1876 and 1877, showing that the will to resist worsening conditions was present.

The general character of all the dockers' activity of this decade was, here as well, its persistent sectionalism. Cotton-porters, provision- and grain-warehouse porters, in seeking parity of wages with general dock labourers, acted in isolation from each other. The spread of improved wages from dock to dock was haphazard and uneven. This reflected the immobility of the workforce, which, as in London, was accustomed to seek employment only at a dock, or a group of docks, where the men were known. The prevalent sectionalism also accounts for the failure of the 1870s movement to produce a stable and lasting trade union.

Rivalries and jealousies were reflected in the small and transient societies which appeared, confined to either the North End or the South End Docks. Eric Taplin comments that

A further divisive factor resulted from religious differences among the dock workers. A large proportion of Liverpool dockers were Irish Catholics. The recruitment of Irish labour was not a peculiarity of Merseyside but it took an acute form in that no other large urban area in nineteenth century England was so divided between Catholics and Protestants. It entered into most aspects of Liverpool's business, political and social life and the docks were no exception. Broadly the Protestant dockers were to be found at the south end docks, the Catholics at the north end. It is, however, no more than a rough generalisation as there were substantial enclaves of Protestants at the Bootle end of the docks and Catholic groups at the Toxteth end. Although the line of docks from south to north was unbroken, in practice there was a sharp labour division between the two. South end labourers rarely sought work at the Bootle end or vice versa . . . The walking time from the north end to the south end, different types of job specialism, smaller docks at the south end, different types of vessels, different types of employers all played their part, but the division between Catholics and Protestants may have been one feature . . . an undercurrent of petty argument and recrimination . . . weakened unified action but in the event of a major conflict the labourers acted together and religious differences were subsumed for the more important immediate issue at stake.[38]

Taplin also finds that the absence of strong local trade unionism outside
the docks – a reflection of the frail manufacturing sector in the city,
which rendered the Liverpool Trades Council a weak reed – were
factors helping to explain why the dockers' organizations were so
ephemeral. Further, and related to this, was their dependence upon their
patron Simpson, a philanthropic middle-class extrovert who rigidly
discouraged self-help through unionization. In London the dockers
freed themselves from similar tutelage at an early stage, and had the
benefit of leadership from Hennessey and Keen, who although not
dockers were trade unionists and political radicals.

Sectionalism in Liverpool, however, did not give rise to the permanent
division between stevedore and docker which rooted itself in London.
The explanation seems to be that Liverpool was, at an earlier date than
London, dominated by the major shipping companies to which both
stevedores and dockers looked for employment. Quayside and shipboard
workers thus had more mutual affinities than in the capital. The same
was true, as we shall see, of Hull. When trade unionism became
permanently established in the northern ports, the fragmentation of the
workers into groups and specialisms, although it created obstacles to
unity, was less deeply entrenched than the institutionalized segregations
in London. After the formation of the TGWU, of course, the London
stevedores found themselves the magnet for all subsequent dissaffec-
tions, including the provincial ones, which plagued the general union for
generations.

## The Mersey Struck

After the recession of the mid-1870s, Liverpool docks exploded in mass
strike action in 1879. The whole docks complex came to a standstill in a
dispute that lasted three weeks and involved the seamen as well as the
dockers. The spark was a planned and announced wage cut, concerted
by all the port employers. It was enforced at first at the North End, where
the dockers struck, to be followed in sympathy by the South End – an act
of solidarity without precedent in the port. The seamen joined the
stoppage with their own grievances, and by that stage no fewer than
35,000 were on strike. The leaders, though still including Simpson and
Samuelson, now counted rank-and-file dockers in their numbers. The
strike occasioned some violence, and the artisan-dominated Trades
Council withheld its support. The numbers out of work because of the
stoppage reached 60,000. Blacklegs were imported from Hull and
elsewhere, but they refused to work when they understood the situation.
There was large-scale police mobilization and troops were also drafted
into the port. After three weeks the dockers capitulated.

Yet, amazingly, the dockers regrouped their forces, formed unions in both Liverpool and Birkenhead,[39] and renewed their effort to advance wage claims. The two unions formed a joint committee and presented a single claim for the restoration of previous wages. At arbitration the union case prevailed, following which triumph the dockers' union sought vainly to persuade the employers to establish a Board of Conciliation. The wage settlements of the 1880s in Liverpool remained unchanged until 1915, when a war bonus was added.

But three unions emerged from this conflict: the two dockers' organizations and one of the seamen. Their success followed recourse to arbitration in 1879–80, a move reflecting their defeat in the previous year's strike, and the continuing influence of Samuelson and Simpson. The unions created at that time were modelled on artisans' methods, and they did not survive the later depression of the 1880s. But the movement was not a purely local event, for Hull too saw a serious dock strike in 1879.

During the depression years of the 1880s, the American Knights of Labour carried on some clandestine work on the Liverpool docks, in which the young James Sexton was involved. The Knights of Labour had been founded in the United States in 1869 by a group of garment workers led by Uriah Stevens. Because they were convinced that trade unions were handicapped in a prejudiced environment, they 'imitated capital' by organizing in secret. The society was not referred to by name, but was usually called 'the Five Stars'. The result was slow growth: eighty assemblies by 1875 and 52,000 members in 1883. But by 1886, secrecy set aside, membership rocketed to more than 700,000. By then the union had already crossed the Atlantic to Liverpool; later it was also to appear elsewhere. The Knights' organization harked back to Robert Owen and the Grand National Consolidated Union of the 1830s in Britain. 'An injury to one is an injury to all,' they proclaimed. The union was open to all races, to men and women equally, and to skilled and unskilled workers. Only bankers, lawyers, traders in alcoholic liquors, and stockbrokers were excluded. Terence V. Powderly, Stevens's successor, was a pioneer of the concept of 'One Big Union', including all who laboured. This idea later found room enough to grow in Liverpool.

Meantime the Liverpool Union of Stevedores, Labourers and Quay Porters played a large part in relief work for destitute port workers. Neither this organization nor the Knights survived for long, and the Birkenhead union also failed, leaving the Mersey with no dockers' unions at all. The seamen's union formed in 1879 disappeared from the records after 1880.[40]

## The Third Port: Hull's Dockers

The third great estuarial port of the industrial revolution was Hull, whose merchant class had already between the sixteenth and eighteenth centuries built a thriving network of trade with northern Europe, to which was added, in the nineteenth century, intercontinental trade, including imperial raw-material imports and the vast exports of the new industries of West Yorkshire and the Midlands. This growth sparked a huge population explosion – from 28,000 in 1801 to 122,000 in 1871. In the last quarter of the century the population again more than doubled, reaching 240,000 in 1901. By the mid-century the transport trades engaged 23 per cent of the male working population, and the complex of docks, largely augmented by investment from the railway companies – eager to create trade and cargo movements from the industrial heartlands – grew until it eventually extended over 7 miles of the north bank of the Humber, completely dwarfing the pre-industrial harbour at the mouth of the river Hull.

Alongside the docks grew up a range of industries for handling and processing the raw materials which formed a large proportion of Hull's trade: cement, flour-milling, seed-crushing, animal feedstuffs, chemicals, timber storage and processing, warehousing, and paint and dyestuffs. All were characterized by the same heavy manual-labour needs as were required on the docks. To this extent Hull was typical of other ports. Its relative isolation from other urban and industrial centres also left it surrounded by a hinterland of arable, and therefore labour-intensive, agriculture. The Hull employers drew on these sources of casual and seasonal labour, which rose to an immigrant flood during the agricultural depression of the 1870s and onwards. This workforce added to the sizeable migration from Ireland, which became as large, proportionately, as that into London and Liverpool. The Irish often arrived as 'navvies', to dig out the new docks, and stayed on to become dockers.

Although, therefore, Hull provides another classic case of a pool of casual, 'unskilled' labour for the tasks of cargo-handling, the student of the period, Raymond Brown, is as concerned as Lovell in London and Taplin in Liverpool to dispel the stereotypical picture.

> There has usually been a tendency to think of the dockers as a homogeneous group of men with common aims and ideals shaped by their environment of mean living conditions, low and irregular pay, casual employment, and unskilled work which they or anyone else with reasonable strength could do . . . This is much too simplified, and dockers have very properly always regarded themselves as in some measure specialists . . . There was a tendency to emphasise the social rank of, say, a deal carrier as opposed to a lumper or a raff-yard labourer although all were involved in the same sort of work, namely carrying timber. This insistence upon the slightest difference in skill and experience of one group of dock workers as against any other was, of course, to add to the more obvious problems of union organisation.[41]

Hull's skilled workers, who dominated the Trades Council, took their full part in the national nine-hours' movement in the early 1870s. Their example was quickly followed by raff-yard labourers (timber-porters) on the Hull docks, and by dockers in Grimsby, on the south bank of the Humber. Several new unions appeared: Grocers' Assistants, Chemists' Assistants, and Hairdressers, calling for reduced shop hours. The following year, marine firemen on both banks struck for improved pay and conditions, and in the important adjacent agricultural districts trade unionism was spreading rapidly in rhythm with Joseph Arch's national movement. The Hull Labourers' Union and the Hull Dockside Labourers' Union were formed at this time. The Dockside Union drew up rules to limit working hours, which it submitted to the employers along with a wage claim.

A port-wide strike was staged in support of these demands, and during it the quays were 'almost at a standstill'. The strike collapsed at the end of three weeks, after an influx of blacklegs: seamen and farm workers from Lincolnshire. Some of these rural immigrants were subsequently enrolled by the Lincolnshire Labourers' League, which claimed to have 700 members in Hull in 1873.

There were further dock strikes in 1872 and 1877, and again in 1879. Throughout this period, and also through the 1880s, a local Dock Labourers' Union continued in existence. Local unions of seamen and ships' firemen also came and went, and conducted a series of strikes. The year 1881 was climactic in Hull's trade-union history, as wave after wave of strikes swept through both skilled and unskilled trades, and a reconstituted Trades Council now included dockers' and seamen's representatives. Amongst the major strikes was one by the dockers, who demanded that the basic wage of 5*d*. an hour be raised to 6*d*. – another move anticipating the cause of the men of 1889 in London. Despite the records of previous unionism on the docks, this strike threw up an evident need for concerted leadership, and a Hull Labour League was formed, which, as well as assuming responsibility for the conduct of the strike, intended to work for the amalgamation of dockers, seamen and firemen. Although all three groups were on strike together, in the midst of the dispute the seamen announced the formation of their own Hull Seamen's Union. Fighting between dockers, blacklegs and police was followed by serious arson on the dock estates, but after three weeks the dockers returned to work at the old rates, as did the seamen. (A section of the firemen gained a rise of 1*s*.) 'But the real significance of the strike is that the three unions which took part did not break up at its conclusion and they were all existing strongly in 1889.'[42]

The end of the period before the 1889 explosion in Hull was marked by a symbolic occasion when the trade and friendly societies clubbed together in 1886 to provide a farewell dinner to honour the local Tory leader A. K. Rollitt, who had played a role in the labour disputes of the preceding years similar to that of the 'outside' sympathizers in London and Liverpool. The next generation of leaders acknowledged by Hull's labourers were to be quite different. They were no longer outside philanthropists, but national, working-class representatives.

## Political Action: Samuel Plimsoll

We have seen how, during the 1870s and early 1880s, port unions in key areas rose and fell with the state of trade. Echoing G. D. H. Cole, we would claim that checks on the industrial plane tended to stimulate political campaigning and vice versa. This process can be clearly seen at work in the movement to defend seamen from unsafe ships and mercenary shipowners.

Samuel Plimsoll was elected as Liberal MP for Derby in 1868, and from the moment of his adoption he styled himself 'the sailors' friend'. For certain, seamen needed friends in the 1870s. The most elementary safety provisions were not simply neglected, but commonly deliberately flouted in order to profit from insurance claims on lost ships and cargoes. Between 1867 and 1882 more than 1,600 sailors perished in collisions; 519 passengers went down with them. But 31,768 crewmen and 5,468 passengers were drowned from other causes. Between 1874 and 1885, 251 steamers foundered, as did 1,657 sailing ships, with a total death-roll of 12,494. Nearly 40,000 deaths in sixteen years, a large proportion of which were due to negligence, and far too many to criminal exploitation of insurances: here was a classic example of Victorian values, fully operational.

The statistics by themselves are too cruel to be understood. George Howell, the TUC's secretary, illuminates them with a single illustration. Visiting Plimsoll at home one day, he found his host was distraught, collapsed on a couch. He rallied himself, and read aloud to Howell a letter he had just received from a new widow. Her husband's ship had gone down with all hands. The man had expected that this would happen: the ship, he knew, was a 'coffin ship'. His wife had begged him not to go, but he had asked, 'What am I to do? If I refuse, there is no other berth.' He hoped against hope that the hulk might struggle through. But on the night he sailed, he sent home his best clothes, his watch and everything of value that he had been carrying. 'His wife knew it,' wrote Howell. 'It was his farewell . . . She, with her two young children, never saw him again.' Howell was shattered. Silent, he blinked back the tears from his eyes. Thinking that his visitor was wanting in feeling, Plimsoll looked up impatiently and saw the distress written plainly all over him. From that moment, the two men shared a bond of commitment which never wavered.[43]

Plimsoll collected a massive dossier about the deployment of unseaworthy ships; about undermanning, overloading, misloading and over-insurance. In spite of every possible litigation, his charges held water. Plimsoll demanded – and, after making a great fuss, got – a Royal Commission to consider his heartbreaking allegations.

At the Leeds TUC in 1873 copies of Plimsoll's book *Our Seamen* were distributed, and George Howell was invited to organize a 'workmen's committee' to lobby for the establishment of an appopriate inquiry.[44] Howell secured the support of Lord Shaftesbury and other peers, and that of his fellow trade unionist George Odger. Behind this team, say the Webbs, he enlisted 'practically the whole force of the trade union movement'.[45] Throughout 1873 a sustained campaign of mass meetings spread throughout the country, from Newcastle-upon-Tyne down to Plymouth, and from Cardiff to Greenock. All major ports were covered, as well as dozens of lesser centres. A great meeting took place in Whitby. The main cities held large rallies. A pamphlet, *Ship Ahoy!*, was distributed in huge numbers. In 1873 the Royal Commission was set up, and it reported in August the following year. Meanwhile, Plimsoll introduced Bills for a Merchant Shipping Survey in 1873, and again in 1874. Both were defeated. After the General Election of 1874, a third Bill was brought in in 1875, only to be abandoned in a great parliamentary scene. At last, in 1876, the Merchant Shipping Act made it through to the statute book. Without doubt, that agitation had its influence on waterfront trade unions. The Webbs record that 'the powerful Shipping Trades Council of Liverpool . . . which played an important part in Samuel Plimsoll's agitation . . . was broken up in 1880 by [a] quarrel' between constituent unions.[46]

Soon, however, trade-union political campaigning was to take on new, direct forms, which would ultimately transform the relationships between philanthropists and their intended beneficiaries. This began during the upsurge of waterfront unions but unlike them political action on behalf of waterfront workers could not be restrained by downturns in the economy, or by the retreat or even collapse of trade-union organizations. Indeed, it came to a head during the middle years of the decade, while such unions as survived along the docks were in greater trouble.

## The Quarries Also Stir

Distanced from the ports, but connected with them by their trade, was another rugged group of workers in the great slate mines of Wales. Events during the 1870s and 1880s led them eventually to become the core of the Transport and General Workers' Union in North Wales in 1923. How did they embark on such a road?

The North Wales Quarrymen's Union was founded in 1874. The industry had enjoyed a boom until 1879, and membership reached 8,000 out of a possible 14,000.[47] Powerful bonds united the communities of this region, who maintained the Welsh language and had no use for

English either in their work or in their union meetings.[48] Immigration was negligible in statistical terms, with the result that social organization was close and homogeneous. (Few Irish had settled in North Wales, despite its nearness; some English professionals joined the town populations, but usually these were people apart, maintaining their own culture and identity.)

The quarries belonged to the super-rich landowners. Lord Penrhyn ensconced himself in a massive castle, as if he were a feudal baron. He employed 2,500 men in Bethesda, and as late as 1899 the Penrhyn quarries earned him a profit of £133,000, which he added to his rental income of between £60,000 and £70,000. In 1869 George William Duff Assheton-Smith inherited 36,000 acres and the Dinorwic quarries, which brought him more than his annual rental income of £42,000.[49]

The intermediaries who managed the quarries, however, were often English. The men distrusted them, the more so because many could not speak Welsh, and lacked all practical skills.

Slate-quarrying was a Welsh-speaking industry . . . consequently the whole terminology of the craft was Welsh[50] and it seemed impossible to the men that it could be practised in English. John Williams, a quarryman, recalled in 1942 how an English manager visiting his quarry saw a man smoking, and asked, 'Do you allow this idleness?' The accompanying agent explained that the man was, in fact, studying the rock as well as smoking. This episode, concluded Williams, proved that 'a quarry cannot be worked in English'.[51] A hundred years earlier, in the 1840s, a David Jones had sung:

> In workplaces here in Wales
> See Englishmen interfering;
> But you must get Welshmen to break the stone,
> For the rock does not understand English.[52]

'The English element', explained Robert Parry to the annual conference of the union in May 1882, 'was . . . very damaging to the success of the quarrymen.'[53] Few present would not have nodded in agreement.[54, 55]

In 1874 the mock-baronial owners and their imported managers confronted an untried trade union which, however, could rely on two advantages – the temporary boom in trade, and the resources of a close community culture as well as the bonds of class. Assheton-Smith's managers at Dinorwic tried to crush the new organization in April by refusing work to those of its members who refused to resign. Only eleven men chose this option; 2,200 loyal unionists were locked out. Within five weeks they had won their point. The contagion spread next to the workers in the Bethesda quarries of Lord Penrhyn who, having already given support to their brethren in Dinorwic, went on to call for higher wages themselves, together with revisions in their contracts. The dispute was a bitter one, but most of the union's programme was conceded in September. However, the local managers (those Englishmen) flouted the new terms, provoking a fresh strike. Three managers were dismissed and replaced. This was an astonishing demonstration of the union's power. It was in the aftermath of the drama that the union's membership rose to more than 8,000 in 1878.

The gains were shortlived. The boom gave way to a slump in the following year: it lasted until the late 1890s, and 'the union came perilously close to extinction.'[56] Membership slid to under 3,500. But it survived, and the triumph of 1874 had created an indelible trade-union tradition on which to draw in the turbulent years which lay ahead.

## III

## *Out Into the Open*

The sum of these experiences seems perfectly clear. Port labour was not easy to organize, but it operated under conditions which made trade unionism seem necessary to increasing numbers of workers. Other groups of allegedly 'unskilled' people shared this dilemma. As the first unions formed ranks, they commonly encountered fierce opposition from employers. That opposition led the dockers, and many other groups in the 1870s, into much more frequent strikes, which were used as a means of developing organization. The 1870s witnessed the first of a series of 'strike waves' which accompanied – indeed promoted – the spread of trade unionism to wider and wider sections of the working class right through to the 1920s. An early statistician of strikes wrote in 1880 of strikes as 'a disease, and a very grave disease [which] shows no sign of having run its course', whilst George Howell, reviewing the 1870s, spoke of 'a period of strike epidemics'.[57]

Trade upturns made association a practical option, increasingly inevitable. Downturns sometimes smashed, and always greatly enfeebled, the new associations, just as they commonly eroded union support in other industries and trades. Employers had not yet learned to live with organized labour. But as the idea took hold, trade unionism became a continuing commitment, more and more rooted among workers even when it was difficult, if not impossible, to proclaim it openly. This is why the semi-clandestine Knights of Labour put out its links in the Liverpool docks, having traversed the Atlantic to do so. By the late 1880s the Knights had discarded secrecy in America and were leading mass struggles. And at that point in Britain, the hour of new unionism, out in the open and defiant, had finally come.

# Notes

1  We shall analyse the composition of the membership fully in vol. II. It is indicative of the immense structural changes through which the TGWU has lived that in December 1986 the membership of its Docks, Waterways and Fishing Trade Group had shrunk to just 28,000 out of a total of 1.4 million.

2  Writing in 1926, while the TGWU was consolidating its merged ranks, and trying to cope with the tumult of the General Strike, Kondratieff stimulated a very active debate. But his diagnosis of capitalism's trajectory did not commend him to Soviet leaders. He was arrested in 1930 and figured in the show trial of the mythical Peasant Labour Party. Subsequently he was deployed as a 'witness' in the equally rigged trial of the Menshevik 'conspiracy' a year later. He was finally rehabilitated in 1987.

3  N. D. Kondratieff, 'The Long Waves in Economic Life', *Lloyds Bank Review* no. 129, (1978), pp. 41 and 42.

4  Michael Barratt Brown, *What Economics is About* (Weidenfeld and Nicolson, 1970), pp. 170–1.

5  There is an extensive discussion among economists about 'long waves'. See in particular Ernest Mandel, *Long Waves of Capitalist Development* (Cambridge University Press, 1980), and the same author's *The Second Slump* (New Left Books, 1978). But although the empirical evidence for the existence of long waves is very strong, it is much more difficult to explain them satisfactorily. The most important recent attempt to do so is to be found in Joshua Goldstein, *Long Cycles* (Yale University Press, 1988). This provides a comprehensive summary of the debate, together with a careful analysis of the evidence. See also James E. Cronin, 'Stages, Cycles and Insurgencies: The Economics of Unrest', in T. Hopkins and I. Wallerstein (eds), *Processes of the World System* (Sage, 1980), where the author identifies the Kondratieff long wave as an influence upon those patterns of labour unrest in Britain with which we shall be concerned throughout this book. The three great strike waves of pre-war Britain occurred in 1871–3, 1889–90 and 1911–13.

6  Henry Mayhew, *Mayhew's London: Selections from London Labour and the London Poor*, ed. Peter Quennell (Pilot Press, 1949), pp. 544–5.

7  H. J. Dyos and D. H. Aldcroft, *British Transport: An Economic Survey from the Seventeenth Century to the Twentieth* (Leicester University Press, 1969), pp. 247–55.

8  Mayhew, *Mayhew's London*, pp. 545–7. Dennis Mayhew, coincidentally a namesake of the London chronicler, joined the Hull dock labour force in 1951, a century after Henry Mayhew wrote. He became a member of the unofficial Port Workers' Committees on the Hull docks in the 1950s and 1960s, and a student in Hull day-release extra-mural classes. When he read this chapter for us, he commented that the nineteenth-century Mayhew's description of the 'call-on' could readily have been taken as a description of the scene on Hull's docks in the 1950s.

9  Ibid.

10  Ben Tillett, *A Brief History of the Dockers' Union* (Twentieth Century Press, 1910), p. 89.

11  Ibid., p. 12.

12  Beatrice Webb, Diary, May 1887, in *My Apprenticeship*, vol. II (Penguin, 1938), p. 345.

13  Ibid., p. 345.

14  Ibid., p. 486.

15  W. J. Fishman, *East End, 1888* (Duckworth, 1988), p. 16.

16  Ibid.

17  James Sexton, *Sir James Sexton, Agitator: the Life of the Dockers' MP* (Faber and Faber, 1936), pp. 74–6. It is a further indication of the neglect of safety standards at that time that winch-driving, regarded by a twentieth-century docker as a highly responsible and adult post, should then have been 'a lad's job'.

18  Henry Pelling, *A History of British Trade Unionism* (Penguin, 1963), p. 76.

19  The figures are given in G. D. H. Cole, *An Introduction to Trade Unionism* (Allen and Unwin, 1953), appendix 1, p. 289. The source is not disclosed, and all other historians commence comparable statistical series in the 1890s. '1892 is the first year adequately covered by official statistics of trade union membership' (H. A. Clegg, Alan Fox and A. F. Thompson, *A History of British Trade Unions since 1889*, vol. I: *1889–1910* (Oxford University Press, 1964), p. 1). Pelling, *History of British Trade Unionism*, p. 261, commences his series with the 1893 membership of 1,559,000. These statistics were first compiled following the appointment of John Burnett as Labour correspondent to the Board of Trade in 1886 – itself a highly significant moment, since he had been the president of the Nine-hours' League, and a leading member of his Tyneside branch of the Amalgamated Society of Engineers, who had published an account of the nine-hours' strike in that region. In 1875 he was elected general secretary of the ASE, on the death of William Allen. He was promoted to chief Labour correspondent at the Board of Trade when it established its Labour Department in 1893 (see Sydney and Beatrice Webb, *The History of Trade Unionism* (1894; WEA edn, 1912), p. 300).

20  Histories consulted include Pelling, *History of British Trade Unionism*; Clegg, Fox and Thompson, *History of British Trade Unions since 1889*, vol. I; Webb, *History of Trade Unionism*; G. D. H. Cole, *A Short History of the British Working Class Movement*, vol. III (Allen and Unwin, 1927).

21  See John Lovell, *Stevedores and Dockers: a Study of Trade Unionism in the Port of London, 1870–1914* (Macmillan, 1969); E. L. Taplin, *Liverpool Dockers and Seamen, 1870–1890* (University of Hull, 1974); Raymond Brown, *Waterfront Organisation in Hull, 1870–1900* (University of Hull, 1972). The account of the three ports' historics through the pre-1889 years presented here draws heavily on these three studies.

22  Refrigeration was introduced by Sir Alfred Haslam of Derby in 1880 to bring mutton from Australia and New Zealand. It caught on very quickly. By the time of the First World War there were more than 200 insulated steamers in the British merchant fleet alone. (See Adam Kirkaldy and A. D. Evans, *The History and Economics of Transport* (Pitman, 1927), pp. 309ff.)

23 Henry Mayhew, *London Labour and the London Poor*, vol. III; cited in Gordon Phillips and Noel Whiteside, *Casual Labour: The Unemployment Question in the Port Transport Industry, 1880–1970* (Oxford University Press, 1985), p. 22.

24 Weston lives on as the partner addressed by Marx in his famous pamphlet *Wage-Labour and Capital*, prepared during the heyday of the International Working Men's Association.

25 See Henry Collins, 'The English Branches of the First International', in Asa Briggs and John Saville (eds), *Essays in Labour History* (Macmillan, 1960), pp. 247ff. See also Henry Collins and C. Abramsky, *Karl Marx and the British Labour Movement* (Macmillan, 1965).

26 'The central government of the League must have found itself in a situation similar to that described by James Sexton . . . In his autobiography he recounts how when he took over the leadership of the Liverpool union in 1893, he found himself at the head of what was virtually a federation of "almost innumerable small clubs and societies all hostile to each other" ' (Lovell, *Stevedores and Dockers*, p. 71).

27 Ibid., p. 91.

28 Harry Gosling, *Up and Down Stream* (Methuen, 1927), p. 1.

29 Ibid., p. 16.

30 Ibid., pp. 17–18.

31 Ibid.

32 Ibid., pp. 18–19.

33 Ibid., p. 19.

34 Lovell, *Stevedores and Dockers*, p. 73.

35 Taplin, *Liverpool Dockers and Seamen*.

36 Ibid., p. 10.

37 Ibid., pp. 19–20. See also entries for both men in J. M. Bellamy and J. Saville (eds), *Dictionary of Labour Biography*, vol. II (Macmillan, 1974).

38 Taplin, *Liverpool Dockers and Seamen*, pp. 10–11. See also P. J. Waller, *Democracy and Sectarianism: A Political and Social History of Liverpool, 1868–1939* (Liverpool University Press, 1981), pp. 509–10 and 511.

39 They were called the Birkenhead Amalgamated Dock Labourers' Union and Benefit Society, and the Liverpool Union of Stevedores, Labourers and Quay Porters.

40 The Liverpool unions of this period do not seem, even in their heyday, to have achieved mass membership. The Liverpool stevedores' and dockers' union's best year was 1881 when its membership was a mere 403 (Eric Taplin, *The Dockers' Union: A Study of the National Union of Dock Labourers, 1889–1922* (Leicester University Press, 1986), p. 26.)

41 Raymond Brown, *Waterfront Organisation in Hull*, pp. 8–9.

42 Ibid., p. 32.

43 See George Howell, *Labour Legislation, Labour Movements, and Labour Leaders* (Fisher Unwin, 1905), p. 266.

44 Ibid., chapter XVIII.

45 Webb, *History of Trade Unionism*, p. 370.

46 Ibid., p. 354.

47 R. Merfyn Jones, *The North Wales Quarrymen, 1874–1922* (University of Wales, 1981), p. 106.

48 Ibid., pp. 57ff.
49 Ibid., pp. 11–12.
50 Some words were originally English, for example *rybelwrs*, derived from 'rubbelers'; and some English terms were used – the classification of slate sizes according to the noble hierarchy (e.g. duchesses) – but most quarry words were Welsh. For a glossary see Emyr Jones, *Canrif y Chwarelwr* (Gwasg Gee, 1963).
51 John Williams, 'Atgofion chwarelwr', *Y Llenor* (winter 1942), pp. 129–35.
52 British Museum, *Welsh Songs 1767–1870* (n.d.), p. 69.
53 *Y Genedl Gymreig*, 24 May 1882.
54 The feeling was mutual: 'these Welshmen', wrote E. A. Young in 1900, 'are so childish and ignorant'.
55 R. Merfyn Jones, 'Y chwarelwyr: the slate quarrymen of North Wales', in Raphael Samuel (ed.), *Miners, Quarrymen and Saltworkers* (Routledge and Kegan Paul, 1977), pp. 123–4.
56 Jones, *The North Wales Quarrymen*, p. 107.
57 James E. Cronin, 'Strikes and Power in Britain, 1870–1920', in Leopold H. Haimson and Charles Tilly (eds), *Strikes, Wars and Revolutions in an International Perspective* (Cambridge University Press, 1989), pp. 80–1.

The statistician was G. P. Bevan, whose study for the Royal Statistical Society in March 1880 included tabular data indicating a tenfold increase in numbers of strikes between 1870 and 1872, which was sustained through most of the following years to 1879 (ibid., p. 82). Cronin suggests that 'beneath the considerable variation over time in the incidence and scale of strikes there was a fundamental continuity to strike movements before 1914. What united these several outbursts of conflict was a broad effort to enrol ever larger sections of the workforce into stable unions. This *de facto* objective seems, in retrospect, to have overshadowed issues of wages, hours, working conditions, and job control, however important these may have been at the moment or in specific conditions . . . the early 1870s probably were years when strikes became the dominant form of workers' collective activity' (ibid., pp. 81–3). What follows in our subsequent chapters certainly upholds this thesis.

# 2

# The New Socialists, and the Way to a New Unionism

## I

### *Educating a Militant*

Tom Mann was twenty-four years old in 1880.[1] His father was a colliery clerk at the Victoria pit near Coventry, and at the age of nine Tom went to work down the mine. Four years later, a fire forced the permanent closure of the pit, and the family was compelled to move to Birmingham in search of work. There, when he was fifteen, Tom was apprenticed to a firm of toolmakers. His chosen new vocation entailed a standard sixty-hour, six-day week, but 'frequently we were called upon to work overtime, usually two hours of an evening.'[2] A year later, in 1871, the engineers' 'society' negotiated the establishment of a nine-hour day.[3] For Tom this was a true liberation. Characteristically, he began to use his new free time to gain some access to the world of letters, from which he had been kept apart: 'Three evenings a week for five years I attended classes . . . In addition I attended a Bible class one evening a week.'[4]

Tom Mann was growing up to be a skilled man, but also, thanks to the 'society', an educated man. He was never to forget that, in the agitation for shorter hours, the trade union had given him the key to learning. Younger children were more fortunate than the teenagers of Tom's generation: they were able to benefit from compulsory, if minimal, schooling as a result of the 1870 Elementary Education Act. Through the last decades of the nineteenth century, therefore, literate working people were becoming more and more common, and it is unsurprising that they began to find interesting things to read.[5] Tom Mann read Henry George,[6] took keenly to his message about land reform and briefly found employment in the United States in 1883 while hoping to meet fellow disciples.[7] On returning to London he graduated from George's radical influence to that of the economic historian Thorold Rogers, whose *Six Centuries of Work and Wages* gave powerful historical authority for the idea of an eight-hour working day: 'The artisan who is demanding at this time an eight hours' day in the building trades is simply striving to recover what his ancestor worked for four or five centuries ago'.[8] And, he asked, were not the cathedrals better built than modern industrial towns?

In 1884 it was a short step from the study of Thorold Rogers to that of Karl Marx, who had pointed out that new inventions were not deployed in order to save the time of working people. A searing chapter on the length of the working day appears in *Capital*.[9] 'A horse . . . can only work from day to day, eight hours', Marx insists, but machinery ensures that there is a continuously applied pressure to lengthen the working day for people. The longer machines are operated, the sooner their investment costs can be recovered.[10] It was not strange that this message gripped Tom Mann, and soon enrolled him as a reader of *Justice*, the journal of the new Marxian Social Democratic Federation (SDF), whose Battersea branch Mann quickly joined.[11] John Burns, then also a colleague in the ASE, belonged to the same branch. Among the regular speakers at Battersea Park Gates and other local meeting places were Henry Mayers Hyndman and H. H. Champion. Hyndman, a wealthy stockbroker, cut an imposing and even lordly figure, resplendent in top hat and whiskers. He was the first well-known English publicist to popularize some of Marx's ideas although he did not improve his stock with the master by plagiarizing him without acknowledgement.[12] Champion was formerly an artillery officer, and the proprietor of a print-shop. 'He approved', wrote Mann in his *Memoirs*, 'my ardent advocacy of the eight-hour day, and urged me to write a pamphlet on the subject which he would print'.[13]

This was the first blow in a campaign which was to lead the doctrinaires of the socialist movement into a direct relationship with trade unionists, and with many thousands of working people as yet unorganized.

## *'Isms' and Schisms*

The socialists were not a united force. All their groups fizzed with argument, and not only on matters of high theory. When Tom Mann outlined his ideas about the eight-hour day at the Battersea SDF branch, he met vigorous opposition from his friend Burns, who believed that the 'time had long passed for such trivial reforms'; it would be a better notion, thought Burns, 'to seize the whole of the means of production and wipe out the capitalists altogether'.[14] Battersea plumped overwhelmingly for the Burns prospectus. Yet not many years were to pass before both groups in this controversy were working side by side in the struggle for the very 'palliatives' that Tom Mann was pursuing.

At the end of 1884 William Morris, the most famous member of the SDF, led a breakaway Socialist League opposed to electoral dealing.[15] Some of the members of this distinguished group opposed all parliamentary action on principle, while others were concerned only to build sufficient strength to act independently, eschewing compromises and pacts with established political parties. With Morris went Eleanor Marx, the daughter of Karl, who was to play a major part in the upsurge of trade unionism.[16] She was soon to part company with the Socialist League, however.

Remaining with the parent body was a key group of young workers: Harry Quelch, who was to become a leader of the dock workers on London's South Bank;[17] Will Thorne, the gasworker who was tutored by Eleanor Marx in reading and writing;[18] James MacDonald, who was to become secretary of the London Trades Council. George Lansbury joined in 1892; he was to become leader of the Labour Party in the early 1930s. A later recruit was Ernest Bevin.

## Unions and the Vote

In Britain in 1880 the large majority of adults, and all women, were voteless; the suffrage extended to less than 3 million men only.[19] A man in middle years might have childhood memories of the People's Charter; no one younger could recall those days, but all had spent their lives under a political system in which voting was a middle-class perquisite, shared by only a minority of labour 'aristocrats'.

From the beginning of the 1880s, the argument for independent political organization of the working-class movement began to gather force and influence. Friedrich Engels drafted a series of articles which appeared in the *Labour Standard* in 1881.[20] Even the restricted extension of the franchise of 1867, which added some 1 million male voters to the electoral register, mostly in urban constituencies, had been inadequately grasped by the trade unions, wrote Engels. Now, with a mounting agitation for wider democracy throughout the civilized world, it was clear that 'in England, where the industrial and agricultural working class forms the immense majority of the people, democracy means the dominion of the working class, neither more nor less.'[21]

But while other socialists were either impatient or contemptuous of the unions, for Engels they were the very foundation of any alternative politics. Whilst consistently arguing for a socialist goal ('there is no real redemption for the working class until it becomes the owner of all the means of work'), he did not share the view of such converts as Burns that all lesser objectives were merely 'palliatives'. On the contrary, he argued that without trade-union action 'the labourer does not even receive what is due to him according to the rules of the wages system. It is only with the fear of the Trade Unions before his eyes that the capitalist can be made to part with the full market value of his labourer's power.'[22]

Even with the 1867 electoral rules, Engels believed it quite possible to secure the election of forty or fifty working-class Members of Parliament. Instead, development was very slow, and those Labour Members who were elected up to this time invariably enjoyed the patronage of the Liberal Party.[23] The reason for this was more to do with arithmetic than pessimism, because the absolute numbers of workers with votes mattered less in Britain than their distribution in the wider population. (We return to this question in chapter 7.) It was precisely in that 'pool of stagnant misery', London's East End, that Engels's followers were to arouse a real challenge to this state of affairs. And this particular political response was to depend on the effort to extend trade-union powers to the 'numberless' trades outside their remit. Of course, the further extension of the vote in 1884 imposed its own discipline on the established parties. Now they had to pay attention to all kinds of people whose wishes might never have been given a thought in earlier days. That is why, in Eric Hobsbawm's judgement, 'the 1880s and 1890s, far more than the earlier years, are the real heyday of "Liberal–Labourism" '.[24]

For the Liberal Party, these were difficult times. They needed the votes of working people newly enfranchised, but their constituency included big employers who had no desire to see trade unions forming among the dispossessed. Around these great fish were many minnows, such as the small shopkeepers who feared and detested the uppity lower ranks.

## II

## *Labour and the Liberals*

In the beginning of this phase, however, these polarities were by no means clear to those who were to suffer them. While the old parties were seeking to attract supporters among recently enfranchised voters, so the newly awoken spirits of formerly excluded people were, at first, often disposed to look for support among existing establishments. A notable example was provided by Ben Tillett, who, when he set out to create a trade union among his tea coopers on the London docks, actively sought assistance from prominent Liberals. We shall turn to this episode in chapter 3. Tillett's 'conversion' to socialism was to follow the dramatic lessons of the experience through which he lived, and it was to become so influential that he has often since been represented as a born revolutionary. But of course his politics were not congenital: he grew into them,[25] and a more natural evolution than that which followed his exploration of the scope and limits of liberal radicalism could hardly be found in East London during the late 1880s. Tillett learned new ideas quickly. Others were not so quick to adapt.

Standing on the brink of a wider franchise on the eve of the 1884 Act, the infant workers' movement faced a natural division. There were those who sought to increase their influence by cultivating Liberal sponsorship or support; others, meanwhile, with Engels, were looking for means of gathering independent scope, without which it would be impossible to go beyond partial, ameliorative demands to the 'abolition of the wages system itself'.

## The Political Economy of Labour: Shorter Hours

For this second group, no demand could possibly have greater relevance than the simple call for the reduction of working time. Marx, writing decades earlier, had celebrated the victory of the ten-hours' movement in 1848 as the 'first great victory of the political economy of labour over the political economy of capital'.[26] In another work which was not to see the light of day until many years after his death, he had written: 'the true economy is economy of labour time'.[27] Quite obviously, this had direct appeal for the exploited wage-slaves who toiled for wretchedly long hours in the sweatshops of London. The great release felt by Tom Mann and his brother engineers with the nine-hours' victory could represent, for all these abject victims of Victorian values, a tremendous promise of freedom. At the same time, with the expansion of the franchise, there could be no proposal more calculated to prise apart likely independent Labour voters from the long hegemony of the Liberal Party. Liberal capitalists might be willing to accept many things, but most of them were hardly enthusiastic for a diminution of the hours of work. Like their Conservative colleagues, they had laid out good money on machines and plant, and they wanted to get it back quickly. Shortening the burden of labour would not help this. By mobilizing and demonstrating for an eight-hour day, Tom Mann and his colleagues were simultaneously recruiting their army, and beginning to separate it from the adversary.

This campaign was to grow continuously, and the demand for a legal restriction of hours, joined to that for a statutory minimum wage, was to attract widespread and committed support.[28] By the end of the decade it had become an international commitment, and the platform of the original May Day demonstrations.[29]

But these years were not marked only by the extension of the franchise, and a concomitant political agitation. The new voters were not as numerous as all that, and even by the end of the century, the total electorate numbered only a little more than 6.7 million. The vote was extended to 58 per cent of adult males, but they made up only 27 per cent of the adult population. Certainly the working class could now find space in the parliamentary struggle, although there were large and intractable obstacles.

Meanwhile, the position of old-style trade unionism was less than rosy. A slight economic upturn followed the slump at the end of the 1870s, but by 1884 shipbuilding was in deep crisis and the Boilermakers' Society reported widespread destitution in the yards.

Two years later, reported the Webbs, James Mawdsley of the Lancashire Cotton Spinners' Union told an International Congress that workers in Britain were suffering great privation:

> Wages had fallen, and there was a great number of unemployed . . . Flax mills were being closed every day . . . all the building trades were in a bad position . . . iron foundries were in difficulties, and one third of the shipwrights were without work . . . Steam engine makers were also slack . . . the depression affecting the great leading trades was felt in a thousand and one occupations.[30]

Mawdsley, a confirmed moderate, felt that there was no way out within the present state of society:

> He did not understand their socialism; he had not studied it as perhaps he ought to have done. The workmen of England were not so advanced as the workmen of the Continent. Nevertheless they, at least, possessed one clear conception: they realised that the actual producers did not obtain their share of the wealth they created.[31]

Yet official trade unionism, squeezed between declining resources and expanding obligations, seemed less and less credible as an effective opposition, let alone defence. The old leaders were intellectually in thrall not only to the established parties, but, more damagingly, to *laissez-faire* philosophy. (There were among them many Liberals, together with not a few Conservatives. Of course, *laissez-faire* as a philosophy was easy to endorse, but as a practice it might often give trouble to a Labour representative.) Neither on the political nor on the industrial plane could this hold out any reasonable prospects of advance for the poorest workers in the sweated trades.[32]

## Criticizing the Old Unions

For the unorganized workers, this framework was distinctly unappealing. But even for the organized it was a stimulus to dissent and, in the end, rebellion. After all, Burns and Mann, who were both uninhibited critics of the old trade-union order, were themselves products of the

Amalgamated Society of Engineers, and among the new generation of craftsmen there were numerous audacious spirits who found it easy to respond to such clarion appeals as this justly famous outcry from Tom Mann:

> How long, how long, will you be content with the present half-hearted policy of your Unions? I readily grant that good work has been done in the past by the Unions, but, in Heaven's name, what good purpose are they serving now? All of them have large numbers out of employment even when their particular trade is busy. None of the important societies have any policy other than that of endeavouring to keep wages from falling. The true Unionist policy of *aggression* seems entirely lost sight of: in fact the average Unionist of today is a man with a fossilised intellect, either hopelessly apathetic, or supporting a policy that plays directly into the hands of the capitalist exploiter . . . I take my share of the work of the Trade Union to which I belong: but I candidly confess that unless it shows more vigour at the present time [1886], I shall be compelled to take the view – against my will – that to continue to spend time over the ordinary squabble-investigating, do-nothing, policy will be an unjustifiable waste of one's energies. I am sure there are thousands of others in my state of mind.[33]

John Burns, speaking from within the same craft union, developed a specific criticism of the mutual insurance methods of the old unions. Writing in *Justice* in 1887, he said:

> constituted as it is Unionism carries within itself the source of its own dissolution . . . Their reckless assumption of the duties and responsibilities that only the State or whole community can discharge, in the nature of sick and super-annuation benefits, at the instance of the middle class, is crushing out the larger Unions by taxing their members to an unbearable extent. This so cripples them that the fear of being unable to discharge their friendly society liabilities often makes them submit to encroachments by the masters without protest. The result of this is that all of them have ceased to be Unions for maintaining the rights of labour, and have degenerated into mere middle and upper class rate-reducing institutions.[34]

## Mobilizing the Unemployed

The socialists had an analysis of economic crisis and of the debility of working-class institutions, but they had more: they were full of youthful fire and audacity. A major agitation against unemployment was set in motion.

London during the winter of 1885–6 was so cold that in February 1886 outdoor work became nearly impossible. The depression had already struck home, and this was now joined by bitter weather, driving distress in the docks and on the building sites beyond endurance. Throughout East London, hunger ruled. On 8 February a rally against unemployment, called by the Fair Trade League, was the subject of organized heckling by the SDF, who led part of the crowd out of Trafalgar Square in protest at Tory manipulation of the issue of jobs. On the way to Hyde Park, some clubmen in Pall Mall jeered at the demonstrators, who replied with a volley of stones. Soon a full-scale riot was raging through the West End, with breakages everywhere and sporadic looting of shops. The SDF leaders realized that things were beyond control, and they withdrew. But the angry crowd did not disband, and looting began in earnest. Carriages were overturned in Hyde Park, and their owners were levied a toll in money and jewels.

The result was a mood of hysteria among the well-to-do. Fog on ensuing days only intensified the jitters. 'Not since 1832', writes Gareth Stedman Jones in a graphic account of this turmoil, 'had private property in London been so disturbed'.[35]

Burns was indicted for sedition, and his answer to the charge, *The Man with the Red Flag* (published as a penny tract), served only to widen his influence.[36] By 13 November 1887 the unemployed were ready to join with the radical left in a huge rumpus in Trafalgar Square, and both Burns and his parliamentary comrade Cunninghame Graham were sent to prison for six weeks for breaking through a police cordon.[37] Far from discouraging his supporters, this punishment did not prevent them from electing Burns to the London County Council in January 1889.

As this agitation developed, it was accompanied by new political initiatives. In 1886 the Trades Union Congress had resolved to respond to the post-reform successes of 1885 by founding a Labour Electoral Committee, even while seeking not to break its protective association with the Liberal Party. George Howell claimed sixty-nine beneficial statutes between 1868 and 1889, enacted as a result of the interactions between Labour and the established parties.[38] The following year the committee changed its name, styling itself 'Association', and claiming to emulate the Irish in becoming the 'centre of the National Labour Party'.[39] H. H. Champion, tired of the wrangles in the SDF, sought to use this association for more independent purposes and was soon joined by Burns and Mann, and then by Eleanor Marx and her husband Edward Aveling after their secession from the Socialist League. Champion began to publish a newspaper called the *Labour Elector*, which became the voice of the eight-hours' movement.[40] Soon, after heavy intervention from the dominant Liberal faction of the Labour Electoral Association had failed to dissuade Keir Hardie from contesting the Mid-Lanark by-election against a Liberal barrister, Champion's journal was to provide the core of a campaign not only for Hardie himself (he lost very damagingly) but for the principle of truly *independent* Labour representation.[41]

## The Pedagogy of the Oppressed

The pedagogy of this campaign was direct and practical. It dealt in simple issues, and it kept on about them. For example, in the course of an agitation to enforce a law restricting juvenile hours to seventy-four per week, a famous scandal about conditions of work came to light in the Northwich alkali plant of Brunner, Mond and Co. 'The head of the firm was a Member of Parliament, being reported to be an advanced Radical and a keen sympathiser with the poor'.[42] The *Labour Elector* published a succession of devastating exposures of appalling standards. Handling red-hot lime for twelve hours at a stretch using only wheelbarrows; exposure to alkaline poisoning which affected the hair, blackened the gums and caused the teeth to fall out; gassing by soda fumes: a range of such dreadful practices turned out to be 'normal' operating standards in this enlightened firm which yielded a 49 per cent dividend to its philanthropic shareholders.

The mechanics worked a customary nine-hour day; but the most vulnerable workers – those who actually manufactured the most noxious substances – found themselves not only doing regular twelve-hour shifts, but also reporting seven days a week. Champion duly recorded these facts, and was promptly served with a writ for libel which could have destroyed his newspaper. He refused to withdraw and resolutely carried on his offensive, while Tom Mann stepped in to secure the evidence to answer a lawsuit. Mann's account is still richly appropriate to everyone who wishes to understand the resource and courage of those who had taken up the fight for honest trade unionism:

I decided to apply for a job as labourer, and dressed the part. Since caution was necessary, I adopted the name of 'Joe Miller'. I learned the customary time and place of taking on, etc., and applied. The second morning I was started as a general labourer, and put with a gang emptying trucks of slack. I was not on the 'process' but on general works, so I was liable to be moved about to any rough job; also, I had meal hours. I was 'posted' as to what departments to take stock of, etc., and in about ten days I had all the confirmatory detail required. Just at this time a public meeting was advertised a few miles distant chiefly political in character, really to serve the political interests of the head of the firm. I had now left the firm as an employee, and attended the meeting where eulogies of the firm were indulged in largely. When question time came I took part in a manner that caused some consternation; but very few knew me by sight, and not more than two knew me by my own name. Suffice it to say that in a few months all legal proceedings against the *Labour Elector* were suspended, and the eight-hour day was established at the works of Messers. Brunner, Mond & Co., Cheshire.[43]

This was some achievement, and it had a sequel. A few weeks after the inauguration of the eight-hour day, Mann received an invitation to attend a meeting to be held by the employees of the firm in a schoolroom adjacent to the works.

The meeting was to celebrate the inauguaration of the eight-hour day, which had resulted in starting one-third more men. The letter inviting my attendance referred to various other advantages of the change, now that the men had some leisure. I accepted gladly, and I duly presented myself at the committee room a little while before the appointed hour. Not more than one on that committee had an inkling that the 'Joe Miller' who had taken part in the public meeting of some weeks earlier, and who had made comments upon the firm, was really Tom Mann. One member of the committee was a trade union official who, doubtless, knew me by reputation; but he had never seen me before except at the public meeting previously referred to, and he had not appreciated the part I had taken in it. His astonishment when he realized that 'Joe Miller' was none other than Tom Mann was so pronounced that it took him some time to get over it.[44]

But all these initiatives, the exposés, the thousands of meetings, the demonstrations and police charges, the pamphlets and the electoral thrusts, all were building a new kind of awareness, a new questioning, and an unprecedented courage. Masses of people, toiling in dank sweatshops and living in sunless slums, were only waiting for a glimpse of hope.

The first great flash in London was lit in Bow, at Bryant and May's match factory.[45] Here the workers, most of them very young women, finally rose up against dreadful health risks and poverty wages. In June 1888, at a Fabian meeting called to discuss female labour with Clementine Black, the first woman to join the factory inspectors, H. H. Champion produced the first spark. Lighting his pipe at the end of the lecture, he flourished the match. Were the Fabians aware of Bryant and May's dividends? These ran at 20 per cent. Bryant and May were also, of course, strong supporters of the Liberal Party.[46] Their employees could not vote, and neither were their dividends very large:

Girls who filled the coils were paid a shilling for one hundred coils, those who cut the matches down got twopence-three-farthings the 'duck' [three gross of small boxes or two-and-a-half gross large]. The wax taper makers earned about ten or twelve shillings a week. Wax box fillers got five shillings per hundred frames, and packers got one and ninepence per hundred gross of boxes wrapped.

These wages were low enough, but the girls complained that they rarely saw the whole of their money. You could be fined for dropping matches, fined for answering back, fined for having dirty feet, fined for leaving burnt matches on a bench. The fines varied from threepence to a shilling. The girls engaged in making the phosphorus matches complained less about the fines than of the risk of getting what they called 'phossy-jaw'. This was a necrosis of the jaw which often set in because the girls' hands became infected with phosphorus through handling the freshly made matches. Phosphorus got on to the benches, and as the girls brought their dinner to work and had nowhere to eat it except the workrooms, the food itself was often contaminated.[47]

Phosphorus poisoning creates terrible debility, sometimes rotting the entire lower face. 'Bryant & May admitted that between 1880 and 1900, 51 employees contracted the disease and nine died from it.'[48]

But the immediate grievance of the girls was very different. There are some grounds for believing that, contrary to the report of Ann Stafford, health hazards were, to far too great an extent, seen as part of the 'natural' order of things. When Annie Besant, hot with anger from the Fabian meeting, presented herself at the factory gate and offered to write down their grievances, she was immediately assailed with the story of 'the statue'. A statue of William Gladstone had been erected in the factory forecourt as a monument to the employers' loyalty. But the girls had been told to subscribe to it, had contributions docked from their wages, and were compelled to take an unpaid holiday for the unveiling. They rebelled, throwing rocks, and mobbing the statue, cursing it and screaming, 'and some girls twined their arms round it and cut themselves so that their blood dripped onto its stony plinth.'[49]

Mrs Besant's exposure was carried in *The Link*, a little weekly newspaper which she edited. The revelations produced threats of litigation by the directors and a solid strike of all the girls. The leaders were Alice France, Kate Slater, Mary Driscol, Jane Wakeling and Eliza Martin: their names are preserved in the company's files, and their picture was reproduced in Annie Besant's *Autobiography* (see plate 1);[50] but nothing else is known about them.[51] To maintain spirits and gain publicity, a march was arranged on 11 July to meet MPs at a committee room in the House of Commons:

Mrs. Besant gave Mr. Cunninghame Graham a list of the girls who had been fined in the past six weeks. He at once asked:
 'Any other stoppages?'
 The girls spoke up: 'Yes, we have to pay for paint for the matchboxes, and also for brushes.'
 The two Members of Parliament asked them all sorts of questions, and 'they showed sharp wits, directness and frankness in answering'.
 Then a little girl, aged fifteen and earning four shillings a week, pulled off her shawl and displayed her nearly bald head; she had lost her hair, she said, through carrying boxes on her head. The sight of this little girl seems to have made an immediate impression on the hard-headed MPs and reporters. Of all the girls there she probably had the least real grievance; her plight was so much less pitiable than that of the girls who contracted

'phossy-jaw'. And yet there was something about her baldness so painful to the eye that it stirred uneasy consciences.[52]

Not only did the matchgirls win: their example shocked the comfortable, who learned the fates which Royal Jubilee London was offering its poor. More significantly, the girls' action inspired fellow sufferers who knew only too well the bitterness of semi-starvation and of subjugation. Now, at last, they could also see hope, and with it came the will to struggle against intolerable inhumanity.

# Notes

1   Tom Mann, *Memoirs* (1923, reissued McGibbon and Kee, 1967), p. 9.
2   Ibid., p. 4.
3   J. B. Jeffreys, *The Story of the Engineers* (Lawrence and Wishart, 1945), pp. 79ff. See also E. Allen et al., *The North East Engineers' Strikes of 1871* (Frank Graham, 1971), pp. 98ff.
4   Mann, *Memoirs*, pp. 5–6.
5   Their reading matter is set in its context in Raymond Williams, *The Long Revolution* (Chatto and Windus, 1961), pp. 156–213.
6   Henry George, *Progress and Poverty* (Dent, n.d.). In *The History of Trade Unionism* (1894; WEA edn, 1912), pp. 375–6, Sidney and Beatrice Webb wrote: 'If we had to assign to any one event the starting of the new current of thought, we should name the wide circulation in Great Britain of Henry George's *Progress and Poverty* during the years 1880–82. The optimistic and aggressive tone of the book, in marked contrast with the complacent quietism into which the English working-class movement had sunk, and for the force of the popularisation of the economic Theory of Rent, sounded the dominant note alike of the "New Unionism" and of the British Socialist Movement.'
    George proposed to appropriate all land rents by taxation, and abolish all other taxes. In the United States as well as in Britain this was a popular call among the trade unions, who persuaded him to run for Mayor of New York in 1886. He would probably have won if the votes had been counted properly (*Encyclopaedia of the Social Sciences* (Macmillan, 1938), vol. VI, p. 635).
7   Mann, *Memoirs*, p. 21. He found only one fellow disciple during his trip to the USA, and that was a Scotsman.
8   J. E. Thorold Rogers, *Six Centuries of Work and Wages* (Swan Sonnenschein, 1884), p. 542.
9   Karl Marx, *Capital* (Dona Torr edn, Allen and Unwin, 1946), p. 215.
10  Ibid., chapter X, pp. 214ff.
11  Mann, *Memoirs*, p. 25. The early days of the Social Democratic Federation are described in A. L. Morton and George Tate, *The British Labour Movement, 1770–1920* (Lawrence and Wishart, 1956), pp. 166ff. See also H. W. Lee and E. Archbold, *Social Democracy in Britain* (Social Democratic Federation, 1935).

12  Franz Mehring, *Karl Marx* (Allen and Unwin, 1951), pp. 525–6.

13  Mann, *Memoirs*, p. 27.

14  Ibid., p. 44.

15  Its manifesto, published in January 1885, is given in full in Yvonne Kapp, *Eleanor Marx: The Crowded Years, 1884–1898* (Lawrence and Wishart, 1976), pp. 63ff.

16  See Chushichi Tsuzuki, *The Life of Eleanor Marx* (Oxford University Press, 1967), pp. 127ff.

17  Quelch's activities are reported in Lee and Archbold, *Social Democracy in Britain*. Some of his statements on behalf of the dockers are reproduced in J. T. Ward and W. H. Fraser, *Workers and Employers* (Macmillan, 1980), pp. 122 and 130.

18  This relationship has been differently reported. Olga Meier, in her notes to *The Daughters of Karl Marx: Family Correspondence, 1866–1898* (Penguin, 1984), p. 221, says that Eleanor taught Thorne to read and write. Giles and Lisanne Radice, in *Will Thorne, Constructive Militant* (Allen and Unwin, 1974), p. 25, say that she taught him 'to write correctly'.

19  In addition to its restrictive scope, the 1867 Reform Act remained far short of democratic standards. As D. L. Keir put it in his *Constitutional History of Modern Britain* (A. and C. Black, 1943), pp. 466 and 470–1: 'The reform of 1867 had made an immensely larger addition to the electorate than the Act had intended. Even so, the process of change was far from being arrested at the point now reached. The new democracy in the first place had to emancipate itself from the coercion and bribery still prevalent in the electoral system. Secondly, defects in the method of registration, which impeded many voters from establishing their qualification, had to be eliminated. Thirdly, the electoral franchise itself had to be made simpler and more uniform, and the qualification lowered. Finally, the discrepancies between population and representation which the redistribution of 1868 had served rather to emphasize than to cure still called for remedy.'

Bribery was indeed widespread, and Keir documents only the more sensational cases. Registration was incredibly complex: 'Alike in the boroughs and the counties a variety of different qualifications existed. In the former, besides a surviving remnant of ancient-right franchises, there were both the £10 occupancy qualification of 1832 and the householder and lodger franchises of 1867. In the latter, besides a substantial proportion of ancient-right voters, amounting to a fifth of the aggregate county electorate, and those qualified by the various franchises introduced in 1832 and modified in 1867, there were also those qualified by the new £12 rateable value franchise created in the latter year. These complications were perhaps less effective in stimulating the demand for reform than the anomaly that the franchise was notably less democratic in the counties than in the boroughs.'

The struggle for the extension of the franchise was to continue; not until 1928 was an adult suffrage established, and even this was marred by plural voting, which remained in force until 1948. The problem of unequal representation arises again in chapter 7.

20  Reprinted in Friedrich Engels, *The British Labour Movement* (Lawrence and Wishart, 1936).

21   Ibid., p. 34.

22   Ibid., p. 14.

23   Cf. Ross H. Martin, *TUC: The Growth of a Pressure Group* (Oxford University Press, 1980), chapter 3, 'The Politics of Deference'.

24   Eric J. Hobsbawm, *Labour's Turning Point, 1880–1900, History in the Making*, vol. III (Lawrence and Wishart, 1948), p. xvii.

25   The evidence for this has been documented by Jonathan Schneer, *Ben Tillett: Portrait of a Labour Leader* (Croom Helm, 1982), chapter 2, pp. 24–38. In greater detail, the same author covers the same ground in 'Ben Tillett's Conversion to Independent Labour Politics', *Radical History Review*, 24 (fall 1980), pp. 42–65.

26   Karl Marx, *Address to the Inaugural Meeting of the International Working Men's Association*, Marx–Engels Selected Works, vol. I (Lawrence and Wishart, 1942), p. 347.

27   Karl Marx, *Grundrisse: Foundations of the Critique of Political Economy* (Penguin, 1973).

28   Morton and Tate, *The British Labour Movement*, pp. 187ff.; Kapp, *Eleanor Marx*, pp. 389ff.; Mann, *Memoirs*, chapter IV.

29   Kapp, *Eleanor Marx*, pp. 368ff.

30   Webb, *History of Trade Unionism*, p. 379.

31   Subsequently it became crystal clear that Mawdsley 'did not understand their socialism': he finished his political career not even as a Liberal, but as an active Conservative.

32   Not that this appreciation came easily, either to trade unionists or to non-unionists. Other issues, especially that of the Irish question, ensured that Liberal influence over working people, and radical opinion, remained a hardy growth for a long time. But it was always disengaged from the core social issues, to which only a committed fringe of the party made any sustained contribution.

33   Tom Mann, *What a Compulsory Eight-hour Day Means to the Workers* (1886; reissued Pluto Press, 1972), pp. 22–3. Introducing this text, Richard Hyman highlights its 'flaws', and judges Mann to have been completely wanting in revolutionary consistency. After all, was it not inconsistent to 'appeal for a major legislative initiative' without considering 'at all the question of the class character of the state'? That Mann was engaged in a political struggle, as well as in a series of industrial engagements, seems not to weigh in this judgement. True, Friedrich Engels made several waspish comments about Mann, and these were collected in the introduction to Mann's *Memoirs* (Ken Coates, 1967), but on this issue of substance, Engels gave total support to Mann's initiatives.

34   Webb, *History of Trade Unionism*, p. 385.

35   Gareth Stedman Jones, *Outcast London* (Penguin Books, 1971), p. 292.

36   Webb, *History of Trade Unionism*, p. 374.

37   Ibid.; and G. D. H. Cole, *John Burns*, Fabian Biographical Series; reprinted in Michael Katanka, *Radicals, Reformers and Socialists* (Charles Knight, 1973), pp. 163ff.

38   Martin, *TUC: The Growth of a Pressure Group*, pp. 28ff.

39   Morton and Tate, *The British Labour Movement*, pp. 179–84.

40   Ibid., p. 182.

41  Kenneth O. Morgan, *Keir Hardie, Radical and Socialist* (Weidenfeld and Nicolson, 1975), chapter 2.

42  Mann, *Memoirs*, p. 54.

43  Ibid., p. 57.

44  Ibid.

45  Ann Stafford, *A Match to Fire the Thames* (Hodder and Stoughton, 1961).

46  Champion could have learned about this scandal from Tom Mann's pamphlet, *What a Compulsory Eight-hour Day Means to the Workers*, which he had published himself only eighteen months earlier.

47  Stafford, *A Match to Fire the Thames*, p. 66.

48  David Keys, 'Statue to Strike that Lit the Way for Unions', *Independent*, 12 October 1988.

49  Stafford, *A Match to Fire the Thames*, p. 67.

50  Annie Besant, *An Autobiography* (Fisher Unwin, 1908), facing p. 336. See also the photograph facing p. 338.

51  An exhibition was organized in 1988 by the archives department of Hackney Public Libraries. This was reported in the *Independent*, 12 October 1988.

52  Stafford, *A Match to Fire the Thames*, pp. 74–5.

# 3

# The Great London Dock Strike

## I

### A Centenary

There is magic in numbers. The year 1889 was the first centenary of the great French Revolution. 'Scientific' though they may have been, the early socialists were as impressed as anybody else by round figures. H. M. Hyndman thought that the Revolution would echo along the years:

> Noble Robert Owen, seventy years ago perceived 'the utter impossibility of succeeding in permanently improving the condition of our population by any half-measures'. We see the same truth if possible yet more clearly now. But the revolution which in his day was unprepared is now ripe and ready . . .[1]

Warming to this theme, he later named the date:

> Let our mission be to help to band together the workers of the world for the great class struggle against their exploiters. No better date could be chosen for the establishment of such international action on a sound basis than the year 1889, which the classes look forward to with trembling and the masses with hope. I advocate no hasty outbreak, no premature and violent attempt on the part of the people to realise the full Social-Democratic programme. But I do say that from this time onwards we, as the Social-Democratic Labour Party of Great Britain, should make every effort to bear our part in the celebration by the international proletariat of the First Centenary of the great French Revolution, and thus to prepare for a complete International Social Revolution before the end of the century.[2]

The time arrived. To begin with, things were quiet.

## 'Terrible Dreams'

That summer, during a prosperous interlude in the long recession, work was brisk in the London docks. The dock companies' directors were away on holiday in, amongst other places, Russia and Cornwall.

Ben Tillett,[3] secretary of the recently formed Tea Operatives' and General Labourers' Union and himself a dock worker in London, was reflecting on the lessons of a disastrous strike recently concluded at the Tilbury dock. He had begun what he called a 'hole-and-corner' trade-union agitation in the depth of the 1880s depression. The tea coopers' tiny organization had in the beginning met with sympathy from some of the interested outsiders to whom Tillett appealed. Samuel Montagu, later Lord Swaythling, sent a donation of £5, and Professor Stewart, MP, wrote in praise of 'combination'; but the London Trades Council blew cold, in spite of initial encouraging words from George Howell and George Odger. When the employers brought in farm labourers as blacklegs, the Tilbury strike collapsed. Tillett knew that, to succeed, his small union needed a more general scope. In the aftermath of defeat he wrote:

> The brutal condition of our class, the squalor and misery of their homes and lives, is a bitter proof of how terribly it is used. How long the aristocracy of labour will hold aloof, how long our mistaken philanthropists will ply with impracticable charity, how long the world will be dead to the wants and wrongs of a neglected class of unorganised labour – and that only so because of the general indifference – I cannot tell; but this must be patent to all, that unless combination on constitutional grounds is encouraged, the country will have to face a graver danger than bludgeons will be able to suppress.[4]

Tillett had other problems. Bogus unions, little short of criminal conspiracies, abounded. His meetings were disrupted and even broken up by hired bullies. He himself was assaulted and badly beaten. Insults and intimidation were rife. Stones and 'filthy refuse' were thrown at union organizers. Tillett was not easily dissuaded. He drew strength from the adult-education movement, which influenced him in ways that were never intended by its initiators. In the days after the Tilbury defeat, he attended a lecture by Cosmo Gordon Lang (later Archbishop of Canterbury), during one of his visits to the Bethnal Green Settlement of Oxford University; the subject was 'The Strategy and Tactics of Napoleon'. As a result, Tillett found his mind engaged on the problem of conquering the world of shipping. Setting off for work in the foggy London mornings, he chewed through all the problems of creating 'a colossal picketing system', neutralizing every wharf in the docks. His minuscule organization was an embryo, but because he could imagine its growth, 'I saw how the Thames might and would be made idle . . . a thousand million pounds of financial power brought to a standstill. These were my dreams, my terrible dreams.'[5]

With these great issues boiling in his head, he would walk the 20 miles from the East End to Tilbury, where the rate was 4d. an hour. Sometimes he would be disengaged after thirty minutes, with 2d., because of the rain. In 1888 the strike for 5d. an hour at Tilbury collapsed disastrously. Tillett's exertions during the strike led to the first of his many physical breakdowns; when he recovered he came back to a Tea Operatives' Union reduced to less than half of its initial enrolment, although the precise numbers involved are a matter of dispute.[6] What is not in doubt is that the union was small: the maximum claim was that it enrolled 2,400 people; hostile witnesses put the figure as low as 300.

Little wonder that the solid craftsmen of the London Trades Council thought that organization of mere 'casuals' was a quixotic labour.

## Help at Hand

Fortunately, Tillett had other moral resources upon which to draw. He had already befriended Tom Mann and John Burns, and was drawn to Annie Besant by the example she set in her intervention in the matchgirls' dispute. He had also come to know and work alongside Will Thorne, with his gasworkers' union.

In 1882 Will Thorne had walked to London from Birmingham after various abortive efforts to organize a trade union of gasworkers in the Midlands. An old friend who had been employed with him at Saltley helped him to get a job with the Gas, Light and Coke Company in its works at Beckton in the East End. In 1884 he settled in Canning Town, joined the Social Democratic Federation, signed the pledge and began the work of proselytizing for a gasworkers' union. As a socialist activist, he soon found himself presiding over Tom Mann's meetings, marching through the West End in the demonstrations against unemployment and joining forces with Ben Tillett in his little union.

On the last day of March 1889, a Sunday and 'a lovely sunny morning', all Thorne's canvassing at Beckton bore fruit: 2,500 workers attended a mass meeting to announce to the world their decision to form an organization, the Gasworkers' and General Labourers' Union. The title was highly significant – the first moment of general, new unionism. Thorne, Tillett and William Byford were elected to a provisional committee and charged with drawing up rules. Thorne made a powerful speech: 'I pledge my word that, if you will stand firm and don't waver, within six months we will claim and win the eight-hour day, a six-day week, and the abolition of the present slave-driving methods . . .'[7]

The gasworkers did stand firm, and their union began to shape itself.

A delegate meeting held that May launched a ballot for the new general secretaryship, in which both Thorne and Tillett stood for the office. Thorne won a large majority, with over 2,000 votes. Tillett took his defeat with good grace, since he had always had reservations about leaving his dockers in order to represent the gasmen. As things turned out, the dockers were to rally to trade unionism within three months. But before then, on 11 July 1889, the London gasworkers had achieved their famous and peaceful victory with the establishment of the eight-hour day.

As well as being able to call on other trade unionists for support, Tillett had got to know Cardinal Henry Manning, Archbishop of Westminster and head of the Roman Catholic Church in England. More than half the dock workers in London were Irish or of Irish extraction, and the Cardinal was a major influence among them. He was also an astute and sympathetic listener, and he took to Ben Tillett as father to son. Tillett wrote:

> In that time, I met with the kindliest and greatest man it has been my good fortune to encounter, Cardinal Manning. In my despair and pessimism I had sought advice from him. I was discouraged and in doubt about the future. 'Hope deferred maketh the heart sick.' It was deferred hope which brought about my sickness of heart, and the consciousness of the futility of my endeavours . . . left me in a thoroughly discouraged state of mind. What the Cardinal told me was of the sternest, simplest, and most practical character, couched in the tersest terms . . . Its essential message was that if a thing was worth doing at all it was worth doing well, whether it brought success or failure. A commonplace and a platitude perhaps, but it was for me not merely a slogan but an inspiration. As I recall the numberless people who have offered me advice in the different stages of my career, I think that Cardinal Manning's influenced me most.[8]

## II

## *The Worm Turns*

On 12 August 1889, two members of Tillett's union came to him with the request that support should be given to a dispute at the South West India Dock concerning the sailing ship *Lady Armstrong*. Tillett's shock was evident:

> I could hardly believe my ears. Months of heart-breaking effort and organisation amongst the poverty-stricken and dispirited dock workers had not encouraged me to expect any such manifestation. Had the worm indeed turned? Was it possible to strike with men who shivered with hunger and cold, bullied and intimidated by the petty tyrants who took a delight in the brutalities of the 'call-on'?[9]

The spark which fired the ensuing strike was a local argument about the distribution of the 'plus' – the bonus paid on tonnage for particular jobs. This was a much-hated system, since the basis of its calculation was concealed from the men; Tillett himself had called it 'systematic robbery'. In this case the initial contention was about a piece-rate of ½d. an hour, but once the dispute had broken out, it provided a platform for the thousand other cries from the victims of the dock world. It was agreed to present the employers with a comprehensive programme of demands. These included not only the famous 'dockers' tanner' (the raising of the base-rate from 5d. to 6d. an hour), but also the end of both the contract and plus systems. The dockers also insisted on a minimum of four hours' work, a reduction in the number of call-ons to two each day, and an overtime rate of 8d. an hour.[10]

Tillett tried to restrain any action on the *Lady Armstrong* until the employers had replied, but impatience ran away with the men. Within forty-eight hours they had walked out and the strike was spreading rapidly. Tillett did not instantly turn for help to Cardinal Manning. Instead, by telegram, he summoned Tom Mann and John Burns to his aid.

## *Enter Tom Mann . . .*

Mann appeared within a few hours on the same day – 14 August – that the men walked out. As a result of the battle which followed, he and Tillett were to become lifelong friends. Their love for one another survived intense political differences, and a worldwide split in the socialist movement. Tillett was later to describe Mann as 'a giant, a power'. Will Thorne spoke of him as 'a streak of human quicksilver, here, there, and everywhere, commanding, pleading, cajoling, enthusing'. When, half a century later, death parted the two dockers' leaders, Tillett delivered a valediction of haunting beauty. None who heard it ever forgot it.

Initially, John Burns had been cautious. But by Friday, the 16th, he had committed himself and was leading a demonstration of 6,000 men. Burns was very well known in the docks, not only as the recently elected socialist county councillor, but also as a stump-orator at the gates. He had helped form a branch of the Gasworkers' Union at Vauxhall, and so he had friends in Thorne's union as well. In addition to these qualifications, in 1887 he had himself put in a brief spell as a docker. Burns had a genius for publicity. He was a natural leader for these demonstrations, and, wearing a straw hat which enabled the constabulary to identify him as the responsible chief marshal, he became a highly visible symbol. The hat passed into legend. Its material remains vanished when it was thrown overboard during a celebratory boat trip on the Thames, after the great victory.

## . . . and Other Reinforcements

The strike was quickly reinforced by the invaluable official support of the two stevedores' unions, who had no immediate grievance of their own but who felt 'our duty is to support our poorer brothers'. Tom McCarthy, secretary of the Amalgamated Stevedores' Labour Protection League, became a key leader on the Strike Committee.

In addition to the stevedores, the lightermen joined the movement. The Seamen's and Firemen's Union, formed in 1887, committed itself in support. In the first days of the strike, Will Thorne thought of trying to recruit the men from the docks directly into his own gasworkers' ranks, but, after flirting with a bid to lead the conflict himself, he decided against the idea and threw his weight wholeheartedly behind Tillett's union. All, it seemed, were now happy to work within this new convergence of forces. Tillett had assembled a strong team, and he himself rapidly put aside his initial doubts and surprise. This, he saw, was to be an historic movement. Within days it was clear that the strike would indeed encompass the whole port. No section held back; at its height, 100,000 workers were involved, and the army of pickets numbered 15–16,000.[11]

So it was that between 14 and 22 August, the entire port stopped. Initially there were two Strike Committees, of the Stevedores' and of the Tea Operatives' Unions. Soon, however, they were merged into a single body, much to the benefit of the dockers, who lacked the administrative skills and experience of the stevedores. The South Side, with its separate Labour Protection League, proved difficult to co-ordinate, and later Tom Mann was sent there to organize and to raise morale. Outstanding sectional claims were advanced there, from corn-porters, deal-carriers, stevedores, trimmers, weighers, warehousemen, granary workers and steamship workers.

## A Pageant of the Oppressed

The noise of the daily marches of dockers and their families, with their bands and banners, filled all the streets of the city. Converging on Hyde Park, the marchers attracted huge crowds to listen to Tillett and his colleagues – above all to Burns. The two contemporary historians of the strike, Llewellyn Smith and Vaughan Nash, have left us a vivid picture of this carnival of the most downtrodden people of the capital, which reflected all the complexity of East London society.

First came a posse of police, behind whom the marshals of the procession, with axes and scarves, reserved a clear space for the leaders. With them sometimes walked Superintendent Forster, a familiar figure in the strike. His solicitude for the comfort and passage of his convoy was unmistakable, and the man in the straw hat [Burns] at his side, deep in consultation, might have been a brother officer in plain clothes. Next came a brass band of the stevedores, following which streamed the multitude whose calling lay at the docks and riverside. Such finery as they boasted in the way of flags and banners had been lent by friendly and trade societies, and this gave the procession the appearance of a great church parade or demonstration of foresters. There were burly stevedores, lightermen, ships' painters, sailors and firemen, riggers, scrapers, engineers, ship-wrights, permanent men got up respectably, preferables cleaned up to look like permanents, and unmistakable casuals with vari-coloured patches on their faded greenish garments: Foresters and Sons of the Phoenix in gaudy scarves: Doggett's prize winners, a stalwart battalion of watermen marching proudly in long scarlet cloaks, pink stockings, and velvet caps, with huge pewter badges on their breasts, like decorated amphibious huntsmen: coalies in wagons fishing aggressively for coppers with bags tied to the end of poles, a brother coalie in effigy attached as figure-head to one of their vehicles, placarded with the announcement that he wouldn't go a step higher up the ladder on which he sprawled till the docker got his tanner: skiffs mounted on wheels manned by stolid watermen: ballast heavers laboriously winding and tipping an empty basket, Father Neptune on his car in tinsel crown and flowing locks, surrounded by his suite, – Britannia in a Union Jack skirt, the doctor in a faultless hat . . . and the barber brandishing a huge razor, ready for the victims of the equator on the other side of the car. Emblems quaint and pathetic were carried in the ranks, the docker's cat and the sweater's cat, the docker's dinner and the sweater's dinner, the docker's baby and the sweater's baby, diminutive and ample, respectively: Sir Hardwood (a gentleman understood to be connected with the Joint Committee), attired in mortar board, gown and mask, gravely saluted the bystanders and bowed low in front of Dock House. The bass dressers, locked out for forming a union, brought up the rear, carrying their bass brooms like lictors.

Such was the strike procession. It had its moods – was merry on some days, taciturn on others, laughed at the Dock House sometimes, howled at it at others, but it never lost command over itself or caused serious anxiety to its leaders or to the citizens of London.[12] (See plate 5.)

'Sir Hardwood' was in fact generally understood to represent the chief dock director, C. M. Norwood. He was also given a harsher character-ization: the dockers referred to him as 'Jack the Ripper', who was at the time vividly present in the minds of all East Enders. The *Star* newspaper said of him: 'He is in appearance the very embodiment of the insolence of capitalism. He is stout, well-fed and arrogant.'

The pageant was compelling, but its significance was even more moving for the old men who remembered the legendary years of

Chartism. One of these was George Julian Harney, who was still young enough, at seventy-one years of age, to compose a memorable description for the *Newcastle Chronicle*:

> The strike has recalled the memory of other great labour struggles . . . But all strikes, turn-outs and lock-outs of the past must pale their ineffectual fires in presence of the great revolt at the East End of London . . . Not since the high and palmy days of Chartism have I witnessed any movement corresponding in importance and interest to the great strike of 1889. How poor and paltry in comparison, appear the make-believe Caucus-manufactured 'movements' of recent years . . . Whatever the immediate issue, the strikers have 'felt their strength and made it felt' and it is safe to predict that this will not be the last revolt of the East End.[13]

These public rallies owed much to the experience of the earlier socialist demonstrations against unemployment. They enabled sympathetic journalists to generate over the condition of the dockers a public sense of shame without precedent in the history of labour struggles. The ground had been cleared for this understanding presentation by the social studies of the London poor, and of dockers' conditions specifically, carried out by Charles Booth and Beatrice Webb, and by the Fabian and Social Democratic Federation agitations during the preceding years. In the end (after an initial humanitarian lapse) *The Times* was the only major newspaper to oppose the strike.

A major influence was the newly founded evening newspaper, the *Star*, created by T. P. O'Connor, Irish Home Rule MP. O'Connor was to be the only Irish Nationalist member to hold a seat at Westminster on the votes of a constituency in England.[14] He sat for Liverpool Scotland from 1885 to 1929, and represented a massive concentration of port workers throughout that time. But in 1888 he had opened the *Star* with the assistance of H. W. Massingham, as much as for the radical as for the Irish cause. His first article in it was composed 'in a white heat', and it made a very firm commitment: 'The charwoman that lives in St. Giles, the seamstress that is sweated in Whitechapel, the labourer that stands begging for work outside the dockyard gate in St. George's-in-the-East – these are the persons by whose condition we shall judge the policy of the present political parties . . .'[15]

The judgement was a forthright one. The new paper was innovative in style: short, punchy articles, many crossheads and bold typography, strong coverage of items of popular interest – all features which were soon to become staple components of mass-circulation newspapers.[16] Yet, unlike its successors, O'Connor's *Star* was truly a radical journal. It began with a circulation of 140,000, and levelled at 130,000. George Bernard Shaw was among the first contributors, but he resigned because he thought socialist affairs were inadequately treated. Even so, he was to return as music critic, replacing a fellow socialist, Belfort Bax, at his own request.[17] Engels's letters are full of references to the *Star*: he clearly found it more sympathetic and perhaps more important a forum than did Shaw.[18] Be that as it may, the dock strike was a perfect issue for such a newspaper, and it campaigned ceaselessly to present the dockers' case.[19]

Tillett was familiar with the socialist agitation of the day. Its activists had already shown their readiness to leave their drawing rooms and studies in order to help the struggles of people who were trying to league themselves into unions. Annie Besant of the Fabians and Herbert Burrows of the SDF had both given selfless help, without seeking to impose direction, in the 1888 Tilbury strike.

The alliance which gathered round the dockers to organize the vast enterprise of the 1889 upheaval comprised people from every part of the new spectrum of radical socialist thought in the capital.[20]

Prominent among them were H. H. Champion and Eleanor Marx. Harry Quelch had been elected to the secretaryship of the South Side Labour Protection League. He was a controversialist and, in spite of his unsparing polemics about the weakness of trade unionism, he made an important mark administering a part of the old, decentralized, job-oriented London port unionism. Will Crooks, the cooper, had been conducting his 'college' of regular agitational meetings at the dock gates. His lectures were Socratic. The students argued back, and his answers were down to earth and spiced with Cockney wit. He 'gave both day and night to the dockers', wrote his biographer.[21]

## Pickets and Strike-breakers

Harry Orbell, president of Tillett's union, played a role which could fairly be called heroic, out of the limelight, in organizing the strike and the picketing at Tilbury docks, 26 miles from the main port. When he was assigned this job, Orbell was diffident. 'I don't think I can do it, Ben', he said.[22] But he did. More, he maintained some loyal union men on the job as 'blacklegs', and their intelligence ensured that the union could intervene effectively when, as was expected, the company brought in outside strike-breakers. A group of labourers was imported from Liverpool, having been untruthfully informed that the strike was finished. Once in place, the employers tried to persuade them to stay on by alleging that the union would 'skin them alive' if they caught up with them. No, we 'will take you by the hand', Orbell wrote to them. That weekend they took the train home, paying their own fares. Harry's pickets provided a friendly protective escort.[23]

On another occasion, getting wind of a carriage-load of blacklegs due at the docks, Orbell mustered some four hundred men, and started with them in procession, nominally to Gray's, near Tilbury – for he was closely watched by the agents of the company – but making a detour, they worked round, with lowered banners to the north gate of the dock, where the men concealed themselves under the embankment. As the train drew near and slowed down, the men started up and wanted to push it back into the station. There was no occasion for this, however, as twenty-seven of the men came out on getting Orbell's message, for the crowd of dockers made it clear that they had been inveigled there under false pretences. The Tilbury men boast that they succeeded in detecting and frustrating an ingenious device of the company for passing blacklegs through the gates. It was found that a large number of individuals, with black coats and bags, and sticks, were daily entering and leaving the docks. The company, so the story runs, had dressed up the labourers in this fashion, hoping that they would run the gauntlet of the pickets without notice. To the dismay of the black-coated blacklegs, and of the dock officials, an effigy, inscribed 'the new docker', and correctly attired with bag and stick was hoisted up to a prominent place. Thus the new dockers were check-mated.[24]

Overall, picketing was organized by Tom Mann. This crucial responsibility kept him largely out of the attention of the newspapers, but it was absolutely vital to the solidarity of the resistance. The sum of £1,200 was expended by the strike fund on picket duties and banner carriers.[25] But, for this incredibly modest amount, at least 15,000 men were organized under 'picket foremen' to patrol the rivers, police the railway stations from which invariably blacklegs might arrive, and, of course, control the docks. At the Albert and Victoria Docks the pickets were paid in food tickets. Often women would be encouraged to enter the wharves, ostensibly to take in lunches. Then they would 'fairly nag' the blacklegs to leave.[26]

> The pickets on night duty at Tilbury received 9d. each; by day they were relieved every two or three hours, and did their turn gratuitously. About one thousand dockers were out at Tilbury and two thousand of their allies, not reckoning the women, or the Chinamen who were locked up in Gray's police station for refusing to coal their steamer. 'Daddy' Rooark, the second in command at Tilbury, a stevedore from head-quarters, said of the Tilbury strikers that he never knew such men – they were as good as gold.[27]

If such efforts largely contained the threat of imported strike-breakers, they did not succeed in breaking down skill barriers, and the division between 'old' and 'new' unions. Even if Mann and Burns had a wide following in the Amalgamated Society of Engineers, their influence was not enough to bring about solidarity on the Commercial Docks, where three engine-men of the ASE kept the cranes running in spite of all efforts to persuade them to stop.[28]

The employers found this blockade intolerable. Norwood maintained a consistent volley of anguished letters, badgering the Home Secretary,

Henry Matthews. As a result, the Metropolitan Fire Brigade was kept on constant alert to inhibit fictitious arson attempts. The police were pushed to send 2,000 constables for the same reason.

> John Burns gave them a great welcome; he said he was glad they had been taken away from the hard duties of the West End to come to the East End, where he could promise them they would have nothing to do. He liked to have them there; they were friends; and he knew every one of them would drop a tanner into the collecting boxes on the sly.[29]

## The Role of Tom Mann

Smith and Nash, in their vivid chronicle of events, appreciated the less flamboyant style of Tom Mann, who took over the responsibility for organizing with the South Side strikers once the picketing had been regulated and rendered lethally effective.

> [Tom Mann] supplied an element in the councils of the strike leaders in which otherwise they would have been weak. He was the eyes of the strike, always ready to see where there was necessary work to be done, and to set to work to do it. Strong and wiry, and capable of great physical endurance, and withal cool-headed and quietly energetic, he applied himself to the details of organization, which frequently carry with them the success or failure of a movement, and yet are so often over-looked by those who are great at beating the big drum. When occasion required, however, he would beat the big drum as well as any, and with all these qualities he combined an unswerving loyalty to his comrades, and an absence of all attempt to gain credit for himself, which are only too rarely met with in the history of labour movements.[30]

Mann himself unselfconsciously corroborates this view in his *Memoirs*:

> I can honestly say that I cared nothing at all for the public meetings, whether on Tower Hill or elsewhere, or for what was thought of the fight by the public. I concentrated on the work of organization and was indifferent to outside opinion. I had been at it about three weeks, and was now dealing specially with the south side of the Thames. One day I realised that my boots had become so worn out that I must get others or go barefoot (we always had long marches, and I invariably marched with the crowd). I slipped away from the marching column as soon as I noticed a boot shop. Hastily buying a pair of boots, I put them on and hurried to catch up with the crowd. When we reached Sayes Court, Deptford, I spoke as usual . . . A few days later, we were marching again along the thoroughfare where I had bought the boots. My eye lighted on the shop window and to my amazement I noticed my name on a card . . . to my still greater astonishment . . . the card bearing my name was on the pair of old boots I had shed a few days before: The writing on the card ran: 'The

boots worn by Tom Mann during the long marches in the Dock Strike'. I was positively flabbergasted to think that importance of any kind could attach to such articles or to me . . .

I . . . felt so completely a part of everything that was taking place, that I had left work, home, and all else and paid no regard to anything other than the fight I was in.[31]

## Liberal Support

Others besides the socialists were also to rally round. Liberals often helped. As we have seen, the Liberal Party needed to worry about votes, because a wider franchise meant that hitherto unheard interests now required consideration. But many Liberals were moved by the experience of the strike, and gave open-hearted support. The Roman Catholic Church was also concerned, because a core constituency within its flock was directly involved.

Sydney Buxton (later Sir Sydney, later still the Earl Buxton), the radical Liberal MP for Poplar, who was to become Postmaster-General in Sir Henry Campbell-Bannerman's first ministry of 1905, befriended the strikers from the outset. Tillett had written to him enlisting his support before the strike, as part of his long-term strategy for the Tea Operatives' Union. When the strike broke out, Buxton cut short his holiday and returned to London to speak at the mass strike rallies. He sat on the Conciliation Committee which sought a solution to the strike, and when the men repudiated its first recommended terms, he stuck by them, refusing to play the middleman or to seek a broker's role. He worked in close partnership with Cardinal Manning in the search for a peace formula, and did indeed produce one proposal for compromise which proved unacceptable to the men and their leaders. When Tillett and Mann showed their embarrassment, however, Buxton loyally withheld his public endorsement of the offer. His 'fidelity as a mediator was as heroic as [Manning's]', and he 'never lost the confidence of the men, as the Cardinal so nearly did'.[32]

After the strike, Buxton remarked: 'For my part I have never been so proud of being an Englishman and a Londoner, as during the past few weeks. Fancy 100,000 hungry men in the streets with nothing to do from morning to night, and never a row of any sort or kind, never so much as an apple taken from an old woman's stall.'[33] If this was obviously a spontaneous and unaffected tribute, behind it ran the still-fresh memory of the far from tranquil events of two years earlier, which had terrified the respectable classes. Riot was still a live memory in London.

Smith and Nash believed that Buxton 'was largely instrumental in bringing about' the eventual settlement of the 1889 strike. Moreover, he raised a fund of £2,300, 'which was chiefly applied to helping the families of the strikers in the Poplar district. Mr. and Mrs. Buxton worked unremittingly, distributing in all some 100,000 meals and grocery tickets'.[34] To set this contribution in context, we should note that a total of £21,396 was paid to tradesmen for redeeming food tickets issued by the Strike Committee from several centres. This commissariat took a lot of organizing. At the beginning of the dispute, 4,000 men besieged the picketing headquarters asking for money, and it was Tom Mann who braced himself at the door of Wroote's Coffee House, his back to one jamb, and his foot against the other, to pass each claimant in, one by one, to receive his ticket. Chatting affably with the crowd, he rapidly cooled the temper of the occasion. But at the end of the day he had lost the skin off his back. Immediately afterwards the distribution was decentralized, so that stewards could recognize their own local strikers, and thus restrict payment to those entitled to it.

## The Clergy Lend a Hand

Tillett also records the important contribution, in raising funds and offering encouragement, of the clergy of the East End, notably the Oxford House and Toynbee Hall clerics, who were often Christian socialists.[35] At the climax of the strike the mediating role of Cardinal Manning became crucial. His interest in the dispute, and his effectiveness in it – greatly enhanced by his influence with the preponderantly Irish Catholic dockers[36] – never detracted from the friendly personal relationship he had established with Tillett and Mann, in spite of their distinctive appeal to his own flock.[37] Manning left a brief summary of his part in the difficult to-ing and fro-ing of the negotiations, passed on to us by his biographer:

On 5th September Miss Harkness came to me from the leaders of the strike to tell me that the coal heavers who had returned to work would strike again at noon the next day, if the dock directors did not grant the demands of their men. If the coal supply had failed, the railroads and the gas factories would have been affected. I went at once to the Home Office; both Secretary and Under Secretary were out of London. I went to the Mansion House; the lord mayor was in Scotland. But I found the deputy lord mayor and the second chief of police. We went together to the directors. They received us courteously but nothing came of it. This was Friday. The lord mayor and the bishop of London came to town. Saturday we met the leaders of the strike at the Mansion House, and drew up terms to be laid before the men, i.e. 6d. from January. We waited for an answer till ten o'clock. No answer was ever given. But next morning, Sunday, appeared a manifesto repudiating terms, negotiations and negotiators. In the afternoon in Hyde Park the meeting passed a resolution, accepting the terms, to begin on 1 October. This the directors rejected, and next,

Monday, the leaders met at the Mansion House, and it was arranged that Mr. Buxton and I should meet the strike committee at Poplar next day, Tuesday. We did so at 5 o'clock, in the Wade Street Schools. The conference lasted three and a half hours. About sixty-five men were present. For two hours there was little hope. I had proposed that the difference of time between then and 1 January should be split, fixing 4 November. Gradually a change came, and Mr. Champion moved a resolution adopting my proposal and empowering me to treat with the directors. This was at last carried by twenty-eight to fifteen, nineteen Surrey men not voting, their demand being distinct from the north.

Next day, Wednesday, we saw the directors. The lord mayor, by telegram, empowered me to urge the proposition of the men upon the directors. They gave no definite answer. We saw Mr. Norwood in private, and things seemed more favourable. The directors said they were bound in honour not to come in, until the wharfingers, and lightermen, and Surrey men came in.

The next days were spent in dealing with the two first, but until Saturday we could not get an agreement. It was five o'clock before the lightermen gave in, and six o'clock before the directors signed.

The strike then ended.

The lightermen then came to the Mansion House to thank us and to shake hands.[38]

## Feeding the Families

During the period when the strike was just beginning to attract support from outside, the *Star* had reported that 'Cardinal Manning and the Salvation Army' shared the credit for feeding the hungry, clothing the naked, and visiting the sick.

But the real story of the funding of the stoppage depends on forces far apart from the Liberal and Catholic influences on London's docklands. Of course, Church funds could be applied directly to the relief of distress, and would not necessarily pass through the hands of the Strike Committee, so that their full extent cannot be calculated. But the evidence we have shows very clearly that the main support came from elsewhere.

At the end of August, the flow of British relief funds was desperately short of the amount needed to sustain the action. Close at hand though they were, the Church and the Liberals had by then made relatively scant financial contributions. The problem of blackleg labour was ominous, and there were rumours of the diversion of ships to other ports. The general trades of London had withheld all but financial support, and negotiations with the employers were in deadlock. The men and their families were hungry.

In these critical circumstances Tom Mann felt that new initiatives were vital. He proposed that a call be made for a general sympathy strike of the whole of the London trades. What became the famous 'no-work' manifesto was hurriedly drawn up and signed by the Strike Committee. Tillett, completely exhausted, returning to his bed after long hours convincing the Wapping dockers not to return to work, was persuaded to sign without fully realizing the significance of what he was doing. Fortuitously, on the very same day, the first meeting of the dockers of Brisbane had been summoned to organize practical support for London. They immediately sent a telegram to communicate the good news. Australian funds began to arrive soon after, and they came in a flood. Beyond doubt this was providential for the dockers.

## A General Strike?

The manifesto, dated 29 August, was issued from the strike headquarters at the Wade's Arms. It read, in part: 'We now solemnly appeal to the workers in London of all grades and of every calling to refuse to go to work on Monday next unless the directors have before noon on Saturday, 31st August, officially informed this committee that the moderate demands of the dock labourers have been fully and finally conceded'. Once he had time to weigh up this attempt to call a general stoppage, over the heads of the cautious leaders of the other unions, Ben Tillett was deeply troubled. He rightly doubted whether such an appeal could be heard. If it failed, it would certainly alienate the established union officers and isolate the dockers. Engels shared Tillett's view, on wider grounds. He wrote at once to Eleanor Marx, asking her to oppose 'such a desperate game', because it would foreclose the support of the 'great mass of the bourgeoisie who all hate the dock monopolists'.[39] In some anguish, the call was withdrawn and its possible effect was thus never tested.

Notwithstanding the prudent influence of Eleanor Marx, masses of unorganized workers from outside the docks did nevertheless flock to join the dockers' marches and so promote their own disputes:

As soon as it became obvious that the Strike was not merely a local dispute, but would be carried on with courage and energy and on a very large scale, numberless trades threw in their lot with the Strikers, abandoned their work, and joined the processions. Men who had been working for years with every appearance of being resigned to their lot suddenly discovered that they too had grievances, and must have an increase of wages or reduction of hours. So rapidly did the discontent spread that the Committee were seriously hampered by the applications to them for advice, encouragement, and assistance by workmen whose precipitate action hindered rather than helped the Dockers' cause ... it is certain that a very large number of East London workmen, who took occasion by the hand and demanded a higher wage, obtained it after stopping work for a few hours, as an indirect result of the Dock Labourers' action. Nor can it be doubted that amongst such men the principles of Trade Unionism will find countless adherents, and that in the next few months the lessons they have learnt will bear fruit in a great increase of organisation amongst them. The Committee were obliged to refuse to assist such Strikers, since it was obvious that the funds with which they were entrusted were meant by the donors exclusively for the benefit of the Dock Labourers. On dozens of occasions we were obliged to advise men who came to tell us of their intention to come out on strike, to refrain from doing so unless they were prepared to fight their own battle alone. At last it became necessary to publish a manifesto warning the discontented that if they came out on strike without the authority of the Committee, they must do so at their own risk.[40]

But, of course, none of this uprush of action among the East End poor would have engaged the older unions in supporting strikes. The level of their sympathy was not negligible, but we can measure it in cash. Checkmated in efforts to spread the strike, only new monies could sustain the dockers in what was becoming unendable hardship.

## Funding the Strike

The final balance sheet of the strike fund covering the period from 14 August to 16 November, showed that out of a total income of £46,499, the 'colonies' remitted £30,423,[41] whilst from all sources in Britain came £16,075. Trade unions gave something over £4,000: the 'public generally' remitted by letter and otherwise £10,661. Of this, £6,723 was collected by the *Star*. Street-box collections yielded £1,039.[42] Without the Australians, the outcome would have been completely different. But with their help, the strikers held out and won. Within two years the Australian waterfronts were themselves in tumult. The defeat of the maritime strike of 1890 has been seen as the turning-point in Australian labour history. After it, political action and the establishment of arbitration became a priority for most trade unionists.[43] None the less, the London dockers were fondly remembered. Cardinal Manning's portrait still decorated at least one Labour Hall in Australia in the late 1960s, where Tom Mann is similarly and widely commemorated.

## III

## Recognizing a New Power

The strike lasted from 12 August until 14 September. The strikers' demands, we should recall, had been for an increase in the hourly rate from 5d. to 6d., the ending of contract work and the plus system, and for taking-on times to be limited to two per day for a minimum of four hours' work. The settlement finally agreed conceded the hourly 6*d*., and 8*d*. per hour overtime (defined as from 6 p.m. to 8 a.m.). It established 2*s*. – i.e. four hours at time rates – as a minimum wage for any call-on. The contract system was converted to piece-work, and the surplus was to be equally divided amongst the gangs under the joint supervision of both company and dockers' representatives. These people, in negotiating the price for their jobs, acquired a role which would later be familiar throughout industry as that of the shop stewards.

During the strike, the Tea Operatives' Union rose in numbers from a few hundred to 18,000. Immediately following the strike, it was reorganized as the Dock, Wharf, Riverside and General Labourers' Union (DWRGLU), and by the end of November had grown to 30,000 members. Branches were set up in Bristol, Southampton, South Wales and Hull, as well as in Rotterdam and Amsterdam, Ipswich, Harwich, Gloucester and the Medway ports. But it was the leadership of the London men which officered the new union. Tom Mann was elected president, Tillett continued as secretary, and Tom McCarthy and Harry Orbell were appointed organizers.

That these leaders understood that the strike settlement must be vigilantly defended and generalized in all its ports is evident in the rules of the new union. Rule 1 established its name. Rule 2 fixed its objects to be:

1  To control the system of boy labour.
2  To abolish the present system of sub-contracts.
3  To regulate hours of hiring.
4  To enforce a minimum of four hours. (Minimum rate of pay to be 6*d*. per hour ordinary, and 8*d*. per hour overtime.) Working in stream 7*d*. ordinary, and 9*d*. overtime.
5  To establish a general fund for the protection of trade interests, for the recovery of compensation in cases of accidents, and for the provision of a 10*s*. weekly payment to members on strike.
6  To abolish extra work and overtime.
7  To establish a labour bureau.

Contributions were fixed at 2*d*. per week, with an entrance fee of 2*s*. 6*d*., and a quarterly charge of 4*d*. for management expenses. It is noticeable that the only money benefit at the outset was strike pay. The real incentive to join the union was, however, the recognition of its card by the employers, who granted work preference to members.

## Central Power and Sectional Division

The constitution of the union centralized power in the hands of its executive, which was appointed by a Delegates' Council comprising two representatives from each branch. (Branches had a maximum of 500 members, and were grouped under District Committees, which could appoint paid secretaries.) The National Executive had nine members, presided over by Tom Mann. It collected *all* the funds received by the branches, and decided on *all* disbursements. It held the authority to sanction strike action. (In constitutional matters the Delegates' Council functioned as an ultimate court of appeal.)

Tom Mann undoubtedly had great influence on this centralized constitution. Lovell speaks of his policies as being

> sweeping and sometimes high-handed. As an outsider, and an impulsive one at that, he occasionally encountered the most ferocious opposition from port workers and on one occasion he told Burns that he was forced to carry a revolver to protect himself. Nevertheless his personality was such an engaging one that he won in the end the whole-hearted support of his members.[44]

It is improbable that Mann's need for weapons stemmed from any need to defend himself from ordinary port workers, but it would be a very probable precaution when confronting the professional strike-breakers. But Lovell is right about Mann's influence: so great was it that when he resigned for a short time in 1892, it was feared that the organization would break up.

Lovell contrasts the centralizing initiative of Mann, whose motivations were 'his passionate concern for downtrodden labour generally', with the approach of Harry Quelch, the South Side's Labour Protection League leader. Both had come from the SDF, but Quelch followed and embodied the traditions of the 1870s dock unionism, localized, sectional and autonomous.

Waterfront trade unionism in London remained divided after the great strike, between the new union, the South Side Labour Protection League, the Stevedores, the Watermen and Lightermen, and numerous smaller sectional bodies such as the Non-Freemen's Society, the Ballast Heavers' Society, and the Coal Porters' Winchmen's Association. Among these, the Amalgamated Stevedores' Labour Protection League and its general secretary Tom McCarthy had played a key part in the strike. Their branch headquarters at the Wade's Arms had been the main organizing centre. McCarthy had always held a wider view of waterfront unionism than was expressed in the separatism of the stevedores, and had supported Tillett's organizing efforts in the Tea Operatives' Union for months before the strike. It will be recalled that the second union formed by the stevedores in the 1870s, the United Stevedores' Union, had also supported the strike. In 1890, overcoming a history of mutual tension, the two stevedores' unions merged in the Amalgamated Stevedores' Labour Protection League. This step, whilst an advance on their previous division, none the less represented a solidification of their shared sectionalism in the face of Tillett and Mann's new union, and was in this sense a retreat from the outward-looking commitment of McCarthy.

The perpetuation of the old corn-porters' branch in the Surrey docks as the South Side Labour Protection League (SSLPL), further entrenched divisions in the port. The great strike was a fillip to the LPL, which added 'South Side' to its name in 1889 and modelled itself deliberately on the 1872 union. It remained separate from the Dockers' Union (as we shall henceforth refer to the DWRGLU) until the amalgamation of 1922, when it brought its 2,500 members into the TGWU.

Following the strike, partial attempts were made in London to overcome these divisions. The Wade's Arms Strike Committee was used as the basis for a United Labour Council (ULC). Most of the smaller occupational unions joined, as did the seamen, but not the Dockers' Union or the SSLPL. In staying out of the ULC, the Dockers' Union hoped, by its numerical dominance, to absorb the smaller unions in the port. In pursuit of this objective, in 1890 it formed its own federation with the seamen and the SSLPL, and in September 1891, as we shall see, it merged this federation with the ULC of the smaller unions. These initiatives demonstrate that there were strong currents flowing for wider forms of unity in London's dockland, and that the formation of the Dockers' Union was never likely to be the last word on the structure of waterfront unionism.

# IV

## *Evaluation*

How then should we evaluate the great dock strike? Before it, as Engels wrote to Edward Bernstein while it was still running its course:

> the East End was bogged down in passive poverty. Lack of resistance on the part of those broken by starvation, of those who had given up all hope was its salient feature. Anyone who got into it was physically and morally lost. Then last year came the successful strike of the match girls. And now this gigantic strike of the lowest of the outcasts, the dock labourers – not of the steady, strong, experienced, comparatively well-paid and regularly employed ones, but of those whom chance has dumped on the docks, those who are always down on their luck, who have not managed to get along in any other trade, people who have become professional starvelings, a mass of broken-down humanity who are drifting towards total ruination,

for whom one might inscribe on the gates of the docks the words of Dante: Lasciate ogni speranza voi che entrate! ['Abandon hope, all ye who enter here!'] And this host of utterly despondent men . . . this motley crowd thrown together by chance and changing daily in composition has managed to unite 40,000 strong, to maintain discipline and to strike fear into the hearts of the mighty dock companies.[45]

It is easy to share Engels's exultation:

How glad I am to have lived to see this day! If this stratum can be organised, that is a fact of great import. However the strike may end . . . with the dock labourers the lowest stratum of East End workers enters the movement and then the upper strata must follow their example. The East End contains the greatest number of common labourers in England, of people whose work requires no skill or almost none. If these sections of the proletariat, which until now have been treated with contempt by the Trade Unions of the skilled workers, organise in London, this will serve as an example for the provinces.[46]

At the same time the novelist Olive Schreiner was staying in London. She wrote to the poet Edward Carpenter, who had inspired Annie Besant:

Isn't the strike splendid. You ought to see the East End now. The strange earnest look in the people's faces, that sort of wide-eyed look. You look straight into their faces and their eyes look back at you; they are possessed with a large idea. It's very wonderful. I went yesterday to the place where the Salvation Army are giving away tiny packets of tea. About 500 men were there . . . waiting. The serious, silent, elated atmosphere, the look in the face of the most drunken old man was wonderful. I think I never felt so full of hope as yesterday.[47]

Another witness who was deeply moved was eighteen years old at the time. Soon he was canvassing in Whitechapel, discovering the depths of its squalor and misery. 'I was appalled by what I saw,' he wrote in his memoirs. 'The contrast between what I was seeing day by day, and what I found when I returned home . . . to our too opulent household, upset my equanimity altogether'. Thus it was that Herbert Samuel, future leader of the Liberal Party, go-between in the General Strike of 1926, and Home Secretary in the National Government of Ramsay MacDonald, came to write his youthful manifesto against those who rode in 'glittering carriages' in Hyde Park:

All these callous, unthinking folk live on, unmoved, untouched by any thought of those millions, whom in contempt they unite to form the collective masses . . . The masses! – what a tale in one word. To be one of them – what a hopeless, endless fate; what a stifling of impossible ambition, still-birth of ideals . . . And what are they, dull, short-visioned, who see not the ground shaking beneath their very feet, and angry voices, quiet, marvellously refraining yet, that are soon to rise, in ever-swelling clamour. Short-lived was the warning of a hundred years ago* . . . Let there be but one bad King, one unscrupulous minister, and down will crumble your monarchy and your upper classes. May it be well led, our English revolution . . . Have you ever thought – upper classes, of a humble workman's daily life, its sorrows, its hardships . . .[48]

In time, Lord Samuel learned how to bring his views into somewhat closer conformity with the forces of order. Others proved less adaptable.

Yet adaptation there was, and it did not take all that long. Only a few months later, the same Engels who had welcomed the 'example' of the strike was bemoaning the respectability of the new leaders of these outcasts of London. Burns, he told F. A. Sorge on 7 December 1889, was 'secretly prouder of his popularity with Cardinal Manning . . . than of his popularity with his own class'. Champion had intrigued with the bourgeoisie. 'Even Tom Mann . . . the finest of them, is fond of mentioning that he will be lunching with the Lord Mayor'. Hope sprang eternal with Engels, though: 'It will not help the bourgeoisie much if they do succeed in enticing some of the leaders into their toils. By that time the movement will have become strong enough to overcome this sort of thing'.[49] None the less, 'If one compares this with the French, one sees what a revolution is good for, after all'.[50]

Engels had been right first time. A new constituency had announced itself. Its potential power could not be disputed.

Yet the established order had indeed noticed what was going on. The Liberal Party had a suitably ambivalent structure, and a division of forces which could connect with even the most intransigent rebels. Shortly Tom Mann was to find himself serving on a Royal Commission. This was not to prove fatal, either to him or his supporters. But in due time, the 'man in the straw hat', John Burns, was to arrive in a Liberal Cabinet. Generations of socialists have seen this simply as an apostasy. So it was: but was it not also the beginning of a great process of deliberate incorporation, in which trade-union militancy was to become simultaneously a protest against and a bid for a place in established society?

## Recognition: the Magic Word

Everything turns on what happens when a hitherto unorganized section of people obtains 'recognition'. With hindsight, recognition may appear to be the first step to 'incorporation'. Certainly once class divisions are not only intuited but also organized, it becomes possible to devise

* The French Revolution of 1789.

structures for regulating and controlling their interconnection. This is the basis for all the various institutions which have since been described as 'corporatist'. To look at the problem in the light of its resolution is signally to misunderstand it in its origin.

For the leaders of the dock workers in 1889, things appeared in a very different light. They had been part of a momentous upheaval. Most of them had stepped into the waterfront arena from outside. Burns and Mann were highly skilled engineers, with a long tradition of craft unionism behind them, even where they rejected it. Champion and Eleanor Marx, and a small host of others, whose influence was vital in the conduct of the strike, were highly qualified professional people acting in the interest of the socialist movement, seeking to proselytize. The skilled workers on the waterfront itself carried an immense burden, and without Tom McCarthy and his supporters no rebellion would have been possible. Lastly, there were those who could truly be identified with the hitherto unorganizable 'dock rats': most notably, Ben Tillett himself.

The mutinous workforce had few points of community reference. Ill- and often impermanently housed migrants, refugees from different forms of oppression and poverty, they were less tractable to permanent organization than any other group which had hitherto atttempted it. Before 1889, and since, there have been innumerable explosions of rage among oppressed populations, which have given rise to a few days or weeks of ferocious combat, only to be followed by the restoration of 'order', and the rebirth of apathy, quiescence and hopelessness.

In the United States, during the great days of the Industrial Workers of the World (IWW) from 1910 to 1922, city-wide stoppages of work could be organized – even up to the point of physical battles – as the union message spread. But once a year had elapsed, the IWW could often muster the merest handful of members among those once 'vanguard' populations. (The military image in such cases is almost appropriate.) In short, nothing could guarantee the continued association of the London dock workers once their claims had been satisfied. Organizing on the day was one thing: organizing a continuous presence was quite another.

But then the concept of recognition comes into play. If the employer 'recognizes' the association of port workers, he does far more than agree to deal with a group of workers' representatives. Now the members of that group can recognize their own collective identity through his opposing eyes. Their personal separateness is overcome, not only by their own efforts to join together but by the concession of collective status on the part of the adversary. If the adversary, in his own newly perceived weakness, seeks to associate himself with others of his class, so much the better: this means that the realities of class have now entered into the formal structure of social relations, so that the words describing it take on a new and deeper meaning.

Long before the complete transformation of our vocabulary, however, we may expect the intervention of a third party. If the state intervenes, whether to 'hold the ring' or for some more direct engagement to uphold its rule, this too may easily offer the prospect of recognition. Class relationships, in short, are built through interaction, and are not simply self-ascribed. Recognition is one of the boundaries evolved in interaction, and becomes a major determinant in the development of trade-union organization.

The events of 1889 were crucial in this process. In them was born a persistent effort, which would survive brutal countermeasures. Recognition could be withdrawn, but the will to establish it could not be cancelled so easily. Its effect would bring vast changes in industrial life, and a transforming influence in politics.

This is an argument about which much was to be heard for almost 100 years afterwards. On the day after victory, the situation was differently perceived.

What, after all, had happened to the people of dockland? They had been pushed to the outermost fringes of rejection by Victorian society. Crowded a dozen at a time into squalid tenement rooms, exhausted, starved, forced to fight one another for a few hours' work which commonly they were too enfeebled to perform: these wraiths had joined forces, recovered strength in their solidarity, and, at last, won. Their message had gone round the world. They had got their sixpence; but more, they had regained their self-respect, and with it their human powers, by daring to rebel. The evolution of 'dock rats' into 'new unionists' turned whole lifetimes of personal subjection and defeat into a wild joy of collective triumph. Could this inspire further victories? Would the union continue? Might it, indeed, become the foundation for all the wider changes in the political order which had seemed so necessary to all those who had rallied to give help? By the time of the opening of the dock strike, Parliament was old, but modern democracy was waiting to be born. At the end of that strike, its healthy embryo was beginning to grow, and nothing would ever be the same again.

# Notes

1   *Justice*, 18 July 1885; cited in Sidney and Beatrice Webb, *The History of Trade Unionism* (1894; WEA edn, 1912), pp. 410–11.

2   Ibid., 6 August 1887.

3   Benjamin Tillett (1860–1947), born in Bristol, ran away from home as a child, joined a circus, then entered the navy at the age of thirteen, where he learned to read and write. He transferred to the merchant marines in 1876 and gravitated to London's East End, seeking work on the docks, in 1885.

4   *Justice*, 24 November 1888; quoted in Jonathan Schneer, *Ben Tillett: Portrait of a Labour Leader* (Croom Helm, 1982).

5  Ben Tillett, *Memories and Reflections* (John Long, 1931), pp. 112–13.

6  John Lovell, *Stevedores and Dockers: a Study of Trade Unionism in the Port of London, 1870–1914* (Macmillan, 1969), p. 97, puts the membership at a maximum of 800 and a minimum of 300, and gives two sources, one of which is Tillett's *Memories and Reflections* (p. 113). But this is inaccurate, and Tillett gives no such figures. He does, indeed, speak of a 'tiny' union (p. 118), 'my own feeble union' (p. 110) and 'our small union' (p. 112). But the only figure we can trace to Tillett himself is 2,400, which is the membership he claimed on 20 November 1888, during cross-examination at the Select Committee on the Sweating System, (Second Reports, p. 111, Parliamentary Papers, 1888, V, XXI). Lovell's second reference is to George Howell, *Trade Unionism New and Old* (Methuen, 1891; 3rd edn, rev. to 1990), p. 153. In fact this reference is to a markedly hostile source, as we shall see when we examine the controversy which gave rise to this report. Of course, the boasted 2,400 might have been a propaganda exaggeration. But in July 1887 Tillett invited MPs and other public figures to an open meeting of 2–3,000 dockers (*Memories and Reflections*, p. 99). Perhaps this is connected with his claim during the Select Committee hearings? In any event, Colonel George Raymond Birt, manager of the Milwall docks, strongly contested Tillett's estimate of the number of dock workers in London, but made no attempt to challenge his statement about union membership. (Tillett said there were 100,000 dockers in London; Birt put the number at an absolute maximum of 75,000.)

7  Yvonne Kapp, *The Air of Freedom: The Birth of the New Unionism* (Lawrence and Wishart, 1989), p. 53. While this book offers an incomparable story of the day-by-day struggles of the gasworkers, for an analysis of the social and technological context of their union it is still necessary to go to Eric J. Hobsbawm's remarkable work, *Labouring Men* (Weidenfeld and Nicolson, 1968), pp. 158–203.

8  Tillett, *Memories and Reflections*, p. 119.

9  Ibid., p. 91.

10  Tillett claimed in retrospect that this programme represented the first challenge to the whole casual system of employment (*Memories and Reflections*, p. 120).

11  The figure of 100,000 workers is Tillett's, supported by Jonathan Schneer, *Ben Tillett*, p. 42. The estimates of picket numbers given here are higher than those of Ann Stafford and other historians.

12  Llewellyn Smith and Vaughan Nash, *The Story of the Dockers' Strike* (Fisher Unwin, 1890), p. 84.

13  Eric J. Hobsbawm, *Labour's Turning Point, 1880–1900*, History in the Making, vol. III (Lawrence and Wishart, 1948), pp. 85–6.

14  F. W. S. Craig, *Minor Parties at British Parliamentary Elections, 1885–1974* (Macmillan, 1975), p. 47, gives details of all contests.

15  T. P. O'Connor, *Memoirs of an Old Parliamentarian*, vol. II (Ernest Benn, 1929), p. 255.

16  Cf. Raymond Williams, *The Long Revolution* (Chatto and Windus, 1961), pp. 198ff.

17  G. B. Shaw, *Collected Letters, 1874–1897*, vol. I (Max Reinhardt, 1965), pp. 183ff.

18  Friedrich Engels, Paul and Laura Lafargue, *Correspondence* (Foreign Languages Publishing House, Moscow, n.d.), vol. II, pp. 239–57, 260–8 and 402; vol. III, pp. 78–82 and 92.

19  Ann Stafford, *A Match to Fire the Thames*, makes extensive use of *Star* reports. This gives a clear impression of the scale of the newspaper's coverage and commitment.

20  Their principal press officer was H. H. Champion. From him, at strike headquarters, the regular newspaper journalists received daily briefings and releases. Eleanor Marx worked 'unceasingly, literally night and day, at our headquarters' (Tillett, *Memories and Reflections*, p. 135) as minute-secretary, counsellor and treasurer. She had already helped greatly in the formation of the Gasworkers' Union during the previous year. Her work earned deeply affectionate tributes in the subsequent memoirs of both Tillett and Mann, who remembered, in their old age, how much they gained from her sparkling intellect and her great force of character. Alas, they also had to record how much they had been moved by her tragic fate. There is copious evidence of the frequency of the meetings attended jointly by Eleanor Marx and Tom Mann during the 1880s in the correspondence of Eleanor, in Olga Meier (ed.), *The Daughters of Karl Marx: Family Correspondence, 1866–1898* (Penguin, 1984), part four, pp. 163–219.

21  George Haw, *From Workhouse to Westminster* (Dalton, n.d.), p. 68.

22  Ann Stafford, *A Match to Fire the Thames* (Hodder and Stoughton, 1961), p. 106.

23  Ibid., p. 117.

24  Smith and Nash, *The Story of the Dockers' Strike*, pp. 104–5.

25  Not £12,000, as Stafford erroneously reports (*A Match to Fire the Thames*, p. 116).

26  Stafford, *A Match to Fire the Thames*, p. 116.

27  Smith and Nash, *The Story of the Dockers' Strike*, p. 105.

28  Friedrich Engels, letter to H. Schluter, 11 January 1890, in *Karl Marx and Frederick Engels on Britain* (Foreign Languages Publishing House, Moscow, 1953), pp. 523–4.

29  Stafford, *A Match to Fire the Thames*, p. 119.

30  Dona Torr, *Tom Mann and His Times*, vol. I: *1856–1890* (Lawrence and Wishart, 1956), pp. 295–6.

31  Ibid., p. 296.

32  Stafford, *A Match to Fire the Thames*, p. 198.

33  Ibid., p. 142.

34  Smith and Nash, *The Story of the Dockers' Strike*, p. 97.

35  Alan Fox analyses the role of these groups in the evolution of the British system of industrial relations in his *History and Heritage: The Social Origins of the British Industrial Relations System* (Allen and Unwin, 1985), pp. 235–55.

36  John Lovell reports that the close-knit, kinship-dominated trades and trade unionism of the Port of London, produced by the Irish immigrants, were more marked in the South Side Labour Protection League (SSLPL), and the Stevedores' Union, than amongst the dock labourers who constituted Tillett's union and who later formed the membership of the DWRGLU. He ascribes the father–son succession practices specifically to the Irish: 'In the London dock area of the 1890s the story was told of a foreman named

Donovan, who was said to have taken on 57 Donovans for work one day, and was only stopped by the men threatening him with violence if he took on any more relations! Tom McCarthy, himself London Irish, recorded that "they collared the corn portering and the stevedoring and being very clannish have kept it in their families ever since. Thus the second generation of Irish got the pick of the work" ' 'The Irish and the London Dockers', *Bulletin of the Society for the Study of Labour History*, no. 35 (autumn 1977), pp. 16–17.

This was precisely the kind of unionism which rejected, and was rejected by, the new unionism which arose out of the London dock strike. Yet we need not follow Lovell in supposing that the Irish – who may well have established this pattern in the SSLPL and the stevedores' unions – necessarily *invented* it: the much older and indigenous practice of the Thames lightermen existed to set an example of clannishness.

37    Tom Mann, *Memoirs* (1923; reissued MacGibbon and Kee, 1967), p. 85, wrote, 'As the Cardinal had been so closely identified with the wind-up negotiations of the dock strike, he maintained his interest in the welfare of the dockers, and on a number of occasions he wrote asking me to call on him to tell him how matters were developing. I have before commented upon his wonderful features, and upon the ultra-refined manner that always characterized him. He was perfectly natural, and simple, and I was entirely at ease with him'.

38    E. S. Purcell, *Life of Cardinal Manning* (1896; 2nd edn, 2 vols, 1985), vol. II, pp. 662–3.

39    Engels and Lafargue, *Correspondence*, vol. II, p. 317.

40    H. H. Champion, *The Great Dock Strike in London: August 1889* (Swan Sonnenschein, 1890), p. 169.

41    P. F. Donovan has analysed the Australian contributions to the dockers' fund ('Australia and the Great London Dock Strike, 1889', *Journal of the Australian Society for the Study of Labour History*, no. 23 (November 1972), pp. 17–26). He shows that there was very widespread support for the strikers, involving extensive middle-class contributions. Not only the unions, but the overwhelming majority of the Australian press, took part in a truly massive campaign. Donovan reports, however, that 'an analysis of the subscription lists that were published [in Australia] suggests that the total was nearer £37,000' than the £30,000 recorded in the British accounts. Donovan offers the following breakdown:

| | |
|---|---|
| Queensland | £2,135 9s 2d |
| New South Wales | £8,386 5s 7d |
| Victoria | £22,569 5s 4d |
| South Australia | £3,073 9s 9d |
| | £36,164 9s 10d |

These figures are based on reports in the *Brisbane Courier*, *Sydney Morning Herald*, Melbourne *Age*, and Adelaide *Observer* between 24 September and 24 October 1889. In addition, the Tasmanian government had sent £500 to the dockers by 11 September, and the New Zealand unions had each forwarded £200. This 'means that the total from the Australasian colonies must have stood at least at £37,064 9s. 10d. The probability is that the final total was even greater than this'. The dockers' balance sheet (*The Great Dock Labourers' Strike, 1889, Manifesto and Statement of Accounts* (Green and McAllan, 1889)) carries a note to the items recording 'colonial' contributions, explaining that certain sums had been sent directly to the Lord Mayor of London for the relief of 'distress' during the strike, without passing through the hands of the Strike Committee. These, of course, were unrecorded in the dockers' accounts. It thus appears that the Lord Mayor handled a minimum of £7,000 from Australia, in addition to whatever was collected in London or the rest of Britain.

Not all these monies reflected the appeal of solidarity, however. Various other motives intruded. They have been discussed and analysed by Humphrey McQueen, *A New Britannia* (3rd edn, Penguin (Australia), 1986), pp. 221 and 259.

42 See Smith and Nash, *The Story of the Dockers' Strike* appendix E, pp. 186–7.

43 'The great turning point in the history of Australian labour was undoubtedly the maritime strike . . . in 1890 . . . The effect of . . . defeat was to galvanise into life the hitherto latent idea that voting power carried with it not only the choice of the Parliamentary representative, but also of the work he was expected to do . . .' (W. G. Spence, *Australia's Awakening* (1909), pp. 94 and 185). See the discussion of this claim by June Philipp and Jean O'Connor in *Historical Studies*, second series, (Melbourne University Press, 1967), pp. 126–50.

44 Lovell, *Stevedores and Dockers*, p. 115.

45 Engels, letter to Edward Bernstein, 22 August 1889, in *Karl Marx and Frederick Engels on Britain*, pp. 520–1.

46 Ibid., p. 521.

47 Cited in Chushichi Tsuzuki, *Edward Carpenter, 1844–1929* (Cambridge University Press, 1980), p. 90.

48 The Rt Hon. Viscount Samuel, *Memoirs* (Cresset Press, 1945), p. 7.

49 *Karl Marx and Frederick Engels on Britain*, p. 523.

50 Ibid.

# 4

# The New Unionism Arrives

## I

### *Nothing Succeeds Like . . .*

If we say that the dock strike was to become the symbol of an uprising of the poorest workers, we are saying that it was not an isolated event. It was by no means the first event of its kind: but it happened in London, at the centre of a national media network, under the noses of national political spokesmen. That London poverty was merely a concentrated example of nationwide deprivation meant only that the news of the uprising of the London poor electrified the slums of the North, and the dockside tenements of ports all around the country. Equally, it inspired the conscientious middle classes, the active Christians, and that part of the intelligentsia that was already beginning to think about socialist ideas. Unions had already been forming during the earlier months of economic upturn, and their further mushrooming could only be encouraged by the dockers' success. Indeed, in the minds of its beholders that success grew to assume almost mythic proportions. The prosperity of the affluent classes in late Victorian England was constantly reproached by the squalor and destitution they engendered all around them. Any challenge to this polarity was bound to arouse wide moral support, and so stiffen the will to resistance. As hopes rose, so the stature of the dockers' heroes rose with them.

Havelock Wilson, the seamen's leader, wrote:

Demonstrations became very frequent. Every branch of a union felt it must have a banner. The silk industry and the painters had quite a boom in trade . . . everyone's portrait had to be painted on the banners. The national men (that is to say, the leaders of national importance) had first place, such men as John Burns, Tom Mann, Ben Tillett, Will Thorne and myself.[1]

In fact these were remarkable men, but they were plainly incapable of fulfilling the legendary tasks which were to be laid upon them. Having been set to long hours of work in early childhood, each was responsible for his own education, and even if rich experience was a fine instructor, none the less there were bound to be important gaps in learning. To a great extent the social and strategic goals of such leaders had to be formed in reaction to the heaving flux of events. It was necessary to think on one's feet.

And for all the great men whose pictures were carried in procession, there were hundreds of others whose role was equally indispensable. A giant wave of unionization broke over the country in the years between 1888 and 1890. People who had previously been thought incapable of organization were suddenly in the forefront of turbulent trade-union actions. Of these struggles, those concerned with the seamen and with dock workers outside London are closest to our concern. But others were also very significant.

## The Seamen

A loosely federated union of seamen had existed as far back as 1851, with branches in thirty ports. It won some concessions from the shipping companies, but, having no central government, it collapsed in 1860.[2] The seamen had formed a number of local associations in the 1870s, mirroring the state of unionism in dockland at that time. Having been a member of one such union in the North-east, Havelock Wilson formed the National Amalgamated Union of Sailors and Firemen in 1887.[3] In 1889 the seamen struck for wage increases in all the principal ports. In most cases they were successful. These stoppages ranged over the first six months of the year, thus preceding the dock strike.[4] By the time the dockers were out, the seamen had formed forty-five branches nationwide.

## The National Union of Dock Labourers

In Glasgow, two craft unionists, the compositor McHugh and the engineer McGhee, formed the National Union of Dock Labour in February 1889, and rapidly spread its recruitment to Liverpool. Soon they had reached out to other ports in the North-west and throughout Scotland. Glasgow dockers joined in strike action with the seamen in that port in June, following an appeal for support from Havelock Wilson, who urged them to form a dock-workers' union which could then federate with his seamen's organization. The new union did not have the impetus that was afforded to London by the great strike. After the collapse of the seamen's strike in Glasgow it led a shadowy existence, and owed much of its survival to the skill and persistence of McHugh, its first general secretary, and McGhee, its first president. McHugh was a personal friend and follower of Henry George, a supporter of the Scottish crofters' Highlands agitation, and already a well-known Scottish radical. McGhee had similarly close relations with Henry George, and with Michael Davitt, the Irish land-reformer. He had participated in the Knights of Labour agitation in the Midlands in 1887, on behalf of the nail- and chain-makers, and the Knights had nominated him to organize in Glasgow. However, he acted independently of them in the NUDL, and worked as a commercial traveller whilst serving the dockers. These two leaders shared the advantage – in dockland – of Irish origins. They were also committed to Irish Nationalism. Their adherence to Georgeism drew no less popular support from the people, many of whom had desperate experience or memories of injustice in the severance of their families from the land.

The full title of their union became the National Union of Dock Labourers in Great Britain and Ireland. Its national aspirations were new to dockland: its specific remit to organize across the Irish Sea had a special significance, with consequences which were to reach far into the twentieth century. Glasgow dockers had a spasmodic record of unionism going back to the 1850s, and one small body continued to challenge the monopoly of the NUDL for some years. Before 1889 had passed, organizers had established the new union in Belfast and, most significantly, Liverpool. Derry, Dundee and Leith followed quickly behind. In Liverpool a strike was provoked during the course of the London strike, 'deliberately inspired . . . by the employers, who hoped to stamp out the union before it attained its full strength, before we ourselves, indeed, could realize the full measure of our strength', reported James Sexton, who joined the union at once, even though he had already been victimized and was forced to earn his living as a coal merchant outside the docks.[5] He bankrupted his new business giving aid to the strikers.

## The Birth of Ca'canny

A three-week strike for higher pay in the Glasgow docks in 1889 collapsed because the employers made ruthless use of blackleg labour. The inefficiency of the substituted workforce was highlighted by the union, and the employers responded by declaring themselves well satisfied with it: whereupon McHugh seized his opportunity. The dockers returned to work, and McHugh advised them that if the employers were satisfied with incompetent cheap labour, and unwilling to pay for work of better quality, then it would be a mistake to give them more than the value of their offered rewards. He told the workers:

> We have seen them [the blackleg farm workers], we have seen that they don't know how to walk on a boat, that they have dropped half the stuff they carried: in short that two of them can't do the work of one of us . . . Work like the farmworkers worked. Only it happened that several times they fell into the water: it is useless for you to do the same![6]

In this way, McHugh invented the tactic of 'ca'canny'. The Glasgow employers were soon driven to appeal for normal work effort, and to get it they conceded the wage increase which strike action had failed to win. Ca'canny thus became an official expedient of the NUDL. It emphasized amongst other things that dock labour was *not* unskilled, and this undoubtedly must have initially contributed to that self-confidence and sense of pride which are important ingredients in developing loyal commitment to trade unionism.

The union's first Annual Report elevated this tactic to a philosophy, based on a reading of contemporary political economy, the law of value and price; in simple terms, 'you get what you pay for'. After invoking the classical economist W. S. Jevons in support, the report concluded: 'If employers of labour or purchasers of goods refuse to pay for the genuine article they must be content with veneer and shoddy'.

The NUDL made the claim to be 'the pioneer organisation of what is called the new Unionism' in its executive report of December 1892. This challenge to the hegemony of the Dockers' Union was often to be repeated in the years down to the 1922 amalgamation. Yet the NUDL, which certainly competed with its London-based rival in the ports (particularly, in its later years, in those of the Humber), never sought members beyond the waterfront: unlike the dockers' organization, it never aspired to be a general union.

In the matter of ca'canny, however, it was a pioneer, and the practice soon spread unofficially to the London docks. There the Dockers' Union Executive, nursing its newly won recognition, met it with scant enthusiasm. Within months of the great strike it put out a 'Manifesto urging members of the Union to work Energetically'. It began:

> Fellow members, – complaints have been made by the Dock Directors that the men are not working as energetically and heartily as in times past, and in consequence they are not only put to a very considerable expense, but very serious delays are brought about in the departure of vessels.
>
> The Union will, of course, at all times and places, protect its members against anything in the nature of nigger-driving [sic], but we regret to know that at some of the docks the men are not working with that hearty goodwill and efficiency that is necessary to make our position strong . . .

We therefore most earnestly appeal to all our members . . . to work in a smart and workman-like manner.[7]

The Webbs, in *Industrial Democracy*, sternly disapproved of ca'canny. Tom Mann's was of course the presidential signature on the Dockers' Union manifesto, and Ben Tillett subsequently opposed the adoption of such working practices by the International Federation of Ship, Dock and River Workers in 1896. It is clearly therefore mistaken to see ca'canny as a 'method' of the new unionism: and even in the NUDL it was not carried on by James Sexton, the successor to McHugh and McGhee. In his memoirs, he described it as a 'boomerang'.[8] For all that, the call to work to rule, to husband energy, to deliver only the effort for which one was being paid, was to recur over and over again, and to be denounced over and over again. Sometimes people who called its genie out of the bottle were the same people who tried to persuade it back in again. Sometimes, indeed, they succeeded in the beginning, only to fail in the end. Yet ca'canny does tend to emerge during times in which employer recognition and bargaining relations are of secondary concern, or simply unobtainable. It sat uneasily with the general, mass-union ambitions of the new unions, and only tended to recur when these ambitions were frustrated by employer recalcitrance.

## Organizing Liverpool

The NUDL's rise in Liverpool, in the climate of trade expansion and the aftermath of the London strike, was rapid. Ben Tillett made an early visit, and newspapers were reporting anything between 10,000 and 18,000 members by March 1890. The union was able to sweep aside the rival Knights of Labour, which had established a Bootle branch in 1885 with the active participation of James Sexton, then thirty-three years old. Sexton's parents were both Irish, and he records that the family inherited memories of 'the pitch-cap and the gibbet . . . the certain fate of any priest caught celebrating Mass', which had been the British rulers' revenge for the Irish Rebellion of 1798:

> The story of those days was handed on to the children of all who endured their agony . . . and engendered in the mind of every Irishman and every Irishwoman who heard it hatred – bitter and boundless hatred – of everything connected with the Briton and the British. That, so far as my mind was concerned, was my principal political and spiritual inheritance.[9]

Sexton tells of his early activity as an agitator, which culminated in his helping to form the Knights of Labour branch. 'We met like conspirators hatching a second Guy Fawkes plot, gathering together in a gloomy cellar with only the flickering half-lights given by tallow candles thrust into the necks of pop bottles'.[10] The picture, and the analogy with the Catholic gunpowder plot, are revealing, for Cardinal Manning, as we have seen, had determined to identify his Church with the cause of labour, especially that of the unskilled, and to this end he had given active encouragement to the Knights. Thus the cause of Irish Nationalism, reinforced by the folk memory of an oppressed and persecuted Church and embodied in the person of the 'saintly old priest' of London, was harnessed in the cause of trade unionism. That it did not stagnate in the clandestine and sectarian forms adopted in Bootle, but was swept up in the powerful current of new unionism, deliberately open and public, is a testimony to the force of that upheaval. But the impetus, the tradition, of the Irish Catholic stream were fused into the new flood to provide much of its vital dynamism. Manning's intervention in London can now be seen as the most public manifestation of a consistent policy, which reached to the heart of the international Catholic Church in the years to come. The famous papal encyclical, *Rerum Novarum* of 1891, which determined Church initiatives in the promotion of confessional trade unionism throughout Europe and beyond, were 'to some extent' the work of Cardinal Manning.[11] Forty years later, *Quadregesimo Anno*, promulgated by Pius XI, was to continue in the same vein.

Manning was hated and feared by the conservative, property-owning wing of his church, who regarded him as a traitor to his class – for his father had been a director of one dock company and his brother of another.[12] But like the papal edict which followed the dock strike, Manning's influence recognized the corporate interest and status of labour, whilst explicitly opposing any transformation of its power from negative protection to positive initiative. His influence on labour extended, and was indeed at its greatest, in the American circles of Henry George and the Knights of Labour. An Italian cardinal wrote of him: 'Manning, living as he did in the midst of the independent and tenacious English people, did not hesitate to put himself at the head of Christian "Socialism"'.[13] The influence reaches down through the union's later history, notably in the docks. Tim O'Leary, London–Wapping Irish Catholic, presided over the docks section of the TGWU throughout the 1950s and 1960s, his faith arming him for his running war against the communists and other dissidents in dockland. A Hull docks officer, appearing before the resolutely secular leadership of Jack Jones and Bill Jones in 1966 to plead his case against dismissal, held up two books, the Bible and the union Rule Book, and declared that he had lived his whole life by these two infallible guides.

## The 'Button' Strike

The docks of Liverpool flared up in mass strike action in 1890. At first McHugh and McGhee sought to contain it – they certainly did not promote or call it. The demands were many and varied: wage increases were called for; hours of work and meal breaks were issues; but the most common demand was for union control of work, which in the NUDL took the form of a dockers' coat-lapel button to be displayed by members, who should receive preference at the call-ons. The union also drew up port working rules, which it sought to negotiate with the employers. In these ways, the union aimed to gain control of the strike, which had begun in a spontaneous manner. The larger employers, formed into the Employers' Labour Association, resisted union recognition and insisted on their right to employ non-union labour. The smaller employers, independent of this association, were prepared to make concessions. The union's official policy was to settle and return to work in these cases, but the men rejected this advice in the name of solidarity. After three weeks, the strikers could hold out no longer, and McHugh called on Michael Davitt's services as mediator. He achieved little, and the terms of settlement were a victory for the big employers. Union members had to agree to work with non-unionists, and could wear their union buttons at the call-stand but not at work.

Yet the union itself survived without discredit, although it remained heir to many sectional and occupational divisions in the port, and in spite of the fact that relations with the seamen's union, which had not supported the strike, had become strained. 'By the end of the dock strike sectionalism at all levels was as prominent as ever. To eliminate the "caste" system endemic to the docks would clearly be a task of heroic proportions'.[14]

For Liverpool, as elsewhere, after the events of 1889 there followed a period of guerrilla war between union and employers, with victory going to the employers, who successfully reneged on their agreement that the union button could be worn at the call-on, which had made recognition instant. Initially, the button had been a powerful weapon in the union's struggle to win members and enforce preference of employment. Cunard set the employers' pace by banning the button, followed widely by other firms. McHugh's response was to enjoin permanent ca'canny on the men, but this failed to prevent a decline of 50 per cent in membership after the ban.

McHugh also sought wider union alliances. There were abortive proposals for an alliance with the seamen, for affiliation with the Miners' Federation, and for a federation with the Tyneside and National Labourers' Union, which had docker members in the North-east. (It was the NUDL which rejected this particular link.)

In 1892 Richard McGhee opened a widespread recruitment campaign for an Ulster Labourers' Union, aimed mainly at rural labourers and built around a strike at a waterworks scheme in Lurgan, where labourers did not even receive the 15s. a week which had been agreed. In England the same work would be rewarded by £1, or 1 guinea, a week. The connection between 'the low pay of agricultural labourers in neighbouring counties and the rates for unskilled labour in the city [was] well understood' by the NUDL organizers, writes the Belfast historian John Gray.[15]

After Tillett's 1890 visit to Liverpool, he claimed that his Dockers' Union could shortly expect 'an addition of 30,000 members from Liverpool and district'. In fact, such a departure was never contemplated by McHugh, who held together a union of 25,000 members, half of them on the Mersey, and the rest in thirty-four other branches.

Although Tillett's overtures in Liverpool had no success, meeting as they did a union with origins outside London, a strong Celtic loyalty and national aspirations, his recruitment tours of the English east, south and south-west coasts and South Wales were accorded enthusiastic responses. A line drawn across the map from mid-Wales to north of the Humber, then to its south and east outlined Tillett territory, whilst to the north and west of it lay the NUDL ports, with the exception of the North-east (the Tyne), where indigenous unions for dockers and labourers grew up independently of either of them.

## Organizing the Humber

In Hull the effects of the London dock strike were felt before the year was out. Tillett visited the port on 5 December 1889 and addressed a mass meeting. The local press found him 'a most reasonable man', and the dockers abandoned their former local union for his card. The shipping magnate and dock employer Charles Henry Wilson granted wage increases and union recognition without industrial pressure. By September 1890 the Dockers' Union had 12,000 members and thirty-one branches in Hull, and by December it was a 100 per cent union port, Tillett's pride and joy, the best-organized port in the land. The dockers' delegates outnumbered all others on the Hull Trades Council. Wilson's attitude was crucial to this success, his pro-union stance being unique amongst the port employers. He told the men that 'they ought to be very proud of the success they had attained by taking the management of their own affairs into their own hands', though advising them simultaneously to 'act with moderation'.[16] An early skirmish with the newly formed Shipping Federation's Free Labour Bureau, involving the dockers in blacking a non-union ship, resulted in an isolated victory over the anti-union cause in the port at that time, many Hull employers following

Wilson's lead in deciding that the counterforce of 'free labour' was unnecessary. Three years later, it was to be a very different story.

A succession of campaigns based on Hull sought to reach out to farmworkers in the region. Tom Mann toured north Lincolnshire early in 1891, speaking to 'a largely attended' meeting at Binbrook, and to other gatherings in Market Rasen, Brigg and Normanby. 'Some half a dozen branches will be formed in the course of a week', reported the *Eastern Morning News.*[17] This tour was the subject of a meeting in Hull, where 'the large audience' received the news of its successes with enthusiasm. By 1892 eleven agricultural branches of the Dockers' Union from this one region were listed in its Annual Report. Two others may have belonged to Lincolnshire, but may have been located in other regions.[18] They did not last for long, quickly disappearing from subsequent Reports.

In shipping, Havelock Wilson's union smoothed out differences with a locally based Humberside seamen's union to achieve high levels of organization. Will Thorne visited Hull in January 1890 and negotiated the merger of a local gasworkers' union with his own, though membership before and after this move remained modest. Thorne launched a drive for recruitment in both town and port, clashing with the Dockers' Union. The National Labour Federation, from its Tyneside base, also founded general worker branches in Hull in 1889. Other local unions were formed that year and through 1890, for tramwaymen, carters, furniture workers and shop assistants. But the dockers dominated the town and applied a policy of not working with non-unionists. The *Hull News* reported that 'the blackleg is about a non-entity in Hull docks'. The extension of this policy to a refusal to work with *any* labour apart from members of the Dockers' Union provoked an outcry from other unions, however, threatening the harmony of the local trade-union scene. The Hull dockers' euphoria was set against a national background of mounting employer attacks on the union. But 'dismal reports' from elsewhere failed to discourage the 'union bastion' of Hull: 'At this particular point of time [the end of 1890] for an unskilled unionist, Hull must have been one of the better places in Britain in which to work'.[19]

## . . . and Bristol

In Bristol, the London dock strike produced an immediate response. The local gasworkers' union (formed in 1888 and merged with Thorne's union in 1889) organized a march to raise funds for the London dockers. They followed this with a spectacular and hugely successful strike of their own, which ended in excited and delighted proclamations of the triumph of the poor over the rich. The dock workers followed with a spontaneous strike, which quickly won the 'tanner' for them, together with 8*d.* overtime rates. Altogether 2,300 dockers were involved, one-third of whom were employed by Bristol Corporation, which had developed and owned the port installations. On 26 October, Tillett, Thorne and Mann addressed a victory rally of 15,000: 'The new unions, the bootworkers, and the bricklayers provided the bulk of the procession, the socialists the bulk of the platform party'.[20]

Just as was happening throughout the country, the success of gas- and dock workers triggered off a wave of disputes in many unskilled Bristol trades during 1889. Amongst these were oil-cake millers, sawyers, cotton operatives, tobacco workers, carters, warehousemen, scavengers, brush-makers, hatters, tailoresses, cigar- and pipe-makers, oil- and colour-mixers and charcoal workers. Being non-unionized, their efforts were co-ordinated by a Strike Organization Committee dominated by socialist activists: 'The socialists were important in the success of new unionism in Bristol'.[21]

All the new unions registered membership gains, the Dockers' Union reporting 2,544 members in March 1890. Whilst the gasworkers and the seamen quickly adopted a policy of support for a conciliation and arbitration scheme in the city, the dockers held back from it until 1892.

## A Sectional Success

In the South Wales ports, it was a rather different story, for two local unions were formed in the wave of new unionism. These were the Cardiff, Penarth and Barry Coal Trimmers' Association, established in 1888, and the National Amalgamated Labourers' Union of Great Britain and Ireland, which was founded in Swansea in 1888 and reached Cardiff in 1889. The former was an exclusive, closed union, rejecting general aims, confining itself to regular workers and their foremen. Whilst paying death and accident benefit, it made no provision for strike pay. Coal exporting was an important element of the Cardiff docks business, and the trimmers were specialists. Their job was to 'trim', or level, the cargo of coal in the ships' holds after it had been tipped from the quayside into a heap on the floor of the hold. For this purpose they used their own shovels, which were large with pointed ends. To fill the corners and extremities of the hold, the trimmers were often forced to work on their stomachs, and clearly required great physical prowess, as well as the knack which comes of experience and tradition. They evolved an elite status. Since they were difficult to replace, it paid the employers to develop good, stable relationships with them, and so they could command high differentials over general dock-labourers' pay. Their mode of unionism reflected all of these characteristics, and did not square with the general methods and objectives of new unionism. The work was hazardous, with the continuing dangers of gas and possible explosions; much of the effort of the union was concerned with safety and ventilation. These issues were highlighted when the union appeared before the Royal Commission on Labour in 1892, but several examples of union action to improve working conditions were also recorded. The Cardiff, Penarth and Barry Coal Trimmers' Association maintained its exclusiveness for eighty years; its entry into the TGWU was delayed until 1968. By this time, it had become one of the six smallest unions in the TUC, but its traditions were so well established that the TGWU welcomed it into the ranks by printing a full-colour photo of its expensive and richly coloured banner in a subsequent Annual Report.

## General Unions in Wales [22]

The Trimmers' Union was in part protected against the encroachments of the Dockers' Union through the controls exercised by their foremen, who deducted union dues from the men's pay. Many trimmers would have preferred membership of the Dockers' Union, and some in fact held membership in both organizations. In Newport, the trimmers and tippers initially joined the Dockers' Union, and throughout the South Wales ports there was frequent inter-union conflict, leading eventually to a mutual recognition agreement between them.

The National Amalgamated Labourers' Union (NALU) was formed in Cardiff by an official of the Seamen's Union. This is yet another example of the formative influence exerted by seamen over new union evolution. NALU enrolled several classes of general labour, including dockers. It quickly spread to other South Wales ports, and immediately won wage increases. It was a hybrid form of union: whilst having a strike fund, its leaders eschewed militancy, and its rules provided for several other cash benefits, including grants to members travelling in search of work. Its officials were elected by its Annual General Meeting.

Despite the prior existence of these two unions, the Dockers' Union opened a Cardiff branch in November 1889. Its first recruits were general labourers, including those at Spillers' Flour Mill; the dockers enrolled when Tillett came to the port later in the month. In 1890 they won a substantial wage increase without a strike. Union members at the Graigola Fuel Company did strike – successfully – and also won an advance. Patent-fuel production was an important industry in Cardiff, and its organization in the dockers' ranks reinforced the idea that general organization could be both practicable and effective.

Thereafter, Tillett and Mann argued for conciliation and arbitration boards in the locality, and for the avoidance of strikes. They sought recognition agreements, and work preference for members, to be achieved by card-checks by foremen members at the call-on. Despite the leadership's pacific method, the dockers struck more than once in 1890 in protest at the hire of non-unionists.

In Swansea the growth of the Dockers' Union to a membership of 4,650 in November 1890 was achieved in part at the expense of the National Amalgamated Labourers' Union. Most port workers transferred: they had seen the gains won by the new union, but they were also aware that it refused to recognize the NALU card. In the hinterland of Swansea, the Dockers' Union organized copper, chemical and steel-tube workers, Harry Orbell and Tom McCarthy being frequent visitors. Wage increases were obtained in all these industries, in the case of the copper workers through arbitration. In Newport, the Dockers' Union had less success against the NALU in the docks, but in the Gwent valleys behind the port it established branches in the steel industry. At the height of its initial burst of success, before the employers' counterattack, the Dockers' Union had 6,000 members in Swansea, 3,000 in Cardiff and 800 in Newport. The union claimed 57,000 members nationally in 1890.

## The National Amalgamated Union of Labour

On Tyneside, a series of attempts at organizing the labourers began in February 1889, producing the Tyneside (quickly renamed the National) Amalgamated Union of Labour (NAUL), with membership in the docks, shipyards and sundry other industries, and the National Labour Federation, with similar coverage.

## The Cabmen Follow On

The example of new unionism was not lost upon workers in the capital city's road-transport systems. Both in the cab trade and amongst bus and tramway workers, trade-union organization and strike action were soon to follow the dockers' 1889 victory.

The nineteenth-century London cab trade was turbulent, and trade-union organization comparatively unstable. There had been strikes as early as 1853, then in 1867 and again in 1868. In 1894 one cabby claimed that he had been a member of eight different cab unions in thirty-four years. The cabmen suffered from a number of oppressive conditions peculiar to their trade. The London police authority was responsible for issuing licences, which were necessary either to own or to hire out a cab. Separate licences were needed to operate as a cab-driver. Police returns in 1890 showed that there were 11,700 licensed cabs but over 15,000 licensed drivers. In addition, the cabbies complained of 'butterflies' – illegal, summer-season drivers who infiltrated the trade.

This situation led to chronic destructive competition between the drivers. Most operated under a 'hire-and-reward' system, paying a daily hire-charge to cab-owners, who could therefore rack up this charge to cabbies desperate to secure a cab. There were 3,599 cab-owners in the capital, of whom 2,500 owned only a single vehicle (plus the necessary horse and equipment); 450 of them owned more than five cabs, and a dominant handful of companies owned up to 400. Unregulated, competitive and individualistic, the system forced cabbies into excessive hours of work to earn even a pittance over and above the daily hire-charge and their other expenses, including stable charges and the licence fee.

Their work brought them under constant harrassment by the police; cabstands were few and ill defined, so that cabbies were regularly summoned for 'loitering'. The railway companies withheld permission for ordinary cabbies to ply for customers on their mainline station forecourts, thus preserving their monopoly for a fleet of railway-owned cabs. The London streets were overcrowded with horse-drawn vehicles, private and public, passenger and freight, and the accident rate was high. Acrimonious disputes between passengers and cabbies were an everyday occurrence, as fares, tips and waiting times were contested at the journey's end; these conflicts led with distressing regularity to the courts, and to costly and demoralizing petty litigation.

What stirred the cabbies' accumulated sense of grievance and fed a special form of class consciousness was the character of their customers – the London rich, both the aristocratic and the bourgeois. The cabby, in an age of mass domestic servitude, was regarded as an extension of the feudal system which prevailed 'upstairs and downstairs' in the households of the prosperous; and he was expected to behave with the deference of a vassal towards m'Lord and m'Lady, whilst accepting without complaint whatever manners they displayed towards him. He was by turns insulted and patronized as a simple, potentially villainous, but vaguely romantic character of London life, known sentimentally as the 'gondolier of the London streets'. He, his vehicle and his horse provided the colourful background for the adventures of Conan Doyle's contemporary hero, Sherlock Holmes. In 1890 the 'gondolier' was labouring, under a heap of grievances, for anything up to twenty hours a day, and he had had enough.

When in 1890 the Prince of Wales joined a charitable party of peers, judges and diplomats in a charade depicting – in grossly patronizing terms – the cabbies' way of life, one of those pilloried sent a protest to the *Star*:

> Ah! Noble sirs and princes, what to you
> The bitter work of working lives, whose rue
> You do but dream of in your festal halls,
> Where mirth runs riot and fat plenty stalls.

You come amongst us with your oily speech,
And eat a banquet in pretence to reach
Those dull, dreary deeps in which we moil,
Some false and foolish patronage of toil.

Back to your places sirs, whilst we keep ours,
We do not play, like you, through God's stern hours;
So keep your idle pity – we'll have none;
There's nought in common twixt us; Get you gone.[23]

The cabmen established their Metropolitan Cab Drivers' Trade Union in 1890, and by October of that year, at a mass meeting in the early hours of the morning, heard from a Mr Walter Drummond of the Dockers' Union a speech in praise of their initiative, which had brought 1,000 into membership already, and was still drawing fifty new members a week. The principal grievance they set out to redress was the hire-charge of 16s. a day, which Drummond characterized as 'sweating'. Their programme also sought to reduce the number of licences issued, to secure the designation of adequate numbers of cabstands, and to break the railway-cab monopoly at stations. In addition, they wanted the issue of licences to be taken from the police and managed by the London County Council.

Drummond told the rally that, just as the dockers had won £300,000 in increased wages, so 12,000 London cabmen could, by similar united action, win £150,000 by forcing a reduction of 1s 6d. a day in the hire-charge. 'The meeting ended shortly before 5 a.m.'[24]

Organization, and the further elaboration of a programme, continued through the following months until, in March 1891, the union was busy pressing the Royal Commission on Labour to hear its grievances, and had prevailed upon the most famous member of the LCC, John Burns, to address a mass rally in Hyde Park on Good Friday. Burns rose to the occasion; the 'Season' was beginning, the moment was right. The call for strike action was taken up immediately, on 3 April, by the cabbies of the Shrewsbury and Talbot Cab Company, owners of 400 cabs, the first of whose proprietors was none other than Lord Shrewsbury himself. The strike was in resistance to a proposed 1s. increase in the hire-charge.

The company's several yards were vigorously picketed, and washers, horse-keepers, yardmen and other employees were thrown out of work. The directors refused to meet the union. They put out a statement justifying the increase on the grounds of the superiority of their rubber-tyred cabs, with which any competent cabmen could, they claimed, earn a living (The 'S and T' was itself the proprietor of a subsidiary rubber-tyre-making company!) The employers' intransigence was carried to the extreme: the company began to sell off its horses by public auction. At first the union interpreted this as an intimidatory bluff, assuring the members that only old horses were being weeded out. But by the end of

May it was evident that the 'S and T' had indeed gone out of business, being content for the future to hire out its cabs to other, horse-owning, companies. On 30 May the *Star* commented sardonically:

> Of course, a company the individual members of which for the most part derive their incomes from ground rents and other agrarian iniquities; and who, as much for pastime as for profit, come down from their high estate to compete with legitimate traders, can readily close the shop when their sweating practices are objected to. Therefore the Shrewsbury company has, in part at least, disappeared – a benefit for which the other proprietors are indebted to the men.

But the withdrawal of the 'S and T' did not subvert the strike, which surged, wave on wave, from one company to the next. Pickets moved in on a company, the union presented its demand for a reduction in the hire-charge, the proprietors vainly set up an association and a defence fund, but one by one they negotiated the required reduction, following which the union allowed a resumption of work and moved on to the next target.

For sixteen weeks, into early August, this tidal action was sustained, cheered along by marches, rallies and speeches. John Burns, chief spokesman for the strikers, was reported to have 'worked like a Trojan night and day, in meetings in halls and in the open, and the wholehearted way in which he has thrown himself into the struggle has been both a help and a source of inspiration to the cause.'[25] At one meeting, held outside the St Pancras Station arches, Burns addressed the rally from the top of a hansom cab.

From spring through the summer, the pressure was all on the proprietors to yield, for the Season, with its high-society events – Ascot, Epsom, the Eton and Harrow and MCC matches, the balls and garden parties – was the most lucrative time of the year for their trade. Public sympathy swung towards the strikers, as the press gave their grievances extensive and sympathetic coverage. The radical *Star* was prominent, but the *St James Gazette* was not far behind in its coverage.

The Metropolitan Union did not consist entirely of John Burns and Dockers' Union sympathizers. During the strike, membership rose to 4,000. With it rose income. The union's president, John Beasley, was probably a cabman, but its treasurer was a Mr W. Everitt, the proprietor of the Guardsman Coffee House in Buckingham Palace Road. There the union had its headquarters, its 'business-like' offices, and its executive meetings. The address itself intrigued the *Star*: '. . . almost within smelling distance of the Royal Stables themselves!'[26]

On 7 August Burns presided over a wind-up meeting of the strikers. He reported that up to 2,500 cabmen had been on strike during the previous four months, but never more than 300 at any one time. Thirty-five different companies had been visited by the action, and the hire-charge reduced by between 1s. 6d. and 3s. a day. The cabmen had largely helped themselves to this victory; the accounts of the Strike Committee and Mr Everitt showed that donations of £3,480 had been received by collections from the public, but also £3,400 from cabmen themselves, helped by only £70 from 'other unions'. One of the biggest cheers at the wind-up meeting greeted the announcement that Mr Sydney Buxton, MP, had intervened with the judges to secure twenty-one days' remission of sentence on three cabmen pickets sentenced for 'initimidation'.

After the strike, the Metropolitan Union turned to its campaign for the regulation of the cabmen's trade by the LCC. The union expired in 1894, but continuity was hardly broken, for the London Cab Drivers' Union set up shop immediately afterwards, in the heat of a four-week strike. In turn, this body was transmuted into the London and Provincial Union of Licensed Vehicle Workers in 1913, extending its recruitment into the bus and tram industries. Before the First World War, it earned the nickname the 'Red Button Union', because of its consistent militancy and its radical syndicalist politics.

So began an experience and a tradition which reaches down from the 1891 strike almost to the present day. In 1987, we interviewed the veteran trade unionist Sid Easton, whose family's knowledge of the London cab trade, including his father's experiences, reaches back to the Edwardian period. Sid Easton had been an active communist, working at one time as chauffeur and bodyguard to the late Harry Pollitt, general secretary of the British Communist Party, and he served on the TGWU executive during the 1970s. He recalled his experience behind the wheel before the Second World War:

> except for the occasional wedding or Christmas time, the only people who could afford to ride in cabs were the rich folk. You then came into contact with the worst elements of capitalism directly. I mean, if you work in a factory, you are one of many, you know there is an employer, [but] it's a thing, a company. But when you get a man or a woman who has no thought about cost, merely about your behaviour towards them, it changes your regard for them, whether your forelock is long enough for you to pull or not. And I believe that was the reason why we had something in excess of 120 members of the London cab section members of the Communist Party, which was a higher figure by ratio than in almost any other industry.

## Tramwaymen and Busmen

The London County Tramway and Omnibus Employees' Trade Union was formed in 1889, under the presidency of Thomas Sutherst, a young barrister.[27] One of its initiators was William Collison, who will reappear in our story in a more sinister guise, following his quarrel with the busmen.[28] In June 1891 between 8,000 and 10,000 London busmen struck, ostensibly for a twelve-hour day, but in fact more because of the introduction of tickets, which controlled the conductor's returns. These had hitherto been based on a highly informal system, in which the companies got that proportion of the fares which could be sustained by custom. This tradition dated back to the coaching system and was tolerated by the London General Omnibus Company, the largest undertaking, until the retirement of its managing director in February. His successor imposed ticket machines, alongside a wage increase of 1s. a day for drivers and 6d. for conductors in compensation for lost perquisites.

The tram and busmen were expected to buy their own uniforms and to contribute to an accident-repair fund. They perceived their status, like the cabmen's, as being more akin to vehicle hirers than employees, and saw in the imposition of ticketing a severe change of status. Their strike received the enthusiastic endorsement of the Metropolitan Cab Drivers' Union. Mutual support, to curtail unregulated competition and excessive working time, made every kind of sense to passenger carriers of all modes of transport in the metropolis. They carried the members of the most prosperous ruling class in the world, as well as, increasingly, a new mass public which was creating heavy demand.

Sutherst argued for municipalization of the omnibus industry and for reduced hours: 'The county council should buy up the whole of the tram lines and the rolling stock, and lease them out to companies who should be under their control, and the control of the men as well.'[29] Workers would be entitled to seats on the board, and after making interest payments, profits would be 'divided between the ratepayers and the men'. This was the system applied in Huddersfield, 'with admirable effect'.

In spite of Sutherst's advocacy, the tramway and omnibusmen did not maintain the impetus of their new union. Their strike resulted in an ostensible victory in that shorter hours were conceded, alongside pay cuts; but the workday was soon extended piecemeal as union members traded their new-found leisure for more pay.[30]

## The Gasworkers

In London itself, of course, the gasworkers had set the example of new unionism, ahead of the dockers, with their successful campaign for the eight-hour day in 1889, and with the formation of the Gasworkers and General Labourers' Union. Will Thorne maintained his leadership of this organization, whose rules were drafted by Eleanor Marx.

Eric Hobsbawm has drawn attention to the special features of the gas industry at that time, which help to explain the relative ease with which the union established and maintained itself through all the vicissitudes which fell upon less stable organizations, such as the dockers. The gas industry enjoyed monopoly status, and depended upon a body of workers who had real technical skills. Its technology remained constant at a time of large expansion of domestic demand for its product. Commonly it was organized under public, municipal ownership or control; hence it was exposed to public and consumer opinion. For these reasons, 'unlike so many other unions of the 1889 vintage, the gasworkers were never effectively dislodged from the positions they occupied then'.[31]

In Birmingham the Amalgamated Society of Gas-workers and Brickmakers dated also from 1889. We should add to this list two latecomers to the role-call of the principal new unions: the Workers' Union of 1898 and the National Federation of Women Workers of 1906. But these arose out of developments which will receive attention later.

# II

## *Results: Quantity and Quality*

What, then, was the overall result of this novel explosion? From the great London dock strike through to its early successes in other ports, from the pioneering work in the gas industry, and amongst general labour in a multitude of industries over a wide area – within two short years the reach of labour organization had been extended further than anyone before had imagined to be possible. The membership of the six principal new unions in 1890 totalled some 326,000; their affiliation figures to the TUC in that year are shown in table 4.1.

Table 4.1 *Membership of New Unions, 1890*

| | |
|---|---|
| Dock, Wharf, Riverside and General Labourers' Union | 56,000 |
| National Union of Dock Labourers | 50,000 |
| National Amalgamated Union of Sailors and Firemen | 60,000 |
| National Union of Gasworkers and General Labourers | 60,000 |
| National Amalgamated Union of Labour | 40,000 |
| National Labour Federation | 60,000 |

*Source:* TUC Reports

London labourers' hourly rate of pay averaged 5½d. in 1881 and 6d. in 1891, whilst the index of food prices had fallen in the same period from 140 to 109 – (1900 = 100). These gains rode on the back of the trade cycle: industrial production (1880 = 100) from a trough of 101 in 1886 climbed to a peak of 122 in 1891; it was to collapse to 113 in 1893. Unemployment stood at 9.6 per cent in 1886 and fell to 6 per cent in 1891. Productivity (1850 = 100) rose from 159 to 186 between 1886 and

1891.[32] In all these quantitative economic respects, the years with which we are concerned here were auspicious ones. But the new unionism involved more than statistical growth of membership: it also signified a qualitative, moral change.

The London dock strike occupies a special place in trade-union history not only because it was a spectacular, public upheaval, but because it happened when and where it did. London was the capital. It could focus metropolitan comment and attention, and thus appeal to every province. That the London industrial scene was so out of phase with the provinces could mean only that *this* movement would exert a singularly powerful influence. London disputes were necessarily rare, exceptional; their impact could energize others far afield. The extension of the franchise had created political uncertainties of great complexity. The cumulative results of the growth of poverty in urban concentrations were bursting into the consciousness of people who were themselves comfortably secure. The increase in literacy and in the media serving it ensured that communication was instant and effective.

It is this social context which explains why the dockers' initiative is widely taken as the founding moment and symbol of new unionism. This was what made possible a deliberate rejection of older models and of various attempts to depart from the norms of pre-existing unions. The young men of 1889 aimed at the creation of a new type of organization. A number of characteristics are associated with this aim: modern historians accept none of them without argument, but all would accept that new unions involved at least five innovations, even if some were less significant than others, or less consistently practised. They were:

1   The organization of workers deemed to be 'unskilled'.
2   The recruitment of members from a wide range of industries and occupations, which is to say that, commonly although not always, they were open, general unions.
3   The commitment to be 'fighting unions', charging low subscriptions, avoiding heavy friendly-society benefits, and using their funds primarily for strike pay.
4   Militancy.
5   Political radicalism, often embracing socialism and questioning the older unions' adherence to the Liberal Party.

To these five generally accepted qualities we would add:

6   They made space for the organization of women, and indeed the whole movement drew an example from the matchgirls' strike (see chapter 2). Other unions, like the Boot and Shoe Operatives' Union and the cotton unions, did this. But women workers in general trades were to offer a special challenge to union organizers.

## Helpers from Outside

The seventh innovation is both a weakness and a strength. Of all the qualities which marked the new unions, perhaps the most remarkable was the extent to which outside helpers could be assimilated into their structures, providing a whole range of specialized services and skills. We have already seen how skilled engineers like Burns and Mann stepped into the roles of spokesman and organizer during the dock strike, and how Champion furnished the new Dockers' Union – as well as the Gasworkers' Union – with their press office during disputes and with an 'official journal' in the shape of the *Labour Elector* immediately afterwards. In the same way, Eleanor Marx gave crucial assistance to both dockers and gasworkers and helped organize the women at the Silvertown rubber works during their strike in 1889. But these were the stars of the socialist movement, and all eyes were upon them in 1889. Outside London the story followed the same trends, but often the volunteers were not socialists, or at any rate not seen as socialists. The Birmingham Amalgamated Society of Gas-workers and Brickmakers was organized by the Lib.–Lab. City Councillors Eli Bloor and Allan Granger;[33] Bloor was a glassworker and Granger a printer. James Bartley, a journalist on the *Workman's Times* and a socialist, carried this same union to the Bradford area with the active help of the trades council. In 1888 E. R. Pease became the first secretary of the National Labour Federation in Tyneside, before he took over the same office in the Fabian Society.

When the London omnibus companies were organized during their strike in June 1891, their first spokesman, as we have seen, was the barrister Thomas Sutherst, who soon stepped aside to assume an advisory role. (His testimony at the Royal Commission on Labour took place some months later.) Sutherst was joined in the work of creating a permanent union by a nominee of the London Trades Council, Fred Hammill, an engineer, who was paid a monthly wage of £10 to establish an organization for the busmen.[34] Hammill had been the socialist candidate for the secretaryship of the Trades Council in 1890, during a heated controversy about the commitment (or lack of commitment) of the incumbent, George Shipton, to the dockers' cause in the great strike. Trades Councils took similar action in many parts of the country, with the result that many skilled men became involved in the disputes of their hitherto unorganized colleagues.

If it is not surprising that inexperienced workers should welcome help during the time that they found themselves actually out on strike, it remains true that similar assistance was frequently needed for considerable periods afterwards in order to establish and stabilize the habits of organization. Thus in September 1889 the Rev. John William Lewis, curate of Bow, became the chairman of two branches of the Dockers' Union for the first year of its existence; he remained chairman of one branch for a further year. If he taught his members something about the rules of procedure, they also contributed to his education.

Questioned in 1892 by the Royal Commissioner, Michael Austin, about how far the conditions of dockworkers had altered since the strike, Lewis replied, 'No doubt it was on the whole very much worse than it is now.' 'Therefore the Union has improved the conditions of the men?' 'I believe it has. It is, however, a long and slow work, and one cannot expect very much in the course of two years.'[35] The curate of Bow had learned his lessons well, because he not only defended the achievements of his dockers, but went on to embrace the aim of general membership. Indeed, he informed the Commission that 'every man throughout the country . . . should join a trades union'. 'You would have no non-unionists?' responded Lord Derby, incredulously. 'None at all anywhere,' came the firm response.[36]

## Centralizing

Although Tom Mann is rightly credited with many of the innovative features of the Dockers' Union, Ben Tillett was also driving in the same direction, in respect both of the centralization of executive power – initially for 'fighting' purposes – and in seeking the widest possible national scope for his organization. These strategies stemmed from his own experiences in London. The Tilbury strike in 1888 had been defeated by the use of blackleg labour from the farms; in the immediate recruiting drive after the great strike, therefore, the union's efforts to recruit in agriculture and among general labourers around the ports was a conscious policy. Moreover, Tillett had sought to hold central control of union funds even in the days of his Tea Operatives' Union, with the object of preventing autonomous branch strikes from dissipating them. Tillett's policy was further determined by his own sceptical opinion of his members' wisdom in their use of trade-union powers. An article in the *Labour Elector* after the 1889 strike expressed this attitude:

> Today it [the Dockers' Union] is numerically the strongest trade organization in the metropolis. But the 18,000 men who have flocked to it are ignorant of the rudiments of trade unionism, are flushed with their sudden success, and are unaware that unless their society is at once thoroughly and closely organized every advantage they have gained must inevitably be taken from them in a few years – perhaps a few months.[37]

Tillett's and Mann's drive for centralization caused much ill-feeling amongst the London membership. The roots of twentieth-century conflict between Ernest Bevin, and later Arthur Deakin, and their docks' membership, may indeed lie in the origins of London dockers' unionism. Harry Quelch's opinion was that the authoritarian tendencies of the new union leadership guaranteed the continued existence of his own South Side Labour Protection League.

The expansion of the union outside London is reflected in the organizing tours undertaken by the leaders. Immediately following the London settlement, Tillett set off for Hull, Gloucester, Bristol, Sharpness, Southampton, Ipswich, Liverpool, Harwich amongst other ports, whilst Tom McCarthy and Harry Orbell covered still more. Sixty-three new branches were formed in the first quarter of 1890 – an unprecedented and truly astonishing achievement. Yet after the initial enthusiasm, some of the provincial members also found the dominance of the London leadership irksome.[38] At times the resentment exploded, as we shall see when we examine the events at Southampton in chapter 5.

The leadership's concern for central control was dictated by anxiety to conserve funds, and to ensure stability and longevity for their new creation. It was an outlook shared by Burns, Tillett and Mann, and was sharply reinforced by the downturn in the trade cycle which began in late 1890. This goes some way to explain how, in South Wales and elsewhere, the initially militant new-union leaders could become the pioneer advocates of conciliation and arbitration. The simplistic view of the new unions solely as a proto-revolutionary development – for which many of Tillett's own fiery utterances have been responsible – obviously required drastic amendment, which it received with interest from the Labour historians of the 1960s and 1970s. But there is a case for believing that these modern accounts have bent the stick too far.

## The Long View

Both Tillett and Mann held a long view of the prospects for political action offered by the new unionism. Both had lengthy and uninterrupted careers, in which the militant industrial phases of 1889–90 and 1910–14 have naturally attracted most attention in popular history and myth. They never doubted that they had created something new in 1889, but they also never hesitated to act to preserve it from collapse when circumstances – particularly those created by the ebb and flow of the trade cycle – required prudent, conservationist policies.

But in the ups and the downs alike, a core requirement of the new unions was that of recognition. Centralization helped. Recognition ensured that the hitherto unorganized masses saw their leaders' perceptions of their own role reflected back in the responses of their adversaries.

The Webbs were soon to identify three main trade-union methods:

mutual insurance, collective bargaining and legal enactment. Downgrading the importance of mutual insurance was not perhaps the central defining characteristic of the new unions, and an extensive literature shows how, at different times, new unions were willing to return for this piece of forgotten baggage, which in varying degrees was found to contain useful elements.

This should not inhibit us from registering what was really going on: the upgrading of collective bargaining and legal enactment. In different ways, both methods extended the crucial principle of recognition. Recognition for bargaining purposes may surely be a means of regulating conflict; but it is also a powerful reinforcement of labour solidarity, since it compels employers to define the social world in the same terms as does the trade union. Wages, hours and conditions – all the most important dimensions of life at work – owe their shape to a collective process. Even if he hates it, the participating employer has sanctioned it. The organized working class thus draws strength from its adversaries, even when it is under attack. Political reform involves a wider social recognition of the same divisions. New unionists, then, ceased to be 'the poor', atomized, rejected, starved. In becoming 'the union', their strength went beyond the scope of their actual organization. Organization could be beaten back, and even temporarily extinguished; but to the extent that society recognized it, the union could burst back into full flame whenever social pressures passed a certain point.

## The 'Old' Unions Take Umbrage

The new unionists were instantly assailed by the old. The most concerted onslaught came from George Howell, who raised a whole series of objections to the new doctrines, most of which were codified in a sour little book, *Trade Unionism New and Old*, first published in 1891.[39] In it he attacked the new unions' drive for the closed shop, their 'needless public display', their quest for legislative rather than self-reliant friendly-society protections, and their overreadiness to support strikes. Howell did have his own loyalties, which he was not shy to affirm: 'In its old age, even in its ruins, perchance, the old trade unionism is not unlike some of the old medieval structures, worthy of veneration by reason of its age and its present uses'.[40]

From such a gothic standpoint, it is not surprising that Howell found the more rudimentary and functional organizations of dockers, seamen and carters indecorous and uncouth. 'In all the earlier battles of trade unionism', he wrote, 'the fighting garrison had this advantage, they were fighting an attacking or besieging army from without . . . [now] the attacks come from within'.[41]

From this point of view, the new leaders were all much the same: their distinguishing trait 'has been, and is, their persistent, cowardly and calumnious attacks upon the old leaders'. Such criticisms, said Howell, had brought about various early retirements and resignations: 'There is . . . scarcely a secretary of long standing who has not had to endure abuse, misrepresentation, and calumny from some of the new leaders or their satellites'. Worse, the Labour Members in Parliament have received 'the extreme violence of the abuse'.[42]

'The culmination of vulgar abuse', Howell went on, 'was reached at the Liverpool Trade Union Congress . . . According to one "leader", tall hats and black coats and also the size and stature of the delegates from the old days, were indications of a frightful state of decay, in the policy and management of the old trade unionism'.[43]

John Burns was the culprit in this once-famous case. After the Congress he had recorded his impression of the difference between the old and new unionists, and had registered the striking fact that the craftsmen's representatives were physically taller, more robust and more comfortable in every aspect of their appearance than the representatives of the dockers and transport workers. Such an observation can hardly, in itself, be interpreted as derogatory, although it is evident that the trade-union establishment found it so. It was intended as a sociological observation, and indeed as such it was acute.

Some societies upheld codes of conduct on dress, even incorporating them in rules. The Phoenix Society of Compositors excluded from its meetings all those members who were improperly dressed: correct attire was a tall hat and evening dress.[44] This rule cut two ways. To those above the line, it registered that deference which cannot be surpassed, since imitation is the ultimate in flattery. To those below, it revealed a chasm of separation: no entry into this artisan universe could be afforded to those too poor to wear the uniform. With such badges of rank went a set of attitudes. Harry Quelch raged against them:

> Can there be anything more exasperating than to hear a skilled artisan, who ought to know that the whole of society is living on the labour of himself and his mates, skilled and unskilled, talking of his home as 'not bad for a working man', his set of books as 'quite creditable for a working man', his children as 'a good-looking lot of kids for a working man', and so on? You never hear this abominable servile cant in any other country. Nor before the old Chartist movement died down was it nearly so common here. The systematic and degrading respect for their 'betters', inculcated into the workers from their childhood upwards, tells its tale in after years.[45]

Burns, who provoked such disapproval among the craftsmen, was himself a craftsman engineer, and no doubt it was his intermediate status as someone identified as a public spokesman of the dockers, many of whose own leaders were far from able to afford to dress in the approved

TUC manner, which made him sensitive to the differences which he recorded.[46] More understandable than the objections to Burns's article, perhaps, is the resentment of the craftsmen over the uninhibited behaviour of the new delegates, prone as they were to heckle or even interrupt ceremonial speeches. 'The loud voice, impatient gestures, persistent interruptions,' thought Howell, rendered the 1890 TUC 'sad and pitiful to behold'.[47]

Secondly, the old-union men objected very strongly to the doctrine that the new organizations should be 'fighting machines'.[48] Howell saw the friendly-society benefits of the old unions as a factor in their self-reliance, and deeply resented any effort to downplay them, let alone manage without them.

But, thirdly, Howell especially objected to the antagonism of the new unions to non-union workers. 'It was reserved for the recent development of the new trade unionism to systematically revert to terrorism, and brute force, to compel non-union hands to leave their employment'.[49] Such infractions, he alleged, accompanied the dock strikes in London, Liverpool, Cardiff, Southampton and other places; the strikes of gas-stokers in South London, Manchester and elsewhere; and various outbreaks of industrial action by the seamen.

Picketing, he went on to argue, gave full scope to this coercive trend.[50] Therefore he was entirely scandalized when the TUC, following the experiences of the dock strikes, instructed their Parliamentary Committee to seek the entire repeal of the clause of the Conspiracy Act of 1875 'making picketing illegal'. At the same Congress, there was a move to abolish Clause 7 of the Conspiracy and Protection of Property Act, as being dangerous to the liberties of the working classes. This clause outlawed 'watching and besetting', and interference with tools, as well as violence or intimidation. That the Congress should record this prohibition as being capable of repressive interpretation was a scandal to some of its elder members. They were even more distressed when the same delegates voted to censure the Irish Constabulary for shadowing participants in a tailors' strike in Derry. The Congress, alleged Howell, now approved of 'shadowing' when it was employed by trade unionists against strike-breakers, but disapproved of it when the Constabulary employed it against trade unionists.

In the same vein, Howell inveighed against 'popular demonstrations'.[51] Parades cost money, which should be laid up for strike benefit, he thought. Yet the dockers' parades had raised far more money than they could ever have put by, even if their membership had in fact been far higher than the 300 (out of 100,000) which he alleged in the same tract.

'The new unionists have also a weakness for federations', he continued. They believe that a grouping 'of weak societies will supply . . . aggressive strength'.[52] All this is a foible, and if general *amalgamation* were achieved it would level down and crush emulation, undermining skill and personal character.

Had Howell's admonitions been heeded, no attempt to organize the so-called 'unskilled' could ever have got off the ground. Of course, general organization could not be easily or quickly achieved: but the goal imposed itself as the only constructive response to the free-for-all that brought masses of starvelings and displaced people to fight for a few hours' labour at the dock gates. Picketing was not a principle, but an expedient. It could provide temporary support, but only if behind it lay an appeal to wider solidarity. Mere force could always provoke answering, and more lethal force.

## Mann and Tillett Reply

Howell's books had been preceded in June 1890 by an article in *Murray's Magazine*, written by George Shipton of the London Trades Council land and entitled 'Trades Unionism: The Old and the New'. Tom Mann, from his presidential position in the Dockers' Union, joined with Ben Tillett in responding in a penny pamphlet entitled *The 'New' Trades Unionism – A Reply to Mr. George Shipton*. In it their 'long view' is clearly discernible:

Many of those who are identified with the 'new' trades unionism have been connected with their own trade societies for many years past, and it was a continual source of bitter grief to them that so much poverty should exist amongst workers of all sections, but especially among the unskilled and unorganized, and that the old Societies should be so utterly callous to this poverty as not to make any special exertion to alter matters for the better . . .

The methods adopted by us of determining a change in our present industrial system, are on a strictly trade-union basis. All our public utterances, all our talks to our members, have been directed towards cultivating a sturdy spirit of independence, and instilling a deep sense of responsibility. In fact we have been at pains to discredit appeals to the legislature, contending that the political machine will fall into our hands as a matter of course, so soon as the educational work has been done in our labour organizations. We are convinced that not until Parliament is an integral part of the workers, representing and responsible to industrial toilers, shall we be able to effect any reform by its means . . .

The statement that the 'new' trade unionists look to Governments and legislation, is bunkum: The keynote is to organize first, and take action in the most effective way, so soon as organization warrants action, instead of specially looking to Government. The lesson is being thoroughly well taught and learned that we must look to ourselves alone, though this, of course, does not preclude us from exercising our rights of citizenship.

It is quite true that most of the newly formed unions pay contributions for trade purposes only, leaving sick and funeral benefits to be dealt with by sick and insurance societies. The work of the trade unionist is primarily to obtain such a re-adjustment of conditions between employers and employed as shall secure to the latter a better share of the wealth they produce, in the form of reduced working hours and higher wages, and our experience has taught us that many of the older unions are very reluctant to engage in a labour struggle, no matter how great the necessity, because they are hemmed in by sick and funeral claims, so that to a large extent they have lost their true characteristic of being fighting organizations, and the sooner they revert to their original programme the better for the well-being of the working masses . . .

Our ideal is a Co-operative Commonwealth. This we believe will be reached by honest effort in various directions, chief among which will be the efforts of the trade unionists: and while striving for the ideal, we are glad to know that we need not wait for years before further advantages can be obtained, but that by discreet conduct on our part, we can be continually gaining some advantage for one or other section of the workers.

While in the heat of this polemic Mann was anxious to refute the 'bunkum' of overreliance on legislation, he and the wave of new-unionist delegates to the 1890 TUC congress in Liverpool led the successful fight for the adoption of an eight-hours' Bill as a campaigning demand of the whole movement. This was not inconsistent: what is clear from the pamphlet is Mann's understanding of the need to 'walk on two legs'; and also that, of the three classic modes of trade-union action delineated by the Webbs – mutual insurance, collective bargaining and legislation – the new unionism discarded the first as an encumbering constraint, adopting collective bargaining as the immediately available method, viewing legislation as a vital support and ultimately as an element in a *socialist* strategy.

If Tom Mann would not subordinate trade unionism to state intervention, he was not, in the 1890s, willing to walk away from any possible source of help. This explains why for a long time he kept some very elevated company indeed. Because hundreds of strikes had erupted during 1889 and the following year, the Conservative government of Lord Salisbury announced that it intended to probe the causes of this unprecedented unrest. On 21 April 1891 it duly appointed a Royal Commission on Labour.

## The Royal Commission

The Commission was constituted under the chairmanship of Spencer Compton Cavendish, Marquess of Hartington, soon to inherit the dukedom of Devonshire. Its terms of reference were to 'enquire into . . .

the relations between employers and employed', to examine the combinations of both sides, and 'the conditions of labour which have been raised during the recent trade disputes'. The Commission was charged to report on proposals for legislation which might 'be directed to the remedy of any evils that may be disclosed'.

It laboured on for nearly three years, into the succeeding Liberal administration, Gladstone's fourth, and beyond it after the old man withdrew in favour of Lord Rosebery in March 1894.

The Royal Commission was, wrote Beatrice Webb, 'a gigantic fraud ... made up of a little knot of dialecticians plus a carefully picked parcel of variegated Labour men, and the rest landlords or capitalists, pure and simple'.[53] The Labour men were Thomas Burt and William Abraham, Liberal MPs from the Northumberland and South Wales coalfields respectively; the Irish typographical worker, Michael Austin; Henry Tait of the Scottish Railwaymen, who had been involved in an epic strike which was extensively raked over in the Commission's hearings; the Darlington Ironworker, Edward Trow; the Conservative leader of the Lancashire Cotton Spinners, James Mawdsley; and Tom Mann, still, of course, president of the Dockers' Union. Mann accepted the appointment after consulting his union and the London Trades Council. He held it 'during their pleasure' as he put it. He found the work 'interesting ... but [was, in the end] unable to point to any legislative measures as a direct result' of his three years' stint.[54] By the time the Commission reported, the Liberal government was in decline and hastening towards an early General Election, which it was to lose. Tom Mann had used the proceedings to table his appeal for an eight-hour day, 'by trade and local option', and to advocate measures to 'dockise the river Thames' under a unified port authority. He advocated improved facilities by cutting a canal across the loop from Limehouse to Blackwall, thus providing space for 9½ miles of 'scientifically arranged warehouses, to which any vessel could get right up'.[55]

Whatever might have been the intention of the Salisbury administration, or of the Liberals, in establishing the Royal Commission, as it continued its long and extensively documented hearings, the results were largely rhetorical. Among the final paperwork was a minority report written by Sidney Webb and signed by Mann (who initiated the project), Mawdsley, Austin and Mabon (Abraham). Beatrice Webb wrote whimsically about the efforts which brought about a joint report from such widely different sectors of the trade-union movement:

This report was produced at yesterday's sitting of the Commission (the *Westminster Gazette* of March 16, 1894, reports), and it created (says the *Manchester Guardian*) almost as much consternation as if a bomb had been exploded in Westminster Hall. The Duke of Devonshire was clearly unprepared for it. It altered the whole situation so far as his draft recommendations were concerned, and he suggested that the Commission should have time to consider the new report, for which purpose he then adjourned the Commission until after Easter. The minority report, it is reported, will propose among other matters a legal eight-hour day, with certain limitations, the amendment of the Factory Acts in the direction of the abolition of home work, the relief of the unemployed by empowering Boards of Guardians to acquire land and to till it by the labour of persons temporarily unemployed, the improvement of the lot of the dock labourers and other casual workers, and the amelioration of the condition of the agricultural labourer. The same report will also express regret that the nationalisation of the land cannot be dealt with. These questions bristle with opportunities for controversy, and it will not be possible to conclude the work of the Commission by the end of the month. It is expected that five members of the Commission at least will subscribe to this report.

Apparently Mawdsley was under no delusion about the authorship of the report. When a number of the majority of the Royal Commission observed with a sneer that the signatories had obviously not written the report, Mawdsley answered sharply: 'Certainly not: nor has the Duke or any of you written the majority report. The only distinction between us and you is that you have paid your man, and we have been sharp enough to get it done without payment, and better done too'. On the close of the Commission, Mawdsley insisted on the three Labour members, Tom Mann, Michael Austin and himself, signing a formal letter of thanks to Sidney Webb for enabling them 'to submit a report which we believe will prove to be of great value to the cause of Labour in the future, also in some sense a guide to the industrial and political policy to be endorsed by the workers'.[56]

Tom Mann sat on the Commission, so his interventions were of a special kind. But his colleagues could, and did, appear as witnesses. A whole procession of port workers gave testimony.

## Municipality versus State

Tillett's own programme was laid out before the Royal Commission at an early stage.[57] He first called for regulation of labour to prevent the exploitation of young people and to prevent strain and injury. He then argued what was to become the classic new-unionist case for municipalization of dock plant and installations, and 'an absolute popular control of the docks'. This entailed the exclusion of subcontracting middlemen. The state should legislate for and finance local-authority ownership and control, buying out existing owners over twenty-five years at the gross rateable values of their properties. The development of democratic local-government machinery was creating the possibility of decentralized state economic intervention, through a variety of 'enabling' measures which did not impose identical responses to problems, but called forth local initiative and inventiveness. In seeing these opportunities, the new unions were developing, with great prescience, an important agency of reform.[58]

Lord Derby immediately counterattacked. First he raised the question: 'You said that the docks were to be worked on the principle of employing the largest number possible?' If that principle were applied, 'would they pay very well?' Tillett replied:

> I think so. Why I would say so is this, that we are quite prepared to admit of the most effective machinery being brought into use, and the best class of labour procured providing that the result of that class of labour's efforts went to support their fellows, and the municipal powers generally. At the present moment, every advantage in the direction of effective machinery and effective labour goes into the pocket of the private owner of the company. Under the other control it would go for the general benefit.[59]

But would it 'be cheaper to employ, say, 12 men where you now employ 10?' asked Lord Derby. 'It would be cheaper to the municipality, but not . . . to the private employer,' said Tillett. And at this point he began to invoke the principle of social costs: 'the municipal power would be responsible as much for the poverty of the community as for the wealth of the community . . . [while the] employer is not responsible for the poverty of the community . . . [if the municipality gave] men employment in one direction, they would not have to give them charity in another.'

But, came the inevitable response, is this not turning the docks into a system of outdoor relief? Tillett thought not, but could easily overcome overmanning problems in municipal docks if the state could be persuaded to co-operate with local bodies in establishing municipal workshops

> to find employment, to provide means of technical education for youths and for men, if they so desire, to provide them all with the necessaries of life, providing them with work; and I would go so far as to say that the man who would not work should not eat . . .
>
> I would say that the Government recognises the necessity of teaching their convicts trades; they understand it, I believe, as the best means of giving the men a fair start in life and allowing them to be honest. If we could get the State to recognise the poor man as it does the convict, to recognise the incapable man as it does the convict and the criminal, if we could get the State to further that idea and to increase the facilities to give every man a chance to learn a trade, then I think one of the most serious labour problems would be grappled with.[60]

Tillett's workshops would, he said as he warmed to his theme, be locally and democratically administered. They would 'select their own officials', maintain access to the accounts and operate under local or district control. This prospectus was no more appealing to the Royal Commission's majority than it was to Margaret Thatcher's administration when it was revived by the Greater London Council and the Greater London Enterprise Board nearly a century later. But in the effort to combine public enterprise with decentralized initiative, it showed a bold imagination which was unfortunately missing when later Labour leaders began to blueprint the idea of the public corporation which was, for long years, to be synonymous with socialism in Britain. Tillett's successors in the TGWU were to become notable among the critics of this model and of its architect, Herbert Morrison.

But this was not all that Tillett had to tell the Royal Commission. He went on to outline a comprehensive framework for industrial relations, which involved far-reaching national proposals.

To deal with labour unrest and to avoid the ill-effects of disputes, Tillett proposed an integrated package of governmental initiatives: 'There should be a ministry of labour; a state board of arbitration; and the men should be bound as well as the employers by any suggestion that the board might make.'[61] The functions of a Ministry of Labour would involve data-collection and the appointment of inspectors to enforce relevant legislation on safety, equipment maintenance and the proper working of shifts.

Government presence in industrial relations was a novel idea, even though Arbitration Acts in 1867 and again in 1872 had made provision for voluntary conciliation. There was no organizational basis for the enforcement of any but the most limited legislation. Neither the government nor the civil service had disposed of any cadre for dealing with labour matters before 1886. After an agitation by Charles Bradlaugh, a Bureau of Labour Statistics was established to inquire into organization, pay and spending patterns of working people. But by the early 1890s all this added up to the most rudimentary provision. Tillett's proposals, therefore, amounted to a comprehensive reform.

Sidney Webb and Tom Mann also ventilated the idea that a Labour Department could arbitrate in industrial disputes. There were differences in the details of their proposals. Tillett wished his arbitrators to be empowered to issue legally binding awards, equally applicable to both parties. Sidney Webb suggested that arbitrators should work by appealing to public opinion: they should inquire into the reasons for disputes and publish their findings. Tom Mann thought that mediation should be organized by a central board with national coverage, and should offer a last court of appeal to which voluntary arbitration boards might have recourse. Mann's proposal was a sensitive compromise. It did not seek final arbitration lightly, but provided for the agreed regulation of disagreements, wherever this was possible.

Not long after the Royal Commission had concluded its work, Sidney and Beatrice Webb published their lectures at the London School of

Economics under the title *Industrial Democracy*. They showed that compulsory arbitration was by no means a popular demand among many established trade unions. It would, they said, amount to the state regulation of wages, and would no longer be restricted to 'the patching up of a quarrel between capitalists and workmen'.[62]

The pressure of unnumbered casual workers undoubtedly confirmed Ben Tillett in his pursuit of the social regulation of both wages and employment. Similar pressures were at work on the other side of the world. In 1894, an Arbitration Court was established in New Zealand, and by 1896 arbitration had spread from New South Wales (1892) through South Australia (1894) to Victoria (1896). The working of this style of government intervention naturally interested the dockers' leaders, and it is not an accident that both Tillett and Mann were to be found in Australia and New Zealand within the next few years.

## The Case for General Unions

Both Tillett and Mann went out to study the effects of the new system. That they drew different and opposed conclusions was to counterpoint the union agenda during the next great upsurge of transport workers a generation later.

Among the other first-generation new-union leaders, Will Thorne also saw clearly the necessity for the new organizations to be all-grade, all-industry, general unions. He went before the Royal Commission in 1892: 'If we should confine ourselves to one particular industry, such as gasworkers alone, and if those other people in various parts of the country are let go unorganised, then, if we had a dispute with any of the gas companies, these men would be brought up to be put in our places'.[63]

Thorne, Burns and Mann had all, as we have seen, been members of the Social Democratic Federation, which had this to say on the question of trade unionism:

> The real emancipation of labour can only be effected by the solemn binding together of millions of human beings in a federation as wide as the civilised world ... The day has gone by for the efforts of isolated trades ... Nothing is to be gained for the workers as a class without the complete organisation of labourers of all grades, skilled and unskilled ... We appeal therefore earnestly to the skilled artisans of all trades, Unionists and non-Unionists alike, to make common cause with their unskilled brethren, and with us Social-Democrats, so that the workers may themselves take hold of the means of production, and organise a Co-operative Commonwealth for themselves and their colleagues.[64]

Thorne's union, whose original preamble to its rules had reflected 'the language of the old unionism', changed it to that of 'the class war' in

1892, when it decided to admit 'every kind of "unskilled" labour . . . on an equal footing'. Eleanor Marx had a hand in this important amendment.[65]

The naming of the new unions reflected, with noticeable consistency, the notion of 'general' unionism. The most famous cases, of the dockers and the gasworkers, added 'and General Labourers' to their titles from the outset. The move away from local to national scope was reflected in other cases. Thus, as we have seen, the Tyneside Labour Union soon became the National Amalgamated Union of Labour, a similar South Wales body soon called itself the National Amalgamated Labourers' Union of Great Britain and Ireland, and the Lancashire Labour Amalgamation became the British Labour Amalgamation.

Of the new unions founded in the late 1880s, only the Sailors and Firemen were untouched by socialist thinking amongst the leadership, and only they and the Glasgow-originated, Liverpool-dominated National Union of Dock Labourers of Great Britain and Ireland sought no recruits outside their original industrial base. Even so, Havelock Wilson had envisaged a federation between his union and the National Union of Dock Labourers in Glasgow in its initial phase. It is true that McHugh and McGhee were Georgeites, not Marxists of the SDF, but both they and Sexton, who succeeded to their leadership, were followers of some brand of socialist thought, since Sexton's and McGhee's membership of the Knights of Labour brought them in touch with an order which 'had an ambitious programme of social and political amelioration . . . [which] may be compared with the grandiose schemes of trade unionism in Owen's day rather than with the cautious and exclusive societies of Gompers's American Federation of Labour, or the British Trades Union Congress before the advent of "new unionism".'[66]

Sexton's instinct to move into politics from his trade-union base was evident from his earliest days of activity, pre-dating the Liverpool strike of 1889 and his entry into new unionism. Following an initial campaign against jerry-building in the city and related corruption on the Liverpool City Council's Health and General Purposes Committee, he recalled in his memoirs:

> From that time onwards some of us banded together to wage open and unceasing war on the jerry-building crew . . . We fought municipal election after municipal election on purely labour principles in the teeth of my old enemies the Unholy Alliance of the official Irish and Liberals, to whom another Unholy Alliance was now attached – that of the Liberal and Tory jerry-builders.[67]

(Sexton maintained that some of his fellow Irishmen, having won council seats, became involved in the corruption.)

In pursuing municipal Labour politics, Sexton was committing himself to a strategy which was also followed by the Gasworkers' Union, which sought council seats where the municipalities owned the gasworks. Later this course was taken by such waterfront leaders as Harry Gosling, the London lighterman, who became a prominent member of the London County Council, as John Burns had done before him. Later again, in the twentieth century, Sexton, Tillett and Gosling, like their opposite numbers Thorne and Clynes of the Gasworkers' Union, were to combine high union office with parliamentary careers. Tom Mann was never elected, although he stood several times on the ticket of the Independent Labour Party. As early as 1890 he was offered, anonymously through his lawyer, a grant of £2 a week to present a candidature.

## New Unions Seen By Others

If these were the politics and the strategies of the leaderships of the new unions, we can turn now to discuss the responses of other parties – the contemporary historians, the radical sympathizers and mediators, and the employers.

But we should begin with the workers who were involved – the members of the new unions. The evidence lies in the statistics: here was spectacular, almost overnight, growth. Quite simply, in the years 1889 and 1890, previously unorganized workers – whole sections of the Victorian underclass of the poorest employees – flocked to the new organizations in their hundred of thousands. This, at the very least, demonstrates a felt need on their part for association and action. They were responding to, and at the same time encouraging, the initiative of a new type of leader. This had been for some time the age of working-class autodidacts, who won their influence on the basis of their own studies. Now the new ideas of socialism helped such men to evolve a deliberate strategy of trade unionism. It was the interaction between such leaders and the mass of members and potential members that produced new unionism. Significantly, those members were largely indifferent to the structure of the unions which emerged. Often, indeed, they sought to break through occupational and industrial boundaries in their eagerness for inclusive forms of organization. Thus the Glasgow dockers initially sought to be enrolled by the Sailors' and Firemen's Union; the Welsh dockers transferred in large numbers from a local to a national union; and, also in Wales, many groups in hinterland industries joined up. In Hull the dockers promptly abandoned their earlier local union for Tillett's new national one, and, as we have seen, agricultural workers joined in from Lincolnshire and East Yorkshire. Inland transport trades such as the carters, usually displaced from the land and closely associated with the docks, made members for the Dockers' Union. The tramway-men were often distanced from this process, having a more separate industrial conception of their identity, and they created their own unions. But at this point neither road-passenger transport nor commercial road haulage was a mass, labour-intensive industry in its own right, the railways still dominating in both passenger and freight traffic. The carters and hauliers who were drawn in to the Dockers' Union were those working alongside the union's founders on the dock and in its immediately surrounding warehouses and markets. Comprehensive statistics of vehicles in use exist from 1904. In that year, there were a mere 5,000 buses, coaches and taxis, 4,000 goods vehicles and 7,000 tramcars, compared to 75,000, 101,000 and 13,000 in 1920.[68]

We should also note that Sexton and his fellow trade unionists readily abandoned the clandestinity of the Knights of Labour (the equivalent in Liverpool of Tillett's 'hole-and-corner' Tea Operatives' Union before the great strike in London) in favour of the open, bands-and-banner-waving public demonstrations of the new unions, which so scandalized the decorous old unionists like George Howell.

## Sectionalism and Generalism

Of course, not all the old sectionalisms gave way before the new upsurge, particularly in London. We have seen that the stevedores, although swept along in the generous wave of sympathetic action which characterized the great strike, preserved their separate identity thereafter. Striking testimony to the tug-of-war between sectional and general impulses is given by Harry Gosling of the London Lightermen's Union, the very embodiment of craftlike organization in the port. In his memoirs he recalls:

We, too, benefited enormously by 1889: it practically revolutionised our industrial outlook. All through their history skilled rivermen had been craft unionists out and out. Even in my early days a riverman was a craftsman, and that only . . . But now, after 1889, for the first time these same skilled rivermen began to feel a half-conscious groping, an urge . . . towards a new group life for themselves. Somehow it came to them, vaguely at first and helplessly, that they could no longer stand each craft for itself, but that all the men engaged in waterside transport work – seamen, dockers, carters, lightermen, coal-porters or whoever they might be – fundamentally belonged together as members of one body and must assert themselves as such. And this new idea was an immense triumph, though it took fully twenty years before it matured, and the first live federation of transport workers came into existence . . . Even the strong impulse they received in 1889 did not convert them to the forward policy of more active groups of workers, and it took years of propaganda before they could be persuaded to join forces with other organisations . . . At times I admit I used to get rather impatient with this attitude, and I remember saying to Tom Mann once in my early days as a trade union official: 'Well, shall I leave them, and come along with the others?' . . . 'No' he said, 'stay where you are, and bring them along with you'. Strangely sober advice from one who has always been branded as an extremist.[69]

Gosling of course followed the advice and, as the only president successively of the National Transport Workers' Federation from its inception in 1910, and then of the newly formed Transport and General Workers' Union, had the satisfaction of 'bringing them along' into the 1922 amalgamation – which he even then saw as simply a further stage in the long march towards total unity. At the TGWU Rules Conference in 1921, which prepared the way for formal amalgamation the following year, in his presidential peroration he spoke thus of unfulfilled hopes: 'But this was the beginning: they had to get an alliance with the railwaymen and then get towards the point when one card would represent trade unionism'.[70] These words were greeted with applause – they echoed what Ernest Bevin had said earlier in the proceedings. One is tempted to add: strangely revolutionary hopes from those who have always been praised as moderates!

In a later volume, we shall see that the tug-of-war between general and craft unionism for the London lightermen was not finally resolved in 1922. Nevertheless, we can legitimately take this case as symbolic of a force, an impetus towards wider and wider association, which ebbed and flowed in the decades succeeding the formation of the Dockers' Union, not only down to 1922 but beyond it to the present day.

This logic was to assert itself again and again. True, immediately following the first triumphs, new unionism shrank back into dependence on more stable employment groups outside the casual docks industry. In an era of unregulated boom and slump, the wider the association, the more prone it was to instability of membership and allegiance. A period of decline, retrenchment and caution was to follow, covering almost two decades from 1891 to 1910. Yet when revival came, it immediately promoted the trend to federation, universally seen by the participants as a prelude to amalgamation.

That this was a resumption of previous tendencies is seen in the federation of the 1870s – of London dockers, carmen, watermen, lightermen and railway servants' unions; in the formation of the United Labour Council arising from the Joint Strike Committee which ran the great strike of 1889; and in the federation formed by the Dockers' Union, the Sailors' and Firemen's Union and the South Side Labour Protection League in London in 1891. This is the record for London alone. The federal process is also very marked in the North-east and in Hull (to take just two more examples) at the height of the first wave of new unionism. Finally, we have already noticed that the NUDL, too, sought wider alliances in 1889–90.

## III

## *Academic Appraisals*

What did contemporary opinion outside the ranks of the new unions make of the phenomenon? The most weighty, and subsequently influential, account comes to us from Sidney and Beatrice Webb, the first edition of whose *History of Trade Unionism* was completed in 1894. It benefits not only from the all-round scholarship of the authors, but also from the specific social studies which Beatrice Webb had undertaken in London's dockland for the studies of Charles Booth.

It is from the Webbs that the first attempt to identify the character of the new unions comes. They point to the common features of low subscriptions and concentration on a single benefit – strike pay. They recognize the tendency to general recruitment – what they call 'comprehensive membership' – and to the concomitant emergence of federations, and also of new Trades Councils, together with the formation of local joint committees of unions in kindred trades, all of which are part of a general 'sinking of rivalries'. They demonstrate the link between socialist propaganda of the previous decade and the leadership of the new unions. They relate this to the conflict between the 'old' and the 'new' unionism and to the triumph, even within the old, of the new unionists' call for the legal limitation of the hours of labour, as the engineers, the carpenters and the London Trades Council (including its secretary George Shipton) became the converts who helped to secure its adoption by the 1890 TUC Congress. They cite John Burns's résumé of that formative Congress. 'Out of . . . sixty resolutions', he declared, 'forty-five were nothing more or less than direct appeals to the State and Municipalities of this country to do for the workman what Trades Unionism, "Old" and New", has proved itself incapable of doing'.[71] They show that this impulse was already, by 1894, producing 'Collectivist victories on the London School Board and County Council, the steady growth of municipal activity and the increasing influence exercised by working-men members of representative bodies'.[72]

The Webbs acknowledged that they were too close to the events 'to estimate the precise character of the new movement itself'. Yet they offered an historical appraisal based on a comparison between new unionism and its only preceding counterpart in Labour history, the Owenite wave of the 1830s, in which mass enrolment in a trade union with large social goals took place – in a matter of months – with similar explosive force to that of 1889. The Webbs continue:

But however strongly the outward features of the wave of 1889–90 may remind the student of those of 1833–4, the characteristics peculiar to the new movement significantly measure the extent of the advance, both in social theory and social methods, made by the wage-earners in the two intervening generations. Time and experience alone will show how far the empirical Socialism of the Trade Unionist of to-day, with its eclectic opportunism, its preference for municipal collectivism, its cautious adaptation of existing social structure, may safely be pronounced superior in practicability to the revolutionary and universal Communism of Robert Owen ... To the great majority of the Trade Unionists the theories of the leaders at either date did but embody a vague aspiration after a more equitable social order. The practical difference – the difference reflected in the character and the temper of the men attracted to the two movements, and of the attitude of the public towards them – is the difference of method and immediate action. Robert Owen . . . despised and rejected political action . . . In this disdain of all existing organisations, and the suddenness of the complete 'social revolution' which it contemplated, the Owenism of 1833–4 found . . . an echo in much of the Socialist propaganda of 1884–9. The leaders of the New Unionists, on the contrary, sought to bring into the ranks of existing organisations – the Trade Union, the Municipality, or the State – great masses of unorganised workers who had hitherto been either absolutely outside the pale, or inert elements within it. They aimed, not at superseding existing social structures, but at capturing them all in the interests of wage-earners. Above all, they sought to teach the great masses of undisciplined workers how to apply their newly acquired political power so as to obtain, in a perfectly constitutional manner, whatever changes in legislation or administration they desired ... To Robert Owen, whose path was blocked on the political line by the disfranchisement of five out of six of the adult male population, open voting under intimidation, corrupt close corporations in the towns and a Whig oligarchy at the centre, the idea of relying on the constitutional instrument of the polling-booth must have appeared no less chimerical than his own programme appears today. The New Unionists of 1889–90, on the other hand, found ready for their use an extensive and all-embracing Democratic social structure, which it was impossible to destroy, and would have been foolish to attempt to ignore.[73]

Despite a substantial attempt at a 'revisionist' version of the import of new unionism, which has appeared in our own times at the hands of H. A. Clegg, Alan Fox and A. F. Thompson, supported by John Lovell,[74] the Webbs' assessment, made so close to the events, still has a loud ring of truth. The traditional view has in fact been reinforced by some important subsequent historical studies, including the recent spate of regional histories on which we have drawn. Of twentieth-century historians, Eric Hobsbawm's findings mostly serve to underscore the Webbs' version. He finds that:

The theory in the mind of the founders of the general unions (and of their predecessors), was fairly simple. The 'labourer', mobile, helpless, shifting from one trade to another, was incapable of using the orthodox tactics of craft unionism. Possessing 'merely the general value of labour' he could not, like the 'skilled man', buttress a certain scarcity value by various restrictive methods, thus 'keeping up his price'. His only chance therefore was to recruit into one gigantic union all those who could possibly blackleg on him – in the last analysis every 'unskilled' man, woman or juvenile in the country: and thus to create a vast closed shop.[75]

Hobsbawm also insists that:

the large national and regional 'general' unions of 1889 were the offspring of a marriage between the class unionism of the socialists and the more modest plans of the unskilled themselves. (The only general union with a really national network, the Gas-workers, secured this largely through the help of local socialist groups.) The expansion of the early 1870s, in other respects an important – and neglected – forerunner of the 'New Unionism', produced unions of a far more sectional type.[76]

## The Liberal Sympathizers

There was another, contemporary, view of the new unionism which was as influential in ruling-class circles and in particular in Whitehall as was that of the Webbs in the Labour movement. It was also sympathetic, welcoming of the new movement, but sought to harness it in the interests of social peace and class harmony. It is embodied in the work and writings of Llewellyn Smith and Vaughan Nash, of Sydney Buxton, Lord Askwith, and Cardinal Manning. It has been given modern appraisals by Gareth Stedman Jones, Roger Davidson and by Alan Fox.[77]

Hubert Llewellyn Smith (later Sir Hubert), was only twenty-five years old in 1889, when he co-authored the first account of the great dock strike. Of middle-class Quaker extraction, he joined the New Oxford Movement of enlightened liberalism, nourished at Balliol College, Oxford, by the philosophers Benjamin Jowett and T. H. Green. He was patronized by the Webbs, and gravitated to the study of East End poverty through Toynbee Hall. He became a university extension lecturer, and a researcher for the Booth inquiries. He espoused the cause of new unionism, helped to publicize the plight of the matchgirls, worked for agricultural trade unionism in 1890, and with John Burns co-ordinated picketing in the London bus strike of 1891. He became Commissioner of Labour at the Board of Trade in 1893, Controller-General from 1903, and Permanent Secretary from 1907 to 1919. He was one of the archetypal figures (George Askwith being the other), representing a continuous strand of enlightened liberalism, which, in pursuit of the preservation and reinforcement of ruling-class hegemony, sought to encourage state–employer–trade-union relations, in particular through the leaderships of the new unions.[78] Smith's co-author of the first history of the London dock strike, Vaughan Nash, became secretary of the Cabinet Reconstruction Committee concerned with post-war social policies in 1916.

These two draw an unexpected lesson from the success of the London dock strike. They predict and hope that it will transform the casual labour force into a disciplined, regular workforce, free of the encumbrance of

the loafer, the cadger, the failure of the industrial race – the members of 'Class B' of Mr. Charles Booth's hierarchy of social classes. [This subclass will] find another door closed against them, and in many cases the last door to employment . . . the difficulty which the loafer will find in competing with the higher class labourer under the new regime will be the exact measure of the success of the strike. Hitherto, all these grades of labour have jostled each other at the dock gates, and the standard of life of the lowest has set the standard of all. Now they will be more sharply divided . . . The problem of dealing with the dregs of London will thus loom up before us more urgent than in times gone by, but it will be simplified by a change which will make it impossible, or at least unpardonable, to mix up the problem, which is essentially one of the treatment of social disease, with the radically different question of the claims of labour.[79]

Sydney Buxton, in his introduction to Smith and Nash's history, reinforces the point: 'in the past, the Docks have formed a "gigantic system of out-door relief" – a huge pauperising agency, planted in the heart of London; a centre from which have been recklessly recruited the ranks of unskilled labour in the Metropolis'. He rejoices that the 'labour question', the 'condition-of-the-people question', has been placed so forcefully before public attention by the dock strike. It is not difficult to sympathize with his enthusiasm: like Smith, he had been working away in obscurity on that very question in his constituency to no avail, and now, suddenly, his constituents had achieved dramatic publicity for themselves.

Buxton's other expectation and hope was that the settlement would be followed by the generalization of the spirit and practice of conciliation and arbitration boards, which he notes were common in many industries in the North, but hitherto unknown in London and in dockland: 'Thus, the formation of a strong Trades Union tends on both sides to bring about that which is the most desirable of all ends, in disputes between labour and capital; a permanent and recognised Board of Conciliation; a Board that shall consist partly of masters, partly of men, with, perhaps, an impartial outsider as final arbitrator'.[80]

Askwith, in his monumental study, *Industrial Problems and Disputes*, also links the dock strike with the spread of conciliation:

It was then too, that efforts at conciliation were found not to be without result, a belief fostered by the closing of the long six weeks' coal dispute in the Midlands, under the chairmanship of Lord Rosebery, in 1893; the national agreement established, through the Board of Trade, in the Boot and Shoe trade in 1895; and the reference of the North-Eastern Railway dispute to Sir Henry James in the same year. The dockers' strike, it seems to me . . . marked a great epoch in the relations of Capital and Labour.[81]

Askwith was writing long after the event, and was able to put the earlier optimism of the social engineers such as Smith and Buxton into a somewhat bitter perspective, as he pointed to the unsolved problems of casualism in the docks industry of the twentieth century, and to his own frustrations at the hands of the dock employers over years of conciliation in the industry.

Not only was the settlement of 1889 inadequate to solve the structural problems of port labour: it was a failure in material terms as well. Pay, conditions and the new call-on system were soon undermined. The power of the Dockers' Union to secure preference of employment for the union ticket lasted just fourteen months through the continued trade boom. As trade turned down, the employers took the opportunity to break the men's dependence on union-preferred hiring by introducing a measure of 'decasualization' which switched dependence to a system of preference lists operated by the companies, through their co-ordinated Joint Docks Committee, which amalgamated the separate dock systems. To the existing 'permanent' men, the companies added the categories A-, B- and C-men. The A-men got some of the 'perms' conditions, but not sick pay or pensions; B-men were registered, with a ticket, but moved up and down the preference list according to their attendance records and performance. C-men were engaged only when all A- and B-men had work. Booth found that 'whatever has been gained by the men on the "B" list has been lost by those on the "C" list and outsiders . . . ultimately they must surely decrease in number if less and less work is offered to them, but the process is a painful one and some of the distress from lack of employment in East London . . . is probably attributable to this cause'.[82] Stedman Jones comments: 'The casual poor had played a full part in the strike of 1889, but for them at least, the experience of victory had been vicarious'.[83]

## A Temporary Settlement?

This sobering picture, of the dockers divided by employer devices which were to play so prominent a part in labour relations and trade unionism in the industry for the next eighty years, and which preface the full-scale assault on new unionism by the Shipping Federation in the 1890s, is perhaps the point at which to close this review of the first phase of new unionism, poised on the eve of its greatest trials.

In 1889, the employers were divided. Mr. Norwood, their spokesman in London, represented intransigence. So did the large shipping companies in Liverpool. The railway company in South Wales adopted similar attitudes. But in all ports there were significant bodies of smaller employers willing to compromise and offer concessions and recognition, and this, as we have seen, was true of a genuine shipping magnate in Hull. In the next phase, the employers presented a united, fighting front, and a pre-planned strategy. Conciliation was no part of it: it was to be outright battle, red in tooth and claw.

# Notes

1 Havelock Wilson, *My Stormy Voyage Through Life*, vol. I (Co-operative Printing Society, 1925), p. 176.
2 Havelock Wilson's evidence to the Royal Commission on Labour, 1892, Minutes of Evidence, Group B, Vol. I, Qs. 9176–88.
3 See Arthur Marsh and Victoria Ryan, *The Seamen: A History of the National Union of Seamen, 1887–1987* (Malthouse, 1989).
4 The Board of Trade recorded 40,000 days lost in each of two major shipping disputes in 1889, making them larger than the Board's figure for the London dock strike (H. A. Clegg, Alan Fox and A. F. Thompson, *A History of British Trade Unions Since 1889*, vol. I: *1889–1910* (Oxford University Press, 1964), p. 55.
5 James Sexton, *Sir James Sexton, Agitator: the Life of the Dockers' MP* (Faber and Faber, 1936), p. 94.
6 Geoff Brown, *Sabotage: A Study in Industrial Conflict* (Spokesman Books, 1977), p. 6.
7 Reprinted in an appendix to Llewellyn Smith and Vaughan Nash, *The Story of the Dockers' Strike* (Fisher Unwin, 1890), p. 190. For ca'canny in Glasgow, see Brown, *Sabotage*, pp. 3–8.
8 Sexton, *Sir James Sexton, Agitator*, p. 104. Sexton thought that 'the policy had some success for a time', but because it backfired 'it was eventually abandoned'.
9 Ibid., p. 18.
10 Ibid., p. 80.
11 Vincent Alan McClelland, *Cardinal Manning: His Public Life and Influence, 1865–92* (Oxford University Press, 1962), p. 141.
12 Manning's father, William (1763–1835), was a West India merchant with large plantations on the West Indian island of St Kitts. He was a founder member of the West India Dock Company in 1797, which was the first wet dock built outside the control of the City and of existing labour customs. He was an MP, Governor of the Bank of England, married twice and fathered seven children. He was bankrupted in 1831. (Information supplied by Rodney Mace.)
13 McClelland, *Cardinal Manning*, p. 149.
14 Eric Taplin, *Liverpool Dockers and Seamen, 1870–1890* (University of Hull, 1974), p. 38.

15    John Gray, *City in Revolt: James Larkin and the Belfast Dock Strike of 1907* (Blackstaff Press, 1985), p. 5.
16    See Raymond Brown, *Waterfront Organisation in Hull*.
17    7 February 1891.
18    Cf. Rex C. Russell, *The 'Revolt of the Field' in Lincolnshire* (Lincolnshire County Council Committee, National Union of Agricultural Workers, 1956), pp. 152–4.
19    Quotations in this passage are from Raymond Brown, *Waterfront Organisation in Hull, 1870–1900* (University of Hull, 1974), pp. 50–1.
20    Brian Atkinson, *Trade Unions in Bristol* (Bristol Branch, Historical Association, University of Bristol, 1982), p. 9.
21    Ibid., p. 10.
22    This section draws upon Phillip J. Leng, *The Welsh Dockers* (G. W. & A. Hesketh, 1981), pp. 13–34.
23    The *Star*, May 1891.
24    *Evening Standard*, 3 October 1890.
25    The *Star*, 30 May 1891.
26    Ibid.
27    Sutherst's evidence to the Royal Commission on Labour, Minutes of Evidence, Group B, Vol. II, Qs. 743–17, 197.
28    See William Collison, *The Apostle of Free Labour* (Hurst and Blackett, 1913), pp. 24–37.
29    Royal Commission on Labour, 1892, IUP, p. 508.
30    See Kenneth Fuller, *Radical Aristocrats* (Lawrence and Wishart, 1985), pp. 22–3.
31    Eric J. Hobsbawm, *Labouring Men* (Weidenfeld and Nicolson, 1968), chapter 9: 'British Gas-workers, 1873–1914', pp. 158–79.
32    These statistics were supplied by Michael Barratt Brown.
33    Clegg, Fox and Thompson, *History of British Trade Unions*, vol. I, p. 65.
34    George Tate, *The London Trades Council, 1860–1950: A History* (Lawrence and Wishart, 1950), p. 73.
35    Royal Commission on Labour, Minutes of Evidence, Group B, Vol. II, Qs. 13,169–13,170.
36    Ibid., Qs. 13,037–13,038.
37    Quoted in Jonathan Schneer, *Ben Tillett: Portrait of a Labour Leader* (Croom Helm, 1982), p. 47.
38    Ibid., pp. 48–9.
39    George Howell, *Trade Unionism New and Old* (Methuen, 1891; 3rd edn rev. 1900).
40    Ibid., p. 131.
41    Ibid., p. 133.
42    Ibid., pp. 134–5.
43    Ibid., p. 136.
44    Zigmunt Bauman, *Between Class and Élite: The Evolution of the British Labour Movement, a Sociological Study* (Manchester University Press, 1972), p. 73.
45    H. M. Hyndman, *Further Reminiscences* (Macmillan, 1912), pp. 249–50.
46    See Ben Tillett, *Memories and Reflections* (John Long, 1931), p. 93: 'John Burns ... felt entitled to jibe at the delegates to the Trades Union Congress because so many of them looked like respectable City gentlemen; wore very

good coats, large watch-chains and high hats; and in many cases were of . . .
splendid build and proportion . . . When I became the organiser of a union,
I fell far short of these sartorial standards.'

47  Howell, *Trade Unionism New and Old*, pp. 136–7.
48  Ibid., pp. 137–9.
49  Ibid., p. 139–42.
50  Ibid., pp. 142–8.
51  Ibid., p. 224.
52  Ibid., p. 225.
53  Beatrice Webb, *Our Partnership* (Longman, 1948), pp. 40–1.
54  Tom Mann, *Memoirs* (1923; reissued MacGibbon and Kee, 1967), p. 75;
    also Tate, *The London Trades Council*, pp. 80ff.
55  Mann, *Memoirs*, p. 78.
56  Webb, *Our Partnership*, p. 41.
57  Royal Commission on Labour, Minutes of Evidence, Group B, 3 July 1891,
    p. 142.
58  This was to be developed, with great panache, by the Greater London
    Council and its offshoots – especially the Greater London Enterprise Board
    – during its last years of existence. No doubt this is one of the reasons why a
    Conservative administration under Margaret Thatcher resolved to do away
    with the GLC.
59  Royal Commission on Labour, Minutes of Evidence, Group B, Vol. I,
    Q. 3582.
60  Ibid., Q. 3594.
61  Ibid., Q. 3615.
62  Sidney and Beatrice Webb, *Industrial Democracy* (1897; reissued Longman
    Green, 1926), p. 245.
63  Quoted in Hobsbawm, *Labouring Men*, p. 181.
64  From the manifesto of the Social Democratic Federation to the Trade
    Unions, September 1884; quoted in Sidney and Beatrice Webb, *The History
    of Trade Unionism* (1894; WEA edn, 1912), p. 396.
65  See Clegg, Fox and Thompson, *History of British Trade Unions*, vol. I, p. 92.
66  Henry Pelling, 'The Knights of Labour in Britain, 1880–1901', *Economic
    History Review*, second series, vol. IX (1956), pp. 313–31.
67  Sexton, *Sir James Sexton, Agitator*, p. 92.
68  B. R. Mitchell and P. Deane, *Abstract of British Historical Statistics*
    (Cambridge University Press, 1962), p. 230.
69  Harry Gosling, *Up and Down Stream* (Methuen, 1927), pp. 144–5.
70  TGWU *Record*, vol. I, no. 3 (October 1921), pp. 22–3.
71  Webb, *History of Trade Unionism*, p. 395.
72  Ibid., p. 399.
73  Ibid., p. 404.
74  In Clegg, Fox and Thompson, *History of British Trade Unions*, vol. I, chapter
    2; and John Lovell, *Stevedores and Dockers: a Study of Trade Unionism in the
    Port of London, 1870–1914* (Macmillan, 1969), *passim*. See also Lovell,
    'The New Unions', *Bulletin of the Society for the Study of Labour History*,
    no. 36 (winter 1977), pp. 15–16, in which he makes his own comments on
    the large controversy amongst historians on the significance of the new
    unionism: 'There are those who see 1889 as the great watershed or turning

point in the history of British labour, and there are those who play down the significance of the new unionist phase and suggest that the periods 1872–4 and 1910–14 were no less important than 1889–92. This paper subscribes to the latter viewpoint'.

The separation of 1889 from the 1910–14 period, as though the latter was a fresh phase with no roots in the new unions, is, it seems to us, erroneous. It leads to a 'playing down' of the new unions by isolating what is really their first phase, and then focusing upon all their subsequent and subsidiary errors and reverses. Thus, after tracing the severe collapse of membership in the 1890s, Lovell declares that 'The impact of the new unions upon the composition of the total movement was thus a fleeting one', a truly astounding judgement. In what looks like an attempt to correct it, he concedes their subsequent growth after 1910, which 'made a lasting impact upon the composition of the movement'. Recognizing the contradiction between the two statements, he seeks escape by (i) putting quotation marks – 'new' unions – around that term *only* when referring to the later stage of revival; and (ii) finding it 'worth noting, however, that the most remarkable gains in membership after 1910 were made by an organisation that was not of 1889 vintage, namely the Workers' Union founded in 1898'. To which we must respond: (a) the Workers' Union was founded in a very personal campaign by Tom Mann, one of the fathers of new unionism, on new union lines, as a socialist, class union; (b) its growth up to 1914, the period chosen by Lovell for comparison, was in industries and occupations untouched by the Dockers' Union, much of it in virgin territory; (c) the Workers' Union, struggling with difficulties more acute than those facing the ultimate product of new unionism – the TGWU – in 1929 was taken over by that union, thus completing a process which was surely inherent in its logic and history.

Lovell's solid achievement in his history of trade unionism in the London docks demands recognition. But this assessment of the broad sweep of events is more questionable.

Clegg, Fox and Thompson express a similar view, in seeking to make final judgements on the new unions on the basis of their first few years' existence. This is reflected in the timespans into which their volumes were divided. It seems to us that the proper periodization is to regard the late 1880s as the beginning of a process of change in trade-union structure and method which was consummated only in the 1920s, with the formation of the two large general unions, the ASE's transformation into the AEU, and the rewriting of the TUC's constitution. Between the two dates lies the equally formative creation – initiated (as we shall see) by new-union influence – of the Labour Party. Clegg, Fox and Thompson, as also Lovell, seek to minimize the role of socialist ideas and of socialists in the formation and evolution of the new unions, even asserting that they played 'no role' in the formation of the NUDL! They give polemical support to their approach by preferring to rely on the opinion of Tillett's greatest enemy, the self-styled 'apostle of free labour', Collison, who called him a 'sybarite; a voluptuary with the hide of an agitator', rather than to make a sober appraisal of his undoubtedly considerable contribution to trade-union history. Fortunately, we now have the biography of Tillett, 'warts and all', by Ben Schneer, to fill the gap.

The dismissal of the 'newness' in the new unions attempted by these four authors is, it seems to us, refuted by the record. For an informed and critical review of the Clegg, Fox and Thompson volume, see Eric J. Hobsbawm, 'Trade Union History', Essays in Bibliography and Criticism, LVIII, *Economic History Review*, second series, vol. XX, no. 2 (August 1967), pp. 358–64.

75 Hobsbawm, *Labouring Men*, p. 181.
76 Ibid., p. 182.
77 Gareth Stedman Jones, 'Working Class Culture and Working Class Politics in London, 1870–1900', *Journal of Social History*, vol. 7, no. 4 (1974), pp. 460–508, Roger Davidson, *Whitehall and the Labour Problem in Late Victorian and Edwardian Britain* (Croom Helm, 1985) and Alan Fox, *History and Heritage: The Social Origins of the British Industrial Relations System* (Allen and Unwin, 1985).
78 R. Davidson, 'Llewellyn Smith, the Labour Department and Government Growth', in G. Sutherland (ed.), *Studies in the Growth of Nineteenth Century Government* (Routledge and Kegan Paul, 1972).
79 Smith and Nash, *The Story of the Dockers' Strike*, pp. 164–5.
80 Ibid., p. 10.
81 Lord Askwith, *Industrial Problems and Disputes* (John Murray, 1920), p. 74.
82 Booth's evidence to the Royal Commission on Labour, 1892, quoted in Gareth Stedman Jones, *Outcast London* (Penguin, 1971), p. 319.
83 Ibid.

# 5

# Defeat: Defence and Defiance

## I

### *Up Like a Rocket – Down Like the Stick*

The explosive uprush of new unionism between 1889 and 1891 was without precedent. In spite of what followed, this was a formative event. In the short run, no one doubted this.[1] Membership of the TUC increased by 80 per cent between 1888 and 1890[2] and there were some 2,400 strikes and 11 million man-days lost between 1889 and 1890. The implosion that followed so swiftly was, however, almost as dramatic, leading some modern historians to question the long-term influences of the upsurge.

By 1893 one-third of the new membership had been lost. The London dockers, who had affiliated 56,000 members to the 1890 TUC, were down to 22,913 by 1892 and dwindled to 10,000 in 1896. Thereafter their union recovered to 13,879 by 1900. The NUDL peaked at 50,000 in 1890, then slumped to 8,463 by 1892, with a recovery to 11,697 in 1896 and 13,388 in 1900. The National Labour Federation, which claimed 60,000 members in 1890, was dissolved in 1894 following heavy costs incurred during the previous year's Hull dock strike.[3] The Seamen's Union was also bankrupted and dissolved after its membership declined from 78,000 in 1891 to only 5,000 in 1894. It was immediately reformed with a new title – the National Amalgamated Sailors' and Firemen's Union became the National Sailors' and Firemen's Union, with strong central control of its funds incorporated in its revised rules. Havelock Wilson's office was changed from secretary to president, but he retained all his powers.[4] The NUDL's Executive Reports record thirty-eight branches in existence in 1891, of which five were on the Mersey, seven in Scotland and fourteen in Ireland. By 1895 there were only twenty-five branches, of which five were on the Mersey, three in

Scotland and four in Ireland. In 1918 branch numbers were back to thirty-six, although Ireland's recovery was minimal, and Hull appears for the first time with five branches.[5]

Beyond the immediate environment of the docks and shipping, many unions which originated in inland transport in the upswing of 1889–90 recorded membership losses of similar proportions. The London Carmen's Trade Union, formed in 1888, lost 4,000 of its original 6,000 members by 1892; its surviving 2,000 represented only 5 per cent of the carmen of the capital at that date.[6] Between 1892 and 1893, the Amalgamated Carters, Lurrymen and Motormen's Association fell from 4,000 to 2,500. The new-union wave undoubtedly stimulated unionization in haulage and road-passenger transport, but it was overwhelmingly sectional and, above all, local. Thus we have such organizations as the Wigan and District Carters and Lurrymen's Association, and the Blackburn and District Tramway Workers' Union. Over a dozen attempts at the unionization of London cabmen have been traced to these years.

The mortality rate amongst new unions of this type was staggering. They were, in the main, 'new' only in the literal sense. Using Marsh and Ryan's invaluable data, we find that, amongst carters and horsemen six unions date from before 1889, whilst twenty-six originate in the expansionary period following 1889. Of these thirty-two unions, twelve were defunct by 1911, unable to participate in the next phase of growth. Of cab, tram and omnibus unions, eight were formed between 1870 and 1888, and thirty-one in or after 1889. Of these, twenty-eight had disappeared by 1911.

If local and sectional unions were still the norm in road transport, they were also widespread in dockland. Twenty-six began life between 1870 and 1888, and no fewer than forty-six in or after 1889. All of forty-four of these had died by 1911. It should be said that in these figures a union which is known to have merged with another and thus to have lost its name and separate existence is not counted amongst those which failed. Information on transfers of allegiance, of course, are normally not documented, so we cannot be sure that the collapse of an organization necessarily involved the loss of its members to the trade-union movement.

Three transport-related unions are, of course, in a distinct category of their own: that which began life as the Tea Operatives' and General Labourers' Union of Great Britain and Ireland; the National Amalgamated Labourers' Union; and the National Amalgamated Union of Labour. Each of these was to endure, in spite of all tribulations. All three had an occupational and local origin, in the London docks, South Wales ports, and among Tyneside unskilled shipyard workers. All expressed in their titles an aspiration to general unionism, reaching beyond their waterside origins. None of them was extinguished in the collapse of the

1890s. The NALU survived, never more than 3,500 strong, as a rival to the Dockers' Union in South Wales, until it joined the TGWU amalgamation of 1922. The NAUL, a much larger body with the bulk of its members in the North-east, was one of the three unions to found the General and Municipal Workers in 1924 (taking its Tyneside dock members with it), along with the other prototypical new union, the Gasworkers', and the Municipal Employees' Association. The Gasworkers' Union, the most substantial of these, exhibited some of the volatility of the transport-based unions in the 1890s, but not to the same degree. It affiliated 60,000 to the 1890 TUC, and reported 36,108 members in 1892, 29,730 in 1896 and 47,979 in 1900.[7] Gas supply always had to be organized with a more stable workforce than that which scrambled for jobs at the dock gates, but improvements in technology reinforced the need for a consistent work organization.

We might add to this list a fourth, marginally general, transport union – the South Side Labour Protection League. It reached a membership of 5,000 after the 1889 strike, but stagnated thereafter. It certainly survived to participate in the amalgamation of 1922. Although it had a branch of labourers at the Woolwich Arsenal, and one of Engineers' Helpers at Deptford, it was predominantly an 'old' sectional union.

How, then, should we account for the substantial collapse of the new unions' membership between 1890 and the middle of that decade? Three types of explanation have been offered, based on respectively, the movements of the trade cycle; the changing structure and technologies of transport and general trades; and the policies of employers and the state towards trade unionism.

## The Trade Cycle

In the overall economy there were short-cycle recoveries at the beginning and the end of the 1880s. The great explosion of new unionism occurred during the second of these upturns. Yet the impact of trade cycles both on the labour market and on the prospects for trade unionism have never been simple.[8] Hobsbawm has pointed to the growth of tonnage passing through the London docks between 1878 and 1888, at a time when key skilled groups such as lightermen were actually falling in number, as a major contributory factor in any explanation of the great strike of 1889. The more general conditions of trade revival in the years 1887 to 1891 may then be invoked to account for the release of a nationwide explosion of visible discontent among general labourers which coincided with the dock strike. In those years the volume of foreign trade rose. Indexed at 1880 = 100, 1887 showed 114, and 1891, 130. During the whole decade there was a shipbuilding boom, and a great growth in the production and export of farm machinery.

By 1892 depression had resumed its course. It was pushed on its way by a famous scandal at the beginning of the decade: the Baring crisis.[9] The nadir of decline was reached in the middle of the decade: thereafter an economic upswing became evident, gathering strength until 1901–2. The established evidence has been tabulated by Clegg, Fox and Thompson, as shown in table 5.1.

Table 5.1   *Trade Union Membership, Strikes and the Trade Cycle, 1889–1910*

| Year | Total Union Membership (000s) | Number of stoppages beginning in year | Total working days lost by all stoppages in progress during year (000s) | Average retail prices (1850 = 100) | Average money wages (1850 = 100) | Percentage unemployed |
|------|------|------|------|------|------|------|
| 1889 | 679   | 1,211 | 3,730  | 91 | 156   | 2.1 |
| 1890 | 871   | 1,040 | 7,473  | 91 | 163   | 2.1 |
| 1891 | 1,109 | 906   | 6,809  | 92 | 163   | 3.5 |
| 1892 | 1,576 | 700   | 17,248 | 92 | 162   | 6.3 |
| 1893 | 1,559 | 599   | 30,439 | 89 | 162   | 7.5 |
| 1894 | 1,530 | 903   | 9,506  | 87 | 162   | 6.9 |
| 1895 | 1,504 | 728   | 5,701  | 84 | 162   | 5.8 |
| 1896 | 1,608 | 906   | 3,565  | 83 | 163   | 3.3 |
| 1897 | 1,731 | 848   | 10,327 | 86 | 166   | 3.3 |
| 1898 | 1,752 | 695   | 15,257 | 87 | 167   | 2.8 |
| 1899 | 1,911 | 710   | 2,503  | 86 | 172   | 2.0 |
| 1900 | 2,022 | 633   | 3,088  | 89 | 179   | 2.5 |
| 1901 | 2,025 | 631   | 4,130  | 90 | 179   | 3.3 |
| 1902 | 2,013 | 432   | 3,438  | 91 | 176   | 4.0 |
| 1903 | 1,994 | 380   | 2,320  | 92 | 174   | 4.7 |
| 1904 | 1,967 | 346   | 1,464  | 93 | 173   | 6.0 |
| 1905 | 1,997 | 349   | 2,368  | 92 | 174   | 5.0 |
| 1906 | 2,210 | 479   | 3,019  | 92 | 176   | 3.6 |
| 1907 | 2,513 | 585   | 2,148  | 95 | 182   | 3.7 |
| 1908 | 2,485 | 389   | 10,785 | 97 | 181   | 7.8 |
| 1909 | 2,477 | 422   | 2,687  | 97 | 179   | 7.7 |
| 1910 | 2,565 | 521   | 9,867  | 98 | 179.5 | 4.7 |

*Source:* H. A. Clegg, Alan Fox and A. F. Thompson, *A History of British Trade Unions since 1889*, Vol. I: *1889–1910* (Clarendon Press, 1964), p. 489.

(Reproduced by permission of Oxford University Press.)

These swings correlate well with the specific trends of the major new unions' membership given above, as well as with the movement of steamship prices, specific to the fortunes of the port industries (see figs 5.1 and 5.2). They also accord with the tramp shipping freight rates for the period (see table 5.2).

Table 5.2  *Index of Tramp Shipping Freight Rates, 1869–1900*

| | |
|---|---|
| 1869 | = 100 |
| 1886 | = 59 |
| 1887 | = 65 |
| 1888 | = 76 |
| 1889 | = 75 |
| 1890 | = 64 |
| 1891 | = 63 |
| 1892 | = 55 |
| 1893 | = 60 |
| 1894 | = 58 |
| 1895 | = 56 |
| 1896 | = 56 |
| 1897 | = 56 |
| 1898 | = 68 |
| 1899 | = 65 |
| 1900 | = 76 |

*Source:* L. Isserlis, cited in B. R. Mitchell, *Abstract of British Historical Statistics* (Cambridge University Press, 1962), p. 224.

(Reproduced by permission of Cambridge University Press.)

The imprint of the pattern of boom and slump on the waterside labour market was considerably more marked than it was in industry generally, because of the sensitivity of foreign trade to that cycle, and – overwhelmingly – because of the dominance of the casual-hiring system. By contrast, although the gas industry suffered seasonal fluctuations of demand, it experienced neither the full impact of trade swings nor the rigours of casual employment. The relative stability of the Gasworkers' Union through the 1890s, noted above, is largely explained by this.

## Changing Technologies

The major technological change affecting the port industry at this time was the displacement of sailing ships by steamships. This was of course a long, if inexorable, process. It experienced no particular moments of intensity, so it does not help explain the rapid shifts in the fortunes of the new waterside unions. Certainly the conversion to steam was in full swing over the period 1889–95 (see table 5.3).

The changeover did not lead to economy in the use of labour in the

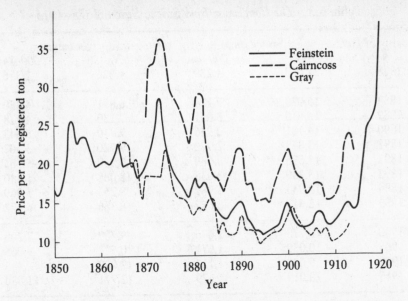

**Fig. 5.1** Steamship prices, £ per net registered ton, present estimate, Cairncross's, and Gray's series, 1850–1920

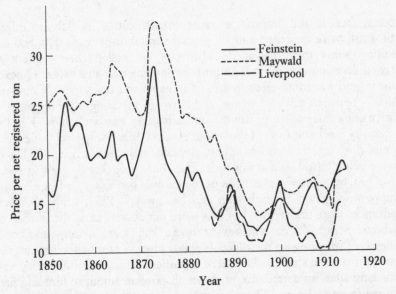

**Fig. 5.2** Steamship prices, £ per net registered ton, present estimate, Maywald's series, and prices paid by Liverpool shipowners, 1850–1913

*Source:* Charles H. Feinstein and Sydney Pollard (eds), *Studies in Capital Formation in the United Kingdom, 1750–1920* (Oxford University Press, 1988), p. 343. (Reproduced by permission of Oxford University Press.)

Table 5.3    *The Conversion from Sail to Steam, 1878–1915*

| | Sailing Ships | | Steamships | |
|---|---|---|---|---|
| | No. | 000 tons | No. | 000 tons |
| 1878 | 21,058 | 4,239 | 4,826 | 2,316 |
| 1888 | 15,025 | 3,114 | 6,871 | 4,350 |
| 1889 | 14,640 | 3,041 | 7,139 | 4,718 |
| 1890 | 14,181 | 2,936 | 7,410 | 5,043 |
| 1891 | 13,823 | 2,972 | 7,720 | 5,307 |
| 1892 | 13,578 | 3,080 | 7,950 | 5,565 |
| 1893 | 13,239 | 3,038 | 8,088 | 5,740 |
| 1894 | 12,943 | 2,987 | 8,263 | 5,969 |
| 1895 | 12,617 | 2,867 | 8,386 | 6,122 |
| 1900 | 10,773 | 2,096 | 9,209 | 7,208 |
| 1905 | 10,059 | 1,671 | 10,522 | 9,065 |
| 1910 | 9,090 | 1,113 | 12,000 | 10,443 |
| 1915 | 8,019 | 779 | 12,771 | 11,650 |

*Source:* B. R. Mitchell, *Abstract of British Historical Statistics* (Cambridge University Press, Cambridge, 1962), pp. 218–19.

(Reproduced by permission of Cambridge University Press.)

ports, but it did impose a great intensification of labour effort. Steamships represented a much greater capital investment than had the sailing ships they displaced. This fact compelled their owners to schedule minimum periods in port for loading and discharge. Quicker turnround was more effective use of an expensive investment. Competition – between sail and steam, and between the shipping companies – intensified this pressure. But the intensification was not achieved, in the main, by mechanization of the labour process. In a few special trades, like grain-discharge and coal-handling, elevators and steam-driven machinery were being introduced at this time. Elsewhere productivity grew in sweat and toil, by greater exploitation of the manual processes and by allotting more work-gangs to each ship and hatchway.[10] True, some technical advances were under way; but they were not about easing the burden of labour. Steam-driven winches on board ship were a new, additional means of speeding up the manual-labour process of transferring cargoes to and from the ship's hold. There remained, through all this period and for long after, an abundance of cheap, disposable labour to hire and fire, to maim and discard. There was simply no incentive for employers to rationalize on labour use, or to cut down the potential dock labour force. The difficulties encountered, even by skilled groups such as stevedores, in maintaining closed and restricted entry to their jobs, reinforced this employer indifference, which was indeed aggravated by the depression of the early 1890s.

## The Employers' Counterattack

The pressure for greater work intensity was redoubled as, after the prosperous years of the late 1880s, the squeeze on prices and profits in the fiercely competitive shipping business resumed. Spurred by competition, the industry gave a classic response: the strong ate the weak. Larger and larger units of ownership emerged, leading to oligopoly. In 1889 the figure who symbolized opposition to the new union during the great London strike was Mr Norwood. He stood for the purely local, fragmented capital as a member of the Joint Committee of London dock companies, wharfingers and stevedoring contractors. Within two years, labour policy had fallen under the domination of the great shipping magnates, who, although often based in the major provincial ports of Liverpool, Hull and Southampton, represented the new, internationally orientated concentrations of maritime capital. Even in London the dock companies after 1889 moved to hand over their cargo-handling function increasingly to the ship-owners.

In all ports, regardless of their peculiarities, the combination of trade-cycle downswing and competitive pressures ensured that the employers' tolerance of the new unions would be shortlived. The force of new unionism was to be confronted by the counterforce of a fighting, militant, anti-union employers' organization: the Shipping Federation, formed just twelve months after the 1889 strike. Its purpose was to break the recently created union controls by the forcible introduction of what it called 'free labour', but which was really quite simply non-union labour. This process was not confined to the waterfront, but it achieved its most open and brutal expression there.

'Formal organisations of employers', reported the Royal Commission on Labour in 1894, 'usually make their appearance at a later date than those of the workmen and arise for purposes of joint resistance, when individual employers find themselves too weak to cope with the growing strength of trade unions.'[11] The historian Elie Halevy was impressed with this judgement, even though he had no illusions about employer pacifism in the years following the birth of the new unionism. By 1892, he reported, there were seventy associations of employers, a dozen of which had been formed since the beginning of the decade. The oldest local association originated in 1865. The first National Federation had been brought together in 1873 'in consequence of the extraordinary development, oppressive action, far reaching but openly avowed designs, and elaborate organization of the trade unions'.[12] It had withered away after a few years, but its revival was proposed amongst employers in the early 1890s, once the agenda of the new unions had made itself understood in the boardrooms:

Already there were many districts completely industrialised, where the employers' sole resource, when the union had declared war upon them, was to introduce labour from outside. They found such labour in the eastern counties – Norfolk and Suffolk – where trade unionism hardly existed. They found it in Ireland which for a century past had furnished British capitalism with the 'reserve army', to use Marx's phrase, which it needed. The new hands thus engaged were brought by railway and taken to barracks where they were confined, out of reach of the strikers' persuasions and threats, so long as they worked . . . but was it impossible to improve on this makeshift? The employers . . . were asking themselves whether it would not be worthwhile to form from the ranks of non-unionist labour, a permanent 'reserve', a 'reserve' in the strict sense, ready to give their assistance the moment they were called up.[13]

The state, and the press, would need to adopt new roles appropriate to the reinforcement of this strategy if it were to succeed. *Laissez-faire* had to be reaffirmed in Labour affairs. In its cause, the judiciary would be required to remove the limited legal supports afforded to strikes and picketing. The police and military would need to be deployed to protect the free labourers and harass the pickets. Newspapers, in which shipping magnates acquired large interests, could usefully assist in turning the sympathy engendered during the great London strike into anti-union, anti-socialist alarm. It is this consciously chosen line of march which, more than any other factor, determined the experience of the new unions during their first decade of existence, including their sharp turn to political action.

## Honeymoon in London

In the London docks, the reorganized Dockers' Union's first task after the strike was to secure its control over the labour supply – in other words, to enforce a closed shop. The blacklegs who were in place after the strike were paid off with a week's wages by the union itself, and then allowed to join the union and take their turn as casuals at the call-on. The majority of the 1,100 treated thus prudently disappeared from the waterside. The companies actually facilitated this process, and at least two managers/directors symbolized their support by joining the union themselves. The union's card became 'the only passport to work',[14] and enrolled not only the permanent and casual labourers, but also many officials and foremen. Yet some foremen, conscious of their ambiguous role, formed their own union; they also had grievances, which they felt required separate representation. Of this honeymoon period, Smith and Nash enthuse: 'It is greatly to the credit of the Companies that they have so heartily recognised and encouraged the Union'.[15]

The problem of the casual docker – the irregularity of work and income – was not of course solved by the settlement of the strike. By the standards of unskilled labour, the dockers did regard their hourly rates as high, but 'tolerably steady employment' was as remote as before. Harry Quelch, the leader of the South Side Labour Protection League, thought that in 1891 25 per cent of dockers earned £1 a week, 25 per cent earned 5s., and 50 per cent earned less than 5s.[16] Joseph Falvy of the Rotherhithe and Bermondsey corn-porters thought that of the 2–3,000 corn-porters involved, only 20 per cent put in a full week's work, and that many did not average one full day per week.[17] Tom McCarthy, in his evidence to the Royal Commission on Labour in 1891, thought that 6 per cent had permanent, year-long work, 10 per cent got ten months' work, 12 per cent averaged eight months, 16 per cent worked only six months, 20 per cent got four months, while 36 per cent found three or fewer months' work in a year. McCarthy also estimated that the average improvement in earnings flowing from the strike and unionization was about 4s. a week.

At this time – 1891 – the employers still engaged a majority of union members, according to several witnesses before the Royal Commission. But they did so with growing reluctance, and were beginning a long-drawn-out process of cutting back on the dockers' gains. Joseph Falvy was asked if it were not true that 'the attitude of the employers towards the unions is one of passive hostility and in some cases of active opposition?' He answered:

> Quite so. While we have the majority with us it will be so, but the moment the employers get the majority it will be the other way. Seeing that in nearly every case we are unionists, at present we have the whip hand . . . I will give you the words of one employer . . . He said: 'I am with you, because you have the majority, but the moment that you are in a minority, I shall be against you'. Those were the words of a very large employer of labour.

The question was followed up: 'The employers now will only take on union men?' 'Yes, in the majority of cases.'[18]

A balance of forces which both sides knew to be precarious was tipped against the union by trends in trade and in technology, and above all by the employers' intent. The new unions were squeezed out of their strong points in London over a period of some years, not, as Clegg and his colleagues were to claim, 'eased out' in twelve months 'with scarcely a ripple of public interest'.[19] The Dockers' Union retained 10,000 docker members in London down to 1891, and 8,500 in 1892.[20]

## London Employers Turn the Screw

From November 1890, in their war of attrition, the employers reverted to the old plus system, cancelling the access of workers' representatives to the books by which, since the strike, they had been able to check the bonus for their jobs. The employers also stopped the agreed payment for a half-hour meal break. They reimposed the foremen's choice of workers, and the practice by which a foreman could engage 'outsiders' – his friends, lodgers, men who bought him beer in the pubs – once again became rampant. Royal Commission witnesses, both union officials and working dockers, insisted that this was a deliberate policy: those engaged commonly had no background in the docks and the purpose was the weakening of the union. Ben Tillett confirmed the trend to renege on the 1889 agreement 'in so far that they close the books against us . . . [and] have also ignored the right of the men to choose their associates in working'.[21]

The erosion of the so-called co-operative system had not been uniformly achieved by all employers at the time the Royal Commission took evidence. Tom McCarthy reported that the big shipping companies were operating as follows:

> The system that now obtains is the union placing itself in the position of the middleman and giving work to the men, though it takes no profit, and does not immediately supervise the work. The men themselves elect their own foremen, bosses, and superintendents, and the Union does not interfere except to see generally that they carry out their contract.[22]

A stevedore who ignored his union's decision not to appear before the Commission told yet another story which illustrates the climate during that same year. His union had traditionally enjoyed a closed shop, had entered into only one dispute in twelve years (with the exception of their sympathetic participation in the dockers' great strike) and had enjoyed peaceful bargaining relations with their employers, 'but in the last fifteen or eighteen months we have been continually in hot water.' He ascribed the change, startlingly abrupt, to 'the action of nothing else but the Shipping Federation': after the great strike 'we had a comparatively quiet time till the formation of this Federation'. A major dispute leading to a strike of the 'coalies' (who bunkered steam ships whilst the stevedores were loading the vessels) had prompted the Shipping Federation to introduce free labour to embark the coal: 'They are keeping these men, supporting them in some shed in one of the docks'.[23] In their incompetence, the free labourers dropped coal on and around the stevedores working below them. After an abusive exchange with the stevedores, the coalies began hurling lumps of coal, while the dock police looked on without intervening: the blackleg coalies were seen as privileged and protected *provocateurs*.

The stevedores' problem with the 'federationists' – free labour brought in by the Shipping Federation, and regarded by unionists as 'the riff-raff of the world'[24] – was confined to those operations where the shipowners or brokers undertook loading. Their relations with the dwindling numbers of small master-stevedores remained one of mutual recognition and respect. The other problem they faced in common with the dock labourers was the spreading use of 'permanent' men, engaged on weekly contracts by the employers. It was not an entirely new practice, but in the climate of mass unionization the unions had a much stronger motive for overcoming this division of status within the workforce; and the employer had an equally strong instinct to divide and rule through conferring enhanced security on a minority of the men. We shall examine the operations of the Shipping Federation in detail later, because they affected not only the Port of London, but new unionism throughout provincial docklands. First, it is worth looking at the threat to the unions' near monopoly posed by permanents and other grades of preferred labour under the classification system developed by the London Dock Companies.

## The London Classification System

The companies issued a directive to their officials and foremen in September 1890 requiring that men engaged for work should be 'carefully selected, physically strong, and the permanent men are only to be within the years of twenty-three and thirty'.[25] Bills to this effect were fly-posted all over the East End. Obviously they implied a direct challenge to union policies of work-sharing with the old and sick, which persisted down to modern times. The chosen permanents were worked for up to eighty hours a week, and as the 'co-operative' system and union control of hiring outside the dock gate was eroded in this period, it became increasingly difficult for it to police and frustrate this development. Harry Quelch explained the effect of the system to the Royal Commission, and to a bewildered Professor Alfred Marshall, one of the Commissioners. 'Witness after witness', said the Professor, 'has admitted that the rates of pay per hour are so very high, that if tolerably steady employment could be got the condition of the dockers would be thoroughly satisfactory.'[26] Since the weekly wage system improved regularity of earnings, he went on, why on earth did the dockers and their union oppose its extension? Quelch replied:

It only tends to increase steady employment for a few, and it reduces the number of men employed, because a weekly man has to do anything. A weekly man dare not refuse anything that he is asked to do. A casual man will not do it: a casual man will not work under price . . . being casual men they [say]: 'We do not depend upon you for employment, you can either pay us the extra halfpenny or pay us our money, and we will knock off if you like.'[27]

Quelch went on to argue that a tradesman with a scarce skill might retain a measure of independence whilst working on a weekly engagement, but that the unskilled could not: 'I do not object to casual employment if there were more of it, but it is so exceedingly limited.'[28]

## The Dockers' Dilemma

This posed a fundamental dilemma for the new unions in dockland. They sought a union monopoly, which could be achieved in theory either by the widest possible enrolment of all potential, casual labour, or by pursuing the stevedores' road of restricting entry to a smaller, more regularly employed force. In time, the dockers came to learn that the latter was not an option for the mass of non-specialists who comprised the bulk of the Dockers' Union membership.

But the other route to control was frustrated by the employers' recruitment of 'outsiders'. At the retail level, these might be farmworkers or the foreman's friends. Wholesale, far more sinister, collectively and aggressively, they were found by the Shipping Federation's deployment of 'free labour'. The restrictive policy had been tried: Tom Mann issued an instruction to the London docks branches of the new union in 1890, calling on them to cease further enrolments. In the same period, the union advised branches to enrol only able-bodied men who were fit and strong, and to exclude 'weaklings'. This was intended as a conciliatory gesture to the employers, who complained consistently that productivity had collapsed as the power of the union had grown. We have already noted this consequence of the great strike (see chapter 4) and seen how the union had then felt obliged to exhort its members to provide 'a fair day's work for a fair day's pay'.

Harry Quelch's answers to the distinguished economist (who was clearly no sort of sociologist) underlines the problem facing both employers and union. Quelch, though a paid official of a docks union, articulated the rank-and-file response of the older, more sectional docks tradition. The responses to the dilemma from the new, inclusive and potentially general union, seeking to consolidate its precarious hold in dockland by wider recruitment at one stage, and by restricted entry at another, were full of inconsistencies. Some spokesmen at the Royal Commission found themselves advocating the extension of the permanent force, while others wavered, as the Commissioners pressed home the virtue of that system from the labourers' point of view. The dockers' grievance was irregularity of work and earnings: why not then accept the spread of permanent employment? The union recognized the Catch 22 in the question and had no official and consistent answer.

A working docker who testified before the Royal Commission summed up all this ambivalence:

I believe myself that this classification system that they have with the joint committee is for their [the dockers'] benefit, because there is a greater number of men employed now working more regularly than what there were then. But if they were to carry it out in its entirety it would be better: they do not do so. They bring favoured individuals in between the classified men, so that it actually leaves the outsiders, or the remnant, far worse off even than the favoured few. But, of course, there are a greater number of men regularly employed than there used to be.[29]

At this point, a Commissioner, Sir Michael Hicks-Beach, asked: 'Do you consider it, so far as it goes, a good thing or a bad thing?' The docker replied: '*If they could all be employed*' (authors' italics). Hicks-Beach pressed his point: 'But I want you to speak of the actual state of things: do you consider it better in that respect, or worse than it was?' 'For the remnant that is outside, it is far worse, but for those employed it is better, and there are more of them employed now than what there used to be.'[30]

Amongst dock-union officials, the inconsistency of approach to the problem was all too plain. Harry Quelch, as we have seen, came closest to expressing the men's position. 'There is a strong feeling amongst waterside labourers generally against the making of permanent men as they are termed.'[31] Tom McCarthy found himself defending the union against the charge that it had discouraged the spread of permanent employment:

*Taking things as they are, do you think that it would be a good step, to start with, to reduce the number of men who are employed at the docks, and to get for those men more regular employment?* – I do: always remembering there is a big surplus of unemployed. *Has not the action of the Trades Unions been in the opposite sense?* – I do not think I can say so: so far as I have known, no. If it appears to have been so, it has always been because of having to look after those who could do little work. *Why are you obliged to look after them?* – If I spoke in a bare business-like sense, I would say because they are members of a Trade Union: but generally speaking, because they remember that their own position as workers is unsafe, and that they at any time may become recruits in the ranks of the unemployed . . . *Do you see any reason why the old traditions of the docks should be maintained, and the docks should continue to be a last recourse for those who have been unfortunate elsewhere?* – I do not see why that should not be altered. *And is not the right way to do that to increase the number of permanent men?* – Undoubtedly it is: it is the best means. *But have you not passed a resolution against that?*–Not that I am aware of.[32]

Finally, we may overhear Ben Tillett attempting to cope with similar questions:

*is it your opinion that if the dock authorities settle on a certain number of men as available for employment in the docks, that would stop the influx?* – It would stop it, or would go a long way towards stopping it. *Men knowing they were not on the staff, so to speak, and could not get a job, would not go there?* – That is so. *Do you think, if by that means you could raise the wages and conditions of a limited number of men, that would be better than having an unlimited number of men who get starvation wages?* – Yes, there would be better organisation. *And would you recommend that?* – I would recommend that. Only in admitting that I would point out that the Dock Companies are not in the position to absolutely guarantee a large number of men work. It is work that is of so fluctuating a character that they may employ 4,000 one day, and require 15,000 the next. So that unless we could make them responsible for the difference between 4,000 and 15,000 it would be an advantage to them, because they could introduce fresh men constantly, and it would be to their benefit to have a drifting number of workmen going to the docks, so that those in will be anxious to keep their place, and those out anxious to get in.[33]

This problem was to live on, albeit in modified forms, until the 1967 decasualization scheme. The reason is evident: the employers' approach to decasualization was always partial. It was in the highest degree convenient to have both a staff of permanent men and a casual pool to call upon when traffic was heavy. A total decasualization, with the maximum coverage, would have represented a heavy economic cost to the industry, and at the same time solved the union's problem, giving it vastly greater power. It is not at all difficult to discern the motivations of the employers in maintaining those conditions, and hence the historical intractability of the issue.

## Casualism and Social Reformers

The social reformers Charles Booth, Sydney Buxton, Smith and Nash, however, were continually pressing their nostrums on the employers. The influence of a public opinion which had been awoken by the dock strike became, as the strike receded in time, an asset for this lobby. By invoking the motive of social reform, the employers appealed to humanitarian sentiment. But their purpose was to reimpose control over their labourers, and their reforms were always partial and directed to the unspoken goal. The public view is clearly expressed in the Commissioners' questions to the trade-union witnesses, on the subject of reform of the casual-labour system.

The employers' responses varied. The use of the classification system was confined to the Dock Companies and their Joint Committee. These sought to capitalize on the reforming schemes of Booth, which they could turn to advantage in two ways. They could use them, as we have described, to divide the labour force, and to smash union controls. At the same time, by appealing to the apparent social benefits of such schemes, they could disguise their real motives and assume the mantle of morally responsible reformers. Very soon they were to move decisively in this direction.

On 24 November 1890 the secretary of the Employers' Federation issued a public statement: 'It is the object of my directors to reduce the amount of casual employment at the docks, and secure as far as possible regular work for all classes of labourers in each department. My directors will always be ready to investigate grievances, and redress them whenever they are proved to exist.' The dockers knew only too well that this last sentence was sheer humbug, and that those who complained, or were visible as union activists, were already subject to transparent discrimination at the call-stands. As the companies' use of casuals diminished, their numbers seeking and failing to find work actually expanded, making such victimization all the easier.

Secondary instruments in the companies' struggle to undermine the union monopoly came to hand when, in the aftermath of the great strike, the foremen and permanent hands formed their own unions: the Association of Foremen and Clerks of the Docks, Wharves and Warehouses, and the Permanent Labourers' Mutual Protection Association. Both groups were segregated from the dock communities. The Permanent Labourers' Association was regarded by the dockers as a company union.[34]

The success of the 1889 strike, and the resultant publicity, had allowed the reformers to separate out the 'legitimate' claims of labour from the 'social disease' of casualism, and to define and isolate a destitute stratum, identified by its moral as well as its physical decay. If separated from a stabilized and unionized workforce, this stratum ceased to appear as a political threat and became a social problem, for which Booth's solutions were the formation of 'labour colonies', the poorhouse or prison.[35] Booth's counsel boiled down to three steps: restrict admission to the docks, increase the internal mobility of the workforce and allow the casual element to 'drift away'. According to D. F. Wilson, it was Booth himself who drew up the companies' classification scheme.[36] (Booth's family business was in Liverpool Shipping.) This advice was adopted and followed through persistently, with the result that, by 1904, less than 2 per cent of the Dock Companies' daily employed workforce was made up of casuals. The full record is shown in table 5.4.

## Enter the Shipping Federation

The scheme applied, of course, to a dwindling sector of the labour force as the Dock Companies yielded more of their cargo-handling function to the shipowners, who were ready with their own, much blunter, response to new unionism, in the shape of the Shipping Federation, formed in

Table 5.4    *London and India Docks: Percentage of Engagements Given to Weekly and Preference Men, 1887–1904*

|      | Weekly | Preference |
| ---- | ------ | ---------- |
| 1887 | 17.0   | n.a.       |
| 1891 | 33.5   | n.a.       |
| 1894 | 65.6   | 28.8       |
| 1900 | 62.7   | 23.8       |
| 1904 | 78.4   | 19.7       |

*Source:* Gordon Phillips and Noel Whiteside, *Casual Labour: The Unemployment Question in the Port Transport Industry, 1880–1970* (Oxford University Press, 1985), p. 50.
(Reproduced by permission of Oxford University Press.)

September 1890. The immediate stimulus to its creation was the setting up of a Union of Shipmasters and Officers, of which Havelock Wilson became 'general manager' with autocratic powers. Wilson's main union – the NSFU – then struck against ships on which, before sailing, the master and officers refused to join the new body, members of which were expected to engage only Seamen's Union members as crew. The Seamen's Union was already applying other pressures at many ports to establish and enforce its closed shop, often with the assistance of dockers and their unions, who became involved in a series of blacking actions against non-union ships in dock.

The objects of the Shipping Federation were formally described to the Royal Commission by its general manager, George Laws, as being:

> for the purpose of maintaining liberty of contract and resisting the new union methods of coercion, more especially the tactics adopted by the National Amalgamated Sailors' and Firemen's Union . . . whose instructions to members are entirely subversive of discipline in the merchant service, and have resulted in a degree of insubordination seriously menacing the security of life and property at sea.[37]

The official historian of the Federation, L. H. Powell, acknowledges the militant spirit of the founders, who regarded it as 'a "permanent battle-axe" . . . against "oppression and abuse" '.[38] 'From the first,' he goes on, 'the Federation was founded as a fighting machine to counter the strike weapon, and it made no secret of the fact.'[39]

Within a month Federation membership, augmented by the adherence of the great liner companies such as the P. & O., represented 6.5 million out of a total of 7.4 million of British merchant tonnage. It set up offices in the principal ports, at which it issued its 'Federation ticket', entitling the holder to preferential engagement in return for a promise to work alongside both union and non-union crew members.

## Free Labour and Unfree Unions

As its coverage extended throughout Britain's ports, the Federation organized large mobilizations of strike-breakers, transported and accommodated them, and provided strong-arm protection squads to break the strikes of both seamen and dock workers. The whole operation was systematically planned. Ex-police officers were often engaged as organizers and recruiting agents. Some of their methods were reminiscent of the press-gangs – they were quite capable of taking away by the cartload men whom they had first made drunk.

The Federation had enormous financial resources, raised through a levy on the tonnage owned by the affiliated companies. 'The funds at its disposal . . . could certainly buy up any trade union in England over and over again'.[40]

A series of strikes, involving either seamen or dockers, and frequently both, swept round the country immediately following the Federation's formation. The list of their locations reads like a roll-call of Britain's ports. All concerned the issue of free labour. In most cases, the *casus belli* was the presence of a non-union crew in a ship due to be loaded or unloaded, which was blacked by the dockers. This provoked the importation of more free labour to break the resulting dock strike. In the period between September 1890 and April 1891, there were strikes of this character at Leith (where the shipowner became the first to apply to the Federation, then just three days old, for a supply of free labour, which performed both ship and dock work for him); Bowness (dockers versus a free crew); Grangemouth (a pay strike broken by free labour); Dundee (dockers versus free crew – strike broken); Garston; Barrow (from whence came the 'blacked' ship which provoked the Garston strike); and then, in December, a major conflict in London, to which we shall return below.

Next came a small dispute involving the Federation in Hull, met by imported free labour from Liverpool. The union retreated, but in good order; Hull's great trial of strength was postponed for two more years. The London stevedores failed to carry their members in resistance to free labour in March, whilst in February there had been a major strike of seamen and dockers against the Federation ticket in Aberdeen. Newry dockers struck against the employment of a single free-labour stevedore in March. The list also included a Dublin dockers' strike over the method of discharge and manning of a ship. In that case, free-labour intervention generated a wave of strikes, as lightermen would not handle the corn discharged by the blacklegs, the railwaymen would not touch it either, and finally the millers and the bakers would not grind the corn or bake the flour which reached them from the free-labour vessel. At Bristol, free labour was supplied by the Federation from London in June, and succeeded in breaking a dockers' strike occasioned by the engagement of non-union dockers. This concluded the catalogue proudly presented by George Laws to the Royal Commission.[41]

The Federation responded in every one of these cases with the despatch of free labourers to the point of the dispute; violence was a common consequence and police protection was always afforded to the strike-bearers. Laws's account gives a vivid impression of the extent of the resources available to him, as well as of the vast logistical scale of the operation. Of the Aberdeen strike he reported:

> We had to send men up at considerable expense, and when the dockers saw that, they also came out in what they called a sympathetic strike, and we had to supply dockers. I may say that at that time there was, and at the present there is, any amount of free labour in the country to be had at any time, at any rate, and good labour too. At any rate, the work of the port was done, and the strike after about a fortnight or three weeks collapsed.[42]

He might have been speaking of the supply, quality and price of potatoes.

## The London Strike, 1891

We must now retrace our steps to the London strike of December 1891. In 1890 three major shipping lines in the upstream docks made a determined drive to break the Seamen's Union control by shifting the place of hiring from the shipping offices, where union officers could check on union membership, to the ships themselves. At the same time, they insisted on the men's taking up the Shipping Federation ticket, with its commitment to work with non-unionists. The United Labour Council as we have seen (chapter 3) was by no means a representative federation. Nevertheless it called for united action against the Shipping Federation's attack, with the publication of the famous 'Wade's Arms Manifesto', which called on all port workers to strike on the vessels of the shipping lines involved. At first, only the coal-porters responded, the Dockers' Union not having participated in the decision, and only a minority of the stevedores' branches having attended the decisive meeting of the ULC. The Shipping Federation installed free labourers from Kent to do the coaling, housing them in sheds and ships at anchor. Eventually the dockers and stevedores joined the stoppage, and the docks were flooded with free labour, although the dispute never reached the proportions of a port-wide strike.

The powerful, aggressive tactics of the Shipping Federation, coupled with the Dock Companies' breach of the 1889 settlement, brought the Dockers' Union and the SSLPL together into a representative body, the Federation of Trade and Labour Unions connected with the Shipping, Carrying and other Industries, in January 1891. It affiliated twenty-five unions in 1890–1, rising to forty-two in 1895. It appointed Clem Edwards[43] as general secretary, and he had now the assistance of Tom Mann, Tom McCarthy and Thomas Walsh (of the Seamen's Union) in conducting the 'Wade's Arms' dispute and negotiating with the Shipping Federation. The owners' Federation conducted the conflict with total intransigence. Indeed, the contrast with the employers' defensive postures of two years earlier was complete. George Laws ensured an appropriate supply of strike-breaking labour. Moreover, using all the weight of his status, he secured the collaboration of the top Police Commissioner to protect the strike-breakers when the dock police force proved inadequate.[44] Laws, or at least his enthusiastic dockside agents, also appears to have armed strike-breakers with revolvers, some of which were discharged in the mêlées which ensued between pickets and free labourers. Clem Edwards told the Royal Commission of many incidents, including this:

> during the dispute in progress at Wapping there was [a] man seen with a revolver. The police refused to interfere with him, and at least in ten or twelve cases men have appeared at loop-holes at the Carron and Hermitage Wharves, have presented revolvers at the pickets outside and have threatened to shoot them. We have approached the police officers in charge, and in every case they have declined to interfere in the matter, saying that they have no right on the wharf, and so on.[45]

The authorities' response to Laws stands in marked contrast:

> I . . . saw Sir Edward Bradford and the other Commissioners, and I am bound to say that they quite realised the position. I pointed out that these men should be got into the docks, and on board these ships, in a condition to work . . . the most effective arrangements were made by the police. They adopted our plan . . . and everything was done in the most quiet and orderly way.

After the police withdrew:

> a mob of coalies whose places had been taken assembled . . . and commenced to hoot and ill-use and to stone the men in the barges below. We again had to apply to Scotland Yard, the dock police being utterly useless . . . but the Metropolitan police cleared the docks and the work went on. Then we enabled all these vessels to sail.[46]

With these forces at its command, the Shipping Federation's 'negotiation' with the union federation was perfunctory: Edwards and Mann made concession after concession, only to be met with escalating demands, including the full withdrawal of the Wade's Arms Manifesto and the surrender of their whole position on the disputed liners. The strike petered out, and the ship-owners retained the imported free labourers, not only as coalies but also as general dock labourers and as stevedores, engaged by a Federation office on the Albert Dock. The strike, said Laws, was 'utterly defeated'.

This disastrous episode laid the foundation for the subsequent decline of London port unionism for the rest of the decade. The stevedores, still having a (dwindling) enclave of recognition with the small masters, withdrew from further sympathetic actions, having lost much in the Wade's Arms affair through their support for the seamen. The lightermen reacted in similar fashion. The hopes of 1889, that sectionalism might be washed away in the tide of new unionism, were disappointed. The Dockers' Union now moved to alleviate its exposed and weakened position by effecting, in September 1891, a merger of Clem Edwards's federation and the United Labour Council.

An appeal from the dockers for solidarity action in a strike at Wapping wharf followed immediately, but was rebuffed by the stevedores, intent on preserving their closed shop in the upstream part of the port even though their problems at Tilbury, where cement combines forced the master-stevedores to break their traditional relations with the union, came more and more to resemble those of the dockers. Faced with the choice of responding to these trends in either 'open' or 'closed' ways, the stevedores chose to retreat into their laager, even whilst trade continued for the rest of the decade to move away, downstream. In the Royal Docks group, the Dockers' Union maintained its status as the biggest British district in the union until 1900. In 1895 it sought without success to form a new tripartite federation with the South Side Labour Protection League and Sexton's National Union of Dock Labourers. The following year, it had more success in initiating the International Federation of Ship, Dock and River Workers.

None of these initiatives created an effective weapon with which to combat triumphant free labour, and the hegemony established by the Shipping Federation. Instead, the London scene was further clouded by accusations of poaching levelled at the stevedores by Ben Tillett.

## Examining Free Labour – Under the Stone

Before turning to review the provincial defeats inflicted on the unions by the Shipping Federation, it is relevant to notice some further features of the free-labour movement. We have noted the Shipping Federation's command of resources – one source suggests that its funds ran to £100 million[47] – its ready access to blackleg labour, its willingness to arm it, and the ease with which it called up weighty police protection.

Further evidence is available on the unscrupulous nature of its operations. A 'crimp' is defined in the Oxford English Dictionary as 'an agent who procures seamen, soldiers, etc., especially by decoying or impressing them'. Crimping houses had long existed in the seaports of Britain and the agents of the Shipping Federation used them to recruit blackleg crews. At the same time, the Federation officially discouraged the use of this source of labour, preferring the crimps to bring their recruits directly to the Federation hiring offices. But this was simply a new, higher form of crimping, since the Federation, not being itself a shipowner, had no more right than the backstreet crimps to issue an engagement to a seaman. Only the *bona fide* servant of an owner had such a right under the Merchant Shipping Act.

When the Federation sacked an agent for practising his crimping unofficially, he left in disgust, asserting that 'the officials of the Federation are as great crimpers as anybody else'.[48] Needless to say, a summons brought in 1908 by the Seamen's Union against the Federation for breach of the crimping section of the Merchant Shipping Act was dismissed.[49]

The Federation's own advice to its members often included the use of the courts to enforce the disciplinary and contractual aspects of the same Act on to their employees. As John Saville has shown, the Federation's militant anti-unionism campaign, directed against the picketing, blackings and strike methods of new unionism, was reinforced by a wave of hostile judicial findings which came to a climax in the Taff Vale case of 1901.[50]

Nor was the Shipping Federation without imitators. The Engineering Employers followed its lead later in the decade. The Liberty and Property Defence League and the National Free Labour Association emerged at this time to add their choruses of praise for 'freedom of contract' and the virtues of *laissez-faire* – the former from the perspective of High Tory landed and Liberal commercial interests,[51] the latter as the voice of anti-union, right-wing working-class men.[52] *The Times* inveighed persistently and at length against the 'tyranny' of new unionism and its socialist leadership in a sustained campaign consciously aimed at shifting public, judicial and political opinion in favour of all-out war against the unions.

Campaigns for tariff-reform began to win working-class sympathies, and were taken up by the free-labour movement. There was mounting evidence that the great Liberal Party industrialists had turned against trade unionism where it challenged them in their own mills, quarries and waterfronts. Rosebery's administration was no model of competence. In the summer of 1895 it resigned, and the alienated mood of Liberal supporters ensured it had no chance of holding on to office. A Tory government took power: whatever reforms in labour relations might have emerged from the copious inquiries and publications of the Royal Commission on Labour, which completed its string of volumes in 1894, were now stillborn. The only legislation conceded by Salisbury's administration was the weak, voluntaristic Conciliation Act of 1896. In this climate, the mildly corporatist wing of opinion within the Board of Trade, which issued the first of its Reports on Profit Sharing in 1894, went without any real hearing.

Although the Royal Commission produced no results as such, it had afforded to a great coalition of ruling-class forces, political, commercial and academic, a unique insight into the minds of the new unionists and into the links that were established there between unionism and socialism. The ruling classes did not always understand what they heard, but they knew that they did not like it: they knew that it was different from the old unionism with which they were familiar. (Even the Shipping Federation protested that it was not anti-union, only that it required port and seaboard unionism to conform to the 'old model'.)

## William Collison and the National Free Labour Association

William Collison formed the National Free Labour Association (NFLA) in May 1893, by which time the Shipping Federation was two and a half years old. He was an East Ender, the son of a policeman, and had drifted into casual labouring work in and around the London docks. He joined the socialist and trade-union agitations of the late 1880s and came to know intimately the principal leaders of that movement. He became a bus-driver and initiated the organization of the passenger-transport workers of London.

In his autobiography, an extraordinary study of a larger-than-life character, he displays a pugilistic, egotistic, yet oddly sensitive personality. In his bid to dominate the meetings of the busmen's union, he clashed with its president, Thomas Sutherst and was expelled from the union's meetings and deprived of office in 1891. The experience undoubtedly led him to revise his pro-union views, though he claimed that his conversion to the cause of free labour came from reading Charles Reade's novel *Put Yourself in his Place* (1870). Collison recounts how, following his humiliation at the hands of Sutherst, he determined to 'escape all thoughts of Trade Unionism, all consideration of the problems of capital and labour, all questions of industrial collectivism and individualism'. In this mood he read the novel, picked up at a second-hand stall. 'The message of that book to me was that the best retreat from Trade Unionism lies in attack. The book said: "Fight the Unions", and from the moment I realized the possibility I saw life anew'.[53] Collison, from this moment, did indeed become a fervent, dogmatic and energetic advocate of all the values and ideology of *laissez-faire*. He was always more than a mere labour agent for capital, though he fulfilled that function readily. His strange personality is illustrated by his account of his last meeting with Eleanor Marx, worth quoting at length:

When I first met Eleanor Marx at the Democratic Club – a place where the people of high ideals and low morals used to congregate in a cellar – she asked me, as she was fond of asking young people, what goal I was aiming for, what end I hoped to attain.

I told her I could not tell. My mind was drifting then. I admitted I was drawn at times to Socialist theories, but always repelled by Socialistic personalities.

Afterwards, about a year before her death, I met her when her face had faded and all the brilliance had died out of her wonderful eyes. In very truth, I think she was dead then, dead in heart and all womanly hope. Many things had happened since we last met. I had found my goal and my mission in life. I knew what I was doing and why I was doing it. I was as fixed in purpose as I am today. The National Free Labour Association had not only been started, but was working with astonishing success. I was doing what I had vowed to do when I felt for the first time in my heart and soul – as I feel now while I am writing – that modern Trade Unionism is an accursed thing, a greater enemy to this country than any foreign power, a greater enemy to you and me than the bitterest individual enemy of ours that exists; I was not only speaking and thinking against it, but I was actively fighting it.

I was breaking strikes.

I knew the heart and spirit of Eleanor Marx, and I knew how unhappy she would have been to know that I had put an unbridgeable eternity between myself and all those 'democratic' forces, no matter what phase or form they took, which she loved so dearly. I was even uncertain as to whether or not she had heard that the young Collison of old had come out, had taken the sword in his hand and was breaking strikes and the strike-makers. So I said little as we stood in the windy twilight at the corner of Chancery Lane, while I noticed the faded beauty of her face and hopeless eyes and the grief inscribed in deep-drawn lines about the mouth. She seemed a little nervous also. She had a fur or a boa, or a clinging scarf of lace round her neck, and she played with it nervously. Then she said presently with her old laugh, and her old infinite grace:

'And what are you going to do now?'

I shook my head.

'I don't know,' I answered.

'But where are you going to? what are you going to be?' she asked again.

I thought I would break the news very gently.

'I think I am going to be a Conservative – one day,' I said half humorously.

She looked at me very seriously, even steadfastly.

'Well,' she said, 'you will find a refuge there; it will be very quiet.'

'Not for me, never,' I answered, with my hand in my coat pocket, feeling a ship's rivet that a Trade Union picket had hurled at my head a week before.

Again she looked at me steadfastly – rather pathetically, and nodded at last in a sort of resigned, serious fashion.

'No,' she said at last, 'you are quite right. You will never be quiet, for they will never forgive you; they would forgive others – but not you.'

And her words were prophetic. And I am exceedingly glad. On the day that the Socialists and the Trade Unionists forgive me I will write out my own memorial card with a steady hand, for my part in life will be finished and the time for rest at hand.'[54]

Collison's National Free Labour Association arrived on the scene fortuitously for the Shipping Federation, as well as for employers in many other industries, intent on following its example. The Federation was finding legal and administrative disadvantages in running its own direct supply of blackleg labour through its network of offices. It therefore subsidised Collison's initiative, thus giving itself the option of using the NFLA as a sub-contracting agent.[55] In this capacity, Collison established his own Free Labour Exchanges and offices in the principal centres of industry and trade, employing local agents – often ex-police officers – who maintained a register of workers who had signed the Free Labour pledge, a promise to work with union or non-union workmates.

But Collison did not confine his role to that of strike-breaker, though he relished the physical conflict involved like a professional soldier. His Association became a propagandist for the crude, individualist philosophy, the *laissez-faire* counterrevolution, which rationalized and underpinned its direct intervention in strikes and the labour market.

Amongst other initiatives, the NFLA was an active promoter of the trend towards restrictive legislation aimed at the freedom to picket and against the whole liberal settlement of trade-union law of the 1870s. In both roles, however, Collison was inevitably the servant of big capital. 'In the 'nineties the NFLA was the creature of the Shipping Federation: in the early years of the new century the role of puppet-master was taken over by the Railway Companies'.[56] Although Collison claimed to have engaged in over sixty strike-breaking incidents, his was not the only free-labour association in a period when, said Tillett, 'Trade Union wrecking and strike-breaking became almost a science'.[57] Collison's personal, and wholly eccentric, relish for his apostolic campaign against trade unionism and socialism survives, in his own words, to re-create for us a lost world of absolute certainties, political pugilism and sheer thuggery. In retrospect he wrote:

the very worst of them who live by the sweat of their jaw have shot their last bolt in invective. No words of theirs can harm me now. In the twenty years' war that has composed the last twenty years of my life, the whole armoury of abuse has been exhausted against me. Their sweetest phrase is to call me 'The King of Blacklegs' or 'The Prince of Scabs'. Even in the obituary notices which the Trade Unionists used to send me to correct before I died, there was a wealth of fiery phraseology, trying in its warmth perhaps to acclimatize me to the heat of the Hades to which demagogues, assuming for the moment the offices of Amateur Destinies, had consigned my soul. The general reader . . . may find it hard to understand all this bitterness . . . Remember that for twenty-one years I have stood up against my own class. I have not argued with Strike leaders, I have broken strikes.[58]

A man of this kind of crazed integrity was an asset to the employers. Earlier forms of strike-breaking organization, especially in London's dockland, had plagued Tillett's efforts before 1889 and had re-emerged in the early days of the Shipping Federation to colour its own efforts with corruption and criminality. Collison's movement represented a different phenomenon, and, unlike the villanous gang-masters of what the dockers called 'bogus' unions, provided valuable and usable copy for *The Times*.

Yet another form of free-labour organization appeared in purely local initiatives, such as the Free Labour Association in Southampton, which emerged from the confused and disastrous strike in that port in October 1890.

## A Disaster: Southampton

The Dockers' Union in Southampton had enrolled the majority of the port's labour force in 1889–90, and in August 1890 the employers had conceded a wage increase. The union nationally was content with that settlement, but the Southampton men, led by local lay officials, also demanded full recognition for the union. At the same time, according to Tom McCarthy, a rumour circulated that the wage increase was to be withdrawn. A section of the men came out, and on 7 September the strike spread to the whole port. (Presumably this was just too early for the Shipping Federation, formed later in the month, to intervene.) In London the union's national leaders had refused to sanction strike action only two weeks previously; Tom Mann and John Burns now sent personal apeals to Southampton for a resumption of work, and their executive voted by eleven to four to withhold strike pay. Tillett ignored telegram appeals for support, and Tom McCarthy called for the maintenance of the executive's authority 'at all hazard'.[59]

Mass meetings at the docks erupted in violence, the Mayor

lost his head, telegraphed to Portsmouth for 250 troops, the fire brigade was called out, the police in the neighbourhood were called in to help the Southampton police; people were driven at the point of the bayonet from the dock gates, telegrams were despatched to us in London that a serious riot had taken place, and that the people were being beaten by the soldiers.[60]

Tom McCarthy was sent by Mann to Southampton, solely to persuade the men to return to work. Shorn of national union support and intimidated by the force used against them, the men ended their resistance, and their local leader, who had been disowned by the national union, got a three-month prison sentence for a common law offence.

The union in Southampton collapsed, in this case not through the actions of strike-breaking free labour but through disenchantment with its national leaders. We have seen that the union did in general adopt a conciliatory policy in the aftermath of the 1889 strike, and also that it was intent on establishing its central authority everywhere. But it behaved in a wholly inconsistent way over the Southampton dispute. It had recently sanctioned a local wharf dispute in London and it was to engage wholeheartedly in arousing support for the Cardiff dockers in their struggle with the Shipping Federation shortly after the Southampton affair. Tom McCarthy told the Royal Commission that the executive simply decided that it was unnecessary to push the Southampton employers on the recognition issue so soon after they had conceded a wage increase.

However the incident is to be explained, the result was that the Southampton men felt betrayed, tore up their union cards and entered – willingly in many cases – into the Southampton Free Labour Association, set up by the local employers immediately after the strike. Its honorary secretary was the president of the Southampton Chamber of Commerce, and it adopted an elaborate, corporatist constitution, with membership sections for both the employers (forty-four of them) and the dockers (2,200 of them).[61] In 1891 it set up an accident fund, a sick fund and a savings bank, all administered by members' committees.[62] A handful of men retained their union membership, but were deterred from active opposition to the Free Labour Association: the employers took on no one who did not carry its ticket. Tom McCarthy, asked if relations between employers and workers had 'been harmonious of late in Southampton', replied, 'Well, there is order in Warsaw. They must be harmonious, the men have no alternative'.[63]

Tom Mann, as a Commissioner, sought to demonstrate the consequences of the triumph of free labour and elicited from McCarthy an adverse comparison between the conditions and wages at Southampton under its free-labour regime and those at all other major ports. Yet McCarthy finally made a damaging admission: that the union is 'entirely broken up', that it was

practically broken up before the Free Labour Bureau was instituted ... for the reason that the men left it because the executive would not pay strike pay, contrary to rule. You see the organisation had not taught them: there had not been sufficient time to show these men what organisation was properly, and they had not been accustomed to the discipline and order and rule of a union. [So the] 'chief reason' [for the débacle was] the quarrel with the executive in London.[64]

The Southampton affair had far-reaching consequences. Within a month a Plymouth coal-trade dockers' strike had been broken by blacklegs under heavy police protection and a Free Labour Association formed, the secretary being the secretary of the Coal Merchants' Association. It took members away not only from the Dockers' Union but also from the Bristol and West of England Labourers' Union and the Gasworkers' Union. There then followed, in February 1891, the Cardiff strike, the first major engagement of the Shipping Federation with the Dockers' Union outside London.

## Free Labour Goes to Wales

Just as throughout the rest of the country, the fortunes of the new unions in South Wales depended in large part upon the employers' attitudes, and these varied from port to port. Capital for port development in South Wales came from a variety of sources, but was dominated by the wealth of the land-owning class, swollen by its ownership of mineral rights. The Bute Dock Company in Cardiff, financed by the Marquis of Bute, became the principal owner of the port. In 1894, following its diversion into railways, it changed its name to the Cardiff Railway Company. It resisted the demand of Tillett's union for recognition, the closed shop, or union preference, throughout the period under review. It was supported in this policy by other railway companies which had interests in the docks – the Rhimney, Taff Vale, and Barry railway companies. It conceded recognition to the DWRGWU only in 1915. It was more conciliatory towards the Trimmers' Union.

In Newport the dock had been developed by Sir Charles Morgan, prominent Glamorgan landowner, for mineral exporting; in the 1890s it was under the control of the Alexandra Docks and Railway Company. Swansea was developed by its Harbour Trust, on which sat the Duke of Beaufort. Colliery-owners built the Barry Dock and its associated railway as late as 1889. Port Talbot followed this pattern, opening its Railway and Dock Company in 1898.

These groups of employers and landlords had an obvious mutual interest in resisting the encroachments of new unionism, but also faced each other in the competition for export trades in coal, minerals and the products of the iron and steel industries. Within this competition, unions sometimes found space to put down roots. Bute and his Cardiff Railway

Company set the example of intransigence, whilst at Newport similar interests conceded a preference for employing union members.[65]

Following the initial recruitment of members by new unionism, these employers collectively formed the Bristol Channel Association, embracing both banks of the estuary, and fought a joint campaign for wage cuts. This Association was almost as strong as the Shipping Federation, consisting chiefly of the dock companies, especially the timber importers. In South Wales, the new unions formed their own Federation of Trades and Labour Unions for mutual defence against the regional employers. As late as 1891 some wage increases were still being won; but a Swansea strike in 1892 against the free-labour office set up by the employers failed to win union support and its officials, led by Harry Orbell, negotiated what amounted to an acceptance of free labour. The strike collapsed after six weeks and the union went into a severe decline. Between 1891 and 1893 the income of its Swansea branches fell from £2,600 to some £300.[66]

Newport avoided any catastrophic industrial war and, although its membership declined by some 50 per cent, it retained recognition from some of the employers. The leadership was relatively content with the situation there, the chief problem of the period being inter-union rivalry and poaching by the National Amalgamated Labourers' Union.

In Cardiff, the Shipping Federation launched a powerful attack against the Seamen's Union, and the dockers struck in sympathy, at the same time advancing grievances of their own against the sub-contracting system. In February 1891 Tillett, Orbell and Clem Edwards were all in the town, organizing and expressing support for the struggle. Tillett interpreted the strike as 'a struggle for our very existence . . . they meant to fight it to the bitter end'.[67] Whilst he and Havelock Wilson predicted sympathy strikes spreading from Cardiff to Hull, Liverpool and London, John Burns strongly advised that the conflict be confined to Wales. Although Burns had little formal status, being only a trustee of the union, his advice carried the day with Tom Mann, and Mann carried the union. Nevertheless, for the seamen and dockers of Cardiff the struggle assumed the proportions of a general strike. Tom Mann appealed in vain for sympathy action from the South Wales miners and railwaymen. He had envisaged that with their participation in a South Wales Labour Federation enough potential power could be mobilized to succeed 'without resorting to the arbitrament of a strike'. Whatever might have happened if regional unity had come about, in its absence the dispute was doomed. Even the coal-trimmers withheld their support. The Dockers' Union was isolated within Cardiff, and though Tillett made three or four speeches a day, predicting that 'there will be a complete reorganisation of labour in South Wales and we shall have a unification in trade unionism', his expectations were no longer realistic, and on 16 March 1891 the strike was called off. 'Tillett then collapsed. Exhausted and ill, he was too weak to lift a spoon to his lips. In the absence of Wilson, who was in jail for "intimidating" free labourers, Mann made the journey to Cardiff to nurse his friend.'[68]

The union was reported as 'moribund' in Cardiff by 1894.[69] In Swansea, making concessions to free labour, the union retained a measure of recognition with some employers and survived, relying heavily on peaceful use of conciliation procedures. The NALU, which had never espoused the methods of new unionism, maintained a relative degree of stability throughout the 1890s, falling from 3,914 members in 1892 to 2,823 in 1895. By the end of the decade, it had recovered to 3,695.[70]

## How Tinplatemen Came to the Rescue

The Dockers' Union lost its Welsh membership in copper and gasworks after its defeats in the docks, but its officials made what became a critically important strategic gain, when the South Wales, Monmouthshire and Gloucestershire Tinplate Association dissolved in 1899. This union's demise followed its failure either to resist wage cuts through the slump or to impose effective output restrictions. It had been a closed, skilled craft society, with a hierarchical seniority system similar to the steelworkers' unions. Yet in the inter-union contest to enrol its former members, whilst the Steel Smelters' Union attracted the millmen and some joined the Welsh Artisans' Union (established in 1888), the majority joined the Dockers' Union, after fierce competition from the Gasworkers' Union. Tillett's superior oratory was ascribed a key influence in this success: Will Thorne was no match for him.

Within months of the tinplate union's collapse, the Swansea district of the Dockers' Union claimed 2,500 tinplate members and twenty-four new branches. Tillett proceeded with a scheme to protect these all-important gains. He proposed to the tinplate employers a system of mutual recognition and protection, in which his members would work only for employers who entered into a cartel arrangement to control prices. In return, he sought a closed shop and a wage increase. Although the employers rejected this scheme, they did set up a very advanced form of conciliation board, stabilized wages and agreed to refer disputes to independent arbitration. Four other unions were included in the scheme: the Gasworkers', the Steel Smelters', and the Tin and Sheet Millmen's Unions. (Tillett and Hodge of the Steel Smelters' Union made a demarcation agreement.) Here, in embryo, and before its time, was a model for a Joint Industrial Council.

The significance of the tinplate section in Wales for our unfolding story is hard to exaggerate. Its full import becomes evident only in the first decade of the twentieth century, which we follow in chapter 8. We may anticipate, however, to point to the fact that in 1908 the tinplate members contributed more to the Dockers' Union's income than all other districts combined.

## II

## *The Shipping Federation's Second Offensive*

In 1892–3, the Shipping Federation gathered its forces for two crucial onslaughts on the remaining provincial strongholds of the Dockers' Union – Bristol and Hull. At that time, and whilst still surrounded by the aura of success associated with 1889, Tillett joined the political wave of new-union leaders seeking parliamentary advances. His Bradford campaign of 1892 (see chapter 6) is seen by his biographer as 'in one sense, a desperate attempt to break the circle drawn by the Shipping Federation around the Dockers' Union.'[71]

### *Bristol*

The Bristol docks were regarded with special esteem by the union leadership. They had established a closed shop, and the municipal ownership of the port provided a model much celebrated in socialist agitations. The Town Council was not, however, a principal employer of port labour, which remained in the hands of master-stevedores and shipping companies: the municipality simply owned the port and its physical facilities.

It was the timber merchants who provoked the strike of November 1892 by engaging free labour. When the dockers walked off in protest at this breach of their closed shop, the employers rejected recourse to the local Arbitration Board and summoned the Shipping Federation to their aid, declaring at the same time a general lock-out, pending the men's acceptance of the Shipping Federation ticket. The employers' intention to smash the union was obvious.

McCarthy and Tillett both hastened to the town, where street-fights between blacklegs, police and strikers had already erupted. McCarthy sought to conduct the strike (which had been made official) on the lines of the great London strike of 1889, with daily street-processions, some of them at night by torchlight. Tillett's first speeches urged caution, 'sober and prudent conduct'. But the physical conflict escalated (Tillett had no doubt that this was deliberately provoked by the Federation) and troops and cavalry were called in. Still Tillett advocated pacifism: he advised the dockers to go to church to pray for the conversion of the employers to 'nobleness', and advocated the formation of a Labour party. The mood of the strikers was quite contrary to all this: local leaders, addressing mass meetings, recalled the Bristol reform riots of 1831, drawing on the memory to call for 'a second or third revolution if necessary'. At this point Tillett caught the crowd's mood, as he so often did, and launched into incendiary speeches of extremely violent import: 'if it came to guns they could pick them up also.'[72]

The high drama of the strike reached its climax when Tillett led the crowd at a mass meeting in the taking of an oath, which it repeated after him: 'if the necessity demands I will protect my home, my interests, my wages, by means of violent or pacific measures'. Whilst this was in the highest degree inflammatory, the speaker distinguished between individual acts of violence, and concerted action led by himself and the union: 'they should intimidate by the crowd . . . the leaders should organise it'.

Tillett was later prosecuted on a charge of sedition; he was acquitted, but not before further scenes of mass street-warfare had swept through Bristol, as the police and the dragoons broke up one of Tom McCarthy's processions. On that occasion, fifty-seven civilians and fifty-one police were injured. Meanwhile, Tillett himself had moved on from his 'oath' speech to advocate, before another crowd of thousands, that 'they must [make] the workers of Bristol the controllers of Bristol's destiny', and 'It must not finish at trade unionism – it must not finish until the workers of all grades and degrees commanded absolutely the whole machinery of the state, the whole machinery of government, of production, control and distribution'.[73] This was the language of Marxism, of socialist revolution. Edward Aveling stood by Tillett's side in Bristol and himself made a speech. We can account for Tillett's extremism as the product of the fiery mood of the strikers, his emotional identity with the suffering of the people of his own home town, the evident intransigence of the Shipping Federation, and possibly also the strong socialist influence which, as we have already observed (see chapter 4), was a notable feature of new unionism in Bristol in particular.

Whatever the causes of this intransigence, all Tillett's exertions could not prevent the total defeat of the strike. There was one last mass march and demonstration, of heroic proportions, on 4 February 1893. Fifty trades took part, the skilled and unskilled, and men from London and South Wales were amongst the procession of 30,000 people. Thereafter, the strike petered out, weakened by the drain on union finances as, from April, these were diverted to the Hull dockers' struggle, and by the sustained intransigence of the employers. By June, union and 'free' blacklegs were working side by side, and the Shipping Federation's contract with the employers could safely be allowed to expire.

Through the rest of the decade, the story of the Dockers' Union in Bristol is typical. From a peak 1891 membership of 2,500, it declined to 1,250 in 1895, and to possibly no more than 800 in 1905 – these survivors being from the corn-porters, who enjoyed a degree of sectional security. It avoided strikes, and in 1900 made an arbitration agreement at the docks, setting up boards of conciliation, winning a wage increase and obtaining employer recognition. The *Dockers' Record* reported satisfaction with the system.[74]

## . . . and Humberside

Hull, Britain's third port, as we saw earlier (chapter 4), had become the jewel in the crown of the Dockers' Union by 1890. The following year the port was still registering record levels of foreign trade. The Dockers' Union held its second annual national conference there, and the National Labour Federation its fifth, both in 1891. The benign influence of the port's largest shipping firm, C. H. and Arthur Wilson, was unique to Hull. It employed only union labour, including its own foremen and shipping clerks, and assisted in the collection of union dues. In January 1891 Tillett proclaimed: 'No town stood higher in the ranks of trade unionism than Hull, for they had not been able to find a blackleg there'.[75]

George Laws, general manager of the Shipping Federation, came to Hull to complain that it was the only port where the dockers persisted in supporting the Seamen's Union's opposition to free labour. He opened a Free Labour Registry on Humber Dock, but it was hardly functional and in time failed. T. Kelly, one of the leading architects of the bogus unions of London, tried his hand at creating a similar organization in Hull, but failed. Tom Mann attended the branch dinner of the foremen's and clerks' branch of his union, a unique occasion. Tillett and Charles Wilson made speeches of mutual admiration at a union dinner.

Pay increases were won on the docks during 1891. The boatmen of the Aire and Calder Navigation Company, members of the union, struck, but they were restrained by Tillett, who negotiated a return to work.

The Hull Trades Council represented 20,000 members in 1891, a gain of 15,000 on its 1889 strength, and was very active in municipal politics, lobbying for free libraries, public parks, standard wages for Corporation contractors, codes for building regulations, and reforms in the Boards of Guardians. Debate between old and new unionists, on the legal eight-hour day and on Independent Labour politics, was fierce. In the building trades, Hull was a 100 per cent union-organized town.

When the Shipping Federation tried to use blacklegs to load a blacked coal ship, it was astonished to find that the Hull Dock Company refused to allow the free labourers to use their cranes!

During 1892, trade in Hull turned seriously downwards and this, together with the countrywide defeats inflicted on the union by the Shipping Federation, led Tillett to speak of caution and restraint in the port, to audiences not at all appreciative of this change of heart. In August 1892 he was loudly heckled by the Hull dockers when he spoke out against strike action to win the Saturday half-holiday. His estrangement from the local leadership may be gauged from a speech by Thomas Chesterfield, secretary of the Hull Dockers' Union, in which he said that 'it was most regrettable that a cloud of distrust had gathered round the name of Ben Tillett'. In this climate, Havelock Wilson mounted a campaign in Hull and throughout the country for a national strike against the Shipping Federation, which was meanwhile exerting severe pressure on the C. H. Wilson shipping company to toe the line of its policy: it organized a boycott of the company by the shipping insurers. Clouds were gathering around the port, which, by early in 1893, represented the bulk of the union's remaining national membership – an asset which Tillett was loath to risk.

The crucial moment came when C. H. and Arthur Wilson joined the Shipping Federation. Charles Wilson claimed that the union's 'dictatorship' could no longer be tolerated: yet after the great struggle which his decision unleashed was over, he stated that 'it had been a fight against the grain with me throughout . . . I may have been compelled to co-operate with those who had some such wish, [to destroy the Dockers' Union] but such co-operation, if it existed, was forced upon me.' This confirms the union view that Wilson was coerced by the Shipping Federation and other local employers. (Wilson was, of course, a prominent Liberal politician and MP in Hull, and this always gave him a strong motive for retaining labour sympathies.)

In March 1893 the Shipping Federation opened its Free Labour Bureau in Hull with a promise of preference of work for those who joined. Wilson's company also ended its practice of deducting union dues from the pay of those dockers who were in arrears, and required its foremen and clerks to leave the union. These combined pressures led Tom Chesterfield, the local docks union secretary, to issue a manifesto entitled: 'Will you walk into my Parlour, said the Spider to the Fly?', warning unionists not to register at the 'Labour Exchange'. Tillett issued a series of statements urging restraint by the men, reinforced by the 'moderate' leader of the Trades Council, W. G. Millington. Havelock Wilson, however, made an inflammatory speech, calling for a general strike of Hull labourers, thus providing the employers with the excuse they needed to import the first 400 free labourers to unload Wilson's ships. Emigrant sheds on the docks were equipped to accommodate them, *The Times* cueing in with a report on the 'splendid sheds' and praising the importation of cooking staff and orderlies to look after the creature comforts of the men. 'Their engagement is for fourteen days certain, with a prospect of permanent employment'. *The Times* failed on this occasion, as it did consistently, to report on the violence of the 'federationists', one of whom fired a revolver at the pickets. On 5 April, more than 100 free labourers returned home after being addressed by union officials.

The national press seized on these opening skirmishes to spotlight the conflict, and the Hull magistrates (some of whom were port employers) called for reinforcements. On 6 April 160 Royal Scots, 90 Dragoons and massive police reinforcements from as far afield as Nottingham arrived in the city, and two Admiralty gunboats appeared in the estuary facing the waterfront. On 11 April the special correspondent of the London *Daily News* referred to 'this preposterous display of force in a town which is as quiet as a Sunday congregation in church.' H. H. Asquith, the Home Secretary, pressed by Keir Hardie in the Commons for an explanation, placed the onus for the authorities' militancy on the City Council and magistrates. The effect was to shift public sympathy towards the strikers, and to augment anti-Liberal, Independent Labour sentiment in the Hull trade-union movement. Above all, it thoroughly alarmed the skilled unionists, including the engineers, who poured large financial contributions into the strike fund. A national response brought over £12,000 to the Hull Trades Council by the second week of the strike, and led Fred Maddison of the Hull Trades Council (a prominent Lib.–Lab. politician) to claim that 'this has certainly been even a more striking rally of the older unions to the aid of the new than was that of 1889'.

The solidarity of the dockers was evident in the results of a ballot announced on 6 April: 3,500 for the strike, with 5 votes against. *The Times* called the result the product of the 'terrorism' practised by the union's officials. In fact, Tillett approached Charles Wilson on 8 April to concede the main point – the ending of the closed shop. He offered an agreement that union men would work with free labour, that clerks and foremen could withdraw from the union and that any disputed items should be referred to arbitration. His only reservation was that free labour should not be given preference of work. Wilson rejected the offer, although what Tillett was conceding was what he had led the men of Cardiff against with such vigour only shortly before. From this point on, the conflict is properly to be regarded as a lock-out. The men had nowhere to go: their backs were firmly pinned to the wall.

Havelock Wilson continued his challenge to Tillett's moderation with a call to 'light the torch at London, Glasgow, Liverpool and Cardiff . . . to prevent them from collecting men to send to Hull'. When he finished speaking, Shipping Federation cards and an effigy of Charles Wilson were burnt. The possibility of the strike's spreading was a real one: Cardiff ship-repairers struck in sympathy, and reports from Middlesbrough, the Hartlepools, the Tyne ports, Swansea and London all suggested willingness to take action on behalf of Hull. It may be that this caused the Shipping Federation to go farther afield for its strike-breakers. Certainly they shipped over free-labour reinforcements from The Netherlands and Sweden: by 11 April they had a force of 1,000 strike-breakers at work.

Tillett began to change his position, joining the speculation about a general strike. Resolutions in support came from seventy-six branches of the shipping trades in London, and from a mass meeting in the London docks. Tillett rushed to Hull on 18 April, fresh from his court acquittal over the Bristol sedition charge, and now spoke in the tones that the dockers wanted to hear:

> That day, right up and down the length and breadth of England, the dockers were preparing for what would be one of the greatest strikes in history. The strike of the London dockers would sink into insignificance by comparison . . . when constitutional methods were useless, they must resort to the fierce arbitrament of a strike, that should be widespread . . . that should shake even the government . . . There was no other way.

Yet behind the scenes, Tillett's old associate John Burns was working hard for a settlement and cautioning against any extension of the strike. He obtained a postponement by proposing, in meetings with Tillett and Havelock Wilson, a national emergency all-union conference, and then prevailed on the leader of the seamen to go with him to meet Charles Wilson and government officials in the House of Commons. Also involved in the mediation was Sir A. K. Rollitt, the Hull Tory MP, who will be remembered as a former patron of Hull's local port unions during their formative period. The ship-owning Wilson, in taking part in these exchanges, was guilty of breaching a week-old resolution of the Shipping Federation that 'no further communications should be held with the union leaders'. Therefore this meeting gave Tillett some hope of a compromise, and he now sought to confine the conflict to Hull. Fund-raising resumed top priority. A national appeal was signed not only by the dockers' leaders, but also by Michael Davitt, John Burns and George Shipton. Always prone to think in military analogies (emulating his early hero, Napoleon), at a May Day rally in Hull Tillett repeated the American Civil War hero General Sherman's famous message: 'Hold the fort, for I am coming.'

At the heart of the conflict, Hull was now a city in rage and turmoil. On 3 May one Hull gunsmith reported that he had sold 200 revolvers in three weeks, as well as large numbers of knuckle-dusters and life-preservers. Each night there was disorder on the streets. Two divisions of cavalry paraded through the town daily. Stone-throwing and police baton-charges were a daily event. Women tore up the paving stones for their men to hurl at the police and military. Railway carriages carrying blacklegs to the Alexandra Dock were stoned. Attempts were made to obstruct trains, and there is evidence that an attempt was made to blow up a bridge carrying the Hull and Barnsley railway line over Beverley Road. Free labourers from Scarborough were met at the railway station and stoned all the way to the docks. The most spectacular event was the great fire of 23 April, visible 20 miles away, which destroyed the Citadel timber yards on the docks. Firemen found their hoses cut when they sought to douse the blaze, and strikers stood around, refusing the fabulous offer of 10s. an hour to help in firefighting. No one has ever established the true cause of the fire. Tillett blamed blacklegs, allowed by the employers to smoke, but arson seems by far the most likely cause.

Agitation by Havelock Wilson for a general strike gained some support from these events, and Tom Mann came close to endorsing it, as did Clem Edwards. Burns, working quietly behind the scenes, had his way when the national conference which he had proposed met on 22 April and rejected the call by forty-five votes to twenty-seven. Burns addressed the conference, speaking 'vigorously against the policy of attempting for so small an issue so great a risk'. Tillett swung round again into line with this decision, but had to exert himself greatly in the next two days, facing spontaneous mass meetings of dockers in London, who denounced it. At one sympathetic walk-out in London's Victoria Dock, Tillett was howled down: after repeated interruptions, ending with a voice shouting 'a strike made you, and if you don't fetch us out the union will be smashed up', the disorder became so great that Tillett, the greatest of mob orators, was forced to abandon his speech before his own London members.

Throughout the strike, no negotiations were possible between the official Strike Committee and the Hull employers. The latter, and particularly Wilson, made several informal attempts in the House of Commons to agree terms. A remarkable and highly significant element in the Hull dispute was that three of the key personalities were at the time Members of Parliament – Charles Wilson represented the Liberal interest for West Hull, Havelock Wilson had been elected in 1892 for Middlesbrough, and at the same time John Burns had won Battersea. Burns, as we have seen, was entrusted by Mann and Tillett with an insider role during the dispute, and was instrumental in arranging the private meeting in the House attended by A. J. Mundella, president of the Board of Trade, C. H. Wilson, J. H. Wilson, Llewellyn Smith (Labour Commissioner), Mr Hopwood (secretary to the Board of Trade), Sir Albert Rollitt, Alderman Woodhouse of Hull and John Burns himself.

The two Wilsons and Burns accepted the terms offered as a basis for settlement. Whilst conceding the entry of free labour to the port, and the severance of the foremen's and clerks' union membership, they stipulated that the free-labour ticket should carry no right to preference. The Shipping Federation rejected the terms, and brought Charles Wilson sharply back into line: he subsequently failed to attend a reconvened meeting of the group of mediators, writing instead to say that 'the York terms were absolutely irrevocable and final'. (York was the venue for the Shipping Federation meetings throughout the dispute.) Other efforts at a settlement were made by Mr Grotrian, a local shipowner and member of the Shipping Federation, in consultation with Tom Mann. To the York terms, which essentially required 'unionists to agree to work with non-unionists', and that 'the British Labour Exchange be kept open, the employers insisting on entire freedom of contract in employing such men as they deem suitable', these two proposed an addition to the last clause. This read: 'But neither registration at the British Labour Exchange nor membership of any union shall in itself carry with it either preference or prejudice, in regard to employment'. By this time, in mid-May, the Borough Justices, the Watch Committee, the Mayor and Council (and behind them the anxious and angry voices of the rate-payers, tradespeople and the local press) were urgently calling for settlement, their pressure being directed solely at the Shipping Federation, which was widely perceived as responsible for the continuance of Hull's distress. The Shipping Federation finally yielded to the point of meeting the Strike Committee and, though dragging its feet for some further days, on 19 May signed an agreement which included the Mann–Grotrian clause. The strike/lock-out had lasted for seven weeks.

The settlement in fact represented a mere tactical shift by the Federation, an adjustment clearly intended to prevent its further isolation as local employers and commercial interests moved away from it. Not only did the Free Labour Exchange remain in being, and the foremen and clerks leave the union (which they themselves did not wish to do), but under the terms of the settlement also dock gatemen, weighers, bookers, gangsmen, berthing masters and assistant berthing masters would sever their connection with the Dockers' Union. No 'external emblem' was to be worn by any member of a union (or of the Labour Exchange) at work or applying for work, and union offiicals were banned from visiting ships whilst the men were at work. Tom Mann was responsible for accepting these terms, and won much praise for his steadying influence, which was contrasted to Tillett's volatility. Yet the terms were similar to those which Tillett had offered, and seen rejected, weeks earlier.

Fred Maddison put them to a mass meeting of dockers on 14 May. He asked if they would be satisfied with the new clause banning preference for either union or Federation tickets. Greeted with loud cries of 'No!', he then sought to win approval by arguing that, since there would be no preference, the Free Labour Exchange would be redundant, as 95 per cent of the men were trade unionists. He pressed the point: since the Federation had accepted the 'no-preference' clause, the men 'had advanced towards ultimate victory'. This interpretation carried the day, dubious as it was.

It very soon became clear what the settlement had conceded. The Free Labour Exchange remained, and within weeks it was obvious that C. H. Wilson and other firms were indeed giving preference to non-unionists.

Fred Maddison at once asked the Mayor to intervene, but he was powerless. A further strike was proposed, but it was unrealistic: the men were exhausted from their ordeal, and the deceit of the employers, now revealed, only enhanced their demoralization. They rushed to join the Free Labour Exchange: 2,000 had registered by 9 June, although many were unemployed at a time of depressed trade. The Shipping Federation had triumphed.

The last act of violence in a violent conflict was, ironically but tragically, self-inflicted. The Dockers' branch secretary Tom Chesterfield tried to commit suicide by cutting his throat, and was for some time desperately ill. He had loyally gone along with every union concession until the end, even though a 'moderate' like Millington, the Trades Council secretary, had found them unacceptable and withdrawn from the negotiating team at local level.

In retrospect, it seems reasonable to ask whether the leadership's acceptance of the outcome as inevitable was justified. The cynical casuistry of the Federation's concession of 'no preference' must have been apparent to acute and experienced men such as Mann. Against the unbending stance of the Federation was set the matching solidarity of the Hull dockers: there is no evidence of any drift back to work during the whole affair. Could fund-raising have been intensified at a national level? Could the test have been made of a national docks and shipping strike? We have cited some evidence to show that dock workers in many ports were aware of the issues involved, and also that the Federation was becoming increasingly isolated, even in relation to local port employers and perhaps to C. H. Wilson himself. The outcome of a national strike could hardly have been worse than the consequences of the settlement.

Of course, this is to speak with hindsight, in the knowledge of what followed for Hull and for dock unionism generally. The union had already suffered the defeats in Southampton, Cardiff, Bristol and half-a-dozen smaller ports before it confronted the Federation in Hull. The scale of the Shipping Federation's resources, and the ruthlessness with which they were deployed, had been fully demonstrated. And the economic climate was adverse for any prolonged industrial warfare.

The leaders' inner defeatism, from an early stage, seems evident in the influence which Burns was allowed to exert from the distance of the House of Commons. Tillett's biographer has made a nice attempt to understand the relationships, at this critical moment, of the triumvirate which had led the London dockers in 1889:

> Tillett's formulation did not represent the softening of Shipping Federation attitudes that he and other advocates of caution had expected. Yet wishful thinking on the part of the Dockers' Executive transformed it into a major concession, and the basis for a settlement. At first Tillett demurred: did he resent the interference of Burns and Tom Mann who

also seemed instrumental in arranging the 'new' situation? If so, a sharp note from Burns brought him around. 'Let there be no fooling about the strike and its termination, and don't allow personal feeling to stand in the way of a settlement . . . Settle at once ere disaster awaits you and your men secede'.[76]

Why did Tom Mann conduct the final negotiations in Hull's Guildhall yet leave the signing to Tillett and three local leaders? (Equally, why did Charles Wilson depute his younger brother and junior partner Arthur to sign for his company?) And why did Tom Mann totally ignore the Hull strike in his *Memoirs*, while Tillett in his gave a competely false account, expressing his distaste for the episode and darkly hinting that Havelock Wilson's malign influence was the cause of an 'unnecessary' strike?

The role of Havelock Wilson must indeed be weighed. His was the union originally targeted by the Federation, and it is true that it was reduced to bankruptcy in 1894. But whilst he made the running in militant rhetoric, most notably in the case of Hull, it was the dockers and their union who bore the brunt of the fighting, and their leaders who carried the heavy task of seeking either genuine mass mobilization or a face-saving settlement which might rescue something of their former positions.

The effects of the defeat in Hull were disastrous. Within a few years William Collison could boast of the town as 'a stronghold of free labour',[77] his own National Free Labour Association having more members than the Dockers' Union during most of the rest of the decade. He staged the national annual dinner of the NFLA in Hull in 1899, and spoke of the useful work his Hull branch (3,977 strong) had done on the Clyde, and as far away as Christiania (the former name of the port of Oslo in Norway).[78] Two years later, Hull blacklegs from the NFLA were working for the Taff Vale Railway Company, to whose aid Collison rallied with the enthusiasm of an old campaigner.

The effect of the Hull collapse on the Dockers' Union's finances is some measure of its importance. Income from contributions from Hull fell by £1,000 out of a total income of £4,000. Bristol, despite its own defeat, now became the best organized port for the union.

Tom Mann came to Hull in 1898 to castigate the dockers for their position as 'the worst organised of any of the considerable ports'. Fred Maddison argued in his new magazine the *Trade Unionist* that a new union – he meant a new *local* union – should be formed, a proposal attractive even to George Belt, who had been Tom McCarthy's election agent at the 1895 General Election in Hull (see chapter 6) and was therefore politically quite opposed to Maddison. Tillett came to Hull to head off this idea, and was back the following year, 1899, with Tom McCarthy in the chair, to berate the 'dirty filthy wretches [who] went blacklegging to other ports'.[79]

But the tide turned, and sooner in Hull than elsewhere. In 1900 trade in the port was booming, and the South African war had caused temporary labour shortage on the docks because some dockers were army reservists. Two spontaneous one-day strikes by 'holders-on', joined by 700 grain workers, raised their wages from 5s. to 6s. a day. Just as he had done before, Tillett raced up to Hull and gave a fortnight's notice of strike action. His claim sought to raise the port's daily wage to the national average: Hull at the time lagged 1s. 6d.–2s. behind the rates of 6–8s. paid elsewhere.

Anticipating a trade-union revival, Wilson's company moved quickly to negotiate an acceptable improvement of wages and hours with an unofficial deputation of dockers, cutting the ground from under Tillett's feet whilst he dutifully waited out the fourteen days' notice. Other firms conceded similar gains, thus avoiding recognition of the union. Yet membership of the Dockers' Union advanced in that year to 4,000, a figure which topped the membership of the NFLA. (Free labourers had been a mixed blessing for the employers: in 1894 they successfully struck against Wilson's for an extra half-day's pay!)

Havelock Wilson's union fared no better than the Dockers' Union during the period following the 1893 strike. Nationally, the union was dissolved and reconstituted in 1894. The local Hull Seamen's and Firemen's Amalgamated Association consistently undercut the national union when pay claims were presented in 1898, 1899 and 1900, and Hull was as infamous for supplying blackleg seamen as for providing strike-breaking dockers. Further humiliation was caused by the evolution of Albert Anlaby Bird, one of the founders of the Independent Labour Party (ILP) in Hull in the 1890s. He had been active in the Hull branch of the national Seamen's Union, had become secretary of the Humber Lightermen's Union, but then defected to take a post with the Shipping Federation.[80] More seriously, the Hull coal-porters broke from Tillett's union to form their own, and Hull Trades Council endorsed a move to found a general, separatist docks' union.

Local distrust of the national union centred round the high ratio of working expenses to income. In Grimsby, this feeling was exploited by A. L. Edwards, founder of the Ipswich Mutual Working Men's Independent Federation, who charged that many unions were 'impudent frauds . . . perpetrated upon the working man'.[81] He had founded his Federation in 1893, at the instigation of the Conservatives in East Anglia, to 'get the labourers divided so that they may get a political advantage at the next General Election',[82] and to supply free labour in opposition to George Edwards's genuine Agricultural Labourers' Union. He succeeded in winning the secession of all the Grimsby branches of the Dockers' Union, and in forming a Grimsby General Workers' Friendly and Protective Society. The National Amalgamated Union of Labour also wound up its Grimsby branches, and in Hull the National Labour

Federation collapsed, being replaced with a new Hull and District Labour Federation. The National Federation of Fishermen also disappeared in 1894, and even the more stable Gasworkers' Union had to send Pete Curran, Tom Maguire and others to Hull to boost morale and hold its organization together.

It is clear that the 1893 defeat triggered off a general revulsion towards Tillett's union and the formation of a series of local, non-political, non-militant unions. Clem Edwards was surely whistling in the dark when he suggested that the national impact of the Hull strike was positive, in that it had given a sense 'of "oneness" to the Labour Movement throughout the country'.[83] Later in the decade he himself produced a study of 'free-labour frauds', which listed fifty bogus trade unions – some measure of the underworld offensive against new unionism which flourished in the 1890s.[84]

Beyond the waterfront, the Hull builders' unions, in alliance with the nine Labour councillors who found themselves on the City Council by 1897, developed a remarkably strong position in a growing 'direct-labour' scheme of the corporation. As we shall see in chapter 7, it is in the formation of Independent Labour politics allied to trade unionism that the genuinely positive lessons of the Hull strike were learned.

## Sexton and Liverpool

The National Union of Dock Labourers moved its headquarters from Glasgow to Liverpool in 1890: half of its national membership of 25,000 worked on the Mersey. Following the strikes and compromise settlements of 1889–90, the dockers were preoccupied, as in Tillett's union, with the problem of establishing and maintaining union control over labour supply.

At the South End Docks, where the employers were mainly small master-stevedoring firms (and the dockers were mainly Protestant), there was relative harmony. Union labour and the uncontested wearing of the identifying Dockers' Button prevailed. At the North End, dominated by the big shipping companies, and by Catholic–Irish dockers, the employers recruited 'preferred', non-union men, and, led by the Cunard line, banned the wearing of the Button at the call-on. Their campaign succeeded: by 1891 'the public presence of the NUDL virtually disappeared'.[85]

Whilst the Liverpool shipping firms pursued the same objective as the national Shipping Federation, they did so independently of it. A Merseyside Employers' Labour Association was formed in 1890 to fight the new unions and the lightning strikes which took place to defend the Button. It was regarded as ineffective by the large shipowners, who defected to fight their own battles. Nevertheless, the Shipping

Federation did make an arrangement with the ELA to supply blacklegs, and to act as its agent in other ports.

The response of the NUDL was to advance ca'canny as the main plank of resistance – a method now elevated to the status of a panacea. Its other response was to seek local and regional federation, and it succeeded in establishing a Federation of Trades and Labour Unions in connection with the Shipping, Carrying and Other Industries. Fifteen unions from Liverpool and Manchester affiliated on its formation in 1893. It was dissolved in 1899, 'having achieved nothing of consequence'.[86]

The large firms' success in banning the Button, according to George Milligan (who started dock work in 1890 and subsequently became the union's deputy general secretary), rang 'the death knell . . . to the unity of organisation in Liverpool'. Between 1891 and 1911 'the twelve thousand and odd men working for the great companies were in the industrial wilderness'.[87] The union's total membership fell to 8,463 in 1892, stabilizing thereafter at around 10,000.

Although not faced by the acute problem of the Shipping Federation's Free Labour Exchanges, the union's decline drove it in upon itself, and exposed a bitter internecine warfare amongst its branches and against the leadership of McHugh and McGhee. The president, general secretary and vice-president (this last was Michael McKeown, a Birkenhead docker – hence 'the three Macs') were elected along with a lay executive but, unlike the centralized power and funds of Tillett's union, the branches retained large proportions of the subscriptions, as well as a wide autonomy. This reflected the sectional and local 'caste' system of which Sexton complained:

Not the least of our manifold difficulties arose from the prevalence of what I can only describe as the caste system throughout the dockers' fraternity, which led to the creation of almost innumerable small clubs and societies all hostile to each other . . . quite frequently religious and political differences kept these bodies apart, and indeed alive. Thus the coal heavers had one society at the North End, another at the South. The leader of one was a North of Ireland Orangeman, the leader of the other an equally perfervid Irish Home Rule Catholic . . . The only point on which they were united was a mutual objection to mere cargo hands handling coal. Salt heavers took up the same attitude as to the exclusiveness of their job: if you weren't one of them you couldn't touch bulk salt . . . Being what were known in the vernacular of the port as 'good earners', salt and coal heavers alike were greatly desired by the other sex as life partners . . . those whose work was the loading and discharging of railway bars to and from barges and steamers – in which at that time enormous traffic – had their two societies. One was the 'Cabbage Club' . . . the other, the 'Clarence Dock Club', was for men engaged only in the coasting trade . . . in those days, Liverpool had a caste system quite as powerful as India's. The hand busheller of grain – now displaced by the elevator – looked with scorn upon the man who did the donkey work on the quay: the grain carrier who could easily sling a four bushel sack weighing a couple of hundredweights across his back and shoulders, and run along a swinging plank, thought himself the master workman of the ages: the stitcher of the bags used in the bulk salt trade, a veritable artist in his craft, had a most colossal contempt for the man who merely handled bags filled at the salt factory, whilst the tallyman who weighed and checked the bags considered himself the best and most important of all the 'casual dock labourers'.[88]

In this climate, branch corruption flourished, as did intrigue and office-seeking against the leadership of McHugh and McGhee, who had the great disadvantage of never having been dockers. Scandal surrounded them, following accusations in 1890 that they had misappropriated union funds in both Glasgow and Liverpool. In the ensuing libel action, their accuser, a union activist named Kierman, was found guilty, but the jury recommended mercy. McHugh supported this plea. The affair badly damaged the leadership's reputation, and in 1893 McHugh and McGhee jointly resigned, amidst continued rumours of dissension and intrigue. (They both remained devoted and active Georgeites, and McGhee was twice elected to Parliament for Irish constituencies as a Nationalist.)

James Sexton, bone of the bone of the Merseyside dock and labour community, was elected to the general secretaryship on 1 January 1894. He was thirty-seven years old, and his credentials for the post were impeccable. He had abandoned his early Fenianism and revolutionary Irish politics in Merseyside and had become a Home Ruler under the influence of T. P. O'Connor. He had early experience as a trade-union agitator, in the Knights of Labour's Bootle branch, and as a practical docker. The severe accident he had suffered on the docks and the inhumane treatment he had received (see chapter 1) had taught him a bitter lesson about dock employers. His patient, unspectacular administrative abilities and his preference for the legislative path to reform were assets to the NUDL, in dire need of internal reform, regularization of procedure and restoration of propriety. Even Sexton's evident political ambitions chimed with both local and national tendencies, and helped the Merseyside union to overcome an isolation from the mainstream of British affairs. He was a founder member (with just six others) of the Liverpool branch of the ILP, and was its delegate to the Bradford conference of 1893 which established the party nationally. He wrote for the *Clarion*, and was president of the Liverpool Trades Council in 1894. There he clashed with the old guard of skilled Lib.–Lab. unionists, who could not accept his ILP stance. In consequence, he withdrew the NUDL's affiliation to the Trades Council, and did not reaffiliate until 1906. He represented the union at the TUC from 1894, winning a seat on the Parliamentary Committee in 1900.

Whilst pursuing all this extra-mural activity, Sexton was fighting to rid the union of petty corruption and lax discipline. He suspended the Cork branch and sacked the Glasgow secretary for this type of offence. His strict administration, combined with his cautious and conciliatory policies towards the employers, did not make for popularity with his members. Whilst Tillett (and Mann, more consistently) pursued similar goals in the 1890s, seeking consolidation, they kept to a more populist style. For the most part, this held firm their support in the rank and file, at least until after the Hull defeat. Sexton, however, lacked the colour and the platform skills of someone like Tillett, but he was undoubtedly a better administrator and held his union together not by mass appeal but by efficient management. Like the Dockers' Union, the NUDL was in any case in no position to issue major challenges to the employers' ascendancy: its membership had fallen and was relatively stagnant, but recovered from its low point of 1892 to a figure of 14,900 in 1899. There were few disputes to record: industrially the remainder of the decade was without spectacle. An attempt to form a branch in Manchester when the Ship Canal opened in 1894 failed after the collapse of a strike for recognition. (Early in the new century, Tillett was more successful there.)

Shorn of industrial muscle, Sexton and the NUDL pursued a series of political campaigns, backed up by fact-finding and patient lobbying, relating to the problems of industrial accidents, employers' liability and the need for an adequate and knowledgeable inspectorate for the industry. Even in this, Sexton won little popular support, for the dockers, he found, were careless and fatalistic about their own safety – attitudes reinforced by a misguided masculine pride in their 'toughness'. Sexton's campaigns were directed upwards, through the TUC, at the Board of Trade. He won a series of partial advances for his chosen causes. First, the Board issued a directive to dock employers to notify accidents, under the Notice of Accidents Act (1894). In 1895 docks were included for the first time for inspection purposes in the Factory Acts. Yet ships themselves, even when tied up, were still excluded. There were too few inspectors, and the employers found ways to frustrate their orders and instructions. Helped in Parliament by T. P. O'Connor, Sexton won some new regulations – on the fencing of machinery, lighting, gangways, testing and improving of ladders, and similar matters. He complained regularly that the educational qualifications required for the inspectorate prevented knowledgeable but unschooled dockers from becoming inspectors.

He conducted a parallel agitation for improvements in workmen's compensation law. The employers constantly evaded their obligations in this field. They had the resources to fight their cases in the courts, and made full use of the pernicious doctrine of 'common employment', under which an accident occasioned by the negligence of a fellow worker rendered an employer immune from liability. This whole area was a very large issue for new unionism in general, as witness after witness demonstrated before the Royal Commission on Labour. The Workmen's Compensation Act of 1897 went as far as to lay down standard terms of compensation, but prolonged litigation remained a frequent necessity.

Sexton plodded on at this string of reforms, meagre though some of them were, a frequent commuter from Merseyside to Westminster, where he was sometimes received more congenially than he was at the dockside. The men disliked this: often they disliked *him*, and began to call him a 'bosses' man'. But by cultivating a close relationship with the employers and a 'moderate' image, Sexton might perhaps have claimed that he enabled the NUDL to come through both the depression of the early 1890s and the phase of hostility from employers better than other new unions.[89]

## Federation? Towards the Greater Unionism, at Home and Abroad

One recurring response to the defensive position into which the new unions were pushed in the 1890s was to seek wider association with each other. This tendency was not new: as we have seen (chapter 1), it reached back to the earliest period of waterside unionism in the 1870s. Port-level federations reappeared in the struggles against the Shipping Federation in London, Hull, South Wales and elsewhere. Clem Edwards's Federation assumed national dimensions, with an affiliated strength of more than forty trade unions. Like most such bodies up to this point, it was essentially a defensive response to an employers' offensive, seeking strength from solidarity. But it also made an early attempt to solve the running problem of inter-union relations through the mutual recognition of union cards amongst the affiliated organizations.[90]

In 1894 Sexton and Tillett brought their two unions together in a joint conference, which resolved that 'an amalgamation of the two unions should be brought about as speedily as possible'.[91] But nothing came of this portentous resolution. Sexton, in particular, may have found it impossible to overcome the sectionalism of which he never ceased to complain.

A more significant and ambitious initiative, attributable, as so many innovations were, to Havelock Wilson and Tom Mann, was the formation in 1896 of the International Federation of Ship, Dock and River Workers. This followed the strategy first practised by Tillett's new union in the immediate aftermath of the 1889 strike, when contacts were established in various northern European ports.[92] The issue of international co-operation surfaced again during a Swedish dock dispute of 1896. Then again, new conflicts broke out in The Netherlands. An appeal was adopted by the British Dockers' Union Conference.

Beginning on domestic ground – 'We of the Dock, Wharf, and Riverside Labourers' Union, in Delegate Meeting assembled, earnestly desire to call the attention of all right minded persons to the conditions under which we, and many thousands of others, are compelled to exist' – it went on to recall the results of the 1889 strike: 'the conditions of labour were improved in many departments of industry'. However:

> many of the conditions then obtained have since been lost, this is in part due to the fact that many of the workers, having been gulled by specious promises of employers and their agents, have acquiesced in conditions that have gone from bad to worse, until now, the conditions in many departments are in every whit as bad as they were seven years ago.

Noting that the wealthy were flaunting even greater extravagances, it linked its call for remedial action quite firmly to international movements:

> Under these circumstances surely it behoves us to take immediate action for a considerable improvement in our conditions . . .
> Let the magnificent stand made by the Rotterdam Dockers serve as an incentive and an example, and remember the blacklegs there went from this country . . . let us at once resolve to formulate our demands, to consult with all kindred Unions, and, if possible, secure common action for the common good. Let us dare to be true to our own manhood, and to have right regard for the women and children.

The resolution ended by authorizing the Executive Council of the union to 'forthwith open up negotiations with other Unions with a view to concerted action'.[93]

The International Federation elected Tom Mann as president and Ben Tillett as secretary. For the next year in the case of Tillett, and the next two years in the case of Mann, this international work occupied much of both leaders' attention. But it was to become more than simply the international arm of the Dockers' Union. Sexton immediately affiliated the NUDL, on the invitation of Havelock Wilson, who also came in.[94]

The short-term objective of the International Federation was to achieve standardization of wages in waterside and shipping employment – in effect a 'levelling-up' of European wages to British standards. In this way the British unions sought to meet a constant complaint levelled at them by the shipowners. Thus, the formal objectives of the International Federation were defined in their rules to include, 'as far as possible, a uniform rate of pay for the same class of work in all ports, and to establish a recognised working day and other regulations in the ports of the world'.

That autumn 19,000 Hamburg dockers struck. They stayed out for nearly three months, and then 'did not win, but they fought splendidly and are now well organised and steadily preparing for another struggle, this time under the auspices of the International [Federation]'.[95] Before, Mann reported, 'they acted independently, and the [International] Federation were not in a position to block vessels loaded by blacklegs . . . The next fight will be . . . scientifically conducted on a scale of unprecedented proportions.'[96]

Rotterdam and Antwerp docks had also been on strike, and had received assistance at the hands of Havelock Wilson from the National Sailors' and Firemen's Union.

In his 1896 Report to the British Dockers' Union, Tom Mann promised 'special attention' to the French ports, including Le Havre, Nantes, Bordeaux, Marseilles, Paris and Dunkirk. Already, he was widening his horizons: 'The French railway workers, who have a splendid Union and are federated with several other countries, are taking a keen interest in the International movement, and ere long we hope the Amalgamated Railway Servants and the General Railway Workers' Union of this country will also join the Federation.'[97]

Quite evidently, both Sexton and Tillett aimed to use the new international body to heal breaches of organization within their own British territories. Mann shared such concerns, but was none the less much more committed to international work for its own sake. At his suggestion, McHugh was enrolled for the task of reviving longshoremen's unionism in New York, using funds from the International Federation; however, he had only a shortlived success there.[98] Mann, Tillett, Sexton and Havelock Wilson, as well as lesser-known figures, visited Hamburg, Antwerp, Rotterdam, Paris, Malmo, Bilbao, Copenhagen, Christiania (Oslo), Bordeaux, Le Havre, Nantes, St-Nazaire and other centres. The bulk of these travels were undertaken by Mann, with a zest and energy which are evident from his later account of the period.[99]

The British leaders addressed mass meetings, and for a time became notorious with the authorities wherever they went. Strikes were generated in several ports, the most important being that already mentioned in Hamburg – a prolonged and ultimately unsuccessful struggle which extended from October 1896 to February 1897. Sympathy action was requested in British ports, but it did not materialize. Tillett, Mann and Sexton were successively arrested and deported, as the continental police in one or another centre sought to prevent them addressing mass meetings. On 24 August 1896, Tillett spent a particularly distressing night in a filthy jail in Antwerp and would have made a diplomatic crisis of the incident had he not been prostrated with illness following the affair.[100] He then departed to convalesce in New Zealand.

Tom Mann was more robust, and clearly enjoyed the cat-and-mouse game which he played with the Paris police in order to address a clandestine gathering of trade unionists and socialists. In 1897, undeterred by the defeat in Hamburg, the International Federation called a conference in London which, although dominated by the British delegates, did bring representatives of the port workers of Antwerp, Rotterdam and Marseilles to confer with them. Tom Mann published his pamphlet, *The Dockers and Sailors in 1897*, in which he elaborated the future goals of the International Federation, particularly the need to combat the common waterfront problem of casual and irregular employment. Yet his personal drive was to substitute for mass participation, and the International Federation did not long survive when he turned his attention to yet another path-breaking movement in Britain: the formation of the Workers' Union.

The International Federation had introduced trade unionism to unorganized continental dockers, and had prepared the way for the next and more durable international organization: the International Transport Workers' Federation, launched in 1908. But it had clearly been too dependent on the British, and on the individual commitment of a few people – particularly Mann, the most genuine internationalist in the leadership. There were two possible responses to unfair foreign competition. International trade-union co-operation was one. The other was xenophobia, protectionism and discrimination. Chauvinism was to emerge at a later stage as a characteristic problem in Britain's ports, not only at rank-and-file level, but sometimes in trade-union leadership.

During all these continental forays, the news for the Federation from Britain had been fairly dismal. In Hull 'a great amount of work yet remains before the Union can exercise a proper influence in the port'; in Bristol 'there is room for improvement'; in Gloucester, likewise; by the time the Dockers' Union Report was prepared for 1896, Bridgwater had just come out of a five-week strike in which 'the men were worsted'. The union had too many officers, and needed a massive recruitment if it was to maintain all its paid officials. None the less, because of the international developments, Mann thought 'that the outlook for Port Workers is brighter than it has ever been before'.

Tillett was still in the Antipodes a year later, so it was again Tom Mann who signed the 1897 Report to the British Dockers. This was not printed until the following year. News on the home front had not improved significantly, although there was some recovery in Middlesbrough and Cardiff, while other districts marked time, and the wound in Hull remained open. In 1897 there was defeat of cataclysmic proportions. The Amalgamated Society of Engineers was locked out by the Engineering Employers' Federation in a contest over trade-union rights. After a long struggle the engineers were forced to submit to a humiliating peace formula which reaffirmed 'management's right to manage', and particularly its right to man new machinery with semi-skilled labour. The employers' victory was an object lesson to other unions. Mann hammered it home:

It behoves all other Unions to seriously consider the reasons that led to such results. Beyond any doubt one of the reasons why the Engineers received such determined opposition from the employers was the fact that the Amalgamated Society was not Federated with any other Union . . . The defeat of the Engineers has stimulated discussions in favour of federation.

The Dockers' Union was already federated with the International Federation of Ship, Dock and River Workers, and 'the Germans, Swedes, Danes and Norwegians are definitely federated with us on a financial basis.'[101] The French and Belgians were poorly organized on the water front, although they remained in 'constant communication'. In Spain there were many women dockers and wages were low, but a nucleus of people was organized. In the United States, McHugh had still been doing his best among longshoremen on the Atlantic coast.

Moving from the universal scene, Mann then retreated to the national dimension:

> The Unions of Britain must turn in a more determined fashion to Parliament, and demand therefrom reductions of working hours, extension of Factory Acts to Docks . . . an effective manning scale, adequate accommodation for Sailors, give proper attention to unemployed problem . . . To make this possible all members should endeavour to take a lively interest in political matters, and force on Industrial questions through Parliament.[102]

There is an apparent disjunction here, which reflects the problems arising, not only in choices between different modes of struggle, but also between theatres of action. International co-ordination was to hold a magnetic attraction for transport workers, and for no one more than for seamen and dockers. In co-operation with continental colleagues, it was easy to think that direct action might be raised to a sufficient intensity to defeat recalcitrant employers, whose strike-breakers already ranged freely across frontiers. Such action positively implied the deliberate use of sympathetic strikes. These, however, did not easily fit national structures for bargaining. International action fitted the framework of the international economy, but of itself it offered no direct leverage on political structures, which were all articulated at the level of the nation-state.

The 'battle for democracy', which Marx had long ago established as the first item on the agenda of proletarians, was, therefore, from the beginning a battle for recognition by and representation in national structures. By force of inertia, it would also become Labour's goal to supplant its opponents in those structures, and rule in their stead.

Internationalism was, by contrast, something of an alternative perspective. Since there were no democratic institutions fixed on a global scale, workers could not possess them or subvert them. They would need to develop their own frameworks, starting from scratch, and it was natural for them to attempt such a project from within the industrial space they already occupied. Federation, in these early days, was seen as naturally international. If it worked, it would amount to a radically new approach to democracy. Each alternative strategy generated a proliferation of variant approaches: yet neither could be sundered permanently from the other. These conflicts within the commitment of the waterfront workers were to be amplified on a vast stage, during the ensuing years.

## Notes

1  Eric J. Hobsbawm, *Worlds of Labour* (Weidenfeld and Nicolson, 1984), p. 157.
2  Ibid.
3  H. A. Clegg, Alan Fox and A. F. Thompson, *A History of British Trade Unions since 1889*, vol. I: *1889–1910* (Oxford University Press, 1964), p. 83.
4  Basil Mogridge, 'Militancy and Inter-Union Rivalry in British Shipping, 1911–1929', *International Review of Social History*, vol. VI (1961), p. 379.
5  E. L. Taplin, *The Dockers' Union: A Study of the National Union of Dock Labourers, 1889–1922* (Leicester University Press, 1985), pp. 168–9.
6  Arthur Marsh and Victoria Ryan, *Historical Directory of Trade Unions*, vol. III (Gower, 1987), p. 257.
7  Clegg, Fox and Thompson, *History of British Trade Unions*, vol. I, p. 83.
8  Hobsbawm, *Labouring Men* (Weidenfeld and Nicolson, 1963), chapter 8.
9  This was an international debt crisis, triggered by insolvency in Latin America. The public debt of Argentina had risen from £10 million in 1875 to £70 million by 1889. Speculation ran ahead, until, in November 1890, the bubble burst, and as a result 'the great city firm of Baring's went on the rocks'. Its liabilities were more than £21 million. Had it simply sunk, the City itself would have been imperilled. But the Governor of the Bank of England, William Lidderdale, mounted a spectacular rescue with the help of Rothschild's. There was no bank liquidation and Baring's was reborn as a joint-stock company.
10  John Lovell, *Stevedores and Dockers: a Study of Trade Unionism in the Port of London, 1870–1914* (Macmillan, 1969), pp. 28–9 and 38–9.
11  Royal Commission on Labour, Fifth and Final Report, 1894, 581,. p. 31.
12  George Howell, cited in Elie Halevy, *History of the English People in the Nineteenth Century* (Penguin, 1939), book 2, Epilogue: '1895–1905', p. 190.
13  Ibid., p. 192.
14  Llewellyn Smith and Vaughan Nash, *The Story of the Dockers' Strike* (Fisher Unwin, 1890), p. 160.
15  Ibid.
16  Royal Commission on Labour, Minutes of Evidence, Group B, Vol. I, Qs. 2452–60.

17  Ibid., Qs. 2612–14.
18  Ibid., Qs. 2634–6.
19  See Tony Corfield, 'Early Trade Unionism in London', TGWU *Record*, September 1964, p. 36, for a critical commentary on Clegg's account of the union's decline in the Port of London.
20  Ibid.
21  Royal Commission on Labour, Minutes of Evidence, Group B, Vol. I, Q. 3877.
22  Ibid., Q. 526.
23  Ibid., evidence of J. Donovan, Qs. 2452ff.
24  Ibid.
25  Ibid., Q. 3180.
26  Ibid., Qs. 2461–2.
27  Ibid.
28  Ibid., Qs. 2462–4.
29  Ibid., evidence of W. Salter, Q. 2832.
30  Ibid., Qs. 2833–4.
31  Ibid., Q. 2366.
32  Ibid., Qs. 472–7 (authors' italics).
33  Ibid., Qs. 3684–7.
34  Lovell, *Stevedores and Dockers*, pp. 130–1.
35  For a thorough analysis of the positions of employers, labourers and unions on casualism, see Gordon Phillips and Noel Whiteside, *Casual Labour: The Unemployment Question in the Port Transport Industry, 1880– 1970* (Oxford University Press, 1985), in particular chapter 2. They express the trade-union problem thus: 'Trade union leaders straddled the two worlds, of reformer and labourer, and displayed an ambivalence on the question of decasualization which was a mark of their frontier existence' (p. 62). On this question see also Gareth Stedman Jones, *Outcast London* (Penguin, 1971), in particular chapter 17.
36  David F. Wilson, *The Dockers: The Impact of Industrial Change* (Fontana, 1972), p. 26.
37  Royal Commission on Labour, Minutes of Evidence, Group B, Vol. I, Q. 4925.
38  L. H. Powell, *The Shipping Federation: a History of the First Sixty Years, 1890–1950* (Shipping Federation, 1950), p. 1.
39  Ibid., p. 5.
40  J. Stafford Ransome, *Master and Man versus Trade Unionism* (London, 1891).
41  Royal Commission on Labour, Minutes of Evidence, Group B, Vol. I, Qs. 4948–57.
42  Ibid.
43  Clem Edwards, 'Labour Federations' (two articles), *Economic Journal*, vol. III (1893), pp. 205–17 and 408–24.
44  Royal Commission on Labour, Minutes of Evidence, Group B, Vol. I, Q. 4954.
45  Ibid., Q. 8640.
46  Ibid., Q. 4953.

47  Jonathan Schneer, *Ben Tillett: Portrait of a Labour Leader* (Croom Helm, 1982), p. 52.
48  Royal Commission on Labour, Minutes of Evidence, Group B, Vol. II, Q. 14491.
49  L. H. Powell, *The Shipping Federation*, p. 20.
50  John Saville, 'Trade Unions and Free Labour: the Background to the Taff Vale Decision', in Asa Briggs and John Saville (eds), *Essays in Labour History, 1886–1923* (Macmillan, 1960), pp. 317–51.
51  N. Soldon, 'Laissez-Faire as Dogma: The Liberty and Property Defence League, 1882–1914', in K. D. Brown (ed.), *Essays in Anti-Labour History* (Macmillan, 1974), pp. 208–23.
52  For the National Free Labour Association, see William Collison, *The Apostle of Free Labour* (Hurst and Blackett, 1913). On right-wing 'labour' organizations generally, see John Saville, 'Trade Unions and Free Labour'.
53  William Collison, *Apostle of Free Labour*, p. 44.
54  Ibid., pp. 83–5.
55  John Saville, 'Trade Unions and Free Labour', p. 336.
56  Ibid., p. 339.
57  Ben Tillett, *Memories and Reflections* (John Long, 1931), p. 176.
58  Collison, *Apostle of Free Labour*, pp. v–vi.
59  Schneer, *Ben Tillett*, pp. 53–4.
60  Tom McCarthy, Royal Commission on Labour, Minutes of Evidence, Group B, Vol. II, Q. 12,276.
61  Ibid., evidence of Thomas Morgan, Q. 12,164.
62  Ibid. for the rules of these bodies, reproduced at appendices LXXVI and LXXVII.
63  Ibid., Q. 12,280.
64  Ibid., Qs. 12,392–6.
65  See Phillip J. Leng, *The Welsh Dockers* (G. W. and A. Hesketh, 1981), *passim*; and Stan Awberry, 'The Story of the South Wales Ports', in the TGWU *Record*, May, June, August and September 1931.
66  Leng, *The Welsh Dockers*, appendix 2, p. 108.
67  Schneer, *Ben Tillett*, p. 54.
68  Ibid., p. 55.
69  Leng, *The Welsh Dockers*, p. 30.
70  Ibid., p. 39.
71  Schneer, *Ben Tillett*, p. 79.
72  Ibid., pp. 81ff.
73  Ibid., pp. 82–5.
74  For Bristol in the 1890s, see Brian Atkinson, *Trade Unions in Bristol* (Bristol Branch, Historical Association, University of Bristol, 1982).
75  The Hull strike has been extensively researched and written about. The quotations used in this account (pp. 156–65) are drawn from: Raymond Brown, *Waterfront Organisation in Hull, 1870–1900* (University of Hull, 1972); Edward Gillett and Kenneth MacMahon, *A History of Hull* (University of Hull, 1980); Clem Edwards, 'The Hull Shipping Dispute', *Economic Journal*, vol. III (1893), pp. 345–57; John Saville, 'Trade Unions

and Free Labour'; Schneer, *Ben Tillett*; and the columns of the *Hull Daily Mail* for 1893.

76   Schneer, *Ben Tillett*, p. 93.
77   Collison, *Apostle of Free Labour*, p. 275.
78   Raymond Brown, *Waterfront Organisation in Hull*, p. 91, recounts that free labour in Hull 'was not always tractable, as may be instanced by their successful strike for an extra half-day's pay in 1894 against Messrs. Wilsons'! He also notes 'a curious feature is that even in the period when Free Labour was strong in Hull the rest of the labour movement always referred to the Free Labour Association with amused contempt, rather than fear and hatred'.
79   Brown, *Waterfront Organisation in Hull*, p. 92.
80   Ibid., p. 94.
81   Ibid., p. 95.
82   Ibid., p. 95n.
83   Clem Edwards, 'The Hull Shipping Dispute', p. 351.
84   Clem Edwards, 'Free Labour Frauds: A Study in Dishonesty', reprinted from the *Critic* (1898), 24 pp.; cited in Saville, 'Trade Unions and Free Labour', pp. 317–57.
85   Taplin, *The Dockers' Union*, p. 40.
86   Ibid., p. 43.
87   TGWU *Record*, June 1923; cited in Taplin, *The Dockers' Union*, p. 43.
88   James Sexton, *Sir James Sexton, Agitator: the Life of the Dockers' MP* (Faber and Faber, 1936), pp. 111–12.
89   Sources for this account of Sexton's union include: Taplin, *The Dockers' Union*; Sexton, *Sir James Sexton, Agitator*; Sexton's evidence to the Royal Commission on Labour; and the NUDL Annual Executive Reports, 1893–9.
90   Clem Edwards, 'Labour Federations', p. 214.
91   Taplin, *The Dockers' Union*, p. 63.
92   Smith and Nash, *The Story of the Dockers' Strike*, p. 161.
93   DWRGWU Annual Delegate Meeting, 1896, Minutes, pp. 37–8.
94   Sexton's autobiography, *Sir James Sexton, Agitator*, pp. 176–80, contains a description of Wilson's role in these events, and of his own adventures. Sexton was imprisoned in Ghent, and deported.
95   DWRGWU Annual Report 1896, p. 7.
96   Ibid.
97   Ibid.
98   Ibid., p. 64.
99   Tom Mann, *Memoirs* (1923; reissued MacGibbon and Kee, 1967), pp. 106–17.
100  He was released after Dilke and Rosebery intervened with Salisbury. Upon his deportation he was informed that he was 'banished from Belgium for seven years'. Tillett, *Memories and Reflections*, p. 181.
101  DWRGWU Annual Report, 1897, p. 6.
102  Ibid., pp. 6–7.

# 6

# Hanging On

## *Horsemen in General*

Some surviving unions in the field of inland transport made steady progress in the 1890s; others were subject to the same destructive forces which visited the new unions in port transport. The Northern Counties Amalgamated Association of Tramway, Hackney Carriage Employees and Horsemen in General (the Tramway and Horsemen here, for short), formed in 1889 with 400 members, had its headquarters in Manchester and branches throughout Lancashire, Yorkshire, the Midlands and South Wales. It recorded 3,799 members in 1894, and closed the century in 1899 with 7,356.[1]

The Tramway and Horsemen's Union's Reports for the 1890s were compiled by a general secretary, George Jackson, who combined cautious Christian sentiment and piety with a deep and consistent sense of outrage at the appalling conditions of work and wages of his members. Nor was he averse to leading vigorous strike action for cuts in working hours and for pay increases, as at Preston in 1894 and Oldham in 1900.

In Preston, carters' hours ranged from 77 to 100 a week (this was quite 'normal' in the industry), for which labour they received from 14s. to 23s. 6d. (from 70p to £1.17). Wages of 2½d–5d. an hour were common amongst horsemen, but it was the long hours that most moved George Jackson, for they prevented carters

from giving that care and attention to their children which, as a father, they ought to bestow on them. [Moreover, they are] prevented from taking any part in the welfare of their country . . . are practically disfranchised; and when the wife is debarred of the company of her husband, and her life is made a life of solitude and misery, we say there is a necessity for them to organise in order to free themselves from a life of industrial slavery.[2]

He records the regular appearance of carters before the courts, fined for being asleep whilst in charge of a horse and cart, after starting work at 3.30 in the morning. He told the Royal Commission on Labour that the lack of meal-breaks obliged men to eat with reins in one hand and food on their knees, and that 'when nature calls . . . they cannot obey the call and . . . we find that it affects the men in Manchester very much indeed.'[3]

Although the 1890s were generally a period of weakness for the new unions, Jackson was able to report a series of successful claims for shorter hours, increased wages and recognition, particularly in the tramway industry. Meal-breaks, and in one case three days' annual holiday, were amongst the improvements won by his union. Jackson mirrored new unionism's wider goals in campaigning for the municipalization of tramways and for federation and amalgamation of sectional unions, and customarily wrote of 'the labour movement' as the vehicle for a wider emancipation. During the 1890s he absorbed the Bolton Tramways Union, the Manchester, Salford and District Lurrymen and Carters' Union, the Edinburgh Tramway and Carmen's Union, the Belfast Carters' Union, and the Huddersfield Carters' Union.[4]

Recognition and reduced hours, conceded by the Manchester Carriage and Tramway Company in 1896, gave Jackson particular satisfaction:

> As regards the reduced hours of labour, the men speak very highly of the same. It hardly seems conceivable that such a great change could take place in the conditions of the men in so short a time. From fifteen and a half hours per day to ten hours, exclusive of one hour per day for dinner, is indeed a wonderful record, and sufficient to persuade any man of the advantages of trade unionism.[5]

The following year, the union reported gains of 1s. a week for corporation drivers in Portsmouth, Colne and Birmingham, and reduced hours in Nottingham and Cardiff.

The defeat of the engineering unions in the lock-out of 1897 drew a prescient comment from Jackson, who, on the strength of his surviving Reports, deserves to be recognized as a pioneer campaigner (in an industry then characterized by highly fragmented and sectional unionism) for One Big Union:

> After the failure of such a powerful organisation as the Engineers and Allied Trades, one is bound to admit that some stronger defence is required than many of us can offer in our sectional unions, and that something will have to be done before long in the way of forming a more solid body of trade unionists than we have at present. Whether it shall be federation or amalgamation I am not at this stage prepared to say, but I am strongly of the opinion that all those sectional unions representing kindred trades or occupations should at once be amalgamated into one solid

society, which would go a long way in assisting to bring about an amalgamation or federation of all trade unionists.[6]

Jackson also embraced the co-operative ideals of the anarchist Prince Peter Kropotkin. A full-page report of the Russian's London lecture on 'The Development of Trade Unionism' (at the Memorial Hall in 1897) was included in the union's own proceedings:

> His advice was now to go on steadily with trade unionism and co-operation and . . . to bring into more effective use the municipal powers which already existed, and enlarge them to the possession of buildings, land and machinery. As to 'management' he supposed that English workmen would be quite as capable of managing their own business, if they got the chance, as the old Craft Guilds, which had no capitalists or wealthy directors to guide them.[7]

A final extract from these reports concerns Jackson's appreciation of the connections between urban overcrowding, slum clearance and the rehousing of the working class in more dispersed suburbs, and the resultant need to expand tramways and cheap public transport generally:

> To spread out the community it is necessary that the tramway system should give a cheap, rapid and comprehensive service. In England the uniform fare for long distances as well as short has always been objected to, but it is essential for the extensive use of the system that the uniform fare should be adopted. It is the 'penny all the way' that induces passengers to travel long distances, and to travel in large numbers. The low cost of working electric trams as compared with horses makes it possible to have receipts per car mile and get a much larger profit. The service must be rapid . . . it must be comprehensive . . . so that a working man living in any one part can readily reach another.[8]

## Dockers' Leaders in the 1890s

In chapter 5 we followed the story of the Dockers' Union through the shocks it suffered from the attacks of the Shipping Federation. These, as we saw, provoked attempts to respond through wider association by seeking federation, both national and international. Now we must look at the internal government of the Dockers' Union, and at the evolution of its leadership during the 1890s. There are several garbled stories about this in the existing literature, and some of them are generally believed.

Tom Mann's precise role in the union during the 1890s has not been adequately recorded. Tony Corfield, who wrote a series of historical essays for the TGWU *Record* in the early 1960s, did draw attention to it, however. 'It is not widely known', he wrote, 'that [Mann] officially led the Dock, Wharf, Riverside and General Workers' Union during the period when Tillett was abroad in Australia and New Zealand."[9] In spite of this (quite accurate) report, the idea is widely current that Mann had largely disengaged from the Dockers' affairs when he took up the general secretaryship of the Independent Labour Party (ILP) in February 1894. Thus, the Concise version of the *Dictionary of National Biography* says of him: 'helped in London dock strike, 1889; first president, Dockers' Union, 1889–93; member of royal commission on labour, 1891–4; signed minority report; secretary, Independent Labour Party, 1894–7'.

The truth is much more complex. Mann's doings at this time were very newsworthy indeed. He thought for a brief moment of taking orders, and discussed the idea with Cosmo Lang, who believed he had netted a fish of great prize for the Church. No sooner had the idea dawned than it was the talk of the town. While he nursed the new ILP, he fought for the leadership of the Engineers' Union, and ran for Parliament in Colne Valley, Halifax and Aberdeen. All these contests attracted attention. This was a busy life, and when he spoke about resigning (as he did more than once) at a Dockers' Union conference, no doubt this would have been strongly noised about. So, at the time, many people believed Mann had moved on. Most historians have reflected that belief. Roger Moore, however, was right when he wrote that Mann was the dockers' president, 'first in the full-time capacity from 1889 to 1892 and then honorary until 1900.'[10] It is worth tracing this evolution, and its interplay with the career of Tillett.

To those who think of trade-union democracy in twentieth-century terms, conferences are a matter of mass gatherings of delegates, large seaside convention halls, television cameras and screeds of (usually none-too-friendly) coverage in the press. Debates will be closely structured around resolutions which have been composited into clear choices from a multitude of proposals received from hundreds of branch meetings. Discipline will show itself in crisp, short interventions, seldom taking longer than five minutes and frequently lasting only three.

Things were not quite like that in 1890. The dockers gathered for their first Annual Delegate Meeting in the Great Assembly Hall in Mile End Road. Sixty-three people were present, of whom eleven were officers or executive councillors. Tom Mann presided. He asked his colleagues to behave in a dignified and calm manner. This, apparently, they did. The press were to be admitted during the presidential address, but not for the rest of the proceedings.

John Burns was then introduced, and it was resolved that he be invited to stay after addressing delegates for a quarter of an hour. Burns too asked delegates to behave in a 'calm, peaceful and dignified manner'. After this, the presidential address was pronounced from a printed copy, already circulated to the press. None of the rest of the deliberations was to remain so easy to read, since the records were written into a very large minute-book in a flowing copperplate, which gradually became less and less calm and dignified, more jagged and, in the end, spidery, as the minute-writer got tired. The meeting itself seems to have remained very orderly, working day by day through all the draft rules and a series of resolutions.

By the time of the second Annual Delegate Meeting in Hull, in late September 1891, participation had diminished to twenty-five delegates plus officers. Four delegates turned up from Hull; Swansea and Bristol were each represented by three; one apiece came from Medway, Cardiff, Newport, Northfleet, Grimsby and Gloucester; and the remainder were from London.

Once again, Tom Mann gave the presidential address, which was described as 'perfectly unique', and which evidently covered a very much wider area than was customary at the time in trade-union orations. Judging by the discussion which was then aroused, Mann's statement covered the question of temperance; Brother Whitehead, of Grimsby, said that there had been a 'wonderful decrease of drunkenness on the part of the men, but a terrible increase on the part of the women'. Mann evidently also spoke about co-operation, since delegates from Swansea and London were moved to comment on co-operative ideas in the speech.

Tantalizingly, as soon as the minutes have recorded agreement on the publication of the president's speech, alongside the general secretary's report, there is an item which reads 'Resignation of President'. Then almost an entire page is left blank, as if the minute-secretary had intended to seek advice on what precisely to record about this matter. In the event, nothing was recorded, and the conference moved on to debate sub-contracting, the inspection of dockside equipment, and the legal eight-hour day. Tom Mann was still signing each day's minutes as a true record right through to the end of the conference.

The third Annual Delegate Meeting brought a couple of dozen delegates to Swansea in September 1892, plus another dozen associates, including officers, executive members and trustees. At an appropriate moment, the delegates left their committee room for a larger hall in order to hear the presidential address, which once again is missing from the ledger which served as a minute book. It was, however, printed in the published record of proceedings, which contains a preface by Ben Tillett, in which he regrets 'that our President has withdrawn from active leadership, although still with us as trustee'.

Tillett's Report to the conference refers to painful internal arguments within the union, and 'the hostile attitude taken up by the districts'. Cliques and factions had emerged. 'In the interest of the union', said Tillett, he had met all this bad blood 'with courage'. There was a special need for an organizational drive in London, where 'revival meetings' were 'imperative'. Other districts 'may be said to be holding their own'.

The printed minutes reproduce Tom Mann's presidential address in full, and show why it again drew many enthusiastic comments. It ranges from a consideration of John Stuart Mill's treatment of the relation between individual initiative and common ownership to an examination of the different roads which were available to secure trade-union goals:

> our ideal is the same as Mill's, viz., 'to unite the greatest individual liberty of action with the common ownership in the raw material of the globe, and an equal participation of all in the benefits of combined labour' – combined labour meaning the organised energy of the workers producing in the most effective fashion – whilst this is our fixed aim, it is a very secondary matter, indeed, as to what precise institution shall be used for its realisation. There is no especial virtue in Trades Union action as against municipal action, or in voluntary co-operative effort as against Parliamentary effort; they are all good when rightly used, and they should all be used to realise the object already set forth. The end is what is required. The means to reach the end must never be treated as the end itself. Thus, given universal co-operation on the voluntary basis, we should then reach the first of our ideals, and there would be but little necessity for Trade Unionism, or given effective action through the municipalities with an effective understanding between each, we should be in the same position, or if as the result of a high level of intelligence it was decided to secure the end in view through the agency of Parliament, the results would still be the same. We must be guided largely by expediency in these matters, and given the temperament of the British people with the existing British institutions it is pretty clear that we must use each and all of the institutions named, but use them all for the purpose declared by Mill.

In following through this diversity of paths, Mann singled out some for special attention:

> The plan proposed by Mr. Mather, M.P., of Manchester, is a bold one and a good one. He proposes to incorporate the trades unions properly representative of their trades, empowering them to deal with the force of law with all matters relative to working hours. But these matters ought not, and must not take the whole of our time; the democratic control of industry in the interests of all is to be brought about, and the principle and practice of co-operation can supplement our trade union work in a splendid fashion. Trade unions enable us as wage earners to secure fair conditions for the time being, but we require to organise also as wage spenders, otherwise it is quite possible to retard trades unionism by neglecting as spenders to see that trades union principles have been complied with as regards the whole of the commodities we obtain by our wages. This can be secured by dealing with the distributive stores which enable us not only to deal exclusively in articles produced under fair conditions, but place a power in the hands of the organised consumers to establish and conduct in their own interests the entire manufacturing departments that are required to supply the distributive stores, and to this

extent we get industry organised under democratic control, and can conduct the same on lines that shall set an example to ordinary capitalistic enterprises.

Many co-operative manufacturing establishments are now working successfully, and during the next ten years we may expect to see a very great spread of the principle . . . In municipal life, also, is to be found many opportunities for spreading the principles we have at heart, and to help on the ideal set forth, a true trades unionist who is also a member of a co-operative society, should not be indifferent to the policy endorsed by his fellow-townsmen.[11]

The printed minutes then diverge from the handwritten ledger account. Some pages of the ledger are not filled, and at least one page has been removed. In moving the vote of thanks, Tillett is reported in the printed minute as reading 'a resolution' (from Bristol) 'begging Mr. Mann not to carry out his intention of retiring from the presidency'.

Clearly Tom Mann had intended his presidential statement to be his swan song among the dockers. It was followed by another long debate on rules revision. After this had continued for a considerable time, Tom Mann

rose and said that it was his fixed determination to comply with the intention already sent out to the delegates. He handed in his resignation [(12 months ago) – this is deleted in the ledger by the minute-secretary, but remains quite legible] at the last annual delegate meeting when it was understood that the governing body would consider the length of time that his notice should expire. He valued the many kind expressions of opinion that had fallen from the lips of several delegates and friends. He could not alter his previous decision; he would not alter it. Whilst however highly appreciating the motives of those who were asking him to reconsider his decision he could not depart from his previous intention.

One delegate after another then spoke, in a chorus of dismay. J. Harrison from Hull was 'sorry that the President had a mind of his own' on this matter. The president had a 'thoroughly democratic, broad, charitable and progressive mind'. Because of this 'he appealed to him from the bottom of his heart to reconsider his decision'. J. Johnson of London said that all his colleagues 'would deeply feel the loss of his splendid services'. Ben Tillett then read out a string of resolutions, from every district in the union, urging the president not to resign. H. G. Spencer from Hull 'animadverted on the work done on behalf of trade unionism and on the dockers in particular by Brother Tom Mann'. J. Morgan from Newport feared that if the president left the union, it would 'break up into sections'.[12] Almost everyone said his piece, and almost all said the same thing.

At the end of the day, exhausted, the conference unanimously carried a motion giving Tom Mann 'until tomorrow morning to reconsider his decision'. But the minute-book then deserts us. It tells us that the 'fourth day's meeting was held on Thursday at 9.30, with the President in the Chair'. And that is all. Three pages are left blank, and we tip straight into yet more debates upon the rules.

The fourth Annual Delegate Meeting met in Bristol for five days in September 1893. It tells us that present was Mr Tom Mann, *Treasurer*. But at the end of the opening address by the Bristol District chairman, Mr Tom Mann 'was unanimously elected to the Chair'.

Ben Tillett reported on the employers' offensive against the union, above all in Hull. John Burns delivered a public oration at a mass meeting on the Grove. It was not until the fourth day that Rule XIX was debated, and Tom Mann was then asked 'whether he would act as Honorary President to the Union'.[13] He asked for time to consider the matter. As the vote was taken on the job descriptions of the various posts listed in the rule, Brothers Frith and Krone (of Hull and London) moved that Tom Mann be 'asked to undertake the position of Honorary President'.[14] After he explained that 'he could not undertake any particular work', Mann accepted. When he left early 'to another engagement', there was a vote of thanks for his efforts during the days he had been present.

The ledger book has blank pages which were presumably intended for the fifth Annual Delegate Meeting; there is, however, a printed record. The dockers gathered in Grimsby Town Hall at the end of May 1894. The fourteen delegates came from London (five), Bridgwater, Newport, Hull (two), Gloucester, Swansea, Bristol (two) and Grimsby. A dozen officers and fraternal observers were also present. Although Tom Mann presided, he declined to give a full-scale presidential speech, saying that 'the time of the meeting was valuable'. But the mood of the time can be caught in the remark 'if their meetings did little to push forward the movement it could not be said they hindered it'.

As if to underline its concern for recognition after the débâcle in Hull, much was made of the hospitality of the Grimsby Council in offering their Town Hall as the seat of the conference. The demonstration, for sure, would have been seen across the estuary! The Lord Mayor then made a welcoming speech. It is easy to read all this, in later times, as formality. But it may be truer to see in it an attempt to recover ground which had been burnt flat by the hired men of the Shipping Federation. Be that as it may, the fifth meeting offers a tantalizing picture of a power-struggle in the working of the union.

Why, asked a London delegate, were two minute-secretaries present? Tom McCarthy had been detailed by the Emergency Committee to take the minutes, 'while Bro A. J. Tomkins was here solely on the authority of the General Secretary'. Tillett defended this decision because Tomkins was aware of all the necessary documentation for the work of the ADM. 'If his action . . . was not confirmed,' he said, 'he would take it as an expression of censure on himself'. There followed a brisk scrap, in which only Swansea came out in support of Tillett. Tom McCarthy, Tillett's close friend, spoke: 'The real question was whether any one man should rule the Union; if this was so there was an end to democratic control'.[15] The present work of the general secretary, he went on, took him so much away from the central office that others constantly had to act in his place. Therefore the decisions of the Emergency Committee 'should be obeyed'.[16] The vote went against Tillett: twelve to nil, with two abstentions. To rub it in, it was then unanimously agreed to send Brother Tomkins back to his desk in London the following day.

The more that his people were moved to criticize Tillett, the more insistently they pressed Mann for his attention. Of course, through all this time he was acting as general secretary of the Independent Labour Party, so that, when he met the demands of the docks with the defensive cry that he was busy, we may very well believe him.

In May 1895 the Annual Delegate Meeting was held in Gloucester, with a dozen representatives, plus three Emergency Committee men and four officers. The following year delegates moved to Newport, and the roster increased by one. Tom Mann presided over both meetings, and delivered an important speech to the earlier one. He also remained in office to chair the seventh meeting: but this, which met in Middlesbrough in May 1899, was the first of a new series of conferences to meet triennially. As a result of this changeover, the detailed affairs of the union are chronicled only in a series of Annual Reports, for the years 1896, 1897, 1898 and 1899.

Tillett was very much a sick man, and largely beaten. In 1897, as we have seen, he was advised by his doctor to take a rest, and he set off for New Zealand. It was to be a long stay. He moved on to Australia in the summer of 1897, and then back to New Zealand. An American interlude was proposed, but the voyage never took place because of illness. It was not until October 1898 that Tillett came home to England. This is how it came about that Tom Mann signed the 1896 and 1897 Reports: 'I have stepped in', he wrote, 'to present the report on behalf of the General Office'.[17]

As we have already seen, the port workers were being heavily intimidated during these years. It showed. 'A general dead level of apathy seemed to characterise the vast majority of Port Workers at the beginning of the year', wrote Mann.[18] It implied efforts to join forces with others in the field, and Mann lost no time in seeking to do just that.

Motions encouraging amalgamation with other unions had been approved in 1893 and 1894. Two Hull delegates had moved two motions on federation in 1893. The first proposed joining up with the American Knights of Labour and other dockworkers' unions internationally. It was amended, to be referred to the TUC. The second motion from Hull urged consideration of the need to federate with the Liverpool dockers and the Miners' Federation.[19] This proposal was reaffirmed in 1894, and it was also reported that overtures had been made to the miners and to the American Federation of Labour, without producing a response.

## The Workers' Union

Tom Mann's creative energy had one more moment during this decade: the formation of the Workers' Union in 1898. Its origins lay in the defeat of the engineering unions in the 1897 lock-out, which was attributed – in a widespread debate in the Labour movement – to the sectional, craft structure of the industry's unions. Tom Mann, in calling for the formation of a new union, spoke specifically of the need 'to avenge the engineers' defeat'. In working on the organizational problem, Mann had two models in mind. One, industrial unionism, 'was only just emerging. Scarcely anyone gave serious attention to the matter, as it was felt there was no prospect of success in that direction.'[20] The other, which was also at the time only at an embryonic stage, was an authentically general unionism, and this, in Mann's fertile mind, fitted the need revealed by the structural defects in engineering unionism:

> In the engineering industry, a workman who was on a job for which the recognised union rate was neither paid nor expected was looked upon by the members of the union as an outsider. They made the machine, they would not work the machine, neither would they broaden the basis of their union so that the man who had to work it could be organised in relationship with them. It was the same in every trade, and not more than one-fourth of the adult male population was organised. The proper course, had commonsense prevailed, would have been for the existing unions so to broaden the basis of their organisations as to welcome every worker that came into the industry, and elastic enough for the admission of all. Instead of this, not only was there no provision for an ever-growing number of handy men, which the changing methods made necessary: but between existing unions, each catering for highly-skilled men, there existed an absurd hostility . . . Resolved to face whatever of approval or disapproval it might bring, I determined to attempt at any rate to draft the rules and to prepare the framework of a union that should be open to any section of workers of either sex for whom no proper union already existed.[21]

The objective thus defined by Mann (and it must be stressed that the union was very much his creation from the top down) went far beyond filling the vacuum in the engineering industry. At the founding conference, the object (drafted by Mann) was declared to be: 'The organisation of all sections of the community on an Industrial and Political Basis for the purpose of raising the standard of social life of the workers, and the ultimate realization of an Industrial Commonwealth'.[22] These were the terms and the ideology of the Social Democratic Federation, which had advocated One Big Union for socialist purposes from the 1880s. But the methods of the Workers' Union were to include electoral activity more akin to the ILP. Tom Mann, having been general secretary of the party, had obviously brought over from it not only contacts, but also the skills he had acquired. The union would 'support . . . Labour candidates at all Parliamentary, Municipal, School Board, and other elections'.

To run the provisional machinery of the union, Mann brought in Tom Chambers, an ILP activist, who was by then the secretary of the International Federation in Tillett's absence. Mann left Chambers to organize the central office, whilst he stumped the country to recruit members and found branches. But his lofty and ambitious hopes were frustrated. Many in the ILP and in the existing general unions, such as the National Amalgamated Union of Labour and the Gasworkers' Union, resented the intrusion of a rival union in their fields, and the union commenced business with only a few hundred members. Sustained for a time by Mann's voluntary labours in the field, and by a short trade boom, it reached over 4,000 members by the end of 1899. Thereafter, it went into sharp decline in the early years of the new century, as economic conditions turned downwards again.[23] Its story will be resumed in subsequent chapters, for it was to play a significant role in influencing the future shape of the TGWU after it joined the general union in 1929.

The Workers' Union was not the only response to the defeat of the engineers. The employers, too, drew their own lessons from that episode. After their victories over the engineers in 1897 and the Welsh miners, forced back on the coalowners' terms after a five-month lock-out in 1898, the Employers' Parliamentary Council was formed on 15 November 1898. This council sought to become a national analogue to the Trades Union Congress. At its head stood an executive of eleven people, charged with the monitoring of legislative proposals, and the organization of appropriate lobbies.

## The Long Hunger in the Quarries

The Conservative victory in the General Election of 1895 seemed to the more intransigent employers to be a licence for heightened aggression against trade unionism. Lord Penrhyn's slate quarries at Bethesda were to be chosen as the stage for an exemplary disciplinary sacrifice. The quarrymen had elected a committee to negotiate with Lord Penrhyn, but he declined to recognize it. When, in September 1896, the committee sought an improvement in working conditions, Penrhyn dismissed them.

A strike inevitably followed. It was to last for nearly two years, becoming a *cause célèbre* for trade unionists throughout the kingdom. The *Daily Chronicle* campaigned for the strikers and raised £7,500 for the relief of distress. The Board of Trade made repeated efforts to mediate, but Penrhyn refused any offer of arbitration.

The 1890s had already seen widespread turbulence in the North Wales quarries, but the dispute in Bethesda overshadowed every other strike or lock-out in the region. By January 1897 'more money was coming from outside than from the quarrymen'.[24] Liverpool building workers imposed a levy on themselves and brought their Trades Council into solidarity. The sum of £150 was collected from a teachers' conference. Bethesda choirs went on tour and raised almost £2,500 in collections. Taken together, the strike funds generated almost £20,000.

Lord Penrhyn made four separate attempts to re-open his quarries: in November 1896, and in January, February and April 1897. No local people reported for work, and the only fear that the Bethesda strikers admitted was that outside strike-breakers might be imported. But it was unthinkable that outsiders could be found with any of the requisite skills to produce slates.

The quarry manager, E. A. Young, tried to bring mounted police into the area, and wrote more than once to the chief constable with this aim in view:

> But his evidence was somewhat impressionistic: on a bicycle trip he had noticed that 'some of the men near Bethesda were very sullen', while some strikers . . . had seen fit to shout at him as he rode by. More alarmingly, he reported that when his name had been mentioned at a mass meeting there had been calls of 'shoot him' and 'kill him', while a Welsh newspaper had printed the suggestion that his teeth be knocked out and a knife be stuck in his bowels.[25]

Even without the police, Young's teeth and bowels survived intact through an endless round of completely fruitless negotiations.

Despite the long hunger, the quarrymen remained firm, but their union finally succumbed to political pressures and agreed to settle the strike. The quarrymen's historian tells us that 'it was with some justification . . . that the Bethesda men felt that the agreement had been reached behind their backs.'[26] The manager saw the settlement as 'a complete victory on every point . . . I have no doubt [that] the result of such a beating will be a lesson to have to be content in future when they are well off, but unfortunately, they never seem to realise when they are well off.'[27]

After the return to work, Young set out upon a campaign of victimization and intimidation of the men's leaders. Their chairman was dismissed in December 1898 and the following year another of their spokesmen was victimized. Holidays were annulled by fiat, and a peace offering from the men's committee (in the form of a present for Lord Penrhyn) was peremptorily refused. In these circumstances, it is not altogether surprising that a new leadership began to form among the quarrymen, and that a further round in their long-running struggle with the owners would not long be delayed.

## The Foundation of Ruskin College

On the eve of the new century, another development took place which was to bring about important changes in the recruitment of trade-union personnel, and to change the lives of some trade unionists.

Ruskin College was inaugurated in February 1899, John Ruskin's eightieth birthday. Its founder, Walter Vrooman, an American socialist, was inspired by Ruskin's *Unto this Last*, which made a passionate argument for the improvement of the poor through education: 'Either these poor are of a race essentially different from ours, and unredeemable . . . or else by such care as we have ourselves received we may make them as continent and sober as ourselves – wise and dispassionate as we are – models arduous of imitation.'[28]

At the meeting in Oxford City Hall, a considerable crowd included Ben Tillett, James Sexton and Dan Irving of the Social Democrats. Numerous trades councils and co-operative societies were also represented.[29] The new college was to enjoy a tumultuous existence, and some of its graduates were to have an influence on the future conduct of the TGWU.

## Adapting – and Reacting – to Adversity

The new unions went through their most severe defeat in the decade under review. In the docks and in shipping they nevertheless survived, wherever they had a national dimension. Local and sectional unions, whether in docks or in inland road transport, often collapsed, except amongst specialist groups such as the London stevedores, and amongst watermen and lightermen generally. Their adaptation to adversity took various forms. They created federations at regional or port level nationally and internationally. These never achieved an adequate degree of mobilization against a ruthless, well-financed and above all national employers' body. In any case, in a time of slump, defensive sectionalism, reinforced by the economic climate, was stronger than the instinct of mutual help. Nevertheless, the experiences of federation went into the pool of inheritance waiting to be analysed and drawn on in future. Clem Edwards made a thoughtful appraisal for this purpose.[30]

The new unionists tried, particularly in the case of the Dockers' Union, to broaden the field of recruitment, but they lacked both the resources and the power to persuade large numbers of potential blacklegs in the fields and pastures of Kent and Lincolnshire to make common cause with urban labourers. In South Wales, where the ports had extensive heavy-industrial hinterlands, they had more success – particularly towards the end of the century – in extending recruitment into manufacturing industry, as well as into general labouring – a development full of meaning for the future general union.

Before the Royal Commission, they argued the case for municipal workshops to absorb the labour surplus which sapped their industrial effectiveness, and for municipal ownership and control of the ports. They put forward embryo schemes of planning and rational use of the ports. They sought to practise and develop local schemes of conciliation and arbitration, and, in Tillett's case, proposed a drastic form of compulsory state arbitration. Most of these strategies would be taken up, with more effect, when the economic and political climate changed in the new century.

But above all, the industrial weakness which they now experienced impelled them to use their own influence in changing the political circumstances in which they worked. To this momentous evolution we must now turn.

## Notes

1 Tramway and Horsemen's Half-yearly Reports, 1894 and 1899.
2 Ibid., 1894, p. 3.
3 Royal Commission on Labour, 1892, Q. 17,893; quoted in Arthur Marsh and Victoria Ryan, *Historical Directory of Trade Unions*, vol. III (Gower, 1987), p. 230.
4 Marsh and Ryan, *Historical Directory of Trade Unions*, p. 232.
5 Tramway and Horsemen's Half-yearly Report, 1896, p. 9.
6 Ibid., 1897, p. 10.
7 Ibid., pp. 108–9.
8 Tramway and Horsemen's Half-yearly Report, 1899, p. 127.
9 Tony Corfield, 'The History of the Union: The Metal and Engineering Group', TGWU *Record*, December 1961, p. 37.
10 Roger Moore, *The Emergence of the Labour Party* (Hodder and Stoughton, 1978), p. 45.
11 DWRGWU Annual Delegate Meeting, 1892, Minutes, pp. 18–19. Mather was a liberal employer who actually came to endorse the proposal for the legal eight-hour day; see Henry Pelling, *Social Geography of British Elections* (Macmillan, 1967), pp. 245–6.
12 Ibid., pp. v–31.
13 DWRGWU Annual Delegate Meeting, 1893, Minutes, p. 24.

14   Ibid., p. 25.
15   DWRGWU Annual Delegate Meeting, 1894, Minutes, p. 6.
16   Ibid., p. 7.
17   DWRGWU Annual Report, 1896, p. 5.
18   Ibid.
19   DWRGWU Annual Delegate Meeting, 1893, Minutes, p. 28.
20   Tom Mann, *Memoirs* (1923; reissued McGibbon and Kee, 1967), p. 18.
21   Ibid., pp. 118–19.
22   *Weekly Times and Echo*, 6 February 1898; cited in Richard Hyman, *The Workers' Union* (Oxford University Press, 1971), p. 7.
23   See Hyman, *The Workers' Union*, chapters 1 and 2.
24   R. Merfyn Jones, *The North Wales Quarrymen, 1874–1922* (University of Wales, 1981), p. 188.
25   Ibid., p. 190.
26   Ibid., p. 194.
27   Ibid., p. 195.
28   John Ruskin, *Unto this Last* (Blackfriars, 1862), pp. 111–12.
29   W. W. Craik, *Central Labour College* (Lawrence and Wishart, 1964), p. 35.
30   Clem Edwards, 'Labour Federations', *Economic Journal*, vol. III (September 1893), pp. 408–24.

1 The youngest
pioneers: the
Match-girls of
Bryant & May,
1888.
*Annie Besant,
An Autobiography*

2 The banner of the Social
Democratic Federation.
*National Museum of Labour
History*

Eleanor Marx

3 Eleanor Marx: unpaid strike secretary. *National Museum of Labour History*

Will Thorne

Ben Tillett

Tom Mann

Harry Orbell

4 Leaders for a Generation: Will Thorne, Ben Tillett, Tom Mann and Harry Orbell in 1889. *National Museum of Labour History*

5 The Coal-heavers' Float: demonstrating for the Dock Strike through the City of London, 1889.

6 John Burns addressing the dockers on Tower Hill, 1889 strike. *National Museum of Labour History.*

7 William Collison: Apostle of
Free Labour.

8 Havelock Wilson, an
early portrait.

| District. | Name. | Trade Union. | Address. |
|---|---|---|---|
| **List of Persons willing to speak as advocates of Industrial Syndicalism in their respective districts.** | | | |
| GATESHEAD-ON-TYNE | NED SCOTT | Railway Servants | 3, Fenwick Terrace. |
| SUNDERLAND | WILLIAM KEY | Government Contractor | Walworth Street. |
| MIDDLESBORO | Cr. J. B DAVIES | Dockers Union | 97, Commercial Street |
| HUDDERSFIELD | E. J. B ALLEN | Gasworkers | New Street, Honley. |
| SHEFFIELD | T. J. RING | Cabinet Makers | 138, Scotland Street. |
| OLDHAM | "PIONEER" | Railway Servants | Carr Farm, Diggle. |
| MANCHESTER | HARRY GREEN | Engineers | 122, Heald Pl., Rusholme. |
| Do. | A. A. PURCELL | French Polishers | 142, Gt. Clowes Street, Broughton. |
| Do. | F. W. SANDERSON | Lecturer | 26, Boston Street. |
| LIVERPOOL | FRANK PEARCE | Ships' Stewards | 6, Spekeland Buildings, 22, Canning Place. |
| Do. | PETER LARKIN | Dockers | 36 Gadsby Street. |
| Do. | F. BOWERS | Stonemasons | 11, Ebsey Street. |
| Do. | S. H. MUSTON | Lecturer | 266. Smithdown Lane. |
| NEWPORT (Mon.) | GEORGE JACKSON | Sailors and Firemen | 31, Ruperra Street. |
| Do. | ALFRED COX | Dockers' Union | 49, Raglan Street. |
| Do. | GEORGE COX | Do. do. | 20, Lewis Street. |
| SOUTH WALES — MARDY | NOAH ABLETT | South Wales Miners' Fed. | 97, Griffith Street. |
| SOUTH WALES — PORTH | W. F. HAY | Do. do. | 28, Mount Pleasant. |
| SOUTH WALES — YNYSHIR | GEORGE DOLLING | Do. do. | 11, Upper Gynor Street. |
| SOUTH WALES — CWMPURE | TOM EVANS | Do. do. | 157, Pure Road. |
| SOUTH WALES — CLYDACH VALE | W. H. MAINWARING | Do. do. | 3, Llwynceln Terrace. |
| SOUTH WALES — PONTYPRIDD | JAMES RIGG | Brassfounders | 20, Brookes Terrace, Tower Street. |
| PORT TALBOT | Cr. JONAH CHARLES | Dockers' Union | 20, Station Road. |
| LONDON | A ELSBURY | Tailors | 51, Jamaica Street, Stepney, E. |
| SOUTHAMPTON | R. W. STORRY | Ships' Stewards | 8. Terminus Terrace |
| Do. | THOMAS GARNETT | Moulders | 39. College Street |

9 (above) Advocates of syndicalism: from the first issue of *The Industrial Syndicalist*, July 1910.

10 Strike-breakers and their Protectors. Free labourers and police escort waiting for action on the *Lady Jocelyn* during the Liverpool strike, 1911 (see text, p.244). *Reproduced by permission of the General Council of British Shipping*

**11** The Liverpool strikers on 'Bloody Sunday', 13 August 1911, in St George's Square. *Reproduced by permission of the General Council of British Shipping*

**12** Police, cavalry and soldiers with fixed bayonets escort a convoy past a strikers' meeting: Liverpool 1911. *Press Association*

**13** A Liverpool docker confronts the young soldiers sent to break the strike, 1911. *TGWU*

**14** Out in Sympathy: Cardiff coal-trimmers march in support of the dockers, 1911.

# 7

# Independent Labour Politics

## I

A whole decade was to elapse between the birth of the new unions and the formation of the Labour Party, or, to be more precise, its foreshadowing Labour Representation Committee, in 1900. During that time, as we have seen, the employers mounted a ferocious counteroffensive, which, conjoined with severe unemployment, weakened all unions in some respects and hit some of the newest unions particularly hard. Notwithstanding this fact, overall union membership grew, and the Trades Union Congress, although it was never controlled by new unionism, found itself under relentless pressure, from new and old unions alike, to adopt a more committed political posture.

### Government (and Empire) in the 1890s

Most of the first half of the decade saw a weak Liberal government becoming increasingly feeble and beleaguered. During the second half, the Conservatives ruled. The Liberals had regained office in 1892 after careful attempts had been made to attract and hold the Labour vote. In their 'Newcastle Programme', aimed directly at working-class voters, it was pledged that plural voting would be eliminated, and implied that action might be initiated on the question of shorter working hours. Other ameliorative measures were also promised.

In retrospect, the resultant administration of 1892 was often described as 'an interlude' during what would otherwise have been two decades of Conservative hegemony. Gladstone, who resumed the premiership more than halfway through his eighty-third year, was to be haunted from start to finish of his new term by the question of Ireland. Because Liberal Unionists had rebelled and found their own identity, he was now dependent on Irish support. Irish Nationalists numbered eighty-one in the new Parliament. New unionists – or rather spokesmen for new unionists, as distinct from old trade unionists running on a Liberal ticket – had won three seats. Of these, only one was solidly committed to independent Labour action. Gladstone, the Grand Old Man, still towered over rivals, but neither parliamentary arithmetic nor the calendar was on his side. Home Rule dominated his agenda, and he succeeded in completing his Bill, through all stages, only to encounter a resolute veto from the House of Lords.

Having failed to disengage from Ireland, British colonists fanned out on other fronts. Imperialism continued to roll over Africa, assimilating Uganda and following Cecil Rhodes into the Transvaal, Mashonaland and Matabeleland. Machine-gun bullets were traded against diamonds and gold. The Boer War was being prepared, inexorably. As the Liberals were about to fall in 1895, W. T. Stead reported a conversation in which Rhodes told him:

> I was in the East End of London yesterday and attended a meeting of the unemployed. I listened to the wild speeches, which were just a cry for 'bread', 'bread', 'bread', and on my way home I pondered over the scene and I became more than ever convinced of the importance of imperialism . . . My cherished idea is a solution for the social problem . . . to save the 40,000,000 inhabitants of the United Kingdom from a bloody civil war, we colonial statesmen must acquire new lands for settling the surplus population, to provide new markets for the goods produced in the factories and mines. The Empire is a bread and butter question . . . If you want to avoid civil war, you must become imperialists.[1]

This shameless utterance was seized upon by socialist writers and has remained well remembered because it found its way into Lenin's little book on *Imperialism*. But in reality, Rhodes's colonization was an idea most imperfectly realized. To be sure, American immigration was being wound down in response to the economic squeeze: ostensibly it was possible to argue that the British 'surplus population' needed somewhere else to go.[2] But no such large-scale movement of people towards Southern Africa was actually to follow, partly because demographic changes in the home territory eased migratory pressures, but also in large part because the African annexations were not undertaken to deal with population overspill: they were almost entirely the result of greed for mineral resources. By the same token, new markets would be somewhat slow to materialize in this region. Neither of these facts prevented the expression of imperial 'concern' for the relatively few British migrants, and this solicitude was to puff itself up into the provocation of actual war before the end of the decade.

What was really going on was a helter-skelter competition to grab whatever territory was not already taken. Each European power was chiefly concerned to plant its own claims before the others. In Britain successive governments, of both parties, gave their blessing to this enterprise. While the accompanying noise of jingo patriotism was often deafening, costing them some damage in moral terms, the tangible benefits to the London poor (or indeed to the submerged third of the population in all Britain's major cities) were absolutely negligible. However, no worry on this account emerged to prevent Lord Rosebery, Gladstone's Liberal successor (who took office in March 1894), from embracing the imperial ethos with all possible fervour. In some ways he outdid Cecil Rhodes. On Irish questions this mattered considerably. Rhodes, for all his imperial fervour, had not only endorsed Parnell, but had actually contributed a cheque for £10,000 to his campaign in 1888.[3] Rosebery showed no such weakness. Indeed, this contributed to the short life of his administration, because once the Lords had seen off Gladstone's Irish Bill, Rosebery's studied equivocations about Home Rule brought mutiny among a vital contingent within his majority. In June 1895 he was defeated on a snap vote. The election which followed produced a decisive turn to the Conservatives, and Lord Salisbury became Prime Minister.

The main domestic achievement of the Liberal administrations of 1892–5 had been in the field of local-government reform. The Fowler Act of 1894 established a tier of urban and rural district councils which was to endure until 1974. For the first time a handful of women were actually allowed to vote, and stand for office, in local elections, without any marriage bar. This was to give a notable impulse to the movement for women's suffrage.

Apart from this, the House of Lords killed off an Employers' Liability Bill which had been energetically promoted by Asquith. Death duties were introduced in Harcourt's budget. Nothing much happened about the balance of the Newcastle Programme. Both of the key questions which mattered to Labour, concerning plural voting and shorter hours, were shelved as soon as the votes were in the tin. For all those concerned with the interests of Labour, or with the Irish question, this cumulative record may well have seemed less than inspiring. Only among the miners, whose resistance to a general lock-out in 1893 was strong enough to bring in Rosebery as a government mediator, was there anything to rejoice about.[4] That Lord Rosebery's lucky horses went on to win two successive victories in the Derby, after he had become Prime Minister, probably estranged a greater number of nonconformist voters than those who admired his good fortune with the turf accountants.

## Turning to Politics

As we have seen, the industrial luck of the dockers and other waterfront unions did not endure for long. Not only did the employers counterattack with great brutality, but in many places the unions were trodden flat. Some of the most belligerent of the bosses were shipowners and prominent Liberals. Such local tycoons did not scruple to provoke disputes and then call upon their town mayors for full police and military support. Even had they not been predisposed to political action, the dockers' leaders would have been forced into it by the resulting shocks.

Weakened as they were by the loss of membership which we have already reported, these leaders none the less had star quality, not only because each was a remarkable personality, but also as a result of the public impact which their conduct of the great strike had made.

Paul Thompson, the historian of the London socialist movement, recognizes the importance of Burns, Mann and Tillett in the struggle for Labour representation, but believes that their influence 'was reduced by their political inconsistency'. They were socialists, he writes, 'but of a peculiarly individualistic kind. Burns' egotism was already drawing him towards the Liberal Party.' Mann, he sees as being no better at all: 'restless and erratic', indeed, turning 'from the Dockers to the London Trades Council', then agitating for the reform of the Amalgamated Society of Engineers. 'Between 1891 and 1894', continues Thompson, Mann

> worked as a member of the Royal Commission on Labour, at the same time acting as secretary of the L.C.C. Progressive Party organisation. After announcing that he was considering ordination as an Anglican priest, he became secretary of the Independent Labour Party in 1894. Three years later he returned to trade unionism to work for the International Federation of Ship, Dock and River Workers, but this required much time abroad, and after a brief return to politics as secretary of the radical National Democratic League, he set off in 1901 for nine years in Australia and South Africa.

Then there was Tillett, who

> kept to his post of Dockers' secretary, but he too was abroad between 1895 and 1898 on account of ill-health, and proved a somewhat erratic political rebel. He stood as an independent Labour candidate at Bradford in 1892 and soon dropped out of the L.C.C. when he realised its dependence on the progressives. He was 'never a Lib–Lab'. But his socialism was based on confused emotion, and his exhortations in the union's annual reports on 'the ethical conception of duty', and a trades unionism 'not limited to the mere sordid sphere', obscure his protests against the status of the worker as 'a mere wages slave'.

All this, the indictment continues, disrupted the organization at lower levels:

> As a result of this lack of an effective lead from Burns, Tillett and Mann, other leading officials of the Dockers can be found playing somewhat

contradictory political roles. Harry Kay, the union treasurer, after dabbling in Fabianism turned to the I.L.P. and eventually became a Social Democrat. Clem Edwards, an early independent Labour man, became Labour editor of the radical *Sun* in 1893 and stood as a Liberal–Labour candidate for Tottenham in 1895.[5]

## The Scope and Limits of Inconsistency

It would of course be difficult, and even pointless, to deny inconsistencies in some of these actions. To seek to impose too much order on this record would be to misrepresent it. But if we examine these events with care, it is arguable that there were fewer contradictions in them than some historians have believed: and that these were far from disabling. First, however, we will look at the element of truth in the indictment.

Tillett's politics in the late 1880s were fluid, as we have already pointed out. In the beginning, he was something of a Lib.–Lab.: but he changed his mind. During this later time, into the 1890s, we might be excused the claim that he had found, for a short but crucial period, a framework of independent Labour action and advocacy which was both resilient and influential. In his later life, Tillett certainly allowed his earlier flamboyance to run unchecked, and he was often wildly unpredictable. Inconsistency, during these convulsions, would come to seem the least of his various vices. His more dramatic twists and turns ensured that he would be right at least some of the time. Now and then the clouds parted, and the sun shone through. What seems very evident is that Tillett's younger days were clearer, and less steamy, than his middle age. Throughout most of the 1890s he followed a relatively steady course, in spite not only of illness but also of the most vigorous assaults from his union's many adversaries. Tillett, like others of his generation, was not only himself self-educated, but was also operating among people who had been denied any chance of instruction and who were prone to respond to all the more crude appeals of demagogy. Continued melodrama sustained a whole generation of leaders who were indeed considerably larger than life. When we come to meet rogues like 'Captain' Tupper, we shall appreciate this: but we need to examine Tillett's contribution before judging it.

As for Burns, his egotism may be recognized, but his move towards the Liberals represented more than personal ambition. The thought of breaking the Lib.–Lab. integument presented real problems for the socialist new unionists. What were men like Burns to do? Their Fabian advisers encouraged them to rely on the goodwill of the younger Liberal radicals, which was not illusory. At the same time, old 'liberal' employers had not the least intention of encouraging their employees to think very actively about their rights. Without independent political organization there could be no change of social direction, but to bring about a new alignment was no simple matter. That this task made it necessary on the Labour side to persuade colleagues in the old organizations to adopt a new style, from the TUC Congress Hall outwards to the branch rooms, meant that dialogue was, for the new leaders, unavoidable. But in the absence of a firm and established centre, the socialist argument needed a more than resilient faith to endure the oppositional pressures to which it would be subjected. Notwithstanding his considerable flair for dramatic action, John Burns lacked the kind of compass which could help him steer through this terrain.

Burns, however, was to end his direct association with the Dockers' Union, if not a lifelong interest in its fate, when he ceased to be its trustee. While no one can deny his part in the events of 1889, his personal engagement thereafter was transitory.

Tillett, by contrast, was to remain general secretary of the Dockers' Union right up to the moment of amalgamation in 1922. Mann became founder of another major organization, the Workers' Union, which was also later to merge with the Transport and General Workers' Union; he also stood in for Tillett when he was forced to convalesce in New Zealand after 1896. If this were not enough, he was again to stand at Tillett's side throughout the formation of the Transport Workers' Federation in 1910, the upheavals of 1911 and the volcanic subsequent reappearance of all the aspirations of 1889. In all the dawn years of independent Labour representation, the big three leaders of the dock strike had a magic appeal: but twenty years on there was still a powerful duo, and their alliance was still enough to shake the complacency of some very powerful people and give heart to all the outcasts living in the margins of the world of labour. Some people will think that there is some consistency within this whole span.

## How to Look for Consistency

But we are here concerned with a shorter timescale, and it is in the career of Mann during the initial struggle for Labour representation that we may see the most steadfast continuity, if only we appreciate the task he had in hand. This was precisely to join together the many strands of action and argument which could integrate a new political force. For this reason we are bound to fault the accusation of inconsistency in his case: it makes no sense to present his different fields of work as areas of conflict in his own commitment. His project was one of linkage and persuasion. He had to organize the unorganized, but also to win over his colleagues in the established movement. He had to co-ordinate the most systematic use of the wider franchise and of the extension of local democratic powers. He had to engage with all the currents of thought which moved other social forces in the same direction as that which he had chosen for himself.

It is therefore hardly reasonable to reproach Mann for 'turning from the Dockers to the London Trades Council'. In fact he was the natural spokesman of no fewer than thirty-two of the Dockers' branches which affiliated to the Trades Council in 1890,[6] by which time Mann himself had already been elected to the executive. The decline of the union under the combined weight of recession and the employers' backlash lapsed twenty of these branches in 1893. But it did not lapse Mann, who had already played a major role in reshaping the policy and action of the Council. In doing so, he was making space for a whole generation of new activists. That he coupled this role with his campaign for office in the Amalgamated Society of Engineers speaks of his considerable energy, but betrays no inconsistency at all. The new unionists were seeking to win over the old, and Mann's election organizer among the engineers, George Barnes, was himself to win the general secretaryship only five years later. The dalliance between Mann and the Church followed its active role in the dock strike, but also registered the involvement of concerned young clergymen in the efforts to structure the Dockers' Union.[7] His secretaryship of the Independent Labour Party we shall consider later; it is enough here to say that it gave the new party a decisive push towards the unions, without which the ILP could never have broken from the ghetto surrounding a smallish socialist society into the new milieu of a Labour Party representing the interests and at times shaping the hopes of an entire social class.

The effort to persuade the craftsmen's societies involved the new unionists in active participation in every forum in which they were to be found associated. Inevitably this argued for all-out participation in the work of the Trades Councils and of the TUC. Since so much of Tom Mann's earlier work had hinged around the campaign for a legal eight-hour day, it was unsurprising that the base of the new large-scale associations of dockers and gasworkers should be seen as home ground from which to widen out the attack. The campaign fanned out in a variety of linked assaults. Local agitation, often through Trades Councils, sought to establish the eight-hour day in local-government employment of all kinds. Later, Burns was to add the support of his local-government constituency by monitoring new contracts agreed with the London County Council. At the same time, local campaigning could be linked with national and international issues, first by organizing support for the institution of May Day as a celebration of the worldwide Labour movement for shorter hours, and then by seeking their acceptance of parliamentary and local electoral contests around the same theme. This pattern repeated itself in towns all across the country. In London, Tom Mann went to the Trades Council to form a succession of instruments to help the work forward.

The general platform of this strategy was outlined in the pamphlet on the new unionism which Mann and Tillett had drafted in reply to Shipton, the secretary of the Council: 'Our contention is that at least 500,000 of London's Workers might be organised in bona fide labour organisations, that they might be affiliated to the London Trades Council, and that if this were so, an enormous change for the better might come about.'[8] This 'parliament of London Labour' would give assistance to every union which needed it. It would discharge a series of educational and organizational responsibilities to service all affiliates. Even though efforts to replace Shipton were beaten off from 1890 onwards, until he finally resigned in 1896 with 'a glowing testimonial on vellum and a cheque',[9] the composition of the executive was radically changed. In 1890 a lecture bureau was established to proselytize. Sub-committees to deal with problems in groups of similar trades were set up. Thousands of pounds were collected and distributed in mutual aid for strike and distress funds. Very substantial sums were sent to Australia to support the maritime strikers, in gratitude for their earlier help to the London dockers. As we have already seen, the Council seconded Fred Hammill to help organize the busmen during and after their 1891 dispute.

## The Legal Eight-hour Day

The Socialist International had launched the call for the legal eight-hour day at its first Congress of 1889. It was to form the platform of an international demonstration on May Day 1890. Eleanor Marx set about organizing a rally in Hyde Park, and the Trades Council was invited to join. It proposed instead, on Tom Mann's suggestion, to organize the event itself. But the Council favoured only the principle of the shorter working day, 'leaving the precise method to the future', and the Demonstration Committee did not find this acceptable. Consequently there emerged instead a double demonstration, half a million strong, where a series of platforms put the case for the legal eight-hour day, or for shorter hours, according to the convictions of the various organizers:

> Eleanor Marx made one of the most widely reported speeches. 'We have not come to do the work of political parties, but we have come here in the cause of labour, in its own defence, to demand its own rights. I can remember when we came in handfuls of a few dozen to Hyde Park to demand an Eight Hours' Bill, but the dozens have grown to hundreds, and the hundreds to thousands, until we have this magnificent demonstration that fills the park today. We are standing face to face with another demonstration, but I am glad to see that the great masses of the people are on our side. Those of us who have gone through all the worry of the Dock

Strike, and especially the Gasworkers' Strike, and have seen the men, women and children stand round us, have had enough of strikes, and we are determined to secure an eight hours' day by legal enactment; unless we do so, it will be taken from us at the first opportunity. We will only have ourselves to blame if we do not achieve the victory which this great day could so easily give us. There is in the park this afternoon a man whom Mr. Gladstone once imprisoned – Michael Davitt; but Mr. Gladstone is now on the best of terms with him. What do you suppose is the reason for the change? Why has the Liberal Party been so suddenly converted to Home Rule? Simply because the Irish people sent 80 members to the House of Commons to support the Conservatives; in the same way we must kick these Liberal and Radical members out if they refuse to support our programme. I am speaking this afternoon not only as a Trade Unionist, but as a Socialist. Socialists believe that the eight hours' day is the first and most immediate step to be taken, and we aim at a time when there will no longer be one class supporting two others, but the unemployed both at the top and at the bottom of society will be got rid of. This is not the end but only the beginning of the struggle; it is not enough to come here to demonstrate in favour of an eight hours' day. We must not be like some Christians who sin for six days and go to church on the seventh, but we must speak for the cause daily, and make the men, and especially the women that we meet, come into the ranks to help us.

> 'Rise like Lions after slumber
> In unvanquishable number,
> Shake your chains to earth like dew
> Which in sleep had fallen on you –
> Ye are many – they are few.'[10]

'We' were indeed many, and the euphoria of the event convinced Shipton himself that this was 'a brilliant success'.[11] It was brilliant enough to mandate the Council's TUC delegates to abandon their caution about how to approach the goal, and to plump for the legal eight-hour day without reservations. Mann was thus enabled to win a major victory at the Congress, and Broadhurst, the very figurehead of the old guard, resigned from his secretaryship of its Parliamentary Committee.

But the eight-hour-day campaign was not unreservedly popular among casual, low-paid, seasonally employed people. It was reported that members of the Dockers' Union went so far as to vote against it, on the grounds that it was 'not appropriate for dock work', to the great delight of George Howell, who celebrated this decision with a considerable fanfare in the book he wrote to attack the new unions.[12] Even among the gasworkers, Eleanor Marx had to enter a public exchange of letters with George Elleston, a branch secretary of her own union. Elleston wrote:

It seems to me that the legal eight hours' day has emanated from the mechanical class. It will, I think, suit them well. Their wages average from

38s. to £2. 10s. per week. They would save in one week as much as some unskilled labourers earn, our expenses are as great as theirs, the same amount of food and clothing are required for us. There are hundreds of very intelligent men among the unskilled labourers who would not be slow to avail themselves of anything that would tend to better their condition, and it would not be necessary to be continually trying to knock the legal eight hours into their heads. I have not heard one advocate it yet, and until I do, I have not much faith in it. First of all let us, through our organisations, get a sufficient wage to live without working overtime, and then we can see about the legal eight hours.[13]

In reply, Eleanor Marx was disappointingly formal. She showed that indeed the measure was official policy, but she did not give George Elleston an answer to his arguments. There followed a correspondence in the *People's Press* in which other members took Elleston's part, so much so that he himself wrote to express his very good opinion of Eleanor Marx and his pleasure at having provoked a discussion. That his views had wide support was to be shown again the following year, when the London busmen struck for shorter hours, won, and shortly afterwards bartered them away for increases in pay.

Yet many of those dockers, gasworkers and busmen would have been present in the Hyde Park festival of May Day 1890, and most would have been touched by its effect. The political claim for shorter hours was not unpopular, to put it mildly: but it was not easy to realize. The industrial claim for decent minimum earnings was equally difficult to assert, as the economic tides turned against Labour, while strike-breakers were marshalled behind forces armed with truncheons, pistols and bayonets. And it was against this bitter reality that the banners of the new unions regrouped for a counteroffensive aimed at the political powers. The turn to politics, as often happened before, resulted from industrial weakness, not strength.

For this, Tom Mann and Fred Hammill prepared the London Trades Council by establishing in 1891 its own Labour Representation League, with a fund to give it reality. By the 1892 LCC elections, not only were several candidates elected, but factory collections were instituted to maintain them while they performed their new duties. Amongst these duties was the promotion of the eight-hour day.

## II

### Founding the Independent Labour Party

'The ILP was founded, I think, in 1892. It was founded, or started, by seven men. I believe I was one of the seven; but I am not sure and it does not matter.'[14] Such modesty was not characteristic of everyone who took part in this process, and there is no doubt that Robert Blatchford could afford modesty, because his role could never plausibly be gainsaid. His newspaper, *Clarion*, became far more than a broadsheet. *Clarion* vans and *Clarion* cycling clubs carried the socialist message from town to town, and far out into the villages. Blatchford, however, had perhaps forgotten the date of at least this of his good works, which began in Bradford on 13 and 14 January 1893. Perhaps, of course, he was referring to the foundation during the previous year in Manchester of the local ILP. If we agree that the names of the 'seven' do not matter, it is still very necessary to remember where they came from. Whichever way we look at the question, we find that all the possible candidates were profoundly influenced by the new unions. We also find that the dockers' leaders were in the front rank of these.

It would hardly be an accident if Blatchford's memory tripped him. The year 1892 was indeed the one during which Labour burst in upon Parliament. Previously, Lib.–Lab. members had been elected as part of the Liberal slate, and were therefore subject to an external discipline. But the entry to Parliament of Keir Hardie, John Burns and Havelock Wilson in the General Election of 1892 was something different, and it was instantly symbolized by Hardie's alleged 'cloth cap', when he presented himself in Westminster in what was considered unconventional dress. Myth apart, the election of Burns and Wilson was only a partial discontinuity in the Lib.–Lab. tradition, and the subsequent careers of the two men have persuaded most historians that it was a lesser matter than it seemed at the time. But it is important to recall the circumstances of the early 1890s. Both these men stood as intransigent new unionists, and were seen as having dislodged an avalanche which was to transform the prospects of the Labour movement. As is often the case, however, the real changes lay further below the surface.

Keir Hardie won the seat of West Ham South. No one denies that he, at least, stood for a new beginning. Yet at first 'He was a total stranger with an almost strange programme', wrote Ben Tillett. 'Mann, Thorne, Burns or myself could have been chosen in place of the young Scotsman who was to make political history; but we felt that our work at that time called us to another stage.'[15] During the dock strike Tillett had been approached by the Liberals to contest Battersea, but he had declined. Burns won the nomination, and the seat, in his place.

## The New Unions and Local Government

But the spade-work in both constituencies owed much to the organized effort of the new unions. The month after the dock strike, the Gasworkers' Union won two seats on the Barking School Board, and held a torchlight rally of 10,000 people to mark the occasion.[16] Before the end of the year West Ham Council had four new unionists, among whom were Thomas Walsh, the London secretary of the Sailors' and Firemen's Union, and George Lambert, a Canning Town docker who had been supported by the gasworkers. William Athey, of the General Railway Workers' Union, made a third. Three more candidates were elected in 1890, in Kensington North, Camberwell and Mile End. Eleven followed the next year, after Tom Mann joined forces with Will Steadman of the Bargebuilders' Union to promote their political campaign under the sponsorship of the London Trades Council, which, greatly reinforced by new Dockers' and Gasworkers' branches, set up the Labour Representation League to which we have already referred. In November 1891 candidates of this body polled more than 10,000 votes in eleven wards. Nine Labour men followed through on to the London County Council in the election of 1892. Ben Tillett was then co-opted as an alderman.

## Parliamentary Campaigning in London

West Ham contained a large population of dockers, gasworkers and Irish people. By 1892 Will Thorne and six other Labour men sat on the Municipal Council. In short, this was one of the few areas where the new unions could make an important difference. Hardie came to it through contact with Burns and with independent radicals like the Christian Socialist Frank Smith.[17] His programme included a strong commitment to the eight-hour day, and his campaign involved a whole series of dock-gate meetings and trade union rallies. At one of these, 'The platform was a full-sized lifeboat, rigged with mast and ropes and gay with streamers and manned by a crew in uniform. I understand it came from the Tidal Basin branch of the Seamen's and Firemen's Union.'[18]

The banners and insignia of the new unions were everywhere during the rallies before polling day, alongside those of the Temperance movement, which also gave its strong support. It is necessary to add that the suicide of the prospective Liberal candidate, Hulme Webster, and the disarray of his local supporters contributed much to Hardie's victory, and that he was careful to tread a conciliatory path during his speeches on the hustings. None the less, alongside him on these platforms stood Thorne and Tillett, who must have struck fear into the hearts of the Liberal 'shopocracy', who had already expressed misgivings because their former candidate had, they thought, given too much support to the dockers only three years before.

John Burns had already been elected to the London County Council before he became the star of the dock strike. He nursed the Battersea constituency carefully, and kept up a constant dialogue with his supporters, reporting back profusely. In 1890 Lord Rosebery, a great power in the LCC, had offered him the Liberal candidature in Bristol.

He declined, as he also declined the Liberal nomination in Battersea itself. He was determined to stand, he said, as a socialist. In the 1892 LCC elections ten Labour candidates were given a free run against the Conservatives, the Liberals having stood down. Seven of these went to the polls with active support from the Liberal organization in their areas. Burns relied instead on his own caucus, the Battersea Labour League.

Whilst this group was solid enough to organize a London election and subsequent victory, it was severely stretched by a parliamentary campaign. Already it carried the burden of raising Burn's weekly salary as a London spokesman, which cost £2 10s. a week. For a national contest, £300 were needed. Burns rejected various offers of Liberal money, but accepted £100 from Champion, having satisfied himself that it was untainted: the 'Tory gold' furnished to socialists in the 1885 contest was still a live stigma, and was to burst into very real flames early in the life of the infant ILP.

Burns's campaign opened in June 1892. It was nothing if not catholic in sponsorship. Messages of endorsement came from Engels, Kautsky and the Marx-Avelings. On the inaugural platform sat the outgoing Liberal Member, O. V. Morgan, alongside George Bernard Shaw and Will Crooks, recently elected as the Woolwich councillor, for Labour. 'Burns's programme was equally mixed. As he told one audience, "in things electoral he was a Radical, in things dealing with Government a Republican, in things social and economic he was a socialist, but in all things he was for Labour night and day".[19] All this scandalized the opposition, and provoked cries of foul play. But the result was a clear and unquestionable victory: a majority of more than 1,500 in an electorate of less than 10,000.

Burns's parliamentary career thus began on 5 August 1892, and was to take him to great heights. But his involvement in the cause of the socialist movement was to become more and more attenuated, and his main radical achievements during the following years were in the fields of local government and the trade unions, notwithstanding his new parliamentary limelight. On the London County Council he pioneered an intervention-ist policy of what would later be called contract-compliance, direct-labour and fair-wages resolutions. Each of these was to have considerable influence in the world of local government during the following years. But the scope for such measures in an overwhelmingly indifferent or hostile Parliament was, to put it mildly, limited. Burns's repeated forays for eight-hours legislation were largely propagandistic, and those concessions he could secure were entirely dependent on the goodwill of sympathetic Liberals. So it was that, while Keir Hardie was moving round the country to recruit an Independent Labour Party, John Burns was invited to a dinner with Gladstone and offered a junior portfolio (which he declined) when Lord Rosebery took over the premiership in 1894.

In this evolution, Burns maintained a cordial and respectful relationship with Havelock Wilson, but became daily more estranged from Keir Hardie.

In 1890, after repeated urging from his friend and ally Samuel Plimsoll, the Seamen's Union leader, Havelock Wilson agreed to seek election to Parliament. Highly articulate shipowners were already strongly represented, and their immense wealth ensured that they were a doubly effective lobby. Plimsoll wanted a counterweight in order to press forward his own campaign for reforming legislation, which was contested every step of the way. A by-election in East Bristol provided an opportunity. 'I made what I now look back upon as one of my great blunders . . .' wrote Wilson. 'The result gave me a first-class shock. The Radical candidate was returned with about three thousand majority . . . and I had to be satisfied with six hundred and fifty votes . . . each vote recorded for me cost about one pound three shillings and sevenpence-halfpenny'.[20]

From the vantage-point of experience, Plimsoll thought this 'a magnificent show'. Clearly Wilson was not discouraged, because after two years he became Member for Middlesbrough: 'Much of my success . . . was due to the fact that I was sentenced to six weeks' imprisonment, and I often remarked . . . after, "If you want to get into Parliament get into gaol first." '[21]

Wilson's imprisonment had followed a strike-breaking attempt by the Shipping Federation in Cardiff. Sixty-two seamen had been recruited at North and South Shields on the false prospectus of jobs in Tilbury. When they entrained they found themselves *en route* for South Wales. They cabled strike headquarters during the journey, and were met by more than 1,000 pickets. Almost all of them immediately joined up with the union men, and paraded the city with Tom Mann, Ben Tillett and Wilson himself. It was, it seemed, a famous victory. Then Wilson was charged with unlawful assembly and riot, and subsequently he was sent to prison. This provoked a general sense of outrage in the Labour movement, since the charges had no reasonable foundation. Wilson entered the Middlesbrough contest as hero of the hour.

Militant though he was, however, Havelock Wilson had no socialist sympathies, even if, at the time, he had many socialist friends. Yet we should not ignore the fact that he was the only one of the three victorious Labour independents who actually stood against, and defeated, a Liberal opponent.

## Tillett's Campaign in Bradford

A different story was unfolding in Bradford, where Ben Tillett himself was standing.

Bradford was quick to feel the influence of the new unions, but although union membership rose sharply under their influence, and notably under the weight of the Gasworkers and General Labourers, headed by Paul Bland, there were other forces leading to the radicalization of the Labour movement:

Ironically, it was the older crafts which provided substantial support and leadership for the independent movement – and this despite the obvious difficulties and splits within their own ranks. The changing economic circumstances, technological threats, the menace of new industries and new ways of making standard products, and perhaps as important though less explored, the polarisation of the classes achieved in the more stable circumstances of late-nineteenth-century Bradford provided the backdrop to a rapid succession of events.[22]

Already in 1889 a running battle had opened in the Trades Council, in which its more conventional Liberal leaders were acrimoniously challenged. This might have spent itself in a long faction fight but for the effect, in 1890 and afterwards, of the general import taxes imposed by the United States, under President William McKinley, to stimulate its own industry. In Bradford this meant trouble. On 16 December 1890, S. C. Lister and Co. of Manningham Mills announced reductions in wages ranging between 15 per cent and one-third, hitting the silk- and plush-weavers with various degrees of severity.[23] Tariffs notwithstanding, and strikes notwithstanding either, the company was later to pay an 8 per cent dividend to shareholders on the results of that year's work. But the workers, who were completely unorganized at the moment that the cuts took effect, promptly struck and maintained a remarkable strike right through Christmas and on to April 1891. By the time it ended, sympathy action and lock-outs had combined to secure the complete stoppage of all workers at the mills. Over nineteen weeks, more than £11,000 was raised in strike funds by the Trades Council itself, the Yorkshire Miners' Association and trade unions all around the country. Quickly the spokesmen of independent Labour action became acknowledged leaders of the dispute. Their names were to have national impact, in some cases for decades: they included W. H. Drew, F. W. Jowett and Ben Turner. For the most part, the local Liberal establishment rallied closely around the mill-owners, with the result that the conflict involved not only industrialists but also the political leadership of the district, the 'Millocracy'. This was a close-knit and powerful Liberal mafia. Policing was tough, and when the military were called in crowds were driven at bayonet-point down the narrow streets, reminding one witness of 'scenes from the French Revolution'.[24]

At a great protest rally the idea of the Bradford Labour Union came into existence. Even the Power Loom Overlookers' Union, a typical craft organization if ever there was one, subsequently issued a strong formal condemnation of the Town Council for calling in the troops. Charlie Glyde summed up the mood: 'We have had two parties in the past; the can'ts and the won'ts and it's time we had a party that will.'[25]

It was in this heady atmosphere that the *Yorkshire Factory Times*, announcing on May Day 1891 that the strike was over, gave it the warning epitaph: 'Labour has so associated itself that even defeat must be victory'.[26]

The Labour Union formed itself officially on 28 May, and within a little more than a year its supporters had taken over the Trades Council. Ben Tillett was a natural candidate for such a group. But he declined the offer when it first came that May: it had to be pressed home repeatedly before he accepted it three months later.[27]

Initially it was proposed that the dockers' leader should contest Bradford East, where he could have a clear run without Liberal intervention. But his sponsors, and he himself, preferred a challenge and opted instead for a real confrontation with the Liberals in Bradford West, the seat of Alfred Illingworth. Illingworth was not only the party boss; he was also Bradford's largest employer. This contest was, at the local level, to divide the Labour supporters from any lingering Liberal affinities which may have survived the shock of the strike; and nationally it was to cause some embarrassment to those Labour supporters who did not wish to burn their bridges to Liberalism. Sidney Webb wrote to Beatrice to say that he could 'see no alternative' to supporting Tillett.[28] He and Bernard Shaw both made the trip to Bradford in the first months of 1892. So did Tom Mann and Tom McCarthy of the Dockers' Union. But while the Fabians travelled in some apprehension, the new unionists were spoiling for a fight. Thus we find Webb speaking in Bradford about his own membership of the National Liberal Club and a variety of other well-known Liberal organizations, and begging votes for Tillett, whose candidature was best not merely for Labour, 'but for Liberalism itself'. By contrast, Tillett laid about himself with a stout stick: 'Fifty years ago the land owning interest was opposed to the middle class capitalists. The former had either died out or gambled away their wealth . . . The rich capitalist was now replacing the old landlord, and he generally took into possession of the land less conscience . . . There was then no Liberalism or Toryism, but there was capitalism.'[29]

'Cheers,' reported the journalist who transcribed these remarks. Illingworth had little enough to cheer, however. Forced on to the defensive, he had to explain why he did not support the raising of the school-leaving age to twelve, but would compromise by agreeing that children might remain in school until they were eleven. That he was himself a large-scale employer of child labour would have been known to all the members of his audience, although it might have been thought impolite to say so. Tillett, however, was an uninhibited campaigner.

It is not difficult to imagine his joyous response to Illingworth's announced belief that wages were perfectly adequate, but for the demon drink. In opposition to this, Tillett was for a bold legislative programme of reforms:

> He wanted factory legislation. He wanted machinery to be protected, proper sanitary arrangements to be made, the separation of sexes, the appointment of women as inspectors, and an obligation on the part of the employer to supply an exact statement of work given out and the wages paid for it without being asked for it . . . He wanted the people to have the land and the money.[30]

At Bradford, in sum, the cutting edge of the campaign drove in the direction of separating Labour voters from the Liberal influence. Whilst Keir Hardie and John Burns remained unopposed by Liberal candidates, their appeal sought to occlude divisions and to mobilize as many Liberal voters in their cause as possible. In this sense Tillett's defeat – by no great margin (557 votes) – marked an extraordinary breakthrough. 'The light will come', he told rejoicing crowds. 'We shall not be long before we shall . . . shout "Glory Hallelujah" for the Democracy.'[31] The following January, the founding conference of the Independent Labour Party convened in Bradford, not West Ham. And this was hardly an accident . . .

## Problems of Independent Labour Organization

The day after his election victory at West Ham, Keir Hardie told the *Daily Chronicle*: 'I hope that we shall soon see the beginning of a new and thoroughly independent Labour Party in the House of Commons. We may be few at first, but we shall attract to us a large number of the new Radicals who have shaken themselves free from laissez-faire Liberalism.'[32]

There were many forces ranged against Keir Hardie's plan, however. Firstly, some new unionists nursed serious hopes of Liberal support for some of their aims, and were by no means ready for a complete breach with the Liberal Party. Thus, John Burns quickly came under the influence of those Fabians who adopted a strategy of 'permeation'. If this sounds uncomfortably like the idea of 'entry' as practised by various left-wing groups in the Labour Party during the 1960s and 1970s, it was none the less defended quite openly by most of the best-known Fabians during the early 1890s. The election of Labour Members of Parliament was seen as a bridgehead to influence within the Liberal Party, rather than as a challenge to the old political alignments.

On the other side, Hardie faced a growing problem with that section of the socialist movement which had, originally, Conservative allegiances and which was now willing to play the old parties off against each other.

He himself had worked closely with H. H. Champion, and merged his newspaper with Champion's *Labour Elector*. Champion was well liked and influential among the dockers, and his organizational talents won him high respect. But he maintained a close liaison with a strange political adventurer, J. Maltman Barry, who had been a Conservative candidate for Banff in 1892. Barry had been an admirer of Karl Marx, and always spoke of him with unbounded enthusiasm. But it is clear that he had also been quite prepared to act as a conduit for Conservative funds, wherever the intervention of Labour candidates might seem likely to damage Liberal electoral prospects. Since Hardie had taken money from Champion during his first contest in Mid-Lanark, he was vulnerable to the charge of receiving 'Tory gold'.

The *Labour Elector* folded in April 1890 and Champion went to Australia – though he was to return in time to conduct a running faction-fight with Hardie during the earliest days of the Independent Labour Party.[33] Meanwhile, on 29 August 1890 Joseph Burgess launched the *Workmen's Times*, which was to play an important role in developing Labour activity, especially in the North.

A third group of adversaries with which Hardie was compelled to contend consisted of the socialist purists, who articulated strong doctrinal objections to co-operation with anyone but themselves. The core constituency of this grouping was, of course, the Social Democratic Federation, but there were some members of that body who were far more tolerant than others.

## Crowds and Orators

Among the new unions, the gasworkers undoubtedly had the greatest national reach. But Will Thorne remained loyal to the SDF, and tirelessly exploited its network to build his own union. The dockers had less scope for national recruiting and were more vulnerable to the counterattack of their employers; but in the short term their leaders were the heroes of the great Labour rebellion of 1889. Wherever they went, crowds were attracted. Their speeches were carefully written down by scores of local newsmen, so that their opinions were very widely read and understood. More, they were passionately eloquent, and capable of arousing real fervour among their listeners.

Here, for example, is a gifted journalist's account of one of Tom Mann's flights of oratory:

> To the usual fierceness of his swarthy face, to the habitual menace of his facial gesture, he was led on this occasion to add the airs of a mountebank – shrugging his shoulders, spreading his arms, distorting his mouth and exciting roars of laughter by his whining parody of the Liberal workman.

He laid himself out to split the ears of the groundlings . . . And then he played to the passions of the gallery. He spoke here with terrible method and terrible intention. He knows all the hardship of a labouring life; he knows the discontents and resentments that labour broods over most sullenly; he knows how frequently workmen hate the very ideas of having 'a master'; and in this knowledge he deliberately touched his hearers on the raw, until they bayed with rage in response to the fierce, rancorous, sullen voice that seemed to be giving concentrated utterance to the deepest class-passions of their nature. He spoke of the machine-minder 'afraid to straighten his back lest it should be marked down against him by a man with a watch, employed to follow him up like a sleuth-hound' . . . He denounced nationalism, he denounced the navy; he declared the navy to be an obstacle to the fraternisation of all workers. But Mr. Tom Mann's incendiary invective gradually passed into finer thought and not less effective appeal. In rapid and dark lines he sketched the intolerable fate of an Elswick labourer, whom he called 'a 17s. and 10d. a week man with a small wife and a large family'. He denounced that, he denounced all life on such terms. He called upon his audience to dare to be men; and 'Now young chaps,' he trumpeted, flinging up to the crowded galleries and side elevations an incitant gesture. 'Now young chaps, what are *you* going to live for?' The 'young chaps' were electrified.[34]

Such a powerful performer was in demand all over the country, constantly requested to speak for all the causes, and against all the injustices, to which Labour was prone. Tillett, also, acquired a truly national following. The early conferences of the Dockers' Union became events at which he was lobbied to give his support to a whole variety of campaigns. At the second conference of the Dockers' Union, delegations from Bradford were so insistent in pressing him to accept their parliamentary nomination that the conference formally debated their invitation, which was accepted by twenty-two votes to three.[35]

## The Birth of the Independent Labour Party

Tillett's campaign established Bradford as the most propitious centre from which to convene the new Independent Labour Party. Provincial socialists were profoundly wary of London influence, which they saw as prone to elitism and manipulation. Hardie represented a constituency in which he was beholden to the dockers and other new unionists, but he did not have there, or anywhere else in London, the kind of organizational base from which to establish a national network. Burns blew cold on the whole project. Havelock Wilson had entered on a maverick course and was not a volunteer. But the Bradford Labour Union had struck deep roots since the Manningham strike and had no encumbering ties with any part of the political apparatus of either of the two main parties. In 1895, two years after the ILP had been established, Bradford was to provide one-sixth of all the affiliation fees received by the new party. Indeed, it provided one-thirteenth of the entire income of the National Administrative Council during those early days.[36]

Around Bradford, of course, there was strong socialist support in Huddersfield, Dewsbury, Keighley, and the Colne and Holme Valleys. These, too, after an initial pause, made their strong contribution to the new party's organizational base. In a famous passage, E. P. Thompson told us that

> The ILP grew from the bottom up: its birthplaces were in those shadowy parts known as 'the provinces'. It 'was created by the fusing of local elements into one national whole. From the circumference its members came to establish the centre . . .' Its first council seat was won in the Colne Valley: its first authentic parliamentary challenges came in Bradford and Halifax: its first conference showed an overwhelming preponderance of strength in the North of England: its early directories show this strength consolidated. When the two-party political structure began to crack, and a third party with a distinctively socialist character emerged, this event occurred neither in Westminster nor in the offices of Champion's *Labour Elector* but amongst the mills, brickyards, and gasworks of the West Riding.[37]

The element of truth in this contention speaks for itself. But the judgement is rounded out when we examine the organization of the party in areas which were not so successful. John Kelly of the carters' and lurrymen's new union and his colleagues hammered away in Salford, with G. T. Jackson of the tramwaymen and other socialist activists, but the message did not take and the Salford Labour Union would not stick.[38] Instead Salford nourished a strong group of SDF members.

Local leadership is just as necessary to successful organization on the ground as national leadership is to the shaping of overall direction. Without it, grassroots will not grow. Of course, there are many circumstances in which grass is hard to cultivate, even by exemplary gardeners.

On 13 and 14 January, 124 delegates, most of whom came from the industrial North, mustered in Bradford for the ILP's founding conference. More than a third of the delegates came from Yorkshire, while Hardie's Scottish Labour Party provided the core of the eleven delegates from Scotland. Fifteen came from London, representing fourteen different societies. Thirteen Fabians, mostly from the North of England, included George Bernard Shaw. Shaw, however, was equivocal about the idea of an Independent Labour Party and the northern socialists went in terror of his influence.

One of the delegates in Bradford was James Sexton of the Liverpool Branch, soon to become general secretary of the National Union of Dock

Labourers. He had replied to Joseph Burgess's original invitation in the *Workman's Times* to meet to consider the formation of the new party. In his memoirs he describes the trepidation with which Shaw's arrival in Bradford was greeted:

> Both in the press before the Conference, and at the conference itself, he declaimed with all his power against what he called the 'unnecessary and mischievous intervention of a new Party', which was bound, he feared, to queer the pitch for the Fabians and their policy of peaceful penetration of the enemy's ranks . . . Hyndman demanded a scrutiny of credentials and those of GBS were challenged on the ground that he was presumably a self-elected delegate. Thereon it was held that he could take no part in the proceedings . . . But it was no easier then than it is now to make Shaw go the way you want him to go, and though we decided that he was not of us, he certainly remained with us . . . He promptly took up a strong enfilading position in the gallery, from which he bombarded us so violently with his interruptions that on the following day we admitted him to our deliberations in sheer self-defence.[39]

When Sexton came to compose his memoirs in 1935, he sent Shaw a copy of his reminiscences of the Bradford conference. The result was a spicy response, in which Shaw reaffirmed all his old views.[40]

If Shaw was the most famous delegate, the conference included many others who were already well known. Tillett represented Bradford as its former parliamentary candidate. Alongside him was Fred Jowett, later to become a Labour Cabinet Minister. John Mahon and Tom Maguire came from Leeds, Ben Turner from Batley, Robert Smillie from the Scottish Labour Party, and the gasworkers' Peter Curran represented Croydon.[41] Hardie was voted into the chair after the meeting was opened.

The first issue to be resolved concerned the name of the new organization. Two Scottish delegates proposed that it be called the Socialist Labour Party. To this, Ben Tillett was strongly opposed.

> Alderman Ben Tillett could not understand why their friends should apply the term Socialist to their party. One speaker seemed anxious to accord support to their continental brethren, but in practical democratic organisation there was nothing like this old country. It was a lesson to every one of the continental bodies, which although they had so much chatter and blabber, had no real effective detail. For pluck and determination to fight out their details English trade unionism was the best sort of socialism and labourism he knew. He desired to capture the trade organisations of the country, for they were a body of men well organised and were willing to pay their money in order to secure their ends. They were men who were not merely Socialists on the platform but Socialists at their work. They were men who did not advocate blood-red revolution and when it came to a revolution sneak under the first bedpost. (A voice,

'Shame.') These vast organisations of men in this country were working out their own economic salvation, and for work could compare favourably with any of these chatterers. As a trade unionist with a little experience and knowledge of the Labour movement he was glad to say that if there were fifty red revolutionist parties in Germany, he would rather have the solid, progressive, matter-of-fact fighting trade unionist of England, and for that reason he desired that they should keep away from their name any term of socialism. He preferred a man who had spent his life in the Labour movement to three chattering magpies who had neither the courage of their convictions nor the capacity to deal with details of their opinions. He himself was anxious that they should not claim any other power than what they possessed, and he desired that they should respect trade unions. There was not a Socialist party in the world who could show the effective organisation of these men and women in Lancashire. He had become thoroughly sick of people who bore on their foreheads 'socialism' and who were no more Socialist than Bismarck. In conclusion he said that he wanted to keep the organisation out of the hands of the wirepullers, and to keep it in the hands of work-a-day men, work-every-day men, who were anxious to do what was right . . .[42]

Tillett's remarks caused an immediate scandal, which has gone on reverberating through the next century.

His biographer, Jonathan Schneer, rightly reminds us that the Bristol docks were out on strike even while the ILP was gathering for its foundation meeting: 'Tillett wanted, and obtained, from the conference a resolution supporting the strike; but he wanted also hard cash for the strike fund. The fledgling Party was in no position to make such a donation, but the trade union delegates in attendance were.'[43] Be that as it may, the blatant chauvinism of this speech brought about an instant repudiation from Edward Bernstein and was registered as a scandalous affront to the German Social Democratic Party, at the time by far the most impressive detachment of the international socialist movement.[44]

The argument about the title of the party was virtually the only issue confronting the 1893 conference which was finally, and – Tillett notwithstanding – amicably resolved on the spot. The programme of the party was agreed on a consensual formula, supporting every extension of electoral rights and all measures to democratize the system of government. But a fierce dispute broke out over the 'Fourth Clause', which sought to pledge all members of the new organization to refuse votes to all other parties, even where there was no Labour candidate available. Sexton proposed an amendment to devolve this decision on party branches. He was ruled out of order, and the clause was defeated by a majority of almost two to one, to Bernard Shaw's immense satisfaction. (He was to recall this triumph of Fabian realism in his comments on Sexton's autobiography more than forty years later.) But the Fourth Clause would not lie down. Some local groups implemented it in spite of the national decision, and it became a perennial at party conferences, where it was defeated by diminishing majorities year after year. Indeed in 1895 it briefly triumphed, only to be rescinded again just before the election. Finally it faded into irrelevance with the formation of the Labour Representation Committee in 1900.

The new party closed its first deliberations having elected a National Administrative Council. The historian of the ILP, David Howell, describes it as 'very much an ILP second eleven'.[45] In fact it had fifteen members, chosen on a regional basis and therefore packed with local activists lacking any national reputation or experience. Moreover, it lacked money. Consequently it met only twice, costing £48 out of a total income of £130. Factional squabbles were ominously present, and for this reason infrequent meetings were seen by some as a blessing in disguise. At the 1894 conference all this was shaken out. Three members of the old Committee survived: John Lister, the Halifax squire, who was treasurer; Pete Curran of the gasworkers; and George Christie from Nottingham, a veteran of the First International.[46] The newcomers included Ben Tillett, and also Leonard Hall of the Lancashire and Adjacent Counties Labour Amalgamation, another new union. But more significantly, Keir Hardie was elected president and Tom Mann became secretary. The party was preparing itself for the next General Election. This came early, in 1895.

## Tom Mann Becomes the Secretary . . .

The circumstances of Tom Mann's election as ILP secretary are not entirely clear. In the discussion after the founding conference, George Bernard Shaw had made much of Mann's absence, claiming that this was a token of weak trade-union support. In January 1894 Russell Smart wrote to the *Workmen's Times* to advocate that Mann should be elected secretary, and later he claimed to have organized a caucus of delegates from Lancashire and Yorkshire to bring about a purge of the National Administrative Council and Mann's appointment.[47] Some recrimination followed, but the decision to field a 'first eleven' was by no means unpopular.

Mann once again applied himself to centralize key powers, while instituting regular monthly circulars to improve membership contact. ILP branches were not keen to surrender power to their national centre, and they were often decidedly reluctant to part with money which they wished to devote to local campaigns. The centralizing pressures were most successful immediately before the 1895 election, and became notably more contentious in succeeding years.

In 1893 and 1894, after the constitution of the ILP, there were by-elections in Halifax, Sheffield Attercliffe and Leicester. In the best of these, John Lister, drawing on his local connections, polled a quarter of the votes in Halifax. But all the results were respectable, given the very slender resources available to the infant party. Joseph Burgess was running against Henry Broadhurst, the scion of Lib.–Lab. conformity, who was teamed with a Liberal capitalist in a two-member constituency. Burgess polled almost 4,500 votes in Leicester, whilst at the same time provoking no small recrimination among the old unionists. Hugh Holmes Gore, an independent with some ILP support, entered the field in a Bristol by-election, following in Havelock Wilson's footsteps. He very nearly won, running his Liberal opponent within 130 votes.

By the 1895 General Election, twenty-eight ILP candidates were in the field. They included Ben Tillett in Bradford, James Sexton in Ashton-under-Lyne and Tom McCarthy, the dockers' organizer, in Hull. They also included Tom Mann in Colne Valley.

Tillett's result fell some considerable distance short of his 1892 performance; he polled only 23.4 per cent of the vote. Thereafter he took a back seat in ILP affairs, dropping out altogether during his convalescence in New Zealand and Australia from 1896 to 1898. But since the dockers' flag was also being carried by others in the 1895 contest, it is interesting to look in closer detail at the campaigns of his two colleagues, Tom Mann and Tom McCarthy.

The parliamentary division of Colne Valley, spread across the Pennines in the West Riding from Huddersfield to Oldham, came into existence in 1885. Its first Liberal Member dissented from Gladstone's policy on Home Rule for Ireland and was again returned, unopposed by the Conservatives, at the next election in 1886. But by 1890 discontent among Liberals had become irresistible, and an orthodox Gladstonian businessman from Leeds was selected. Sir James Kitson then reclaimed the seat in 1892, holding it until after 1906, when he was elevated to the peerage as Lord Airedale. Throughout this time only 59 per cent of adult males possessed the vote nationally. Plural votes included, the proportion in Colne Valley ran to higher levels, and by 1911 they had reached 75.5 per cent,[48] although there is no reason to doubt that the true register enfranchised rather fewer individual electors if duplicate voting were separately identified. In 1895, after the declaration, Mann published an analysis of the result in which he referred to 'six hundred property owners resident in Huddersfield who had helped to swell the Liberal majority, for not one of them had voted for the Labour candidate . . . It would be silly to complain of defeat by such forces.'

## . . . and the Candidate

The Colne Valley Labour Union was established on 21 July 1891, and its first meeting, in a Slaithwaite cottage cellar, instructed its secretary to write to Tom Mann to ask him to become their parliamentary candidate.

Mann's first response was cool. In an interview given to a representative of the *Yorkshire Factory Times*, he said:

> I do not concern myself much about Parliamentary parties. My aim is to spread amongst workmen a knowledge of industrial economics, and the channels for the diffusion of this knowledge are the trade union and the co-operative movement, especially the productive branch of co-operation. This knowledge, as it obtains, will soon assert itself in municipal life, and then the workers will take care to put upon local bodies men who are in sympathy with their aims. We want all our energy for these things; by them we shall improve our capability; and until then it is a waste to attempt Parliamentary work. I am, therefore, not anxious to run Labour candidates for Parliament.[49]

None the less, Slaithwaite invited both Tom Mann and Ben Tillett to come up and speak, and a big meeting took place on 24 October, at which Mann repeated his refusal. Continuous representations from all over the area failed to change his mind, although at the time, notwithstanding his responsibilities to the Dockers' Union, he was also a candidate for the office of general secretary of the Amalgamated Society of Engineers. The election of 1892 duly arrived, without a Labour candidate in place. Afterwards, Mann revealed that he had been invited to stand in no less than fourteen constituencies, five of which had guaranteed the necessary funding to finance a campaign. But in the end Yorkshire persistence paid off: the last half of 1892 found Tom Mann delivering monthly speeches in the constituency and finally accepting the task which was pressed upon him.

Colne Valley was not a strong trade-union area. Less than 2 per cent of its population were organized in unions, which ranked it far behind the national average. Even the handful who did hold cards were highly concentrated – in Mossley, right at the seat's western end. If they were excluded from the calculation, in the rest of the division less than 0.5 per cent of the population were trade unionists. This situation was not unique to Colne Valley, but also applied in Bradford and throughout the wool-textile regions. Half-time working was common and child-labour survived, notwithstanding the Education Act or the Factory Acts themselves. E. P. Thompson reports an old lady's reminiscence: 'The mill-owners were very cute in dodging the factory inspectors . . . they had a big whisket handy in the sheds, and when they expected the inspector, we young girls were popped underneath the blankets until he had gone'.[50] Yet the constituency organized itself very competently indeed in its own way. A network of Labour Clubs was created. Extensive social functions raised funds and bonded people together; women played an active part in this. As a result, the constituency elected one of the first Labour county councillors, and began to mount a steady challenge in local elections and for membership of school boards. Nonconformity was a strong and steady influence, and both Mann and Tillett were at the time deeply interested in religion.

None the less, Tom Mann saw trade-union recruitment as the main duty of his long campaign. Early in 1893 he wrote in the *Yorkshire Factory Times*:

> First I have long contended that attention to Parliament is not the first duty of workmen, but that Parliament should receive attention at the hands of those who have already been at work using the agencies that lie ready to hand. Now I am a firm believer in the efficacy of trade unionism, not merely for raising the standard of living of the workers, but for increasing the general industrial prosperity of the country, and I have never yet been able to respect a constituency where the workers clamour for Parliamentary action unless they have made a good show by means of the Trade and Labour organisations. Now the Colne Valley contains some twenty industrial centres where the textile trade is carried on. Have the operatives become identified with their trade unions? No they have not; only a very small proportion have become members, and this proportion is not increasing very rapidly, and unless this changes pretty quickly for the better I shall consider myself at liberty to withdraw my conditional promise.[51]

Had Westminster been his target, he continued, he could have found a compact constituency in London:

> but it does so happen that my attitude towards Parliament today is what it was years ago, when I many times said Parliamentary effort should follow upon, not precede, trade union effort. Now I desire to say that irrespective of cost in time etc, and inconvenience, as Colne Valley is to me a representative manufacturing district, where the operatives are badly paid, I shall have much pleasure in remaining with them and doing all that any one person can to help them up the hill that leads to better conditions, but then they will have to make an effort, and prove to me they make it by their behaviour as trade unionists.[52]

Sir James Kitson was not pleased by all this. On 23 April 1893 he wrote to Herbert Gladstone to decline some preferment or other, acceptance of which might have left the field open to Tom Mann during the subsequent General Election:

> if I am correct in believing that a certain possible appointment might be made having in mind the suggestion that Tom Mann would be an acceptable candidate for the vacancy, and that hereby I should at a future election be placed in a most favourable position in a contest . . . but as I should consider it a calamity if Tom Mann had a direct interest in organising Labour in Leeds for the purpose of combating capitalists, I should not wish to see him in Leeds. My interest, and that of my partners

have suffered by his actions. Today we are almost without work and our men will be without employment. We shall pay £1,000 a week less in wages than a year ago.

I ask you therefore not to consider me in any transactions.[53]

Herbert Gladstone, as Commissioner for Public Works, disposed of some patronage. But while the surviving half of this exchange of letters does not allow us to speculate about what offers had been made to Sir James, it does give rise to the suspicion that the Liberal Party was apprehensive about its prospects if the vote was split.

However, Tom Mann did not confine himself to propaganda and exhortation. While his opponent was biting his nails about the spectre of trade unionism, Mann was using his access to the evidence of the Royal Commission on Labour to compose in 1893 an *Appeal to the Yorkshire Textile Workers*. Within weeks 2,000 copies were sold, all adding specific weight to the general incitement to the people of the West Riding to build the strength of their appropriate unions.

None the less, recruitment remained slow, and by the end of the campaign in 1895 combined union membership was still little more than 1,500.[54] Mann's vote weighed somewhat less, at 1,245, or 13.4 per cent of the electorate.

## Tom McCarthy in Hull

Tom McCarthy's campaign was altogether a tougher problem than Tom Mann's. In November 1893 he was selected as ILP candidate for the lion's den – to fight Charles Wilson on his home ground. West Hull, Wilson had said when he first entered the field, had been the favoured spot of the local Tories 'because of the presence in it of large numbers of the upper classes'.[55] There were others, including fishermen and railway workers; but, Henry Pelling tells us, very many people were 'in more comfortable occupations'.[56] The Hull Trades Council balked at Independent Labour representation by a small margin (sixty-four to fifty-two) but two ILPers won local council seats soon afterwards. The editor of the *Railway Review*, Fred Maddison, had fought as a Lib.–Lab. in Central Hull in 1892, and was ferociously engaged to use his extensive influence to prevent the polarization of the Hull unions by an ILP candidature in Wilson's constituency. All the factors which most urgently impelled the Dockers' Union to seek a contest worked equally powerfully against Maddison's powerbroking in the interest of his own chosen political future.[57]

The Trades Council was kept out of the battle under this influence. The Irish National League also stood aside – an especially painful blow to McCarthy, since only two years before they had pressed him to accept a Nationalist nomination. The Social Democratic Federation added their penn'orth of commination, because they did not 'concede . . . the right of choosing a candidate' to the non-socialist ILP.[58]

Little money was available for the election campaign. As late as 5 July 1895 the local press was speculating that McCarthy's nomination might not go ahead for lack of funds, and pointing out that the candidate had 'not yet arrived in Hull'.[59] The Conservatives stood down in favour of Charles Wilson, having warned him off trespass in adjacent constituencies.[60] Wilson attacked union tyranny and beat the drum of foreign competition. He invited those of his employees who had grievances to see him at his office.

When McCarthy did arrive in Hull, he entered immediately on a heated controversy. He was presented as 'a man born amid poverty, a worker since he was eleven years of age' opposing 'a gentleman who owned vast wealth'.[61] The class lines already clear, he then took the platform and announced that 'he was opposing Mr. Wilson because he was the representative of a system which . . . was the cause of poverty, and . . . that while men occupied a position similar to that of Mr. Wilson, there would be poverty, suffering, misery and destitution'. For fifty years, he went on, 'the working men had clamoured for one man one vote, and that reform was still a promise'. The Liberals were resisting the payment of Members 'because it would lead to the complete disruption of the Liberal Party. But they would disrupt it'.[62]

On the plane of real politics, this complaint raised a crucial problem. If the Liberals could resist the widening of the franchise, then it would always remain difficult to get rid of them. We shall return to this question, which needs to be understood if we are to make sense of what happened to the ILP, and to the Labour Party itself in its earliest days. At the more artificial level of the hustings, however, no one needed to organize the 'disruption' of Wilson's campaign. The outraged dockers did that quite spontaneously. Here, for instance, is an account of just one meeting:

Mr. Wilson was received with hisses, cheers, and cries of 'Retire at once'. It was several minutes before Mr. Wilson could make himself heard, and during the greater part of his speech there were frequent interruptions and uproar. He said that at every meeting he had addressed there had been some opposition, but on the whole the opposition had been of a good-natured character. They came to a political meeting for a certain purpose, and ought to behave themselves. They were not there to listen to discordant shouts, which any child or a person wanting in intellect could easily send forth (cries of 'blacklegs'). Now, what did that man mean by that term? He meant a fellow labourer like himself (hear, hear, and uproar). If his platform and views did not agree with those of Mr. McCarthy, they had their remedy in their own hands. Some of them were excited and irritated, because they thought they had a grievance against his firm; or was it against him personally ('No')? Naturally there was still a considerable amount of friction on account of what happened two years ago, and that feeling had, unfortunately, not yet been removed (a Voice: 'It would be if you was to shift Ritson and Knowles'). He had talked the matter over on many occasions, and had come to the conclusion that had there been a little more tact on both sides and a little more listening to reason that strike might have either been quickly ended or prevented. They must always remember that it could not possibly be any advantage to his firm, having all their work to do, to have the men knocking off work and leaving them in the lurch as they did. His own feeling had always been that the strike ought never to have occurred. Whether right or whether wrong, they had got past that state in the history of Hull, and it was now his duty to do all in his power to prevent a recurrence of that deplorable calamity (applause). The duty of all should be to improve the position of the people (a Voice: 'Why don't you do it?'). How was it to be arrived at? Not by quarrelling with themselves. Whether they voted for or against him – (a Voice: 'You will get in') – it would not be because of any ill-feeling on his part (a Voice: 'You'll fly in, Charley'). It occurred to him from what he could see that his party were going to be in a minority . . . What he knew of the [Tory] party was that they would want watching (a Voice: 'You want watching an' all') . . . A Voter: Mr. Wilson, are you in favour of seamen, marine firemen, marine engineers, sea fishermen, and other classes being brought under the Employers' Liability Act (applause). Another Voter: I want you to stop a list of names being sent from your office at the arrival of every ship and a foreman being obliged to start these men and then call to his own men. Another Voter: I wish to ask you if you have the same opinion as you had years ago, for the abolition of the law for distraint for rent. A voter in East Hull desired to ask a question but was not allowed to do so . . .[63]

Earlier, Tillett had written to the *Hull Daily Mail* to denounce the behaviour of the Hull employers after the strike. The settlement, he said, promised absolute freedom to join trade unions, and to withdraw support and recognition from 'any employers' free labour association'. But

not a single condition has been upheld. Messrs. Wilson have organised a staff of clerks to ascertain the name of every trade union man, to pay visits as spies to all labour meetings . . . and have, besides, a paid organiser to blacklist trade unionists. No promise has been kept, and the agreement is not worth the paper it is written on, and has been repudiated by the Union.[64]

On polling day Wilson 'was well supplied with carriages' while Tom McCarthy 'had but a solitary cart to rely on'.[65] West Hull had never been propitious ground for a Labour candidate, but even so, McCarthy polled 1,400, or 17.4 per cent, of the votes.[66]

Tom McCarthy's defeat was shared by Fred Maddison, who lost by a handsome margin to his Conservative opponent. It is at least conceivable that many Hull dockers voted against the Lib.–Lab. precisely in order to register their disgust about a Liberal Party which included the shipowner Charles Wilson on its lists. Be that as it may, historians have considered it 'certainly unusual to find a city where the customary political order of things is reversed, and the working class appears more Conservative than the middle class'.[67]

## James Sexton's Campaign

Sexton's campaign had followed the prosecution of some tailors who had been picketing a shop which had been putting work out to Manchester sweat-shops; they were sent to prison for non-payment of fines. Ashton trade unionists were scandalized. Keir Hardie protested in Parliament. The local Trades Council paraded in front of the offending premises with a band playing the Death March. Whilst this issue aroused some sympathy for Sexton's cause, Sam Woods, the miners' leader, stumped the constituency pleading the Liberal cause, and James Mawdsley, the cotton spinners' secretary, campaigned for the Conservatives.[68]

The dockers' leader was thus hemmed in by trade-union opponents. The ILP in Ashton was broke. Sexton's meetings were held on streetcorners. Publicity consisted of chalked slogans on streets or walls. For want of carriages, he sent out bands of ragged children to chant for votes. In the circumstances 415 votes (6.4 per cent) were seen as quite a lot, but the Conservatives walked home with a majority over all opposition candidates combined.

After the dust had settled, Sexton concluded:

> The real lesson of the Election . . . was that the foundation of the movement was insecure. The effort had not got the support of those for whose benefit it was primarily intended. The workers, sectionalised in their trade unions, which themselves were too often embroiled in domestic squabbling, had not realised that their hope and strength lay in their own unity.[69]

## Coping with Defeat

For the ILP as a whole, the 1895 election was a fierce setback. Twenty-eight candidates polled less than 50,000 votes. Hardie, in a straight fight with the Conservative, was defeated: a bitter blow to the new party, even if Beatrice Webb told her diary that this might mean that his influence would now diminish – in her opinion, much to the good. Other socialist and Labour candidates went down. The Social Democratic Federation ran four people and of these George Lansbury came out with 203 votes, while Hyndman got 1,498. Lib.–Labs did worse than before. Burns and some of the miners held on, but George Howell lost his seat, in part because of the defection of new-unionist voters following his onslaught against them.[70] Altogether nine Lib.–Labs were elected, five of them miners. By-elections brought in W. C. Steadman at Stepney, Maddison in Sheffield Brightside, and the miners' leader Sam Woods, whom we have already met in Ashton, in Walthamstow. Before the end of the century, then, there were a dozen Lib.–Labs in Parliament, half of whom came from the miners.

Independent Labour representation had been annihilated. Labour members who survived in 1895 were all, still, dependent upon the Liberals. But the Liberals themselves were in a poor way. Gladstone had withdrawn, and with him went a strong commitment to the incorporation of Labour in the Liberal alliance. Engels, had he survived, might have wished to qualify his optimism about the effects of the extension of the franchise, to which we referred in chapter 2. What had become clear was that Labour could win with Liberal support or neutrality, and come near to winning in strong new union territory without such endorsement. This lesson was reinforced by Tom Mann's powerful campaign in Aberdeen North in 1896, to which we shall return shortly. But the new unions were under the hammer. They still had influence, but in many areas they were fading fast.

How had this electoral reverse come about? Tom McCarthy provided the answer during his campaign speech, when he accused the Liberals of inspired tardiness in the extension of the suffrage. During all these years, something like 5 million male workers were denied votes, either because they were lodgers, or paupers, or servants living in, or because, as happened in 1905, they were deprived of the franchise for claiming school meals for their children under a local-government order.[71]

## The Politics of the Franchise

Speaking just before the 1867 Reform Bill, Gladstone had revealed the ambiguity of his attitudes quite precisely. Firstly, he accepted that the franchise was too restricted: 'I believe that a smaller portion of working men enjoy the franchise now than enjoyed it thirty years ago after the Reform Bill [1832] was passed.' Yet the working class had been enlarged, it was better off, more educated, and more 'loyal'. 'I must say that proofs of competency such as those ought to have some influence on the spirit of privileged classes, and to induce them . . . with a view of strengthening the laws and institutions of the country, to make some sensible, ay, some liberal, though some safe extension of the franchise'.[72] That same year, he advocated a fair, and liberal, and sensible, though not a sweeping, nor an overwhelming, admission of our brethren of the labouring community to the privilege of the suffrage . . . I should earnestly desire to see an extension . . . not wrung, not extorted as it was in 1832 . . . but given freely . . . in that way which excites confidence and gratitude, instead of engendering something, perhaps even much, of reasoning or even disaffection . . .[73]

At the turn of the century, Gladstone's close friend Alexander Murray, the Master of Elibank, wrote to *The Times* to warn the Liberals to be more accommodating to Labour in case the division between capital and labour should be enlarged to dominate the electoral choices. Gladstone, he thought, 'with his wonderful intuition', whenever labour democracy appeared to be gathering support 'took it by the hand, and led it into gentler paths'.[74]

Max Beer, the socialist historian, noted Gladstone's skill in the management of workers' movements. Gladstone, he pointed out, unlike Disraeli:

had nothing of the social romanticism which lent so much attraction to his great adversary. He perceived with the utmost clearness, in the rise of labour as a class, a danger to the power of the classes. On the one hand therefore, he encouraged the manufacturing, and generally the capitalist, class to allow the wage-earners a larger share in the national income, while, on the other hand, he went warily and acted parsimoniously when it was a matter of granting them political and economic rights. His policy was directed towards their political education . . . it was Gladstone who raised working men to the rank of members of the government; and, whenever he saw labour moving towards political class warfare, he spared no effort to lead it back to middle class paths.[75]

But it was the last Gladstone administration which itself contributed to the calling of this great bluff. Even while efforts were made to 'take by the hand' Lib.–Lab. heirarchs and such new agitators as Burns and Havelock Wilson, the Liberal manufacturers and shipowners began to wage outright battles against their beleagured employees and constituents. A picture in the official history of the Shipping Federation says it all: the depot ship *Lady Jocelyn* 'was the ship most extensively used for housing and accommodating strike breakers, and she was towed round to whatever docks were experiencing trouble'.[76] The picture shows rows of bestriped police officers, resolutely basking in the camera's eye, some reclining on deckchairs while others are more formally seated in postures of controlled dignity. Behind them, bowler-hatted and spruce, as if readying themselves for church, stand the masses of 'free labourers' who are about to be deployed in yet another industrial counterinsurgency. The very fact that these strike-breaking armies were private served to emphasize their political origins. And the fact that the uniformed servants of the state afforded every protection to these strong-arm squads, bashing and battering their way round all the ports of the island, argued the necessity of changes in the state itself.

It has been calculated that as late as 1910 4,665,000 men were excluded from the registers. There were, throughout this time, half a million people with more than one vote. Plural voting was mostly based upon the ownership of property. It produced freak voting registers: 548 per cent of the male population of the City of London had the right to vote there. In Pudsey, 112 per cent could vote. But in the seven parliamentary seats of Tower Hamlets in 1911, an average of 35.7 were enfranchised, and this does not discount the people who had two votes, each of which counted in the total. In Sheffield, Hanley, Stoke, Cardiff, Salford and Manchester less than 60 per cent of men could vote, again without making allowance for plural voting. In Liverpool, the figure for all nine seats was less than 50 per cent. Hull and Birmingham enfranchised 62 per cent of their men. Rural seats did much better, and the seven Lincolnshire seats averaged 84 per cent of all their men enregistered, not allowing for their share of plural voters.

Class voting was to become normal, once nearly everyone could vote after 1918. Before the universal suffrage it was seriously inhibited by tactical considerations. These prevailed throughout the whole period between the 1884 legislation and the First World War, during which time there had been very little improvement indeed in the extension of the franchise, as is clearly shown in table 7.1.

Of course, even these figures exaggerate. It is not difficult to assess the handicaps under which Mann in North Aberdeen, Tillett in Bradford, or Hardie in West Ham were operating. On anything like manhood suffrage, they might have been home and dry; but Labour was not making the rules.

This is not to say that a wider franchise would automatically engender class voting. Duncan Tanner has calculated that many of the voteless men were middle-class lodgers, sometimes from comfortable occupations.[77] Yet, allowing for this, there were certainly many voteless workers and trade unionists. Given access to the ballot, these men and women would need to be persuaded to vote for the Labour Party before it could win. Large numbers of them were not so persuaded even in 1918, and indeed arguments about 'deference' voting were still lustily pressed right into the 1960s.[78]

However, notwithstanding Tanner's elegant reasoning, the core fact is this: the 'social context' of solid Labour voting was, first and foremost, the approach of universal suffrage. Of course, this did not directly entail solid political support for Labour: none the less, without it such political support was far more difficult to achieve. There are strong grounds for offering a formula: trade unionists who could all vote might well be readier to support trade-union candidates, thinking they might win, than

Table 7.1  *Percentage of Adult Males Enfranchised in England and Wales, 1892–1915*

|  | England and Wales | Counties | Boroughs |
|---|---|---|---|
| 1892 | 66.9 | 73.2 | 59.7 |
| 1901 | 63.0 | 68.1 | 56.9 |
| 1911 | 65.6 | 69.9 | 59.9 |
| 1915 | 68.1 | 72.8 | 61.9 |

'Made up from the 1891, 1901, 1911 census tables, pp. 1893–4 xx.675, which allows comparison of the 1892 electorate with the 1891 population, and pp. 1914–16 lii.596. The England and Wales column includes university voters. The 1915 figure is calculated on the basis of the 1911 census using an adult male percentage of 57%. On the basis of the 1914 male population estimate of Michell and Deane, *Abstract of British Historical Statistics* (1962), p. 10, the England and Wales figure is 66.4% (i.e. below the 1892 figure); no estimates for the 1914 borough and county populations have been found. Because of the rapidly declining birth rate throughout this period, it is important to calculate the *adult* male percentage; comparison on the basis of the all-male population is misleading. The following have been taken as the percentages of males ages 21 and over: 1891, 51.7%, 1901, 54.5%, 1911, 56.0%, 1915, 57.0%, 1921, 59.5%.'
*Source:* H. C. G. Matthew, R. I. McKibbin and J. A. Kay, 'The Franchise Factor in the Rise of the Labour Party', in J. M. Roberts and G. A. Holmes (eds), *The English Historical Review*, vol. XCI (1976), p. 726.

(Reproduced by permission of the authors and Longman Group.)

they would have been when many of their colleagues were known to be disenfranchised. The fewer they were in the general electorate, the more attractive might tactical voting appear. Of course, the stronger the unions became, the greater the influence which they might expect to exert on their members' thinking, especially when all shared full electoral rights. In this respect, the emergence of the TGWU in 1922 was to represent a great potential advance for Labour: it annulled the ill-effects of fragmentation between the myriad of lesser, often local, trade-union bodies. At the same time it offered powerful encouragement to seek a common political expression.

However, in the 1890s Labour still had far to go before it could ponder these problems of success.

## *How to Oppose?*

Does this mean that John Burns and George Bernard Shaw were right to embrace the doctrine of 'permeation'? Was it necessary to cuddle up to the Liberal machine before Labour could win? Yes and no. Without a Liberal alliance, in practice, Labour representation would be small. But with it, it would tend to irrelevance. Until well into the twentieth century, unless the Liberal boat could be rocked, no beneficial reforms of the electoral law were remotely conceivable. Without some confrontation, nothing would move. With it alone, not much more could be shifted. Insofar as new-union politics were 'inconsistent', this is why: they sought to resolve profound and ample ambiguities in the very narrow space which was open to them. The new unions gave the ILP's activists a real opening. With a trade-union base, it was possible to win some elections, especially at local level. As the new-union presence diminished, a trade-union alliance would involve a more timid orientation, because even where 'new' men had been elected to high office in old unions, the majority of their members had a place in society which was far more comfortable than that of the dockers, carters or general labourers.

## Mann's Aberdeen Campaign

Immediately after the dust had settled on the wreckage of Independent Labour hopes in 1895, the party set about its recovery. The opportunity arose in Aberdeen North in 1896. This has been described by David Howell as 'perhaps the most successful of the ILP's Scottish campaigns',[79] and indeed it figures statistically as the party's most successful attempt anywhere.[80] Tom Mann polled 46 per cent of the votes cast, which was 0.4 per cent more than Keir Hardie had drawn in his defeat at West Ham South. It was streets ahead of all the others. Mann was opposing a Liberal in a straight fight, and thus came within 430 of ousting an industrialist who was trespassing in a constituency which was a pillar of the Gladstonian establishment. Mann won the support of the Trades Council at the beginning of his campaign, and was enthusiastically welcomed in the dock areas. He campaigned for dock municipalization and supported the demands of the local fishermen. His election oration was published as a popular pamphlet, and was both rousing and intransigent.[81] David Howell reports that: 'Mann's post-poll euphoric meeting ended with the singing of "Will ye no come back again?" '[82]

He never did. None the less, his candidature achieved that unity of trade-union response which he had sought in vain in Colne Valley, and strengthened the understanding that trade-union support was crucial to Labour success. Within a few years, the dockers of Aberdeen were to be recruited not to Mann's own union, but to the NUDL.

Mann stood again, the following year, in a by-election in Halifax. But he did not repeat his success in Scotland, polling 1,000 fewer votes than 'Squire' Lister had done in 1895. In part this could be explained by Lister's absence; but it was also due to an open squabble with Lib.–Lab. trade unionists. In this way, the lesson of the Aberdeen contest was reinforced by negative example.

## The New Unions and Socialist Unity . . .

During these years, active new-unionist participation in the government of the Independent Labour Party gradually fell away. So did the party's overall claims of membership. Tillett did not offer himself for re-election to the ILP leadership in 1895, perhaps in part because of the acrimony caused by his criticisms of the German socialists. Mann had left the secretaryship at the end of 1897. He had been involved in abortive fusion negotiations with the Social Democratic Federation, after a long internal wrangle. Clearly he saw socialist unity as one necessary dimension in the recovery of the political initiative by socialists. It is also clear, from his subsequent actions, that he was willing to conceive a strategy of co-operation with Liberals for at least some specific objectives. If socialist unity had not been a matter of either/or, it is possible that it could have been combined with a new offensive to divide the Liberal forces, thus offering a different perspective from the conformity which marked the earliest days of the Labour Party.

At the ILP Nottingham Conference of 1896, delegates had voted down Hardie's opposition to merger talks with the SDF. His reproach that the SDF had contributed to his defeat in West Ham went unregarded. Talks were in fact stalled when the TUC Parliamentary Committee rejected a tripartite initiative, but the 1897 ILP Conference returned to the agenda of unity and carried a motion for fusion. Hardie, Mann, Ramsay MacDonald and Russell Smart were delegated for the ILP, to meet Hyndman, Quelch, H. W. Lee, George Lansbury and J. T. Barwick of the SDF. The ILP then balloted to accept unity proposals, later in 1897.[83] So did the members of the SDF. Fusion was ditched only in a complex of manoeuvres at the 1898 ILP Conference. These culminated in a declamation by Bruce Glasier, which suffocated all hopes of a united party in a fog of mystical rhetoric:

> Socialism is a very great and a very marvellously pervading and encompassing power. It is the most human spirit that has grown up in the world, and it is the divinest of all things we have ever had vision of with our eyes. We who call ourselves Socialists cannot ourselves comprehend its might or magnitude. We are as reeds shaken in the wind of its coming. We can only receive knowledge of it so far as the space and peculiarities of our minds will allow . . . Is it not, think you, better for a land that there be many pleasant rivers and brooks – yea, and mountain torrents – of socialism . . .[84]

The ILP Executive had commissioned this elegant metaphor in putting up Glasier to offer reasons for reneging on plans for the merger. Such rhapsodies were to become a stock-in-trade of the Independent Labour Party in later years, under the competing influence of Glasier himself, Philip Snowden and Ramsay MacDonald. The effort to straddle a party dependent upon socialist radicals on the one side and craft-union traditionalism on the other called up a remarkable new Muse – demagogic obfuscation.

## ... and Discord

But Tom Mann had also encountered unpleasant controversy within the party after the March 1897 Halifax by-election. Acrid comments on his private life had been made by various members of the NAC. A slime of prurient gossip resulted. Pete Curran's defeat in a by-election in Barnsley in October 1897 had been worse than expected. Curran, the gasworkers' leader, was another new-union stalwart, but he came third, after a powerful intervention by Yorkshire miners' leaders on behalf of the Liberals. Mann had also been involved in a sharp exchange with James Sexton, who had backed Fred Maddison in the by-election in Sheffield that August. Maddison, it will be recalled, had been the most vigorous opponent of Tom McCarthy's intervention in West Hull, and his subsequent victory in Sheffield Brightside did not make him any more acceptable to the dockers. That Sexton, a dockers' leader, should be prepared to endorse the dockers' antagonist as 'a pronounced trade unionist . . . instead of the nephew of a duke' seemed to Mann to be 'sheer rebellion'.[85] It in no way wiped away the memory of Charles Wilson's onslaught upon, and destruction of, the Dockers' Union in Hull, and Maddison's ambivalence was seen as willingness to condone strike-breaking and strike-breakers. All of this implied future rivalries over who might win access to organize the Humber again. Sexton was, this time round, admonished by the NAC.

## The Lessons of Defeat

If the first reaction of the ILP campaigners was one of dismay at the scale of the 1895 defeat, there were also other important lessons to be drawn from that experience. Liberalism, after all, had been hit even harder than the infant Labour slate. Labour had lost one seat, but the Liberals had lost few short of 100. On the one hand it made sense to see the Labour débâcle as part of the wider swing to the Tories; on the other it was clear that Labour interventions had cost the Liberals very heavily, and that the doctrine of abstention under the Fourth Clause, where it was applied, had also taken its toll:

> The Liberals lost all three seats in Bradford, one seat in Halifax, one seat in Otley, one seat in Shipley, and regained the Huddersfield seat lost at a byelection in 1893. Although there had been a national swing against the

Liberals, it did not go unnoticed that some of the most significant local losses occurred in areas where the Labour challenge was strong . . .[86]

This perception by a contemporary scholar gives us a remarkable echo of Ben Tillett's 'victory' oration after his 1895 defeat in Bradford: 'They set out upon the task of soundly thrashing one of their enemies. They could not take them both on at once . . . They had not been spreading their forces for nothing, and if the Liberals did not come to their side, and fight side by side with them, they would keep them out.'[87]

## The National Democratic League

Tom Mann, although he never wavered in his prior commitment to trade unionism as the base of all Labour organization, clearly drew from these experiences the related conclusion that changes in the franchise would be necessary before there could be any parliamentary breakthrough. It was the South African War which highlighted this question.

Sir Alfred Milner, the British High Commissioner, had demanded a universal male franchise in the Transvaal for all British immigrants who had completed five years' residence.[88] Neither blood nor treasure was to be stinted in this cause, given that its victory would also bring the Witwatersrand Gold reefs and Johannesburg into the comfortable folds of the empire. But W. C. Steadman, speaking at the TUC, pointed out that Her Majesty's domestic subjects, living at a great remove from all gold mines, were equally or even further distant from the civic rights and duties which Britain now sought to impose upon the Boers: 'With our present electoral system not one-half of the million and a quarter workers whom this Congress represents would have a vote if an election took place on the morrow.'[89] It was left to the editor of *Reynolds's Newspaper*, W. M. Thompson, to draw the moral about this widely detested war: 'It will at least have taught people the great lesson – that where in any country the franchise is denied, even to foreigners, it is not only just, but it is an absolute duty to use force to acquire it.'[90]

In order to remedy this deficiency the National Democratic League was initiated by Thompson, together with Tom Mann, who became its founding secretary. The new organization involved, among others, David Lloyd George, John Burns and other radicals, together with Bob Smillie and Charles Duncan, the secretary of the new Workers' Union. John Ward of the Navvies' Union also took part.[91] So did stalwart Lib.–Labs such as George Howell.[92] The platform of the League was that 'a man should have the right to vote because he was a man, and that it should not depend upon the house he occupied or the rent he paid'.[93] Besides universal male suffrage, it demanded payment of MPs and the abolition of the House of Lords. 'For a time', wrote G. D. H. Cole, the new organization 'had much more of the limelight than the Labour Representation Committee . . . it gradually lost its importance, but not without playing a highly significant part in the leftward re-orientation of the Liberal Party and thus checking considerably the movement towards Labour independence. It was undoubtedly a factor in the great Liberal victory of 1906'.[94]

The NDL platform launched itself when the Boer War was beginning; it was not to be implemented until the altogether more cosmic mayhem of the First World War made it unavoidable, and Tom Mann's old arguments could still be heard right up until 1918 when the new electoral arrangements were introduced. Then the 'missing men' were finally enfranchised. The vast carnage of young men – many of whom could die for their government but were not allowed to join in electing it – seems to have killed off the argument against giving votes to the soldiers who survived. By that time, a new political order was emerging.

# III

## International Socialism

We should not leave the story of the transport workers in the ILP without dealing briefly with their international connections. These were to have a certain influence on subsequent happenings.

Unlike many of his colleagues, Tom Mann was to become closely familiar with the French unions, partly because of his experiences in the Socialist International and partly because of his simultaneous efforts to organize the International Federation of Ship, Dock and River Workers.

While he was still responsible for the organization of the Independent Labour Party, as its secretary, Mann found himself in charge of the various arrangements for the housing and administration of the 1896 International Socialist Congress in London. This convened on 27 July and immediately erupted into a famous controversy about the seating of trade-union delegates who were also anarchists, or at any rate anti-parliamentarians. A boiling row between constitutional socialists and anarchists had already broken out in the Zurich Congress of 1893, resulting in the exclusion of a couple of dozen delegates, including the young Rosa Luxemburg.[95]

Anarchism was a frightening concept because it was associated with direct action, which for most trade-union members meant straightforward support for strikes and boycotts: but for that public which was uninformed about the details of labour and socialist organization it invariably implied bomb attacks and senseless terrorism.[96] By 1896 the French trade unions in particular were largely aligned in support of direct action, even though they were obviously far removed from terrorist commitments. As Tom Mann remembered it in his memoirs, fifty-one of the French delegates to the London Congress were of one view about parliamentary methods of work, and the other fifty favoured the other view. He could not remember whether the direct-action school was in the minority or not: but he knew that the majority, whichever way it ran, consisted of one vote only.[97] Partly because the division was so narrow and partly because it was the main force of the trade-union movement in France which was so strongly involved with the allegedly 'anarchist' current, Mann and Keir Hardie voted for the seating of the anti-parliamentary delegates, much to the annoyance of some of the would-be parliamentarians.[98]

In fact there had been five distinct groups, not just two, in the French delegation to London. Parliamentary socialists ranged themselves in two factions, one led by Jules Guesde, Paul Lafargue and M. Deville, and the other by Jean Jaurès and Alexander Millerand. Anti-parliamentarians came from three tendencies: the Blanquists, led by Edouard Vaillant; the followers of Jean Allemane; and the anarchists, grouped around Fernand Pelloutier and the trade-union radicals. Taken together, these trends divided into two broad groups of roughly equal size, as Tom Mann rightly recalled. The contemporary French chronicler A. Hamon gives the syndicalists a majority of two over the parliamentarians.[99]

The three big delegations in London came from England, France and Germany. The Germans were orthodox parliamentarians. The historian of French anarchism, J. Maitron, wrongly records that Tom Mann alone among the English supported the anarchist participation:[100] Mann, of course, was a determined supporter of all trade-union colleagues, regardless of their reported political allegiances – not least because he was busy assembling support for the Transport Workers' International. But Keir Hardie also spoke out alongside his general secretary, against 'state socialism of the German type'.[101]

The two ILP leaders provoked widespread recriminations among supporters of the SDF, who remained sternly opposed to dalliance with anarchism or any other unorthodoxy. From its beginning to its end, the International Congress was an almighty rumpus, which spilt over from the meeting hall into the columns of the London press. The newspapers had a field-day ridiculing the socialist scrimmages. George Bernard Shaw wrote a long apologist essay, making the best of what he clearly saw as a bad job.[102]

The cause of all the aggravation was Pelloutier, the spokesman of the three non-parliamentary caucuses: 'He it was to whom the anarchist mandates had been given at the London Congress; in a word, he was the most conspicuous protagonist of anarchism among the unions'.[103]

Having provoked such paroxysms, Pelloutier was to die within five years, at the age of thirty-four, 'leaving behind an indelible memory of energy, goodness and devotion.'[104] We shall meet his ghost when we come to look at what was to happen in 1910.

## IV

## *Independent Labour and the Trades Union Congress*

We have already described the establishment in 1887 of the TUC's Labour Electoral Association, and H. H. Champion's subsequent espousal of its cause. This, however, was to prove shortlived and, as we have seen, Champion's own *Labour Elector* ceased to appear in 1890.

That year saw a set-piece debate on the eight-hours' question at the TUC, and in spite of Hardie's altercations with the old guard during earlier Congresses, the combined weight of new-union affiliations and old-union converts was enough to carry the question. The debate had clearly swept through the old-established organizations. The stonemasons were for the eight-hour day, and repudiated Broadhurst, the TUC secretary, who represented them at Congress. The carpenters and joiners also overruled the strong objections of their secretary. The cautious majority at the AGM of the railway servants in 1889 turned down a proposal to introduce a new class of membership with a weekly contribution of 3*d*. Existing members paid 5*d*. Their reluctance to acknowledge the needs of less-affluent fellow workers produced a speedy reaction. Within two months, the General Railway Workers' Union was founded, and the poorest-paid railwaymen, including porters and platelayers, were swept into its ranks in support of militant new unionism. The new union also recruited amongst van-men and lurrymen, grades neglected by the Amalgamated Society of Railway Servants. Here it could not be accused of poaching. In November it resolved 'that the union shall remain a fighting one and shall not be encumbered by any sick or accident fund.'[105] Both the new General Railway Workers' Union and the old ASRS lined up for shorter hours. The compositors and the ironfounders also joined in.[106]

Broadhurst had had enough, and he stood down as TUC secretary; Charles Fenwick was elected in his place. Even more spectacular was the election of John Burns to the Parliamentary Committee, albeit as runner-up, after not one but two successful though disgruntled Lib.–Labs had withdrawn.

By 1892 the last pockets of resistance to the eight-hours' movement had been brought round by membership revolts in their own unions. Birtwhistle and Mawdsley, of the United Textile Factory Workers' Association, were key cases: 'No trade union leaders reacted more violently' to the 1890 decision than they did,[107] but their joint organization voted by 132 to 21 to join the eight-hours' movement.

In 1891 Congress threw out a scheme for the establishment of a political fund to meet election costs, and to maintain elected members.

But the following year the Parliamentary Committee was mandated to prepare proposals for such a project.

In 1893 Hardie stood against Fenwick for the TUC secretaryship and was defeated. His amendments to the new scheme for Labour representation were accepted, however, committing TUC-sponsored candidates to independence of the established parties, and the public ownership and control of the means of production, distribution and exchange. This, however, was a paper victory, since contributions to the new fund were voluntary. Volunteers were soon found to be wanting.

The year 1894 saw a debate on land and mines nationalization. Hardie, supported by Burns and Mann, put forward an amendment to add the means of production and exchange to this list, and it was overwhelmingly carried, by 219 votes against 61. That year there were three candidates for the secretaryship of Congress: Fenwick, the incumbent; Sam Woods, another miner; and Tom Mann. Woods won on a second ballot, after Mann withdrew, having won one-third of the votes.[108] During that Congress, Mann claimed at least eighty delegates who were supporters of the ILP. Since the dockers were already at a very low ebb, and other new unions were suffering heavy losses, it is quite clear that this tally, and the large support for Independent Labour policies, reflected serious changes of opinion (and personnel) in the established organizations.

The result was a heavy counterblow. In 1895, hot on the adverse election results, Congress was persuaded to accept new standing orders. The block vote was introduced, Trades Councils were henceforth to be excluded, and only those who were working union officers or actively employed at their trade were to be admitted as delegates. Out went Keir Hardie, at whom the blow was aimed. Burns had aligned with Mawdsley in order to bring about the change, but doubtless it was reinforced by the hurt reactions of Lib.–Lab. supporters to the part played by the ILP in their electoral discomfiture. Paradoxically, the bar on Trades Councils was to exclude many Lib.–Lab. centres of influence, as well as the few socialist enclaves. To add to the general sense of rout, Ben Tillett was voted off the Parliamentary Committee, since the Dockers' Union membership was now so diminished.

## Tories and Liberals in the Unions

Now Congress seemed almost a fiefdom of two great blocks: the cotton workers and the coalminers. The cotton workers included many traditional Conservative supporters, and the miners were still over-whelmingly Liberal – partly because their geographical concentration meant they could relatively easily drive a hard bargain with the Liberal machine, unlike dockers, for instance; and partly because of a visceral antipathy to landowners, and hence Tories. We have already seen that Rosebery's intervention as a governmental mediator during the miners' lock-out had, in some of the coalfields, done the Liberals no harm at all. Nor did the killing of two miners, shot by soldiers at Featherstone during the same dispute, appear to damage them. The sad intervention of Pete Curran in Barnsley in 1897, which brought about a derisory result for the ILP after powerful intervention by the miners' leaders, only underlined this message. Not only Hardie was out under the new rules: so too was John Burns, for the same reason, but his political position was already secure.

And yet, only four years on, the TUC was to approve its momentous resolution to form the Labour Representation Committee, and at the end of February 1900, 129 delegates were to gather at the Memorial Hall in London to establish it on completely new foundations. How did this come about?

The apparent defeat of the socialists at the 1895 TUC was nothing if not impermanent. The employers' offensive was shaking out older unions, and the lock-out of the engineers served not only to radicalize the activists, but also to make space for Tom Mann's last major initiative of this phase – the Workers' Union. This was much reinforced by new technological developments, which undermined the security of craftsmen and created large bodies of semi-skilled employees. A revolution was brought about in the metal trades with new processes, concentration and mergers, and intensified foreign competition. Upturn or not, 10 per cent of the workers in engineering and shipbuilding were unemployed. The printers and the boot and shoe workers met similar upheavals. Railwaymen were becoming more and more aware of the deterioration in their conditions. Given the continued withholding of recognition, they needed political action. The dockers, in both Tillett's and Sexton's organizations, were no less committed to political action because it proved difficult; and they had gained some real ground in local government. Even more was this true of the gasworkers. By 1898 Keir Hardie claimed that three-fifths of TUC delegates belonged to the ILP. There was certainly a socialist majority, because a motion in favour of support for the 'working class socialist parties' was emphatically carried.

In June 1899 James Mawdsley stood as Conservative candidate in Oldham, and was defeated after heavy Lib.–Lab. intervention. This gave strong support to the notion that independent action was necessary, since Labour would otherwise remain for ever a cat's paw in other people's quarrels. James Sexton was to refer to it, in scathing terms, when seconding the motion at the 1899 TUC for the creation of the Labour Representation Committee. It was necessary, he said, 'to end the present disgraceful confusion in which prominent Labour men . . . opposed each other on separate platforms'.[109]

## Taking the Plunge

On 12 October 1899 the South African War broke out. The Liberals were still further divided by it. Liberal imperialism was now compelled to occupy a subaltern role, since the Conservatives were manifestly in charge. Liberal opponents of the war were compelled to run for cover under a literal hail of jingo missiles. That the TUC was already estranged from the established parties was plain from their resolution of the previous year: but now the Liberals offered little credible support to any Labour aspirant, in their obvious confusion and demoralization. Paradoxically, having digested its own experience of the difficulties of independent action, the ILP was much more ready to meet and treat with the Lib.–Labs than at any time in its short history.

The text of the 1899 motion, which it took three hours for the Plymouth Congress to debate, looked a bit like a committee product:

> That this Congress, having regard to its decisions in former years, and with a view to securing a better representation of the interests of Labour in the House of Commons, hereby instructs the Parliamentary Committee to invite the co-operation of all the co-operative, socialistic, trade union, and other working organisations to jointly co-operate on lines mutually agreed upon, in convening a special congress of representatives from such of the above-named organisations as may be willing to take part to devise ways and means for securing the return of an increased number of Labour members to the next Parliament.[110]

One thing, however, was quite clear: while the Parliamentary Committee was to take the first initiative, the new 'congress' would, if it could agree on anything, carry on the baton for the next length. There is some disagreement about how this rather clever formula was evolved. The Webbs report that it was 'drafted in London by the members of the Independent Labour Party'.[111] Henry Pelling doubts this, and tells us that 'It appears rather to have been drafted by Thomas R. Steels, a member of the [Railway] union's Doncaster branch and of the ILP'.[112] Certainly the motion was proposed by the railway servants. Max Beer records that 'in the office of the *Labour Leader*, the organ of the ILP, a resolution was drafted . . . and handed over, through the executive of the Amalgamated Society of Railway Servants, to James Holmes . . . [one] of the delegates'.[113]

James Sexton's memoirs, however, contain a quite explicit account of the matter, which is consonant with both stories once it is realized that there were in fact three motions on the TUC's original order paper: one from the railwaymen, one from the London dockers, and the third from Sexton's own National Union of Dock Labourers. These were composited for debate at an informal meeting in which Keir Hardie participated:

'He, as a visitor, with "Jimmy" Holmes, Ben Tillett and myself, had fashioned the three resolutions of our respective unions into one.'[114] The initiators of the Labour Party, in other words, included two of the most important unions which later founded the Transport and General Workers' Union. They also included the one (in the shape of the NUR) which, later, got away.

The Parliamentary Committee, in its majority, had but small appetite for this decision, even though Congress delegates received its victory with unrestrained jubilation. Four members of the committee were delegated to sup with the socialist devil, in the general supposition that nothing much would come of it. The four people chosen were Sam Woods, W. C. Steadman, Will Thorne and Richard Bell. They represented the miners, the bargebuilders, the gasworkers and the railway servants respectively; but they were also drawn from different allegiances. Woods was a Liberal and rather a progressive one at that; Steadman was a Fabian and a Radical; Thorne a longstanding Social Democrat; and Bell, for the moment, a hostage if not exactly a follower of the ILP. The railway servants would not send him to Parliament unless he stood as an Independent.

Woods it had been who in 1892 had moved the censure of the Parliamentary Committee for failure to act adequately to implement Congress wishes on the legal Eight-Hours' Bill; and it was after this dispute that Woods succeeded Charles Fenwick as secretary of the Parliamentary Committee. Having been defeated as Lib.–Lab. MP for Ince in the landslide of 1895, he had won his way back into Parliament in the 1897 Walthamstow by-election. None the less, his politics were consistently at the Labour edge of the Lib.–Lab. spectrum: he not only campaigned for the legal eight-hour day, but for Irish Home Rule, payment of Members of Parliament, compulsory employers' liability, and nationalization of mining royalties. Like Tom Mann, he was among those who after 1900 joined in the National Democratic League to work for franchise reform. It was useful, to say the least, to have support from such a man, given the general sentiments of the majority of his colleagues among the TUC leadership.

Sexton reported the last act of the Parliamentary Committee in this drama with some wry detachment:

The Special Conference was held in the following year, and was attended by Michael Davitt as a visitor. The Parliamentary Committee . . . gave their report and then left the platform, believing that without their official countenance the whole attempt would fizzle out. No nominally representative body of men can ever have been more totally unable to read the signs of the times or appreciate the mood and spirit of those they were supposed to represent.[115]

So it was that the Trade Union Congress sired the Labour Party, even before the age of artificial insemination, at a distance somewhat greater than an arm's length.

# Notes

1  V. I. Lenin, *Imperialism, the Highest Stage of Capitalism*, Selected Works V (Martin Lawrence, 1936), p. 72.

2  See Michael Barratt Brown, *After Imperialism* (Heinemann, 1963), pp. 90ff.

3  R. C. K. Ensor, *England, 1870–1914* (Oxford University Press, 1936), p. 189.

4  R. Page Arnot, *The Miners*, vol. I (Allen and Unwin, 1949), p. 252. It is very likely that this intervention strongly delayed the Liberal decline in the coalfields.

5  Paul Thompson, *Socialists, Liberals and Labour: The Struggle for London, 1885–1914* (Routledge and Kegan Paul, 1967), pp. 52–3. Tom Mann had not, in fact, left trade unionism: this view reflects a general misapprehension about which we wrote in chapter 4.

6  George Tate, *The London Trades Council, 1860–1950: A History* (Lawrence and Wishart, 1950), p. 70.

7  It contributed, as well, to the growth of the quite separate Labour churches. These preached an ethical socialism, of which E. P. Thompson claims, 'It is . . . difficult to describe them as Christian or religious in any sense except that of the broad ethical appeal of the "religion of socialism" whose text was Morris's "Fellowship is Life" ' (E. P. Thompson, 'Homage to Tom Macguire', in Asa Briggs and John Saville (eds), *Essays in Labour History, 1886–1923* (Macmillan, 1960), p. 291.) Without doubting this, Stanley Pierson provides a more detailed account of the Labour church movement, tracing its origins in unitarianism, and following its doctrinal evolution in *Marxism and the Origins of British Socialism* (Cornell University Press, 1973), pp. 226–45.

8  Cf. Tom Mann and Ben Tillett, *The New Trade Unionism* (London, 1890).

9  Tate, *The London Trades Council*, p. 72.

10  Yvonne Kapp, *Eleanor Marx: The Crowded Years, 1884–1898* (Lawrence and Wishart, 1976), pp. 735–6.

11  Tate, *The London Trades Council*, p. 77.

12  Ibid., pp. 201ff.

13  Kapp, *Eleanor Marx*, p. 370.

14  Robert Blatchford, *My Eighty Years* (Cassell, 1931), p. 199.

15  Ben Tillett, *Memories and Reflections* (John Long, 1931), p. 190.

16  Paul Thompson, *Socialists, Liberals and Labour*, p. 101.

17  Kenneth O. Morgan, *Keir Hardie, Radical and Socialist* (Weidenfeld and Nicolson, 1975), pp. 44–9.

18  *Workman's Times*, 25 June 1892; cited in Fred Reid, *Keir Hardie, The Making of a Socialist* (Croom Helm, 1978), p. 130.

19  Kenneth D. Brown, *John Burns* (Royal Historical Society, 1977), p. 65.

20  Havelock Wilson, *My Stormy Voyage Through Life*, vol. I (Co-operative Printing Society, 1925), pp. 202–3.
21  Ibid.
22  J. Reynolds and K. Laybourne, 'The Emergence of the Independent Labour Party in Bradford', *International Review of Social History*, vol. XX (1975), pp. 326–7.
23  See Cyril Pearce, *The Manningham Mills Strike* (University of Hull, 1975).
24  Reynolds and Laybourne, 'The Emergence of the Independent Labour Party in Bradford', p. 329.
25  Ibid., p. 329.
26  Ibid., p. 327.
27  Jonathan Schneer, *Ben Tillett: Portrait of a Labour Leader* (Croom Helm, 1982), pp. 62–3.
28  Sidney and Beatrice Webb, *Letters*, ed. Norman MacKenzie, (Cambridge University Press, 1978), vol. I, pp. 419ff.
29  Schneer, *Ben Tillett*, p. 71.
30  Ibid., p. 72.
31  *Bradford Observer*, 6 July 1892; cited in Schneer, *Ben Tillett*, p. 77.
32  Reid, *Keir Hardie*, p. 134.
33  This and other once-famous squabbles are documented in A. E. P. Duffy, 'Differing Policies and Personal Rivalries in the Origins of the Independent Labour Party', *Victorian Studies*, vol. VI (Indiana University, 1962/3), pp. 43–65.
34  J. L. Garvin, 'A Party with a Future', *Fortnightly Review*, September 1895; cited in Eric J. Hobsbawm, *Labour's Turning Point, 1880–1900*, History in the Making, vol. III (Lawrence and Wishart, 1948), p. 146.
35  David Howell, *British Workers and the Independent Labour Party, 1888–1906* (Manchester University Press, 1983), p. 116.
36  Ibid., p. 17.4
37  E. P. Thompson, 'Homage to Tom Maguire', p. 277.
38  Jeffrey Hill, 'Manchester and Salford Politics and the Early Development of the Independent Labour Party', *International Review of Social History*, vol. XXVI (1981), part 2, pp. 186ff.
39  James Sexton, *Sir James Sexton, Agitator: the Life of the Dockers' MP* (Faber and Faber, 1936), pp. 129–30. Sexton was wrong about Hyndman, who was not present. His recollection of the argument with Shaw is also faulty: the objection to his presence was not based on his 'self-selection' but on his presumed antipathy to Independent politics.
40  Ibid., pp. 135–40.
41  G. D. H. Cole, *British Working Class Politics, 1832–1914* (Labour Book Service, 1941), pp. 138ff.
42  David C. Douglas (ed.), *English Historical Documents*, XII, 2 (Eyre and Spottiswood, 1977), p. 666, Document 172, 'Trade Unions and Socialism'. Douglas uses the report in *The Times*, 14 January 1893.
43  Schneer, *Ben Tillett*, p. 100.
44  Bernstein had many British defenders, and indeed Tillett attracted strong criticism from them. The issue did not go away quickly. (As late as 1965 it became an important part of the indictment of Labour Party provincialism published by Tom Nairn in the New Left broadside *Towards Socialism*.

This sparked a heated exchange among Labour historians: Perry Anderson and Robin Blackburn, *Towards Socialism* (Fontana, 1965), pp. 171ff.; E. P. Thompson, 'The Peculiarities of the English', in Ralph Milliband and John Saville (eds.), *The Socialist Register* (Merlin Press, 1965), pp. 340ff.; Jonathan Schneer, 'Ben Tillett's Conversion to Independent Labour Politics', *Radical History Review*, 24 (fall 1980), pp. 42–65).

There can be no doubt that Tillett's lapse in Bradford was only one of many. Beatrice Webb, in her diary, 27 November 1887, paints a picture of a dockers' meeting in East London, at which Tillett 'ranted against white slavery, sub-contract, and irregular hours'. A stranger entered, and pressed forward to the platform: 'No one knew him except the secretary. He took the seat nearest to me, and asked the chairman to give him the resolution to look at. Then in a stage whisper to the secretary, "I will give you twenty pounds but don't let my name appear. I don't want it to be known. Of course you will support me about foreign immigration"'

No one has been able to show that this donation to his union brought undue influence to bear upon him; but Tillett's condemnation of unrestricted immigration was none the less to be vigorous and outspoken. Thus his pamphlet *The Dock Labourers' Bitter Cry* (London, 1887) argued: 'The influx of continental pauperism aggravates and multiplies the number of ills which press so heavily on us . . . Foreigners come to London in large numbers, herd together in habitations unfit for beasts, the sweating system allowing the more grasping and shrewd a life of comparative ease in superintending the work.'

These and other instances have been documented by W. J. Fishman, *East End Jewish Radicals, 1875–1914* (Duckworth, 1975), pp. 76ff. At the same time, Fishman notes a number of utterances by Tillett which quite contradict these sentiments. Racism and anti-semitism were intricately embroidered on the social fabric of the East End and, says Fishman, 'To most trade unionists, the alien Jew meant sweating'.

45  Howell, *British Workers and the Independent Labour Party*, p. 302.
46  Christie's activities are documented in Peter Wyncoll, *The Nottingham Labour Movement, 1880–1939* (Lawrence and Wishart, 1985), pp. 115–18, 123–5 and 130–5.
47  Howell, *British Workers and the Independent Labour Party*, pp. 306 and 457.
48  David Clark, *Colne Valley, Radicalism to Socialism* (Longman, 1981), pp. 4 and 197.
49  Ibid., p. 30.
50  E. P. Thompson, 'Homage to Tom Macguire', p. 283.
51  Clark, *Colne Valley, Radicalism to Socialism*, p. 39.
52  Ibid., p. 40.
53  Ibid., p. 56.
54  Ibid., p. 89.
55  Henry Pelling, *Social Geography of British Elections* (Macmillan, 1967), p. 294.
56  Ibid.
57  Maddison's biography is to be found in J. M. Bellamy and J. Saville, *Dictionary of Labour Biography*, vol. IV (Macmillan, 1972), pp. 119–22.

58  Statement by F. W. Booth, *Hull Daily Mail*, 10 June 1895.
59  Ibid., 5 July 1895.
60  Ibid., 27 June 1895.
61  Ibid., 12 July 1895.
62  Ibid.
63  Ibid., 16 July 1895.
64  Ibid., 26 June 1895.
65  Ibid., 17 July 1895.
66  Pelling, *Social Geography of British Elections*, p. 295, gives a figure of 10 per cent, but this is of the electorate, not of those voting.
67  Ibid., p. 295.
68  J. Carter, 'The ILP in Ashton-under-Lyne 1893–1900', *Bulletin of North-West Group for the Study of Labour History* (1977), p. 76.
69  Ibid., p. 77; and Sexton, *Sir James Sexton, Agitator*, p. 145.
70  Cf. F. M. Leventhal, *Respectable Radical – George Howell and Victorian Working-Class Politics* (Weidenfeld and Nicolson, 1971), p. 212.
71  H. C. G. Matthew, R. I. McKibbin and J. A. Kay: 'The Franchise Factor in the Rise of the Labour Party', in J. M. Roberts and G. A. Holmes (eds), *The English Historical Review*, volume XCI (Longman, 1976), p. 726.
72  W. E. Gladstone, *Speeches and Addresses Delivered at the Election of 1865*, pp. 47–9; cited in Alan Bullock and Maurice Shock, *The Liberal Tradition* (A. and C. Black, 1956), pp. 143–4.
73  Ibid., p. 145.
74  Max Beer, *Fifty Years of International Socialism* (Allen and Unwin, 1937), p. 140.
75  Ibid., pp. 141–2.
76  L. H. Powell, *The Shipping Federation: A History of the First Sixty Years, 1890–1950* (Shipping Federation, 1950), p. 8.
77  Duncan Tanner, 'The Electoral System and the Rise of Labour', *Bulletin of the Institute of Historical Research* (1983), pp. 205–19.
78  See R. McKenzie and Allan Silver, *Angels in Marble* (Heinemann, 1968), for a convenient account of this phenomenon.
79  Howell, *British Workers and the Independent Labour Party*, p. 169.
80  The figures for all ILP contests are to be found in F. W. S. Craig, *Minor Parties at British Parliamentary Elections, 1885–1974*, pp. 39–40.
81  It has been reprinted in John Laurent (ed.), *Tom Mann –\Social and Economic Writings* (Spokesman Books, 1988), pp. 63ff.
82  Howell, *British Workers and the Independent Labour Party*, p. 171.
83  David Kynastone, *King Labour: The British Working Class, 1850–1914* (Allen and Unwin, 1976), p. 149.
84  Quoted in E. P. Thompson, *William Morris: Romantic to Revolutionary* (Lawrence and Wishart, 1955), p. 702.
85  Howell, *British Workers and the Independent Labour Party*, p. 121.
86  Keith Laybourn and J. Reynolds, *Liberalism and the Rise of Labour* (Croom Helm, 1984), p. 70.
87  Schneer, *Ben Tillett*, p. 110.
88  G. M. Trevelyan, *British History in the Nineteenth Century and After* (Longman, 1923), p. 420.
89  Henry Pelling, 'British Labour and British Imperialism', in Henry Pelling

(ed.), *Popular Politics in Late Victorian Britain* (Macmillan, 1968), p. 83.

90  Ibid.

91  G. D. H. Cole, 'John Burns', in Michael Katanka, *Radicals, Reformers and Socialists* (Charles Knight, 1973), p. 190.

92  G. D. H. Cole, *The Second International*, part I (Macmillan, 1956), p. 195.

93  Tom Mann, *Memoirs* (1923; reissued McGibbon and Kee, 1967), p. 125.

94  Cole, *The Second International*, part I, pp. 195–6.

95  James Joll, *The Second International* (Routledge and Kegan Paul, 1975), p. 72.

96  It also had other sinister overtones, brilliantly lampooned in G. K. Chesterton's novel *The Man Who Was Thursday* (Arrowsmith, 1908).

97  Mann, *Memoirs*, p. 105.

98  Ibid., p. 104.

99  A. Hamon, *Le Socialisme et le congrès de Londres* (Paris, 1897), p. 124.

100  J. Maitron, *Le Mouvement anarchiste en France* (Maspero, 1975), vol. I, p. 293.

101  Morgan, *Keir Hardie*, p. 88.

102  G. B. Shaw, 'Socialism at the International Congress', *Cosmopolis*, September 1896, III, p. 658.

103  Maitron, *Le Mouvement anarchiste en France*, p. 295.

104  Joll, *The Second International*, p. 61.

105  Philip Bagwell, *The Railwaymen* (Allen and Unwin, 1963), pp. 132–3.

106  A. E. P. Duffy, 'New Unionism in Britain, A Reappraisal', *Economic History Review*, vol. XIV, no. 2 (December 1961), pp. 313–14.

107  Ibid., p. 314.

108  Henry Pelling, *The Origins of the Labour Party* (Oxford University Press, 1966), p. 192.

109  TUC Report, 1899, p. 65.

110  Ibid.

111  Sidney and Beatrice Webb, *The History of Trade Unionism* (1894; WEA edn, 1912), p. 684.

112  Henry Pelling, *Origins of the Labour Party*, p. 205.

113  Max Beer, *History of British Socialism*, vol. II (G. Bell and Sons, 1921), p. 316.

114  Sexton, *Sir James Sexton, Agitator*, p. 194.

115  Ibid., p. 194.

# 8

# In Transition: 1900–1910

## I

### *The Struggle to Survive*

When all the bells stopped ringing, and the new century was installed, all the new unions, including those in the 'carrying trades', seemed to have opted for the quiet life. Some had been beaten flat by the mercenaries of the Shipping Federation. Others had survived by adopting the lowest of low profiles. It was to be eleven years before a new 'long hot summer' revived the old hopes on the waterfront.

During those years of apparent torpor, however, the struggle for survival continued. It demanded a high order of courage and commitment, not least because those exposed to its perils were unprotected by wider publicity. The anonymity of trade-union actions during these difficult years has lent superficial credibility to the notion that the 'great unrest' of 1911–14 was a new beginning, rather than a renewal within a continuing process stretching from the 1880s to the 1920s, in which the industrial and political purposes of trade unionism underwent a profound and permanent alteration.[1] We shall return to this academic debate later.

By 1900, in many areas every sign of independence, let alone purposeful protest, had been overwhelmed. This is not to say that all turbulence had evaporated.

### *Jingo Bells*

The year 1900 was that of Mafeking, when Colonel Baden-Powell's beleaguered forces were relieved after an Afrikaner siege of 217 days. This was celebrated in a 'crazy and rather unlovely carnival' throughout

London's streets.[2] 'No one', wrote Gareth Stedman Jones, 'who saw the crowds on Mafeking night ever forgot them'.[3] Bunting and flags and people erupted everywhere in Whitechapel and Bow; more flags sprouted on the trams and buses; the rich threw fivers or sovereigns at the tumult all around them; crowds rejoiced in every street, in song and drink, much of which was distributed free. 'Hundreds of cyclists wearing photographs of Colonel Baden-Powell formed in procession and paraded the principal thoroughfares of Poplar and Stepney', reported *The Times*.[4] Euphoria at the defeat of the Boer set ringing all the jingoistic echoes which dismayed radicals and socialists, but which signalled the presence of a strong patriotic affinity in the East End population. By no means was this attributable to any whiff of prosperity.

In 1902 Jack London, the popular American socialist writer, set out from Stepney Station on his journey of exploration among the London poor. He had originally stopped over *en route* to South Africa. He had a contract to write a book on the Boer War, but after the war ended it was cancelled. He decided instead to record his impressions of London slum life, which became *The People of the Abyss*, his favourite among his own books. Squalor and raw want were still the entire condition of the East End. Jack London began by kitting himself out in second-hand rags, and then dossed his way round all the spikes and Salvation Army hostels of the district. The spirit of Mafeking was, he found, very much abroad: the death of the old Queen had brought in its wake a Coronation, a celebration to unite the nation. So it did, bridging the great social divide with a vast ostentation of artificial pageantry on one side and a wild heave of drunken debauch on the other.

Standing in Trafalgar Square, walled in by a double file of soldiers, and overwhelmed by the sheer power of the well-fed legions of lifeguards, blue-jackets and metropolitan constables, Jack London, visiting from a more democratic world, felt that he could never have understood the stunted toilers of his 'abyss' until he had also seen the strapping Guards in the royal procession 'and come to know that the one must feed and clothe and groom the other'.

There is cheering down Whitehall; the crowd sways, the double walls of soldiers come to attention, and into view swing the King's watermen, in fantastic medieval garbs of red, for all the world like the van of a circus parade. Then a royal carriage, filled with ladies and gentlemen of the household with powdered footmen and coachmen most gorgeously arrayed. More carriages, lords and chamberlains, viscounts, mistresses of the robes – lackeys all. Then the warriors, a kingly escort, generals, bronzed and worn, from the ends of the earth come up to London Town, volunteer officers, officers of the militia and regular forces . . . there they come, in all the pomp and certitude of power, and still they come, these men of steel, these war lords and world harnessers. Pell-mell, peers and commoners, princes and maharajahs, colonials, lithe and hardy men . . .

and now the Horse Guards, a glimpse of beautiful cream ponies, and a golden panoply, a hurricane of cheers, the crashing of bands – 'The King! the King! God save the King!' Everybody has gone mad. The contagion is sweeping me off my feet – I, too, want to shout, 'The King! God save the King!' Ragged men about me, tears in their eyes, are tossing up their hats, and crying ecstatically, 'Bless 'em! Bless 'em! Bless 'em!' See, there he is, in that wondrous golden coach, the great crown flashing on his head, the woman in white beside him likewise crowned.[5]

## A Docker from the Abyss

Leaving the celebrations, Jack London visited the home of a docker, not far from Leman Street in Whitechapel:

It was not a room. Courtesy to the language will no more permit it to be called a room than it will permit a hovel to be called a mansion. It was a den, a lair. Seven feet by eight were its dimensions, and the ceiling was so low as not to give the cubic air space required by a British soldier in barracks. A crazy couch, with ragged coverlets, occupied nearly half the room. A rickety table, a chair and a couple of boxes left little space in which to run round. Five dollars would have purchased everything in sight. The floor was bare, while the walls and ceiling were literally covered with blood marks and splotches. Each mark represented a violent death – of an insect, for the place swarmed with vermin, a plague with which no person could cope single-handed.

The man who had occupied this hole, one Dan Cullen, docker, was dying in hospital. Yet he had impressed his personality on his miserable surroundings sufficiently to give an inkling as to what sort of man he was. On the walls were cheap pictures of Garibaldi, Engels, John Burns, and other labour leaders, while on the table lay one of Walter Besant's novels. He knew his Shakespeare, I was told, and had read history, sociology, and economics. And he was self-educated.

On the table, amidst a wonderful disarray, lay a sheet of paper on which was scrawled: Mr Cullen, please return the large white jug and corkscrew I lent you – articles loaned, during the first stages of his sickness, by a woman neighbour, and demanded back in anticipation of his death. A large white jug and a corkscrew are far too valuable to a creature of the Abyss to permit another creature to die in peace. To the last, Dan Cullen's soul must be harrowed by the sordidness out of which it strove vainly to rise.

It is a brief little story, the story of Dan Cullen, but there is much to read between the lines. He was born lowly, in a city and land where the lines of caste are tightly drawn. All his day he toiled hard with his body; and because he had opened the books, and been caught up by the fires of the spirit, and could 'write a letter like a lawyer', he had been selected by his fellows to toil hard for them with his brain. He became a leader of the fruit-porters, represented the dockers on the London Trades Council, and wrote trenchant articles for the labour journals.

He did not cringe to other men, even though they were his economic masters, and controlled the means whereby he lived, and he spoke his mind freely, and fought the good fight. In the 'Great Dock Strike' he was guilty of taking a leading part. And that was the end of Dan Cullen. From that day he was a marked man, and every day, for ten years and more, he was 'paid-off' for what he had done.[6]

Many parts of the country followed East London into quiescence. Stronger men than Dan Cullen were steamrollered. If the name for such conditions be 'peace', then peace reigned widely while they buried the old century with the old Queen, and installed the new King with his informal but dazzling court of plutocrats and swingers.

But the decade we are considering was not wholly pacifist in its industrial temper. The Homeric qualities of the Penrhyn Quarry strikes in North Wales spread over from the 1890s. The 1907 upheaval in Belfast, which gave James Larkin the impetus to introduce general unionism into Ireland and to invent 'Larkinism', surely prefigured the rising of all the transport workers in 1911. Both disputes fall in this interim period. While Belfast in 1907 anticipated by four years the characteristic militancy of the general labourers in the 'syndicalist' years, the railwaymen also voted by a massive majority for a national strike in 1907: this 'first' was only averted by government intervention to force a conciliation scheme on the reluctant railway companies.[7]

## The Roots of Industrial 'Peace'

The general impression of industrial peace is not, however, a false one. In the decade 1890–9 there was an average of 804 strikes per annum. Between 1900 and 1909 the figure almost halved, to 464.[8]

Three reasons may be advanced to account for the relative quiescence of the period. The Taff Vale and other subsequent judgements of the courts in 1901 made serious inroads into the hitherto assumed legality of strike action. Trade-union leaders were certainly constrained to withhold official support for strikes, after heavy financial penalties imposed on the rail union in the Taff Vale case. But this influence could have been operative only for the years 1902–6, after which the incoming Liberal government reversed the judges' rulings in the 1906 Trades Disputes Act (see p. 302). Yet the number of strikes in all industries remained low for the rest of the decade. In any case, the Taff Vale effect, where it operated, served only to reinforce a much longer-held predeliction for peaceful settlements which had been pursued by most new-unionist leaders from the early 1890s onwards – an attitude stemming most obviously from their reduced bargaining, numerical and financial strengths, brought about by economic depression and high unemployment.

We saw in chapter 5 that the long slump ended in the mid-1890s and that an upswing ran through to the turn of the century. Unemployment fell from 7.5 per cent in 1893 to 2 per cent in 1899; but thereafter it rose again to 6 per cent in 1905, fell to 3.6 per cent in 1906, and climbed again to 7.7 per cent in 1909. This perennial instability of the labour market, affecting 'unskilled' and casual labour most acutely, was a constant constraint on new-unionist activities.

The third factor inhibiting union initiatives was the attitude of the employers. The Shipping Federation's onslaught had won the field for its free-labour method of curtailing union power: from the mid-1890s and throughout the 1900s such strikes as occurred on the waterfront were regularly met by the employers with the importation of free labour: it is noticeable how often the reports refer to Hull (Collison's 'stronghold of free labour') as the source of the strike-breakers. In other industries, notably engineering and footwear, strong employers' federations pursued the same methods. In this climate, unions 'kept their heads down', husbanded islands of recognition and existing conciliation procedures, and awaited better times. Equally, most employers, finding themselves in control of the situation, refrained from further union-smashing campaigns, and consequently the unions were not compelled to enter further desperate defensive struggles. Away from the battlefields of the waterfront, Tillett found grounds for satisfaction in 1901, in the tolerance and encouragement offered by those employers who had continued to accept trade unions: 'I am glad to recognise the growing confidence of employers in Trades Unionism, the more practical seeing the need of closer association and discussion with the workers' representatives. This has resulted almost in the abolition of strikes, greatly to the credit of both sides'.[9]

## Union Membership

The workers, for their part, had by no means abandoned trade unionism. Membership figures showed a steady, even substantial recovery from the nadir of 1895. In rounded numbers, total membership in Great Britain grew from 1.5 million in 1895 to 2 million in 1900 and to 2.5 million in 1910, only faltering in this trend in the recession of 1904–5. This is an increase of 67 per cent between 1895 and 1910. However, within these totals, the fortunes of transport and general unions varied significantly. 'All-grade' transport unions – the London Carmen, the Amalgamated Carters, the Amalgamated Tram and Vehicle Workers, the Municipal Employees (which had members in municipal transport undertakings) and the NUDL – together registered only a 27 per cent increase in this period. Even that result was beyond the 'general' unions – the London Dockers, the Gasworkers, the NAUL and the NALU – whose combined growth was restricted to a mere 7 per cent. And the 'aristocratic', sectional unions – including the London Stevedores, the Thames Watermen, the Cardiff Trimmers, the Mersey Quay and Rail Carters, and the Winsford Saltmakers – registered no increase at all.[10] This stagnation, most evidently for the London Stevedores and Lightermen, represented an actual retreat, as less formally qualified labour encroached on their territories. We shall see later that this experience contributed significantly to their crucial conversion to the cause of federation at the end of the decade.

## Transport Technology

The transport industries continued their technological evolution during this period, largely by substituting steam and electricity for wind- and horse-power. (The full impact of the internal combustion engine came later.) As we have seen (chapters 3 and 5), these changes were hardly ever labour-saving, nor did they enhance the technical sophistication of labour in transport, except where horses were displaced on the roads by electricity, steam and later by the petrol motor. Indeed, in the case of the switch from sail to steam in shipping, the old sailor's old skills in seamanship were displaced, and the ordinary deckhand became more of 'a cleaner and polisher'.[11] However, in the booming passenger-liner trade, a new semi-skilled group emerged, including ships' cooks, butchers, and stewards, with a status superior to the deckies. The number of seamen of all grades increased by 32,000 to 205,000 during the decade.[12] In 1900 the number of sailing ships was still greater by 1,500 than the number of steam ships, but the latter accounted for 7.2 million tons of a total merchant tonnage of 9.3 million. By 1910 sailing ships numbered 9,000, which was then 3,000 fewer than ships under steam power: steamships then accounted for 10.4 million of a total fleet of 11.5 million tons.[13]

On the docks, hydraulic cranes and steam winches had been replacing human lifting power since the 1890s. This change, characteristically, made no impact on the rate of increase of the dock-labour force, which grew by almost 23,000 between 1901 and 1911, to a total of 123,000.[14] This represented a comparable rate of growth to that of the previous twenty years. Similar rates of growth were registered amongst ware-housemen, porters and messengers, who totalled 232,000 by 1911.[15] Significantly, watermen and bargemen, having held their numbers at 29,000 for twenty years, lost almost 2,000 between 1901 and 1911 – further evidence of the shrinking base on which their sectional unionism rested.

In road haulage, the decisive displacement of the horse and cart by the motor lorry was still some decades distant (see table 8.1). Road haulage employed a total of 238,001 employees in 1911. Of these, 58 per cent were engaged by haulage contractors; overwhelmingly these were small-scale capitalists. Of the rest, 26 per cent worked on vans and delivery carts in food and drink. Carters were also employed in large numbers by the railway companies, coal merchants and mining companies, brewers, and in local government. The numbers seeking carting work were constantly reinforced by surplus farmworkers, who were well qualified in the management of horses. Booth had calculated that, in 1890, 43 per cent of all heads of families engaged in carting in London were born outside the capital.[16]

Table 8.1   *Commercial Road Vehicles, 1900–1920*
*(Nos in 000s)*

|  | 1900 | 1910 | 1920 |
|---|---|---|---|
| Horse-drawn | 680 | 830 | 430 |
| Motor-driven | 2* | 50† | 142 |

*1902
†1911
Source: Charles H. Feinstein and Sydney Pollard (eds), *Studies in Capital Formation in the United Kingdom, 1750–1920* (Oxford University Press, 1988), pp. 322 and 326.
           (Reproduced by permission of Oxford University Press.)

Horse-drawn buses, mainly developed by large but localized private companies, fulfilled a role in the development of urban passenger transport in the late nineteenth century, but had to compete with trams (which were powered successively by horse, steam and electric power) and later with motor buses. The figures tell the story (see table 8.2).

The dominant era of the electric tram ran from the 1880s to the 1920s. Between the 1870s and 1914, route mileage rose from 100 (or a little over) to over 2,500.[17]

Table 8.2   *Horse-drawn and Motor-powered Omnibuses, 1900–1920 (Nos in 000s)*

|  | 1900 | 1910 | 1920 |
|---|---|---|---|
| Horse-drawn | 35 | 10 | – |
| Motorized | 0* | 3† | 10 |

*1902
†1911
Source: Charles H. Feinstein and Sydney Pollard (eds), *Studies in Capital Formation in the United Kingdom, 1750–1920* (Oxford University Press, 1988), pp. 322 and 326.
           (Reproduced by permission of Oxford University Press.)

In London the first motor bus began the run from Charing Cross to Victoria before the turn of the century, but its schedule was much disrupted by mechanical hiccups. By 1903 there were thirteen London motor buses, out of a total of 3,636. But six years later more than one-third of London buses had been converted, and General Omnibus sacked its last horse bus in 1911. Others followed more slowly, but the changeover was remorseless, and virtually complete by the middle of the war. Traffic increased proportionately. In 1902 the London buses carried 280 million passengers. By 1913 there were 736 million. After the war there were legions of soldiers who were qualified as drivers, and there followed a big increase in the services run by large companies, together with a mushrooming of little firms run by one or two people. By 1929 London buses carried 1,912 million passengers in the one year.[18]

The overall workforce employed on buses actually declined slightly between 1901 and 1911, from 11,974 to 11,442.[19] The fashionable technology in urban passenger transport at this time was the tram, the first means of transport to exploit recognizable twentieth-century power in the form of electricity. The first decade saw a near-trebling in the value of net capital stock in the industry, from £15 million to £42 million. Thereafter, investment declined, partly through wartime neglect and partly through belated competition from the motor omnibus. In 1920 the tramways' capital stock had fallen to £24 million.[20] The most striking evidence of the tramway 'boom' lies in the numbers employed, which more than doubled in ten years, from 18,244 in 1901 to 42,095 in 1911. (In 1881 there had been a mere 2,650 tramwaymen.) The tram industry was dominated by municipal ownership in the large towns. Municipal 'socialism' was often initiated by local politicians of all colours. It fed local pride. It also made a contribution to the ranks of transport trade unionism.

The changeover from horse-power to the internal combustion engine in the cab trade, whilst in full swing in our period, also climaxed in the following decade (see table 8.3).

The total occupied population grew from 11.2 million in 1881 to 14.3 million in 1901, an increase of 28 per cent. In the same period, the transport trades – that is, all the industries reviewed above – grew by 56 per cent to a total of 817,193. By 1911 the total occupied population had increased to 16.3 million, a gain of 13 per cent for the decade. Transport in 1911 employed 982,344 – a leap of 20 per cent. Between 1881 and 1911 transport employment grew from 4.6 per cent to 6 per cent of the working population.

Table  8.3  *Horse-drawn   Cabs   and   Motor   Taxis,
1900–1920 (Nos in 000s)*

|  | 1900 | 1910 | 1920 |
|---|---|---|---|
| Horse-drawn | 90 | 95 | 50 |
| Motorized | 3* | 31† | 79 |

*1902
†1911
Source: Charles H. Feinstein and Sydney Pollard (eds), *Studies in Capital Formation in the United Kingdom, 1750–1920* (Oxford University Press, 1988).
(Reproduced by permission of Oxford University Press.)

## 'Residual' Labour in Transport and Its Employers

The increase in transport employment fuelled by the Industrial Revolution had generated faster growth than that in manufacturing employment from the mid-nineteenth century onwards. By the beginning of the twentieth century it was by no means over. Almost all transport trades seemed, during the early decades of the 1900s, to have an insatiable appetite for labour. In this they were comparable with the textile-factory trades, mining and metals, during the first stages of industrialization. Thus, although transport was clearly a *group* of industries or services with wide heterogeneities within it, rather than a single industry, its distinct sections had this in common: the workforce was continually reinforced by new recruits as its number expanded. Phillips speaks of it as seeming to be a 'residual' form of employment.[21] (Irish and displaced agricultural labourers made up a large element of the inflow.) This gave to its workers a certain community of outlook, a sense that they were indeed 'general labour', casual, or irregular, or hyper-exploited. Outsiders would characterize them as 'lower', or even 'brutish' classes.[22] Low-level technology prevailed. It is very significant that in the developing struggle towards federation, amalgamation and the ultimate achievement of the unified TGWU, the one branch of transport with an advanced technology – railways – developed a unionism which could not ultimately bring itself to submerge its identity with carters, busmen and dockers. Dislocation of status can be a very painful prospect, and the fear of it must have been a powerful influence.

Matching the complexity of transport labour was the confusion of different kinds of employers. They ranged from the great capitalists of the shipping companies, international in scale, through the large national capitalism of the railway companies – which were taking over more and more dock property (especially in the Humber, the South Wales ports and Southampton) as the new century advanced – to the municipal tramway companies, and the diminutive haulage and cab proprietors. Small capital still held a place in dockland, too, and would continue to do so right down to the Devlin reforms of the 1960s.[23] Whilst there was no simple correlation between scale of ownership and attitudes to unionism, it is true that the shipping magnates and railway-dock owners, together with the major dock companies in London, continued to show the most consistent hostility, whilst small master-stevedoring companies in both London and Liverpool established a much more tolerant relationship with the unions. Private bus companies, notably in London, opposed trade unionism, whilst municipal tramways encouraged it. In carting, the small-scale employers and the larger capitalist brewers shared opposition to recognition, which was not to be overcome until the First World War, and indeed persisted beyond it.

## Two Necessities: Recognition and Amalgamation

To grow and prosper, after their setbacks of the 1890s, transport unions (and those general unions which enrolled in the transport trades) needed recognition from the employers. They could compel that recognition against the intransigent sections of the employers only by a show of strength and by the enrolment of a larger proportion of the labour forces. The economic situation was slowly restoring a climate in which such strength might be restored to its 1889 dimensions. But it was borne in upon the trade-union leadership, and ultimately on the membership, that an essential requirement, if their potential strength was to be realized, was to overcome the variety of forms of sectional isolation into which the depression and the Shipping Federation had driven them. Of course, in inland transport, there was no model of previous unity and national organization, such as the dockers inherited from 1889–91. Yet they had their own impulsion, centred round the need to overcome the great regional and local disparities of earnings and conditions which character-ized their industry. As with the seamen, their aspirations were directed towards the achievement of national, standard wage-scales. On both the waterfront and the roads, a convergence towards federation and ultimate amalgamation was possible and necessary.

## Upstairs, Downstairs

The social condition underlying the great unrest of 1910–14 has commonly been taken to be the decline in real wages which preceded it during the first years of the century. This analysis, nowadays contested, has owed much to the influential work of George Dangerfield, whose book *The Strange Death of Liberal England, 1910–14* was first published in 1935. (It is still a resonant and exciting work.) The Edwardian era was an age in which ostentatious consumption, the crude public display of wealth by a plutocracy growing fat on the profits of imperialism, was given sanction and licence by court circles, and reached levels which positively provoked the proletarian distemper of the great unrest. This was the world of Upstairs, Downstairs.

The case of the millionaire Wilson brothers, shipping magnates of Hull, is characteristic. Already in 1876 they were declaring gross profits of 51 per cent. By the turn of the century they had amassed the largest privately owned merchant fleet in the world, and their business was worth £2.5 million. They monopolized the Baltic trades, driving away potential competitors with notorious ruthlessness. They warred incessantly, and very publicly, with the Hull Dock Company, and also – as we have seen – with the Dockers' Union, after an initial period in which they patronized it. The historians of Hull have written:

> While it had long been the custom of Hull magnates to live in the country, no one had yet displayed the baronial splendour of Charles Wilson, M.P., at Warter Priory, bought from Lord Muncaster, or of Arthur Wilson, his brother and master of fox-hounds, at Tranby Croft. [Charles] married his eldest son to the daughter of a Duke, setting them up in The Cottage, Cottingham (now part of a University Hall of Residence). In 1905, he was ennobled as Lord Nunburnholme . . .[24]

Arthur Wilson was host to a notorious house party at Tranby Croft at which the Prince of Wales (the future King Edward VII) was a guest. A scandal of national proportions arose out of accusations of cheating at baccarat by one of the guests.

## Wages Down Below

At the same time, it was believed by a whole generation of historians that the real wage of the working class was actually falling from about 1900 onwards, as the cost of living outpaced money wages. Those price and wage statistics which were available to Dangerfield confirmed this view. The statisticians A. L. Bowley and G. H. Wood produced a series of figures, used subsequently by Layton and Crowther in a study published in 1938.[25] No regular official indices for our period were produced. Bowley's and Wood's work shows that average retail prices rose by some 10 per cent between 1900 and 1910, falling only once in that time, by a single point in 1905–6. During the same period, average money wages fell by 3.3 per cent from 1900 to 1904, recovering only to their 1900 level by 1910. Thus, a fall in real wages of some 10 per cent was demonstrated. Dangerfield accepted this conclusion: 'Society in the last pre-war years grew wildly plutocratic . . . only the workers seemed to be deprived of their share in prosperity: in 1910 the English worker was a poorer man than he was in 1900'.[26]

Sydney Pollard, using more recent statistical research, however, has produced a series showing that the real wage rate rose by 6 per cent between 1900 and 1910.[27] Whilst this may appear to undermine the 'Dangerfield interpretation' of the causation of the great unrest, Pollard has also shown that *wages as a share of national income*, which had held up during the depression, began a decline which took them from 41 per cent in 1896 to 36.6 per cent in 1913 (see fig. 8.1).

E. H. Phelps-Brown, in his examination of industrial relations between 1906 and 1914, relies on Bowley's and Wood's series, but asserts only that 'in several countries, economic forces were *checking the rise* in real wages'.[28] In speculating on why the industrial protest against this trend was so long delayed and confined, when it came, to the 'unskilled', the railways and mining, he reflects: 'One reason may be sheer unawareness of the change. By present standards it was an age of statistical darkness: increasing attention was being given to the cost of living, but if the change in the course of real wages was estimated by one or two specialists, that was as far as knowledge of it had gone.'[29]

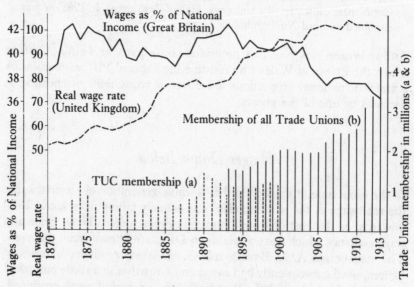

**Fig. 8.1**   Trade Union Membership and Wages, 1870–1912

*Source:* Sydney Pollard, 'Trade Unions and the Labour Market, 1870–1914', *Yorkshire Bulletin of Economic and Social Research*, vol. 17, no. 1 (May 1965), pp. 101–2. (Reprinted by permission of the Trustees of the *Yorkshire Bulletin of Economic and Social Research*.)

A more recent historian is aware that the statistics involved here were all people, some of whom knew from their own experience what scholars have since had to learn from afar: 'The likelihood is that even had the cost of living remained stable the lower paid would have gradually realised that they were not getting enough. The primary poverty that went with regular wage-earning could hardly be explained away in terms of the 1s. or 2s. in the pound rise in the cost of living'.[30]

The Board of Trade, in response to public concern, reported belatedly on the cost of living for the first time only in 1913, suggesting that it had risen by 14 per cent since 1906. This information clearly came too late to influence pre-war trade-union responses.

But important pioneering work on the distribution of income, and on the statistical evidence of inequality, was emerging in the publications of the Fabians, and in the work of L. G. Chiozza Money, whose *Riches and Poverty* was first published in 1905; it subsequently ran through many editions. He showed that at the income-tax exemption limit of just £160 a year, the national income divided into two equal parts. One-half was shared by 38 million people below the limit, and one-half by just 5 million above it.

Whatever the precise nature of the relative movements of wages and prices, which may remain uncertain, the average movements would, as they always do, conceal from view what was happening to particular groups. Given the expansive growth of their numbers, the frail condition into which their unions had fallen and the absence of negotiating machinery to compel their employers to make standard increases in wages, the general labourers and the transport workers may safely be assumed to have suffered disproportionately from the rise in prices. This combined with the decadent displays of the wealthy, many of whom were directly profiting from the misery of the poor, was the source of the slow build-up to the revolt of the labourers. Alongside it went a degree of disillusionment with the performance of official Labour in Parliament. This was very strong on the political left, and can also be found in more moderate quarters. The Webbs commented in 1912: 'The manual working wage-earner has lost faith in the necessity, let alone the righteousness, of the social arrangements to which he finds himself subjected.'[31]

How general were these sentiments? It is not easy to determine. What is plain is that, whatever people expected from the Labour Party in Parliament, they did not defer to its judgements and would not be restrained by its opinions. The sense of relative deprivation was undoubtedly more consciously experienced at this time, and it combined with the vivid presence of absolute poverty to provide a spur to action.

But first the transport and general unions had to work through a decade of less spectacular recovery and transition, in an economic and social climate which was engendering profound discontent among the mass of the workers. At the same time, trade-union leaders such as Tillett showed evidence in their public utterances and Reports of a mounting apprehension at the growth of trusts, cartels and monopolies: the sheer scale of early twentieth-century capitalism seemed positively to menace labour organization.

## II

## A Disastrous Strike

In London, the new century opened with further disaster for the Dockers' Union. In a short phase of brisk trade, the dockers at the Royal Docks struck for the stevedores' rate of 8d., with 1s. overtime, at the same time demanding that taking-on be transferred outside the dock gates where they could enforce union control. The union supported the strike, but sought backing from Stevedores' and Lightermen's Unions in vain. The Shipping Federation deployed its tried and trusted method, importing strike-breaking labour. The union was once again humiliated, and lost all influence in the Royal Docks. At the same time, the shift of trade downstream to Tilbury, where the union's presence was marginal, accelerated. The Dockers' Union in London was reduced to minuscule proportions. In 1901, the union's total income from its London districts was £344 11s. 11d., out of a total income for the whole union of £8,033 13s. 9d.[32] Tilbury's two branches returned just £17 10s. 3d.! Little evidence of recovery was forthcoming throughout the decade. In 1910 the Loondon district's income was £551 2s. 1d., out of the national total of £11,391 11s. 0d., with Tilbury hanging on with £25 0s. 11d. In 1891 there were sixty-five branches of the Dockers' Union in London. In 1901 there were only fifteen. At the end of 1910 there were twelve.[33]

## Stevedores and Lightermen

The Stevedores' union presided over a shrinking enclave of recognition and security. The cement combine and the large shipping companies were joined by Scruttons', a larger than average stevedoring company, in breaking the union's controls downstream. Yet the union clung to its isolation, refusing participation in the federations initiated by Tillett and Mann in the 1890s. It began to repair links with the wider movement by joining the General Federation of Trade Unions in 1899, it affiliated to the Labour Party and participated in local government. It also held discussions with James Sexton on safety regulations for the industry.[34] But it was belligerently antipathetic to industrial alliances. An undated pamphlet of the Amalgamated Stevedores' Labour Protection League, in which a reformed rule book is proposed, advanced the following Rule 1: 'That there shall be no person enrolled as a member of this Society until occasion demands. That the Transport Workers' Federation be totally ignored'.[35] This attitude, we shall see (chapter 9), was overcome; in the event, the stevedores' joined the National Transport Workers' Federation (NTWF).

Through the decade 1900–10 the isolationists held sway, however, strongly motivated by the memory of their losses in the 1891 conflict with the Shipping Federation. In particular they were estranged from Tillett's union, which had not only encroached on their territories, but had also accused them of blacklegging in the 1900 strike in the Royal Docks.[36] Yet the stevedores' leadership, especially that of James Anderson, its outward-looking secretary, understood that the mere defence of a shrinking specialism could no longer serve as an adequate strategy. Demarcation boundaries had been breached by the major employers, and the union itself had begun to enrol shipboard dockers engaged in discharging, thus abandoning its exclusive concern with loading. The steamship required less finesse in the loading operation, anyway, than had the sailing ship. Since the Dockers' Union was moribund, it could have fallen to the Stevedores' union to initiate any general move to re-create general organization in the port in these new circumstances, which included the acute problem of Tilbury, where employers' dominance was becoming a threat to unions throughout the whole port. Thus, in 1909, Anderson proposed to his executive that 'the necessary steps should be taken to enrol as members all men engaged in the operations of loading and unloading vessels, or handling cargo on dock, wharf, or quay, in the Port of London, and strongly recommends that these steps be taken at the earliest opportunity.'[37] This proposal, had it been implemented, would have transformed the union into an all-grade dockers' body akin to Sexton's union. Powerful, conservative influences in the branches prevented any action to apply it. The logic which had produced it, however, was finally to be acknowledged when the union joined the NTWF.

Similar pressures were impelling the Lightermen's Union to reconsider its exclusivity. The trade's Conciliation Board had collapsed in the 1890s, and it had faced strikes in 1900 and 1909. It opened its membership to non-freemen in 1900, and in 1910 brought in the Medway bargemen, hitherto a grade beneath the watermen's notice. Its relations with increasingly hostile employers were deteriorating, adding further weight to Harry Gosling's long struggle to bring his traditionally aristocratic membership to an acceptance of the need for wider industrial association. In these ways the two sectional, but stable, port unions of London were prepared for the Federal initiatives which were shortly to mature.

Meanwhile, the Dockers' Union stagnated, Tillett's Annual Reports extracting what significance he could from the union's participation in the campaign for government inspection and regulation of safety conditions on the docks, a matter in which Sexton made all the running.

## Port Ownership: the Port of London Authority

One structural reform in London might have given dock unionism an opportunity to restore and extend some of its influence. In 1908, the Port of London Act established the Port of London Authority (PLA), a public trust, as the sole owner and manager of all the riverside and docks, though not the wharves. This was part of a general tendency towards sole ownership and management of port installations everywhere. Indeed London had survived longer than other ports as an unplanned, multiple-owned agglomeration of docks and quays. Liverpool and Glasgow had well-established public utility trusts – the Mersey Docks and Harbour Board, and the Clyde Navigation Trust – which had taken over from the civic owners half a century earlier. In Bristol the municipality had acquired sole ownership of the port in 1848. In Southampton, the Humber ports and South Wales the railway companies had financed, and finally acquired control of, port installations over a longer period. In South Wales the Great Western Railway Company completed its regional ports monopoly in 1923, when it took over the Swansea docks from the Swansea Harbour Trust. The Manchester Ship Canal Company raised private capital, and also became a monopoly owner of its docks. The London reform was thus overdue, and followed a series of private mergers which had left all the docks on the North Bank in the hands of a single 'joint docks' committee'.

For the unions, the PLA became a hope frustrated. The idea of public ownership harmonized with their consistent campaigns of the 1890s for municipalization. A public authority such as the PLA might be expected to recognize the status of labour and the unions, and to give its attention to decasualization. But only two labour representatives were initially appointed to the Authority. They were Harry Gosling and James Anderson. (The omission of Tillett from the appointees was in itself a clear indication of his union's condition in the port.) The PLA, far from meeting the union's programmes on labour practices, took over the old Joint Dock Companies' classification system (see chapter 5) and conceded nothing to the unions.[38] Governmental attempts to use legislation to compel the port employers, through the PLA, to plan labour engagement more rationally and to institute daily notifications throughout the port to unemployed dockers, informing them where jobs might be obtained, were totally frustrated by the port's major users of labour – the shipping and merchant interests which dominated the Authority. Only one-third of the port's labour force was in the permanent employment of the PLA: the rest continued as before to fight at the call-stands for the attention of foremen representing the big shippers, stevedoring companies and merchants.[39]

## Dockers and Tinplatemen

In the other ports where Tillett's union retained membership, the period was one of modest overall growth (although Bristol doubled its membership) and heavy dependence upon the South Wales (especially the tinplate) districts.

South Wales, as can be seen from table 8.4, saved the Dockers' Union from virtual extinction during the lean years. Much depended on the attitude of the employers. In Newport the dock company and other port employers, largely involved in the expanding coal export trade, recognized and bargained with the union. They established the Newport Coaltipping

Table 8.4  *DWRGWU District Income, 1901–1910*

| | 1901:£ | % | | 1910:£ | % |
|---|---|---|---|---|---|
| Bristol | 831 | (10.3) | | 1656 | (14.5) |
| Gloucester | 727 | (9.1) | | 762 | (6.7) |
| London | 334 | (4.2) | | 551 | (4.9) |
| Hull | 368 | (4.6) | | 63 | (0.6) |
| North-east* | 339 | (4.2) | | 543 | (4.8) |
| Newport† | 1336 | (16.6) | | 847 | (7.4) |
| Swansea† | 3989 | (49.7) | transit | 1850 | (16.2) |
| | | | tinplate | 2198 | (19.3) |
| Barry† | | | | 739 | (6.5) |
| Cardiff† | | | | 311 | (2.9) |
| Midlands‡ | | | | 453 | (4.0) |
| Misc.** | 107 | (1.3) | | 148 | (1.3) |
| Total: | 8033 | (100.0) | | 11391 | (100.0) |

*Confined to Middlesbrough (dockers) and Teesside.
†Swansea was divided into separate transit and tinplate sections in 1907. The tinplate income is incorporated in the 1901 general Swansea total, by which time the tinplate branches of 1910 had already been formed. In 1901, branches in Barry and Cardiff were included in the Newport and Swansea Districts. The combined Welsh contribution to the union's income was 66.3 per cent in 1901, and 52.3 per cent in 1910. Including Bristol, the whole Bristol Channel region contributed 76.6 per cent and 66.8 per cent.
‡A miscellaneous group of branches administered by District offices in Stalybridge and Salford, they included the Manchester Ship Canal dockers, and branches in Walsall, Widnes, Wolverhampton, etc.
**Included branches in Arbroath, Ipswich, Bridgwater, Mold, etc., in 1901. Two Southampton branches had reappeared by 1910, one of which dated from 1905.

*Source:* DWRGWU Annual Reports, 1901–10

and Trimming Conciliation Board, which maintained industrial peace – at least until 1908, when a brief strike was directed against the hiring of Chinese sailors to load general cargo.[40] The National Amalgamated Labourers' Union continued with its attempts to poach the Dockers' members, despite a formal agreement of 1905 between the two unions.

In Swansea, too, employers in the patent fuel and timber trades held to their recognition of the union, and in the docks conciliation was employed to preserve wage levels: a union representative, Tom Merrells, was appointed to the Swansea Harbour Trust. A major strike broke out in 1900, directed against the use of free labour. It spread to Weaver's flour mills nearby, and the Shipping Federation brought in strike-breakers from Hull. Tillett sanctioned the strike and organized a picket on every shop where Weaver's flour was sold. The strike ended with the capitulation of the employers. Elsewhere in Swansea, the union made substantial wage gains in the patent-fuel industry and in the docks between 1900 and 1910. As at Newport, the union clashed with NALU over recruitment rights, in 1908.

In Cardiff the union was faced with opposition from the Cardiff Railway Company, which owned the docks. Deal-runners were defeated in a strike, which again involved the deployment of strike-breakers from Hull. Some union enclaves were created, in iron-ore labouring (1901), pitwood yards (1904) and dry-dock workers (1907). But Cardiff's poor state in 1910 may be seen from table 8.4.

At Barry docks, the union won recognition in 1906 and established a separate district, which also recruited in the flour mills.

Only at Port Talbot did the Dockers' Union prevail against the Cardiff, Barry and Penarth Coal Trimmers, the aristocracy of the waterfront, to recruit this grade of workers.

The NALU preserved its total membership throughout the decade, which it entered with 3,505 members. By 1910 it had retained 3,549.

In the tinplate section, established in the 1890s (see chapter 5), Tillett himself took a special interest and used his influence to ensure that peace and conciliation prevailed, despite several disputes which originated in sectional claims by other unions. No wage gains were pressed, despite the spectacular growth of tinplate exports to Europe, which all but doubled in the decade. The tinplatemen's importance to the union can be seen from table 8.4: their contributions in 1910 were four times as great as the whole of the London district, amounting to almost one-fifth of the union's total income. As well as their own district secretary, the tinplatemen had three representatives on the National Executive in 1910. This representation became a traditional one, and at least one tinplateman was always elected to the General Executive Council of the TGWU until the 1970s. The union's only problem with the tinplatemen arose over politics: it became so involved in promoting Labour Party activity in Swansea and Newport that in the January 1910 General

Election Tillett was selected to fight the Swansea seat against Alfred Mond, the chemical manufacturer, who stood for the Liberals. The tinplate members of Tillett's union backed the Liberals, Mond himself and free trade: they had suffered from the effects of the Americans' McKinley tariff. And their Welsh sabbatarianism was outraged when Tillett held two election meetings on a Sunday. They threatened to leave his union, but were mollified by the result: Tillett lost by a margin of four to one.

## The Newport Dispute

In Newport, at the end of the decade, a serious strike erupted, with syndicalist overtones. The shipping firm of Houlder Bros sought to substitute day-wages for the traditional piece-work, giving the men the prospect of reduced earnings and hiring for the day only, instead of for the duration of the job. When the dockers struck against the new system in May 1910, the firm used Shipping Federation strike-breakers from London. This provoked a general dock strike in the port. After fighting between blacklegs and strikers, the 'free' men returned to London. Houlders persisted: the Shipping Federation supplied replacement strike-breakers from its depot ship, the *Lady Jocelyn*, moored in the Bristol Channel. Houlders rejected arbitration and also the negotiated settlement offered by the union's district secretary: the fighting resumed. Frank Houlder demanded, in the most militant and arrogant terms, police and military protection for his labour. The Board of Trade (in the person of Sydney Buxton), the local authority, and the Home Office, turned him down. Sir Edward Troup, Permanent Under-Secretary at the Home Office, was buried in telegrams from the Shipping Federation, the Mayor and Chief Constable of Newport, demanding government reinforcements. He was also subjected to heavy pressure by Houlder himself, as he reported to his political chief, Churchill:

> About 10.45 p.m. last night Mr. Houlder called at my house about the Newport disturbances. He seemed to have dined and was much excited . . . [he claimed that] 40 of his men were at that moment being murdered and he demanded that I should instantly take steps to save them. He said that he held the government responsible; that I was the government, and that I should stop it! . . . I said that we were sending 300 police by special train tomorrow. He said that was no use; they must be there tonight and stop the murder . . . He said that in the Argentine they managed things better; they would send artillery and machine guns, and give proper protection to their subjects . . . He had, about this time, been joined by his Secretary, who assumed the same offensive and bullying manner as his chief. They finally left saying that they were going to the Admiralty to demand assistance . . .

In a covering note to Churchill, accompanying this report, Sir Edward commented: 'If Mr. Houlder bullied his stevedores as he tried to bully me, it is no wonder there was a strike!' He also obtained assurances from Newport's Chief Constable that Houlder's report was grossly exaggerated, there being few police and fewer strikers on the dock at the time.

Churchill followed the dispute at some distance, whilst he was on the move: Troup's telegrams were addressed to him successively at Canford Manor, Winborne, Folkestone, Lucerne, Lugana and Venice! The Home Secretary's replies called for restraint in the use of force, condemned the provocative use of free labour by the Federation and Houlder, and urged the deployment of Board of Trade staff to effect an arbitrated settlement.[41] Houlders were forced to accept arbitration, yet promptly won the case, the arbitrator awarding that day-wages might be paid in the port. Tillett insisted on the men's accepting the decision: when they persisted in the strike, he withheld further strike pay.

At this point, the unofficial leadership of Alf Cox, a docker and 'an avid reader of Karl Marx',[42] came to the fore, supported by his brother George, and a following of other dockers and seamen. One of Houlders' ships was diverted to Bristol, despite the availability of labour from the *Lady Jocelyn*. Bristol dockers responded to Cox's personal appeal and blacked the ship, turning down an appeal to work it from the Dockers' Union Bristol district secretary, William Gorman. Eventually he regained control after a port-wide stoppage, and negotiated a return to work. But in Newport the unofficial blacking of Houlders' ships was sustained through the year, following which the dispute was subsumed into the much wider general industrial conflicts of 1911.[43]

In Bristol, the Dockers'.Union had entered the new century with a small, hard core of members in the corn-portering section of the docks – only 800 strong. This it protected with an elaborate arbitration agreement, conciliation boards and union recognition. By 1910, when the Houlder dispute ruptured the long peace which had prevailed under this system, the district had doubled its 1901 income. That the dockers of Bristol had not become inured to pacifism in these years is attested by their impressive solidarity in the Houlder affair, when 3,000 dockers struck, unofficially, in a dispute centred around a single ship. The dispute spread to the Avonmouth dock, and the membership boom which accompanied it included the carters, recruited by the branch chairman Ernest Bevin.[44] The Dockers' Union took part in the general revival of membership in 1910 which presaged the unrest of 1911–14, adding 5–6,000 to its total, to end the year with 18,000 members. Tom Mann spearheaded this growth with a nationwide organizing tour.

## The Fortunes of Sexton's Union

As we have seen (chapter 5), the NUDL had been reduced from a union with thirty-eight branches at its high point in 1891 to only fourteen by 1895. The principal Irish ports of Belfast and Dublin had been lost to non-unionism, and only in Cork, Drogheda and Londonderry did small struggling branches remain. In Scotland, the principal Glasgow branch was a source of constant complaint in the National Executive reports between 1900 and 1910, arising from its instability, lax administration and fractious, corrupt officials. It was suspended from the union more than once. In Dundee and Aberdeen, the inroads of the Free Labour Association also made for instability and defections. The union made two appointments, in 1904 and 1908, to the post of national organizer, designed to remedy this state of affairs and to advance organization into other major port areas. Sexton clearly aimed to challenge the DWRGWU in Hull from an outpost his union had established in Goole. In 1908 he wrote:

> I must remark that the port of Hull, with its 11,000 dockers, still remains in a complete state of disorganisation, and as such, is a menace to the best interests of us as an organised body, in many ways. If we are not in a position to organise this port, we should insist that those who are in a position to do so either ought to do it, or, if they are unable, to step out and allow someone else an opportunity.[45]

The two new appointments were of James Larkin, a Liverpool Irish dock foreman, and O'Connor Kessack, a Glasgow Scottish labourer and socialist agitator. The NUDL's history in this decade might be written around the contrasting activities of these two men. The union's contribution income was some £4,500 at the beginning of the century. By 1910 it had risen to £6,300, suggesting modest and steady progress.[46] It made the union about half the size of the DWRGWU, but by now most of Tillett's union's membership came from outside the docks. Only in Bristol and South Wales could it make any claim to representative status in the ports.

At the end of the decade, Kessack was called on to make good, as best he might, some of the ravages suffered by the union in Scotland. He struggled once more to restore the union's fortunes in Glasgow and Aberdeen, but found Glasgow 'a heart-break'. The dockers there resolved the problem by declaring their independence in 1911, establishing the Scottish Union of Dock Labourers, which returned to the fold of British docks unionism only when it amalgamated with the TGWU in 1922. Even then, its stay was to prove temporary. Kessack found Dublin equally dispiriting. In Goole and in Preston, twentieth-century branch formation was more successful. Liverpool's branches closed the decade in a weak condition. Sexton wrote in 1910:

> The real reason of the whole unrest in the trade union movement today lies deeper down than the mere bread and butter reason. There is a spirit of revolt against general conditions and against the conspiracy to drive trade unions out of the political arena . . . the sheer force of circumstances . . . are contributing to the revolution in trades unions.[47]

In an important sense, the revolution which Sexton foresaw had been set in train across the Irish Sea by his own national organizer, James Larkin, during his hectic progress between 1905 and 1909. It is to this explosive episode that we now turn.

## James Larkin Arrives

In January 1907, Belfast, the most rapidly growing city in the United Kingdom, was the somewhat indifferent host of the Labour Party Conference: 'As the gangplanks went down at the cross-channel quays, just short of the Queen's Bridge . . . unusual visitors could be seen disembarking. Within a few days Keir Hardie, Ramsay MacDonald, Arthur Henderson and others . . . stepped ashore.'[48]

One of the others was James Larkin, delegated by his union to represent it at the conference, but also to seek ways to organize the dockers in the port.

Larkin, a Liverpool Irish man, had a background quite remarkably similar to that of James Sexton. In 1903 he became a foreman dock porter on Liverpool's South End Docks. A socialist since his youth in the 1890s, he was a skilled soap-box preacher. Liverpool was the home of a group of followers of the American Industrial Workers of the World, including Fred Bower, the syndicalist stonemason, a childhood companion of Larkin.[49] The young agitator stayed largely clear of trade-union activism until 1905, when the NUDL became involved in a rearguard battle to defend union recognition against T. and J. Harrison's, where Larkin worked. The firm not only withdrew recognition after an unofficial stoppage, but brought in strike-breakers to defeat the official dispute which inevitably followed. Larkin became involved and established a strong following. He was a dramatic orator and was quickly marked down for victimization. By the same token, he was offered first a temporary and then a permanent job with the union.

That November Larkin ran Sexton's campaign for election to Liverpool Corporation (in which Sexton distinguished himself by his xenophobic remarks about Jewish and Chinese immigration).[50] This was successful, so Larkin was then called upon to organize Labour's forces in the contest for Parliament, in the West Toxteth division. It was, wrote Fred Bower (who took on the job of assistant to Larkin), 'a bigoted orange district', so that Catholic, socialist Sexton was 'perhaps the worst man we could have selected'.[51] The Conservative candidate, R. P. Houston, was a millionaire shipowner. He had voted for the introduction of Chinese labour into South Africa. Now the Chinese issue had been stood on its head:

> so Chinese Slavery was the battle-cry against him. Larkin had got a glass-sided hearse and several cabs. The Labour women had worked all the hours they could spare from home ties, in making loose-fitting, over-all pants and coats, out of a cheap yellow cloth material. I had cadged a dozen picks and a dozen shovels from a friendly contractor in the neighbourhood. Some fifty members of the Dockers' Union, who were unemployed, were garbed à la Chinese. Heralded by a brass band, playing the Dead March in Saul, the pseudo Chinamen trailed with their shouldered implements, behind the hearse, in which a coffin-shaped box, draped with the Union Jack, reposed. And so, on the election eve, the cortege wended its way through the main streets of the constituency. It was supposed to represent the burial of Freedom. To make it more realistic, Larkin had got hold of some decoction which he got the men to put on their faces and hands, which gave them a yellow countenance, and he himself had made them pigtails, out of oakum, the which they had pinned to their caps.
>
> At last they returned from the tour, and were paid off for their three hours' work, at trade union pay. But when they came to be paid, the fifty had grown to a hundred. Some had only the pigtail to show, some a pick or shovel, some a coat or a pair of pants. They had shared the gear with their mates, and as no names had been taken, Jim couldn't tell whom he had engaged, and whom he hadn't. It was twelve o'clock at night when I left them barging, and went home to bed. And there were some two or three score of men who didn't dare to go to the docks and look for a job unloading Houston's boats, for a week after, when the yellow dye had worn off their faces.[52]

Soon Larkin carried the union to Preston, Ardrossan and Aberdeen.[53] It was perfectly natural to seek to take it to Belfast.

## The Belfast Strike

Boom notwithstanding, the condition of the Belfast labourers was dire – 'bordering on starvation', in the words of Thomas Carnduff, a young Protestant worker from Sandy Row, and at the time an active sectarian zealot in the Pass Gang, a Belfast Protestant group noted for its stridency.[54] Respectable official reports were saying much the same thing, and the historian of the Belfast strike, John Gray, cites damning evidence to that effect.

There were 3,100 dockers in the city. Larkin started work on his soap-box. By mid-February 1907, he had won 400 to the NUDL. In March he put on a conference about dockers' problems; next month he had 2,000 members and two offices. Police reporters, who had dogged Larkin carefully from the first moment of his arrival, put his score at 2,978 dockers by the end of April, with the 'infection . . . spreading to the 1,500 carters'.[55] Orangemen among the workers welcomed Larkin's departure, in June, to support Pete Curran's by-election campaign in Jarrow, in which he opposed an Irish Nationalist. But Catholics were equally happy about Michael McKeown's appointment as branch secretary for the dockers, since he was a councillor for the United Ireland League.

The first skirmish on the docks followed a (non-union) engineering strike. Kelly's coal quay tried to sack union members, and faced a virtually complete stoppage. This alerted the Shipping Federation, which sent a representative to investigate on 6 May; he was prepared 'to act immediately should the necessity arise'.[56] It would. Meantime, as the warning bells sounded in Northern Ireland, 'thousands of Shipping Federation blacklegs were finishing off a mass strike in Hamburg. Later in the year, the same organisation was to be bloodily engaged on the streets on Antwerp'.[57]

Larkin tried to avoid the next strike, which erupted spontaneously against the Belfast Steamship Company. But the chairman of the company, Gallaher, the 'Tobacco King', was spoiling for a fight, and even after the union had called upon the men to return to work he flatly denied it recognition. Larkin turned the other cheek yet again, and sent the men back regardless. They returned to find themselves locked out, and to discover fifty-three strike-breakers deployed from SS *Caloric*, courtesy of the Shipping Federation. From that point on, things escalated. Altogether 140 Steamship Company dockers joined those locked out. More strike-breakers were imported, and some were set to work at Kelly's coal quay. A pitched battle drove them off, overwhelming the Harbour Police along the way. Talks followed between the union and the blacklegs, some of whom reformed and spoke at dockers' mass meetings. They came from Liverpool, where they had been offered £1 10s. a week, plus 1s. an hour overtime, to cross the Irish Sea and break the strike. Shortly afterwards, all the interlopers agreed to go home, and were seen off by enthusiastic strikers and a flute-and-drum band.

Kelly gave in. A victory parade, led by the Union Jack, sang 'Rule Britannia'. The Orange establishment took fright and offered mayoral arbitration in the remaining dispute, which Larkin accepted. Gallaher refused, and demanded police protection.

At this point, Larkin raised the temperature. Gallaher, he said, was an obscene scoundrel, and if St Patrick had banished the snakes from Ireland, 'there was one he forgot and that was Gallaher – a man who valued neither country, God nor creed'.[58] Later, Larkin returned to this theme with the thought that Gallaher could not be hung 'for no honest rope would do it'. The dockers did not seem to be distressed by this hyperbole.

By now there were 250 strike-breakers on SS *Caloric*, which had to be moored out in Belfast Lough to prevent union approaches to them. A force of up to 300 constables was required to march the blacklegs into work at Donegall Quay. Larkin now sought to recruit Gallaher's tobacco workers to a union, and the employer promptly dismissed seven of them simply for attending the meeting. One thousand women walked out to a mass strike meeting of dockers. The crowds refused to disperse and some windows were broken. The Lord Mayor called in the troops. Two hundred men of the Royal Sussex Regiment now confronted 200 dockers.

Belfast Steamship Company ships were blacked on other docks, and because the police were stretched in defending the Donegall Quay they were unable to prevent the *Caloric*'s being stoned when it tried to disembark strike-breakers elsewhere. In June the coal-heavers on quays other than Kelly's demanded a weekly rise of 2s. and won it. The Dublin Steamship Company also capitulated. More disputes mushroomed all around. To co-ordinate them, on 20 June the NUDL put a claim for £1 7s. 6d. minimum to all the cross-channel shipping companies. Larkin endorsed a claim by the seamen, which won 5s. a month for them. By 26 June 'all the dockers at Heysham, Barrow and Fleetwood berths came out'. The Royal Sussex now sent 500 more soldiers to defend the quays. Fires had already broken out.

Next day the carters began to strike. Blackleg carters were imported from Glasgow; the first cart to venture out under such a driver was followed by 2–3,000 jeering people. That afternoon the Glasgow men asked to go home. On the following day the carters filed a claim for a minimum of £1 6s. a week, with a maximum sixty-hour week. On 4 July the remaining carters joined the strike: 1,000 men employed by sixty companies.

Food began to rot. Quantities had to be destroyed. Polarization was far advanced, and the coal companies now locked out the very workers with whom they had so recently settled. With some apprehension, the strike leaders faced the fact that 12 July was bearing down upon them, with all its potential for sectarian division. A Protestant NUDL delegate to the Trades Council, Walter Savage, wrote an appeal to counter this threat: 'Our fervent prayer is that James Larkin may long be spared, by the help of God, to work for the emancipation of the unskilled workers in his native land.' He claimed that he could 'get 1000 Old Orange Order [union men] to sign this letter'. In the event, both Orange Order processions bristled with pro-strike insignia.

Violent action against strike-breakers was now widespread. The police were impotent. Their commissioners tried to offload the problem on to Dublin Castle, since 'only cavalry' would serve to protect the motor lorries the employers wished to bring in. Traction engines were used, heavily guarded by police, but they were ambushed. One had its cargo discharged into the Connswater river. Another was destroyed by a crowd of 200 in the very centre of Orange loyalism in East Belfast. Sometimes cargoes were destroyed, but sometimes they simply disappeared into people's houses. The strikers were, to say the least of it, undaunted by the prodigious force ranged against them.

It was money, or the want of it, that broke this upsurge. By mid-July 1,000 men needed £400 a week. By the 24th of the month there were 3,500 to be maintained. On the 19th, James Sexton arrived from head office full of good news. 'Every penny' of the NUDL's reserve of £20,000 'should be spent for the benefit of the locked out men', he told them.[59] Other unions would help, too. There was word of '£48,000 by noon on Tuesday next'. In fact, Sexton had brought £200 with him. Worse, he was evidently concerned that Belfast might prove a bottomless pit in which to lose all his union's reserves. He had no wish to explore the possibility. Altogether, John Gray estimates, he spent less than £5,000 on the strike from first to last. Sexton himself claimed it had cost £7,000.[60] The General Federation of Trade Unions, upon whom heavy calls were entirely in order, was even more parsimonious. In all, it spent £1,692 in Belfast. Alarmed at what they saw as a financial burden of unlimited scope, they pressed their Northern Irish affiliates to settle.

Settling was precisely what Sexton had in mind. On 20 July he met the Lord Mayor to seek a 'friendly conference'. With him went Gee and Mitchell of the GFTU. Mitchell then went forward on 25 July to negotiate a 'settlement' of the coal dispute. This proved to be a total disaster: nothing was agreed in writing, and although extravagant and windy promises were made, the coalmen went back to work on a false prospectus. Gee and Mitchell remained in Belfast to 'interpret' their settlement, and consistently ruled in favour of the masters. Although initially Larkin accepted the judgement of his general secretary and the two GFTU spokesmen, within a fortnight he was complaining that the dispute 'had been settled by three Englishmen in his absence, who knew nothing about the situation.'[61]

While the English labour leaders were bending their best efforts to get Belfast's coalmen back to work, the constabulary in that city was bearing the full brunt of the disorders and recalling its own ample grievances. From 10 July to 16 July, and again on the 22nd, an anonymous correspondent, signing himself 'Willing to Strike', began to air police complaints in the *Irish News*. It seemed clear that this correspondent had inside information. Soon others joined in. A delegate conference of policemen was announced for 24 July. This was duly banned by Acting Commissioner Morrell; however, it took place. Two or three hundred men turned up, defying a verbal ban delivered, as it opened, by a head constable. The Acting Commissioner then entered and sought to bully some of the men individually. Fisticuffs ensued. As the meeting was about to form up to march to a protest meeting, Morrell promised to meet a deputation, provided the demonstration did not take place. His offer was accepted, but before the meeting happened the whole story broke in the *Irish News*, and thereafter became sensational copy throughout the province.

Morrell went public, with an 'official' version of events. Constable Barrett, a spokesman for the men, then wrote to the *Irish News* contradicting his chief and confirming every detail in that newspaper's original report. Barrett was promptly suspended. Between 500 and 800 Belfast policemen, out of a total strength of 1,000, then attended an 'illegal meeting' at the Musgrave Street Barracks. Morrell appeared and tried to persuade the men that he would seek permission for a 'legal' gathering if only they would disperse this one. The men shouted him down and called for Barrett. He proposed that written demands be agreed, and that the chiefs be given eight days to respond, during which time police duties would be carried out normally. The loud cheers which greeted agreement on these proposals provoked a press on the gates giving access to the barracks, as hundreds of waiting trade unionists outside pushed forward to hear what was going on. Police and strikers were now intermingled in a stormy enthusiasm, and Barrett was carried in triumph to a mass meeting at Euston House steps, then back to a confrontation at the office of the Commissioner. By now the only 'police' in sight were arm-banded union pickets, who marshalled the crowds impartially, whether they were constables or civilians. Indeed, it was the union officials who finally persuaded the crowds to disperse, as Morrell stalled for time while the Assistant Inspector General voyaged up from Dublin. Even so, many waited. James Sexton spoke to the mixed crowd, urging the formation of a policemen's union. 'You will have fifty Labour men behind you', he told them.

Now the authorities had on their hands a strike and a mutiny. Accordingly, 2,500 soldiers were sent for and emplaced. They were joined by others. By 5 August *The Times* announced that 7,000 troops 'and maxim guns' were deployed in the city.[62] Once they were on the spot, Constable Barrett was summarily dismissed and those other colleagues who had endorsed the men's negotiating agenda were all suspended. 'Almost the entire force' in Belfast was dispersed to country beats in the hinterland.[63] Spectacular meetings and processions of trade unionists followed, and Barrett toured the city to a vast demonstration of solidarity.

But with this firm crackdown, the mutiny was ended. The arrival of so many troops now re-opened the question of national loyalties and the ever-present sectarian schisms which lay not far beneath them. As things were, the pressures of the strike-breakers, the increasing privation and the frustration of all these events combined to trigger an epidemic of riot throughout the Catholic areas. Bayonets were fixed, and deployed. On 11 August troops opened fire in the Falls Road. Two people were killed and many wounded.

In mid-August George Askwith was sent from London by the Board of Trade to mediate, and he has left a controversial account of what happened.[64] After shuttling between Larkin and the men, and the employers, the carters were offered a pay increase, though not the closed shop they demanded, while the dockers were told that settlement might follow a return to work. A meeting was summoned, with the carters in the body of the hall and the dockers in the balcony, to hear this message. Sexton arrived nervously, with not one but two revolvers in his breast pocket. Perhaps they were a testimony to a kind of uneasy conscience.[65] It might be that Sexton feared that his intervention might not be appreciated by his new members. Needless to say, the guns were never used, because Larkin soon had 'the men throwing up their caps and roaring applause.'

Because of their faith in Larkin, the dockers survived the humiliations of what, on most quays, was capitulation. In November 500 coalmen stopped work again, followed by thirty carters and fifty crane-men. Newry coalmen joined in sympathy action. Sexton hurried over and took the dispute out of Larkin's hands. Larkin would have permitted a re-opening of the general, port-wide stoppage, but Sexton foreclosed and ordered everyone back to work.

The predictable result was not long in following. The sense of betrayal which festered was soon to corrode the solidarity which had marked the union's confident beginning. For a brief while, people were willing to be union members first, and Green or Orange afterwards. When James Sexton went home to Liverpool, those days were but a memory of what might have been.

If Sexton was now in a cold fury with Larkin, another political leader – less conspicuous, to be sure – was deeply impressed by the Belfast events. John MacLean, the Scottish socialist, visited Belfast at the beginning of August during a speaking tour. He 'found the situation electrifying', wrote his biographers.[66] Moreover, it upended his previous view of the processes of social change, which had been set in a conventional mould, much influenced by the thinking of Hyndman. Now he addressed audiences of thousands. The labourers were 'mad to join trade unions'. Hitherto, MacLean's perception of trade unionism had been coloured by his experience of the Labour aristocrats of the Clyde: highly skilled, exclusive, cautious. Now he became a partisan of organization among unskilled workers, even while he upheld the primacy of political process.

This distinctive view began to separate MacLean from political orthodoxy, and represents the thin end of an important wedge of Irish influence, or rather of the influence of Irish experience, over in Britain. Particularly in Scotland, this was to carry a long way. The later mixture of the revolt of the labourers with the cause of Irish Nationalism was, perhaps, not inevitable, and it was certainly to inhibit the Belfast workers in later years. But among Irish migrant labourers in Scotland and the British ports, it was undoubtedly an explosive combination. (The first communist MP, Walton Newbold, was later unhesitatingly to attribute his 1922 election victory in Motherwell to this constituency: by then, John MacLean was already dead, after suffering prolonged and brutal imprisonment during the war.) Be that as it may, MacLean's 'conversion' was no small matter, and represents an important achievement by Larkin.

At the time, however, the weight of James Sexton would have seemed heavier than that of an obscure Scottish agitator. This weight was abruptly used.

## The Genesis of the Irish Transport and General Workers' Union

Larkin was relegated – sent to spread the NUDL's influence first in Dublin, then in Cork. Whilst happy to bank the new members' subscriptions, the NUDL leader was mainly concerned to box in and limit Larkin's influence. When the Dublin dockers were on the brink of a modest victory in July 1908, Sexton intervened to negotiate a defeat for them. Locked out, they won, with Larkin, arbitration and an agreed return to work. It was Sexton who quite gratuitously conceded that the men would not wear union badges at work. All future disputes were, it was agreed, to be arbitrated nationally, between the employers and Sexton personally.

Clearly, Larkin was on the way out. In short order he was sent on from Cork to Aberdeen. Before he could get to Scotland the Dublin carters struck and Larkin went to them instead. This was seen, in Liverpool, as insubordination.

By 7 December 1908 Sexton had informed his too-able adjutant that he was suspended from office. But Larkin was not disposed to go quietly. He took this disciplinary action to mean that British unions would never represent the true interests of Irish workers, and drew some logical conclusions. Three days after Christmas the Irish Transport and General Workers' banner was raised, and the NUDL had ceded its most exciting prospects over the Irish Sea. The adventures of this new organization are part of another story, of which the great Belfast strike was only a precursor.

## A Learning Phase

The first decade of the twentieth century marked a learning phase for dockers' unions of all three types. Tillett's union's harsh experiences demonstrated that dockers needed their own, 'industrial' unity, even though they may be part of a general union. (The tinplatemen might give the union financial security, but had no obvious role in any industrial revival in the ports.) Without the adherence of the specialists – stevedores and lightermen in London, coal-trimmers in Wales, and other specific groups amongst corn-porters and timbermen – their organization would remain partial and vulnerable. The dockers who were enrolled in other general unions were also reaching out for an inclusive dockers' alliance. Such were the gasworkers' docks branches in the North-east and on the Humber, in the National Amalgamated Union of Labour on Tyneside, and in the National Amalgamated Labourers' Union in South Wales. Wherever they were to be found, the dockers, fragmented into a dozen or more unions, were vulnerable to free labour, the infiltration of non-members and inter-union rivalries.

The 'all-grade' dockers' union, exemplified by the NUDL, was faced with the same obstacles to effective progress: but in that case there arose an additional challenge from James Larkin and the special needs of Ireland. Neither type of union was allowed respite from the remorseless and often brutal deployment of strike-breakers from the Shipping Federation and from Collison's free labourers. From Hull, a union 'no-go' area, and to a lesser extent from London, came an endless flow of recruits to break strikes. Evidently nationwide unionism was the only available means to counter this weapon. After all, had not this been the drive behind all previous attempts at federation in the 'carrying trades' in the 1890s?

The specialist unions were also discovering the disadvantages of separatist traditions. The dilution of the special skills of stevedoring and lighterage threatened their established roles in the labour process, and therefore the trade-union method which they had adopted. We have seen that in London adaptation had begun in both these cases. In Cardiff, the Coal-trimmers' Union reached the point at least of affiliating to the new Labour Party, as did the London Cranedrivers. In the North-east, a Trimmers' and Teemers' Association joined a regional federation of shipping and general labour unions, and in Liverpool the North End Coalheavers merged with the NUDL in 1911.[67] These moves are seen by Gordon Phillips, the historian of the National Transport Workers' Federation (NTWF), as the preliminary steps towards a wider association. All were occurring during these formative years.

# III

## *The Seamen*

The Seamen's Union, at the receiving end of the Shipping Federation's nationwide free-labour strategy, which had, as we have seen, an international dimension, were natural advocates of waterfront federation. The union recorded growth of membership from 7,000 in 1906 to 12,000 in 1910. It had pioneered the all-grade, national model of port-based unionism, with one exception: it had neglected to organize the growing catering section of the merchant navy. In May 1909 the National Union of Ships' Stewards, Cooks, Butchers and Bakers was formed in Liverpool, where the growth of the passenger-liner business quite obviously underlined the failure of Havelock Wilson's union to meet the needs of people in these occupations. It was led by Joseph Cotter, a ship's cook from Liverpool, a socialist agitator who was an early convert to syndicalism. He was known as 'Explosive Joe'. Four thousand members were enrolled in the new organization.

This nascent division in the ranks of the seamen was to have far-reaching consequences for the future prospects of an inclusive transport unionism. From its foundation in 1887, Wilson had foreseen that the future of his union lay in co-operation with the shipowners. Denied this relationship by the big, anti-union shipping firms, he pursued a policy of national-level militancy, directed to obtaining standard national rates at all ports and the exclusion of non-unionists. 'An alliance with the shipowners remained his ideal, if not his practical policy, for most of the next thirty years.'[68]

## *Carters*

Horse-drawn road-haulage workers, the carters, wherever they had established any organization, were fragmented into local associations, or membership in one of the general unions. The Dockers' Union enrolled them in Bristol and South Wales, the NAUL on the Tyne, and the Gasworkers' Union on the Tyne and the Wear. All these were tiny and scattered minorities. The ports were their main bases of both work and unionism: cartage was a universal requirement between the dockside and the rail terminals. Toiling alongside the dockers meant that some learned the virtues of wider alliance, at least in London, where the Carmen's Union had a tradition of collaboration in union matters.

In Scotland, a future stronghold of 'industrial unionism' in road haulage, the Scottish Carters' Association, formed in 1898, had a former railwayman, John Sampson, as its first general secretary. He had been associated with new unionism in the 1880s and saw the need to organize carters on a national (Scottish) basis, at a time when the English carters' unions were confined to single towns or regions. In 1902 the union sacked Sampson and appointed a Falkirk iron-moulder, Hugh Lyon, to replace him.

> The next ten years are a story of slow recruitment on a narrower basis and the patient organisation of the carters to fight for . . . a standard working day and the limitation of the shocking hours, for trade union recognition, for the right to payment for overtime, for the abolition of unpaid Sunday stable duties, and for improvement of wages, which had shrunk below the levels of 1889.[69]

That programme was common to carters' needs throughout Britain: their organizations would eventually utilize the NTWF to pursue it jointly. At this stage, the appeal to them of federal bodies was limited, and they were in no position to influence the pace or form of federalism.

## Road-transport Mergers

Only in the North of England were there signs that the carters were moving out of their localism: the Manchester, Salford and District Lurrymen and Carters' Union, the Huddersfield Carters' Union, and the Edinburgh and District Tramway and Carmen's Union had already, in the 1890s, merged with the Tramway, Hackney Carriage Employees and Horsemen's Association. This was the former Northern Counties Amalgamated Association of Tramway and Hackney Carriage Employees and Horsemen in General, which adopted its new title in 1892. (See p. 178.)

These pioneering mergers prepared the way in the North for the creation in 1901 of the Amalgamated Association of Tramway and Vehicle Workers, which, in a development of great potential, overrode the division between freight and passenger unionism in road transport. In the post-war period this union became known as the 'Blue Button Union', in contrast to its rival, the London and Provincial Union of Licensed Vehicle Workers, the 'Red Button' or militant union, which had pursued a parallel but separate series of mergers to arrive at its form and title in 1913. It had originated as the shortlived Metropolitan Cab Drivers' Trade Union in 1890, reformed in 1894 as the London Cab Drivers' Trade Union, with 3,000 members. In 1911 it merged with the Motor Cab Drivers' Protection Association, which had been formed in 1907. In 1910 the National Union of Carriers was formed to cater for the employees of the removal firm of Carter Paterson.

This whole evolution pointed away from local, sectional road-transport unions, through complex mergers which gradually overcame both their geographical and trade separatism. From the North came the streams which merged into the Amalgamated Association of Tramway and Vehicle Workers in 1901. It could claim a genuinely national status in its tramway section. It had no competitors in that field, and there was no national employers' association to offer resistance. However, that absence also signified that the union was unable to concert wage movements at a national level. In 1910 it was still dominated by its northern membership: six of its executive places were occupied by the northern branches, against only two for the South and Midlands. Its policies were cautious: hence its nickname, 'the Blue'. Inspired by the traditional militancy of the London cabmen, the London and Provincial Union of Licensed Vehicle Workers, like its provincial counterpart, had begun the process of organizing the neglected and newly emergent section of road-passenger transport, the buses, in about 1910.

A further pointer to future trends in this section came in 1908, when the AATVW became a founder affiliate of the General Labourers' National Council.[70]

## New Troubles for the Quarrymen

Another, very different, sector entered the century in an embattled state. In mid-October 1900 the Penrhyn quarries entered a new phase of troubles. Fourteen men at Ponc Ffridd were victimized for refusing work in defence of two colleagues. After being suspended, they were told that they would be split up and that their own previous work would be contracted out. Upon his arrival on the site, the contractor was beaten up and thrown out. Another similar incident followed within a few days. Three hundred dragoons were called in, and twenty-six quarrymen were prosecuted.

On Guy Fawkes' Day the case came up at Bangor. All the workmates of those charged struck and marched to court to protest their colleagues' innocence. Twenty of those tried were found not guilty of the affrays, but the entire workforce was suspended for a fortnight. On 19 November the resumption of work was made a pretext for an all-round reassignment of tasks, in which 800 people were not given their places. On 27 November the majority insisted upon the reinstatement of these workers and were told to leave if they were dissatisfied: 2,800 men took up their tools and went. Of these, 1,000 never returned and a further 1,000 were kept out of work until after November 1903.

At Easter 1901 Ben Tillett voyaged up to Bethesda and spoke to a mass meeting on Easter Monday. He pitched into Lord Penrhyn: 'a cross between Pharaoh and Nero', a brute who had ignored people's basic rights; he likened the quarry-owner to Kruger, and his victimized workpeople to 'economic Outlanders'. He told them not to blame the manager of the quarry, who was 'only Lord Penrhyn's jackal'. 'Although he spoke in English, a language "strange" to most of his hearers, his comments were greeted with laughter and applause.'[71] After Tillett had returned to England, those who had condoned his verbal assaults on Lord Penrhyn were subject to continued reprisals. At least one of his Lordship's tenants found himself in trouble for sponsoring the Easter gathering.

As the months wore on, many drifted south in search of jobs in the pits. Some few found work in a co-op quarry which was re-opened by W. J. Parry; but meanwhile Lord Penrhyn's factors made sporadic efforts to inveigle groups of men to return to his own quarry on his own strict terms. In June 1901, 242 succumbed, alongside roughly similar numbers of outside strike-breakers. Violence stewed and brooded beneath the surface, occasionally erupting into open public riot. By July, 200 footsoldiers and 60 cavalrymen were billeted to keep order; 100 more infantrymen and 30 dragoons quickly followed them into place in Bethesda. By September there were more union men up before the courts in Bangor, and by New Year's Eve there were several more affrays and many more soldiers in place.

Peace moves by the County Council failed to take effect, and in 1902 efforts to arbitrate were coolly turned down by both Lord Penrhyn and his manager, the stolid E. A. Young. Hardship clamped down upon the townships. A few more miserable people were tempted back to work. More than 2,000 still stood firm, however, and the lock-out entered its third year. That March, there were impassioned voices raised in Parliament, including that of Lloyd George. The Conservative government was widely criticized for laxity and failure to invoke the 1896 Conciliation Act. But in reality that Act could bring no relief, since its powers of arbitration were restricted to purely voluntary invitations, and Lord Penrhyn was quite determined never, but never, to volunteer. Pleas were made to the Prime Minister, to the new Prince of Wales, to anyone people could think of. Nothing moved. Quarrymen began to emigrate to the United States, and the General Federation of Trade Unions cut off its funding.[72]

'By December the situation in Bethesda was "no work, no union, no fund . . . every fountain has dried up". The traditional Saturday Market closed down; and as the year drew to a close, poverty intensified and fever shut the schools.'[73] The 2,000 were sustained, with their families, by contributions from all over Britain. Their choirs toured the island, raising support wherever they could. At home, comfort came from the chapel. Each mass meeting ended with the hymn 'Rwy'n gweld o bell y dydd yn dod' – 'I see from afar the day that is coming':

> The beautiful light of the dawn,
> From land to land now proclaims,
> That daybreak is at hand;

The tops of the hills rejoice,
As they see the sun draw nearer,
And the night retreat away.[74]

Lord Penrhyn's victory was the result of his power to inflict continuous deprivation upon his workpeople, culminating in their actual starvation. But the North Wales quarrymen had become the living symbol of sheer courage, tenacity and good faith. Their struggle to maintain trade unionism was to continue and, uncannily, even to prosper. As Lord Penrhyn's business declined, the union grew.

## The Workers' Union Endures

The historian of the Workers' Union, Richard Hyman, entitles his chapter on these years 'Endurance, 1898–1910'. Founded with ecumenical aims, as we have seen (chapter 6), in this first decade it failed entirely in their realization. Tom Mann had hoped to create for it a leading *political* role, but the formation of the Labour Party in 1900 displaced this possibility completely, and the union, which participated in the foundation of the then Labour Representation Committee, fell into line with its leadership. Industrially, it ebbed and flowed in numbers with the short-term trade cycle, reaching a first peak of 4,172 members in 1899. Thereafter it collapsed in the short recession of 1903–4 to just over 1,000 members. The resumption of the trade revival brought renewed growth by the end of the decade. Later this was to be followed by spectacular expansion.

Tom Mann having departed in 1901 for Australia, and Chambers, the first secretary, leaving to work full time for the Dockers' International, Robert Morley, a skilled iron-moulder from Halifax became president and Charles Duncan, a skilled engineer from Middlesbrough, became secretary. Both were active socialists, Morley for the ILP. These two men dominated the union's policies for the next twelve years. Power gravitated towards them, and to the district full-time officers, as the membership was in the highest degree unstable. In the first eighteen months 3,000 members lapsed and nearly forty branches closed.

The union's recruitment pattern in these years was haphazard. In London, its first base, the 'unattached labourer' proved hard to identify and organize. Membership was established at the Army and Navy Stores, where Duncan's union competed with the Shop Assistants' Union. After an unsuccessful struggle against the employer's opposition, this branch had to close in 1899. The union next formed a branch at Lipton's tea warehouses, where genuine sweated conditions prevailed. These efforts also met with defeat, in 1900, and thereafter the union's membership was predominantly provincial.

A Middlesbrough branch was now its largest outpost, members being drawn from amongst the corporation's workers, but the sacking of unofficial strikers and internal problems led to the branch's closing in 1902. Corporation workers were also recruited in Coventry, with the active assistance of the Trades Council secretary. Again, the branch closed after only a year's existence.

More stability attended the union in West Yorkshire, where there was a mass of unorganized general labour. The union registered its first success when it obtained a wage rise for the workers at the Halifax municipal gasworks. Morley made a personal organizing drive in Manchester, where a branch of 300 existed by 1907. Further successes included the formation of branches in Preston and Halifax, which became the base for the wider organization of welders in the boiler industry, including branches in Derby, Rotherham and Glasgow. In the South Wales iron and steel industry, the union put down early roots and experienced the same swings of fortune as elsewhere. By 1909 it had become one of the union's major centres.

In these early years, the union was active in rural Shropshire: again, initial agitation and organization amongst farm workers were followed by employers' resistance and the closure of branches, all of which had ceased to operate by 1901.

In Birmingham the union found its eventual *métier*, enrolling the machinists in the BSA arms factory, a pioneer site of mass-production techniques. From its base of 600 members here, the union moved on to enrol in the same city's Cadbury's Bourneville factory, amongst the maintenance men. Having attained an engineering membership of 1,000 by 1907, the union was admitted into the local Engineering Workers' Federation, which adopted an official wage-scale for semi-skilled workers. The union had by that time amended its rules to exclude recruitment of workers eligible for membership in the craft unions.[75]

## IV

## *Federation Again*

In tracing the chronology of successive attempts to renew the process of federation amongst transport and general unions, we must glance first at the General Federation of Trade Unions, which was formed in 1899, although it did not arise in the transport field. It was born on the initiative of the TUC, as a generalized defensive response to the employers' offensives of the 1890s, especially that of the engineering employers' lock-out of 1897. By 1904 it had affiliated unions with membership totalling 424,000, including both Tillett's union and the NUDL. Its purpose was to provide mutual assistance to unions involved in expensive strikes, through financial supplements to the unions' own dispute benefits. Whilst this might appear to be an incentive to militancy, in practice the GFTU was an extremely cautious body, intent on preserving its funds, and a fervent advocate of conciliation and industrial peace. This is not to say that it shirked the necessity to provide support where this was judged appropriate: it contributed £9,000 to the aid of the Penrhyn strikers, and over £1,000 to the NUDL in the Liverpool strike of 1905. In commending the Federation's work in 1901, Tillett saw it as standing 'for the new development in Trades Unionism, whose evolution has been necessarily slow.' He saw symbolic importance in a body which expressed the unity of purpose of the movement, when faced with the development of capitalism of trusts and cartels.[76]

The GFTU failed to secure the affiliation of several key unions, including the miners and railwaymen. Since it would only admit organizations which were not federal, the miners could not join, and their absence hurt. The GFTU had a limited, insurance function, not adaptable to the development of organizational change and amalgamation, or to the formation of common trade policies. Its message of cautious conciliation was discarded in the turbulent years – from 1911 to 1914 – which lay immediately ahead. Its role became more and more limited as the century advanced.[77]

The need for federal links between unions in the transport and general fields became more urgent as the decade went on. Quite apart from the consistent conviction with which this goal was held by the principal new-union leaders, Mann, Tillett, Sexton and Gosling, pragmatic considerations now pushed the cause to the forefront. These included the growing problem of inter-union rivalries and relations. In municipal employment, the Municipal Employees' Association was involved in a series of poaching disputes with the Gasworkers' and Dockers' Unions, a problem which was instrumental in prompting the formation of the General Labourers' National Council in 1908. Ten affiliates participated in its foundation, including the Dockers' Union, the Gasworkers, the NAUL, the Amalgamated Tramway Workers, and the Workers' Union. The object of the new body was specifically to foster good inter-union relations by arranging for the mutual recognition of cards, transfers of members and spheres of influence. This was a more concrete advance than had hitherto been possible, but it fell short of attempting the co-ordination of industrial and trade policies and movements.

Tillett's union had founded the International Federation of Ship, Dock and River Workers and campaigned all round northern Europe to build it. The decline of dock representation nationally was accompanied by a falling-off of support for the International. But, consistently with their own long-term goals, the dockers reaffiliated to the replacement International Transport Workers' Federation when it emerged in 1908. This timing allowed transport workers to join in the debate on the

international workers' movement's response to world crisis on the eve
of the First World War.

As the end of the decade approached, a whole series of threats and
opportunities pointed forcibly to the need for the greater integration of
transport unionism. The GLNC's formation had not catered specifically
for transport workers, and had in any case a narrow remit in the general-
worker field.

## Sounding the Alarm

Tillett interpreted the Houlder dispute in South Wales and Bristol, and
the renewed aggression of the Shipping Federation in that affair, as the
forerunner of another major assault. Moreover, the NALU in South
Wales had been drawn closer to the Dockers' Union by the Houlder
dispute. The London stevedores faced the prospect of wage-cutting
from non-union labour employed directly by the shipowners. The
lightermen on the Thames were still struggling to maintain their
agreements against the larger firms which were taking over their
industry, and their ancient licensing system was under threat from new
powers granted to the PLA. Sexton's union had just lost its major battle
against Larkin's breakaway in Belfast and Dublin, and needed allies in
the rest of the British trade-union movement.

Havelock Wilson was sounding justifiable alarm bells at the formation
of the International Shipping Federation in October 1909. In Amsterdam,
Antwerp, Copenhagen, Marseilles, Naples, Paris and Dunkirk, employers'
federations on the lines of the British Shipping Federation, founded to
do battle with 'workmen's syndicates', had been proposing an international alliance since 1902. In 1907 the British Federation had hosted a
London conference of these bodies to discuss 'the maritime labour
problem both in England and abroad in all its bearings, more especially
with a view to arranging a scheme of co-operation between the various
organisations for the mutual support of their members at any time the
trade unions should attempt to give effect to their declared intention of
themselves concerting attacks upon an international basis.'[78] This
conference led to detailed committee planning, and the fully fledged
International, complete with plans to maintain employment bureaux
'throughout the world', was ready for business at the end of 1909.

> The newly-formed organisation concentrated . . . upon dealing with
> strikes both of seafarers and of dock labour – but mostly the latter. Too
> often in the past, while the national employers in a port might be
> determined to resist what they considered to be unjustifiable demands, the
> front was broken – often in ignorance – by a foreign shipmaster anxious to
> get his ship to sea again.[79]

The Seamen's Union had by now tabled a comprehensive programme of national demands: for a standard wage, new manning scales and an end to the Shipping Federation's ticket of preference. Havelock Wilson presented this to the Shipping Federation in July 1910, but the owners were in no mood to respond. Wilson appealed in vain to the International Transport Federation for an international strike: only the Dutch and the Belgians made positive replies. Sydney Buxton at the Board of Trade was asked by Wilson to persuade the Shipping Federation to accord recognition to his union. It refused. The NSFU was therefore on a collision course at the very moment of formation of the National Transport Workers' Federation, to which it was bound to appeal for support.

The general industrial temper in the transport industry was showing signs of the coming turbulence. Between 1902 and 1905 there were eighty-eight strikes in transport, involving 8,000 workers and occasioning the loss of 146,000 working days. Between 1906 and 1909 these figures rose to 20,000 workers and 242,000 working days.[80]

This was the industrial situation when the Dockers' Union sent their circular inviting unions to a conference on the question of federation. The Dockers' Union had renewed expectations, not just defensive reasons, for its initiative. We have seen that its numbers had improved in the last half of the decade, particularly in the last few months. New groups, such as Bevin's Bristol carters, were joining. The formation of the PLA had also generated an initial optimism. Harry Orbell came to represent the union on its Board: surely here was a return to the status the union had not enjoyed since the early 1890s? At this moment, Tom Mann was to embark on the campaign to spread syndicalism throughout the trade-union world.

# Notes

1 H. A. Clegg, Alan Fox and A. F. Thompson, *A History of British Trade Unions since 1889*, vol. I: *1889–1910* (Oxford University Press, 1964), placed much emphasis on the thesis that such a transformation was illusory. They see the upheaval of 1889–91 as having been absorbed and neutralized in the succeeding years, and in the upsurge of 1911–14, therefore, recognize a different phenomenon. The assumption is that the new unionism's intermittent progress proves the superficiality of its 'newness', and that older, less radical, pre-socialist modes of trades unionism provide the underlying, 'real' continuity.

In contrast to this view, Eric Hobsbawm has sketched out a perspective much closer to our own: 'As applied to its period of origin, the 1880s and early 1890s, the term "new unionism" suggests three things to a British labour historian. It suggests, first, a new set of strategies, policies, and forms of organisation for unions, as opposed to those associated with an already existing "old" trade unionism. It suggests, in the second place, a more radical social and political stance of unions in the context of the rise of a socialist labour movement: and in the third place, the creation of new unions of hitherto unorganised or unorganisable workers, as well as the transformation of old unions along the lines suggested by the innovators. Consequently it also suggests an explosive growth of trade-union organisation and membership. The dock strike of 1889 and its aftermath illustrate all these aspects of the "new unionism", and therefore it provides the most popular image of the entire phenomenon. It is interesting that the very similar union upsurge and transformation of 1911–13 has never generated any similar label, though it was quite as innovative and much more radical. This suggests that even at the time it was regarded as a continuation, or a second instalment, of the process initiated in 1889. I believe that this is in fact the best way to see it' (Eric Hobsbawm, *Worlds of Labour* (Weidenfeld and Nicolson, 1984), p. 1,152).

The only qualification which we might make to this judgement is to question why it says '*even* at the time'. Is this intended to imply that those involved were not fully aware of continuity in their struggle? But of course the second wave of new unionists knew perfectly well that in its origins and its nature it was a renewal and further development of their original organizations and long-term purposes. For the most part the same actors were involved, on both sides. In 1911 Mann, Tillett, Sexton, Havelock Wilson on the one hand, and the port employers and the Shipping Federation on the other, renewed conflicts which had been fought to a standstill in the mid-1890s. Then one side was exhausted and the other triumphant. Here we are anticipating the 1911–13 uprising. For the most part, the preceding years were quite different.

2   R. C. K. Ensor, *England, 1870–1914* (Oxford University Press, 1941), p. 255n.

3   Gareth Stedman Jones, 'Working Class Culture and Working Class Politics in London, 1870–1900', *Journal of Social History*, vol. 7, no. 4 (1974), p. 460.

4   *The Times*, 21 May 1900; cited by Jones, 'Working Class Culture', p. 461.

5   Jack London, *The People of the Abyss* (Journeyman, 1977), pp. 62–3.

6   Ibid., p. 68.

7   See Lord Askwith, *Industrial Problems and Disputes* (John Murray, 1920), pp. 115–25.

8   Board of Trade *Abstracts of Labour Statistics*, as digested in Clegg, Fox and Thompson, *History of British Trade Unions*, vol. I, p. 489. The figures for numbers of separate strikes are taken in preference to numbers of working days lost, since the latter can be dramatically inflated by one or two very large and protracted strikes.

9   DWRGWU Annual Report, 1901, p. 4.

10  Eric J. Hobsbawm, *Labouring Men* (Weidenfeld and Nicolson, 1968), p. 180.

11  Gordon A. Phillips, 'The National Transport Workers' Federation, 1910–1927' (unpublished PhD thesis, Oxford University, 1968), pp. 20–1.

12  Ibid., p. 5, table I, based on the 1911 Census figures.

13  B. R. Mitchell and P. Deane, *Abstract of British Historical Statistics* (Cambridge University Press, 1962), pp. 218–19.

14  Phillips, 'The National Transport Workers' Federation', p. 5.
15  Ibid.
16  Cited in Phillips, 'The National Transport Workers' Federation', p. 25.
17  Phillip Bagwell, *The Transport Revolution from 1770* (Batsford, 1974), p. 153.
18  F. Sherwood Taylor, *The Century of Science* (Heinemann, 1942), pp. 44ff.
19  Ibid.
20  Charles H. Feinstein and Sydney Pollard (eds), *Studies in Capital Formation in the United Kingdom, 1750–1920* (Oxford University Press, 1988), p. 330.
21  Phillips, 'The National Transport Workers' Federation', p. 9.
22  Ibid.
23  Just prior to the Devlin reform of the Dock Labour Scheme in 1967, there were 300 registered employers of dock labour in London, and 90 in Hull. A government report in 1956 estimated the UK total at 1,248. See Tony Topham, 'The Dockers', in Ken Coates (ed.), *Can the Workers Run Industry?* (Sphere Books/Institute for Workers' Control, 1968), pp. 157–81.
24  Edward Gillett and Kenneth MacMahon, *A History of Hull* (University of Hull, 1980), pp. 335, 349 and 392.
25  Sir Walter T. Layton and Geoffrey Crowther, *An Introduction to the Study of Prices* (2nd edn, Macmillan, 1935).
26  George Dangerfield, *The Strange Death of Liberal England, 1910–14* (Constable, 1935; reissued Perigree Books, 1980), p. 219.
27  Sidney Pollard, 'Trade Unions and the Labour Market, 1870–1914', *Yorkshire Bulletin of Economic and Social Research*, vol. 17, no. 1 (May 1965), pp. 101–2.
28  E. H. Phelps-Brown, *The Growth of British Industrial Relations: a Study from the Standpoint of 1906–14* (Macmillan, 1960), p. 336.
29  Ibid.
30  Rodger Charles, *The Development of Industrial Relations in Britain, 1911–1939* (Hutchinson, 1973), pp. 46–7n.
31  Sidney and Beatrice Webb, *What Syndicalism Means* (London, 1912).
32  DWRGWU Annual Report, 1901.
33  John Lovell, *Stevedores and Dockers: a Study of Trade Unionism in the Port of London, 1870–1914* (Macmillan, 1969), pp. 219–21; and the DWRGWU Annual Reports, 1901 and 1910.
34  Lovell, *Stevedores and Dockers*, pp. 148–9.
35  *Amalgamated Stevedores' Labour Protection League, Past and Present* (n.d.). The original is in Tim O'Leary's private collection.
36  Lovell, *Stevedores and Dockers*, p. 149.
37  Ibid., p. 152.
38  See Gordon Phillips and Noel Whiteside, *Casual Labour: The Unemployment Question in the Port Transport Industry, 1880–1970* (Oxford University Press, 1985), pp. 64ff., for a study of this episode.
39  Ibid., p. 84.
40  Phillip J. Leng, *The Welsh Dockers* (G. W. and A. Hesketh, 1981), p. 36.
41  Randolph S. Churchill, *Winston S. Churchill*, vol. II (Heinemann, 1969), companion part II, pp. 1,164–75.
42  Leng, *The Welsh Dockers*, p. 50.

43  This account of the Welsh sections of the Dockers' Union is drawn from Leng, *The Welsh Dockers*.

44  This account is based on Brian Atkinson, *Trade Unions in Bristol* (Bristol Branch, Historical Association, University of Bristol, 1982).

45  NUDL Annual Report, 1908.

46  Ibid., 1901 and 1910.

47  Quoted in Eric Taplin, *The Dockers' Union: a Study of the National Union of Dock Labourers, 1889–1922* (Leicester University Press, 1986), p. 79.

48  John Gray, *City in Revolt: James Larkin and the Belfast Dock Strike of 1907* (Blackstaff Press, 1985), pp. 1–2.

49  Bob Holton, 'Syndicalism and Labour on Merseyside', in H. R. Hikins (ed.), *Building the Union: Studies in the Growth of the Workers' Movement, Merseyside, 1756–1967* (Toulouse Press, 1973), p. 133.

50  See P. J. Waller, *Democracy and Sectarianism: A Political and Social History of Liverpool, 1868–1939* (Liverpool University Press, 1981), p. 217.

51  Fred Bower, *Rolling Stonemason* (London, 1936), p. 168.

52  Ibid., pp. 169–70.

53  Emmett Larkin, *James Larkin, Irish Labour Leader, 1876–1947* (Routledge and Kegan Paul, 1965), p. 18.

54  Gray, *City in Revolt*, pp. 13 and 15.

55  Ibid., p. 56.

56  Ibid., p. 59.

57  Ibid., p. 60.

58  Ibid., p. 63.

59  Ibid., p. 100.

60  Clegg, Fox and Thompson, *History of British Trade Unions*, vol. I, p. 451.

61  Gray, *City in Revolt*, p. 107.

62  John McHugh, 'The Belfast Labour Dispute and Riots of 1907', *International Review of Social History*, vol. XXII (1977), p. 10.

63  Emmett Larkin, *James Larkin*, pp. 32ff.; Gray, *City in Revolt*, pp. 111–36. McHugh, 'The Belfast Labour Dispute of 1907', p. 12, cites a report in the *Labour Leader* which speaks of 253 such transfers.

64  Askwith, *Industrial Problems and Disputes*, p. 109; also Gray, *City in Revolt*. pp. 171–3.

65  Askwith, *Industrial Problems and Disputes*, p. 111.

66  B. J. Ripley and J. McHugh, *John MacLean* (Manchester University Press, 1989), pp. 30–3.

67  Phillips, 'The National Transport Workers' Federation', p. 4.

68  Ibid., p. 46.

69  Angela Tuckett, *The Scottish Carter* (Allen and Unwin, 1967), p. 25.

70  This survey of road-transport unions draws on Arthur Marsh and Victoria Ryan, *Historical Directory of Trade Unions*, vol. III (Gower, 1987); Phillips, 'The National Transport Workers' Federation'. See also Part II, Appendix: Profiles of the Unions.

71  Jean Lindsay, *The Great Strike* (David and Charles, 1987), pp. 128–9.

72  The quarrymen had wisely affiliated in May 1899, in time to benefit from GFTU support when Lord Penrhyn struck his blow.

73  R. Merfyn Jones, *The North Wales Quarrymen, 1874–1922* (University of Wales, 1981), p. 215.

74  Ibid., p. 285.
75  This account of the Workers' Union's early years is drawn from Richard Hyman, *The Workers' Union* (Oxford University Press, 1971), pp. 12–35.
76  DWRGWU Annual Report, 1901.
77  See A. Prochaska, *History of the General Federation of Trade Unions, 1889–1980* (Allen and Unwin, 1982).
78  L. H. Powell, *The Shipping Federation: A History of the First Sixty Years, 1890–1950* (Shipping Federation, 1950), p. 109.
79  Ibid., p. 111.
80  Clegg, Fox and Thompson, *History of British Trade Unions*, vol. I, p. 329; source: *Sixteenth Abstract of Labour Statistics*, 1913.

# 9

# The Political Challenge: From Above, or From Below?

## I

### *Transport Workers and the Labour Representation Committee*

On 27 February 1900 129 people gathered in the Memorial Hall, in East London's Farringdon Street. They stayed for two days, and at the end of their labours was born the Labour Representation Committee, soon to become the Labour Party. Just over half a million members belonged to the assembled organizations, if their claims can be believed. The three political groups appeared to have exaggerated somewhat: the Independent Labour Party claimed to represent 13,000 members (there were actually 6,084 fee paying members of the ILP in 1900), the Social Democratic Federation claimed 9,000, and the Fabians 861. But the ILP had only 5,000 members the following year. Shrinking though it was, there was no special reason for it to shrink that much in twelve months. But there is good reason to believe that, even with only 5,000 members, it was almost certainly the largest of the socialist groupings. Be that as it may, it was no small achievement that all these different bodies were now sitting down together.

Without the initiative of the two dockers' unions and the railwaymen, none of them would have been there. But the transport workers were now divided and enfeebled. Tillett's union paid its bills only because of the loyal efforts of the South Wales tinplatemen. Along the waterfronts of southern England, the union was at a low ebb. Things were not much, but a little, better in the North. The port workers' memories remained, but it was not possible to organize a political response on memory alone. The clever young men of the ILP needed, and were courting, other trade-union allies, even if they were more staid, better-heeled, less turbulent, than their own founding union fathers. The pioneers were moving on. Burns was now firmly with the Liberals. Tom Mann was soon to leave for Australia. His influence on the dockers would not be replaced, try as Tillett might.

None the less, five waterfront trade unions were represented at the conference, and between them they said they mustered a little over 34,000 members. The representation of the new unions taken together was greater: the Gasworkers and General Labourers claimed 48,000, the Workers' Union clocked in at over 4,000, and a variety of other societies could add something like 10,000 members to the 'new-union' tally. Allowing that problems of definition are intransigent, it is therefore safe to say that approximately one-fifth of the trade unionists represented at Labour's founding conference had been mobilized by the new unions.

The Parliamentary Committee of the Trades Union Congress was not anxious to be dragged into the formation of an independent political body, and it therefore proposed, as a controlling measure, that the trade-union element in the new committee should be represented by – itself. This suggestion was politely declined by Ben Tillett: he thought that to accept their offer would deprive the LRC of 'all its meaning and all its character'. The intention was to create an alliance between the trade unions and a variety of progressive bodies, and he did not believe that the Parliamentary Committee could 'assume a responsibility and an authority it had no right to'.[1] The gasworkers were willing to have the seven representatives of the trade-union movement chosen by the Parliamentary Committee, but a card-vote went with Tillett, and the conference elected representatives of the Lancashire Miners, the Railway Servants, the Gasworkers, the Textile Workers, the Shipwrights, the Steel-smelters and the Vellum Bookbinders to form the trade-union section of the new organization's Executive.

## The Options

The political perspectives open to the new party turned around three distinct platforms. The SDF wanted a party organization 'separate from the capitalist parties based upon a recognition of the class war, and having for its ultimate objective the socialisation of the means of production, distribution, and exchange'. The Party, they went on, should 'formulate its own policy for promoting practical legislative measures in the interests of labour, and . . . co-operate with any Party that will support such measures, or . . . assist in opposing measures of an opposite character'.[2]

The shipwrights wanted none of this. A. Wilkie, their delegate, proposed that a Labour Group be formed in Parliament, based on a platform 'composed of, say, four or five planks, embracing questions upon which the vast majority of the workers in the country are in agreement . . .'.[3] Wilkie did not want Labour representatives to be bound to any overall political philosophy, and once they had pledged themselves to promoting Labour's interest, he thought they should be 'left entirely free on all political questions'.[4]

Two dockers' leaders got into an immediate spat on different sides in this confrontation. James Sexton thought that the SDF resolution was 'magnificent, very heroic but . . . not war'. It was divisive, and though he agreed with it he could not vote for it at this conference. Harry Quelch of the SDF denounced Sexton's view as 'humbug', and robustly cast doubt upon all those who proclaimed themselves in favour of a principle which they intended to vote against. Keir Hardie then came through with a third proposal which steered straight down the middle. He wanted a distinct Labour Group in Parliament with its own whips. He chose as many as possible of the words of the SDF motion, including their commitment to the promotion of legislation in the interests of Labour and their opposition to measures 'having an opposite tendency', but carefully filleting out their socialist pronouncements. Hardie received support from Pete Curran of the gasworkers, John Burns and Ben Tillett. His proposal then carried unanimously. Hardie also succeeded in keeping open the question of whether the new group would, or would not, work with the Liberals: 'If he saw anything which Labour had to gain by that, nothing would hinder him from agreeing to it. But every day tended more and more to confirm his belief in the folly of any such a course.'[5]

In reality, the new party was very vulnerable to offers of co-operation with the Liberals, even though its own emergence owed much to the intransigence of local Liberal associations, in refusing to accommodate to electoral change by adopting trade-union-supported candidates. But those Labour men who were elected on a Liberal ticket were still able to bar the road to fully independent action for a number of key trade unions, above all the miners.

## Empire and Protection

The General Election of 1900 had confirmed the Conservatives in office, still with a bone-crushing majority. While 334 MPs directly accepted their whip, a further 68 were elected on the allied Liberal–Unionist ticket of Joseph Chamberlain. In opposition there were 184 Liberals and Lib.–Labs; 82 Irish Nationalists; and 2 Labour Representation Committee members, each at odds with the other. Westminster was by now commonly referred to as an 'imperial' Parliament, although it was by no means representative of the subject peoples either abroad or at home. It was still elected on a purely national franchise, excluding all British women – and many British men who happened to be working class – from the right to vote. If it was imperial, it was not as a voice of the peoples of the empire but as the embodiment of authority, the source of the writ which ran around the world. But the old century, and with it the 'Pax Britannica', had really gone.

This peace had been far from absolute, but such as it was, it had

> depended less on Britain's absolute strength than on the absolute weakness of others. This thought was expressed . . . by Ernest Bevin . . . 'What astounds me about the history of the Navy is how cheaply we policed the world for three hundred years. I often think, when I read this history, that it is a good job no-one called our bluff very often . . . the world was policed largely by the British Navy with less than one hundred thousand men'.[6]

In the twentieth century the others' absolute weakness was at an end. Commercial and military competition were already rampant. Imperialism as a British policy was to face a serious political test, which was not at all diminished by the fact that the Conservatives had begun with a notable victory by winning in the so-called Khaki Election, named in honour of the Boer War. The war, which dragged on long after its end had been anticipated, was far from universally popular, but even those who enthused about it were about to be tested by other problems. British industrial supremacy now faced highly effective and sustained challenges from the United States, Germany, France and Japan. Productivity was increasing at double the British rate in each of these countries. Thus, each new recession brought increased unemployment to Britain, and increased the pressure on the poor.

Joseph Chamberlain, from May 1903 the voice of Protectionism, was to be much more than a junior partner in the Conservative administration of Salisbury. As Michael Barratt Brown tells us:

> It is sometimes supposed that his re-entry to the Cabinet as Colonial Secretary was a downgrading. The fact is that he could have chosen any office that he had wanted, and the Prime Minister allowed him 'usually the power of a co-premier and on some rare occasions more'.[7] His choice of the Colonial Office was deliberate, and was central to his plans for a new economic policy for the country.[8]

From this base, Chamberlain eventually developed his proposals for tariff reform, protecting home-based agriculture and industry, but negotiating a system of imperial preferences which would defend British exports and grant privileged access to empire suppliers. Chamberlain did everything he could to win over working-class endorsement of his campaign, but the Labour Representation Committee, under the influence of the doctrines of free trade, moved continuously closer to the Liberals.

## Labour and the Liberals

Although the Independent Labour Party had established an impressive support network, capable of damaging the Liberal interest, it had not created a basis for widespread alternative representation. The failure of attempts to unify the two main socialist parties was accompanied by continuous erosion of the ILP. The political intellectuals who supported the ILP felt that a fusion with the SDF would abort any chance of creating a wide alliance with trade unions. Yet, as their own membership declined, they began to seem less than adequate to fulfil the project they had taken on. The departure of Tom Mann, seen by Keir Hardie as 'a strong personality', was accompanied by the rise of Ramsay MacDonald, who was certainly a personality, whether strong or not. With this wordy fellow emerged a style of leadership which was to debilitate the Labour movement for many years. It combined a melodious line in pseudo-millennarian rhetoric with a practical capacity for compromise and short-sighted duplicity, which still has the power to shock when one reads about it at the other end of a century much versed in the finer arts of hypocrisy.

'If I had the power and the authority, I have no doubt that I could come to terms with the leaders of the Labour Party in the course of half a morning,' said Herbert Gladstone, the liberal Chief Whip, in October 1901.[9] Within two years a secret pact had indeed been stitched together. This had been seen as the foundation of the Liberal recovery of 1906, and the simultaneous birth of the Labour Party. But perhaps, had the impact of the issue of Protection been foreseen by Gladstone, he might have been able to think of managing without it.

Back in 1900, eight months after the foundation of the LRC, the railwaymen's leader, Richard Bell, and Keir Hardie gained seats at the General Election. Bell had spent £900 during his campaign in Derby, while Hardie had disposed of £300 to win Merthyr Tydfil. Half of this last sum had been advanced by George Cadbury, the Liberal chocolate king, in opposition to the South African War. Hardie had contested two seats simultaneously, and had not believed that his chances were very good in Merthyr. Accordingly, he campaigned most energetically in Preston, which he failed to win. But one of the two Liberal candidates in Merthyr had been pro-war, and had roundly attacked Hardie as a 'pro-Boer'. It has been alleged that this abusive campaign gave Hardie the seat, so alienated were the South Wales voters by Liberal imperialism. Doubt has been cast on this interpretation. Was the victory simply a reaffirmation of Welsh radicalism? Whatever explanation we choose, the split in Liberal affinities could not have been made plainer.

Fifteen other Labour candidates failed, including Fred Jowett, Ramsay MacDonald, Philip Snowden and Will Thorne. Thorne lost in

West Ham South, where the socialist forces had been doing extremely well in local-government elections. The prospects of the Labour Party were clearly influenced by the Liberal split about the war, and Lib.–Lab. contenders, who still included the miners' MPs, sought to bridle the 'independence' of the LRC by building upon the recognition of this fact. First, they tried to recover lost ground by repeating their attempt to bring all trade-union representatives on the LRC under the control of the TUC's Parliamentary Committee. Beaten in 1902, this ploy was replaced by a variant tactic, seeking affiliation of the National Democratic League, which, as we have seen, had been founded for the purpose of electoral reform by a coalition of Liberals and Socialists, in which Tom Mann had at first played a major role. By this back door, it was thought, all the radical Liberals would enter; the 'independence' of Labour would thus be tidily disposed of.

This initiative was defeated at the 1903 conference of the LRC, and provoked Pete Curran of the gasworkers and James Sexton of the dockers to propose firm measures by which the new LRC might obtain financial independence which could underpin their desire for political autonomy. In 1904 a voluntary levy was agreed and each affiliate was requested to pay a penny per member to a central treasury. In 1905 this levy was made compulsory. All candidates would receive 25 per cent of their election expenses from this new fund, which would also pay Members of Parliament an annual sum of £200. Central funds in 1900 had allowed the expenditure of a princely £33 during the whole election campaign. From now on, however, the LRC would dispose of adequate resources to render the financial blandishments of the Liberals far less influential than heretofore.

Three new Labour MPs arrived in the House of Commons in the by-elections which followed 1900. They were David Shackleton, Will Crooks and Arthur Henderson. Each of the new members, for different reasons, had strong Liberal affinities. Hardie began to weaken in his proclaimed independence. He sought to bring John Burns into the leadership of the Labour faction. In March 1903 he wrote to Burns: 'With your magnificent voice, your rich imagination and attractive personality, you would rouse your fellows as no other man in public life could.' Roger Moore, who has highlighted these events, points out that the 'very fact' that this offer was made 'is indicative of the uncertain future of the Labour Party'.[10]

## The Impact of Taff Vale

By 1901 forty-one trade unions with a membership of more than 350,000 had affiliated to the Labour Party. More than 100,000 other trade unionists were additionally affiliated during the following year.

They belonged to 65 separate trade unions. The growth of affiliated membership followed directly on the celebrated (or infamous) Taff Vale case. By 1903, 127 unions with nearly 850,000 members had joined up. In 1905, the total reached 158 unions and 73 Trades Councils. These accounted between them for the lion's share of a total affiliated membership of 900,000.

The Taff Vale strike broke out in the summer of 1900 because John Ewington, a signalman employed by the Taff Vale Railway Company, was victimized. The men were fractious because wages had not risen to meet the rise in prices which resulted from the Boer War. Claims for recognition of their union, the Amalgamated Society of Railway Servants, were rejected. The company blustered, and was accused of dictatorship by the union. When the strike erupted, Ammon Beasley, the railway manager, sent for Collison's free labourers to break it. Two hundred practised blacklegs duly materialized. Beasley went to law to stop the counter-picketing, and was given an injunction against the ASRS. This was quashed in the Appeal Court, but re-established at the House of Lords in July 1901. The Lords further decided that in such a case as this, the union's funds did not enjoy immunity. Given this green light, Beasley pressed ahead to secure damages from the railwaymen and was awarded £23,000 plus costs.

The House of Lords was in a gung-ho mood in 1901, and a couple of weeks after it had ploughed trade-union immunities into the ground, it interdicted boycotts, in the case of *Quinn v. Leathem*. In this case, the Lords sanctioned the principle, first established by the Court of Appeal in the earlier case of *Temperton v. Russell* (1893), that a conspiracy to injure was cause for an action against a union. The government peremptorily rejected Keir Hardie's appeal for legislation to restore protection to union funds.

At the beginning of August, the LRC's secretary, MacDonald, wrote to every union emphasizing the significance of the Taff Vale judgement in particular, which, he said, 'should convince the unions that a Labour Party in Parliament is an immediate necessity.'[11] The LRC agreed to establish a sub-committee to explain the consequences of the Taff Vale judgement; it went to work immediately. As invariably happens during such legal upheavals, union leaders saw the point much quicker than their members. An engineers' ballot on affiliation to the LRC touched only 7,000 members in total. But some leaders took steps to divest themselves of their personal property in order to avoid possible confiscation in subsequent disputes.

Not all full-time officers shared this apprehension. Richard Bell himself actually welcomed the judgement, on the grounds that it would reinforce trade-union discipline and facilitate recognition. It would be 'a useful influence in solidifying the forces of trade unionism', he thought.[12] James Sexton went further along the same line of argument:

'There are those in the Labour Movement sanguine enough to hope that the decision in the Taff Vale case will be a blessing in disguise, and will tend to strengthen executive control and minimise, if not entirely kill, irresponsible action in the localities', he wrote.[13] (Disguised or not, this blessing was to fall well short of the hopes placed in it by the Liverpool dockers' spokesman.) Sexton lost no opportunity to preach this message, and in his 1902 Annual Report he wrote:

> the whole mischief was caused by the first initial step taken being contrary to the rule of the Society itself. Had the action of the men and the Executive been governed by the rules of the Society there would have been no Taff Vale case today, and the Railwaymen's fund would have been richer by £23,000 than it is, while the legal position of trades unions would have remained what it was understood to be previous to the now historic decision. It will, therefore, we hope be fully recognised by our members the absolute necessity of a strict observance of the rules, as any lapsing from them would place us in the same position as the Railwaymen.[14]

## Tillett: Arbitration and Recognition

Ben Tillett also saw Taff Vale as an unexpected boost for his policy of compulsory arbitration. Shortly before the House of Lords delivered its judgement, Tillett opined that 'it would do a world of good and stir up those who had got an easy belief in things.'[15] Later, in 1903, he told the TUC that the Taff Vale judgement should stay in place. Of course, he said, the judgement was a threat to Labour; but he could not support the campaign to reverse it. He was strongly critical of the leaders of unions who opposed the judgement and yet paid without demur the legal penalties which were imposed upon them: 'Mr. Bell's society had tamely paid £40,000 or so. If Mr. Bell and his colleague . . . had done six months in prison it would have been better for them all.'[16]

In a more flamboyant mood, speaking to the conference of his own union in 1902, he said that he himself was quite prepared 'to go to the stake, the gallows or jail'. But in spite of his intransigence, Tillett's priority during these years was to establish governmentally regulated binding arbitration. His biographer tells us that he

> began advocating this practice for dockers just as it was falling into general disuse. Tillett could plausibly argue to his own rank and file, for whom trade unionism was a comparatively recent development, that it was a great advance for their representatives merely to appear before an arbiter on equal footing with the employer. The novelty of this sort of equality, however, had long since worn off among craft unionists.[17]

No doubt this is true, but it does not face up to the real meaning of Tillett's policies. Schneer quotes a miners' spokesman: 'He says the capitalist system is wrong. Then why is he creating an Arbitration Court to perpetuate it?'[18]

Schneer believes that Tillett 'no longer seemed interested in replacing capitalism with socialism'. Instead, his disapproval of strikes, and his impulse to maintain the organization of his union, totally dominated his thinking. Schneer is quite right to say that 'probably he was correct in thinking that the Shipping Federation had become too strong for the Union'.[19] But it was not necessary for compulsory arbitration to bring instant success to union claims before it could offer some very real hope to a Labour leader with his back against the wall. What arbitration brought with it was *recognition*, and it was recognition which could reinforce the continuous solidity of class opposition, and therefore the continuity of organization (as we have argued in chapter 3). If a third party, the government, mediated between the forces of labour and capital, whether the decision went ill or well for Labour, all the forces of society were none the less conspiring with Labour to reinforce its self-awareness and its evolving sense of its own identity.

Schneer himself shows how skilfully Tillett argued the case of the Swansea tinplate workers during an arbitration at the beginning of 1904. His cross-examination highlighted all the grievances of the men he represented. He lost his case. But he had persuaded his members of their common cause, at a time when, quite evidently, it was beyond their powers to win their demands in any more direct way.

It is true that Tillett was floundering, because, as we have seen, his union had been gravely weakened in the ports and no longer constituted an important power-base for intervention in the affairs of the rapidly growing Labour Representation Committee. In 1903 he entered into a dubious relationship with Horatio Bottomley, a racketeering business-man with a sleazy reputation, who was seeking to ingratiate himself with Labour leaders as part of his plan to enter Parliament in the Liberal interest in Hackney. Tillett's Annual Reports to the dockers, however, maintained, year by year, a constant flow of class-war commitments.

In 1900, regretting the lack of unity among the waterside unions, he drew a dismal balance sheet of the defeats of the dockers' and lightermen's disputes. Their disunity made it highly unlikely that they could ever force conditions upon the employers.

> For myself, [said Tillett,] I have at all times taken full responsibility for disputes even . . . when these have taken place against my advice . . . I have never thought to save my neck . . . by repudiating the action taken by our members, but have associated myself with them at all times . . .
>
> During the years I have taken an active interest in Labour movements, I have advocated Arbitration and Conciliation; since my visit to the Antipodes, I am convinced that compulsory arbitration is essential to the well being of the worker and the welfare of trade. At present all the law is on the side of the Capitalist who makes as much use of the law as we

should, were we the dominant factor . . . Lord Penrhyn, the great Coal and Shipping millionaires, Dock Directors, Engineers, and others, have at all times power to throw industry out of gear without a murmur from the public, and a public that would go frantic with rage at a dislocation of trade caused by a dispute of the workmen, the press even siding with the employers when screwing the wage earners.[20]

This unequal relationship was aggravated by the confusion of the port industry:

London is the great unmanageable. Here social economy is in confusion, here government tangled, and even the Port itself is controlled by a muddled confusion of authorities, its working bungled and costly, while labour is starved and demoralised instead of being healthy and efficient. The toilers of London make millionaires by the score, but thousands even fail to recognise the commercial character of a trade union.[21]

If all this implied the acceptance of arbitration machinery, it also implied centralized union discipline and the rejection of 'hare-brained' action. 'Strict adhesion to rule', ballot votes and constitutional behaviour were to be enforced, 'while the strikes in sympathy should be given a wide berth.'[22]

All this reorientation was accompanied by a strong statement of continued loyalty to

the great international movement. Labour must be as international as capital. The great trusts, the combines, the fact that New York is fast becoming the successor of London as the money mart of the world, indicates such a shifting of controlling centres as will make for change in the humblest industrial calling of the world. Capital speaks all languages; let labour speak the language of universal brotherhood, and we shall be able . . . to check the forces which are driving the . . . producer to beggary and starvation.[23]

There is a confusion here which harks back to the problem of choice we identified in Tom Mann's words to the Dockers' Union, spoken only a few years earlier (see chapter 5). International action implies sympathetic action, which frequently cuts across the rules agreed within permanent national structures for bargaining. The injunction to eschew 'the strikes in sympathy' was calculated to ease new agreements into being. International action might ease them out again. National democratic advance and internationalism might, in theory, be reconcilable: but they were certainly not identical processes, and at times one could conflict with the other.

For the time being, Tillett's main activity was concentrated on a national stage. He had been elected to the Executive of the Labour Representation Committee in 1901. His stay there appears to have been turbulent, and he certainly quarrelled repeatedly with Keir Hardie. By 1903 Hardie thought that 'it would do others of the wavering brotherhood a world of good [if] an example could be made of . . . Tillett'.[24]

## Wheeling and Dealing

During all the years in which Tillett was becoming increasingly estranged from the predominant leadership of the LRC, the Committee was growing continuously. (His membership of the Executive was an early casualty of this growth.) The effects of the Taff Vale judgement brought one union after another into the fold. At the same time, efforts to restore direct control by the TUC were recognized as fruitless. In 1904 Richard Bell, now TUC president, and also by now estranged from the LRC, ruled that the Congress had no control over the LRC because it was 'an organisation'. The ILP politicians had thus succeeded in attaching to themselves a growing, and soon to be preponderant, body of trade-union opinion.

Undoubtedly, this was eased by the agreement with the Liberals. Keir Hardie prepared this in a series of appeals to Liberal leaders: first to John Morley, then to Lloyd George. But a secret agreement had been finally concluded between Ramsay MacDonald and Herbert Gladstone, the Liberal's agent, in August 1903. Negotiations had dragged on for several months, with Jesse Herbert representing Gladstone. According to his biographer, MacDonald excelled in these talks:

> He held one or two good cards – notably the Parliamentary Fund – but on the whole his hand was not a strong one. In effect, he was asking the Liberals to allow the L.R.C. to establish itself in Parliament, but he had little to offer in exchange. The L.R.C. had a large affiliated membership, but no one who knew the Labour movement would imagine that the trade unionists affiliated to it could be 'delivered' in a parliamentary election. Many were Liberals already: their votes would go to Liberal candidates without any special arrangement between the Liberals and the L.R.C. Others were Conservative, notably in Lancashire, but it was far from clear that Conservative working-men would vote for Liberal candidates merely because the L.R.C. asked them to. Yet all this was obscured in a tantalizing cloud of promises and threats. The L.R.C., MacDonald claimed, had a membership of a million and a political fund of £5,000 a year. Its candidates were 'in almost every instance earnest Liberals who will support a Liberal Government'. Liberal opposition to these candidates would 'not only lose the possible accession of the erstwhile Tory working man, but will inevitably estrange the hitherto loyal Liberal working man'.[25]

Jesse Herbert received this news impassively, and said nothing very much. But he did ask MacDonald for specific proposals, and he sent post-haste to Gladstone a detailed report which showed that he had missed none of the potential of MacDonald's offer:

'The LRC can directly influence the votes of nearly a million men. They will have a fighting fund of £100,000 . . . Their members are mainly men who have hitherto voted with the Liberal Party. Should they be advised to vote against Liberal candidates, and (as they probably would) should they act as advised the Liberal party would suffer defeat not only in those constituencies where L.R.C. candidates fought, but also in almost every borough, and in many of the Divisions of Lancashire and Yorkshire. This would be the inevitable result of unfriendly action towards the L.R.C. candidates. They would be defeated, but so also should we be defeated.'

Shortly afterwards MacDonald discussed the proposed arrangement with Gladstone and in the next three months he had at least seven further meetings with Herbert.[26]

David Marquand reports an undated note from MacDonald, probably written three years after the event:

Before the General Election of 1906 I saw Mr. Gladstone, the Chief Liberal Whip, twice and his confidential secretary, Mr. Jesse Herbert, several times. There was no bargain struck. I told them what seats we were determined to fight. They were friendly & no doubt expected their friendship to influence our policy. They never asked that it should however. The impression they gave me was that they [agreed] that we should have a fair chance of representation. Their attitude no doubt did influence me in opposing wild-cat candidatures, & in one or two constituencies I told them there would be no Labour candidate because there was no Labour organisation. I repeat, however, that information was not given in any way as a *quid pro quo*. A case in point was Walsall when it was proposed to make Sir Arthur Hayter a peer. I said there would be no Labour candidate. There could have been none.[27]

In the middle of these negotiations, the LRC published a resonant declaration entitled 'Why We Are Independent'. This was dated April 1903 and signed, on behalf of the Committee, by J. Ramsay MacDonald, secretary. It said:

Upon this conflict between Capital and Labour, neither a Liberal nor a Conservative Ministry can be trusted to stand by the workers. The nation is called upon to settle economic and industrial difficulties for which neither of the old political parties offers any definite or satisfactory solution. Would it not, therefore, be futile to commit this new movement to parties which neither understand nor sympathise with its aims?[28]

The document continues with a declaration on 'The Wisdom of Independence', which says:

WE ARE INDEPENDENT, THEN

*Because* we must unite the democracy;

*Because* we must have the support of all sections of the Labour movement;

*Because* if we are Liberal or Conservative, the Trade Union movement cannot unitedly support us;

*Because* this policy has already secured the support of about 1,000,000 Trade Unionists;

*Because* we raise new economic and industrial issues, upon which the old political parties speak with an uncertain and hesitating voice;

*Because* we must be free in Parliament to lay down our Labour policy and adopt the most effective means for vindicating the rights of Labour and improving the social conditions of the people.[29]

For fifty years this declaration was the public face of Labour in Britain. MacDonald's secret accord was effectively blotted out, until it was rescued from Gladstone's archives by Henry Pelling and reprinted by Frank Bealey in 1956.[30]

No one can doubt the electoral significance of this accord. Yet Labour was acting independently in an important sense: campaigns about unemployment, the Poor Law and poverty drew thousands of workers into street demonstrations and made an important impact on public opinion.

## Taff Vale Recruits for Labour

And all the while, the shadow of Taff Vale hung over the unions.

On 1 August 1902, David Shackleton, the representative of the United Textile Factory Workers' Association, was elected as Labour member for Clitheroe. His victory brought his union into the Labour Representation Committee the following January. This accession marked a major gain for the Committee; the Textile Workers were its largest affiliate up to that time, and adherents of an 'old' trade union, of a classic type, to boot. No one could doubt the concern of Shackleton's members about Taff Vale, and he was quick to table a very qualified Bill for the restoration of immunities, which would have lifted union liability except, as the Bill had it, 'in cases where the damages were the result of action which had not been authorized by the Union executive'. His measure would also have legalized peaceful pickets. This bill failed, partly on a technicality, and partly as a result of an adverse vote. Subsequently, a Royal Commission was announced, but no trade unionists were appointed to serve on it. Small wonder that unions now flocked to support the LRC, and that their members began a systematic lobby, first of sitting members and then of candidates, to pressure for reform.

## The Conservative Split

Chamberlain's criticism of the Balfour government in May 1903 had split the Unionist Party from top to bottom, and in the course of the argument it was 'reduced almost to a rump'.[31] Balfour's administration was already under sustained attack for sanctioning the deployment of Chinese labour in the Rand, under conditions which were very oppressive. The defection of Chamberlain was a fierce blow. It began with a powerful speech in Birmingham, denouncing the continuation of free trade and demanding a system of imperial preferences. It went on to insist upon retaliation against foreign tariffs. The Unionist rank and file responded warmly, but the Cabinet was frigidity itself. Its predominant membership was firmly committed to free trade, while the Prime Minister was concerned to find a compromise and reunify his divided forces. There followed some months of manoeuvre. The Cabinet was reconstructed in order to straddle the issue. Uncertainty grew and grew. The Liberals were overjoyed at their good fortune, finding in the defence of free trade an issue strong enough to dissolve their former divisions on the Boer War. Two popular slogans confronted each other: the Liberals denounced taxes on food, 'The Big Loaf and the Little Loaf'. Chamberlain insisted that 'Tariff Reform Means Work for All'. Balfour got squeezed.

The dockers' unions did not stand on one side in this argument. Sexton, indeed, surpassed himself: the most notable events of the trade-union year, he thought, had been the defeat of the Penrhyn quarrymen, the Taff Vale agitation, and

the protectionist theory raised by 'Joseph and his brethren'. Thanks to the firm attitude taken by the Trade Unionists on this question this attempt to again fool the British workman utterly failed. Joseph himself took flight to the land of the Pharaohs, and returned to find that a host of Pharaohs had arisen that knew not Joseph. It is a source of satisfaction to know that our resolution at the Leicester Trades Union Congress was the means of setting the opposition going in the Trade Union world. A complete answer to the theory of Mr. Chamberlain that protection would find work for everybody is found in the fact of the introduction of cheap Chinese labour into South Africa. Let it not be forgotten that there are hundreds of thousands of persons in this country willing to work but cannot get it, while the country purchased at the cost of many thousand British lives and expenditure of British treasure is now being given over to hordes of Chinamen at 1s.6d. per day. And what can be done in South Africa is also likely to be done here, when under the policy of protection, even were it possible, everybody found work and higher wages.[32]

## The General Election of 1906

During the first year of the split in the Unionist forces, unemployment ran high. Had this continued, Chamberlain might have created a bandwaggon of support for his views: but trade picked up subsequently, so that as the country moved towards a General Election the Unionist appeal to public opinion was losing momentum. The election of 1906 decided this argument very clearly. The Conservatives secured the election of 130 Members, and the Liberal Unionists suffered a loss of 40, so that their total was now 28. The Irish Nationalists won 83 seats, with 375 Liberals, 24 Lib.–Labs and 29 candidates of the Labour Representation Committee. One miner joined them after the election.

The twenty-nine now recognized their victory, and assumed the designation of 'the Labour Party'. They had polled 321,663 votes out of a total of 5.6 million.

All shared in the Liberal consensus on free trade. What bonded them as a special group was the commitment to reverse the Taff Vale decision and restore the right to strike. By far the majority of Liberal MPs had pledged themselves in the same sense: but for the Labour Party this was, of course, a core issue. Home Rule remained the banner of the Irish contingent, which Labour supported. Outside Westminster there was a rising clamour of women's voices, demanding admission, and this was to reach deafening volume within a short time. The Labour manifesto had been short, sharp and sweetly compatible with the Liberal ascendancy. It read:

> This election is to decide whether or not Labour is to be fairly represented in Parliament.
>
> The House of Commons is supposed to be the people's House, and yet the people are not there.
>
> Landlords, employers, lawyers, brewers, and financiers are there in force. Why not Labour?
>
> The Trade Unions ask the same liberty as capital enjoys. They are refused.
>
> The aged poor are neglected.
>
> The slums remain; overcrowding continues, whilst the land goes to waste.
>
> Shopkeepers and traders are overburdened with rates and taxation, whilst the increasing land values, which should relieve the ratepayers, go to people who have not earned them.
>
> Wars are fought to make the rich richer, and underfed school children are still neglected.
>
> Chinese Labour is defended because it enriches the mine owners.
>
> The unemployed ask for work, the Government gave them a worthless Act, and now, when you are beginning to understand the causes of your poverty, the red herring of Protection is drawn across your path.

Protection, as experience shows, is no remedy for poverty and unemployment. It serves to keep you from dealing with the land, housing, old age, and other social problems!

You have it in your power to see that Parliament carries out your wishes. The Labour Representation Executive appeals to you in the name of a million Trade Unionists to forget all the political differences which have kept you apart in the past, and vote for . . . . . . . . [here was inserted the name of the Labour candidate][33]

Of the twenty-nine Labour candidates who were elected on the LRC ticket, only four had faced official Liberals. Twenty-five had been given a clear field by the Liberal Party, so that they had only to beat the Conservative or Unionist contenders. Keir Hardie faced no Tory opponent, by contrast, but he had to beat one of the two Liberals offering themselves in this two-Member constituency. Twenty-six Labour men failed to secure election, and eighteen of these faced three-cornered contests. The gasworkers' Pete Curran was opposed only by a Liberal and he lost. All others were beaten by Conservatives in straight fights. One of these was James Sexton, who gained 2,592 votes, as opposed to his Conservative opponent's 3,373, in Liverpool West Toxteth. Ben Tillett came third in Eccles. He had been ill and absent, but he also felt that the intellectuals of the ILP were deliberately neglecting to press his case. Among new unionists who were actually elected were J. R. Clynes and Will Thorne of the gasworkers, and Charles Duncan of the Workers' Union. Harry Quelch stood in the two-Member Southampton constituency for the Social Democratic Federation, polling just over 2,000 votes and coming last. Two Liberals were elected there.

There were big regional influences on this representation. Thirteen of the Labour Party's seats were in Lancashire and Cheshire, and all of these resulted from the withdrawal of Liberal candidates. The traditional strength of Conservatism among parts of the working population persuaded the Liberals to be magnanimous in their negotiations with Labour. If they could not expect to win themselves, generosity was a prudent gesture, especially if it might then remove troublesome splits in what they saw as 'their own' votes elsewhere. Yorkshire, by contrast, saw the Liberals in a more secure situation, which made them less flexible. The trade-union movement was weaker there than in the adjacent counties; so there was scant Lib.–Lab. trading. Eight LRC candidates ran, but only three were elected. Jowett won in Bradford against both established parties, building on his own previous campaign and on the earlier trail-blazing contests of Ben Tillett. The other two victorious candidates were the ones who had not been opposed by Liberals.

## *Taff Vale Reversed, Immunities Established*

It was not simply the disposition of candidates and Labour's electoral success, however, that set the framework of the new administration. The TUC had run its own preparatory lobby, to great effect, throughout every constituency, up to polling day itself. Two and a quarter million affiliated members had been asked to withhold votes from every candidate whatsoever who would not pledge himself to work for the complete removal of trade-union liability in disputes. Gone was the caution of Shackleton's defeated Bill. Now Taff Vale was to be totally annulled with the exact restoration of the status quo ante. A number of Conservatives, counting their margins, gave their word. But at least three-fifths of all Liberal candidates signed up in support, and, in contrast to their Tory co-thinkers, a very large proportion of them was elected. Among them was Sir John Walton, who was later entrusted with presentation of the Liberal government's original proposals in the Commons. These were far from satisfactory to the TUC.

After the election, the Conservative-appointed Royal Commission reported, broadly in favour of the 1903 Shackleton halfway-house. The new government moved to legislate accordingly, but by now it was too late for half-measures. The new Labour Members tabled their own Bill for the restoration of full immunity. Premier Sir Henry Campbell-Bannerman gave his support. In the debate in the Commons, Keir Hardie showed that Sir John Walton himself had issued an election poster pledging his unequivocal support for the Trade Union Bill. The heart went out of the campaign for a compromise reform. So it was that there emerged the Trades Disputes Act of 1906, carried through its second reading by 416 affirmative votes to 66 against. Shackleton was given a celebratory banquet by the TUC, the GFTU and the Labour Party.

The Trades Disputes Act of 1906 was an unqualified victory for the trade-union movement. It established that no act done 'in pursuance of an agreement or combination by two or more persons' should be actionable unless it would have been so if done individually. Henceforth it was not open to the courts to regard unions as 'civil conspiracies'. It restored and augmented the rights of peaceful picketing. It brought into force a major concession, legalizing actions 'in restraint of trade' whenever they arose in the course of a trade dispute. And, lastly, it explicitly protected union funds from claims 'in respect of any tortious act'. Some commentators have maintained that this immunity was too far-reaching to be wholly for the good of the unions themselves.[34]

After this 'signal triumph', however, most Labour MPs did not quite know what to do next. The Parliamentary Labour Party, wrote Henry Pelling, 'seemed for a time thereafter to have lost its sense of purpose'.[35]

Different factions pulled in different ways. The party in the country became more restive. There were other lesser gains,[36] most notably an act enabling the provision of school meals (except in Scotland), which, during the depression which followed, brought aid to children in a number of areas with high unemployment. But although the Liberals brought in other measures of reform, they successfully held up or diluted any new proposals from the Labour Party, with the result that criticism mounted as unemployment rose.

## Victor Grayson: Voice of the Unemployed

By 1907 there was visible unease, which expressed itself in the election of a young and unendorsed socialist fire-raiser, Victor Grayson, for the division of Colne Valley, which had been contested by Tom Mann in 1895 (see chapter 7). Grayson scandalized his new parliamentary colleagues by a succession of indecorous acts. He ran an open skirmish with Ramsay MacDonald, refused to sign the Labour Party's constitution, and rumpussed continuously about unemployment. As a one-man band, he made more noise than all the Labour MPs put together, and this stimulated some considerable response from people outside Westminster. John Lister of the Halifax ILP summed up the mood of many older socialists in a jingle entitled 'The Lost Party':

> Oh! Where can it be – the old ILP?
>   The party of sinews and brawn?
> Oh! Where is the muscle, that once used to tussle
>   With foes in the days that are gone?
>
> The days that have been – will their like ne'er be seen?
>   When courage and candour stood tall
> Ere we entered the ways – yes the policy ways
>   And hearken to history's warning!
> 'Tis this – that to laike with the old yellow-shirted 'snake'*
>   Is a spree you may rue in the morning.
>
> Anything! Anything! just to get in –
> Any tale! Any tale! so you may win –
> All the false lying spirits unchain,
> Barter your soul man, your voter to claim.[37]

## Accountability

All sorts of controversies began during these experiences, and many of them have run on throughout the ninety years which have followed. One

---

* Alternative version: with Whig or with Liberal to jig

of the most notable concerned the question of who was to call the tune in the new party. The Parliamentary Labour Party which came into existence in 1906 had much to play for along the margin of the Liberal Party, and in fact it made considerable gains within the strategy of covert alliance, the most notable of which was the detachment of the mineworkers from the organizational framework of the Liberals, and the incorporation of the Miners' Federation into the Labour Party's own structure. But the price in conformity was more than many wished to pay.

As early as January 1905 Ben Tillett had moved a motion at the LRC Conference 'That it be an instruction to the Executive of the LRC to enforce the hearty adoption by LRC candidates of all legislative proposals emanating from the Trades Union Congress. In view of the refusal of candidates, that it be the peremptory duty of the Executive to refuse or discontinue support financially and morally.' Tillett was seconded by J. N. Bell of the National Amalgamated Union of Labour, and supported by Harry Quelch, speaking on behalf of London Trades Council. Quelch widened the question, by insisting that the 'Party as a whole' should formulate policy, which the candidates 'would have to accept or stand down'. On a show of hands, Tillett's proposal lost by 148 to 84. A card-vote being called, it was finally defeated by 537 to 245.[38]

James Sexton took the view of the majority, and a year later he reported to the NUDL: 'At the time of the Election this LRC, Labour Party had formulated no official programme. Its first and all-absorbing object is to be – to exist – in independence of all other parties.'[39]

The honeymoon following the victories of 1906 (in the election and then in the enactment of the Trades Disputes Act) did not endure long beyond the year. Even at the 1906 Conference, the first to convene under the name of the Labour Party, attempts were made to 'instruct' the parliamentary party on its Trade Union Bill. By 1907 Keir Hardie complained of seventeen separate resolutions containing 'instructions to introduce this and that'.[40] An attempt was made by the National Executive to direct the Standing Orders Committee to rephrase these motions in order to uphold the autonomy of the parliamentary party. It soon became clear that this would not pass the Conference, so a compromise formula was submitted. This left the PLP and the Executive to decide between them the timing of action upon such instructions. Even this was too bitter a pill for some to swallow, although in the end it was accepted.

Unintimidated, Ben Tillett returned to the attack, moving that

The Executive is instructed to secure united and consistent action on the part of its representatives in Parliament. For the aforesaid object the Committee should be sole authority granting the right to back Bills, or support measures, directly or indirectly affecting Labour. The Executive shall organise a Committee within the House of Commons, of Labour

Party Members, to instruct and advise its fellow members on all Parliamentary work.[41]

This uncompromising prescription once again went to a card vote, and lost by 590,000 to 229,000.

Tillett's biographer, Jonathan Schneer, believes that his critique of the Labour Representation Committee had 'so far . . . come from the right'. This hardly fits the evidence. Undoubtedly it is true, as Schneer insists, that personal acrimony between Hardie and MacDonald on the one side, and the dockers' leader on the other, ran at a very high level. In such a scrimmage, people might not worry overmuch about which cudgel to use, in which hand. Neither would they be squeamish about where their blows landed. But although Tillett's dubious friendship with Horatio Bottomley was close enough to permit him to accept financial help to enable him to voyage again to Australia, his overall political commitment had remained very strongly on the left throughout this period. We can see it in the Report to his union in 1905:

> Mr. Charles Booth indicates 4 per cent of the criminal and wastrel class as being voluntary agents of their own downfall by drink, yet a criminal class of less than 1 per cent of the whole population, and only 4 per cent even of this class, are indicated as offering a cause of poverty to the other 99 per cent. It is a pity that so-called leaders of labour subscribe to this mendacity, which only ignorance or wilfulness would ever stoop to make use of.
>
> The restoration to the people of the confiscated thousand millions, the recovery for the community's benefit, of lands, capital, and industrial machinery, will find ample scope for the services of those who claim to serve the country.
>
> Nothing but an economic adjustment can ever suffice as a remedy. I have carefully investigated the services and bonafides of the persons preaching thrift, etc. and without an exception, not one of them has ever done, or even desires to render, service to the community, aiming at least at the abolition of poverty. We ought not to be the victims of time-servers, or permit our sacred cause to be side-tracked by charlatans or incompetents. To create an environment making possible the development of the best types of humanity, with all the aids of civilisation generously at command, and equality of opportunity, with working, sleeping and living conditions, conducing to efficiency; by these means, and these only, can we make for happiness or goodness. There is already a change in thought, and my wish is, that we may have a change in action, in methods making for the acquisition of all the powers ensuring for political and social justice.
>
> Any change in government ought not to act as a soporific, for it is still the same class struggle, whichever party may be in power.[42]

In Australia, Tillett met up again with Tom Mann, and caught some of the feverish *élan* which accompanied his crusade in the Antipodes. He did not return until early 1908.

## Abusing and Accusing

Tillett's next onslaught began straight away as an exchange of letters about the need to campaign against unemployment. The Dockers' Union Executive was moved to complain that a number of Labour members had been appearing with Cabinet ministers and prominent Liberals 'on platforms all over the country, in some cases consorting with well known union-smashers'. In particular, the dockers called upon the Executive 'to request explanations of Messrs. Henderson, Shackleton, Richards, Crooks, Duncan, Snowden and others, whose expenses . . . have been met by the Temperance-Liberal party over the last 12 months.'[43]

Shortly afterwards the Willesden Labour Party wrote urging support by the Parliamentary Labour Party for an initiative by Victor Grayson demanding immediate attention to the problem of unemployment. The Oldham Branch of the Social Democratic Party wrote in similar terms. Ramsay MacDonald replied to both letters in a strangely abusive style. To Willesden he said:

> If you understood the methods of getting things done in Parliament you will see that the very last thing to be done in the interest of the unemployed is to adopt your . . . resolution . . . there is nothing more disheartening to our Parliamentary work than the way that well intentioned supporters like yourselves are misled by proposals that appear to be energetic, but which in actual fact are utter rubbish.

In his reply to the Oldham SDP, MacDonald's low threshold of courtesy was lowered even further:

> I am in receipt of yours of the 18th which, knowing as I do the general stupidity of the SDP . . . gives me no surprise. It is perfectly evident that your members, or, at any rate that part of them which voted for the resolution, care nothing for doing anything for the unemployed, but prefer to gas copiously about them . . . The stupid tub-thumpers who compose the SDP glorify an exhibition of weakness and incompetence.

MacDonald wrote in a similar vein to correspondents in a number of other cities, and Tillett gathered some of the replies and published them. They made his point more convincingly than his own arguments, which were equally strident. He also published an abrasive exchange in which, writing on behalf of the union, he accused leading members of the Labour Party in Parliament of giving temperance priority over employment, and strongly hinted that this decision had come about because some Labour leaders had been subsidised by Temperance money.

If MacDonald had been rude in his answers, Tillett was not exactly polite in his accusations. In a pamphlet provocatively entitled *Is the Parliamentary Labour Party a Failure?*, he hit out:

Why should not the unemployed demand food, the right to live, with vehemence commensurate to the tragedy, and resent with physical violence the callous fate the rich leave them to? There is no argument against the 'right to live', with wealth and production so far advanced as at present. Something must be done to make the rich think over the murderings and starvings under the system which gives them plenty and the wealth-maker nothing at all of the wealth produced.

What forces, he continued, can cope with the increase in unemployment?

In the House of Commons, flatulent paunches shake under dress waistcoats in laughter at the sally of a Minister utilising some heartless gibe against the Labour Party. On the boards of guardians, hell's own conspiracy is at work to circumvent the law, inadequate though it be. Relief committees spend 80 per cent of their income in expenses, turning out of their mean minds drivel and lies to excuse their wickedness, and damning the poor all round. Political parties edge and shuffle; the Labour Party is not seriously awake to the evils . . .

Echoing Tolstoy, Tillett continued: 'The army of central and local government officials will not get off the backs of the poor, but pile themselves as comfortably as possible with the rest of the thieves.'

From this appreciation he went on in the same vein to denounce Temperance Liberalism as humbug, and to allege that Labour leaders had been suborned by Temperance bribery to forget their true social commitments.

The duties of the Labour Party should be to look to the purely economic interests of the workers, and avoid as contagion any form of 'red-herring' politics. If liberty be given one section, the movement will be faced with divergent groups of Tariff Reformers, Free Traders, Disestablishers, House of Lords Reformers and Abolitionists, Educational hair-splitters, the while such an important matter as Unemployment is neglected. Poverty is due to the lack of means to live, and as the means of life is the property of capitalists, the Labour Party should exist to combat the system whereby the many are deprived of the means and rights of existence.[44]

## Tillett and the SDF

Shortly after the pamphlet was published by the SDF's Twentieth Century Press, Tillett became a regular contributor to Harry Quelch's newspaper, *Justice*. In its columns he continued to berate 'the Temperance bleating martyrs'.

All this helped the majority of the SDF to keep their members out of the Labour Party. The 1908 Labour Party Conference at Hull had carried an ASE motion fixing the party's objects, which included 'the Socialisation of the means of production, distribution and exchange, to be controlled by a democratic State in the interests of the entire community, and the complete emancipation of labour from the domination of capitalism and landlordism'.[45]

Since this declaration of faith precisely mirrored that of the SDF, it is hardly surprising that some of the Federation's members sought to reaffiliate to the party. Dan Irving, of Burnley, was a consistent supporter of affiliation, as well as a great admirer of H. M. Hyndman. In 1908 Hyndman himself came down on the side of rejoining the Labour forces. But the opposition, led by Tillett's friend Quelch, defeated the reunion by a majority of 100 at the Federation's conference.[46] Evidently Tillett's pamphlet caught a mood of intransigence and helped ensure the continued separation of the social democrats.

Hyndman had already embraced Tillett in 1906, when, after the General Election, he travelled to Eccles in an effort to persuade the local Labour movement to re-adopt Tillett as a candidate, following his defeat earlier that year. He had come third, with almost 4,000 votes, in a seat won by a Liberal. The voters of Eccles did not think their Labour candidate was a man of the right, and the local ILP reflected their fear of extreme rhetoric by threatening to withhold support if he were re-adopted. The following year saw the Stuttgart Congress of the Socialist International, which was attended by sixty-one SDF delegates, together with thirty from the ILP and nine from the Labour Party. There were also sixteen Fabians.

When a delegate of the Dockers' Union was debarred from speaking on the question of 'blackleg' labour at Hamburg, 'the British section rose en masse in their seats to protest, Hyndman . . . acting as protestant-in-chief':

Hyndman, with his locks, flowing beard, and waving arms, hurled unparliamentary imprecations at the chair. He shouted out that he and his fellow-British delegates had been supremely self-effacing at the congress, that the German and French speakers had, by their long-winded orations . . . monopolised and dissipated the time of the congress. Cries of 'Order, order! Chair, chair!' in a dozen different languages rose simultaneously in the hall. But Hyndman stood like Casabianca on the burning deck, amidst the flames of Continental wrath, and would not sit down. He was flatly and transparently out of order; he was wildly and shamelessly anarchistic; but the British delegates abetted him in his 'manifestation'.[47, 48]

Tillett's adherence to the SDF was, in the light of these events, not the most unlikely event of the year. Meanwhile, Bruce Glasier wrote that

Tillett 'should be forever disqualified from comradeship in the ranks of self-respecting members of the Party.'[49]

While all this was going on, a new talent was beginning to assert itself.

## A New Star Appears

Ben Tillett, thought the historians of the Social Democratic Federation, was not very closely embroiled with the Bristol branch, even though he was born in the city and maintained some family connections; but 'In a later period Ernest Bevin was much more closely associated with the Bristol organisation, and fought his first contest as a candidate for the Bristol City Council in 1909.'[50]

Born in 1881, Ernest Bevin had a hard childhood. He never knew his father, and his mother died when he was eight years old, after which he was cared for by his half-sister and her husband, George Pope, a railwayman. He went to school in Crediton, in Devonshire, and within a year he had reached standard IV and was thus entitled to claim a Labour Certificate and leave; but he stayed on for almost one full additional year, until March 1892. At the age of eleven he started work as a farm boy, living in, with a wage of 6$d$. a week. After moving from one farm to another for a couple of years, he decided to explore the golden streets of Bristol, and at the age of thirteen he went to live with his brother Jack, a butcher. He sold pies, then became a van-boy delivering mineral water. By 1897 he was a tram conductor, and at the turn of the century he was earning 12$s$. a week. When his brother moved, he had to find lodgings, and he also found himself out of work. For two months before the relief of Mafeking he was amongst the unemployed. Then he got work with another mineral-water manufacturer, who also employed his brother Fred. After a year, he had become a permanent driver. By now he was earning 18$s$., plus a commission of 1$d$. a gross on empty bottles. He worked from six in the morning until six at night, after which he groomed the horse. But 'once he had loaded up at the York Street yard . . . he was his own master. The job, in fact, gave him the independence and out-of-doors life which he wanted'.[51]

Alan Bullock tells us about Bevin's tour of the adult-education institutions of Bristol, and his training in nonconformity. But by 1905 he had become a socialist. The Bristol Socialist Society was an outpost of the Social Democratic Federation, and co-existed, at times uneasily, with two branches of the Independent Labour Party. Bevin joined the SDF. To be precise, 'he joined the Bristol Socialist Society, which affiliated to the Federation during 1906'.[52] Bullock reports the reminiscence of Bristol Alderman Milton: 'I think the first time Ernest Bevin spoke was at St. George's Park Gates [an ILP patch] but he did not like the ILP too well. He thought they were social reformers and preferred the Bristol

Socialist Society, who had now become affiliated to the SDF, and who, Ernest thought, had more of the revolutionist spirit.'[53]

Bevin rapidly became a stump-orator. For a time he ran a café and a coffee stall, but by 1908 he was once again working as a carter. This and the following year saw very bad unemployment, and indeed it was at this time that Bevin cut his teeth as a political organizer, as the secretary of a new Right to Work Committee, which lobbied and deputized on behalf of the unemployed. He worked to considerable effect. Very likely he would have used Ben Tillett's new pamphlet on the failure of the Parliamentary Labour Party, precisely inasmuch as it roasted the shortcomings of parliamentarians as agitators for jobs. Because of the skills he showed in this campaign, Bevin was asked to organize a relief fund for the dockers when they came out on strike at Avonmouth in June 1910. At this point he was spotted by Harry Orbell, the Dockers' Union national officer. 'On behalf of the Executive Council', Orbell invited Bevin to become 'delegate for the Carters and Warehousemen of Bristol, and so successful was the appointment that the General Secretary soon called upon him to accept responsibility for much greater efforts than he had anticipated in Southampton, Cardiff, and the whole of the west and other ports of England.'[54]

Bullock describes how members of the ILP had tried to organize the carters into the Workers' Union, and how Bevin outmanoeuvred the opposition to bring them into the Dockers' Union instead. The technical argument concerned whether the Workers' Union was affiliated to the local Trades Council, and it gave Bevin the victory. But we are bound to suspect that here, as in other sectors, there was stiff in-fighting between adherents of the ILP and supporters of the SDP (the Federation changed its name to 'Party' in April 1908). The carmen promptly designated him their first chairman. He was twenty-nine years old.

In short order, Bevin negotiated recognition for his branch, and by March 1911 a Joint Arbitration Board, consisting of seven people from the union and seven employer-representatives, was in place. The union leadership was impressed. That spring Orbell invited Bevin to join the staff of the Dockers' Union on a salary of £2 a week.

Tillett was later to claim that he had 'spotted' Bevin and marked him down for promotion. In the late 1930s he would hold forth in the Trade Union Club about all the victories and traumas of his life, and about the wickedness of Bevin, whom he had 'found and made' and who had 'pushed him to one side'.[55]

## A Red Cell?

In truth, Bevin's emergence almost certainly involved a more collective process of 'discovery'. As an effective campaigner in Bristol, he would have met Tillett during his public meetings there. Tillett would have been arguing the cause of the SDP, and his weekly journalism on behalf of the party would certainly have been read by the young activists of the West Country.

But Orbell, too, was an SDP member. George Lansbury, originally from the same school of thought, remembered him as a 'happy, full faced, fresh-coloured man, always cheery, and in the most depressing circumstances quite undismayed and confident that the workers' cause would triumph'. He was, said Lansbury, a 'professional agitator'. Like Lansbury himself, he was a Christian.[56]

As national organizer, Orbell was in a position to ensure that the activists of his small party extended their influence in the Dockers' Union.[57] As Eric Hobsbawm has pointed out, the Gasworkers' Union was 'the nearest thing to a "red" body conceivable before the foundation of Communist Parties . . . virtually all its national and district leaders were Marxian social democrats.'[58] By the time of the great unrest, the nucleus which guided the Dockers' Union was no less 'red'. It joined with Lansbury in promoting the *Daily Herald*. Ernest Bevin's commitment to this long outlasted his apprenticeship to Ben Tillett. We shall examine this a little later in our narrative.

'Meanwhile, the education of the upper strata of the working classes grew apace. Elementary education, continuation schools, debating societies, cheap reprints of some of the best books, socialist propaganda, the classes conducted by the Workers' Educational Association . . . and Ruskin College at Oxford have produced a young generation of working men responsive to the mental currents of the time.'[59] All this led Max Beer to conclude that 'Great Britain possesses now what it never possessed: Labour intellectuals with a healthy desire for the study of economics, social history and science.'[60]

## Socialist Agitators and Educators

The election of 1906 had provoked a surge in expectations, and, when these were not met, an outright rebellion. This was soon to rage across the entire economy, and nowhere more violently than in the transport industry. But it began with a mutiny in workers' education, when the students at Ruskin demanded classes in Marxian economics, formed the Plebs League and then broke away, in 1909, to set up a Central Labour College, first in Oxford, then in London.

A considerable effort had developed the thinking of this revolt. The Labour press, especially the newspapers the *Labour Leader*, *Clarion* and *Justice*, underwent a rapid growth. But book publishing also transmuted, with cheap editions of radical classics from the Rationalist Press Association, and Kerr's editions of the writings of Marx and other socialists, imported from Chicago. Hostile witnesses greeted this cultural revolution with dismay:

> At the present time the Socialists are spending between £250,000 and £300,000 every year on organisation and propaganda. In a word, incredible as it may seem, they spend more money, hold more meetings, and circulate more political literature than the Liberal and Conservative parties together. These things could not be done if there were no movement among the people . . . It is estimated that more than a million working-men have been through the branches of the Independent Labour Party and the Social Democratic Party, and assimilated their confiscatory doctrines; and it is certain that fully five or six million others have been influenced by the incessant meetings . . .[61]

No doubt these guesses were far from accurate. But it was not the inflated statistics of revolt which frightened the anti-socialist propagandists so much as the growth of 'extremism' around the fringes of the new movement. The SDF had twice split in the earliest years of the century, to give rise first to the Socialist Party of Great Britain and then to the Socialist Labour Party, based in Scotland but inspired by the doctrines of Daniel De Leon from the United States. 'They are, as a whole, the best-informed Socialists in the Country, and would make incomparable soldiers, or desperate barricadists. As revolutionaries they deserve no mercy: as men they command respect.'[62]

Now they were to be rejoined by two giants, Tom Mann and James Connolly. Both were incorruptibles, both were committed internationalists, and both were to be completely identified with the transport workers, in thought and in deed. And the deeds which followed were to shake the world.

## II

### *Tom Mann Is Back!*

On 16 May 1910 the Tom Mann Reception Committee assembled 250 of its supporters and mustered at the dockside to meet their comrade, returning from his long voyages to New Zealand, Australia and South Africa. Ben Tillett and Guy Bowman waited inside a roped enclosure. 'Almost his first words when we met him were: "let's go and see the men of the Direct Action" '.[63]

A fortnight later Mann and Bowman were in Paris, meeting with the leaders of the General Federation of Labour. Within six weeks they had produced the first of a series of penny pamphlets, under the title the *Industrial Syndicalist*. Number 1 was on sale in July, edited by Mann and published by Bowman. Its title was 'Prepare for Action'.[64] Prepared in an especially thin format, designed to fit into an overall pocket, it was a little bomb; in its twenty-four pages Tom Mann distilled his entire experience as a trade-union organizer. Gone were the appeals for arbitration. Experience in Australia and New Zealand had persuaded Mann that state intervention was normally to Labour's detriment, and that only organization, and then better organization, could win for the unions. 'Chief among our faults is our remarkable gullibility. We have been singularly ready to take the word for the deed – and take it with a degree of gratitude and enthusiasm that has gladdened the hearts of the capitalists'.

'Many sops', wrote Mann, 'have been thrown to the snarling Demos. The earliest on record were "bread and circuses". The latest are profit-sharing and Old Age Pensions. But never before have the masters been face to face with a literate and coherent democracy.'

Such a democracy had built trade unionism, powerful co-operatives, and political and municipal organizations. Through these agencies, workers had participated in educational and administrative bodies, and elected, around the world, 'hundreds of members of Parliaments and thousands of municipal councillors'. Too often these representatives had been overcome by the logic of detailed reform, losing sight of the fundamental objectives of the movements which had brought them to office. There had arisen a self-serving discussion on the merits of revolution or evolution, which sought to displace the one by the other. 'You can't', said Mann, 'change the world and yet not change the world. Revolution is the means of, not the alternative to, evolution'. Yet the call of this clarion was carefully composed. It did not refuse political action. What it did was to extol direct industrial action, and organization on the industrial plane.

Here is an example from the first pennyworth:

## Direct Action and Syndicalism

. . . what will have to be the essential conditions for . . . success . . .?

*That it will be avowedly and clearly Revolutionary in aim and method.*

Revolutionary in aim, because it will be out for the abolition of the wages system and for securing to the workers the full fruits of their labour, thereby seeking to change the system of Society from Capitalist to Socialist.

Revolutionary in method, because it will refuse to enter into any long agreements with the masters, whether with legal or State backing, or merely voluntarily . . .

Does this mean that we should become anti-political? Certainly not.

Let the politicians do as much as they can, and the chances are that, once there is an economic fighting force in the country, ready to back them up by action, they will actually be able to do what now would be hopeless for them to attempt to do.

This view of the political process was one that Mann would soon abandon. But he did not abandon his principal commitment to the view that change would come only when working people began to appreciate their own strength:

> The curse of Capitalism consists in this – that a handful of capitalists can compel hundreds of thousands of workers to work in such manner and for such wages as please the capitalists. But this again is solely because of the inability of the workers to agree upon a common plan of action. The hour the workers agree and act they become all-powerful. We can settle the capitalists' strike-breaking power once for all. We shall have no need to plead with Parliamentarians to be good enough to reduce hours – as the workers have been doing for fully twenty years without result. We shall be able to do this ourselves – and there will be no power on earth to stop us so long as we do not fall foul of economic principles . . . Police and Cabinet alike become powerless to enforce the dictates of the bureaucracy when the workers are united.[65]

Was this the classic statement of syndicalism? Tom Mann himself had produced a pamphlet on industrial unionism in Australia in 1909, a few days before he received a copy of James Connolly's fervent pamphlet *Socialism Made Easy: The Industrial and Political Unity of Labour*.

A great deal has been written about the alleged inconsistencies of syndicalist doctrine. In point of fact, there are at least two kinds of inconsistency that can arise within any political doctrine. Its followers may be led, in the test of practical action, to adopt views which are not consonant with their own principles: or, more seriously from the point of view of the logic of the doctrine, contradictory facets may be discovered within the original fabric of thought itself. There were many syndicalists, who drew their ideas from many sources. At one extreme, there were ethical socialists upon whom the main influence came from Christian writers of various kinds, culminating in the modern writings of Chesterton and Belloc, whose *Servile State* (1912) was a warning to many. It expounded the dangers of state socialism, but it could also be read as an indictment of many lesser encroachments of government intervention. Connolly was a Catholic, and had called down on his own head the anathemas of his Church, and the stern admonitions of the leader of his party, the Socialist Labour Party of the United States. Mann, as we have seen, toyed with the ideas of taking orders in the Anglican Church. Another wing of the movement was sternly secular, influenced by Darwin, and to a lesser extent by Marx, and by the numerous rationalist booklets of the time. Rational, it may have proclaimed itself. Tolerant, it was usually not.

The idea of workers' control stimulated men's imaginations, so that they not only began to think and act for themselves but also found that their thoughts and deeds brought them up sharply against widely diverse features of the industrial order to which they were reacting. It would be astonishing if all responded in the same way to these different shocks. A live movement *lives*. As Goethe told us, 'grey is every theory, but green is the living tree of life'.

## Some Roots of Syndicalism: Marx

And yet there was a remarkable continuity between the ideas of Tom Mann and those he accepted as his tutors. Marx, for instance, drafted a widely published resolution for the International Working Men's Association:

Trades' Unions. Their Past, Present, and Future
(a) Their past.
   Capital is concentrated social force, while the workman has only to dispose of his individual working force. The contract between capital and labour can therefore never be struck on equitable terms, equitable even in the sense of a society which places the ownership of the material means of life and labour on one side and the vital productive energies on the opposite side. The only social power of the workmen is their number. The disunion of the workmen is created and perpetuated by their unavoidable competition amongst themselves.
   Trades' Unions originally sprung up from spontaneous attempts of workmen at removing or at least checking that competition in order to conquer such terms of contract as might raise them at least above the condition of mere slaves. The immediate object of Trades' Unions was therefore confined to everyday necessities, to expedients for the obstruction of the incessant encroachments of capital; in one word, to questions of wages and time of labour. This activity of the Trades' Unions is not only legitimate, it is necessary. It cannot be dispensed with so long as the present system of production lasts. On the contrary, it must be generalised by the formation and combination of Trades' Unions throughout all countries. On the other hand, unconsciously to themselves, the Trades' Unions were forming centres of organisation of the working class, as the mediaeval municipalities and communes did for the middle class. If the Trades' Unions are required for the guerilla fights between capital and labour, they are still more important as organised agencies for superseding the very system of wage labour.
(b) Their present.
   Too exclusively bent upon the local and immediate struggles with capital, the Trades' Unions have not yet fully understood their power of action against the system of wages slavery itself. They therefore kept too much aloof from general and political movements. Of late, however, they seem to awaken to some sense of their great historical mission, as appears,

for instance, from their participation, in England, in the recent political movement . . .

(c) Their future.

Apart from their original purposes they must now learn to act deliberately as organising centres of the working class in the broad interest of its complete emancipation. They must aid every social and political movement tending in that direction. Considering themselves and acting as the champions and representatives of the whole working class, they cannot fail to enlist the non-society men into their ranks. They must look carefully after the interests of the worst paid trades, such as the agricultural labourers, rendered powerless by exceptional circumstances. They must convince the world at large that their efforts, far from being narrow and selfish, aim at the emancipation of the downtrodden millions.[66]

## *Annie Besant as an Influence*

To a remarkable extent, this view was carried down the years, so that it was still contemporary at the time of the great dock strike. Annie Besant, a staunch Fabian, echoed it the year before she set out to organize the matchgirls:

Why would it be worse to have one's labor controlled by the State than to have it controlled by the individual employer? A workman does not control his labor now; he must sell it for what he can get for it. His labor is controlled by the individual manufacturer, who controls it for his own advantage; whereas the State would control it for the corporate advantage in which the worker would share. But it is, of course, not practicable that the State, as a whole should direct and control the labor of each individual. For what is the State? It is the people, organised as a community. As a whole, the State could not control the labor of each citizen; but when the people are organised in groups of workers, each group can very well control its own labor, and elect its own superintendents, as well as elect such representatives as might be necessary to constitute boards of management to keep group in touch with group. The Trades Unions have in them the germs of the necessary organisation. If every miner were in the Miners' Union, then that union, with its branches in every coal district, would be the body which would immediately control the production of coal in a Socialist state. Can Radicals, who have fostered Trades Unions and urged the workers to combine, oppose a development of them? Can they, who have so preached self-reliance and self-government, maintain that men must always work for masters, and that they are not competent to control their own labor and to regulate their own production?[67]

For Tom Mann, doctrine was always intimately related to practice:

My industrial and political faith is as follows: (1) Industrial solidarity is the real power to effect economic changes. By this I mean that even though resort be had to Parliament it is only effective when the demand is made as the result of intelligent and courageous industrial organisation. It was thus that the Factory Acts were obtained and all other legislation that in any degree is economically advantageous to the workers. (2) The chief economic change must be the reduction of working hours. All through our industrial history nothing stands out more clearly than this, that the reducing of working hours is a genuine method of raising the standard, economically and ethically correct. (3) By a drastic reduction of working hours we can absorb the unemployed. The cure for unemployment is the chief concern of revolutionaries and reformers, and the most natural, most simple, and most effective of all methods is by absorbing them into the ranks of the employed, so apportioning the work to be done over the total number to do it. (4) By removing competition for work we gain the power to get higher wages. (5) It is necessary for every worker to belong to a union, and for every union to unite with every other union in the same industry. (6) Unite to fight, fight to achieve your economic emancipation. (7) Under existing circumstances it is not desirable that membership of an industrial organisation should pledge one to specific political action. (8) Parliamentary action is secondary in importance to industrial action; it is industrial action alone that makes political action effective, but with or without Parliamentary action, industrial solidarity will ensure economic freedom, and therefore the abolition of capitalism and all its accompanying poverty and misery. (9) To ensure industrial solidarity it is necessary that the finances of the unions should be so kept that the Friendly Society benefits should be kept entirely separate from the industrial, so that every union on its industrial side may amalgamate with every other union in the same industry.[68]

None of this said anything about syndicalism.

## The French Connection

Tom Mann himself was always at pains to point out that 'syndicalism' was no more than an anglicized version of the French word meaning 'trade unionism'. Even in France, as its historian insists:

Syndicalism was a movement rather than a theory. It was a general trend within the French labour movement, a range of ideas rather than an agreed body of doctrine. Primarily, indeed, it was a way of looking at politics, a temper which was expressed in action, rather than in clearly formulated ideas. The C.G.T. [Confédération Générale du Travail] adopted a number of principles, never a philosophy. Nor did its theorists produce a really unified body of thought. They wrote for the worker rather than the social philosopher. They dealt with issues of the moment. Their ideas were scattered in newspapers, pamphlets and speeches. Nowhere did they attempt to bring these ideas together within the covers of a single book. It would have been difficult for them to do so. Their views changed;

they did not always agree. Even at the level of the printed word, therefore, no integrated system of ideas, certainly no definitive philosophy, was produced by the syndicalists themselves.[69]

Revolutionary syndicalism in France based itself on the ideas of Fernand Pelloutier, and his disciple Émile Pouget. The conditions to which they were responding were different, in a wide range of ways, from those confronting Tom Mann and his colleagues. The French trade unions had polarized in an acrimonious debate about the role of the general strike in their strategy. The first May Day demonstrations, in 1890, had been organized by two separate groups, one favouring the perspective of a revolutionary general strike, the other strongly opposing it. This dual sponsorship persisted, but in 1891 there were serious clashes at some of the demonstrations, and a girl was killed when soldiers fired on a demonstration at Fourmies. In the angry reaction, the militants gathered strength.

In 1892 a new federation was formed – the Bourse du Travail. Pelloutier became the secretary and spokesman of this federation in 1893. English syndicalists were to translate the term 'Bourse du Travail' as 'Trades Council', although this description greatly underrepresented the range of functions undertaken by the French organizations. In origin, they were indeed labour exchanges, as their name implied. They were set up in opposition to the private employment offices which had been established to serve the employers. These private agencies had a dual role: on the one hand they charged applicants for placing them in jobs. On the other, they exercised strong discrimination against trade unionists and maintained lively blacklists. Initially, the Bourses du Travail developed in response to the pressures of the moderate trade unionists, and frequently called upon institutional support from local authorities or the prefectural administrations. But once the Bourses became associated in a national network, the debate on the general strike swept into their forum and carried all before it. It was this commitment which so shocked the parliamentary wing of the Socialist International, back in 1896, when Tom Mann was organizing the London Congress.

Pelloutier began his short political life as a journalist working for Aristide Briand, who, during the early 1890s, was passing through a phase of leftist extremism; later he was to occupy a quite different place in the political spectrum. But Pelloutier was not content with the often demagogic invocation of the general strike. For many of its advocates this was a secular version of the second coming. It would happen spontaneously, of its own accord: and as a result of it, all would be made anew. 'Not at all,' argued Pelloutier. Such a strike would not happen without organized preparation, and even if it did its outcome would be in doubt, unless the workers knew what to do when it happened. It was necessary to have a precise vision of the kind of society which the workers wished to bring into being. For this vision, Pelloutier called upon a rich anarchist tradition in the French Labour movement. He developed the notion of a federation of communes, from a self-regulating community of free individuals to a focus of producer co-ops. Every working collective would be associated in a local syndicat, which would include all the various trades and crafts employed within it. The management would be elected by the producers, who would work for the commune, in which the ownership of the enterprise would be vested. The commune itself would be administered by delegates from all the syndicats within its area. Where more general administrative problems arose, they would be confronted by wider, federated agencies, representing at a higher level, of region or nationality, the primary communes of producers.

All this echoed previous discussions, going back to the days of the First International, founded in 1864. But Pelloutier was completely unambiguous in his blueprint. For him, the heart and soul of the new society was the local trade-union organization. Within the framework of workers' control, all the conventional tasks of trade unionism could be subsumed. Unions must control hiring and firing, apprenticeships, training and promotion. To discharge these functions, and thus monopolize labour supply, they must take on profound educational functions. Managers must be educated from within a trade-union academy. Every Bourse would thus maintain its workers' college, library and educational circles.

## Anarchist Overtones

Pelloutier died in 1901 at the age of thirty-four. His book on the history of the labour exchanges was published the following year. Far more widely read was a popular tract, half novel, half programmatic statement, by his followers Émile Pataud and Émile Pouget. This was translated into English under the title: *Syndicalism and the Co-operative Common-wealth (How We Shall Bring About the Revolution)*.[70] It appeared in Britain in 1913 with a foreword by Tom Mann, a preface by the Russian anarchist Prince Peter Kropotkin, and a series of striking cartoons by Will Dyson. In so far as British workers came under the direct influence of French syndicalists, this book was undoubtedly a main source. Most British activists, however, were responding to a message from sources nearer to home.

The French syndicalists were far more consistently hostile to political, or parliamentary, forms of action than was Tom Mann in 1910. One of his first actions then was to join up with the SDP, alongside his comrade Tillett. Later he left the organization, and he was to become more distinctly reserved about parliamentary politics; during the war he was actively hostile to the Labour Party for this reason. But his judgements on parliamentary politics throughout this period seem to have been more tactical than strategic. For the French, political sociology argued a more fixed course:

> the proletariat did not form a majority of the electorate in France at the turn of the century. The socialist party must therefore make electoral agreements: the class enemy becomes the friend of the polls. The same thing necessarily occurs in parliament. The socialists' only hope of ministerial office lay in collaboration with bourgeois parties. Policy degenerates into bargaining, concessions and ultimately a betrayal of the working class. The parliamentary milieu is itself bourgeois and thus a further corrupting influence.[71]

This coloured a series of consequent attitudes:

> Whatever benefits may be gained for the working class as a result of compromise, they cannot compensate for its dangers. Democracy is a system designed by the bourgeoisie for bourgeois domination. It is a façade to hide the real nature of social conflict; its ideology – universal franchise, equality before the law – distracts from the real economic inequality that it protects. The parliamentary game is, in the last analysis, but a means of diverting the energy of the proletariat into harmless channels.
> Social legislation is part of this attempt to stifle the class war. Reforms do not alter the fundamental property relations and concede nothing of real importance. They do, however, undermine the class struggle by creating an impression of benevolence and social harmony. They are the crumbs the rich man throws from his table to satisfy the hunger of a proletariat that would otherwise be driven to revolt. Genuine concessions are never achieved through parliamentary action but only through the direct action of the workers themselves.[72]

For this reason, French syndicalists identified with their unions, not with parties. Bowman was more 'French' than Mann about this, but less able to draw support from British unions, so that, within a year or so, the two men were to find themselves at odds. What is clear is that if Mann had simply sought to become the evangelist of a cross-Channel creed, his impact would not have been at all comparable to what it actually was. Bowman's influence, by contrast, is a matter for the footnotes.

## Connolly Comes Home

While Tom Mann was arranging the publication of his monthly letters on syndicalism in 1910, another wanderer was coming home, this time from the United States. On 26 July, James Connolly arrived in Derry. His mission was to superintend the publication of his journal the *Harp*,

recently transferred from America to Dublin. The Irish edition was to
have been edited by James Larkin; however, Connolly disembarked in
time to find that his colleague was otherwise engaged. To see him it was
necessary to go to Mountjoy gaol: he had been sentenced to one year's
imprisonment with hard labour on a baseless charge of fraud.
Meanwhile, his new union, the Irish Transport and General Workers'
Union, was being hammered by employers on the one side and
obstructed by some of the related English unions on the other.

James Connolly was born in Edinburgh in 1868, the third son of Irish
immigrants. His father was a manure carter, working for the Edinburgh
Corporation. James himself became a compositor's labourer on the
*Edinburgh Evening News* after his tenth birthday. Since even the factory
inspector thought this was too early for the boy to be employed, the
discovery of his age led to his dismissal. He then found work in a bakery,
and later in a tiling factory, until at the age of fourteen he enlisted in the
King's Liverpool Regiment.

This regiment was heavily infiltrated by Fenians, so much so that it
had been disarmed during the Fenian uprising for fear that it might take
its weapons and join the rebels. Its guns were likewise confiscated and
locked away during the Land League troubles of 1881: but by the
following year the trouble was deemed to be under control, and when his
battalion was sent to Ireland that year James Connolly paid his first visit
to his family's homeland. It was a long tour of duty, lasting until the
beginning of 1889.

At the same time that Connolly's regiment was recalled to Aldershot,
his father was injured at work and consequently dismissed. Deeply
worried, James deserted from the army and went to Scotland. Within a
few months he had married and had become a socialist. He started to
write for *Justice*, the journal of the social democrats, and began to speak
at meetings of the Scottish Socialist Federation, of which his brother
John became the secretary. By 1894 he was a candidate in the Edinburgh
Municipal Elections. Then he was victimized. Without work, and with
three daughters to care for, he was greatly relieved when in May 1896
the Dublin Socialist Club offered him a position of paid organizer.

In Dublin he formed the Irish Socialist Republic Party and began a
programme of writing which was to have an enduring influence on the
Irish Labour movement. The salary of Ireland's socialist organizer
proved intermittent, and to eke it out Connolly did labouring jobs, found
employment in the shipyard and became a publisher's proofreader. Even
so, money was short and the family found the way to the pawn shop often
enough.

Under such dire conditions were published the first essays which were
to become *Labour in Irish History*. But although Connolly was from the
beginning deeply involved in the movement for Irish independence, he
was also, from the beginning, a committed internationalist. He became a

correspondent for the American socialist *Weekly People*, the journal of the aggressively doctrinaire Daniel De Leon. In 1898 Connolly spent weeks in County Kerry reporting on the famine for this newspaper, and later the same year he was to launch a newspaper, *The Workers' Republic*, in Ireland.

All this agitation brought on the pronounced dissatisfaction of the Roman Catholic Church, which did not approve of socialism. When Connolly stood for election to the Dublin Municipal Council in 1901, priests told their flocks that no Catholic should vote for him, under pain of excommunication. After lecture tours in England and the United States, the hardship of life in Dublin became too much, and Connolly decided to emigrate to the United States. Here it was that he met the Industrial Workers of the World (IWW), the apostles of One Big Union for workers' control.

## The American Experience

Daniel De Leon expressed the original idea of the IWW in a pamphlet entitled *The Socialist Reconstruction of Society* which first appeared in 1905.

> Political power is reached through the ballot-box. But the ballot-box is not an open field; it is a veritable defile. The defile is held by the agents of the Capitalist Class. The election inspectors and returning boards are capitalist appointees; they are veritable garrisons with which the Capitalist Class holds the defile. To imagine that these capitalist garrisons of the election defiles will complacently allow the candidate of the Revolution, whose programme is the dismantling of the political burg of capitalism, peacefully to file through, is to indulge in a mooncalf's vision. The revolutionary ballot of Labour is counted out now; it has been counted out from the first day of its appearance; it will be counted out even more extensively in the future. This fact is taken by some as a sufficient ground from which to conclude that the political Movement is utterly useless. Those who arrive at that conclusion fall into the error of failing to realise that correct conclusions never flow from single premises. They can be arrived at only by considering all the premises in the case . . .
>
> Without political organisation, the Labour Movement cannot triumph; without economic organisation, the day of its political triumph would be the day of its defeat.
>
> Industrialism means Might. Craft Unionism means impotence. All the plants of production, aye, even the vast wealth for consumption, is today in the keeping of the Working Class. It is workingmen who are in charge of the factories, the railroads, the mines; in short, all the land and machinery of production, and it is they also who sit as watch-dogs before the pantries, the cellars, and the safe deposit vaults of the capitalist class; aye, it is they who carry the guns to the armies.[73]

## One Big Union

Connolly shared this view, and indeed never diverged from it. But De Leon's concept of politics was rigidly intolerant, and in 1908, while Connolly was still in the USA working with the IWW and the Socialist Party of Eugene Debs, it resulted in one of those resoundingly acrimonious splits for which the American Labor movement was to become so famous. Connolly drew the conclusion

> that since the political party was not to accomplish the revolution but only to lead the attack upon the political citadel of Capitalism, there no longer existed the same danger in the unclearness of its membership, nor compelling necessity for insisting upon its purification . . . it is our belief there will evolve . . .
> One Socialist party, embracing all shades and conceptions of Socialist political thought.
> One Socialist industrial organisation drilling the working class for the supreme mission of their class – the establishment of the Workers' Republic.[74]

In *Socialism Made Easy*, first published in Chicago after the dispute in the De Leonite ranks (and, as we have seen, coming into the hands of Tom Mann while he was still in Australia), Connolly set out his vision with limpid clarity:

> social democracy, as its name implies, is the application to industry, or to the social life of the nation, of the fundamental principles of democracy. Such application will necessarily have to begin in the workshop, and proceed logically and consecutively upwards through all the grades of industrial organization until it reaches the culminating point of national executive power and direction. In other words social democracy must proceed *from the bottom upward*, whereas capitalist political society is organized *from above downward*.
> Social democracy will be administered by a committee of experts elected from the industries and professions of the land;
> capitalist society is governed by representatives elected from districts, and is based upon territorial division.
> The local and national governing, or rather administrative, bodies of Socialists will approach every question with impartial minds, armed with the fullest expert knowledge born of experience; the governing bodies of capitalist society have to call in an expensive professional expert to instruct them on every technical question, and know that the impartiality of said expert varies with, and depends upon the size of his fee.

This conception of socialism, thought Connolly, 'destroys at one blow all the fears of a bureaucratic State, ruling and ordering the lives of every individual from above.' It would ensure that 'the social order of the future will be an extension of the freedom of the individual, and not the suppression of it.' Connolly continued:

> To focus the idea properly in your mind, you have but to realize how industry today transcends all limitations of territory and leaps across rivers, mountains and continents; then you can understand how impossible it would be to apply to such far-reaching intricate enterprises the principle of democratic control by the workers through the medium of political territorial divisions.
>
> Under Socialism, States, territories, or provinces will exist only as geographical expressions, and have no existence as sources of governmental power, though they may be seats of administrative bodies.
>
> Now, having grasped the idea that the administrative force of the Socialist republic of the future will function through unions industrially organized, that the principle of democratic control will operate through the workers correctly organized in such industrial unions, and that the political territorial State of capitalist society will have no place or function under Socialism, you will at once grasp the full truth embodied in the words of this member of the Socialist Party whom I have just quoted, that *'only the industrial form of organization offers us even a theoretical constructive Socialist programme'*.[75]

## Syndicalism: Cause, Effect or Catalyst?

One historian after another has told us that such notions as these were 'an effect rather than a cause' of the great unrest, which was so shortly to follow.[76] Tom Mann, wrote Dangerfield, 'was one of the most successful and intelligent agitators in British Labour history', but for all that he could not shape his times. No one will deny that the syndicalists failed to reach their ultimate objectives. But their influence was direct and immediate, and men and events followed and reflected their counsel far more closely than is generally appreciated.

While their impact on the state and the social–economic order was contained, their interaction with the trade unions produced a result which was anything but neutral. Connolly played his part in the development of the Irish Transport and General Workers' Union, and this is the subject of our chapter 13; but he found himself learning from the members he led, and the mistakes of American industrial unionism were largely avoided in this process. The historians of the IWW tell us that 'For nearly a decade the IWW made little headway in organising basic industry. Landmark strikes in scattered geographic areas did little more than establish an IWW presence and style. Even the momentous 1912 victory at Lawrence failed to lead to permanent mass organisations in textiles.'[77]

Revolutionary unionism often sits uneasily with recognition, representation and the to-and-fro of collective bargaining. Strikes explode, organizers arrive to help them win, members are recruited and the agitators move on. Maybe more agitators are recruited, and maybe they move on. It is difficult enough to establish a stable, self-governing, continuous organization, even when you are trying to do so. To succeed without trying calls for a truly exceptional amount of luck.

Tom Mann always tried. That is why, however he changed his strategic view about the role of the state, and however the shifting power-balance moved to the combines, or to the workers, he always eschewed dual unionism.

For him, if workers were not strong enough to maintain control of their unions, they would never recover control of anything else. Breakaways might be quick, but they were always likely to prove brittle. To penetrate Tom Mann's thinking, it is always necessary to go to specifics. For him such universal ideas as he would embrace must always reveal themselves in particular, real, practical experience.

## *One Big Port Union?*

The second penny number of the *Industrial Syndicalist* appeared in August 1910. It was entirely devoted to the transport industry. No other country had so large a proportion of its workforce engaged in this sector as Britain, wrote Mann. This resulted from British pre-eminence in shipping, carrying half the world's oceanic trade, and from a dominant position in export trade. As a result, Britain was surrounded by ports, with easy access to all sea-lanes. 'I was brought into close contact with the men in the carrying trades', he went on,

> when, as a social-democrat in the years 1885–8, I did my share of propaganda work among these men, but it was not until the London Dock Strike of 1889 that I became really intimate with . . . [their] conditions. And when I once grasped the full meaning of 'casual' labour . . . it gave me revolutionary stimulus . . . to do all that could be done to abolish such a system.

Now, twenty years on, it was time to take stock. In London the number of permanent men had increased and wages were a little higher. But the conditions of work had deteriorated with speed-up, while casualism was still the rule. 'The conditions of the *pre*-strike days obtain at present.' The cutting of the size of work-gangs had once again become the rule:

> Since the '89 period many changes have taken place in the method of unloading vessels. In the discharge of grain in bulk, for instance, which

prior to '89 in all the London docks except Millwall was done by hand; since that time the suction elevator or else the cup elevator, have been in general use, which has added enormously to the unemployed. A very moderate statement is that two men out of every three formerly employed in the discharge of grain are now dispensed with, i.e. thrown into the ranks of the unemployed. The system now resorted to is to have as few handlings of cargo as possible, and as little storage as possible. Thus at the Victoria Docks there are two flour mills. The grain is hauled in at one side of the mill from the vessel or lighter, and it goes through all the necessary processes almost without the aid of man. It is then lowered as flour from the other side of the mill into the barge ready for delivery; and every time an improved method of handling is resorted to, it means more profit for the Capitalists and more starvation for the Workmen.

In the discharge of bags of flour from a ship's hold, formerly there would be nine men in a gang in the hold, four men on each side of the boat and one man to hook on the sling. Now the pace is set so keenly that there are only three men on each side, that is, seven men instead of nine, to do the same work. This is when working under the crane. When working under the winch, less powerful than the crane, formerly they had six men in a gang, now only four, but there is the same amount of work to be done.

The same slave-driving was general in the discharge of cargoes of American flour. Mann gave a wealth of detail on working practices:

To sum up, on the average there are twenty thousand employed each day in the Port of London; but there are quite 40,000 more left out. It does not mean that 20,000 get regular work. It means that it is shared in an uneven way between the 60,000, only the permanent men getting regular employment.

It should not be necessary to urge that these conditions should be altered without delay.

Then comes the question 'who is to alter them?' And to that there is only one reply: The men themselves must do it. Ah, but How? There is only one way: viz. by proper Industrial Organisation.

'Now,' he continued, 'it is necessary to ask if the workers are properly organised.' The answer could only be 'No.'

one is compelled to admit that organisation is very far from being efficient.

The Dockers Union, with headquarters in London, has a membership in London and provinces of 14,000; and in the Bristol Channel ports many of the men are receiving 25 per cent, better conditions than before they were organised. But improved methods of doing the work are constantly being employed, resulting in more profits and less wages, and this is universally operative.

In the country generally, there are some twenty different Unions connected with the Transport or carrying Trades.

The Dockers Union, with headquarters at Liverpool, has also about 14,000 members, but as yet there is no real working arrangement between these two, or between these and either of the other Unions in the Transport Industry. The effects of this sectional unionism can be seen by what has just happened in the Welsh ports.

Here, Tom Mann drew the lessons of the struggle among trimmers and tippers for a half-day on Saturdays. The workers were in four separate unions, two being London-based, one being situated in Cardiff and another in Swansea:

I propose giving a few details in connection with this matter, because it serves well to illustrate the impossibility of effective action with the multiplicity of Unions, working each independent of the other; and in doing so I have one object only, and that is to bring to a head what I am sure is the desire of all the better men in each of these Unions, viz. the unifying of these respective organisations so that they shall become powerful for good, instead of being powerless as they are at present.

The ports where the men desired to get the Saturday half-holiday were Cardiff, Barry, Penarth, Swansea, Port Talbot and Newport.

Now to show the complexity of the situation:

In Cardiff, the Trimmers belong to the Coal Trimmers Union, but the Tippers belong to the A.S.R.S. In Newport, the Trimmers and Tippers belong to the Dockers Union. In Barry, the Trimmers belong to the C.T.U., but the Tippers belong to the A.S.R.S. In Port Talbot, the Trimmers and Tippers belong to the Dockers Union. In Penarth, the Trimmers belong to the C.T.U., but the Tippers belong to the A.S.R.S. In Swansea, the Trimmers and Tippers belong to the N.A.U.

Several Conferences were held between the delegates of these respective Unions, and it was agreed that notices should be given in as a preliminary to action to obtain the Saturday half-holiday. Then it transpired that one of the Unions was not prepared to give in notices. Another Conference was held and then it was found that another of the Unions was not prepared to take any action beyond informing the Shipowners and Brokers they would like to have the half-holiday; by which time the owners on their side, knowing perfectly well the sectional nature of the men's organisations, rode the high horse and declared that such a claim as that put forth for Coal Trimmers and Tippers to finish the week on Saturdays at 1 o'clock could not be entertained. If vessels needed coals the men must work till 5 o'clock, and if it was a case of getting the boat out by next tide, they must work till 8 o'clock on a Saturday; and so the matter is supposed to be settled.

This has just happened, the Owners had no reason to advance other than that the corresponding men in the North of England, at Hull, Shields, etc., worked these hours, and, therefore, they must continue so to work in Bristol Channel ports.

Now the Saturday half-day has been established over 40 years in many occupations, and there is no reason why men connected with coal loading should not have this condition as well as others. Ships are loaded now in half the time they were a few years ago, and there is no reason why Saturday afternoon should be worked any more than Sunday . . .[78]

## Founding the National Transport Workers' Federation

Only sectional divisions, and the chaotic proliferation of unions, gave the employers the initiative. If the unions could work together, they would win: 'It is not necessary to dwell at greater length upon the necessity for unity. It is self-evident to every thoughtful person'.[79]

Ben Tillett was one such thoughtful person. He engaged with the doctrine immediately, above all for its advocacy of larger union unity for fighting purposes – whether in the form of industrial or general unionism. Tom Mann recorded his historic intervention without sensation. But in truth it was a momentous event:

> Having been invited to attend an executive meeting of the Dockers' Union by the general secretary, my old colleague, Ben Tillett, I submitted a proposal urging that invitation be sent to the various Transport Workers' Unions with a view to forming a 'National Transport Workers' Federation'. This was done, and a conference, held in London, achieved the object.[80]

The invitation sent in the name of the Dockers' Union, July 1910, read:

> The conditions of port workers in the United Kingdom, in common with all other workers, leave very much to be desired . . . . In common with others we of the Dockers' Union desire to do all that is possible to bring about changes for the better: and we are glad to know that other unions are wishful to be at the work also . . .
>
> We are of the opinion that there is urgent need for a genuine federation of all unions connected with the carrying trades and that this should be attempted without delay. The Executive of the Dockers' Union therefore respectfully make this overture to each of the other unions in the transport industry, and ask: – Will your organisation take part in a conference having in view the unifying of the transport workers' organisations in a genuine federation, for the purpose of taking such action as may be necessary for improving the standard of the workers in the transport industry, and to enable us to ally ourselves with all other industrial organisations for fighting purposes?[81]

Fifteen unions sent delegates to the founding conference, held in the Compositors' Hall, London, from 22 to 23 September 1910. They resolved to form a federation for the purposes of 'controlling and conducting disputes in the trades covered', preventing 'unwarrantable competition between unions for members, and . . . the overlapping of unions'.[82] They also agreed upon an immediate, combined, recruiting campaign. In November, seventeen unions took part in appointing a Rules Committee; in December the committee drafted a constitution; and fourteen unions attended the inaugural conference in March 1911.

Twelve unions sent delegates to the first General Council held three months later in Liverpool's Engineers' Hall. By June 1911 the following unions had affiliated: the Amalgamated Society of Watermen, Lightermen and Bargemen (2,244 members); the National Union of Dock Labourers (12,000); the National Sailors' and Firemen's Union (10,000); the National Union of Ships' Cooks, etc. (3,000); the Amalgamated ·Stevedores' Labour Protection League (4,000); the Upper Mersey Watermen and Porters (986); the Dock, Wharf, Riverside and General Labourers' Union (8,000); the National Union of Enginemen, Firemen, etc. (2,000); the National Union of Gasworkers and General Labourers (5,000); the London Carmen's Trade Union (4,000); the National Amalgamated Labourers' Union (2,096); and the South Side Labour Protection League (1,390).

Amongst unions withdrawing from the negotiations between November 1910 and June 1911 were the Amalgamated Society of Railway Servants, the General Railway Workers' Union, the National Amalgamated Union of Labourers, the Workers' Union, the London Cab Drivers, and the National Coal Porters. The Irish Transport and General Workers' Union attended the March conference, but was refused permission to affiliate on the grounds that it originated in a breakaway from the NUDL; the NUDL had submitted an objection to its membership and, at the June council meeting, it was resolved 'that the entrance fee of the Irish Transport Workers' Union be returned', Joseph Cotter and Frank Pearce, the delegates of the Ships' Cooks' Union, dissenting from the decision.

We shall have cause to review the affiliations again at later stages of the NTWF's history. At this stage we should note the absence of the largest inland transport unions: the Amalgamated Tramwaymen did not enter until 1918, following the lead of the London and Provincial Licensed Vehicle Workers, who joined in 1916. The road-passenger unions' initial judgement was that the Federation was weak in substance and potential; the rail unions came to similar conclusions.

Thus the NTWF in its initial form was overwhelmingly based on the waterfront unions. It was this which prompted the gasworkers and NALU to affiliate only their dock memberships in order to protect them from poaching. A rule declared: 'Where in any industrial undertaking there is a union already catering for men and having a branch or branches in existence for enrolling such men as members, no other affiliated union shall attempt to cater for members of that undertaking.'[83]

The NAUL, significantly, later affiliated only its London and Liverpool members, not its Newcastle dockers, 'who were unlikely to desert it',[84] since neither the Dockers' Union or the NUDL had a presence in the North-east. Rule XIII, moreover, stipulated that a member of a union with 'a controlling interest' in an area should have preference of employment, followed by members of other affiliated unions. This rule embodied the dockers' aim to deny the mass of general labour access to port employment. It resisted strongly, throughout the NTWF's existence, the idea of the single 'Federation ticket'. The general unions, on the other hand, were strong advocates of the ticket.

Harry Gosling, general secretary of the lightermen, was elected as the NTWF's first (and as it transpired, its only) president. The first secretary was James Anderson of the stevedores. These appointments emphasize the critical importance of the 'craft' unions' conversion to the cause of federation. It is certainly true to claim that 'without the adhesion of the Stevedores and Lightermen, the National Transport Workers' Federation could never have got off the ground in London'.[85] Yet Gosling later, with characteristic modesty and generosity, gave the credit for the NTWF's birth to Ben Tillett, who, he said, 'had long been urging closer union between the many organizations catering for transport workers'.[86] Tillett's understanding of the need for the goodwill of the specialist London unions is evident in his move to nominate Gosling for the presidency, and in stepping aside from the secretaryship to allow Anderson of the stevedores to take that post. Clearly, in its origins the NTWF was dominated by the London waterfront, the main outside lever being of course the Mersey-based NUDL, which had taken no part in the preliminary gatherings. (Sexton does not mention the 1910 meetings in his Annual Report for that year, nor does he refer to the NTWF in his memoirs.)

It remains to emphasize that, whilst the concept of the NTWF came from Tom Mann, and the organs and conferences of the Syndicalist League gave every encouragement to its formation, the NTWF was not 'a syndicalist artifact'.[87] It was formed for pragmatic reasons by trade-union leaders seeking solutions to both immediate and long-term problems of organization and effectiveness. Yet would it have been formed so soon if Tom Mann had stayed in Australia? With his encouragement, it was born on the eve of the greatest upheaval that the labouring people had ever created: and the fortunes of the NTWF were, for the next four years, intimately bound up with the elemental flux of militancy associated with the syndicalist spirit.

None the less, the NTWF's first contemplation of militancy – over the gathering crisis in the shipping industry – was quickly set aside. At the June Council meeting, the delegates 'regretted' the attitude of the International Shipping Federation towards the request of the seamen's two unions to the establishment of a Conciliation Board. The motion containing this regret concluded that 'All unions affiliated to this Federation are hereby requested to do their utmost to assist the National Seamen's and Firemen's Union, and the National Union of Ships' Stewards, Cooks, Butchers and Bakers.'[88] This sentence was deleted from the motion, on an amendment! It was too early to risk a test of the new body's cohesion in a pending industrial conflict.

But, if the leaders were rightly apprehensive about going too far in front of their men, who, after all, had two decades of endurance and quiescence behind them, this condition was not to last long. Soon they would have to run to catch up with a workforce intent upon action, action and more action.

And what of the syndicalists? They were not about to topple the throne. Nor, for sure, would they overthrow the plutocracy that surrounded it. They could not even persuade trade unions to do many of the things that would have prepared them better to look after themselves in a still profoundly unfriendly world. But they were forming close and even brotherly alliances with other trade unionists, embracing old adversaries, and in the process bringing new courage to formerly defeated men and great hope to a completely new generation. As the time came near, the image of what was to happen is clear in the deeds of two men. Havelock Wilson, hero of an older Lib.–Lab. age and villain of an age to come, is laying the fuse. And it is Tom Mann who brings the spark.

## Notes

1 LRC Report on the Conference on Labour Representation, 27 February 1900, p. 11.
2 Ibid.
3 Ibid., p. 12.
4 Ibid., pp. 11–12.
5 Ibid., p. 16.
6 L. C. B. Seamen, *Post-Victorian Britain, 1902–1951* (Methuen, 1966), p. 3.
7 W. Scovell Adams, *Edwardian Heritage* (Frederick Muller, 1946), p. 83.
8 Michael Barratt Brown, *Global Imperialism: 1870–1914* (Mimeo, 1989), p. 13.
9 Frank Bealey and Henry Pelling, *Labour and Politics, 1900–1906* (Macmillan, 1958), p. 131.
10 Roger Moore, *The Emergence of the Labour Party, 1880–1924* (Hodder and Stoughton, 1978), p. 84.
11 Ibid., p. 87.
12 Mark Stephens, *Roots of Power* (SPA Books, 1986), p. 65.
13 Ibid.
14 NUDL Annual Report, 1902, p. 10.
15 Jonathan Schneer, *Ben Tillett: Portrait of a Labour Leader* (Croom Helm, 1982), p. 125, from the TUC Annual Report, 1903, p. 69.
16 Ibid.
17 Schneer, *Ben Tillett*, p. 122.
18 TUC Annual Report, 1901.
19 Ibid.
20 DWRGWU Annual Report, 1900, p. 5.
21 Ibid., p. 6.

22  Ibid.
23  Ibid., p. 9.
24  Schneer, *Ben Tillett*, p. 127.
25  David Marquand, *Ramsay MacDonald* (Jonathan Cape, 1977), p. 79. For the full text of Jesse Herbert's memorandum, see Keith Laybourn, *The Labour Party 1881–1951: A Reader in History* (Alan Sutton, 1988), pp. 61–2.
26  Marquand, *Ramsay MacDonald*, p. 79.
27  Ibid., p. 80.
28  Laybourn, *The Labour Party 1881–1951*, p. 60.
29  Ibid., pp. 60–1.
30  Henry Pelling, *The Origins of the Labour Party* (Oxford University Press, 1954), p. 227. Cf. *Bulletin of the Institute for Historical Research*, 1956; cf. also Bealey and Pelling, *Labour and Politics, 1900–1906*.
31  R. C. K. Ensor, *England 1870–1914* (Oxford University Press, 1936), p. 355.
32  NUDL Annual Report, 1903, pp. 15–16.
33  F. W. S. Craig, *British General Election Manifestos, 1900–1974* (Macmillan, 1975), pp. 9–10.
34  Sidney and Beatrice Webb, *The History of Trade Unionism* (1894; WEA edn, 1912), p. 606, wrote that this was 'an extraordinary and unlimited immunity, however great may be the damage caused and however unwarranted the act, which most lawyers, as well as all employers, regard as nothing less than monstrous.'
35  Henry Pelling, *A History of British Trade Unionism* (Penguin, 1963), p. 126.
36  G. D. H. Cole, *British Working Class Politics, 1832–1914* (Labour Book Service, 1941), p. 191.
37  Keith Laybourn, *The Labour Party 1881–1951*, p. 64.
38  LRC Conference Minutes, 1905, p. 52.
39  NUDL Annual Report, 1905, p. 14.
40  R. T. McKenzie, *British Political Parties* (Heinemann, 1955), p. 392.
41  Labour Party Annual Conference Report, 1907, p. 58.
42  DWRGWU Annual Report, 1905, p. 6.
43  Ibid., 1908.
44  Ben Tillett, *Is the Parliamentary Labour Party a Failure?* (London, 1908).
45  London Municipal Society, *The Case Against Socialism* (George Allen and Sons, 1908), p. 38.
46  Walter Kendall, *The Revolutionary Movement in Britain* (Weidenfeld and Nicolson, 1969), p. 31.
47  *Labour Leader*, 30 August 1907.
48  Chushichi Tsuzuki, *Hyndman and British Socialism* (Oxford University Press, 1961), p. 165.
49  Schneer, *Ben Tillett*, p. 131.
50  H. W. Lee and E. Archbold, *Social Democracy in Britain* (Social Democratic Federation, 1935), p. 92.
51  Alan Bullock, *The Life and Times of Ernest Bevin* (Heinemann, 1960), vol. 1: *Trade Union Leader: 1881–1941*, p. 8.
52  A. L. Morton and G. Tate, *The British Labour Movement, 1770–1920* (Lawrence and Wishart, 1956), p. 225.

53 Bullock, *The Life and Times of Ernest Bevin*, vol. I, p. 15.
54 DWRGWU Triennial Delegate Meeting, Official Souvenir, 17–21 May 1920, p. 16.
55 Schneer, *Ben Tillett*, p. 218.
56 George Lansbury, *Looking Backwards – and Forwards* (Blackie and Son, 1935), pp. 191–3.
57 At a municipal binge given by William Devenay on the occasion of his selection as first Labour Mayor of West Ham, in 1919, Tillett, Bevin, Thompson, Kay and other dockers' leaders all took part in the conviviality. The dockers' *Record* (November 1919, p. 4) reports that the proceedings were enlivened by songs from the Mayor's daughter, and the general secretary, 'who gave us "cockles and mussels" '. A good many toasts were drunk, and the 'Labour movement' was toasted on the proposal of Mr W. J. Barwick. 'He said he looked back with a certain amount of pride on being one of the earliest members of the old SDF, with which were associated many members who were also associated with the Dockers' Union. He recalled such stalwarts as Tom McCarthy, Jack Williams, Pete Curran and Harry Orbell.'
58 Eric J. Hobsbawm, *Labouring Men* (Weidenfeld and Nicolson, 1968), p. 327.
59 Max Beer, *History of British Socialism*, vol. II (G. Bell and Sons, 1921), p. 352.
60 Ibid.
61 W. Lawler Wilson, *The Menace of Socialism* (Grant Richards, 1909), pp. 315–16.
62 Ibid.
63 Guy Bowman, Foreword to Tom Mann, *From Single Tax to Syndicalism* (Guy Bowman, 1913).
64 Reprinted with a Foreword by Geoff Brown (Spokesman Books, 1974).
65 *Industrial Syndicalist*, Documents in Socialist History, no. 3 (Spokesman Books, 1974), pp. 19–20.
66 *Documents of the First International* (Progress Publishers, Moscow, n.d.), vol. III, pp. 290–2.
67 Anne Besant, *Essays on Socialism* (Freethought Publishing, 1887), p. 16.
68 J. H. Harley, *Syndicalism* (T. C. and E. C. Black, 1912), pp. 44–5.
69 Ridley, *Revolutionary Syndicalism in France* (Cambridge University Press, 1970), p. 170.
70 A modern edition was published in 1989 by Pluto Press.
71 Ridley, *Revolutionary Syndicalism in France*, p. 172.
72 Ibid.
73 Daniel De Leon, *The Socialist Reconstruction of Society* (Socialist Labour Press, n.d.), pp. 27–9.
74 Cited in Bernard Ransom, *Connolly's Marxism* (Pluto Press, 1980), p. 58.
75 Peter Berresford Ellis (ed.), *James Connolly – Selected Writings* (Penguin, 1973), pp. 151–2.
76 George Dangerfield, *The Strange Death of Liberal England, 1910–1914* (Constable, 1935; reissued Perigree Books, 1980), p. 232.
77 Stewart Bird, Dan Georgakis and Deborah Shaffer, *Solidarity Forever* (Lake View Press, 1985), p. 8.

78  *Industrial Syndicalist*, pp. 58–66.
79  Ibid.
80  Tom Mann, *Memoirs* (1923; reissued McGibbon and Kee, 1967), p. 207.
81  Letter from Ben Tillett, DWRGWU, 7 July 1910; NTWF Inaugural Conference Minutes, 1911.
82  Ibid., 22 and 23 September 1910, Agenda.
83  NTWF Annual General Council Report, June 1911.
84  Gordan A. Phillips, 'The National Transport Workers' Federation, 1910–1927' (unpublished PhD thesis, Oxford University, 1968), p. 71.
85  John Lovell, *Stevedores and Dockers: a Study of Trade Unionism in the Port of London, 1870–1914* (Macmillan, 1969), p. 150.
86  Harry Gosling, *Up and Down Stream* (Methuen, 1927), p. 147.
87  Phillips, 'The National Transport Workers' Federation', p. 57.
88  NTWF Annual General Council Report, June 1911.

# 10

# 1911: Big Bang

## I

### *Spontaneous Combustion?*

Ignition was planned for 14 June 1911. But Southampton seamen stopped work on 9 June, five days in advance of the chosen date for the national strike. Others followed. Suddenly all around were involved. Seamen inspired seamen, and together they fired the dockers. Dockers provoked carters. In almost no time, and in every major port, nothing could move.

Those who live or holiday in the Mediterranean and Adriatic regions will know that in the 1980s a series of summers hotter and dryer than usual produced devastating outbreaks of forest and brush fires. They erupted without warning in areas far apart from one another, each within days of the other. Every fire was a separate event, not contiguous with the others. Emergency after emergency, each demanded its own mobilization of services, firefighters, ambulances. Yet no one supposed that all these fires broke out at the same time by coincidence, or through divine intervention. We all knew that the same climatic conditions, the same sun, prepared the tinder-dry conditions in which any carelessly discarded match, bottle or cigarette could ignite the trees in their distinct and distant habitats.

So it was in the British ports in 1911. Decades of pain and intimidation were, in an instant, overcome. Now, unbelievably, the workers in this abused and impoverished world had the initiative, and in that initiative the power to turn all things upside down. The upsurge of 1889 had been the pride of the unskilled trades of East London; but now the entire subjected kingdom stood tall at the same time. Historians took their revenge upon the insubordination of the oppressed by describing these events as an 'unrest'. But its sheer scope was so awe inspiring that it is even now remembered as the *Great* Unrest.

What provoked this elemental uprising?

## Economic and Social Conditions, 1911

The spreading fires of the transport strikes in 1911 were part of an even wider conflagration covering the years 1911–14 which burst out at the juncture of very powerful social and economic pressures. We have already discussed some of these (see chapter 8, pp. 252–6) in our survey of the first ten years of the new century. We must now resume these themes.

From about 1900, real wages stagnated while prices rose easily and continuously, and money wages staggered feebly after them. This rising cost-of-living curve (see fig. 8.1, p. 254) coincided with a time of high and flaunted fashion. The Edwardian rich threw off the constraints of Victorian respectability to indulge a new taste for open, and often crass, ostentation. The combination of decadent waste and struggling poverty served to provoke an unprecedented sense of social injustice among working people.

Then, crucially, the short slump of 1908–9 suddenly gave way to a trade boom the following year. Unemployment fell, confirming the general upward trend of the economy.

The number without work fell to 4.7 per cent of the working population in 1910. The figure stayed low throughout the years of unrest down to the outbreak of war in 1914. Might Labour once again ride the back of such a boom to make real wage gains, as it had done twenty-one years earlier? Several key leaders of the general workers were certainly astute enough to entertain the thought. Yet, although 1911 heralded a true renewal of new unionism, the port workers' strikes of that year were not at all a carbon copy of 1889. Then, orderly processions, well marshalled and peaceful, had presented the main face of the strike. The middle classes were sympathetic, and the press reflected that sympathy. Now there was to break out a passion amounting to rage, which bewildered many commentators, and indeed many participants. Surely this wild outburst must require explanations other than economic rationality? Some later historians have reflected this feeling. One who emphasized an instinctive element of revolt in the movement was the influential French observer Elie Halevy, whose studies were first published in English in the 1930s.

## Disillusion and Injustice

Halevy charts the disillusion with the social-reform programme of the Liberal government between 1906 and 1910, which had won the well-behaved support of the new Labour Party in Parliament. But 'Ramsay MacDonald was not the man to give the impression . . . that the advent of the Labour Party meant the birth of a new world'.[1] Moreover, he points out, largess, in the form of new administrative and official jobs, was now sufficiently obtainable to influence the behaviour of numbers of people. Under the Trades Boards Act, in the new labour exchanges and under the National Insurance Act, many relatively secure and well-paid posts became available. These were systematically distributed among hundreds of trade-union officials. The introduction of salaries for MPs pointed in the same direction, towards the incorporation of the new political and industrial forces in an arrangement which was not open to the mass of workers.[2] To a growing sense of exclusion was added resentment against conspicuous upper-class over-indulgence. This stimulated commentary from all sides, not least from apprehensive Labour leaders, fearful of the alienation of their followers in a revolt against the still fragile political structures which they had helped to create, in a toil which had cost two decades of intensive effort. Writing on the eve of the strikes, Phillip Snowden said:

In 1910 . . . with stationary wages, the real condition of the workers is one of diminishing power to satisfy desires . . . With the spread of education, with the display of wealth and luxury of the rich, it is certain that the workers will not be content. It is the duty of statesmanship to acknowledge the justice of the desire of the workers for a more humane and cultured life, and to satisfy this unrest by concessions of reform. If employers and politicians are so unwise as to ignore the demands of labour, then what might be done by safe and constitutional methods will, by great suffering and loss, be accomplished by industrial strife, and through social anarchy . . . The year upon which we have just entered is likely to be a momentous one for Labour. There is trouble brewing in a number of trades which may break out into open hostilities. Labour has become aggressive, and is not merely opposing attack, but is determined upon advances.[3]

Snowden's fellow parliamentarian, Ramsay MacDonald, made a characteristically muddled attempt to understand the revolt of labour in an essay published in 1913. A brief extract is enough: 'The education and experience of the workman had led him to discover many economic flaws in society, and he challenged it. But there was something more that was wrong. Society was not merely a poor inefficient thing, it was an irritatingly vicious thing.'[4]

## Tom Mann at Work

Tom Mann carefully nourished this growing awareness of injustice in all his eager audiences. He railed against all forms of subordination and supplication. In the face of avarice and neglect by capital and the legislature, he called for revolt, and nothing less than revolt. In 1889 John Burns and Ben Tillett had held the spotlights on themselves. They were the orators of the great dock strike, while Mann was the officer in charge of organization, even if this task ensured that he was not to be without his own share of platform time. But now, in the Great Unrest, it was Mann's voice which gave tongue to the entire mute mass. His technique was direct and simple. Jack Jones has given 'a youngster's impression' of Mann's oratorical style, recalled from the inter-war years:

> Tom Mann, first of all, was a good powerful speaker, but he also had a bit of acting ability. He was the sort of man who would walk up and down the stage declaiming and then would suddenly sit down – 'Come up and have a cup of tea, don't bother about it!' In other words, he was denouncing those who wanted to stay at home and have a cup of tea, and not do anything about reforming the world.[5]

Another eye-witness of Mann's meetings has told of the same element in his speeches. He would berate the members of his audience for their meekness before the parliamentarians: 'You petition them for pensions . . . for jobs . . . for food . . . for houses . . .', and at each item in his list of pleas he would literally grovel, kneeling on the stage, hands together, eyes raised in prayerful supplication. In peroration, as he swung over into the opposing message of self-help through direct action, he would raise himself and stand upright and four-square.[6] In an age of mass politics governed by more professional and, it must be said, less honest forms of public television 'performance', the impact of Mann's speeches, no less than that of his organizing and writing, is hard to recapture. But it cannot be lightly dismissed.

## 'Sectional Unionism Is Our Curse!'

There are many other witnesses to Tom Mann's eloquence. But it was *what* he said, not how he said it, which ran in front of him around the ports, and through all the arteries of trade within the kingdom.

'Sectional unionism is our curse', he trumpeted to all the members of every little provincial section:

> The ability to act trade by trade, occupation by occupation, each independent of the other, may have been of some service a couple of generations ago. But it is no use now! Let us see!

Miners are organised in a given district. Engine drivers at the hauling engines are organised. Miners have trouble with the Masters. They strike. They ask the Engine drivers to help them by refusing to lower blacklegs into the mines, or to haul any stuff whatever that is detrimental to the Miners' interests. The Engine drivers take a vote of their members. They decide it is not their quarrel – why should they risk good jobs? A big majority against the miners decides the latter's fate . . .

The Shipping Federation systematically supplies British workmen as 'scabs to order' in this or any other country. It is no use objecting that these miserable wretches ought not to be called British Workmen. The facts are too palpable. And these blacklegs, with all their necessary food, liquor, bedding . . . are shipped and conveyed over hundreds of miles by rail and road, as well as water, by other Union men. The drivers of locomotives, conveying them in batches of a hundred to the port, carry their Union card. The Engineers on the boat belong either to the Marine Engineers' Union or the Amalgamated Engineers. The carman, carrying food stuffs for the scabs, is a member of his Union. The carpenters who make to order the fittings to house them, are Unionists.

It is these Union men, and not the capitalists, who beat the other Unionists trying to resist reduction or obtain increases. And so it must continue until we can organise by Industries and not merely by Trades. Until we can unify the Industrial Movement into one compact fighting force.

Comrades, we have got to face the fact that Sectional Unionism is played out.[7]

## Quiescent Port Unions . . .

Sectional or not, trade unionism was not played out. Overall trade-union membership had already registered substantial growth in the years 1906 and 1907, increasing by half a million its long-fixed total of approximately 2 million. The rise was checked in the short recession which followed, but resumed, with a further gain of 4 per cent, in 1910. Was the prescience of the syndicalists, who had sharpened up their doctrine before the Great Unrest came to demonstrate its power, based on an apprehension of the effects of the boom in trade?

In the ports, however, there was no immediate rush to join this surge of membership, despite Tom Mann and the NTWF's recruitment drive, even though the trade-cycle upturn was, as always, to show itself in a new burst of traffic. London's port unionism remained moribund, and elsewhere the DWRGWU was simply hanging on. Ben Tillett's Annual Report for 1910 (in which he celebrated his return to work 'after my last protracted illness'[8]) contained no hint of what was to come: it was preoccupied with parliamentary matters, with the Osborne Judgement of 1909 (in which the Law Lords had ruled that trade unions must not spend their funds on political activity), with old-age pensions, labour exchanges, increased taxation, the increased cost of living, invalidity and unemployment insurance. Tillett did express himself sceptically about the efficacy of the reforms, and shared the mood of syndicalist rejection. The NUDL, though more prudently administered, lay similarly flat. Sexton, in that same year, wrote simply. 'We do not propose to labour the report this year for more than one reason, but the main one is to let those who have had the actual experience in the various localities speak for themselves.'[9] (The regional reports which follow this cryptic introduction, sent in by loyalist and aggrieved officials, make very plain that Sexton's reticence had much to do with his sense of injury over the 'Larkin affair'.)

## ... Elsewhere, Portents

In 1908 the number of strikers doubled over 1907. There was a pause in the following year. Then, in 1910, the number of workers involved in strikes more than doubled again over those of 1909 (see table 10.1). The trend of strike figures is also evident in the number of stoppages, rising from 346 in 1904 to 521 in 1910, and in the totals of working days involved, growing from 1.5 million in 1904 to 9.9 million in 1910. In all these series, the same escalation is visible, interrupted alike in 1908–9 by a downturn in the trade cycle, during which unemployment temporarily doubled, from 3.7 per cent in 1907 to 7.8 per cent in 1908 and 1909. But the number of strikers in 1910 was the highest since the great defensive struggles of 1893. In that year, the *casus belli* had been the defence of trade-union membership against free labour. It is highly significant that in 1910 the Board of Trade Report remarked that 30 per cent of those who struck work had come out in protest at the engagement of non-union labour. In that year, too, the troops fired on the miners of

Table 10.1  *Number of Workers
Directly Involved in Strikes,
1904–1910*

| | |
|---|---|
| 1904 | 56,380 |
| 1905 | 67,653 |
| 1906 | 157,872 |
| 1907 | 100,728 |
| 1908 | 223,909 |
| 1909 | 170,258 |
| 1910 | 385,085 |

*Source:* Labour Department of the Board of Trade, *Reports on Strikes and Lock-outs.*

Tonypandy, engaged in the great Cambrian coal strike in South Wales, killing one striker. In the ensuing riots, over 500 were injured. The ostensible cause of the strike was a disputed wage rate for coal-getting in a new seam which the Cambrian Coal Combine had opened in the Rhondda Valley. But the whole industry was tinder dry for revolt, with the possibility of an industry-wide stoppage never far from men's minds.

Tireless, busy everywhere, Tom Mann was present. The ebullient and combative Home Secretary, Winston Churchill, followed up this act of class warfare in South Wales two months later by personally supervising, in London, the direction of rifle and cannon fire against two Russian anarchists at the 'siege' of Sydney Street. Tom Mann's journal, the *Industrial Syndicalist*, saw this in a symbolic light: it offered a 2-guinea prize for an essay of 3,000 words on the question: 'If two men can keep two thousand men employed and hold them at bay on one street, how many men would be required to defeat two or three million men, spread over the area of Great Britain?'[10] No one knew the answer to that question.

The new spirit of rebellion, fostered and expressed by young men in the coalfields, in cotton and elsewhere, was lovingly nurtured by the syndicalist agitation. Tom Mann's tours and publications took him everywhere. The worker-students and Marxist tutors of the newly formed Central Labour College had already touched the dockers in South Wales in 1910 (see chapter 8, pp. 261–2). In that dispute, at Houlders' ship in Newport, the sight of the blacklegs brought in from London to break the strike provoked a violent cry from one of the strikers: 'You bloody bastards . . . Are we going to let them take the bread out of our mouths? Let's go for them!'[11] The offensive flavour of the language, captured for history in the Arbitration Board's Report, should not obscure for us the rage of that man, expressing the dockers' long years of humiliation at the hands of free labour. Tom Mann, as we saw in chapter 8, had preached his message in the South Wales ports just prior to the Houlders' dispute. Amongst the converts who came to him was the strikers' unofficial leader, Alf Cox. He represented a new generation, touched by the influence of the syndicalist spirit. At the height of the unrest to come, a shipowner remarked to Lord Askwith, 'The dockers . . . had new leaders, men unknown before; the employers did not know how to deal with them'.[12]

Tom Mann's evangelizing tour of the ports followed the formation of the National Transport Workers' Federation; but it was also co-ordinated with Havelock Wilson's campaign to revive the Seamen's Union and to prepare for a major strike. Alone amongst the affiliates of the NTWF, the NSFU had adopted a programme of demands, intended for national and even international application. A team of NSFU speakers, led by Wilson, canvassed the idea of an international seamen's strike right across the trading world, from New York to Norway.

As applied to British owners, the union's demands were comprehensive:

> The claim was for a conciliation board, a national minimum rate of wages, a manning scale for stokehold, deck, and galley, the abolition of medical examinations by doctors privately appointed by the Shipping Federation, abolition of engagement of seamen at Shipping Federation offices, the right of seamen to a portion of their wages while in port and to have a representative present while signing on, the fixing of working hours and overtime rates and improved forecastle accommodation.[13]

Behind this impressive shopping list, of course, and crucial in all that followed, lay the demand for recognition, which was anathema to the anti-union moguls of the Shipping Federation. This recognition was pursued at *national* level, for standard national, if not yet international, terms and conditions. It was ambitious beyond the dreams of the more sectionalized and localized, and, be it said, more timid, leaders of the dockers, carters, tram and bus workers enrolled in the NTWF. But out of the turmoil to come, it was recognition, even more than wage increases, which ultimately emerged as the dominant objective of those occupations, inspiring them, and belatedly their official representatives, to follow the seamen's lead.

## The Role of Havelock Wilson

It has been said that the strike wave of 1911 was largely leaderless, or (more plausibly) that its leaders were local men, not the national union hierarchs. There is some truth in this. But clearly there is another figure, besides Tom Mann himself, who provided a vigorous national lead. Havelock Wilson has been remembered in Labour and trade-union lore as the author of various betrayals and some degree of corruption, and it is clear that his union suffered during decades of his autocratic rule. In 1911, however, this evolution could scarcely have been predicted, and even in retrospect Tom Mann (admittedly ever generous) paid his own very real tribute to him. Speaking of the events of 1911, Mann writes:

> the shipowners, over a period of many years, with the aid of clever lawyers, did their utmost to make Havelock Wilson a bankrupt. In the whole history of the trade-union movement of Britain, there is no case of such persistent, systematic, and venemous persecution of a union official as that to which Havelock Wilson was subjected by the shipowners of this country.
>
> In ultimate ideals and objectives, Havelock Wilson and I have nothing in common, but I have had occasion to work in close relationship with him in trade-union affairs, and we have been colleagues in many industrial disputes. I have always found him a straightforward, honourable and loyal

comrade. Moreover, he was always at his post early in the day, tackling the most difficult tasks with the utmost readiness. I take the opportunity of saying this because there is considerable feeling against Wilson for certain of his activities. I like to dwell upon other phases, and especially upon what happened in 1911, in the industrial arena of Britain, and particularly in connection with the transport industry . . .

Tom Mann's remarkable nose for action had undoubtedly helped him to identify the scent of trouble brewing:

I had faith in Wilson's ability to seize the opportune time for vigorous action, knowing that he was in deadly earnest and above all anxious to make no mistake when the right time came. I was informed of conferences held quietly in the chief ports. Wilson told me he was convinced that the summer of 1911 would be the time . . .
I readily agreed to identify myself with the intended effort, for I shared Wilson's hopes and beliefs, though all the time eager for a broader and bigger outlook to prevail . . .

The great strike of miners in South Wales had already impressed port workers all round the Principality:

in the ports, solidarity with the miners had been earnestly advocated. Some union officials, however, positively refused to participate in the effort, which they regarded as untimely. In some cases they went further and tried to stultify the movement. In May 1911 it became evident that the time for action was at hand. We decided to approach the shipowners through the Shipping Federation . . . The reply . . . was of that haughty type characteristic of dominant Capitalism. This left us no alternative but drastic action. The Sailors' and Firemen's Union therefore had another conference, and decided to call a strike for the middle of June.[14]

When the call came, the International Transport Workers' Federation failed to evoke the planned international action. German, Danish and Norwegian shipowners quickly made concessions to their seamen, and international solidarity as quickly collapsed.[15] Nearer home, the NTWF wavered.

## 'Suspicion Brooded Melancholy'

The first Annual General Council Meeting of the NTWF was held only two weeks before the seamen's strike call, yet it side-stepped a direct call for federal support for the looming conflict. James Anderson, the NTWF secretary, expressed his anxiety about Wilson's 'bull and rush' mood. Harry Gosling recalled: 'Havelock Wilson's task was no easy one, but in spite of his growing physical disabilities he conducted it with amazing energy. The blaze spread rapidly . . . though at one moment we were all saying more or less volubly that he could not possibly succeed, the next we found ourselves travelling along behind him.'[16] Robert Williams said of the NSFU and their 1911 strike: 'It certainly appeared to those who knew that this Union's fortunes were at a very low ebb, that this proposed international strike was a gambler's last chance.'[17] The NSFU was reported to owe its bank £6 13s. in 1911.[18]

Ben Tillett reported, of the founding of the NTWF: 'Following the trend of the general working class moving towards solidarity, the Transport Workers themselves, encouraged by the movements initiated in other directions, came together almost stealthily with much caution and with much fear. Suspicion brooded melancholy over the most optimistic anticipations.'[19] But, says Tillett, it was Havelock Wilson, 'although crippled with rheumatics, sick and enfeebled', who 'struggled bravely to the middle of the summer'.[20] Gosling says quite precisely: 'It was J. Havelock Wilson who actually set fire to the heather.'[21]

## The Mystery Explained

The heat generated in that fire was more than metaphorical: the English summer of 1911 was the hottest for forty-three years. Under a remorseless sun, one by one, the ports burst into flames. And this is not simply a metaphor; all too often the fires were real ones, not moral upsurges. In the immediately preceding months, militant – even riotous – strikes, which were widely reported and debated, had set the scene in the coalfields and in the cotton towns. In Ireland (all of which was still a province of Great Britain), a convulsive industrial struggle in Belfast and a colourful revolutionary trade-union leader, James Larkin, had already given a premonition of all of these trends and had shaken the staid leaders of the National Union of Dock Labourers. In 1911 'the transport workers disturbed, emotionally and physically, not just their industry, but society at large.'[22] A leading Labour politician told Askwith, 'I don't know what has come over the country. Everyone seems to have lost their heads.'[23]

In that summer of 1911, then, trade was booming, there was a rising sense of social and political injustice among the workers, there was syndicalist agitation, a rising tide of militancy was already apparent, and there was a conscious plan for a national seamen's action. Finally, and if we are to give due weight to the remarkable testimony of Tom Mann himself (who speaks consistently of 'we' and 'us' in his memoirs, in recalling the joint planning of the seamen's campaign by Wilson and himself), there were two highly experienced men giving practised and dedicated leadership and coherence to the movement in the ports.

In short: opportunity, provocation, incitement, example and leadership. Some historians have felt that the uprising of the ports in 1911 remains mysterious.[24] The only mystery is why it took so long for this convergence to generate itself. Now at last, action against the long-standing abuse of human beings in the ports was not only possible, but real. After years of privation and oppression the seamen, dockers and carters left their work in droves and together took to the streets. The all-powerful Shipping Federation and its Free Labour Battalions were rendered impotent. So forceful was the revolt that all opposition was lightly brushed aside.

## II

### *Jumping the Gun*

A short strike by the Southampton coal trimmers, supported by the Dockers' Union, provoked the stoppage by seamen in that port, which, as we have seen, anticipated the official national seamen's strike.

Meanwhile, amongst the transport workers solidarity was being earnestly advocated in all ports, and for all sections, but not by any means by all Union officials; on the contrary, some of these declined to be identified with the effort, declaring it to be 'altogether untimely,' etc., etc.

The deciding factor that fixed June as the best month in the year for the struggle was that trade was exceptionally busy, that the Coronation [of George V] would take place in that month, and that an exceptional number of over-sea visitors would be making their way to this country. June was therefore beyond question the best month in the year for the struggle, and at the conference of sailors, the 14th June was ultimately decided upon as the particular day on which to commence hostilities.

The largest ocean liner ever built up to that date was lying in Southampton, and making ready for her maiden voyage across the Atlantic; it was the SS *Olympic*. The first shots were fired by the coalies who refused to load the vessel except under improved conditions. It looked as though there would be a serious delay in the departure of the big boat, but the public generally little thought that the vessel would be absolutely tied up, especially as she was to bring back a special contingent of American millionaires to join in the Coronation junketings. But so it was; the *Olympic* could not get away, and on the 14th war was declared in all the chief ports of the country, and the men responded in magnificent style.

Even now the Capitalist press was utterly unable to calculate the forces at work, and tried to laugh down what they called 'the wicked and insane attempts to hold up the shipping'. In three days' time it dawned upon them that something quite out of the ordinary had taken place; they saw that every vessel, as it came into port, had to remain there, and that there was a strong indication on the part of dockers and others to make common cause.

The experience was unique in industrial battles. Shipowners who had absolutely refused to have anything to do with the workmen, now earnestly wrote to get a conference. The Shipping Federation proved utterly incapable of helping its clients, and after having dictated conditions for over twenty years they had in a single day lost all power whatsoever. The workmen simply folded arms, saying that they were 'quite willing to return to work when their demands were granted, and not before'. Shipowners begged of Union officials to 'instruct the men to take out the mail boats and others,' on the assurance that they would meet in conference without delay, and discuss all points desired. But it was too late to discuss; the situation had now reached a point when discussion was out of the question, and the actual granting of the demands should be complied with'.[25]

## The Seamen's Demands Conceded

We have already itemized the official programme of seamen's demands (p. 342). It was a truly formidable claim, but, 'to the surprise of everyone,' concluded Tom Mann, 'all these demands were complied with in a few days'.

The seamen, although summoned to the contest nationally, on a national programme, fought and negotiated port by port. This was inevitable, since the Shipping Federation had rejected any kind of formal bargaining relationship with the unions. The settlements forced out of local groups of shipping companies reflected this: Cardiff seamen won a 30s. increase, but in Hull only 5s. were conceded.[26] The same was true of the strikes by dockers and carters. Having received no national call, either from their unions or the NTWF, the local unions formed ad hoc strike committees in attempts to focus and express the initially inchoate demands of the strikers. The National Transport Workers' Federation role was marginal: it lent its name and some shape to the Strike Committee in Liverpool and – later in the summer – much more substantially in the London strike. In the Humber and the Bristol Channel, its existence may have helped local co-ordination.[27] Nowhere in the provincial settlements of 1911 did the employers recognize the NTWF as a bargaining agent. In London things were different. Consequently, the dockers and carters also came out of the strikes with a wide variety of wage increases – though some were very substantial, in the range from 30 to 40 per cent.

One consistent demand was presented everywhere: for union recognition, and preference of employment for union members. And one consistent and permanent result of the strikes was the flood of new recruits who flocked to join – or rejoin – the waterside unions. The events of 1911 permanently transformed the fortunes of the new unions in transport. Though they were to face declining numbers in the 1920s, there was ñever, after 1911, any equivalent setback to match that of the 1890s. No counterattack by the employers ever again reduced the general union and its associated organizations in transport and general trades to the impotence of 1893–1910.

## Liverpool Epic

The Liverpool strikes were an epic complete in themselves. They reached into the imagination of the age. Indeed, long afterwards their dramatic overtones moved Trevor Griffiths to make them the subject of a major television script. This was commissioned in 1971 by the BBC as one of a series on *The Edwardians*; but it proved too raw for the modern age, student demonstrations and UCS work-ins notwithstanding, and it was filleted out of the series by the Corporation's controllers. By 1990 it had still never been seen. Fortunately, British publishing has until recently been largely free of such self-censorship and the drama of Tom Mann's impact on the Liverpool scene of 1911 can at least be read.[28]

On 13 June Mann arrived at the Liverpool Exchange Station by train. He had come to help the seamen. Although the NTWF gave belated support to the ensuing stoppage, Mann held no national office in that body. He was given a district responsibility. Yet he was immediately elected chairman of the Joint Strike Committee, presiding over the officials of the unions of seamen, dockers (James Sexton himself), ships' stewards and Liverpool carters, whose vice-president, Billal Quilliam, was a local solicitor.[29] Of these leaders, Sexton was of course the general secretary of a national union, and the Ships' Stewards' Union also had its national headquarters in Liverpool. Its two representatives on the committee, Frank Pearce and Joe Cotter, were both syndicalists. Was there perhaps some flicker of doubt in Sexton's mind over the propriety of these arrangements? What were the apprehensions of a moderate and financially prudent leader, confronted with the national spokesman of the syndicalists surrounded by his strong supporters? And such a fire-eater given the authority of the chair . . . ? If these questions troubled him, they never showed in Sexton's public role during the strikes. He and Mann negotiated jointly, and spoke unanimously on the public stage – a remarkable partnership of opposites.

The committee concentrated its first attentions on the big, independent passenger-liner companies at the Liverpool North End Docks, rightly judging them most vulnerable. Cargo-shipping, controlled by smaller firms affiliated to the intransigent Shipping Federation, was less vulnerable. Imperishable cargoes, at least, could await shipment or discharge for a time, but passengers who had booked an expensive trans-atlantic crossing could not. The liner firms faced severe international competition and, in addition, had mail contracts to fulfil. Several such sailings were scheduled, and were duly stopped by the strike on 14 June. Mann instantly translated the theory of class solidarity into action, calling 'upon all departments of the transport trade – the dock labourers, the carters, the coal porters, the bargemen and the railwaymen . . . to rally to the support of the seamen . . . the object aimed at . . . was to unite the transport workers on the sea with those on the land.'[30]

Within days, and following the capitulation of the Blue Funnel line, in succession the White Star, Canadian Pacific, Cunard and Booth lines had ceded. Breathtaking victories, these, to the strikers. All grades of seamen won an increase of 10s. a week, the abolition of the company medical examination, no victimization, and recognition of their appropriate union. The long contraband union badges could now be worn in public, and union officials could board company ships. The unions' demand for a Conciliation Board was waived for the moment. The NSFU and the Stewards' Union were promptly flooded by thousands of new members.

The local press identified the decisive factor in the astonishing breakthrough: 'for the first time in the history of the port of Liverpool, yesterday saw "all hands" throwing sectionalism to the wind and joining hand in hand for the furtherance of a common cause. It was a remarkable – even an historic – event in trade union progress.'[31] Up to this point, the dockers' and the carters' unions had held back from direct action on behalf of their own causes, although some unofficial dockers' action in sympathy with the seamen had already occurred.

But Mann judged that the smaller cargo firms, buttressed by the Shipping Federation, would require a more general mobilization to ensure a comparable success. He issued 50,000 copies of a manifesto calling a seamen's and catering-staff strike in these firms for Monday, 25 June, at the same time calling on all dockers and other cargo-handlers to black the goods of the firms. 'All eyes are now turned upon Liverpool men, anxiously watching whether they will exhibit solidarity or whether the evils of sectionalism shall curse our movement once more'.[32]

On the day before the strike, between 3,000 and 4,000 workers attended a mass meeting at St George's Plateau. It resolved on support for the seamen. Blacking was then endorsed by the NUDL and the Carters' Union. The dispute became, in effect, a total stoppage, since no cargo was to be moved in or out of ships which had been tied up, and no ship could move. In the face of this action, the dockers were prompted to remember their own grievances and assert their own demands: for union rates of pay and recognition of the NUDL. Hitherto such a mutiny would have been an unthinkable affront to bosses who were affiliates of the Shipping Federation. But, faced with such solidarity, the employers caved in, again one after another. During a single day Mann and Sexton went together to the offices of four cargo-shipping companies, obtaining union recognition in every case. As they emerged from each office, they made impromptu speeches to crowds of cheering dockers. 'Tell your readers,' said Tom Mann to a local journalist, 'that never in the course of my career have I seen so successful a fight for labour accomplished in one day. We have given wonderful proof of the unity existing between all the affected unions. We have broken the back of the opposition to trade unionism along the line of docks'.[33] Sexton was, characteristically, more laconic: 'It has been a good day, a very good day. I am satisfied with it'.[34]

The demand for union recognition now spread to the dockers working for the large liner companies. Seamen began to give thanks for the solidarity shown to them by striking in sympathy with the dockers. Two thousand coal-heavers downed shovels to join the union and the movement. Boiler-scalers and cold-storage men in turn came out to join the strikes. The South End men joined with the North Enders in common cause, after all those years of separation. Sexton and Mann negotiated union recognition from Cunard on behalf of all the Liverpool liner firms. The union badge was to be worn once again. When Mann and Sexton accepted the companies' wish to defer implementation of the union's port-working rules, including payment of union rates, the men revolted against their own leader. George Milligan, secretary of No. 12 Branch and an active member of the NUDL who at the time shared the dockers' old suspicions about Sexton, led the protest. At the men's insistence, Milligan was co-opted on to the Joint Strike Committee, which was now in danger of losing control of the strike.

The big firms gave varied and equivocal answers to the men's demands, submitted to them by Mann, Sexton, Cotter and now Milligan. When presenting compromise settlements for acceptance by mass meetings, Mann was heckled, even though Milligan supported his plea for a return to work. Cotter tried his persuasive powers, as did Sexton, who told strikers: 'If you don't take our advice today, I can do no more for you'. But the recommendations were rejected. The Strike Committee then offered the following resolution to the men:

> we, the joint committee advise those employed at the firms mentioned on the White List [i.e. those firms who had agreed to the recognition of all unions] to return to work at once pending the Dockers' Union port rules being granted during the coming month, and pledge ourselves that, should the north end not receive the full recognition of union rules at the end of the month we shall fully support their activity to obtain such.[35]

Mann addressed mass meetings to win support for this advice. Despite Milligan's and other local leaders' support, the vote was evenly split. The union threatened the expulsion of members for defying what was now an instruction to return to work. Union officials toured the docks to persuade the men, who finally conformed to their pressures: union discipline had prevailed.

The tugboat men now struck, winning a wage gain in a few days. And though the dock strikes were now apparently over, the men's truculent responses to foremen who failed to implement all the details of the settlement led to daily walk-outs, at which Milligan appeared as the over-worked troubleshooter. The union preached order, discipline, loyalty, and Milligan became a firm supporter of Sexton and his policies. Soon he was appointed deputy general secretary of the NUDL. (In 1922 he became the first area secretary of the TGWU for Area No. 12 on Merseyside.)[36]

After many meetings, on 4 August the conference of shipowners and unions signed the White Book Agreement. All the major employers of port labour signed. For the men outside the NUDL, the separate coal-heavers' unions of North and South Ends signed for their dockers. The settlement provided for the union button to be worn at the call, agreed that employers would not discriminate in favour of non-union labour, and established a Conciliation Board. In practice, preference for union labour was decisively imposed, in return for a union commitment to maintain work in any dispute whilst it was before the Board. This was the constitutional settlement of which Sexton had dreamed, and he set himself thereafter to deliver the union side of the deal.

He and the employers expected that the agreement signalled the end of the dock strikes. But on 7 August the railway-goods porters struck for reduced hours and increased pay. Although the ASRS condemned the strike, Mann's Strike Committee supported it, co-opted local officials of the ASRS and the General Railway Workers' Union, and called on all transport workers to black goods moving to or from rail depots and stations. This, of course, reactivated the dockers. The shipowners were outraged and threatened a port lock-out unless the NUDL prevailed on its members to work normally. But other forces were propelling the city towards a general transport strike. Some sporadic violence and arson had already occurred and the authorities mobilized extra police and the military on the very day that the Strike Committee summoned 80,000 people to a demonstration at St George's Plateau in support of the railwaymen.

Joe Byrne, later to be a branch official of the TGWU on Liverpool docks, had childhood memories of that day:

We lived at Seaforth (it's all docks now, but then it was sands and the townies would flock down there at the weekend). Nearby was a barracks for the Scots Greys and one Sunday I saw the Scots Greys mounted with lances and flags ride past the end of the road. Some women came to my mother and asked 'Has Patrick gone to the meeting in town?' She said he had. 'Oh God', they said, 'I hope he won't get hurt.'

Tom Mann had come to be Number One speaker that day. There had been religious trouble and Tom Mann marched up William Brown Street with a green and orange sash to the Plateau to symbolise Liverpool united, Protestant and Catholic.[37]

This picture of Tom Mann sporting the colours of both communities, striding out to heal sectarian divisions, inspired 'Nemo', who is better remembered as Robert Blatchford, to write an imaginary dialogue between Order and Conscience:

*The Old Order:*– Surely, we as reasonable men cannot be governed by this fellow, Tom Mann. Who is he? Is he not a discredited agitator, expelled from England, from Australia, who must inevitably be found out?

*The New Conscience:*– Tom Mann was loved and honoured by Cardinal Manning, the greatest Christian since the time of Francis of Assisi. He was admired and loved by Archbishop Benson, one of the greatest Churchmen of the Church of England, who offered him Orders without the preliminary examination. He had the hearts of the workmen of London and of Broken Hill, just as he has the hearts of the workpeople of Liverpool. He voices the voiceless wrath of the wretched, and their unlearned discontent. Say he is another Attila, who styled himself the Scourge of God. Could Attila have ravaged Europe unless his warriors believed in him? Could Mann hold up the port of Liverpool unless the docker, the carter, the seaman and fireman, the cook and steward, the coal-heaver, the tramwayman, believe that through the solidarity of whose mighty wave he is the crest, that they will be able to get an extra slice of bread for their children, an extra hour's leisure for their wives, even if it is expressed only through an increase of wages?

*The Old Order:*– The men could have had all this gradually. Why couldn't they agitate resonably?

*The New Conscience:*– Do you mean by that they should have waited for their claims to be settled by arbitration?

*The Old Order:*– Certainly. It takes time for all claims to be settled. They cannot be adjusted in ten minutes.

*The New Conscience:*– It does not take much time for men to starve. The Conciliation Board took an average of sixteen months to settle claims. A man can die of hunger in three days.'[38]

Sectarian violence was always a possible risk. But the forces which drew blood in Liverpool were entirely secular, as Joe Byrne recalled many years later:

The police were waiting inside Lime Street Station, and my Dad who was on the Plateau said to Tom 'Looks as though there's going to be trouble'. There were thousands out, it was like a Sunday outing, all in their straw hats.

The mounted police sailed out of the station and drove them right off the Plateau so they ran into the troops coming up Dale Street. The fighting went on all Sunday night and the best part of Monday. Wherever people gathered they attacked them.

Years later, I was asked to chair a meeting for Tom Mann . . . I'll never forget it: the place was packed with women in shawls, sitting on the window sills. When I introduced Tom Mann, they got off their seats and hugged and kissed him. When I got home, my Dad told me all about 1911 and Bloody Sunday: that's what they called it. Those women remembered all about it and Tom Mann leading the men.[39]

The police and the troops between them put over 350 people in hospital on Bloody Sunday. Two thousand more soldiers were brought to the city, and the shipowners did close the docks, putting 15,000 out of work. The Strike Committee promptly called for a general strike, and 66,000 responded. Military escorts were needed for any movement of goods, which the Strike Committee sanctioned by issuing permits; only bread and milk received such permits. At this point, the railway strike had become national, but was resolved in just three days, when the railway companies – which had traditionally opposed union recognition with the same vehemence as the Shipping Federation – agreed to meet the unions.

In Liverpool, violence continued. Troops shot and killed a dock labourer and a carter during an obscure tumult involving a prison van on a dockland street. On 17 August the city tramwaymen, power-station workers and dustmen all struck. The Corporation dismissed the tramwaymen, and only a threat by the Strike Committee to renew the general strike secured the promise of reinstatement. (In the event, this was long delayed.) Finally, on 25 August, the NUDL and the shipowners agreed terms for a return to work at the docks. The great strikes were over. All sections had made advances except the tramwaymen.

## Conflagration in Hull

For the first time, during the 1911 strikes the NUDL became deeply involved in the Humberside ports. As we have seen it had established a branch at Goole as early as 1902, and had chafed at the failure of the DWRGWU to take back into its fold the 11,000 Hull dockers who lapsed their union membership after its collapse in 1893. The Goole men were the first to strike on 14 June, in harmony with the seamen, although only one-third of them held union cards before the strike. In Hull, too, despite the almost complete absence of organization, the dockers' sympathy action with the seamen was total. The NUDL sought to solidify the strike into a permanent association and its national organizer, O'Connor Kessack, hastened from Leith to the Humber, where he was active in both Goole and Hull during the strike.

As elsewhere, the seamen's strike in Hull had been well prepared.[40] The NSFU had appointed John Bell as its Humber organizer in 1910.

Planning meetings began in February 1911 and the NTWF seems to have played an active role in promoting them. They were addressed by Tom Mann, Ben Tillett, Havelock Wilson and his extraordinary organizer, the 'sky-pilot' Rev. A. B. Hopkins.[41]

Throughout the spring new members flocked into the unions: fish-dock workers, grain workers, checkers and weighters. The DWRGWU began its own recruitment drive in May. This came just too late to prevent a formation which ever after impaired the monopoly of the TGWU in the port: the Fish Dock Workers' Protection Society was supported by the Gasworkers' Union in its struggle with the trawler-owners, and this paved the way to their eventual merger into what became the General and Municipal Workers' Union, which retained the membership of the fish 'bobbers' down to modern times.

Madame Sorgue, the French syndicalist leader, made appearances in Hull in the build-up to the strike. On 14 June a crowd of 4,000 gathered in Paragon Square to hear the strike declared by John Bell. A rocket-flare confirmed the decision that evening at 8.30. (This signal was used to start the strike in other ports too.)

Initially, the success of the strike was not guaranteed. Hull, of course, was a stronghold of Collison's Free Labour Association, which had some success in bringing strike-breakers from Europe, Wales and Lancashire. And a long-established local seamen's union, the Hull Seamen's and Marine Firemen's Amalgamated Association, was strongly represented in the port, with 800 members. Its secretary, J. Butcher, was a 'moderate' who valued his intimate relations with the shipowners; the NSFU organizer called him 'a tool of the Federation'. Butcher railed at the 'agitators' who had 'warped' his members into a strike mood, but when they walked out and joined the stoppage it became clear that he had lost control. (The Hull seamen merged with the national union only in 1922.)

The battle between pickets and free labourers in transit to and from their depot ship, moored in the Humber, was reminiscent of the 1890s. It was no less bloody. A striker was shot and seriously wounded by gunfire from a strike-breaking cargo ship as she put to sea. Its captain was arrested when he docked in Rotterdam. Hamburg dockers sent a telegram to report that they were refusing to unload ships from Hull. Far from being intimidated, the resolve of the seamen was strengthened. It spread when the dockers made their first gesture of solidarity with a one-day strike at the Alexandra Dock. This prompted Tillett to send a telegram: 'No instructions from the Dockers' Executive to Hull dockers to cease work.' But in fact 90 per cent of them were non-unionists, and they went right on to extend their strike. Tillett's message did, however, register. As a result the Hull dockers denied a platform at their mass meetings to the local dockers' secretary and took their lead instead from a young, hitherto obscure docker, John Burn, a non-unionist who nevertheless, reported the local press, 'had always believed that the salvation of the working classes did not lie in politics, but in their industrial organisation, by means of which they could obtain anything they liked'.[42]

This strongly suggests a young man under the influence of the months of syndicalist advocacy. He rapidly assumed the chairmanship of the Joint Strike Committee, which included Kessack, representing the Goole dockers for the NUDL. Significantly, Burn proposed that a regional committee of the NTWF be formed, independent of other bodies. This was taken to be a rebuff to Tillett's union, as well as to the Hull Trades Council, whose response to the strike had been cool. That Burn seized on the idea that the NTWF should be strike co-ordinator suggests that its role was seen much more in 'syndicalist' terms in the provincial ports than at the centre, where it remained low-key, if not exactly inert, until August and the London strike.

For a time the shipping lines, including C. H. and Arthur Wilson's, were able to get some ships away, with the aid of non-English-speaking and untrained crews. Even so, this usually meant defiance of Board of Trade regulations. Clerks and warehousemen continued to break the strike of the dockers. The Shipping Federation adopted postures and issued statements strongly reminiscent of 1893, and began to incur criticism from the press and from local traders. The owners claimed that, since the strike leaders were unofficial, no meeting with or recognition of them was possible.

Want and hunger amongst the strikers and their families became a threat to the solidarity of the strike: except in the seamen's case, no union strike-benefit was available to allay it. To aggravate matters, food prices rose, as supplies, most of which arrived by sea, were cut off. Charities made some contribution and the *Hull Daily Mail* ran a fund to relieve the suffering. The Strike Committee now sought to extend the strike, to increase pressure on the owners. One thousand lightermen came out and the railwaymen acted outside their union's authority to take sympathy action. Picketing was increased and became more effective. The scent of perishable cargoes rose over the port and flattened out on the city in the summer heat. It was estimated that some 300,000 pounds of rotting produce was held up by the strike.

Other ports throughout the country were settling: the absence of any gesture of conciliation from the shipowners in Hull led the Strike Committee – and the strikers spontaneously – to press for a general strike of the whole city. On 27 June thousands of strikers stormed a ship which was being unloaded by female stewards. Evidently the new Liverpool-based Ships' Stewards' Union had established no presence in Hull. From that moment the action became more directly violent and intimidatory. The strikers compelled a shut-down at Reckitt's factory, and flying pickets then quickly brought out the flour-millers, the timber-porters and the boiler-scalers at the Fish Dock. Daily police baton-charges became ritual. The constables were very busy: all traffic had to be escorted. This was not enough for the shipowners, who pressed the government to be more assiduous in its efforts at repression. The Home Office responded: 'Mr. Churchill is in telegraphic communication with the Mayor of Hull and has reminded him that it is his duty to maintain order and take adequate measures to secure the landing of perishable cargoes.'[43]

The Board of Trade finally stirred itself to break the impasse: George Askwith, the chief conciliator, set off for Hull armed with a concession from the Shipping Federation nationally. Some 'moderate' advance in wages, they now admitted, might be justified, although they would not concede recognition of the unions.

The scene which met him almost unnerved him: 'There was no doubt about the upheaval. Employers were greatly surprised by the developments. The strike-leaders were men unknown to them, the violence unexpected, and the strait-jacket attitude of the Shipping Federation rendered them quite inadequate to the task.'[44]

Askwith was able to achieve a series of concessions immediately. In the case of the seamen, whose strike was official and who had a national programme of demands to work to, wage increases were granted, the 'Federation ticket' was withdrawn, the medical examination modified and an arbitration procedure agreed. But no settlement was attempted in the whole complex of claims which had been voiced by the 'sympathy strikers' on and around the docks. In spite of this the Strike Committee endorsed the settlement. Askwith reported that the violence and desperation of the dock communities, aggravated by near-starvation, had petrified the local leadership of the committee. Yet it was surely predictable that violence might be provoked, rather than discouraged, when the shore-workers' grievances were denied a settlement. Failure to agree was announced to a crowd of 40,000 outside the Royal Station Hotel, where Askwith was staying.[45] The strike leaders' performance verged on the irresponsible. Kessack told the angry crowd to go back to work because the town's tradesmen faced ruin. He then begged them to think of the welfare of the country. Burn said that, as most strikers were unorganized, his committee could not advise them. Askwith wrote a classic report which many historians have chosen to symbolize the temper of the Great Unrest:

It was estimated that there were fifteen thousand people there when the leaders began their statement. They announced a settlement; and before my turn came, an angry roar of 'No!' rang out; and 'Let's fire the docks!' from the outskirts where men ran off. The crowd surged against the platform in a space below the hotel; women who had come to see the show shrieked with alarm . . . I heard a town councillor remark that he had been in Paris during the Commune and had never seen anything like this: the women were worse than anything he had ever seen, and he had not known there were such people in Hull – women with hair streaming and half nude, reeling through the streets, smashing and destroying.[46]

Although the docks were not fired that night, 2,000 dockers rampaged through them, wrecking the offices of Wilson's line, and the depot of the British Free Labour Association. They used paving slabs, wood, even gravestones; 1,300 policemen were mustered in baton-charges. The following day the shops were shuttered, the town crouched in fear. Five hundred men of the Metropolitan Police arrived, and more troops were deployed. In fact, as The Times reported, 'Hull is in far greater danger of famine than of mass violence'.[47] In comparison with the wild abandon of the police in Liverpool, the Hull authority's action was almost benign: only seventeen people received hospital treatment.

After a weekend's pause (Askwith sought peace at the seaside: he went to Bridlington), the Strike Committee and the conciliator did what they should have done initially: they held sectional negotiations for all groups on strike, and exacted concessions. First among these was a wage increase of a halfpenny an hour for the dockers. Work was then resumed on Tuesday, 4 July.

Although Askwith's famous account of events has been used to exemplify the general mood of the working class in 1911, there were in reality very specific causes for the frustrations and rage of the Hull dockers. On the employers' side, there was the embattled posture of the old warriors of the Shipping Federation, blind even to their own long-term interest. The vestiges of free-labour strength were particularly strong in Hull, whose union structures and loyalties had been so vitally enfeebled in the dismal years since the 1890s. Local disillusion with Tillett was particularly strong. Conciliatory unions had filled the vacuum for almost two decades. When the strike broke out, Mann was tied up in Liverpool and Tillett offered no leadership at all. On the contrary, he actually sought to discourage action. He was personally preoccupied with the pending London strike. In their absence, leadership devolved on inexperienced men who had organized relationships with neither the strikers nor with the national offices. At the crisis of the movement, these spokesmen lost their nerve. The only officer involved who had any experience of national union affairs was O'Connor Kessack, and he took after James Sexton rather than Tom Mann.

The Hull dockers were, in short, not well served by the unions or their leaders, and they won their own victory unaided by either. Skilled strategic and tactical leadership did not prevent violence in Liverpool, but there it was visited on a peaceful rally by an unprovoked police charge. In Hull, it was the workers who initiated the violence, in sheer frustration and despair. Belatedly, it won them a settlement which they could accept. Tillett's neglect of Hull came home to his union when, after the strike, John Burn was able with Kessack's help to form branches of the NUDL, in direct opposition to the DWRGWU. The lightermen, too, went their own way by forming a branch of the NSFU. Harry Orbell and James Anderson, for the NTWF, finally came to Hull, and worked to re-form Tillett's union and a regional federation. The DWRGWU benefited to the tune of 1,000 new members enrolled in July 1911, but the majority were now in the NUDL. Rivalry between them found a morbid expression outside the TUC conference hall that autumn, when Tillett and Kessack exchanged blows![48]

Apart from the NUDL, the other beneficiary of Tillett's weakness in Hull was the Gasworkers' and General Labourers' Union. It had, of course, held a position there since the 1880s. Its membership was always more stable, and it had not suffered catastrophic rout in the 1890s. At the beginning of the 1911 strikes, on 17 June, Will Thorne had spoken in Hull and offered mature counsel on the real possibilities for concerted action of the kind then under way in Liverpool: 'He spoke at length about the "mechanics" of a general strike of all transport workers, stressing the need for scientific organisation. It was this lack of organisation and permanence he said, which had made the Shipping Federation reluctant to negotiate . . . but now all workers must unite.'[49]

We have already seen that the gasworkers won over the specialist Hull fish-dockers, the 'bobbers', in the spring of 1911. Through July and August, coal-heavers, timber workers, cement workers and flour-millers, all of whom had been brought into the Hull strikes by the dockers' picketing, were represented not by the Dockers' Union but by local officials of the gasworkers. Their Hull district secretary, Councillor R. H. Farrah, had established himself on the City Council in the 1890s as a member of the 'progressive group' sponsored by the Trades Council. He won union recognition and a wage increase for each of these groups, despite the autocratic opposition of Joseph Rank, the largest mill-owner in the town.

What was at work in this complex process, of course, was a competition between separate new unions to recruit membership among the hitherto unorganized strikers. In Hull, Tillett's union was poorly placed, because of its past defeats and recent abstentionism. Its failing image was reinforced by the absence of its leaders at the critical time. Little progress came its way. The NTWF had, in principle, been formed to police the process of recruitment. A similar role was envisaged for the General Labourers' National Council. At this stage neither body was effective in preventing fragmentation. Enclaves of membership were thus built almost at random, and these perpetuated the divisions of the future general unions. The split between the NUDL and the DWRGWU was, of course, to be healed in 1922; but the seeds of distrust of national dockers' leaderships, so powerful in later twentieth-century history, were sown in part by the Hull dockers' experiences from 1893 to 1911.

## Strikes and Conciliation in Manchester

Lord Askwith had barely finished his work in Hull when he was summoned to Manchester. Here, the seamen's strike had also called down a dockers' stoppage on 27 June, which closed the Manchester Ship Canal docks. On 3 July all the city's carters had struck, not only those employed by the carting contractors but also those who worked for the railway companies. Manchester was thus gripped by a total transport strike. Eighteen unions were involved, and each was pledged not to return to work until the demands of all had been satisfied. Police were drafted in from Birmingham and troops were stationed in Salford. The Lord Mayor organized a vast conciliation operation, using every room in the Town Hall. Lord Askwith described the process:

> In every room . . . different trades were closeted, employers and employed, debating, discussing, and almost fighting. Hour by hour, and day by day, it was only possible to go from one to the other, get a dispute upon apparent lines of possible settlement, and then answer a hurried summons to another room to prevent a conference breaking up. For five days, for all the days and nearly all the nights these conferences proceeded, until at last, on Sunday night (July 9), all the trades had come to agreements except two, which would require the acceptance by the seamen of an arrangement slightly modified from one which the men had refused but their leaders seemed inclined to accept, and the consent of the Great Northern Railway Carters to go back to work without any change.[50]

By dint of persuasion, and the attrition tactics of an all-night session behind locked doors, Askwith won the consent of these two groups, and on 10 July the Manchester strikes were over.

They left behind a series of problems, some of which were spelt out by Will Hughes in Tom Mann's new Liverpool-based broadsheet, the *Transport Worker*. Assuming a regular magazine format, this represented great progress beyond the pocket-sized pamphlets of the *Industrial Syndicalist*. The front page bore two legends: 'Circulation 20,000' on one side, and, in capital letters, 'NON-POLITICAL' on the other. Non-political or not, the same front page of the first issue reported on a 'great French Labour Demonstration' under the title 'War Against War'. Unbelievably, Tom Mann had run over to Paris in the middle of the strike to participate in, and give his account of, an anti-war rally of the Confédération Générale du Travail. 'If the Transport Workers on land and sea actually refuse to carry or handle any material,' he wrote, 'government could no longer play at War.'

On Manchester affairs, its reports were severely practical: the United Carters' Union had gained 1,500 members and were exploring amalgamation with the Mersey Quay and Bolton Carters' Associations;

railway allegiances among carters and crane-drivers were complicating the task of rationalization of union structures; the dockers were

> going strong, they have increased their membership by over 100 per cent, making a membership of something like 3,500. This is extraordinary considering the short time since organising was started on a proper basis, viz., at the latter end of last October. Irma Dock is organised to a man. A new Branch has been opened for the Dry Dock Workers, and is doing well. Branches have been opened for Grain Workers and other allied industries.
>
> Practically every man has tumbled into the Branch for the Coal Tippers at Gartington; this, by the way is one of the sections of workers whose grievances were not tabulated in time for discussion before the settlement, but a definite promise has been made by the Ship Canal Company that these demands will be favourably dealt with under present negotiations. The Sailors and Firemen's Unions continue to make good progress.[51]

All this organizing, on the strength of the Manchester victories,

> has put new hopes for the future in the hearts of all the workers, including even the Foreman and Stevedore. Every man appears to be assuming the actions of a man, and now walks erect, I shouldn't wonder if the Death Rates are not reduced 25 per cent during the coming year, owing to the improved physique of the workers' walking attitude. They have at least realised that they have the right to live, and are becoming more determined to live by demanding the necessaries for giving that life.[52]

## The Most Dangerous Man . . .

Leaving Manchester in this high euphoria, Askwith managed to fit in an emergency dash to Leeds to settle – again at 2 a.m. – a strike of the city's tramwaymen, before hurrying on down to London to conciliate in the dock strike there. During that year he was here, there and everywhere. Ben Tillett has left a shrewd and perceptive picture of the man and his role, as observed in the London strike.

> Sir George Askwith, the patient plodding man, with pigeon-holes in his brains; who listened without sign of being bored or absorbed, who concealed his mind like a Chinaman. Emotionless, except that he would peer through his glasses at someone making a statement of moment, never raising his diplomatic voice, or appearing to hurry over anything; guiding without falter or apparent effort the disputants however heated they may be, himself the inscrutable, patient listener. And such patience! It was more than dour in its persistence and calmness; it compelled by its coldness, and saved us from bickerings on occasions when the wisest become puny and spiteful.

He is the most dangerous man in the country. His diplomacy is and will be worse than war. Unless it absolutely succeeds in forcing industrial combatants to appreciate the human oneness of the community it will be a danger, inasmuch as it will make with its great genius for a peace that after all will be artificial.

There is no real peace for the toilers so long as the wage system exists. Men like Askwith might make the more supine and ignorant believe there can be peace without paying the price of war.[53]

Harry Gosling also recalled Askwith's methods: 'He always seemed to be waiting until nobody could think of another word to say and then he would come in . . . but he never decided for you. You always found you had decided for yourselves and he had merely counter-signed your own decision.'[54]

Askwith also seems to have been the originator of the 'smoke-filled room': 'he was more responsible than any other man', said Gosling, 'for introducing smoking at gatherings of this kind.'[55]

## South Wales Catches On

The strikes which erupted in the complex of the South Wales ports were also detonated by the seamen's strike. In common with other ports, they received no coherent and official directives from either the NTWF or the DWRGWU. As a result, their responses were conditioned entirely by local trade-union resources, and by local leadership. The strikes which developed in the Cardiff docks exemplify the problems involved in a proliferation of sectional unions. This debility was never more evident than now, at a moment when port-wide solidarity was essential to success. When would it ever be more reasonable to call for sympathetic actions?

In Cardiff, the port's trade was dominated by coal, exports of which were booming. Two grades of dock workers, the tippers and the trimmers, constituted the key groupings in this trade. Each generated powerful loyalties and traditions. In the initial surge of new unionism during 1889–91, we saw that the trimmers had founded their own, exclusive union, based on tight control of labour supply and a closed, craft outlook (see chapter 4). By 1911, this attitude had become so rigid that the union did not even seek membership of the NTWF. Its leadership was essentially 'moderate', greatly valuing its close relation-ships with the port employers and also with the coal-owners. A mutual dependence had come into being. The coal-tippers, less skilled than the trimmers but still an exclusive, elite band when compared with the general dock labourers, had originally joined the DWRGLU in 1890. But in 1898 they had broken away to join the ASRS, in an effort to win closer relations with the Cardiff Railway Company and to improve their security and status as regular workers. The railway owned the port and was also a principal port employer. The defection of the tippers left the Dockers' Union greatly weakened. Henceforth it had no members in strategically placed occupations, and organized only the general cargo-handlers. In addition, dock membership was shared with the NALU, a purely regional union (despite its title), which had an old-style rule book and upheld the customs of an earlier age.

When the seamen stopped work in Cardiff on 14 June 1911, these divisions on the waterfront threatened them with isolation. Not only was there no call from the NTWF for dock workers' sympathy strikes, but even if such an appeal had been made, both tippers and trimmers were outside its membership. Tillett was far from enthused about the prospects of a wider strike, viewing his base in South Wales in a proprietorial and defensive light. Soon he was sending instructions to his members in the region – for example in Swansea, where the dockers had struck on 23 June – for an immediate return to work. This was of a pattern with his response to the Hull strike. Both decisions reflected a preoccupation with the pending strike in the Port of London.

The chemistry in the provinces and principalities was powerful, however. In South Wales the same yeast was working as in all the other ports around the kingdom. Syndicalist evangelists were hard at work, especially encouraged in Wales by the response they had aroused in the Cambrian coal strike and the success of Houlder dock strike of the previous year. The *Industrial Syndicalist*'s 'List of Persons willing to speak as advocates of Industrial Syndicalism in their respective districts' included George Jackson of the Seamen's and Firemen's Union, as well as Alfred Cox and George Cox, both of the Dockers' Union, and all of Newport. Six persons from the South Wales Miners' Federation, including Noah Ablett, appeared in the same list, as well as Councillor Jonah Charles, of the Dockers' Union in Port Talbot (see plate 9).[56] Madame Sorgue made a tour of South Wales in June 1911 to reinforce local supporters; and Tom Mann was a recent visitor too, rounding the coast from port to port in preparation for the seamen's strike.

But as the seamen began their strike in Cardiff, the coal-tippers and trimmers continued working. Their action was a restraint, holding back any surge of solidarity action which might have flowed from the example of the sailors. Liverpool and Hull were not, it seemed, to be imitated. At one point, it seemed possible that the tippers would break loose of their own accord, in response to their own grievances. They had sought the same status as railwaymen, but their inclusion in the Conciliation Board established in 1907 had not been confirmed; moreover, they now entered a claim for a shorter working week. On the very verge of a strike which would have given the seamen their first backing, Jimmy Thomas hastened to Cardiff for the ASRS, obtained the tippers' admittance to the Conciliation Board and a concession over their hours. He succeeded in his goal of defusing their grievance. And, 'with the tippers apparently bought off, was it likely that those notorious moderates the trimmers would come out?'[57]

## Captain Bombast

One man who knew that drastic action was urgently needed, and was highly qualified by temperament to provoke it, was 'Captain' Edward Tupper, an extraordinary combination of bombast, flamboyance, racialism and alcoholism. He was the Seamen's Union organizer and moved from port to port throughout the year. He had been enrolled, a vigorous thirty-nine-year old, by the fifty-nine-year old, arthritic Havelock Wilson in 1910, specifically to assist in the planned strike and to act as Wilson's emissary. (He had a vague record as a speaker on Liberal Party platforms.)[58]

In early July 1911, Captain Tupper was hopping with frustration and anxiety because the Cardiff dockers' sympathy action had failed to materialize. He later recalled: 'I was getting desperate. Coal was thundering down hour after hour from the coal tips, into ships' holds and bunkers.'[59] On 3 July he proclaimed a general strike of the Bristol Channel ports, but nobody came out. Undaunted, he sustained the work of provocation.

> At his union meetings in Bute Street, Cardiff, he wore a morning coat and a silk top hat, drank large quantities of 'Bass', and frequently challenged Shipping Federation toughs and employers to box against him at the Neptune Park, Cardiff. On 17th July, Tupper issued a challenge to Mr. E. Handcock, a Cardiff tug-boat owner, to fight him for £50, and at the head of a large procession he marched to Handcock's office. The demonstration got out of hand, and coal and jack-knives were thrown through the company's windows. Tupper was arrested, served with sixteen summonses, and appeared at the City Hall the next day.
>
> His presence in court had a considerable effect upon industrial relations at Cardiff. Local members of the Dockers' Union, who until then had declined to strike . . . left work and were joined by workers from all sections of the port. The strikers also armed themselves, and soon many of them 'carried sticks and bludgeons; clubs with knife-blades and cut-throat razor blades set in the end, rope coshes with nails sticking out from the knots and plenty of weapons'. When the court decided to remand Tupper in custody, dockers and seamen stormed the City Hall, but were beaten back by large numbers of mounted and foot police. They retreated to the docks, stole barrels of stout and bottles of whisky from ships and warehouses, set fire to the Dublin and Liverpool warehouse, attacked the Glagow warehouse, and pushed a lorry into the dock. Further damage was prevented only by a fierce baton charge by the Cardiff constabulary. During this riot Tupper was in the cells at the City Hall . . . [he] was

released the next day on bail; according to him, the magistrates realised that he was the only person who could prevent more disorder.[60]

Tupper's incitement included blatant racism, as he attacked the Chinese labour which was being used to man one ship. Recalling this episode, Tupper himself was to write:

That same night Liverpool Chinamen were taken from a train in the village of Marshfield and put into cabs. We knew all about it, and ship's rope was stretched across the Newport road. I had strictly commanded that there was to be no violence, and there wasn't: but those Chinks, on their knees in the road, thought their last hour had come.

'No goee blackee-leg! Wanchee go Livelpool – one time! No goee blackee-leg! Bad men makee talk, send Chinamen in tlain allee-same on piecee. No can do!' There was a terrible screeching, all trying to appeal to me, the 'Serang' – the boss. 'Cardiffi-side no good. Wanchee go back Livelpool! Can do? I solly, solly, solly! Bad men makee talk . . .' We sent them back to Liverpool.[61]

Thus wrote the self-proclaimed 'King of the Bristol Channel', future acting general secretary of the Seamen's Union. This 'leadership' provoked racial attacks on Chinese laundries and shops in Cardiff, and the terrorized Chinese workers required police escorts to go about their business.

One eye-witness, Pat Murphy, a rank-and-file seamen's leader, recorded that

In Cardiff, there were seven ships needing crews but there was no response from the unemployed seamen crowding the street at the Merchant Shipping Office, most of whom were coloured. Captain Tupper, one of the leaders of the union, made a fighting speech appealing for determination, but he made some very nasty remarks about Chinese and Arabs, who had really stood firm with British seafarers . . . Tupper's racialist speech inflamed some men and caused bitter quarrels among the seamen, and agents spread rumours to inflame disunity.[62]

Racial prejudice was a weapon deployed not only by Captain Tupper: it was manifest in the speeches of Havelock Wilson.

After these 'Tupper Riots' the Cardiff dockers, trimmers and tippers now all came out in sympathy action. The last trimmers left work on 20 July, led by Tupper himself, flamboyant to the last, perched in front of the march-out on a bicycle, from which vantage-point he brandished a trimmer's outsize shovel like an emblem of battle. All were then joined by the tippers and trimmers in Barry and Port Talbot.

But there remained serious divisions between the dockers themselves at the different Welsh ports. At Swansea the dockers' unofficial strike in June had won a wage increase, and now they rejected the call for sympathy action with the seamen. The Cardiff seamen won major gains, and the Joint Strike Committee in the port accepted them as a settlement of the whole dispute, just as they had in Hull. This committee included in its ranks the railwaymen's Jimmy Thomas, representing those tippers who were members of the ASRS, and also Ernest Bevin, newly appointed as a Dockers' Union official in Bristol and now seconded to represent the dock labourers' cause in Cardiff. He chaired a meeting of 40,000 in the city. Tupper represented the seamen, and there were representatives of the coal trimmers and of NALU. Bevin was the only member to oppose both the settlement and the return to work; his members had gained nothing from the Cardiff Railway Company. The seamen won a new, fixed port rate, union recognition and a Conciliation Board. These gains were undoubtedly attributable to the support finally given by the dock workers. The Strike Committee had initially resolved: 'That we recommend the men now on strike at Cardiff to remain out until settlement is arrived at affecting every section of workers involved . . . the full settlement to be submitted to a full conference for confirmation. Any section violating this will be repudiated.'[63]

Following the seamen's triumph, the Strike Committee had presented the employers with the dockers' demands – union recognition, no victimization and a prompt meeting to negotiate their grievances. The Cardiff Railway Company set its face against recognition of the Dockers' Union and promised the tippers no more than that they would be treated like other 'railway servants'. The seamen had settled; and the committee, despite Bevin's strong objections, ended the strike on these terms. The Dockers' Union received no reciprocal sympathy support to help break the hostility of the Cardiff Railway Company.

A second, unofficial strike against the Railway Company took place in August, but again failed in its object to win recognition or a bargain over wages. Dockers employed by other companies in the ports, however, won recognition in the July settlement, together with preference of employment. On this base, the union was able to re-establish itself in the port, although no standard port rate was achievable against the intransigence of the Railway Company. Divided rule in the Strike Committee, and the reassertion of sectional interests, produced an untidy and debilitating settlement. Bevin replied to his members' criticisms: 'He denied absolutely that he was a guilty person in bringing about that particularly unsatisfactory settlement. His last appeal in the conference room was to hold out for the sake of his men . . . but he found that he did not succeed so he shut up.'[64] For the young and aspiring Bevin, it was a salutary lesson on the evils of sectionalism.

The fragmentation of the workforce was perpetuated down to the First World War. Tippers had been embraced in the Railways' Conciliation machinery, and remained in the ASRS; the trimmers returned to their isolation, rejecting the renewed overtures of the NTWF. The Dockers'

Union had re-established a presence in the port, but faced the sustained opposition of the Railway Company. Much more could have been won with a united leadership. Less opportunism would have been a welcome asset, too. The dockers clearly felt that they had been exploited by the seamen. It is difficult not to hold Tupper personally responsible for this result.

The union in Newport was stronger, even before the events of 1911. It had a more radical tradition, and had been blooded in the Houlders dispute of 1910, which was still festering. However, Newport men faced employers of a less hostile temper than the Cardiff Railway Company. The strikers looked to the whole Bristol Channel to hold out for an estuarial agreement. They rounded on the Cardiff men's unilateral settlement, which 'sold their neighbours',[65] and they resolved to fight on alone. On 31 July, the Newport Employers' Committee concluded a settlement which gave preference to union workers and substantial wage gains. A comparison of the wages of different grades of docker at the three main South Wales ports after all the settlements shows that at Cardiff, rates were consistently 2–3s. per week less than at Swansea and Newport.[66]

As a final act, the Newport dockers sought to use their strength to resolve the long-standing dispute with Houlder, and to compel him to revert to the piece-work system. A blacking campaign, significantly supported by the NTWF, extracted a wage increase and other concessions from the company, which satisfied both the NTWF and the Newport Strike Committee. But the dockers were appalled by the company's insistence that its long-serving blacklegs should be allowed into their union, with the same rights of preference, as part of the settlement. Alf Cox, who had been up in Belfast, was summoned by the men to resume his unofficial leadership of the conflict. The Executive of the NTWF condemned the men and withdrew all further support. Cox summoned a mass meeting and formed an Emergency Advisory Committee. Among his colleagues and helpmeets was the seaman and fellow syndicalist Percy Knight. Their renewed leadership over the men was to be sorely tested in the following year.

## Action in Bristol . . .

In Bristol, as we have seen, the dockers' exercise of rank-and-file solidarity in the 1910 Houlders dispute had anticipated the great unrest by a year. In that conflict, conducted on behalf of the Newport men, the Bristol dockers had demonstrated great solidarity. They had been backed up by rail and engineering grades in the port. Tillett had sought to restrain the men, and this highlighted the fact that 'there had long been an under-current of rank-and-file discontent with the moderation of the

Dockers' leadership'.[67] The strike of 1910 had already stimulated union growth in other sections of Bristol labour, notably amongst the carters, whose branch chairman was Ernest Bevin.

The initial impact of the seamen's dispute on the Bristol dockers was minimal: the few Bristol-based shipping companies made early settlements in June 1911, and the limited solidarity actions by dockers on their behalf, and in support of a carters' agreement, were shortlived. A spark from a different source fired an explosive strike of Bristol dockers in August. Without union endorsement, they struck solidly in support of the railwaymen, at first in connection with a local dispute and then in sympathy with the national rail strike. The dockers, following the pattern almost everywhere, then drew up their own programme of demands and called out the carters for good measure. Soon 6,000 men were on strike, in addition to the railmen. Some factories, and even two adjacent collieries, downed tools against union advice. The army appeared (what a familiar scene this had become in Britain's ports by August!) and fired over a crowd's heads to disperse them.

The railway strike was settled in days, however, and the dockers returned to work in comparative peace and good order to await the terms of a Joint Conciliation Committee. Union recognition was accorded to the Dockers' Union, victimization was ruled out and wage rates were increased by a halfpenny, to 7d. an hour, with night rates up a penny to 10d. Uncomplicated by association with the seamen's strike, which was resolved before they acted, or by serious inter-union differences or fragmentation, the Bristol dockers and carters had a relatively straight furrow to plough through the year: their victory 'marked the high water mark of the Dockers' achievements in [pre-war] Bristol.'[68] By 1914 their union had established a virtual monopoly of all port labour and was organizing in brickyards and widening its appeal to the carters. In contrast to Hull, the Dockers' Union moved into these new fields at a moment when the Gasworkers' Union in Bristol was dwindling to 'a pale shadow of the Dockers'.[69]

### . . . and in Glasgow

In Glasgow, the seamen appealed to the Trades Council for assistance as soon as their strike got under way on 14 June. A young, militant Co-operative mill-worker (he found the work very dull) was sent by the Council to render support on the Clyde waterfront.[70] In this way, Emanuel Shinwell enters the story of transport unionism for the first, but by no means the last, time. To begin with, he worked voluntarily for the strikers, in the evenings and for two holiday weeks. The Clyde, he reminds us, along with Southampton and Liverpool, was one of the centres of the passenger-liner trade, shipping out thousands of emigrants to Australia, Canada and the USA. Seamen earned £4 a month, firemen £4 10s. They now demanded an increase of £1 a month for both grades. The dockers, by now organized in the Scottish Union of Dock Labourers, their breakaway from the NUDL (see chapter 4), came out in sympathy. Shinwell became involved with them too, addressing their meetings not only on the Clyde but in Leith and Dundee besides.

According to Shinwell, the Glasgow liner companies included amongst their directors some powerful figures who were prepared to be conciliatory, and the sums demanded by the NSFU locally were soon conceded. But Havelock Wilson had made an accord with the Shipping Federation accepting 10s. less, in return for a union monopoly of labour supply. This account is not unique.[71] Wilson's sights were set on winning recognition, and he was prepared to pay the price, in terms both of moderation in wage settlements and in transforming his union into an agent of industrial discipline. In Southampton this had already led to the breakaway of the NSFU branch to form the British Seafarers' Union, an episode which was to cast a long shadow, darkening Ernest Bevin's desk at Transport House in the early years of the TGWU (see vol. II). There is further evidence available of the evolution of Wilson's methods away from militancy and towards a material intimacy with the shipowners: several of the most prominent magnates were present at the union's annual dinner after the 1911 strikes. Captain Tupper tells the story of this bizarre change in his fortunes with evident satisfaction:

> Many of the leading shipowners were invited to the annual dinner of the union, held at the Holborn Restaurant. Havelock Wilson, of course, was in the chair, and amongst us of the Union was the Rev. Father Hopkins, that famous Calcutta Seamen's padre, who had fought valiantly in the fight just won. Havelock Wilson said that the Union did not desire unnecessary trouble in any direction. He declared that, after his experience of the mercantile marine, he would say that he did not believe shipowners had had real value for the money they had paid out – that over twenty-five per cent of the men in the mercantile marine, Asiatics of all kinds, were not fit for the job . . . In replying to the toast of 'The Shipping Industry', Sir Walter Runciman . . . said they had just emerged from one of the most bitter fights – a well-conducted one – that had taken place in his time . . . he did not believe that there was a shipowner present or absent who was not glad of the rise in wages.[72]

The arrangement of such convivial encounters set in thereafter as a standard practice.[73]

In the Glasgow episode, two of Wilson's assistants arrived with the intention of closing down the seamen's branch because it had obtained the higher rate of wage increase. The two were none other than Richard McGhee, now a Nationalist MP for an Irish constituency, and Captain Tupper. Here was a supreme irony: the veteran co-founder of the NUDL in harness with the demagogue of Cardiff, invested with the task of negotiating a wage reduction and the closure of a union branch! The seamen responded by forming the Scottish Seamen's Union, and in 1912 this breakaway merged with its Southampton counterpart to form the British Seafarers' Union.

Meanwhile, the dockers of Glasgow, who had won a wage increase after striking for only eight days, solicited Shinwell's services as their secretary, a post which he declined in favour of the secretaryship of the new seamen's union. This appointment was no sinecure. Neither was it free from hazard. In recalling the temper of this period on the Clyde, Shinwell claims that he was once fired on at a meeting by one of Wilson's hired men, 'with the result that the person standing next to me was killed'.[74] The Scottish Union of Dock Labourers put an end to its own isolation from the rest of dockland by affiliating to the NTWF in February 1912.

## . . . and London Follows On

It is time to turn to the drama on the Thames, where there had been no immediate mass dock strike upon the declaration of the seamen's strike in June. This pause gave Tillett and the other leaders of the NTWF, whose National Executive was dominated by the London waterfront unions, the opportunity to work out a strategy for the coming movement and to present agreed common demands, in the name of the NTWF, to the London employers. In this way they were assured of the leadership of the new upsurge. A public meeting in April in Canning Town had already pledged all port unions to support the simple and long-cherished demand for a 'port rate' of 8d. an hour, 1s. overtime and regular call-times. At the end of June these demands were presented by the NTWF to the PLA, the shipowners and the wharfingers.

Of course, by this time the provincial strikes were well under way (despite Tillett's various efforts at discouragement) and some had even been favourably settled. Tillett claimed that the period of restraint in London was attributable to union and NTWF discipline. This seems a bold claim when set against the fact that, at the outset of the unrest, less than 50 per cent of all types of waterfront workers on the Thames were trade-union members, Tillett's own union being, as we already know, particularly weak. The level of organization had not been greatly improved by the recruitment drive in the months since the formation of the NTWF. When it came, the London dockers' militancy and solidarity were as formidable as elsewhere. The tardiness of their action is nevertheless curious. Tillett himself, although in 1911 wholly engaged with the cause of London, admitted that 'it may be said with safety and due regard to truth that there would not have been a London movement but for the provincial Transport Workers' agitation . . . In nearly all the important ports the movement had progressed with great strides, forcing recognition of trade unions, better conditions of labour, improved rates of pay, and a healthier outlook.'[75] In using capital letters to designate the transport workers in that passage, Tillett was claiming for the NTWF an initiating role which it did not in fact play. (Tillett himself was, we have seen, actually discouraging provincial strikes.) On 27 June it had threatened 'drastic action'. At its executive meeting on 3 July it decided against any kind of national call and, as we know, each port followed its own methods in responding to wave after wave of unco-ordinated strikes.

In London the sequence of events was quite different, with the initiative for a crucial early period in the hands of Tillett. He used it, on the day after the NTWF ultimatum, to dispatch the concerted London demands to the PLA, the shipowners, the wharfingers and the granary-keepers. Uncertain, despite abundant evidence from the provinces, of the temper of his own men, he together with Gosling, the NTWF chairman, and the rest of the Joint Committee nevertheless set a deadline for an employers' response: 3 July, the date chosen by the NTWF for its call for national sympathy action. The Lightermen's Society put in a separate claim, so seamen, dockers and lightermen converged in claims on the London employers. At this point, the employers undoubtedly contributed to the men's decision to hold their hand when, in an unprecedented response, they offered to meet the NTWF committee and discuss its claims. The employers were clearly alarmed by the mass strikes in the provinces. The NTWF then cancelled its plans for a sympathy strike – evidence that its preoccupation was with London. The provincial dockers, whose actions had clearly prompted the London employers' unprecedented readiness to deal, were left without a framework of national support.

For all that, the negotiations in London between the groups of employers led by the PLA, and the NTWF, were the first occasion when something like modern collective bargaining took place in the port, unaccompanied by mediators from outside the industry. In London at least, the NTWF was working. Apart from the PLA, the employers' side included at first the Shipping Federation, the Wharfingers', the Granary Keepers', the Master-Lightermen's, and the Short-Sea Traders' Unions. However, the short-sea traders withdrew from the negotiations, and this had important effects on the course of the subsequent strike and settlements. In their absence it was impossible fully to achieve the goal of a single port rate. Nevertheless, the two sides concluded the Devonport Agreement, named after Lord Devonport, chairman of the PLA. Under its terms, those dockers on 6d. and 8d. got an increase of 1d. an hour on both normal and overtime rates, whilst those already on 7d. and 9d. were to receive 8d. and 1s. Clearly the 'port rate' had not been achieved, and several grades of dockers, including those in the short-sea trades, won nothing. Yet to the negotiators it must have seemed incredible: a wage increase had been negotiated without a strike, after twenty-odd years of trade-union stagnation. The conduct of the negotiations, as recorded by Tillett, had some of the hallmarks of today's collective bargaining, with the unions deploying arguments based on productivity improvements, manning scales and the cost of living. But although they had won some wage increases, no progress was made on union control of hiring, or on the wage claims of many specialist groups, including tugboatmen and coalies.

Now, however, Tillett, Gosling and Will Thorne were to be ambushed by unambiguous evidence of the temper of the men: at a mass meeting on 28 June, their presentation of the Devonport terms was howled down. Tillett recorded that 'Only respect for the Chair and platform prevented a violent antagonism.'[76]

Tillett claimed that the negotiators would not have settled for the Devonport Agreement 'had that spontaneous outburst been given a month earlier [for] it would have been of incalculable value to us. Although we battled with all the courage, persistence, and brains we were capable of, we realized the apparent weakness of our own side'.[77] The contrast between Havelock Wilson's frontal attack – adventurous, officially led from the centre – and the caution of Tillett (and Gosling) could not be sharper. Of course Wilson's militancy, whilst fierce and even unscrupulous, was highly ambiguous. It enabled him first to control his union and then to lead it into the uniquely compromised relationship with the shipping magnates which we have described above. The challenge to Wilson's leadership came only at the edges, in Glasgow and Southampton. Here on the docks the NTWF leaders were given no such latitude. They were ignominiously sent back from the mass meeting, and told to negotiate better terms with Lord Devonport's committee. But the employers would not amend a line of the agreement. Now at last, six weeks behind the provinces, a general port stoppage was inevitable.

The coalies, excluded from the deal, began it on 29 July. Others whose claims were unsettled followed: they were absolutely not prepared to await the results of the proffered arbitration. Gosling and Orbell made one last effort to restrain them, but on 2 August, at a further mass meeting, the leadership caved in, accepting the plain fact that the Devonport 'agreement' was not enough and was not going to be 'agreed'. An official port strike was called. Immediately the lightermen came in with their own demand for a ten-hour day. On 3 August the Port of London stopped. An awe-inspiring collision, this was 1889 revisited, and Tillett did a rapid about-face to claim the leadership of the conflict. The employers were indignant: how was collective bargaining to be conducted in good faith with such a leader? Why, had he not sanctioned the strike's commencement for the very day that Sir Albert Rollitt had been due to perform his official function as arbitrator over the key issue of the port rate, referred to him under the Devonport Agreement?[78] Tillett had displayed great caution, and evidently wished to establish stable permanent-bargaining structures, but the men were urging him to wage intransigent battle instead. He heard them. And he went with them.

The strike had all the colour of its great forerunner, with its marches, rallies and mass meetings on Tower Hill and in Trafalgar Square. But it had a momentum of its own, not determined by leaders but driven forward from demand to demand by the force of the strikers themselves, and by their will that no section should be deserted before a settlement was reached for all of them.

The 1911 strike was different also in that each grade and group acted on its own behalf, and in tune with its separate unions' aspirations, whilst consenting to federal presentation of their case in negotiations. In addition to dock labourers, the lightermen, tugboatmen, ship repairers, sail-bargemen, coalies, carters and stevedores all entered the struggle, wave after wave, each union with its own demands. For the leaders and negotiators, this made a moving and constantly changing picture; consequently, as they sought agreement for one group and at one level of compromise, they found that the impetus had moved on, or that the minimum acceptable terms had increased.

This shifting pattern brought out the contradictory sides of Tillett's leadership and personality. On the one hand, he sought pacific, negotiated settlement. On the other, as always, he was caught up in the mood of the men and driven by his always passionate engagement with the deprivation and suffering of the dock community. He was also excited by the demonstration of the enormous, if negative, power which this overwhelming refusal of labour services meant for London. The capital ran short of food. Perishable cargoes turned rancid, green with mould or infested with flies and vermin in the hot-houses which warehouses and ships became in the heat of the summer. Ice could not be produced to cool the unmoveable wares, as no coal was carried to drive refrigeration plant. As in other ports, the Strike Committee issued permits to ensure essential supplies to hospitals and orphanages. Without such protection, nothing else moved. The general effect was dramatic, and Tillett basked in that drama, enjoying every nuance of its symbolism:

> The number of meetings was increasing, the enthusiasm was spreading, excitement was rising high, there were skirmishes with the police; frantic, panic-stricken officialdom bungling their functions and powers. The Transport Workers' fingers were for the time being on the throat of trade. What a contrast between the squealing, struggling capitalist and well-to-do class, who squirmed and shrieked as they shouted 'Famine!' 'Famine!' and the year-round silent suffering of the 52 per cent of our number who are more or less constantly fighting and facing the grim devils of hunger, misery and death. For a moment the great British public had brains and conscience, not that it cared so much for the hundreds of thousands of our

class, who had endured for months and years and decades and generations, but the public's stomach was being pinched, and there was a wolf-howl as it snarled its hate of possible hunger.[79]

And Tillett undoubtedly meant to preach this lesson more widely to workers who, for so long, had incurred his displeasure for their passivity and fecklessness: 'I want to say that the workers should for ever remember that their hands are on the throat of trade and industry at all times . . . they have only to use their power . . . to bring the whole activities of civilisation to an abrupt standstill'.[80]

The condition of the carmen moved him more than most: at the end, their massive strike, which was the making of carters' unionism in London, won the magnificent victory of a ten-hour reduction in their working week – to a new standard week of seventy-two hours!

In the midst of this turbulence fell the decision of the Rollitt arbitration. He awarded the full claim of 8d. and 1s. to the dockers employed by overseas shipowners and contractors. Nothing moved, none the less. The strike rolled on: the NTWF told all to stay out until every sectional claim was satisfied. The strikes of carmen actually gathered force after the Rollitt award, paralysing all street traffic. Other specialist dock grades joined in even at this late stage. In all, the Strike Committee, assisted by the tireless and dispassionate Askwith as conciliator, made nine separate agreements. Some were so complex that their final details were still being settled in September, long after the dispute was over. Askwith recalled one such agreement, for the sail-barge crews of the Thames, Medway, Sittingbourne and Faversham. The men had gone back to work on the understanding that the new rates would be back-dated to 21 August, the date their strike was called off. The new rates had to cover every class of cargo: 'The completed list contained about 600 items, with rates for cement, lime, bricks, clay, coal, coke, corn and grain, ballast, timber, wood-pulp, manure, flints, oil, and a number of miscellaneous items.'[81] Such were the minutiae, essential matters for the bargemen concerned, of the great upheaval in the Thames.

Around this tortuous and exhausting process of meetings, the lobbying and political pressures swung to and fro. Winston Churchill at the Home Office resisted the mounting demands of merchants, anxious for their cargoes and their businesses, and of the West End, anxious for its stomach, to put soldiers in to move the cargoes. (There was no need to send them in to break picket lines, as there were none. There were no strike-breakers on hand to be dissuaded.) John Burns, as the minister responsible for local government in this Liberal government, met and dealt with his old comrade of 1889. Tillett was not hostile: 'Although the dock agitator was now a Cabinet Minister, he really forgot that at times.'[82]

As the strike extended in scope and duration, so did its organizational reach. By mid-August the London membership of the Dockers' Union had risen from 2,000 to 22,000, and its branches from 14 to 49. The Stevedores' Union grew from 4,000 to 8,000.[83]

The main sectional deals were completed in four hectic days at the Board of Trade, between 8 and 11 August. They covered lightermen, sail-bargemen, carmen, coal-porters. The NTWF and the employers' associations were the signatories. The lightermen alone signed as a separate union. Askwith countersigned them all.

It might have been expected that, following these agreements, which all conceded much on wages, hours and conditions, the strike would at last be over. But in fact no return to work was possible. The PLA refused reinstatement to 3,000 labourers, and the NTWF supported a renewed protest strike of the PLA men, who were also incensed by a second grievance: the PLA alone would not concede the mealtime payment which had been negotiated. (These irritants can be seen in hindsight as portents of Lord Devonport's intransigent behaviour in 1912.) A second set of problems attended the return to work, for the men now eagerly sought to impose union control over hiring. They struck again at the Royal Docks when the call-on continued inside the dock gates, where the union could not control it. Again the NTWF endorsed the men's spontaneous strike – it is noticeable how much more readily the leadership responded to rank-and-file initiative as the year's experience changed its perceptions of what was possible and what was prudent.

The government viewed the prospects in mid-August with renewed alarm. The upheaval in the Port of London had defied every concession and still raged on; Liverpool had now erupted in a general strike, and a national rail strike was in the offing. Whilst the government was prevailing on the railway companies to conciliate, the Home Office also leant on the London port employers: the shipowners were to concede that the call-on should take place outside the dock gates, although the master-lightermen refused an equivalent concession. The men at the short-sea trades had also been excluded from previous settlements, and the variations in the rates they earned from different groups of employers was a classic example of the general case for a port rate for all dockers. In a final effort to achieve a total resumption of work, short-sea-trade men with this outstanding grievance were induced to go back whilst an arbitrator dealt with their case. When he did, in October, he found against the men. The strike, which came to an end for this group only on 31 August, could not be immediately revived; but the decision added provocation to the untidy muddle of sectional settlements which complicated port wage structures. It was to mark a pause in, not a resolution of, the pre-war struggles of the London dockers.

## III

## *The Effect of the Transport Strikes*

What was the sum effect of the 1911 strikes in transport? How did it influence the argument for amalgamation? The scale of the unrest was enormous; the number of workers involved in stoppages during the year was almost 1 million, and the number of working days lost more than 10 million. Nothing remotely like this had happened since 1893. Now, as then, the majority of strikers were port and transport workers. (As many as 80,000 workers were involved in a series of shipbuilding and engineering strikes, and 4 million days were lost in the coal industry.) Excluding the railway strikers, some 120,000 transport workers – seamen, dockers and carters – had been involved in the stoppages.

The effect on union membership was dramatic and immediate (see table 10.2). The main port unions' figures doubled or trebled, compared with an increase – spectacular enough itself – for all trade unions in the same year of 22 per cent, from 2,565,000 in 1910 to 3,139,000 in 1911.

Table 10.2   *Membership of Waterfront Unions, 1911–1912*

|      | NSFU | DWRGWU | NUDL | Stevedores (London) | Lightermen (London) |
|------|------|--------|------|---------------------|---------------------|
| 1911 | 20,000 | 20,000 | 12,000 | 4,000 | 3,000 |
| 1912 | 60,000 | 50,000 | 24,000 | 8,000 | 6,761 |

*Source:* TUC Reports

The annual accounts of the NUDL tell of the impact of the year. Contribution income doubled to £2,475. Expenditure on strike pay had been reported as only £921 in 1907, the year of the Belfast strike, even though James Sexton had claimed in the union's Annual Report to have spent £7,000. It fell to £565 in 1908, £147 in 1909 and a mere 12s. in 1910. But it was £10,886 in 1911. At the same time, the union increased its expenditure on officers' salaries by £1,300 to £3,915. Although his finances were modestly improved by the merger with the Liverpool North End Coal Heavers' Society, which brought £536 9s. 9d. into the coffers, the parsimonious Sexton actually ran down the capital account by £4,462 to finance the strikes.

The real membership of the union at the year end is in some doubt. In table 10.2 we have used the figures of membership affiliated to the TUC, but the union's Annual Report gives its membership at the year end as 'something like 50,000'.[84] Of Liverpool, Sexton writes: 'Suddenly, like a bolt from the blue came the dispute of last July . . . with the result that before the end of August, it might be truly said that there was scarcely a man, either seeking work or employed at the Docks, who was not a member of our organisation.'[85] And he confesses, 'We entered upon that dispute with a feeling of anything but hope, owing to past experience . . . We were very soon convinced . . . that our analysis of the new spirit was not the right one . . . The change, when we come to consider it, is simply marvellous.'[86] Thomas Hutchcroft, branch secretary in Goole, reported that, although the maximum number of dockers did not exceed 1,200, the union ended the year with 1,550 members, the balance being made up of gasworkers and general labourers, who came in after the strike. In Ireland the union 'still seems to lag behind . . . At the present time we occupy the same position only as last year'.[87]

After the strike, Sexton set about establishing greater central control over the funds, attacking the 'out-of-date method of all branches maintaining their own funds'.[88] At the same time, he sought to generalize the new practice in Scotland and Hull of creating District Committees.

Tillett's Annual Report also records the advances of the year, but is less than comprehensive in its accounts of the strikes. Whilst it celebrates the great gains of the London dispute, it refers only to 'a very prolonged lock-out of the dry dock workers in Barry and Cardiff', amongst all the other provincial strikes. Bristol increased its income by £2,000, Cardiff by four times to £1,244, and London from £554 to £6,753. All round the southern and eastern districts, the Report records the renewal of union membership and life, from East Anglia to Plymouth. All districts, except Barry, Hull and Workington, had comfortable excesses of income over expenditure. Of Hull we learn that 'against many difficulties, we succeeded in increasing income . . . from £64 2s. 3d. to £298 0s. 3d. The expenditure was £457 11s. 10d., being £159 11s. 7d. in excess of the income'.[89]

In total, the DWRGWU spent £3,643 on dispute pay. Of this sum, no less than £1,474 was expended in supporting the locked-out members in the Barry dry-dock. (This was an obscure affair, but a lock-out no doubt left Tillett with no option but to finance his members.) In London the union dispensed a mere £656 on strike pay, in Port Talbot £590, in Swansea £511, in Hull £136, in Bristol £66 and in Cardiff £3 10s.

Tillett, despite his ostensible militancy, by refusing to sanction so many of the provincial disputes had spent less than one-third of the sum laid out by his rival, the prudent Sexton. The NUDL's active role in the Humber ports that summer cost Tillett the bulk of those dock members who might have been expected to return to him, as Hull's old hero of 1889–90. Memories proved shorter, going back only to the sad manoeuvres and retreats of 1893. In any event, it was not the record of olden times, but the impact of present activities which brought Hull dockers home to a different union.

The carters in the main ports all took part in the upsurge of trade unionism. Following their participation in the strikes, many flocked to enrol themselves on the union books. Some substantial improvements in terms and conditions were gained. At this time, carters were principally organized in their own specialized unions, the main exception being Bristol, where Bevin brought them into the Dockers' Union. The principal unions present in the ports in 1911 were: the Mersey Quay and Railway Carters' Union in Liverpool; the Amalgamated Carters' and Motormen's Association in Manchester; the London Carmen's Trade Union in London; and the Scottish Horse and Motormen's Association in Glasgow. Their membership performance at this time is shown in table 10.3.

Table 10.3  *Membership of Road Transport Unions, 1911–1913*

|  | 1911 | 1912 | 1913 |
|---|---|---|---|
| Carters and Lurrymen (Bolton)* | 3,000 | 3,000 | 3,000 |
| London Carmen's Union† | 4,980 | 8,000 | 4,000 |
| United Carters' Association (Manchester)‡ | 3,000 | 5,000 | 5,000 |
| Amalgamated Association of Tramway and Vehicle Workers (Manchester)** | 18,000 | 21,000 | 21,000 |

*Joined the NTWF in 1917 and the TGWU in 1922.
†Changed its name from London Carmen's Union to National Union of Vehicle Workers in 1913. Sam March continued as its secretary. Joined TGWU in 1922.
‡Became the United Road Transport Union (URTU).
**Though Manchester-based, took over the London Tramway Employees' Association in 1904 and so had national status. Affiliated to NTWF in 1916. In 1919 joined with the London and Provincial Licensed Vehicle Workers' Union to form the United Vehicle Workers' Union, which joined the TGWU in 1922.

*Source:* TUC Annual Reports, 1911–13.

Hugh Clegg rightly concludes that the actions in which these bodies became engaged were 'a series of organisation strikes, such as had also occurred in 1871–4' and again in 1889, and were to break out yet again in the United States and France during the 1930s. 'Such a series', he writes,

> begins either with rapid recruitment into trade unions in industries where unions have hitherto been weak and unrecognised, or with spontaneous strikes leading to union recruitment . . . The employers are taken by surprise. Some concede quickly. Others resist, but they are ill-prepared . . . Most eventually yield. The new union members are confirmed in their support of their unions, and further recruits flock in. Other ill-organised groups . . . rally . . . and so on.[90]

All these unions benefited from their association with the wider transport strikes. They fitted easily into the strike committees and eventually into the NTWF's structures, being for the most part new and 'open' unions with strongly centralized constitutions, dominated by the full-time officers.[91]

We have acknowledged already the crucial role of the Seamen's Union in precipitating the strike-wave. Its own fortunes improved sharply. Membership, as well as the level of wages, increased proportionately. Militant action paid off. But we have also noted the roles of two distinctly shady characters, Hopkins and Tupper, in these battles: both were unscrupulous adventurers personally deployed by Wilson. At the same time, new patterns of collaboration were for the first time brought into being in Glasgow, Southampton and Manchester. We have noted evidence of the 'deal' which Wilson made at some point in the strikes, to settle for less than the official claim in return for closer relations with the shipowners. Similar reportage suggests dissent at this tactic also amongst the seamen of Goole.[92] Formal relations were quickly established. Before the year was out, Wilson was entertaining Sir Walter Runciman, an archetypal Edwardian Liberal, shipowner and member of the Shipping Federation. Runciman became president of the Board of Education, with a seat in the Cabinet, in 1908, at the same time that Winston Churchill joined him as president of the Board of Trade. Seeds of later bitter conflicts between Wilson and his contemporaries in the NTWF and the wider trade-union movement were sown, albeit discreetly, in the flush of the success which was due to his initial combativeness.

If these were the main components of the waterfront struggles, this port-by-port survey has drawn our attention to many smaller, local, sectional unions. The overwhelming evidence, at least as obvious to contemporaries as to historians, is that these divisions seriously impaired the process of bargaining, co-ordination of strikes and the achievements – in wages, conditions and union recognition – won in the settlements. Of course, 'it takes two to tango', and the other side of this coin is the evident fragmentation, or the complete absence of, employer organization capable of conducting mature, binding and constructive negotiations with the unions.

## The Role of the National Transport Workers' Federation

The young NTWF was intended to solve the problem of fragmentation on the union side. Undoubtedly, it had in this respect stepped out in front of the employers: contrary to some views of the evolution of British industrial relations, a study of the history of transport unionism strongly suggests that the innovators in collective bargaining were the unions. But in 1911 the NTWF was untried, and was top-heavy with London unions. Moreover, it had no regional structures. On top of this it was led by men who commonly looked back in apprehension to the 1890s, while they freely confessed that they had failed to read the mood of the men of 1911 correctly. The result of these impediments was that the NTWF's role in the strikes was minimal – with the important exception of London, where it assumed an advanced role not only as strike initiator and co-ordinator, but as a bargaining agent and signatory of agreements.

Impressed with their own achievements in the capital, NTWF leaders tended thereafter to claim far too much for the federal role in 1911. Gosling wrote:

> The 1911 transport workers' strike was the biggest, sharpest, and most successful dispute that had ever been known. The men had been absolutely loyal, which made it possible for us to get on with the negotiations without unnecessary distractions. The settlement was one quite without precedent, inasmuch as every section involved had obtained at least some concession . . . Of course the secret of it all was the federation ticket, which had cemented the men together as never before. It was their first real taste of solidarity . . .[93]

This claim may have substance in the case which Gosling is describing, the London strike. Elsewhere, however, solidarity actions were the order of the day, and the NTWF often played little part in them.

Nevertheless, the NTWF benefited greatly, both in reputation and in membership, from the actions of the year. In June 1911 it had an affiliated membership of 54,716. By April 1912 this had become 220,000. Up to February 1912, eleven new affiliations had been made.[94]

## Railwaymen and Dockers

The railwaymen touched the dock strikes at many places in 1911. In the ports of South Wales, the Humber and in Southampton, railway companies, as owners or part-owners of the quays, the cranes and the rail links to the dockside, employed many grades of dock labour. They ran carting services to and from the docks, and so were big employers of the carters. Frequently the railway companies offered a form of permanent, as opposed to casual, employment to their 'servants' in the ports. They practised the same paternalism as on the railways proper, and applied similar standards of discipline. The dockside railworkers were consequently induced to join railway unions, such as the ASRS and the Railway Clerks' Association. In Cardiff, we saw that the coal-tippers' membership of the ASRS told against their solidarity with the general-strike movement in that port. The ASRS, and from 1913 the NUR, never did enter the NTWF. Its chosen path was that of the 'one union, one industry' model. That industry was to be the railways, narrowly defined: not the transport industry seen inclusively. Regularly employed rail-company dock porters, carters, crane-men, maintenance-men, and lock-gate keepers, potentially key grades in a strike, were embarked on roads which diverged from those chosen by the general dock labourers. Shipping clerks, many of whom were unionized for the first time in 1911, joined the Railway Clerks' Association in the railway-owned ports but formed their own union in London. Later this was to adhere to the TGWU. The resultant divisions survived in the ports down to modern times.

Yet in 1911 the railmen's intimacy with docks and dockers was still strong enough to generate widespread sympathetic participation, unofficially, in a common struggle. The national rail strike itself had its origins in Liverpool, where Tom Mann's Strike Committee brought the city to a standstill on their behalf. Elsewhere, solidarity actions linking railway-men with port workers were common – almost as frequent as joint action between seamen and dockers. The chosen method of industrial unionism of the railways had not at that time frozen into rigid forms. Participation by the rail unions in the NTWF, and later the TGWU, was widely anticipated and would have enabled waterfront railway employees to build on the links made in 1911, just as the road transport men eventually did. This is one of many 'ifs' on the road to the general union's formation; similar speculation is provoked by the case of the seamen's unions. Road-, rail- and water-transport workers all focused their efforts around the dockside. In 1911 they made common cause in their actions, but they did not press forward to develop a common organization.

## Developing the NTWF

If the railwaymen stayed clear of the NTWF, those who had already moved to join forces in it did derive great benefit; and, indeed, they quickly learned from the experience.

In 1911, however, the leadership drew the appropriate lesson. Gosling told the TUC in September: 'I think it has now been made clear that we must now abandon every form of sectional strike and get the men into much larger federations. In this particular case [the London strike], we were able to drop the individual unions, and speak of the whole of the trades as a federation'.[95]

The Federation embarked on internal reforms. The provincial unions sought to end the London domination on the Executive and, in an important move, District Councils were set up, with financial assistance from the centre. This was a natural development arising from the experience of the *ad hoc* Joint Strike Committees of the summer, and indeed some DCs had been formed before the NEC's decision that they be established. Well designed for the co-ordination of industrial movements, such councils were also much better placed than the centre to adjudicate in poaching disputes and to issue a Federation ticket. They developed considerable autonomy, being enjoined only to 'consult' the NEC in any dispute which was 'likely to cause a national stoppage'.[96] It is significant that, of the present-day regional offices of the TGWU, five of the eleven – in Hull, Bristol, Liverpool, Glasgow and London – were chosen in 1911–12 as locations for Federation district headquarters.

## Bargaining, Conciliation and the State

The impact of the strikes on the development of collective bargaining was most advanced in Liverpool and London, where the White Book Agreement in the first case, and the Devonport Agreement in the second, represented the results of genuine bilateral bargains, the first of their kind. Even in these cases, however, the degree of union recognition involved and the permanence of the relationship were uncertain. Elsewhere (and in the later stages of the London dispute) the intervention of conciliators was often necessary to bring the antagonists to the bargaining table. For the port employers were reluctant, and nowhere more so than in London, to acknowledge that the days of free labour and the depot ship were almost over. In this respect, the changed attitude of the state was critical. The readiness of the administrations of the 1890s to smash picket lines and protect strike-breaking labour with police and troops was replaced by a new caution in the face of massed strikers. This undoubtedly had a profound effect on the outcome. In place of the cavalry – or in some cases, admittedly, in addition to the cavalry – the new response was: send George Askwith! The records of the Shipping Federation are revealing. Writing of the situation at the commencement of the 1911 strikes, its historian relates:

> Although the Federation was in a position to obtain the services of large bodies of men to replace strikers, the necessary protection for them could not be obtained.
>
> As an instance of 'the entire helplessness of the authorities', the Federation reported at the time that during the strikes in London the Federation's depot ship *Lady Jocelyn* lay in the Thames for some days with men on board ready to discharge cargo. Bodies of men were at the same time standing by in various parts of the country in readiness to proceed to London to work where required. The Home Office and police authorities, however, declined to allow the vessel to enter the docks, or to permit the

men who had been engaged to be brought into London. The machinery of the Federation for the supply of dock labour was thus rendered virtually inoperative . . . The records of the Federation at this period dwell repeatedly on the question of picketing. The outstanding feature of the strikes, it is reported, was undoubtedly 'the licence which from the commencement took the form of gross intimidation, which was assumed by union pickets under the Trades Disputes Act', coupled with the attitude of the central authorities which 'appeared to proceed upon the assumption that any attempt to replace men on strike must be regarded as a provocative act – practically justifying intimidation'.[97]

The Shipping Federation sent a deputation to Winston Churchill at the Home Office. He told them that the Trades Disputes Act 'did not directly countenance violence'. He said that he believed that pickets should be limited in number to those sufficient to convey information, and that they should wear a distinguishing badge. He sent a circular to police authorities affirming these points. Churchill, of course, had received a lot of adverse publicity following the action of the troops in Tonypandy, and he was clearly reluctant to add to this stigma by letting loose another bout of repression. Given that Sir Walter Runciman of the Federation was a Cabinet colleague, and that Lord Devonport, before his elevation to the peerage, had, as H. E. Kearley, been a government whip, this mild response to its protests must have shocked the die-hards of the Shipping Federation. John Burns's status in the government was an additional indication of the administration's adjustment to new realities. All this must have had something to do with the presence, after the settlement of the strike, of Walter Runciman at the union's dinner.

Askwith was himself more than just a pioneer of state conciliation. He had, with his evidence to a Select Committee, swung opinion round to the feasibility of the Trades Board system which Churchill, then at the Board of Trade, had introduced in 1909.[98] Further evidence of new forces and new faces at work on labour reforms is the introduction of William Beveridge, again by Churchill, to prepare plans for labour exchanges, aimed to tackle the problem of casual labour. Beveridge, who came from Toynbee Hall (a generation after Llewellyn Smith), was himself highly placed in the Board of Trade as Permanent Secretary. The Board's policy, shaped by these influences but also confirmed by the veritable avalanche of case material it dislodged in this period, was to promote union recognition and collective bargaining. Although they denied it, the 'practical', the pragmatic Smith, Askwith and the rest had clear departmental opinions, and in this represented a new engagement in Whitehall, alien to its older tradition of amateur, gentlemanly detachment. Right-wing Tories and industrial magnates regarded these officials as promoters of socialistic tendencies, while the left saw them as designing bureaucrats who were set upon seduction of the trade unions into a cosy, neutered relationship. The 'servile state' was much criticized not only in literary magazines but also among Labour activists. Trade-union leaders might share this suspicion but, given their own goals, could hardly afford to reject whatever help and support might be forthcoming from this quarter.[99] At the least, the days of thoroughgoing state support for unmitigated capitalist individualism were gone, not to return until the Conservative administrations of the 1980s.

Employers emerged from the experience of 1911 with varied reactions. In Liverpool, far-sighted big capitalists led the way in granting union recognition and control of labour supply. But they won, in return, commitments from the Dockers' Union, and from Sexton personally, to exert a new disciplinary control over the membership and to abide by collective agreements and agreed procedures. The pages of Sexton's Annual Reports in succeeding years are full of exhortation to this end:

> we are gradually getting back to the old spirit of discipline, with the new spirit of vigorous activity to help us on. For our one grave danger was to know how to use the NEW POWER we had gained by the enormous addition to our ranks. A Trades Union is the workman's industrial army, and no army can hope to enter upon a campaign with divided counsel. Its army regulations are the rules of the organisation, and are of such a democratic character that every member of the organisation can participate in the framing of them. But, having done so, they must be administered . . . by legitimately elected officers and committees . . .[100]

In other ports, resistance to change amongst employers was often stronger than in Liverpool, amongst both great employers, like the railway companies, and small. But even the carters' unions obtained three separate formal collective agreements during the year.

## New Leaders

The unions benefited not only from an influx of mass membership, but also from the emergence of a new generation of capable younger leaders. Some, like John Burn in Hull, were unknown before the strike, and held no office at all. Many such volunteers were needed quite quickly to fill new official posts. Others, like Bevin in Bristol and Milligan in Liverpool, through their intense participation in the 1911 struggles rose from voluntary positions as branch officials to become full-time officers and major influences at regional level. Others again, like the Cox brothers in South Wales, took up no formal appointments but continued as goads to local militancy and voices of discontent.

Ben Tillett, in his history of the strike, paid generous tribute to the activists in London. They included many of his own generation, together with important new faces. Amongst these he numbered J. B. Ruark, whose father had been 'one of the great characters of the 1889 strike', from the Stevedores' Union; Sam March, general secretary of the London Carmen's Union; George Grisley, representing the Cranemen and Enginemen, 'young, experienced, strong of limb, lung, and voice ... one feels glad that men as young as Grisley are to the front and helping to make history'; Frank Stillwell, financial clerk of the Dockers' Union, 'among the useful younger men'.[101] Two others selected for Tillett's praises were Bob Merry and John Davenport, the older and younger representatives of the United Order of General Labourers. Clearly a federal, all-union strike leadership had been achieved. And there was Fred Knee, the 'mighty atom', who along with Harry Quelch rendered help from the London Trades Council. Both of them, of course, were political comrades of Tillett's in the Social Democratic Federation and the British Socialist Party.

In 1911 the NSFU also threw up its new generation of leaders, two of whom we have already described as rather dubious members of the new wave. Set against them was the young, pugilistic Manny Shinwell. Joe Cotter, secretary of the new Ships' Cooks and Stewards Union, and Frank Pearce, the union's treasurer, were both syndicalists, and both sat on the Liverpool Strike Committee. (Pearce was shortly to abscond with the union's funds; Cotter evolved, after a post-war period of intense conflict, towards an intimate relationship with Havelock Wilson and much later took office in the Seamen's Union. Adventurism and defection do seem to have been endemic in the history of seafarers' trades unionism. We shall return to this problem.)

Another syndicalist on the Liverpool Strike Committee was James Murphy of the Liverpool Trades Council. With Tom Mann in the chair, it is clear that the doctrine was well represented there. But Mann was the opposite of sectarian in his conduct of the dispute and the Liverpool strike was by far the best directed of the whole series: 'Mann's syndicalism was limited in the short-term to the creation of "industrial solidarity". This was intended as the first step towards fuller industrial unionism, committed to revolutionary industrial rather than Parliamentary methods.'[102]

Outside Liverpool, where local syndicalist propagandists like Peter Larkin (James Larkin's brother) were especially active, syndicalists also came forward as strike leaders in Hull, Manchester and in South Wales. But, as in Mann's case, they were concerned to stay inside the limits set by the strikers themselves and by their local trade unions. The essential advice which they gave was to strive constantly to overcome sectionalism, and to learn unity in action. It was an important message.[103]

# IV

## *The Growth of the Workers' Union*

The Workers' Union had spent its earliest years in struggle with an unfriendly environment. It found progress and expansion most difficult to achieve. By 1910 its membership of 4,500 was little more than it had been at the turn of the century, when it had been only two years old. But all of a sudden, its luck turned: the next four years saw a transformation. Its membership growth was spectacular: entering the Great Unrest in 1911 with 18,000, the figure reached 143,000 in 1914.[104] Now it was to exercise real influence on the growth and potential of general unionism.

This last figure ran the union close up against the gasworkers, then the largest general union. Upon the outbreak of the First World War, the Workers' Union had become the fifth largest in the country. Recruitment on this scale fed further success.

From the first, the union had built its strength from the top down, relying on the appointment of full-time officers who were put to work in the field to bring trade unionism to hitherto wholly neglected areas, industries and occupations. This rather haphazard, but necessary, method now received a huge filip; as the union's contributions income grew, so it ploughed it back in the creation of many more full-time recruiting and organizing officers. In 1910 the union had six officers in the field, plus president and secretary. In 1914 it had more than forty; at that time the gasworkers, slightly larger in numbers, had only fourteen.

These four years saw more than continued random growth. Now there emerged a clear industrial and geographical pattern. Whilst the union had shared to some extent in the catch-as-catch-can expansion of the other general unions in the great revival of unionism, it also acquired its most significant industrial and occupational focus: as a mass organization of the semi-skilled grades in the engineering industry, and as a regional focus in the West Midlands.

## *Early 'Fordism'*

Three factors, two specific to engineering, helped to define its role. The first was the nature of the Workers' Union; as a general union, willing and eager to expand wherever opportunity offered, it was tailor-made for the chance which now opened before it. Engineering unionism was dominated by the craft societies, and especially by the ASE, the original mid-Victorian 'new model' union. The engineering craftsmen had evolved a successful formula of closed, apprentice-based recruitment, based on the twin pillars of yesterday's labour aristocracy, fitters and turners. (Other crafts, the blacksmiths, the boilermakers, the pattern-makers, plumbers and carpenters, followed similar methods in the single-craft unions which abounded in such industries as engineering, vehicle building, construction and shipbuilding.) The craftsmen had no interest in the unionization of the 'unskilled', who were regarded as a sub-class.

Tight craft control on labour supply depended upon two things: the apprenticeship system and the indispensability of particular skills. But in consequence of a profound, transforming technological change, these controls were becoming daily more difficult to uphold. The turner and the fitter used handtools, on the lathe and at the workbench. But more and more automatic, power-driven machines were being invented to do the turner's work without handtools, so that his function, essentially the shaping of revolving metal components, could be performed by a machine-minder, whilst the lathe itself became more versatile. Training for the machine-minders' work was far less exacting than it had to be for the craftsmen. Similar advances were made in automatic, repetitive assembly processes, which undermined the indispensability of the craft fitter. The final element of change was the increasing size and specialization of engineering companies, which enabled small-batch and one-off jobs to be replaced by long runs of standardized products, at which point mass production, and the assembly line, became economic; the requisite inventions were naturally further stimulated by this. Management methods adapted in turn to this evolution. In place of the autonomy of the craftsman came rigid supervision, the elevation of the foreman's discipline, and detailed planning and control of the worker's every move. His speeds were increasingly determined by the machine which he 'minded'.

This change did not happen overnight. As it matured it came to dominate production industry with an all-pervasive engineers' culture, 'scientific management' and 'Fordism'. (The term 'Fordism' refers to the system of mass production – usually based on the assembly-line method of factory layout – in which the operatives' skills are reduced to a minimum, and he/she is required to perform endless, minute, repetitive tasks. It was first developed by Henry Ford at his Model T factory in Detroit, USA, in 1908. The term is now used more generally to denote the whole era of twentieth-century, labour-intensive, mass-production methods, which are now, at the end of the century, being superseded by automated, robotized and computer-controlled factories – hence the concept 'post-Fordism'. We shall deal at length with the 'Fordist' phase of the TGWU story in a subsequent volume.) The Workers' Union was in almost at the start of this profound process and, as its adoption spread further, the union could frequently run ahead of managers who were themselves learning as they went along. By successfully organizing this new, soon-to-be dominant assembly-worker grade in engineering, the

Workers' Union helped to ensure its eventual incorporation into general unionism, as the Dockers' and Gasworkers' Unions did for workers in many other rising mass-production industries such as chemicals, rubber, paint, oil-refining, brewing, flour-milling, food-processing, brick and cement production, and so on. In engineering, both these unions had some presence amongst the purely labouring groups, but it was the Workers' Union which pinpointed the needs of the semi-skilled workers, at the very moment that they were becoming part of a recognizable grade, with its own particular needs in the bargaining and wages structures of the industry.

## Skilled Men and Labourers

The ASE could, of course, have forestalled the rise of the Workers' Union by opening its ranks to the recruitment of non-apprenticed workers. Indeed, it was urged to do so by both Tom Mann, and by Charles Duncan (the union's first president after Mann accepted the honorary title of vice-president. Duncan later became General Secretary). Both men came from the skilled ranks of the ASE themselves, and both had worked together on reform projects within it. Not only did the ASE fail to take their advice, but it also failed in the attempt to prevent the employers from displacing the traditional skills by the use of new methods. Semi-skilled employment grew apace. The 'machine question' lay behind the great national lock-out of 1897–8, and the resultant defeat of the ASE culminated in the employers' reassertion of their managerial prerogative 'to select, train, and employ those whom they consider best adapted to the various operations carried out in their workshops, and . . . pay them according to their ability as workmen'.[105]

Although by 1914 machine-minders made up one-fifth of the industry's labour force, the ASE's reluctance, at branch level, to admit them even after the union modified its entry qualifications, left them with nowhere to go – until the Workers' Union, which had not embarked on this course initially, recognized their needs and swept them into mass membership.

The union's first major advance in the industry was at the Birmingham Small Arms (BSA) factory. From this base, where mass-production methods were already in place, the union's growth was predominantly in engineering, with the result that by 1914 half of the union's hundred largest branches were almost exclusively composed of engineers. They set themselves to promote the claims of the semi-skilled in a wage structure which had at that time little coherence and no national standards, outside the craft rate. As a highly centralized union, seeking to promote the interest of a new grade, it was always likely that it would be a force tending to promote general, standard wage claims over as wide an area as possible. This is exactly what happened in the great Midlands engineering strikes of 1913.

Already in 1911, a significant strike at BSA Birmingham set the pattern for what was to follow. The semi-skilled had followed the craftsmen into a strike with demands of their own, and emerged with much improved relative wages. They made particular gains for the piece-workers. Beginning the strike mainly as non-unionists, their lack of funds and consequent destitution won publicity and public sympathy. It also taught its own lesson, for recruitment enjoyed an immediate stimulus. More WU organizers were appointed, including Julia Varley, the first woman officer, because female labour was common in the Birmingham engineering industry.[106] Of course, the ASE did not admit women members. In 1913 the union raised the banner of its demand for a standard 23s. a week minimum in engineering, with a minimum 12s. for women!

## The Black Country Strikes

The scene was set for the Black Country Strike – a struggle which rivals in significance the more famous epics of the labour movement. The Black Country Strike began as a series of unconnected disputes and culminated in a vast wave of industrial action. There were three main phases. First there was a movement, largely successful, to win the 23/- minimum at the major engineering firms in Birmingham, Smethwick, and West Bromwich. Then came strikes in Smethwick and the Black Country which caused a chain reaction. Finally the strike fever turned into an epidemic, and for six weeks around 40,000 workers were affected.[107]

Avery's weighing-machine factory was the first to yield a new minimum of 21s., union recognition and separate negotiations for the extra 2s. In West Bromwich, United Hinges' women strikers spread their stoppage to neighbouring factories, and John Beard and Julia Varley formulated precise claims. (Beard, a former farm worker, and now a union organizer, was soon to replace Robert Morley as the union's president.) Most of the women earned less than 10s. a week, and the demand was made for a 12s. minimum, for enhanced piece-rates and shift premia. In two weeks the firms affected conceded the bulk of this programme. BSA and the huge Metropolitan Carriage and Wagon Company in Saltley conceded the 23s., and by the end of April most firms had followed suit. As a result, 10,000 workers gained an increase of 2s. a week.

In the next phase, a prolonged strike originated in the Birmingham Carriage Company; as elsewhere, the strikers entered the dispute as non-unionists and were ineligible for strike pay. A massive community effort went into providing relief, with charity shows at theatres, tradesmen donating food, and the Town Council of Smethwick feeding children at school. Varley summoned up the strikers' wives to lend support. They were being sustained, by these means, by only 1–5s. a week.

Wolverhampton Trades Council now led a new agitation for the minimum wage. Its secretary, Harry Bagley, later became a Workers' Union organizer. Women workers again took a prominent part in the town's campaign. Strikes spread throughout the district. In May, tube workers in Wednesbury and Walsall struck for the 23s. Their battle mirrored those that had inspired it: first the strike of non-unionists with vague but strong discontents, then the arrival of the WU organizers and the adoption of the union's programme of demands, then the mobilization of neighbouring factories and of public support. By the end of May, this wave of action involved some 10,000 workers.

At the end of May, the Smethwick carriage strikers, still in deadlock, made a renewed surge towards victory by spreading their struggle to Oldbury and Wednesbury, where the company's workers joined the strike after receiving 1,500 marchers from Smethwick. The tube strikers copied this method, marching from Wolverhampton through Great Bridge, West Bromwich, to Halesowen, where workers at Stewart and Lloyd joined in. The movement was so general that Beard set up, as a co-ordinating body, a Minimum Wage Council, which drew up a more elaborate set of common demands.

During June, strikers numbered between 30,000 and 40,000. As some firms conceded the 23s. and work was restored, new disputes broke out to take their place. The 3,000 workers at GEC, a firm with notoriously bad conditions, made a specially large addition to the total. The union had, until this point, supported every new outbreak; it never initiated claims, but followed them round, articulated the demands and won thousands of members in this process. Now it began to discourage further strikes, but without much effect. Public relief funds raised locally were becoming clearly inadequate; a national appeal produced a good response, but not sufficient to prevent the first deaths from starvation in early June. Strikers now had resort to Poor Law relief. The employers, who had been in retreat since the first wave of strikes, began to show intransigence; they formed a Midland Employers' Federation to stiffen their opposition to the union. In mid-June they conceded some part of the union's claims, but insisted on a differential of 2s. between Birmingham's minimum of 23s. and the Black Country rate. At this point, hunger marchers were dispatched to raise funds countrywide, and more firms conceded when the ASE's craftsmen threatened sympathy action. Other firms sought to break the strike, some trying to reopen with anti-union labour. The levels of violence, stone-throwing and street collisions with police notably increased.

## George Askwith Arrives . . .

The pattern of 1911 in the port strikes, already evident in the recurrent surges of stoppages, was completed when George Askwith appeared on the scene and almost immediately succeeded in opening the process of conciliation. The Midland Employers' Federation accepted his role, and conceded 23s. immediately for Birmingham, Oldbury and Smethwick. Elsewhere the rate went up to 22s., with the last shilling forthcoming in six months' time. Women won a general 12s. minimum. Permanent conciliation machinery was agreed. The MEF was converted to collective bargaining, and Askwith recorded his satisfaction at improved industrial relations in the Midlands following the settlement.

The Midlands strikes embraced boiler and bridge works, metal-rolling firms, tube works, railway-carriage and wagon works, nut-and-bolt works and many related trades. In their midst, a serious but separate dispute occurred in the Midlands firebrick-making industry, and a Wages Board was created as a result. Askwith's role was crucial: the speed with which state conciliation effected settlement was astonishing, given the tough stance adopted by the employers up to the moment of his intervention. He arrived to find the two sides, the MEF and the Birmingham and Allied Trades Societies' Federation, holed up in different hotels. Within three days the conciliation was accomplished, and a disputes procedure was agreed which recognized the union. It 'involved stages of exhaustive discussion, speedy examination of claims, and no stoppage of work while negotiations were pending, together with avoidance of stoppage or suspension of work on account of outside disputes, while at the same time the right to strike or lockout was maintained.'[108]

After the great port strikes of 1911–12, a Birmingham manufacturer had said to Askwith that he just could not understand what had got into port workers. But by 1913 he and his fellows had their explanation. There was, as Askwith recognized, a clear connection: the dock strikes had their demonstration effect on the previously non-union men and women of the Midlands.

The dispute in the Midlands was a sequel to the economic disputes of 1911 and 1912, but it must not be supposed that any of these disputes failed to leave a mark. They indicated to labour the value of organisation, which was being actively pressed throughout the country, and the value of propaganda, which more and more made its force felt; they increased the cohesion of labour, particularly among semi-skilled and unskilled labour; they educated both leaders and rank and file on things to be done and things to be avoided in the course of a strike.[109]

Beard summed up the gain in the union's stature: 'In the Midlands, we can hold our own against craft and sectional prejudice, and we are able to declare that the Workers' Union stands for class as against craft.'[110]

The union continued its progress, across trades and industries, territories and counties, until the First World War. Even a partial catalogue of its conquests makes astonishing reading. In the core Midland towns, membership rose twenty-eightfold. In Coventry, in a highly significant development, a three-day strike brought the cycle and motor-vehicle trade into organization, recognition and a minimum wage of 26s. 6d. The Employers' Federation signed an agreement on Provisions for Avoiding Disputes; amongst the signatories were Daimler and Humber cars. In Swadlincote among the clay and pipe workers, in Burton at the breweries, in Stoke, in Nottingham, in Gloucester and Swindon, the union gained many members and considerable victories. Many of these sectors remained within the TGWU, after the absorption of the Workers' Union into the amalgamation, on into the 1990s.

## Teaching by Example

In Manchester, Cheshire, Preston and North Wales, new groups were organized and wage gains won. In Yorkshire, engineers, foundry and boiler workers, gas, road and other council workers, builders' labourers, brickmakers and quarrymen, textile labourers and maintenance-men, brewery and metal workers came in from Halifax and the Calder Valley to Sheffield and Doncaster.

In South Wales, steel workers joined, struck and won a minimum day-wage. Smelter workers struck for nine weeks and obtained extra Sunday pay, although they did not win alleviation in their working hours, which increased the risks of lead-poisoning. In Cardiff the flour-millers and others formed a regional membership of 12,000.

In Cornwall, an embittered struggle against the clay-pit owners of St Austell resulted in much police violence. Beard was kicked and punched when he appeared on the picket line. Julia Varley was also injured. Eventually, after a year of conflict, even here the union won recognition, wage increases and complete organization amongst the clay workers.

In Glasgow, foundry and building labourers, the herring-barrel coopers, railway shopmen and brewers were organized.

In the South, there was renewal in London and much success in Essex, where Colchester became a major centre for the WU, which also organized a ball-bearing factory in Chelmsford. In Braintree, Courtaulds workers were organized, and in Bedford and Oxford so were the Witney blanket mills.

Such widespread progress was possible because of the boom in trade.

But it was helped by the discovery of 'workers' power' through trade-union success, by new technologies which were grouping new grades of workers together in mass production, and of course because much of the union's drive was directed to non-union, virgin territory.

## Inter-union Rivalries

But not always. Such a rapid progress inevitably gave rise to inter-union problems, and brought the Workers' Union to the heart of the debate on the federation and amalgamation of general workers' unions. Its very success made it suspect in the eyes of some other unions. Inevitably, it was accused of poaching – by, amongst others, the main steel union. Its application to affiliate to the TUC was rejected. Even so, it does not seem to have had a worse-than-average record as a predator among older unions. Doubtless it was also resented because, although it recruited previously unorganized workers, it often seemed to be invading territories which others regarded as theirs. Was it felt to harbour 'ecumenical ambitions' to be itself the 'One Big Union'?

In practice, however, it never sought to invade the area of the great craft societies, and always insisted that it was a union of the semi-skilled. In agriculture, where it genuinely was the industrial union, and in engineering, where it systematically recruited the machine-minders, it had a status and role which were unique. It was in engineering, nevertheless, that for the WU inter-union friction was most intense. Its aim – to represent the semi-skilled in the industry's hierarchy of wage movements – was resented and frequently frustrated by the ASE.

How the union understood its proper place in the whole structure was shown when it took part in the 1902 attempt at amalgamation of the general unions, and when it joined the General Labourers' National Council in 1908. A ballot of its own members in 1911 showed a large majority in favour of the merger of all general unions. Subsequently, it took part in the major debate on amalgamation of both general and transport unions in 1914, a subject to which we shall return in chapter 15.

## V

## The Children Join In

Reverting to 1911, as if to provide a final note to that incredible year, in September, when all the actions were over, the schoolchildren ended their summer holidays and promptly struck school. It had been a holiday during which they had witnessed their fathers joining in massive actions to change their conditions – conditions which their families, young and old, shared. Teachers, parents and the public at large were astonished when, in town after town (at least sixty major urban areas, including all the ports, were affected), school after school broke out of its classrooms at the start of the new term. 'Some of the [press] reports speak of hundreds of children parading through the streets and at Dundee and Hull thousands of pupils defied the school authorities, but it is not possible to give the actual numbers of children who left their classrooms.'[111] But with every major city in the land included in the list of places where *some* children struck – London, Birmingham, Glasgow, Coventry, Newcastle, Nottingham, Manchester, Sheffield and South-ampton amongst them – we are faced with something on the scale of a junior General Strike!

The children organized pickets, bands and marches, stoned school windows, intimidated 'blacklegs' and went from school to school calling out their fellow pupils. Their marching song was 'Fall In and Follow Me'. For sure, the slum schools which engendered these rebellions were grim enough 'work-places', mirroring the harsh environment of adult work which surrounded them. If head teachers were not always sadistic bullies, the teaching was often repetitious and boring. The children invented appropriate demands. Their banners demanded 'No More Stick', 'Payment for Monitors', 'Half-day Holidays'.[112]

These poor, undernourished, undersized children had caught the mood of revolt. They were starting a serious but immensely spirited game: it was played out to the end when the parents, especially the mothers, recovered from the shock and broke the strikes by delivering up their charges to retribution at the school gates. It is an intriguing question: how many of those children, eleven years later, were to constitute part of the first generation of TGWU members?

# Notes

1  Elie Halevy, *A History of the English People in the Nineteenth Century*, vol. VI: *The Rule of Democracy, 1905–14* (Ernest Benn, 1934), book II, p. 445.
2  Ibid., pp. 446–7.
3  Quoted in Lord Askwith, *Industrial Problems and Disputes* (John Murray, 1920), pp. 146–7.
4  J. Ramsay MacDonald, *The Social Unrest* (T. Foulis, 1913), p. 35.
5  Jack Jones, 'A Liverpool Socialist Education', *History Workshop Journal*, issue 18 (1984), p. 4.
6  Recalled by Jim Roche, a veteran militant from the Leeds clothing workers' union. Jim Roche, who was close enough to Tom Mann to be a pall-bearer at his funeral, also recalled that the old man, who ended his days as a publican in Yorkshire (he died in 1940), used to say that there was more sense talked in his bar-parlour in one evening than in a year of parliamentary debate!

7   The *Industrial Syndicalist*, Documents in Society History, no. 3 (Spokes-
    man Books, 1974), pp. 39–40 and 41–2.
8   We have reported several of Tillett's previous bouts of ill-heath, which
    alternated throughout his career with phases of intense activity, in a
    discernible pattern. His biographer has summarized this process: 'When
    healthy, Tillett would work at a feverish, indeed manic, pace. Letters,
    pamphlets, proclamations and articles would flow from his pen; he would
    embark upon ambitious speaking and organising tours, he would take up
    with great energy the cause of the moment, all the while carrying on the
    multitude of administrative tasks which fell to him as general secretary of a
    major union. His activities would reach their climax: a strike would be won
    or lost, a political manoeuvre succeed or fail. Immediately afterwards
    Tillett's health would break, he would be out of commission for months at
    a time, his illness real but accompanied by psychosomatic symptoms and
    depression amounting on more than one occasion to complete nervous
    breakdown' (Jonathan Schneer, *Ben Tillett: Portrait of a Labour Leader*
    (Croom Helm, 1982), p. 114).
9   NUDL Annual Report, 1910, p. 2.
10  The *Industrial Syndicalist*, vol. I, no. 6, p. 48.
11  Phillip J. Leng, *The Welsh Dockers* (G. W. and A. Hesketh, 1981), p. 49.
12  Askwith, *Industrial Problems and Disputes*. p. 149.
13  Arthur Marsh and Victoria Ryan, *The Seamen: A History of the National
    Union of Seamen* (Malthouse, 1989), p. 54.
14  Tom Mann, *Memoirs* (1923; reissued McGibbon and Kee, 1967),
    pp. 207–9.
15  M. J. Daunton, 'Inter-Union Relations on the Waterfront: Cardiff, 1888–
    1914', *International Review of Social History*, vol. XXII (1977), p. 368, and
    L. H. Powell, *The Shipping Federation: A History of the First Sixty Years,
    1890–1950* (Shipping Federation, 1950), p. 21.
16  Harry Gosling, *Up and Down Stream* (Methuen, 1927), pp. 147–8.
17  Report of the International Transport Federation, Berlin, 1913; quoted
    in Basil Mogridge, 'Militancy and Inter-Union Rivalry in British
    Shipping, 1911–1929', *International Review of Social History*, vol. VI
    (1961), p. 381. Williams's comment was made in retrospect, for he
    succeeded James Anderson as General Secretary of the NTWF only in June
    1912, at the age of thirty-one. He had been a cardiff coal-trimmer, President
    of the NALU, and a local councillor. He will occupy centre stage throughout
    Part II of this volume, and continued in his post with the Federation until
    1925.
18  Powell, *The Shipping Federation*, p. 24.
19  Ben Tillett, *History of the London Transport Strike of 1911* (National
    Transport Workers' Federation, 1912), foreword, p. x.
20  Ibid.
21  Gosling, *Up and Down Stream*, p. 147.
22  Gordon Phillips, 'The National Transport Workers' Federation, 1910–
    1927' (unpublished PhD thesis, Oxford University, 1968), p. 84.
23  Askwith, *Industrial Problems and Disputes*, p. 149.
24  G. A. Phillips, 'The National Transport Workers' Federation', p. 78, says:
    'The events of 1911 are still, in large part, inexplicable. To union leaders

they remained as mysterious as they were unexpected. And historians have not come much nearer to establishing their origins.' It is interesting to note that H. A. Clegg, Alan Fox and A. F. Thompson, *A History of British Trade Unions since 1889*, vol. I: *1889–1910* (Oxford University Press, 1964), p. 55, open their account of the great 1889 precursor of 1911 with a similar sense of mystery: 'The "new unionism" stands out as one of the most colourful and baffling phenomena in British trade union history'.

25    Tom Mann, *From Single Tax to Syndicalism* (Guy Bowman, 1913), pp. 68–70.

26    Phillips, 'The National Transport Workers' Federation', p. 95.

27    Ibid., p. 97.

28    Trevor Griffiths, *Through the Night and Such Impossibilities: Two Plays for Television* (Faber and Faber, 1977). The other programmes in the series, all of them screened, were on E. Nesbit, the Countess of Warwick, Marie Lloyd, Baden-Powell, Conan Doyle, Horatio Bottomley, Rolls-Royce, and Lloyd George. As Trevor Griffiths puts it in his foreword to the volume, 'Tom Mann might well have roughed the series up a bit, but it's arguable he might have also done something towards redressing its "balance" too.'

29    The Liverpool carters' chairman was a prominent local Tory. The union was strongly 'Orange' in its image and influence.

30    *Liverpool Daily Post and Mercury*, 15 June 1911; quoted in E. L. Taplin, *The Dockers' Union: A Study of the National Union of Dock Labourers, 1889–1922* (Leicester University Press, 1986), p. 85.

31    Ibid., 21 June 1911; p. 86.

32    Ibid., 26 June 1911; p. 87.

33    Ibid., pp. 89–90.

34    Ibid., 28 June 1911; pp. 89–90.

35    Ibid., 3 July 1911; pp. 91–2.

36    George Millington's obituary notice, TGWU *Record*, June 1925, p. 244.

37    R. A. Leeson (ed.), *Strike: A Live History, 1887–1971* (Allen and Unwin, 1973), pp. 41–2.

38    *The Transport Worker*, vol. I, no. 1 (1911), p. 46.

39    Leeson, *Strike: A Live History*, pp. 40–2.

40    The following passage draws on the account by Keith Brooker, *The Hull Strikes of 1911* (East Yorkshire Local History Society, 1979).

41    Father Hopkins had been the cathedral organist and chaplain in Rangoon, and in Arakan and Calcutta was the founder and Superior-General of the Anglican Order of St Paul. He appeared at Liverpool, South Wales and in London during the 1911 strikes, as well as in Hull. He became a trustee of the union and a strong supporter of Havelock Wilson on its Executive.

42    Brooker, *The Hull Strikes of 1911*, p. 12.

43    Ibid., p. 17.

44    Askwith, *Industrial Problems and Disputes*, p. 149.

45    This is the figure given in Taplin, *The Dockers' Union*, p. 85. Askwith, *Industrial Problems and Disputes*, gives 15,000 and Brooker, *The Hull Strikes of 1911*, gives 'several thousand'.

46    Askwith, *Industrial Problems and Disputes*, p. 150.

47    Brooker, *The Hull Strikes of 1911*, p. 20.

48   The fight is reported in Brooker, *The Hull Strikes of 1911*.

Taplin, *The Dockers' Union*, p. 84, cites an official NTWF source, which reported diplomatically on the inter-union relationship in Hull a year later: 'the two unions have worked as one for the benefit of the Hull dockers . . . and there are over 10,000 dockers enrolled in the two unions' (Humberside Transport Workers' *Gazette and Monthly Record*, 16 February 1912). Tillett's union had a district office and two branches, and the NUDL had a district office and four branches. In 1912 the NUDL's Liverpool branches' contribution income totalled £10,660, and Hull's £2,284. The Hull branches of Tillett's union returned only £438 in the same year. For the NUDL, the figure for 1911 had been £1,112 and for the DWRGWU, £298 (*source:* Annual Reports of the two unions).

49   Quoted in Brooker, *The Hull Strikes of 1911*, p. 11.

50   Askwith, *Industrial Problems and Disputes*, p. 152.

51   *The Transport Worker*, vol. 1, no. 1 (1911), p. 3.

52   Ibid.

53   Ben Tillett, *Memories and Reflections* (John Long, 1931), p. 30.

54   Gosling, *Up and Down Stream*, p. 153.

55   Ibid.

56   *The Industrial Syndicalist*, vol. 1, no. 10 (April 1911).

57   M. J. Daunton, 'Inter-Union Relations on the Waterfront', p. 370.

58   Tupper wrote his memoirs, *The Seamen's Torch* (Hutchinson, 1938), in which, whilst revealing nothing of his life before 1910, he hints at an adventurist past: 'my doings in half the countries of the globe would make a passable book'. His claims to naval or military rank were almost certainly spurious, as was his entitlement to the VC. Basil Mogridge describes him as 'a bankrupt company promoter turned private detective' (*International Review of Social History*, vol. VI (1961), p. 401n.). After his prosecution for incitement to riot, when the Crown was represented by F. E. Smith (Lord Birkenhead), he revelled in Smith's having designated him 'the most dangerous man in Europe'. He was as proud of his strike-breaking activities in the inter-war shipping industry, as Havelock Wilson's principal assistant, as he was of his agitator's role in 1911. In his last years he became an agent for the government's spy system, helping to identify 'bolsheviks' amongst his own members. Yet in 1911 he succeeded in smuggling a pro-union cook on board the Shipping Federation's depot ship, the *Lady Jocelyn*, who then poisoned the strike-breakers and their crew. In addition to his exploits in Cardiff that year, he showed similar intransigence in Liverpool, where on 'bloody Sunday' he appeared on the rostrum with Tom Mann, the Rev. Hopkins and the Strike Committee. In the police-charge that day, he received a truncheon blow on the head from a constable as he joined the fleeing crowd. He survived to participate in a wide range of colourful events, living on until 1942. Four years later, 'his ashes were consigned to the deep from the *Queen Mary* in the presence of the British delegation – Government representatives, shipowners, and seafarers – on their way to the Seattle Conference in 1946. It would no doubt have pleased Captain Tupper, who all his life was a valiant fighter for the cause he had adopted, to have known that even at the last he had the final word; some of his ashes were blown back over the delegates!' (Powell, *The Shipping Federation*, p. 25). See also vol. II.

59   Tupper, *The Seamen's Torch*, pp. 39–40.
60   Leng, *The Welsh Dockers*, pp. 57–8.
61   Tupper, *The Seamen's Torch*, p. 34.
62   Leeson, *Strike: A Live History*, pp. 42–3.
63   Daunton, 'Inter-Union Relations on the Waterfront', p. 372.
64   Ibid., p. 374.
65   Leng, *The Welsh Dockers*, p. 61.
66   Ibid., p. 62.
67   Brian Atkinson, *Trade Unions in Bristol* (Bristol Branch, Historical Association, University of Bristol, 1982), p. 17.
68   Ibid., p. 20.
69   Ibid., p. 21.
70   Emanuel Shinwell, *Lead with the Left: My First Ninety-six Years* (Cassell, 1981), pp. 45ff.
71   Pat Murphy's recorded notes (Leeson, *Strike: A Live History*, p. 43), in a section on the shipping strike in Goole, relate that 'Havelock Wilson issued a manifesto declaring that if the shipowners recognised the union he was prepared to concede more favourable terms, and threatened his members with fines for questioning his actions'.
72   Tupper, *The Seamen's Torch*, p. 63.
73   Mogridge, 'Militancy and Inter-Union Rivalry in British Shipping', pp. 384–5.
74   Shinwell, *Lead with the Left*, p. 49.
75   Tillett, *Memories and Reflections*, p. 4.
76   Ibid., p. 14.
77   Ibid., p. 13.
78   This is the same Albert Rollitt whom we met in chapter 1, when he was Tory MP for Hull and a patron of the earliest Hull dockers' union, and later in chapter 5, mediating in the 1893 Hull lock-out.
79   Tillett, *Memories and Reflections*, p. 69.
80   Ibid., p. 20.
81   Askwith, *Industrial Problems and Disputes*, p. 158.
82   Tillett, *Memories and Reflections*, p. 36.
83   John Lovell, *Stevedores and Dockers: a Study of Trade Unionism in the Port of London, 1870–1914* (Macmillan, 1969), p. 173.
84   NUDL *Annual Report, 1911*, p. 4.
85   Ibid.
86   Ibid.
87   Ibid.
88   Ibid., p. 7.
89   DWRGWU Annual Report, 1911, p. 8.
90   H. A. Clegg, *A History of British Trade Unions since 1889*, vol. II: *1911–1933* (Oxford University Press, 1985), p. 40.
91   Paul Smith, 'The Process of Unionisation in the Road Haulage Industry' (unpublished PhD thesis, Warwick University, 1988), p. 68.
92   See note 71.
93   Gosling, *Up and Down Stream*, p. 157. Robert Williams made a similar claim in his report to the ITF in 1912: 'The phenomenal success of the mass movements of 1911 was due to the existence of the Federation and

the vague recognition or their identity of interest shown by all transport workers'; quoted in Phillips, 'The National Transport Workers' Federation', chapter 2, p. 98.

94  See Phillips, 'The National Transport Workers' Federation', pp. 579–80. The eleven new affiliations were: the Amalgamated General and Warehouse Workers' Union, the Amalgamated Protective Society of Engine and Crane Men, the Boiler Firemen and Wire Rope Makers, the Hull Seamen and Marine Firemen's Association, the Liverpool South End Coalheavers' Association, the Mersey Quay and Railway Carters' Union, the United Carters' Association of England, the United Order of General Labourers of London, the Weaver Watermen's Association, the National Amalgamated Union of Labour, and the Scottish Union of Dock Labourers.

95  Ibid., quoted p. 99.

96  Ibid., chapter 3, contains this discussion.

97  Powell, *The Shipping Federation*, p. 22.

98  Eric Wigham, *Strikes and the Government, 1893–1974* (Macmillan, 1976), p. 22.

99  See Alan Fox, *History and the Heritage: The Social Origins of the British Industrial Relations System* (Allen and Unwin, 1985), pp. 248–9; and Keith Middlemas, *Politics in Industrial Society: The Experience of the British System since 1911* (André Deutsch, 1979), pp. 29–31.

100  NUDL Annual Report, 1912, pp. 4–5.

101  Tillett, *History of the London Transport Strike of 1911*, p. 56.

102  R. J. Holton, 'Syndicalism and Labour on Merseyside, 1906–14', in H. R. Hikins (ed.), *Building the Union: Studies in the Growth of the Workers' Movement, Merseyside, 1756–1967* (Toulouse Press, 1973), p. 139.

103  P. Lloyd has sought to trace 'The Influence of Syndicalism in the Dock Strikes in Hull and Manchester in 1911' (unpublished MA thesis, Warwick University, 1972). He concludes that 'Syndicalism in both Hull and Manchester was only contributory in a secondary and indirect way to the tactical conduct of the Dock Strikes of 1911.' In Hull, only Burn of the dockers and Bell of the seamen, can be found uttering syndicalist sentiment, and though in Manchester there is slightly more evidence of 'institutionalized' syndicalist presences, 'how strong these were is difficult to assess'. Syndicalism never became "institutionalized", but its grapevine, its informal networks, were important contributors to the spirit of independence and militancy which inspired the strikes.

104  In these pages, we have drawn freely on Richard Hyman, *The Workers' Union* (Oxford University Press, 1971), chapter 3; on Askwith, *Industrial Problems and Disputes*, chapter XXV: 'The Midlands, 1913'; and on Clegg, *History of British Trade Unions since 1889*, vol. II, pp. 58–60.

105  Hyman, *The Workers' Union*, p. 41.

106  When the union merged into the TGWU in 1929, Julia Varley, together with Florence Hancock and Ellen McCullough came with it to become successive TGWU National Women's Officers.

107  Hyman, *The Workers' Union*, pp. 50–1.

108  Lord Askwith, *Industrial Problems and Disputes*, p. 257.

109  Ibid.

110   Hyman, *The Workers' Union*, p.60.

111   Dave Marson, *Children's Strikes in 1911*, History Workshop Pamphlets no. 9 (History Workshop, 1973).

112   The historian of the children's strikes, Dave Marson, was – appropriately – a Hull docker, who attended a day-release course taught by Tony Topham, went on to Ruskin College and there researched and wrote his pamphlet (see previous note). He then used the material, with Billy Colville, as the basis of a play, *Fall In and Follow Me*, which was successfully performed at the Half Moon Theatre in Whitechapel, 10–27 July 1973. The script was published as History Workshop Pamphlet no. 13.

# Index

# PART II

## 1912–1922

## *From Federation to Amalgamation*

# 11

# The 1912 London Transport Strike and the Federation

## I

### *Learning by Negative Example?*

Nine complex sectional settlements terminated the London transport workers' strike of 1911. Each had its own inadequacies, all of which were soon to seed further conflict. The port workers were soon out again: within a few months there was another total London port strike. By May 1912 an official inquiry, appointed by the government, had identified seven quite distinct grievances as contributory causes of the new stoppage. Some of these sectional problems would seem at first sight to offer rather flimsy explanations for the very wide scale of the renewed conflict; but behind each of them lay issues of immense significance for the future of general unionism and indeed for the whole system of industrial relations in Britain.

The 1912 strike ended in defeat, and there can be no doubt that this was a serious setback for the National Transport Workers' Federation. Initially, the strike did not have the spontaneous inevitability of its immediate predecessor, or of 1889. Yet, although its short-term effect was to retard the progress of the new Federation, and of some of its most important constituents, it none the less proved, in the middle and long term, to have certain useful consequences. Above all it was an essential forcing ground: the shoots of amalgamation grew more rapidly and with greater strength than might otherwise have been the case, because the demonstration of the apparent weaknesses of mere 'federation' argued the case for closer co-operation between unions and sectors. Ernest Bevin, in subsequent years, never tired of invoking 'the lessons of 1912'.

## Devonport: the Intransigent

Ironically, the unions had their opponents to thank for this outcome. In 1911 the London employers, section by section, had negotiated and jointly signed agreements with a committee of trade-union leaders who spoke and signed in the name of the National Transport Workers' Federation. This was recognition, of a sort, for their new creation, and the experience engendered among all participating unions some strong expectations about its future role. These were not to be directly realized in the strike which followed. By 1912, the same London employers had rediscovered a comprehensive unity. This time they grouped themselves, not under the leadership of the Shipping Federation, but of the Port of London Authority. *De facto*, this was soon to embody the personal authority of one man, its chairman, Lord Devonport. All the rest, from great shipowners to small master-carters, came to cede their own power into his hands and, once he was in control of affairs, his reply to all efforts at negotiation or mediation was consistent and unbending: 'Tell the men to get back to work.' When called upon, he and his committee would elaborate a little:

> They will have nothing to do with the officials of the Transport Workers' Federation, who alone are responsible for the strike and its continuance. It has been their practice to consider any grievances brought before them by the men themselves or representatives of the particular union concerned, and they have no intention of departing from this practice.[1]

On the day that this collective policy was announced, Lord Devonport issued a separate press statement, which concluded: 'Parliament is sovereign, and can do anything – by legislation. Nothing short of that will change the attitude of the Port of London Authority towards those who declared this unprovoked and unjustifiable war.'[2]

How did the members of the NTWF come to face such an impasse? What was the cause of the 'war'? From its opening skirmishes, through its tortuous course, down to the stalemate signalled in July by Devonport, it registered the employers' refusal to live with the agreements they had yielded up under the weight of the dockers' victory of 1911.

## The Employers Go Back On Their Words

From the very moment of the settlements in 1911, different groups of London employers were busily abrogating the agreements they had then made with such evident reluctance. Others were intent on resisting the logical extension of partial agreements which had littered the port with all sorts of anomalies in rates or conditions. Lightermen, stevedores, tugboatmen, sailing bargemen and carters, together with PLA employees, all had their particular experience of what Harry Gosling called 'a growing sense of irritation among the members of the London district [of the NTWF]' arising from 'the general trouble of broken agreements'.[3] The official inquiry in May, in addition to specific grievances, listed 'certain instances of vexatious interference with union workmen'.[4] In all this, the unions discerned a conspiracy by the employers to undermine the gains of 1911.

The most contentious issues at the beginning of the year arose in the specialist trades of stevedoring and lighterage, where both unions concerned had crossed beyond their old frontiers of recruitment without being able to establish in their new territories the superior standards enjoyed in their traditional areas. In the stevedores' case, their union precipitated an inter-union row at the Federation's Councils in February and June, when it sought to establish preference for its new membership in areas where it was in competition with casual workers and their unions.

The stevedores had a dispute with the Short Sea Traders' Association (SSTA), where their new members among the shipmen were denied the elusive 'port rate' of 10*d.* an hour, won for the traditional stevedores in 1911. The short-sea trade members, on only 7*d.* an hour, were even for a time issued with a distinctive coloured union card, at the insistence of old-guard stevedores in the London Master Stevedores' Association (LMSA) territories, to prevent them from claiming parity of engagement in the old, protected area of work. It was argued that men who had been working for 7*d.* could otherwise share the fruits of the union's best rates, whilst those in the old trades could find no equivalent rate if they sought work in the SSTA area.

At Tilbury, the big shipping companies and the major stevedoring company, Scrutton's, began to introduce dockers in place of stevedores in May 1912, supported in this provocation also by the cement and pulp-handling companies, who began to engage members of the National Amalgamated Union of Labour. This produced another inter-union squabble at the NTWF meetings. In May, the stevedores complained to the Federation of encroachments by the United Order of General Labourers (UOGL), the Labour Protection League, the DWRGWU and the NAUL. Clearly, inter-union rivalries were being provoked by employers: whether this was a conscious 'conspiracy' must remain an open question. The effects were not in doubt. The stevedores' inter-union conflicts were generating great tensions in any number of locations.

The lightermen's grievances arose in part also from their expansion into new areas. Their tugboat members were denied their 1911 settlement terms, even though the tug-owners were members of the

Masters' Association. The sailing-barge owners were systematically withholding both the back-pay and the new schedule of rates agreed in the 600–item 'Pink List' drawn up by Askwith in 1911. In the cartering trade, one master, Bissell, had refused point-blank to honour the 1911 terms; when his association brought pressure on him to conform, he left that body in order to persist with the pre–1911 terms.

## The Case of James Thomas

The 1912 version of 'the match to fire the Thames' came in the lighterage trade, where, in April, men employed by the Mercantile Lighterage Company complained about the continued employment of James Thomas. Thomas was sixty-one years old, formerly a foreman, but later, because of his age, engaged as a watchman. He stubbornly adhered to membership of the Foremen's Society (founded in 1889) and refused to take out membership of the Lightermen and Watermen's Union. The masters, who had resisted the union's attempt to bring the foremen into membership of Gosling's union in its drive for union control over hiring in 1911, would neither dismiss Thomas nor yet coerce him into joining the men's union. Consequently the union declared an official strike. The company responded by asking fellow master-lightermen to assist it by handling its trade. The union blacked that traffic, its members were sacked and the union called a port-wide lighterage strike. Neither side had felt it worthwhile to use its established conciliation procedures. The union argued that failure to agree would have been inevitable.

The District Committee of the NTWF, in consultation with the National Executive, called a general strike of the whole port on 23 May, only a week after the commencement of the initial strike at Thomas's company. This decision, to which the response was solid, was probably inevitable. For 'by the summer of 1912 . . . the port of London was visibly on the brink of civil war',[5] as the lightermen's, stevedores', carters' and sundry other overheated troubles rose up and boiled over. The London District Council of the Federation had, in any case, accepted its leading role promptly on this occasion, by sanctioning a federal blacking of the traffic of the Mercantile Lighterage Company on 20 May. No doubt, too, as John Lovell suggests, the leaders recalled the ease of their victory the previous year, and took heart also from the partial success of the first ever national miners' strike, which had recently prompted the government to give legislative force to a settlement.[6] As the port employers' intransigence became more and more clearly demonstrated, indeed, the actions and utterances of the Federation were increasingly directed towards inducing the government to persuade or coerce the employers to concede – a role for the state which was becoming familiar, not only in mining, but in railways and in the ports.

## The Federation's Fears

However, there was a darker side to the outlook of the port-unions' leaders. Many of them could recollect the employers' counterattack of the 1890s, following the new unionism's first triumphs. The behaviour of the London employers in 1912 led them to anticipate a repetition, and they went into the fight with something approaching a desperate, even paranoid, defensiveness. Moreover, they seem to have contemplated the necessity of a national sympathy strike of all the Federation's forces at a very early stage. As early as 25 May Gosling told the Clarke Inquiry into the dispute that 'the matter could possibly become a national matter by carrying the same line of action [the blacking of the London strike] into the other ports, and asking them to assist'. It was for this reason, he explained, that the full Executive of the Federation was called to London, 'and they . . . decided that, as this was an attack upon trade unionism and was a breach of agreement, to call out all the men in the port. They have not gone beyond that at present.'[7]

The government's initial response to the strike had been the convening of this public inquiry, the first of its kind. It was conducted by Sir Edward Clarke with such alacrity that his Report was on its way to Sydney Buxton at the Board of Trade on 27 May, just three days after its first sitting and only four days after the Federation's port-wide strike actually began.

Harry Gosling, as its president, gave all the evidence to the inquiry on behalf of the Federation, tabling and detailing the seven grievances. Gosling's stature, up to this point, had been overshadowed by that of Tillett. As we shall see, on this occasion too Tillett soon took his customary place in the limelight, with some quite extraordinary passages of headline-grabbing rhetoric and various other extra-curricular activities. However, in the public eye, the leadership was now seen as equal. Tillett had to share the glory and the blame with Gosling. The hostile portion of the press referred continuously to the 'Gosling–Tillett dictatorship', and made weak-minded puns on Gosling's name: 'sauce for the goose, sauce for the Gosling', and so on.

Gosling's performance at the Clarke Inquiry was impressive: he began by threatening to withdraw from the proceedings if the employers were allowed to present their case through hired lawyers. He convinced Sir Edward that this would have been contrary to the spirit of collective bargaining and the will to reach bilateral agreement. The burden of his evidence was that, given the accumulation of 'vexatious' provocation by the employers over the observance of their agreements, and given their continuous discrimination against trade-union members, the Federation faced a challenge to its role. This menaced the continuation of trade unionism in the port. He saw the case of Thomas within this wider context:

> If ninety-nine per cent of the men – or a very much higher percentage than that: very nearly the whole of the men – in this port are now trade unionists, and yet this chap comes along and says 'I am going to upset all of you', can he be doing it for himself? Is it common sense that he is doing it for himself? . . . no man can be persuaded to believe that he is doing anything else but being a tool for the Masters' Association. They have backed him up. His own employer has backed him up. Good gracious! If he had come to me and said, 'I cannot afford the money', it is only five shillings, and I would have given him the five shillings to join . . . It is so absurd; yet because the Masters' Association says, 'No, Thomas, don't join, we will back you up, and we will break the necks of these fellows', that is why we are in this ridiculous state . . . he has been used as a tool.[8]

Gosling elaborated the same essential point in all seven of the grievances, with evident and uncharacteristic passion. 'Bissell is a scab, and has employed scab labour . . . '. On the sailing-barge dispute, on which 'Sir George Askwith worked like a trooper' (in 1911), he argued the case for compelling all employers to conform to an agreement intended to cover a whole trade:

> do not allow any scalliwag to get out of it by saying, 'I was not there and I took no part in it.' That is what is going on in nearly all the trades. When the employers are saying to us: 'How can you expect us to obey this agreement when you are allowing so-and-so to do this work at a lower price?' Then if we say: 'We are not allowing it,' they say: 'Why do you not stop him?' which means 'Why do not you strike against him?' Then when we strike against him they take up the cudgels for him and take his part and lock the men out; that is why you get unrest. Once a rate is fairly and securely agreed upon in a trade it ought to be standardised and made the rate for the whole of that trade.[9]

## The Pursuit of Recognition

So cogent did this logic appear to Sir Edward Clarke, that in the disputes involving the question of the standard rate, or where a breach of agreement was proved, he reported in favour of the unions. Where, as in Bissell's case, the problem was the inability of the union to coerce a non-signatory to an agreement into observing that agreement, he reported that the securing of such compliance required legislation, on which he was not asked to express an opinion. But on the question of trade-union membership, he rejected the union's claim that, in the Thomas case, the masters had an obligation to enforce a union monopoly, or to recognize the Federation ticket, from which, in the union's view, only foremen were exempted. George Askwith also criticized both sides for failing to use the conciliation procedures set up in 1911. He later recalled:

> The question of the Federation ticket . . . had not really been fought out and settled in 1911. It was revived in 1912, and the attempt showed . . . the weakness of that union [sic], a lack which they have been working studiously to remedy ever since . . . I was one of those who countersigned the agreement of August 11 [1911] and . . . there was nothing in it about the Federation ticket being obligatory . . . [10]

Although the employers, urged on by Lord Devonport, were quick to reject all the findings of the Clarke Inquiry, they might have been induced eventually to conciliate on the issues of rates and conditions. But the sight of the Federation pressing the issue of the 'Federation ticket' and a closed shop, however imprecisely, undoubtedly transformed their initial resolve into cold intransigence and hostility. In its response to Sir Edward Clarke's Report, the Federation raised its bid to establish itself as the recognized negotiating body for the whole port. Whilst accepting most of his findings, it stated that: 'We are prepared to meet the employers as a responsible body for the purpose of the employers honouring Agreements made with us, we demand that the National Transport Workers' Federation shall be the authority for the workers, [and] we demand the reinstatement of all men involved.'[11]

By the time of the NTWF's second Annual General Council, 4–7 June 1912, the government had made proposals for the establishment of a permanent Joint Board for the industry, comprising unions and employers, with sectional panels for each separate trade, modelled on the lines of the Brooklands Agreement operative in the cotton industry. The AGC debated the idea, which found general favour. After all, this was what they all sought. Gosling had been at pains, in the Clarke Inquiry, to insist that their aspirations were directed to the foundation of stable and enforceable collective-bargaining ageements, and not industrial warfare. Reservations were voiced about the concept of separate sectional bargains; the 'port rate', or standardization of wages, was a major priority. Nevertheless, the Council passed this resolution:

> That this National Council of the National Transport Federation agrees to the formation of a Joint Board, representing employers and employees of the Thames and Medway. The men's side of such Board to be representatives of the National Transport Workers' Federation and the Federated Employers to be representatives of the masters' side. That a sub-committee be selected from such Board to deal with the claims and agreements of the various sections. Agreements reached to be endorsed by the National Transport Workers' Federation as representing the men, and the combined employers representing the Masters, and that a sub-committee be formed to arrange details for carrying this resolution into effect.

## The Employers Dig In

This formula neatly prefigures collective-bargaining machinery and, indeed, the future Joint Industrial Council of the docks industry. It was reasonable, constructive and 'responsible'. Unfortunately, to Lord Devonport and his allies, each of these three proposals was a provocative impertinence. They wanted no Joint Board, they rejected any recognition of the NTWF and roundly declared that they had no intention of forming a counterpart Employers' Federation. (At the NTWF's AGC, Councillor Jack Jones of the Gasworkers' Union had insisted, to general agreement, that 'this Joint Board shall be a Federation on one side, and a Federation on the other side.'[12])

Even as the NTWF was formulating its reply to the government proposals, the port employers informed the government 'that they [would] not, under any circumstances, consent to any recognition of the Union or Transport Workers' Federation ticket, or to any discussion of such recognition.'[13]

## Confusion in Government

The employers' 'passive resistance', as Askwith dubbed their stance, was impervious to appeals. The House of Commons passed a resolution suggesting that a meeting between the protagonists would be 'expedient'. This was rebuffed by the employers. The Bishops of London and Southwark made a futile proposal for 'some arbitrator'. Five Cabinet ministers – led by Lloyd George, eager to win prestige and industrial peace in Prime Minister Asquith's absence abroad – intervened, to no avail, the employers announcing themselves quite unmoved by Lloyd George's 'cajolery'. The professional conciliators were marginalized in this process. Asquith, on his return, was furious. In private, he told his conciliator, Askwith, that these bungling initiatives were 'a degradation for government', whose impotence in the face of the unbending Devonport was made publicly manifest. He ordered all ministers, even those at the Board of Trade, to keep out of all future industrial disputes. Sydney Buxton, President of the Board of Trade in 1912, was already schooled in discretion and, after him, Runciman and Harcourt followed the same policy. (It was Lloyd George, during the First World War, who reversed this posture, intervening both personally and by giving wide powers to departmental ministries. The resultant 'maze of authorities' was responsible for actually generating many wartime disputes.)

All this offended the arch-professional, Askwith, who recorded these twists and deviations in government industrial-relations policy as object lessons in good and bad practice.[14] Conciliation, he knew, depended for its success on its independence from 'politics'. In 1912 the ministers cut the ground from under Askwith's feet, and his role was minimal. He succeeded only in arranging a very private meeting between Lord Devonport, and Harry Gosling and Harry Orbell. These two were the labour representatives on the PLA. Devonport, as its chairman, could hardly refuse to meet them, and he lost no face by agreeing. Nevertheless, it was a clandestine encounter. Askwith took the two trade unionists in his carriage to the steps of Devonport's house in Grosvenor Place and waited to see if they gained admittance. As they did, Askwith, the man who a year ago had been ever present between the two sides, discreetly drove away.

## Devonport Sticks

Askwith had recommended to Gosling and Orbell that they seek from Devonport a minimal public statement, endorsing the view that agreements should be honoured. He advised against raising the red rag of the Federation ticket. In the event, Devonport's statement after the meeting was as unyielding as ever. The PLA told the press that 'Mr. Gosling and Mr. Orbell, who are members of the Port of London Authority, interviewed Lord Devonport, the chairman, at this house, 41 Grosvenor Place, this morning (16.7.1912), with the view of discussing a possible settlement of the strike. After a prolonged discussion, Lord Devonport undertook to submit their views to the Port Authority and the employers.'[15]

On one key issue, the employers' position was disingenuous. They publicly rejected the calls for them to form a federation. This would have looked like a concession, heralding recognition and collective bargaining. Yet they already had their forum, their meeting ground, in the shape of the PLA itself, on which sat representatives of the shipowners, merchants, wharfingers, master-lightermen and master-stevedores, together with Admiralty and Trinity House officers. (Poor Orbell and Gosling evidently hardly counted against these massed ranks of port capitalism.)

It is true that the employers did not hesitate to identify publicly with Devonport's conduct of affairs. Their joint statement on the dispute, on 12 July, was signed separately by the PLA, the Association of Master Lightermen and Barge Owners, the Association of Public Wharfingers, William Cory and sons, the General Shipowners' Society, the Granary Keepers' Association, the London Master Carmen and Cartage Contractors' Association, the London Master Stevedores' Association, the London Shipowners' Dock Labour Committee, the Sailing Barge Owners, the Short Sea Traders' Association, the Steamship Owners' Coal Association, and the Thames Dry Docks. Against this formidable front of employing interests the voices of reason and conciliation prevailed not at all.

The government abandoned the problem, by referring all the intractable questions to the toothless Industrial Council:[16] how to ensure the observance of voluntary collective agreements by the signatories, and how to extend their observance throughout a trade to employers not party to the agreement.

## II

### Counterattack: Policemen and Poverty

Employer solidarity was founded on a simple fundamental. They sought only total surrender. The London unions, grouped into the Federation, were also solid in the sense that they were acting together, but all were engaged to achieve distinct and sectional goals. Each union had backed the strike for its own claims and grievances. They, and not the Federation, had made the strike, though they consented to a federal presentation of their case. Between them, they were responsible for between 60,000 and 100,000 strikers and their families.[17] Strike funds were soon exhausted. Strikers were selling their houses to stay alive, while charities brought daily supplies to the dock communities. The *Daily Express*, scourge of the strike leaders and especially of Tillett, daily announced its own bread van's location, in a shrewd display of contrived philanthropy.

Departing from its view of the previous year, the government was persuaded of the merits of deploying troops and police to handle and protect convoys of essential supplies from the docks. This occasioned much rioting and stone-throwing, and many baton-charges. Thirteen thousand free labourers were brought in to the port, and they, with the trains and the ships conveying them, were received in a spasm of violence. In turn, police methods were brutally aggressive, and the free labourers used firearms against pickets with such alarming frequency that Tillett felt justified in calling for the arming of the pickets. In arguing for this course, he made a quite remarkable appeal to authority:

> As the government has allowed the Shipping Federation to organise a civilian police force, we on our side are equally entitled to organise a civilian police to protect our interests, and unless the strike finishes on Monday night, we are going to organise such a force, and we are going to arm them and give them cudgels. Lord Haldane has told us that if it is fair for the Shipping Federation to have a civilian force, so it is fair for the dockers, and we are going to take him at his word.[18, 19]

## Parson Tillett's Prayer

Tillett's conduct in the strike involved its share of revolutionary rhetoric. But in other ways it was, to sober judgement after the event, over the top. Having at first been reluctant to support the London stoppage, he then pursued it in a display of frenzy which had some other Labour leaders in dismay, the press agog to report his daily theatre on Tower Hill, and the cartoonists and satirists busy with acerbic comment.

He began by sending telegrams all over the country at the end of May, before the NTWF Council had met, announcing the imminence of a national sympathy strike. This provoked protests from O'Connor Kessack at the Council. No consultations had taken place with the Liverpool dockers, he complained, before they had been publicly enjoined to action about which they were completely uninformed, and for which they were quite unready.

Then, in one spectacle after another, Tillett surpassed himself. First, at a mass meeting on Tower Hill, he called upon the dockers to pray with him. They assumed the right reverential posture, whereupon he offered up the solemn entreaty: 'Please God, strike Lord Devonport dead.' The Almighty failed to respond. When this cosmic disobedience became apparent, Tillett threatened to take a revolver and do the job himself. It later became plain that this might prove difficult: the adversary was apparently unwilling to volunteer as a target. So Tillett challenged him to a duel. In fact, he exchanged letters with a hoaxer posing as Lord Devonport. It seems that Tillett did not believe that his leg was being pulled.

More damaging to Devonport than all this bloodthirsty talk might have been Tillett's broadcast intention to stop all dock cargoes being unloaded and transported under police protection: 'We will hold up meat; we will hold up flour; we will hold up the Government,' he said. But in fact, the Federation issued permits to move essential supplies, whilst fiercely picketing other cargoes. Gosling negotiated with the Home Secretary in measured terms, conceding the case for certain foods to be moved, and concentrated his public criticism on imported policemen, in contrast to what he described as the acceptable role of local forces.

## Enter Ben Frascati

If Gosling was treating with authority, Tillett was by now attracting the persistent attention of the press. The Daily Express in particular made him the target of continuous denigration. They reported his threat of mass demonstrations when the King came to dockland, as was scheduled, to cut the first sod in the construction of a new dock. (The

King, on government advice, decided to cut his sods elsewhere.) Next, Tillett made a public apology to Lord Devonport – he had never, he said, intended to offend him. If these tenterhooks were not enough, the *Express* then reported that Tillett had been seen on the previous day (16 July) dining at the fashionable and expensive Frascati's restaurant, drinking champagne and smoking an ample cigar, a few hours after issuing a passionate appeal for charitable aid to feed the strikers' starving children. Moreover, he was also tailed to the most expensive gentlemen's hairdresser in town, where in addition to coiffure, he ordered an electric face-massage.

The *Daily Express* related all these 'scandals' with relish. From now on the dockers' leader was given a new name: Ben Frascati. The *Express* was in attendance each day at Tower Hill to report his defence against its charges, claiming that its campaign brought down on Tillett's head a hail of barracking and heckling when he appeared. One sample of this is quite enough to illustrate a much larger volume of *Express* harassment, which continued day after day:

> At a quarter to five, to the music of bands, Ben Tillett bustled through the crowds, and climbed into the wagon amid an uproar of shouts of 'Where's the *Daily Express*?' and tender enquiries of 'Was the champagne very good, Ben?'
>
> Tillett was smartly dressed. He might indeed have just stepped out of a West End restaurant. He wore a fancy white waistcoat, with a neatly arranged grey silk tie, a dark blue lounge suit, and a green squash hat.
>
> As he heard the constantly repeated cries of 'Champagne' he fanned himself vigorously with his hat, and drew from an envelope some sheets of closely-typed paper.
>
> 'Is it a wine list, Ben?' cried an anxious voice from the crowd, and in the laughter that followed the question, Will Thorne replied 'No boys; it's the menu of the dinner he is going to tonight. Sixteen courses – and plenty of champagne.'
>
> 'I should like a drop of champagne now,' retorted Ben as he climbed on a bench to face his laughing followers. 'No chance whilst we're here,' chanted a docker in reply.
>
> Tillett was interrupted then by the arrival of fresh contingents marching to the strains of 'Boys of the Bull-dog Breed'. He stood with uplifted hand, bareheaded, the wind making play with his artistic hair, and cried: 'That's all champagne, boys. A good brand that!'
>
> Every time there was an interruption there was a cry from the platform: 'Are you paid by the *Daily Express*?' and there were threatening shouts from the Tillettites of 'Where is the *Express* man?'
>
> 'Our answer to Lord Devonport and our detractors in the Press', cried Tillett loftily, 'is that the strike is still very much alive.'
>
> 'Like champagne', came an echo.
>
> Then Tillett became pathetic. 'In the name of the little ones,' he pleaded, 'in the name of the children whose eyes look into yours – whose little hands seek yours in confidence —.

'Champagne!' cried a voice, and the rest was lost.

'Wouldn't you like a drink, Ben? shouted a man from the back of the crowd as Tillett was mopping his forehead after his effort.

'I'd like a bottle,' replied Tillett, as cheerfully as possible.[20]

Tillett aggravated the story of the champagne dinner by issuing more than one explanation. At first, he claimed that the *Express* had invited him to Frascati's, but later wrote to *Reynold's News* to say that he had been the guest of a socialist businessman and a wealthy American lady who wanted to arrange financial relief for the strikers' families:

Wine and cigars were ordered and I shared the same; it would have been discourteous otherwise . . . I should be only too delighted to go to the Ritz, the Carlton, or the Hotel Cecil for the same purpose . . . for I have always believed that for my class the best is not too good. I really want the strikers to invade these places to see for themselves how the rich live.[21]

Unfortunately, this tale was followed, on the same page of *Reynold's News*, by a letter from Cecil Chesterton (brother of the novelist G. K. Chesterton), who claimed that he was a fellow guest at the dinner, along with two unnamed friends, to discuss a policy initiative which would strengthen the hand of Labour. One of these two was Hilaire Belloc, whom Tillett had mentioned as a fellow guest.

Concerning the other extravagance of which he was accused, Tillett claimed that the massage he had ordered was 'a vibro treatment for facial neuralgia and headaches' and nothing to do with cosmetics. He concluded: 'to attempt to make capital of the two incidents I have related is to intensify class hatred and class prejudice.' Coming from one who had been telling his audiences that if justice were to be done, all rich people should be hanged, since it was impossible to have acquired wealth without having committed murder, this was perhaps not completely consistent.[22]

Yet if the *Daily Express* and other newspapers were not slow to advertise Frascati's best customer, Ben Tillett kept his hold over his audiences. R. M. Fox, then a young engineering worker, attended a dockers' meeting on Tower Hill and, with all the differences in perception which obviously separate his account from that of the *Express* reporter, it could easily be the same gathering:

the little man holds up his hand for silence. A heavy lorry rumbles through the edge of the crowd.

'Turn that lorry back!' commands Ben Tillett sharply, waving an expressive hand towards it. A score of men spring to do his bidding. 'I will not have lorries coming through my meetings,' he continues . . .

The lorry repulsed, a foreign gentleman addressed the crowd on the need for revolution, and receives loud cheers. Then Ben Tillett again resumes the platform:

'Boys!' he cried. 'I have something to say to you today. Stick together! Let nothing divide your ranks. We are bound to win. The newspapers are at their old tricks of abusing your leaders. They talk about my wine, my dinners, my face massage. They say I went to the South of France after the last strike. Now I have a few words to say to them! It is quite true you sent me to the South of France for my health, didn't you?'

He paused expectantly and looked at the immense crowd.

'We did!' they shouted in chorus.

'And you'll send me again after this strike, won't you?' he cried.

'We will!' came the answering roar.

'And now,' he said triumphantly, 'if there are any reporters here, let them put that down.'

Ben Tillett played on the emotions of the crowd as if he were seated at the organ in some vast cathedral. Sinking his voice to a whisper that could be heard right to the edge of the throng, he spoke of the barefoot, starving children, blue with cold, shivering with need, selling papers at midnight. 'And the only bare legs objected to by our pastors', he continued, swiftly changing his key to scorn, 'are the well-rounded, well-nourished limbs of chorus girls.'

Flinging a hand upward at the big gloomy building behind, he used it to drive home his point. 'In that building is a caretaker. He is looking after it for the Port Authorities. The Government is the caretaker for the capitalists. It takes care of everything for them. We must rely on ourselves!'[23]

If his audiences often warmed to the fire of Tillett's evangelism, the response of Labour and trade-union leaders to Tillett's hyperbole was mixed. Will Thorne, on the platform, clearly tried to laugh it all off. Will Crookes and several other Labour MPs were on their feet more than once in the House of Commons to dissociate themselves from Tillett's 'blasphemy' and his other offences. Askwith tells an interesting story of this period, which may throw light on Tillett's standing:

He could almost deprecatingly wish the boys good luck in Trafalgar Square, but in the Council Chamber he was not always so effective. 'Where is Mr. Tillett?' I asked. 'I want to see him.' 'Oh, we have put him out of the way, to write manifestos in your room, so that he won't interrupt us,' was the reply. There I found him, with his coat off, his shirt-sleeves rolled up (it was very hot), his long hair ruffled, scribbling for all he was worth, on sheets and sheets of Government notepaper. I watered down that manifesto for him, just as he consented to go back by the next train from Manchester at a crucial moment, when he could only have upset things. Ben Tillett is a far more sensible man than some people think, and, be it said, with a very kindly heart.[24]

If we are to take this evidence at its face value, neither his fellow negotiators nor the government conciliator wanted Ben Tillett around during the intense negotiations which resulted from the Great Unrest. Although he clearly made an appearance at the Manchester negotiations of 1911, he features not at all in the other provincial disputes that year, and in 1912 his appearances were also confined to London. His main impact seems to have been on the public platform.

## A Sense of Desperation

Yet in 1912, this frenetic mood was not confined to the changeable impressionistic leader of the dockers. Other, more sober characters, made pronouncements which showed that a common desperation affected many of the leaders. Will Thorne, MP and an Alderman of the West Ham Town Council, moved the following motion at a Council meeting on 11 June:

> That in consequence of the refusal of the London Port Authority, the shipowners, the master lightermen, the wharfingers and other employers on the Thames and Medway to accept the terms of the settlement suggested by the Government and agreed by the men, this council instructs the borough engineer to pull up immediately those parts of the roads in West Ham that have direct communication with the docks in the borough.

This idea was greeted with some jeering. Thorne cried out, 'I am not bluffing, I am in dead earnest.' The Mayor, from the chair, refused to accept the motion, observing that the roads were the King's. 'The King be hanged!' said Thorne. 'He doesn't pay for the roads and we do. We are perfectly justified in doing all we can to obstruct the Port Authority ... We have a perfect right to pull up the roads, the men themselves will do it if they get instructions.' 'They will do it without,' shouted Councillor Jones.[25]

## The Failure of the National Strike Call

In this heady atmosphere, the Federation Council called out its members on a national sympathy strike on 10 June. The NUDL registered its reservations. O'Connor Kessack went so far as to say that he could not instruct men to break agreements in a cause which was not their own.

Father Hopkins instructed the Liverpool seamen not to strike, and both he and Kessack were rebuked at the NTWF Council. The provincial membership of the DWRGWU in the South-west struck for a few days, as did the Southampton breakaway seamen's union. In Manchester 1,000 dockers struck, in Bristol 8,000. There was some support voiced for a strike in Hull, but none took place. In Liverpool, when the National Executive of the NUDL convened, it resolved that, since the London strike had been called without consultation, and on behalf of a London dispute, the union could not ask men to break their agreements, and 'we cannot accept the responsibility of participating in a national strike'.[26] The NSFU had supported the strike in London, but declined to spread it to the other ports until it had held a ballot. Father Hopkins sent a telegram to the seamen in Manchester and the North-east: '[I] place my honour in your keeping, and beg you to maintain it unsullied by refusing to be either frightened or cajoled into ceasing work.'[27]

The national call was answered by only 20,000 men, who, on seeing the meagre response, themselves went back to work in a few days. On 19 June *Punch* had an apt and ironic cartoon for the day. In it, a man is standing on a barrel, arms raised, in his hand a scroll bearing the words 'General Strike'. He faces a turbulent seascape, labelled 'Labour Unrest'. Lightning flashes across a dark sky. Alongside the man stands Mr Punch. Their conversation in the caption reads:

GLENDOWER GOSLING: 'I can call spirits from the vasty deep.'
HOTSPUR PUNCH: 'Why, so can I, or so can any man, but will they come when you do call them?'

(*Henry IV*, Part 1, act III, scene i)

## Six Sullen Weeks in London

The Londoners sustained their now isolated strike for another six weeks, resisting or sullenly watching the food convoys move through their streets, listening to Tillett on Tower Hill, in increasing despair and bitterness, diverted only by the ribaldry of the exchanges with their leader on the rostrum. Their despair reached out to engulf the leaders. When the union funds ran out, a grant was expected from the General Federation of Trade Unions. Men were told that they could come in to the union offices to collect it. There was a delay in delivering the cash, and it was thought that all the branches had been told of this and that the men knew of it. But Gosling, arriving at his office, saw

two or three hundred members queueing up for their strike pay. On inquiry I found that through some oversight three of the outlying branches had not been written to and the men had come, as usual, some of them having walked as much as ten miles to get there. It was impossible to pay them, and I had to go down the line to tell them so. It was a bitter disappointment to them, but they went quietly away to their homes. I felt sick and miserable about the whole business . . . I passed the weekend in the depths.[28]

## Calling it Off

Without funds and without hope, the Federation at last ordered a return to work on 27 July. There were resounding protests from the men at mass meetings called to announce the decision, and the leadership temporarily withdrew its instruction. It reaffirmed it, however, two days later. Nevertheless there were riots on the day of the return: strikers fought free labourers, and a full, general resumption was not obtained until mid-August. The strike had achieved nothing; no Joint Board, no Federation ticket, and the call-stands reverted to their old position inside the dockgates, outside union control. The men had no guarantee of reinstatement, and many remained unemployed. Union membership was sharply reduced, and Lord Devonport punished his permanent workers – who had struck – by placing them on the 'B' list, giving their places over to free labourers.

The strike had been defeated by a combination of circumstances, of which two were outstanding. The employers rediscovered their nerve rapidly after the defeat of 1911 and found unity under the toughest of leaders. And the issues which engaged the London stevedores, lightermen, bargemen and carters were not such as to engage nationwide support; they appeared to be parochial. The Federation placed too much faith in the success of 1911, which had little to do with its own authority, and upon the government's ability and willingness to coerce the employers as it had done in mining, railways, and to some extent in the docks, in 1911. The government proved impotent against the stand of Lord Devonport and his alliance.

There had to be a stocktaking, and an inquest.

## III

## Consequences

The quantitative effects were evident when the TUC's annual membership figures were published in September 1913. The Stevedores' Union, which had doubled in size between 1911 and 1912, fell from 8,000 to 5,610. The Lightermen's Union was less seriously affected: it had increased from 3,000 in 1911 to 6,761 in 1912; it fell to 5,000 in 1913. The London Carmen's Union was severely afflicted: between 1911 and 1912 it had increased by 3,000 to reach 8,000; the following year, the union's strength was halved, to 4,000. The comparable figures for the principal new unions on the waterfront are shown in table 11.1.

It is evident that the Seamen's Union and the NUDL suffered no after-effects from the London strike or its associated and aborted

Table 11.1 *Membership of Principal New Unions, 1911–1913*

|        | 1911   | 1912   | 1913   |
| ------ | ------ | ------ | ------ |
| NSFU   | 20,000 | 60,000 | 60,000 |
| DWRGWU | 20,000 | 50,000 | 37,000 |
| NUDL   | 12,000 | 24,000 | 32,000 |
| Gas/Gen. | 32,000 | 71,000 | 82,000 |

*Source: TUC Annual Reports.*

national sympathy action. The NUDL had refused to respond to the national call. The NSFU had supported the strike in London, but not its provincial extension. Thus Captain Tupper appeared with his customary enthusiasm alongside Tillett on Tower Hill, whilst Father Hopkins told his northern membership to abide by their agreements, and the National Executive would not back the national call without a ballot, which went narrowly against supporting it. Havelock Wilson returned to Britain from an assignment in the USA in July, and tried, with Tom Mann, to rouse support in the northern ports. But they got no further than Hull before Wilson was convinced of the lack of support and swung his authority in favour of an end to both national and London strikes.[29] The gasworkers were fully committed to the London strike, but their membership spread was diverse and so the union sustained its recruitment through the critical year.

Thus, the blow fell principally upon the DWRGWU, along with the three London-based occupational unions. In Tillett's union, the losses were confined to the London district, whose contribution income fell by more than 50 per cent, at a time when the union's total income (including London) fell by about 8 per cent.[30]

In the NTWF, the combined loss of membership was 30,000, of which we must attribute 13,000 to the DWRGWU and 4,000 each to the London carmen and the stevedores. These losses were not recovered until after the First World War. Two unions withdrew from the Federation – the London Riggers and the National Union of Clerks. Several others declined invitations to join. The defeat marked the end of London's domination of the Federation and its London District Committee was reduced to impotence in the face of indiscriminate poaching, while blacklegs retained their jobs. The PLA removed the ancient legal monopoly of apprenticed lightermen on the barges.

The longest-lasting consequence was to drive the stevedores back into the laager of their traditional, but shrinking, aristocratic domain, covered by the London Master Stevedores' Association, which restored the old conditions of monopoly for them. The Short Sea Traders' Association and the large, downstream employers reversed all the stevedores' vulnerable gains, and Lord Devonport refused their request to arbitrate in these cases. In July 1913, the union had to close its short-sea branch, as the men left. At Tilbury, its insistence on its call-on rules caused the formation of a breakaway London Stevedores' Society, since the union's rigidity meant that many members could not compete against dockers for jobs with shipowners or with Scrutton's. Dockers then took over their jobs. The Stevedores' Union expelled members who conformed to the in-dock call-on, despite the Federation's pleas for flexibility, and the dockers continued to encroach upon the stevedores' jobs, down to the First World War.[31] This proved to be a permanent rift, of enormous consequence for the future TGWU and for inter-union relations in the docks industry. In 1911 the port workers had created a truly remarkable solidarity, but now it was gone, and the seeds of conflict between dockers and stevedores had been sown, to endure for generations. The 1912 defeat and its consequences isolated the stevedores, making them a focus for any future dissent within the TGWU amongst dockers. Eventually this dissent escaped the confines of London (see Vol. II).

The Federation became preoccupied with the controversy of the 'Federation ticket', for which the Gasworkers' and General Labourers' Union and the London Carmen's Union pressed, against the resistance of the DWRGWU, the NUDL and (on this making common cause) the Stevedores' Union. To Will Thorne, it was an affront that his gasworkers, who had traditionally taken dock jobs in the summer months, should be disbarred from what was a way of life, in the sectional interests of more regular dockworkers.[32] Here we find the seeds of another intransigent problem facing those who wished to move on from federation to amalgamation, and we shall explore it more fully later.

## Learning from Defeat

The Federation's more thoughtful leaders, Harry Gosling and Robert Williams, were capable and ready to learn from defeat. Williams, now translated from his post in the National Amalgamated Labourers' Union to the secretaryship of the Federation, recalled in 1914: 'My experience of the Federation . . . has been that before we attempted to promote a national strike everybody believed it was possible . . . and therefore our federation was very strong; but once we attempted and miserably failed, then our Federation fell miserably flat.'[33] Workers on the railways, in the mines and engineering had all achieved deliberate and coherent national actions by this date. What had gone wrong in transport, to render its sole attempt at general action so disastrous?

Clearly, the spontaneous solidarity of 1911 had broken down; the seamen showed no general inclination to respond, nor did the dockers beyond London. The railwaymen had moved goods blacked by the

London strikers. James Sexton probably came closest to explaining why the national call failed to evoke a wide response:

> in order to secure unanimity for a national movement there should be a collective national interest with a well organised national programme in which all should mutually have some at least prospective advantage. In the case of the Thames dispute all these were not only conspicuous by their entire absence, but, in addition, the unions outside London stood to lose all the advantages they had previously gained.[34]

It is hard to quarrel with this. The London strike was in origin a series of sectional disputes, joined together and justified by the London federationists. The attempt to widen it by raising the issue of the Federation ticket failed, since this instrument was hardly yet a popular concept in the minds of the industry's workers. If the Federation had been more comprehensive, and had already evolved an effective internal discipline, it is conceivable that it could have separated each group of employers in a series of specific sectional strikes, which could have been sustained by disciplined blacking and by strike funds augmented from its total, national, federal income. This is the understanding towards which the acute young mind of Ernest Bevin was moving.

> I happen to be where the dockers and carters are in one union (in Bristol) and there the carters have been more successful than in any other town in the country in relation to the conditions they were under . . . I say it is the consciousness of the employer, the whole time that he is negotiating with the coal trimmer, the docker, the carter, or the seaman, that they have a central executive behind them representing the co-operation of their fellows in the same organisation, that gives the power to negotiate. It is not so much a power to attack, as a power to negotiate . . . [35]

Bevin was in an unassailable position to read this lesson into the debate. In 1912 the Federation prepared and distributed a map of the representation of its affiliates in the different British ports (see Fig. 11.1). In the Port of London, the map shows us seven unions in place, although there were actually more if every specialism were to be accounted for. In Liverpool five unions were operating; in Hull and Cardiff four; while, of ports comparable in significance, only in Bristol was the DWRGWU possessed of a monopoly of port labour organization (although, in Glasgow the dockers were represented in the NTWF only by their own Scottish Union of Dock Labourers).

Harry Gosling was honest, if peremptory, in his assessment of the strike, calling it 'the fiasco of the so-called national strike of 1912'. He recalled that 'A sense of defeat and weariness hung over us for many weeks and months after the summer of 1912'.[36]

**Fig. 11.1** NATIONAL TRANSPORT WORKERS' FEDERATION

British Ports and the Trade Unions with Membership in Them, 1912

1 National Union of Dock Labourers
2 Dock, Wharf, Riverside and General Labourers
3 Irish Transport and General Workers
4 Scottish Union of Dock Labourers
5 Amalgamated Stevedores Labour Protection League
6 National Amalgamated Union of Labour
7 National Union of Gasworkers and General Labourers
8 National Amalgamated Labourers Union

9 Cardiff, Penarth and Barry Coal Trimmers
10 North of England Trimmers and Teemers
11 National Union of Railwaymen
12 National Amalgamated Union of Enginemen and Firemen
13 United Order of General Labourers of London
14 Amalgamated General and Warehouse Workers Union
15 North East Federated Societies
16 Amalgamated Protective Union of Engine and Cranedrivers

*Source:* NTWF Annual Report, 1912.

## Tillett Stirs the Pot

Ben Tillett, however, reacted differently. In his Annual Report for the
DWRGWU in December 1912, he wrote a heady account. It was short
on analysis, but effervescent with syndicalist rhetoric. Appalled by the
repeated and brutal baton-charges of the police on defenceless strikers,
he reiterated the call to arms which he had made so often on Tower Hill,
even though this was his considered review of the events rather than a
speech at an excited mass rally: 'The lesson, if any, is, that in future
strikes, the strikers must protest against the use of arms, with arms;
protest against shooting, with shooting; protest against violence, with
violence.'[37]

This revolutionary rhetoric goes far beyond any likely practicable
policy, as may be seen if it is contrasted with the response of Tom Mann
to state violence. After all, Mann had, in 1912, joined the strike
organizers only after a prison sentence imposed not for advocating the
militarization of pickets but for urging the soldiers not to shoot their
fellow workers, in his famous *Don't Shoot* pamphlet. Mann's offence, in
the eyes of authority, was far deeper than Tillett's, who would declare,
before his calls for weapons on Tower Hill, 'this may be sedition but . . . '
There was far more danger, from the viewpoint of authority, that the
army might listen to Mann than that the dockers might take Tillett's
advice. But sedition of Tillett's kind was, however, to become absolutely
practical politics in Dublin, in the course of the elemental struggles of
the following year. The difference between London and Dublin dockers
must surely be sought in the different conjunctions between class and
national claims. To follow Tillett's argument, it is necessary to remember
that he was inveighing not against injuries inflicted by the guns of
soldiers, but against wounds brought about by armed strike-breakers,
none of whom was arrested or punished. These squads of private
terrorists caused real damage and hurt. To that should be added the
weight of police beatings, not one of which brought any prosecution for
violence. This it was that aroused Tillett's rage, which survived the
passions of the strike for many months.

For Tillett there was another lesson, which he expressed in phrases
which have gone down in history as epitomizing both his own firebrand
style, and somehow the spirit of syndicalism: 'The other lesson is, that
Parliament is a farce and a sham, and is the rich man's Duma, the
employers' Tammany, the "Thieves Kitchen", and the working man's
despot'.[38] This angry onslaught was provoked by the inability of
government or Parliament to prevail on the employers to conform to
acceptable collective-bargaining norms: 'The Conciliation Act was
inoperative, the elaborate panels were useless, and legal contracts were
ruthlessly thrown over . . . It is unwarrantable that . . . the Port of London

Authority is allowed to break every bond, to refuse conciliation and recognition'.[39] Whilst this may be true, it also revealed a certain inconsistency on Tillett's own part, since it was scarcely prudent for a declared anti-parliamentarian to expect the state to help him in the conduct of the class war, 'the most brutal of wars and the most pitiless'.

From this moment, it seems that Tillett's influence on the forward evolution of new unionism towards its goal of wider amalgamation and recognized collective bargaining was beginning to wane. He had always had a tendency to seek scapegoats when defeated; he had often castigated the backsliding of his own members and attacked other unions. Now, he returned to this theme:

> So far as the strike is concerned, there is much of a sinister character to regret. Some of the unions with the least responsibility, were frantic for action, for the strike, etc. These, who were lions in the councils and demanded war, were veritable mice in the actual fighting, although they went whining around after the settlement to betray those who had made the fight strong, although some of us had opposed the calling out of the men. Since the strike I regret to report that these same parties are now setting up 'poaching tactics'.[40]

## Robert Williams Speaks Out

For a consistently radical judgement of these events, the dockers and their allies would have been able to turn to Bob Williams, who wasted no words on hyperbole. 'The 1912 Strike left us enervated and well-nigh disconsolate,' he wrote. 'It has called for a considerable amount of effort to maintain the numerical strength left to us. The members of the waterside Unions are still keen on more effective organisation, and something must be done to utilise to the fullest the ever-increasing desire for solidarity.'[41]

Williams recognized that the Federation had lost ground in those provincial ports which had tried to respond to the national strike call. 'Manchester, Bristol, Swansea and Southampton will look with extreme suspicion at any requests . . . for prompt action,' he went on. (We should note that young Bevin had the responsibility for safeguarding union membership in an important part of these territories.)

> We are not dismayed by the facts outlined above. We wish only to point out the rocks and shallows for the purpose of preventing further disaster. We are not deterred even by failure. Today's failure may lead to tomorrow's success. Whatever success the Federation has achieved has been in consequence of the reprisals of numbers of men, who, by continued defeat and humiliation, were driven into universal revolt. Let it be made unmistakably clear, the struggles and accomplishments of 1911, except for a

word of guidance here and there, were from the bottom upwards. Unconstitutionalism, and the driving force of spontaneous action, have done more for Trade Unionism, and in fact, for all other movements, than all the leadership, guidance, and counsel put together.

In 1911, according to the Report furnished by the Registrar of Friendly Societies, the increase in the number of Trade Unionists amounted to half-a-million – an increase that is simply phenomenal. One Union alone within the Federation, the National Sailors' and Firemen's Union, registered an increase of fifty thousand members. This is unparalleled in industrial affairs.

It requires no gift of prophecy to discern on the horizon one of the greatest industrial crises imaginable. For years the workers have witnessed a reduction in their Real Wages, brought about by the rise in prices. For years they have endured it with ox-like patience. But already can be heard the rumblings of revolt. One of the questions for us, now on the threshold of a new year is: How far are we prepared for the storm when it must inevitably break?[42]

Williams's answer was a radical return to an earlier tradition:

The main body of Trade Unionists do not yet fully realise the important strategic position we as Transport Workers occupy. Nor do they see what elaborate preparations the employers and the Government have made, and are making, to prevent a successful stoppage of traffic and transit. Would it be considered a crime were we to suggest that since, as Board of Trade figures testify, a sovereign buys only as much as sixteen shillings bought ten years ago, we should give a diminishing quantity of labour in exchange for the diminishing value of the wages we receive? Perchance it would be called Sabotage? . . . Well, call it what we may, it seems to us eminently practicable that as the price of every commodity tends to rise, except that of the commodity known as human labour, and as the purchasers of human labour – the employing class – steadfastly refuse to raise the price, and we are unable to raise it ourselves, we should give less and less in return for that price, in proportion to the decline in our Real Wages.

Now, this cannot be adopted effectively by one section, not in one district: it must have general application. We commend it to the attention of those who appreciate the gravity of the increased cost of keeping alive. We commend to all those who are mindful of their position as leaders this suggestion. We offer this as a starting-point for a National Campaign in favour of the 'Conquest of Bread'.

Here is a rallying-point for the men who would dare in the New Year 1914. Advise the men who use shovels to lessen the size of them, or to use them slower. Tell those who work with a hook to slacken speed. Urge those who stoke furnaces to bring down steam pressure. Impress upon carters not to overwork their horses. Request all and sundry to go steady, 'Ca' canny'. In value you get less – well, then, give less.

And, maybe, the adoption of this policy will result more to our advantage than all the active strikes ever embarked upon.[43]

## Amalgamate!

The Federation as a whole wasted little public breath on inquest or recrimination. At its third Annual General Council in Newport, in June 1913, Gosling, in his presidential address, set the tone and encouraged a forward-looking response: 'We have at least the great advantage (even if dearly bought), of the mistakes of last year. If we can profit by this experience, and can in future avoid those mistakes, then the sacrifice was not in vain.'[44]

Moreover, in reporting on the Executive's post-strike tour of the country's ports, in which he had taken a full part, Gosling found that 'There is no doubt about it, the men are splendid,' though he admitted that in London 'we met with men embittered and bad-tempered'. These impressions may serve as a balanced assessment of the whole affair, which was deeply damaging in the capital but, for better or worse, made little impact elsewhere upon the minds of the membership. Its lessons were learned by the leaders. And that is really all Gosling had to say about 1912. He hurried on to speak at length and persuasively about the necessity to move towards an amalgamation. Will Thorne helped the mood: 'There was no need to wash dirty linen at that Conference.' Tensions and divisions did appear on that occasion, centred round the Federation ticket issue, but the conference made its mark on history by resolving, after lengthy debate, that 'This Conference recommends that the Executive Council of the Federation be instructed to prepare a scheme for the complete amalgamation of all the unions affiliated to the Federation'.[45] This was carried 'amidst cheers'.

## The Government's Balance Sheet

It remains to add that the government, taxed by the intractable problem of the London strike, had its own lessons to learn. It had been criticized by Tillett for supinely upholding Lord Devonport, and for assisting the strike-breakers with police and troops. It was attacked by a hostile section of the new, Tory, populist press, for not breaking more pickets' heads; for not 'meeting violence with violence' and punitive action. What disturbed it most, in the long-term, were the difficulties thrown up, within the voluntary system of industrial relations which it had set itself to foster, of ensuring observance of agreements and their general application throughout a trade. Both questions have great historic significance. Throughout the twentieth century, a whole range of optional answers have been tried, in law and in practice. For the moment, the government in 1912 referred them to the Industrial Council for a report.[46]

The events of 1912 were a warning and a setback. They did not repeat the catastrophic reverses of 1893; but they did dispel illusions about the industrial clout of the NTWF and induced a permanent caution in the unions' leadership, for never again did the Federation issue a call for a national strike.

# Notes

1  Resolution passed by the principal London port employers and their associations, 13 July 1912.
2  Letter from Lord Devonport to the *Daily Express*, 12 July 1912.
3  NTWF Annual General Council Report, June 1912, p. 5.
4  Report upon the Present Disputes affecting Transport Workers in the Port of London and on the Medway, Cmnd 6229, May 1912 (the Clarke Report), p. 3.
5  Gordon Phillips, 'The National Transport Workers' Federation, 1910–1927' (unpublished PhD thesis, Oxford University, 1968), p. 130.
6  John Lovell, *Stevedores and Dockers: a Study of Trade Unionism in the Port of London, 1870–1914* (Macmillan, 1969), p. 199.
7  The Clarke Inquiry, Minutes of Evidence, p. 28.
8  Ibid., p. 14.
9  Ibid., p. 18.
10  Lord Askwith, *Industrial Problems and Disputes* (John Murray, 1920), pp. 221–2.
11  NTWF Annual General Council Report, June 1912, p. 8. These three demands were formulated by Tillett.
12  Ibid., p. 30.
13  Phillips, 'The National Transport Workers' Federation', p. 134.
14  Askwith, *Industrial Problems and Disputes*, p. 230.
15  Press statement by the PLA, *Daily Express*, 16 July 1912.
16  On the initiative of Sir Charles Macara, a leading and highly influential cotton magnate, Sydney Buxton set up the Industrial Council in 1911. George Askwith was its chairman, and it comprised representatives of big business, employers' associations and trade-union leaders. Of these, Harry Gosling for the NTWF and J. R. Clynes for the gasworkers sat with eleven other leaders – all with craft or single-industry unions. Askwith's verdict on its deliberations, which were intended to foster good relations between capital and Labour, is telling: 'Advice not desired, sought, or taken, and decisions without sanction of possible force, would, after a few failures, have little or no value. Usefulness can only be acquired by success' (Ibid., p. 184).

A detailed study of the Industrial Council over the years 1911 to 1913 is to be found in Rodger Charles, *The Development of Industrial Relations in Britain, 1911–1939* (Hutchinson, 1973), pp. 37–76, in which it is interpreted as the harbinger of the voluntarist tradition in British industrial relations which developed through Whitleyism and the Joint Industrial Councils, the National Industrial Conference of 1919–21, and the Mond–

Turner conferences of 1928–9. The author, and the editor of the series in which the volume appeared, Arthur Marsh, (in a foreword) lament the rupture of this tradition caused by the Industrial Relations Act of 1971.

17  Askwith gives the larger figure, Phillips the smaller. Whichever is more accurate, the strike was enormous in scale.

18  Lord Haldane, a lawyer who had studied Hegel and translated Schopenhauer, had been an MP since 1885. During 1912 he was successively Secretary for War and Lord Chancellor.

19  Quoted in *Daily Express*, 10 June 1912.

20  *Daily Express*, 24 June 1912.

21  *Reynolds News*, 23 July 1912.

22  Tillett's clashes with the *Express* became daily affairs on Tower Hill. On 20 June he called the paper 'a sewer rat's rag . . . and the editor is the chief sewer rat . . . How much is he paid by the Shipping Federation? He is a low scoundrel, a capitalists' pet, a rat, a liar.' On another occasion, he threatened a libel action against the paper, which contemptuously printed his threat and invited him to go ahead. He never did. One day, he claimed to identify 'the *Express* spy' in the crowd, and incited the dockers to seize the man and bring him forward to the rostrum.

23  R. M. Fox, *Smoky Crusade: An Autobiography* (Hogarth Press, 1937), pp. 96–7.

24  Askwith, *Industrial Problems and Disputes*, p. 233.

25  Press reports, 12 June 1912.

26  *Liverpool Daily Post and Mercury*, 12 June 1912, p. 7; quoted in Eric Taplin, *The Dockers' Union: A Study of the National Union of Dock Labourers, 1889–1922* (Leicester University Press, 1986), p. 119.

27  *Daily Express*, 12 June 1912.

28  Harry Gosling, *Up and Down Stream* (Methuen, 1927), p. 162.

29  Arthur Marsh and Victoria Ryan, *History of the Seamen's Union* (Malthouse, 1989), p. 63.

30  DWRGWU Annual Reports, 1912 and 1913.

31  Lovell, *Stevedores and Dockers*, pp. 204 ff.

32  At the NTWF's Annual General Council of 1913, Thorne said: 'It was a well-known fact that men followed two occupations. Members of his own union worked in the gasworks in the winter and in the docks in the summer. It [the rejection of the Federation ticket] would force the men who found work in the gasworks in the winter to join the gasworkers and leave the dockers.'

33  Report to the Joint Executive of the Triple Alliance, 1914, quoted in Phillips, 'The National Transport Workers' Federation', p. 149n.

34  Press report, quoted in Eric Taplin, *The Dockers' Union*, p. 120. Sexton's attitude to the 1912 strike was evident in his next Annual Report. He didn't mention it!

35  NTWF and GLNC Amalgamation Conference, 8 July 1914, pp. 22–3.

36  Gosling, *Up and Down Stream*, p. 164.

37  DWRGWU Annual Report to 31 December 1912, p. 6.

38  Ibid., p. 6.

39  Ibid.

40  Ibid., p. 7.

41  NTWF *Weekly Record*, no. 36 (3 January 1914), p. 1.
42  Ibid., pp. 1–2.
43  Ibid.
44  NTWF Annual General Council Report, 1913, p. 9.
45  Ibid.
46  The report of the Industrial Council's Inquiry into Industrial Agreements, appeared as Cmnd 6952, 1913 (Minutes of Evidence, Cmnd 6953, 1913). Its conclusion was that 'We regard it as axiomatic that nothing should be done which would lead to the abandonment of a method of adjusting relationships between employers and workpeople which has proved so advantageous throughout most of the trades of the country'. There was no help here for Tillett's advocacy of compulsory arbitration, or for radical interventionists like Lloyd George.

# I2

---

# 1912: Registration

## I

### Decasualization? How?

While London's port workers were bandaging the wounds inflicted by
the failure of the 1912 strike, the port of Liverpool was adjusting to an
experience of another kind. It was coping with the manifold difficulties of
the most elaborate attempt yet made to regularize dock labour, through a
clearing-house scheme.

We must remember that in London, after the 1889 strike, the Dock
Companies had followed the advice of the poverty researcher and charity
organizer Charles Booth, and had unilaterally instituted a classification
system creating categories of permanent and preferred dockers (see
chapter 4). The unions saw this as an effort to rule by division. Their
view was reinforced when non-dockers were brought in to take preferred
places. The customary social solidarity of the men, whose whole outlook
assumed work-sharing, with the strong looking after the weak, was
undermined. The unions' evidence to the Royal Commission on Labour
in the early 1890s had consistently advocated municipal ownership of the
ports, and the establishment of municipal workshops to provide work for
surplus labour, as the humane way to overcome casual employment.
Employers, in the main, favoured neither solution. Decasualization was
seen as benefiting only the big companies, disadvantaging all the smaller
fry who could not accurately plan their needs for labour. It was also
suspect to employers, who commonly perceived it as a means for
advancing the power of the union through a closed shop. Most dock
employers thought in the crudest 'man-management' terms. Fear, they
believed, was a necessary stimulus to work, and its discipline was the
main incentive to sustain productivity. The London Classification

Scheme did not extend beyond the Dock Companies; and the big shipping companies, which were taking over larger shares of cargo-handling, produced their own gritty panacea – the Shipping Federation ticket, free labour and the brutal anti-union drive of the 1890s.

Booth took his scheme to Liverpool in 1894, but achieved no results from his conference with charities and the municipality.[1] Eleanor Rathbone, the daughter of a leading Liverpool overseas merchant, who believed that trade unions were an obstacle to her ideas of reform, resurrected his programme in 1904, again without results.[2] The Charity Organization Society tried again, in 1906, but their proposals broke down over the definitions of permanent and preference men; only the large liner companies operated such systems, and in the port as a whole it was desired neither by the men nor by their employers.[3]

Opposition from both sides to all these schemes of partial decasualization rested on a number of considerations, quite apart from the employers' fear of union power and their strong desire to hire and fire at will. To reduce the surplus of labour and end the scandal of destitution associated with casualism, it would be necessary to build in some device which could promote the mobility of workers between docks, between trades and between employers, as seasonal and other fluctuations recurrently created labour shortages here and surpluses there. Abstract mobility schemes to overcome these imbalances assumed what had never been the case, namely the homogeneity of dock labour. We have said enough on this point, in previous chapters, not to need to elaborate it further here. Many dockers were specialists, in the handling of, say, corn, timber or coal. Those trades which were subject to seasonal and cyclical fluctuations in demand solved the problem by maintaining their own, segmented, labour surplus. The men shared what work was going, reaching full employment only at rare peak times. In return, the employers 'looked after' this pool of established 'tradesmen' by giving their small unions recognition, and their members preference of employment. Both sides managed their needs from day to day, often respecting the customs of the trade or the dock. These customs extended from the acceptance of certain manning scales for each cargo, to elaborate 'working rules', which were to become codified in union rule books.[4] These unilateral worker controls gave the older dock unions, based on particular trades, real bargaining power: employers at the South End Docks in Liverpool and in Birkenhead had complained of 'a reign of tyranny' by union rule as far back as 1892.[5] These discrete, trade-bounded practices, and also the looser but still real immobilities which resulted when dock groups and gangs confined themselves to one customary call-stand, were reinforced by a strong communal feeling; no docker felt easy moving into other trades or territories, especially if this meant taking another docker's work from him. Into this world of deep traditions and binding customs stepped rude new forces, in the Liverpool of 1912, which combined in an attempt to break the habits of generations of casual labourers.

## Attitudes in London and Liverpool

The two principal dockers' new unions, Tillett's and Sexton's, both sought an inclusive membership covering all grades and trades. Both, therefore, set out to absorb or put out of business sectional dock unions. We have seen that Tillett's union succeeded in this only in Bristol; in London by 1912 no fewer than twenty-nine unions claimed waterfront members of one kind or another.[6] The National Transport Workers' Federation ticket, which might have helped to draw all unions together in preparation for a jointly regulated decasualization, became instead a bone of contention between port unions, especially in London. Consistent with the relative weakness into which these circumstances drove Tillett, he was a vociferous critic of decasualization schemes; from his perspective and that of his union, such schemes would destroy old and ingrained customs, replacing them with streamlined (and ruthless) employer controls. The formation of the Port of London Authority, moreover, instead of bringing modernization, union recognition and rationality, merely entrenched and oligopolized the power of capital in London, perpetuating preference schemes in which the employers called all the shots.

In Liverpool, things were different. Sexton's union was much more comprehensive; whilst coal-heavers, engine- and crane-drivers, and warehousemen had separate organizations, there was here no equivalent to the South Side Labour Protection League, or the Stevedores', and the Gasworkers' Unions, which cut swathes right through Tillett's territories in the Port of London. Sexton was relatively untroubled, therefore, by inter-union problems, or by the issue of the Federation ticket. None the less, he joined Tillett's opposition to the gasworkers' and the NAUL's claims that their members in other sectors were seasonally entitled to take dock jobs.

## Incorporating the NUDL

If he faced different problems, Sexton's strategy to meet them was also different. He sought a disciplined, tightly controlled and centralized union, guaranteeing stability of membership and income. As we have seen, he further sought to reinforce these aims by close collaboration with the employers, leading to the setting up of joint bargaining and regulatory mechanisms. Thus, one plank of a platform on which to build a decasualization agreement was already in place.

At the same time, the leading shipowners in Liverpool, major employers of dock labour in the transoceanic liner trades, now faced a highly volatile labour force which, fresh from its triumphs of 1911, was on the warpath. Unofficial lightning strikes flared up at every grievance. The major employers reasoned that they might avoid the pressure to buy peace by constant concessions to the men, if they could harness Sexton's parallel instincts for good order and discipline into a scheme to regularize the supply of labour at the dockside itself. They would incorporate the union as a labour agent, give it a new status and rely on its institutional interests to deliver not only labour, but industrial peace.

The union had, in the agreement of 1911, accepted that its officials were expected 'to control their constituents by enforcing decisions of the [Joint] Committee . . . and strict adherence to the terms of the Agreement'.[7] Sexton was already facing accusations from parts of his membership that he was too much of a bosses' man, and his reputation had been bruised by his conflict with James Larkin, so for him this was a perilous formula. Nevertheless, Sexton's standing was not so low that he did not feel confident of taking the union along his chosen course. He had shared the leadership of the successful strikes of 1911 with Tom Mann, and had secured recognition, and the White Book bargaining and conciliation agreement – the most advanced of its kind – as a result. His membership had soared. And he had carefully avoided involvement in the Federation's strike of 1912, so that the cost of defeat was not visited upon his union directly.

## Beveridge Chastises the 'Lazy'

We have already identified William Beveridge as a product of the Oxford–Toynbee Hall tradition. Successively encouraged by the Webbs and Churchill, Beveridge was evolving his ideas on unemployment and the labour market. No doubt he would have recognized his evident debt to Booth in the scheme he evolved at this time. Whilst envisaging 'substantially full employment' as a practical goal, 'those men who through general defects are unable to fill such a "whole" place in industry, are to be recognized as "unemployable".'[8] In 1909 the young administrator's reputation as an advanced social thinker was enhanced by the publication of his book, *Unemployment: A Problem of Industry*, in which he advocated both labour exchanges and unemployment insurance. In the case of the docks, he saw the exchanges helping the employer to nurture preferred and efficient labour by securing, through mobility, more regular work for the best workers. At the same time, he clearly accepted the obverse of this: for 'the man who wants to get a casual job now and again, the exchange will make that wish impossible' . . . 'The lazy and incapable' would be compelled 'to be regular'.[9] Finally, the unfit would be referred to the Poor Law authorities. All this amounted to a belated reworking, in the new century, of the venerable doctrines of Jeremy Bentham, or of the example of Charles Dickens's immortal Thomas Gradgrind: 'a man of realities. A man of facts and calculations ... [discarding] the word "fancy" altogether'.

## II

## *Labour Exchanges*

Under Churchill's management, a Labour Exchange Act was carried in 1909. However, contrary to advice from Sidney Webb, neither employer or worker was compelled to make use of the offices it established, and they were in fact under-utilized. Unemployment insurance was introduced in 1911, but was not applied on the docks; the prevalence of casual work would have rendered it too expensive. The dockers were, however, covered by the health-insurance provisions of the Act. The Port of London employers, led by the PLA, systematically resisted the 'interference' of the Board of Trade, which pressed in vain for a system of labour exchanges in the port itself. In order to overcome employer resistance, Beveridge would have preferred that unemployment insurance be extended to the industry. Employers would then have had an additional inducement to economize on their contributions by regularizing their use of labour, and pooling those costs which the scheme imposed on them. The Cabinet resisted this extension of the system to an industry which would have brought about a heavy drain on the national fund.

## *Richard Williams's Diligence*

Despite these poor auguries, the Board of Trade embarked on its most ambitious test of the labour-exchange concept in the port of Liverpool. Richard Williams was the divisional officer of the North-western Labour Exchanges and Unemployment Insurance Offices, and his enthusiasm and hard work contributed much to the organization and launch of the scheme. He was also an effective and diligent publicist of his work, reading two detailed papers to the Liverpool Economic and Statistical Society in 1912 and 1913, both of which were subsequently published.[10] He claimed that the scheme had attracted interest not only in other British ports, but also in Germany, France and America.

Initially, the scheme which he drafted for the shipowners and for the Dockers' Union drew heavily on the ideas of Booth and Beveridge, incorporating preferential employment for those performing 'hard and consistent work', and for men of 'approved character' who would be selected as the first recipients of the 'tally' of registration. Of these, some would eventually be given 'permanent' status. This draft was vetoed by Sexton, containing as it did all the divisive elements against which dockers had fought in past schemes on the Mersey and in London. It placed all the powers of selection and patronage in the employers' hands. That Sexton's veto was effective is highly instructive; the employers in Liverpool saw him as a friend and ally, and positively welcomed the fullest participation of his union in the administration and control of any scheme for the port. Sexton was therefore in a position to make terms which conferred control upon his organization. He successfully insisted that 'every man earning a living on the Docks should be given a tally, so that he might still have a chance of getting work . . . The entrance to the trade could then be closed, and then gradually the death rate and other causes would weed the men down to a normal level.'[11]

Accordingly, in January 1912, a register was set up, under joint union–employer control. (The companies retained powers to engage their own preference men, but these were not accorded any port-wide preference within the scheme, and did not have 'permanent' status.) Seven clearing houses were built on the docks. To them were assigned the duties of issuing the tallies which entitled men to seek work and the task of collating information about daily labour requirements. (A clearing house was regarded as a sub-labour exchange within the Act.) All dockers were to be registered at the clearing house associated with the firm or firms for which they customarily worked, but were deemed to be available to work anywhere in the port. They would draw the whole of their week's earnings from their particular clearing house, regardless of how many firms had engaged them in the week. This offered a great advantage to the men, who were accustomed to spending much of their Saturday afternoons tramping from one company booth to another, at each of which they would have to queue, to accumulate their week's earnings. Additionally, the clearing houses kept the men's insurance cards and deducted their 4d. weekly health-insurance contributions, apportioning employers' contributions according to their separate engagements of each man.

Thirteen 'surplus' stands were erected, linked by telephone, to arrange labour mobility between docks as surpluses and shortages were reported. At each of the clearing houses a Joint Committee, comprising equal numbers of employers and working dockers – representatives of the union – managed their section of the whole scheme, which was overseen by the Joint Committee established in 1911 in the White Book Agreement. The cost of the clearing houses and their staffs was carried by the Board of Trade, which levied a charge on employers in partial recompense. This charge also went to meet the costs of administering health-insurance contributions. This aspect of the scheme also had benefits for the men, since in its absence, the employer who first engaged a man in any week would have borne the whole cost of the employers' contribution. Thus, dockers who had obtained jobs on a Monday would have had preference for the rest of the week, as their later employers would have been free of any insurance charge. And the full involvement of the union in the Joint Committee and in the Clearing House Committee – which actually issued those workers who were set on with their brass tallies and therefore controlled labour supply and limited it in practice to union members – was an enormous potential advance of workers' control.

## 'Slimy Jimmy' in Court

Yet the scheme met with the resistance of the dockers themselves. Through their union branches, they first tried to prevent Sexton from endorsing the scheme late in 1911. Williams reported to Beveridge that 'the B. of T. is d—d unpopular here . . . you have no idea of the underhand methods that have been used to smash the scheme.'[12] The men feared the loss of their customary controls and of their independence. They suspected that they would be ordered about from one firm to another, probably to do unfamiliar work alongside strangers. Moreover, they believed that, since the labour surplus in the port was chronic, a hidden agenda existed to squeeze out of the industry those men who were old and unfit. They were also wary of tighter supervision, speed-up, and loss of overtime. Before long all these apprehensions found a voice.

A vitriolic broadsheet accused Sexton of a conspiracy 'to hand over the union to the employers to manipulate as they will.' He took proceedings for criminal libel against the author, John Mitchell, who was 'probably' a syndicalist.[13] He was certainly 'an influential militant in the North End Docks' and an associate of Larkin's brother Peter, a coal-heaver and 'prominent anarcho-syndicalist'.[14] The handbill was certainly very, very rude. In it, Sexton was described as a 'trickster', a 'creature', a 'vulture', without principles or morals, 'an unprincipled, lying thug', 'a creature of the employers, an enemy of the working class', and 'Slimy Jimmy'. The text ends with a threat to 'smash the dock scheme'.

The focus of discontent centred repeatedly around Sexton and his high-handed method of getting the scheme adopted by the union. For 'Sexton chose to ignore one of the most sensitive features of the Liverpool dock labourer: his right to be consulted. The procedures adopted paid only lip service to the consultative process.'[15] A correspondent in the *Liverpool Daily Post and Mercury* enquired: 'Will Mr. Sexton kindly give us the dates on which the workers viewed the plan? . . . The workers had no say in the framing of the "White Book Agreement", neither have they had anything to say as regards this scheme . . . They have had quite sufficient . . . of Mr. Sexton's despotism'.[16]

The union's executive had put the plan to the Annual Congress, which had called for a ballot of the Liverpool membership. This never took place because, according to Sexton, he was too busy with other union work and with the London strike, and because union meetings had been disrupted so that no explanations of the scheme had been possible. These were thin excuses.

Given this climate of suspicion, it was not surprising that on and even before the start of the scheme on 11 July 1912, strike actions broke out, to the point when almost the whole port was affected. The union moved swiftly to dispel false rumours about the scheme, and the strike, which lacked leadership or focus, petered out in a few days, except in Birkenhead, where it persisted until mid-August. The return to work followed a threat from the Joint Committee to end the 1911 Agreement.

## The Employers Yield Control to the Union

But already before the strikes, the men's reluctance to register had produced far more damaging effects upon the scheme than their abortive industrial action. On 1 July, registration was supposed to begin. In fact, on that day in the clearing houses 'it was weary work for the Staff waiting all day long in a hut 15 feet by 10 feet for registrations which never came, the while they were subjected to a great deal of insult and unpleasantness.'[17] This spontaneous boycott of the scheme had a profound and immediate consequence, for on 9 July the Joint Committee (of the White Book Agreement) issued a circular stating that:

> In order to ensure that every Docker is able to get a tally, and in order to hasten the process of registration, the Dock Labour Joint Committee have agreed that employers shall issue a Registration Card to any man who produces his Dockers' Union Membership Card stamped by the Branch Office to which he belongs. Employers are requested to give immediate effect to this decision, by notifying their foremen, etc., without delay.[18]

As if this was not enough, a further circular followed two days later:

> The Joint Committee having decided unanimously that it is desirable to do everything possible to hasten the registration of Dockers, I am directed to request employers to give back, on demand, to the Officers of the Clearing House system, a substantial part of the registration cards in their possession. These cards will then be issued to the men *through the Union* under *conditions defined and approved by this Committee* [authors' italics].[19]

How are we to interpret these decisions? Clearly their effect was to give almost exclusive powers to the union in the allocation of tallies, in effect endorsing a union monopoly of labour supply. There is a note of panic in the employers' reaction to the boycott. At all costs, they seemed to be saying, we must get the men registered, even giving the union powers far beyond those envisaged – powers without precedent.

Yet still the men remained unconvinced. For if suspicion of Sexton was a major cause of suspicion of the scheme, then the more that the employers signalled their desperation for it to succeed, and the more they endorsed union powers in order to win over the dockers to registration, the more would dockers' apprehensions grow. John Mitchell underlined the point: 'The very fact that the scheme is put forward by such eminent – dockers please note – men of business as Mr. Harold Sanderson, Mr. A. A. Booth, Mr. H. W. Nelson, and Mr. James Sexton, should be quite sufficient to convince every docker that this scheme will certainly be a boon to the shipowners of Liverpool.'[20] It was not the inducement of union control of the tallies, but a threat by the Joint Committee to abrogate the 1911 settlement which brought an end to the strike, and the beginnings of mass registration.[21]

The dockers, on returning to work, began to develop other means of disabling the scheme. The years 1912–13 marked a trade boom, with plenty of overtime available. There were, on a simple arithmetical count, more than enough tallies issued to meet peak labour demands. Under union control, of course, tally distribution was far less likely to have been restrictive, and in 1912 some 26,500 tallies were issued, whilst even peak labour demand was only 22,000.

## The Mystery of Labour 'Shortage'

The mystery of labour shortages in these circumstances was only to be explained by the dockers' habits. In fact, only two-thirds of the labour force offered itself for hire on any given day. Making sufficient money – including overtime – in just a few days to meet their customary standard of life, they absented themselves for the rest of the week, or longer.[22] They had normally worked in this way, except when necessity drove. Hence, when Sexton claimed in November that discontent with the scheme had melted away, he was right, but it hardly mattered. The docker had by now discovered that he did not have much to fear from a system which disturbed his way of life so little, and which assembled his wages for him conveniently at one booth every Saturday!

In sum, the voluntary and piecemeal nature of the new system meant that, as the union itself had resisted 'perms' and preference categories, and the workers themselves had frightened the employers into giving every union man a tally, the men could ignore its 'improving' features. Most evidently, they made little use of the 'surplus' stands, to which they were supposed to report when no work was available at their own clearing house. They were then supposed to respond to signals, telephoned in from other docks to the staff at these stands, and obediently make the journey to the place of labour shortage, anywhere on the miles of Liverpool docks. Williams tried to make the best of it. 'These stands, although shamefully abused by both employers and dockers alike, at least directed 19,644 dockers in the busy months.'[23] The men suspected the whole philosophy on which the surplus stands were based. They 'seem to have been under the impression that if they went to work in another area they were "blacklegging", and this is an impression from which they must disabuse their minds. Mobility of labour can never be obtained as long as the men refuse to go from one area to another'.[24] This plainly tautological observation is a cry of despair: 'If things don't get better, they'll stay as they are.'

## Mobilizing Against Mobility

So, the men either did not use the surplus stands; or, when they did, failed to turn up at the ship to which they had been directed; or, on turning up, declined the work on offer. Refusal may have been due either to fear of 'trespassing', or because it was an unfamiliar job, or a 'bad job' – either dangerous, dirty, or poorly paid. Likewise, the employers 'abused' the stands. They would frequently order labour from them but, instead of waiting for the arrival of the despatched workers, would engage other men through the traditional, private and informal places of call at the dock gates or in the neighbourhood. This, of course, reinforced the lack of trust in the stands, as the men who had travelled at their instruction then found that the offered job had been manned in the meantime.

The headaches associated with the surplus stands were documented by the earnest Richard Williams in a fifteen-page appendix to his book. It is a diary of woe:

1912. Aug. 7th, Wednesday. Demand received in 'A' Area for 20 shipmen, but the men on the Surplus Stand would not work for the firm owing to some dispute . . .
    Aug. 12th, Monday. – 50 men were demanded in 'E' Area. There was a surplus of 60 men. 2 men were placed, the rest refused to work. There was a demand in the 'D' Area for 39 men to handle pig iron. There was a sufficient number of men on the firm's stand, but they refused to work. The men on the Surplus Stands refused also . . . Aug. 26th, Monday. – Demand received at 'B' Area for 10 coalheavers. The surplus men had dispersed when application was received. Demand was received at 'E' Area for 200 shipmen. There was a surplus of 77 shipmen. 67 were placed. The rest refused to work . . . Nov. 25th, Monday – Demands received in 'A', 'C', and 'E' Areas for 46 shipmen and 44 quaymen, only 36 shipmen and

44 quaymen were placed; unsatisfied demand, 10 shipmen at 'C'. Surplus at 'C' refused to handle cement . . . [25]

So it goes on. Other abuses were candidly recorded by Williams. The brass tallies were bought and sold, loaned, hired and even pawned. Many disappeared without trace.

## Registration In Other Ports

The experience of the Liverpool scheme hardly added up to an encouragement to extend it elsewhere. In Bristol, the employers rejected a scheme proposed by Ernest Bevin because, like Sexton, he insisted on registering all the men and on excluding preference and permanent categories. In Hull, Board of Trade officials could find no representative body of employers with which to deal. In Glasgow, a mass meeting of dockers threw out proposals for a scheme. In London, as we have seen, both employers and union leaders like Tillett were hostile. Tillett reported in 1912 that

> The Government is at present busy on some scheme to dragoon the so-called unskilled workers into 'clearing-house' schemes, which make the employer a greater tyrant than ever, and keep men for ever-lasting at the beck and call of foremen and managers . . . Probably no worse form of slavery ever existed outside of a negro compound than this attempt to enslave the workers. When one realises that the author of the scheme is of the opinion that the surplus labour should be poisoned or shot, or put into a lethal chamber, the brutal sinisterness of the proposal should be obvious. The man employed by the Government is of that opinion, and yet he is allowed to formulate schemes, backed by his inhuman bestialness, to further enslave the toilers.[26]

It is not clear from this fairly purple outburst whether the government man referred to is Williams or Beveridge, or what is the source for Tillett's claim that whoever it may have been had such murderous intentions towards surplus dockers.

In fact, Tillett was expressing, if with typical hyperbole, the standard opinion on the new labour exchanges held in the Labour movement as a whole. The TUC itself had declared its opposition, believing that they could be nothing other than agents of the employer, and that compulsion lay round the corner. On the other side, *laissez-faire* employers, who predominated, saw them as agents of government 'interference' with their prerogatives. Above all, they shrank from the logic of Richard Williams, whose honest appraisal of the defects in the Liverpool experiment drove him to an inescapable conclusion: 'My solution can be stated in two words – permanent employment.'[27]

An academic study at the time extended this devastating thought: 'if the employers of a port state that they require a certain normal maximum of men, they should pay for their labour at such a rate and in such a manner that the total sum of wages is sufficient to provide a fair wage all the year round for each of those men.'[28] Here is formulated the ultimate requirement: work or maintenance on a guaranteed minimum fall-back wage, for which the *employers* should pay, which would ultimately emerge only in the scheme imposed by Ernest Bevin as Minister of Labour during the Second World War. Neither in 1912, nor at any subsequent time, did port employers entertain the thought that *they* might voluntarily carry the costs of the ranks of surplus casual dockers' maintenance. Dockers' – and general workers' – unions were pushed inevitably and eventually into seeking state compulsion applied by their own leader from his post in Whitehall in 1941 to achieve this end. The government in 1912 was also stung by the costs of the Liverpool scheme: its parsimony led it to discourage any general extension, especially since, in terms of greater regularization of work, there was nothing to show for the expense of it. Only Goole and Sunderland, both ports of modest dimensions, adopted similar schemes.[29]

## Sexton's Case

Sexton managed to make a trade-union case for the scheme in Liverpool when he reported on its adoption and early developments.[30] He used two strong arguments: 'the Clearing House system, in spite of the prejudice raised against it, has proved, instead of the prophesied curse, to be a blessing, as the branches of our union practically control by it the supply of labour at the Docks through the Area Committee.' This great advance simply could not be gainsaid by Sexton's critics, who might, however, have gone on to claim that, under Sexton's 'despotism', the question was not whether the union controlled labour, but whether labour controlled the union. His other argument concerned the benefits of having a clearing-house system to administer contributions to health insurance. Without this system, he pointed out, many dockers were obliged to pay their 4d. contribution several times over a week, as they obtained work with fresh employers. This undoubted gain was modified in practice, since, precisely because of the suspicions attached to the clearing houses, only 13,000 out of 50,000 men had joined the insurance scheme, which the union itself administered as a friendly society.

## III

# *A Long Shadow Across the Future of the TGWU*

We have dealt in detail with this moment in the dockers' history, since it contains – like the London dock strike of the same year, though for quite different reasons – the seeds of a whole set of future problems for the TGWU docks section. The question of how far a union should go in collaboration with employers, and/or the state, to regularize port employment, raised in acute form by this case, was to dog the life of successive generations of leaders and members in the TGWU. This was a real dilemma. Collisions and contradictions abounded within it. The dockers' pre-industrial sense of independence, the rejection of factory time-keeping, routine discipline and managerial authority had to be respected if they were not to become a dissident group within the union. Yet those traditions perpetuated both the individual docker's perennial poverty and his unpredictable conduct as a trade unionist. How far could institutional arrangements, jointly administered by unions and the hated employers, be developed without risking the alienation of the members and the incorporation of the union as an agent of the bosses? And how far were these dangers enhanced by undemocratic union leadership? Finally, was it not inevitable, as the state began, tentatively, to attempt the regulation of the labour market, that its purposes would be those of the employing class? All those questions awaited Ernest Bevin, Arthur Deakin, Frank Cousins and Jack Jones, together with their members, in the years ahead.

In 1912 the dockers passed through two formative experiences, each of which would add to their earlier collective memories. The London strike taught bitter lessons, particularly – but not exclusively – to the stevedores. In Hull and some other ports, Tillett's selective support for militancy in London, and cautious quiescence elsewhere, cannot possibly have gone unnoticed. In Liverpool, the dockers had watched and resisted their union leader's evolution towards closer and closer relations with the employers, and his commitment to the employers' goals of stable, disciplined labour.

## *Dock Life and Culture*

It can hardly be doubted that these experiences contributed to the prolonged future tension between members and union, when the TGWU took over as the (almost) all-inclusive dockers' union. This is not romantic speculation. It is essential to appreciate the nature of the dock communities, if we are to understand the intensity of the passions involved and the tensions generated in the relations between future leaders and members in dockers' trade unions. Dockers have lived, until very recently, in tightly knit urban enclaves, which, in their intimacy of scale, resembled nothing so much as mining villages. Yet, alongside them, in close spatial relationship, lived other groups of load-shifting and load-moving, heavy, manual labourers – the millers, the carters, the cement workers, the timber men. So, unlike the miners, they could not build an exclusive unionism. They had to make alliances. But in the organizations they created out of this necessity, they could not forget or neglect their primary loyalties, even as both they and their leaders sought wider alliances. When defeated they, much more than their professional leaders, would retreat into the rooted group from which they had emerged and to which they ultimately referred. These retreats would not serve as a permanent solution, as they did for some of the miners until the 1980s.

Dockers' memories extended far beyond the lifespan of the individual. A docks community was a community of families, in which grandfathers, fathers, uncles, brothers and cousins shared and passed on jobs, connections with an individual employer, and specialist or localized preference of work. This collective memory extends to an endless, unyielding sustaining of the blacking of strike-breakers. In 1989 road-haulage firms which broke the strikes of the 1960s and early 1970s were still blacked on the Hull docks.

Dockers are also unlike factory workers: they worked in gangs and shared decision-making about the working methods they would use. They 'carried' the weaker and older members of the gang. They were pre-Fordist, never experiencing the assembly line.

The upshot of all this is that dockers were not alienated from their work in the way which became 'normal' among factory employees: and in any dockers' gathering – at the call-on, in the pub, around the family table, in their clubs – they 'talk shop'. Endlessly, enjoyably. Dockers' humour enriches all this talk. It often hinges on the observation of the human frailty of, for example, their foremen. On the Mersey as on the Humber, the same jokes are told about the lazy, the fussy and the incompetent foreman. Thus one foreman is known as 'Rembrandt' – 'Let me put you in the picture.' Another is 'the Lawyer' – he is 'always sitting on a case'. A third is 'the Sheriff' – 'Where's the hold-up lads, where's the hold-up?' The son listened to the father and the uncle, and absorbed the talk. Invention was continuous. Later generations met 'Dinner Mint', who 'only showed up after eight'. And that talk included the transmitted folk memories of betrayals, or – at the least – of the *ambiguities* of union leadership and its role, as well as the obverse lesson: that self-reliance, local action, ca' canny and care of the local interest had produced the best defences. The dockers' attachment to the wider, general union, in which they eventually united with other transport and general workers, was therefore necessary but conditional. The future leaders of these men would always have to understand and remember this. Wise leaders did: overbearing or ignorant leaders, whether they worked from local, regional or national offices, would pay dearly for not understanding it, or for attempting to ride over it roughshod.

# Appendix

## *Williams on Williams*

A review by Robert Williams from the NTWF *Weekly Record*, no. 44, 28 February 1914:

*'The First Year's Working of the Liverpool Dock Scheme'*, by R. *Williams*, *M.A. (London, P. S. King & Son.) 2/6 net.*

We briefly referred to this book in a previous issue, and now propose to take a more extended view.

The tone of the book is to be regretted. It is that of the 'superior person'. But this apart, it is an eminently useful and instructive volume, to the compilation of which much care has been devoted. The utmost pains have been taken to give the fullest and most accurate statistical data, with diagrams and tables to illustrate the working and effects of the scheme.

The author (being a Labour Exchange official) necessarily takes on the optimistic view of the official, and to that extent his conclusions are vitiated. Fortunately, it is not necessary to agree with the conclusions at which the author arrives to be able to appreciate the value of the material he has collected.

The history of the events leading up to the establishment of the scheme, and the methods by which the various difficulties in its path were overcome, are given with much detail and not a little self-congratulation in the first chapter. This is, of course, important, and will prove helpful to those who are concerned in launching similar schemes in other Ports. So far, London, Southampton, and Bristol are being tackled by the Commissioners in this respect, and in dealing with these efforts, it must be borne in mind that these present efforts are being made under an Amending Act which gives power to the Commissioners to introduce a daily rate of contribution (though not, we believe, proportionate benefits), and are primarily concerned with the Insurance aspect of the affair; whereas the Liverpool scheme has as its main feature the 'Clearance of Wages', to which the collection of the men's contributions and the pooling of the employers' share is secondary.

Into this Clearance of Wages the author goes with considerable detail. It is a complicated operation which cannot be summarised here.

Concurrently with the Clearance of Wages is made an equitable allocation of the employers' Insurance contributions. (The tables of wages would seem to show that the burden on the employees is far from being equitably allocated, but the author of the book is apparently quite satisfied with the fact that they all pay.)

In outline, the scheme is as follows:

Every worker who could prove that he was a regular worker at the Docks prior to the introduction of the scheme – the National Union of Dock Labourers was strong enough to insist that possession of a Union Card was sufficient proof – received a ticket which he exchanged at a Clearing House for a numbered tally, and after receipt of this tally he deposited his Insurance Card there also. The tally is evidence to the employer that the man's card is at the Clearing House, and will be stamped there.

The employers send to the Clearing House a return of wages due, the officers extract from the various returns the amount of wages due to each man, and pay him each week (weekly payment is an essential part of the Scheme) the total in one sum, less the Insurance deduction. The employers' share of the Insurance contribution is divided according to the number of men employed by each employer who is party to the scheme. A further tally is given to each man when he is taken on, bearing the name of the firm and its Key Number in the Scheme. This is surrendered for wages, and returned to the employer. Thus, it will be seen that the scheme provides against the flooding of the Docks by outsiders, it ensures that no man shall have to stamp his own card in order to obtain work, and that every man, wherever he has been employed during the week, receives his wages at one place – the Clearing House at which his card is deposited.

The scheme is worked in conjunction with a subsidiary scheme for securing greater mobility of labour. The Clearing Houses are in communication with the stands at which the men are called on, and a demand for men at one part of the Docks is communicated by telephone to other parts where there may be a surplus. It is complained that neither the employers nor the men take full advantage of these facilities, which are intended to secure that a smaller number of men should meet the demand for labour at the Port, diminishing casual labour, and a sufficiency of work for each man. Against this contention may be set the fact that a very large surplus is always required to be on hand to meet the fluctuations of trade. Fresh tallies are only issued in special cases under recommendation of the Joint Committee, which is composed of an equal number of employers and Union representatives. This is intended to reduce the surplus to a minimum.

For the Clearing House Committees the author has nothing but praise, and considers that they are a necessary feature of any scheme, which should encourage the members of our own Sub-committee dealing with London, who are demanding that the same basis – equal representation for employers and men in the administration of the scheme – shall apply to the projected scheme for London.

The statistical side of the book is excellently done, as we have hinted above. There is enough cold, hard fact about the bareness of the docker's life, the tremendous insecurity of his existence, to justify a revolution. For instance, a table is given for the month of January, 1913, which shows that the least number of men working in any week during the month was 21,483, whereas the greatest number of men working in each of the five weeks [i.e. working for at least some time in every week] is only 16,258. In another table is a record of the number of men receiving 15/– or less for each week in the year. The percentage of men who receive this sum, or *less*, is never less than 27% of the total wage-earners, and is more often 32%. And one of the excellencies of this scheme is that it ensures that men shall only have fourpence deducted from their miserable wages for benefits they will never get!

Despite his admiration of the scheme, and his insistence of its success – and we are bound to say that, within its limits, it *is* a success, – the author does not regard it as anything more than a temporary expedient, and the few modifications he suggests for the scheme are unimportant. His own personal solution of the problem is Permanent Labour. He thinks that this solution is a long way off, and his immediate practical reform is the putting of all lads employed in Dock work on a regular weekly wage. Little by little, step by step, is his method of going to work. But let us quote:

> Let me postulate an axiom – If a reserve of labour is required by any industry, then that industry should maintain that reserve not only when working, but also when it is unavoidably unemployed.
>
> Granted a small floating reserve, how shall it be paid for? First of all discover from the records of a series of years the average fluctuation and fix the reserve. Then agree to pay that reserve a weekly *minimum wage work or play* . . .
>
> The seasonal reserve would be required to be dealt with in another way. Seasonal employment is well known. The building trade, farm-labouring, to mention only two instances, are always slack in winter. Would it not be possible to recruit a sufficient number of men from these and such like trades to whom a seasonal tally available from October to March might be given? These men to be guaranteed a similar wage under similar conditions to that for the floating reserve, but only for the limited period.

This quotation serves to indicate the measure of his outlook. We confidently recommend the study of this volume to all interested in the problem.

# Notes

1   Report of the Commission of Inquiry into the Question of Unemployment in the City of Liverpool, 1894.

2   See Eleanor Rathbone and G. H. Wood, *Report of an Inquiry into the Condition of Dock Labour in the Port of Liverpool* (Liverpool Economic and Statistical Society, *Transactions*, 1903–4).

3   Gordon Phillips and Noel Whiteside, *Casual Labour: The Unemployment Question in the Port Transport Industry, 1880–1970* (Oxford University Press, 1985), p. 54.

4   See R. Bean, 'Custom, Job Regulation and Dock Labour in Liverpool, 1911–39', *International Review of Social History*, vol. XXVII, (1982), part 3, pp. 271–89.

5   Ibid., p. 275.

6   Noel Whiteside, 'Public Policy and Port Labour Reform: the Dock Decasualisation Issue, 1910–1950', in Steven Tolliday and Jonathan Zeitlin (eds.), *Shop Floor Bargaining and the State: Historical and Comparative Perspectives* (Cambridge University Press, 1985), p. 82.

7   Dock Labour Joint Committee Minutes, 23 December 1912, quoted in R. Bean, 'Custom, Job Regulation and Dock Labour in Liverpool', p. 278.

8   W. H. Beveridge, 'The Problem of the Unemployed', in *Sociological Papers*, 3 (1906), p. 327; quoted in Phillips and Whiteside, *Casual Labour*, p. 79.

9   Royal Commission on the Poor Laws, 1909, appendix to vol. III, Q.78153; Beveridge's evidence cited in Phillips and Whiteside, *Casual Labour*, p. 81.

10   Richard Williams, *The Liverpool Docks Problem* (P. S. King and Son, 1912), and *The First Year's Working of the Liverpool Docks Scheme* (P. S. King and Son, 1914).

11   Quoted by Phillips and Whiteside, *Casual Labour*, p. 91.

12   Ibid., p. 93.

13   Eric Taplin, *The Dockers' Union: A Study of the National Union of Dock Labourers, 1889–1922* (Leicester University Press, 1986), p. 113.

14   Bob Holton, *British Syndicalism, 1900–1914*, (Pluto Press, 1976), p. 128.

15   Taplin, *The Dockers' Union*, p. 112.

16   Ibid.

17   Williams, *The First Year's Working of the Liverpool Docks Scheme*, p. 7.

18   Ibid., p. 8.

19   Ibid.

20   *Liverpool Daily Post and Mercury*, 5 March 1912, quoted in Taplin, *The Docker's Union*, p. 114.

21   Williams, *The First Year's Working of the Liverpool Docks Scheme*, p. 9.

22   Ibid., p. 13.

23   Ibid.

24   Ibid., p. 85.

25   Ibid., pp. 177–92.

26   DWRGU Annual Report, 1912, p. 12.

27   Williams, *The First Year's Working of the Liverpool Docks Scheme*, p. 129.

28  F. Keeling, 'Towards the Solution of the Casual Labour Problem', *Economic Journal*, vol. 23 (March 1913), p. 16.
29  Phillips and Whiteside, *Casual Labour*, p. 95.
30  NUDL Annual Report, 1912, pp. 5–8.

# 13

## James Larkin: Dublin Erupts

### I

### *The Conditions of Dublin*

In 1913 Dublin had a population of just over 300,000. It was a transport workers' mecca, drawing in hundreds of people from the western countryside. However, it was landlessness, not faith, which drove them before it. Shipping and commercial interests dominated everything. So did poverty. In the city 7,600 men were carters. A wage of £1 a week was considered untold wealth, and many thousands of families subsisted on half as much. A handful of craftsmen aside, dockers were the city's elite. They could be paid as much as 24*s*. if they were able to put in a seventy-hour week. Commonly they were not able to do so. On such pay, amidst such crippling toil, social conditions festered: Dublin's death-rate was higher than that of Calcutta. Two-fifths of all deaths occurred in workhouses, twice as high a rate as in England. Infant mortality was higher than in any English city, at 142 per 1,000. Even so, the population of the city leapt up by 55,000 between 1891 and 1911. While the whole of Ireland's numbers shrank (by 315,000), Dublin's grew. Thirty per cent of Dubliners lived in tenements. Four-fifths of tenement families were confined to one room.[1] Prostitution was an industry. On the docks 'women were allowed to board ships . . . to sleep with the crew. Larkin refused to allow his dockers to work a ship where such a state of affairs existed.'[2] Homelessness and vagrancy crowded the streets with infant beggars.

### *Defeat in Cork*

James Larkin was already famous as the hero of the great Belfast upheaval of 1907. His Irish Transport and General Workers' Union

provoked the employers to federate themselves in May 1909. Next
month, when a strike broke out in Cork, the employers imported
Shipping Federation blacklegs. The strike spread to railwaymen and
carters, and by the end of the month 6,000 men were on strike. Larkin's
new union was totally unable to fund so large a dispute; by mid-July the
carters were compelled to return to work, and the strike collapsed. There
followed a nasty court case, in which Larkin himself and James Fearon
were accused of diverting for their own use the sum of £147, donated by
the Cork branch of their union to a Dublin carters' dispute.[3] Fearon and
two others received sentences from one to six months, while Larkin was
given twelve months with hard labour. The resultant protests soon took
effect, however. After three months of intensive meeting and petitioning,
he was discharged from prison by order of the Lord Lieutenant, Lord
Aberdeen. He had undergone 'some disgraceful prison treatment. But
his power for good in the nether Dublin and Ireland had been greatly
increased'.[4]

Defeat in the Cork strike was not the unmitigated disaster which it
might have been in another place, in quieter times. Larkin was
organizing the most downtrodden and deprived workers, victims as much
of neglect by the wider society in which they lived as of the ferocious
rapacity of their direct exploiters. To advertise defeat in such conditions
was to arouse interest, and even hope, among those masses for whom no
choice had ever presented itself.

## Connolly Gets to Work

We have already noticed that, in 1910, James Connolly had arrived home
from the United States. His book, *Labour in Irish History*, applied a
rigorous Marxism to the study of Ireland. 'The Irish question is a social
question,' it said. 'The whole age long fight of the Irish people against
their oppressors resolves itself in the last analysis into a fight for the
mastery of that means of life, the sources of production in Ireland.'[5]

In 1911 Connolly became Larkin's Belfast organizer, with the
responsibility of developing the ITGWU throughout the Ulster region.
Like Larkin, he was a free-thinking and empirical leader. He was not
'imprisoned in an iron cage of doctrine . . . as Larkin once remarked
"why use one arm when we have two? Why not strike the enemy with
both arms – the political and the economic?"'[6]

## The Great Unrest Goes Visiting to Dublin

Both Larkin and Connolly were very happy to campaign electorally, and
neither wished to distinguish himself from the mainstream of European

socialism by standing aside in this respect. Each fought his own corner in local ballots. But the squalor that was Irish urban life would admit of no exclusive dependence on any such patient strategy. When the industrial unrest swept across Britain in 1911, it simply had to go home to Dublin. The ITGWU had 4,000 members in 1911, twice as many in 1912, and 10,000 by the middle of 1913. Most port employers got the message. It was time to yield or break. Larkin negotiatied significant wage increases for his dockers, and their example helped him to recruit farm labourers in the surrounding countryside, so that 'at harvest time they were able to hold the farmers to ransom and extract from them what seemed the princely sum of seventeen shillings for a sixty-six hour week.'[7]

The Great Unrest affected English and Irish ships alike, and the seamen quickly won their victory in Belfast, as elsewhere. The National Union of Railwaymen came together in London in February 1913, after long preparation and much agitation.[8] It had been eased into existence during the August railway strike of 1911, which also spilled out across the Irish Sea and then stalled. Although the Irish railwaymen stopped work in support of their English comrades, when they were called out on their own account in September there was no English support for them. Larkin's loud warnings, that Irishmen could not count on English solidarity, gathered wider currency.

More and more people joined the Irish Transport and General Workers' Union. Throughout 1911, a series of battles erupted. In Wexford, where ironmasters locked out more than 500 workpeople simply because they had joined the union, one worker was killed and many others were disabled in running battles with the police.

Connolly negotiated a settlement which was a major victory for the union: a formally separate, but in fact parallel, Foundry Workers' Union was to be established as an affiliate of the ITGWU. (By 1914 the status of the foundrymen had been rationalized to fit with reality, and the Wexford branch had again become a straightforward component of the parent body.)

Larkin saw the union as an alternative, not only to low wages and miserable exploitation, but to all the bondage of a wage system which restricted the capacities of those caught within it. He echoed the syndicalist ideas of Tom Mann and the Industrial Syndicalist Educational League, at whose inauguration he had been present in 1910; but he also responded to the upsurge of a self-consciously Irish national culture which gripped Dublin during those years. His union quickly blossomed. He told an audience in Liverpool:

> We have our own park of 162 acres, our own vinery and gardens, and we bring our women and men down there on Sunday or Saturday afternoon and teach the boys and girls how to cultivate the garden, and show them the beauty of life in its full expression. They play football too, and no one is

allowed to come who is not either in the union or a wife of a worker . . . We make our family life focus around the union . . . "[9]

Larkin always insisted that he did not like strikes, and preferred to negotiate. Throughout 1912, brisk trade and sharp bargaining ensured that the ITGWU went from strength to strength. The year 1913 continued this trend, but the strike figures increased again and so did the casualties. Galway and Sligo saw pitched battles. In Sligo, the police batoned a striker to death. Thirty work stoppages broke out in Dublin between January and August, and forty strikers were sent to prison for alleged acts of violence or intimidation.[10] The union and some of the key Dublin shippers agreed large increases for dockers, but then the crunch came.

## Larkin's Call to Arms

On 26 August 1913, Larkin called out the tramwaymen of Dublin, because William Martin Murphy, director of the Dublin United Tramways Company, refused them union recognition. Murphy was a powerful entrepreneur. He owned tramways and electric railways in more than one country, a large department store, the Imperial Hotel in Sackville Street (now Connell Street) and the *Independent* newspaper, voice of the well-heeled section of the Catholic and Nationalist community. Murphy had for some time been prudently weeding out supporters of the union among his tramwaymen, so the ITGWU's answer was to launch sympathetic strikes against his other important interests. The *Independent* was blockaded when Larkin's men were locked out of the distribution department. The dockers came in to black Murphy's distributors. The Employers' Federation jumped into the mêlée, locking out ITGWU members wherever they could. Before the end of September 25,000 men were already laid off work, with three times that number of dependants in need of food and provisions.

Larkin rose to the highest passion in denouncing Murphy and all his works. He widened his targets to include the Ulster Unionists and the state itself. Sean O'Faolain has left us an account of some of those fevered meetings: '"Carson is arming in the North", he cried. "If he can arm why shouldn't the Dublin workers arm? Arm yourselves, and I'll arm. You have to face hired assassins. Where ever one of your men is shot – then shoot two of them." '[11] As soon as this report was published, on 28 August, Larkin was arrested and charged with sedition. Once bailed, he repeated all his original accusations: '"Starve us?" he shouted. "Starve us out? If they lock out the Transport Union we'll pay no rent. If they lock out the Transport Union, then, in Kruger's words, we'll stagger humanity. Starve us, would they?" he besought the beast of many heads growling beneath him. "Any man who starves when there's food in a shop window is a damn fool."[12]

O'Faolain goes on to report Larkin's defiance of the Royal Proclamation on the emergency, which he burned in public:

> 'People make kings and people unmake them,' his voice carried over the listening crowd. 'I care as much for the King as I do for the magistrate who signed this paper . . . We have a perfect right to meet in O'Connell Street. We are going to meet in O'Connell Street.' The flames ate through the uplifted paper. 'And if the police or soldiers are going to stop us, or try to stop us, let them take the responsibility.'
>
> His face was in the dark as the last glowing ashes floated down on the faces upturned to hear him. Out of the dark his voice came, strident: 'If they want a revolution, then God be with them.'[13]

Some 10,000 voices, O'Faolain tells us, 'soared in a wordless cheer'. James Connolly was present among the crowd, and O'Faolain records that 'he did not cheer at all'. Riots burst out on all sides. Bricks and bottles were the weapons of the poor, and they were met by systematic beatings, and the 'thud of baton on flesh and bone'. A virtual civil war was raging, and has continued to rage through our literature ever since. Indeed, it came to seem as if the very stones of the city were leagued in conspiracy with the constabulary against an impoverished but insurgent people. Readers of James Plunkett's powerful novel, *Strumpet City*,[14] will remember how, in the midst of street battles and mass funerals, two crumbling tenement houses collapsed, killing seven people outright and disabling many others. The police killed only five people in the events surrounding the lock-out, but thousands were injured and 656 detained.

## Riots and Arrests

Larkin, fearing rearrest, had disappeared, and was secretly resting up at the house of the radical countess, Constance Markievicz. However, he had promised to speak in O'Connell Street on Sunday 30 August, ban or no ban. At the appointed time, heavily disguised, he coolly drove through a cordon of 300 policemen to the door of Murphy's own hotel, entered unchallenged, and calmly appeared on the balcony: 'At twenty-five minutes past one . . . a window was flung open on the second storey and Larkin began to cry out to the mob. From end to end of the street his name rang and the crowds converged to the hotel door. At the same time police rushed upstairs and dragged Larkin inside. Below, outside, the police charged. Rush and counter-rush continued for several minutes.'[15]

Larkin's arrest saw all police caution abandoned, and when the police charged, mayhem followed. The riots continued. Among the young men who took part in these events was Sean O'Casey, who was to become the secretary of the Irish Citizen Army.[16] Many years later, his play *Red Roses for Me* celebrated an image of the transformation of Dublin in a scene of great beauty, in which the familiar landscape of the Four Courts and the river Liffey reflect a surge of rich colours, as the hope generated in the strike lights up the leaden skies of the old decaying town. The play's hero, Ayamonn (part Larkin, part O'Casey?), directly echoes the famous speech of John Burns during the great London Dock strike: 'A shilling's little to me, and less to many; to us it is our schechinah, showing us God's light is near; showing us the way in which our feet must go; a sun ray on our face; the first step taken in the march of a thousand miles.'[17] O'Casey's hero perished in the violence, but Larkin and Connolly were simply arrested.

Other union members, P. T. Daly and William O'Brien, promptly stepped into the breach. An appeal was sent to the Trades Union Congress in Manchester on 1 September. Harry Gosling has left an account of the impact on his colleagues of this call from the Dublin workers. When the delegation arrived, it was greeted by strong speeches of support from Tillett (who asserted once again that the strikers had the right to bear arms), Smillie (who saw a duty to train people to 'defend themselves') and Jack Jones of the gasworkers. Sexton was for compromise, and against Larkin and Connolly. The Congress responded to these disputes by sending a delegation of six people, three from the body of the hall and three from the platform. Gosling himself, J. A. Seddon and John Hill represented the Parliamentary Committee; from the body of Congress came William Brace, John Ward and Jack Jones. They instantly embarked on their journey. When they arrived in Dublin they were summoned to meet Lord Aberdeen, the Lord Lieutenant, and this they did the same night. Then, having asked him to pull back the police, they participated in a great rally at Liberty Hall 'to re-establish the right of free speech', following the fracas in Sackville Street. While Gosling spoke in Dublin, Tillett, at home in London, spoke in strong form in Trafalgar Square, where his militant speech won the attention and the praise of Lenin.[18]

## Food Relief from Salford

The oratory done, however, the next task, said Gosling,

was to get food for the hungry women and children. They were literally starving. Charles Bowerman, who was at that time secretary of the Trade Union Congress, accompanied Seddon [J. A. Seddon, the Shopworkers' Union leader] and myself to Manchester to interview the directors of the Co-operative Wholesale Society, Ltd. We had no money, but we pledged the credit of the trade union movement to the extent of £5,000, and the directors, who were very sympathetic, accepted our word and agreed to supply food and have it ready to be sent across to Ireland during the week-end.

Then we had to get a ship to carry the food. To our dismay we found a strike was pending in the Salford Docks, and the ship we wanted lay loaded with Guinness's stout alongside the quay. To single out any vessel would risk breaking the strike. However, we visited the Salford strike committee and stated our case. The men were obviously struggling between their desire to help the women and children of Dublin and their fear of breaking the solidarity of their own movement in Salford. No one was willing to unload the vessel, but we felt bound to insist on it being done. As is always the case, the better side of the men came uppermost in the end and the women and children won.

This having been decided, the keenest competition took place as to who should have the honour and glory of unloading the vessel that she might be loaded afresh with food. The strike committee thought they ought to do it, but the gang whose job it would have been in the ordinary course claimed their right. The end of it was the work was done in double-quick time and the vessel put into her berth for loading. Sixty thousand packages of food had been prepared by the Co-operative Wholesale Society and on Friday evening the vessel was ready to sail. Representatives of the society, some pressmen, with Seddon and myself, were the only passengers.

We were under a bond to be alongside the quay at Dublin at seven o'clock the following morning. But a fog came down, thicker and heavier – so it seemed to us – than any fog that ever was. It was difficult enough to get down the Manchester Ship Canal, but when we reached Eastham it seemed impossible to attempt the Mersey. The tide was falling, and unless we were through the lock without delay the water would be gone and we should be left till the next day. We prayed for the fog to lift, but as it did not, the captain, in spite of his anxiety, decided to make the venture, and out we went into the darkness. As perhaps the only person on board the ship apart from the crew who realized to the full the great risk we were running, I experienced the voyage of that vessel down the Mersey as one of the most thrilling feats of nagivation I have ever been connected with.

Slowly we crept along, not another vessel under way, every one watching the clock and seeing the chance of carrying out our bond growing fainter and fainter. Only as the day broke did the fog lift at last, and then we set about the task of making up lost time with a vengeance. The men in the stokehold threw the coals on the furnace like demons in hell, until they had the vessel nearly red hot. All rules and regulations for the safety of navigation were discarded and the ship flew along, every one on tiptoe of excitement. Though we knew we could not arrive on time, we were all determined not a moment should be wasted. While these strenuous efforts were being made at sea, the women and children were sitting along the banks of the Liffey all night, singing and praying we might come with the food they so much needed. By the time we entered Dublin Bay the sun was shining. We dressed the ship in all her colours, the lightship hailed us with her siren, and every vessel blew us a welcome with her whistle. We went up the Liffey in the greatest triumph, with cheers and blowing of whistles from every side and we passed the women and children who had waited all night and were still upon their knees.

As we approached, Seddon and I were preparing to make great speeches to the folks assembled, for the quay was crowded. Larkin was there with a great body of men who had volunteered their services to unload the ship. But instead of talking we could only stand dumb, with tears in our eyes. It was the most wonderful sight I had ever seen![19]

Thousands of pounds of relief aid was quickly raised by TUC affiliates alone. In all, around £100,000 was subscribed to the TUC fund. A further £50,000 was collected at meetings and rallies of solidarity. More food ships soon made the journey across the Irish Sea. The first, *The Hare*, was quickly followed by the aptly named *Fraternity*.

## Larkin's Mission to Scotland and England

Connolly was released from prison after a week's hunger strike. Larkin came out on bail of £100, and immediately set off for a round of meetings in Scotland and England. By mid-September he was in Manchester, spellbinding an enormous open-air rally:

I have got a divine mission, I believe, to make men and women discontented ... no Murphy or Aberdeen ... can stop me carrying on the work I was born for ... Hell has no terrors for me ... I have lived there. Thirty-six years of hunger and poverty have been my portion. The mother that bore me had to starve and work and my father had to fight for a living. I knew what it was to work when I was nine years old. They cannot terrify me with hell ... Better to be in hell with Dante and Davitt than to be in heaven with Carson or Murphy ... I am out for revolution, what do I care? They can only kill me, and there are thousands more to come after me.[20]

After a quick dash back to Dublin, where Connolly was controlling affairs, Larkin was in Glasgow on 21 September, and the next day met the NTWF Executive in London.

In Dublin, Liberty Hall, the headquarters of the ITGWU, served as the commissariat. It 'became one vast warehouse and welfare centre. Food packages were made up and food tickets were issued to the men when they collected their strike pay in accordance with the number of dependants they had. Clothes and underwear were also distributed to the needy. Soup kitchens were set up in the Hall and meals were served.'[21] Harry Gosling ate the soup and pronounced it very appetizing. The Countess Markievicz and Delia Larkin (James's sister) organized these extensive welfare activities for the duration of the lock-out.

## Enter Sir George

At the end of September the government announced a Board of Trade inquiry under the chairmanship of Sir George Askwith. Murphy was speaking for the employers, and Harry Gosling, as chairman of the NTWF, for the unions. The inquiry would open at Dublin Castle, 'to enquire into the facts and circumstances of the dispute now in progress in Dublin, and to take such steps as may seem desirable with a view to arriving at a settlement.' The NTWF *Weekly Record* reported:

Having obtained the sanction of the Executive Council, the President and the Secretary attended the Court with a delegation from the Dublin Trades Council. In his opening remarks, Sir George Askwith said that his desire, and the desire of his colleagues, was to obtain a 'picture' of the industrial situation in the City of Dublin.

Some misapprehension was aroused by the President's declaration in favour of a private inquiry rather than a public one. Not, as he said, that he objected to the widest publicity being given to the men's case, but that if the Enquiry were held in private, there would be more likelihood of bringing the disputants nearer to one another, and of effecting an amicable settlement.

At the first day's sitting there were present only three of the employers' representatives, and these seized upon Mr. Gosling's argument as a sign of weakness, and thereupon demanded a 'full and open' enquiry, leading up to, and attendant upon, the whole dispute. They also claimed the right to be represented by counsel. Later in the day's proceedings we were advised in camera that, in spite of their protestations, the employers' representatives would attend a private conference on the following day (Tuesday). These are essentially private details about which the Press was kept entirely in the dark, and are now being placed at the disposal of the active members of the Federation to give an inner light upon the whole of the proceedings. On the afternoon of Monday we were informed by Sir G. Askwith that the employers would not entertain any suggestion of a private conference until the whole matter had been thrashed out in public. They were desirous, they stated, to rebut most, if not all, the statements made public by the Trade Union Congress delegation, and the Enquiry would continue as decided in the morning: that is, a full Court, open to the Press and the public, would resume on Wednesday morning.

After many long deliberations between the representatives of the men it was agreed that we listen to the case put forward by counsel on behalf of the whole of the employers, in conjunction with such witnesses as counsel considered necessary to amplify the statements made by the legal representatives. It may be well understood that we on the workers' side had some slight misgivings in having to face trained and experienced counsel acting on behalf of the employers. Mr. Tim Healy, MP, acted as leading counsel, and spoke for three hours, stating the position as fully as he could from a carefully and elaborately prepared brief. While these learned gentlemen have all the advantages which their training gives them, their position is much more difficult than ours, because of their absolute lack of any technical knowledge of the facts of the dispute. In the presentation of his case, Mr. Healy was continuously interrupted by the various employers' solicitors and barristers who were sitting round and about him, anxious to coach him in his brief.[22]

## Robert Williams at the Inquiry

Robert Williams, the author of this account, had nothing but contempt for Mr Healy: 'He . . . has risen on the shoulders of the workers into a position of legal and political eminence. Not content with raising himself by standing on the workers' shoulders, he now prostitutes his ability by trampling them into the mire.' This, said Williams, was an attitude 'of the blackest treachery . . . Every sweating employer, every would-be Union-smasher; all those who by petty tyranny and victimisation had made it well-nigh impossible for the workers to organise themselves; every slum-landlord and rack-renter; every employer who, by underpaying women and girls drove them on to the streets, found a champion in Mr. Tim Healy.'[23]

Larkin cross-examined Healy's numerous witnesses, all of whom maintained that he had broken every agreement he had made. According to Robert Williams:

Mr. Larkin, who was complete master of all the details, and who had every fact at his finger-tips, put the various employers through a very trying ordeal. He was able to elicit information conclusively proving that the employers had set up every obstacle to impede the progress of Trade Unionism in Dublin, just as, as a matter of fact, they have done elsewhere. Men who were known to be members of the Irish Transport Workers' Union were dismissed on the slightest pretext. The same has happened to girls and women who have been employed in the various factories in Dublin. So persistent has been the persecution of those who were known to be Trade Unionists that this has of itself given rise to what has been called 'Larkinism'. It is to be understood that Larkin *acts* on the precept that 'an injury to one is an injury to all'.

Having formed an industrial union, including all the members of the transport industry, he has employed the weapon of the sympathetic strike in a manner undreamt in this country. Only by the extreme loyalty of the members of his Society has he been able to strike terror into the hearts of the employers. He has not been very much concerned with the sanctity of agreements. Neither has he given the employers very much notice when the occasion demanded prompt and immediate action. He says most emphatically that any Trade Unionist who assists an employer during a dispute between that employer and his workpeople is a scab; and not only is he a scab, but that he is cheaper than a professional scab to that employer. His methods have, in Dublin, met with striking success. This most noticeably so among waterside workers, and transport workers generally.

Having accomplished a great deal for this class of worker, his attention was called to the degrading conditions obtaining at the numerous factories in Dublin. Here again he has been successful in the use of the sympathetic strike. Every employer who would not accede to the reasonable terms put forward, and who in fact, tried to crush out Trade Unionism, was hampered and embarrassed in the conduct of his affairs by the refusal of the transport workers to convey any goods consigned to or despatched from the centre of his undertakings.

The methods adopted by Larkin challenge the very constitution of wagery and capitalism. The measure of the employers' vehement antagonism is the measure of Larkin's success. It may be said in passing that capitalism sets a limit to purely trade union activities, and that the limit to some extent has been reached in Dublin. The employers in Dublin have been compelled to do what the promoters of the fifty-million-pound fund desire on this side of the Channel. They are prepared to throw their all into the melting-pot rather than consent to the further development of a progressive trade union policy. They say, in effect, 'While we are prepared under duress to concede slight increases in the wages and modifications in the conditions of employment, we cannot permit the unions, the officials, or the men themselves to have any determining voice, or any control in the industry in which they are engaged.' We are seeing more and more that the workers are clamouring to be considered human factors in present-day wealth production and distribution, and that in spite of all documents signed, agreements made, and contracts entered into, there will be a steadily-growing reluctance to refrain from the use of the sympathetic strike.[24]

Askwith's report could hardly be expected to condone this view. It condemned sympathetic strikes, saying that no community could survive a general policy of sympathetic action, because of the interdependence of all the branches of industry. Askwith admitted that the conditions endured by Dublin people were deplorable and required action, even drastic action. Accordingly, he recommended the establishment of Conciliation Boards. Both Larkin and Connolly had previously argued for conciliation and readily agreed to restrict sympathetic strikes, if the report were accepted: but the employers rejected it point blank, and left the inquiry.

## George Russell Sums Up

The *Irish Times*, a profoundly conservative journal, printed an open letter to Dublin employers by 'AE', the well-known writer George Russell:

Sirs, – I address this warning to you, the aristocracy of industry in this city, because, like all aristocracies, you tend to grow blind in long authority, and to be unaware that you and your class and its every action are being considered and judged day by day by those who have power to shake or overturn the whole Social Order, and whose restlessness in poverty today is making our industrial civilisation stir like a quaking bog . . .

Your insolence and ignorance of the rights conceded to workers universally in the modern world were incredible, and as great as your inhumanity. If you had between you collectively a portion of human soul as large as a threepenny bit, you would have sat night and day with the representatives of labour, trying this or that solution of the trouble, mindful of the women and children, who at least were innocent of wrong against you. But no! You reminded labour you could always have your three square meals a day while it went hungry. You went into conference again with representatives of the State, because, dull as you are, you know public opinion would not stand your holding out. You chose as your spokesman the bitterest tongue that ever wagged in this island, and then, when an award was made by men who have an experience in industrial matters a thousand times transcending yours, who have settled disputes in industries so great that the sum of your petty enterprises would not equal them, you withdraw again, and will not agree to accept their solution, and fall back again upon your devilish policy of starvation. Cry aloud to Heaven for new souls! The souls you have got cast upon the screen of publicity appear like the horrid and writhing creatures enlarged from the insect world, and revealed to us by the cinematograph.[25]

# II

## Suffer the Little Children

This moment marked the high point of Larkin's leadership, and by mid-October it looked as if he was winning. But then he left for London, for a round of mass meetings, in which his expectations of solidarity were increasingly disappointed, while his language about labour leaders became less and less temperate. At the same time, new snares were set for him, sometimes in the effort to bring help.[26]

At a meeting of the *Daily Herald* League (formed to rally support for the newspaper, with branches throughout the country), Larkin shared a platform with the women's suffrage leader Dora Montefiore, and the Countess of Warwick. Mrs Montefiore wrote:

In 1913 I was on the platform at a meeting at the Memorial Hall, when Jim Larkin came to tell the English workers what straits the Dublin workers were in after seven weeks of slow starvation. As I listened to his appalling story, it flashed across my mind that here was a great opportunity for organised workers in England to prove their solidarity with the locked-out men in Dublin, by taking in to their homes some of the children who were suffering so severely from the effects of industrial strike.

When Larkin had finished speaking I wrote out a slip of paper and passed it across to him, asking him if a plan like this which had already been successfully carried out by Belgian comrades, and in the Lawrence strike, in the United States, could be arranged through the *Herald* League, would it have his backing. He wrote a few words in the affirmative, and I then passed along a line to Lady Warwick, who was also on the platform, asking her if she would act as Treasurer to the Fund, which she agreed to do. With the consent of Mr. Lapworth, the Editor of the *Daily Herald*, I wrote the next day a letter to that paper, setting forth the idea, and in less than two days I had upwards of 110 homes offered by workers in England and Scotland to the 'Dublin kiddies'.[27]

Soon these numbers were greatly increased, and when she had 300 'responsible homes', Dora Montefiore set off for Dublin on the evening of 17 October. At this point, the Catholic church intervened, and Dublin's Archibishop Walsh let it be known that he was concerned about the defence of the faith of Catholic children set loose among Protestant families. On 25 October, the NTWF *Weekly Record* reported:

Events in Dublin, otherwise quiet, have taken an exciting turn by the intervention of the priesthood, led by Archbishop Walsh, in the struggle. By this we mean that they have not made any effort to end the struggle, they have not decided to help the poor of Dublin to resist the unChristian attitude of Murphy, they have not come out, as one might expect, to remind Murphy of the saying of their Lord 'Inasmuch as you did it unto the least of these, ye did it unto Me'. No, they have come out to prevent English sympathisers from feeding and housing Murphy's victims, on the pretext that their religious education might not be in accordance with Catholic ideas. To put it shortly, the Black International cares a great deal about the way by which the children of the workers ascend to Heaven, but it does not care a jot how soon Murphy sends them there.

We confess that we find it hard to understand the frame of mind that can induce a man with human attributes writing such a letter as Archbishop Walsh addressed to the mothers of Dublin the other day. We should have thought that so kind and generous an offer as that made by the English women, to take those who were suffering out of the firing-line, would have appealed to the human instincts of any man above the grade of a South Sea Islander. We were mistaken. The Priesthood, whose power in Ireland we English are so apt to overlook, have determined that the men shall submit or the children shall suffer.

We wish we had space to quote the Archbishop's letter in full, that our readers might see to what lengths religious bigotry can be carried when it is a question of helping the capitalists to oppress the workers. One sentence, that he 'heard with consternation the proposal to send the children to be cared for in England by persons of whom the parents can have no knowledge' stamps the character of the man at once.

He further states that there is no security of any kind that their religious needs will be looked after, and this despite the fact that Mrs. Rand, one of the women organisers of the scheme, told the clericals that the nearest priest would be communicated with. Though she is a Catholic, the priests refused to accept this assurance.

The latest advices are that Mrs. Rand and Mrs. Montefiore have been arrested for abducting the children, and we understand that the charge is brought under a section of the White Slave Act. The whole business stands out as one of the most disgraceful examples of religious bigotry, and ignorance, and venom, that has ever disgraced the Black International in all its long history of effort to keep the poor oppressed and ignorant.[28]

## Purging the Infidel

Robert Williams had overreached himself, however, in thus condemning the Catholic Church. As a propaganda slogan, the 'abduction of children' was effective, and not only in Dublin. At the next meeting of the NTWF Executive, James Sexton arrived in a state of boiling fury, to demand that the anti-clerical excess of the *Record's* editor be moderated. On 1 November, Williams climbed down, although by no means as unconditionally as his critics would have wished:

We should here like to amplify what we said last week in reference to the action of Archbishop Walsh. We are not concerned with anyone's creed in these columns – we are out to improve the standard of life of the workers, and we believe that we have the bulk of the members of the Federation behind us in attacking any menace to the efforts of the workers to obtain a larger share of the wealth they produce, whether that menace comes from the Church, the Press, or the Politician. The fact that the organised Catholic Church has always been against the efforts of the workers to raise themselves out of their environment is a matter of history, which is deplored by many good Catholics who, like ourselves, have, in Connolly's words, 'learned to make a clear distinction between religion and ecclesiastical politics or organised clerical capitalism'. Matters of faith are personal, but we must protest when an organised religious body steps in to help the capitalist class to keep the workers in subjection. Archbishop Walsh may have meant well in the action he took, he may have been sincere in his fears for the religious welfare of the children, but we are only concerned with the practical effect of his action, which was undoubtedly against the interest of the workers, and in favour of the interest of capitalism. For ourselves, we need no more justification for our comments than is contained in the following extract from a speech by Archbishop Walsh:
'The fantastic policy of spending money in taking the children away for what I heard is called a holiday can do no real good. It can have but one permanent result, and that surely the very reverse of a beneficient one. It will but make them discontented with the poor homes to which they will sooner or later return.'
This is where we of the Federation part company with the Archbishop. We believe that the policy of making the poor discontented *is* a beneficient one. The Trade Union movement, the Federation itself, is a result of the discontent of the workers. We believe in fomenting that discontent, in preaching revolt – revolt, organised to remove the cause of discontent; revolt

against the injustice of present-day society to the only useful class in that society . . . [29]

Liverpool's Catholic Irish dockers might have been expected to hear these arguments with keen concern for what was happening in Dublin. But Sexton's fierce reaction indicates that this was not their most widely shared response. Sexton's religion obviously played a formative role in his trade unionism, and his contribution does entitle us to visualize a 'Catholic' presence in the sectors he represented. But by no means all those of his co-religionists with membership in his union were prone to share his immediate reactions.

## Welcoming the Children

Eighteen children were soon embarked for Liverpool, with the written permission of their parents. Fred Bower, the syndicalist stonemason, was among the welcoming committee present at the dock to meet them. There were also several priests.

The time was five o'clock in the morning, when I waited at the Liverpool landing-stage, as the *Carlou* nosed alongside. Detective Inspector McCoy came up to me. We knew each other. 'Hello,' he said. 'What brings you down here so early?' 'The same business as what brings you, I expect, Inspector,' I replied. 'I hope there will be no trouble.' 'There won't be any, if I can help it,' he promised. The gangway was let down, and I went aboard to meet Miss Neale who had charge of the bairns, pinched and ill-clad, most of them barefooted. I set off to board the ferry-boat which was to take us over the Mersey to a beautiful house in Cheshire, the occupant of which had promised to act as host for the children till they had all been fixed up in their respective destinations, when a priest stopped me. 'Where are you going with the children?' he asked. I told him. 'Have you their parents' permission?' 'Not on me,' I replied, 'but it has been given.' 'Then I must give you in charge,' he said, and called a policeman.

I explained to the officer. The detective inspector could vouch that I was known to him. Eventually we were corralled into a customs shed around a fire, and the children were regaled with cakes and hot tea. Another priest, a canon, had now appeared and began asking the scared mites what church they went to, had they attended Mass, and so on. The priests soon had the poor children crying. I said, 'If you please, you might leave the children alone, they were quite comfortable before you interfered.' Other things were said, but Miss Neale soothed the youngsters, and we waited.

In about a couple of hours, Inspector McCoy came back, to report the police had got in touch with the Lord Mayor of Dublin. 'He had the written consent of all the parents in his hands,' he said. So we were allowed to pass on. 'Now,' I said to the two priests, 'they are in my charge and you will have to stop annoying them, or else I shall call a policeman.' 'But may we go with you?' one said. 'I cannot stop you,' I replied, 'the ferry-boat doesn't belong to me.' A Press photographer had come aboard and asked me would I mind posing the children. 'Not at all,' I replied. 'It may evoke sympathy with the plight of their parents, amongst the unthinking general public.' I stood at the end of the line and just as the camera was going to click the priest stood in the centre, and bless me, if the picture didn't appear with me cut off, and an article stating 'our picture shows some of the strikers' children being taken to palatial foster-homes in the charge of Father Walsh of Liverpool.'[30]

Attempts to billet the children with Catholic families in Belfast received no kinder treatment from the hierarchy. But while the 'scandal' of the evacuees was raging, want was abroad in Dublin. On 27 October the *Daily Herald* reported:

To walk in Dublin streets is almost enough to make one despair. Women and children with hollow cheeks and hollow eyes, barefooted, ragged, and splashed with street mud, accost one every few yards, and trot alongside until one is shamed into turning out a coin. The place is swarming with police. Jaunting-cars dash along with loads of laughing R.I.C. men, and laden lorries must have two or three police passengers added to their loads. Capital, the Law, and now the priests, are against the industrial rebels, and yet they refuse to go back to wage-slavery. It is magnificent.[31]

## *Larkin Back in Prison*

The same day, Larkin went for trial, and the day after he was in Mountjoy jail, beginning a seven-month sentence.

A vast protest rally in the Albert Hall heard speeches from Connolly, Delia Larkin and Ben Tillett, as well as from George Bernard Shaw, George Lansbury and Dora Montefiore. George Russell (AE) repeated his excoriation of the Dublin employers. Bernard Shaw was beside himself with anger. Connolly proposed that until Larkin was released, all should work and vote against the Liberal government. This was a shrewd move: Sir Edward Carson (leader of the Irish Unionists in Parliament and Ulster) was incessantly preaching treason, and offering to counter the Home Rule Bill by establishing a provisional government. Most Labour men, and all radical Liberals, were incensed that Larkin found his way to prison while Carson preached sedition with no threat of restraint. By 9 November Connolly's strategy had gained strength when the Liberals lost the Reading by-election. Of course, objective psephology (if such there be) might offer other explanations for this change of allegiance by the voters.[32] None the less, those Labour men in Reading who took Connolly's advice no doubt felt that they had won their point.

Larkin was released the next week, having served only seventeen days of his sentence. At this point, it was Connolly who talked sedition: 'The next time we are out for a march, I want to be accompanied by four battalions of trained men. I want them to come with their corporals, sergeants, and people to form fours. Why should we not drill and train our men in Dublin as they are doing in Ulster?'[33]

Larkin and Connolly then proclaimed that the port of Dublin was closed: 'We appeal to our brethren in Great Britain to second our efforts. We thank them for that cordial support which has made our blow so successful, and we counsel them to go ahead and strike while the iron of revolt is hot in our souls.'[34]

## Manchester Manifesto

This manifesto it was that Larkin proclaimed at a fantastic meeting in Manchester Free Trade Hall that Sunday. Every seat was taken, and 20,000 people stood outside:

> In Dublin men know that what I say is the truth. Do you think I dare come to a country like England, and to Lancashire, where at least one half of every four of you, or a little more, are Irish, and tell you a lie about my own country, a country I love as I love no other land, no other people? A man who won't love his own fireside can have no love for those outside. What I want to do is lift up the class I belong to; I want to improve them physically and mentally, broaden their outlook as human beings, and because of this among the things said of me is that I live in a mansion and drive a motor-car. By God! if ever a man deserved a mansion or a motor-car that man stands here – Jim Larkin, the symbol and embodiment of the working classes in Ireland. (Loud cheers.) I speak to you here as their mouthpiece, the official mouthpiece, the ambassador from the working classes of Ireland, the Chairman of their Trade Union Congress. I do not come with any mandate from a clique, but from the whole working class population.[35]

Larkin's words had an electric impact, not only in Manchester, but in all the other centres where he addressed overflowing mass rallies. But increasingly he found himself at odds with trade-union leaders, who were becoming ever more visibly apprehensive that action in support of the Dublin lock-out might run far beyond their control or influence. Various groups of railwaymen had stopped work, in South Wales, at Briton Ferry and elsewhere, for a mixture of reasons in which sympathy with the Dublin workers certainly featured. Some scholars argue that solidarity was by no means the only motive for these strikes:[36] but they had been preceded by other outbreaks in Liverpool and Birmingham, and the *Daily Herald* was campaigning to spread their example. In London, as Bob Holton, the historian of British syndicalism, records, Harry Orbell found it pressingly difficult to keep his dockers at work:

' . . . In all my experience I have never known a time when there has been manifested a desire to help any union in dispute as there is among dockers both in London and the provincial ports towards their Dublin comrades. . . . '

In London only the most strenuous efforts by union leaders kept men from striking. 'We have had to rearrange the whole of our paid officials in London,' added Orbell, 'placing them in certain centres with the express purpose of preventing any disorganised move . . . It has been with the greatest trouble – and some of us have received rather strong words – that we have so far been able to hold the men in check . . . Should it come to a stoppage I think it will be of such magnitude as has never been equalled in any previous dispute.'

Similar developments occurred on Merseyside, particularly at Garston docks, where boats were arriving from Dublin for coaling. Once again 'union leaders experienced great difficulties in keeping the men at work'.[37]

## Jimmy Thomas Keeps Order

The railwaymen's leader, J. H. Thomas, began to put down warning markers: 'No trade union official, no matter how competent or able or influential, ought to have the sole power of telling men when they must cease work.'[38]

Thomas was still seeking full recognition for his newly amalgamated union, so he was not at all benevolent to the doctrines of sympathetic action. His fluent advocacy was a sufficient impediment to full acceptance by the employers, who lost two significant cases to him. In September the Midland Railway had denied him admittance to an important inquiry on the Aisgill disaster, for fear, said a superintendent, that he might repeat the successes of his earlier cross-questioning. His biographer tells us that the railway companies were slowly coming round to the idea that the unions had something to offer within a stable framework of recognition, while it might be difficult to keep them beyond the pale: 'Thomas did much to promote this admirable trend by his handling of the rebellious during this period. For the strike bug was virile, and there was wide agitation to come out from sympathy for the transport workers of Dublin.'[39] But Thomas stumped his districts, asserting his authority and denouncing sympathetic action: ' "Sympathetic strikes are ruinous," he told them at Swindon, "because as railwaymen no dispute can take place in which you will not be involved." ' The railway directors were listening to these strong warnings against 'anarchy', and in March 1914 Thomas got his first offer of formal institutional recognition. Larkin's revolutionary unionism thus provided the directors with an incentive to treat with the more cautious reformists on their doorsteps. It was the awareness of this conflict of interest which stung the Irish leader into recriminations with Thomas and his colleagues, not simply his personal distaste for them.

## The TUC Prevaricates

Others besides the railway leader dragged their feet. When the Dublin Trades Council asked the TUC to act to impede the importation of non-union labour by Dublin, and to boycott the transit of materials to the city, these requests were not rejected outright, but a Special Session of the TUC was called for 9 December to consider what action might be taken. Undoubtedly this move was prevaricative, and it gave rise to noisy criticisms on the platform of the *Daily Herald*. On 22 November Larkin published a manifesto in that newspaper, in which he made a specific appeal to union members over the heads of their officials:

> Tell your leaders now and every day until December 9th, and raise your voice upon that day to tell them that for the future they must stand for Trade Unionism, that they are not there as apologists for the shortcomings of the Capitalist system, that they are not there to assist the employers in helping to defeat any section of workers striving to be free, nor to act as a brake upon the wheel of progress.[40]

At this point, Havelock Wilson issued a counter-manifesto, denouncing Larkin and all his works. Early next week, 'the proverbial roof came off'.[41] Larkin pitched into Wilson and Thomas with all the acrimony he could summon. They were too big for their boots. Thomas was 'a double-dyed traitor to his class'. The ferocity of this onslaught threw Larkin's supporters among the trade-union leaderships into no small consternation. Bob Williams, up to now his most dedicated supporter, cautioned Larkin: 'this fight and its consequences are immeasurably bigger to us than fifty Larkins'. Larkin responded by widening his fire, and savaging Philip Snowden: 'I am not going to allow these serpents to raise their foul heads and spit out their poison any longer.'

The next day, he spoke about union leaders who had 'neither a soul to be saved nor a body to be kicked'. Even the audiences winced at some of these attacks. Emmet Larkin reports that at Leicester Robert Williams was shouted down for supporting Larkin's criticisms of Ramsay MacDonald (their local MP) and of Philip Snowden. But Larkin 'showed his courage as he faced the hostile crowd and in a few minutes had them cheering'.[42]

The call for a special conference of the TUC had not originated in Dublin. As early as 8 November the NTWF *Weekly Record* had suggested a special conference of the Joint Board representing the TUC, the Labour Party and the General Federation of Trade Unions. In an editorial, Robert Williams had recommended 'cool restraint, well-planned, and co-ordinated action' against the movement of free labour into Dublin.[43] Williams had also proposed systematic action up to and including a boycott of goods from Dublin. A week later, the *Record* returned to this theme:

> The action of the British trade unionists . . . must not be confined to the despatching of ships which are, so to say, running the blockade. We have it within our power to raise the seige . . . We have exercised all our influence to restrain our members from taking part in sporadic and desultory strikes of a sympathetic character. We have been able to do this by an assurance that national action of a far more decisive nature . . . would probably take place.[44]

By 22 November the *Record* was reporting on the TUC's decision to go to a special conference, and recommending transport workers to show further restraint until a combined call could be issued to the trade-union movement as a whole. At the end of November, however, Robert Williams was concerned to identify other targets and other tasks:

> Among the many regrettable features of the Dublin dispute is the fact that as most of our thoughts are centred upon Dublin it leaves us little or no time to deal with our own domestic problems.
>
> It would be idle to pretend that, deplorable as are the conditions in the City of Dublin, our own conditions are in any way satisfactory. The movement in favour of amalgamation is being retarded in consequence of a large portion of our efforts being given up to the Dublin problem . . . [45]

At the same time, it was necessary to learn the lessons of the Dublin struggles:

> The tendency in the modern disputes between capital and labour is for the fight to be extended rather than confined. We shall require more and more to have understandings and agreements between large Unions and Federations for the purpose of defence and aggression. We heartily desire the consummation of the sentiments expressed at a recent conference of the Miners' Federation. At a recent meeting of our own Executive it was urged that we should communicate with the Miners' Federations with a view to promoting such an understanding between ourselves, the Miners' Federation, and the National Union of Railwaymen. It was felt, however, that the approach should be made from the Miners, as we had no record of their resolution than a report in the Press. It will be remembered that during the great Miners' Strike we made overtures to this effect that we were prepared to render assistance if the occasion warranted. The Miners, confident in the splendid organisation to which they had attained, did not deign to accept our proffered assistance . . .
>
> We are living in a period when our Trade Union organisation is in a state of becoming rather than being. We fervently desire that ample opportunity shall be given to those who hold strong opinions on the question of trade union structures and policy to put forward their opinions and ideas with all the clarity and strength of mental conviction that they possess.[46]

## Getting Off the Fence

The special conference of the TUC opened according to plan on 9 December: it was the first occasion upon which the British trade unions had ever convened such a gathering. Connolly presented the view of the Irish Transport and General Workers' Union, about the need to hold out and reinforce the blockading of the port of Dublin. Then Ben Tillett spoke. It was a bombshell. After touring the country, speaking to one mass rally after another, and always outdoing his fellow orators in radical, even incendiary, declamations, Tillett put the motion:

> That this Conference deplores and condemns the unfair attacks made by men inside the trade union movement upon British trade union officials; it affirms its confidence in those officials who have been so unjustly assailed, and its belief in their ability to negotiate an honourable settlement if assured of the effective support of all who are concerned in the Dublin dispute.[47]

As Tillett's biographer rightly comments, this was a strange sentiment to hear from 'the castigator of Hardie, Snowden, MacDonald, Henderson and countless others!'[48] Whatever qualities it revealed, self-criticism was not among them.

All the issues were then immediately lost in a storm of personal recrimination. Jimmy Thomas was not going to 'allow himself to be libelled and slandered'. Havelock Wilson thought that Larkin had been 'blundering from the very beginning' of the Dublin struggle. When Larkin himself obtained the rostrum, it was as a Daniel in a den of lions hungry for his blood. After a brusque exchange of insulting remarks, punctuated with uproar, he shouted:

> Neither you nor these gentlemen on the platform can settle this Dublin dispute. I challenge you to try it. I know, however, that the rank and file of the British trade unionists will support the Dublin men in their battle, and if we do not get that support we will do what we have done before – fight it out (cheers). This is a game of war; it is not a game of beggar-my-neighbour. I know the men we have to deal with. All they want to do is to delay the negotiations in order that they may weed the men out. The ban against the union has not been withdrawn. The employers of Dublin are neither truthful nor honest, and the only way to deal with them is to deal with them with a strong hand. We have always been able to do that. Take away your scabs, out of Dublin; take away the men who are organized scabs, who are acting worse than the imported scabs. The men of Dublin will never handle 'tainted' goods as long as I am an official (cheers).[49]

The Congress broke for lunch. When it returned, Tillett's motion was carried almost without dissent.

This decision could have been cathartic: it was now necessary to focus on the issues, once the personal disputations had been so thoroughly mangled in the morning's exchanges. John Ward, MP, and Ben Turner spoke to a resolution thanking those who had given such generous financial support, and pledged its continuation. It was the fundamental right to organize which was under challenge in Dublin, not a quarrel about personalities. Then one question remained: what, precisely, was to be done? J. W. Kelly proposed another initiative by the Joint Board of British and Irish Delegates to negotiate a solution. George Roberts, MP, drew all the conclusions from this motion, insisting that the financial support of the dispute would have to come to an end sometime. Jack Jones of the gasworkers put an amendment, appealing for an announcement that Dublin traffic would be boycotted after a given date, and initiating a monthly levy of British unions to maintain the Dublin workers. This amendment was lost by a vote of more than ten to one. The original motion, which implied that the men would be willing to ask for terms, was overwhelmingly carried.

Connolly replied for the Dublin delegation. He thanked the TUC for its generous financial support, and added that while it was understood that the decisions of the Congress must stand, 'there were some proposals they would not necessarily accept'.[50]

## Robert Williams Sums Up

The NTWF *Weekly Record* registered its dismay at these proceedings. Its editor had been excluded from them on a procedural technicality.

The greater portion of the day was given up to the indulgence of sordid and petty recriminations and abuse, and it was for this – this! – that we and others strove sedulously for an international expression of solidarity. We have now to regret that an epoch-making movement has been temporarily stultified by Larkin's want of good judgement, foresight, and tact. It is only on rare occasions that principles are able to transcend personalities. In this, a great occasion, need we say that personalities came before principles. It is not altogether unsafe to say that the Agenda was deliberately and consciously rigged for this self-same purpose. What possible need was there for men who feel that they are doing their duty to pass resolutions congratulating one another? One is tempted to quote Shakespeare and say, with respect to each and everyone of the whitewashers, 'methinks he doth protest too much'. One was reminded of a mutual admiration society, where the almost unanimous opinions were confidence in and praise of one another, and extended denunciation of Larkin.

We have said that Larkin has been, and is, to blame, although he is not responsible for the complete futility of the Conference. We are certain that if a plebiscite of the members were taken, the distribution of the votes would not work out in the proportion of ten to one against the systematic boycott of Dublin traffic.

The Secretary of the Federation, who probably knows as much of the facts and circumstances of the Dublin dispute as any other one man in the movement, was deliberately kept out of the Conference because his views were not satisfactory to the members of the Parliamentary Committee. His name was submitted as a delegate from his own Union, and from the Executive of another Union, but because he is a paid official of a Federation of 29 Unions, and not of one separate Union, he is rigorously excluded. And this happened at a Conference where Mr. W. C. Anderson, who joined in the scurrilous abuse of Larkin, boasted that he was not a Trade Union official, and was not in any way connected with a Trade Union. A resolution was moved and seconded by two middle-class members of the Fabian Society, who would not claim the slightest association with a Trade Union. We do not complain, we explain.

In spite of the fact that the main decision of the Conference was cowardly, in that it refused to accept its further obligation to settle the Dublin dispute, we are not without hope for the future. The Conference has established a precedent in industrial warfare. Although we move but slowly, we do move. We are gradually forsaking the politics of the parish pump and are beginning to realise more and more that our industrial concepts must not be that of the shoemaker sticking to his last, nor, as Mr. Thomas and Mr. Williams of the Railwaymen would have it, the guard thinking only of his brakevan and the signalman of his cabin and levers. A large and steadily-growing section of the rank and file are realising the interdependence of the modern labour movement. The members of their Unions, by their constant association with the machine process, know better than the officials that sectional Unionism must give way to the greater Class Unionism.[51]


## Down Again to Hell

One question is bound to be asked during any account of these days. Tom Mann had been touring the United States, but what might his influence have been, had he been at home? It is unthinkable that he would have stayed in Liverpool waiting for reports.

While the British transport workers examined the industrial implications of these events, and reinforced their moves towards their own amalgamation and towards closer co-operation with the other union federations of miners and railwaymen, things were different in Dublin. The industrial battle was losing ground fast. By the beginning of February the Builders' Labourers' Union capitulated, accepting a return to work on the basis of repudiating the ITGWU and every form of sympathetic strike. Levies from Britain died back to a trickle. The relief fund was exhausted by mid-February, and Connolly wrote: 'And so we Irish workers must again go down into hell, bow our backs to the last of the slave drivers, let our hearts be seared by the iron of his hatred and instead of the sacramental wafer of brotherhood and common sacrifice, eat the dust of defeat and betrayal. Dublin is isolated.'[52]

In isolation, the newly formed Irish Citizen Army continued to drill.

## Amalgamation or Revolution?

The revolutionary upsurge in Ireland confronted all the forces of the TUC and the Labour movement. The metropolitan workers, many of whom had never imagined such turbulence as that through which they were currently living, found that there was an even greater disorder across the water. But the Irish had more than one possible target: a new society, yes; but also an independent nation. Back in England, choices were more restricted. The transport workers had made what they conceived to be a profoundly radical decision: to amalgamate their own forces, and to join together in triple alliance with the railwaymen and miners. In this way they sought to shift the balance of industrial power. Across the Irish Sea things moved to a yet more insistent rhythm. Edward Carson, the Orangemen and the Tories were leaguing together for a war of secession. George Dangerfield, in his provocative work *The Strange Death of Liberal England*, asks us to suppose what might have happened if the Ulster Unionists had succeeded in detonating a civil war.

> Would it remain just a civil war? Between Larkin and the Irish Nationalists there was one link, and that link was James Connolly, who had drowned his Syndicalism in the dearer cause of the Irish Volunteers. If Ulster and Southern Ireland ever came to blows, it was far from inconceivable that Larkin would join in, to give this domestic bloodshed the deeper colour of revolution. And if Larkin joined in, how would the English workers behave? One thing was certain – the Dublin transport strike had completed a fatal circle: the Tory Rebellion, and the workers' Rebellion were no longer separate . . . 'Within a comparatively short space of time,' Sir George Askwith said to the members of the Cavendish Club in Bristol, 'there may be movements in this country coming to a head of which recent events have been a small foreshadowing.' And Sir George had never yet been accused of over-statement.[53]

Nor had he. But today we have a longer hindsight than Dangerfield, and maybe we can see the limits, as well as the scope, of national revolution. Two contending nations in Ireland were to duplicate not only aspirations to statehood, but also affinities of class and society. There was, perhaps, a short moment in which civil war might have joined social revolution, keeping together forces which, in the event, were soon to separate. This conjunction, had it been speedily consummated, might have led to something absolutely new. However, its failure would guarantee division enough to control and inhibit social change for years and decades to come.

# Notes

1   W. Moran, 'The Dublin Lockout, 1913', *Bulletin of the Society for the Study of Labour History*, no. 27 (autumn 1973).

2   Peter Berresford Ellis, *A History of the Irish Working Class* (Pluto Press, 1985), p. 184.

3   The injustice of this charge, and the subsequent verdict, is argued in W. P. Ryan, *The Irish Labour Movement* (Talbot Press, n.d.), pp. 185–7.

4   Ibid., p. 189.

5   James Connolly, *Labour in Irish History* (Irish Transport and General Workers' Union, 1934), pp. 167–8.

6   F. S. L. Lyons, *Ireland since the Famine* (Fontana, 1973), p. 281.

7   Ibid., p. 282.

8   See P. S. Bagwell, *The Railwaymen*, vol. 1 (Allen and Unwin, 1963), pp. 309 ff.

9   *Liverpool Daily Post and Mercury*, quoted in Bob Holton, *British Syndicalism, 1900–1914*, (Pluto Press, 1976), p. 188.

10   Moran, 'The Dublin Lockout, 1913', p. 11.

11   Sean O'Faolain, *Constance Markievicz* (Cresset Women's Voices, 1987), p. 111.

12   Ibid.

13   Ibid., pp. 111–12.

14   James Plunkett, *Strumpet City* (Hutchinson, 1969).

15   O'Faolain, *Countess Markievicz*, pp. 114–15.

16   The third volume of Sean O'Casey's autobiography, *Drums Under the Windows* (Macmillan, 1945), gives a somewhat free account of these events (pp. 219 ff.).

17   *Red Roses for Me*, act IV; Collected Plays, vol. III (Macmillan, 1951), p. 211.

18   V. I. Lenin, *Collected Works*, vol. 19, (Foreign Languages Publishing House, Moscow, 1963), pp. 332–6 and 348–9.

19   Harry Gosling, *Up and Down Stream*, (Methuen, 1927), pp. 123–5.

20   *Manchester Guardian*, 15 September 1913; quoted in Emmet Larkin, *James Larkin, Irish Labour Leader, 1876–1947*, (Routledge and Kegan Paul, 1965), p. 128.

21   Ibid., p. 129.

22   NTWF *Weekly Record*, 11 October 1913.

23   Ibid.

24   Ibid.

25   *Irish Times*, 7 October 1913; quoted in Larkin, *James Larkin*, pp. 136–7.

26   Of helpers there were many. One who was missing, however, was Tom Mann, who at the time was on a coast-to-coast tour of the United States, talking to an assortment of IWW, AF of L and other groupings, and linking up with William Z. Foster, who had developed the strategy of 'boring from within'.

27   Dora B. Montefiore, *From a Victorian to a Modern* (E. Archer, 1917), p. 156.

28   NTWF *Weekly Record*, 25 October 1913.

29 Ibid., 1 November 1913.
30 Fred Bower, *Rolling Stonemason*, (London, 1936), pp. 174–5.
31 Montefiore, *From a Victorian to a Modern*, p. 177.
32 Henry Pelling reports that Rufus Isaacs, who was both popular and much opposed by local industrial hierarchs, held on to Reading only by a small margin. Did his loss tilt the balance? (*Social Geography of British Elections* (Macmillan, 1967), p. 111).
33 Larkin, *James Larkin*, p. 144.
34 Ibid.
35 Ibid.
36 David Howell, *A Lost Left*, (Manchester University Press, 1986), p. 117.
37 Holton, *British Syndicalism, 1900–1914*, p. 193.
38 Larkin, *James Larkin*, p. 145.
39 Gregory Blaxland, *J. H. Thomas, A Life for Unity* (Frederick Muller, 1964), pp. 85–6. In his own memoirs, Thomas does not refer to these events.
40 Cited in Larkin, *James Larkin*, p. 146.
41 Ibid.
42 Ibid., p. 147.
43 NTWF *Weekly Record*, 8 November 1913.
44 Ibid., 15 November 1913.
45 Ibid., 29 November 1913.
46 Ibid.
47 Larkin, *James Larkin*, p. 152.
48 Jonathan Schneer, *Ben Tillett: Portrait of a Labour Leader* (Croom Helm, 1982), p. 170.
49 See Larkin, *James Larkin*, p. 153.
50 Ibid., p. 154.
51 NTWF *Weekly Record*, 13 December 1913.
52 Ellis, *A History of the Irish Working Class*, p. 202.
53 George Dangerfield, *The Strange Death of Liberal England, 1910–1914* (Constable 1935; reissued Pedigree Books, 1980), pp. 329–30.

# 14

# The Politics of Revolt

*The seed sown by the pioneers began to bear fruit. The movement became a political power. Whole battalions were shepherded into it, much as the troops of Feng-Yu-Hsiang, 'the Christian General', were baptised with a hose. Thanks to the judges, the unions were the first wave. The war brought another . . .* [1]

## I

## *Internal Dissension in the Labour Party*

Whilst new unions in Ireland were nudging towards a social explosion, the left in the rest of Britain reacted, mostly defensively, to a series of challenges over which it had little or no control. If trade unions were to move closer together, the political left was to become even more divided than before.

In the run-up to the two General Elections of 1910, the Labour Party was in difficulties. The year before, the judges had ruled against political expenditure by unions, and to this, the Osborne Judgement, we shall return shortly. Quite apart from this trauma, the party was already, if not polarized, at any rate subject to rather profound internal dissension. Victor Grayson's maverick campaign against unemployment had aroused very great enthusiasm and, in reaction, many activists were critical of what they saw as parliamentary inertia. If one man could raise hell so effectively, where were all the other MPs? The electoral agreement with the Liberals had provoked much acrimony, although of course it was not officially acknowledged that any such pact existed. However, visible or not, it imposed obvious restraint in by-elections, and there were numerous tussles between resentful local organizations and an increasingly beleaguered head office. In 1909 there were major rows at the conferences of both the Labour Party itself and the ILP. Both leaderships held their ground, but with some difficulty. Rank-and-file dissatisfaction was rising, and nowhere more plainly than in the ILP.

More than 100 Labour candidates had been groomed for the first 1910 contest, but that January only 78 were actually nominated. Money was just part of the problem. None of Labour's leaders, and at the time probably few of its supporters, wished for a Liberal defeat. The Liberal whips knew this, and it must be assumed that they toughened up their attitudes in the backstage bargaining. They were not willing to connive at a growth of Labour influence. J. A. Pease, the Chief Whip (and Chancellor of the Duchy of Lancaster in 1910), delivered an ultimatum, and 'no doubt [the Labour Leaders] took the point'.[2] During all this time the miners were restive, and the hitherto unchallenged position of their cautious MPs could no longer be taken for granted. The ground beneath their feet was moving, and with it they slid into a new allegiance.

Both elections in 1910 'were fought virtually by a Liberal–Labour Alliance'.[3] In January, no Labour members got past the Liberal opposition. Only twenty-six seats were contested by both parties. Eight Labour men went down, while three new ones were elected. Altogether forty Labour Members were elected, but, of course, they now included the former Lib.–Lab. miners, most of which bold leopards had by no means changed their spots. Two further seats were won from Liberals in the December elections. This was Labour's full complement at the beginning of the Great Unrest. Had Labour joined forces with the Irish Nationalists, it might theoretically have held the balance of power, so diminished was the Liberal contingent. Far from drawing encouragement from this, Labour's leaders were paralysed by the apprehension that they might get the blame for breaking ranks.

At the ILP Conference of 1909, MacDonald had found the necessary words to plaster over this programme of conformity to Liberal interests. Minorities, he argued, could not impose their will upon the majority. Even unemployment was less important than was the protection of 'the conditions and the existence of democratic government'.[4] That the Liberal government was elected on a profoundly undemocratic franchise, and that Liberal voters might have been far from hostile to real action against unemployment, was widely understood by MacDonald's critics. There were really two strands to this argument. The lesser strand involved the expediency of agreement with the Liberals, which was still perceived – especially in some key unions – as electorally necessary. The greater one involved a commitment to the myths of parliamentary convention, which were ultimately to involve Labour in wholesale retreat. When the time came to challenge the feudal inheritance of Parliament and reform it in a democratic direction, MacDonald was nowhere to be seen.

## Victor Grayson and Unemployment

Grayson used the short time left to him as an MP to continue his work of confrontation. He was often absent from the chamber, spending most of his time campaigning in the country. His opinion of parliamentary institutions was unflattering in the extreme: 'No man possessing a heart and a conscience could sit in the House of Commons without suffering all the horrors of the damned . . . There is no bond between this respectable assembly of well-fed and well-clothed men and the hundreds of thousands of out-of-work, miserable and famished, who wander about the cities of 'Christian' England.'[5]

This was a message which appealed, not only to some disaffected ILPers, but also to the older men of the left, like Hyndman, Blatchford and Tillett. It was soon to encourage new efforts to create a socialist platform. In the ILP itself, Grayson had a mixed following. At the April 1909 Annual conference, he successfully moved the reference back of that part of the National Administrative Council's report, which confirmed its decision not to invite him to speak on party platforms. Although they had won on every other issue, MacDonald, Hardie, Glasier and Snowden found this affront too much to swallow, and the following morning they dramatically resigned from the Council. Perhaps the resignations were more than drama, even melodrama. Once threatened, the delegates were all too anxious to eat their words. But out went the great men, none the less.

The ILP, in short, entered the General Election year in a mess. Between 1909 and 1911 'over forty branches disappeared'.[6] The Labour Party could now draw on wider institutional supports, but its condition was hardly very healthy. Whilst the Osborne Judgement was not by any means the only reason for this, it undoubtedly played its part.

## II

## The Osborne Judgement

If troubles never come in single spies, the Amalgamated Society of Railway Servants seemed to nourish whole battalions of troublemakers for the Labour Party. First, the Taff Vale Judgement; then the victory and subsequent defection to the Liberals of the railway spokesman Richard Bell; and then, in 1908, the marauding legal action of the Walthamstow branch of the union and its secretary, W. V. Osborne. Osborne it was who went to the High Court for an injunction to stop political payments by his union, because they were *ultra vires*. Two years earlier, a similar action had been brought against the South Wales Miners' Federation by a member called Steele. He lost. So, too, did Osborne. But he appealed, and won. The case toiled through to the House of Lords, where, in 1909, Osborne won again. The immediate effect was a disastrous setback to the finances and morale of the Labour Party. If union money could not be spent on political objectives, then all the elaborate work of persuasion and organization which had banded the unions into a collective political force was, at a stroke, nullified.[7]

The TUC and individual unions insisted that the judgement be overcome by new legislation, specifically restoring full freedom to spend their revenues in whatever way their members determined.[8]

Meanwhile, the December 1910 General Election had seen a marked contraction in the number of Labour candidates in the field, to fifty-six. There was greater anxiety than ever before about state payment of MPs. Lloyd George brought in a measure to award them salaries; but his price was support for his proposals on National Insurance. These were disliked by many Labour MPs, and even more disliked by a great number of those who had voted for them. In the first days, it was thought that those trade-union leaders who sat in the Commons might now be more independent of their unions. Tensions were anticipated by the Liberal managers. After all, their whips knew the foibles of the former Lib.–Lab. members better than anyone. But in fact payment of MPs would not fund their campaigns, and the compulsory withdrawal of trade-union funding was therefore more than a blow against the survival of the new party. More, because it was soon applied more widely, after cases involving Liberal members of the Miners' Federation. Indeed, MacDonald pointed up the irony that, while the judgement minimally affected MPs from the Independent Labour Party, it would strike hardest at the moderate trade-union nominees.[9] The Liberals dragged their feet about rectifying this position, since its advantages must at first have seemed too good to be true. Soon a clearer picture emerged. Liberal trade unionists who had initially gone along with Osborne, a fellow Liberal, soon began to worry about the scatter-shot effect of all this legal action, and became anxious for clarification.

Not until 1913 did the government really move, and then crabwise. It invented the institution of Trade Union Political Funds. These were to be kept completely apart from general funds, which would continue to be restricted for conventional uses, specifically excluding political purposes. A political fund could be set up only after an affirmative vote in a special ballot for the purpose. Even if a 'yes' decision emerged, any member would have the right not to pay, and could sign to 'contract out' of political payments. So ran the Trade Union Amendment Act, 1913. Try as they may, trade-union MPs could not improve on this measure. Cries of anger echoed up to Westminster from annual conferences, from the TUC, and from individuals who were affronted by what they regarded as gross interference in their right to determine how their own funds might be allocated.

In spite of this, as A. J. P. Taylor points out, the invention of a special political fund made the unions more, not less, generous with their party:

> In the old days a union felt generous when it subscribed £100 to the Labour Party. Now it thought nothing of handing over £5,000, if the money were lying idle in the political fund. Not all the political fund was paid to the national Labour Party. Some went to Union MPs; some to assist local associations and to pay the expenses of elections. All the same, the income of the Labour Party multiplied overnight, and it shot up further when unions increased their membership during the war.[10]

## Balloting About the Political Funds

The ballots were conducted with due urgency, as soon as the Act was in force. They provide us with some insight into the state of political commitment during the months immediately before and shortly after the outbreak of the First World War. Tillett's union won a big majority for the new fund, on a low turn-out. While 88 per cent were in favour, only one-quarter of those eligible voted. Surprisingly, the Seamen's Union polled much better, at 37 per cent, and secured 98 per cent in support. But the seamen were accustomed to the parliamentary presence of Havelock Wilson, and they did not employ their mandate to take themselves into the Labour Party. Liberal and syndicalist influences combined to keep them out. Sexton's union voted in broadly the same proportions as their London-based colleagues, but secured a very low turn-out of 9 per cent. Four-fifths of the Carters' Union voted but, apart from the Cardiff coal-trimmers, no one else reached a 50 per cent turn-out. Overall, the transport and general unions in this sample voted by 84 per cent of a 27 per cent turn-out to establish political funds (see table 14.1).

This compares with larger turn-outs by the miners (75 per cent), weavers (57 per cent) and railwaymen (51 per cent). Yet the majorities in favour of the fund were smaller in these unions: 43 per cent of miners voted against, 44 per cent of weavers, and 48 per cent of boilermakers, on another very low turn-out of 13 per cent. The engineers won their fund with 62 per cent of those voting. (See table 14.2.)

It would be a mistake to compare these figures with the very much larger responses secured when recurrent ballots were instituted in the 1980s.[11] The major difference in conditions was, of course, the state of the franchise. Large numbers of trade-union members, including all women, entered the First World War without parliamentary votes. Very probably this fact accounts in part for restricted turn-out in the ballots

Table 14.1 *Political fund ballots: Transport Unions**

| Unions in Transport | Total membership | Voting in political fund ballots | | | | Turnout as percentage of members |
| | | Numbers | | Percentages | | |
| | | For | Against | For | Against | |
|---|---|---|---|---|---|---|
| Dock, Wharf, Riverside and General Workers' Union | 43,691 | 9,729 | 1,350 | 88 | 12 | 25 |
| National Sailors' and Firemen's Union | 55,000 | 19,879 | 329 | 98 | 2 | 37 |
| National Union of Dock Labourers | 51,000 | 4,078 | 501 | 89 | 11 | 9 |
| London and Provincial Union of Licensed Vehicle Workers | 16,000 | 1,609 | 836 | 66 | 34 | 15 |
| National Union of Gasworkers and General Labourers | 134,538 | 27,802 | 4,339 | 86 | 14 | 24 |
| National Union of Ship Stewards, Cooks, Butchers and Bakers | 8,000 | 436 | 148 | 75 | 25 | 7 |
| Amalgamated Society of Watermen, Lightermen and Bargemen | 5,000 | 1,624 | 298 | 85 | 15 | 38 |
| National Amalgamated Labourers' Union | 6,000 | 1,485 | 318 | 82 | 18 | 30 |
| Cardiff, Penarth and Barry Coal Trimmers' Union | 2,050 | 728 | 305 | 70 | 30 | 50 |
| National Amalgamated Union of Labour | 65,000 | 18,214 | 7,470 | 71 | 29 | 40 |

Table 14.1 (*cont.*)

| Unions in transport | Total membership | Voting in political fund ballots | | | | Turnout as percentage of members |
| | | Numbers For | Against | Percentages For | Against | |
| --- | --- | --- | --- | --- | --- | --- |
| Amalgamated Carters', Lurrymen's and Motormen's Union | 5,000 | 2,446 | 1,482 | 62 | 38 | 79 |
| Totals | 391,279 | 88,030[†] | 17,356 | 84 | 16 | 27 |

* These eleven unions are those included in table 17.1 (pp. 612–13), for which full figures are available. They represented 84 per cent of the total membership of those twenty-four transport-related unions.
† Total voting for a political fund represents 22.5 per cent of the membership of these eleven unions.

*Sources*: Membership – TUC Congress Report, 1915. Ballots – Report of Chief Registrar on Trade Unions, 1914, on Ballots as to Political Objects under the Trade Union Act, 1913, up to 15 April 1916 (appendix B).

and, alternatively, for the higher involvement of mineworkers and some skilled groupings. Voteless members had no personal influence in the electoral process and, understandably, might have been more reluctant to pay for participation at one remove. None the less, *The Times* drew the lesson that 'a large section' of Labour's affiliates were 'indifferent, and another large section positively hostile' to the cause of the party.[12]

If some hostility came from the Liberal trade unionists, since we must assume that there were many mute inglorious Osbornes, probably some of it also came from disenchanted socialists. After all, the Parliamentary Labour Party was sustaining the Liberals in office, and it would be very difficult to overlook the loyalty of the new 'Labour' MPs to the government. Rock the boat they would not: their chief concern was to hang on. Some gave the impression that they would rather go down with the ship than swim to leave it. The young men, like Ernest Bevin, were less than enchanted with this performance. They were campaigning against unemployment, and they wanted action.

## Left Unity . . . and Diversity

It was in this context that the Social Democratic Party was offered an opportunity to come out of isolation. In 1907 it had dubbed itself a 'party', abandoning the name 'Federation'. It had then won Ben Tillett, as we have seen, and it was joined in 1910 by Tom Mann for a brief period before he hived off to proclaim a purer syndicalism. Among the leaders of the dockers' union, it had considerable strength. Now it was able to profit from Victor Grayson's insurgency, and profit it did.

With the support of Grayson himself, and of Robert Blatchford, the Coventry Conference of the SDP agreed, during Easter 1911, to convene a United Socialist Party. At the end of September, at a conference in Salford, there gathered the founders of the new party, which called itself the British Socialist Party (BSP). Most of its members (118) came from the Social Democrats, but 41 were delegated from branches of the ILP; 32 from Clarion Cycling Clubs; 48 from local socialist societies and Labour Representation Committees; and 12 from a pre-launched body already calling itself the British Socialist Party. Total: 251 delegates, representing a claimed aggregate membership of 35,000.[13] Quelch moved the constitutive resolution.

Table 14.2: *Political Fund Ballots: Non-transport Unions*

| | | Voting in political fund ballots | | | | |
|---|---|---|---|---|---|---|
| Selected unions outside transport | Total membership | Numbers For | Against | Percentages For | Against | Turnout as percentage of members |
| *United Society of Boilermakers, and Iron and Steel Shipbuilders | 68,000 | 4,752 | 4,404 | 52 | 48 | 13 |
| *National Union of Railwaymen | 267,611 | 102,270 | 34,953 | 75 | 25 | 51 |
| Amalgamated Society of Engineers | ? | 20,586 | 12,740 | 62 | 38 | n/a |
| *Miners' Federation of Great Britain | 607,152 | 261,643 | 194,800 | 57 | 43 | 75 |
| *Amalgamated Weavers' Association | 198,966 | 98,158 | 75,893 | 56 | 44 | 57 |

*Note:* Of the four unions marked °, for which membership figures are available, 41 per cent of the members voted in favour of a political fund.

*Source:* As table 14.1

Tom Mann had already resigned from the SDP before the fusion. Ben Tillett became one of the new party's five most popular speakers. However, it quickly became apparent that the SDP core of the new membership was completely predominant, as all its old quarrels re-emerged in full throat. Funded by Bert Killip's Red Flag Toffee and Chocolate sales, and the distribution of 'Revolutionist' razors of 'finest Sheffield Steel' at 3s. 6d. apiece, together with socialist coffee, tea and tobacco shops, the party maintained its press and a volume of publications. But the young men were now flocking to industrial unionism and the gospel of Tom Mann, while the ancients were quarrelling about the rising German menace, and whether or not to build Dreadnoughts. The party quickly divided into patriotic and inter-nationalist wings, and its latent split was finally accomplished under the pressure of war.

But while the left followed schismatic patterns in its organization, there was one field in which, with union help, more ecumenical thoughts might gain wider influence. This concerned the Labour press.

## III

## *Politics and the Press*

The socialist newspapers in the first decade of the twentieth century were weeklies. Blatchford's *Clarion* was the brightest, reaching a circulation of 70,000 in 1906. Its star was dimmed, however, by its response to the South African War, and its political bite was perhaps less mordant than that of its rivals. The ILP published the *Labour Leader*, which sold about half as many. *Justice* had a presence, and then there was a plethora of factional broadsheets.

The modern daily newspaper had been a product of industrial, commercial and technical concentration. Northcliffe's prototypical *Daily Mail* grew out of the profits of a periodical chain, and was launched in 1896 with a circulation of 200,000. It could be printed in one hour on the new rotary presses which were installed for the purpose. It sold for a halfpenny. Circulation doubled in two years, nudging 1 million at the turn of the century. The respectable papers, *The Times* and the *Daily Telegraph*, were in long-term decline. But Northcliffe's revolution began to establish a mass daily readership, with another journal from the same stable being founded in 1904: the *Daily Mirror* began to sell 1 million during the years of the Great Unrest. The *Daily Express* was launched in 1900 by Pearson. Even taking all the competitors together, total national daily circulation had reached only 5.5 million by the end of the First World War. Evidently many working-class families had still not got the newspaper habit.

Yet, as Raymond Williams has pointed out, this really was a 'revolution'; it took the newspaper 'from its status as an independent private enterprise to its membership of a new kind of capitalist combine.'[14]

## Employers and the Press

Such combines were commonly conglomerates. Since shipping was a strategic, and extraordinarily profitable, industry, shipping magnates were quick to diversify into the field. At the Shaw Inquiry, Bevin presented a complex chart by Walton Newbold, the BSP activist, showing how, among countless other interests, the shipowner Ellerman held more than 60,000 Associated Newspaper shares, and 83,000 shares in the Sphere and Tatler Limited.[15] The Cunard Steamship Company controlled the *Liverpool Daily Post and Mercury* and *Echo*.[16]

On the trade-union side Tillett, above all, had reason to know the power of the press. When once it had offered him sympathy, he had won his greatest victory in 1889. When, over and again, it had subsequently attacked him, he had every reason to understand how wounding it could be.

Numerous proposals were canvassed, in the TUC and in individual trade unions, seeking to establish a national Labour daily. The idea was debated in 1903, and again in 1907. Labour was not alone in exploring this question. In 1901 Lloyd George had 'engineered the purchase of the *Daily News* by the Cadbury family in the Liberal interest'.[17] (Later he was to use laundered funds, garnered from the sale of peerages and lesser baubles, for a similar purpose, in the takeover of the *Daily Chronicle*.) The Conservatives had direct influence on a whole string of journals. Labour seemed badly handicapped in these stakes.

## The Syndicalist

In January 1912, Tom Mann had launched another little paper called the *Syndicalist*. Its first number had appeared with an open letter to British soldiers, which was to become celebrated. It read as follows:

Men! Comrades! Brothers!
You are in the army.
So are we. You, in the army of Destruction. We, in the Industrial, or army of Construction.
We work at mine, mill, forge, factory, or dock, etc., producing and transporting all the goods, clothing, stuffs, etc., which makes it possible for people to live.

You are Workingmen's Sons.

When We go on Strike to better Our lot, which is the lot also of Your Fathers, Mothers, Brothers, and Sisters, YOU are called upon by your Officers to MURDER US.

Don't do it.

You know how it happens. Always has happened.

We stand out as long as we can. Then one of our (and your) irresponsible Brothers, goaded by the sight and thought of his and his loved ones' misery and hunger, commits a crime on property. Immediately you are ordered to murder Us, as You did at Mitchelstown, at Featherstone, at Belfast.

Don't You know, that when you are out of the colours, and become a 'Civvy' again, that You, like Us, may be on strike, and You, like Us, be liable to be Murdered by other soldiers.

Boys, Don't Do It.

'Thou shalt not kill', says the Book.

Don't forget that!

It does not say, 'unless you have a uniform on'.

NO! MURDER IS MURDER, whether committed in the heat of anger on one who has wronged a loved one, or by clay-piped Tommies with a rifle.

Boys, Don't do it.

Act the Man! Act the Brother! Act the Human Being.

Property can be replaced! Human life, Never!

The Idle Rich Class, who own and order you about, own and order us about also. They and their friends own the land and means of life of Britain.

You Don't! We Don't!

When We kick they order You to murder Us.

When You kick, You get court-martialled and cells.

Your fight is Our fight. Instead of fighting Against each other, We should be fighting With each other.

Out of Our loins, Our Lives, Our Homes, You came.

Don't disgrace Your Parents, Your Class, by being the willing tools any longer of the Master Class.

You, like Us, are of the Slave Class. When We rise, You rise; When We fall, even by your bullets, Ye fall also.

England with its fertile valleys and dells, its mineral resources, its sea harvests, is the heritage of ages to us.

You no doubt joined the army out of poverty.

We work long hours for small wages at hard work, because of our poverty. And both Your poverty and Ours arises from the fact that, Britain with its resources, belongs to only a few people. These few, owning Britain, own Our jobs. Owning Our jobs they own Our very lives. Comrades, have We called in vain? Think things out and refuse any longer to Murder Your Kindred. Help US to win back Britain for the British, and the World for the Workers.[18]

This appeal had actually been drafted by Fred Bower, the Liverpool stonemason. It had appeared in various publications, but after it came out in the *Syndicalist* it was republished as a leaflet for distribution at

Aldershot. The culprit was arrested. Then the *Syndicalist's* editor, Guy Bowman, was arrested, and then its printer. Fred Crowsley, who had leafleted the soldiers, got four months. The printer got six. Guy Bowman was awarded nine. That March, once the sentences were known, Tom Mann spoke at a big meeting of the Workers' Union and offered to sell copies of the offending journal at 2*d.* each. They remained with him, he said, after the police 'actually stole' all the others. As chairman of the committee responsible, he went on, 'I don't see how I shall escape arrest'. Nor did he. His trial came just in time to elicit close coverage in the *Daily Herald* (see below). He got six months. The *Herald* lobbied ceaselessly on his behalf, much, as its editor George Lansbury pointed out, to the discomfort of various prominent Labour leaders. Yet some Liberals joined their voices with George Lansbury's. They included Lord Russell, who said that he did not approve of action which might provoke shooting, but he did not approve of shooting either. It seemed reasonable to him that potential targets might think it sensible to ask potential marksmen to refrain from firing at them. Bertrand Russell, the Earl's younger brother, was more vociferous in his defence of free speech. In this cause, the *Herald* never wavered.

## *The Daily Herald*

In January 1911 the London print unions struck for a forty-eight-hour week. They began to print a daily strike bulletin, which swelled out to feature general news and sport. Beginning in London, it soon spread, with the dispute, to provincial cities. It was clear that a Labour daily was possible. When the *Daily Herald* died after the strike, plans were quickly made to relaunch it.

A ten-man committee of management was formed. Two members of the TUC's Parliamentary Committee agreed to serve on it, but the moving spirit was Ben Tillett. In 1911 George Lansbury was elected to Parliament. Tillett went to tea with him on the terrace of the House of Commons, and, using all the charm at his disposal, prevailed upon him to join the team:

> Those who only know Ben by reading about him do not know him as he really is – one of the most persuasive persons to be met with in our Movement. He wrestled with me quite a long time. All through the interview, I felt like a rabbit when a stoat is after it – just mesmerised. All the time he seemed to be saying: 'I will not let you go unless you say Yes'. And at last I agreed to join in what my common sense told me was a madcap scheme, and my name, therefore, remained as a member of the committee, and I was responsible with the others for our fateful start on April 15th, 1912.[19]

An appeal raised £300. With this improbable capital, the new paper was put together, and, on the appointed day, a little late for the trade, it came out. Timetabling was soon improved, but finances remained always impossible. The *Herald* was short of everything, even desks and pencils. The success of the project depended on its vivacity and, above all, on its openness. It was a forum. But it stood at the centre of an upsurge of literally unprecedented proportions. There was the Labour unrest which had given it birth. There was the kindred movement in Ireland, interlaced with a national movement for independence. There was the uprising of women, in the movement for suffrage, in whose interests Lansbury himself was valiantly to provoke, and lose, a by-election. And beneath it all was the sullen, inexorable, drift to war. Such a forum would at times be shrill, even abrasive; but it could never for one moment be dull. As Lansbury himself put it:

'Our weekly Socialist and Labour journals have become far too partisan and have thought very much more of the party they represented, than of the cause itself. The Socialist Movement, especially, has been in danger and is still in danger of being smothered by dogma . . . In the *Daily Herald*, Trade Unionists and Socialists of every creed and kin, Parliamentary and anti-Parliamentary, Syndicalist and Non-Syndicalist, will have room and scope fairly to state their ideas in their own way. No committee and no editor will edit the people's opinions . . . We want to have thrashed out in a perfectly friendly manner, those questions connected not only with the theory of the general strike, or the right to strike, but the fundamental utility of the general strike, as a Labour weapon. We also want thrashed out – and this requires to be done very quickly – the question as to why it is and with what object we send Labour and Socialist members to the House of Commons.'[20]

Debate was not the only strong suit of the new paper, however. What it lacked in news coverage it made up for, with interest, in curiosity, courage, and the capacity to ask and press awkward questions. It began as it meant to carry on:

As the first issue of the *Daily Herald* went to press on April 15th, 1912, the *Titanic* was sinking. The ship had been pronounced unsinkable. On this first voyage it was trying to make a speed record with the Chairman of the White Star Line, Bruce Ismay, on board. At first faked messages of 'all's well' were sent out, but it was soon realised that 1,300 persons were drowned. As soon as it realised this, the *Daily Herald* struck a distinctive note. W. R. Titterton was sent to Southampton to meet the rescued seamen and passengers. On April 18th the following appeared: –
    'Mr. Bruce Ismay, Chairman of the White Star Line, has been saved . . . Why is it that so few of the steerage passengers have been saved?'
    It was not till the 26th that the full story was known, and then, under the 'streamer': 'Women and Children Last!' the *Daily Herald* published a biting analysis. It pointed out that 121 steerage women and children were saved,

134 were drowned; 246 first and second class women and children were saved, and only twenty drowned; fifty-eight of the 173 first-class men passengers were saved. More than half the steerage children were drowned. The following biting words were printed: 'Where were those fifty-three steerage children, Mr. Ismay, when you saved yourself?' The White Star Line's profits were pilloried as follows: 'They have paid 30 per cent to their shareholders and they have sacrificed 51 per cent of the steerage children. They have gone to sea criminally under-equipped with means of life-saving; they have neglected boat drill; they have filled their boat with cooks and valets, with pleasure gardens and luxurious lounges; they have done all this to get big profits and please the first-class passengers. And when the catastrophe came they hastened to get their first-class passengers and their Chairman safely away. Fifty-three children remained to die. They were steerage passengers! One hundred and thirty-four women and children were slain. They were steerage passengers!'[21]

## Free Speech and Strikers

However, it was as a partisan of strikes and strikers that the *Herald* excelled. It did not apologize or equivocate; it simply gave support. In the 1912 London dock strike it solidarized, hectored, collected funds, organized the feeding of the children, and carried black propaganda among the blacklegs. 'Diseased!' ran one stark headline. 'Startling Medical Discovery Among Blacklegs. Wharf Closed':

> Some startling statements respecting the condition of men who are working as blacklegs was given by Councillor C. Smith, of Shoreditch, who presided over yesterday's big gathering of Transport Workers at Tower Hill.
>
> He said, three men among the blacklegs working at a Wapping wharf, were that morning unable to continue their work owing to illness.
>
> The parish doctor was called to them, and they were found to be suffering from a very serious contagious disease.
>
> He ordered their immediate isolation, and gave instructions for all the other men working on the wharf to be isolated for twenty-one days, and for the wharf to be thoroughly disinfected before any further work was proceeded with.
>
> The medical authorities of the Borough of Shoreditch were seeing that these orders were carried out.[22]

Similar forthright coverage was given to every dispute, culminating, in 1913, in a passionate campaign for the victims of the Dublin lock-out.

A galaxy of dissident stars began to write for the *Herald*. There was Tom Mann, of course. Ben Tillett was reported verbatim, day after day, as he took the stand at Tower Hill throughout the 1912 dock strike, but he also wrote continually. Hilaire Belloc and G. K. Chesterton, the Catholic 'distributivists', made war on the 'servile state' and impaled their former Liberal colleagues with fierce barbs in their battle against corruption and the Marconi scandal. Conrad Noel, vicar of Thaxted, preached the gospel of Christian communism with fire and verve. The unruly, brilliant Sylvia Pankhurst and her associates argued impatiently with the less savoury anti-feminist implications of Belloc's doctrine. Soon G. D. H. Cole and William Mellor were to join. Somehow the money was found to keep it all coming.

A nationwide network of *Herald* Leagues was formed. While the men at the top were preoccupied with the problems of how far their alliances and blocs could stretch or bend, some fifty-odd branches, covering many major cities, allowed the *Daily Herald* League to bring into one discourse the different arguments of the ILP, the BSP, the syndicalists, and all the social movements which looked to the paper for a voice and for encouragement.

Financial crisis never abated. On one occasion, when the brokers were in, the paper came out for three days while they were in possession. Lansbury recorded: 'On the third day vans arrived to move our furniture. Robert Williams, Ben Tillett and myself for some time filled the doorway while a parley took place, and from somewhere came the funds to purchase our tables, desks and chairs back again.'[23]

## *Looking for an Editor:*
## *Enter Tillett, with Frank Harris*

These problems were compounded by suits for libel. A succession of editors came and went. Sometimes their passing was acrimonious. Sometimes it caused heartache on both sides. On one occasion, it was nearly a sensation. 'During one period,' wrote Lansbury:

when we were searching for an editor, a friend who, for the benefit of any anti-Catholic, anti-Jew, or anti-Bolshevik readers, I may say was an Englishman, promised us a fairly considerable sum of money as share capital if we could induce a first-class journalist to take charge of the paper as editor. Ben Tillett at once thought of Frank Harris, and before any of us could say him nay, had packed his bag and was on his way to the Riviera in search of that redoubtable journalist. Within a few days they both appeared at our Board meeting. Frank Harris, direct as usual, lost no time in stating his terms and conditions. He required no pay; we must engage a man of his choice who would take orders from him; we must alter our whole policy. What Labour and the world needed was applied Christianity. This was the gospel he would preach daily in the paper. In doing this, he might come up against vested interests, monopolists, sharpers, scribes and pharisees, as did the Founder of the Christian religion 2,000 years ago. Humanity, if it were to be saved, must be made to see that religion consists of doing, not talking. Our task was to make this understood, and, like Jesus of old, go out into the market-places and money exchanges, and into the temples and churches, exposing scribes, pharisees, money-lenders, gamblers and worshippers of mammon. This policy might prove as dangerous to us as to the disciples of old, but we need have no fear of libel actions or anything else – he would take all responsibility and give us an agreement indemnifying us from all the consequences of any actions or writings appearing in the paper which might land us before the judges. Alas! our Board took fright; they could not accept all Frank Harris said as likely to happen. Although we had no money to lose, and were encumbered only by debts, they talked of financial ruin. It is an extraordinary fact that from working men to archbishops few, very few of us, are willing to accept and stand up for all the implications of the Christian religion.[24]

Stability was achieved when Lansbury himself took over the editorial chair in October 1913. Around him grew a talented team, some of whom would have been outstanding anywhere. The typographer Francis Meynell was one of these. Another was the cartoonist Will Dyson, whose work can still elicit a gasp of shock, and who made many of the images through which his age is recognized.

The *Herald* had to fall back to weekly publication early in the war. Its rebirth preoccupied another transport leader, Ernest Bevin. But we shall return to that story later on.

## *The Daily Citizen*

In October 1912, an official Labour newspaper was launched to compete with the *Herald*, not without rivalry and some internecine squabbles. It was called the *Daily Citizen*, and it gained a circulation of 200,000 by the following year. More staid by far than the *Herald*, it depended more on official trade-union funding. It was to become a victim of the Osborne Judgement, because it could be claimed that funding of a political journal was a task for the political funds, and that payments from general funds were *ultra vires*. In 1915 this was argued in a case which arose in the House and Ship Painters' Operatives' Society. Unsurprisingly, the judge was convinced. Where freedom of speech is concerned, judges have proved wary creatures, skittish in the extreme.[25]

Despite the enforced retreat of the *Herald*, it survived as a major influence, even while socialist quarrels raged happily on. As a result, it was able to reflect and serve the impulse to unity among the transport unions.

# Notes

1   R. H. Tawney, *The Attack* (Spokesman Books, 1981), p. 59.

2   Ross McKibbin, *The Evolution of the Labour Party, 1910–1924* (Oxford University Press, 1974), p. 55.

3   G. D. H. Cole, *A Short History of the British Working Class Movememt*, vol. III (Allen and Unwin, 1927), p. 58.

4   ILP Annual Conference Report, 1909, p. 47.

5   Quoted in Reg Groves, *The Strange Case of Victor Grayson* (Pluto Press, 1975), pp. 95–7.

6   Kenneth O. Morgan, *Keir Hardie, Radical and Socialist* (Weidenfeld and Nicolson, 1975), p. 227.

7   Osborne was a very remarkable man, as can be seen in his book *Sane Trade Unionism* (Collins, 1912). It does not seem at all likely that the charge that he was simply a cat's-paw, a tool of the capitalists, could be sustained. He reads like a man of conviction.

8   We have documented this campaign in *Trade Unions and Politics* (Basil Blackwell, 1986).

9   Michael Klarman, 'Osborne: a Judgement Gone Too Far?', in *English Historical Review*, vol. CIII, no. 406 (January 1988), pp. 21–39.

10  A. J. P. Taylor, *English History, 1914–1945* (Oxford University Press, 1965), p. 114.

11  See Coates and Topham, *Trade Unions and Politics*, p. 261.

12  McKibbin, *The Evolution of the Labour Party*, p. 81.

13  Figures from H. W. Lee and E. Archbold, *Social Democracy in Britain* (Social Democratic Federation, 1935), p. 177.

14  Raymond Williams, *The Long Revolution* (Chatto and Windus, 1961), p. 106.

15  Report of a Court of Inquiry concerning Transport Workers' Wages and Conditions, with Minutes of Evidence and appendices, Cmnd 936 and Cmnd 937, Parliamentary Papers, XXXIV, 1920 (the Shaw Report), vol. II, appendix 29. Sir John Reeves Ellerman, head of Ellerman lines, was so wealthy that he was able to buy up the mighty Wilson line of Hull. It was reorganized as Ellerman's Wilson Line Ltd. He was the third largest shareholder in *The Times*, and had large interests in the *Daily Mail*. He was also a brewing magnate, and through interlocking directorships he was connected to the Rockefeller Corporation, a militantly anti-union conglomerate. See J. Walton Newbold, *Solidarity Amongst the Shipowners*, foreword by Tom Mann, Reformers' Bookstall Series, no. 24 (Glasgow, 1918), pp. 7–8.

16  Ibid., appendix 28.

17  James Curran and Jean Seaton, *Power Without Responsibility* (Fontana, 1981), p. 73.

18  Tom Mann, *Memoirs* (1923; reissued MacGibbon and Kee, 1967), pp. 236–8.

19  George Lansbury, *The Miracle of Fleet Street* (Labour Publishing Company, n.d.), p. 10.

20  *Daily Herald*, 16 April 1912; quoted in R. J. Holton, 'Daily Herald versus Daily Citizen', *International Review of Social History*, XIX (1974), p. 351.

21  Lansbury, *The Miracle of Fleet Street*, pp. 89–90.

22  *Daily Herald*, 7 June 1912.

23 Lansbury, *The Miracle of Fleet Street*, p. 14.
24 Ibid., pp. 31–2.
25 Holton, 'Daily Herald versus Daily Citizen'. See also Arthur Marwick, *Clifford Allen: The Open Conspirator* (Oliver and Boyd, 1964), pp. 11–20.

# 15

# The Debates on Amalgamation and Alliance: 1913–1914

## I

### *The Debate on Amalgamation*

Early in 1913 the National Transport Workers' Federation had begun to publish its mimeographed *Weekly Record*, under the editorial control of its secretary, Robert Williams. He proved to be a fluent and persuasive journalist, with an eye for a story. Tact, however, was not his strongest suit. Time after time his forthright style and blunt advocacy provoked protests from his opponents, inside the Federation as well as further afield. His first editorial, in favour of amalgamation, is a case in point. 'We mean to do great things,' he wrote. 'We are aiming high, because we are impelled by a great purpose. The transport workers are appreciably nearer to fusion of their forces than they have been.'[1] The fusion would enable workers to level conditions up, instead of permitting employers to level them down. Amalgamation, following the railwaymen's recent example, could unify effort, as well as bringing agreement on common goals. What, then, was the impediment? 'The rank and file say that they are ready, but the officials stand in the way. The officials declare that they are willing, and even anxious, but the men are unprepared. We shall see.'[2]

See they soon did. Two NTWF Annual General Council Meetings, in 1913 and 1914, and a Special Conference on Amalgamation convened jointly by the General Labourers' National Council (GLNC) and the NTWF in July 1914, brought into focus all the aspirations of the transport and general workers' unions towards unity. At these meetings the main ideas about amalgamation were given their most ambitious and hopeful pre-war expression. Formidable obstacles remained. These included the sectional anxieties of particular unions, and their fear that, in a complete amalgamation, members would lose their sense of identity. Moreover, there was the apprehension that job controls would suffer erosion and dilution. To be sure, amalgamation was nothing if not an ambitious project: reading the debates about it the difficulties seem to be almost insuperable. It is impossible not to be impressed by the combined determination of a whole generation of leaders to achieve it, in spite of every obstacle. Recognition of a common interest was dominant throughout the entire complex discussion. In the end, two unions alone were to withdraw their participation from the scheme, in order to protect entrenched sectional monopolies in specific working territories. The two in question were the London Stevedores' and the Cardiff Coal Trimmers' Unions. Their colleagues all went ahead. New unionism had evidently etched its original purposes deep in the men's minds, through all the decades of experience since the 1880s.

## The Engineers: a Contrast

This makes a striking contrast with the record of a more venerable, if only partial, federation of unions, in engineering. Even though it was established two decades before the NTWF, in the year following the upheavals of 1889, within it the dominant ethos was the much older sectionalism of the craft societies that formed it. General unions organizing that industry felt constrained, in this ethos, to assume a subordinate role as organizers of the labourers. Meanwhile, since the space between craftsmen and labourers, which was taken by workers in the new semi-skilled occupations. Whatever its interrelations, this was undoubtedly a hierarchical structure. Indeed, the two unions of labourers, the NAUL and the gasworkers, were only belatedly and very grudgingly allowed into the then Federation of Engineering and Ship-building Trades. Admission was delayed until 1908 and 1910 respectively. Even then they were required to 'know their place' in the pecking order. The Workers' Union refused to 'give assurances' to the ASE, and was therefore excluded altogether.[3] Radical, egalitarian movements existed in the ranks of the engineers, and in the course of time would grow; but the Transport Workers were far ahead. A comparison of the policies of the leaders of the two federations draws us to the conclusion that we are looking at the difference between an innovative and inclusive strategy on one side, and a conservative and sectional one on the other.

## 'One Union for all Vehicle Workers'

Of course, 'inclusion' was a process in which lesser and greater groupings might join. Of the transport workers, carters and drivers were among the first to try to league together. Urging their fusion, Will Godfrey wrote an appeal for 'One Union For All' in the NTWF *Weekly Record*:

> Wherever one goes, the rank and file of the Trade Union Movement, and especially of the Transport Workers' Movement, are anxious for the formation of one Union to cater for all transport workers. In this connection the vehicle workers are moving towards an amalgamated Society that shall embrace all classes and grades of vehicle workers. A conference of representatives of those Societies which cater for vehicle workers will shortly take place at Manchester, under the auspices of the Parliamentary Committee of the Trade Union Congress.
>
> The old London Carmen's Trade Union, now re-named The National Union of Vehicle Workers, is the pioneer of this conference. This Society has for years advocated One Union for all Vehicle Workers, and its members have gone so far forward with the matter as to have inserted in the Rules governing their Society, a rule to enable the Society to amalgamate with other Unions.
>
> In other vehicle workers' Unions, and other transport workers' Unions, there are no doubt a number of members who think that the present system of a Union for each class or grade of worker is the best, and that great difficulty would be found in framing a code of rules to cover all vehicle workers, or all transport workers, in One Union; also, that confusion would arise at branch meetings of trammen, cabmen, etc, meeting in the same branch room, especially as some of these said workers are licensed men, and others are not.
>
> Personally, I believe that little, if any, difficulty would be found in dealing with these matters if a determined attempt were made to amalgamate into one union all classes or grades of men in a given industry . . .
>
> To my mind the time has come when it is absolutely necessary for a closer understanding to exist between workers if they are to maintain their power as Trade Unionists. Employers and Companies, Corporations and Councils, are entering into, or have entered into, working agreements and understandings with each other, whereby it will be easier for them in the future to help one another. They will take joint action, and the workers will find a far more formidable enemy to fight.
>
> On our side, we have overlapping, waste, and unfriendliness, valuable time being frittered away, and sectional power only; whereas there should be combined strength, service and action.[4]

## Recognition of Cards

The deliberations of the NTWF in 1913 showed the continuing obstinacy with which the sectional issue asserted itself, in many other areas as well as this one. The Annual General Council debated a string of amendments to the constitution. One proposal would have required all affiliated unions to recognize the cards of all other affiliates, so that members of any such union would have had equal rights to employment at any union's workplace. The Mersey Carters' Union representative, W. H. Jones, said that such a clause would not be observed in Liverpool, where men already had to join three unions to obtain work. George Milligan pointed out that, if the amendment were accepted, men would choose to join the cheapest union, which would then give them access to the whole federation territory. Ernest Bevin also opposed the idea. Unions, he thought, must be allowed to retain control over their own members. The stevedores were opposed as well. Their man, J. Wood, emphasized that 'the particular union card was the first consideration'.[5]

Despite these objections, the contested amendment was carried. Yet the Council then went on to an apparently contradictory decision. It reaffirmed a clause guaranteeing preference to other affiliated cardholders, whenever a labour shortage remained, *after* placing in work those local members of whichever union held a controlling interest. It was hard to reconcile such procedures with the earlier amendment, affirming equal rights for holders of any federal union card.

## Spheres of Influence

An attempt was made to delete another rule (Rule 14, clause 1) providing that, where a union had a representative branch for a class of work, 'no other affiliated union shall attempt to cater for members in that undertaking'. This provision anticipated one of the main approaches to the regulation of inter-union disputes within the TUC, laid down in 1924 at Hull and put into the form which survives to the present day in the so-called 'Bridlington Agreement' of 1939. The offending clause imposed restrictions which worried some, such as the Mersey carters, because new unions were already moving in to recruit those of their members who became motormen, as motor vehicles replaced horse-drawn haulage. The carters wanted to retain the freedom to keep their ex-carters as they changed over to become motor-lorry drivers. Most motor-bus drivers, too, had formerly been carters. Another union, the Enginemen and Cranemen, poured oil on troubled waters by announcing that they would not object if the Carters' Union were to enrol motormen. These exchanges illustrate the endless problems thrown up in the Federation whose constitution provided only a halfway house to their favoured solution, which was summed up in the famous slogan 'One Big Union'.

Issues like these bore in on wider questions of status and caste, as Robert Williams recognized in his comments on the NTWF Executive's mandate to prepare for amalgamation by devising a suitable scheme. This would not be easy, he wrote:

The Executive will require to steer clear of any suggestion likely to alienate the rapidly-growing willingness of the better-situated sections . . . from fusion. The critics will say that capitalist development is breaking down all barriers which linger between the various callings . . . This is undoubtedly so, but it is not for us to raise objections among the men.

There are thousands of men, all members of unions whose eyes are turned with envy upon their more regularly employed fellow unionists . . . they begrudge their fellow-workers their two, or perhaps three, pounds a week more than . . . their employers their two or three hundred pounds per week.[6]

In broad terms, the Federation was prone to division. On one side stood those who wished for maximum autonomy, aiming to protect their own chosen territories and structures. Typical of this school were the 'skilled' unions of stevedores, and the other specialist dock groups; they were supported by the inclusive dockers' union, the NUDL. On the other side were the unions seeking to open up all such exclusive preserves, allowing Federation members to move freely between every branch of the port- and road-transport industry. Of this second school, the Gasworkers' Union and the NAUL were most vocal. Tillett's union havered and equivocated between the two extremes. Beyond doubt, it too wished to bar from dockland any new influx of labour, and feared the competition which might result from open access by all Federation affiliates. Yet it could not rest content with the simple demarcation and policing of waterfront territories; its own dock membership was volatile and unreliable, and it had itself, from the 1890s onwards, upheld its status as a dockers' union only by extending into more stable and sustaining areas. Its most notable success had been amongst the tinplate workers in South Wales.[7] More recently it had prevailed amongst carters and general workers in, for example, Bristol.

Such conflicting interpretations of the best interests of different affiliates found expression at first in rather technical debates about the best ways to contain poaching and to define boundaries. Rule-framing can seem a very grey occupation, even neutral. But beneath the boredom it engendered ran passions which became fully exposed when the organization began to consider the best form, not of federation, but of amalgamation.

Facing this question, a considerable number of models were examined and canvassed. These revealed something of the movement's strategic thinking, besides unerringly exposing particular selfish or sectional interests. In its scrutiny of the range of models on offer, the Federation was defining the purposes of the united union which it wished to succeed it, and evaluating the scope of different forms of action. 'Structure is a function of purpose', said a TUC leader in the 1960s.[8] The leaders of 1913–14 had anticipated the significance of this axiom. Accordingly, their deliberations were intense, and aroused equally intense interest amongst observers throughout the Labour movement.

## The Debate in 1913

We have already said that the NTWF debated the form of amalgamation twice, at its 1913 and 1914 Annual General Councils. Each of these occasions helped preparations for a third meeting, the joint conference with the GLNC in July 1914.

At the 1913 Council, the clashes between the proponents of different versions were unresolved because delegates were persuaded by their chairman, Harry Gosling, that they were voting on that occasion not for a specific method of amalgamation but for the general principle. So it was that the vote for amalgamation (undefined) was 'carried amidst cheers'. This celebration was provoked when delegates agreed to instruct their Executive Council 'to prepare a scheme for the complete amalgamation of all the unions affiliated to the Federation'. Nevertheless, the short debate which led to this decision brought into the open some of the deepest anxieties of the dockers. The 'London' union was vulnerable because of its complex membership. Harry Orbell feared that too narrow an amalgamation, confined either to dockers alone or even to all transport workers, would 'nibble away sections from the unions'. (Fifty years later, an attempt by the TUC and its general secretary to reform trade-union structure on 'rational' industrial lines met just as fierce opposition from Jack Jones, who declared that 'trade union members can't be treated like cattle to be bought and sold at the whim of theorists'.[9])

The Liverpool spokesmen for the NUDL were disunited. Sexton announced that he was personally in favour of amalgamation, but that his union was not. Kessack openly rebuked his leader: 'The members' difficulties are that they have been in terror of the universal ticket . . . there should be one union of dock labourers . . . there would be three [sectional unions] only: carters, dockers, and sailors.'

Will Thorne of the Gasworkers' Union expressed similar fears to those of Orbell: 'If amalgamation is brought about in that way, they would be "lopped off". He wanted an amalgamation of the lot.'[10]

J. Wood of the Stevedores' Union said: 'If the resolution meant simply amalgamation of Transport Workers he was prepared to support it, but if it meant amalgamation of all unions he was not.'

Ernest Bevin began with an observation which, in the light of his eventual tactics in 1921, was highly significant: 'the discussion convinced him that the Federation was likely to be used as an obstacle to amalgamation.' In 1921, as we shall see, Bevin master-minded the negotiations for the TGWU amalgamation entirely outside the cumbersome and inhibiting structures of the NTWF. Of course, in 1913–14 he had not by any means achieved the dominance which would have allowed him to do this. But his own model, shared by many of his seniors, had already been formed in his mind by his Bristol experience:

> In the port of Bristol theirs [the Dockers'] was the only union; they had all kinds of men in all classes of work, yet there was no trouble about lines of demarcation, and there had never been any overlapping, and transfers were worked quite smoothly through a departmental system with different officers for each section. If it could be done locally, it could be done nationally.

Bevin was impatient with the prevarications of the Federation: 'He thought it was "the platform" that needed to be convinced of the necessity for amalgamation, and not the rank and file. There ought to be a definite time limit fixed – six months was quite sufficient – for the Executive to produce a scheme, and then we could see who are the enemies of amalgamation.' In his urgency he swept aside all those problems of harmonizing cash benefits which so frequently arise in trade-union mergers. 'As to benefits, the men do not want benefits, they want . . . wages.' And, in another anticipation of his 1921 method, he concluded: 'There may be unions which do not want to come in, but we could afford to let them stop out. Let the big unions come in, and the new generation would come in to us.'[11]

This thinking in 1913 already displayed the tough pragmatism and at the same time the raw boldness which were to become hallmarks of Bevin's leadership. At this time he was thirty-two years old. His trade-union experience was confined to the Bristol Channel and the South-west. At the 1913 AGC, he was representing the West of England District Committee. But his adventurous mind, which shows itself in the breadth of these arguments, already comprehended the problems of organization across the whole field. By the following year he had become the Federation organizer for the West and South-west of England, and in that capacity, young as he was, he did not hesitate to ruffle the feathers of the most senior national leaders. At the same time, he played in a team with Bob Williams, sometimes belling the cat for him.

In his District Report, he spoke of Southampton as 'our greatest bugbear', where 'the employers must be smiling at our stupidity'. The problem that he identified lay in the rivalry between the British Seafarers' Union (BSU) and the NSFU. Bevin asserted that this created non-unionism, access for free labour, low wages and poor conditions, and 'insane rivalry and recrimination'. His realism led him to report that the breakaway BSU was well established, that it had not been destroyed by the Federation's 'frontal attack', that it should therefore be recognized, and that the Federation must take responsibility for achieving unity in the port. In particular, 'the NSFU will . . . have to face the situation'.[12] Bevin's temerity provoked a loud protest from Edmund (Ned) Cathery of the NSFU, who demanded that the BSU should be 'dislodged' by the Federation.

Not content with plain speaking on Southampton, Bevin caused great offence to the NUDL and James Sexton, who was by now a venerable national leader (he was sixty years old), by calling the Federation's attention to the low wages of the Liverpool dockers, which, he claimed, were always being quoted against him by the Bristol employers. Sexton querulously complained:

> the West of England report . . . dealt amost entirely with Liverpool, and it was unfair to Liverpool . . . the men there received from five shillings to eight shillings per day. These rates may appear small, but it must be understood that the conditions were very different from those obtaining in other ports . . . He mentioned these things to show that Liverpool was not as black as Mr. Bevin had painted it.

Bevin was unrepentant, declaring that 'he was getting tired of' the employers quoting Liverpool rates: 'When you mentioned Liverpool to the men in Bristol you raised a laugh . . . when Liverpool was mentioned he had to retort: "Oh, they do it for nothing there." '[13]

There was no doubt of the validity of Bevin's charge, which Sexton hardly denied. The Board of Trade 'Reports on Changes in Wages and Hours of Work 1910–13' listed Bristol dockers as earning 7*d*. an hour in 1913 (an advance of a halfpenny on 1910), which would yield 5*s*. 10*d*. for a ten-hour day. Liverpool was rated at 4*s*. 6*d*. a day, the same as in 1910.

Sexton's reply made a choice which strengthened the case for amalgamation. Bevin's acid comments could be interpreted either as a call for remedial local action, or as a demand for a national movement for standard national rates. Sexton chose to respond to this second question, rather than to the alternative implication that his own union might tackle Liverpool's problem of low wages locally by itself: 'He did not agree that it was time for a national movement in favour of equal rates. If we started that now we should have a big national fight before we had a big national organisation ready for it.'[14]

Bevin may have felt a certain satisfaction when, in 1920, he was able to point out that the Shaw Award, for which he was primarily responsible, gave the Liverpool dockers their first basic wage increase since the 1880s.[15]

Further evidence of Bevin's antipathy to Sexton during this time can be found in a remarkable article he prepared for the *Dockers' Record*, which was promptly taken up and reprinted by Robert Williams in the NTWF *Weekly Record*. This newsletter provoked one scuffle after another with the Liverpool leader, who was recurrently moved to intervene to clip the editor's wings. 'Mr. Williams should not incorporate so many of his personal opinions'; 'the secretary should not give his own views of Federation matters'; complaint after complaint arrived at the Federation's Blackfriars Road office.

The *Weekly Record* consisted of two, three or four cyclostyled pages printed in virulently purple ink. It was nothing if not robust in its advocacy of amalgamation, some forms of sympathy action, and One Big Union. Yet if so minuscule a publication put so much heat into the internal debates of the Federation, Ernest Bevin's proposal, once implemented, might well have raised the temperature still more: he sought to further amalgamation by producing a joint newspaper. He wrote:

> The only way is for all unions to agree immediately to cease publishing their present monthly, quarterly, and weekly journals, as the case may be, and to allow the Federation to run a journal for all affiliated Unions. Take the Seamen; they publish their paper weekly and the docker selc'om sees it, while the inland general workers know nothing of the seamen' difficulty. The same thing applies to the Dockers, Cooks and Stewards, an all other Unions.
>
> There should be no difficulty in the question of editorship or management, or even the allotment of space; and, as pointed out above, the fact that we should through such a medium be able to know the difficulties of each section, would lead to that oneness of feeling which is the very basis of unity. The money now spent on the various productions, a d, I am afraid, in many cases with little result, would go a long way to meet the cost of production, and, coupled with that, the fact that it would be distributed to nearly 300,000 homes should bring in a decent revenue from advertisements.
>
> We are very glad to note that in all directions the importance of keeping the members of a Union or a Federation intimately in touch with everything that happens concerning the movement is being thoroughly recognized. There is no doubt that the splendid organisation of our German brothers has been largely achieved through the valuable aid . fforded by their Press.[16]

Only four of the Federation affiliates produced journals, 'and not one of these is even a weekly'. Smaller unions had no means of communication at all. Without news, the movement was gravely handicapped.

If this idea brought comfort to Robert Williams, it also foreshadowed Bevin's long commitment to the printed word in the later struggle for the continuation of the *Daily Herald*.

In all these conflicts, Bevin's purpose was not merely to shake complacency and confront the facts, but also to call on the Federation collectively to take stock of a problem, face it and act. Of course, in neither of these two cases did action follow. If a certain lack of direction and executive authority were exposed, Bevin's call for a regular journal none the less strengthened the hand of Robert Williams against the critics of his little newsletter.

## Williams's Analysis: the 1914 Debate

The 1914 AGC saw the emergence of Bevin as a formative influence. However, it had another significance as well. The amalgamation scheme, prepared by the Executive in response to the decision of the previous year, was placed before the delegates, and they now had to take clear positions on it. As a preliminary educational contribution to the debate, Robert Williams produced a report and a map showing the multi-union confusions and overlapping which characterized Britain's ports: it was well received and made a deep impression at the Council. (The map appears as Fig. 11.1, p. 441.)

Williams also contributed a trenchant oral summary of his report, in the process adding directly to Bevin's stature by praising the comprehensive coverage of one union in the South-west: 'If two or three unions had been competing in the ports indicated, it would be a policy of mutual extinction.'[17] In South Wales, by contrast, 'we see a frightful example of how not to do it, where there is always rivalry between the Dockers and the NALU'. The Mersey, asserted Williams, 'is very little better than the Thames'; although the NUDL caters for dockers, 'there are four other unions catering for other phases of the transport industry'. And, if territorial organization was rationally pursued, Manchester docks should have been in the NUDL, not in Tillett's union. On the Humber, 'the condition of affairs was no less criminal in character', with four different unions catering for waterside workers. And so on. Williams ranged round the whole coastline to read the same chastening lesson. His own trade had been coal-trimming: he found seven different local or regional, as well as sectionalized, unions in this one occupation. (They had all recently come together to agree a common movement for the Saturday half-day, a meeting convened outside NTWF auspices, as not all the trimmers' unions were affiliated. But that experience was the beginning of the end of their isolationist attitude, as they learned the virtues of co-operation.) Williams's presentation was a formidable indictment of the state of union organization amongst waterside workers, yet – because it would have made his map too crowded for clarity – he had omitted all the carters' and sailors' unions.

## The Greater Unionism

Outside the Councils of the Federation, some other clever people were concerning themselves about transport union amalgamation. At this time the general theme of restructuring union organization preoccupied the whole trade-union movement. Almost all this thinking was generated on the left. Two young writers, both of whom were associated with the *Daily Herald*, were beginning to develop a hybrid doctrine of syndicalism, which left more space for a distinctly political process. It was called Guild Socialism. In support of this new creed, G. D. H. Cole[18] and William Mellor produced a popular manifesto under the title *The Greater Unionism*. In it, they defined the transport industry very narrowly, 'to include only such occupations as are concerned solely with the manipulation of goods and the loading or unloading of ships. It therefore excludes railways, tramways, bus or cab services, and other forms of passenger traffic, which cannot be included in a single effective organisation of transport workers.'[19]

These writers also thought that the railways were self-contained, and that the NUR would never come into a widely defined amalgamation. Writing in 1913, at the very moment of the debates which concern us here, they asserted that the great weakness of the Federation would be compounded by any overall amalgamation of all transport and general unions: 'it would mean the complete swamping [by the general labourers] of the transport industry which is a natural unit.'[20] They recommended that the general labourers should go their own way to another amalgamation and that, for the time being, the NTWF should take steps to strengthen itself by organizing mergers of its definable sections into dockers', carters' and seamen's unions, with the centralization of strike funds and decision-making. Strikes should be subject to rigid central discipline: 'going out and coming in on command are most likely to lead to success, and the Executive Council should be given power to terminate strikes after consultation with the district organisations.'

Complete fusion would be possible only when port labour was decasualized, 'as is already the case in Liverpool'.[21] Cole and Mellor's solution for the general labour unions was for them to amalgamate, and act as a single 'Union Clearing House', with the object of unloading their members on other unions as soon as they became decasualized 'and not to play "finding's keepings"'. This imaginary transit organization would retain close touch with the new transport unions, the ASE, the cotton, railway and coal industries, and all other industries where it would have members, handing over to them relevant groups of unskilled workers. In this way, Labour could carry through the process of working towards One Union, One Industry. (The authors were strongly influenced by the model of German industrial unionism, which was the subject of independent discussion within the NTWF.) 'The function, then, of the General Labour Union is to work for its own extinction, which will also be the extinction of the casual labourer.'[22]

All this meant that the brilliant young Guild Socialists were swimming very much against the drift of pragmatism prevailing within the NTWF. For sure, some of their prescriptions did find responses amongst the 'sectionalists', but the model of narrow industrial unionism and tight centralization was too abstract, at odds with the untidy realities of the organizational inheritance with which the leadership had to deal.

## Theory and Practice: Connolly's Problem

James Connolly was not only embattled alongside James Larkin in the ITGWU at this time (see chapter 13); he was also thinking about his experiences. In April and May of 1914, he published two essays on union organization, in *Forward* and *New Age*.[23] At the same time, he was vainly trying to obtain the Federation's invitation to be allowed to address its 1914 Council.[24] The climate created in the previous year's conflict between Larkin and the English trade-union leadership made Connolly, so close an associate of Larkin's, an unwelcome guest, and his approach to the Federation was ruled out of order. However, his views on the problems of multi-unionism in the transport trades at this time were highly relevant to the Federation's debate, since they were based on close involvement with the actual strike wave of the pre-war years. Their revolutionary perspective was shared by some, at least, of the Federation's leaders.

In one respect Connolly's May article echoed the view of Bevin: that the Federation's processes were themselves often a brake upon decisive action. Connolly, however, was referring not to the prospects of amalgamation, but to industrial action. 'Every appeal to take industrial action on behalf of a union in distress is blocked by insisting upon the necessity of "first obtaining the sanction of the Executive"', a process which Connolly described as slow and cumbersome, to the point that effective responses were delayed until the strikers were bankrupted and beaten. 'The Greater Unionism' (this catchphrase, of course, was also the title of the Cole and Mellor tract) 'is . . . forging greater fetters for the working class'.[25] Connolly supported his critique with a case-study of the Anglo-American Oil Company, whose use of scab labour at Tilbury could not properly be countered by the NTWF because bunkering was carried out by an affiliated union which refused to follow the call for federal blacking of Anglo-American ships. Connolly cited Robert Williams's conclusions on the case:

When co-operation is sought from one union by another, the men involved say 'consult an official'. The official says 'get the consent of my EC'. The Executive Officers say 'communicate with the Transport Workers' Federation'. The Federation waits on the decision of its own Executive, and by this inconsequent fiddling of time and opportunity, a thousand Romes would have burned to extinction. The employers move, strike, turn, strike, move, and strike again with the rapidity of a serpent, while we are turning about and contorting with the facility of an alligator.[26]

Connolly concluded that the working class needed a supreme Cabinet, as powerful and authoritative for offensive purposes as he believed the state's Cabinet to be. Without vesting authority in a central body of this kind, every separate union would normally avoid support for sympathy strikes in order to preserve its financial balances. Mere amalgamation may express the letter of 'industrial concentration', whilst the spirit of working-class solidarity is absent, and 'the spirit of sectionalism still rules and curses our class'.[27]

In the previous month, Connolly had put forward a different argument.[28] He had, that April, insisted that the NTWF had frozen 'the fraternal spirit of 1912'. The cause of this chill was, he thought, that 'Into the new bottles of industrial organisation is being poured the old, cold wine of Craft Unionism'. Here also he referred to the case of bunkering: 'Dublin and Belfast members of the Irish Transport Workers' Union have been victimised ever since the end of the lock-out by the Head Line Company, whose steamers have been and are regularly coaled in British ports and manned by Belfast and British members of the Seamen's and Firemen's Union'.[29] Connolly then took up a position dramatically opposed to the received wisdom of the Federation and to the opinion of Cole and Mellor:

> A main reason for this shameful distortion of the Greater Unionism from its true purposes is to be found in the campaign against 'sporadic strikes' . . . The big strike, the vast massed battalions of Labour against the massed battalions of Capital . . . is seldom successful . . . The sudden strike, and the sudden threat to strike suddenly, has won more for Labour than all the great labour conflicts in history.

This idea seems at first to contradict those put forward by Connolly a month later, advocating an all-powerful Cabinet of Labour, calling strikes at will, rather than at the will of a rank and file suddenly galvanized into action. In fact, the first essay makes it clear that for Connolly, the 'Cabinet' was seen as necessary to ensure swift, unquestioning *endorsement* for 'sudden', or 'spontaneous' actions by the rank and file, in order that there should be both effective sympathy action and adequate funding for the striking section.

Like the recommendations of Cole and Mellor, but for different reasons, these prescriptions could not fit easily alongside the cautious approach of the Federation's leaders. Many of them held a largely administrative, and more or less constitutional, view of the purposes of amalgamation. Neither right nor left wings of the Federation were likely to give their unconditional favour to the advocacy of centrally supported mass sympathy strikes, even when their advocate was as much respected as James Connolly. Robert Williams, from the left, had told the AGC of 1913 that central control over its District Councils was necessary in order to restrict 'sympathetic action whereby every lunatic with an imaginary grievance should hold up a whole port.'[30] True, he had also supported the Dublin workers longer and more resolutely than most of his colleagues in the leadership, and specifically endorsed Larkin's tactics there. But did this amount to the rigorous consistency of policy requested by Connolly?

On the other wing of the Federation, James Sexton revealed his own retrospective distaste for Mann's encouragement of sympathy strikes in Liverpool in 1911 (at the time, he had kept quiet about it). In his memoirs he speaks of 'the blunder of calling out the butcher, the baker, the candlestick maker, who were in no way concerned with the originating dispute!'[31] This is in fact a caricature of the actual coverage of Liverpool's 'general strike'.

## The Enginemen's Dilemma

While Cole, Mellor and Connolly were appealing in these terms to whoever might listen, the two federal bodies, the NTWF and the GLNC, were elaborating their approach to the joint conference planned for July 1914. The dilemma facing them was summed up by George Parker of the Enginemen's and Firemen's Union.

> With all the schemes of amalgamation now being discussed, he and his members were in considerable confusion. They were part of a Federation known as the National Federation of Enginemen and Kindred Trades. They were also closely in contact with the Miners' Federation through their large section of colliery enginemen and stokers. They were also connected with the Building Trades Federation, through their members who work the overhead cranes necessary in modern building construction.'[32]

He was also addressing, at that moment, the NTWF's AGC, of which his union was also a member by virtue of representing crane-drivers on the docks, recruitment of whom was contested with the newly formed NUR, at least in the railway ports. As a result of the ensuing debate, his union became one of the dissentients from the idea of amalgamation. This rejection was sustained up to and beyond the outbreak of war. None of the models on offer satisfied the enginemens' multifarious interests. Later, however, there was a satisfactory model. As the expanded National Amalgamated Union of Enginemen, Firemen, Motormen and Electrical Workers, his union finally did join the TGWU in 1928. But back in 1914, George Parker was asking the right question: what sort of amalgamation should it be?

There is no doubt that the immediate stimulus to the debate had been the failure of the 1912 transport strike. For Tillett this suggested an obvious and simple solution: 'this strike calls for One Transport Union'.[33] This model derived partly from the NTWF's basic character, and indeed from its title. Its protagonists included Williams and Gosling, who went together in the autumn of 1912 to Germany and brought back a glowing account of the effectiveness of that country's industrial transport union. Gosling told the Federation that 'In Germany, the movement is characterised by organisation, intelligence, discipline and restraint'.[34] As a result, various articles appeared in the *Weekly Record*, and a detailed report of the International Federation's meeting in London, at Caxton Hall, highlighted the efficient example of the Germans.[35]

Williams proposed integrating seamen, dockers and road-transport workers into one departmentally administered organization. Gordon Phillips calls this an 'intellectually admirable' model,[36] but it could not be applied in a multi-industrial situation without hiving off those large sections of membership which were extraneous to transport. In some unions, including Tillett's, a majority of members were outside even the broadest definition of transport.

A second model was represented by the recently formed NUR – the sectional consolidation of a single, definable group of grades within a single industry. This was the model favoured by Sexton and the NUDL, the maritime workers' unions led by the NSFU, and by the group of localized carters' unions and societies. Amongst the strong pressures supporting this model were the dockers' recurrent anxieties about 'outsiders' who would acquire a common union card in any wider amalgamation, thus flooding their occupation with even more surplus labour. (The NTWF's card was abolished in 1914 precisely in order to allay this fear.) The NSFU was clearly hostile to any merger other than one embracing all the seamen's unions, which would thus be reassimilated to their rather authoritarian parent body. The carters' separatism was expressed when, in 1913, as we have seen, they invoked the auspices of the TUC to hold their own quite separate discussions on a merger with other road-workers' unions, including the Tramwaymen's Union and the Licensed Vehicle Workers' Union, which was beginning to organize London busmen. Wise heads, like Gosling's, actually welcomed these trends, seeing them as transitional and helpful efforts to tidy up, and not as necessarily entrenching sectionalism for all time. Steps towards One Big Union might be taken one at a time. The different sections could consolidate smaller unifications and still reach out to larger ones at a later stage. This line of thought, patience itself, came most naturally to one who had been in the business of promoting unity ever since the early 1890s.

## The Amalgamation Committee Movement

The advantages of industrial unionism were also pressed home by unofficial rank-and-file Amalgamation Committees. These mushroomed in a number of industries from 1910 to 1917, strongly influenced by syndicalist teaching. The best known of these has been the engineering committee,[37] but there were others in the building industry, printing, furniture and transport. Mann's journal, the *Industrial Syndicalist*, which had carried the campaign through the first 'direct action' phase of the movement, ceased publication in May 1911. Now he turned his energies towards the promotion of a new paper, the *Syndicalist*, which first appeared in January 1912. It was published under the auspices of the Industrial Syndicalist Education League, and quickly threw its weight behind a move to bring the Amalgamation Committees together in their own all-embracing federation. As a result, a conference of Amalgamation Committees was held in London in November 1912. In the same month, the Transport Workers' Amalgamation Committee held its own rally in Canning Town, attended by some 2,000 people.[38] Sam Roden, chairing the meeting, affirmed that 'the object of the committee was the formation of One Transport Union, not by forming any new Union, but by amalgamating the existing ones'. In other words, this unofficial radical pressure group aimed to push the official Federation in a direction which some of its affiliates were already strongly inclined to follow. In craft-dominated industries, such as engineering, there was no such convergence of views between the reformers and their organizations. Moreover, the meeting carried a resolution which reflected the pragmatic conviction of many of the federated unions, that sectionalism should be allowed a constitutional expression within a unified union. The resolution read in part:

> seeing that a lengthy experience has fully demonstrated the lamentable inefficiency of sectional unionism, this meeting of transport workers declares in favour of one organisation for the whole of the transport workers and, to guard against centralised official bureaucracy, urges the immediate necessity for the amalgamation of the existing Unions in the transport industry, *with adequate provision for local sectional autonomy consistent with general efficiency* [italics added].

Mover, seconder and speakers on this motion came from each major section of the transport industry: railwaymen, carters and dockers. All spoke feelingly against the chaotic diversity in which their organizations were toiling: no fewer than fifty-eight unions were struggling, often with one another, to cater for transport workers. Tom Mann, the principal speaker, claimed that the meeting had an historic significance. Drawing on the experience of the 1912 London dock strike, recently concluded in disastrous defeat, 'he was compelled to come to the conclusion that the Federation was hopeless: he was out for complete amalgamation . . . The Transport Unions' officials had all been invited to attend that meeting and support the formation of one union, but they were not present.' But 'he was not out to slate them: he could do more effective work than that.'

## A Third Model

The third model was general unionism, and it was in the meetings of the General Labourers' National Council, formed three years before the NTWF, that this version got the widest hearing. The GLNC was the first to produce a scheme for amalgamation, incorporating a fourteen-point constitution in 1912. The NTWF had to be reminded, when in 1913 it began its own debate, that the GLNC already had a scheme on paper, and that it would be wise to work out one of its own and go on to meet jointly with the GLNC. Coming together would inevitably be necessary at some point, partly because of the overlapping affiliate membership of the two bodies, and partly because the general labourers' debates also aroused the dockers' old fears of the 'single ticket'.

The NTWF Executive did not agree its scheme for amalgamation until 4 November 1913, when it decided to circulate affiliates with a short, four-point proposal which was nothing if not sharply to the point:

CENTRAL FUND: Your Executive recommend the establishment of a Central Fund to be constituted by (a) The payment of a sum of money per head of the whole affiliated membership, supplemented by further periodical payments, OR (b) The institution of a Fund by a specific weekly contribution per member of the affiliated organisations. Payment to a central fund to commence on an agreed date.

CENTRAL EXECUTIVE: We recommend under any scheme the formation of a Central Executive, to be appointed for an agreed period, to control the funds – to administer the national organisation.

INDUSTRIAL ORGANISATION: Your Executive, having taken cognisance of the separate funds, industrial and provident, of the several unions, recommend as a basis central control of a central fund, the central fund to be purely trade union and industrial.

PROVIDENT FUNDS: In view of the widely-varied provident benefits of the several unions eligible to join a National Transport Workers' Union – we recommend that the administration of the same remain under the authority of the respective organisations, until such time (and by agreement) the national Council is prepared to assume responsibility for any provident benefit.

We recommend the submission of these suggestions to the respective Executives of the affiliated organisations, with a view to the same determining an agreement on principle – and further that a national

Conference be called of Unions agreeing to this amalgamation, which shall have power to determine (a) The form of Executive control, and (b) The amount of contribution per member.[39]

## The General Labourers' Scheme

In December 1913, the Executives of the GLNC and the NTWF met, on neutral territory in the board room of the London Society of Compositors, to examine their respective schemes and to plan a joint conference.

The noise of the Dublin strike was still ringing in everybody's ears. In this excited moment, it was necessary to step back and evaluate the relevance of the different models which had been proposed for merger.

The GLNC scheme involved a complete and centralized merger, with an Executive Council having total control over union funds, and with no provision for departmental or trade-group autonomy. District Councils would, however, be formed 'for Administrative purposes'. They would, subject to the decision of their governing committees, be empowered to exercise defined responsibilities for industrial action. In full, the fourteen points of the GLNC ran like this:

GENERAL LABOURERS' NATIONAL COUNCIL
SCHEME OF AMALGAMATION

(1) That the Societies be amalgamated by merging them all into one organisation.

(2) That effect to this course be given after receiving authority from the members, or in compliance with existing rules.

(3) That a Central Fund for dispute, legal aid, victimisation, and administration purposes be formed by means of an equal payment per member from the separate funds of each Union.

(4) That this sum per member be as high as the funds of the least wealthy Union can afford, say 2/– per member.

(5) That balances which the Unions may retain be disposed of for the benefit of present members as the Executives of those Unions may hereafter decide.

(6) That the contributions in the new organisation be settled by an authorised Conference on a scale to be framed in accordance with the wages and requirements of the classes of members covered by the new organisation.

(7) That benefits be proportionate to the contributions, and according to the most appropriate list of benefits provided by any existing organisation.

(8) That provision be made in the new scale for voluntary

payment of extra contributions, covering such extra Friendly Benefits as members may require.

(9) That an Executive Council be appointed, the Common Funds of the new organisation to be under their direct control.

(10) That the Executive Council shall exercise complete control over the business connected with strike, Lock-out, Legal Aid, Victimisation, and administrative purposes in connection therewith.

(11) That the whole of the Officials and Clerical Staff employed by the respective Trade Unions in Trade Union work shall be placed at the disposal of the new organisation, and under the control of its Executive Council.

(12) That for Administrative purposes, District Offices of the Union shall exist in different centres, to be hereafter fixed according to membership and requirements.

(13) That the branches of the Union surrounding those Offices be formed into Districts with Committees having defined powers for management and industrial action.

(14) That other points of detail and of management, including the drafting of Rules, be decided by a National Conference to be called in the event of the Societies taking part in the amalgamation movement approving of this Scheme by a vote of their members.

(This was an uncannily prescient draft of the original constitution of the National Union of General and Municipal Workers (NUGMW) in 1924.) J. R. Clynes, of the Gas and General Workers' Union, taking the chair at the first Joint Executive of the two bodies, immediately went to the heart of the question: 'he would like it to be made as explicit as possible what were the intentions of the Transport Workers towards amalgamation. He interpreted the proposals of the Federation to mean extended and improved Federation and nothing else. If they were not prepared to go further than that the two schemes were not reconcilable.'[40]

## Central versus Departmental Authority

Other voices sought to identify areas of common ground in the two schemes. J. N. Bell of the NAUL and Robert Williams thought that reconciliation of the two schemes was possible. Gosling specifically insisted on the need for departmental autonomy. This the Federation's scheme had to embody, because 'self-centred' sections, 'like my own', would have to be accommodated. This, he maintained, did not exclude a genuine amalgamation, with a central executive having general administrative and financial powers. Clynes would not let go, however, insisting again that the two bodies' different approaches to the degree of central control were incompatible, and he specified: 'If the better-circumstanced grades refused to be associated with those whose position was more precarious, that might be the rock upon which they would split. He hoped that such was not the case.'[41]

At this point Bevin weighed in with his now standard illustration of the possible combination of an all-embracing single union, with real departmental autonomy. This was drawn from the Dockers' Union experience in the South-west. He found, he said, that 'the difficulties raised were more imaginary than real', when, as in his case, 'practically all sections of general labour were under the control of his and Mr. Twomey's Union [the NALU]'. And, in what was becoming characteristic iconoclasm, he said bluntly that 'London was hopelessly behind the provinces'! He concluded by calling for One Great Union. Charles Duncan, MP, general secretary of the Workers' Union, echoed this approach. He cited the case of the tightly organized Middlesbrough dockers, whom he knew well: such groups 'would jealously guard any privileges they had obtained by years of patient organising effort'.

The meeting concluded by resolving to appoint a sub-committee of six, three from each of the two Executives, to draft a joint scheme and to organize a joint conference to debate, amend and approve it. Those chosen were J. R. Clynes, Charles Duncan and J. N. Bell for the GLNC; and Harry Gosling, Ben Tillett and Robert Williams for the NTWF.

Bevin did not yet have the status, either in his national union or in the Federation, to win a place among the six. Even so, we can see the historical lines of development and of division already showing through the exchanges at this meeting.

The option of a dockers-only amalgamation, favoured by Sexton, was flatly unacceptable to his opposite numbers in the DWRGWU, with its large non-docks membership. From then on, Sexton became a secondary figure in the negotiations. He believed in an amalgamation, and had therefore little choice but to support the wider boundaries advocated by Bevin and others. A transport-only union would have meant equally damaging inroads on the membership of the unions of mixed recruitment outside the industry, and so that, too, was not an available solution for the same reasons. A 'transport and general' union was the only acceptable amalgamation. (The very name suggests itself, eight years before the christening.)

The remaining point to determine was that of the constitution. Would the centralizers from the general workers' unions, or the departmentalized model favoured by the waterfront unions prevail? Or was Clynes right to discern an irreconcilability between the two formulae? This matter was to be explored in the NTWF AGC of June 1914, and in the joint conference with the GLNC the following month.

## Preparations for the Joint Conference

The Federation's AGC wasted little time on the amalgamation issue; the scheme drafted by the bipartite sub-committee with the GLNC was approved, in preparation for the joint conference. The advantages of amalgamation cited by different speakers showed various preferences: some, like Kessack and Sexton, emphasized organization, discipline and 'control' of the members by the centre. Williams and Tillett, by contrast, talked grandly of the need to match 'the forces of capitalism' with a labour organization of comparable weight. Others, like Will Godfrey of the National Union of Vehicle Workers,[42] and Will Thorne, were more specific: they highlighted the value of a central strike fund and envisaged powerful, controlled mass strikes as the product of amalgamation. Will Thorne thought that the advantage of the scheme was 'that it was not complicated. It was purely a fighting scheme, and there were no benevolent benefits attached to it'.[43]

While formal exchanges between the two federations were agreed and systematically extended, the informal agitation gathered strength. At the beginning of 1914 Robert Williams opened the *Weekly Record* with an evaluation of the newly fashioned National Union of Railwaymen, which he saw as a powerful example:

> Nothing stimulated the movement for the amalgamation of the various Unions of the Railway workers more than the general campaign which was known as the all-grades movement. The question we now have to ask is – Is the time ripe for a similar movement on the part of the transport workers of the country?
>
> Conditions vary all over the country. One prosperous town pays 6d per hour to its dockers, and an equally prosperous town a few miles away pays perhaps 9d. The wages of carters are as varied as those of any set of men could well be. One has only to consult the files of the 'Record' to prove this. The hours of labour – admitting that the varying cost of living would tend to make differences in wages more or less just – vary enormously. They vary in the same Union, in the same trade, in the same town . . .
>
> We feel that the great stumbling-block to any movement for the general raising of the wages of transport workers, the standardisation of the working-day, the abolition of overtime and Sunday labour, the insistence on the one o'clock Saturday stop, and best of all the exclusion of the non-unionist – is the existence, first of the great number of competing Unions, and secondly, of the number of Unions which have not yet seen fit to come into the Federation. We feel that the latter difficulty will be small if the former one is solved, and the greatest factor, to our mind, in the solving, will be the initiation of a movement destined to raise all sections of transport workers, to give them a reasonable standard of living and a defined code of working conditions and hours. Amalgamation of itself is not an end – it is a means to an end. Give the men – already willing to look favourably upon

amalgamation – something which it is hoped to accomplish as an immediate result of such amalgamation, and it becomes a thing to be striven for, to be enthused over.

The first thing to be done before a national programme can be drafted is to know exactly what are the conditions at present prevailing. And in this, the Unions, if they will, can take the bigger part. We should like to have a complete record of the conditions, hours, agreements, tariffs, and wages of every port in the United Kingdom. This would serve as a basis for the drafting of a programme that would bring men into the Unions by the thousand, would stimulate the officials into amalgamation, willy-nilly, would bring the Shipping Federation, the P.L.A., and similar bodies to a clearer recognition of their duty towards Trade Unionism than any number of threats of strikes, sympathetic or otherwise. While we are split into so many sections – with each section putting forward its own demands in its own way – the employers can smile at us and the men will ignore us. Let us unite on a programme, and the one will fear us, and the other rally to the fight.

We talk amalgamation – some of us. Suppose we talk like this:

Amalgamate! –for an eight-hour day for every transport worker!
Amalgamate! –for the abolition of overtime for all transport workers!
Amalgamate! –for the recognition of the TRANSPORT WORKERS' UNION by
          every employer in the transport industry!
Amalgamate! –for the exclusion of the scab!
Amalgamate! –for a standard minimum rate for all transport workers!
Amalgamate! –for a one o'clock Saturday stop throughout the transport
          industry!
Amalgamate! –for improved conditions of labour in every port!

These are a few of the demands that we might put forward in a National Programme. We have need to build up our forces. We need to put a stimulus into the hearts of discouraged and disheartened men. That stimulus, to be of use, must be conveyed to all men in the industry. The day we launch such a Programme will see the forces of Trade Unionism in the transport industry take on a new complexion. The men will pour into the organisations as they have never done before – even in the palmy days of 1911.[44]

If the railways' all-grades movement might be taken as an example by other transport workers, the newly created fusion of railwaymen itself held out a promise of closer joint collaboration, joint action and even merger. Hope ran through each possibility, and reinforced the idea of unity. Following an initiative from the Miners' Federation, a joint conference of railwaymen, miners and transport workers was convened at the end of April 1914. It was from this conference that the Triple Alliance emerged, and we shall discuss its development later.

## Ten Points

Meanwhile, the two Executives of transport workers and general labourers had met on 25 March. Their joint sub-committee reported, with a new proposal for a ten-point scheme. The rapporteur was J. R. Clynes, and his points were:

(1) That the whole of the members contained in all the Unions affiliated to both bodies, together with any other Unions of a similar kind, be merged into one consolidated Union of Labour.

(2) That effect be given to this immediately by those Unions the members of which are ready and anxious.

(3) That a Central Fund for dispute, legal aid, victimisation, and administrative purposes be formed by means of an equal payment per member from the separate funds of each Union. This sum per member to be as high as the funds of the least wealthy Union can afford, say 2/– per member.

(4) Balances which the Unions may retain to be disposed of as the Executives of these Unions may hereafter decide for the benefit of the present members.

(5) That a graduated scale of contributions and benefits (trade and friendly) be drawn up by an authorised conference, the scale to be framed in accordance with the wages and requirements of the classes of members covered by the new organisation.

(6) That a central executive be appointed, which shall have complete control of the central fund, and shall sanction or withhold any disbursements according to Rules, such Rules to be determined upon later.

(7) That for the purpose of effective administration, there shall be set up district *and departmental* sections [italics added] allowing full free play of initiative and autonomy, consistent with the powers of financial control exercised by the central executive. These departments to make adequate provision for sectional and sub-sectional groupings, where called for and necessary.

(8) That the whole of the officials and clerical staff employed by the respective Trade Unions in trade union work be placed at the disposal of the new organisation, and under the control of the new E.C.

(9) That means must be devised to prevent the unnecessary migration of men from place to place and thereby pressing upon the available amount of employment at certain places at

any given time, while making every attempt to widen the sphere of activity of the new organisation, and consequently creating easy means of transfer from one occupation to another.

(10)  That other points of detail and management, including the drafting of Rules, be decided by a national conference to be called after the Unions have agreed upon the proposals for amalgamation as outlined above.[45]

Only clauses 1, 3, 4 and 7 provoked more than exploratory discussion, and most were easily agreed. The first clause implied the need for some nifty footwork to safeguard certain specialized groups, and the stevedores emphasized the need for this. When James Sexton, who had the capacity to raise awkward problems, made it plain that no one would seek to impede such special arrangements, the clause was adopted. Clause 3 left unresolved the financial detail, but was agreed as a rough guideline. Bevin wanted a different arrangement from that put forward in clause 4, because he did not want residual finances to be left in the control of sectional groups. The new amalgamation should dispose of all funds whatever, he believed. He was outfaced by Clynes, and his objection was not sustained. But Clynes agreed that the funding of 'regional and department sections' was yet to be determined, so that this, for Bevin crucial, issue remained open.

In late April the committee of six reconvened to agree upon a joint conference in July. Each union would send up to ten delegates.

The *Railway Review* announced, at that time, that the NUR had more than doubled its membership since railway amalgamation had been completed. 'Experience proves', it wrote, 'that the larger the body, the greater its recruiting powers, and that success in reducing the number of unions is at once followed by a large accession of members.' The *Weekly Record* concluded:

We think this applies with special emphasis to the work of organising the enormous mass of labour which is included in the classification of general labour. The work to our hands is so vast and potential that it is far and away the most important and consequential to be accomplished by labour within the next generation. We have to create a conception of working-class loyalty and co-operation towards our aims among the unnumbered army of the unorganised, ever-ready to play the part of blackleg because of the lack of that morale which Trade Unionism creates. Give us a united front in the face of the enemy, and the larger majority of those who are now non-unionists will be found within the ranks of an amalgamated general workers' union, while not detracting from the interest of those now fairly well organised.[46]

## Special Conference, July 1914

The climax of all this long debate came on 8 July 1914, when the two federal bodies met in a special Amalgamation Conference at Caxton Hall, Westminster.[47] All the affiliates of both bodies attended, except for the seamen, the crane-drivers, and the Ships' Cooks' and Stewards' Union. In all, thirty unions sent representatives; of these, six – the DWRGWU, the Gas and General Workers' Union, the National Union of Vehicle Workers, the NAUL, the United Carters, and the UOGL – were affiliated to both the GLNC and the NTWF. Six unions with no affiliation to either body attended: both the Cardiff and the North of England Coal Trimmers' Unions, the London and Provincial Union of Licensed Vehicle Workers, the Scottish Horse and Motormen's Union, the Coal Porters' Union and, most significantly, the Irish Transport and General Workers' Union, whose representatives were James Larkin (of 'Liberty Hall, Dublin'), and James Connolly. Overcoming their antipathy towards Larkin, the English union leaders accepted his presence on this occasion. The carters' societies of Manchester and Liverpool attended but abstained from voting.

The joint ten-point scheme agreed in March was presented, with the support of both the GLNC and the NTWF. If it is examined, we see that it goes beyond the fourteen-point GLNC scheme of the previous year in advancing quite new organizational ideas. In effect, these represented a victory for the NTWF over the GLNC, as provision was now made in clause 7 for, in addition to district machinery, 'departmental sections, allowing full free play of initiative and autonomy consistent with the powers of financial control exercised by the Central Executive. These Departments to make adequate provision for sectional and sub-sectional groupings, where called for and necessary.'

As we have seen, clause 1 boldly called for the setting up of 'one consolidated Union of Labour.' Clause 3 provided for a central fund for dispute, legal aid, victimization and administrative purposes, and clause 6 gave complete control of this fund to a Central Executive; however, the composition of such an Executive was not specified. Clause 8 provided job security for all the officers and clerical staff of all the amalgamating unions: each should be taken on by the new union, under the control of its Central Executive. Clause 9 made an important concession to the dockers' fears: 'means must be devised to prevent the unnecessary migration of men from place to place and thereby pressing upon the available amount of employment at certain places at any given time'.

The whole scheme represented a distillation of the accumulated experience of generations of transport and general unionism, and a bold attempt to reconcile the centralizers with the 'departmentalists'. Behind the scenes, great labours had been accomplished.

## Larkin and Connolly Weigh In

The debate on 8 July hardly lived up to the occasion. True, it was much enlivened by the Irish. The first controversy was aroused by Larkin's question of whether the new union would be national or international; both he and Connolly insisted on their enthusiasm for amalgamation, but equally claimed the right to be received as a national, Irish, union, rather than as representatives of an English colony. 'We are a union within our nation . . . [but] we are prepared to sink our identity within an international organisation', he told the conference. O'Connor Kessack rebuked them for 'ranting about nationalism' and reminded them that the Scots had long ago accepted their status within the UK.[48] Larkin was advised to be content with the scheme's provision for district machinery. This was never likely to satisfy the Irish national aspirations, now vividly defended by Larkin. Today, the whole of Ireland constitutes Region 11 of the TGWU, with its headquarters in Belfast, and with Dublin as one of seventeen district offices, most of them in the Republic. These are the descendants of Sexton's union's branches, the survivors of the split of 1908. Alongside them sits the ITGWU, with its headquarters in Dublin.

Larkin was also strongly opposed to the grading of contributions according to the choice of benefits, or to differentials in wages. He was for the lowest practicable flat-rate subscription. And when the absentee affiliates, the NSFU, and the Ships' Cooks' and Stewards' Unions, together with the Mersey Carters' Union, sent a letter to the conference declaring their opposition to the planned amalgamation, it was again Larkin and Connolly who proposed that Havelock Wilson, in particular, had in this way disqualified himself from any future role in the NTWF in its future preparations for the merger. Others, prominent amongst whom were the delegates of the Workers' Union, wished to have the Municipal Employees' Association invited to take part: this was opposed by the majority, as the MEA had a reputation for ignoring existing structures, and was ostracized by all official organizations of the Labour movement.

Despite their absence, the NSFU, Mersey Carters', and Ships' Cook's Unions put up, in their joint letter, a counterproposal that separate amalgamations be arranged to form distinct unions for seafarers, dockers and carters. Connolly found himself in a difficulty over this proposal. He told the conference that 'quite frankly . . . [the NSFU] is inimical to us'. He was a schematic industrial unionist, and said so. Yet he could readily appreciate that, coming from that source, and presented to that congress, the Wilson proposal was divisive. Connolly managed to square the circle by supporting the all-in amalgamation which was intended by almost all unions present, and suggesting that, at a later stage, the new union might dismember itself into a number of rationally established, industrially organized, unions. Of course these would also embrace the craftsmen in each industry.

## An Unwieldy Conference

Other delegates drew attention to the recent formation of a National Agricultural Labourers' Union, and proposed that it, too, be enrolled in the amalgamation process. These and other exchanges clearly show what is also apparent from the frequent procedural dilemmas of the joint chairmen, Clynes and Gosling: that the conference was unwieldy, uncertain of the scope of amalgamation, and unsure of its own status, or of the authority exercised by the delegates from the individual unions present. Some were able to declare that they had a mandate to vote on behalf of their unions; most of the others, although they did vote for the scheme, would have to report back to their executives for an endorsement of their decision. As for what the next stage would be, no one was certain, although all understood that their intention was to proceed eventually, and without prolonged delay, to a ballot of every participating union. The open, all-embracing access to the meeting was long on idealistic oratory, but it prevented horse-trading. The mutual adjustments of discrete interests conducted in small, closed committees might, however, have led more readily to agreement. This was the alternative method which Bevin was able to deploy so effectively after an interval of only seven years. Of course, his chance came after the intervention of a world war and his own rise to dominance in the DWRGWU and the NTWF.

Despite all these drawbacks, the conference revealed that all the most powerful forces assembled in the Caxton Hall were determined and committed to amalgamation. Clynes himself led the way in his chairman's opening address, committing the powerful Gas and General Workers' Union to the scheme, including departmental autonomy and protection for dockers' jobs. Bevin made by far the most cogent speech for both the grand concept and the detail of trade or departmental autonomy. Tillett's speech was general and modest in scale in comparison to that of his young protégé. Tillett's talent for grand, sweeping generalities, quite unsuited to the detailed negotiation of an amalgamation, were not displayed at the conference. His thinking on the subject, in the aftermath of the 1912 defeat, was expressed in syndicalist terms: 'The revolutionary organisation must mean One Union for all Transport Workers, at the very least, with the objective of One Union for all labour.'[49]

A telling intervention came from Gosling, not only as chairman of the NTWF, but as one of the old lightermen, the supreme exemplars of sectional advantage. He told the conference that

I belong myself to one of the oldest organisations here – a set of men who have always had to conduct their business separately and distinct – but I will tell you what their answer is when you talk to them about it. They say: 'We demonstrate together; we fight together; we starve together; and why should not we thrive together?' I find that even the old-fashioned conservative view of some of these old unions is fast disappearing because of the necessity of linking up closer and coming together.[50]

A considerable number of delegates testified to the strong, uncomplicated pressures for amalgamation coming from the rank and file. Equally impressive was the new commitment of the leaders of the NUDL. Everyone knew they had originally been reluctant to accept the general workers into amalgamation. In 1913 Sexton had written that

the carters, dockers, seamen and firemen, vanmen, and all connected with the transport trade should confine themselves strictly to organising and catering for their own class in their own particular industry . . . A system whereby all the employees of a certain industry, irrespective of their grade, either skilled or unskilled, are under the control of one organisation . . . is simply impossible in this country, where the spirit of caste is the growth of nearly a century and the skilled and the so-called unskilled, rigidly separated.[51]

## Kessack Overrides Sexton

Representing the NUDL instead of Sexton, who kept a low profile, Kessack frankly confessed to the conference that he was a recent convert. In 1913 he had spoken of the general workers' unions' 'motley membership [which] ranges all the way from University professors to agricultural labourers, and from suffragettes to sandwichmen'.[52] But in July 1914 he had said, of a dispute with the Mersey Docks and Harbour Board, 'how much easier would it have been if the engineering and shipbuilding men were in one union and we of the general crowd in another! The lesson of this strike, for the men of the whole working class is: Amalgamation!'[53]

At the conference he confessed his earlier adherence to the proposal for separate unions for seamen, carters and dockers only in order now to repudiate it, principally in the name of efficiency and economy. For, he pointed out, a union as small as the ships' cooks' simply had no resources to maintain an officer and an office in every port, with the consequence that non-unionism in those trades persisted. The same was true for all the localized carters' societies. So, 'much against my will at first . . . I was compelled to ask myself was I right or wrong? I am therefore strongly of the opinion that [amalgamation] will lead to economy; and that it will lead to efficiency'.[54]

For the sentimental, it should be recorded that this conference saw Bevin overshadowing Tillett, and Kessack eclipsing Sexton. It also saw a younger man, Clynes, coming forward to outshine Thorne. The original torch of the new unions was passing to another generation, at the moment that both young and old were preparing the transcendence of their established organizational forms.

The voting on clause 1 of the scheme was recorded in detail: twenty-six unions voted in favour; two – the Cardiff coal trimmers and the stevedores – were 'undecided'; and two – the Mersey Quay and Railway Carters' Union and the United Carters' Association – voted against; to these we should add the absentee opposition from the NSFU and the ships' cooks.

The rest of the clauses occasioned debate on detail (notably – and predictably – on the levels of subscription), but all were adopted. The conference finally instructed the sub-committee to proceed to draft detailed rules, and to convene a second delegate conference to approve them, prior to a ballot.

At its close, the conference degenerated into a quarrelsome wrangle about how long the sub-committee should be allowed to draw up rules and convene a second conference. One said one month, others three months, some a year, some three years. Larkin became increasingly impatient, urging minimum delay, against the cautious 'realism' of, amongst others, Tillett. Exchanges between the two became acerbic and personal. Delegates were calling 'Vote!', 'Agreed – Vote!' 'Point of Order!' 'Move the vote!' 'Right of reply!' One can picture the movements for coats and hats, the consulting of watches and railway timetables, hear the scraping of chairs, see the drift towards the exits. In a final burst of frustration and contempt, Larkin threw in, 'I move that it be in twelve years' time.' This was ignored by the chairman, and 'as soon as possible' became the inevitable compromise.

Tragic irony could not have been more heavily rehearsed. No hint of the coming storm of dread and terror had been evident at the conference, but every step of its way had been overshadowed. Archduke Ferdinand of Austria had been assassinated in Sarajevo on 28 June, ten days before the delegates convened. Soon many of them, and thousands of their members, would be killed. On 4 August, one month after the delegates had gone home, Britain and France went to war against Germany and Austria, and the amalgamation process came to an abrupt halt.[55] It would resume after years of hardship and loss.

## II

## *'The Most Successful Campaign'*

We cannot leave the story of the earlier days of the National Transport Workers' Federation without recording the story of its most 'successful', and yet most dubious, campaign. This turned around the issue of cheap labour, especially Chinese labour. We cannot paint a true portrait of transport trade unions without tracing these events, which were truly a corrupting legacy of empire.

For unmixed racial bigotry, there were few who could descend to the standards of 'Captain' Tupper, who came into his own in a truly sordid episode, to which we have already briefly alluded in chapter 10. This involved riotous demonstrations in Cardiff, during the 1911 upheaval, against the employment of Chinese labour. The historian of the Welsh dockers, Phillip Leng, tells us that Tupper 'did not advise such disorder'; but if we were to believe the Captain's own account, he went considerably further than the issuing of advice: 'Men of the Welsh laundries came to me with yarns about the washing establishments run by the yellow men . . . my blood was boiling . . . I arranged a great demonstration outside Roath Dock Gate . . . all the available police mustered'.[56] But this, he boasted, was all a decoy, 'respectable' in that the constables looked on while various orators fulminated against the 'yellow peril'. Meanwhile, says Tupper:

> I was leading my storm troops to the back alleys which house the Chinese laundries and boarding houses. I believe that one of the Chinese bosses . . . had a very bad time that day. A good many of the dives caught fire, too; quite a lot of Chinamen got hurt. But there were little white girls, some no more than thirteen years old, running out of the places when the sailors visited their lords and masters. We cleared the decks – and the Cardiff Chinese laundries shut up shop.[57]

This shameless account is not an invention by some critic, although it may well have been invented. It comes from the Captain's own rather rancid memoirs. Summing up this unwholesome affair, he writes: 'England's conscience wasn't bothered, anyway. I received thousands of letters – many from the Church – blessing us for this bit of riot.'

There is some evidence that Tupper might actually have been speaking at his 'decoy' meeting during the time that he claims to have been rumpusing in the alleys, and was not leading his 'storm troops' at all.[58] However, even if it is fantasy, this story gives us a complete picture of a mentality which could fantasize in such a way.

Alas, Tupper was not alone in the persecution of Chinese immigrants.

Under Liberal and some Labour auspices, a campaign of intimidation had been waged in a number of areas for some years. The general cry for discrimination had featured in the Liverpool elections of 1906, as we have already seen (chapter 8). Then, James Larkin had been the stage manager, although, to his credit, he was later to take up a very different attitude. Xenophobia was widely spread, and the Chinese seamen were a visible and vulnerable target. In the years leading up to the election of 1906 the Liberals had campaigned against the recruitment of Chinese labour for South African mines, but this campaign had two edges, since, while it fed xenophobia, it also opposed the 'slave' conditions in which labourers were confined in barracks, flogged and very generally ill used.[59] There was a wide trade-union reaction against these iniquities, part of which was echoed by James Sexton in a passage which we quoted in chapter 8. But in the early years actual discrimination was hardly organized, sporadic or riotous.

The question of an organized campaign was first raised at the Federation's 1913 AGC, at which the NEC accepted the task of initiating a national campaign. Gosling's presidential address to the 1914 AGC was enthusiastic about the virtue and the impact of this campaign.

> In all the shipping centres of the United Kingdom large and enthusiastic meetings of Transport Workers and other trade unionists have been held. The Secretary has been inundated with resolutions protesting against the apathy of the Board of Trade and the action of those shipowners who threaten the Western standard of life and morals, which have been passed at numbers of meetings of local LRCs [Labour Representation Committees, or Labour Parties], Trades Councils, and trade unions throughout the country. Public indignation has been roused everywhere, and we are fast approaching the stage when drastic action, either politically or direct, must be taken if we are to prevent this growing evil.[60]

The campaign kicked off with a rally in Hull which set the tone for what followed. As the *Weekly Record* reported, all the big names of the Federation were there:

> On Wednesday April 15th, a splendid opening meeting was held at the City Hall, Hull, to inaugurate the Great Campaign against the employment of cheap Asiatic Labour in British ships. Mr. R. H. Farrah, President of the Humber District Committee, presided, supported by members of all the Unions affiliated to the District Committee.

First to speak was Joseph Cotter. He said that this was the pioneer meeting of what 'he hoped would be one of the greatest achievements of the transport workers – the abolition of Asiatic labour on board British ships. The problem was one not only for sailors and firemen, it was also a question for the shore workers. At the present time there were six ships in one of the docks at Hull manned by Chinese labour.'

Next came Harry Gosling. The reason they had come to Hull first, he explained, was that they

knew the importance of the place. They were going to the other Northern ports, and along the Bristol Channel, and so round to London. They had made up their minds that they were not going to tolerate cheap Chinese labour any more than they would tolerate cheap blackleg labour. As a matter of fact, they did not see the difference. If Parliament would do something they would be grateful, but they were not going to take any chances: they were going to do it for themselves. There had always been Chinamen competing with the Sailors and Firemen, but never to the extent that it was done now. Although the Federation was approaching a quarter of a million strong, it was not big and strong enough. Shortly they were going into Conference with the Miners and Railwaymen for the purpose of having an understanding with them that when things like Chinese labour and other matters of that kind had to be considered, they would not have to be considered alone.

Then, Robert Williams took the floor. He said that the employment of cheap Chinese labour was an economic matter. Since labour was the prime charge upon all industry, and because the permanent interest of the employing class was to reduce that charge,

there were two distinct tendencies within the working of modern capitalism. One was the economy of labour by the introduction of mechanical contrivances and devices, and improved processes, resulting in an actual and portentous reduction in the number of men in well-nigh every occupation. The other tendency was to substitute cheap for more expensive labour. The employing class would engage the nimble fingers of monkeys did it but add to their profits and bank balances. We asked for superior organisation of the men in order to grapple with the growingly effective organisation of the employers. The men were asked to become more and more self-reliant. We were at the present moment taking steps to promote amalgamation between 40 and 50 Unions with a membership of 400,000 men. Only by the power of highly effective organisation, utilised in a scientific manner, would the workers be able to cope with the menace of cheap labour in the transport industry.

Havelock Wilson wound up, giving

some remarkable figures in illustration of the growth of the Asiatic menace. Last year the number of Chinese was 9,500, whereas nine years ago the number was 2,000. This was on shore. In the Mercantile Marine the number of Asiatics had risen from 20,000 in 1890 to 56,000 at the present time. He did not believe that Parliament would move unless they saw the danger of the whole of the workingmen ceasing work on the Chinese Labour question. 'We have already waited upon Mr. John Burns, and he immediately took action to apply the language test more vigorously, but we have got to be prepared for something more drastic.' He did not believe in strikes, but there were times when the workers had no other course.[61]

All these sentiments were published in the *Record* under the headline 'The Curse of the Cheap Chinee', with the subtitle 'Hull's Brilliant Send-off to the "Yellow Peril" Campaign'.

Mass meetings were then held, and, it has to be said, aroused some enthusiasm, in Sunderland, South Shields, Leith, Glasgow, Liverpool, Cardiff, Barry, Newport, Swansea and Birkenhead, among other places. At Barry, a short stoppage of seamen and firemen took place, supported by local dock workers, but the union officials prevailed on the strikers to return to work, 'pending the build-up of the national campaign'.[62]

This agitation did not pass unopposed. In mid-May 1914 the Labour Council of Kensington and Paddington wrote to the NTWF enclosing the text of a resolution 'that in asking for the elimination of the Asiatic the Transport Workers' Federation is adopting a method which is detrimental to the International Working Class Movement, and suggests as an alternative that the Transport Workers should demand equal payment and conditions for the Asiatic'.[63] The reply of the *Weekly Record* was that it was as internationalist as anyone else, but 'we do draw the line at fraternising with the scabs of the Shipping Federation'. All men are brothers, continued the *Record*, 'but a scab is less than a man'. On the reasoning of the Kensington Council, went on the NTWF, 'a campaign for the elimination of non-Unionists would also be detrimental' to the international movement.[64] This was a plain *non sequitur*, but it implied a question which was asked by others: if the NTWF wanted to eliminate non-unionism, why did it not take up that very issue, instead of generalizing the agitation about the 'yellow peril'? From Dublin, James Larkin expressed the same view as Kensington. He could solve the Lascar problem in one hour, he wrote, by organizing the Lascars (Lascar was the common term for Indian seamen). The *Daily Herald* League gave its assent to this solution, and provoked a bitter response from O'Connor Kessack, which happily animadverted on all the old rows with that 'curious person from Dublin'.[65]

Bevin, too, said his piece about the 'insidious attempt' of the Shipping Federation to lower the standard of life for the English workers:

I regard the encroachment of the Asiatic as the most formidable form of blacklegging we have yet had to fight, hence the seriousness of the problem. What is there to prevent the Shipping Federation from introducing the Asiatic during periods of strike? You must remember that the present Government have always been ready, and really over anxious to supply thousands of soldiers to protect blacklegs, and in the event of this happening, the Capitalist Press would come out daily, telling us that the British worker is a drunken, wretched person; on strike for a holiday; too lazy to work; etc. etc. Their scribes would write up articles to order and have special interviews with the managers, who would be astounded at the remarkable ability of the Chinaman . . .

Remember that only a fortnight ago there were hundreds of Seamen unemployed at Barry, and several steamers manned with Chinamen. I want to ask my readers to come away from their firesides and stand in the shoes of those seamen; overworked and underpaid, ofttimes with insufficient food when employed, but even that avenue of employment closed. Imagine yourselves going to your factories or workshops, or even offices, on Monday morning, and being told that there was no work, and that Chinamen had taken your places in the land of your birth! That is the position the Seaman often finds himself in when he presents himself at a British Shipping Office, and probably the ship is owned by a patriotic shipowner, who is either a Liberal or Tory M.P. . . . [66]

Strengthened by the responses at the mass meetings, and by 2,000 favourable replies to a circular, from trade unions, Labour Parties, other federations and the TUC, the NTWF then led a deputation to John Burns. Sadly, it is necessary to record that, in the words of Robert Williams, 'On the whole, this is the most successful campaign the Federation has yet conducted.'[67]

The NSFU and the Ships' Cooks and Stewards' Union next sought to move the Federation on, from an agitation confined to propaganda, to outright industrial action by calling for a general ports' stoppage against 'blackleg Chinamen'. The Dockers' Union would not support the seamen's resolution, which was referred to the NEC. This move frustrated the seamen's intentions, for the Federation's rules forbade any affiliate from taking action likely to involve other affiliates without first consulting them. This became yet another source of friction between the seamen and the Federation, which created enough abrasions to influence the shape of any future amalgamation. At this point, it is enough to note that, in the campaign against Chinese labour, the Federation probably reached greater unanimity, albeit only on propaganda terms, than it attained on any other pre-war issue. This very 'success' underlined the federation's fundamental fragility, as well, of course, as the fatal attraction of a racial issue for the Labour movement in the imperial homeland. Chauvinism of this kind was all the more damaging as the European continent drifted closer to a war which would very soon engulf all the world. The passions unleashed in this unsavoury racist lobby were to do great damage to those who took part in it, many of whom, like O'Connor Kessack himself, would soon be swallowed up in the greedy maw of war.

Ultimately, industrial action was ruled out because although this was a national issue, it remained a sectional one. Much as it affected the interests of the two seamen's organizations within the Federation, others were but marginally embroiled. However, the problem did not go away, and was to become the cause of much further contention during the war, as we shall see.

## III

## *The Triple Alliance*

Three pressing priorities gripped all the transport workers' unions in the immediate pre-war years. The first was to overcome their structural divisions, and this involved them in the amalgamation movement. The second was to agree upon, and to prosecute, a national programme of demands, in order to rise above their divisions not only on the structural level, but also on the industrial and strategic fronts. Progress in facing up to either of these two questions would enhance the prospects of resolving the other. But a third project was to emerge, forced to the front of the leaders' agenda by the fierce industrial storms of the years 1911–14, both in transport itself and also in the mining industry. Internal cohesion within transport was no longer enough. A wider industrial alliance was needed, to reinforce bargaining power on sectoral demands, to control conflicts of interest between unions and sectors, and to bring pressure to bear on government to revert to that conciliatory, even-handed stance which had been so helpful in 1911. This was the genesis of the idea of the Triple Alliance.

In pursuit of the first objective, the NTWF and the GLNC had held their amalgamation conference. On the matter of the second goal, neither the NTWF, nor its constituent unions, nor the sectors of which they were composed, made very much real headway before the war. The Seamen's Union pursued, as it was wont to do, its own autonomous course; it did at least have a national programme, dating back to 1908. There were two unfulfilled elements in that programme in 1912–14. The union demanded enhanced manning scales; these had to be pressed far more strongly after the *Titanic* disaster, which cruelly underscored their relevance. Then there was the issue of cheap, Asian labour employed in the British mercantile marine, which we have reviewed above. (It was easy for companies with a global reach to employ Chinese seamen or the so-called Lascars.) Beneath both of these specific issues there lay a general aspiration for national bargaining, and for a national shipping industry conciliation board.

The Shipping Federation had adopted a less unfriendly disposition towards Havelock Wilson and his union in the aftermath of the 1911 strikes. None the less, it withheld recognition from the NSFU exactly because it disapproved of the union's affiliation to the NTWF. Sir Thomas Lane

Devitt, Bart., chairman of the Shipping Federation, in a letter to *The Times* in 1912, explained: 'So long as this connexion [with the NTWF] exists, and so long as the Transport Workers maintain their present policy [of the sympathetic strike], I cannot see how the shipowners can consult or have anything to do with the National Sailors' and Firemen's Union.'[68]

Concerning wages, the Shipping Federation pre-empted an expected action by the NSFU by granting a pay increase of 10s. a week, without any prior bargaining, in January 1913. Wilson's Executive then turned from the direct question of ratés of pay to announce its national campaign against the engagement of Asian labour on British ships, and as we have seen, sought and won the support of the NTWF for a national boycott.

A more permanent and healing common cause, which would have bound the affiliates closer together, if it could have been agreed and promoted, was the much-needed national programme for the dockers, and to a lesser extent, for the carters and vehicle workers. In the dockers' case, early moves were made towards a general agitation for the eight-hour, five-and-a-half-day week – in effect a demand for a forty-four hour week. This programme was agreed at the 1913 AGC, and Tillett proposed that a federal conference on the issue should be summoned. No demand was tabled, however, before the war. Bevin told the Shaw Inquiry in 1920 that a claim was almost ready for submission in August 1914:

> I want to put before you the history of that shorter working week. We had prepared that programme in 1913, and in 1914 as an historical fact, the Triple Alliance was formed of the Miners, the Railwaymen, and ourselves. We had all had bitter experience, and knew the type of fight we would have to meet. We did not want it, I can assure you, and if there had been a ready means of conciliation at our hand at that time we should probably never have thought of it. We had our bitter experience in London in 1912 of people driven to starvation and suicide over the bitter strike, in London particularly; and we had to get the necessary machinery to prevent so prolonged a struggle taking place again. But when the war broke out, we were appealed to by the State to forego all those negotiations. We were asked, 'Do not press your claims now when the country is in the throes of danger', and we said 'Very good', and we withdrew our claim. As a matter of fact we had not actually sent it to the employers but it was ready . . . We did not submit the demand for the shorter working week until after the Armistice was signed.[69]

Gordon Phillips questions this claim: 'No evidence', he writes, 'exists to support this assertion.'[70] However, if the claim was ready, but neither published or publicized, hard evidence would naturally be lacking. The patriotic restraints imposed by the war on union claims (both claims pending and those in the pipeline) were often marked, and quite general in their effect. There seems no reason to doubt Bevin's statement. Why should he invent such a claim? The general intention of the Federation was clear enough. We have already cited Bob Williams's draft for a programme of demands. However, this does not invalidate the point that, up to and including 1914, the NTWF lacked cohesion, both structurally and strategically. This meant that it stood to gain most from any wider support in struggle that the proposed Tripple Alliance might provide for it. Indeed, the very notion of the Alliance afforded an incentive to the Federation to resolve its internal problems. But for all that, it was always likely to be the weak link in any concordat with the miners and the railwaymen.

All three of the parties to the Triple Industrial Alliance had been feeling their way to a link-up before 1913. The rank-and-file railwaymen made the running even before they had overcome many of their own internal divisions by forming the NUR in that year.[71]

The railwaymen had constantly pressed the Executive of the old Amalgamated Society of Railway Servants for solidarity action during the transport strikes of 1911, and it was Tom Mann's Strike Committee in Liverpool which offered them reciprocal support from the dockers, carters and tramwaymen (see chapter 10). The following year, during the national coal strike, a typical mass meeting of railway workers in Sheffield passed a resolution calling upon 'the joint ECs of the railway union and the transport workers to take up the fight for a living wage for all workers in the event of the miners calling them to their aid.'[72] As early as June 1911, Will Thorne had won the Federation's support for 'an instruction to the general council [of the NTWF] to get in touch with the miners' federation with a view to giving whatever assistance they may consider necessary.'[73]

After the miners joined the discussion, Tillett claimed the initiative as his own before the year 1913 was out:

Probably the most momentous development of modern times is the working agreement about to be ratified between the National Transport Workers' Federation, the Railwaymen's Union, and the Miners' Federation. Considerably over a million workers will be involved in a working agreement in case of industrial movement or movements pertaining to industrial action. A committee representing the chief officers of the several organisations has been appointed for the purpose of drawing up a form of Industrial Co-operative Agreement. If the respective organisations are sincere and act with unanimity, the latest development of industrial organisation will spell a great revolutionary movement in the future. This development we are glad to boast of as coming from the Dockers' Union. Its fulfilment will indeed be a great triumph for Trade Unionism.[74]

The other general dockers' union, the NUDL, also ventilated the same idea, but with a twist which was to give their proposal a quality of savage irony. They sought to bring into being a triple alliance among whose objectives would figure objection to war:

> Proposed by J. O'Connor Kessack, seconded by J. Kinsella, 'That this Congress strongly condemns any action likely to lead to war between nations, and pledges itself to do everything possible to make war impossible; and, further, instructs the Parliamentary Committee to confer with the British Miners' Federation, the National Transport Workers' Federation, and the National Union of Railway Men, with a view to opening negotiations with foreign Trade Unions for the purpose of making agreements and treaties as to common international action in the event of war being forced upon us . . .'[75]

It was O'Connor Kessack, a man of great influence among the dockers, who volunteered in November 1914. He was to be slaughtered, at the age of thirty-six, in the battle of the Ancre. 'Had it not been for his untimely death', wrote the Liverpool dockers' historian, 'there is little doubt that he would have played an important role in the creation and development of the TGWU in the post-war years.'[76]

On 9 October 1913 the Miners' Federation carried a conference resolution: 'That the Executive Council of the Miners' Federation of Great Britain be requested to approach the Executive Committees of other big unions with a view of co-operative action in support of each other's demands.'[77]

This was the week in which the Dublin employers rejected any settlement of the lock-out, and peremptorily turned down the Askwith formula. Sympathy action was thus forced into the front of people's minds. The NTWF was immediately interested in the miners' proposal, and convened a special Executive Council meeting to elaborate its response. By April the following year, a joint conference had been agreed between miners' and transport federations, together with the railwaymen. Dublin had already provoked quite serious divergences within and between these bodies, on the very question of sympathetic action. The NTWF agreed to present three proposals to the joint conference. They had been separately formulated by Sexton and Patrick Kean – who represented the General Workers' Union on the Federation Executive – and were joined together to read:

(1) That in the opinion of this E.C. the formation of a working agreement or scheme between the three bodies is very desirable, and that we agree to the formation of a national consultative body in conjunction with the Miners and Railwaymen on all questions affecting the three bodies in all future industrial disputes.

(2) That a sub-committee equally representative of the three bodies be appointed for the purpose of formulating a scheme

> to be submitted to the three E.C.s, and a further conference
> called.
> (3)  That Joint Secretaries be appointed, and instructed to secure
>      from all Societies the nature and terms of all existing
>      agreements and their termination, to be filed for future
>      reference.[78]

The three unions met on 23 April. As Bob Smillie, president of the
Miners' Federation, was to report:

The three bodies have much in common. Their membership is considerable,
the miners numbering 800,000, the railwaymen 270,000 and the transport
workers 250,000. The miners have done much fighting in the past,
sectionally and generally; the railwaymen on more than one occasion have
come through struggles similar to our own; and the transport workers are
famed for their fighting spirit and fighting qualities. But while we achieved a
great deal by our industrial struggles, and while we can hardly calculate the
benefit conferred upon our people by these three bodies, it must be
admitted that a great deal of suffering and privation has been caused. A
strike on the railway system immediately affects the miners and the
transport workers, as well as the others. Though these for the moment may
not have any quarrel with their respective employers, yet within a few days
they are placed in the same position as though they had. They are idle and
are thrown upon the funds of their unions. The same result follows if the
miners or the transport workers are on strike. When the miners struck in
1912 the cost to the railwaymen alone was about £94,000. Whenever any
one of these three great sections have struck the others have had to stand by
and suffer in silence.

The meeting of the three Executives, held in April 1914, to consider ways
and means of working in common and so avoiding the evils of disjointed
action, was enthusiastic and unanimous. It resolved that a working
agreement should be drawn up, and appointed a committee, consisting of
the presidents and secretaries of the three organisations, for the purpose.
The idea behind this agreement is not in any way the formation of a
federation. The new body is not to be a rival to any other. Nor is it to be
sectional in any sense. There is no suggestion, for instance, that if one
section of the miners determines to strike they will receive the assistance of
the new alliance. Action is to be confined to joint national action. Further,
no action will be taken until all three partners have met in conference and
have agreed upon the course to be adopted. Sympathetic action, in fact, is
no longer to be left to the uncontrolled emotions of a strike period, but is to
be the calculated result of mature consideration and careful planning. The
predominant idea of the alliance is that each of these great fighting
organisations, before embarking upon any big movement, either defensive
or aggressive, should formulate its programme, submit it to the others, and
that upon joint proposals joint action should then be taken.

It is clear to everyone acquainted with industrial development that capital
is now organised for the purpose of attacking trade unionism and for

defence against trade union advance. Should the occasion arise, each section of the alliance must be ready to render sympathetic action, deliberately thought out and agreed upon, should any one of the partners in the scheme be the object of attack.[79]

At the conference Smillie's own role was considerable. He was unanimously called to the chair and he made the keynote speech. According to Robert Williams,

> he said some fairly startling things. These remarks are so essentially of a private character that we feel safe in recapitulating the points made by comrade Smillie. He said that no one conversant with the details of modern industry could ignore the fact that the employing classes on all sides were organising themselves not only to resist any encroachments upon their own position and privileges, but would challenge the entire position occupied by organised labour. This being so, we were in duty bound to make such preparations to effect such arrangements and to bring about such understandings as would further equip us in the future conflicts between organised labour and organised capital. There was a natural connection between the Miners and the Unions connected with the transport affairs of our country, and when one considered the interconnection of the three organisations represented, it was a wonder that steps had not been taken much earlier to promote a common understanding.[80]

Without such an understanding, thought Smillie, more money would be spent 'to provide assistance for those who were thrown out of employment than was spent on account of those who promoted the dispute'. J. Bellamy, of the railwaymen, heartily endorsed this view. Gosling then proposed the NTWF's three points, which were substantially accepted.[81] 'It was especially agreed', reported the *Weekly Record*, that synchronization of negotiating timetables was necessary to effective co-operation.

A joint sub-committee was then set up to carry forward the project of the Triple Alliance. For the miners, the representatives were to be Robert Smillie and Thomas Ashton; for the railwaymen, J. E. Williams and J. Bellamy; and for the NTWF, Harry Gosling and Robert Williams.

Shortly afterwards, the leaders of the NTWF debated the matter at its 1914 AGC. The Council endorsed the moves taken by its Executive in April, and instructed 'the new Executive Council to give their closest attention and support to any working arrangement calculated to secure joint action arising from the identity of interests in these three great industries.'[82]

In the debate on this motion, Robert Williams credited Vernon Hartshorn of the Welsh miners with the original idea, conceived 'during a critical time in the dispute of 1912'. He emphasized the function of the

Alliance in preventing blacklegging by rail or transport workers against each other, and against the miners, during sectional strikes:

> They, as transport workers, conveyed the coal to the industrial areas and to the seaboard. When the railwaymen were on strike the transport workers assisted in the diversion of traffic by water, and when they, the transport workers were on strike, the services of the railwaymen were utilised carrying blacklegs and diverted shipping traffic. They did not want any section of organised workers to become strike breakers or blacklegs.[83]

Joseph Houghton of the Scottish dockers thought that the Alliance, 'instead of creating trouble . . . would prevent it'. Godfrey, of the vehicle workers, 'hoped the first object of the new alliance would be the elimination of the scab'. Will Thorne, sceptical of any instant revolution in their fortunes arising from the Alliance, sounded a note of warning:

> Unless they were exceedingly careful, the whole of them might be involved within twelve months in very serious trouble, because, as they were aware, the railway workers would meet in Swansea on Monday, and they were going to agree on a national programme . . . He understood their agreements were about to terminate sometime this year, and if they agreed upon a national strike it would mean that the whole of the transport and the miners would become involved. If that were so, there would be no need for a railway strike. (Applause) But they must not imagine that every time the transport workers were involved in a dispute that the railwaymen would down tools. (Cries of 'Oh'.) Personally he thought it should be an understanding that all agreements should terminate at one time.

To which Sexton added: 'that was one of the objects of the alliance'. Thorne also looked to the Alliance to render 'sporadic' strikes less likely.[84]

The origins of the Triple Alliance lie very clearly in the whole experience of industrial militancy of the Great Unrest. All three partners experienced strikes on an unprecedented scale between 1910 and 1914. In the case of the transport workers, the formative episode was undoubtedly the wave of port and transport strikes in the summer of 1911. For them alone of the three, this encouraging experience was followed by a check to the method of militant mass strikes when they failed to mobilize a national, federal response in support of the London dock strike during the following year.

For much of the leadership of the NTWF, this lesson confirmed a general caution, which was reflected in their interpretation of the purposes and methods of the Triple Alliance. Yet precisely because of the 1912 defeat, these same cautious leaders could not reject the possibility, held out to them by the Alliance, of repairing the weaknesses in their own structure, and reinforcing it by an industrial agreement with two evidently like-minded industrial unions.

Nor, of course, did the initial opinions on the purpose and potential of the Alliance stand still for all the participants. Whilst Robert Williams in 1914 felt that 'they did not want to talk too much about a strike, but they wanted to have the power behind them as a final resort to put the screw upon all the governing classes of society in order to effect such demands as they might find it desirable to make,'[85] by 1920 his voice was raised in an unambiguous support for the general strike: 'When the workers are negotiating with the employers or with the government which invariably represents the employers, they invariably exercise a greater influence when they speak in terms of industrial strength than when they speak politically . . . Before the general strike the general election pales into insignificance.'[86]

It may have taken the First World War and the Russian Revolution to bring Williams to this point, yet even in its formative years the concept of the Triple Alliance as a revolutionary syndicalist weapon was widely advocated in the rank-and-file syndicalist movement in all three of the allied industries. In the syndicalists' local branches, in their journals and at their meetings, railwaymen, miners and transport workers met and made common cause, sending up the line of communications to their Executives and leaders a stream of resolutions calling for joint action. The syndicalists in the British Socialist Party lent their voices to the call, arguing for joint action 'between miners, transport workers, and seamen' in support of each other's claims.[87]

Even O'Connor Kessack, moderate national organizer of Sexton's union, had caught the same mood in a speech to Scottish miners in 1912: 'if at any time the Miners' Federation deemed it necessary, the transport workers would come immediately to their aid. The fight of the miners was the fight of the whole working class just now, and if the miners failed it might be the beginning of war with every section of the workers of the country.'[88]

## 'Rampagious Syndicalism', or 'Trade Unionism in its Right Mind'?

One senses in many of the leaders' pronouncements that an unacknowledged debate was being conducted between radical syndicalists and cautious, pragmatic leaders. Thus Bellamy of the NUR, in June 1914, defended the Alliance from accusations of subversion. The scheme, he said, was 'not . . . rampagious syndicalism, but . . . trade unionism in its right mind'.[89]

None of the definitions of the Alliance's purposes was put to the test before the war, and a dangerous ambiguity slumbered away at the heart of British industrial relations through the period of officially declared industrial truce which commenced in August 1914. On the outbreak of war, the joint board representing the Labour Party, the TUC and the General Federation of Trade Unions resolved 'that an immediate effort be made to terminate all existing trade disputes, whether strikes or lockouts, and whenever new points of difficulty arise during the War period, a serious attempt should be made by all concerned to reach an amicable settlement, before resorting to a strike or lockout.'[90] Lord Askwith recalled: 'At the beginning of August there were 100 disputes known to the Department [of Trade] to be in existence. At the end of the month there were twenty . . . Disputes melted away as fast as the hours of the day, and often of the night, gave time for the hearing of difficulties.'[91]

For Ernest Bevin, the war was to provide a transformed industrial setting in which he strove to exploit the new opportunities for trade-union advance towards national recognition and collective bargaining. For these purposes, he had to hand the NTWF: its greatly enhanced wartime role in turn paved the way for the amalgamation of 1922.

## Assessments

The Triple Alliance has been seen by the majority of labour historians of the period, as well as by much contemporary opinion, as a potential catalyst of even more serious industrial conflict than had given rise to its creation in the years following 1910. However, more recent attempts have been made to revise this view, notably by Gordon Phillips, the NTWF's historian. Elie Halevy's study of the period characterized the Triple Alliance as 'a project . . . typically British in character though suggested by the formulas of French syndicalism'.[92] That is to say, the objectives of the trade unionists who founded it were pragmatic and limited to industrial purposes, but the project was inevitably linked in many minds with the agitation for One Big Union, the general strike, and the overthrow of capitalism. These were widely canvassed in the syndicalist campaign, and their realization was seen as more likely through the proposed Alliance than through the agency of either the TUC or the General Federation of Trade Unions. Halevy suggested that the railway industry, which had an outstanding claim deadlined for 1 December 1914, might have been the trigger for a wider conflagration involving both the other parties.

Another scholar, E. H. Phelps Brown, also identifies the outstanding NUR claim – for union recognition, a forty-eight-hour week and a 5s. pay rise – as the most likely cause of any potential general stoppage. However, he does not, as Phillips suggests, suppose either that the Triple Alliance was conceived as, or that it might have become, the deliberate organizer of such a strike. His judgement rests on the formal rules of the

Alliance appended to this chapter – see pp. 561–2); but these were not agreed until 1915.

> The text revealed the parties' embarrassment, for it laid them under no obligation to strike together, or indeed to do anything save consult one another before proceeding with a major issue: all its other major provisions were designed to limit their obligations and safeguard their autonomy. None the less it was understood to have pledged all to back the cause of each. Nothing could have been less thought out. That it should ever have been adopted can be explained only by the amount of unemployment among railwaymen and other transport workers that the coal strike had caused in 1912, prompting the thought that if all must be in it together in practice they might as well go in with a will; and by the sense of an impending general clash, a civil war between capital and labour, that was strong at that time of so many clashes. J. H. Thomas of the railwaymen asked in the House why, if Ulster could arm with impunity, his union should not spend its half million of funds on arms too.[93]

This is well said. Of course Thomas, an avowed constitutionalist who had chosen a parliamentary career, was speaking here with heavy irony. But the convergence of the labour unrest, along with subversive, extra-constitutional and mutinous behaviour by the Ulstermen, and the crescendo of direct, illegal activities staged concurrently by the suffragettes, generated a climate fervid with expectations of social conflict. This was the theme of Dangerfield's pioneering attempt to explain the whole period in terms of a collapse of liberal social conventions, in his book with the ringing title *The Strange Death of Liberal England*.

Another distinguished historian, R. C. K. Ensor, tells us 'The immediate object [of the Triple Alliance] was to synchronise the expiry of their agreements, so that disputes, if any, might be synchronised also. But it was really a victory for the syndicalist idea.'[94] The first sentence carries conviction; the second needs more extended discussion.

A. J. P. Taylor's reference to the Alliance in its pre-war days is confined to the assertion that it 'had been preparing something like a general strike for the autumn of 1914'.[95] Cole and Postgate assert similarly that 'on the eve of the outbreak of war, the new Triple Alliance ... was just setting about its preparations for the biggest strike of all'.[96]

A much more considered version of the origins and purpose of the Alliance comes from Phillip Bagwell, the railwaymen's historian.[97] He notes that the secondary consequences of strike action in any of the three industries have direct impact on employment in the other two:

> No doubt it was true that a strike of miners, railwaymen or transport workers would, before long, bring about a closure of factories and plants in a wide range of industries through a breakdown in the source of power or

failure to get goods to the markets. But a closure of the pits brought about
an immediate reduction in the demand for rail, road, and water transport.
Likewise a transport strike directly affected employment in the mines since
there were severe limits to the quantity of coal that could be stored at the
pithead. When the railwaymen withdrew their labour in August 1911, the
jobs of many thousands of miners were immediately threatened . . . More
than a quarter of the [railwaymen's] £437,121 union funds at the end of
1911 had been drained away a year later as a result of disputes in other
industries. In view of this uneconomic dissipation of union funds, it is not
difficult to understand why demands were voiced for closer collaboration
between the organisations serving the miners, railwaymen, and transport
workers.[98]

Gordon Phillips notes that other Labour historians, such as John
Lovell and B. C. Roberts, have written of the 'many signs that the winter
of 1914 might well see an outbreak of serious unrest leading to a general
strike'.[99] It is precisely this view that Phillips is at pains to dismiss as 'a
myth' dependent on two assumptions: that one at least of the parties to
the Alliance was preparing a major action, which would have been
effective; and that the Alliance was intended to deliver mass sympathy
action in response, and was capable of doing so. In fact, most of the
historians referred to by Phillips do not make the bald assertion that the
Alliance sought to deliver a general strike, all neatly packaged and led
from on high by its generals. They see the Alliance much more as a
portent, a harbinger, a symptom of labour and capital moving towards
conflict on a larger and larger scale, with a general strike as the likely
climax. The mechanisms of such a strike cannot be extrapolated from the
material events of the last peacetime months of 1914. Equally, the
tendency towards a generalized strike movement cannot be refuted by
reference to the intentions of leaderships, or to their formal politics, or to
the timings of particular industrial movements and wage demands. All
this would be idle speculation, were it not that the Alliance, cemented in
a formal agreement in 1915, was then put on ice for the duration of the
war, only to emerge as a critical agreement involving the transport
workers in the turbulent post-war years, when they were simultaneously
formulating new industrial relations with employers and taking the last
steps towards the coveted goal of amalgamation.

It is therefore worth tracing Phillips's argument in a little more detail.
It is true, as he asserts and as we have said, that the NTWF was a body
with little or no executive control over its affiliates, and that it was
governed by men who showed both caution in endorsing federal action
and a strong surviving concern for the sectional interest of their
individual unions. The evidence which we have reviewed above confirms
the limited progress made by the NTWF towards co-ordinated
campaigns or agreed programmes within their own ranks.

The Miners' Federation, although simpler in structure, shared with the NTWF a weakness at federal, executive level, though some of its constituent parts had shown the most aggressive, militant tendencies of any of the parties to the Alliance during the Great Unrest.

The NUR was the most 'modern' of the three, in both structure and centralized power, whilst being led by more moderate leaders. Moreover, Phillips presents convincing evidence that the national demand for a new agreement with the railway companies was not likely to have reached any definite deadline in the latter part of 1914, and that this industry was not necessarily poised to be the catalyst of the General Strike. This, however, takes the speculations of history, as of much contemporary opinion, to extreme limits and the discussion begins to turn on the question not of whether but of precisely when the brewing conflict on the railways might have produced a major strike.

The Phillips thesis also relies on the evident absence, in the cases of NTWF and the Miners' Federation, of any substantial central strike fund, which he interprets as a defect large enough to have deterred the calling of a strike in the names of these parent bodies. However, the individual unions of the federations could have sustained a strike, if they had felt that vital interests were involved and that claims had matured to the point where strike action was necessary. We have seen that the NTWF was still in the stage of formulating a national joint claim for the forty-four-hour week, whilst the miners' district wage agreements were not due to expire until 1915.[100] Thus, the problematic element in the notion of a General Strike via the Triple Alliance lies in precisely the problem identified in the first conference: that of the timing (and the co-ordination of the timing) of the claims of the three parties. The parties certainly intended that such co-ordination should be organized; but their statements all concur in expecting that such a formidable threat – the presentation of a combined claim simultaneously – would coerce government into a favourable intervention, and compel realistic negotiation and recognition of their bargaining rights. Phillips dismissed this expectation of 'bloodless victories' too easily, as 'facile confidence'.[101] Had the concertation taken place, it might well have succeeded, at any rate in the beginning. New ploys have a good chance of winning, at least once.

The leaderships, especially that of the NTWF, certainly emphasized that the Alliance was not to be used to support purely sectional militancy. In this sense, the Alliance was seen as a means to control unplanned outbreaks of sympathy action rather than to endorse them. But it was also presented as a means of planning controlled joint actions, which might well be 'sympathetic'. Any trade union may simultaneously frown upon 'unofficial' action, whilst not abandoning the use of the strike weapon. There is no doubt that the Alliance sought to arrange for all its agreements to terminate concurrently. In that event, if one may assume employer intransigence and a failure by government to attempt or to achieve a conciliation, the logic would point to a Triple Alliance mass strike. Whilst the leadership hoped for 'bloodless victories', even the moderate Jimmy Thomas was prepared to contemplate the necessity of a demonstration strike: 'I do not hesitate to say that . . . we shall only use this power once. If we use it effectively, the fear of it will be sufficient for all time after.'[102]

George Askwith was as well placed as anyone to gauge the temper of the time:

The comparative placidity of the summer of 1914 seemed in a measure to be deceptive. It was known that the three years' agreement between the Engineers' Employers' Association and the Amalgamated Society of Engineers was drawing to a close . . . The mining industry was also preparing claims for the autumn. The transport industry had been steadily organising. Those unions, which were principally recruited from semi-skilled and unskilled workpeople, were adding daily to the numbers of their members.[103] The cost of living appeared to be on the upward trend. There was a spirit of unrest which vaguely expressed itself in an oft-heard phrase, 'Wait till the autumn.' I had decided to take a long holiday, so as to get some rest before the strenuous time which promised to be forthcoming in the near future.[104]

Phillips has, however, identified an important secondary function of the Alliance, which was used to heighten the pressures for further rationalization of trade-union structure in all three industries:

'The Sub-committee [of the Alliance]', said Smillie, 'thinks it would be a mistake to open the doors of this proposed combination to all and sundry organisations who might feel that they were to some extent connected with the three industries. What we proposed was, that the section of the [Enginemen and Kindred Trades Federation] that is connected in any way with the mine workers might come in through the Miners' Federation into this joint body in some shape or form; that the locomotive people or any other railway organisation might come in through the railway workers in some shape or form; and that the others connected with the transport workers . . . might come in in some way through them.'[105]

All these currents and themes were explored in the debates on the Alliance held by the NTWF in 1914.

# IV

## Looking Ahead

Writing on the eve of the Amalgamation Conference of 1914, Robert Williams had taken stock of the long march which the transport unions had made, in order to arrive at the threshold of amalgamation. 'The Path to Power', he called it.

Compare the condition of affairs obtaining a quarter of a century ago with that of today. There has been a veritable revolution. Nowadays the large offices of the employers are equipped with everything human ingenuity can devise to serve the employers' interests. There are charts on the walls of the inner offices of some of the great shipping companies showing the state of trade union organisation at the various ports where their ships call from time to time. They employ the most capable brains and intelligence they are able to obtain. Books are written specially for them pointing out how to increase profits and bank balances by minimising human labour. Men, specially chosen by reason of their training and organising capacity, are given a free hand and paid handsome salaries purposely to cut expenses in every direction. Others, equally alert and well-informed, are told off to watch every development of trade union organisation. When our Federation was first formed, we were enabled to put something akin to respect, or maybe fear, into the hearts of the employers and their agents. But since our failure to make good our threat of a national transport strike in 1912, the Federation has gone down like the stick of a rocket after the explosion.

Very well, we have now to show that we are on the path to power. We are in a stronger position than men in other occupations, by reason of the interdependence of our labour. A ship loaded in one port is discharged, or calls at, another port within our sphere of influence. When employers learn, as they have learned, that it takes weeks, or months, to obtain the consent and approval of the Executive of a second or a third Union before assistance can be given to a Union waging a life and death conflict, those employers will – nay, they do – treat us with contempt.

Were our forces effectually combined, and our power unmistakably manifest, there would be less occasion to resort to that power and those forces. We are not entitled to the respect of the employing classes for the simple and obvious reason that we do not respect ourselves and one another. How can we hope to deal with a rapidly improving capitalism and industrialism by a stationary unionism? 'Get on, or get out', forcibly, but briefly, expresses the modern trend of events.

This sharp doctrine could spell out a triumph of narrow conformity and greed; but it could also provoke an altogether more radical response. The men who had led this great pilgrimage had gained vastly in experience. But some of them had also gained immeasurably more in another quality. Now they led a great mass of people; but now, as well as potential influence, their new powers also gave them a truly remarkable insight, amounting to a real vision of a different world:

The First Lord of the Admiralty indicated the other night that liquid fuel was destined to take the place of coal in the British Navy and no doubt the Navies of the world. This must assuredly extend to the Mercantile Marine. What will happen to the fireman and the trimmer? What will happen to the seamen at present employed in the coal tramp? What of the thousands employed in trimming and tipping coal in the large coal-exporting ports? What is to become of the miner when coal is no longer required in the Navy and the Mercantile Marine?

Of course, these thoughts may be put off until the certain results become evident, and shriek aloud to be dealt with. This is a policy of cowardice, and the worst expression of the time-serving spirit. In the near future (sooner than a good many of us think) we shall have to make provision for regulating the work of those engaged in Transport by *Aerial Navigation*. Some day a development fraught with incalculable results will find us unprepared. Coal, gas, and oil power will be superseded by atomic or molecular energy, even as hand, wind, and water power gave way to steam. We need a double dose of Trade Union 'Futurism' to dispel the cobwebs lurking in our brains, and to get an adequate sense of the flux of things, which proceeds as certain as it is imperceptible.[106]

All these industrial phantasms were to become real, and in turn to be organized by trade unions. The TGWU was to play a major part in bringing the union spirit to every part of this 'futuristic' realm. But before any of it was to materalize, millions of men and women were to be slaughtered. It was this agenda of extermination, not the friendly agenda of amalgamation and democratic representation, which was now to dominate the trade-union world, while it tore apart the wider society into a frenzy of bloodlust and destruction.

## Appendix: The Constitution of the Triple Alliance

The following rules were adopted by a delegate conference of miners, railwaymen and transport workers on 9 December 1915 at a meeting in the Westminster Palace Hotel:

(1)   That matters submitted to this joint body, and upon which action may be taken should be those of a national character or vitally affecting a principle, which in the opinion of the executive making the request, necessitates combined action.

(2)   The co-operation of the joint organisation shall not be called upon, nor expected, unless and until the matter in dispute has been considered by and received the endorsement of the national executive of the organisation primarily concerned, and each organisation instituting a movement which is likely to involve the other organisations shall, before any definite steps are taken, submit the whole matter to the joint body for consideration.

(3)   For the purpose of increasing the efficiency of the movement for combined action, periodical meetings of the full executives shall be held at least half yearly.

(4)   There shall be appointed a consultative committee of six, composed of two members from each of the three bodies, whose duty it shall be to meet from time to time, and who shall be empowered at any time to call a conference of the executives of the three bodies if, in their opinion, such a conference be necessary. That a meeting be called on application made by any one of the three bodies.

(5)   With a view to meeting all management expenses incurred each affiliated body shall contribute a sum of ten shillings per one thousand members per annum, or such sum as may be decided upon from time to time.

(6)   Simultaneously with these arrangements for united action between the three organisations in question, every effort shall proceed among the three sections to create effective and complete control of their respective bodies.

(7)   Complete autonomy shall be preserved to any one of the three bodies affiliated to take action on its own behalf.

(8)   Joint action can only be taken when the question at issue has been before the members of the three organisations and decided upon by such methods as the constitution of each organisation provides. A conference shall then be called without delay to consider and decide questions of taking action.

(9)   No obligation shall devolve upon any one of the three bodies to take action unless the foregoing conditions have been complied with.

# Notes

1 ˋ NTWF *Weekly Record*, vol 1, no. 1, March/April 1913, p. 1.
2 Ibid., p. 2.
3 H. A. Clegg, *General Union in a Changing Society* (Basil Blackwell, 1964), p. 49; and Richard Hyman, *The Workers' Union* (Oxford University Press, 1971), pp. 70n. and 122.
4 NTWF *Weekly Record*, 5 July 1913.
5 NTWF Annual General Council Report, 5 and 6 June 1913, p. 24.
6 NTWF *Weekly Record*, 28 June 1913, p. 1.
7 Between 1910 and 1914 the DWRGWU's income from its tinplate section in South Wales increased from £2,198 to £3,292, or by 50 per cent. However, whilst in 1910 this represented about 20 per cent of total income, by 1914 its dependence on this section had fallen to 17 per cent. (*Source*: DWRGWU Annual Reports.)
8 George Woodcock, TUC general secretary, in a debate on the reform of trade-union structure in 1962. See Ken Coates and Tony Topham, *Trade Unions in Britain* (3rd edn, Fontana, 1988), pp. 60–3.
9 Ibid.; and also Jack Jones, *Union Man: An Autobiography* (Collins, 1986), p. 157. On an earlier occasion, Frank Cousins had offered similar resistance to the proposal to rationalize union structure on industrial lines. 'I did not become general secretary of the TGWU in order to preside over its dismemberment.' This theme arises again and again in British trade-union history, and is of heightened significance in any study of the TGWU, with its unashamedly multi-industrial structure and membership. This structure was precisely the product of the long evolutionary process which we have been concerned to trace in this volume. The TGWU leadership has held off the attempts of 'social engineers' of both left- and right-wing persuasion, whose schemes would have rationalized the union out of existence by dividing it into its constituent industrial parts. The question must arise: were Cousins and Jones fighting off these schemes from institutional and self-interested motives, or were they acting as guardians of history's bequest of a structure uniquely shaped by the real needs of a very wide, and ever widening, sector of the working class? Have the successors to Gosling, Tillett and Bevin acted well as history's agents to enable a 'natural' evolutionary process, pointing towards a class-based union, to continue? The extraordinary sequence of mergers into the TGWU since 1922 suggests that they do have such an inherited and continuing task, which now, in the 1990s, reaches over on to the international plane.
10 NTWF Annual General Council Report, 1913, p. 43.
11 Ibid.
12 NTWF Annual General Council Report, 1914, p. 27.
13 Ibid., p. 26.

14   NTWF Annual General Council Report, 1914, pp. 26–7.
15   See chapter 18.
16   NTWF *Weekly Record*, 26 July 1913.
17   NTWF Annual General Council Report, 1914, p. 19.
18   For a biography, see A. W. Wright, *G. D. H. Cole and Socialist Democracy* (Oxford University Press, 1979).
19   G. D. H. Cole and W. Mellor, *The Greater Unionism* (National Labour Press, 1913), p. 14.
20   Ibid., p. 15.
21   Ibid., p. 16.
22   Ibid., p. 17.
23   James Connolly, 'The Problem of Trade Union Organisation', *Forward*, 23 May 1914; reprinted in Dudley Edwards and Bernard Ransom (eds), *James Connolly, Selected Political Writings* (Jonathan Cape, 1973), pp. 324–8; and James Connolly, 'Old Wine in New Bottles', *New Age*, 30 April 1914; reprinted in Peter Berresford Ellis (ed.), *James Connolly, Selected Writings* (Penguin, 1973), pp. 175–80.
24   Connolly sent a telegram to the NTWF Council: 'Secretary, Transport Workers' Congress, Hull. – Coming to Hull to explain Irish Transport case to Congress. Can I obtain permission? Will arrive tonight. Connolly.' He wanted particularly to put the case of scabbing by NTWF members in British ports on ships blacked by the ITGWU. He was refused admission to the Council meeting, as his union was not an affiliate. Tillett moved that he should not be heard.
25   Connolly, 'The Problem of Trade Union Organisation', pp. 324–5.
26   Ibid., pp. 326–7.
27   Ibid., pp. 327–8.
28   Connolly, 'Old Wine in New Bottles', p. 177.
29   Ibid., p. 179.
30   NTWF Annual General Council Report, 1913.
31   James Sexton, *Sir James Sexton, Agitator: the Life of the Dockers' MP* (Faber and Faber, 1936), p. 214.
32   NTWF Annual General Council Report, 1914, p. 65.
33   *Daily Herald*, 22 July 1912; quoted in Gordon Phillips, 'The National Transport Workers' Federation, 1910–1927' (unpublished PhD thesis, Oxford University, 1968), p. 174.
34   NTWF Annual General Council Report, 1914, p. 11.
35   NTWF *Weekly Record*, 30 August 1913: 'The report of the General Council is animated throughout by the German desire for centralisation, discipline, and executive control. Everything tending towards German system is praised, and everything approaching the French Syndicalism and direct action is tactfully censured by our German comrades. The logic appears to be with the Germans in that where the nations are organising industrially by amalgamating similar sectional Unions, there the Trade Unions are most powerful and effective in combating the interest of the employing class.'
36   Phillips, 'The National Transport Workers' Federation', p. 179.
37   B. Pribićević, *The Shop Stewards' Movement and Workers' Control, 1910–1922* (Oxford University Press, 1959), chapter IV.
38   The *Syndicalist*, 12 November 1912. See *The Syndicalist, 1912–1914*

(reproduced in facsimile, with an introduction by Geoff Brown, Bertrand Russell Peace Foundation, for the *Spokesman*, 1975).

39  NTWF Executive Committee Minutes. Report on Amalgamation, 4 November 1913.

40  GLNC and NTWF Joint Executive Committee Meeting Minutes, 13 December 1913.

41  Ibid.

42  Ben Tillett, in his book on the 1911 London transport strike, wrote: 'Will Godfrey was the godsend of the strike. A Sam Wellerian capacity for quaint wit and imperturbable spirit and patience . . . Cheerful when all appeared glum . . . I remember him and his courage to face odds . . . In the weariness of . . . prolonged discussion he set eyes dancing with fun by some outrageous joke as innocently malicious as Puck. (*The Story of the London Transport Workers' Strike, 1911* (National Transport Workers' Federation, 1912), pp. 51–2).

43  NTWF Annual General Council Report, 1914, p. 31.

44  'An All-grades Movement for Transport Workers?', NTWF *Weekly Record*, 17 January 1914.

45  GLNC and NTWF Joint Executive Committee Meeting Minutes, 25 March 1914.

46  NTWF *Weekly Record*, 2 May 1914.

47  GLNC and NTWF Special Conference on Amalgamation Minutes, 8 July 1914.

48  Ibid., p. 24.

49  *Daily Herald*, 5 August 1912; quoted in Jonathan Schneer, *Ben Tillett: Portrait of a Labour Leader* (Croom Helm, 1982), p. 164.

50  GLNC and NTWF Special Conference on Amalgamation Minutes, p. 11.

51  *Liverpool Weekly Courier*, 5 April 1913; quoted in E. L. Taplin, *The Dockers' Union: A Study of the National Union of Dock Labourers, 1889–1922* (Leicester University Press, 1986), p. 121.

52  Quoted in Phillips, 'The National Transport Workers' Federation', p. 185.

53  Ibid.

54  Joint Conference Minutes, p. 25.

55  The immediate impact of the war upon trade-union consciousness can be gauged from the fact that, in their respective Annual Reports in December 1914, neither Tillett nor Sexton so much as mentioned the momentous amalgamation conference which has been our subject in this chapter. Their preoccupations are wholly with the 'war-emergency', the need to support 'our lads in the trenches', and to preserve their jobs for their return.

56  Phillip J. Leng, *The Welsh Dockers* (G. W. and A. Heketh, 1981), p. 59.

57  'Captain' Edward Tupper, *The Seamen's Torch* (Hutchinson, 1938), pp. 50–1.

58  Neil Evans, 'A Tidal Wave of Impatience: The Cardiff General Strike of 1911', in Geraint H. Jenkins and J. B. Smith, *Politics and Society in Wales, 1840–1922* (University of Wales Press, 1988), pp. 135 ff.

59  See Henry Pelling, *Popular Politics and Society in Late Victorian Britain* (Macmillan, 1968), pp. 97 ff.

60  NTWF Annual General Council Report, 1914, p. 11.

61  NTWF *Weekly Record*, 16 April 1914, p. 2.

62  NTWF Executive Committee Minutes, and NTWF *Weekly Record*, no. 55, 16 May 1914.

63  NTWF *Weekly Record*, 16 May 1914, p. 4.

64  Ibid.

65  'Joint Action and Chinese Labour', NTWF *Weekly Record*, 9 May 1914, pp. 2–3.

66  NTWF *Weekly Record*, 4 April 1914, p. 2.

67  NTWF Annual General Council Report, 1914, p. 13.

68  Quoted in Phillips, 'The National Transport Workers' Federation', p. 161.

69  Report on a Court of Inquiry concerning Transport Workers' Wages and Conditions, with Minutes of Evidence and appendices, Cmnd 936 and Cmnd 937, Parliamentary Papers XXXIV 1920 (the Shaw Report), Minutes of Evidence, p. 12.

70  Phillips, 'The National Transport Workers' Federation', p. 166.

71  The NUR was formed by the merging of the Amalgamated Society of Railway Servants, the General Railway Workers' Union, and the Signalmen's Union. Although the footplatemen and the railway clerks remained outside as separate unions, the formation of the NUR created an amalgamation more centralized and comprehensive than either the NTWF or the Miners' Federation. See Phillip Bagwell, *The Railwaymen* (Allen and Unwin, 1963).

72  Phillip Bagwell, 'The Triple Industrial Alliance, 1913–22', in Asa Briggs and John Saville (eds), *Essays in Labour History, 1886–1923* (Macmillan, 1971).

73  NTWF Annual General Council Report, June 1911.

74  DWRGWU Annual Report, 1913, p. 7. The Miners' Federation numbered 870,000, the NUR 268,000 and the NTWF about 163,000 – a total of 1,301,000. Total trade-union membership in 1914 (Great Britain and Northern Ireland) was 4,145,000, having grown by 61 per cent since 1910. On the eve of the war, therefore, the Triple Alliance embraced more than one in four of all trade unionists.

75  NUDL Annual Congress, 1913, p. 61.

76  Taplin, *The Dockers' Union*, p. 125.

77  Quoted in NTWF *Weekly Record*, 25 April 1914, p. 1. A slightly different wording with the same drift is reported in R. Page Arnot, *The Miners: Years of Struggle* (Allen and Unwin, 1953), p. 174.

78  NTWF Annual General Council Report, 22 April 1914.

79  Robert Smillie, article in *Labour Year Book*, 1915; quoted in Arnot, *The Miners: Years of Struggle*, pp. 174–6.

80  NTWF *Weekly Record*, 25 April 1914, p. 1.

81  In their modified form they read as follows: 'That the Conference welcomed the action of the Miners' Federation, and agreed upon the formation of a consultative body consisting of the three organisations. That a sub-committee equally representative of the three organisations be appointed to formulate a scheme for consideration at an ultimate meeting of the Joint Conference. That Joint Secretaries be appointed to secure such details and information as would enable the sub-committee to draw up a scheme or proposals to render operative the powers of the triple alliance.'

82  NTWF Annual General Council Report, 1914, p. 32.

83   Ibid.
84   Ibid., p. 33.
85   Ibid.
86   Robert Williams, *The New Labour Outlook* (Parsons, 1921), pp. 139 and 192; quoted in Bagwell, 'The Triple Industrial Alliance', p. 103.
87   British Socialist Party Manifesto to Railway Workers, MS copy, BSP papers, LSE; quoted in Bob Holton, *British Syndicalism, 1900–1914* (Pluto Press, 1976), p. 172.
88   *Glasgow Herald*, 13 March 1912; quoted in Holton, *British Syndicalism*, p. 173.
89   *Voice of Labour*, 26 June 1914; quoted in Holton, *British Syndicalism*, p. 175.
90   TUC Report, 1915, p. 185.
91   Lord Askwith, *Industrial Problems and Disputes* (John Murray, 1920), p. 356.
92   Elie Halevy, *A History of the English People in the Nineteenth Century*, vol. VI: *The Rule of Democracy, 1905–14* book II, (Ernest Benn, 1934), p. 484.
93   E. H. Phelps Brown, *The Growth of British Industrial Relations: A Study from the Standpoint of 1906–14* (Macmillan, 1960), p. 330.
94   R. C. K. Ensor, *England, 1870–1914* (Oxford University Press, 1936), p. 473.
95   A. J. P. Taylor, *English History, 1914–1945* (Oxford University Press, 1965), p. 140.
96   G. D. H. Cole and Raymond Postgate, *The Common People 1746–1946*, (2nd edn, Methuen, 1946), pp. 470–1.
97   Bagwell, 'The Triple Industrial Alliance', pp. 96–109.
98   Ibid., pp. 97–8.
99   John Lovell and B. C. Roberts, *A Short History of the TUC* (Macmillan, 1968), p. 48; quoted in Gordon Phillips, 'The Triple Industrial Alliance in 1914', *Economic History Review*, vol. 24, no. 1 (1971), pp. 55–67.
100  Ibid., p. 60.
101  Phillips, 'The Triple Industrial Alliance in 1914', p. 173.
102  Ibid., p. 65.
103  Membership of NTWF affiliates in 1913–14.
104  Askwith, *Industrial Problems and Disputes*, p. 356.
105  Speech to the Triple Alliance Joint Executive Committee, 23 April 1914; quoted in Phillips, 'The Triple Alliance in 1914', p. 66.
106  NTWF *Weekly Record*, 27 June 1913.

# 16

# War

## I

### *Mobilizing*

Flags, bugles, drums: suddenly all the nations were in a frenzy of mobilization. First the marching, cheering and countermarching. Then the lust for blood. And then, overhanging all Europe, the stench of death.

Labour had seen it all coming. Many unions were pledged to industrial action against the outbreak of war. The Labour Party, and even more, the two largest socialist groups, the ILP and the BSP, were committed to the decisions of the Socialist (Second) International, at Stuttgart in 1907, and then at Basle in 1912.[1] A new Congress was scheduled for Vienna in August 1914. A Bureau meeting of the International was held at the end of July to finalize the preparations. The French leader, Jean Jaurès, was there, with Keir Hardie, Rosa Luxemburg, the Austrian Victor Adler, and Angelika Balabanova, who was later to become famous as the first secretary of the Comintern. Consternation ruled: the Congress was already announced, and yet its venue was in a country already at war. Keir Hardie announced that if war were declared the British unions 'would at once call a general strike'. Balabanova reminded her colleagues that they themselves were all pledged to similar action by Congress decisions; later she reported that they had looked at her 'as if they thought I was crazy'.[2] In any event, they took no notice. Instead, the Bureau agreed to call for demonstrations.

Hardie and his ILP colleagues appealed for action in Britain. But in London itself, on 4 August, war was declared. In France, Jaurès was shot down by an assassin. Hyndman declared not for demonstrations but for belligerence, and *Justice* announced preparations to resume the class struggle after the hostilities, implying its present adjournment. The International, all across Europe, crumbled into fragments, its adherents tumbling every which way. While they were implementing the Bureau's call for mass meetings, those British Socialists who sought to uphold its writ were reading of this collapse. Dismay was complete. A joint board of representatives of the TUC, the Labour Party and the General Federation of Trade Unions, together with a variety of senior personalities, had been convened by Arthur Henderson to set up a Peace Emergency Committee to keep Britain out of war. When it met on 5 August, the deed had already been done. On the same day, Ramsay MacDonald, a pacifist, resigned as leader of the Parliamentary Labour Party and Henderson (known in the Labour movement as 'Uncle Arthur') took his place. 'The meeting wasted no time reflecting upon its original purposes ... It rather addressed itself to the matter in hand, resolving to establish a committee which would be responsible for safeguarding working-class interests during the "Emergency". And it stuck to its last.'[3] So was born the War Emergency Workers' National Committee. The translation of the name was apparently effortless.

From the TUC Gosling was among the nominees who joined the new Committee. Tillett's name went forward from the General Federation of Trade Unions. An inaugural conference nominated six more people to join the nine set in place by the three convening organizations. The new people included Bob Smillie, Sidney Webb, Dr Marion Phillips of the Women's Labour League, Mary MacArthur and H. M. Hyndman. Co-option then began, more than doubling the initial tally of Committee members. Among those to enter in this way was Bob Williams. Later, the BSP said that Hyndman no longer represented them; but because he had been elected at the beginning, the Committee claimed he could not be dropped. Instead they co-opted Tom Quelch (Harry's son) as an additional member to watch the interests of the BSP.

Arthur Henderson was elected chairman at the very beginning. He showed great skill in keeping the Committee together, in spite of all the acrimonious controversies about the war which divided it. In this process he established the ascendancy which made him a natural candidate for co-option into the government in 1915.

## Trade Union Advance

While the other unions were looking to defend their territories from the effects of war, the affiliates of the National Transport Workers' Federation, too, kept a sharp focus on their previous objectives. As a result they made dramatic advances after 1914. The Federation put its head down to pursue recognition, the establishment of national wage standards, greater control in casual labour industries, and the greater centralization of its own powers. Each objective helped in leading towards the eventual amalgamation of 1922. In common with other unions, those in transport gathered membership, and strength. They also won a new status in measuring up to the employers and the state. Total war meant labour shortage. All available labour was deployed either in slaughter, the production and transportation of the means of slaughter, or in the fuelling and feeding of the machines and the people engaged in slaughter. In this macabre landscape, which could have been mapped only by Hieronymus Bosch, lay the devilish forcing ground in which, for better or worse, the main features of modern British industrial relations germinated.

## Casualties

The price of these advances was not small. It was paid in human souls. A lot of them were necessary: from Britain alone 750,000 young men were sent to be chewed up into bones and mud. They came, as Ben Tillett never tired of insisting, overwhelmingly from the working class. In addition to the dead, twice as many others were injured or incapacitated. Eyes, arms, legs were lost. An army of cripples, larger than all the ghostly mutilated hordes of all previous wars, inexorably formed its ranks. Along with the survivors, these Britons helped kill off even greater numbers of German workers. These were the comrades with whom, up until 4 August 1914, many of them had been associated in the recently established international organs of the European labour movement.

Ideas, as well as men, were wrenched and tested in this bloodstorm. Like men, they were also ripped apart. One such casualty was the notion of internationalism. Anti-German sentiment was, of course, carried to obsessional limits. No lie was so preposterous that it could not find believers. Yet the truth was so horrendous and full of dread that even those who knew it dared not entertain it. In Britain, the Germans were not the only sufferers. British labour also responded with a ferocious racism to the accelerated influx of Chinese and 'coloured' labour into the shipping and port industries during the war. 'Social imperialism' flourished in an upsurge of nationalist fervour. And the economic truce declared by the trade unions in 1914, and largely sustained, by at least some of their leaders, throughout the conflict, offered employers the opportunity for some very greedy profiteering.

At the same time the state took its chance to experiment in active intervention, in perfecting means of regulating the labour market and in incorporating the representatives of labour and capital into jointly staffed structures of control. Sometimes the experiments did not work. Often, though, they did. In turn, some trade unions were led to frame counterproposals in the effort to hold off this incorporation, seeking instead genuine advances for controls by the workpeople.

Whilst the transport workers' unions participated in the industrial truce, they neither abandoned their defence of labour's civil liberties, nor in the main did they condone the attempted militarisation of their industries. Their response to state incorporation was watchful and wary: they answered to a series of such attempts by urging an advance in the effective powers of their representatives. These responses came easily to a generation nurtured in the days of syndicalism, and they ensured that within the structures set up for bargaining, arbitration, consultation and the joint management of the wartime labour market, unions retained their independence and kept to their own priorities. For the most part, then, they gained on the industrial dimension even whilst they were offering broad support for the war. Such support was tempered by increasingly critical views of military strategy and of the government's war aims, as the war moved through its wearying length. However, until 1917, they failed to defend real wage rates against rising inflation, even if earnings rose with the regularity of war-generated work. These tensions ensure that we shall need to distinguish different degrees of patriotic commitment, and different degrees of internationalism, amongst the leaders of the transport and general unions, in their conduct of industrial matters no less than in their wider political roles.

It is difficult to provide a chronological story of this fraught time. Life in war is compressed by the continual presence of death and the threats of death. Time shrinks. Days may bring events enough to need months or years to digest. Convulsive adjustments follow hasty and wrong judgements. People snap. At such times, there is a yearning for routine, within which the larger madness can be accommodated. But in the next moment, old conventions may come to seem irrelevant, irrational, unsustainable. We are concerned to follow the sharp shifts in the evolution of trade-union power among the transport workers, but first we need to trace their reactions to the horrors in which they were toiling. This forces us to portray what was really one process as two distinct, political and industrial, trajectories. This is an artificial procedure, but were we not to follow it, the complex interactions which took place would require a whole volume before we could begin to do them justice. We will be forgiven, we think, when it is remembered that grief continually visited the families of those whose witness we record in the effort to regulate the procedures of work, and that legions of good union men were among those who left behind the new industrial institutions as they were drafted into sacrifice in that immense carnage.

The immediate industrial response of labour to the war was to declare an embargo on all current and pending claims and disputes. This was the first result of the War Emergency Workers' National Committee. Its most important effect was to postpone indefinitely any test of the strike potential of the Triple Alliance, whose formal rules were in any case not agreed until 1915. The dockers, as we have seen, had been preparing their claim for a forty-four-hour week, but it was shelved in the atmosphere of war-fever engendered in 1914.

We have already referred to Bevin's account of this development above (chapter 15), but we might recall here his words on patriotism:

> We were asked, 'Do not press your claims now when the country is in the throes of danger,' and we said, 'Very good,' and we withdrew our claim . . . The whole of us worked patriotically, as you know. I do not use the word 'patriotically' in a vulgar sense, and in fact I would like not to use it, it has been so abused, and I only use it for want of another word.[4]

Behind Bevin's distaste for the 'vulgar sense' of patriotism lies a subtle judgement. He was constantly at pains to distance himself from the chauvinism which was defended by some of his closest colleagues in the dockers' unions and beyond them. Indeed, he was himself among the orators opposing the war at a mass meeting on the Bristol docks during the first weekend of hostilities. He called for international action to stop the war, in the spirit of a resolution he had supported at the International Federation of Trade Unions, favouring a general strike if war appeared likely.[5]

Union self-denial in pressing the claim for shorter hours was particularly altruistic, when we recall that the trade union feared that the outbreak of war might bring about economic dislocation and widespread unemployment. This expectation now seems incredible, given what subsequent history has taught us concerning the all-inclusive nature of modern warfare. But in 1914, memories of British involvement in wars between the superpowers of mainland Europe had stopped at Waterloo, almost a century earlier. Then military technology was still simple, and relatively innocent. Slaughter at that time was heavy, tiring manual labour, not a mechanical process. Civilization had now advanced far beyond the Napoleonic Wars, into vast new hecatombs. Its demands for young bodies were insatiable.

But the early months of the war witnessed troubles which seemed to bear out the prediction of gross disruption. In July 1914, trade-union unemployment benefit was paid out to 2.8 per cent of members involved in it; after three weeks of war, the figure had jumped to 7.1 per cent.

## Man- and Womanpower Shortage

However, thereafter unemployment fell, and it then remained at minimal levels throughout the war, while the unsleeping demands of military strategy ate men alive, and also swallowed an uncountable treasure. Out of a total male labour force of 15 million, some 5.6 million were enlisted in the armed forces. Male civilian employment fell by only 2.4 million between 1914 and 1918; in compensation, female employment rose by 1.6 million over the same period, though its contribution to the so-called 'war trades' was certainly more than this, as women not only came fresh, for the first time, into the labour market, but also transferred within it from domestic labour into the munitions – and transport – industries. Formerly unemployed labour was also absorbed, of course.

Whether these shifts and enrolments compensated fully for the withdrawal of 5.6 million men, and whether, therefore, a 'labour shortage' existed in an absolute sense, was a critical question both for the state, intent on total war, and for the trade unions, seeking to protect their independence in the face of all the pressures of the war. The heat was on, from the state, the military, the employers and, not least, the Northcliffe press, which aimed to place the onus for meeting delivery dates, and the ending of traffic congestions, on labour's shoulders.

Lord Kitchener, a soldier somewhat reluctantly transmogrified into Secretary of State for War, discerned early on that the war would run on for years, and not, as was widely hoped, conclude itself after a few intense weeks or months. He demanded the enrolment of 'an army of millions'.[6] When Premier Asquith ruled out conscription as politically unacceptable, Kitchener launched his voluntary recruitment campaign, with that famous poster 'Your country needs YOU!' The initial response was dramatic: '175,000 had enlisted in the single week ending 5 September; 750,000 had enlisted by the end of September. Thereafter the average ran at 125,000 men a month until June 1915 when it slackened off. In all over two and half million men enlisted before voluntary recruitment came to an end in March 1916.'[7]

## Working-class Patriots . . .

In the face of this surge of largely working-class patriotism, the resistance of the Labour movement to the war collapsed. On the eve of its outbreak, Keir Hardie had addressed a mass rally in Trafalgar Square. 'Down with the imperialist war,' he had cried. 'Long Live the Class War!' That rally had been part of a nationwide campaign, spearheaded by local Trades and Labour Councils. But before the end of August, the TUC and the Labour Party had withdrawn their opposition and endorsed the recruitment campaign. Hardie himself wrote that it would be wrong to confront and defy the popular mood. Soon after, his heart broke. Even amongst workers not caught up into the forces, the evidence suggests that people actually competed for the first War Service Badges which were issued to those deemed to be engaged on work of national importance. Such emblems were worn with pride.[8]

For the most part, trade-union leaders went along with this drift in their messages to their members. This did not stop them stressing that solidarity with the armed forces was a class question, because the army was overwhelmingly recruited from among working people. Nor was their message uncritical of the origins of the war, or of its conduct and aims. Rage was directed quite as much against the employers' record profits as against the Germans. Ben Tillett, who was later to become as bellicose as any Blimp, opened his Annual Report of December 1914 with a powerful indictment of militarism:

> Whoever fomented this war could not have counted the cost, let alone estimated the evil. This war is absolutely wanton and brutal in every feature. The greatest argument against militarism is this war . . . The curse of it all is the hypocrisy of diplomacy and intelligent cunning that again assert themselves in our pastors and masters of loud unquestioned authority. As it is, those responsible for the conduct of the war, its risks and sacrifices, are the very men and the very class who are in no way responsible for the war, and appear to have as little desire for a voice and representation as they now possess power to determine policy or the conduct of the war. The measure of the capitalists' exploitation of the war is that in proportion to profits achieved there is an inverse ratio of responsibility and share of the risks and sacrifices of war . . . 96 per cent of the men at the front belong to the great industrial classes . . .

These people had given life and service, willingly 'and almost blindly' in the interest of the country, he said, adding that 'the burdens of war like the burdens of industry fall on the shoulders of the toilers . . . Any action in retarding supplies, ammunition or hospital arrangements acts directly upon men of their own class.' By contrast, Tillett rounded on the men of another class:

> In some cases, capitalists have become carrion crows living on the dead and dying. These thieves would not make decent scavengers. When the history of this war is written it will be shown that our army and country generally has been bled by the most rapacious type of capitalist that has ever cursed the world. Up to now, none of our statesmen in responsible positions or the press have ventured to criticise the greatest gang of thieves and looters that has ever despoiled humanity, and despoiled it, mind you, in a period of war.[9]

Against the rapacity of the capitalist class the dockers' leader counterposed 'the very best of the poorest class, as well as the best of the oldest and so-called highest families, [who] appear to share the duties and responsibilities of the war.'[10]

Tillet was voicing a view which was widely held. His picture of British society was shared by more and more working people. The clouded class structure had been made transparent by the war, particularly to the front-line troops themselves. It was this heightened awareness that lent popularity to the call, which Tillett supported, for 'the conscription of wealth', which was taken up by the TUC itself when people began to be conscripted in 1916. But Tillett became heavily committed to a new role, as an unofficial liaison officer between the army establishment and the patriotic wing of the movement. When not ill, he was frequently to be found 'at the front'. He was taken up and befriended by Lord Kitchener himself, who subtly pointed out to Tillett the new ambivalence of his situation. The Countess of Warwick noted:

> During those early days of the War, my friend Ben Tillett used to visit Kitchener a great deal at the War Office. He told me once, after Kitchener had said that he believed the War would last for years, that he took his arm and led him to the window.
> 'Do you see those lamp-posts?' he inquired, and Ben, amazed at the question, nodded.
> 'I should not be surprised if you and I were hanging from them before this thing is over,' said Kitchener gravely.[11]

Kitchener perhaps had a better appreciation than his new friend of the social implications of diplomacy.

## . . . and Internationalists

Other transport leaders sought to sustain internationalism and to question the war's legitimacy and purpose. In the first week of war, Robert Williams opened the NTWF *Weekly Record* with this plea:

> We know full well that the German working men hate war as much as we do ourselves . . . Let us who can, be calm during the next few weeks. Let us rigorously suppress the blood lust in ourselves, and among those whom we can influence . . . These myriads of Russia, France, Austria, Germany, – what quarrel can they have amongst one another? What sympathy has the French peasant and the French industrial worker with Russia that in order to support a tottering despotism, they shall attempt to butcher other German workers, who are divided from them by an imaginary line called a frontier? Why are hundreds of British transport workers torn from their occupations and their little homes to join the naval reserves . . . in anticipation of a naval engagement the carnage of which will blacken our reputation for centuries? This German fleet may easily contain reservists from the German working class who contributed £5000 to the London Transport Workers when they were fighting the 'patriotic' London Employers . . . [12]

Yet in spite of this call for calm, Williams none the less found something to support in the nationalist programme of Hyndman, who called for the government to 'resolve itself into a "Committee of National

Security"'. The state should, said Williams, 'in its corporate capacity, assume complete responsibility' for the prosecution of the war, on communistic lines, exacting payment 'from each according to his or her ability', and giving 'unto each according to his or her needs'.[13]

This was the agonized social and industrial programme which the left wing of trade unionism presented as a response to the moral dilemmas created by the war. Robert Williams, like some others, adopted this stance with deep misgivings and continued all the while to take part in anti-war, pacifist movements and initiatives. Williams managed to raise a most courageous voice for peace, even whilst he himself was engaged in the administration of the war-effort as a (very capable) troubleshooter in the transport industry (see chapter 17). Bevin was of this same school of thought. He sought out every means to extend trade-union power, wherever unions were called on to assume greater responsibilities for keeping industrial peace and for labour supply in the ports and inland transport.

## Other Trends of Thought

A few 'super-patriots', led in the transport field by Havelock Wilson, regarded the argument for equality of sacrifice as subversive. In 1916 Wilson threatened to secede from the NTWF because its Annual General Council had opted for the mobilization of wealth. The Executive had no difficulty in rejecting the criticism, pointing out to Wilson that the TUC itself had made a similar call, and that the Prime Minister had promised that he would, 'if necessary', consider a special capital levy to help finance the war. Wilson's anger was not assuaged. His attitude was later characterized by Royden Harrison as typical of the 'hun-hating jingoes' who led the trade-union war party.[14]

In addition to these super-patriots, Harrison discerned three other trends: a 'sane patriot' tendency, the pacifists like Williams, and the revolutionary defeatists. Among the members of the group of restrained patriots he included John Bromley of the railwaymen, as well as Tom Mann. To support this judgement, which he qualifies by saying that 'Mann's attitude . . . is difficult to discover', he cites a report in *The Times* of a speech on conscription to the Scottish TUC: 'He would do everything possible to make ourselves and our allies more efficient in the conduct of the War, but no definite facts had been placed before the country to show that compulsion was necessary.'[15] We have uncovered much more evidence than this to authenticate Harrison's hunch, but it makes it more difficult to separate one kind of patriot from another.

In fact, Tom Mann also spoke on conscription to the NTWF AGC which debated the subject in 1916, and we shall consider his intervention shortly. It is enough here to say that it confirms Harrison's view. But we must not overlook the fact that Mann's relations with Wilson were, at this time, very close indeed. In January 1915, at the Sailors' and Firemen's Union Conference in the Caxton Hall, Wilson delivered what, for him, was a measured statement on the war: 'My feeling is that we had but one course to pursue in this country, and that was to maintain our honour and integrity.'[16] It was necessary, however, 'to crush this damnable military system which . . . [the Germans] have been certainly the foremost nation in creating'.

The bulk of Wilson's speech, however, concerned the measures taken by his Executive to share responsibility for the internment of hundreds of German seamen who were, at the outbreak of hostilities, employed in the British merchant marine. Half of them were loyal union men. Tom Mann, as an executive councillor of the union, delivered a speech of thanks for Wilson's address. He was glad, he said, to have been identified with Wilson:

> The Chairman has made some very wise remarks concerning the war. I am glad he did not touch upon it more, but I am exceedingly glad he touched upon it as he did, with a complete absence of any silly racial animosity, and with a frank and manly recognition of the organization for those men who stood by us when times were exceedingly trying. (Hear, hear.) It was nice to hear how his remarks were received. If that spirit could only prevail throughout now where difficulties take place, we should very soon have a termination of this nasty war. (Applause.) It is pleasing that the initial steps taken here, should have been of that manly character. It is nice to me to be identified with men who preach that sort of genuine brotherly fraternity; and in spite of all the papers have been doing, and others in high places, it is pleasing to find that they have not succeeded in poisoning the minds of men against the men who have lived like ourselves, but in other circumstances. But the spirit of genuine fraternisation has manifested itself throughout this organization in the attitude of the Union, shaped by its President largely, and to him be very largely the credit.[17]

(Later in the same conference Tom Mann threw his considerable influence into the argument against affiliation to the Labour Party, speaking from a syndicalist position.)

The British seamen very quickly abandoned all the finer sentiments about internment expressed by the leaders, as the torpedoes began to claim a grisly toll in sailors' lives.

By the time of the next Conference, on 26 September 1916, attitudes had polarized, and Wilson's position on the war had become much more embittered. But Tom Mann still moved the vote of thanks 'for that magnificent address [which] I very much wish could be delivered a thousand times over throughout the country'. Wilson, he thought, should write his memoirs. His health and mental vitality had 'delighted' the delegates.[18] Few more gracious thanks-offerings have been moved, and it hardly surprises us that the Conference went on to elect Tom Mann, alongside Captain Tupper, as an honorary member.[19]

If it is difficult to sustain the division between extreme chauvinists and 'sane' patriots, there was, for all that, a discernible difference. War worked away to erode it. The climate in which judgements were made was often far from reasonable, and the 'facts' upon which they were based were often corrupted or even false. It is easier to demarcate the division in the anti-war camp, between pacifists like Williams and Charles Ammon, (secretary of the clerical workers' union for dock staffs in London), and revolutionary defeatists like James Connolly, or John Maclean in Scotland. But even this could be occluded, and as war-weariness developed, opposition became more self-assured, intransigent, even defiant.

Few sets of opinions can be more vigorously advanced or contested than those involving war and peace, which imply death or life. But war brings vast uncertainties within its turbulence, and thought can shift swiftly between extremes. The four trade-union 'schools' were not exempt from the traumas in which people learned, and unlearned, their attitudes.

For trade unions, there were the bitterly established affinities of class, won in prolonged struggles; there also remained a variable but strong allegiance to nationality. These commitments could clash, or could appear to run concentric one with another – it all depended where you stood. If you saw it all with a dispassionate eye, the whole picture showed a violent incompatibility. Miracles of production created uncountable piles of corpses. But living close to the ground, far from the mayhem, it could seem that war meant more considerate bosses and a higher level of earnings, because of longer hours in more secure jobs. Given that the dead cannot vote, patriotism was an option that might last out. Given that the living might rebel, it was by no means securely established.

In one zone of the world, the war was late to arrive. The United States was in no rush to enter the destruction, and its neutrality excited willing belligerents and pacifists alike. Trade unionists, too, maintained a keen interest in American attitudes.

## Braving the U-boats

Ernest Bevin was a delegate to the 1915 TUC, where he moved a resolution to press for the appointment of a fully fledged Minister of Labour with an appropriate department. He was also appointed fraternal delegate to the American Federation of Labour (AFL), whose Congress was to be held within a matter of weeks in San Francisco. This responsibility was normally considered a plum, and competition could therefore be stiff. But in 1915 the Atlantic was full of U-boats, and volunteers were markedly more difficult to find. He went along with Charles Ammon, who is remembered for his work for Post Office trade unionism, but who was to become, as a result of wartime victimization because of his pacifism, acting general secretary of the National Union of Docks, Wharves and Shipping Staffs. This organized clerical, administrative and supervisory personnel in the London docks,[20] and was to be one of the key unions participating in the 1922 amalgamation which brought the TGWU into being. It was significant that these two leaders stepped forward to brave the siege of the submarines: certainly this was an act of solidarity with the seamen, but it was also extremely hazardous. Ammon was a pacifist, no doubt keen to meet American neutralists.

There are various detailed accounts of the work of the American delegation, including descriptions of Bevin's cordial relations with the cigar-makers' leader, Samuel Gompers.[21] There is no doubt that the two men got on well together. They continued to do so, and many years later Bevin sealed the North Atlantic Treaty with the gold ring Gompers had given him in 1915. 'What have you got there?' the American had asked when he had been unable to get his gift to fit over Bevin's sturdy finger: 'A bunch of bananas?'

Most accounts of the visit naturally dwell on what Bevin learned from his hosts in the AFL. Naturally, this was a lot. Not the least lesson was the value of a solid and impressive headquarters office, since at the time the AFL was feverishly building on a lavish scale. It is very probably the AFL example which inspired the tremendous effort which was to create Transport House, an office which was not only to house the TGWU, but also, for many years, the TUC and the Labour Party as well. But the United States was also the home of the idea of One Big Union and of its defenders, the Industrial Workers of the World. This abrasive campaigning group was never popular in Gompers' office: however, Gompers' strong opposition to revolutionary syndicalism would, contrary to the suppositions of some of Bevin's biographers, have been greatly muted in the autumn of 1915.

## 'One Big Union' Martyr

This was the year in which the AFL rallied to the defence of Joe Hill, a Swedish American who had been 'railroaded' on a murder charge during his union recruitment campaign among copper-miners in Utah. Joe Hill was an archetypal 'Wobbly', who tramped the entire area of the United States with a union tract in one hand and a songbook in the other. He wrote innumerable ditties for the Wobblies and, after his execution, was himself the subject of a famous ballad. Legions of trade unionists have been moved to tears by the great American bass Paul Robeson singing 'I dreamed I saw Joe Hill last night / Alive as you or me.'

At the San Francisco Congress that year another later IWW martyr,

Tom Mooney, made an impassioned plea for action in defence of Joe Hill.[22] Bevin cannot have missed this event, which impelled Gompers and his associates to a whole series of desperate efforts to save Hill's life. Telegrams went to President Wilson, the Swedish Ambassador and all the relevant judicial bodies. The President responded, but he could not win a reprieve. All these fraught activities were, after many years, to inspire the lyrically beautiful Swedish film by Bo Widerberg, *Joe Hill* (1971).

Joe Hill sacrificed his life in the cause of One Big Union. Warmly though Bevin may have responded to his more respectable American host, it is inconceivable that he did not also hear the echo from the firing squad at Joe Hill's execution. 'Don't mourn – organize', were the victim's last words to Bill Haywood.[23] His own will he composed in a short poem:

> My will is easy to decide
> For there is nothing to divide.
> My kin don't need to fuss and moan
> 'Moss does not cling to rolling stone'.
>
> My body? Oh! If I could choose,
> I would to ashes it reduce
> And let the merry breezes blow
> My dust to where some flowers grow.
>
> Perhaps some fading flower then
> Would come to life and bloom again.
> This is my last and formal will
> Good luck to all of you.
>
> JOE HILL

## A Labour Peace Conference?

Whatever the British transport workers' leaders thought about these tragic events, there were two important consequences of this visit.

First, when Gompers invited the 1916 TUC to join a Labour Peace Congress, to be held concurrently with the Congress of Nations which would finally settle the issues at stake at the end of the war, Bevin bravely defended this proposal at the same time that he reported back on his journey. Gompers' appeal had the qualified support of the Parliamentary Committee, but it could not carry, because of the fierce heat of anti-German feeling. Delegates were enraged at the very idea of dialogue with Germans. 'You have got to take the Germans into consultation after this war,' argued Bevin:

Everybody in this Congress will agree that the present war has largely arisen as a result of the settlements of every other war in Europe . . . It has not come about . . . because a certain monarch's son was killed by a Serbian revolutionist. I stand here for a republic of Europe . . . for the complete democracy ruling throughout Europe; but that seems impossible for the moment . . . [24]

None the less, he thought, 'the attitude of organised Labour towards the peace is worthy of a special Congress.' The courage of this utterance is matched only by the breadth of its vision. The American delegation had widened Bevin's outlook, and carried him to new perspectives. He was still stirred by these many years afterwards.[25]

The second consequence led to success. Bevin and Ammon must surely have come very close together, not only in their exciting tour of the United States, but even more in the ordeal of their voyage. Surely it is not an accident that the Staff Union was so early to join the last push to amalgamation, even before Sexton and his colleagues had been finally brought to agree?

## Prices and Profits Rise: the Federation Protests

The cost of living rose by 25 per cent in the first year of war, with food prices escalating by 32 per cent. From November 1915 until April 1916, the index held steady at 35 per cent above its pre-war level, but by June it leapt to 45 per cent over 1914. By the war's end the pound had lost two-thirds of its pre-war purchasing power, and wage-rates did not overtake this inflation until 1917, although overtime earnings afforded some compensation. Caught between these averages, of course, were seriously deprived groups. There were others who enjoyed sizeable sectional gains in their real wages. Working-class discontent was fired above all by exorbitant food prices and house rents, both of which triggered serious strikes and demonstrations. Food shortages in 1917–18 created further unrest and a political crisis for government, as front-line troops reacted to the news from home with real hostility and anger.

The greatest wrath was directed against war profiteering. The very term 'profiteering', coined at this time, suggests the abiding sense of 'fairness' – described in some areas as the principle of 'fairation' – with which the working class and the soldiers expressed their demands for 'equality of sacrifice'. The NTWF reflected this feeling in constant complaints directed against maritime profits in particular: of all trades, the shipping industry became the most notorious for its exploitation of the war emergency to inflate charges without scruple. The official figures of average dividends throughout industry had been rising steadily since 1908, when they were 6.3 per cent. By 1916–17 they had reached 10.2 per cent. But within this figure were concealed the much higher-than-average earnings in shipping, where dividends reached 13.1 per cent in

1916 and for several years thereafter. Moreover, shipping firms put large sums to reserve; dividends by no means reflected total profitability.[26]

The Executive of the NTWF presented an analysis of shipping freight charges and profits to the 1916 AGC, which occupies nine pages of tabular and statistical material. Nevertheless it opens by asserting that 'It would require an encyclopaedic volume to deal adequately with an analysis of freight change effected during the war'.[27]

We may cite some examples from the Report. Freight charges per ton from Bombay to the UK were 11s. in 1914, and from Burma to the UK 19s. 6d. By mid-1916 they had reached 150–80s. From the Welsh ports, charges for outward cargos to French ports before the war ranged from 4s. 6d. to 7s. 6d. By June 1916 they had reached, in one case (to Rouen), 46s. 6d. Charges to Genoa rose in the same period from 7s. 6d. to 100s. The report also cites a *Times* survey which gives an example of a shipping company making £5,000 profit pre-war on a single ship, which increased to £89,248 in 1916: 'Of this amount, the State, at this period, would take Excess profits Duty of 50%, £44,629, leaving the owners the handsome sum of £44,624 for a year's working on an estimated value [of the ship], of £35,280.'[28] The Oceanic Steam Navigation Company did not even try to conceal its rapacity: it declared an actual dividend of 65 per cent in 1915, but the available profit would have sufficed for a bonus, additional to that dividend, of 100 per cent.[29]

The Board of Trade *Labour Gazette* for June 1916 produced figures to show that the retail price of food had risen by 59 per cent since 1914, and that the combined costs of food, rent, clothing, fuel and light had risen by 40 per cent, 'disregarding increased taxation'. But, commented the NTWF, 'the officials of the Board of Trade may afford to disregard increased taxation, but the workers cannot . . . The tea consumed by the workers pays 50 to 60 per cent tax; that consumed by the rich pays not more than 25 per cent.'

Harry Gosling's presidential address that year reflected on these figures:

whilst the Central Powers have been blockaded by our matchless Navy . . . we in this country have been blockaded by the power exercised by the shipowners . . . Had we, on behalf of the transport workers . . . taken advantage of the monopoly of our labour power as the shipowners have taken advantage of the monopoly of their ships, we could have doubled, trebled, or increased more than tenfold the wages of our labour, as the shipowners have multiplied by more than twenty times the freight rates for the use of their ships. Now, as in all other instances, we have manifested a patriotism far higher and more self-sacrificing than those who live on the labour of the common people.[30]

Freight charges were belatedly brought under government control in 1917. Perhaps the NTWF protests helped to provoke this measure.

Certainly the reports of civil servants, arbitrators and spies, which reached government ears, indicated the strength of feeling which was building up on the question. But the Federation, in promoting 'patriotism', was arguably failing in its trade-union duty to protect its members' living standards. Money wage increases, it claimed in 1916, had not advanced by as much as 40 per cent: a decline in real wages was the result of both the profiteering, the inflation and the extreme reluctance of the unions to pursue wage claims which might appear 'unpatriotic'.

## Closing Time and the Birth of the 'Welt'

Because of this caution, the government was slow to move in controlling rents, prices and profits. It was also tardy in recognizing labour's right to participate in controls over the supply of labour, materials and transport, and reluctant to treat the unions even as junior partners in the war-effort. The attitude of government and ruling class towards the working-class war-effort can be seen in the early legislation which limited the opening hours of the public houses, and which decreed, quite literally, that the workers' beer should be watered down in strength. This was supposed to curtail alleged drunkenness in the munitions factories and other essential war-work. It was widely resented, and Tillett, among others, took it as just one more insult to his class, and one more curtailment of civil liberties.[31] Whilst King George V announced that he had taken 'the Pledge' for the duration, his example was not always followed, either by the peers of his realm or by his government.

An unforeseen and permanent consequence of the new licensing law – which imposed an afternoon closure of the pubs and gave rise to the cry 'Time Gentlemen Please!' at 10 p.m. – was recounted at the Shaw Inquiry in 1920. Sir Alfred Booth, a leading Liverpool port employer, told the story. In 1919 the employers reached agreement with the NTWF for a forty-four-hour week. In implementing this in Liverpool, the negotiators wished to preserve the practice of dividing the work into unbroken four-hour spells. Before the war a 'half-night', or evening, overtime shift had been worked, from 6 to 10.30 p.m. The men would commence work at 1 p.m. and take an hour's break for tea from 5 to 6 pm. They then worked through until 10.30, but,

> During the war, owing to the alteration in the hours when public houses were closed, the men adopted the alternative arrangement . . . of working through, as we call it, from 5 to 9 instead of going away to tea; so that the men were actually supposed to be at work from 1 o'clock until 9 o'clock without a break. Obviously this was an impossible engagement from any decent working point of view, but the men insisted on working that

engagement in order that they might get through their work early and the employers had to fall in with that arrangement in spite of the obvious objection to it being physically impossible to give good work for such a stretch without slipping away for refreshment. More and more the practice of slipping away for twenty minutes or for ten minutes or half an hour for tea in the afternoon while work was kept nominally going crept in, and grew to be an established practice. It had to be recognized, because, obviously, no man could work from 1 o'clock in the afternoon until 9 o'clock at night without a break at all. The great objection was that they had a recognized slip-away time at this time, and it became almost impossible to prevent unrecognized slipping away at other times.

The employers sought to end the practice by paying overtime rates for the evening work and cutting the finishing time from 10.30 to 10 p.m. They laboured for weeks with the union negotiatiors, and, Booth said, 'I thought myself that I had never done a better three-weeks' work in my life, because here we had a process of working which would promote efficiency and output, and treat the men as they ought to be treated, as human beings. They would not be expected to work for impossible spells without going away'. But the men refused to work the new hours. The employers, in desperation, said they would modify the system 'in any way the men might suggest. We would make it from 5.30 to 9.30, so that they could get out to the public houses before they closed at 10 o'clock'; they offered other variations to the same purpose, 'but it was useless.'[32]

In order to curtail the working man's drinking habits, the government had inadvertently provoked what was to become the famous (or notorious) dockers' tradition of 'the Welt', under which half the gang works whilst the other half goes 'welting', which means that it 'slips away' to the coffee shop! Sir Alfred's story ends sadly:

So that the whole work which we had done in arriving at an agreement which I hoped was going to lead to efficiency and good work in the docks was thrown away, and we had to go back to the old arrangement of working through from 1 o'clock until 9 o'clock with the men slipping away for their tea as before, with the natural consequence that the men slip away at all times of the day, and we cannot help it.[33]

This might be thought to have constituted an object lesson to government in how not to treat free, civilian workers in a national emergency.

## Responsibility . . . and Power?

Under Lloyd George's premiership, which, in December 1916 succeeded that of Asquith, Labour, in the shape of Arthur Henderson, was co-opted into the War Cabinet, albeit as a rather junior partner. This move was strongly opposed by Ernest Bevin. The TUC was now consulted on general labour matters, and trade unions in key industries – ranging from munitions to mines, railways, and transport – were invited to place nominees on a plethora of government committees. Initially they were offered minority roles; the NTWF pressed again and again to be accorded power, as well as responsibility. Some concessions in this direction were forthcoming. The Prime Minister received deputations from both the Triple Alliance and the Federation. In 1915, of course, as Minister of Munitions, he had already handled the more famous meeting with thirty-six unions, including the Federation as well as Beard and Duncan of the Workers' Union, from which arose the Treasury Agreement terminating strikes and pre-war restrictive practices.

But the agreement was soon to be followed by compulsion. The Munitions of War Act, 1915, prohibited strikes and ushered in compulsory arbitration. This edged in the direction of military discipline over the civilian workforce. Munitions Tribunals, acting with less formality than courts of law, and with a labour representative on their panels, nevertheless afforded employers powers to impose new disciplines on workers and to administer fines for drinking, gambling and other shopfloor offences: 'men could be fined . . . for using more than peaceful persuasion in trying to persuade workmates to join trade unions.'[34] The *ASE Journal* warned that the Tribunals might supplant the trade-union machinery in grievance handling and trade disputes.

## Conscription

In 1916 military conscription was introduced amidst a storm of protest from trade unionists, and the direct militarization of munitions and transport workers was threatened.

The Western Front had devoured so many volunteers that the army, by late 1915, feared that it might become unable to maintain the slaughter. A scheme was initiated by Lord Derby, inviting men to register for military service so that they could be enrolled and trained when they were needed. Thus, they would remain 'volunteers'. Notwithstanding fervid attempts to intimidate them, with white feathers and charges of cowardice, young men were increasingly reluctant to offer themselves. Word was getting round. The popular press launched an attack on professional footballers who declined to volunteer, and wanted to know why the fans were not in the trenches as well. This campaign failed. In January 1916 conscription was introduced for single men. By 21 March Sir William Robertson was telling the Cabinet that, of 193,891 called up under the new scheme, 57,416 had failed to appear.[35] Compulsion was accordingly applied more widely, and on 25 May

married men of military age were included in the call-up. The unions
had been strongly opposed to this measure, partly because it was a blow
against the civil freedom of those pressed into service, but also because
they feared the militarization of industrial life.

In Hugh Clegg's words, 'the labour movement was in a turmoil' when,
on 5 January 1916, the government presented its Military Service Bill.
Lord Derby's attempts to avoid conscription had provided for men to
'attest' that they were willing to serve. Lists of reserve occupations were
drawn up, and the scheme was controlled under a National Registration
Act to standardize the process of granting exemption from the moral
obligation to enlist, and to conserve essential civilian labour supply. The
whole Labour movement had seized on the Derby scheme as an escape
from conscription, but it failed the test. It was announced by the
authorities that over 1 million unmarried men had not 'attested', and the
prospect of calling up married men who had offered themselves was too
much for the government to accept. Compulsion for single men, it was
judged, had to follow. An immediate wave of official Labour Party and
TUC protest was met with Asquith's promise that conscription would for
ever be limited to single men and that it would end immediately after the
war.

A meeting of the TUC and the Labour Party had resoundingly
declared its opposition to the Bill the day after its introduction, and
called on Labour's ministers to resign. Asquith's promise, however, was
enough to save the ministers' faces and, more important, to keep their
bottoms on the front bench. They remained in office, and the Labour
Party conference on 27 January confined its opposition to a protest vote.
There would be no Labour campaign against conscription.[36] In April,
Asquith's pledge was withdrawn; the Bill to extend conscription to
married men was introduced, and the TUC advised the unions to
support it.

## The Call-up and the Transport Workers

On 8 and 9 June the NTWF Annual General Council took place in
Glasgow. Gosling, in his presidential address, conceded that whilst 'we
are carefully watching every tendency in the direction of industrial
conscription, military conscription has been reluctantly agreed to'.
Samuel March moved, on behalf of the National Union of Vehicle
Workers, the London and Provincial Union and the NALU, that the
NTWF

'views with deep misgivings the introduction of compulsory military service
into Great Britain. This country has been regarded as the chief stronghold
against tyranny and oppression of every kind, and should lose no single

opportunity of re-establishing individual liberty and the right voluntarily to refrain from organised destruction. It therefore calls upon the EC to press for the repeal of all Acts of Parliament imposing compulsion, especially in view of the very definite promise of the Government that it would be limited to single men, and this Conference pledges itself to oppose Conscription with all its power until it is coupled with the conscription of the wealth of the country. We particularly protest against the compulsory retention of time-expired men. We ask all Affiliated Societies supporting this resolution to press for a national conference to support these demands.[37]

Conscription had not come about from military necessity, he began. (About this he was not wrong. There were more men in the army than it could equip.[38]) The capitalists wanted conscription, he said, because they did not like the way trade unionism was growing, and because workers were demanding more of the wealth they produced: 'They were more afraid of the worker getting his rights than they were of losing the war.' The forceful organizer of the LPU, Ben Smith, seconded, with a strong call for the conscription of wealth. The workers were 'giving their all', their lives. The wealthy were simply enriching themselves:

They lent their money at huge interest, the Government spent it with the people who lent it, and they made a further profit out of that. The result of this was that the wealthy class sacrificed nothing; they got their money back, they got their interest and they got huge profits as well. It had to be remembered that money would be dearer after the war, and that this would lead to unemployment for the workers, but he had hopes that this would eventually lead to the repudiation of the debt altogether.[39]

After George Grisley (general secretary of the Cranemen and Enginemen's Union of London) had spoken in opposition, on grounds of patriotism, Ernest Bevin intervened. His was a swingeing contribution, forthright in the extreme. First, he impeached the Labour Party for reneging on its clear mandate:

Reference had been made to the conduct of the Labour Party in dealing with the Government in connection with the passing of the Act. It would be remembered that when the first Act was before the country a national conference was called, which declared against the Act. He would respectfully suggest that those who conducted the negotiations had been jockeyed into undoing the work of the conference. The second Act was introduced, and he had heard suggestions that in secret conclave representatives of the Labour movement met the Government and agreed that a second conference should not be held.
Mr. Sexton: That is not true.
Mr. Bevin: If it is not true, it should be contradicted. I have made the suggestion that it was true in more than one place, and I have never had a contradiction.

Then he rounded on the general staff of the army:

He had to suggest that the higher command of the British Army had not been all that it might be. He objected to the right of the military authorities to continue to call upon the country for more men while men were sacrificed through the bad strategy of the Staff. The closer they got to grips with the enemy, the more their strategy seemed to consist of sacrificing lives, and he had yet to learn that those who had been responsible for disasters where thousands of lives had been sacrificed had been punished or seriously dealt with at all.

Moreover, there was another reason to oppose conscription:

The people who advocated conscription were doing it with the intention of leading up to industrial conscription, and before the Act had been in operation three months they would find that the Northcliffe Press and their tools would be clamouring for the extension of the Act to industry, and they would find Labour men agreeing with it on the ground of military necessity. He wished that these Labour men had to come down amongst the men themselves and settle the troubles that arose. He believed that if there was not a lead given on this question there would arise a kind of blind action on the part of the men themselves which would disorganise the Labour movement. They had a conflict of evidence on the part of the Government. At one moment it was munitions that was wanted, at another men. At another time the difficulty was shortage of transport labour, and incidentally it was drunkenness – he was sure that whatever Grisley's opinion on other subjects, he was opposed to the compulsory powers of the Liquor Control Board – they were never sure what it was. There was a doubt in his mind whether the Government had any co-ordinated policy on the war at all: there were the differences between the Army Council and the Munitions Ministry. Again he had to express surprise at the action of the Labour men. One Liberal politician had told him that he could not understand why the Labour men had allowed themselves to be so easily twisted to suit the whims of the Government.

James Sexton opposed the motion:

He was never fond of militarism; on the contrary, he had opposed it always. If anyone had told him before the war that he would be advocating a big army and a big navy, that he would be advocating war to the finish, he would have told them, quite politely, that they were liars. What had happened to change his opinion? What had happened to change Tillett's? Nobody could accuse Tillett of being in favour of the capitalist class. What had changed the president's opinion? Nobody could accuse the President of being in favour of militarism; all his thoughts and inclinations had been in the opposite direction. The thing that had changed their opinions was the unmistakable fact that Germany had been deliberately preparing for this war for thirty or forty years.

Then Tom Mann intervened. He favoured the resolution, because it was neither a pacifist nor an anti-war declaration. Sexton erred to see in it a pronouncement on the merits of the war. What were the national duties in the conflict? There were three:

We had to provide men, munitions, and money. They were told they must maintain on behalf of themselves and their Allies the magnificent Fleet which had swept the seas. They had to supply the Allies with munitions. They had to maintain the trade of the country in order to finance the Allies. That meant that men had to remain at home to produce the wealth to cover the expenses not only of ourselves but of our Allies. Could that be done while they depleted the country of wealth-producers? They declared that the men could not be got. A call was made for three millions of men. Three millions came forward. A call was made for more, and more came forward. The question was not one of men. Their Allies had millions of men. Russia had its millions of men who wanted arms and equipment, who wanted big guns, and who wanted finance. There was France, which had its millions of men, who also wanted arms, equipment, and guns. It was our duty to provide the arms, the equipment, and the money, and he repeated that there was no military necessity for the conscription of men in this country while the Allies were possessed of millions of men whose chief requisites were the arms and the money that this country alone could provide. And he was there to declare that Lord Kitchener could not, and no man could, make out a case for conscription. Russia's man-power was nineteen million men of military age. France's man-power was five and a half millions. Britain had six millions, and, with the dominions, eight millions. Did that look like deficiency of men? Italy had five millions. Was that a reason for taking a few hundred thousand more men from the trades essential to the financing of the Allies? It amounted to this: that Russia alone had as large a man-power as the whole of the enemy countries. The plea of military necessity could not be substantiated. The one thing that animated the conscriptionists was the fear of organised Labour. Immediately the Triple Alliance came into being the Press was full of articles demanding that it should be controlled in the interests of the country. Conscription was the gateway to industrial compulsion. Sexton had quoted Lord Kitchener, but how many times had Lord Kitchener said that he thought voluntaryism would fill the bill. He [Tom Mann] said that this country must win the war; he would declare that to the conference, but he was also one who said that he was in favour of a settlement by negotiation as early as possible.

At this point, Ben Tillett had the last word. He had been at the front. The nearer he got to the front line, the more the soldiers supported conscription:

Mistakes had been made, that was true, but was there a man there who had not made a mistake? Was there ever a strike conducted in which blunders had not been made? And in a strike they were conscriptionists; they were more than conscriptionists, they were coercionists, and God help the conscientious objectors. Let them all realise that this was something more than a strike; it was a world-war, and although he could feel and endorse the anti-compulsionist point of view, he did not want the country to get the impression that the transport workers were pacifists and anti-warites.

A card-vote followed. The vehicle workers lost their motion by 100,000 to 81,000. This was some measure of the movement of opinion; but it was more. By far the most radical statement had come from Ernest Bevin. Around him were crystallizing the hopes of the younger men, the idealists and the radicals. More and more 'mistakes' by the generals were, alas, guaranteed. But now there were men who were unafraid to challenge them.

## Chinese Labour Again

While more men were to be marched off to the trenches, the extended use of Chinese and 'coloured' labour from the colonies in the Merchant Service and elsewhere fanned pre-war racial antagonisms to a fierce heat. Opposition to this practice became general across the whole spectrum, right and left, of the transport workers' leadership. Earlier we dealt with the campaign of the pre-war Federation against the 'yellow peril'; in 1915 the matter recurred, and there were deputations to the Board of Trade which exacted a promise of full employment for British seamen. Not all the general unions maintained their anti-Chinese xenophobia. To its credit, the Workers' Union opened a campaign in Birmingham to recruit Chinese workers. It published leaflets in Chinese. John Beard contributed an article to the Workers' Union *Record*, seeking to convince members to welcome this step.[40] But here we must take note of an important fact. Besides their political and racialist effects, these issues lit up, for both government and labour, the understanding that modern war was insatiably dependent on man- and increasingly woman-power. Between the morbidly competing needs for soldiers, weapons, transportation, food and fuel, priorities had to be established.

## 'There Is Not Enough Labour to Go Round'

Lloyd George gave a confidential interview to the leaders of the Triple Alliance in December 1916. It made these dilemmas crystal clear. It also showed how they issued from an uncritical acceptance of the military priorities of his generals, mindless and profligate though these were.

There is not enough labour to go round. There is not enough material to go round. I hope there will be enough food to go round . . . The Army wants labour . . . and I shall uge this in public – the more you can give to the Army the shorter will be the war . . . let us talk here in the Cabinet room and under Cabinet conditions. There is going to be very big fighting . . . the question of whether those attacks are to be decisive depends entirely upon the number of men that you can throw in at the decisive moment. That is one of the elementary propositions of war which any man reading history can ascertain for himself . . . Therefore to undersupply the Army with men is to damage every trade which you are here representing, to damage the whole of the country . . . you increase the bloodshed instead of diminishing it; you increase the cost, you increase the burden . . . you increase the risk of disaster . . .

Having thus turned the screw of this moral blackmail to its limits, the Prime Minister made his play for an end to the Alliance's resistance to further 'combing-out' of men for the forces:

Men are being taken from every trade and substitutes are being put in. Now I am told I must not get any men from agriculture . . . Mr. Gosling says: 'You must not take any men from the docks'. Mr. Smillie says, and quite properly, 'If you take any man from the mines, very well, we cannot produce coal for you.' Mr. Thomas and Mr. Bellamy will say the same thing about the railways, and Mr. Williams will certainly say the same thing . . . I want to find a trade from which I can get them . . . It is a problem of war. You may say: You ought not to go to war. That was not our choice, and the trade union organisations of the country have supported us in that view.[41]

By 1918 'Britain had fully exhausted her manpower reserves',[42] with serious effects upon the output of munitions, food and coal, as Lloyd George did indeed proceed to call up more farm workers, miners and engineers. (So acute was the coal shortage that some miners were actually brought back from the army to the pits in the summer.) The casualty toll, as we have seen, was immense. Yet it was not the butchery alone which caused the labour shortage, for before the war some 300,000 young men had emigrated annually from Britain, and that drain was actually stopped by the war.[43] The war was sustained by full employment and inflation yet, by dint of the constant appeal to their 'patriotism', the trade unions were inhibited from maintaining wage rates at the level of inflation until its very last year. Of course, working-class family earnings, bolstered by women's work, by overtime and bonuses, and by the elementary fact that work which had been irregular was now available seven days a week, meant that poverty was more than held at bay.[44]

Government intervention was central to this sea-change in the labour market. Quite simply the state became the largest employer of (or contractor for) labour in the country. It therefore became the largest influence on industrial relations, and on the growth of neo-corporatist structures of control. We seek to explore this influence in chapter 17. It is clear enough, however, that labour shortages gave working people a chance to build up their rights and to insist on a more dignified space in the world. If their expectations were not met, the resulting truculence brought big problems for the war-planners. Through 1916 the stakes were all raising themselves. Then, in an instant, a new force emerged.

# II

## *Revolution in Russia*

On the evening of 27 February 1917, according to the old, Byzantine (Julian) calendar, after several riotous days in Petrograd, the Soviet of Workers' Deputies proclaimed its summons to a meeting in the Tauride Palace. Mutinous troops were already opening up the prisons and liberating the inmates. Some tsarist ministers had been arrested; others took refuge in the Admiralty offices. The constitutive meeting was joined not only by representatives from the factories, but also by delegates from the rebellious regiments. Accordingly it became the Soviet of Workers' and Soldiers' Deputies. The sailors at the naval base of Kronstadt declared for revolution. The Tsar was lost. Shunted around the railway network, he dithered for some days and then abdicated. A few days later, he was under arrest.

In Britain this news engendered fear and hope, in a turbulent mix. But in the first days optimism predominated. Part of the government hoped that the Tsar's displacement would now lead to a vigorous prosecution of the war. Patriotic Labour men shared this expectation. Others were convinced that the Revolution would bring nearer that peace for which they were becoming daily more concerned. For the socialist community, the Revolution came as a moment of revelation. Years later, in the midst of a bitter struggle in the Labour Party, Aneurin Bevan was to recall that moment:

> I am now 53 years of age. I was coming to adult life at the end of the 1914–18 war. I remember so well what happened when the Russian revolution occurred. I remember the miners, when they heard that the Tsarist tyranny had been overthrown, rushing to meet each other in the streets with tears streaming down their cheeks, shaking hands and saying: 'At last it has happened.' Let us remember in 1951 that the revolution of 1917 came to the working class of Great Britain, not as a social disaster, but as one of the most emancipating events in the history of mankind.[45]

In retrospect, George Lansbury also saw these events as 'the dawn of a new day'. He 'cared not whose revolution it was . . . whether Menshevik or Bolshevik: for us it was enough that the Tsardom had fallen'.[46]

## Transport Workers and the Support Network in Britain

At the end of March – on the Western (Gregorian) calendar – the minority socialists in Britain convened a great rally in the Albert Hall, using the title 'Russia Free'. An *ad hoc* body called the Anglo-Russian Democratic Alliance, based on the staff of the *Daily Herald*, distributed more than 12,000 tickets. The hall was packed, and perhaps 8,000 people were unable to gain admission. Robert Williams was a keynote speaker. Bertrand Russell sought to persuade John Burns to chair the meeting, but he declined.[47] Clara Butt sang 'Give Us Peace in Our Time', and the meeting ended with 'The Red Flag'. Bob Smillie and Williams, wrote Russell, 'were admirable as regards Labour'.[48]

Charles Ammon organized the tickets. Some of the transport workers' leaders were involved from the first day of the new mobilization. Soon the unions of their federation were invited to a follow-up, which was to be a major conference, in Leeds.

The Leeds Convention met on 3 June. It gathered 1,150 accredited delegates, but the attendance was much larger. It was convoked by the United Socialist Council, which had been formed in July 1913 when the Socialist International Bureau convened a meeting of British socialist organizations to discuss the possibility of unity. Émile Vandervelde and Camille Huysmans had attended for the Bureau, and delegates had been assembled from the Independent Labour Party, the Fabians and the British Socialist Party.

The spokesmen of the International had recommended a dual solution to British disunity: the ILP and the BSP should fuse, and the BSP should affiliate to the Labour Party, following which, pending further development towards unity, a United Socialist Council was to be set up comprising all three bodies, under the chairmanship of Beatrice Webb.[49] At a subsequent conference attended by many international delegates, the BSP put forward four conditions for unity with the ILP. Keir Hardie agreed to three of these: that the party should be free to proclaim its socialist goal; that it should recognize the existence of the class war; and that it should be free to carry on extra-parliamentary activity, including intervention in trade-union struggles. The fourth, that BSP parliamentary candidates should stand on an explicitly socialist ticket, was met by Hardie with a compromise proposal that the United Socialist Council should ask its members to request the Labour Party to amend its constitution to permit candidates to describe themselves as 'Labour and Socialist'.

The next year, 1914, the BSP held a referendum which revealed agreement on affiliation.[50] Application was made, and accepted unanim-

ously at the 1916 Labour Party Conference. The Russian Revolution of
March 1917 brought left and right close enough together to permit the
BSP and the ILP to revive the United Socialist Council, and organize the
Leeds Convention.

It seems probable that the Council was deliberately resuscitated to
replace the Anglo-Russian Alliance, which now disappeared. But
Ammon was still present at the hub, as one of the convenors. The
organizing committee included Smillie, Williams and Lansbury. On the
day, Lansbury was too ill to attend and Smillie took the chair. The first
motion, proposed by Ramsay MacDonald, welcomed the Revolution.
The second proposal called for a peace without annexations or
indemnities, and was presented by Phillip Snowden for the ILP and by
E. C. Fairchild for the BSP. The third resolution, on civil liberties,
demanded an amnesty for political prisoners, and freedom for trade
unions; it was moved by Ammon and seconded by Mrs Despard, the
women's suffragist. She was supported by Bertrand Russell. The
speakers included Bevin, Mann and – in a storm of protest – Captain
Tupper.

W. C. Anderson moved the most controversial resolution of the day,
calling for the establishment, at home in Britain, of Workmen's and
Soldiers' Councils. Robert Williams, in seconding, showed himself fully
familiar with Russian developments. 'The resolution,' he said,

if it means anything at all, means that which is contained in the oft-used
phrase from Socialist platforms: The *dictatorship of the proletariat*. (Cheers.) I
am glad that the Press, the competent Press, the subtle Press, the sinister
Press which represents the proprietary interests of this country, have
allowed their case against the first three resolutions to go by default, in order
to fix themselves steadfastly to the implication of the fourth. My friend
Smillie said we have come here to talk not treason but reason; but I would
remind Smillie, if he needs it, that under the Defence of the Realm
Regulations reason has become treason. (Cheers.) We stand steadfastly by
this resolution, and we are not going to weaken it by one jot or tittle. If the
governing classes in this country are convinced that you are going to give full
adequate effect to this resolution, they will give effect to resolutions one,
two, and three in order to defeat you. You have got the most competent, the
most capable governing class of the whole world in this country. (A voice:
'We have beaten them.') You have not beaten them. They have taken your
own leaders from your ranks and used them against you. (Voices: 'Not
Smillie.') After they found that Lord Devonport was unable to deal with the
profiteers of this country, they wanted to cover up their slimy tracks by
putting Bob Smillie into Grosvenor House. They will make every
conceivable sacrifice and concession short of getting off your backs.
(Cheers.) Mr. Tupper demanded that we should fight for indemnities in
order to provide adequate sustenance for the dependants of men who have
lost their lives in the mercantile marine. If you want restitution, reparation,
and guarantees, in God's name get it from the profiteers of your own

country. (Cheers.) We want a mandate from you to proceed with this resolution, and if there are many amongst you who have got cold feet about this, slip out before the resolution is put. (Laughter.) We want to break the influence of the industrial and political labour 'machine' – (cheers) – and this Convention is our attempt so to do. Today hundreds of thousands of miners, engineers, transport workers, railwaymen, and the rest are represented here through their Trade Union lodges. We want these men to go back to their constituents and convince them to use the power that lies in their hands to give or withhold their labour in the place where wealth is produced. Parliament will do nothing for you. Parliament has done nothing for you for the whole period of the war. The workpeople have sacrificed in blood and treasure at all times for their country, and the country is theirs by right of those very sacrifices. They say that you will hamper the production of munitions, that control by the workpeople would mean that our national affairs would be less well managed. Smillie referred to Mr. Lloyd George's indictment of the old gang; but every word of Mr. Lloyd George's indictment of the old gang applies even more pertinently to the new gang. (Cheers.) The workpeople have been called upon to make sacrifice after sacrifice; the engineering and highly-skilled occupations have had to dilute and water down their highly-skilled labour; you have been called upon to forego your holidays and work long, tedious hours of overtime. We want to assert our right to the ownership and control of the country. We want to demand the representation of the soldiery, of the millions of organised working people in the Army, which, in the words of Mr. Ben Tillett, contains 95 per cent of the working classes of this country. We are competent to speak in the name of our own class, and damn the Constitution. (Loud cheers.) Had the Russian revolutionaries been disposed to be concerned with the Constitution of Holy Russia the Romanoffs would have been on the throne today, and I say to you: Have you as little concern for the British Constitution as the Russians you are praising had for the dynasty of the Romanoffs. (Cheers.) You have a greater right to speak in the name of our people, civilians and soldiers, than have the gang who are in charge of our political destinies at this moment. It has been said by a German intellectual that the proletariat is the rock upon which the church of the future shall be built. It is the rock upon which the reactionary forces will break themselves. (Cheers.) If you are really sincere in sending greetings to Russia, I say to you: 'Go thou and do likewise'. (Cheers.)[51]

It was not easy to 'do likewise'. There is some considerable doubt whether all the Leeds participants were entirely familiar with exactly what had been done, and what precisely was to be imitated. Lord Bullock, in his life of Bevin, tells us that the Convention was 'a preview of the British Left between the wars, anarchical, Utopian, already fascinated by and profoundly ignorant of the Russian experience.'[52] Another historian, Stephen White, is perhaps nearer the mark: the Convention, he thought, 'reflected the preoccupation of minority Labour with the achievement of an early and negotiated peace. This concern preceded the February Revolution; and what was welcome in that revolution was less the emergence of a Soviet system and "dual powers" than the support it soon began to provide for a renegotiation of war aims and . . . a "people's peace".'[53]

It is true that Bertrand Russell was cheered by the echo when he spoke up for the conscientious objectors. But it is also true that the King was deeply worried, as he told Will Thorne shortly afterwards. Nothing would come of it, Thorne assured him. 'This seemed to relieve his mind, and he spoke to me in a most homely and pleasant way. I was very pleased.'[54] Whether the King would have been pleased if he had understood the depth of feeling against the war is another matter.

The Leeds Convention rumbled on in the arguments of the transport unions.

At their Triennial Delegate Meeting, in London at the end of May, the Dockers' Union had carried a resolution moved by its chairman, W. Davidson of Bristol, and seconded by Stan Awbery of Swansea. It pledged opposition 'by economic action' to 'any further war promoted by autocracies, junkers, or capitalists,' and called upon the workers of the world to 'unite in close international brotherhood'. An enthusiastic message to the revolutionaries was approved and sent to the British Foreign Office for forwarding. Then Awbery and Fred Thompson, of the London dockers, proposed that two delegates be sent to the Leeds Convention the following week. Their motion was carried unanimously, and Bevin and Tillett were elected.[55]

Immediately after the Convention, Tillett contributed a report on it to the Dockers' *Record*.[56] The names of people like Lansbury, he said, had given reason enough to participate. But the meeting had been unrepresentative, dominated by the two socialist parties. The resolutions had been 'jockeyed'. Between 400 and 500 delegates had been 'under twenty-six years of age' and some of these had been 'of alien origin'. MacDonald, he complained, had 'delivered a revolutionary speech'. Tillett launched then into a patriotic diatribe, culminating in the charge that 'the blunders of our Government and the malignity of these new revolutionaries(?) have resulted in the loss of a million Russian lives and half a million of our own soldiers'. Connolly's memory had been invoked (he had recently been shot after the abortive 1916 uprising in Ireland) but it had been 'dishonoured'. 'Connolly died . . . for his country, but these people have no country'. In conclusion, the dockers' secretary argued that 'some of those who spoke [had] begrudged the meagre allowance to the soldiers' dependants'. Further, other supporters, he charged, had 'fought against women's wages being fair'. Here Tillett was clearly wrong: the resolution put forward by Anderson and Williams had specifically charged the proposed workers' and soldiers' councils to

watch diligently for and resist every encroachment upon industrial and civil liberty; shall give special attention to the position of women employed in industry and generally suppport the work of the Trade Unions; shall take active steps to stop the exploitation of food and all other necessaries of life, and shall concern themselves with questions affecting the pensions of wounded and disabled soldiers and the maintenance grants payable to the dependents of men serving with the Army and Navy; and the making of adequate provision for the training of disabled soldiers and for suitable and remunerative work for the men on their return to civilian life.[57]

## Greetings to Butcher Haig

The same issue of the *Record* contained, verbatim, a message signed by Tillett and Davidson expressing 'heartfelt gratitude to the Services' which had been sent on 1 June to Field Marshall Haig, together with the commander-in-chief's reply, of 7 June, ordering that a copy of the resolution be published in General Orders to 'strengthen the bonds' between 'all serving [and] their comrades of the Dock, Wharf, Riverside and General Workers' Union at home'.[58] At the end of the following month Haig showed how he would use these bonds. He launched what Lloyd George was to call the 'battle of the mud', and what the poor victims knew as Passchendaele. For 4 miles of slime, he paid some 320,000 young British men. They claimed a couple of hundred thousand German casualties. Solidarity with all those doomed soldiers was very much in order. It required very different attitudes to the mass murderers who organized the carnage.

It is a million pities that Ben Tillett could not have read the private thoughts of Lloyd George, locked as he was in a bitterly frustrating tussle with Haig about a project in which he lacked any confidence whatever. The French army was already in mutiny, as the Prime Minister was to recall when he later composed his memoirs:

Camps were placarded with notices declaring the intention of the soldiers to refuse to go back again to the trenches, whilst their fellows were earning 15 to 20 francs a day, working in safety in the factories. A battalion ordered to the front refused to proceed and dispersed into a wood. Soldiers coming home on leave sang the *Internationale* in the trains and demanded peace. Mutinies occurred in 16 different Army Corps, the mutineers alleging that they had been sacrificed by treacherous or inefficient Generals. A force of 15,000 Russians which had been sent to France to fight on the Western Front, openly revolted and had to be bombarded with artillery fire into surrender. A number of young infantrymen marched through the streets of a French town 'baa-ing' like sheep to indicate that they were being driven like lambs to the slaughter. The ominous symptoms which preceded the Russian Revolution, and later on the German, appeared in the French Army in 1917.[59]

Tillett would not have known what the Premier knew; but both his article in the *Record* and his message to Haig indicate that he was preparing his positions for a major struggle in the union. Within a fortnight battle came, at the NTWF Annual General Council in Bristol on 15 June. It did not, however, turn out to vindicate Tillett's own position. Patriots most transport workers may have been; none the less, the war-weariness was beginning to reach them. The first shot came from Ned Cathery, who took the floor to propose, on behalf of the sailors and firemen, a protest against Williams's abuse of the name of the Federation in the cause of the 'peace and bogus meeting', and a demand that Williams either resign his secretaryship or pledge himself not to use the NTWF's name 'outside of NTWF business'.

## *The Stockholm Mission: Wilson versus Williams*

Cathery's union had itself just become the object of hot controversy: it had, a week earlier, blacked a ship which was due to sail from Aberdeen to Stockholm and Petrograd, carrying a number of Labour leaders on a delegation to Stockholm and then scheduled to continue to Russia on a mission of goodwill and investigation. MacDonald, Fred Jowett and Smillie were among those prevented from sailing. So, also, was Tom Mann. Williams had given a statement to the *Daily News*. The seamen had blacked the voyage until those taking part agreed to call for indemnities for the victims of submarine attacks. Williams, as he had already told the Leeds meeting, thought that British shipowners should pay:

> It is quixotic that Mr. Tom Mann is to be sent to Petrograd and to Stockholm as a representative of the National Sailors' and Firemen's Union. Mr. Tom Mann was the ablest supporter of the resolution calling for 'no annexations and no indemnities' who spoke from the floor of the Leeds Convention; so that the seamen will paradoxically prevent their own representative from sailing to Stockholm and Petrograd if he does not recant.'[60]

This stung Cathery. Tom Mann had indeed opposed annexations and indemnities at Leeds and Cathery protested:

> when the Mersey Report comes up I am going to ask who paid for Tom Mann and Mr. Cotter to go to Leeds. I understand they went to hold a watching brief. Did Tom Mann hold a watching brief? He was one of the strongest supporters of the 'no indemnities' resolution. When the Seamen's Union appointed Tom Mann to go to Petrograd we knew nothing of his activities at Leeds. I tell this Conference that the matter has aroused a storm of indignation among our branches, and my blood boils . . . [61]

Havelock Wilson's blood was not exactly tepid, either, and he seconded his union's motion with a scalding attack on Williams himself, and 'Shinwell, that jew tailor who has been turned down by every national body in this country'. 'I am told', said Wilson, 'that one thing that made Mr. Williams' face beam with delight was when Shinwell got up and jeered at the poor sailors who have been murdered, and I am here to say that if Shinwell's company is good enough for Williams, then Williams' company is not good enough for the Sailors' Union.'[62] There is no record of Emanuel Shinwell's having jeered at anybody, and this story is bound to be thought doubtful. But Shinwell had further enraged Wilson by offering an alternative crew to take MacDonald and his colleagues from Aberdeen to Russia.[63]

James Sexton then proposed an amendment to the sailors' motion, insisting that Williams seek the approval of the NTWF Executive or Conference before allowing his name to be associated in an official capacity with such gatherings as that at Leeds. 'I want Williams to give us some encouragement to believe that in the future he will not compromise the Federation,' he said.[64]

Tillett immediately asked if Sexton wished to abrogate 'the ordinary rights of a man to hold his own opinions'. 'No,' came the reply. So Tillett seconded the Sexton proposal, repeating his own arguments in his union's *Record* and adding, for good measure, an onslaught against Havelock Wilson ('the biggest despot of them all') and 'Captain' Tupper ('no other union would have Tupper with all his ability'). But then, in yet another of his famous turnabouts, Tillett went on: 'I don't want the Secretary's brains and manhood to be set aside from his proper person. We are all growing old in the work, but what is the use of the work if we cannot have men like Williams to carry it on?'[65] The amendment was 'a fair statement of fact' to be supported if it did not 'impair or imperil the personal freedom of the individual'. Williams should give the pledge, and the resolution should be withdrawn.

By contrast, Tom Mann, who still retained his association with Wilson's union, began by supporting the resolution. He explained how he had been appointed to attend at Leeds by the Mersey District Committee of the Federation, with a watching brief. His expenses had been met by the district treasurer. His position on indemnities was that 'no power should come out of this war as a conqueror', and he saw no more in the Leeds proposal than that. 'I have intolerance for no one,' he said. 'I respect those who differ from me.' To forbid Williams to speak would be 'resorting to the very Prussianism you claim to oppose'. Tom Mann hoped Williams would make his statement so that both proposals might then be withdrawn.

Will Thorne, who had already been to Petrograd with James O'Grady, MP, secretary of the National Federation of General Workers, at the end of April, at Henderson's request (on behalf of the government), spoke at some length about the unrepresentative nature of the Convention, whilst denying that it was 'bogus'. Rather, he believed it was inflated. The nub of the question, he thought, was that there was a straight choice between the Allies and the Central Powers, and no alternative. There is little doubt that this was the view he had been charged to carry to Russia, like others after him. If in Britain he remained plausible, in Petrograd his arguments were to prove less than persuasive.

Ernest Bevin began a long and considered statement by hoping that Williams's case would be cleared up 'without carrying any resolution'. Leeds had been a political demonstration. The seamen's action was equally political. 'Both have gone outside the etiquette of the Trade Union Movement'.

It must not be forgotten that Williams is the servant of the organisation, and to that extent is identified with the organisation in whatever he does. I can speak with some feeling on this matter. I largely agree with Williams. He knows that. I objected to the foreign policy of this country for many years before the war. I regarded the Russian Alliance as likely to lead to war. I did not change that view when it did lead to war. It came to this: when the psychology of two forms of organisation clashed I had to ask myself the question of what was to be my attitude. Tillett and I had some discussion, and I came to the conclusion that I would do my best to preserve the economic unity of the men I represent and to accept passively the opinions of the majority of men.[66]

Tupper's speech at the Leeds Convention, thought Bevin, had been a provocation. Had Wilson himself tried to speak there, he would have got a hearing. Wilson demurred. 'I can tell you,' rejoined Bevin, 'that if Tupper came to Bristol, my men would not listen to him.' There was 'a feeling of repulsiveness' about Tupper, he went on. (Tupper had recently led hooligan disruption of a peace meeting in Cardiff.) But if the sailors and firemen were not innocent of political motives, there was all the more reason for Robert Williams to tread carefully.

Now I said that the Leeds Conference was a political move. I am on the Federation Executive. If Mr. Williams believes that something could be done to bring this awful Armageddon to an end, I am willing to support him inside the organisation. Instead of jumping off to a political organisation, why not give us a chance of expressing our views inside the organisation? I say the same to our friend Smillie. Our friend Smillie is on the Parliamentary Committee, he is President of the Triple Alliance, President of the Miners' Federation. Friend Williams is on the Triple Alliance, he is Secretary of the Federation. I do ask Williams and Smillie why they do not try to move that great Labour machine. I thought and hoped that men like Williams and Smillie would try, in the light of the entry of America and the Russian Revolution, to get a great national conference, in order to get down to ways and means. I don't agree with Thorne that you must be either pro-

Ally or pro-Central Powers. I look upon this war as one brought about by the force of trade competition. Now, whatever our opinions of MacDonald might be, the fact is that he was asked for by the Russian Government, and the fact that he did not go may mean the loss of another half-million lives. The step taken by the Seamen's Union is as ill-advised as the Leeds Conference. Williams is a man of my own age; we are trying to do things together inside the movement, and I am hoping that we shall take on the work that the older men are leaving, and that this Federation will be made a mighty force. I might ask whether he could accept as a policy for his own future guidance that no new organisation should be started until the old ones have failed. It stung me a good deal when Williams said at Leeds that a new organisation was wanted strong enough to break the present political and industrial machine. A number of his best friends in the country have been alarmed by that statement. He says it means an organisation strong enough to get rid of reactionary officials and executives. I don't believe there is any need of another organisation outside of the Trade Union movement.[67]

At this point, Havelock Wilson interjected again, to deny political motives for his union's refusal to sail with MacDonald. 'Do you think you could have held up the ships if the shipowners had not been with you?' snapped Bevin. 'If you could, you could revolutionise the conditions of the Seamen.'

I have had circulars sent to my members in Bristol, and I object to Mr. Wilson usurping the functions of the Trades Union Congress just as much as I do to the Leeds Conference. If it is necessary to get a plebiscite as to whether Ramsay MacDonald can secure 500,000 votes, why is not the Trades Union Congress asked to do it? The Seamen's Union is overriding the Executive of all the Executives. There is another point I want to make regarding the resolution. If it was carried, Williams could do nothing but resign. It means, if it means anything, that Williams organised that Leeds Conference knowing it to be a fraud. I don't believe he did that. I don't believe he had any intention of its being a fraudulent conference. I disagree with some of the matter of the resolutions, but so far as Williams was associated with it I don't believe it was bogus. I would rather see us settle the whole matter by leaving it to Williams' word of honour . . . [68]

After this statement, although the debate wound on repetitively, the argument was clinched.

Williams's critics on the pro-war wing found it impossible to press their demand either for his resignation or for any promise of future discretion. Williams himself, in a courageous and defiant, but calm and dignified reply, insisted that he did not use the Federation's name in his peace campaigning, or in his work for the Union of Democratic Control. He apologized for once having used Federation notepaper 'as being nearest to hand', and promised that this would not happen again. He catalogued some of his many functions as Federation secretary. He had been steadfast in carrying out its policies energetically and faithfully, but with his own initiative prominent in everything he did:

> as Tillet said to me when I assumed office: Do you want to be an automaton or a man? Tillett then advised me not to be an office-boy or even a secretary, but to be a man. That I have been and shall, I hope, remain . . . I have challenged on many occasions Government Departments in a way that Executive resolutions would not perchance have allowed, perhaps in some cases would not give me authority to do, but I have always sought to safeguard Labour interests, and that surely no one here can deny.

They couldn't, and they didn't. He went on:

> I must ask you not to call for pledges under duress because under those circumstances it is frankly impossible. If I was amenable to pressure of that kind, the Government Departments have a stronger form of duress that you can exercise. I said I have challenged Government Departments, and you do not suppose that the Government Departments are fond of the way in which I have tackled their ineptitudes. They can look up the records of the War Office and easily discover my eligibility to military service . . . Moreover, if I am to become clay in your hands, what reliance could the membership have in me when I have to meet various employers . . . I will tell you what will happen if you force me to resign. In a month or six weeks I shall receive a calling-up notice. A few days after that I shall be in Wormwood Scrubs . . . (Mr. Grisley: Shame!). You may say shame, but those are my deeply held convictions. Your duress and threats cannot alter them. I have contributed my best service to assist the Government in a civilian capacity in the transport service and its efficiency. I have gone down into various ports to ask for the relaxation of rules and customs against the wishes of many of my old friends. I have done my best in a civilian capacity to assist the country without prejudice to the interests of Labour . . . But don't ask me to forego my civil, personal, and political rights.[69]

Williams's rhetoric surely contributed to the decision, but it was none the less Bevin's logic which won. His stance, claiming to accept 'passively' the pro-war position 'of the majority of the men' in order to serve the cause of their 'economic unity' was apparently simple, but had complex results. The war was not 'passive' in its reach. It challenged the 'economic unity' of the men at many points. Wherever it did, Bevin took their side.

The Federation was not the only trade union or labour organization where this tension was felt, of course. But Bevin recognized what was happening on this occasion and broke his 'passive' silence to help save his contemporary, his friend and – be it said – his potential rival for the future leadership. Williams was saved by his own and his supporters' advocacy, and by his acknowledged indispensability. At the end of the debate, Wilson himself led the stampede with which movers and seconders of the motion and amendment 'withdrew'.

## Learning from Controversy

If Williams survived, it was Bevin who triumphed. When he objected 'to Mr. Wilson usurping the functions of the Trades Union Congress just as much as I do to the Leeds Conference . . . The Seamen's Union is overriding the Executive of Executives',[70] his concept was clear. The trade unions represent the single channel through which their political as well as their industrial powers should be exercised. Williams's response was to point to the apparently war-induced constraints which prevented this happening. But there was another, structural inhibition: the nature of leadership and authority in a purely federal constitution. The resolution of political differences is impossible within such a framework. The Confederation of Shipbuilding and Engineering Unions to this day remains a purely industrial alliance, encroaching upon the wider political issues of the times only when they concern its own industries directly. Bevin looked forward to a 'mighty force'. The whole drift of his thought suggests that this force might channel and express not only narrow industrial questions, but also the great political issues, through a centralized, loyal and disciplined authority. This is a wider version of the purpose of the future amalgamated TGWU. And at that moment Bevin, quite personally and intimately, associated Williams and himself together as those who would 'take on the work that the older men are leaving'. It is a vibrant, even (with hindsight) a poignant moment.

The impact of the Leeds Convention did not, as has usually been maintained by historians, peter out. Various attempts were made to establish regional councils along the lines of the fourth resolution. But they were subject to heavy government pressures, and to intense hooligan disruption incited by the popular press. The most infamous of these affrays took place at the Brotherhood Church in Southgate Road, London, where participants were attacked by men wielding boards with rusty nails. Bertrand Russell was there, and he recorded the experience:

> The mob burst in led by a few officers; all except the officers were more or less drunk . . . Two drunken viragos began to attack me with their boards full of nails . . . one of the ladies went up to the police and suggested that they should defend me. The police, however, merely shrugged their shoulders. 'But he is an eminent philosopher,' said the lady, and the police still shrugged. 'But he is famous all over the world as a man of learning,' she continued. The police remained unmoved. 'But he is the brother of an Earl,' she finally cried. At this, the police rushed to my assistance.[71]

Assistance was not vouchsafed to less well-connected people, whether they may have been trade unionists or pacifists. In Swansea, at the end of July, a crowd of rowdies invaded the Elysium Hall and beat up all who remained there. Arthur Horner 'had his teeth punched out of his head and his eye and upper face badly bruised'. Ted Ascott of the ILP lost a pint of blood. Ted Davies of Aberdare was hit by a pole spiked with steel prongs and received nine punctured wounds on his neck.[72] Meetings were also broken up in Newcastle and prohibited in Glasgow; 4,000 Glaswegians demonstrated in protest.[73] Birmingham's meeting was banned by the Chief Constable and the Lord Mayor acting together, with the approval of the Home Office. We do not know what pressures secured the cancellation of meetings in Leeds, Southampton and Manchester.

The Leeds initiative, in short, did not 'fizzle out'. It was repressed by the use of naked force and official discrimination.

## Uncle Arthur's Voyage to Russia

Although they succeeded in stopping MacDonald's voyage to Russia, Wilson's sailors had not been able to prevent Arthur Henderson from going to Petrograd. He was sent by the government to follow up the intiative in which Will Thorne had been involved. It was feared that the proposed international socialist congress in Stockholm might bring a German socialist delegation to Sweden to fraternize with the Russians. The War Cabinet felt 'that there might be an advantage in sending a strong British delegation [to Russia], even one headed by Mr. Arthur Henderson.'[74]

In the end it was decided that he should embark alone, on a special mission. For a time it was thought he might be designated British Ambassador in Petrograd, but he was unwilling to accept this role. He did not mind, however, the given assignment: to keep Russia in the war. He left Britain in May, and he did his best to find those who might support this unlikely project. His speeches were noted by N. Sukhanov, the Menshevik spokesman:

An extraordinary amount was done to influence the chauvinistic atmosphere by the Entente agents who had arrived in Russia . . . [Henderson's] policy speech . . . shed an unexpected light on his . . . naiveté . . . Calling a spade a spade [he] expounded the war programme of British finance – including the liberation of Mesopotamia, Africa, Constantinople and Armenia from the German or Turkish yoke. For all these idealistic purposes he demanded from the Russian Revolution cannon-fodder and practical self-immolation.

Sukhanov was no extremist. After the Bolshevik November Revolution, seven volumes of his diaries were published and they remain an extraordinary source of material about those turbulent days. But their author was soon to fall foul of Stalin; and in fact he became a prime figure in the first show trial of 1931, in which Menshevik leaders were paraded in front of a mock court before disappearing, for ever, from public life. If such a man found the appeals of Henderson unconvincing, so too would every other educated Russian, from those standing on the left to those at a fairly rightward centre. The British Labour leader may have seemed naive to such an audience, but he was by no means stupid. He came home persuaded that the Russians were in earnest about the proposed Stockholm Conference, and that British and Allied socialists would have to participate if the middle ground of Russian opinion was not to make rapid transit towards an alignment with the Germans.

He returned to London a convinced supporter of the Stockholm Conference. The Cabinet was appalled. Henderson went before the July Executive of the Labour Party and told them the Russians would surely go to Stockholm, whether the Allies would or not. Labour, therefore, had to go. A delegate meeting was agreed for early August. Four Soviet spokesmen who had come to London with Henderson were so impressed by this decision that they went to Paris to arrange a similar outcome. Henderson went with them, accompanied by MacDonald and Wardle. By now, the War Cabinet was in a paroxysm. Their emissary had been turned round by the Russians. He was therefore humiliated by being kept waiting outside a Cabinet meeting which he was entitled to attend while his colleagues animadverted about what he had done.

In fact, things had not gone smoothly in Paris. But Henderson was now convinced of his right course of action, and he went before Parliament to argue that what he did as general secretary of the Labour Party was not a matter affecting his status in the War cabinet. On 10 August the special Labour Conference met. Henderson made a passionate appeal for participation at Stockholm, to help the Russians and to 'secure a lasting, honourable and democratic peace'. James Sexton opposed any delegation, and any meeting attended by 'enemy representatives'. Barnes supported the Liverpool dockers' leader. But first MacDonald and then J. H. Thomas gave their support to Henderson. Sexton was defeated, crushingly, by 1,846,000 to 550,000. The moment came to choose the delegates. William Adamson, the Fife miner, proposed that once the twenty-four recommended people had been chosen, eight apiece from the Conference, the Labour Party and the TUC, 'no further additions thereto shall be permitted from any other affiliated or unaffiliated body in this country'. This was seconded by Ernest Bevin and carried by an even larger margin.

Henderson's very strong personal influence accounted for the size of the vote. The railwaymen endorsed the Stockholm Conference simply because he had, while the miners waited until he had spoken before they would commit themselves. Then they made up their minds. They were with him.

## *The End of the Lib.-Labs*

Now Henderson's boats had been burned. An abrasive press campaign had already been unleashed against him. On 11 August he resigned from the Cabinet. Lloyd George appointed Barnes in his place, thinking he had made a new 'king' for the Labour Party. 'Nothing of the kind,' wrote A. J. P. Taylor. 'Henderson remained the Labour Leader, and he had learnt his lesson. Never again, he declared, would he join a government in which Labour did not predominate. From this moment, "Lib–Lab" was dead.'[75] But for some days this was a close call. The frenzy in the press rose and rose. A further Labour Conference was scheduled for 21 August. There the decision to support Stockholm was reaffirmed but with a much smaller majority.

The Labour opposition between conferences was led by Tupper, Sexton and Thorne. They quickly organized to ensure that the recall meeting would be an about-turn. Lansbury's *Herald* was the campaign-sheet of those who were determined to prevent reversal. The miners wavered. Attempts were made to persuade the ILP to forego its right to be represented in Stockholm: if the pacifists were not present at the International Conference, perhaps the miners' delegation would confirm its original decision. Now it became plain why Bevin had supported Smillie's motion to send twenty-four, and only twenty-four, delegates, excluding representation for socialist societies. But the ILP accepted self-denial only after prolonged appeals and fraught negotiations. By the time they came into line, it was too late. The miners had decided, and their vote would go against. Sexton's 'patriots' had equipped themselves with handkerchief-sized Union Jacks to wave when the vote was taken, presuming the defeat of the 'pro-Germans'. But Henderson won, even without the miners. It was a narrow shave: his majority was only 3,000 in a vote of 2.5 million.

Now Lloyd George felt strong enough to follow his instincts. It was announced that no passports would be issued to intending participants in the Stockholm meeting. The socialist parties of the Allied powers were not there, when the Germans went to meet the Russians. Alexander Kerensky, leader of the Russian Provisional Government, failed to secure the peace, and by November he was gone. Now it was to Lenin and Trotsky that the powers, and the oppositions, in the West had to measure their responses.

Had the planned meeting taken place in Sweden, would it have prevented the Bolshevik seizure of power? This is highly doubtful; but in any case, the facts speak loudly: there was no representative peace conference, and there was a successful Bolshevik Revolution.

Such speculation apart, we should not forebear to think on the meaning of Henderson's dramatic decision on his home territory. Now there was a framework for reconciliation of pro- and anti-war socialists in Britain, and for drawing unions and socialist societies back together. It would take time, but Henderson had time. He also had a message from Petrograd, which was in a short time to become Leningrad. That message hastened the process of reforming the Labour Party Constitution and of drafting its famous clause IV. Henderson was undoubtedly afraid of Bolshevism, and he drew from this fear an enhanced impetus towards 'a powerful parliamentary and socialist alternative':

> But fear of Bolshevism and the needs of international socialism were arguments which could only go so far with the unions. Henderson rather appealed to their self-esteem: he noted the immense advance made by the unions in size and importance. They had felt the powers of the State, now they must be able to control the state.[76]

With a new electoral law and a wide new franchise impending, they had to create a political force which could stand on its own.

Their adversaries had been induced to move over, making a new space within which might be shaped a developing democracy. The cost of this concession had been high. It had been paid by the slaves in blood, and by their masters in fear. Frenzied conflict between the old empires had brought them all to the very edge of destruction, and, as a result, in Britain Labour had now been recognized as a national force. It would, henceforth, seek to realize national aims within a national constitutional framework of collective bargaining and representation which it had itself helped to establish. It would also be invited to join the political process through the extension of a universal (or nearly universal) suffrage. Flawed and hobbled though the new democracy might be, it would ensure a preoccupation with the national dimension for decades yet to come.

International aspirations, which had encouraged and inspired the socialist trade-union movements in their earliest days, had received a crippling blow with the outbreak of war. The painfully established machinery of the Socialist International had collapsed. Nothing remained of its former powers, and its resolutions were merely pious memories. Now the new political reforms drove active democracy into the shells of the old national structures, blocking off attempts to create new global, co-operative, democratic institutions, however powerful the blandishments of internationalism might be on one day or on one issue, from time to time. In orations on May Day, the brotherhood of man would remain an inspiration. But on the grey normal working days, votes would be counted within the walls of the nation-states, and governments would be made or unmade in the light of perceived national interests.

# Notes

1 A. L. Morton and G. Tate, *The British Labour Movement, 1770–1920* (Lawrence and Wishart, 1956), p. 255.
2 Cited in Walter Kendall, *The Revolutionary Movement in Britain* (Weidenfeld and Nicolson, 1969), p. 86.
3 Royden Harrison, 'The War Emergency Workers' National Committee, 1914–1920', in Asa Briggs and John Saville (eds), *Essays in Labour History*, (Macmillan, 1971), p. 211.
4 Report of a Court of Inquiry concerning Transport Workers' Wages and Conditions, with Minutes of Evidence and appendices, Cmnd 936 and Cmnd 937, Parliamentary Papers, XXXIV, 1920 (the Shaw Report), Minutes of Evidence, p. 12.
5 Alan Bullock, *The Life and Times of Ernest Bevin*, vol. I: *Trade Union Leader, 1881–1940* (Heinemann, 1960), p. 45.
6 A. J. P. Taylor, *English History, 1914–1945* (Oxford University Press, 1965), p. 20.
7 Ibid.
8 Bernard Waites, *A Class Society at War: England 1914–1918* (Berg, 1987), p. 188.
9 DWRGWU Annual Report, 1914, pp. 5–7.
10 Ibid.
11 Frances, Countess of Warwick, *After Thoughts* (Cassell, 1931), p. 222.
12 NTWF *Weekly Record*, 8 August 1914.
13 Ibid.
14 Harrison, 'The War Emergency Workers' National Committee' pp. 219–24.
15 *The Times*, 1 May 1916.
16 NSFU Annual General Meeting Report, 26–7 January 1915, p. 8.
17 Ibid., pp. 16–17.
18 NSFU Annual General Meeting Report, 1916, p. 25.
19 Ibid., p. 56.
20 See TGWU, *The Growth of the Trade Union Idea and Spirit among the Staffs of the Port of London*, May 1923.
21 Francis Williams, *Ernest Bevin: Portrait of a Great Englishman* (Hutchinson, 1952), pp. 58 ff.; J. T. Murphy, *Labour's Big Three* (Bodley Head, 1948), pp. 37–9; Trevor Evans, *Bevin* (Allen and Unwin, 1946), pp. 63–5; Mark Stephens, *Ernest Bevin – Unskilled Labourer and World Statesman, 1881–1951* (TGWU, 1981), pp. 29–31; and, most comprehensive, Bullock, *The Life and Times of Ernest Bevin*, vol. I, pp. 52–6.
22 Philip Taft, *The AFL in the Time of Gompers* (Harper Bros, 1957), pp. 372–3.
23 Bill Haywood presided at the founding of the 'Wobbly' trade union, the Industrial Workers of the World, in Chicago in 1905. He became well known to British trade unionists when he made a lecture tour of Britain in 1910. Tom Mann publicized this in the *Industrial Syndicalist*, and doubtless

the tour would have come to the attention of Ernest Bevin at the time. Did Haywood's invitation to Tom Mann to return the compliment by visiting America account for Mann's absence from the domestic scene during the Dublin lock-out of 1913? Or are there other reasons why Mann stayed in the USA? It is a fascinating question, if one thinks of what Mann might have been able to do, alongside Larkin and his colleagues. Haywood later became associated with the Communist International, and when he died he was buried under the wall of the Kremlin.

24  Bullock, *The Life and Times of Ernest Bevin*, vol. I, p. 61.
25  See Bevin's book of speeches, *The Job to be Done* (Heinemann, 1942), for evidence of this.
26  Bernard Waites, *A Class Society at War*, p. 100.
27  NTWF Annual General Council Report, 1916, p. 55.
28  Ibid., p. 56.
29  See also Arthur Marsh and Victoria Ryan, *The History of the Seamen's Union* (Malthouse, 1989), p. 78.
30  NTWF Annual General Council Report, 1916, p. 13.
31  DWRGWU Annual Report, 1915, p. 6.
32  Shaw Report, Minutes of Evidence, p. 94.
33  When we recounted this story to Brian Barker, regional docks' secretary of the TGWU in Hull, in 1989, he recalled that Hull dockers who were directed to work in Liverpool during the Second World War picked up the custom of welting, and brought it back to Hull docks in 1945; it had been unknown there previously!
34  Bernard Waites, *A Class Society at War*, p. 201.
35  Dennis Hayes, *Conscription and Conflict* (Sheppard Press, 1949), p. 213.
36  H. A. Clegg, *A History of British Trade Unions since 1889*, vol. II: *1911–1933* (Oxford University Press, 1985), pp. 153–4.
37  NTWF Annual General Council Report, 1916, p. 94.
38  Taylor, *English History, 1914–1945*; cited in Clegg, *History of British Trade Unions*, p. 154.
39  NTWF Annual General Council Report, 1916, pp. 95–102.
40  Birmingham Labour History Group, *The People's Century* (Birmingham Trade Union Research Centre, 1989), p. 9.
41  NTWF Annual General Council Report, 1917, pp. 64–5.
42  Chris Wrigley, *A History of British Industrial Relations*, vol. II: *1914–39* (Harvester Press, 1987), p. 51.
43  Taylor, *English History, 1914–1945*, p. 120.
44  Waites, *A Class Society at War*, p. 51.
45  Labour Party Annual Conference Report, 1951, p. 194.
46  George Lansbury, *My Life* (London, 1928), p. 186.
47  Jo Vellacott, *Bertrand Russell and the Pacifists* (Harvester Press, 1980), p. 155.
48  Ibid., p. 157. Another eye-witness at the Albert Hall reported: 'Ordinary speakers could scarcely be heard – there were no microphones in those days. Three voices only rang plainly through those vast heights – the chairman, George Lansbury's, the transport worker, Robert Williams's and Clara Butt's, whose singing called . . . all the audience to its feet to join with her – all those who could control their emotion and were not already in

tears of relief and joy.' (Raymond Postgate, *The Life of George Lansbury*, Longman, 1951, p. 166).

49 Beatrice Webb was very flattered to be chosen, according to Margaret Cole, *The Story of Fabian Socialism* (Heinemann, 1961), p. 170.

50 For an account of this episode, see H. W. Lee and E. Archbold, *Social Democracy in Britain* (Social Democratic Federation, 1935), pp. 210–17.

51 *Daily Herald*, 'British Labour and the Russian Revolution', Documents on Socialist History, no. 1 (Spokesman Books, 1974), pp. 31–3.

52 Bullock, *The Life and Times of Ernest Bevin*, vol. I, p. 75.

53 Stephen White, 'Soviets in Britain: The Leeds Convention of 1917', *International Review of Social History*, vol. XIX (1974), pp. 165 ff.

54 Will Thorne, *My Life's Battles* (Lawrence and Wishart, 1989), p. 195.

55 DWRGWU Triennial Delegate Council Minutes, 22–6 May 1917, pp. 58–60. Stan Awbery was to become the TGWU's Barry District Secretary. Of Fred Thompson's dissident career in the TGWU we shall hear much more; see p. 842, and volume II.

56 DWRGWU *Record*, June 1917, pp. 10–11.

57 *Daily Herald*, 'British Labour and the Russian Revolution', pp. 29–30.

58 DWRGWU *Record*, June 1917, p. 3.

59 David Lloyd George, *War Memoirs*, vol. II (Odhams, 1956), p. 1,260.

60 NTWF Annual General Council Report, 14–15 June 1917, p. 26.

61 Ibid., p. 27.

62 Ibid., p. 30.

63 David Marquand, *Ramsay MacDonald* (Jonathan Cape, 1977), p. 215.

64 NTWF Annual General Council Report, 14–15 June 1917, p. 32.

65 Ibid., p. 33.

66 Ibid., pp. 36–7.

67 Ibid., pp. 37–8.

68 Ibid., p. 38.

69 Ibid., pp. 40–3.

70 Ibid., pp. 37–8.

71 Bertrand Russell, *Autobiography*, vol. II (Allen and Unwin, 1968), pp. 31–2.

72 David Egan, 'The Swansea Conference of the British Council of Soldiers' and Workers' Delegates, July, 1917', in *Llafur*, Journal of the Society for the Study of Welsh Labour History, vol. I, no. 4 (summer 1974), pp. 12–37.

73 White, 'Soviets in Britain', pp. 188–9.

74 Lloyd George, *War Memoirs*, vol. II, p. 1,121.

75 Taylor, *English History, 1914–1945*, p. 90.

76 Ross McKibbin, *The Evolution of the Labour Party, 1910–1924* (Oxford University Press, 1974), p. 92.

# 17

# Change: Power Without Glory

*Of all human activities, war is most inextricably linked to the extremes of misery, suffering and human degradation. To demonstrate how, at the same time, the war of 1914–18 was accompanied by important social change is in no sense an attempt to glorify or condone war.*[1]

## I

## *Technological Changes*

During the war, the technological changes in transport which we have followed in previous chapters continued full blast. The number of motor vehicles in the UK rose from 271,000 in 1914 to 294,000 in 1917 and to 476,000 by 1920. The value of the stock of motor vehicles (at constant 1900 prices) was £17.1 million in 1910 and £60.9 million in 1920. Of these values, passenger vehicles accounted for more than twice the stock of goods vehicles. The new generation of road-transport workers was increasingly motorized. The number of horse-drawn carts and wagons fell from 830,000 in 1910 to 430,000 in 1920. Sizeable though this number remained, it had none the less almost halved in a decade. Horse-drawn buses, however, were harder hit. None survived to 1920. Tramways were giving way to the omnibus. (Their capital stock halved between 1910 and 1920, when its value was £24.1 million.) The horse was not yet driven from our roads, which were nevertheless being better prepared to receive their increased traffic – the net value of road investments was £132 million in 1910, and £139.5 million by 1920. Though not a dramatic rise, this increase compares with a noticeable decline in the railways' capital stock, which fell from £651.5 million in 1910 to £600.3 million in 1920. This contrasting experience was full of portent for the future balance of trade-union forces, as the road-transport section of the future TGWU gathered strength and the railways began the slow, drawn-out decline from dominance in the field.

In the docks and harbours there was a small disinvestment between 1910 and 1920, capital stock falling by almost £3 million to stand at £95.9 million. We have already noticed the inflationary effects of the war in shipping; earnings by steamships rose from 104 in 1914 to 198 in 1918 and to 236 in 1920 (1900 = 100). The average steamship was valued at £18.2 per gross ton in 1914, £33.4 in 1918 and £49.3 in 1920.[2] On the docks the last burst of major investment had been in the Edwardian years, to accommodate the modern steam vessels and ocean liners. The docks apart, then, the NTWF's forces were concentrated in expanding services.

## Trade Union Membership

The growth in trade-union membership, which had been as high as 21 per cent in 1913, was halted in 1914. Then it resumed: 5 per cent in 1915, 6 per cent in 1916, and then, under the impact of Lloyd George's policies of total war and an alliance with Labour, it leapt by 18 per cent in 1917 and by 19 per cent in 1918 to a total of 6,533,000. (The figures for individual transport and general unions' membership are shown in table 17.1.) The affiliated membership of the NTWF rose from 162,000 in 1914 to 236,000 in 1918, partly as a result of union growth and partly by the affiliation of nine more unions (see below).

The relative passivity of the transport workers in the war years stands out when we look at the strike statistics (see table 17.2).

## State Intervention

In industrial relations, the growth of the state's economic role promoted a strong trend towards national bargaining, through the awards of the Committee on Production, the official arbitration body. Inflation, which affected all alike, tended to generate the same wage claims from all sections of an industry or trade. Instead of settling each claim locally or regionally, the Committee built up the practice of awarding standard settlements, pooled and co-ordinated by the trade unions concerned. This gave such unions a new role, and it was this which so greatly enhanced the status of the Federation in the transport industry. Ernest Bevin, in particular, played the game with great effect. He sought continually to advance the concept of the national wage and standard hours, and at the same time to establish the central authority of the Federation over its constituents. Incidentally, of course, this advanced

Table 17.1 *Trade Union Membership in Transport, 1913–1918*[*]

| | 1913 | 1915 | 1916 | 1917 | 1918 |
|---|---|---|---|---|---|
| Dock, Wharf, Riverside and General Workers' Union | 37,000 | 43,691 | 44,934 | 47,881 | 80,000 |
| National Sailors' and Firemen's Union | 60,000 | 55,000 | 55,000 | 55,000 | 65,000 |
| National Union of Dock Labourers | 32,000 | 51,000 | 47,000 | 47,000 | 45,000 |
| London and Provincial Union of Licensed Vehicle Workers[†] | 6,000 | 16,000 | 16,000 | 16,000 | 20,000 |
| Amalgamated Association of Tramway and Vehicle Workers[†] | 21,000 | 28,000 | 28,000 | 23,584 | 31,770 |
| National Warehouse and General Workers' Union | – | – | 5,000 | 12,000 | – |
| National Union of General Workers (ex-Gas) | 82,135 | 134,538 | 131,711 | 164,681 | – |
| National Union of Ships' Stewards, etc. | – | 8,000 | 7,000 | 7,000 | 7,000 |
| Scottish Union of Dock Labourers | – | 5,000 | 5,000 | 6,000 | 6,000 |
| National Union of Vehicle Workers[‡] | 4,000 | 6,000 | 6,000 | 6,000 | 11,000 |
| Amalgamated Society of Watermen, Lightermen and Bargemen | 5,000 | 5,000 | 4,651 | 4,578 | 4,865 |
| Amalgamated Stevedores' Labour Protection League | 5,610 | – | 4,000 | 4,000 | 4,300 |
| National Amalgamated Labourers' Union | 5,000 | 6,000 | 5,372 | 6,000 | 6,000 |
| Cardiff, etc., Coal Trimmers' Union | 2,050 | 2,050 | 2,050 | 2,018 | 2,025 |
| United Carters' and Motormen's Association | 5,000 | 5,000 | 5,000 | 5,000 | 8,000 |
| Amalgamated Union of Engine and Cranemen | – | 1,000 | 1,000 | 1,000 | 3,000 |

| | 1913 | 1915 | 1916 | 1917 | 1918 |
|---|---|---|---|---|---|
| National Amalgamated Union of Labour | 51,000 | 65,000 | 75,000 | 95,000 | 100,000 |
| Labour Protection League | 3,000 | 3,000 | 3,000 | 3,000 | 3,000 |
| Amalgamated Carters, Lurrymen's and Motormen's Union** | 3,000 | 5,000 | 7,000 | 6,000 | 5,000 |
| Hull Seamen's Union§ | – | – | – | – | 1,750 |
| Mersey River and Canal Watermen's Association | 2,000 | 2,000 | 1,440 | – | – |
| North of England Trimmers and Teemers | 1,580 | 1,500 | 1,502 | 1,478 | 1,436 |
| National Amalgamated Union of Enginemen, etc. | – | – | – | – | 28,000 |
| River Weaver Watermen's Association | 402 | 405 | 409 | 407 | 405 |

\* Unions listed here were all members of the NTWF by 1918, but some affiliated to the TUC for the first time only during the war, and some remained unaffiliated to the TUC down to 1918. The unions listed here are placed in rough order of the size of their affiliation to the NTWF in 1918, but some large unions, notably the NUGW (ex-Gasworkers) and the NAUL, affiliated only a portion of their membership (that involved in transport) to the Federation. (See the appendix to this chapter, p. 674, for the NTWF affiliation fees of 1918.)

† These two unions merged to become the United Vehicle Workers in 1920, and then reaffiliated to the Federation.

‡ Originally the London Carmen's Union, until 1913.

**The Bolton based Union featured in the Scarborough Brewery case (see below). It affiliated to the NTWF and became the Northern Section (Commercial) of the United Vehicle Workers in 1920.

§ Merged with NSFU in 1922.

*Source*: TUC Annual Reports.

his own towering personal influence. 'Bevin complained at this time that he lived on the doorstep of the Committee on Production.'[3]

The state machine expanded in all directions. In addition to the Committee on Production and the Ministry of Labour (founded in 1916), the War Office, the Admiralty, and the Board of Trade (through the Coal Controller and the Railway Executive Committee) all developed industrial-relations functions. Predictably, their initiatives frequently conflicted, greatly to the annoyance of Sir George Askwith. Before the war he had blazed trails towards state arbitration and conciliation. Now, under his chairmanship of the Committee on Production, these became standard practice and his committee was the national arbitration tribunal. He had a mandarin's contempt for the blundering and, in his eyes, irresponsibly generous settlements which ministers offered to unions in essential trades.[4] Eventually, in 1919, he was removed from office and sent to the House of Lords.[5]

Whitehall became the scene of many other conflicts between members of the mandarinate and the inexperienced new directors of services. Some of these were patricians and some were Labour gatecrashers.[6] They included Lord Devonport, Food Controller; John Hodge, Minister of Labour; G. H. Roberts, who succeeded Hodge; and David Shackleton, Permanent Secretary at the Labour Ministry. William Beveridge, Permanent Secretary of the Board of Trade's Labour Department, who resented the post of chief official going to Devonport and coveted that given to Shackleton, was scarcely less antagonistic than was Askwith to these upstart Labour Party appointments. The powerful Llewellyn Smith, Permanent Secretary of the Board of Trade, the same man who had written the story of the 1889 dock strike, was now dug into the Labour Department of the Munitions Ministry, from where he opposed the new Ministry of Labour. His co-author, Vaughan Nash, became Secretary of the Cabinet Committee on Reconstruction. Thus the state and its servants groped and stumbled their way into a vastly extended economic and industrial-relations role.[7]

Table 17.2 *Number of Strikes, Numbers Involved (000s) and Total Days' Duration (000s), Transport and All Industries, 1914–1918*

| | No. of strikes | % | No. workers involved (000s) | % | No. of days lost (000s) | % |
|---|---|---|---|---|---|---|
| Transport 1913 | 115 | 8 | 84 | 13 | 1,184 | 12 |
| All industries 1913 | 1,459 | 100 | 664 | 100 | 9,804 | 100 |
| Transport 1914 | 53 | 5 | 13 | 3 | 87 | 1 |
| All industries 1914 | 972 | 100 | 447 | 100 | 9,878 | 100 |
| Transport 1915 | 75 | 11 | 25 | 6 | 152 | 5 |
| All industries 1915 | 672 | 100 | 448 | 100 | 2,953 | 100 |
| Transport 1916 | 44 | 8 | 28 | 10 | 103 | 4 |
| All industries 1916 | 532 | 100 | 276 | 100 | 2,446 | 100 |
| Transport 1917 | 32 | 4 | 26 | 3 | 184 | 3 |
| All industries 1917 | 730 | 100 | 872 | 100 | 5,647 | 100 |
| Transport 1918 | 48 | 4 | 59 | 5 | 277 | 5 |
| All industries 1918 | 1,165 | 100 | 1,116 | 100 | 5,875 | 100 |

*Source:* Christopher Wrigley, *A History of British Industrial Relations*, vol. II: 1914–39 (Harvester Press, 1987), pp. 13–15. (Reproduced by permission of Harvester Press.)

Ben Tillett, for all his patriotic fervour, did not like it at all. Writing in his Annual Report of December 1916, he exclaimed:

The country found our capitalists and our banks bankrupt within a week of the war; to prevent scandal and ruin, banks were closed until the State guaranteed the banks, the employers, the ship-owners. Capital and commerce was at once made secure, but so far as labour is concerned, every ciliery [sic] of the Civil Service, of the ramifications of capitalist control, was organised against labour. The complex and labyrinthine machinery of control has been at work with sordid thoroughness ever since.[8]

An official report described chaotic relations:

Thus, the Ministry of Munitions and the War Office were concerned with the settlement of disputes on munitions work; the Admiralty, as regards war vessels and other Admiralty contract work; the Board of Trade as regards the coal-mining industry and the railways; the Ministry of Shipping with merchant vessels; the Air Ministry with the building of aeroplanes, the construction of aerodromes, etc. All this had a tendency to result in lack of uniformity and absence of co-ordination.[9]

From our perspective, one irony is that no Ministry of Transport was created until 1919, just as the 'bonfire of controls' got under way in the post-war government. But the Port and Transit Executive Committee became a central influence on the evolution of the transport unions. We examine it in more detail below.

## National Agreements and Arbitration

Before Askwith was expelled, he presided, as Chief Industrial Commissioner at the Ministry of Labour, and as the principal arbitrator of the Committee on Production, over the creation of the first genuinely national agreements in British industry. The pioneer settlement was the national Wages Agreement of 1917 in the engineering industry. With its provision for continuous four-monthly revisions (to anticipate and accommodate the predictable inflation), it set the pattern for other industries, including transport. Askwith proudly recorded the comment of 'a critic', whom he did not identify: 'This award is in many ways a "record" in wage arbitrations. For the first time, a uniform advance of wages has been given to the whole of the men in the engineering workshops of Great Britain, nearly a million in number, they and their families representing one-tenth of the whole population.'[10]

Cotton and shipbuilding had established national bargaining before the war; the railways achieved it in 1915. In 1917, the engineering national example was followed by chemicals, mining, shipping and wool.

Agriculture was a special case. The government established statutory wages boards in the industry in 1915: 'Including agriculture therefore, by the end of 1917 national collective bargaining had been adopted in industries accounting for at least a third of the employed labour force, a larger share of the manual labour force, and well over half of total trade union membership.'[11]

The effect on wage rates was substantial. Between 1914 and 1916, their real value fell by 30 per cent. Already in February 1916, trade unions had protested to Asquith that his government was using the Committee on Production to freeze wages, Bevin leading a series of walk-outs from arbitration hearings.[12] After Lloyd George's succession, however, the gap between wage rates and prices was reduced to 15 per cent in 1917.[13]

The pace of work of the arbitration service during the war was hectic. Askwith tells us: 'The Committee on Production was simply overwhelmed with the number of cases, each of which required a large amount of correspondence. Its staff was ludicrously small. Visits to the North of Scotland by a single member could only alleviate, not meet, the number of pressing cases. A glut of cases was dealt with as speedily as possible'.[14] Of course, there had been a dizzying speed of growth:

> In 1913, the number of cases referred to arbitration was about forty-five. In 1918, the figures referred to the Committee on Production and other arbitrators was more than 3,500. During the five years of its existence, either with three members or, latterly, with several courts, the total nearly reached 8,000 cases; and, says the Twelfth Report under the Conciliation Act, 'the awards were almost universally accepted'.[15]

Appendices I–VIII of the Twelfth Report of Proceedings under the Conciliation Act, 1896, contain accounts of all the wartime arbitration awards; they were published in two volumes, each exceeding 900 pages.

## Leadership Responses

How did transport unionism respond to all these pressures and opportunities? Their industrial scene was reshaping itself in the fires of war. We have already noticed some of the quantitative changes: the growth in membership of both individual unions and of the Federation. Its leaders maintained their different opinions and policies throughout this period of growth, although Robert Williams became noticeably more self-confident as the war ground on. Without abandoning the defiant support for pacifist campaigns and the cause of socialist internationalism which we reported in the previous chapter, he developed formidable administrative and organizing skills to advance the industrial powers of the Federation.

His colleagues in the NTWF, including his bitterest 'patriotic' opponents, were compelled to acknowledge his indispensability, when they learned that he had accepted nomination from his own union, the NALU, as a parliamentary candidate. Whilst acknowledging his right to stand for Parliament, they begged him not to do so, in terms which speak volumes about Williams's wartime industrial role. The Executive Committee resolved:

> That having full regard to the growing activities of the Federation in conducting national wage movements, and the increasing need on the part of the Federation to maintain its economic and industrial influence in all the general policy and programme of reconstruction, this Executive Council strongly recommends the General Secretary to concentrate his efforts upon his industrial duties. While agreeing on general grounds that the Secretary should have equal rights with other trade union officials to his full political freedom and when desirable to accept nomination as a Labour Candidate, this Executive Council trusts that during the stress of the transitional period before and following the resumption of peace, the General Secretary shall devote himself to his industrial activities.[16]

Bevin stood at some distance from Williams; he took no active part in anti-war activities, though he shared most of Williams's criticisms of British foreign and military policy. In industrial matters, these two worked in close and harmonious partnership to resist incorporation in the state machinery of labour controls and to advance – within the limits set by the overall support for the war emergency adopted by the Federation – their pre-war policy of national bargaining, recognition and greater centralization of Federation power, as a preliminary to amalgamation. But Bevin's political commitment, though shaped in his union, was none the less firm for that. He, too, became a candidate in the 1918 election.

Tillett's role in the NTWF, and indeed in his own union, declined sharply. He was frequently absent from the EC of the Federation, pursuing his self-allotted duties in the war-effort, and in 1916, in a significant moment, he resigned from its vice-presidency and from its Executive. The vice-presidency passed to Sexton, and more importantly, his executive seat was taken by Bevin.

Now the younger man began to gather power into his hands. In the Federation he shared the initiative with Williams, but in the DWRGWU, where he remained formally subordinate to Tillett, he assumed the effective leadership. Together, with their joint authority secure, Williams and Bevin shaped the Federation's wartime policies.

Gosling, a war supporter, retained his presidency of the Federation; the rest of the leadership, with the exception of Havelock Wilson and Joe Cotter, whose excessive chauvinism was a general embarrassment, took up their industrial positions behind these two. Sexton's patriotism was less strident than Wilson's but the issue of civilian conscription of dock labour led him into isolation from the mainstream, as we shall see.[17]

The trend to national settlements, though imposed by all that new and overworked machinery of state arbitration, was of course welcomed by the unions in the fragmented structures of the NTWF. It was given permanence by the reports of the Whitley Committee, part of the government's Reconstruction Committee, which recommended the creation of voluntary Joint Industrial Councils composed of representative bodies of trade unions and employers in each industry. Its recommendations went beyond the idea of national wage bargaining alone, for it proposed that these JICs should afford a consultative function to the unions in matters of production and the general welfare of employees. In this, it reflected and sought to head off the mounting demands for greater powers of control, or even for joint management, that came from shop stewards in engineering and from trade-union representatives on the state control bodies that were managing mines, munitions factories, ports and railways. By this time, too, the influence of the Russian Revolution was beginning to be felt in the Labour movement, not least in its industrial aspect: in Russia, Workers' Councils were deciding the destiny of a whole nation and their example was not lost on the British Labour movement, involved as it was in more and closer corporate relations, in a war with which it was increasingly disenchanted.

Most British Labour history for this period has concentrated naturally on the munitions industry and engineering. In these trades disruptive strikes and unrest built up to a frontal challenge to government during the later phases of the war. It had become possible to question the war itself, but the industrial unrest was not about the war, as such. Rather it confronted the effects of war. The munitions industries, of course, involved the Workers' Union, whose membership rose from 140,000 to 379,000 between 1914 and 1918, making it the second largest union in the country, as it swept up into membership the swollen ranks of semi-skilled workers in the munitions, engineering and the new aircraft industries, recruiting widely among women, as well as extending its former enclaves elsewhere, as in agriculture.[18]

## Who Led the Federation?

Conditions in transport were different. The government was extremely sensitive about the need to keep all channels open. The NTWF, for all the reasons we have surveyed above, had entered the war in a cautious mood. It was unsure both of the appropriate strategy to pursue on industrial matters and of its own authority over its affiliates. A study of the Executive minute-books shows that, from 1914 until 1916, it tended to refer back to individual unions their requests for advice, leadership or co-ordination. For example, in January 1915 the Executive, on being informed that various ports had given notice of demands for increased wages, resolved 'that no specific action be taken by the Federation as a whole, but that Unions should get the best terms they could in their individual capacities, and report.'[19] Again, on 29 October, the EC, in response to an appeal from its Humber District Committee for federal action in support of claims for further war bonuses, replied to both the Humber and London districts that 'the matter of further war bonuses must be left with the Unions concerned, leaving them to take action either separately or in co-operation with other unions in the same districts as conditions might determine.'

Sexton proposed that the secretary should collate the agreements of the affiliated unions, 'with the length of term, period of notice, date of expiry, and so on, and present them to the Executive with a view to action after the war. There would be a big economic fight going on after the war, and they would have to be prepared for it. The Federation ought to have a set policy'. However, Robert Williams had to report that the response to his circular requesting this information from the affiliated unions had been 'somewhat meagre'.

During this time, the Federation began to show an increasing reliance on the Triple Alliance on questions of high policy, such as conscription, post-war aims and programmes, the Chinese labour issue, and a number of other political matters. At first sight these might have seemed appropriate for reference either to the TUC, the Labour party, or the War Emergency Workers' Committee;[20] but the liaison between the NTWF and the leaders of the railwaymen and miners in the Triple Alliance occupied much EC time and attention. Clearly it was thought to be useful.

Another Executive response to issues which came before it was reference of the question to the Federation's appropriate District Committee. This was an expanding practice. The circumstances of war raised their own problems. There were the twin needs of co-ordinating wage movements and of nominating and controlling union representation on governmental regulatory bodies such as the Port and Transit Executive Committee and its local Port Labour Committees. These gathered a welcome accretion of authority for the NTWF districts. Of course such authority contributed to the will towards amalgamation, and developed a foretaste of the model of district government which was to mark the future TGWU.

But the most strikingly significant development was that the Executive increasingly took its own initiative on a widening range of issues. Inter-union demarcation and poaching disputes between affiliates were dealt with at regular intervals, with evident decisiveness. As the state arbitration process developed on a huge scale, the Federation's officers found themselves more and more involved as bargainers for groups of affiliates. They spoke for their people in road haulage, passenger transport and docks; they represented coal-trimmers, pilots and many others. The seamen's unions, however, stood apart. They retained almost total autonomy in their negotiations with the Admiralty and the shipowners. Across the rest of its field, by 1917 and 1918, the Federation was presenting or preparing in its own name a whole range of co-ordinated, standard national demands for wage agreements. In these matters, it was already acting *de facto* in the same way as the executive of a trade union.

There were some areas where it declined to take action, however, on the grounds that the issue was properly one for its individual affiliated unions. These questions served to underline that the Executive retained the sense that it was still a federal body, rather than the governing body of a unified organization. This reluctance to encroach powers from constituent bodies was very marked. Thus, the Executive referred a request to affiliate to the Railway Nationalisation Society, and an invitation to attend a Ruskin College conference, to the affiliated unions and decided to take no action 'as a Federation'. In a similar vein, it turned down an invitation to attend a conference of the Workers' Suffrage Federation, on the grounds that it was 'political' and therefore 'outside the scope of the Federation'.[21]

It must be said that this self-denying ordinance was applied with no apparent consistency, since a vast amount of the Federation's work was inevitably 'political', while the government was intervening with such wide-ranging powers in the transport industries. It was, however, a constraint which fell with particular severity upon the left, and particularly upon Robert Williams. In the debate at the 1917 AGC, as we have seen, Bevin had spoken in defence of Williams, and stuck his neck out to do so. But he felt it necessary to reproach him for his criticism of the established trade-union movement, delivered at the high point of the Leeds Convention that June. Bevin called on Williams, with whom he sympathized, to take his arguments into the trade-union movement rather than engaging in extra-mural activities. Williams replied: 'I am told by Bevin that I ought to try to convert those inside, and especially to influence the Triple Alliance with the principles of internationalism and working class solidarity. But whenever we raise controversial matters inside the Federation, for example, the cry is: Don't let us raise contentious matters; let us keep to our industrial purpose and work. I have therefore taken my views and advocacy outside.'[22]

This is a rather clear example of what was a general political problem for the Federation. Short of amalgamation, it was impossible for its Executive or Council either to pursue a collective policy on politically contentious matters, or to insist on its chief officer's accountability for his personal conduct in the political arena, since this was an area largely outside the collective domain. It was especially difficult to bridle a general secretary whose prosecution of the Federation's 'legitimate' concerns during the war was exemplary, as even political opponents such as Havelock Wilson acknowledged. Tillett, who violently disagreed with Williams about the war, remained personally loyal to him. At the same time, Bevin's insistence that the politics of labour should be determined in the organizations of labour, carried weight and conviction.

In wartime, the trade-union distinction between 'industrial' and 'political' roles is much more difficult to trace than it is in times of peace. Government is everywhere. As the war progressed, the Federation in its industrial role did indeed assume more and more functions of a unitary trade union. This is particularly true of its Executive Committee, and of its District Committees. The Annual General Council, although fulfilling the constitutional, policymaking function of a membership conference, was an assembly of the chief officials of the constituent unions, not a collective of rank-and-file delegates. Total attendance at the AGC in 1917 was an intimate forty-six, representing twenty-one unions; a further seven affiliated unions did not send delegates that year.

The Executive Committee at the beginning of the war consisted of J. Anderson of the Stevedores' Union; E. Cathery, general secretary of the NSFU; J. Cotter, general secretary of the Ship's Cooks' and Stewards' Union (headquarters Liverpool); Joseph Houghton, general secretary of the Scottish Dockers' Union (from Glasgow); P. Kean of the National Warehouse and General Workers' Union (headquarters Liverpool); G. Parker, general secretary of the National Amalgamated Union of Enginemen, Firemen, Mechanics, Motormen and Electrical Workers (headquarters Rotherham); S. March, general secretary of the National Union of Vehicle Workers; Harry Gosling, president of the NTWF, of the Watermen's and Lightermen's Union; J. Twomey, general secretary of the National Amalgamated Labourers' Union (headquarters Swansea); J. Sexton, general secretary of the NUDL (headquarters Liverpool); Ben Tillett, vice-president of the NTWF; and Robert Williams, general secretary of the NTWF and a member of the NALU. It can be seen that to the London-based unions there was now added a stronger leavening from the Mersey and South Wales. This group sustained the work of its monthly meetings throughout 1914, being joined in July by W. H. Jones, general secretary of the Mersey Quay and Railway Carters' Union (headquarters Liverpool). Given that the formidable Tom Mann spent the war as the Mersey district secretary of the NTWF, the Liverpool weighting becomes even more pronounced.

In July 1915 J. T. Clatworthy, of the Cardiff Coal Trimmers' Union, was elected to the Executive, increasing the Welsh presence. Ernest Bevin was elected at the 1916 AGC, coming from nowhere to second place in the poll, marginally behind Cathery (161,000 votes, against 160,000 for Bevin). The following year he headed the Executive poll by a margin of 5,000 votes over Twomey in second place (170,000, against

175,000 for Bevin; Cathery fell to sixth place). A very few others came and went: R. H. Farrah of the Gas and General Workers' Union came on in 1917; he was NTWF district secretary for the Humber.

This small group of men sustained the heavy wartime agenda of the Federation with real diligence; their attendance records testify to this, and also to the key importance which the Federation had now achieved in the affairs of their unions. Sexton was content to offer a full contribution to EC debates, whilst playing only a small part in implementing its decisions. Whenever the EC required a delegation, a deputation, a troubleshooting team, or a sub-committee, as distinct from action by Williams alone (whose labours were prodigious), the usual practice became to appoint 'The President, the Secretary, and Mr. Bevin', except when the affairs of a particular union were involved, when its representative on the EC would be nominated. But to the Triple Alliance, to the Boards of Trade, to the Ministry of Labour, to the Committee on Production, to the War Office, to the Ministry of Reconstruction, or wherever, went Gosling, Williams and Bevin, who thus became *de facto* an executive officer. His duties in the Federation also extended to the District Committee for the Bristol area, and he was a national organizer of the DWRGWU, working out of London. He also made a weekly journey to Bristol for his own union as well as for the Federation. In 1917 the National Council of General Labourers was transformed into the National Federation of General Workers, and Bevin played a prominent part on its Executive as well.[23] Little wonder that, towards the end of the war, he suffered a nervous breakdown. He had to be relieved of most of his duties for two or three months from July 1917.[24]

Bevin's rise had a certain inevitability about it. The war, and the increased influence and widening roles of the NTWF and the NFGW which it occasioned, created for him a unique opportunity to dominate events and to shape the future structures of trade unionism. Alan Bullock's monumental biography stands, of course, as the definitive account of Bevin's life and should be read by all who wish to know about this remarkable man. Here we are concerned with the collective history of the union. Yet it must be said that Bevin's massive influence, which erupted during the war, would remain evident in everything which followed.

In addition to the functions described above, the wartime transport workers' EC continued to promote mergers amongst its sectional affiliates where possible. A new and less stringent Trade Union Amalgamation Act was conceded to the movement by the government in 1917 – the Act under which the great post-war amalgamations would eventually take place. Lloyd George intended it as another favour in his sustained bid for union support, and in its final form – more stringent than he had planned, but amended by the Commons – it required that 50 per cent of the membership should vote, and that those in favour of merger should exceed those against by 20 per cent.[25] The 1876 Act, which it replaced, had required a two-thirds majority. The new law was timely, for the war prompted a flood of mergers and federations across the whole field of trade unionism.

## Rationalizing Transport Unionism

With the Federation, it was in the road-transport field, both commercial and passenger, that the greatest degree of rationalization was still required. We have seen in earlier chapters that a plethora of local and regional unions had existed since the outburst of new union formations in the late 1880s. Harmony sometimes eluded them. However, the Federation found an increasing authority and was often to adjudicate their disagreements during these years. When, for instance, the London and Provincial Union of Licensed Vehicle Workers (LPU) applied to affiliate to the NTWF in February 1916, its acceptance was opposed by the National Union of Vehicle Workers (NUVW) (formerly the London Carmen's Union), on the grounds that, since the applicant union catered only for passengers, it was not a transport union.[26] The EC took a larger and more balanced view, admitted the LPU and admonished the NUVW; moreover, it went on to urge that the new affiliation should help to pave the way for early amalgamation of all road-transport unions.

This issue was pressed more firmly in the following year, by which time, as we shall see, co-ordination of wage movements in the vehicle workers' sector had begun. The EC recommended that, in this setting, the three competing vehicle workers' unions in London should compose their differences and at least come to an agreement on spheres of influence. The unions' response was to propose instead a national conference to consider a merger. A pencilled draft resolution in the margin of the minutes, the status of which is obscure, records that the EC was 'convinced that a National Union of Transport Workers is both desirable and necessary to meet changing industrial requirements and after-war problems. It further declares that no efforts to define spheres of influence can be entirely satisfactory unless and until all the transport unions are under one banner.'[27]

From time to time the EC used its power to accept or reject applications for affiliation, in order to promote mergers. The Wigan and District Carters' Association and the Halifax and District Carters' Association applied simultaneously in September 1917 to affiliate. Both were told that the EC would prefer them to join the Federation by amalgamating with an existing constituent union.[28] The Wigan union entered negotiations with the Mersey Quay and Railway Carters' Union, whose secretary, W. H. Jones, was on the Federation EC. The Halifax union declined a similar approach from Jones, and was in fact then allowed to affiliate directly.

Another route used to encourage regional mergers was taken in the case of the Amalgamated Horsemen's Union of Glasgow, whose application to affiliate was referred to the Clyde District Committee of the Federation.[29] In 1918 the Grimsby General Workers' Friendly and Protective Society resolved 'to recommend to our next Members' General Meeting, the desirability . . . of our amalgamation with a National Organisation, with a view to our being affiliated to the National Transport Workers' Federation.'[30] G. Parker, the Rotherham-based Executive member, visited this little society in Grimsby – which had been founded as a client union with employer intervention in the aftermath of the collapse of Tillett's union on Humberside in 1893 – to arrange a merger with his union.

The organization of tramway workers in Liverpool called for the intervention both of the local EC members, led by Jones of the Mersey Quay and Railway Carters' Union, and of the EC's 'big three' – Gosling, Williams and Bevin, who went to Merseyside as a Federation deputation. With these steady but unspectacular initiatives, the Federation quietly gathered to itself more and more of the fragmented unionism in road transport and general labour.

The EC was involved, too, in an attempt to merge the London Stevedores' Society and the Amalgamated Stevedores' Labour Protection League in 1918.[31] The latter was an affiliate, and it will be recalled that the London society had been formed in an unhappy breakaway of the Tilbury branch of the Amalgamated League in 1912, resulting from the different policies (open versus closed craft unionism) pursued by different groups of stevedores on the London waterfront.

## Inter-union Conflict: the Scottish Carters

Not all inter-union conflicts were resolved by the EC's intervention. The North of Scotland Horse and Motormen's Union had a long-standing rivalry with the Scottish Horse and Motormen's Union. The efforts to resolve this recur in the EC minutes from 1915 through to 1918. The two organizations collided in a dispute in Dundee in March 1915 and the EC attempted conciliation. The North of Scotland Union, the smaller of the two bodies, was a breakaway from the Scottish Union, and had been an affiliate of the NTWF since it was formed. The parent body had attended a national conference of carters' unions in Manchester in that year, to discuss closer unity and the role of the NTWF, but Hugh Lyon, general secretary of the Scottish Union, recalled in his memoirs that 'there were a hundred and one English carters' unions, "and that the officials are all jealous of one another".'[32] His union consequently remained outside the Federation, although willing to discuss amalgamation with any other Scottish carters' unions, including the Northern Union with its headquarters in Dundee. Peter Gillespie, its general secretary, was urged by the EC to negotiate a merger with its larger rival in 1916, despite what was admitted to be 'a good deal of recrimination between these two societies',[33] so bringing about the entry of the Scottish society into the Federation. At that stage, Lyon changed his stance, following his union's decision to affiliate. He reported that 'This combination, if properly guided, should be of immense value and importance to the workers' future progress.'[34]

Lyon's union thereupon affiliated, after marathon efforts by both Williams and the Scottish TUC to reconcile the two unions. Lyon's decision was undoubtedly influenced primarily by the launching at the conference in Manchester of the Federation's national carters' 'movement' – a six-point programme of wage demands, shorter hours, etc. This was important evidence of the growing effectiveness of the Federation as a national bargaining agency; it was enough to overcome the parochial and nationalistic barriers to co-operation between the fiefdoms of the scattered carters' unions. The most nationalistic of all, Lyon's union, affiliated its 8,000 members in 1917.

However, Lyon may have had secondary motives for moving in to the Federation. He lost no time in tabling a motion at his first AGC, in 1917, calling upon the EC to compel the North of Scotland Union to go back into his union, which he called 'the parent organisation', or – failing willingness of the Dundee union to obey – to expel it from the Federation. The debate which ensued between him and Gillespie vibrated with ill-will, as accusation and counter-accusation flew back and forth. Lyon claimed that Gillespie had only 3–400 members; Gillespie claimed 2,500. Each argued that the other's terms for a merger were bogus and illicit. Gillespie was accused of 'wanting to be the general secretary'. Lyon was accused of strike-breaking in 1911 in Glasgow, and of neglecting the needs of his Dundee members. After listening to all these recriminations, the AGC promptly referred the dispute to the EC.[35]

Williams and Bevin went up to Dundee, and obtained the agreement of the Northern Union to a joint effort to bring about amalgamation with the Scottish Union. Failing agreement, the Federation would have the right to arbitrate and determine the outcome. No amalgamation followed on this initiative, however. Instead, the Northern Union was found complaining of the resistance of the Scottish Union to the formation of a Joint Industrial Council in road haulage for the Scottish area, and of 'discrediting the Federation in the matter of national negotiations'. Lyon's union, although a participant in the carters' national 'movement', now aimed to establish separate negotiations for Scotland.[36] Even whilst the EC was considering its response to these developments, Lyon was persuading his union's Annual Conference to withdraw from the Federation.[37] He never explained his motives; it would seem quixotic to have withdrawn at the very moment that centralized bargaining and the wartime arbitration machinery was combining to grant much-improved, standard wages for all carters. But Lyon, throughout his long career as general secretary, would ultimately oppose either amalgamation with any non-Scottish trade union, or participation in joint-bargaining machinery with other unions. Immediately after the war he resisted yet further efforts by both the Scottish TUC and the United Vehicle Workers' Union to achieve a merger, his Executive resolving that it would 'take no part in any scheme of amalgamation or fusion which involves the handing over of their funds and the relinquishing of their independence and individuality as a Scottish Union to any Executive with headquarters in London or in any part of England.'[38] Lyon's hostility seems to have been compounded of nationalism, the desire to maintain his own powers, and a backward-looking conservatism about the carters' job. To the end of his career, when his Executive compelled him to retire in 1937, he continued to think of the motorized lorry as a temporary intruder.

The Northern Union retained its membership of the NTWF and joined the TGWU at its foundation. Another Scottish carters' union, the Associated Horsemen's Union (of Greenock), was kept waiting for its affiliation to be approved whilst the conflicts with Lyon rumbled on, but it also joined the TGWU in 1922. Lyon's idiosyncracies, which undoubtedly reflected genuine sectional nationalism, had the result that the principal Scottish road-haulage union remained separate from its UK counterparts for the next fifty-three years, until Alex Kitson and Jack Jones brought about a successful, and very harmonious, merger in 1971.

## Conflict Between Seamen

In its handling of inter-union conflicts in the shipping industry, the Federation betrayed no sign of consistency in its attitude to another breakaway union, which had originated on the Clyde in 1911. Whilst Lyon's union, only 8,000 strong and outside the Federation, was unable to blacklist the North of Scotland Horsemen's Union, Havelock Wilson's union easily achieved the outlawry of the British Seafarers' Union. The process engendered no little venom.

It will be recalled that both the Southampton and Glasgow seamen had contested Wilson's judgement in 1911, and that the resultant breakaway branches had united to form the British Seafarers' Union, with Emanuel Shinwell as its secretary. The wartime shortage of seamen, and the national feeling of sympathy towards them, strengthened the BSU's position, and in Glasgow some shipowners entered negotiations with it.[39] This recognition was anathema to Havelock Wilson, and he won Federation support in his campaign to ostracise the BSU. Joseph Houghton, Scottish dockers' secretary, Federation district secretary for the Clyde and member of the EC, reported in 1915 that the NSFU had complained that the BSU had blacklegged during an NSFU strike in Leith. The Glasgow Trades Council investigated and 'found by a small majority that the BSU had not blacklegged'.[40] 'We seem as far off as ever of getting one Seamen's Union for the Clyde, and every now and then we hear of the shipowners playing one Union off against the other. If this is the case now, what will happen after the war? . . . there is not room for more than one Union for seamen in this country.'[41]

In December 1916, the Admiralty, which was harassed throughout the war on the question, invited the Federation, the NSFU, the Ships' Stewards' Union and the BSU to a conference on the use of Chinese labour: 'The parties concerned had refused to be associated with the BSU in this matter . . . Mr. Cotter explained that he had at first accepted the invitation of the Admiralty . . . of course, when the facts were available, [he] refused to associate with the BSU'.[42] The Admiralty dutifully forwarded another, acceptable invitation, and Havelock Wilson, Cotter and Williams agreed to it.

In 1917 the Labour Party requested the guidance of the Federation on the propriety of accepting the BSU's application to affiliate. The Executive replied that it would like time to consult the NSFU.[43] In the following February the Executive resolved to advise the party 'that it was undesirable that this union be affiliated to the Labour Party.'[44]

## Havelock Wilson: Maverick

In his role as super-patriot, Havelock Wilson sustained a running campaign against any Federation involvement in politics critical of the war-effort. Twice his union submitted four months' notice of impending withdrawal from the Federation, on the ground that 'pro-German' sentiments had been expressed in resolutions or by individual leaders. It was Robert Williams, of course, who most frequently offended. The Executive responded in conciliatory vein. Wilson complained that the AGC in 1917 passed a resolution critical of the National Alliance of Employers and Employed, but Gosling assured him that, although tabled, it had been withdrawn without debate. A second complaint that the Seamen's Union was inadequately represented was met with the suggestion that the union should propose an amendment to the rules at the next AGC. A demand that the Seamen's and Firemen's Union be accorded separate representation on the Joint Executive of the Triple Alliance received the same soft answer. The seamen, said the Executive, should raise this in the proper constitutional quarters. Their union took this advice literally: in 1918 it tabled a motion for the AGC requesting that the Triple Alliance 'so to alter its rules and constitution as to admit the NSFU as a section of the Alliance, and that afterwards the title shall be "The Quadruple Alliance".'[45]

The Executive agreed to present Wilson's case to the Alliance, and he withdrew the motion. Conciliatory behaviour had its limits, however. The Executive drew the line at the final charge, that the Federation had endorsed a joint call in the Triple Alliance demanding the conscription of wealth. Gosling pointed out that this 'fault' was one the Federation shared with the whole Labour movement, including the TUC, and that even Bonar Law, for the government, had promised that a capital levy, or the conscription of wealth, would be considered 'if the necessary money was not forthcoming voluntarily'.[46]

Wilson's treatment of the Federation reflected his union's enhanced autonomy, now that wartime recognition was in force. The government and the shipowners set up the National Maritime Board in 1917. It included representatives from Wilson's own union and from the Ships' Stewards' Union. Wilson had finally got his national bargaining machine, and thereafter he felt able to treat the Federation frivolously. In its turn, its Executive seemed deferential towards his outbursts, maintaining all possible courtesies in the face of sustained bombast. The consequences, for the future unity of all shipping, port and transport unionism, were none too healthy.

## Difficulties with the Railwaymen

There were different problems in the relations with another powerful, autonomous union; but they were not one whit less difficult. The National Union of Railwaymen, like the seamen, consolidated its recognition through the war, in spite of the old intransigence of the railway employers. From its foundation in 1913, the NUR had not affiliated to the NTWF. Its new status under the regime of the government's Railway Executive Committee, which took over railway management in 1915, for the war period and beyond, served to reinforce the NUR's sense of independence from its fellow transport unions. As in the shipping industry, capital concentration, together with wartime exigencies, pointed to a centralized system of bargaining and made it convenient to recognize a centralized trade union. The fact that, in the docks, road-passenger transport and road haulage, progress towards a single or at least one dominant union, together with similar organization on the employers' side, lagged behind these developments in shipping and railways, had a decisive effect upon future trade-union structure and frustrated hopes for a unified organization covering the whole transport field. Recognition for the NUR and NSFU, at an early stage in the war (the seamen were granted a national increase on Admiralty-requisitioned ships within a fortnight of the declaration of war)[47] had the effect of pulling them away from closer association with the NTWF, which struggled on with local wage bargaining until 1917–18.

Government management of the railways had permanent effects which reinforced this trend; before the war there were five main railway companies specific to Wales, at least thirteen main companies in England and five in Scotland. After the war all these were consolidated by the Railway Act of 1921 into the 'Big Four': the London Midland and Scottish, the London and North-eastern, the Southern, and the Great Western Railway Companies. (The ports owned by the Victorian railway companies came with them into these amalgamations. All the South Wales ports, for example, came into the ownership of the Great Western Railway, the last – the Swansea Harbour Trust – in 1923. By similar means, the LNER acquired the Humber ports, and Southampton went in with the Southern Railway.) As in the mining industry, wartime state management stimulated the demand for railway nationalization, thus reinforcing railwaymen's perception of their autonomy. But, as in mining, private ownership survived until after the Second World War. Nationalization of the pits took place in 1947, while the railways were to follow in the next year. The very nature of many railway workers' jobs, which entailed daily travel linking the great conurbations of the whole land, had taken their unions towards a national structure some time before the carters and busmen and dockers became aware of how necessary it would be to reach this stage.

Whilst the NUR, which dealt with the Railway Executive Committee, remained outside the Federation, which related to the Port and Transit Committees, the two bodies could not avoid a constant problem of 'overlapping' and rivalry in the ports. The railway companies owned vast areas of dockland, which they had developed in the nineteenth century in consequence of their competitive drive to control freight movement to and from the ports. This was especially true of the Humber, the South Wales ports and Southampton. The Midland Railway held interests in the London docks, and elsewhere the several railway companies owned harbours and quays in Dover, Harwich, Folkestone, on the Tyne, Wear and Tees, and in Leith, Grangemouth and Bo'ness. In all, railway ownership covered fifty-one separate docks or harbours in 1919.[48]

In all these locations, the NUR had membership amongst the more permanently employed staff in a diverse group of occupations, including crane-drivers, porters (who did dock work where the cargo came or went by rail wagons on quayside railway lines), lockgate men, tugboat men, shunters, weighbridge attendants, berthing masters, horse-keepers, and many others. These workers had the status of railway 'servants' rather than of casual labour. A gulf was already fixed between their perceptions of interest and those of the dockers. And in the war, labour shortage, the ban on strike action, patriotic relaxation of union controls and the

Railway Executive's drive for maximum through-put, in which it was expressing military priorities, meant that NUR members were often used to undertake genuine dockers' work.

Although led by Jimmy Thomas, in politics a 'super-patriot', the NUR was less scrupulous than the Federation in its readiness to exploit any sectional advantage offered by the war. In the ports, it bargained aggressively. Inter-union disputes became endemic in this situation. In 1917 the Federation was provoked to complain:

> As is known, the National Union of Railwaymen cater for transport workers in a few isolated ports where docks are owned by railway companies. This has resulted in a certain amount of friction and an appreciable prejudicial effect upon other workers in the same classes of work who are employed by private firms. Efforts have been made to induce the NUR to arrive at a mutual agreement to co-operate in such cases. So far, the NUR executive has not yet seen its way clear to do this.[49]

Bevin sought to create machinery with which to handle the demarcation disputes, and the Federation invited the NUR to confer.[50] Bevin also pressed the NUR to approve joint action by port workers in the NTWF and the NUR on general district wage questions and conditions.[51] In the following year, the NUR took the initiative in proposing 'a joint meeting of the two Executive Councils . . . to go fully into the possibilities and prospects of joint action or ultimate amalgamation.'[52] This invitation was accepted. The Joint Standing Committee which arose from these talks was charged not only with adjusting demarcation on the docks, but also to examine 'the whole possibility of a Transport Workers Union' and to confer on 'all questions of State ownership and regulation of transport, inland, coastal, and overseas'.[53]

Despite this initiative, the Federation continued to receive from its districts complaints of NUR members taking dockers' work. In 1918 the Federation gave the tireless Williams the mammoth task of collecting and collating 'all information available regarding transport developments'; the NUR would meet half the costs of this survey work.[54] As we shall see, hopes of eventual amalgamation persisted down to 1922 and the conference which inaugurated the TGWU. Perhaps it was this expectation which led the NTWF in 1919 to enter into an elaborate and truly voluminous agreement with the Railway Executive Committee, the NUR and the National Union of General Workers. This was to settle 'the arrangements made at the Railway Ports of the Country for segregating workers between the National Transport Workers' Federation and the National Union of Railwaymen'.[55]

Whatever was in the minds of the Federation's representatives, the effects of this agreement froze the lines of permanent division of trade unionism in the railway ports, which were further reinforced when the Dock Labour Scheme of 1947 excluded all the NUR grades from its coverage. Attitudes hardened, post-war discussions aimed at including NUR members in the scheme always failed, and the division remains to this day.

## Merging with the General Workers?

Another great step towards unity, a merger between the National Union of General Workers and the DWRGWU, came tantalizingly close to realization in 1916–17. (The National Union of Gasworkers and General Workers became the National Union of General Workers in 1916.) Tillett reported to his members in December 1916 that such an amalgamation would be achieved 'within a few months . . . I am sure we shall be the better for the new organisation. Careful estimates have been made, the constitutions of both unions examined, and a very anxiously sincere effort has been made to blend the better parts of both rules and experiences into a composite whole'.[56] Will Thorne, general secretary of the General Workers' Union, confirmed this optimistic expectation a few months later in a debate at the 1917 AGC of the Federation: 'Bevin has mentioned that we are negotiating with the Dockers, and if the same good feeling prevails during the rest of the negotiations, the Dockers and the Gasworkers will be here next year as one organisation.'[57]

In the event, the ballot which would have consummated this profoundly important fusion was delayed until 1919, when the dockers' vote, although in favour, failed to produce the legally required turn-out. The general workers voted for the merger.

## Comprehensive Amalgamation?

The momentous issue of a general amalgamation, either of the transport unions or of transport and general unions, had been left in abeyance after the grand eve-of-war Special Conference in July 1914. In the early war years, the NTWF Executive had no heart for a revival of the project, nor was there any general enthusiasm among the constituent unions. It will be recalled that the NTWF and the GLNC had established a joint sub-committee to process the results of the 1914 conference. In March 1915, the Workers' Union approached the Federation to propose that this sub-committee should be reconvened 'to draft Rules and Constitution'. The Executive decided that the matter would be 'held over for the time being'.[58]

During the early years of the war Jack Twomey, secretary of the NALU and its representative on the NTWF Executive, was a persistent, lone voice in favour of reviving the amalgamation process. He was told on more than one occasion in 1915 and 1916 that 'further action would be ill advised', because of the poor response to the sub-committee's last circular to the affiliates of both the NTWF and the GLNC:[59] 'The replies to this circular were of such a character as to prevent us from proceeding. Thirty-one unions were circularised, and of these fifteen did not even go to the trouble of making a reply, eight were in favour of proceeding at once, seven were against any action being taken during the war crisis, and one was ambiguous.'[60] In this climate of apathy, warned the Executive, 'any attempt which we make at the present time, being as it seems foredoomed to failure, would have the most disastrous effect on future efforts to bring the unions together'.[61]

At that time the requirement of the 1876 Act, for a two-thirds majority in favour of a merger, was a formidable block to successful amalgamation. This lesson had recently been pointed up in London, where the United Order of General Labourers and the United Building Labourers' Union were prevented from joining forces because they failed to obtain the necessary majority.[62]

Jack Twomey, however, was not finished with the subject; his next approach to the EC in June 1917 met with the now standard reply: that 'the matter be held over for further consideration'.[63] But Twomey was indefatigable. In July he returned to the subject and now 'a long discussion as to ways and means took place'. And this time the response was quite different. Ultimately the following resolution was moved by Patrick Kean of the National Warehouse and General Workers' Union (headquarters Liverpool) and carried: 'That in the opinion of this Executive Committee, recognizing the growing demand of our members for amalgamation of all the Unions attached, such matter be immediately entered upon by this body, and a sub-committee be appointed immediately to put into circulation a scheme to be put before our affiliated societies.'[64]

It is highly significant that this new initiative was to be confined to the NTWF unions; the 1914 conference and its sub-committee had involved, of course, the GLNC as well. At this very moment, as the NTWF set out on its own road, that Council was transforming itself into the fully fledged National Federation of General Workers whose inaugural conference, with Clynes in the chair, was held in July 1917. This does not imply the hardening of the lines which were to bring us, in 1922 and 1924, to fix in place our two great general unions, the TGWU and the NUGMW. Their shapes were only beginning to emerge from the haze. The ballot attempt between the dockers' and the general workers was still a distant prospect – it actually took place in 1919 – and there was still much overlapping on the Executives of the two federations.

But it was the rapid drive for national bargaining, conducted industry by industry, which brought the Federation of General Workers into existence.[65] As one group of employers after another during the final phases of the war came to accept the wisdom of agreeing national pay scales and conditions, and accorded unions recognition for this purpose, the centralization of union authority along industrial lines became a powerful trend. In the general workers' case the two dominant unions, the NUGW and the NAUL, thought initially of their federation's taking advantage of the new national procedures in engineering.[66]

## New Thinking in the NTWF

As with the general workers, so with the transport workers: the new thinking which emerged from the Executive sub-committee on amalgamation in 1917 (a sub-committee of Gosling, Williams, and Sexton; no space was found for Bevin, surprisingly enough) derived from the relationship between structural transformation of the Federation, and the growth of sectoral, national industry bargaining. Could all these leaders hear the spectral pre-echo of George Woodcock's voice at the TUC rostrum in the 1960s declaiming: 'Structure is a function of purpose'?

The new thinking was reported with firmness and conviction by the sub-committee when it came back to the Executive in September 1917. The team declared with a solemnity appropriate to the occasion:

Arising from the instruction received from the Blackpool meeting of the Executive Council, we, the undersigned, have met to consider and frame recommendations upon the subject of amalgamation.

In our judgement, the Federation is adopting the best line of policy on conducting the series of geographical conferences covering the whole country. This must inevitably lead to the assumption on the part of the Federation of a good deal of the work hitherto performed by the affiliated Societies. It becomes increasingly clear that the Federation must tend to absorb the work of the respective organisations, and perhaps perform that work in a more effective manner than has hitherto been the case because the Unions have not been able to exert the influence exerted by the Federation . . .

We feel that, much as we desire to bring about the amalgamation originally intended by the ten-clause scheme of the London Conference of July 1914, the problem becomes less susceptible to that form of solution as time proceeds. It is with no desire to put off the discussion and determination of the amalgamation problem that we suggest the foregoing tentative policy. We, on our part, are strongly convinced that it is absolutely essential in the interests of the workers we are serving to bring about a more concentrated form of organisation and to prevent the wastage of effort implied in a plurality of Union organisation. We conclude by repeated affirmation of the collective opinion of the sub-committee that the policy outlined in the national programme and passed so enthusiastically at Bristol is the line for the Federation to take, and is certainly the line of least resistance.

(Signed): Harry Gosling, James Sexton, Robert Williams.[67]

This is portentous stuff. If the evolution of the Federation had proceeded smoothly as envisaged in this statement, its own central authority, Executive Committee, Annual General Council and its officers – above all its general secretary – would have held all the power in the eventual amalgamation. There would have been no rupture: the Federation would have undergone a metamorphosis, from which the TGWU would have emerged, with all the former constituents reconstituted in the new form. Conceivably, Robert Williams would have been seen as architect and titular leader. In the event, as we shall see, the regenerative process resembled more the division of cells, albeit an unequal separation. Williams was left in control of the weakling, shrunken part, while Bevin marched off with all the more confident and best-integrated forces. But this is to anticipate.

## The Bristol Policy

The new policy which caused the leaders to rethink the strategy of amalgamation was launched at the NTWF's Bristol AGC in June 1917 and became known as the 'Bristol policy'.

On the Council's first day, Ben Smith of the London and Provincial Union of Licensed Vehicle Workers moved: 'That the policy of the National Transport Workers' Federation shall be to use their influence to bring about complete amalgamation of all societies catering for transport workers in the United Kingdom, based on Industrial Unionism.' This led to a debate which, because of its last four words, lacked all conviction or consensus. These served only to revive old doctrinal divisions between the industrial unionists and the proponents of general unionism – or One Big Union.

Contributors included Havelock Wilson, whose speech contained both a complaint that the motion, in using the 'industrial union' formula, was contaminated with 'a taint of Germanism . . . ; it comes from Berlin', *and* an assertion that 'seamen would only merge with other seamen'. His xenophobia and his hatred of Williams blinded him to such an obvious inconsistency.

> A certain gentleman connected with this Federation went to Berlin and spent a week there, and he came back and told us we were all wrong about Trade Unionism. Well, Mr. Chairman, it is twenty-seven years since I taught the Germans what Trade Unionism was. For what purpose do they want this resolution passed? For the over-man! The over-man – Germany all over! I believe in the under-dog, and I am going to support him all the time.[68]

After this tirade, Ernest Bevin destroyed the motion, for a different purpose, with a cool and prescient speech:

If this resolution is carried here today I am afraid it may interfere with some progress which is being made in regard to amalgamation in other directions . . . Rightly or wrongly, our Unions have developed in a dual form. In my own Union we have two departments – broadly dockers and general workers. We have developed in consequence certain forms of organisation, and the only possible way to amalgamate with other Unions is to retain some of the old forms and to graft new ones on them. We have been in negotiation with Thorne's Union, and we are getting nearer to amalgamation . . . Industrial Unionism is a catch phrase, and it is nearly time we got to business. Industrially, every carter in the transport trade ought to be with the Dockers, and according to Godfrey every docker ought to be with the Carters. Industrial Unionism was all right in theory, but if you developed your Unions on industrial lines you would not reduce the number of Unions but increase them, mainly because Unions like Thorne's and my own cover hundreds of industries, and everyone would argue they were industries in themselves. Necessity is driving us to amalgamation, but not in the form proposed by this resolution.[69]

This speech really ended the long debate in the Federation. Industrial unionism had appeared and reappeared on the agenda ever since 1910.[70] The defeat of the motion was overwhelming: 26,000 votes for, 155,000 against. In this decision might be read the symbol, if not the shape, of things to come: One Big Union.

The necessity which Bevin saw as requiring invention in this matter came out vividly the following day in the AGC's debate on the EC motion for a national wages' and hours' policy. This was the 'Bristol policy', and we shall look shortly at its significance for collective bargaining; but first we must examine its influence on the choice of structure. It called on constituent unions to 'abstain from all negotiations except they be of a national character'. It empowered the Executive Council to convene a series of district conferences to give effect to nationwide understanding of the national programme and to win support for it in the regions. Six districts were defined for this purpose and, in addition, 'consideration [should] be given in as far as the problem affects Ireland'.[71]

## All Power to the Federation

Bevin proposed the motion for the EC. His speech was a succession of calls for centralized power in pursuit of standard, national wages, hours and conditions. The same themes echoed through it: 'empower the Executive', 'have confidence in the Federation', 'agree to prosecute a policy on national lines', 'no separate negotiations', 'loyalty to the Federation':

When the employers know that if they attack, say, Bristol, the local officials will say, 'You must approach the Federation', there will be less likelihood of any of the ports being tackled singly. There must be co-ordination and a national policy . . . I believe that the adoption of this policy will be the first real landmark in the history of the Federation, because for the first time we shall be meeting our opponents as a national entity.[72]

With this hammering, insistent repetition of the call for national unity and discipline, Bevin was not only laying his claim on the future; he was also intent on laying every last ghost of the past – of 1893, of 1912, of the miseries of sectional divisions and regional defeats. The debate which followed him was cursory. The motion was already nearly consensual: it was carried with only three dissentients.

In pursuance of its policy, the EC proposed a new clause to the federal constitution in 1918. It read:

There shall be appointed trade advisory committees to consider all matters relating to joint movements and joint action in particular sections. They shall be called together from time to time to advise the Executive Council and the Officers of the Federation on matters relative to their respective trade sections . . . Among the sections to be represented on trade advisory committees may be included the following: coastal and overseas transport, inland waterways (river and canal), road vehicular traffic (passenger and commercial), coal export, general cargo, export (piecework and timework), pilotage, boatmen, and riggers.[73]

An amendment to these groupings was suggested some months later – the export and import trades might, the EC thought, be combined in one group. Whilst the 'coalies' preserved, to this point, their sectional autonomy from other dock workers, the stevedores' claim to separateness in loading for export was here overridden. These are the first essays in structuring the eventual trade groups of the TGWU, the first time they were teased off the blueprint sheets into life as substantial bodies, with real, if at this stage limited, functions.

Twomey's last wartime assay at promoting the One Big Union amalgamation came at the 1918 AGC, when he moved a motion calling for new talks with the GLNC. (He seemed unaware that it had converted its name to the National Federation of General Workers in 1917.) He said that 'what the Unions wanted was One Union and one card'.

The debate was interesting for two reasons. For the first time, the frustrations of the delegates turned inwards, so that several speakers blamed trade-union officers 'afraid for their jobs' for hindering progress. Of course this was not a new charge, but previously it had been coupled with assertions that the members were too conservative to press for change. Of course, full-time officers could undoubtedly constitute a vested interest in the structural conservatism. This kind of institutional, bureaucratic inertia has always been a factor in social organization, and it remains so. Countless negotiations about mergers and takeovers in the trade-union movement have been preoccupied with safeguarding the positions and the fortunes of the chief officers involved. This was true among the transport unions before 1922, and it was to remain true throughout the subsequent history of the TGWU. We shall have plenty of occasion to illustrate the problem in vol. II.

But Bevin's speech broke new ground, both in tackling this problem (and turning it to advantage) and in revealing that he had moved away from the grand design of 'all-in' amalgamation achieved in one move, towards the method he was finally to lead, using the dominant numbers and the role of the DWRGWU in the ports to negotiate a deal, or a series of deals, with other unions, largely ignoring the processes of the NTWF. This now seemed to him the way of breaking the deadlock. The speech is so significant that we quote it in full:

The position was that the members were pressing the officials for amalgamation, and the officials – to avoid an unthankful task – always talked of a general amalgamation, and he was forced to the conclusion that the resolution before the Conference was more or less window-dressing. In South Wales, there was the Coal Trimmers' Union, with a couple of thousand members, the Amalgamated Labourers, with about four thousand, and his own Union with about sixteen thousand, and every wage movement in South Wales had had to be carried on the backs of the Dockers. The whole weight of the general cargo movement had to be carried by his own Union, as far as South Wales was concerned. He had made it clear, in reply to assertions that the Dockers' Union wished to absorb these other Unions, that he was prepared to make a business-like bargain with them – but he was not encouraged to go any further with the matter. He was always told that the members would object to joining forces with an individual Union – but if the little pill could not be swallowed, how could it be expected that the bigger one would be? His union was prepared to talk business on the matter of amalgamation, and he for one was not going on a platform to pay lip-homage to the principle. They were prepared to offer the small Unions – not absorption, but the negotiation of an amalgamation on a fair basis and offering conditions which would protect the officials and the members. If it was right for the coal-trimmers of Newport to be in the Dockers' Union, why was it wrong for the Cardiff coal-trimmers? When the Joint Committee in South Wales met with the employers they met as one body, not as individual Unions. He was prepared to go anywhere in South Wales and place the difficulties of a general amalgamation before all or any of the three Unions there.[74]

In this statement Bevin let the cat out of the bag. He also chalked up his own writing on the wall and Sexton read the message. Immediately he leapt in to assert that, in himself, 'there was at least one official who subscribed to the principle of a general amalgamation honestly and without camouflage'. He declared his support for inclusion of the NUR, and for a 'departmentalised Union'.

What was the cause of his conversion from his previous goal of a single Dockers' Union? 'If the London Dockers and the rest came together there would be a general workers' Union outside. He thought the Federation itself ought to be the pivot on which the amalgamation could move.'[75] It was evident: under Bevin's 'amalgamation by accretion', the DWRGWU – and Ernest Bevin – would be dominant. For Bevin deployed not only superior numbers, but the multi-industry membership which all other contenders for leadership, including the NUDL, lacked. On the Federation Executive, Sexton, March, Clatworthy, Houghton and the rest had an equal voice with Bevin. But what if Bevin decided to carve up the Federation taking the 'little unions' with him? This accomplished, might he not then seek to attract the rest? And since the Federation's own cherished 'departmental' model had originally been established in the Dockers' Union, in Bevin's equally cherished Bristol District, might he not revert to that example, powerfully reinforcing the magnetic attraction of his new amalgamation? Indeed, for unions outside transport, might not such a framework hold a special allure? The Federation after all, had deliberately restricted its own limits. It lived only within the transport industries.

Moreover, Bevin had, with great candour, publicly announced his sensitivity to the self-interest of full-time officials and offered to buy out their opposition to mergers. Unlike the Federation, which did not have a penny for such a purpose, the DWRGWU had full coffers, thanks to the stable membership and industrial quiescence of groups like the Welsh tinplate section, and the wartime recruitment of members everywhere. The union's annual income leapt in a single year from £60,000 in 1917 to £83,000 in 1918, and its total assets at the war's end were £86,000. Of this, £16,500 was its salary bill, and it paid £12,000 in expenses to its officials. The Federation's income in 1918 – half from union affiliation, half from bank interest – was £6,600. It had one full-time official, Williams, a clerk and a junior, who between them received £466 19s. Its largest affiliation fee, of £710 (see appendix, p. 674), came from the DWRGWU!

But Sexton was prescient: Bevin's magnet would not be strong enough to attract Thorne's union, and would perhaps be inadequate to draw to itself the NAUL and others. Thus, to abandon 'general amalgamation' under the auspices of the two federations was to ensure that 'there would be a general union outside'. Only general amalgamation, or the combined will of leaders and members of the two unions, could ensure the adhesion of the DWRGWU and the NUGW. These extrapolations occur naturally to us in hindsight, though Sexton read them into the immediate situation instinctively. Would Bevin have replied that, in time, his influence would be strong enough to bring them all into one union, through successive 'deals'? We shall learn some, but perhaps not all of the answer, as events unfold. Certainly, the model of growth by deals, with attractive roles on offer to full-time officials, was to become a familiar pattern in the TGWU, particularly in the era of Jack Jones.

One official, however, having no constituency, no members, and no interest to buy out, was the servant of the Federation, Robert Williams. For the future, his role was tied to the fortunes of the Federation. The seeds of his later profound misfortune lay in Bevin's speech that day. Twomey's resolution for One Big Union was defeated by 140,000 votes to 90,000, and a second resolution moved by the vehicle workers, echoing its call of the previous year, to convert the Federation into a single transport union, received the same treatment.[76]

All this time, the Federation itself added to its strengths through new affiliations. In 1915 the Glasgow Ship Riggers' union joined up, as well as both the Cardiff, Barry and Penarth Coal Trimmers' Union, and the North of England Trimmers' and Teemers' Association. In 1916 the London and Provincial Union of Licensed Vehicle Workers enrolled: as we have seen, its origins lay in London cab drivers' unions, which now reached out into association with the omnibus and tramway industries. Shortly afterwards it merged with the Amalgamated Tramwaymen, who joined the Federation in 1918 and reaffiliated with them under the name of the United Vehicle Workers in 1920. We have already noticed the late entry of the Scottish Horse and Motormen's Association in 1917 and its precipitate exit a year later. The Amalgamated Association of Carters and Motormen joined in 1918, as did the Midlands-based Amalgamated Society of Gas, Municipal and General Workers. This was one that 'got away': in 1921 it merged with the National Union of General Workers (Thorne's union), and so ended its life as part of the NUGMW. Finally, the NTWF's wartime haul included in 1918 the Amalgamated Carters, Lurrymen and Motormen's Union, which became the third wing of the mini-amalgamation of 1920 that produced the UVW. In summary, the pace of new affiliations quickened notably in the later years of the war, as the extension of national bargaining in the vehicle sector, both commercial and passenger, provided just the right incentive for ending the fragmentation of unions in those industries.

## Executive Self-denial

More curious than the affiliations, however, were the frequent occasions of self-denial by the Executive. In 1915 the North Wales Quarrymen's Union's application to affiliate was turned down. In 1917 the Amalgamated Union of Co-operative Employees (AUCE) – a future section of the Union of Shop, Distributive and Allied Workers (USDAW) – which had a portion of its members working in transport, received the same treatment, the Executive writing to the AUCE that 'it was impossible to consider the question of their affiliation'.[77] In June, the Amalgamated Society of Farriers was rejected too: 'It was decided that these workers could not be considered transport workers, and that the application could not be entertained.'[78] Curious! Farriers may indeed work in agriculture, but at this time, if we map out the horse population of the country, their principal industrial location must have been in transport.

An application from the Cumberland Iron Ore Miners' Association was referred dutifully to the Miners' Federation. The National Union of Clerks had affiliated in 1912, but had withdrawn the following year amidst the noisy recriminations provoked by the London dock strike of 1912. In 1918 it applied for readmission; the application 'could not be entertained' because only a small minority of its members worked in transport.[79] The Hull Stevedores' Mutual Aid Society was rejected at the same time after receiving an unfavourable report on its constitution from the Humber District Committee.

It seems that the Executive took its definition as a transport federation seriously, and that this was interpreted in a restrictive sense. Indeed, at the 1918 AGC it adopted a long schedule of occupations eligible for affiliation. This was confined to maritime, port, road-passenger and commercial transport. All this amounts to a sort of self-enforced acceptance of inter-union boundaries, foreshadowing the Bridlington Agreement. This understanding, which was never debated, none the less seems to have prevailed over any doctrinal pursuit of the One Big Union. In these few years, the NTWF passed up the chance of associating with the future USDAW, and also with the Clerical and Administrative Workers' Union (CAWU) – now the Association of Professional, Executive, Clerical and Computer Staff (APEX) – which merged with the General, Municipal, Boilermakers' and Allied Trades Union (GMBATU) in 1989. In one case, however, the rigidity of the policy had no permanent effect on the TGWU, which received the North Wales Quarrymen into its folds in 1923.

## Bargaining Policy

Strengthened numerically by recruitment and affiliation, and structurally by the 'Bristol policy', the NTWF moved centre-stage in wage bargaining as the war entered its last two years. Its ambition to negotiate for all its sections was not uniformly fulfilled. In particular, the seamen, under the influence of the separatist Wilson, who was in any event disaffected, and in consequence of their winning national recognition without Federation intervention, decided upon their own path to national bargaining.

'Seamen were the only major group of employees to have received general pay increases that fully compensated for rising prices' after the first year of war.[80] It was Tom Mann, a member of the NSFU Executive, who pushed the union into an 'endeavour to secure uniformity in the various ports'.[81] And in July 1915, the second general increase agreed by the Admiralty gave seamen a rise of 30–40 per cent over pre-war wages. This was unprecedented success, and Wilson, despite his pro-war stance, had no scruples in defending the wartime labour shortage on which it was based, both by redoubling his opposition to Chinese labour in shipping (in which policy he was supported both by popular opinion and by the other leaders of the Federation) and by threatening, through his mouthpiece Captain Tupper, a national strike if the government imposed the disciplines of the Military Service Act in the merchant marine.[82] The union's bargaining power was further reinforced in a fortuitous way, when in 1916 America legalized the 'right to quit' for foreign seamen in US ports. This led to a huge exodus of British seamen to the American fleet, which paid almost double the British seamen's rates.[83] It was also less likely to be torpedoed. This placed the government under enormous pressure to concede Wilson's dream of national recognition, and a union monopoly of labour supply.

We have already referred to the setting up of the National Maritime Board, which was established in November 1917. The shipowners' final price included a union commitment to suppress the strikes which were erupting on all sides over the wage differential with America. The new Board was constituted of the NSFU, the Ships' Stewards' Union, the officers' representatives, and the representatives of the government's Controller of Shipping. The registration of seamen under the Board gave Wilson the controls he had sought. After the war, the Board reverted to bipartite representation of the unions and the shipowners, as the government withdrew from intervention. The NTWF played no part whatsoever in this process, except on the Asian labour issue. Wilson's union's loyalist xenophobia climaxed in its participation, complete with banner, in the Victory Peace Parade, held in London in 1919: 'This was the first time in history that a trade union banner had been borne aloft in a great military and naval display'.[84]

In its other industries – road-passenger transport, carting and docks, together with the production industries in which unions like the DWRGWU were involved – the NTWF was not at first to find progress easy. Steady efforts towards co-ordinated wage claims, national bargaining and recognition were none the less maintained. In the early war years, as we saw above, the Executive itself was reluctant to accept the mantle of co-ordinator of such claims. When it began its attempt to document the range of sectional and district claims in 1916, at first it met with indifference and apathy from its constituents. Most of them failed to respond to Robert Williams's questionnaires. His report complained with some bitterness:

It is humiliating to have to state that very little response has been made to the appeals sent out from time to time. The Unions are very anxious to receive information from the Federation when such information is clearly to their advantage, but it is becoming a matter of reiteration to state that the Unions rarely accept their responsibilities and obligations to supply this information. No phase of the work of the Federation is really of more importance than that relating to the Wages and Conditions Intelligence Department. Is it too much to hope that the constituent bodies of the Federation will bestir themselves and place every single item of knowledge at the disposal of the head office?[85]

At this stage of the war, the kind of information for which the Executive was asking lay in the offices of the individual unions at local level, although the District Committees had already begun to record and report on a range of matters in their own annual reports to the AGC. Typical, though more thorough than the rest, was Tom Mann's report from Merseyside in 1916.[86] He noted over forty different wage gains made in the previous twelve months by the Mersey Quay and Railway Carters' Union alone. They included a gain of 3s., to 39s. a week, for motor drivers, in a working week of 55.5 hours. Heavy-traffic teamsmen (horse drawn) gained a 4s. war bonus, to 34s. a week. Other sections with gains included corporation carters, Co-operative coal carters, mail-van drivers, and mineral-water drivers. He documents the current rates for the seamen and ships' stewards, and for a wide range of occupations in the Gas and General Workers' Union – sweepers, canal men, ship-repair men, etc. Finally come capstan men in the pay of the Mersey Docks and Harbour Board, and steam-crane drivers. It is all very mundane, very fragmented and localized; but it shows, at that level, that local unions or the branches of national organizations were commonly making two or more successful claims a year.

## National Action: Buses and Trams

In road-passenger transport, London commanded much attention and was an area of consistent militancy during the war. The London and Provincial Union of Licensed Vehicle Workers had inherited the spasmodic militancy of the London cab-drivers' organizations, but now also spoke for the majority of London's busmen. It shared representation of the tramwaymen with the Manchester-based Amalgamated Association of Tramway and Vehicle Workers (AAT), which had established four London branches by 1914. The busmen were employed almost wholly by the London Traffic Combine, comprising the London General Omnibus Company and the Underground Electric Railway Company. Tram-ownership was more fragmented amongst the London boroughs and the

LCC. Although the LPU affiliated to the NTWF in 1916, the AAT stayed out until 1918. The LPU organized in branches based on the bus depots, the AAT's branches being more conventionally geographical in coverage.

In 1915 the LPU supported a strike of its tramway workers, who wanted a shorter spread-over (the time between signing on and signing off). The tramwaymen were accused of dragging their feet before endorsing the LPU action and, following the strike, members and at least one officer transferred from the Blue to the Red Button Union (see part I, p. 274). By 1918 the LPU had more than doubled its founding membership, to a total of 20,000.

The union had obtained its first ever agreement with the London General Omnibus Company and Tillings, one of the largest private bus companies, in 1914. In 1916 further gains were made, though confined to the same company. Neither agreement commanded rank-and-file enthusiasm, and the London busmen formed the first of a succession of unofficial committees, the Vigilance Committee, in 1916. Here they were foreshadowing the sustained conflicts with the leadership of the TGWU which prevailed through decades, until the era of Frank Cousins.

In May 1917 the LPU brought out all its then 10,000 members: 98 per cent of the workforce employed by the London General. Their agreement had contained a clause guaranteeing the company against sympathy strikes, and the LPU now proposed to annul this clause; simultaneously it submitted a claim for a war bonus of 10s. a week. The company refused to meet the union's officials, and the ensuing strike lasted five days.[87] But now the men had the backing of the Federation.

The Federation's Executive gave full support to the busmen, calling for union recognition and negotiations. Gosling and Williams were placed at the disposal of the union, and Arthur Henderson was called in by them to pressurize the company. It then recognized the union, and agreed that the war-bonus claim be submitted to the Committee on Production, which awarded a 5s. increase for both bus and tram workers. Women, however, were excluded from the award.

By 1918 the 'Bristol policy' was in full operation, and the Executive showed its ability to exploit the multi-industry nature of the Federation: it used the agreement of £1 a week war bonus in the carters' national settlement (see below) and immediately sought its extension to the passenger workers. The benefits of a national programme, through federal co-ordination, were becoming evident to the sections. In this case, George Askwith responded to the demand, arranging a conference of both sides of the whole road-passenger industry. Bevin, Williams and Gosling attended.

This was the beginning of national action in passenger transport. The Tramway and Light Railways' Association, the Municipal Tramways Association, the Omnibus Associations and the London General

Omnibus Company all declared that they would negotiate only with the individual unions, and would not recognize the NTWF. The two main unions, the LPU and the AAT, representing 80 per cent of the workforce, gave seven days' notice to cease work. The Executive endorsed this decision and, after bureaucratic delays, the Committee on Production awarded the £1 increase, but again not to women workers. In March the EC 'heartily' congratulated Bevin and the officers on the settlement of the dispute at the Committee on Production.[88]

Further strike action took place in 1918, embracing both London and provincial towns, led often by women workers, for the outstanding grievance remained that of equal pay for the many women now employed as conductors on London buses and trams, which the companies refused to concede. The Committee on Production made a fresh award in the industry in July 1918, and the Federation convened a joint meeting of the LPU, the AAT, NUGW and the NUVW, with Robert Williams in the chair, to demand the extension of the award to the women. The meeting registered 'its intense dissatisfaction with the terms of the Supplementary Award, as far as it affects the position of women tramway and omnibus employees doing the work of the men whose places they have so well filled'. It spoke of their 'unfair and inferior position', and warned of their 'growing discontent' and of 'the support given by the men workers'. The meeting called on the Executive to demand a meeting with the employers. However, even after the strike action in London, the Executive reported that 'the general principle of equal pay for equal work had still not been decided'.[89]

London's passenger workers continued to suffer from the multi-union division which prevailed. The AAT and the LPU complained about each other to the Federation in November 1918. The AAT, in particular, accused the London and Provincial of failing to sustain the equal pay demand, called on the EC to censure its rival, and announced that it was withdrawing from discussions on amalgamation of the two unions. Robert Williams was impartial: both unions 'had embarked wholesale on the policy of admitting each other's members . . . both unions were ignoring the Rules and Constitution of the Federation, and until such regrettable internecine conflict ceased, the Federation could take no action'.[90]

## Sectional Successes – the Coal-trimmers

Another, and vastly more successful, group of militants were the coal-trimmers on the docks, particularly in South Wales. Dockers' and Coal Trimmers' Union leaders urged restraint, but a number of unofficial strikes emphasized their bargaining advantage, compelling arbitrators to deal speedily and generously with their claims. On the ships of neutral countries they succeeded in extracting twice the pre-war wage as early as 1915. The *Dockers' Record* was embarrassed: 'Power of organisation should be used where necessary, but not abused'. A 12.5 per cent war bonus was awarded in 1915, followed by a further 25 per cent in 1916, 22.5 per cent in 1917 and 20 per cent in 1918. Overtime rates were correspondingly generous. In 1919 it was reported in the local press that some trimmers were earning between £2,000 and £3,000 a year! Other sources made similar estimates: wages of £60 a week were not uncommon.[91] Here was a closed-shop sectional unionism, pursuing higher wages in almost total isolation from the more modest general wage trends in dockland. Militancy paid off.

But the trimmers also provided an early model showing how to co-ordinate movements at national level. This was overseen by the Federation. As we have seen, both the South Wales and the north-east-coast trimmers' unions affiliated in 1915. They brought with them previous experience of concerted national action from the year before the war, when they had united to establish the Saturday half-day. (Under intense pressure, they suspended this during the war.) There is evidence of federal attempts to combine the trimmers' claims in 1915, but the effective movement was initiated by the Federation in September 1916 at a conference in Salford. It involved the NALU, the Scottish Dockers' Union, the NUDL, the two trimmers' unions, the DWRGWU and the NUGW. The conference acted to assemble comprehensive data on wages and conditions in the different ports, and discussed the problems arising from the use of out-dated coal ships (brought into re-use because of wartime shipping shortages), in which bulkheads slowed down the work and led to complaints of slow work from the employers. It also dealt with 'adequate ventilation, escape holes, and the abolition of middle-men ... It is hoped that similar sectional conferences affecting other classes of work will be held as the resources of the Federation permit and as the sections themselves require.'[92]

Robert Williams became involved regularly thereafter in assisting the coal-trimmers' claims,[93] and the Federation was evidently delighted at the example of co-ordination which this section of its affiliates had provided.

The general cargo dockers had some of the advantages of the trimmers in wartime bargaining, but their co-ordination into a national force was more difficult to achieve, and their monopoly of labour supply was by no means so secure. The industry was not for some time recognized as an essential 'war trade', and many dockers rushed to join the forces in 1914–15 (see below). With a tight labour market and congestion of shipping in the docks (see below), the dockers were early among beneficiaries; the result was an average increase in their rates of 11 per cent in the first twelve months.[94]

At this stage, however, the federal role in advancing claims was confined to the pooling of information: 'letters were read from Glasgow, Liverpool, and Hull, notifying intention to apply for increases in wages. The secretary announced that he had information that London was moving in the same direction. Discussion on these was held over.'[95] There was evidently nothing for the Executive to do. Reports continued in the same vein; Glasgow won a 1*d*. an hour increase; Liverpool sent news of a strike over the interpretation of an arbitration award and sought the EC's adjudication over its wording.[96]

## Unity of Action for Dockers

In November 1916, however, the South Wales, Bristol Channel dockers showed the way. They met in joint conference to discuss 'the diversity of rates for general cargo and iron ore in the Bristol Channel ports . . . It was resolved that unity of action on wages questions was desirable.' The conference agreed to seek Board of Trade assistance towards setting up a Channel Conference of unions and employers, 'to bring about uniformity of tariffs and wage rates . . . Conferences of this character prove extremely useful, and it is hoped to cover other districts and other occupations in the same manner.'[97]

From district co-ordination, in 1918 the Federation moved on to the national level. In January the EC convened a conference of its general cargo group in Manchester, where it was agreed to demand a general increase of 8*d*. an hour.[98] Disciplined adherence to a national movement did not come easily: the Humber District complained that the NUDL in Liverpool was pressing for a separate arbitration, contrary to the intention of the Manchester conference. The Executive congratulated the Hull membership on sticking to national policy and urged the deferment of all separate claims pending a national settlement.[99] Problems existed on the employers' side as well. Lord Devonport was unable to adapt to the new climate of union recognition, so he carried on in the old way, refusing to attend the arbitration hearings. All other port employers complied, but their fragmentation was very evident: seventeen local port associations were named in the award, whilst on the workers' side there appeared a single body, the NTWF.

There was general unrest at the delay in the arbitration, quite apart from this problem, and the Executive cabled all ports urging them to refrain from strikes. In fact, several strikes did occur after the award was made, over interpretations of the overtime provisions, or of the application of the findings in London, or over its effect upon the permanent men. In the London case, Lord Devonport's obduracy could be overcome only by 'proclaiming' the award: that is, the government was compelled to use its powers of wartime compulsion under the Munitions of War Act. This, the first national standard increase (not yet a national standard rate), gave the dockers a rise of 2*d*. an hour. The arbitrators decreed that four-monthly revisions should occur, and in October 1918 a second national award brought a further 1½*d*. improvement.

At the Shaw Inquiry in 1920, Bevin documented the complex story of dockers' wages in great detail, reaching back to 1911, and including a port-by-port account of wartime increases.[100] Most of the major ports obtained six or seven increases during the war years, but until the two national arbitrations of May and October 1918 these were all negotiated at port level; the differing dates in Bevin's table make this very clear.

The data furnished to the Shaw Inquiry also highlights the wide variety of rates still prevailing two years after the war's end, and after the first national increases of 1918. Day rates varied from 11*s*. 8*d*. in Hull and Liverpool to 16*s*. in Belfast. Other high rates – 14*s*. or more – applied in Bristol, Plymouth, Glasgow, Grangemouth and Middlesbrough. These rates were tabulated alongside those prevailing in 1914. The largest gains in the period were of 166 per cent in Belfast and Avonmouth; the lowest, of 65 per cent in the London stevedores' rates. They do not reflect earnings, which were favourably affected by overtime and also often (though not universally) by piece-work earnings. The average increase for all ports over 1914 rates was 113.4 per cent. But the Shaw figures relate to 1919, after a further national increase in April of that year. Hugh Clegg tells us that by July 1918 the average wage rates of railwaymen, miners and dockers had risen by about 90 per cent over pre-war.[101] The wartime inflation of food prices reached 111 per cent.

It is significant that Bevin's detailed statistics were not challenged by the employers at the Shaw Inquiry. No alternative source of information was available within the industry. The court accepted and published the data without question. This has several resonances for our story. It speaks volumes for the new respect with which both the judge and the port employers now treated the port unions and their instrument, the Federation. It also demonstrates how much more closely the unions had prepared for national bargaining, by assembling vital data, than had the employers. In front of Shaw, and in the face of the unions', and Bevin's, masterly case, the employers were seen to be amateurs. The Federation had seized the chance offered by wartime circumstances to drive for its twin goals of recognition and national bargaining, and, assisted by state arbitration, it had succeeded in dragging the employers into conceding both objectives. Yet only four years earlier, Williams had been compelled to utter all those heartfelt complaints about his constituents' apathy in the vital business of gathering intelligence. The unions' evidence before Shaw was the fruit of a long and ceaseless process of 'bringing the unions along' to meet the new conditions and goals. Bevin taught employers and arbitrators the business of professional preparation of a case, but he did not do this alone. Behind him lay Williams's long, pioneering effort, and also the matching professionalism of George Askwith, who had set out on the road in 1911.

As a postscript to these events, we should note Bevin's use of the Federation's statistics to reinforce his pre-war attack on Sexton's performance in Liverpool. We anticipated this story in chapter 15. The wages table which Bevin laid before Shaw carried the evidence. One column is headed 'Year of Last Increase granted prior to 1914'. Down two pages the eye runs, reading off the 'Big Bang' year of 1911 against the name of every port in the land – except Liverpool, where the entry reads '1889'! It will be recalled that in 1911 Sexton and Mann negotiated recognition from the Liverpool employers, not wage increases. That is, recognition was used purely in the institutional interests of the union, not for its fruits in increased wages for the membership. The implied indictment is serious. Only the war brought the Liverpool men four local increases between 1915 and 1917, before they were subsumed into the national awards negotiated by the Federation before the Committee on Production.

Bevin was not content to leave the statistics to speak for themselves. He could not resist drawing attention to their meaning in his oral evidence to the Shaw Inquiry. His summary of the history of wages in London from 1889 onwards ended: 'That briefly is the story of London'. He went on without pausing for breath:

> but when we turn to Liverpool things are even worse. The Liverpool rates of 4s. 6d. and 5s. per day, which were the base pre-war rates, were fixed in 1885,[102] and there was not a penny advance in wages from 1885 until after the outbreak of war, and the whole base rate conditions of Liverpool upon which war bonuses, war wages and the rest of it have been built, as I say, go back to that date. You will find in 'The First Year's Working of the Liverpool Dock Scheme', by R. Williams, on page 173, a reference to the 1885 period when these rates were fixed; this is in Appendix 4. So you have a period from 1885 until 1915 in Liverpool without a single advance to meet either the growing aspirations or even the development of the cost of living which had taken place in the meantime.[103]

Bevin sustained a consistently hard line against Sexton, in both industrial and political matters. It was not a merely personal vendetta, although there was in it more than a hint of the contempt which a bold and forceful personality may feel towards the pusillanimous. With hindsight, it should be seen as part of the struggle being played out over the future inheritance of power in the pending amalgamation of dockers' – and transport – unions. In this game, Bevin was a master player, of ruthless instinct and intelligence.

## *Carters' Wages*

The story of the carters' wage advances during the war follows that of the other sections. In the beginning, the Federation received reports of local deals and merely recorded them. But in March 1916 we find the Mersey Carters' Union sending its thanks to the president and secretary of the Federation 'for their good offices in the negotiations', which had brought George Askwith to Merseyside to award an advance in wages: 'The terms were submitted to a mass meeting of the men, where they were agreed upon, and were in operation the following day, except in one firm, where after a stoppage of a few hours, this firm had agreed to the terms of settlement'.[104]

The carters had more need of Federation aid than most others, and more to gain from it, as the state arbitration system swung into gear. We have seen something of their fragmentation, into over more than 100 local societies, and the efforts which were made to overcome it. As elsewhere, the demands of the war greatly accelerated the process.

A fascinating correspondence between the Scarborough branch of the Amalgamated Carters', Lurrymen and Motormen's Union, its general secretary John Parr, and the Scarborough and Whitby Brewery Company, covering the years 1914–17, has survived.[105] The union, based in Bolton, had been formed, in common with so many other carters' societies, in 1890 and had since spread outwards in the North of England. The Scarborough branch was formed only in 1914; its appearance led all employers of carters in the town to summon a joint conference, in some alarm. The first demand from the union to the brewery was for a minimum rate of £1 4s. (single) and £1 6s. (teams) for horsemen. The brewery was reminded that several local employers had already conceded the claim, which for draymen amounted to a 1s. rise on the 1913 rates. (They also received a half-gallon beer allowance per day.) Parr threatened a strike if the brewery resisted this claim.

By June, when the brewery had still not settled the claim, Parr told the directors that 'the men are getting out of hand', and a collection of individual 'notices to cease work on Saturday, the 23rd June', signed by the members, are attached to his letter. A concession of 1s. followed. In 1915 Parr demanded a further rise to £1 6s. (single) and £1 10s. (teams), just twelve months after the previous rise. The branch secretary, John Appleby, assumed responsibility on this occasion. He reminded the brewery both of the general movement of wages in the country, and of the increased cost of living. The demand was conceded on this occasion too.

In 1916 the branch was back with a demand for a 3s. a week increase and John Parr resumed the correspondence, calling the attention of the brewery to 'the terrible increase in the cost of living'. The union dismissed the brewers' plea that winter was coming, meaning trade would be much diminished: 'that cannot be helped by your carters,' wrote Parr; 'the cost of living will meet [them] every week'. Finally, Parr deployed the argument of comparisons: 'We trust your Directors imitate the Railway Companies in giving something to these low paid workmen to help them to meet the daily claims of life ... All over the country, men following laborious occupations have been forced to ask for higher rates ... Carters [elsewhere] are now being paid 30/– for single and 34/– for teams.' On this occasion we find a pencilled note on the union's letter: 'Memo: Meeting of Nov. 3/16. Decided to make no reply.' There is no indication of the outcome. But in May 1917, John Parr wrote to the brewery again:

Acting on the instructions of the men in your employ, expressed by ballot vote, we apply for a 5/– a week advance on present wages. You are fully conscious, because you are a purchaser, of the continual rise in everything the workman and his family require. There is no reason to argue the point why this advance is required. We are sure you must agree that hitherto the amount paid by your firm to your carters is inadequate, the 26/– and 28/– not being worth more than 14/– in the market today. Because Employers have recognized the position of the carters to be serious, they have advanced his rate to 36/– and 40/– a week ... P.S. We shall be pleased to submit this application to the Board of Trade for arbitration, if you can't reach a settlement at once. You are asked to give your immediate attention to this matter as the men are pressing strongly.

John Appleby wrote to the brewery in June:

I am instructed by the local members of the above Society to comply with the request of the Head Quarters for an advance of wages. Another refusal of this will mean that you absolutely ignore us. We therefore ask you not to force us to take extreme measures but rather we prefer to meet you to discuss matters. May we ask you to comply with this request not later than Thursday's post, otherwise it will mean us tendering our notice to you which we should very much regret ... P.S. We have full liberty from H.Q. to take this action.

Two days later came the reply: 'We have been waiting to receive the Government's expected decision with regard to State Control of our Trade ... but if we do not hear as to this by 1st July, we shall be pleased to discuss the matter you refer to, with our men.' Two days later (16 June) Appleby replied: 'we are sorry you are delaying the matter as the money is now three weeks' overdue. We do not think it is your wish that the men should lose anything in the event of the Government taking control.'

Here the correspondence ends. The picture it presents is incomplete, but it reflects a number of factors in the carters' situation. Their poverty wages are evident. (Overtime was very limited in this non-essential, seasonal, trade.) If the 1917 increase demanded by Parr was granted, the rate for a single horseman would have been 31s. per week. This compares with a 1914 day rate for dock labour in Hull (the nearest port to Scarborough) of 6s. 3d. in the summer months, 5s. in the winter. The Scarborough case illustrates also the local and regional nature of carters' unionism, and the disparities in wages which were partly consequential on this. It shows us the impact of inflation and the escalation of claims on that score as the war progressed. And, towards the end, it shows the long arm of the state, arbitration and state control reaching out to affect even an isolated, seasonal workforce such as the seaside brewers' draymen.

At national level, the Federation was working hard to bring that arm into play to full effect. By 1917 the Bolton union was not the only one to call in arbitration on carters' pay. The Mersey carters summoned Gosling and Williams to accompany the union before the Chief Industrial Commissioner in May. By September, however, the Federation made its move for a national policy. The carters' first national conference was held in Salford; the outcome was the first national carters' award, in January 1917. Such carters' sectional conferences became regular events, and their sub-committee acted as an Executive, submitting the conference resolution of August 1917 for a £1 advance to Askwith in October. On 8 January 1918, he awarded the Federation's claim in full.

Later in 1918, the Federation was demanding a further flat 5s. weekly increase. The cartage industry formed its own employers' association, the National Alliance of Commercial Road Transport Associations and Federations, but the Liverpool employers did not affiliate to it. The Federation agreed to tolerate separate negotiations in that city, since its cartage firms paid substantially above the new national rates. Williams, in line with the four-monthly revisions which were now common throughout industry, submitted two separate 5s. claims to the national employers during the war's final months. At its 1918 AGC, the Federation was 'looking forward' to the creation of a National Joint Industrial Council (NJIC) for the industry.

## The Federation and Municipal Employees

There was one curious case in which the Federation, for purely inter-union reasons, withheld its support for a concerted national wage campaign. It concerned the municipal workers. In May 1918, the National Federation of General Workers proposed a joint action with the NTWF for a national 'movement' for municipal workers. The initiative had in fact been put forward by the vehicle workers' unions during the carters' Salford conference. The Executive agreed. But in July the joint meeting resolved that 'the present method of working upon the lines of national movements for the various trades – tramway workers, gasworkers, carters, etc. etc., – be continued, and that a national movement for municipal workers as such was impracticable.'[106]

The reason given was that such a movement, by recognizing the municipalities as units of organization, would encourage the policy of the Municipal Employees' Association (MEA). A national movement was impossible without the co-operation of that union, but any encouragement of it would embarrass the National Federation of General Workers. The MEA was, for organizational reasons ('the restricted scope of its organisation'),[107] excluded from both the TUC and the Labour Party. Hence it was ostracized in the movement. Its exclusion from the movement for joint wage bargaining was one of the forces which impelled it into alliance with the Workers' Union and the NAUL in the shortlived National Amalgamated Workers' Union. Eventually, after many other liaisons, it became one of the main constituents of the merger which gave birth to the NUGMW in 1924. Yet another sectional rupture had prepared the ground for the big division into two general unions after the war.

We must not leave this question without noting an important feature of all these settlements. All the wage increases conceded, at all levels, during the war, were styled 'war bonuses', or 'war wages'. One of the principal purposes of the NTWF's 'Bristol policy' of 1917 was to prepare for the defence of these enhanced rates when the war came to an end and to consolidate them into new, negotiated national scales of pay. Otherwise the employers were universally expected to withdraw the bonuses once peace was announced. 'No separate negotiations on reductions' became Bevin's constant instruction; it was a major factor reinforcing understanding of the need to restructure union authority around central, departmentalized trade groups.

## II

## Labour Supply and State Control in the Docks

The government was slow to recognize how far the transport industry would be essential to its war-effort. In the initial phase of patriotic voluntary recruitment, many dockers and carters joined the forces and were drafted indiscriminately into infantry, artillery, the navy. Sexton reported in 1915 that 7,600 of his members had joined 'the colours'. He was preoccupied with 'the enormous liability of keeping the 7,600 in benefit, which carries with it the payment of death benefit for all these men'.[108] By 1917 15,000 NUDL members had joined the forces, and 481 had been killed.[109] In Wales, 1,500 members of the DWRGWU from Cardiff and over 1,000 from Swansea joined the army.[110] Merchant seamen often joined the Royal Navy. Carters, keen to forsake the lowest-paid occupation in transport, flocked to join up, and their skills, either as horsemen or motormen, were welcomed by the generals. Others with experience of horses followed them on to the docks, attracted by the higher pay; the shortage of carters and wagons was to be exposed by the Federation as a major cause of traffic congestion in and around the docks.

The existence of an absolute labour shortage in docks and shipping remained a matter of dispute between the unions, the employers, and the military and state authorities throughout the war. The government and shipowners used it in order to justify the increased use of Chinese labour in the merchant navy, and, as we have seen, their response provoked a united, and racist, opposition from the Federation's leaders.

Women workers were, of course, extensively deployed in the munitions factories and this, as we have noted, resulted in a large enrolment of women into the Workers' Union. One or two attempts were made, in London and the South Wales ports, to introduce women workers on the docks. The unions were outraged, and made their opposition so effective that the practice ceased and no attempt was made to spread it. The Executive gave its opinion that women were unsuited for work in the docks for both 'physical and moral reasons'.[111]

In road-passenger transport, the LPU, representing the 'radical aristocrats' in the London bus service, put up vigorous opposition to a Home Office proposal that women should be granted drivers' licences. The busmen's threat to strike on the issue, on the grounds that 'the work is highly strenuous and sufficient to try the strongest of men' was effective, and the proposal was dropped.[112] The men also feared a permanent dilution of their closed labour market. However, the unions, including the AAT, did enrol the large influx of women conductors, who came to provide some 75 per cent of the platform staff in the capital during the war. The AAT, indeed, claimed to have been a more consistent advocate of equal pay for these women than was the militant LPU.

On the whole, transport and its associated waterside-process industries, most of which involved heavy manual work, retained their all-male character.

## Militarization of Labour?

With foreign labour excluded by what amounted to a colour bar, and with women confined to the passenger section of transport, the government and the port employers were squeezed. They were strongly tempted to militarize the dock labour force. Certainly they protested their enthusiasm for this temptation. But the dockers were having none of it, and a prolonged struggle broke out as the unions summoned all their forces of resistance. The unions also opposed the thin ends of its wedge: state control of labour deployment and other forms of domination. They resisted incorporation in new state machinery, seeking instead to register their own authority over the supply of labour.

In all these areas, it was the unions which took the initiative, and the government and employers who dragged their feet. As early as January 1915 the Liverpool District Committee of the Federation proposed to the Executive that it should 'draw up a scheme for the organisation of transport workers to facilitate transportation of troops and supplies, and invite the government to receive a deputation. Mr. Sexton said there were plenty of men available; it was the machinery which was at fault. It was absolutely chaotic.' So the Executive wrote (again) to Sir George Askwith, 'reminding him that we had had no reply to our previous letter, and that we are still open to consider with the Government measures to effect improvements.'[113]

Was the Federation here seeking a corporate embrace? Hardly. But it was looking for a real response. As often happens, pressures for subordinate 'participation' and demands for effective workers' control enjoyed an uneasy co-existence.

After two more months, following the Treasury conference between the Prime Minister and the unions, at which Gosling and Williams had been present, the Federation renewed its initiative: 'it was resolved that the Secretary write to the War Office, the Board of Trade, the Admiralty, and the Chancellor of the Exchequer again offering co-operation in forming an advisory Board for Transport Affairs.' This should be 'separate and distinct from the Advisory Committee on Production'.[114]

## Robert Williams Tours the Ports

Nine months later, the government belatedly set up its Port and Transit Executive Committee to deal with congestion at the docks. It excluded any labour representation. Robert Williams promptly sent a letter of protest to the Prime Minister and reported to the Executive. Sexton thought that 'the Secretary's association with certain anti-conscription campaigns might have influenced the Prime Minister and to that extent prejudiced the claims of the Federation.' Williams returned the point: 'the President had signed the letter also, and as the Prime Minister had recently given public praise to the efforts of the President, he could scarcely resort to discourtesy.'[115]

Williams's protest had certainly been forthright. He accused the Prime Minister of 'again studiously ignoring the claims of organised labour', and pointed out that the new committee was a powerful, executive body, authorized 'to give directions . . . for carrying their decisions into effect', that the Federation learned of its formation only through the press, and that the 'arbitrary confinement of its personnel to proprietary and administrative interests and influences' was extremely damaging: 'The present time of national tension is scarcely one in which to make invidious class distinctions, and we should heartily welcome a real exhibition of the cohesion of all classes and interests calculated to protect and promote the well-being of the State'.[116]

A few days later, Asquith's Private Secretary telephoned his response: 'it had been the intention to suggest a name of a Labour nominee, but that under pressure of work the matter had been overlooked'! There followed an official invitation to Harry Gosling to join the Committee. Williams, it may be said, had taught the PM to mind his corporate manners – but this was just the beginning.

Gosling was well aware of the ambiguity of his new and isolated role:

> were I possessed of the power to determine otherwise, I should have at least half a dozen colleagues as fellow-members of this Committee . . . I know only too well that all of what has happened in the work of the Committee has not met with the support of the members of affiliated Unions. It must be made quite clear to those who criticised the actions of the Committee that I was alone as representing organised labour . . . There is an idea prevalent in the minds of some of our officials that I, on the part of the Executive, in some way countenanced the employment of military labour. That is totally wide of the mark . . . My one wish has been to avoid the use of military labour. If I have asked our members . . . to relax certain of their Trade Union practices, it was because I wanted to maintain the work entirely within civilian bounds . . . [117]

Moreover, Gosling claimed for Labour the expertise which government lacked and had ignored: 'had we been consulted twelve months before we were, we should have been able to suggest means of avoiding many of the blunders into which the nation drifted during the first fifteen months of the war.' During that period, the Federation had repeatedly 'implored' the government to do something. Dockers were, after all, the eye-witnesses of the congestion. Their knowledge, their 'patriotism' and their interest constituted the grounds for their participation, but it was precisely this claim to a share in control which was resisted: not overtly, but by default.

The need for vigilance in face of the threat posed by military labour was real enough. In July 1915 the NALU went on strike at Fishguard over the refusal of the Great Western Railway to increase wages on their cargo traffic with Ireland. The government promptly sanctioned the use of soldiers to act as strike-breakers. The strike collapsed in consequence. In other incidents of this kind, however, the systematic use of the military as strike-breakers was frustrated by the protest and counterstrikes of the unions – for example, in Glasgow or, again, in Hull.

More insidious was the emergence of the so-called 'Khaki Battalions'

– dockers within the armed forces, constituted as special Mobile Transport Battalions to undertake dock work when labour shortage was held to be responsible for congestion and delay. This issue was intimately bound up both with the question of who controlled the method of working in the ports, and with the controversy over the call-up, reserved occupations and conscription. The dockers and their unions readily recognized a menacing sequence: dockers were called up, a labour shortage at the docks was then proclaimed, and the soldier dockers, identified as experienced port labour, were then returned to the work under military discipline to threaten civilian, trade-union controls in the industry. In the face of this threat, union resistance, both in the corporate machinery and outside it, stiffened and grew. On the inside, the Federation fought a successful battle for enhanced representation and veto powers on the Port and Transit Committee; on the outside, and with federal sanction, dockers struck more than once in local disputes over the use of the Khaki Battalions.

The Port and Transit Committee launched the Khaki Battalion scheme with the approval of the War Office, claiming that congestion in the ports was traceable mainly to labour shortage. It estimated that the peacetime labour requirement of the industry was for 100,000 men, and that by 1916 there was a deficiency of 20,000. The Battalions should initially number 3,000, with a deferred target number of 10,000. It was

> essential that the new battalions thus formed shall remain part of the armed forces of the Crown, charged with the duty of supplementing any deficiency of labour which may exist for any work anywhere in the United Kingdom . . . A recognized military force is necessary in order that the Government may convince the existing supply of labour that these transport battalions are formed through national necessity and not for commercial convenience.[118]

The Port and Transit Committee made a serious concession at this point, agreeing that the deployment of the Khaki Battalions would depend on the agreement of Local Consultative Committees in the ports, on which the Transport Workers would be represented. These committees would also include a military and naval officer, and the Port Authority's representative. The soldier dockers would be paid at the port or district rate, having their military pay deducted whilst engaged in dock work.

Local Consultative Committees were then set up. They included: for Bristol, Ernest Bevin; for Liverpool, James Sexton; for London, Alderman Devenay (DWRGWU); for Glasgow, J. Houghton; and so on. But the civil servant who acted as the Port and Transport secretary, F. G. Dumayne, addressed these officials in terms that provoked the wrath of the Federation:

labour remaining in some of the ports is no longer sufficient to deal with all the cargoes . . . When this is the case ports become congested . . . causing a block in the flow of traffic both as regards necessary overseas supplies for His Majesty's armed forces and the food and other supplies of the population of these islands . . . Bearing these facts in mind, my committee is of the opinion that the most economical form of labour . . . is to form a mobile battalion of transport workers, who can be moved to any port where for the time being the existing supply of labour is unable to cope . . . [119]

Williams's reaction was swift and angry. The government may have 'sanctioned' the Mobile Battalions, but the Federation most certainly had not: 'we have insisted time and again that there is sufficient civilian labour if such be used to the fullest advantage'. The 'alleged shortage of labour . . . was quite contrary to the facts of their own experience'.[120]

Williams had good grounds for this assertion. The Port and Transit Committee had complained that iron ore, essential raw material for the smelting mills which supplied the steel for the munitions factories, was held up at the ports due to labour shortages. The NTWF secretary demanded to be supplied with a list of the ports where this was alleged. They were Barrow, Heysham, Glasgow and Ardrossan, whilst Manchester and Leith were also cited as ports where general cargo was held up.

Williams went on a tour of every one of these locations, conducting a severe personal investigation. He was met at each site by local union officials and accompanied on foot to the quaysides. He reported back to the NTWF Executive. In Salford, 'work appeared to be proceeding with due celerity', and indeed on Tuesday, 7 February, he found 600 men without work at the Manchester Ship Canal. He then 'proceeded' to Barrow. Here he found 'clear evidence of a shortage of labour'. Soldiers were working one hold of an iron-ore ship with 'a very perceptible lack of capacity to deal with the arduous work'. (Williams, as a former coal-trimmer, was an expert on arduous work.) The civilian dockers at Barrow, he discovered, were not unionized, and were employed by a contractor who 'had knocked all the spirit out of them'. In consequence, and observing his large profits, the men were 'indifferent to the needs of the country'. They were 'hopelessly demoralised' – in a word, alienated. Moreover, alongside the shortage of labour, Williams discovered an ore ship wholly idle 'because of there being no empty wagons'.[121] Finally, he drew attention to the obsolescence of the ore ships, against which the trimmers' unions had launched a national campaign. Williams found the ships in Barrow 'ill adapted to modern requirements of promptness in . . . discharging'.

Williams then visited Glasgow. The dockers at the Clydebank docks had to travel many miles to work, starting at 5 a.m., and travelling in 'deplorably evil circumstances, the workmen's trains being almost universally without light of any kind'. At the 'place of call' there were 'many more men than were required'. Moreover, the men were

employed by the hour and were discharged 'whenever there was a
shortage of wagons, which, be it noted, is quite frequently the case'.
They were miles from home and

> it can easily be imagined that when the men are told to stand off because of
> a lack of wagons there is every inducement for them to leave their work and,
> during non-prohibited hours, adjourn to the nearest public-house, from
> which, during the remainder of the day, it is almost impossible to recall
> them. In this bleak, inhospitable district of the Clyde there is no sort of hut
> accommodation to which the men may resort for meals, or during any delay
> awaiting empty wagons. This is an evil calling for instant redress on the part
> of the Clyde Trust or such other authority as may be responsible for the
> totally inhuman conditions under which the men are expected to work and
> have their being.

Did ever the dockers have a finer champion than Williams? It is hard to
think so.

On the whole of the Clyde, he reported, 'there was no visible evidence
of a shortage of labour'. At Ardrossan there were 'obviously plenty of
men to meet all the demands'. At Leith 'there was a sufficiency of men',
but there was a dispute over the customary contract with the employer
over the discharge of grain. The men, enjoying the bargaining power of
wartime full employment, were determined to prevail in this dispute, the
origins of which lay in events of 1913. 'This difficulty is quite susceptible
to adjustment . . . There are sufficient men to man all the work of the
port.'

Williams concluded his report with an aggressive flourish. The
congestions were 'not in the main, due to any shortage of labour. Of
course it must be agreed that periodically there may not be all the men
required at a particular place . . . But this is almost entirely due to the
anarchical methods of the employers and the want of managerial capacity
at our large dock and harbour centres.' This incompetence was caused
by the tradition of casual labour, because port employers were
accustomed to a queue of unemployed dockers waiting for the call. For
this reason they had never developed any skills in manpower planning:
'The employers feel that they have not quite so much control as they had
in normal times, when there was a large surplus of unemployed labour.'

The only solution was for the employers' and workmen's representatives
to establish joint co-ordination of labour supply. To this end, Williams
invited the Port and Transit Committee to join with the Federation in a
tour of the ports. He warned them of the threat of strikes if the Mobile
Battalion was deployed in the face of his evidence:

> Military labour must only be used . . . after consultation with and agreement
> on the part of the Trade Union representatives . . . The NTWF will at all
> times be prepared to place the services of their officials at the disposal of the

Port and Transit Executive . . . to help in all matters of labour co-ordination . . . in order to facilitate the work of transport, upon which the nation and its Allies so closely depend.

Williams returned to the attack in a letter to the NTWF representatives on the port Local Consultative Committees:

congestion is the result of causes over which the workmen and their representatives have had, and still have, no control . . . The Prime Minister himself has stated . . . that it costs from £200 to £300 per year per unit to drill, maintain and equip our soldiers. It seems the most extravagant expenditure imaginable to bring them back to their civilian occupations where, on the facts of the case, such is neither desirable nor necessary . . . The present method of employing our members is wasteful, and . . . the bulk of the congestion has arisen through the employers' interest being unadaptable . . . The authorities are attempting to obtain more and more men from the reserved occupations in order to release them for military service, while at the same time they are releasing more and more men from military service to use them in civilian occupations under military discipline.[122]

This complaint was heard far and wide, from the engineering industry to the mines. No one analysed the phenomenon more trenchantly than Robert Williams. Neither did anyone labour so hard and successfully to expose it. Fittingly, his strategy for combating it rested entirely on workers' control.

The vast majority of the Federation and its leaders followed Williams's lead and gave his view unqualified endorsement. There was one exception: the NUDL and James Sexton. Sexton went so far as to support the formation in Liverpool of a local dockers' battalion. In this he was alone: even the NSFU had threatened to strike if the seamen were brought under military-service conditions. Hand-picked dockers were enrolled to work under military discipline at any dock where they were required in Liverpool. Three 'companies', totalling 375 officers and men, were formed in 1915; by 1917 they had been increased to a second battalion and a total of 2,000 men. Its commandant was Lord Derby, who later became Secretary of State for War; its adjutant was Richard Williams of the labour exchange (author of the pre-war Liverpool registration scheme); and its sergeants and corporals were union officials, working at higher rates of pay than the 'privates'. Sexton became its unpaid adviser. He was alone in the NTWF Executive in accepting that the blame for congestion in the ports should fall on the dockers themselves, bound, as he claimed them to be, by ancient customs and immobilities. Lloyd George recorded his appreciation many years later: 'it was James Sexton whose loyal co-operation made possible the success of this scheme'.[123]

The battalion did well for its members in terms of high wages and regularity of work. Milligan, Liverpool district secretary of the union, hoped that it could be transformed after the war into a self-managing co-operative labour agency. The scheme aroused jealousy amongst the other dockers, but Milligan joined Sexton in the Honours List for 1917 (they received an OBE and a CBE respectively). Lord Derby took a great interest in the battalion, hoping that it could serve as a model to be transposed to many other war industries; Lloyd George, grappling with the problem of shell supplies, agreed. But it remained unique, except for an imitation unit at Leith, where the NUDL was also the dominant union.

The Mersey Carters' Union found itself under intense pressure to accept an imitation of the battalion in its own trade. There was a genuine shortage of carters during the war, not confined to Liverpool. As well as men, the industry surrendered thousands of horses and wagons to 'the colours'. Here was another classic example of chaotic *laissez-faire* in the management of an essential industry. The employers in Liverpool demanded militarization as a remedy for these shortages, but the union offered 'strenuous resistance to any form of military discipline for their members'.[124]

Congestion at the Liverpool docks persisted throughout the NUDL experiment, and even Tillett, than whom no union leader could be more fervid in his patriotism, was scandalized by the Liverpool union's collaboration in militarization. 'Since the war,' he wrote at the end of 1916:

> we have been successful in maintaining in each port where our members are situated a free and independent labour stand, without resorting to mobilisation of Khaki battalions. In some cases other Unions have lamely submitted to the regimentation of labour with very wretched results. The congestion of traffic has been a scandal to the country ... The only reply we have had to our offer of help in a practical manner is the plea of industrial conscription which we have and shall fight against, equally as we fought against military conscription.[125]

The last phrase in that quotation is misleading, to say the least. We dealt with this issue in chapter 16, in which Tillett's real position is adequately explained. As we noted there, the NTWF voted not to initiate the proposed campaign against conscription.

However, the Council went on to approve the summoning of a special TUC Conference 'to safeguard all Trade Union rights likely to be involved in the application of the Military Services Acts'. Before and after this debate the key struggle for labour representation in the control of the docks continued unabated.

## Military Strike-breaking

On the very eve of the Federation debate on conscription came powerful evidence of the need for vigilance on this front. The Manchester dockers were negotiating for a wage increase, and a strike was possible. R. Blundell, the Federation's district secretary, reported that 'right in the midst of the negotiations came a letter from the Port and Transit Executive', claiming that

> The question of whether there is a deficiency of civilian labour is a matter of fact. If the civilian labour in the port is not prepared to work there is clearly a deficiency. It is neither desirable nor necessary for the Local Committee to postpone obtaining help from the Transport Workers' Battalion until the port is congested or until vessels are held up for indefinite periods . . . it is only failure on its [civilian labour's] part to handle effectively and promptly the traffic through the port which will necessitate the withdrawal of the Transport Workers' Battalion from their military duties.[126]

No clearer threat to use the Battalions for strike-breaking could have been delivered.

The Annual General Council debated the letter and heard an accumulation of evidence, from Hull, Glasgow and Tyneside, of its replication around the ports; in every case the ruling was the same, that 'where the men refused to work there was clearly a shortage of labour'. Sexton, characteristically, 'wanted to know what they were to do where the men refused to agree to the results of the negotiations conducted by their own officials? Was the port to be held up? His own men had refused to work two transports unless they were paid more money . . . What were they to do in such cases?'

Blundell went straight to the point: addressing Gosling – who sat on the central Port and Transit Committee – he asked: 'whether you have been a party to a policy which . . . is meant to coerce us?' The president replied that this was the first he had heard of the letter, and rehearsed the function and powers of the Local Consultative Committees, who were empowered to decide on whether there was a labour shortage. The trade-union representatives on these committees had, he implied, the power of veto over the calling in of the Battalions, and this should be exercised. Dumayne (Sir Frederick, secretary of the Port and Transit Executive Committee) and the Manchester Ship Canal Company had tried to by-pass this machinery; but the duty of the Port and Transit was to keep the flow of traffic through the ports, and the men should keep working during a dispute.

However, as other speakers pointed out, in the case of the PLA for example, employers could refuse to go to arbitration. And others were manipulating the Military Service Acts to force dockers into the army, in the expectation that they would then return to the docks as military labour. One firm in London employing over 1,000 men had applied for only forty-eight of them to be granted exemption from the call-up. Gosling promised to take up the matter at the Port and Transit, and the exchanges ended with the tabling of Blundell's letter of protest to the Ship Canal Company, about 'a communication so threatening and coercive in character'.[127]

The Federation sustained its complaint at being held at arm's length by the government in the management of the ports. Gosling discerned in this the hand of the Shipping Federation, 'the one organisation of international capital which maintains in peace-time a professional army of strike-breakers . . . The Government has not dared to exercise complete control over shipping affairs because of the formidable character of the political and financial influence exercised by the shipping fraternity', which was used to deny Labour nominees their place in 'the counsels of the nation'.[128]

In November 1916 *The Times* announced that the government planned an increase in the Khaki Battalions to 20,000 men. Williams leapt to protest: 'we have not been consulted in this huge extension . . . and we will accept no responsibility if and when the civilian workers take action as a protest . . . Those who fondly imagine that these encroachments upon the civilian status of the working people will be allowed to continue unchallenged are living in a fool's paradise'. Dumayne replied that the extension would be limited to a new total of 10,000![129]

The NTWF District Committees stepped up their vigilance during 1917, and the Annual Report was able to claim that numerous threats by employers to bring in the Khaki Battalions had been countered by 'prompt action' in the ports to enforce adherence to the terms under which it could acceptably be deployed. But a more subtle ploy made its appearance in Hull, where the army had held 'private talks with one or two leading labour men', who had offered to withdraw opposition to the Battalions if 3*d.* per head was deducted from its pay and handed over – as union subscriptions – to union funds. Gosling's response was to tell the colonel in charge that 'it would certainly not do to stop any money from the men's wages, particularly to be stopped by any representative of the military', but that 'the officer in a friendly way might remind the men that their Unions will be wanted after the war is over, and therefore they should not lapse membership.'[130]

The cat-and-mouse game continued. Indeed, it was stepped up while the committees proliferated. The port Local Consultative Committees were empowered to determine when the Battalions could be used, and by 1917 the Federation was satisfied that this machinery, on the whole, was working satisfactorily. Local Labour Committees were empowered to release men for military service. Both these bodies contained union representatives. But a third committee, the Port Co-ordination Committee, which ordered the traffic, the berths and the diversion of ships, 'studiously excluded' labour representation and consequently 'these Committees could only work to the disadvantage of the workers and the Federation'. The interdependence of the three functions was illustrated by Williams. The trade of a port falls suddenly, and there is a temporary labour surplus. There follows pressure to release men to the army. Then comes a glut of shipping back to the port, civilian labour is now inadequate, and the call goes up for the Battalions to be brought in: 'if the men are provoked by what appears to be a deliberate policy, [the Federation Executive's] counsel and advice will be of no avail in restraining the more impetuous'.[131]

Joseph Houghton's District Report from the Clyde for 1917 exemplified the problem:

> Like other ports, we have had to call in the aid of the Mobile Dockers' Battalion, but they have been a mixed blessing indeed, as the five days' work guaranteed, when once being started, has meant a week or a fortnight, and before the military have half finished a bout, our men are walking about in scores looking for employment . . . Again, the clause . . . which says a stoppage is a deficiency of labour is enabling the shipowners to use the military as blacklegs . . . [132]

Faced with the presence of the Battalions, the Federation began to look more favourably on schemes of registration for dockers. In Hull a scheme was established for the first time, to obtain a reliable count of the number of dockers, in order to prevent both excessive demands by the army for the release of dockers to it, and the incursion of the Khaki Battalions.

The unbelievable jumble of authorities threatened further confusion when, in 1918, the Ministry of National Service, 'with its usual lack of perspicacity . . . evidently regarding dock labour as a mobile commodity, prepared a scheme to transfer labour from one port to another.'[133] The Federation rejected it out of hand and prepared its own proposals. They amounted to the first programme for comprehensive registration of dock labour, controlled by the unions, in history:

> All dock labour in the ports which adopt the scheme to be registered and classified. The registration authority shall be the Union or Unions affiliated to the Federation . . . Men so registered present themselves for work at periods . . . agreed upon, at the ports . . . Men shall undertake to conform to reasonable requests for transfer . . . All men registered shall be guaranteed for each day they present themselves and are not employed, a retaining fee of 75 per cent of . . . the day rates . . . Men conversant with the organisation of labour shall be appointed to allocate the gangs when there is a shortage of labour and shall . . . be paid by the Registration Committee.[134]

The Minister of National Service, J. W. Balfour, on receipt of this scheme, wrote to Robert Williams: 'it would be impossible to give effect to the proposals set forth therein, and it has consequently been decided to abandon the attempt to establish any Dock Labour Transfer Scheme at the present time.'[135]

## Resigning for Victory

The accumulated frustrations of the Federation reached breaking point in the same year. It presented a demand (to yet another ministry, of Shipping, which had jurisdiction over the ports) for increased representation on the central Port and Transit Committee, and for the functions of the three separate local committees to be combined in a single comprehensive body. The ministry refused these changes. Promptly Gosling resigned from the central Port and Transit Committee, and so did all the Federation's representatives on the Local Consultative Committees. This abrupt reaction worked wonders. The War Cabinet conferred, and announced the reconstitution of the entire system, largely in accordance with the wishes of the Federation.

The NTWF Annual Report recorded this victory with restrained pleasure:

> The President resumed his membership of the Committee, reinforced by Mr. Sexton, Mr. Bevin, and Mr. Ben Tillett, M.P., (with the Secretary as an alternate member). In addition, Mr. J. H. Thomas was selected to serve on the Committee as representing railway port interests. The local representatives resumed their membership of the Local Committees, and it is pleasing to report that, generally speaking, matters connected with labour in the ports are proceeding smoothly.[136]

In addition to the reformation of the Central Committee, the unified committee structure desired by the Federation at port level was introduced, and an additional power was conferred on Harry Gosling: 'In the event of any difference of opinion between any Port Labour Committee and any local Port and Transit Committee as to the granting or withdrawal of exemptions, the matter shall be decided by the Board of Trade after consultation with Sir Norman Hill and Mr. Gosling.'[137]

Yet still the conflict went on, for the Board of Trade continued to cancel the exemptions of large numbers of dock workers over the heads of the Port Labour Committees, despite the new agreement. Whole categories of grades and ages were affected, in so-called 'clean-cut comb-outs'. Williams fulminated in a letter to Garnham Roper at the Board of Trade: the Port Committees are treated with as little respect and consideration as though the members were enemy prisoners of war. It must surely be patent to the Board of Trade officials that the successful carrying on of the transport trade necessitates the work of the manifold sections of transport workers – dockers, stevedores, warehousemen, cranesmen, trimmers, capstanmen, and other sections too lengthy to enumerate. The Board of Trade and the Ministry of National Service, hiding themselves behind the profound character of their ignorance of water-side occupations, appear fondly to imagine that all these highly technical and complex grades are interchangeable . . . The clean-cut, for an entire occupation so complex as transport, is a clean cut to madness and desperation . . . I am advising the Labour Members of the Port Labour Committees to resist strenuously the despotic action of the officials of the Ministry of National Service. In certain districts our Labour representatives have resigned or threatened to resign. We shall certainly refuse point-blank to accept any responsibility for the muddle in which the country is being placed by these arbitrary proceedings.[138]

Once again, the censorious tone, the expert contempt of a practical trade unionist for the ignorant government department, and the prediction of chaos if he were ignored, produced results. Williams deployed these weapons consistently in this struggle. He also warned of impending 'unrest' among the dockers. A positive avalanche of telegrams and letters followed, from the Board of Trade (Public Utilities and Harbours Department), the Ministry of National Service, and ultimately from the War Cabinet, reaffirming the sole authority of the Port Labour Committees over exemptions – the most satisfactory one being to Robert Williams from Downing Street: 'War Cabinet has ordered that for the present no further recruitment of Dock Transport Workers is to take place in any Ports. Men at present under call may be posted. No more calling-up notices may be issued to Dock Transport Workers until further notice.'[139]

It was May Day 1918, and it was the last exchange in the long-running saga.

This whole experience demonstrated the persistence of the attempts by both state and employers to break into the stronghold which the dockers had established in the ports. By direction, by military labour and by indiscriminate conscription – no approach was to be ignored. It also illustrates the quite extraordinary degree of bureaucratic confusion in which the greatest imperial power on earth sought to conduct its total war. And, most significant for us, it paces out the exciting strides which the transport workers made towards unified action and centralized authority. Finally, it shows authority reposing more and more in the personal hands of the Federation's secretary. Nobody dictated Robert Williams's letters, or his initiatives, which often preceded Executive decisions; its meetings invariably endorsed what he had done. The man was, we now know, at the peak of his influence and authority, and using them to advance what were, in effect, demands for co-management powers in the industry on behalf of transport workers and their federation.

## The Labours of Williams and Bevin

The Federation's tiny resources were stretched beyond their limits by the accumulation of a wide and growing range of duties, all devolving either on Williams, assisted by his clerk and a junior, or on a tiny cadre of executive members, of whom Bevin carried the most onerous workload. In 1918 the AGC considered a motion from Sexton to increase the complement of officials, at the discretion of the Executive Committee. There was, he argued a crying need for a Bureau of Information, and the Federation should have its own statistical staff.

Others who supported him stressed the unbelievable workload of Williams, and called for the appointment of a national organizer. Bevin contributed personal evidence:

Take the previous Monday: there were four hearings in connection with the carters' demands. For his own part that meant that he had to finish his own work by twelve o'clock, attend those hearings and then go back that same night by the eight o'clock train. That had been going on a long time. The tramwaymen's delegates would remember that their negotiations were spread over four days.

Williams spoke feelingly of the size of the task before them, arising simply from the Labour Resettlement Committee on which he served: 'the labour movement neither had the staff to do such work nor could the present staff find time to do it. It required a fortnight's preparation sometimes for a conference or an arbitration that lasted perhaps two hours . . . What was wanted was a general staff, men to do the thinking for labour.'

Wilson asked whether he was to understand that the general secretary was requested to deal with arbitration cases by the unions, and that the Federation had to deal with them. Williams answered, 'Yes, scores of them.' Why, asked Wilson, did the unions put out to the Federation work which they should do themselves? Williams replied as modestly as he could: 'I do not want to say anything about myself, but a Union thinks it can do better when it has the services of a skilled advocate like Bevin or the President.'

Yet on the pretext that the Council was unclear whether the motion called for more officials or more staff, the reference back was successfully moved, and Williams was left to carry his burden, with the inevitably part-time assistance of Bevin.[140]

The struggle over the control of the ports had an equally important sequel, as the Federation turned to draw up its proposals for demobilization. Here, the design and the initiative came from Bevin, who had been responsible for drafting the Federation's Port Transfer Scheme which had so frightened the Board of Trade.

## Demob and Registration

However, Tillett had, as early as 1916, given voice to a widely felt apprehension about the impact of eventual demobilization on unemployment and poverty. In his Annual Report to the DWRGWU for that year, he had written of the 6–8 million men and women in the armed forces, the munitions and 'war-trades' industries, and of temporary government staff, amounting altogether to half the working population, who would be released on to the civilian labour market. The government had promised one year's leave with pay to demobilized soldiers; Tillett raised the demand for the same terms to be offered to all 'war workers'. Further, he called for the unions to be designated as employment agencies; the government should send copies of all its individual discharge notices to the head offices of the men's unions. The employment exchanges (against which the same Tillett had raged in pre-war days as an instrument of state oppression) should be run by national and local committees with 50 per cent of their seats allocated to the unions, the rest going to Board of Trade representatives – the Ministry of Labour not having then been created.[141]

By 1917 this campaign was under way, both in the NTWF and in the Triple Alliance. In the docks industry, it became linked with the NTWF's conversion to a comprehensive registration scheme for dockers, and with its rejection of surrogate state-imposed registers administered by the Board of Trade.[142] The Triple Alliance adopted a general version, calling for 'registration bureaux' with trade-union representatives making up half of their management boards, which would have 'full executive power'.[143]

The Alliance's leaders met Asquith to table this demand. He was cautious and non-committal, but was extremely careful not to appear dismissive. He did undertake to continue wartime arbitration powers for the munitions industry and its 4,000 controlled factories. Unemployment insurance on the scale envisaged by the unions, which amounted to full maintenance by the state, he would not pledge, hoping instead that demobilization would be a gradual, and therefore non-disruptive, process. Answering the crucial demand for full executive powers for joint labour–state registration bureaux, which he most certainly regarded privately as outrageous, he preferred to duck, offering a general hope that 'labour will be strongly represented' on local committees.[144]

The Ministry of Labour created a Demobilisation and Resettlement Department in 1918, and invited the Federation to submit proposals for the port industry. The Port Labour Committees conferred, and suggested that they should be retained in existence in peacetime to deal with demobilization and the re-absorption of discharged dockers, 'with the proviso that their constitution was amended with the object of securing equal representation of employers and employed'.[145] There should also be a Central Advisory Committee having the same balance, plus non-voting representatives from government departments.

Now Bevin drove for a harder bargain still. The Ministry of Munitions had announced a scale of minimum payments to which redundant munitions workers would be entitled for a year following their dismissal – a major but incomplete concession. Bevin demanded that these also apply to all registered dock labour, in the form of the retaining fee which had featured in the Port Transfer Scheme. Here were the origins of the 'Fall-back Pay' of the 1947 Dock Labour Scheme; in its turn, the idea looked back for inspiration to the dockers' demands for 'work or maintenance' before the Royal Commission of 1891–3. A further demand was added to the port-transfer model: that no man be registered who was not, prior to August 1915, a member of the union or unions with a controlling interest in the port of his registration. And finally, 'in order to absorb the discharged and demobilised workers, a systematic shortening of hours should take place in all ports, and weekend work should be abolished'.[146]

## Whitleyism

Another theme of subsequent evolution which originated in the war years was Whitleyism, the concept of a national industry-based system of union–employer councils to create a permanent machinery for bargaining, conciliation and consultation. This, embodied in the reports of the Whitley Committee in 1917, was at first approached by the transport and general unions with caution, even hostility. Certainly they did not greet it with the enthusiasm which was later celebrated. But then it became evident that the proposals could readily be incorporated and adapted by the unions to harmonize with their own cherished twin ambitions: permanent recognition and standard, national wages and conditions. Moreover, the machinery was as applicable in the industrial sectors into which the DWRGWU and other transport unions had penetrated as it was in the service sector of transport. At the same time, in framing its proposals in terms of organization by industry, Whitleyism fitted the strong industrial-union strand within the general unions, thereby reinforcing the need for 'departments' – for which read 'Trade Groups' in the final architecture of the TGWU.

One industry in which the future TGWU was to have a major interest was agriculture. It had, as a consequence of the wartime price guarantees to the farmers, which required a corresponding guarantee of farmworkers' wages, acquired its first Agricultural Wages Board in 1917. Its first national, legal, minimum wage award was for £1 25s. a week, which was, even then, an abysmal standard.

National bargaining, as we have seen, was advancing steadily under the influence of compulsory state arbitration; but most industries lacked permanent machinery for this purpose. The Whitley Committee originated in the government's anxiety about rising industrial unrest in the engineering industry, culminating in the widely reported strikes of May 1917.[147] Its recommendations set the framework for the industrial relations system which survived down to recent times. They were for the creation of Joint Industrial Councils of employers' and workers' representatives, 'to deal with issues affecting a whole industry', for the extension of the Trade Board system of legal minima where the conditions for collective bargaining did not exist, for joint consultative and welfare committees at the plant level, and for a permanent, but non-compulsory system of state arbitration.

Within months, and pressed forward by the Federation of General Workers in particular, talks about forming JICs were in train in cement, chemicals, chocolate manufacture, flour-milling, fertilizers, rubber, sugar-refining and other industries.[148] These were and remain, recognizably, the industries in which new unionism, and the general unions which derived their origins from it, had the deepest roots: industries characterized by heavy male manual labour, in which the craft element was minimal, and in which, consequently, labour's need to concentrate its bargaining strength in national structures was most acute.

For the institution of JICs to flourish, however, national organization was also necessary on the employers' side, and this had lagged noticeably behind that of the unions. Once again, it was the war, and the enhancement of labour's strength and status which followed from it, that impelled the employers to follow the trend and to create, in industry after industry, national industry-level associations to counter and meet the unions' challenge.[149] Finally, to crown the generalization of the process, the civil service and postal unions demanded, and won, the government's acceptance of Whitley machinery in the public sector, in the first place in government industrial establishments.[150] The Whitley Committee, be it noted, had included four trade-union representatives, and the scheme's promoter in government was George Roberts, a right-wing trade-union leader of the Typographical Association, Minister of Labour from August 1917, and uncritical supporter of the war.[151]

In 1918 twenty JICs were founded, in 1919 a further thirty-two, and in 1920 another sixteen; six followed in 1921. As an index of their significance for a general union with members spread across many industries, we might take the experience of the Workers' Union, which found itself represented on no less than fifty JICs. Even its large complement of full-time officers was heavily stretched in the effort to staff all those places.[152]

What part did transport play in this process? Surprisingly, perhaps, the initial response, supported by Bevin, was hostile. The NTWF Executive resolved on 29 June 1917

> to take no part in the Enquiry now proceeding into the causes of industrial unrest realising that to give Labour responsibility without power is merely a farce. Further, we consider the respective Commissions were unconstitutionally appointed without consulting Labour officially and the great Labour organisations generally. It is moreover well known to the Government that the causes of industrial unrest are in the main food profiteering and irksome and irritating legislation.[153]

By July, when the first Report had appeared, the tone was different. The EC accepted its broad principles, 'subject to the right to withdraw labour being unimpaired'. Williams wrote in these terms to the Ministry of Labour, throwing in a sharp protest about the traditional hostility of the shipowners to union recognition. In November the EC was asking the ministry to convene a conference of transport employers and unions to secure the foundation of a transport JIC.[154]

The following month, the EC requested Roberts to assist in setting up separate councils for waterside employment, docks, canals and river traffic, road haulage, road-passenger transport, and inland warehousing and distribution. This was an important refinement; the NTWF was seeking to shape the JIC structure to its own national design of departmentalized programmes and 'movements'. This was a novel sectionalism, within a co-ordinated whole. In effect, the Federation took over Whitley's proposals and adapted them to its own, already structured, plans. (We must note, however, that these plans excluded the merchant service; Wilson's ambivalence towards the Federation, and his success in obtaining autonomous machinery in the National Maritime Board, meant that there was no role here for the Federation.)

The Federation (and Williams was its scribe in this, as in so much else) maintained a sceptical and critical stance, making clear that it approached Whitleyism in a pragmatic and instrumental mood, being not at all persuaded of its ability to transform antagonistic relations into harmony.

> The Whitley Report has met with much criticism, but like all other expedients to which resort has to be made to further the interests of the workers and to facilitate smooth working, much depends on the power of organisation responsible for selecting the workers' side of any prospective industrial council . . . long and costly fights . . . would have been avoided if

there had been some machinery by means of which employers and employed could meet round a table without prejudice to each other's right to resort to the arbitrament of direct action . . . So long as that right remains unimpaired . . . we are of the opinion that the establishment of Joint Industrial Councils will be of advantage to our membership. We must not, however, delude ourselves that these or similar projects will or can do anything for us we could not do in the main for ourselves.[155]

The secretary had to defend the Executive for this statement at the AGC in June 1918, for its endorsement of the general principle of Whitleyism. The passenger-transport unions' criticism was met by Williams: 'The Executive's endorsement of the principle of the Whitley Report had considerably helped . . . the Licensed Vehicle Workers and the Amalgamated Association in the national negotiations which had been set on foot, and at the moment the Licensed Vehicle Workers and the Amalgamated Association were engaged in negotiations tending towards the formation of a Joint Standing Industrial Council for the Tramways industry'. So had not the unions committed themselves to the principle?[156]

Will Godfrey of the NUVW, argued, however, that Whitley Councils would be used against the unions 'in the same way as the Insurance Bill was used', and R. H. Farrah, district secretary for the Humber, representing the General Workers' Union, said that 'he did not favour workshop committees'. He was against the Welfare Committees being put forward as the equivalent of the Workshop Committees. Havelock Wilson asked 'where the Government official came in . . . ?' Williams assured him that 'the whole business should be conducted without any interference from the State'. S. J. Wright of the General Workers' Union had an existing Council as evidence: 'in the Building Trades' Industrial Council the representation was ten employers and ten trade union representatives. No government official had anything to do with the business of the Council.' Will Thorne wanted strenuous resistance to any suggestion that non-unionists might sit on the local committees of the Councils.

Bevin's thoughts were more subtle. He was a member of the government's tripartite Reconstruction Council, and had sought for ways of combining state intervention – on the lines of the Trades Boards – and the JICs, where there was a low level of organization:

The Government official was a bugbear to some people . . . but was there any union represented here that did not fly to some government department or other when it was in a difficulty? The State, by the sheer virtue of the tasks imposed upon it during the war, was bound to play an important part in industrial life for the next fifty years. He for one, was not prepared to agree to the government giving up control of raw material, in the allocation of which there was ample scope for the work of Whitley Councils.

Here was a bold attempt to convert the JIC into an instrument of workers' control.[157]

Consistently with the Federation's general design, it expressed reservations about the Report's emphasis on

> devolution from the centre to the circumference, providing for district committees of management and a measure of shop control between the shop stewards and local managerial sections. In the case of the Federation, with its scattered and diverse units, the desire at the moment was the achievement of a larger measure of national organisation and co-ordination by creating uniformity between the various sections performing similar work.'[158]

A pregnant statement, this, foreshadowing the direction of TGWU policy from Bevin, through Deakin, which persisted until the Second World War and the devolution policies of Jack Jones.

In 1918 the Federation took part in the formation of the Furniture Removal and Warehousing Industry JIC, and exerted its powers to exclude the outlawed Municipal Employees' Association from the JIC for the Electric Power Industry.

## Nationalization and Joint Control

Whitleyism was the official, concessionary response of government and the employers to labour unrest and self-confidence, which was born in the Great Unrest of 1910–14, when it was accompanied by syndicalism, and nurtured in the war, when it was influenced by Guild Socialism. The Guildsmen taught the doctrine of industrial self-management, based upon social ownership and elected management councils. Their constitutional model-making, outlined in pamphlets describing ideal management structures in a number of industries, later came to appear abstract and contrived. Often they were styled as a 'diversion from the class struggle'. In fact, considered in their true context, they relate very closely to the actual experience of state control with which the trade unionists of the period lived in daily contact during the war. This it was that generated the counter-claims for industrial democracy which we have documented in the case of the dockers. Influential numbers of active trade unionists, including experienced officials and executive members, enrolled in the National Guilds' League or read its literature sympathetically.[159]

At the 1918 Annual General Council of the NTWF, George Sanders of the London and Provincial Licensed Vehicle Workers' Union proposed the following motion:

That this Annual General Council Meeting calls upon the Executive
Council to approach the National Union of Railwaymen and the Postal
Workers' Association with a view to making joint representation to the
Government to form a National Board for Communications, with equal
representation of the employees and the State, which will take over and
administer the whole of the inland passenger, mail, and goods transport of
the country – road, rail, air, and water – in the interests of the nation.[160]

We shall have occasion to meet George Sanders later, as a leading
sceptic about the value of the 1922 amalgamation, and a harsh critic of
Bevin's 'ambitions'. He was a London busman, at this time an organizer
for the 'Red Button' Union, the journal of which carried a regular
column written by 'Members of the National Guilds' League'. Sanders
later joined the Communist Party and was an active promoter of the
Comintern's Red International of Labour Unions (RILU) and of the
party's Minority Movement in the London bus section of the TGWU.
Speaking to his 1918 motion: 'He said that there could be little
misunderstanding about the resolution; it aimed at the control of
industry by the workers.' The debate on the motion was very brief;
Havelock Wilson dissociated himself from it and Bevin proposed that the
question be made the subject of a report by the Executive – it was too big
a subject to resolve at the Council, and he did not want to vote against it.
The meeting agreed, and carried the resolution on that understanding.
The resolution was debated again at a special AGC in 1919 and its
demands tabled for the Labour Party Conference in that year.

Its significance is clear. The war had forced a further giant move in the
direction of 'homogenization' of labour[161] and contributed immensely to
a growth of confidence amongst very large numbers of the so-called
'unskilled' workers, who had met and confronted not only employers but
the state itself in a daily struggle for control of work. The resulting self-
assurance, which Robert Williams articulated so well on behalf of
dockers and drivers, was matched at the economic level by a sharp
reduction in the differential income gap between the general workers and
the craftsmen and salariat. Economic claims, and those for a new status,
the quantitative and the qualitative, now went hand in hand in wider and
wider trade-union alliances.

The fact is that both the postal workers and the railwaymen, invoked
as partners in the busmen's resolution, were heavily influenced by the
Guildsmen. Both were the subject of Guild League publications
advocating a Guild government for their industries. The LPU, we have
seen, promoted Guild Socialism. Moreover, the other member of the
Triple Alliance, the Miners' Federation, was also pressing for nationalization with workers' representation. So there came together a
dominant section of the Labour movement, espousing a common
programme of industrial democracy, which, in all these industries,

complemented and took further the strides which were then being made in recognition, in national wage advances, and in the creation of permanent bargaining structures. This process was all congruent, and all integrated in a consistent view of the necessary direction of its march. It had, we must always remember, cost the deaths of millions in a hopeless war to allow Labour to reach this point in so few years.

# Appendix

## Affiliation Fees – NTWF 1918

| | |
|---|---|
| Amalgamated Association of Carters and Motormen | £14 5s. 0d. |
| Amalgamated Association of Tramway and Vehicle Workers | £144 17s. 6d. |
| Amalgamated Carters', Lurrymen's and Motormen's Union | £33 15s. 0d. |
| Amalgamated Union of Engine and Crane Men, etc. | £7 10s. 0d. |
| Amalgamated Society of Salt Workers, General Labourers, etc. | £10 13s. 0d. |
| Amalgamated Society of Watermen, Lightermen and Bargemen | £56 6s. 6d. |
| Amalgamated Stevedores' Labour Protection League | £49 16s. 1d. |
| Cardiff, Penarth and Barry Coal Trimmers' Union | £30 18s. 4d. |
| Dock, Wharf, Riverside and General Workers' Union | £710 14s. 4d. |
| Glasgow Ship Riggers' Protective Association | £3 19s. 7d. |
| Hull Seamen's Union | £24 6s. 0d. |
| Labour Protection League | £13 15s. 0d. |
| London and Provincial Union of Licensed Vehicle Workers | £249 6s. 8d. |
| Liverpool and District Carters' and Motormen's Union | £98 10s. 10d. |
| Mersey River and Canals Watermen's Association | £1 9s. 2d. |
| National Amalgamated Labourers' Union | £47 11s. 6d. |
| National Amalgamated Union of Enginemen, Firemen, etc. | £46 17s. 6d. |
| National Amalgamated Union of Labour | £31 5s. 0d. |
| National Seamen's and Firemen's Union | £625 0s. 0d. |
| National Union of Dock Labourers | £500 0s. 0d. |
| National Union of General Workers | £125 0s. 0d. |
| National Union of Ships' Stewards, Cooks, etc. | £93 15s. 0d. |
| National Union of Vehicle Workers | £81 15s. 5d. |
| National Warehouse and General Workers' Union | £155 4s. 2d. |
| North of England Trimmers' and Teemers' Association | £20 6s. 2d. |
| North of Scotland Horse and Motormen's Association | £23 8s. 9d. |
| Scottish Horse and Motormen's Association | £25 17s. 6d. |
| Scottish Union of Dock Labourers | £93 15s. 0d. |
| United Carters' and Motormen's Association | £25 13s. 9d. |
| United Order of General Labourers | £15 12s. 6d. |
| United Society of Boiler Scalers, etc. | £3 2s. 6d. |
| Weaver Watermen's Association | £5 9s. 6d. |

*Source*: NTWF Annual Report, June 1918.

# Notes

1 Arthur Marwick, 'The Impact of the First World War on British Society', *Journal of Contemporary History*, vol. III (1968), p. 63.

2 Charles H. Feinstein and Sydney Pollard (eds), *Studies in Capital Formation in the United Kingdom, 1750–1920* (Oxford University Press, 1988), pp. 313–53.

3 Alan Bullock, *The Life and Times of Ernest Bevin*, vol. I: *Trade Union Leader, 1881–1940* (Heinemann, 1960), p. 82.

4 Lord Askwith, *Industrial Problems and Disputes* (John Murray, 1920), pp. 412–13.

5 Eric Wigham, *Strikes and the Government, 1893–1974* (Macmillan, 1976), p. 38.

6 Lord Devonport – chairman of the PLA, of course – was head of a grocery business. He was an inept bureaucrat, but in his short career as the first Food Controller, he filled the seats on the Local Food Committees with fellow food-traders and anti-union interests; see Bernard Waites, *A Class Society at War: England 1914–1918* (Berg, 1987), p. 227.

7 The role of that first generation of reforming civil servants, of whom Llewellyn Smith and Lord Askwith were most representative and influential, had from late Victorian times been directed towards a consensual accommodation with trade unionism. In the conditions of war, the limits of that tradition were tested and its continuity threatened, both by the escalation of trade-union demands and by the growth of emergency state powers, which confronted each other. Social reform and social control, as alternative state policies, co-existed uneasily until the post-war slump dispensed with the necessity to treat with the then withered power of the unions. For an important discussion of this issue, see Roger Davidson, *Whitehall and the Labour Problem in Late-Victorian and Edwardian Britain: A Study in Official Statistics and Social Control* (Croom Helm, 1985).

8 DWRGWU Annual Report, 1916, p. 6.

9 Twelfth Report of Proceedings under the Conciliation Act, 1919, pp. 37–9; quoted in Chris Wrigley, *A History of British Industrial Relations*, vol. II: *1914–39* (Harvester Press, 1987), p. 61.

10 Askwith, *Industrial Problems and Disputes*, p. 421.

11 H. A. Clegg, *A History of British Trade Unions since 1889*, vol. II: *1911–1933* (Oxford University Press, 1985), p. 168.

12 Ibid., p. 145.

13 Ibid.

14 Askwith, *Industrial Problems and Disputes*, p. 421.

15 Ibid., p. 386.

16 NTWF Executive Committee Minutes, 31 August 1918.

17 None of the transport leaders seem to have gone so far in military enthusiasms as John Beard, President, and Charles Duncan, MP, Secretary, of the Workers' Union. Having started his career on the left, Beard in the war joined his Local Volunteer Force, and attended union meetings in uniform. He resigned from the ILP in protest at its anti-war stance, and both he and Duncan were associated with the British Workers' Defence League, a dedicated pro-war faction, and the Alliance

of the Employers and Employed. In industrial matters they adopted an extremely conciliatory attitude to the employers in the munitions industry. (Richard Hyman, *The Workers' Union*, Oxford University Press, 1971), p. 82.

18  Hyman, *The Workers' Union*, chapter 4.
19  NTWF Executive Committee Minutes, 24 September 1915, p. 2.
20  The sub-committee of the Triple Alliance met regularly. In February 1916 the NTWF proposed that it should draw up a comprehensive programme on demobilization and the crisis which was expected after the war (NTWF Executive Committee Minutes, 25 February 1916). The Prime Minister himself met the Alliance leaders on the subject – see pp. 589–90, above.
21  NTWF Executive Committee Minutes, 25 August 1916.
22  NTWF Annual General Council Report, 1917, p. 42.
23  Bullock, *The Life and Times of Ernest Bevin*, vol. I, p. 83.
24  Ibid., p. 87.
25  Clegg, *History of British Trade Unions*, vol. II, p. 201.
26  NTWF Executive Committee Minutes, 25 February 1916.
27  Ibid., 13 November 1917.
28  Ibid., 28 September 1917.
29  Ibid., 11 December 1917.
30  Ibid., 22 March 1918.
31  Ibid., 31 August 1918.
32  Angela Tuckett, *The Scottish Carter* (Allen and Unwin, 1967), p. 126.
33  NTWF Executive Committee Minutes, 25 January 1916.
34  Tuckett, *The Scottish Carter*, p. 138.
35  NTWF Annual General Council Report, 1917, pp. 107–8.
36  NTWF Executive Committee Minutes, 24 May 1918.
37  Tuckett, *The Scottish Carter*, p. 140.
38  Ibid., pp. 142–3.
39  Arthur Marsh and Victoria Ryan, *The History of the Seamen's Union* (Malthouse, 1989), p. 393.
40  NTWF Annual General Council Report, 1915, p. 67.
41  Ibid.
42  NTWF Executive Committee Minutes, 20 December 1916.
43  Ibid., 11 December 1917.
44  Ibid., 27 February 1918.
45  Ibid., 27 July 1918.
46  Ibid., 18 December 1917.
47  Clegg, *History of British Trade Unions*, vol. II, p. 120.
48  Report of a Court of Inquiry concerning Transport Workers' Wages and Conditions, with Minutes of Evidence and appendices, Cmnd 936 and Cmnd 937, Parliamentary Papers XXXIV, 1920 (the Shaw Report), Minutes of Evidence, p. 177.
49  NTWF Annual General Council Report, 1917, p. 53.
50  NTWF Executive Committee Minutes, 13 October 1916.
51  NTWF Annual General Council Report, 1916, p. 105.
52  NTWF Executive Committee Minutes, 28 September 1917.
53  Ibid., 11 December 1917.
54  Ibid., 27 February 1918.

55 Shaw Report, appendix 133, pp. 176–94.
56 DWRGWU Annual Report, 1916, p. 17.
57 NTWF Annual General Council Report, 1917, p. 19.
58 NTWF Executive Committee Minutes, 26 March 1915.
59 Ibid., 25 February 1916.
60 NTWF Annual General Council Report, 1916, p. 45.
61 Ibid.
62 Ibid.
63 NTWF Executive Committee Minutes, 29 June 1917.
64 Ibid., 27 July 1917.
65 Clegg, *History of British Trade Unions*, vol. II, pp. 202–3.
66 Ibid.
67 NTWF Executive Committee Minutes, 28 September 1917.
68 NTWF Annual General Council Report, 1917, pp. 17–18.
69 Ibid.
70 The industrial union question of course continued to be debated in the TUC throughout the 1920s, and on down to 1962.
71 NTWF Annual General Council Report, 1917, p. 98.
72 Ibid., pp. 97–9.
73 NTWF Executive Committee Minutes, 22 March 1918.
74 NTWF Annual General Council Report, 1918, p. 84.
75 Ibid.
76 Ibid., pp. 86–7.
77 NTWF Executive Committee Minutes, 26 January 1917.
78 Ibid., 29 June 1917.
79 Ibid., 22 March 1918.
80 Clegg, *History of British Trade Unions*, vol. II, p. 141.
81 Ibid.
82 Marsh and Ryan, *The History of the Seamen's Union*, p. 79.
83 Ibid., pp. 80–1.
84 Ibid., p. 83.
85 NTWF Annual General Council Report, 1916, p. 27.
86 Ibid., pp. 72–3.
87 Account based on NTWF Executive Committee Minutes and on Ken Fuller, *Radical Aristocrats: London Busworkers from the 1880s to the 1980s* (Lawrence and Wishart, 1985), pp. 32–43.
88 NTWF Executive Committee Minutes, 22 March 1918.
89 Ibid., 8 August 1918.
90 Ibid., 13 November 1918.
91 Phillip J. Leng, *The Welsh Dockers* (G. W. and A. Hesketh, 1981), pp. 78–9.
92 NTWF Annual General Council Report, 1917, pp. 45–6.
93 NTWF Executive Committee Minutes, 1 September 1917.
94 Clegg, *History of British Trade Unions*, vol. II, p. 141.
95 NTWF Executive Committee Minutes, 29 January 1915.
96 Ibid., 31 March 1916.
97 NTWF Annual General Council Report, 1917, pp. 52–3.
98 NTWF Executive Committee Minutes, 22 January 1918.
99 Ibid., 27 February 1918.

100  Shaw Report, appendix 3, table A/4, p. 1.

101  Clegg, *History of British Trade Unionism*, vol. II, p. 186.

102  Bevin's wages table gave 1889 as the year of Liverpool's 'last increase' prior to 1914. Yet here, in his speech to the Inquiry, he refers to 1885. His source for the latter date, and the wages for that year (Richard Williams, *The Liverpool Docks Problem* (P.S. King and Son, 1914, p. 173) is authoritative). Bevin referred again to the 1885 date in 1931 (TGWU *Record*, 1931, p. 336).

In 1889, according to Eric Taplin (*The Dockers' Union: A Study of the National Union of Dock Labourers, 1889–1922* (Leicester University Press, 1986), pp. 32–7), dock strikes in Liverpool won some wage increases, but as the strikes were defeated, 'all claims were abandoned except those relating to hours of night work and a regular meal hour'.

It is curious that Bevin, and his researcher Walton Newbold, did not trouble to explain the discrepancy in the dates given for 'the last increase'. Whether it was 1885 or 1889, Bevin's point remains substantially intact. He used figures from the Ministry of Labour for the 1914 wage, of 4s. 6d., and 5s. (overtime). They were the same as at *some* date in the 1880s (given by Williams as 1885), and from 1s. to 2s. a day less than the July 1914 wage in other principal ports. Sexton sat with Bevin at the Shaw Inquiry and would have corrected any error which tended to undervalue his union's achievements. It is also certain that Liverpool was alone amongst the main ports in securing no increase in 1911.

103  Shaw Report, Minutes of Evidence, p. 6.

104  NTWF Executive Committee Minutes, 31 March 1916.

105  Our thanks are due to J. E. Constantine of Scarborough, who forwarded the collection to us in 1987.

106  NTWF Executive Committee Minutes, 27 July 1918.

107  Hyman, *The Workers' Union*, p. 124.

108  NUDL Annual Report, 1915, p. 6.

109  Ibid., 1917, p. 7.

110  Leng, *The Welsh Dockers*, p. 77.

111  NTWF Executive Committee Minutes, 29 June 1916.

112  Fuller, *Radical Aristocrats*, p. 42.

113  NTWF Executive Committee Minutes, 29 January 1915.

114  Ibid., 3 March 1915.

115  Ibid., 8 December 1915.

116  NTWF Annual General Council Report, 1916, p. 29.

117  Ibid., p. 14.

118  Statement of the Port and Transit Executive Committee; reported in the NTWF Annual General Council Report, 1916, pp. 36–7.

119  NTWF Annual General Council Report, 1916, pp. 39–40.

120  Ibid., p. 41.

121  Ibid., pp. 32–6.

122  Ibid., pp. 42–3.

123  Eric Taplin, *The Dockers' Union: A Study of the National Union of Dock Labourers, 1889–1922* (Leicester University Press, 1986), p. 128.

124  NTWF Annual General Council Report, 1916, pp. 24–5.

125  DWRGWU Annual General Council Report, 1916, pp. 15–16.

126  NTWF Annual General Council Report, 1916, p. 79.

127 NTWF Annual General Council Report, 1916, p. 83.
128 NTWF Annual General Council Report, 1917, p. 12.
129 Ibid., pp. 56–7.
130 Ibid., p. 76.
131 Ibid., p. 80.
132 Ibid., p. 112.
133 NTWF Annual General Council Report, 1918, p. 53.
134 NTWF Executive Committee Minutes, 27 February 1918, pp. 3–40.
135 NTWF Annual General Council Report, 1918, p. 54.
136 Ibid., p. 56.
137 Ibid., p. 57.
138 Ibid., p. 58.
139 Ibid., p. 59.
140 Ibid., pp. 16–20.
141 DWRGWU Annual Report, 1916, pp. 9–11.
142 NTWF Annual General Council Report, 1917, p. 46. William Beveridge, at the Board of Trade, was responsible in 1916 for a draft Bill to extend unemployment insurance to dock workers in a scheme coupled with registration. In this he had the support of Llewellyn Smith. The NTWF was far from complaisant, Bevin in particular referring to 'that sinister crowd of civil servants, the Labour Exchange crowd'. See Gordon Phillips and Noel Whiteside, *Casual Labour: The Unemployment Question in the Port Transport Industry, 1880–1970* (Oxford University Press, 1985).
143 NTWF Annual General Council Report, 1917, p. 47.
144 Ibid., pp. 47–50.
145 NTWF Executive Committee Minutes, 13 November 1918.
146 Ibid.
147 See Clegg, *History of British Trade Unions*, vol. II, pp. 168–74.
148 Ibid., p. 205.
149 See Chris Wrigley, *History of British Industrial Relations*, vol. II: *1914–39* (Harvester Press, 1987), pp. 54ff.
150 Clegg, *History of British Trade Unions*, pp. 206–7.
151 See Wigham, *Strikes and the Government*, pp. 41–4.
152 Hyman, *The Workers' Union*, p. 115.
153 NTWF Executive Committee Minutes, 29 June 1917, p. 2. The NTWF is here referring to the Commission of Inquiry into Industrial Unrest, chaired by George Barnes, which recommended the adoption of Whitley's reforms.
154 NTWF Executive Committee Minutes, 11 November 1917.
155 NTWF Annual General Council Report, 1918, p. 51.
156 Ibid., pp. 78–9.
157 Ibid., pp. 78–80.
158 Conference with George Roberts, 18 December 1917; reported in the NTWF Annual General Council Report, 1918, p. 50.
159 A notable case was that of William Straker, secretary of the Northumberland Miners' Association, whose evidence to the Sankey Commission in 1919 amounted to a Guild blueprint for industrial democracy in a nationalized coal industry.
160 NTWF Annual General Council Report, 1918, p. 89.
161 Bernard Waites, *A Class Society at War*, p. 337.

# 18

---

# 1919

## I
## *Uprising*

All over Europe, millions of men were going home from the war. That January, Rosa Luxemburg and Karl Liebknecht, leaders of Germany's communist movement, were murdered in Berlin. Revolts and uprisings were boiling not only in Germany, but across the whole landmass. The red flag, said the *Daily Herald*, 'is actually flying in Petrograd, in Moscow, in Budapest . . . Its shadow, brighter than the daylight, is over Berlin . . . It will fly in every city.'[1]

Even the placid Dutch rose up in Rotterdam. Switzerland was aflame with mass demonstrations, with the result that President Wilson's Peace Conference was displaced from Geneva; it went instead to Paris. John Maynard Keynes, who was there, wrote that in Continental Europe 'the earth heaves but no one is aware of the rumblings. There it is not just a matter of extravagance or 'labour troubles'; but of life and death, of starvation and existence, and of the fearful convulsions of a dying civilisation.'[2] Others shared the opinion, but embroidered it further:

We are standing on the threshold of a new age. We are entering into the period of the emancipation of labour from the thraldom of wage slavery. It is the time of which poets have dreamed, the time for which in every country men and women have striven, have gone to prison, have sacrificed their lives. Thrones are tumbling like skittles. Revolution like a cleansing gale sweeps through Europe. Say! British and American soldiers, what are you? Are you just dull clods? Are you not stirred by the throb of new life that pulses through the veins of your fellow-workers?[3]

In Britain, demobilization was so far bungled that delays triggered one mutiny after another.

The War Cabinet opened the year in fine style, on 10 January, with a meeting with three key generals, including the Commander-in-Chief of Home Forces. General Sir William Robertson was sent 'to meet the delegates of the soldiers assembled in Horse Guards' Parade, and to inform them that officers will be sent at once to Park Royal to investigate their alleged grievances.'[4] Two days later, Field-Marshal Sir Henry Wilson told the Cabinet that he could not relieve British forces in Siberia or northern Russia because of the turmoil of discontent throughout the army. Strict censorship was enjoined, but the news got around. In several army and navy depots there were sharp confrontations, even mass defections.

## A Brief Boom

Yet this upheaval did not immediately produce the predicted outbreak of unemployment. Neither did it bring the revolution which was feared or hoped for. The country enjoyed a brief boom in trade, during which a volcano of labour unrest rocked the very foundations of the state. In this great bending of the strata were shaped the last, decisive moves towards the creation of the TGWU. Unemployment, standing at an average of 2.4 per cent in 1919, remained steady through 1920. Then it rocketed upwards. Disaster passed all forecasts, as the figures rose to 14.8 per cent in 1921 and to 15.2 per cent in 1922. The TGWU was to be born in the comfortless wastes of the post-war slump. But all its activists had won their experience in the new conditions established during the war, and sharpened their skills and expectations during the brief boom in which the thought and action of both members and leaders was audacity itself. Yet their new organization was to be compelled to learn the cautious, defensive arts, and to learn them quickly. Soon it was ducking and weaving to protect the gains of recognition and status which had been won in the battles of the preceding decade.

## Union Membership

Total union membership climbed to 6.5 million in 1918, to 7.8 million in 1919 and to 8.3 million in 1920. It then fell to 6.5 million in 1921 and again to 5.6 million in 1922. In 1920, union density reached the unprecedented figure of 48.2 per cent – a concentration not to be achieved again until the 1970s.[5] It dropped, catastrophically, to only 32 per cent in 1922.

Table 18.1 gives the comparable figures for all the TUC-affiliated unions in the fields of transport and general organization, whether or not they eventually joined the TGWU amalgamation. This enables us to give

Table 18.1 *Trade Union Membership in TUC-affiliated Transport and General Unions, 1919–1924 (000s)*

| | 1919 | 1920 | 1921 | 1922 | 1923 | 1924 |
|---|---|---|---|---|---|---|
| Dock, Wharf, Riverside and General Workers' Union | 98 | 80 | 119.5 | – | – | – |
| National Sailors' and Firemen's Union | 65 | 75 | 75 | 60 | 60 | 60 |
| National Union of Dock Labourers | 40 | 50 | 65 | – | | – |
| London and Provincial Union of Licensed Vehicle Workers | 20 | – | – | – | – | – |
| Amalgamated Association of Tramway and Vehicle Workers | 38 | – | – | – | – | – |
| United Vehicle Workers' Union | – | 109 | 100 | – | – | – |
| National Union of General Workers (ex-Gas) | 384 | 444 | 490 | 300 | 235 | – |
| National Union of Ships' Stewards, etc. | 7 | 10 | 12 | – | – | – |
| Scottish Union of Dock Labourers | 6 | 9 | 9 | – | – | – |
| National Union of Vehicle Workers | 15 | 30 | 28 | – | – | – |

| | | | | | | |
|---|---|---|---|---|---|---|
| Amalgamated Society of Watermen, Lightermen and Bargemen | 6 | 6.7 | 5 | – | – | – |
| Amalgamated Stevedores' Labour Protection League | 4.2 | 6 | 5.6 | 5.6 | 5.6 | 15.7 |
| National Amalgamated Labourers' Union | 10.6 | 10.8 | 9.3 | – | – | – |
| Cardiff, etc., Coal Trimmers' Union | 1.9 | 1.8 | 1.6 | 1.6 | 1.7 | 1.8 |
| United Carters and Motormen's Association (later URTU) | 10 | 10 | 10 | – | – | – |
| Amalgamated Union of Enginemen and Cranemen | 3.6 | ? | ? | ? | ? | ? |
| National Amalgamated Union of Labour | 150 | 170 | 143 | 85.5 | – | – |
| Labour Protection League | 4 | 2.5 | ? | – | – | – |
| National Warehouse and General Workers' Union | 80 | 96 | ? | ? | ? | ? |
| Amalgamated Carters', Lurrymen's and Motormen's Union | 6 | 6 | ? | – | – | – |
| Hull Seamen's Union | 2 | 2 | 2 | 2 | – | – |
| River Weaver Watermen's Association | 0.405 | 0.350 | 0.350 | 0.350 | 0.350 | 0.350 |

Table 18.1 (*cont.*):

| | 1919 | 1920 | 1921 | 1922 | 1923 | 1924 |
|---|---|---|---|---|---|---|
| North of England Trimmers' and Teemers' Association | 1.4 | ? | 1.3 | – | – | – |
| National Amalgamated Union of Enginemen, etc. | 30 | 40 | ? | – | – | – |
| National Amalgamated Coal Porters (later 'Workers') Union | 6 | 10 | 6 | 6 | – | – |
| Workers' Union | 331 | 495 | 450 | 247 | 140 | 140 |
| Municipal Employees' Association | – | 60 | 65 | 30 | 30 | – |
| National Union of Railwaymen | 416.5 | 481 | 457.8 | 341 | 327 | 327 |
| National Federation of Women Workers | 30 | 30 | ? | ? | ? | ? |
| United Order of General Labourers | ? | 15 | 15 | 12 | ? | 2 |
| Liverpool Carters' and Motormen's Union | ? | 8 | 10 | 10 | 10 | 10 |
| North of Scotland Horse and Motormen's Union | ? | ? | 2 | – | – | – |

| | 1919 | 1920 | 1921 | 1922 | 1923 | 1924 |
|---|---|---|---|---|---|---|
| United Road Transport (later Union) Workers' Association | – | – | – | 10 | 10 | 10 |
| North Wales Quarrymen's Union | ? | ? | 7 | 7 | 8 | – |
| National Union of General and Municipal Workers | – | – | – | – | – | 255 |
| Transport and General Workers' Union | – | – | – | 300 | 300 | 300 |
| Totals | 2,706 | 3,627 | 2,099 | 1,418 | 1,138 | 1,122 |
| All TUC Membership | 5,284 | 6,506 | 6,418 | 5,129 | 4,369 | 4,328 |
| of which | | | | | | |
| (a) percentage in Transport and General Workers' Union* | – | – | – | 5.8 | 6.9 | 7 |
| (b) percentage in all transport and general unions listed here† | 51 | 56 | 33 | 28 | 26 | 26 |

*Note:* * As the slump progressed, and the TUC membership fell, the proportion organized by the TGWU rose substantially, demonstrating the anticipated benefits, in greater stability, of the new and wider association. In 1989, the proportion of TUC membership in the TGWU was approximately 14 per cent.
† The relative instability of the general unions is demonstrated by the declining proportion of TUC membership in them, as the slump progressed. This tendency would have been even more marked had we deducted the figures for the TGWU from the total of all transport and general unions, but this would not have made a valid comparison over these years possible.

*Source:* TUC Annual Reports, 1919–24.

an overall picture of not only the eventual, but also the potential, size and nature of the TGWU. At the same time, we have chosen to present the statistics over the period of the first six full post-war years, spanning the formation of the TGWU in 1922, so that the reader may have them available as the story of these few years unfolds from this point on to the amalgamation. We have also extended them beyond that, to 1924, in order to demonstrate some of its quantitative effects.[6]

Inflation, on whose upsurge the war had been financed, continued to increase: taking 1914 as 100, the cost of living index stood at 203 in 1918, and thereafter went through 215 and 249 in 1920–21. But a long deflationary trajectory, lasting into the 1930s, began in 1922, when it fell to 226. The index of wage rates followed a similar curve, up and down.

Table 18.2 *Weekly Wage Rates, 1918–1922 (1914 = 100).*

| | |
|---|---|
| 1918 | 195–200 |
| 1919 | 215–220 |
| 1920 | 270–280 |
| 1921 | 231 |
| 1922 | 191 |
| 1923 | 188 |

*Source:* H. A. Clegg, *A History of British Trade Unions since 1889*, vol. II: *1911–1933* (Oxford University Press, 1985), p. 568.

## Not the Best Time . . .

These were the very least propitious times in which to achieve the second 'social miracle' of our story. If, in 1889, the first miracle achieved organization of the unorganizable, the outcast poor, then to found what was to become the largest British trade union from a heave of disparate sectional bodies was to perform no meaner magic. The first miracle was performed during a brief boom at the end of the 1880s. The second, in the earliest 1920s, was achieved while wages, prices and membership were falling, even while prices were historically inflated. Less favourable conditions for making wine out of water would be hard to find.

It is hardly surprising, given the volatility of the economy and the revolutionary political climate of the period, that industrial unrest was so intransigent in 1919–22. The overall figures are awe-inspiring. The numbers of working days of strike action or days 'lost', in the conventional jargon, rose from 5,875,000 in 1918 to 34,969,000 in 1919. They fell back to 26,568,000 in 1920, shot up to 85,872,000 in 1921, and retrenched again to 19,850,000 in 1922. Yet, strangely, the battlegrounds of the period, in industrial disputes, including as they did the mines, railways and engineering, did not encroach on transport. There, the NTWF pursued its wartime methods of seeking and obtaining recognition, JICs and other bargaining structures, wage gains, the shorter working week, and national standards, without committing itself to a single official national stoppage. Its members were far more inclined to contemplate strike action for political purposes, particularly in 1919 and 1920, as we shall see.

## Changes in the Labour Movement

Structural and constitutional change in the trade-union and labour movements was the order of the day, affecting not only the transport and general unions, but the TUC and the Labour Party.[7] The TUC replaced its Parliamentary Committee with a new General Council, structured around 'Trade Groups'. This was intended as a 'general staff of labour', but in fact it fell well short of real executive authority. The Labour Party became a double federation of trade unions and constituency parties and adopted the socialist objective expressed in clause 4(4) of its 1918 constitution, drafted by Sidney Webb.

The Communist Party of Great Britain began to emerge from a complex grouping of shop-steward activists, trade-union leaders and rank-and-file members, together with a sprinkling of intellectuals and some feminists. From the left-wing parties it was to draw core support from the British Socialist Party, and to include part of the Socialist Labour Party and some other regional groups.

The Triple Alliance geared itself up for joint action on a number of fronts. Not the least of these involved some of its members in an initiative of great significance.

In March 1919 the *Daily Herald* was reborn. Gerald Gould (as associate editor) joined Lansbury in the editorial office. The TUC and the Labour Party were not ready to give official support to the relaunch. Perhaps they remembered the fate of the ill-starred *Citizen*;[8] certainly some were still sore from the well-aimed barbs of Lansbury and his colleagues. By no means all the opposition came from the ranks of Labour's officialdom. Distributors did not want to know about the new paper. Paper manufacturers refused to supply it. Robert Williams was compelled to threaten the Newspaper Proprietors' Association with a strike at the mills, before the ban was lifted; even then, supplies were insufficient and irregular, and often had to be secured by orders under invented names, spread around the country.

In November, a trade-union support committee for the paper was launched. Ernest Bevin initiated it, and he became the secretary. The sum of £100,000 was raised. Three new directors joined Lansbury, Williams and Meynell. Bevin was the most energetic of the new men, and he remained at his post until he became Minister of Labour in 1940. To launch his appeal for the paper, he contributed to the DWRGWU *Record* an article under the title 'The Written Word'. This roundly objected to the bias of the existing press, pouring out wealth and influence to maintain the present order of capitalism:

> with all its terrible consequences, manufacturing as it does millionaires and paupers, building palaces, preserving slums . . . dividing the world into financial and economic spheres; keeping the people in a state of suspicion and hatred of each other; maintaining its great offspring militarism, fomenting war and expending enormous energy to maintain the right to idleness and luxury for the privileged few![9]

To defeat this vast power, the 'first and most important thing is to . . . stir the minds of the people. Physical poverty will remain as long as there exists mental poverty.'

The spoken word was not enough to enable Labour to win. Only the written word could reach deep enough to 'influence the public mind'. The 'power of the press' was as essential as the strike or the vote to Labour's success. But having deployed all the arguments for a daily press as a political advocate and industrial mobilizer, Bevin went deeper:

> Thousands of our people . . . cannot conceive any other conditions under which industry could be organised and managed for the benefit of the community . . . the enjoyment of literature, poetry, understanding of scientific investigation, and all the arts which would bring greater joy into the lives of the people, are limited to the few. There is a great yearning for the Arts among the rising working classes . . . There is more latent talent in the workshops than in the Universities.[10]

In these difficult days, the *Daily Herald* did, indeed, bring some of the brightest young talents into the direct experience of the Labour movement. None the less, the continuation of the paper was a giant task, and it required a tireless commitment. Without doubt, Bevin was the dynamo. He it was who ensured that the Labour movement could generate its 'written word', creating a press upon which later generations can only look back with envy.

Far away on the map, but intimately close in the minds of the people, was continuous revolution and civil war in Russia, and a storm of insurrections and *coups* across Central and Eastern Europe. Down went the old empires. A new world struggled into shape.

## The Coupon Election

The British coalition, led by Lloyd George, had won a snap General Election in 1918 for its alliance of coalition Liberals and Conservatives.

This, the 'Coupon Election', filled the backbenches full of 'hard-faced men who looked as if they had done well out of the War,' as Baldwin said.

Throughout the Labour movement the election result was widely seen as fraudulent. Lloyd George feared that, given the violent anti-German sentiment in the country, the Conservatives could well run away with the vote, destroying the Liberal Party in the process and letting Labour gain a stronger foothold in the Commons.[11] Accordingly, he made a deal with Bonar Law, leader of the Unionists (Conservatives), which spared a selected 150 Liberal candidates from Unionist opposition at the polls. In return, those Liberals pledged support for a Coalition government. Asquith, leader of the independent Liberals, dubbed the Lloyd George–Law endorsement of Coalition candidates 'the coupon', echoing the coupons in ration books, and thereby giving the election its pejorative name. Asquith saw the agreement as an attempt to destroy the Liberals; Lloyd George later pointed out that, under it, more Liberals were elected than ever after. The two statesmen would find little to agree about after 1919, and the Liberal decline was now beginning its rapid downward glide.

The Unionists ran 410 candidates, and the Liberals of both persuasions 425. The Labour party endorsed 363, and 10 were separately fielded by the Co-operative Party. Thirty-six ran for Coalition Labour, and a number of others were independent left-wingers.[12] Less than 25 per cent of the armed forces voted, and less than 60 per cent of the whole electorate. This electorate was the first to approach suffrage for all males, and 10.8 million actually took part in the election out of 21.3 million who were eligible. For the first time, women over the age of thirty were entitled to a vote. We do not know how many used it, but we do know that, even with the restrictions on the age of entitlement to vote, women now comprised two-fifths of the total electorate.[13] Entitlement to vote was henceforth to be determined by residence, although vestiges of a property qualification still persisted in the 'business premises qualification' which conferred a double franchise on shopkeepers and other small entrepreneurs.[14]

The result was that the government Coalition benches contained 484 MPs, and Labour 59. Radical Labour candidates, who included Bevin at Bristol, and apparent pacifists such as Ramsay MacDonald, did badly and lost, whilst the patriotic wing of Labour – which included such former new unionists and NTWF stalwarts as Tillett, Sexton, Thorne, Gosling and, in a category of his own, Havelock Wilson – was returned. The 'class of '89' were now reunited almost *en bloc* in parliamentary politics, in the twilight of their careers. The exception was Tom Mann, who, emerging from the wartime cocoon in which Havelock Wilson had contained him, tired of a brief spell of chicken farming in Kent and won election as general secretary of the ASE. When he was ready to contest a parliamentary seat a few years later, it was as a contender for the Communist Party, which did not secure his election.

Henderson was not elected but came back in August 1919, in a by-election at Widnes. He did not resume his position in the leadership, however. The Parliamentary Labour Party was weak, not only in numbers. In 1920 it elected J. R. Clynes as its chairman, so the new unions were briefly represented at the head of the party they had done so much to found.

Lloyd George met the threats of unrest and his fear of revolution with an inventive combination of concession, conciliation, counterthreats and, ultimately, of duplicity and deception. This manipulative mix was particularly evident in his handling of successive crises in the mining, railway and transport industries. Initially, the new Ministry of Labour (which Churchill, at the War Office, thought an unnecessary piece of government) pursued corporate policies, promoting the formation of Joint Industrial Councils, extending Trades Boards, and sponsoring an Industrial Courts Act to provide a permanent court of voluntary arbitration. Lloyd George's response to the demands of the miners for national wage increases, a six-hour day and nationalization of the mines was to establish a Royal Commission (the Sankey Commission) on these matters as a delaying tactic. Whilst the temporary boom lasted, he avoided direct conflict and waited.

## Changes in Transport

From the end of the war until two years after the formation of the TGWU, our running series of statistics on transport are, again, helpful in trying to picture the manpower climate in the industry. Registered shipping grossed 10 million tons in 1918 and curved upwards to 11.8 million tons in 1922. Thereafter a stagnant period set in, and tonnage was down to 11.7 millions in 1924. This represented 18,355 vessels, of which 5,842 were sailing ships. These, however, accounted for a mere 522,000 tons in all.[15] It could therefore be said that one great transport revolution, from sail to steam, was completed just as the new union was launched in dockland. But it was completed during a commercial disaster, as the index of tramp-shipping freights collapsed from 751 in 1918 to 130 in 1922 and to 121 in 1924 (1869 = 100).[16]

On the railways there was similar stagnation, especially on the passenger side. Whilst in 1919 305 million tons of freight was carried by rail, in 1922 the figure was 301 million, only rising to 335.5 million in 1924. But 1,523 million passenger miles were travelled by rail in 1919, and 1,195 million in 1922; in 1924, the figure was 1,236 million. Of course, the railway directors were nervous at this moment, about to feel the full force of road-transport competition in both passenger and freight traffic.

The number of private cars on the road increased six and a half times between 1919 and 1924, from 78,000 to 474,000; and the number of motorcycles by almost equal figures. Buses, coaches and taxis together rose from 42,000 to 94,000 in these years, and road freight vehicles from 41,000 to 203,000. So the total of all kinds of motorized vehicles rose from 229,000 to 1,300,000. Trams, however, had reached their peak of 14,000 in 1921, and remained there until a decline set in during the 1930s.[17]

All this was worked out against a background of post-war boom (1918–1920), economic crisis (1921) and recession (1922). In 1923–4 a modest upswing briefly reappeared. We shall trace the fortunes of the TGWU during the later years touched on here in vol. II.

## Electoral Weakness, Industrial Strength

The year 1919 was marked by an unprecedented combination. Labour suffered from considerable electoral and parliamentary weakness, and at the same time had gathered formidable industrial strength. This juxtaposition held explosive possibilities in a time when revolutionary fervour gripped half the European continent, while at home an immense dissatisfaction was rising. Small wonder that there was widespread debate about the need for 'direct action' to achieve a wide range of objectives, including political goals.

Yet most progress was made in the achievement of more orthodox trade-union aims. Among these were the formation of new Joint Industrial Councils; the achievement of shorter hours and wage gains; the defence of wartime wage levels; and the registration or retention of basic trade-union recognition. Moving through a spectrum of demands, the transport and general unions joined with many others, notably the miners and railwaymen, in demanding nationalization with joint state–union control of the envisaged management boards. But things did not stop at this level. Leaders and rank and file alike, throughout the transport industry, shared a profound distrust of government, and particularly of the Prime Minister, Lloyd George. Whilst Bevin and the rest in the NTWF pursued their purpose of establishing JICs for particular industries, they boycotted the National Industrial Council, which Lloyd George summoned into being in February. So did their fellows in the Triple Alliance, the miners and the railwaymen, as well as the ASE. All agreed that the new body had been summoned as an exercise in window-dressing.

Some delighted in their capacity to stand outside and watch it all going on. Robert Williams exulted:

Mr. Lloyd George, who had condemned and vilified the workers' Representatives at the polls two months before, was now on his knees begging the trade unionists and the employers to settle their differences amicably through the hastily-empanelled National Industrial Conference. Who can forget the plaintive appeal made by the Premier, speaking with sobs in his voice, asking that all efforts possible should be made, and promising that all should be done to make this 'a country fit for heroes to live in'? The Triple Industrial Alliance, however, comprising between a million and a half and two million mine workers, railway workers and transport workers, would have nothing to do with this body.[18]

## Rejecting the NIC

When the Council met, however, there were 800 delegates representing 'moderate' trade unions, employers and Joint Industrial Councils. Arthur Henderson was made chairman for the trade-union side. Lloyd George was all sweetness and light: 'You will get this land into such conditions of happiness and contentment as it has never seen', he told the assembly.[19] Happiness and Contentment were not so easily obtained, in the opinion of the National Transport Workers' Federation. Harry Gosling's presidential address that year was forthright. Whilst asserting support for single-industry JICs, he declared that 'any effort like the Government's Industrial Council – which in the judgement of your Executive was only a temporary expedient to check-mate the workers' demands then fructifying – we shall not associate ourselves with.'[20] The AGC, on the day following his address, confirmed this position, carrying a resolution from the LPU which affirmed 'that no useful purpose could be served by such an assembly unless and until the workers are assured of more democratic control of industry, with the object ultimately of eliminating rent, interest, and profit.'[21]

This verdict on the usefulness of the project proved accurate, for the NIC was unable to agree on the content of its proposed Forty-eight-hours Act, or on its Minimum Wages Act. Neither was it able to determine a permanent constitution for itself. When the government's domination over labour was restored by the slump, it abandoned the National Industrial Council, and its shadowy existence was terminated in 1921.[22]

In this matter, as in all others during 'the most remarkable year in the history of our Federation',[23] the transport unions stood firmly with the majority, left wing, of the trade-union movement. The police strikes of 1918 and 1919, together with serious disaffection in army camps, the restless militancy of the mass of trade-union members (to which their leaders made constant reference in NTWF Executive Minutes, and in speeches to the Annual General Council), put in question the ability of the state to manage industrial affairs by legitimate means.

## Opposing Bolshevism

The government was particularly alarmed about trade-union growth and success. It needed, above all, to divide if it was to rule. The historian of corporatism, Keith Middlemas, has probed the government's methods. He reports on the frantic search for an antidote to public resentment against profiteering. Both Tory ministers and the FBI joined in this quest, and in the effort to pressurize newspaper editors to present capitalists in a favourable light. At the time of the rail strikes of 1919, Lloyd George set up a secret organization, 'concerned with anti-Bolshevism and Increased Production propaganda'. Amongst other establishment figures, the Coalition's Chief Whips were participants in this work, which was designed to generate antipathy of trade unions and the left. 'Sidney Walton, a former undercover agent and government fugleman, was appointed to run it, with a fund of £100,000 subscribed, not from government funds, but industrial sources, chiefly members of the Engineering Employers' Federation, headed by Sir William Caillard.'[24]

Walton followed the models of wartime organizations such as the British Empire League, the British Workers' League, the National Democratic and Labour Party, and the National Unity Movement. These had all been financed by industrialists, but now Walton was able to draw on the utterly secret sources of the Special Branch and Secret Intelligence Service. His grapevine grew and grew, to embrace journalists and MPs, 'until Walton claimed to be able to put "authoritative signed articles" in over 1,200 newspapers. The effect was prodigious, and even allowing for exaggeration, its returns can hardly be ignored.'[25]

Stoking up the mood of panic and apprehension came a long series of reports 'on Revolutionary Organisations in the United Kingdom', from Sir Basil Thomson, former head of MI5, which added colour to the fantasies. For spies are for ever prone to feed the paranoia of their paymasters.

This does not mean that the fears were absolutely baseless. In June the *New Statesman* put its finger on the really new element which troubled authority: 'The greatest barrier to labour unrest before the war was the widespread conviction that capitalism was inevitable – that it had been in possession ever since the workers could remember, and that there were no signs that it was likely to come to an end. Today the world, and the workers perhaps most of all, have lost the feeling of certainty about anything'.[26]

## II

## *The Drive to Establish Joint Industrial Councils*

So the government, fighting for time, passed its Wages (Temporary Regulations) Act to restrain employers who might provoke unrest by premature attacks on wartime wage gains.

This Act, passed just ten days after the signing of the Armistice, ended the ban on strikes and lock-outs, and forbade wage cuts, as well as replacing the Committee on Production by an Interim Court of Arbitration.[27] The government deployed its swollen army of civil servants at the new Ministry of Labour, which handled 1,370 industrial relations cases in 1919.[28] The Ministry, either on its own initiative or in response to Federation requests, was hyperactive, too, in promoting and facilitating the formation of legions of Joint Industrial Councils. These were intended, in the Ministry's scheme of things, to give workers a semblance of 'control' within the restrictive ministerial view of that concept. In fact, however, they conferred a heightened degree of recognition on the unions. But the Federation, spurred by the supreme initiative of the DWRGWU, behind which lay the immense personal commitment, drive and energy of Ernest Bevin, pursued the creation of JICs with conviction and success. It distinguished very clearly and consciously between false images of power offered by the amorphous National Industrial Council and the real, practical gains to be made from recognition, and a permanent machine for national-level collective bargaining, represented by industry JICs.

Thus, we find the Federation Executive dealing with JIC matters at eight of the twelve meetings it held in this crowded year. On 8 January it discussed the Ministry's proposal that, in response to the Federation's request for a JIC for the whole transport industry, there should be established instead Sectional Councils for the various branches of transport. The Executive concurred, but added that joint meetings of such sections could be arranged. The Port of London Staff Association wanted its own JIC, but was advised that this would be too narrow a base for such a body.[29]

## *Road-passenger Transport*

In road-passenger transport, historically determined divisions in the bargaining structures of the industry cast their evident shadows on the developments of 1919. On the trade-union side, divisions had been all too common between provincial and London-based unions. (We deal with these in chapter 19.) The divisions were effectively overcome, for bargaining purposes, in the Federation, to which all unions were affiliated. They naturally sought a single, comprehensive agreement for passenger workers in whatever branch of the industry they worked.

The employers, on the other hand, had divisions but no encompassing organization within which to subsume them. The Federation, accordingly, had to submit its claim for a national wage advance in 1919 to three bodies simultaneously: the London companies, the Tramways and Light Railways' Association, and the Municipal Tramways' Association.[30] The London bus companies were willing to negotiate jointly, but the tramway associations would not agree. Separate bargains resulted, and the earliest joint negotiating machinery for the industry was the National Joint Industrial Council (NJIC) formed in 1919, exclusively for the tramway industry, covering both local-authority and private operators of tram and trolleybus services.

Bus services eventually split three ways, into London, provincial private and provincial municipal bargaining units, and did not come under comprehensive JICs until 1937 (municipal services) and 1940 (provincial companies); this will concern us in vol. II.

A further anomaly in the industry, undoubtedly in this case trade-union determined, separated municipal busmen from all other municipal workers, who evolved what would otherwise have been comprehensive Whitley Council machinery. This was to cover, in Sectional Councils, all grades, occupations and services. On the manual side, these Councils have been dominated not by the TGWU, which is the main union only in the passenger-transport JICS, but by the NUGMW. This case illustrates the general proposition that there are many ways of defining an industry for bargaining purposes, and that actual structures have been determined by institutional divisions on both trade-union and employers' sides, rather than by economic needs or central bureaucratic logic. On the whole, however, in those formative years the trade-union influence, exercised first through the NTWF and then by the TGWU, was exerted to achieve the most comprehensive possible unity, rather than a multiplication of Sectional Councils.[31]

## Road Haulage

The carters and motormen, or, to give them now their modern title, the commercial road-haulage workers, encountered even greater difficulties in the operation of the NJIC for their industry. Such a Council came into existence on 11 March 1919. The union side came exclusively from the NTWF, which nominated nine members from its affiliates. They were the Amalgamated Tramway and Vehicle Workers (AAT), the London and Provincial Union (LPU), the National Union of Vehicle Workers (NUVW), the National Union of General Workers (NUGW), Tillett's

Dockers' Union, the United Carters' Association, the Amalgamated Carters' Union, the North of Scotland Carters' Union and the Liverpool Carters' Union. But the employers were represented by three bodies: the National Alliance of Commercial Road Transport Associations and Federations, the National Union of Horse and Motor Vehicle Owners' Associations, and the Motor Transport Employers' Associations. The vice-chairman of the new Council was Ernest Bevin.[32]

Almost immediately following its formation, the employers' organizations began to make sustained objections to the implementation of its decisions. They refused to refer matters in dispute to arbitration or to abide by its findings.[33] In July, outstanding Federation claims were addressed to the employers' associations because of the continued failure of their local constituents to respect the authority of the JIC.

On 11 August Robert Williams reported that:

> arising from a Conference of the Vehicle Workers' Unions in the Lancashire area, relative to the failure of the employers in that area to carry out the Awards of the Court of Arbitration and to apply the recommendations of the Joint Industrial Council, communications had been addressed to such employers asking for a reply within fourteen days as to whether the Awards and recommendations would be honoured.[34]

On 18 December the Executive learned that the employees' side had been convened in order to discuss 'the employers' desire to exclude questions of wages and working conditions from the purview of the Council.'

These difficulties, in an industry marked by fragmented, small-scale ownership, were followed by the breakdown of the JIC in 1920. Voluntary collective bargaining withered, finally to be replaced by a statutory Wages Board in 1938. These developments will concern us in vol. II.[35]

## Manufacturing JICs

Both in the passenger and haulage sections of inland transport, industrial relations were dominated by the Federation's efforts to impose a uniform and effective JIC machinery upon reluctant and divided bodies of employers. These union pressures were supported by the Ministry of Labour. (We deal with the formation of the ports JIC, which was postponed until 1920, in chapter 19.) But we should notice how much greater success the Federation, and its counterpart National Federation of General Workers, had in the field of manufacturing industry.

Here the pace was set by both Will Thorne's NUGW and the industrial sections of the DWRGWU. Bevin's influence was again

1 The Dockers' Call-on, Liverpool. A South End dockers' stand, 7 a.m. The foreman putter on chooses men for work. Those selected are on the right of the picture. The men around the lamp post are NUDL members who have preference of employment over the non-union men who are standing on the left.

2 Glendower Gosling and Hotspur Punch! (see text, p.436) *Reproduced by permission of Punch*

PUNCH, OR THE LONDON CHARIVARI.—June 19, 1912.

NO ANSWER.

Glendower Gosling. "I CAN CALL SPIRITS FROM THE VASTY DEEP."
Hotspur Punch. "WHY, SO CAN I, OR SO CAN ANY MAN:
BUT WILL THEY COME WHEN YOU DO CALL FOR THEM?"
(*Henry IV., Part I., Act III., Scene I.*)

3 James Larkin. *Reproduced by kind permission of Emmet Larkin*

4 James Connolly. Frontispiece photograph in *The Life and Times of James Connolly, 1960* by Desmond Greaves. *Reproduced by permission of the publishers, Lawrence and Wishart.*

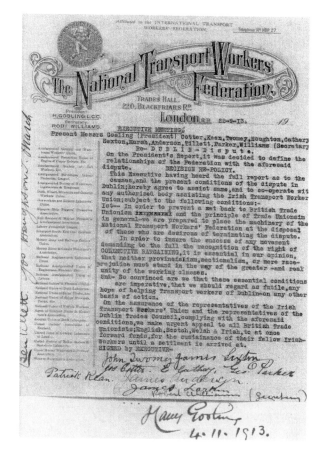

5 An appeal for Dublin, from the Federation. *Reproduction of a letter of the National Transport Workers' Federation, 1913, signed by the leaders.*

6 Front row, left to right: James Sexton, Ben Tillett, Ernest Bevin and Joseph Houghton, at the Shaw Inquiry, 1920. *Reproduced by permission of The Hulton Picture Company.*

7 Soldiers camped out in Kensington Gardens in preparation for the 1921 Coal Strike. *The Hulton Picture Company*

8 'One Big Union': handbill advertising an amalgamation meeting, 1921. *TGWU*

Sam March

Alfred Short

Jack Twomey

Peter Gillespie

John Parr

R.T. Jones

**9** Some of the founders of the amalgamation. Cameo portraits of Sam March, MP, (NUVW), Alfred Short, MP, (NUDWSS), Jack Twomey, (NALU), Peter Gillespie, (NSMA), John Parr, (ASCLM), R.T. Jones, (NWQU). Transport House Official Opening Booklet, 1928. *TGWU*

**10** International Transport Leaders: Robert Williams, Harry Gosling and Hermann Jochade.

**11** A regional leader: George Milligan. Dock porter 1890-1911; Secretary No.12 Branch, NUDL, from 1909; Mersey District Secretary, NUDL, from 1912; Deputy General Secretary, NUDL, 1919-22; First Area Secretary, TGWU Merseyside, 1922-5.

Stanley Hirst

John Cliff

Ernest Bevin

**12** The First Executive Officers: Stanley Hirst, Financial Secretary; John Cliff, Assistant General Secretary; Ernest Bevin, General Secretary. Offical Opening of Transport House booklet. *TGWU*

**13** The Amalgamation Conference, Leamington, 1921.

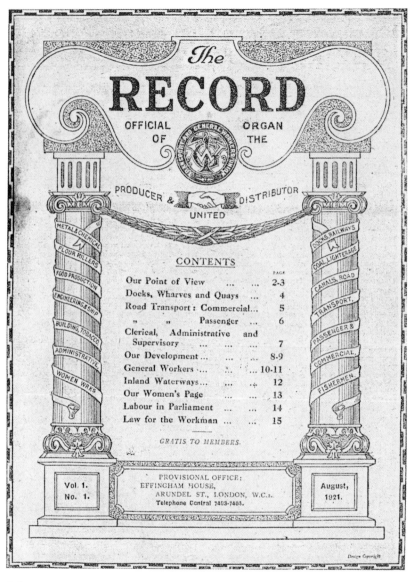

# The RECORD

### OFFICIAL ORGAN OF THE

PRODUCER & DISTRIBUTOR
UNITED

METALS & CHEMICAL · FLOUR MILLERS · FOOD PRODUCTION · ENGINEERING & SHIP · BUILDING, TOBACCO · ADMINISTRATIVE · WOMEN WRKS

DOCKS, RAILWAYS · COAL, LIGHTERAGE · CANALS, ROAD · TRANSPORT · PASSENGER & · COMMERCIAL, · FISHERMEN.

## CONTENTS

*GRATIS TO MEMBERS.*

PROVISIONAL OFFICE:
EFFINGHAM HOUSE,
ARUNDEL ST., LONDON, W.C.2.
Telephone Central 7403-7403.

Vol. 1.
No. 1.

August,
1921.

*Design Copyright*

**14** A New Record begins: Cover page of the first issue of the TGWU *Record*, August 1921.

prodigious. He was involved in his capacities first as the Dockers' National organizer up to 1920, and thereafter as DWRGWU Assistant General secretary. We have seen that this great initiative had already commenced in 1917–18. Amongst JICs established after the war, the most significant were those for chemicals, confectionery and flour-milling. Industries like rubber, heavy chemicals, and paint, varnish and lacquer had achieved JIC status in 1918. Soap, candles and edible fats followed with a JIC the year after. The NJIC for the flour-milling industry was established in 1919 and, although, as we have said, it received Bevin's special personal attention, at first he had to share the workers' side with thirteen representatives of other unions, some of which eventually joined together to become, respectively, the NUGMW and USDAW. On the employers' side, no divisions developed, and a single association represented them.

At the beginning of 1920, Bevin was sitting on fourteen JICs, being chairman of two and vice-chairman of three.[36] He himself regarded the flour-milling JIC as a model. Indeed, it was to become a textbook case, a prototype to which reference would regularly be made in order to explain the working of JICs. It carried the stamp of Bevin's personal involvement and support. Therein he advanced schemes for technical education, a pension fund, compensation for redundancy, and workplace health and safety. When the National Union of Millers merged with the DWRGWU in 1920, and after the greater amalgamation two years later, his organization held a clear majority of the seats on the workers' side of the Council.[37] Joint consultation, in such a setting and with such leadership, was at times a good deal more than a cosmetic exercise.

Remarkably, all this work of peaceful construction, of what was to become a bedrock foundation for industrial-relations practice over the next sixty years, was conducted by unions and union leaders who were simultaneously in a running conflict – indeed, an open war – with the state. On profound international, military and civil-rights issues, the unions faced the government eyeball to eyeball. We must look at this confrontation; but first we need to examine the uses to which the unions put the new machinery in their pursuit of the more limited objects of standard, reduced national hours and common, enhanced wages.

## Shorter Working Time

The opening moment of the 1919 campaign for shorter hours, in industry generally, was anything but tranquil. General strikes on the Clyde and in Belfast engulfed their regions in January. During the war the Clydesiders had set up a Workers' Committee, recruited from engineering shop stewards. Now they called for a complete stoppage to enforce a forty-hour week, when 'faced with the problem of absorbing demobilised soldiers into the Glasgow workforce.'[38] There were mass demonstrations, followed by street violence. An army of policemen and soldiers was emplaced, while tanks rolled into the city centre. The government was the more nervous because it could not be sure that the army would do as it was told. The strike leaders, Willie Gallacher, David Kirkwood and Emanuel Shinwell, who was the chairman of the Glasgow Trades council, were arrested.

Jim Gardner, who became secretary of the Foundry Workers' Union in later years, was present in Glasgow:

I was there on what was called 'Bloody Friday'. The police attacked the marchers who were massed outside the Municipal Buildings. I was standing several yards away from Gallacher and saw him running forward to try to stop them hitting David Kirkwood. Both of them were batoned. I saw Gallacher go down. Jock McBain, from my union, got a beating as well and Kirkwood must have taken it badly. I went into the Municipal Buildings and saw Kirkwood lying flat out and groaning. Gallacher was sitting up with bandages round his head, smoking his pipe.'[39]

Another eye-witness allows us to follow the story:

I marched with the Clydebank contingent eight miles to George Square on 'Bloody Friday'. We walked on the tram lines and never let a tram-car pass us. When we reached George Square, the baton charge had taken place, and we marched through the Square on to Glasgow Green. The tram-cars were halted in the centre of the city, because the marchers pulled down the arms that linked the trams to the electric cable and bent them. There was a lorry which had been carrying lemonade bottles lying across the road and people grabbing bottles and stones to throw at the police. The police would charge, the crowd would scatter, then reform and the police would charge again. I was 17 at the time, an apprentice, and vividly remember the whole business, above all the fact that we hadn't eaten since the morning and were starving.'[40]

The objective of the forty-hour week had been originally agreed by the Federation of Engineering and Shipbuilding Trades. The Clyde Workers' Committee, dominated by the stewards from the same industries, dropped their own demand for thirty hours in order to throw their weight behind the official target.[41] This was also endorsed, though not without dissenting voices, by the Parliamentary Committee of the Scottish TUC. However, the Glasgow dockers were also fully involved, as were the members of the Scottish Horse and Motormen's Association, whose secretary, Hugh Lyon, was a member of the Strike Committee and chairman of the Scottish TUC.[42] The Lanarkshire miners stopped work unofficially in sympathy. This was the beginning of a radical upsurge in their coalfield, which was to have long-term effects.

Lyon used the occasion to make separate forty-eight-hour agreements with the Scottish Co-operative Wages Board, and with Glasgow Corporation, the railway companies and local contractors, following which his members returned to work, and he offered to resign from the Strike Committee.

The conflagration spread to Belfast on 25 January, when twenty-six unions joined together on a Strike Committee, including municipal transport workers. As on the Clyde, the majority of the strikers were from shipbuilding and engineering. The Chief Secretary for Ireland warned that 'The Workmen had formed a "Soviet" Committee, and this committee had received forty-seven applications from small traders for permission to use light.'[43]

A London engineering Strike Committee attempted to broaden the movement into a countrywide general strike, but the Executive of the ASE suspended the District Committees in all three cities, and the strikes were then called off. Belfast was the last to return to work, on 19 February. The engineering industry officially concluded a forty-seven-hour agreement. This set its stamp on a new tradition: that of the supremacy of national over local or district negotiations. It was a pattern which the NTWF was keen to imitate, yet its Executive and leaders won reductions in hours without mass strike action, and without much resistance from employers' associations, except in road haulage. The Federation joined strategic and tactical discussions on this programme with their partners in the Triple Alliance, and reported back at each stage of negotiations. One of the demands of the Miners' Federation before the Sankey Commission was for the reduction of the working day from eight to six hours. The railwaymen won their eight-hour day within one month of the Armistice, following a government wartime pledge.[44]

## Shorter Hours in Transport

The NTWF Executive showed what it was made of in February, when it rebuked its Newport district for concluding a purely local agreement for a forty-eight-hour week for the tramway workers. Robert Williams was told to circulate all affiliated unions, instructing them not to conclude such local agreements, on 'matters upon which National negotiations were being conducted or unless provision was made that such settlement was without prejudice to the claim made nationally'.[45]

The same meeting heard extensive news of those national claims. Williams reported a forty-eight-hour settlement in commercial road haulage;[46] the Trimmers and Bunkering Unions' Conference's joint application with NUR trimmers for a forty-four-hour week; the tramwaymen's application for forty-four hours; and similar demands on behalf of canal workers, and, of course, the dockers. The Executive decided there and then to summon a Special General Council on 10 March to deal with all these claims, emphasizing the importance of ensuring the attendance of the NTWF district secretaries.

When this Council convened in Central Hall, Westminster, Gosling had first to announce that the Seamen's Union, and Cotter's Ships' Stewards' and Cooks' Union were absent, attending 'a conference in Paris'. This was symptomatic of the growing autonomy of the seamen's wing of the Federation in trade matters and the beginning of what was subsequently to become a permanent parting of the ways.

The Executive's Report of proceedings contains forty-two pages of reports on progress towards shorter hours, wage increases and the establishment of negotiating machinery in various sectors. These include canals, docks, commercial and passenger road transport, coal-trimming and bunkering, in which last group the Federation joined forces with the NUR. Closely detailed, it represents the highest point of practical achievement reached by the NTWF in its short life. This Report reflected the maximum degree of centralized decision-making which was realizable within the federal form of organization.

In presenting the draft agreement for the dockers, for example, Harry Gosling drew attention to a clause asserting that the NTWF would 'undertake to provide for the strict observance by the workmen of the agreement arrived at', and confirmed: 'Well, that is an obligation that we are prepared to undertake'.[47] But one anonymous delegate is recorded as commenting on this undertaking, in an aside, 'Pious, purely pious!' The delegates worked their way more or less patiently through the tedious details of adapting starting and finishing times to the new hours and, in the case of the road-passenger workers, the technically complicated but essential adjustments to 'spread-over' duties. Ken Fuller, the historian of the London busmen has accepted that this '1919 agreement was a milestone – one to which London busmen would look back fondly during the employers' offensive which, commencing in 1921, continued into the 1930s . . . It was also the last agreement negotiated by the LPU, and thus would become associated in the minds of the rank-and-file militants with the "red button" image.'[48]

But we should not ignore the essential role in all this of the Federation, nor of its officers, Williams and Bevin. Fuller also believes that this was the agreement which strengthened the busmen's view of themselves as an 'aristocracy': 'from 1919 onwards, London busworkers were paid more, and worked shorter hours, than most groups of semi-skilled workers. They had arrived.'[49]

## Triple Alliance: When to Agree?

A critical moment in the Council meeting came with a question from J. R. Clynes, who wanted to know whether, when terms satisfactory to the NTWF had been achieved in any or all of its sections, 'we are not to settle until we have received the sanction or approval of the other two parties in the Triple Alliance?'[50] Robert Williams gave a somewhat convoluted answer. Certainly, the Alliance Executives had agreed very recently that

> no section of the Triple Alliance shall agree to any action or settlement until this Conference is again called, such Conference to be held before March 15th . . . We felt . . . that mass negotiation, apart entirely from mass action, is better than partial or sectional negotiation, and we felt that a ponderable, very intangible, weight was always behind us in our association with the Triple Alliance . . .

Williams argued, consequently, that the NTWF had an obligation to go to the Alliance for its 'formal endorsement or ratification' of settlements, even those which the transport workers themselves deemed satisfactory. This step he saw as simply reflecting the procedures applying between the carters, the dockers and the rest, inside the Federation itself.

Clynes accepted the value of the 'moral pressure' which the Alliance had exerted on employers, but remained uneasy about the extent of its executive power: 'Have we, as a Transport Federation, handed over our executive function and our right to settle industrial questions . . . to some other body – namely the Triple Alliance Executive? That is a plain question to which I would like a plain answer.' He might not have been mollified when Williams responded: 'we are not handing over our power to any of the other organisations, but we are deriving as much strength as the Alliance will give us, and then we must at a later stage report the stages of our negotiations. I am always convinced of this, that what will be satisfactory to us will be satisfactory to them.'

With hindsight, it is easy to see that the problematic case would not be that in which the negotiating party was 'satisfied', because such a case would entail no supporting action by the Triple Alliance. The problem of autonomy versus dependence, which was to destroy the Alliance two years later, would arise when one party, in its own sectional negotiations, reached impasse on terms which remained 'unsatisfactory' to it. Were the other parties then uncritically committed to its support in those circumstances? Crucially, would such support involve sympathetic strike action? Ernest Bevin gave a less equivocal interpretation of the high degree of commitment involved in the Alliance's constitution, and also approached this critical question directly, with a caveat:

> So far as I understand the position it is this: that if the miners get what they want, and the railwaymen get what they want, and we do not, then, according to the constitution, those two bodies refuse to ratify their decision and support us . . . there is no interference with the negotiations; no

interference in what we say is satisfactory to ourselves. The railwaymen cannot say your settlement as a transport worker is not right; they cannot even criticise it; we determine that . . . *The only point is that if the power was being exploited to an extent which either of the other parties thought unreasonable, then only to that extent, where a dispute was involved, would there be any consideration of the merits of the claim* [italics added].[51]

Clynes was grateful for this statement, which, he recognized, gave powerful executive functions to the Triple Alliance Executive:

I confess that I have never seen . . . in minutes or any recorded statement, declarations to the effect that this Triple Alliance had those executive functions and powers to which brother Bevin has referred . . . If [they] do exist in the hands of the Triple Alliance, what I said with regard to an instrument of mere moral pressure ought to be eliminated from any record of this meeting, as I would not like such a remarkable statement [he means Bevin's] to get into the hands of the employers, who might think that we have less powers. [Here he means his statement on moral power.] As now explained by Mr. Bevin, we have those powers.[52]

## *The Shorter Working Week: Some Gains*

In 1919 'those powers', however defined and interpreted, were not put to the test. The shorter working week, whether of 48, 47, 46 or 44 hours (as in the dockers' case) went through for miners, railwaymen and every section of transport workers without employer resistance. There was therefore no need to strike, singly or jointly.[53] The working week had been reduced, for different occupations, by anything from six to sixteen hours; it was a remarkable and, for the most part, an enduring advance. Similar gains were made by the National Federation of General Workers. Here we should remind ourselves of the overlapping personnel in the leadership of the two federations, for Bevin was also prominent in this other team, which secured reduced hours from twenty-six employers' federations.[54] In all, some 6.5 million workers gained enhanced leisure in the settlements of 1919.[55] The government did not feel able to obstruct this process, and indeed promoted a Bill for a legal forty-eight-hour week. The NTWF Executive gave its support to a motion from the NSFU that seafaring workers should not be excluded from this measure.[56]

## *Wage Improvements*

Concerning wages, the Federation provided the basis for the joint strategy to be adopted by the Triple Alliance. The Executive tabled a motion for their AGC as follows:

That this Annual General Council Meeting pledges itself to use every means in its power to maintain the monetary advances in wages gain by its affiliated unions during the war. In the event of any material reduction in the cost of living, the existing money wages shall be maintained to provide for improvement in the status of the working class. It furthermore instructs the Executive Council to take immediate steps together with the other two constituent organisations of the Triple Alliance, to declare in favour of the complete conversion of all increases obtained during the War into actual wage rates.[57]

This was the baseline of policy; in practice many positive wage claims were made in this self-confident year, notably of course the claim for a 16s. national rate of time-wages for the docks industry, and a corresponding (20 per cent) improvement in piece-rates which was to be 'tried' in public the following year at the Shaw Inquiry. And the movement for reduced hours was invariably accompanied by successful demands that these be awarded without loss of pay. The trimmers' programme followed that of the dockers – a demand for a 20 per cent rise in piece-rates. In June, unusually in this year, the salt workers reported to the Executive that they faced a cut in wages: 'the Secretary was instructed to write to Messrs Brunner Mond and Company on the subject'.[58] We do not know what the outcome was in this case.

Cotter of the ships' stewards, true to the policy of independent action, informed the Executive that, in winning an improvement in overtime pay, 'the matter had been settled and that it would not be necessary for his members to call for the assistance of the Federation'.[59]

In July the Executive was told of Williams's initiative in summoning yet another conference of tramway and omnibus workers' unions to prepare an application for another increase in wages. The whole process resembled a rerun of the events of 1918 when national 'movements' were first successfully carried through.

Reading these minutes, and the Annual Report, we sense a swing, a rhythm, about the Federation's work. A sectional conference of unions is called, a claim is formulated, presented, negotiated, settled, reported back, a JIC is set up, the result is ticked off in a Minute: the attention moves on to another section. Robert Williams initiated and organized, Ernest Bevin led the negotiations, first here, then there, and, in the final outcome, almost everywhere.

Alan Bullock cites Bevin's own evidence on his workload at this time. It was given in a report to the Dockers' Conference in July 1919: 'Many of the workpeople have now secured a 44- or 48-hour working week with enhanced rates of pay. In my own case I estimate my hours of labour average about eighty per week of six days and, in addition to this, I devoted, last year alone, thirty-eight Sundays to work away from home, for which I was paid nothing.'[60] It is not altogether surprising that Bevin's doctor warned his union's Executive that his health was seriously threatened by his pace of work that year.[61]

An interesting case is that of the joint application by the Federation and the Irish Transport and General Workers' Union for a pay increase for the dockers of all Ireland.[62] On receipt of information that the Irish District of the NUDL had submitted its own claim, Williams took the step of inviting Jimmy Sexton to co-ordinate it with that of the ITGWU.

By the end of the year, the Federation was preparing its case, and deploying its forces, for the major public trial of bargaining skills and advocacy which was to take place before the Shaw Inquiry. This was due to sit early in 1920. It was the NTWF, of course, which had presented the claim, to no fewer than 200 employers and employers' associations. The unions stipulated that the claim incorporated an 8 a.m. – 5 p.m. standard working day, with a one-hour break for a meal, 8 a.m. – 12 noon working on Saturdays, and a wage level of 16s. per day. The forty-four hour week was conceded by the employers in March 1919. The wage claim, submitted in October, included a demand for time-and-a-half overtime during the week, and double-time at weekends.

This comprehensive package compelled the employers to overcome their own divisions and to form, in November, the National Council of Employers of Dock and Riverside Labour. In December talks on the pay claim broke down, and the employers proposed that it be submitted to a Court of Inquiry, such as the government had recently given itself the power to appoint under the Industrial Courts Act, 1919. The case was to be the first heard under that legislation. The NTWF accepted the proposal. Harry Gosling, Ben Tillett and Robert Williams were nominated to sit representing the trade-union interest as members of the court, whilst Ernest Bevin and Jimmy Sexton were to prepare and submit the claim. This was the NTWF's first team, indeed, deployed in its most effective formation.

The Mersey District Report to the Federation's Annual General Council contained, as it always did (in a tradition started by Tom Mann and continued by the new secretary, C. McVey), a detailed list of gains achieved during the previous twelve months. Mann's reports had always been more detailed than those from other district secretaries; they reflected his commitment to the development of a strong sense of mutual interest in the unity of the Federation. This could not be done better than by demonstrating its effectiveness in achieving results section by section.

In 1918–19 the Mersey made gains for all its sections. The seamen won a monthly base pay of £11, plus £3 war bonus, an unprecedented fixed working day and overtime conditions, both at sea and in port. The coastal trade was on £4 7s. 6d. a week. The ships' stewards won a £3 a month war-risk bonus, and 10s. a week for men on weekly articles. During the last months of the war, the well-run and tightly organized

Liverpool and District Carters' and Motormen's Union won advances of 9s. and 5s. a week, and 4s. 6d. for youths.[63] Satisfaction was expressed, too, at the national award of the forty-eight-hour week. Two-horse men in 1919 earned basic pay of £3 7s. per week, while drivers of motors over two tons were on £3 12s.

The Mersey branches of the NAUL won a 5s. a week increase, but the tramway vehicle workers were content to record gains achieved nationally by the Federation. The enginemen dealt with anomalous overtime and shift-pay premiums, improving and standardizing them. The National Warehouse and General Workers' Union had obtained, through national processes as well as by their own efforts in Liverpool, the forty-four hour week, basic pay of £3 6s. and increased overtime rates: 'It is safe to say that this Society has benefited as much as, if not more than, any other Society in the Federation.'[64]

The canal porters had won a forty-seven-hour week, and a 'big increase' in overtime rates, 'and it goes without saying that what has been accomplished by the Transport Workers' Federation has acted as a great lever in securing better hours and conditions for our Members engaged in sections of industry other than Transport.'[65] And C. McVey, honorary district secretary, dated his signature in May: there were still months of advance to come before the slump ended the festival.

## Equal Pay?

The year saw a significant postscript to the 1918 London bus strike, which, it will be recalled, was led by women conductors demanding that the Committee on Production reverse its finding that their case for equal pay had not been established. The Federation pressed successfully for a Committee of Inquiry into women's wages. This the Cabinet duly set up. It reported six months after the Armistice, by which time the women were in an advanced state of 'demobilization'. Once again the buses were being restored to the men who had driven and conducted them before the war. The Federation reported, in June 1919, that:

> Neither the Majority Report nor the Minority Report (signed by Mrs. Sidney Webb) admits to the full the principle of equal payment to both sexes for equal work, although there is general agreement upon the principle in the form as it would affect the members of the Federation. It is not anticipated that women will be retained in the industry, and the issue must now be fought out by the women's organisations.[66]

Thus, whilst endorsing the cause of equal pay, the NTWF Report appears to resign, or hand over responsibility for the struggle for it, to 'women's organisations'. The time in which this might have been embarked upon was quickly running out.

## The NUR Goes It Alone

Before the year was through, however, there was one very important strike over wages. This involved not the NTWF, but the NUR.

The government was heavily involved in the railways. It still retained its wartime powers of management over the industry, so that the union was therefore essentially negotiating with the state. But that state had already built and indeed exercised in Glasgow and Belfast, an extensive strike-breaking machinery of special constables, troops and civilian 'volunteers'. And throughout this whole period its Ministry of Labour was offering mediation, whilst from another eyrie the Prime Minister and Cabinet watched the battlefield for mistakes by the adversary, and waited for a decisive foray by the Triple Alliance.

In the second quarter of 1919 Lloyd George was not ready for a showdown. He accordingly bought off the threat from 'the weakest link' in the Alliance, the railwaymen.[67]

> J. H. Thomas, like many trade union leaders of the time, was shocked by the grass roots militancy of 1919; Beatrice Webb noting in her diary in January that he was 'considerably alarmed at the insubordination and always increasing claims of the railwaymen'. So, in March 1919, when the threat to the Government of a Triple Alliance strike was greatest, the War Cabinet determined to make as generous concessions to the railwaymen as possible in view of the intransigence of the miners.[68]

Reflecting upon the conduct of the railwaymen's leader, Lloyd George was to say in Cabinet a couple of years later: 'I have complete confidence in Mr. Thomas's selfishness.'[69]

The miners were given the Sankey Commission, and the railwaymen money and a shorter week.

By the autumn, the government felt stronger, and proposed a new wage settlement which amounted to a completely unexpected wage cut, deploying all its strike-breaking and public opinion-forming machinery to undermine the strike that followed. Lloyd George's strategy of divide and rule included a prior deal with the train-drivers' union ASLEF. However, when the NUR called its national strike on 26 September, ASLEF loyally joined in. There had been no reference of the dispute to the Triple Alliance, because, Thomas claimed afterwards, there had been 'no time'. But rank-and-file busmen and dockers, in London and throughout the districts, were vociferous in their demands that the NTWF call them out in sympathy action. On 29 September, three days into the strike, the Federation's Executive met, in difficult circumstances – they could not raise a quorum, since members outside London were stranded by the strike. If the bodies were absent, the spirit was not. Overwhelming intelligence testified to it. The affiliated unions were experiencing 'great difficulty in restraining the men from joining in the struggle immediately'. The Executive hastily issued a call for restraint, and sought out the Executives of the NUR and ASLEF. At that meeting, Thomas explained that the NUR sought no assistance from the NTWF or the Miners' Federation.

The NTWF itself, however, without consulting the miners, took the initiative in calling an emergency conference of all 'representative trade union organisations', and declared:

> the position is rapidly becoming untenable in consequence of the attempted diversion of goods and passenger traffic . . . no efforts of the Federation can definitely restrain the members from taking drastic strike action in support of the NUR . . . the motives of the rank and file are warranted and justifiable, and we will stop at nothing in order to defend the long-established principles of Trade Unionism, and the right to defend wages constitutionally secured.[70]

## Bevin Mediates

The call to the special trade-union meeting went out over the names of Gosling, Sexton, Bevin and Williams. It is not hard to see the hand of Williams in the fiery statement, and that of Bevin in the idea of a conference.

The Federation Executive reconvened its meetings on 6 October. Even then, 'Mr. Houghton was unable to reach London [from Glasgow] owing to the railway dispute.'[71] By then, the *ad hoc* conference of unions had met in Caxton Hall, and appointed a Mediation Committee, on which the initiative was all Bevin's. Negotiations with Downing Street agreed a settlement of the strike, avoiding either its extension or a wage cut. By 6 October, as the strike was being wound up, the Executive found itself writing to the unions which had participated in the mediation, and, on a motion by Ned Cathery of the NSFU, thanking the president, secretary and Mr Bevin for their services on the Mediation Committee: 'He said that Mr. Bevin in particular was the prime mover in the idea of calling the conference and he felt the movement owed a debt of gratitude to him.'[72] The *Daily Express* was impressed: 'Hitherto he has been regarded as an extremist, but he has played a great part in bringing about a settlement of one of the most threatening industrial disputes the country had ever experienced.'[73]

Bevin himself registered his anxiety to avoid a situation which, he feared, could lead to 'civil war'. He also expressed his ill-disguised contempt for the two principal actors in the drama, Lloyd George and J. H. Thomas. He did not know, he said, which of them was the more devious and deceitful.[74] His mediation had held them both at bay, for the railwaymen avoided a pay cut in spite of Thomas's tactics, which had isolated his members from officially led sympathy action by the Triple Alliance, while the Prime Minister was, for the time being, dissuaded from entering a showdown.

## Guilds and Industrial Democracy

So much for the transport unions' initiatives in the formation of Joint Industrial Councils, the reduction of hours and the defence of wages. We must turn now to an area where history has – as in other fields – given more attention to the demands of other groups of workers, particularly miners and railwaymen. This concerns the demand for nationalization with some form of industrial democracy.[75] In fact, during the immediate post-war years, the transport unions shared in the insistent and almost universal campaign in the trade-union movement for a decisive advance in labour's status in industry. At this time, the National Guilds' League, driven by restless intelligences amongst which that of G. D. H. Cole was outstanding, was flooding the Labour movement's bookstalls with its programmes for self-managed socialized industries. Cole's *Self-Government in Industry*, an influential and extended tract for the times, had first appeared in 1917; it was reprinted in 1920.[76] Its influences tempted a wide movement to exercise itself in two separate directions. In engineering, the expression of workers' control demands was made through the shop-stewards' movement, and in 1919 this approached its near-revolutionary climax. The leading participants in that movement went over not quite *en bloc* to the nascent British Communist Party, some of whose members were eventually persuaded that their espousal of libertarian demands in those early years had been a mistake, a 'diversion from the class struggle', after 'one-man management' succeeded Workers' Councils in the administration of embattled Soviet industry. Others were happily more difficult to teach, and continued to preach their heresy of workers' control for long enough to disaffect new generations of libertarians decades later.

In the mining, railway and transport industries, and in the post office, a different strand of the doctrine took hold. In the first three, the wartime experience of state control was profoundly influential. In the post office there was, of course, a permanent state administration. These all offered the syndicalist and Guild Socialist advocates a golden opportunity. It was seized, and the trade unions concerned were persuaded to embrace, in officially adopted programmes, precise demands for nationalization with various kinds of joint union–state management. All shared the common view of the Guildsmen, that neither the return to *laissez-faire* capitalism in these industries, nor the imposition of 'state capitalism' through bureaucratic state ownership were at all acceptable. Wage slavery resulted from both conditions, and it was wage slavery which must be replaced. It was wage claims, not workers' control, which, whilst necessary, obscured the true class struggle, the 'real root' of which was 'the straining of the spirit of man to be free'.[77] This phrase, which was widely quoted after it was used during the meetings of the Sankey Commission by a working trade-union official of the Northumberland miners, actually derives from a passage in the writing of Cole:

We have too long repeated the Marxian phrase that the emancipation of Labour must be the work of Labour, without understanding it. The Syndicalists and the National Guildsmen are fundamentally right in regarding the industrial consciousness of the workers as the pivot on which the whole social system swings. The fundamentally important thing about the various forms which the capitalist organisation of industry assumes is not whether they are harsh or gentle, whether they feed the workers well or ill, but whether they foster or destroy the spirit of liberty in men's hearts.[78]

The National Guilds' League produced pamphlets for these industries: *Towards a Miners' Guild* (1917), *Towards a National Railway Guild* (1917) and, in 1921, *Towards a Postal Guild*, written by Milne Bailey. At the height of the agitation, Frank Hodges of the Miners' Federation published *The Nationalization of the Mines*, in which he detailed the union's demands as tabled before the Sankey Commission, for 'a Mining Council, consisting of a President and twenty members, ten of whom shall be appointed by his Majesty and ten by the association known as the Miners' Federation of Great Britain'.[79]

In the building industry, the unions adopted the concept of Guild management and translated it into practice by establishing a working Guild of House Builders in Manchester. The *Guildsman* celebrated with an announcement in its columns:

BIRTH – January 1920, at Manchester, Building Trade Unionists and the National Guilds League, of a Guild. Parents and Child both doing well.
MARRIAGE – January 1920, at Manchester, a marriage has been arranged between the labour-power of the building workers and the credit of the public.
DEATH – January 1920, at Manchester, the theory of the necessity of capitalism passed painlessly away. No flowers by request.[80]

The transport workers, like all others, breathed this heady air of freedom. Expectations rose and rose. The miners' demands, including the programme outlined by Hodges, were tabled in February. The government took the unusual step of replying to them in large newspaper advertisements, urging the miners to vote against strike action.[81] The transport workers could draw on their own long tradition: the demands for municipalization of the ports, and for municipal labour agencies in dockland, tabled before the Royal Commission in the 1890s; the early expectations for significant trade-union representation on the Port of London Authority; union control in dockers' registration schemes; union representation (and the demand that this should be 50 per cent) in the wartime Port Labour Committees, and on the Port and Transit Committee; municipal ownership and management of tramway undertakings in the provinces, in which trade unions had won recognition and in which trade-union-sponsored councillors played a big role; and, of course, municipal ownership of the port of Bristol, Tillett's and Bevin's home territory. The Guildsmen's doctrines and demands came as no novelty to them, harmonizing naturally with all their experience. All their aspirations for the dignity and status of labour were consonant with the new doctrines.

## A National Board of Communications

Such was the transport workers' scepticism, born of experience, concerning the waywardness of public officials. Only when they were tempered by labour's countervailing power could they be expected to behave differently from other employers, and even then the slightest abatement of pressure would see them revert to type. The wartime control mechanisms had given the unions the opportunity to put a foot in the door; now they tabled demands which would have pushed it wide open for their entry. We saw in the previous chapter that the Federation began with the widest practicable vision of all, for a National Board of Communications, 'with equal representation of the employees and the State, which shall take over and administer the whole of the inland passenger, mail, and goods transport of the country – road, rail, air and water – in the interests of the nation.'[82] The NTWF Executive was instructed in this resolution 'to approach the National Union of Railwaymen and the Postal Workers' Associations with a view to making joint representations to the government'.

At that time, a Bill was before the Commons to establish a Ministry of Ways and Communications. The NTWF sent a resolution on the Bill to the Labour Party, requesting it to draft amendments in the House:

> this Executive Council of the NTWF protests against the establishment of bureaucratic control of Transport under the Bill setting up a Ministry of Ways and Communications. It demands that the powers of the proposed Minister shall be vested in a Board of Communications composed of equal numbers of representatives of the State and of the Unions catering for transport work. It moreover demands that each separate section of the Ministry shall likewise be controlled by a Railways Board, a Canals Board, a Harbours Board, etc., with direct representation in Parliament by an official

responsible thereto. It further resolves to communicate with other Unions affected with a view to joint action in furtherance of this resolution.[83]

The Federation passed this resolution after a debate in which Bevin, in particular, sought to harden the stance of its MPs in dealing with the Bill in the Commons, but there was no dissent whatever from the principle of nationalization with joint worker–state control.

The following year's AGC contented itself with reaffirming its policy by passing, without debate, a resolution from the LPU, the 'Red Button' Union, which again called for 'the means of Transport by Road, Rail, Air, and Water' to be owned by the Nation and be controlled jointly by the State and the employees'. But the resolution concluded tamely, as though the movers were unsure what to do with it: 'and urges the Executive Council to make representation in the appropriate quarters towards securing this end.'[84]

This hesitation before the fact of the movement's parliamentary frailty reflects the earlier timidity demonstrated at the TUC in 1919, after the August announcement by the government that it would not implement the Sankey Commission's recommendation to nationalize the mines. The miners themselves had voted by six to one to strike in support of the package of demands they had tabled in February. But, despite the TUC's total support for them in September and talk of 'compelling' the government, the Annual Congress decided on nothing more fearsome than a propaganda battle around the slogan: 'The Mines for the Nation', and the Miners Federation followed suit. Lloyd George, by astute timing, had successfully called the bluff of miners, TUC and Triple Alliance.

## Port Labour Committees and Workers' Control

The docks were a special case where public ownership and workers' control were concerned, for this almost universal formula could not be expected directly to solve the problem of casualism, for which a registration scheme and an institution to administer labour supply were necessary. At port level, experiment and persistent attempts to render registration schemes amenable to union control continued into the post-war years. In London, J. T. Scoulding of the Dockers' Union, and NTWF District Secretary, reported that the wartime Military Service Committee had been transformed into a Port Labour Committee, and that he had obtained ten seats on it for union representatives:

Its functions are to deal with unemployment and to devise ways and means to enable men seeking employment to go to the places of call where they are most likely to be required, instead of the old system where men went to a calling on place without knowing how many men were likely to be required, and possibly lose an opportunity of obtaining employment elsewhere. The Committee have power to deal with the Government out-of-work donation . . . [85]

(The 'out-of-work donation' was the forerunner of the dole, designed to assuage social unrest in the transition to a peacetime labour market.)

In Scotland, Joseph Houghton, NTWF district secretary, reported that 'The Scottish Dockers have announced that they are applying for a Stevedore's Licence, as they are out to abolish the Master Stevedore entirely, and stop that part of the exploitation of their labour.' And he added with a flourish: 'Meanwhile, we stick loyally by our Federation until we devise something better to take its place.'[86]

The idea of a self-managed labour agency in dockland, which echoes the Building Guild initiative, recurs at times throughout the modern history of dock labour, reaching down to a scheme in Hull as recently as the 1970s, influenced by the modern Institute for Workers' Control.

London's Port Labour Committee made significant strides in the next twelve months, for in his next Annual District Report, Scoulding was able to announce its transformation into a Port Registration Committee, with parity representation: seven NTWF members and seven employers. It was early days for him to report on its achievements, 'Owing to the enormous area to be covered it will take some considerable time to get the scheme into proper working order,' but 'much is expected of the scheme'.[87]

In Bristol, 'Work in the docks was but normal during the first six months,' reported A. Despres, South-western district secretary, in June 1920, 'since when it has been below the normal. Due to the registration scheme for the docks having been kept in operation, the Dockers' Union has been enabled so to regulate the number of applicants for dock work that a semblance of economic security now appertains to this class of work.'[88]

On the Mersey, McVey's usual comprehensive report in mid–1920 includes this significant testimony to an effective 'closed' union use of registration to cope with a labour market in downturn: 'I may add that this week we have closed down the registration of Dockers on the Mersey in order to stop the inflated surplus of labour.'[89]

The whole question of casualism and labour controls was to make its impact on the Shaw Inquiry, as 1919 closed and Bevin prepared his case. It was to exert an immense influence on conditions in the industry, and on the future shape of transport trade unions.

## III

## *Direct Action*

Such was the strength of the NTWF industrially, that the major trial of will and strength between Lloyd George and the transport unions came over other issues. On industrial questions, there was to be 'no contest'. Contest there was, in abundance, however. Conscription, British military intervention in Russia, the threatened use of troops to break strikes, 'prisoners of conscience' (conscientious objectors) still held in British gaols in 1919, and the raising of the blockade against Germany: these were the issues on which the unions of the Triple Alliance joined in a combined assault on the government's authority.

The sequence of events in this crisis was well summarized in a circular which accompanied a ballot form on direct action, sent out by the Triple Alliance to the members of the constituent unions in July.

On 3 April a representative conference of the wide Labour movement was held at Caxton Hall to debate its attitude to the new League of Nations. The meeting passed a resolution calling for the withdrawal of a new Conscription Bill then before Parliament, the withdrawal of troops from Russia, the raising of the blockade and the release of political prisoners. But it was ruled from the chair that that conference had no authority in these matters to enforce implementation of the resolution.

Shortly afterwards, the joint Alliance Executives met at Southport and resolved to urge upon the Parliamentary Committee of the TUC the need to summon a 'Special National Conference of the Trade Union Movement' to determine how to implement the Caxton Hall resolution. A deputation in the form of a sub-committee of the three Executives waited upon the TUC on 15 May to press the case for a conference. At this point, they also took up, and added to their bill of complaints, the issue of a secret circular from the War Office, which had asked commanding officers to report whether their troops could be relied on in the case of civil disturbance, for strike-breaking, or for service in Russia.[90]

The Parliamentary Committee of the TUC, however, dominated by the moderate wing, settled for a private meeting with Bonar Law, the Lord Privy Seal, on 22 May. They decided, 'in view of the nature of his reply, a National Conference should not be held.' There followed the Annual Conference of the Labour Party on 25–6 June, at which decisive majorities were recorded for resolutions supporting the points at issue and 'if necessary', for the use of direct action to force them on the government. The Labour Party NEC then requested the TUC to summon a special conference, and again 'the Parliamentary Committee refused to give the Trade Union Movement an opportunity to declare what action they would take'.

Accordingly, the Triple Alliance Executives resumed the initiative, and summoned a full delegate conference, again in Caxton Hall, on 23 July. This carried, by 217 votes to 11, a resolution recommending 'all its constituents to take such action, in accordance with their respective constitutions, to ascertain whether their members are prepared to take industrial action to enforce these demands.'

## The NTWF Ballot

The miners were required to ballot under their rules, but the NUR was not: its Executive had standing authority to decide such matters. In the NTWF each of the constituent unions would proceed according to its own Rule Book. Some rules enjoined a ballot, some did not. But the circular enclosed a uniform ballot paper which would be used wherever balloting was mandatory (see fig. 18.1).

---

As explained in the attached circular, the Government have refused to abolish:

1 CONSCRIPTION.

2 MILITARY INTERVENTION IN RUSSIA.

3 MILITARY INTERVENTION IN TRADE UNION DISPUTES.

Are you in favour of withdrawing your labour to enforce the abolition of the foregoing?

| Yes | |
|-----|---|
| No | |

Please place your X opposite 'Yes' or 'No' in the space provided for the purpose.

---

**Figure 18.1**   NTWF Ballot

Within a week of the issue of the circular and ballot paper, Winston Churchill announced in the Commons that all British troops would be withdrawn from Russia by the end of the summer, and that conscription would stop by the end of the financial year. On 12 August the Triple

Alliance Executives met and resolved that 'Bearing in mind the changed circumstances . . . and the proposals of the Triple Alliance having been further considered by the Government and the House of Commons', the ballot should stand postponed. It had been a remarkable demonstration of the potential power of direct action, and encouraged the movement to far more united efforts in the same field in the following year.[91]

## Churchill versus the Alliance

Historians have tended to play down, curiously, any connection between the pending ballot and the government's change of military policies. Such a connection seems plain enough, although it should be said that the real struggle was that between the Triple Alliance and Winston Churchill (who lost no opportunity to harass and bombard the Bolsheviks), rather than between the unions taken together on one side, and the Cabinet and Prime Minister on the other. Indeed, the Lloyd George administration was at sixes and sevens about how to contain revolution abroad, and not entirely at one about how to exorcise it at home. The Premier had profoundly held reservations about Churchill's stridency since early in the year. In February he said to Lord Riddell: 'Winston is in Paris. He wants to conduct a war against the Bolsheviks. That would cause revolution.'[92] He sent Churchill a telegram: 'I beg you not to commit this country to what would be a purely mad enterprise out of hatred of Bolshevik principles . . . Were it known that you have gone to Paris to prepare a war against the Bolsheviks it would do more to incense labour than anything I can think of'.[93]

Whatever the disagreements in the Cabinet, in public Lloyd George temporized to the manner born. After Churchill had been pushed into announcing the withdrawal of troops from Russia, and a further series of concessions had been made to the Labour Party, the Prime Minister set about isolating the rebels:

> First, then, they must recapture the public mind, and counter 'that formidable body of young men whose aim it is to destroy the present industrial and parliamentary system and replace it by a workers' state' – and whose advocacy of Soviet government drew strength from popular impatience with the parliamentary mode of government. Grievances, principally profiteering, must therefore be met: 'the making of money has become a craze, like an alcoholic craving, which could not be resisted. But it had got to be stopped. The working classes would not tolerate it . . .'[94]

High-sounding though his argument was, it disguised another instalment of the plan to split the Triple Alliance from the main body of trade unions. This accelerated after 25 July because of the Triple

Alliance's decision to go ahead without the support of the full Labour movement, setting August for their ballot on the general strike.[95]

What was the role of the Transport Workers and their leaders during these events? Within the Federation's Executive there was serious conflict, more so than on any industrial matter. The protagonists were Cathery of the NSFU and Sexton on the one hand, Williams and Bevin on the other. On 17 April Cathery complained that Robert Williams was conspiring with Bob Smillie of the miners to commit the Triple Alliance to a policy of industrial action for political ends. Mr Farrah, district secretary for the East Coast, and a Boston official of the NUGW, agreed with Cathery.[96] Cathery repeated his complaints at an NTWF Executive meeting following the decision of the Triple Alliance at Southport, on 22 May. On each occasion Williams was able to maintain Executive support for his actions.

The argument about direct action was clearly bubbling up from below, and it was to spill over at the earliest opportunity. It has been remembered selectively, and not only by historians.

## Are You Ready? Bevin Is – Sexton Isn't

Aneurin Bevan more than once alluded to a famous confrontation, reported to him by Bob Smillie, between the spokesmen of the Triple Alliance and Lloyd George in 1919:

'He said to us: "Gentlemen, you have fashioned, in the Triple Alliance of the Unions represented by you, a most powerful instrument. I feel bound to tell you that in our opinion we are at your mercy . . . If you carry out your threat and strike, then you will defeat us. But if you do so . . . have you weighed the consequences? The strike will be in defiance of the country, and by its very success will precipitate a constitutional crisis of the first importance. For, if a force arises in the State which is stronger than the State itself, then it must be ready to take on the functions of the State, or withdraw and accept the authority of the State. Gentlemen, have you considered, and if you have, are you ready?" "From that moment on", said Robert Smillie, "we were beaten and we knew we were." '[97]

But, on 5 and 6 June 1919, a more acid exchange took place at the Federation's AGC in Swansea. James Sexton took the floor to warn against abusing the power of the Triple Alliance:

The opinions of a powerful body like that will carry influence and there is every possibility if a resolution had been carried in favour of a national strike, it would have meant the end of constitutional rule in this country. Suppose we succeeded in a National Conference in deciding to fight the Government, and suppose we won, where would that land us?

Ernest Bevin sharply interrupted: 'Then you might be President of the Board of Education.' Sexton replied, 'You would require more than one Board of Education to get out of the devil of a mess we should get into.' 'While you were President?' asked Bevin. Reassuming his composure, Sexton continued:

> It would be all right if the rank and file were capable of running the country, but they have a long way to go and they have not got there yet. Some of the rank and file I know who talk about running the country could not run a potato machine. Whatever the Government is to-day the rank and file of Trade Unionists have made it, and having made it they must take their share of responsibility in having helped to make it what it is. We ought to protest on the floor of this Conference against outside irresponsible busybodies using the name of the Triple Alliance without anyone's authority. (Hear, hear.) We have men going about advocating a policemen's Union and they are not policemen, and they are using the name of the Triple Alliance to fortify the police in striking. I have my own opinion on that. I have been a member of the Police Committee for the last four months in the House of Commons which is inquiring into the police matters. No matter what conditions have been created in the police I am not going to trust anybody with a baton in their hands. A baton, like the rain from Heaven, falls on the just and unjust alike.
> A delegate: Take the baton out of their hands.[98]

Bevin's lack of fear, and matter-of-fact acceptance of the logic of direct action, reflects the mood of his members during this extraordinary year. He was not a man to romanticize, and this exchange surely reveals the same pragmatic attitude to power and its transfer that was later admired by iconographers and others in quite different circumstances.

The militant position was, however, successfully challenged, on more constitutional grounds, later on that June at the NTWF Executive meeting:

> Mr. Sexton moved, Mr. Cathery seconded, that when the Triple Alliance meeting discussed the action of the Parliamentary Committee in refusing to call a national conference, the Federation representatives should move: – 'That the fit and proper place to discuss the action of the Parliamentary Committee is at the Trades Union Congress'. This was carried – 6 voting for and 5 against.[99]

Bevin then intervened, with a motion calling for a Triple Alliance instruction to be sent to members of the three bodies, calling for a 'limit to production, pending the withdrawal of the Secret Circular, the abolition of conscription, and the cessation of intervention in Russia. This was lost.' Undeterred, Bevin followed this with a further motion – which he believed was sanctioned by the recent Conference decision to back strike action – calling for a special Delegate Conference of the

Alliance. This motion was, however, withdrawn, and the Executive ended inconclusively.

In sequence thereafter, the Southport meeting of the Triple Alliance called for a full delegate conference on 24 June, the Labour Party Conference followed in the same town on the next two days, and the Delegate Conference of the Alliance, which adopted the ballot, was on 23 July. The National Conference of Bevin's Dockers' Union fell in between, on 7–9 July.

Bevin did not speak in the heated, indeed, momentous debate at the Labour Party Conference. He explained why, in a speech to the Dockers' Conference: 'the question has been taken too lightly. It is of no use to keep on threatening. We know what it means, we know what is involved.'[100] He went on to argue that the correct place for a decision was not the Labour Party Conference, but the TUC, where any decision to strike should be followed by balloting by individual unions.

But of course we know that the Parliamentary Committee had consistently blocked this, Bevin's favoured route to a decision. Moreover, Bevin went a crucial step further in opposition to any action outside the TUC. 'In asking the Parliamentary Committee to call a conference, that step was taken because we agree that the Triple Alliance must not usurp the functions of the Trade Union movement.'[101]

Bevin could read the mind of the Prime Minister. Lloyd George sought to divide the Triple Alliance from the TUC, and to isolate 'the formidable body of young men' calling for direct action. Bevin favoured direct or any other action, but he insisted upon its being *joint* action, in common cause.

Remarkably, Bevin does not appear to have attended the Alliance's Delegate Conference on 23 July; he certainly abstained from speaking as he had done at the Southport Labour Party Conference.[102] It is hard to imagine him sitting silent throughout its passionate length.

Some comment on his behaviour is obviously justified. There was inconsistency, surely, between what he told the Executive in June about the Alliance initiating ca' canny, or work to rule, in this cause, and his later position on the Alliance's duty 'not to usurp' TUC functions, at his union's conference, just two weeks later. His second position, advancing the thesis of the supremacy of the TUC in matters affecting the whole movement, was in fact more consistent with the view we have encountered from him in an earlier clash with Havelock Wilson, over Wilson's actions in sabotaging the Stockholm Peace Meeting during 1917.

Why, then, did Bevin play with the idea of an Alliance initiative at the Federation Executive Council? He lost the vote on that proposal. Did he know from the beginning that he would lose it? For it is that motion, and not his subsequent explanations to his union, which was inconsistent with his powerful doctrines of centralized, constitutional authority, reaching up a pyramid of union structures to the TUC. That position was his lifetime motif, governing his strong influence in the NTWF, and supremely relevant throughout his leadership of the TGWU.

Yet Bevin's response to the call for direct action was not a ploy. He, and not the TUC leaders, had correctly caught the mood of the membership. This was fully demonstrated when Congress voted to refer back the Report of the Parliamentary Committee, which attempted to justify inertia through these events. By an overwhelming majority, of 1 million plus, the TUC leaders were invited to eat rook pie.

The Parliamentary Committee was seen to have shirked any leadership role on this occasion. It was surely one of the formative episodes, leading Bevin and others to examine the TUC's constitution and to set about reshaping it. The concept of a General Council as the 'general staff of labour', which was accomplished with the ending of the Parliamentary Committee, followed the grain of Bevin's proposals, as did the creation of combined constituencies of Trade Groups for the election of the General Council in 1920.

As things stood at the close of 1919, the higher instruments of policymaking and co-ordination in the trade-union movement all looked inadequate. To a leadership and a membership which had felt their own strength to shape events in pursuing a wide range of issues during that momentous year, from reducing hours of work to opposing Churchill's military adventures, this would not do. The tasks before them defined themselves very readily. They must strengthen the central authority of the TUC. They must streamline the Triple Alliance, for its industrial purposes (in Bevin's view). Likewise, the NTWF needed more teeth. Beyond that goal lay the still cherished, and now maturing, target of full amalgamation in the field of transport and general unionism.

For the moment, the district secretaries were euphoric on the subject of the Federation, whilst calling with equal fervour for rapid progress towards amalgamation: 'this has been our most successful year': J. Powesland, South Wales district secretary; 'the past year has been the most remarkable in the history of our Federation': R. H. Farrah, Humber district secretary; 'the past year has been the most successful in history of the Federation, and on behalf of the Committee I desire to thank all the members of the National Executive (and also the officials)': C. McVey, honorary secretary, Mersey District.

## Football and the King Keep Order

There was something else to thank for all these advances. The powers that be were scared. So scared, indeed, that the head of Intelligence, Basil Thomson, prepared for the Home Office a 'Survey of Revolutionary

Feeling During the Year 1919'. Eight subversive social influences were charted, in descending order of importance:

1   Profiteering and high prices.
2   Insufficient and bad housing accommodation.
3   Class hatred, aggravated by the foolish and dangerous ostentation of the rich, the publication of large dividends, and distrust of a 'Government of profiteers'.
4   Education by Labour Colleges, schools and classes and better circulation of literature on Marxian economics.
5   Influence of extremist Trade Union leaders – Mann, Cramp, Smillie, Hodges, Bromley, Hill, Williams, Turner.
6   Unemployment.
7   Labour press, particularly the 'Daily Herald', 'The Workers' Dreadnought', and 'The Worker'.
8   External influences – Russia, Ireland, Egypt, India.

Balancing these disturbing forces were:

1   Popularity of the Royal Family.
2   Sport.[103]

Football and the King notwithstanding, it had been a close call for authority. But a giant ally was about to join them. Its name was Slump.

# Notes

1   David Mitchell, *1919: Red Mirage* (Jonathan Cape, 1970), p. 66.
2   J. M. Keynes, *The Economic Consequences of the Peace* (Macmillan, 1920), p. 2.
3   From a Bolshevik leaflet addressed to marauding Allied soldiers in Russia; quoted in Mitchell, *1919: Red Mirage*, p. 11.
4   War Cabinet 514, 8 January 1919; cited in Mitchell, *1919: Red Mirage*, p. 371.
5   H. A. Clegg, *A History of British Trade Unions since 1889*, vol. II: *1911–1933* (Oxford University Press, 1985), p. 568. For union densities from 1969 to 1984, when (for the years 1975 to 1980) density exceeded 50 per cent, see Ken Coates and Tony Topham, *Trade Unions in Britain* (3rd edn, Fontana, 1988), p. 23, table 1.1.
6   The TGWU has always been amongst the most scrupulous affiliates of the TUC in returning realistic membership figures. This tradition was established at the outset. The first Annual Report (p. vi) notes that 'When the amalgamation was promoted in July 1920, the membership of the majority of the Unions was at its peak level. Due mainly to the slump, however, it was found that from the date upon which the first returns were submitted until the date of the actual consummation of the amalgamation, the membership in the case of some of the Unions had fallen by at least 50

per cent, and the slump, with consequent loss of membership, was still in progress . . . It was decided to write off all paper membership . . . for the purpose of ascertaining exactly how the membership stood and to build up from that figure. As a result of writing down the membership to its proper basis, and the efforts put in during the past year, the figures were, at January 1st, 1923, 297,460. This figure, it should be borne in mind, does not include the membership of the Scottish Union of Dock Labourers, the North Wales Quarrymen's Union and the North Wales Craftsmen and General Workers' Union. Also, that from January 1st 1923, up to the time of writing this report, there has been a considerable revival, and the actual membership figures at the moment are considerably higher than as stated above.'

7  C. J. Wrigley, *1919: The Critical Year* (Loughborough University, 1979), p. 14, cites Lansbury's call: 'The whole structure of Trade Unionism will have to be rebuilt from top to bottom, and . . . thoroughly democratised by taking the workshop as a basis and vesting important decisions in delegates drawn for each occasion directly from the rank and file'. By these criteria, Wrigley is correct in adding: 'However, radical reform of trade union structure was not to be'.

8  *The Citizen* finally expired in June 1915, after it became insolvent. The flow of funds to sustain it was cut right back after a judgement in March 1915. This ruled that trade union subsidies to the maintenance of newspapers supporting the Labour Party were, themselves, political expenditure. Consequently, they could only be financed from their political funds.

9  DWRGWU *Record*, vol. V, no. 7, November 1919, p. 10.

10  Ibid., p. 11.

11  See Trevor Wilson, *The Downfall of the Liberal Party, 1914–36* (Collins, 1966).

12  A. J. P. Taylor, *English History, 1914–1945* (Oxford University Press, 1965), pp. 126–7.

13  Only one woman was elected, and she was the Countess Markiewicz, Larkin's lieutenant in the great Dublin lock-out. As an Irish patriot, she refused to take her seat. In all, seventeen women presented candidatures. See J. F. S. Ross, *Elections and Electors* (Eyre and Spottiswoode, 1955), pp. 252 ff.

14  Ivor Jennings, *Party Politics: I Appeal to the People* (Cambridge University Press, 1960), p. 60; David Butler and Jennie Freeman, *British Political Facts* (Macmillan, 1963), p. 122.

15  B. R. Mitchell, *Abstract of British Historical Statistics* (Cambridge University Press, 1962), p. 219.

16  Ibid., p. 224.

17  Ibid., p. 230.

18  Robert Williams, *The New Labour Outlook* (Leonard Parsons, 1921), p. 110.

19  Eric Wigham, *Strikes and the Government, 1893–1974* (Macmillan, 1976), p. 50.

20  NTWF Annual General Council Report, 1919, p. 16.

21  Ibid., pp. 50–1.

22  Wigham, *Strikes and the Government*, p. 90.

23  NTWF Annual General Council Report, 1919, p. 101.

24   Keith Middlemas, *Politics in Industrial Society: The Experience of the British System since 1911* (André Deutsch, 1979), pp. 131–3.

25   Ibid.

26   Quoted in C. J. Wrigley, *1919: The Critical Year*, p. 16.

27   Wigham, *Strikes and the Government*, p. 47.

28   Ibid., p. 49.

29   NTWF Executive Committee Minutes, 8 January 1919.

30   Ibid., 11 August 1919.

31   See *The Industrial Relations Handbook* (Ministry of Labour, 1961), pp. 56 and 117.

32   NTWF Annual General Council Report, 1919, pp. 29–30.

33   NTWF Executive Committee Minutes, 24 June 1919.

34   Ibid., 11 August 1919, p. 5.

35   See also Paul Smith, 'The Process of Unionisation in the Road Haulage Industry' (unpublished PhD thesis, University of Warwick), 1987.

36   Alan Bullock, *The Life and Times of Ernest Bevin*, vol. I: *Trade Union Leader, 1881–1940* (Heinemann, 1960), pp. 94–5.

37   Ibid., pp. 95–6.

38   Keith Jeffery and Peter Hennessy, *States of Emergency: British Governments and Strike-breaking since 1919* (Routledge and Kegan Paul, 1983), p. 10.

39   R. A. Leeson, *Strike: A Live History, 1887–1971* (Allen and Unwin, 1973), pp. 60–61.

40   Ibid., p. 61.

41   Clegg, *History of British Trade Unions*, vol. II, p. 270.

42   Angela Tuckett, *The Scottish Carter* (Allen and Unwin, 1967), pp. 146–7.

43   Quoted in Wrigley, *1919: The Critical Year*, p. 9.

44   Clegg, *History of British Trade Unions*, vol. II, pp. 194–5.

45   NTWF Executive Committee Minutes, 26 February 1919.

46   The problems for the unions in road haulage at this time are illustrated by Smith, 'The Process of Unionisation in the Road Haulage Industry', p. 70: 'In December 1918, an NTWF sectional conference of road haulage unions agreed a claim for the establishment of a Joint Industrial Council . . . a forty hour week, a 10s. wage increase, payment for Sunday stable duties, and overtime rates. The settlement of January 1919, negotiated with various employers' organisations, fell short of this to give a forty-eight-hour week and prohibited unpaid overtime; but the employers' organisations refused to ratify the agreement without the approval of their district bodies. Many firms were not members of employers' organisations and so the Wages (Temporary Regulation) Act 1918 was used to enforce the agreement.'

47   NTWF Special General Council Minutes, 10 March 1919, p. 18.

48   Ken Fuller, *Radical Aristocrats: London Busworkers from the 1880s to the 1980s* (Lawrence and Wishart, 1985), pp. 44–5.

49   Ibid.

50   NTWF Special General Council Minutes, 10 March 1919, p. 22.

51   Ibid., p. 25.

52   Ibid., p. 27 (authors' interpolations).

53   The most heated conflict actually recorded was that between Robert Williams and George Milligan of the NUDL, over an intemperate accusation which Milligan had levelled against Williams at the Special

General Council, that the latter had consorted with the Dublin employers during negotiations on the shorter week in that city, and undermined his, Milligan's, position. Gosling, in the chair, was aghast at the idea! Williams demanded a full inquiry into the allegation, and an EC report. Subsequently, at the Executive, Sexton advised that Milligan should be sent a sharp note and invited to retract, implying that he knew his man and that retraction would follow. It did. Milligan wrote to Harry Gosling, as president, on 12 September, saying: 'I am sorry that through stress of work and as a result of sickness I have delayed replying to your letter in the matter of Mr. Robert Williams and myself over the Irish ports 46 hours question. Mr. Williams has been such a brick since and before in helping us out of our over-rising [sic] difficulties that I can do no more than withdraw unreservedly any charges I made against him at our last Conference. I am heartily sorry, and make this apology for you to use as you like. I feel no sentiments other than respect and admiration for Mr. Robert Williams. Yours fraternally, George Milligan.'

This incident, and all the accompanying chorus of praise for Williams at the Conference and the EC, underlines once again for the historian the almost invulnerable position in which Williams's qualities placed him during these years in any controversy. Time and again, his political opponents – and Milligan was an extreme 'patriot' – were discomfited and forced to confess William's indispensability, incorruptibility and value to the NTWF. See NTWF Special General Council, 1919, pp. 53–8, and NTWF Executive Committee Minutes, 23 July and 6 October 1919.

54  Bullock, *The Life and Times of Ernest Bevin*, vol. I, p. 94.
55  Wigham, *Strikes and the Government*, p. 51.
56  NTWF Executive Committee Minutes, 6 October 1919.
57  Ibid., 17 April 1919.
58  Ibid., 4 June 1919.
59  Ibid., 24 June 1919.
60  Bullock, *The Life and Times of Ernest Bevin*, vol. I, p. 93.
61  Ibid.
62  NTWF Executive Committee Minutes, 11 August 1919.
63  Paul Smith, 'The Process of Unionisation in the Road Haulage Industry', pp. 69–70, provides an interesting commentary on the evolution of this union. Originally, as we have seen, it was the Mersey Quay and Railway Carters' Union, heavily influenced by conservative, Merseyside-Orange leadership. It 'for the most part threw off its sectarian origins in a transformation that began in 1908, and was consolidated through the development of a class-based trade union consciousness in the upheavals of 1910–11'. Later, during 1918–19, 'the LDCMU [Liverpool and District Carters' and Motormen's Union] constructed a comprehensive range of working rules which embodied the collective presence of the union at the point of hire over the terms of the wage-effort bargain, and were enforced against both employers and members alike. In 1919, the LDCMU imposed a second man on vehicles carrying more than three tons, and a third man when a trailer was used within a radius extending ten miles from Birkenhead and Liverpool town halls. It was this measure of workers' unilateral job regulation which made the LDCMU distinctive among

carters' unions. The strength of the LDCMU caused the employers to organise in the Liverpool Conference of Road Transport Employers'.

64 NTWF Annual General Council Report, 1919, p. 106.
65 Ibid.
66 Ibid., p. 28.
67 Wrigley, *1919: The Critical Year*, p. 9.
68 Ibid., p. 10.
69 Cabinet Meeting, 5 April 1921, cited in R. Challinor, *The Origins of British Bolshevism* (Croom Helm, 1977), p. 202.
70 NTWF Executive Committee Minutes, 29 September 1919, p. 2.
71 Ibid., 6 October 1919, p. 3.
72 Ibid., p. 6.
73 Quoted in Bullock, *The Life and Times of Ernest Bevin*, vol. I, p. 109.
74 Ibid., p. 108.
75 The first major historian of the movement, Branko Pribićević, wrote in 1959 that 'The Miners, the railwaymen and the engineers played by far the most important role in the movement for workers' control. Of the workers in other industries only the builders and the postmen need be mentioned here' (see *The Shop Stewards' Movement and Workers' Control, 1910–1922* (Basil Blackwell, 1959), p. 9.) It is not pedantic to seek here to redress the neglect of the transport unions' equal commitment to industrial democracy at this time, for otherwise we miss an important strand in the inheritance and subsequent contributions of the TGWU. These reached through the debates of the 1930s, in the TUC and the Labour Party, over Morrisonian versus worker-representative boards in nationalization statutes. In these, John Cliff and Harold Clay were prominent spokesmen for the union in Bevin's day. The tradition extended to the individual and collective input of leaders such as Jack Jones, Bill Jones, Moss Evans, Alex Kitson, Ron Todd, Jack Ashwell, John Miller, Walt Greendale and others, and to the 1960s working groups in docks, chemicals, agriculture, passenger transport and motor industries. These have inspired the movement for industrial democracy in the past three decades. This is a theme we shall develop in vol. II, of course.
76 G. D. H. Cole, *Self-Government in Industry* (1917; reissued by G. Bell and Sons, 1920).
77 William Straker, secretary of the Northumberland Miners' Association and member of the Executive Committee of the Miners' Federation. He led for the Federation in its evidence to the Sankey Commission. He went on, in the passage from which we have quoted here, to conclude: 'This ideal [of industrial democracy under social ownership] cannot be reached all at once owing to the way in which private ownership has deliberately kept the worker in ignorance regarding the industry; but as that knowledge, which has been denied him, grows, as it will do under nationalisation, he will take his rightful place as a man. Only then will labour unrest, which is the present hope of the world, disappear. The mere granting of the thirty per cent and the shorter hours demanded will not prevent unrest, neither will nationalisation with bureaucratic administration. Just as we are making political democracy world-wide, so must we have industrial democracy, in

order that men may be free'; Coal Industry Commission, Minutes of
Evidence, vol. I, Cmnd 359, 1919, p. 324. Straker was not alone in using
this language: Hodges' text *The Nationalization of the Mines* (see note 79)
includes this passage: 'only through the removal of the influence of the
capitalist in industry can the workers experience the gratification of that
impulse for freedom for expansion, and for self-expression, which they
feel in their inmost beings.'

78  Cole, *Self-Government in Industry*, p. 160.
79  Frank Hodges, *The Nationalization of the Mines* (Leonard Parsons 1920), p.
    117. All the quotations from Cole, Straker and Hodges cited here are
    included in more extensive extracts from their works in Ken Coates and
    Anthony Topham, *Industrial Democracy in Great Britain: A Book of Readings
    and Witnesses for Workers' Control* (1st edn, MacGibbon and Kee, 1968;
    2nd edn, rev., as *Workers' Control*, Panther Modern Society, 1970; 3rd
    edn, rev. in 3 vols, Spokesman Books, 1975).
80  Quoted in M. B. Reckitt and C. E. Bechhofer, *The Meaning of National
    Guilds* (Cecil Palmer, 1918), p. 179. See Coates and Topham, *Industrial
    Democracy in Great Britain*, 1st edn, pp. 54–60.
81  Wrigley, *1919: The Critical Year*, p. 11.
82  NTWF Special General Council, 10 March 1919, p. 42.
83  Ibid., p. 43.
84  NTWF Annual General Council Report, 1920, p. 88.
85  Ibid., 1919, p. 97.
86  Ibid., p. 96.
87  Ibid., 1920, p. 169.
88  Ibid., p. 172.
89  Ibid., pp. 173–4.
90  This was leaked, and found its way into the *Daily Herald*. Socialist stump-
    orators made effective play with the news. One such was John Paton. For
    an account of his use of the news, and of the trouble he got into as a result,
    see his *Proletarian Pilgrimage* (Routledge and Kegan Paul, 1935), pp.
    306 ff.
91  Gordon Phillips, in his comprehensive 'The National Transport Workers'
    Federation 1910–1927' (unpublished PhD thesis, Oxford University,
    1968), vol. II, p. 456 ff. tends to the view that direct action was an incubus,
    weighing down upon the movement. But he rightly points out that two
    reasons were given for opposing it: one, it might fail; two, it might succeed.
    Its opponents, he thinks, feared success far more than failure.
92  Quoted in Wrigley, *1919: The Critical Year*, p. 5.
93  Ibid., p. 5.
94  War Cabinet 606A.
95  Middlemas, *Politics in Industrial Society*, p. 149.
96  NTWF Executive Committee Minutes, 17 April 1919.
97  Aneurin Bevan, *In Place of Fear* (Heinemann, 1952), p. 20.
98  NTWF Annual General Council Report 1919, p. 77.
99  NTWF Executive Committee Minutes, 24 June 1919, p. 3.
100 DWRGWU recalled Triennial Delegate Meeting Minutes, 7–9 July 1919,
    pp. 37–8; quoted in Bullock, *The Life and Times of Ernest Bevin*, vol. I, p. 105.
101 Ibid.

102   Triple Alliance Report of Proceedings at a Conference, Caxton Hall, Westminster, 23 July 1919.

103   Cited in James E. Cronin and Jonathan Schneer (eds), 'Coping with Labour, 1918–19', *Social Conflict and the Political Order in Great Britain* (Croom Helm, 1982), p. 120.

# 19

# 1920: The Shaw Inquiry

## I

### *The Dockers' Lingering Power*

Some time during the late summer of 1920, Lloyd George sensed that there was a new current in his sea of troubles. Perhaps, after all, he might be able to ride over the tide of labour demands which had pressed so hard against 'normalcy' during the post-war months. In fact, 1920 was to be the last year in which economic forces favoured the unions. Until the onset of the Second World War the annual average of unemployment was to rise and stay at over 10 per cent of the insured population. After 1920 the workless numbered never less than 1 million. Through boom or slump, Labour's task would never be easy. But for a brief moment, and even while the storm was gathering towards the year's end, the transport unions made further gains. Wage negotiations went reasonably well. They consolidated their hold on Joint Industrial Councils in most of their territories. True, they lost out in road haulage, but on the other side of the coin, there was the triumphant affirmation of the demand for civilized standards and bargaining rights in the port transport industry at the Shaw Inquiry. After this began the final dash for the long-expected, long-delayed amalgamation which was to produce the TGWU a year later.

During the year, the miners' crisis, and the campaign against government intervention in the Russo-Polish War, again exposed the weaknesses in labour's organizations: the TUC, the Triple Alliance and the National Transport Workers' Federation. Attempts to reform and centralize authority in all these bodies made only meagre progress. These failures, together with the prestige won for it by Bevin at the Shaw Inquiry, gave Bevin's own union, the DWRGWU, both the spur and the impetus to drive ahead for amalgamation.

Customarily prone to precarious and unstable membership from their infancy, the dockers' unions rose in 1920 to achieve a membership density of over 90 per cent, matching that in coal, printing and the postal services.[1] The slump was to force them back, savagely: but for the moment they aroused respect. A national hearing for their case would enhance public concern to a degree not seen since the great dock strike of 1889. That respect was not at all diminished by their commanding, if temporary, hold on the nation's booming trade. In February, at the Shaw Inquiry, the NTWF's Humber district secretary, R. H. Farrah, described the scene in the Hull docks: 'All the quays are blocked with timber, the warehouses are full of grain, all the river craft are full, they are simply using them as warehouses, and if we had anything like normal facilities, as in pre-war days, I do not think we should have a very large amount of casual labour in the transport industry.'[2]

## The Federation Opts for Inquiry

The NTWF Executive had decided in December 1919 to take their demands for the dockers before a Court of Inquiry. The employers had already broken off bilateral negotiations on the claims, and the union leaders were alarmed at the militancy of their own members. They chose not to give this expression by declaring a strike, but to go down the untrodden path of public examination. Gordon Phillips has suggested that the decision was influenced by doubts concerning the likely support of both the Triple Alliance and the marine and road-transport sections of the Federation.[3] At the same time, they also knew that they had a strong case. Moreover, their sights were set on the winning of Joint Industrial Council status in the industry, as the employers would be induced by the court procedure to organize themselves into a national Port Employers' Association. On both counts, they were right.

Ironically – for its results were to speed the dismemberment of the NTWF – the Shaw Inquiry marked the zenith of its achievements. Historians have properly accorded Bevin the credit for a notable triumph at the Inquiry, but it was the Federation which selected the representatives who would sit on the court, and made the choice of Bevin and Sexton as its spokesmen. The Federation also carried the whole burden of financing what became a most elaborate operation, including the marshalling of the witnesses for the workers' side. The whole case was conducted by the Federation, not the dockers' unions.[4]

## Preparing the Case

Bevin set up a team of researchers, including Walton Newbold of the British Socialist Party and Labour College movement (later to achieve fame as a Communist Member of Parliament),[5] and his tireless secretary, Mae Forcey. They put together an overpowering case, neutralizing the shortage of time by sheer hard work. Newbold had, he later wrote, been summoned by Robert Williams to meet himself and Bevin. He was asked to 'prepare detailed and documented material' on the port employers and their subsidiaries and allies. He and his wife began feverish enquiries at Somerset House. They were not the only people working under pressure: 'A Bristol docker, Harry Tomkins, hurriedly summoned overnight to London to give Bevin detailed local information, remembers lights still burning in Effingham House [headquarters of the Dockers' Union] in the early hours of the morning and Bevin and his secretary hard at work preparing for the next day in Court.'[6]

The employers preferred to hire a prominent lawyer to lead for them. Sir Lynden Macassey was 'acknowledged to be the most experienced counsel then practising in industrial cases', and 'they prepared to bring up expert witnesses to overawe their working-class opponents'.[7] Lord Shaw, who presided, was a Law Lord who had previously been a radical member of the Commons. Dockers crowded the public gallery throughout the court's sittings, and the press reported it fully, sometimes with panache. Bevin knew that at the Sankey Commission the previous year the miners had made a powerful impact on public opinion. He therefore set out to speak not just to Lord Shaw, but over his head to the wider tribunal of the public outside the courtroom, and to instil into working people that same sense of outrage against their conditions which he himself felt so passionately. To the power of his argument he joined a clinically lethal documentation.

## Bevin's Statement

Bevin's opening speech ran on for two whole days and into a third; it took eleven hours. He marshalled compelling statistics to show that the dockers' wages had fallen behind the cost of living. He went further, to claim that the docker was entitled to more than a mere subsistence wage, so that he must now receive a real increase in his standard of life. To this point, he held the sympathy of Lord Shaw. But when he moved on to an examination of the high wartime profits in the industry, Shaw tried to rule him out of order: 'I myself would have thought that . . . you would not base your claim upon whether persons made a profit, because you would then be in a position of claiming to share profit. If you are out for profit-sharing that is another inquiry'.[8] He wished, he said, to avoid a diversion of the inquiry into profit-making or 'profiteering', as this would introduce 'what we are all anxious to avoid, prejudice, into this case, because you must know that prejudice is the foe of fair judgement.'

Bevin, clearly with some sense of apprehension, resisted this judgement, which itself was hardly innocent of class prejudice.

'Ability to pay' may have been a novel concept for Lord Shaw in 1920, but it was to become a standard trade-union plea as the world of collective bargaining developed. Bevin put it so:

> With great deference, we were met at the preliminary negotiations by the argument of the inability to pay, and at the risk of losing all, I intend with your permission to show not on the basis of profiteering – I am not debating it, I am not arguing it . . . that the dismissal of our case behind closed doors was because they said that they could not pay it without passing it on to the public, and the public are, I think, expecting me to show (because there is a greater Court than this Court in this case, and it is to that Court that I am going to appeal in this case in addition to this Court, so convinced am I of the justice of the claim), that these wages can be paid and that the standard of life can be increased without adding one particle to the cost of food . . .

To challenge the authority of the chair was indeed to risk 'losing all', and this was boldness on Bevin's part. He prevailed, as Shaw found himself eventually conceding the relevance of the evidence on profits. This was as well, for Bevin succeeded in inundating the Inquiry with such material. Indeed, had the case been decided only by the physical volume and weight of written and statistical evidence submitted by the two sides, Bevin would have won hands down, as his documentary submissions (thirty-three in all) piled up over the days of the hearings.


## Bargaining: an Exemplary Exercise

Bevin was setting the highest standard for what were to become staple labours of trade-union officials in the modern world. He proved his case by reference to the cost of living and he firmly established the profitability of the employers. In 1988 we interviewed the eighty-year-old Tim O'Leary, national docks officer of the TGWU in the 1950s and 1960s. He produced his beautifully bound copy of the Shaw Report for us with every show of reverence, calling it his 'bible'. From it he claimed to have learned the art of bargaining, as well as the history of wages and conditions in the docks industry. And indeed Bevin conducted a very full history lesson, ranging all the way back to the London settlement of 1889.

Walton Newbold was called by Bevin to present evidence not only on shipping-company profits, but also on the vast and complex interlocking of company directorships both within and beyond the industry. These were the early days of the Labour Research Department, yet Newbold's evidence reads like the very modern exercise which is now standard practice for LRD and trade-union research officers. A short sample of his evidence may be quoted: the whole repays study today as a classic example of radical research directed towards the 'opening of the books'. Bevin asked him:

> You heard Sir Alfred Booth's statement re the Cunard rate of profit . . . and that he found it difficult to give the actual trading profits. A. Yes. Q. Can you help in that direction? A. I again have the same difficulty as Sir Alfred Booth in that I find it extremely difficult to separate his trading profits from his profits from investment, because I can never get to the end of the investments of the Cunard Company, just as I can never get to the end of the investments of the Anchor Line. I find these companies owning one another backwards and forwards, until one loses oneself completely in a maze of interlocking ownerships . . . it would be quite impossible, I should imagine – I have consulted a chartered accountant on this matter – to discover what were the actual trading profits, unless an impartial chartered accountant could be put on the books of the company.[9]

Newbold had been thorough; he had consulted, he told the court, 'the Directory of Directors of 1919, the Stock Exchange Year Book, Stock Exchange Official Intelligence, and other papers on the Stock Exchange. I never use any others.'[10]

Amongst other titbits, this search revealed that shipping directors were amongst the directors of the *Liverpool Daily Post and Mercury*, and the *Echo*. Newbold offered the court an ironic comment on Sir John Ellerman, the millionaire shipowner and newspaper magnate, whom he described as 'that champion friend of . . . the docker'.

## Roche and Registration

One of Bevin's submissions was a copy of the year-old report of the Roche Committee into decasualization in the London docks.[11] By agreement with Lord Shaw, Bevin was able to extend the case he had made there, and in several draft schemes during the war, for a scheme of registration for dockers combined with the payment of a fall-back 'maintenance' wage for men temporarily without work. This, he insisted, was a special scheme, adapted to the nature of the industry, in place of the inappropriate provisions of the national unemployment insurance scheme. The report of the Roche Committee had been inconclusive, as the employers represented on it would neither accept compulsory registration, nor any special out-of-work payment for which they would have been financially liable. The voluntary registration scheme introduced in London following Roche, was a failure: 61,000 registration tallies were issued under it, against a maximum labour requirement in the port of some 30,000.

But Bevin's evidence to Roche revealed much of his thinking on the subject of the dockers' status. He told the Committee that 'if we are to develop the right kind of citizenship and good discipline for all those engaged in this trade', then it became necessary

> for us to have something to lose. The present position is that the main bulk of casual workers have nothing to lose . . . Therefore I think some form of registration will build up a kind of status in the trade which will make a man feel that if he is thrown out of the trade and loses his position in the calling through being guilty of some kind of misdemeanour . . . he is really losing something.

And he demanded that the registration scheme, including this implied disciplinary function, should be administered on the workers' side by 'actual workmen'. Roche recommended this principle, but confined it to a purely voluntary process, and ducked the question of maintenance.

## Bevin versus Bowley

But first Bevin had to establish his case for 16s. a day, and his argument for its application to be standard throughout all the ports. In the first case, his advocacy became famous, then and ever after, for his scathing treatment of the distinguished academic statistician A. L. Bowley, who was brought on by the employers to demonstrate how cheaply might be bought the necessities adequate for the docker's standard of life. Bevin had said that £6 a week was necessary for a family of five to live on. Bowley claimed that £3 12s. 6d. was enough. Bevin, assisted by Mae Forcey, went down to Canning Town market and bought the exact amount of vegetables and cheese allowed for in Bowley's diet. He presented these in court, divided on to plates in five portions. He solicited a predictable response from the Birkenhead docker in the witness stand who was asked to comment. Could such a meal sustain a working docker? Not at all. He then rounded on Bowley himself, by presenting him in court with the scraps of bacon, fish and bread which the Professor had allowed for, asking whether a Cambridge don breakfasted on this diet, in these amounts. Bowley protested. Bevin then displayed a Savoy Hotel menu, for which a shipowner, he said, would expect to pay 7s., compared with Bowley's 40s. a week for five people. Did the Professor ever carry 5-hundredweight bags for eight continuous hours? Evidently not. Bowley and his statistics had been hijacked, because his testimony now brought great support to the dockers. The press rallied. Photographers rushed to display Bevin's plates of food. The argument was in the headlines.

## A National Standard

Bevin was concerned, however, not only to achieve the level of the wage claim, but also to establish it as a national standard. He did this by drawing dockers' union witnesses from different ports to testify to the detrimental effects which the low-wage ports had upon the higher paid, and further to insist that those on higher wages would accept a proportionally lower increase under any award which established a national standard wage.

Liverpool wages were his particular target, as we have seen they had been in previous exchanges with Sexton over the years.[12] Bevin called W. Paul, Dockers' Union secretary in Southampton, to testify that the employers 'have always insisted . . . that you should not go above the Liverpool rate', and that 'if Liverpool's wages went up they would have no objection to Southampton's wages going up'.[13]

Joseph Houghton, general secretary of the Scottish Dockers' Union, was summoned. Bevin elicited from him the fact that the opposition of the Glasgow port employers to the forty-four hour week in 1919 was argued on the basis of the threat of competition from Liverpool, where wage rates were 2s. 4d. a day lower than in Glasgow. Sexton, sitting by Bevin's side as his 'junior' throughout these proceedings, might have been excused if he found this leitmotif played on his men's pay scales distinctly galling! Bevin then won from Houghton the critical commitment to support for a standard wage. Since Glasgow men were then on 14s. and Liverpool men on 11s. 8d., Liverpool would win a larger increase than Glasgow if 16s. were established as the national rate. Would they, he asked, 'for the purpose of making common cause . . . accept the 16s.?' Yes, indeed, was the answer.[14]

R. H. Farrah, NTWF Humberside district secretary, and an official of the NUGW, who had been a docker in Hull for sixteen years and an official for ten years, held to the same position. The wage in Hull was 11s. 8d., with no piece-rates to compensate for the fact that Hull's dockers worked at piece-work speeds. It was a very important grain port, supplying the flour mills which lined the river Hull by transferring the cargo 'overside' from ship to barge for conveyance to the mills. Despite this natural advantage, nearby ports on the Humber were enjoying higher wages. Given their currently strong bargaining position, Hull's dockers had made a claim for £1 a day, and struck for its achievement on the eve of the national claim's presentation. Bevin led Farrah into an account of how the Federation had persuaded the Hull men to return to work. He, too, insisted that they would loyally accept a reduction of their demand to 16s.[15]

These exchanges illustrate both the advantages and the sacrifices for the dockers, in adhering to the concept of the national wage, for which the Federation and Bevin in court drove so hard. But Farrah was able to demonstrate the strength of the case for national rates, from Hull's industries which were ancillary to the docks; on the JIC for flour-milling and the JIC for paints and colours, he had negotiated inclusive rates of 76s. plus two weeks' holiday with pay, and 63s. plus two weeks' holiday, respectively.[16] Bevin did not fail to draw out these comparisons.

## *Decasualization*

Bevin, as we have seen, was the principal architect of the transport workers' schemes for decasualization of the dock labour, and we must revert to this question in looking at the use which he made of the platform now available at the Shaw Inquiry to develop his case. This issue has been extensively researched by academic commentators, and none have been more thorough than Gordon Phillips and Noel Whiteside.[17] They have been chiefly interested in the role of state intervention in this field, which reaches back, as we have seen, to the Liberal administrations of late Victorian and Edwardian times, in a tradition of state paternalism about the casual labour problem, which, as we shall see in vol. II, was almost abandoned in the inter-war years. Their findings coincide with ours, and with generations of labour historians. In the period from the 1880s to the 1940s it is true to say that 'the constraints on state intervention in industry proved as striking as its extent: schemes for the reform of port employment rarely produced the effect that policy makers intended, since dockers and employers alike turned out to be adept at modifying official initiatives to suit their own ends.'[18] This was certainly true of the pioneering clearing-house scheme in the Liverpool docks of 1912 (see chapter 12.)

Bevin's contribution to this story is of course uniquely important. As a radical trade-union leader, he sought in all his proposals for decasualization to extend union control, and to make the employers responsible for financing minimum fall-back maintenance payments, thus excluding, as far as possible, direct state regulation. He was a bilateralist, rather than a proponent of corporate tripartite solutions. And if the state would not legislate in this spirit, he fell back on collective bargaining to achieve his ends. He was also hardly unaware that his advocacy enhanced the role and the potential for leadership of his own union, the DWRGWU, in the struggle for hegemony between rival port unions.

The dock registration schemes in existence in 1920, at the time of the Shaw Inquiry, were not working effectively, for they were all entirely voluntary.[19] Both employers and unions, from entirely different motives, encouraged the over-generous distribution of the tallies entitling their holders to work on the docks. The problem was only aggravated by inter-union rivalries. On the one side stood the principal dockers' unions, seeking to enforce a closed shop, whilst on the other were the general unions demanding recognition of their union cards for access to dock work. This was the rock on which the attempted merger between the dockers' unions and the general unions would very shortly founder. Partly for these reasons, and partly because the slump came to reinforce the employers' resistance to an effective, bargained scheme, and allowed the state to revert to a *laissez-faire* posture, at no time in the whole inter-war period did registration schemes make any significant impact on .the casual nature of port employment.[20] But this is to anticipate the outcome.

## Opposition from the Dockers

In 1920 the state, through its civil servants, was still pressing vigorously for registration. The Ministry of Labour urged Lord Shaw himself to take a wide view of his terms of reference and allow Bevin to develop the case. But Bevin was faced from the outset with opposition from some dockers themselves. A tough resistance came from the men of Glasgow, who had successfully stopped the extension of the Liverpool scheme before the war, and who had also opposed wartime controls.

Bevin pressed Joseph Houghton hard at the Inquiry, in order to elucidate the men's position. It was rooted in pre-industrial attitudes to work discipline, and to regulated systems of payment. Houghton explained that one objection was that registration would mean a transition to weekly, as opposed to daily, payment of wages. But at the heart of the matter was their fear 'of losing what they call their liberty and their freedom so far as selecting their work is concerned . . . at the present time, they have a right either to work or not, as they like.'[21]

Houghton reported overwhelmingly adverse votes by his members to registration, first in 1912 and then again in 1919. These decisions had been taken in spite of the fact that, on both occasions, he and his Executive had endorsed the proposals. Resistance was also opposed to the vesting of any power of discipline in a Board, even one constituted with 50 per cent union representation. (Bevin, we recall, had envisaged such powers in his submission to the Roche Committee.) The men, Houghton was quite adamant, would not have a government-imposed scheme. What then, asked Lord Shaw and Bevin, if the NTWF came to Glasgow to recommend such a scheme? Houghton tried hard to envisage its acceptance: 'It would certainly be more likely to have a better effect; it would be more likely to succeed than anything emanating from the employers' side, or the Government.' Lord Shaw wanted cast-iron assurances, however, and immediately followed with: 'So that if the Court recommended a scheme of registration, with an indication of its leading to subsistence . . . and the Federation was responsible for its acceptance or rejection, and the Federation accepted it as a Federation, there is not much likelihood, judging from past experience of the Federation's activities, of your district turning down the Federation?' But this was too much for Houghton to endorse. He replied: 'On everything else, I do not believe they would, but on this question of registration, I believe they would defy the Federation. I am speaking plain.'[22]

This position was not universal, as Farrah demonstrated in respect of Hull, where, he reported, there was a functioning registration scheme administered by a Port Labour Committee. It worked well, he contended, because to obtain registration a man had to produce a union card (and there were at least three unions involved – the DWRGWU, the NUDL and the NUGW). The unions could, in this way, stop 'every Tom, Dick and Harry' from coming on the docks. There were 9,000 effectively registered dockers, who averaged at that time four days' work a week. Some were, admittedly, unwilling to work more than this. The unions also had a Disputes Committee jointly with the Chamber of Commerce.

Dissatisfaction in Hull centred on the employers' resistance to reforming the 'tin-pot system' of calling-on. There were no call-stands, either in or out of the dock gates: 'our men are started at the ship's side'. (This system prevailed through the inter-war years, and gave rise to the cheerful title of 'gangway-enders' for the veterans of those years, who now run their own retired dockers' club in Hull.) The Federation had asked in vain for the provision of call-stands and linking telephones to facilitate mobility. The Hull dockers could depend only upon an informed grapevine to learn where, on Hull's 7 miles of dock fronts, there might be work. Many used to take evening walks to the riverside to spot the arrival of ships.[23] Farrah had ascertained that the Ministry of Labour would have paid for stands and for 'stamping cards', but some of the employers had frustrated all reform.

At Bristol, the Inquiry heard, a Port Labour Committee with 50 per cent union representation had co-opted a Ministry of Labour official as its secretary. The union, however, was solely responsible for issuing the tallies of registration.[24] Concerning Southampton, the court learned of a problem endemic in the ports owned by railway companies. The railway dock company there refused to operate a registration scheme for casual dockers. But they provided permanent employment for their own staff of porters, who worked cargo on the quay, wherever it was moved in and out of railway rolling-stock. These men were members of the National Union of Railwaymen.[25]

Sexton, working alongside Bevin at the Inquiry, had by this time discovered a sympathy for the old dockers' spirit, which had not been evident in the pioneering days of Liverpool's own clearing house, or during the war. He wrote in his 1920 Annual Report of 'the obstacles in the way of establishing a scheme of maintenance', which included the very humane [*sic*] and natural fear of the older men being crushed out, and the practice and experience of over half a century of the free and easy Bohemian spirit of the workman being at liberty to choose his own employer, and to take a day off without running the extreme risk of the permanently employed man of being thrown out of employment ... In the case of the casual labourer this spirit is stronger than in any other workman, owing to a long-established custom, and must be considered and reckoned with in any contemplated change.[26]

## Shaw Condemns Casualism

The Shaw Report found in favour of registration and also endorsed the principle of employer-financed maintenance, without specifying the details of a universal scheme. But this was no more than Bevin asked for. In his closing speech he had spoken pragmatically. Trial and error was the expected road.

> You, with your experience in Parliament, know that in shaping Bills you have never been able to see, My Lord, the exact structure and organisation that is going to develop ... You agree to the principle; you place it in a Bill and your structure begins to grow and you change it with experience until you finally get the right method to solve your problems.[27]

The court's general condemnation of casualism could scarcely have been more forthright: 'labour frequently or constantly under-employed is injurious to the interests of the workers, the ports, and the public ... it is discreditable to society. It undermines all security, and is apt to undermine all self-respect on the worker's part ... it must be torn up by the roots. It is wrong.'[28]

Quite evidently, the court had been influenced by Bevin's opening peroration, which deserves to be remembered:

> If your Court refuse our claim I suggest that you must adopt an alternative. You must go to the Prime Minister, you must go to the Minister of Education and tell him to close our schools, tell him that industry can only be run by artisan labour on the pure fodder or animal basis, teach us nothing, let us learn nothing, because to create aspirations in our minds, to create the love of the beautiful and then at the same time to deny us the wherewithal to obtain it, is a false policy and a wrong method to adopt. Better keep us in dark ignorance, never to know anything, if you are going to refuse us the wherewithal to give expression to those aspirations which have thus been created.[29]

## Sixteen Shillings (and a JIC)

The employers accepted for the time being the 16s. a day as had been expected, and organized themselves into their own National Council of Port Labour Employers to negotiate its implementation. True, this process went through thanks to past pressure from the Ministry of Labour. They also agreed to the formation of the National Joint Industrial Council for the industry, through which to conduct regular collective bargaining. The NTWF sent an urgent message to port unions and districts, that on no account were they to settle for any local variation on the Shaw findings which undercut the national standard so established. It is a supreme and bitter irony for the present authors that, as they were drafting this chapter in 1989, the contemporary press was reporting the abolition of the National Dock Labour Boards which had decasualized port labour in 1946. Worse, most newspapers were celebrating the employers' unilateral termination of the NJIC and nationally standard wages and conditions.

The Shaw Report carried a sting in its tail. The employers had made much in their evidence not only of slack time-keeping – whereby, they claimed, they lost an hour a day of the men's forty-four-hour contracted labour – but also of consciously slow work, or 'ca' canny'. On this practice, the majority Report was severe:

> The system known as ca' canny is loss on every side. The workman gains nothing in time. Even with regard to his habits and character as well as the dignity of his calling, the things which to every decent man are really precious, loss and deterioration and injury occur. It must be so under a system which substitutes for honest work a scheme of make-believe . . . it is time adulterated . . . there is only one answer, to all such devices; honesty forbids.[30]

For Bevin, of course, the Shaw Inquiry was a personal as well as a trade-union triumph. He was fêted at union conferences and at a special celebration rally at the Albert Hall. He chose to use these gatherings to speak of grand concepts and to lift his audience to a sense of its own dignity and pride:

> Before our movement developed . . . you responded to the whip; I want you to respond to the call of liberty. I want self-discipline, self-sacrifice, self-control, to take the place of the whip . . . There are ninety-nine per cent of the men and women in this audience tonight who believe they are of a lower order than the other class. You accept it, and I want to get rid of it.[31]

## II

## *Maintenance or Insurance?*

The NTWF lost no time in placing its demands for a maintenance scheme before the new NJIC, on which Bevin and Lord Devonport sat as joint chairmen. In September 1920, the Federation asked for a guaranteed minimum income of £4 a week, equivalent to five days at the new standard wage, for all registered dockers. The Federation wanted registration to be made compulsory, and union membership to be obligatory for registration as a docker. To qualify for maintenance pay, dockers would be required to report at call-stands at designated hours. The scheme would be financed by a levy of £4 a ton on all cargoes passing through British ports, together with a state contribution in lieu of its otherwise standard obligations under the new (1920) national unemployment insurance scheme. The administration of the whole scheme would be by joint committees of employers and unions in the ports, but the unions would retain sole power of discipline over dockers for breaches of the scheme.[32]

The unions had long regarded state intervention in the industry with suspicion. Tillett had inveighed against labour exchanges as symbols of state oppression in pre-war days. Now they sought to exclude the unemployment insurance scheme from the port industry for similar reasons, as an intrusion on men's privacy. More, they saw the scheme, with its waiting days and contributory elements, as quite inappropriate for an industry working with casual labour.

Sexton, from his seat in the Commons, was shadowing the passage of what became the National Insurance Act of 1920. He demanded the substitution, right across industry, of a non-contributory scheme:

On the second reading of the Bill, I took the opportunity of moving its rejection, and suggested the setting up of an Act by which unemployment and under-employment became a charge upon the industry without the workman or the employer being asked to contribute directly; and in the course of a speech which follows I gave the following example of what would happen [under the government proposals]: The figure 0 means one day idle, and X means one day employed. Thus, 0X0 means the first three days of the week, and as the man must be unemployed for two days continuous he does not qualify under the Act at all. Again, the last three days of the week may be the same as the first, 0X0, or he may get only a half-day on the fifth day, which again disqualifies him. Even though he fully qualifies as thus, 00XX00, he is only entitled as a probationary to one day's unemployment at the end of the week though he has been idle four days. True, this is only for the first week; but the casual's first week may be his last for he may again get his 0X0 the first three days of the following week, so that the under-employed man's industrial OXO has quite the opposite effect than has that very nourishing food one sees so extensively advertised.

Sexton concluded that the Act was 'pernicious' in its application to docks.[33]

## The Employers' Comeback

But in 1921 there was a calamitous collapse into slump. Now the employers felt quite strong enough to resist the Federation scheme. They claimed that their contributions under the National Insurance Act fulfilled their obligation to the industry's unemployed, and moreover that the escalation in the numbers out of work in 1921 had doubled the reassuring estimate of the costs of Bevin's scheme, which he had submitted in the previous year. And in purely actuarial terms, there was no gainsaying the truth, that as the need for maintenance grew with the slump, so did its costs to the employers. Given these calculations, and the new balance of forces through the rest of the 1920s and 1930s, the high hopes and expectations of 1920 faded from view and attention. The dockers were compelled instead to turn to desperate attempts to defend themselves against wage cuts, as we shall see in vol. II.

The Shaw Report's 16s. did not survive the slump by more than two years. Its recommendations on decasualization were brusquely set aside by the employers. Its wage award, and the pacific manner of its achievement, have been seen by some as yet another government-established device to keep the partners in the Triple Alliance divided and preoccupied with their own sectional affairs. There is truth in this. Writing of the government's fears of a united labour insurgency in 1919–20, James Cronin remarked: 'The government was particularly concerned at the prospect of a generalised transport stoppage and so granted wage increases to the railwaymen and set up the Shaw Inquiry for the dockers, whilst simultaneously perfecting its strike-breaking apparatus.'[34]

## Neglecting the Lightermen

Not the least gain, however, was to have compelled the port employers, after a struggle stretching back over forty years, to accept national bargaining and national rates. Bevin's advocacy had also advanced collective negotiating techniques, and in the process put beyond challenge his own – and his union's – bid to lead the push for docks amalgamation. For the unity of the Federation's constituents before the Inquiry had been only barely preserved. Sexton was marginalized. The watermen and the stevedores felt that their cases had been hardly recognized in Bevin's presentations. Bill Lindley, leader of the Watermen and Lightermen's Union after the Second World War, told us in interview in 1988 that Tom Condon, who became the district docks officer of the TGWU for the London region, had confided in him about the causes of the break between lightermen and the TGWU in 1922 'when the ink was hardly dry' on the amalgamation agreement (an important story to which we shall revert in vol. II). Lindley told us:

The break came when Ernie Bevin got the Shaw Award; it meant that lightermen, who were always higher paid than the dockers, didn't get anything, but the dockers got their one-and-sixpence. That put dockers on a par with lightermen. Now Tom Condon, a great old character – I used to get along well with Tom, never mind about the enmity between the two unions – he was telling me when we had a break one day at a meeting we were at, and he said . . . 'You know what happened, Bill? . . . Well, I was there,' he says, 'you take it from me. During a break in that Inquiry, when Bevin was making his name as the Dockers' KC, Gosling had a row with Bevin. He said: "You're not putting the lightermen's case as well as you should." And Bevin said: "I'm here for the dockers, and if you want to put the lightermen's case over, you go and bloody well put it over." In other words, he was anxious to get this dockers' thing. And Condon said: 'Well, Gosling had his say, but didn't do anything like Bevin, and so you [the lightermen] didn't get anything,' he said, 'and that caused the break.'[35]

There is some ring of authenticity in this story. Undoubtedly Bevin's sights were firmly set on the case of the dockers; he had his head down and was going hard for his people. That he was capable of treading on other sectional corns in that process, as in the subsequent drive for amalgamation, is not to be doubted.

Was Gosling making an oblique reference to these divisions when he opened the inaugural meeting of the TGWU at Leamington Spa in 1921? Extracts from his speech were reported in the TWGU *Record*:

What seemed to him the real declaration of need [for amalgamation] occurred at the great dockers' inquiry, where it was found that, amalgamated or not, they must appear united and put up a strong front to the employers. But – he did not think he was giving away secrets – they went into the inquiry with a very thin front. Fortunately they held together, and a great deal of credit for keeping it together was due to friend Bevin, who dealt with the problem in a very masterful way, but he at the time was probably trembling in case he had to admit the weakness of the solidarity he was supposed to represent. This brought clearly to them the necessity for closer co-operation.[36]

Was 'masterful' an unambiguous word of praise, or did it have a critical undertone? We can read the speech, but we cannot hear it, so we do not know.

## 'More Than a Penny an Hour'

Gosling's commitment to amalgamation was certainly strong enough to suppress any temptation to wash dirty linen in the public forum of the Leamington Spa conference on the very eve of unity. There is no doubt that Bevin's model was of a docks industry administered jointly by a centralized and disciplined employers' federation, and an equally centralized port-workers' union with a closed shop. He did not want a loose alliance of unions in which the 'Federation card' allowed all and sundry from transport and general unions to encroach on that preserve. This will become clearer when we examine the pre-amalgamation conflict over dock work in which the DWRGWU collided with the NUGW. In the moment of his triumph, however, Bevin was conscious of having made the public impact he had planned. Much later he told his friend, and later biographer, Francis Williams: 'People thought all that business with plates was just a clever stunt. It wasn't. These fellows quote statistics but they forget about human beings. I had to make 'em remember they were dealing with human lives – it's terribly easy to forget that when you're sitting in a Court or on a Government Commission.'[37]

And there need be no doubt that Bevin's wider compassions and radical visions, to which he gave expression after the Inquiry, had the sound of conviction in them. He told the Albert Hall rally that the Inquiry 'had been an opportunity to unfold the great human tragedy of men and women fighting year in and year out against the terrible economic conditions with which they are surrounded. Although my speech lasted eleven hours, let me say that no tongue exists, no voice is capable, no pen can write, no artist can paint, the real human tragedy that is behind it all.' And he went on: 'when the time comes, if it ever does, for a great struggle between Capital and Labour, I want it to be for something bigger than a penny an hour . . . I want it to have a definite object – that of achieving for those who toil the mastery of their own lives.'[38]

One morsel of life mastery survived the combined onslaughts of a slump economy and the employers through dismal years ahead. Bevin clung to it tenaciously even whilst negotiating wage cuts (the national rate was to fall to just 10s. by 1923, amidst great controversy for the leader of the new TGWU). This was the 1919 gain of the forty-four-hour week. It was won by centralized bargaining and without benefit of Courts of Inquiry. We may let Sexton, by now Bevin's shadow and no longer a serious rival for leadership, have the last word amongst his contemporaries: 'it must be admitted that it was a great achievement to so concentrate the power of transport workers, scattered about and mixed up with general labourers in at least 33 unions, as to establish a minimum uniform rate of 16/– a day.'[39]

We shall come upon other key moments at which it is fitting to reflect upon the nature of port unionism in Britain. But the Shaw Award certainly represents one such moment, as did the 1889 strike and the strikes of 1911–12. Whilst the dockers formed the essential base upon which the wide general unionism of the TGWU was to be built, reaching out into hundreds of industries, they were always to be the most difficult to integrate into that broad unity.

## *The Dockers and Trade-union Unity*

The dockers' needs varied according to the state of trade and the economy, and, over longer years, with the secular changes in both transport technology and the ownership patterns in their industry. When these factors rendered the supply of dock labour over-abundant, they needed to make common cause with general labour and to form the widest possible political alliances, to win by peaceful and legislative means what bargaining and industrial militancy could not deliver. When trade boomed, and their hold on their labour supply was more secure, and when eventually a statutory scheme of labour control was won, then their methods changed dramatically, and trade-union organization and leadership either had to change with it or risk internal conflict with its docker members.

In addition to these swings of fortune, the port membership was spatially and occupationally fragmented. Sexton's reference to the '33 unions' of 1920 says it all. Only a determined, visionary, and at times ruthless, exercise of central union control, impervious to sectional sensitivities, could have welded these disparate elements – corn-porters, coalies, stevedores, lightermen, deal-carriers, lumpers and the rest, into a coherent force. In 1920–1 Bevin judged that restraint and subtle diplomacy might, at this moment, be supplemented with decisive initiative. As a result he was to shape a very strong trade union and, for himself, a position of remarkable authority. H. A. Turner coined the phrase 'popular bossdom' to describe this kind of leadership.[40]

But the force of organization, and the will of one man, could not permanently suppress sectional interests. They needed their own space within the whole. Lindley's story about the breakaways of lightermen and stevedores in London was repeated more than once in the following years. The Scottish dockers' long insistence on independence, the secession of Hull and Liverpool dockers from the TGWU in the 1950s: these and more examples illustrate the dilemma – that whilst 'popular bossdom' might be successful in unifying a wide section of working-class occupations and industries, it could not always find reserves of tolerance with which to meet the needs of the stronger groups under its sway.

This volatility led John Lovell, for example, to conclude that port unionism in its historical trajectory reveals no 'meaningful pattern of growth'.[41] Of course, Lovell's subject was London, the most volatile of all the ports. Hobsbawm, on the other hand, discerns clearly enough a progressive movement towards national, industrial, unionism within the context of general unionism.[42] This is surely right. This movement did not follow a straight line: it was a contradictory and embattled process, and a highly uneven one at that. But there are obvious moments of qualitative change, in 1889, 1911, and the point at which we make this digression from our narrative: the Shaw Inquiry and the now clear pre-eminence of Bevin, equipped through this triumph with the power to force through amalgamation.

Not everyone saw things this way at the time. From the far past there was to come a mordant comment on the meaning of the Shaw Inquiry. In 1928 Walter Citrine, recently appointed general secretary of the TUC, went to visit John Burns at his house on Clapham Common. He wanted his autograph on a history of the Congress, so he went along with Alf Purcell and George Hicks to request it. Burns cross-questioned Purcell about the Russian Revolution, for which he expressed himself in warm support. Then he turned to Citrine:

'I want to ask you something, Citrine. Why is the trade union movement moving over to the Left?'

I said, 'I think it is merely a reaction to the political situation generally.'

Burns continued: 'Do you think, Citrine, that the trade union movement has passed the stage at which it must continue to lose members?'

'Yes,' I replied, 'positively. The reports from the unions indicate a definite increase.'

Burns went on: 'Well, I am a trade unionist of forty years' standing, and I think I am in a position to speak. I think you are making a big mistake in the trade union world. You are devoting too much of your time to charts and plans and statistics. Good God! When I see the General Secretary of the Glass Dolls' Clothing Weavers' Union going to a labour conference he carries a dossier with him. You are trying to turn out records and reports like Government Blue Books. You are neglecting getting out to the street corners. And the men are getting fed up with it too. You will be losing them. Look at Bevin. He goes to the dockers' inquiry, and he puts on a plate so many pennyworths of bread and potatoes and cabbages and God knows what else, and thinks he is winning his case. Why? I went to that inquiry. Practically every man on the Court asked me to go and sit with them on this dais, as an old organizer of the '89 dock strike. But I said: "No, it is not my job. I am merely here to look on." And I told the employers who spoke to me that they were going to get it in the neck. Why? Because Lord Shaw – one of the most incapable of judges – was out to get his name down on the pages of history as the man who gave the Shaw Award. I told the employers that he would give the dockers £5 a day, never mind 16s.. You don't know what men will do to get themselves into the picture. There are too many cinematograph leaders in the trade union movement – too many of you want to be in the picture.'[43]

But we now return to the wider context of 1920.

# III

## *The Case of the* Jolly George

At the end of April 1920 the Poles set out upon their invasion of Russia. It was widely felt that their inspiration in this attack came from London, Paris or both. In Britain, left-wing groups had established a 'Hands Off Russia' Committee in the summer of 1919.[44] It included the *Daily Herald*, and it also knit together activists from the British Socialist Party, the Socialist Labour Party, the Workers' Socialist Federation (led by Sylvia Pankhurst, the suffragist leader who was extremely active in East London), and the Shop Stewards' National Committee. Among union leaders giving support were Tom Mann, who had now become, after a lifetime of membership, the engineers' secretary; C. T. Cramp of the railwaymen; Straker of the miners; and Purcell of the TUC. A hitherto unknown boilermaker, Harry Pollitt, became national organizer.

On 10 May 1920, the Polish expedition reached Kiev. During that same day, the Watford line steamship, *Jolly George*, was waiting to be loaded in the East India dock. Its intended cargo arrived bearing labels saying 'O.H.M.S. Munitions for Poland'. Would the dockers load such freight? A deputation went off to the London district secretary, Fred Thompson, and then to Ernest Bevin, who was deputy general secretary, the national officer in charge. It was established that the men would receive union support if they declined to continue loading the ship. Straightaway the arms shipment was blacked. Coal-heavers also refused to charge the ship. It was strikebound. After five days, the shipowners conceded. The *Jolly George* discharged that part of its cargo which had already been loaded, and left it all on the dockside. This strike, wrote Pollitt, 'was the result of two years' tremendously hard and unremitting work on the part of a devoted band of comrades in East London.'[45]

Whilst there is every reason to accept that the intensive agitation by London socialists had come home to the dockers, it would be a mistake to downplay the part played by the Dockers' Union itself in the whole matter. True, Fred Thompson was a member of the BSP, soon to become a founder of the new Communist Party. But the deputation of dockers went also to see Bevin. It was, after all, a highly centralized union. 'Without hesitating,' wrote Alan Bullock, 'he told them they could count on the union's backing'.[46] Only a week later, the union gathered for its Triennial Delegate Conference, which took place on 18–22 May in Plymouth. First item of all was an emergency motion, presented by Bevin himself:

> That this Triennial Conference records its emphatic protest against the export of arms to Poland and other border States, which enables the Junkers of those countries to set the people at war in the interests of their financial paymasters. It congratulates our London members in refusing to have their labour prostituted for this purpose, and calls upon the whole of the movement to resist their labour being used to perpetuate these wicked ventures. We further demand the abolition of secret diplomacy, on the grounds that it will be impossible to maintain the peace of the world while the differences between peoples are dealt with behind closed doors, and decisions binding peoples arrived at without their knowledge and consent.

In opening, Bevin came straight to the point: 'I want to take the opportunity in the early part of the Triennial Conference to move this resolution.' He could not have been earlier: the doors were hardly open. He went on:

> You have an admission in the Press from Mr. Bonar Law that the munitions for this recent Polish war have been supplied by the British Government. I do not believe that the present Government has the authority of the democracy of this country either to lend a single penny or to supply a single gun to carry on further war against Russia. Whatever may be the merits or demerits of the theory of government of Russia, that is a matter for Russia, and we have no right to determine their form of government, any more than we would tolerate Russia determining our form of government. My sympathy goes out to the Poles and Ukrainians. Here are a people who have been promised their freedom, promised their liberty, now being conscripted by the thousand to start another war against Russia, and the poor Pole is being driven into that war again and he has no desire to fight. I am talking about the common people of Poland. They have no quarrel. Peace has been offered to the border States. A satisfactory peace can be arrived at with the border States, but the whole policy of the peace diplomacy appears to be one of the most sordid materialism that the world has ever seen. Here you set these peoples at each other's throats again, not because there is any people to free, not because you are going to save the Poles or save the Russians, but in order that the Western financiers can regain the grain belt of Southern Russia. I think, and I hope you think with me, that the time has come for the more advanced democracies of the Western world to raise their voices in protest against our or any other Government inspiring these people to fight their battles for them and supply them with munitions to shoot one another in our own financial interest.

Bevin was evidently not going to drift into any replay of 1914.

> I was glad that when the London dockers realised that the *Jolly George* was to go to Poland with munitions, they absolutely refused to load her. When

the shipowner got on the telephone to me and said, 'What about my ship?' I told him to ask Bonar Law or Lloyd George, as I was not going to ask the dockers to put a gun in a ship or to carry on these further wicked ventures and wars among people in the East. If they had opened trade with Russia after the second revolution, Russia would have been settled down long ere this, and the world would not be lop-sided from the point of view of exchange, as it is at the present moment. I think the working people – I have not talked about direct action and general strikes – have a right to say where their labour and how their labour shall be used, and if we are being called upon either to make munitions or transport munitions for purposes which outrage our sense of justice, then I think we have a right to refuse to have our labour prostituted to carry on wars of this character.

Having firmly endorsed the principle of action for peace, he went on to advocate the cause of open diplomacy, so strenuously developed by the anti-war lobby of the earliest war years, in the pamphlets of the Union of Democratic Control:

Just a word on the second part of the resolution. Away down in the south of England at a great financier's house, Sir Philip Sassoon's, at the present moment, the fates of peoples are being decided. Nobody knows what is happening except the great financial and capitalist interest. Very meagre reports are placed before the House of Commons itself. Parliament is having little or nothing to say on the great question, which must determine at least for a century to come what the conditions of the world are going to be. As I have indicated in all the speeches I have made on this problem, if anyone attempted to shut Parliament up in your own country and to decide the laws which should govern the destiny of the people of this country behind closed doors, you would be outraged. You would say, 'Throw open the doors of Parliament. Let us see what our representatives are doing in the light of day.' In the Courts of Law you insist that the doors shall be open, and I say it is a thousand times more important where millions of people are involved. I think the Labour Party itself might be a little more emphatic on this point than they are at the present moment. I believe the people of the world want their differences discussed in the light of day, and I believe there is very little difference between us when it is discussed in the light of day.

To hammer this point home, he skilfully deployed the most convincing industrial analogy, which his audience could immediately comprehend:

One of the greatest features of the Dockers' Inquiry was that it was conducted in the light of day, and it has done more to create confidence than if we had had a million arbitrations behind closed doors. As far as I am personally concerned, I say emphatically, with a full sense of responsibility, wherever a man is called upon to make munitions, ship munitions, or do anything else to enable the Junker people, who are in the pay of the financial houses of France, America, and Great Britain, to set these people as mere pawns or tools to fight one another in various parts of the world, I will not be party to it.[47]

For the time being, the British Government 'was content not to force the issue'.[48] Kiev surrendered to the Poles in early June. The British posture of 'neutrality' was reaffirmed by Curzon, content to see events unfold by proxy. Soon, however, the Red Army began to recover ground. By August the Poles were running, and soon they were defending Warsaw. Now neutrality was not enough. *The Times* called for war.[49] The *Jolly George* had become the symbol for an altogether more general confrontation.

Bevin's ascendancy in the movement, established at the Shaw Inquiry (the dockers' national minimum wage became operative in May), was further enhanced by this firm endorsement of the *Jolly George* strike. All remembered that in the previous year 'direct action' had been advanced by the leaders of the Triple Alliance, Hodges, Smillie and Williams, to compel the withdrawal of British forces from Russia and an end to conscription. Now, while the Poles were marauding in Russia, the *Jolly George* incident – direct action in miniature – revived Labour's wider, extra-constitutional challenge to British government policy in Eastern Europe. It was certain that the transport unions and their leaders would again play a crucial role in this campaign.

## *Labour Decides for Recognition*

The government, whilst it had withdrawn from direct intervention in Russia, was feeding the Poles with the instruments of war, and adding diplomatic cover for them besides. At the same time, it resisted pressures to restore trading relations with the Russians. Lloyd George raised evasiveness to a new art-form, while Churchill intrigued behind the scenes.

By the time the Labour Party Conference met, on 22–5 June in Scarborough, a Russian counterattack had forced an initial retreat by the Poles, who were nevertheless still on Russian territory. The conference received a report from a joint TUC–Labour Party delegation recently returned from Russia, on which Robert Williams had been one of the Labour Party's Executive representatives. It recommended that the Bolshevik government should be accorded unconditional recognition, and demanded the end of all allied intervention. The conference debated a resolution endorsing these recommendations, and insisting that the British government should end all assistance to the Poles, and resume trade relations with Russia. A Russian Economic Mission was in London at the time. Its team was headed by Leonid Krasin and Lev Kamenev, who met with Labour leaders while this crisis developed.

The British Socialist Party, still affiliated to the Labour Party, moved an addendum calling for the convening of a National Labour and Trade Union Conference to organize a general strike which could force these demands on the government.[50] Colonel l'Estrange Malone, MP, a delegate from the BSP, rose to speak on this addendum. There followed an immediate storm of protest from some quarters, in which Bevin was prominent. They challenged the Colonel's right to speak, since he was still accepting Asquithian Liberal whips in the Commons. The debate was interrupted whilst the Standing Orders Committee investigated Malone's credentials. It found that his status as a BSP delegate was valid, although it deplored that party's choice of such a delegate.

## Bevin Reserves His Position

Malone's speech was an indictment of the pusillanimous stance of the movement; only direct action would shift the government, and it should be adopted immediately. Bevin replied, at first by recalling that Malone had fought the last election on the slogans 'Hang the Kaiser' and 'Make Germany Pay'. This provoked disorder in the conference: Malone's supporters protested, and the chairman had to call on Bevin to stick to the resolution. Bevin was undeterred; he had made a damaging attack on his antagonist. But he went on to argue that the addendum should be defeated 'because he wanted the movement to take the requisite action at the proper time when circumstances determined. If they continued to debate the theory of Direct Action versus Political Action they would cripple both.'

His intervention was therefore not a condemnation of direct action as such, but a characteristic reservation of positions until such time as the circumstances warranted it. Moreover, he always resented those who, from outside the trade-union movement, sought to tell it when and how to act. But he also went to the heart of the problem of credibility; the continental movement was looking to them for light and leadership, and to threaten strike action at this stage would mislead Lenin and Trotsky. In June, the military situation in Russia was not critical, but it was very shortly to become so and to precipitate a crisis which made 'the requisite action' appropriate.

In early July, the *Daily Herald* published a confidential document which reawakened Labour's apprehension that Churchill had not abandoned hopes of supplying the White Russian leaders with 'volunteers'.[51] As the Polish army went into headlong retreat, even to the gates of Warsaw, the British government announced that further advance by the Soviets would call forth its direct assistance to Poland. By early August a full-scale war emergency was on hand, with *The Times* pronouncing on the 6th that 'we must face it with the same courage with which we faced the crisis of 1914'. The *Daily Herald* countered with a famous headline: 'Not a Man, Not a Gun, Not a Sou!'

## Councils of Action

Trade-union and Labour leaders issued, on 7 August, a manifesto against war, and Bevin led the list of signatories. Besides Tom Mann and Robert Williams, this included such moderate leaders as J. R. Clynes and Arthur Henderson, together with a galaxy of other influential names. The manifesto accused the 'war party' of using 'supreme efforts' to 'involve us in a war against Russia'. Like the special TUC, it approved of 'any and all action' to maintain the peace. Thousands of resolutions poured into the head offices of the Labour Party and the TUC.[52] Now Bevin, changing gear sharply from his June speech, took the initiative in calling a conference of the TUC, and the Labour Party Executive and parliamentary wings, which met on 9 August. It was Bevin again who there proposed the formation of a Council of Action, which the conference endorsed, together with a statement that 'the whole industrial power of the organised workers will be used to defeat this war'. Following this central lead, some 350 local Councils of Action were formed.

The Prime Minister acknowledged the power of the movement his government had provoked; he received a deputation from the Council the following day – 10 August. Bevin was chosen to state its case to Lloyd George; his words were recorded by the deputation's own shorthand writer and published the following day in the *Daily Herald*.[53] He spoke at length, affirming Labour's opposition not only to direct war, but to blockades and the supply of munitions to Russia's enemies. He challenged the right of any state to take up arms against a revolutionary regime abroad, and condemned the reactionary, dominant influence of Britain's ally, France. He went on:

> if the war with Russia is carried on directly in support of Poland, or indirectly in support of General Wrangel [leader of the last remnant of the anti-communist White Russian army in the Crimea], there will be a match set to an explosive material the result of which none of us can foresee today . . . We are ready and determined to resist the triumph of reaction and war . . . It is not merely a political action, but an action representing the full force of Labour and we believe it represents the desire of the great majority of the British people.

In reply, Lloyd George used soft words.[54] But he cast doubts on Russia's defensive purpose in carrying the war into Poland, whose independence he judged to be threatened. Bevin countered by proposing that the Council of Action should itself meet the Russian representatives Krasin and Kamenev to establish that Polish independence was secure. Later that same day, the Russians published generous peace terms which included such a guarantee. When Lloyd George expressed continued suspicion of the Russian offer, Bevin conducted a series of meetings with Kamenev and Krasin, followed by another visit to Downing Street. The Council of Action also sent its own direct messages to Moscow, urging Soviet adherence to the published terms.

## Bevin Endorses Direct Action

Whilst this remarkable Labour diplomacy was under way, a mass delegate meeting representing the entire Labour movement gathered on 13 August in Westminster Hall to reinforce its words with the threat of action. Bevin delivered a report of the Council's negotiations, and provided a rallying call: 'I hope Labour is going to fight this to the bitter end . . . Our great work in life until now has been mainly wages, but . . . this question you are called upon to decide today – the willingness to take action to win world peace – transcends any claim in connection with wages or hours of labour.'[55]

The Special Labour Conference then resolved to authorize the Council of Action 'to call for any and every withdrawal of Labour which circumstances may require.'[56] It also invited the membership 'to act swiftly, loyally, and courageously in order to sweep away secret bargaining and diplomacy', and to ensure 'an end to war and the interminable threats of war'.

Support for this dramatic declaration came from all wings of the movement at the rally, including such pillars of the Labour establishment as Clynes and Thomas. The Council of Action should remain in being until its objectives had been achieved.

In the event, the Council did not need to carry out its threat. The Polish army rallied in front of Warsaw, and drove the Russians out of its country; an armistice on 12 October ended the crisis, but throughout those months the Councils stayed in being, monitoring signs of munitions movements. It had been a remarkable moment in Labour and trade-union history; all shades of opinion had swung behind their own leadership in a clearly unconstitutional, but overwhelmingly popular call to direct action. Bevin's leadership, including above all his important decisions about timing, had been crucial.

'There can be no gainsaying the fact', wrote Robert Williams a year afterwards, 'that Labour in its industrial sphere is far more ready to take revolutionary action than would appear . . . the formation of the Council of Action in 1920 was the result of the painstaking and serious propaganda in favour of revolutionary direct action throughout 1919 on behalf of the Triple Alliance.'[57]

## IV

## *The Fortunes of the Triple Alliance*

In fact, however, things were not to continue in the same vein. It is necessary to examine the fortunes of the miners and the Triple Alliance, and the NTWF's internal conflicts, section by section, as it moved towards amalgamation. The dockers may have been in the limelight, but the movement for unity had many other voices to hear, and interests to reconcile, both within the NTWF and between the three wings of the Triple Alliance.

We saw in the previous chapter that the NTWF, under Bevin's influence, had met the failure of the NUR to involve the Triple Alliance in the railway crisis of 1919 with a most effective initiative of Bevin's own. His *ad hoc* Mediation Committee had in effect substituted for both the Alliance and the TUC, neither of which would or could effectively intervene. Now, in 1920, the miners precipitated a further test of union cohesion in a crisis.

Lloyd George had, with complete impunity, abandoned his commitment to implement the Sankey Report on nationalization. The trade-union movement had shied away from a general strike in 1919. There was little the miners could do. In 1920, without consulting the Triple Alliance, they announced a ballot on strike action over a pay claim. With a two-thirds majority in favour, the Miners' Federation named 25 September for the start of the strike. The government was still in control of the industry and with the owners it made a further offer on a new 'datum line'. The Miners' Federation therefore postponed the strike and called a new ballot, which again supported strike action. The reluctance of the Triple Alliance partners to call for sympathy action, and the pressure exerted by them to persuade the miners to go before a government-offered Tribunal of Inquiry, led them to postpone the strike until 16 October. In this interval, the NTWF debated its attitude and studied the likely effects of the strike on its membership in transport.

Williams canvassed the affiliated unions and reported to the EC, no doubt with personal reluctance, that only ten out of thirty unions were prepared to give his Executive plenary powers to declare supporting action. Bevin was amongst those counselling pacific responses; at a special Triple Alliance conference on 23 September, he had argued that the reluctance of the miners to take up the offer of a Tribunal Inquiry into their claim flew in the face of the evidence of the Shaw Inquiry, that such a procedure could be successful. In fact, Smillie, the miners' president, was in favour of the Tribunal, but Hodges, the secretary, was opposed to it. Triple Alliance support also wilted because the NUR unsuccessfully bid to persuade the miners that the other partners should have a share in the conduct of the dispute.

The NTWF's Executive met frequently throughout the crisis, and the six-man sub-committee of the Triple Alliance was in continuous session from 27 August, awaiting the outcome of a special miners' conference on 2 September. The Transport Workers' Executive roundly declared its support for the justice of the miners' claim from the beginning, yet it had decided already, a week earlier, to make no recommendation to its affiliates about whether they should take action in this cause. Williams reported that some affiliates were urging the miners to resort to the Tribunal which had been offered, whilst others sought a Federation-wide ballot on industrial action.

On 14 October, the Federation received a formal letter from Hodges, telling it that the strike would start 'on Saturday next' and adding, 'in accordance with the constitution of the Alliance, I am informing you of the whole situation'. There was no call here for supporting strikes. The miners in 1920 had exactly followed the example of the NUR in 1919, in acting unilaterally.

The NUR immediately laid plans to call a Special General Meeting; the Federation (with no centralized executive authority like that of the railwaymen) did nothing, beyond recording events and noting the effects of the strike in its districts. No action was discussed, and there were no reports of rank-and-file pressure for supporting action, such as had been boiling up everywhere during the railway strike one year previously. The economic tide was turning, and with it went down any surviving insurgency amongst the transport workers, first in line to feel the effects of a downturn in trade.

On 21 October, the Executive heard that the TUC was to call a special meeting of Congress, and it agreed that, following that, its own General Council should be summoned. 'No good purpose would be served', it resolved, 'by taking action in regard to the mining dispute until after the special meeting called by the TUC'. Thereupon, the transport leaders adjourned their meeting until 27 October, which is to say for six days, in the midst of the crisis.

## A Paper Alliance

But on the very day that the NTWF Executive resolved to postpone action, the NUR conference declared that it would strike if negotiations were not resumed within three days. Lloyd George immediately found an extra 2s. a shift for the miners; the strike was over, the crisis punctured. This was, as it proved, a false dawn. In it, the Triple

Alliance's weaknesses had been concealed rather than overcome. And in it, the NTWF had played no part.

Bevin was, in fact, as we shall see, well advanced in his negotiations for the TGWU amalgamation at this time; neither this episode nor the following year's Black Friday were decisive events in determining either the conviction or the timing behind his drive for the new union. Nevertheless, these events on the widest stage served well to underline his consistent theme that without organization there could be no effective action, and organization must carry executive authority, comprising more than mere alliances or federations.

Bevin had voiced this conclusion already at the height of the crisis, on 24 September, at a Triple Alliance conference: 'My charge is that the six men who are at the head of affairs have not constructed an organisation that is capable of working when the test comes . . . I have said over and over: "When the test comes, if you do not make a real organisation it will be found to be a paper alliance." By God, it has revealed itself to be a paper alliance this week.'[58]

Thereafter, Bevin did not exert himself in the NTWF to promote supporting action for the miners, and Williams, partly in consequence of this and partly because he perceived the evident reluctance of his affiliates, was cribbed and crippled. Locked in the inertia of his organization, all he could do was cajole, exhort, report and comment. That Williams was indeed personally anxious to win his affiliates to action is revealed in the contents of a telegram he sent to a Special District Secretaries' Conference of the DWRGWU, held in Bristol on 2–3 October. It read:

> Greetings to your conference of District Officials – glad to know you are making preparations for all emergencies likely to arise in the near future – possibility miners' strike now postponed for further fortnight – I am convinced transport workers will not contribute to defeat miners' just and equitable claim – courage and steadfastness never more essential than now – hope your conference will exhibit preparedness and solidarity. Robert Williams.

The note of apprehension in this attempt at a rallying call was to be justified by the terse, single word in the Conference minutes which follows it; it says simply: 'Noted'. This was the moment, perhaps, when the delicate fabric of the industrial and political partnership of Williams and Bevin began to tear, with consequences fatal to the Federation and personally tragic for Robert Williams.

The dockers' district secretaries did not discuss preparations for action, but listened dutifully to accounts by Tillett and Bevin of their roles in the crisis, resolving thereafter not upon immediate industrial responses, but upon an endorsement of their leaders' positions, and upon a call for the reorganization of the Triple Alliance, reflecting Bevin's critical stance on its current 'paper' constitution. It read:

> This conference of Officers of the Dockers' Union accepts the report of its representatives on the Triple Alliance.
>
> In view of the weaknesses revealed in the Triple Alliance, and the fact that the whole of the forces of the Government and Capitalists are being organised to resist the efforts of the Labour movement to improve its position, we call upon the component parts of the Triple Alliance to reorganise the Alliance, with a view to creating such a machine as will be capable of functioning in a manner which will lead to success; that the constitution provide for the promotion of agreed programmes and policies; that proper and adequate methods be adopted to influence the public in support of the claims, and that such financial arrangements be made as will secure the necessary funds to carry on the work of the Alliance in a practical and scientific manner.[59]

The conference agreed to submit this resolution to the Executive of the Dockers' Union, for forwarding to the NTWF and the Triple Alliance, but not to publish it. Two constitutional points arise from the resolution and its intended use. Bevin, tacitly supported by Tillett, incorrectly designated the two as representing the Dockers' Union on the Triple Alliance, when in fact he represented the NTWF. This provides a further illustration, along with the attitude he took at the Shaw Inquiry, that Bevin was now putting his weight behind his own union, rather than behind the wider grouping through which he had worked hitherto. This, we shall see, was storing up antagonism to his personal drive for power across the whole field of transport unionism. Increasingly, he came to be seen by his rivals as usurping the functions and authority of the Federation for his own purposes.

Secondly, the district secretaries in conference – a captive group from Bevin's perspective – had no constitutional status in the union, yet were here being used to advance, through the Dockers' Union Executive, a policy directed at the heart of the NTWF and the Alliance. Surely Bevin's purpose may have been a worthy one, but his respect for constitutional niceties was less than rigorous.

The content of the resolution, however, shows that despite his preoccupation with the pending amalgamation (we shall show in the next chapter how endless meetings and the preparation of a ballot to this end were proceeding simultaneously with the wider crises) and despite his disillusion after the events of 1919 and 1920, Bevin did not propose summarily to abandon the Alliance. Consistent with his long-term theme, he sought instead to turn the organization of the Alliance outward to the public which he had so effectively influenced at the Shaw Inquiry, and also to solve the problem of its lack of executive coherence.

This was becoming an urgent defensive need. It was no secret that the government wanted to de-control the mines and that, when that happened, the owners would be back with demands for wage cuts, especially as the slump bit into coal prices. In October 1920 the government bought time, to hone further its strike-breaking weapons and to equip itself with new powers; the Emergency Powers Bill, which had been on and off the stocks for some time, was, in the aftermath of the miners' strike and the threatened rail strike, rushed through its final stages to receive the Royal Assent on 29 October.[60]

Whilst 'the Triple Alliance's inherent weaknesses scarcely showed in October 1920',[61] as the government withdrew from a fight with the railwaymen, the background economic situation, as it worsened, guaranteed that the balance of forces would be different in 1921: 'The coal strike of October 1920 just caught the flood; that of April 1921 ran out on the ebb of government de-control of the mines, and unemployment.'[62]

## Putting Teeth in the TUC

The leaders of the NTWF, who had been responsible for calling the *ad hoc* Mediation Committee in the railway strike of 1919, turned their attention in this hectic year of 1920 to the reform of the TUC. Once again Gosling acted as Bevin's junior partner in a joint enterprise. The *ad hoc* Committee articulated afresh a long-held view on the left of the movement that the Parliamentary Committee was another 'paper tiger', in need of teeth if it was to become a 'General Staff of Labour'. (The military analogy was much in evidence throughout this whole debate.)

Through the rest of 1919 and up to the Congress meeting in 1920, a Co-ordination Committee composed of representatives of the Mediation Committee, the Parliamentary Committee and the trade-union side of the National Industrial Conference met to thrash out a new TUC constitution. Prominent amongst the draftsmen was G. D. H. Cole, from the National Industrial Council's provisional trade-union committee, the only member who was not a trade-union leader. A core scheme of reform had been tabled at the Co-ordination Committee within a week of its formation in November 1919, authored by Bevin. V. L. Allen reports that 'The document reflected an acute emphasis on the industrial solution of trade-union problems. And although Bevin's ideas were not accepted in their entirety they formed the genesis of the final reorganisation.'[63]

The drafters sought to give expression to the concept of a General Council becoming 'a real co-ordinating body for the industrial side of the whole Trade Union Movement.' This reflected the prevalence of syndicalist-tinged tendencies, compounded by the actual frequency of major industrial disputes and by the relative impotence of the political wing of the movement.

Yet in the event, the attempt to vest industrial executive powers in the new General Council faltered before the instincts of individual unions to preserve their autonomy in industrial disputes. Opposition came not only from the cautious and conservative; Frank Hodges for the miners was equally opposed.[64] The Congress did agree to a grouping of unions according to industry, so that an electoral system for membership of the new General Council would more accurately represent the different trade groups affiliated. The extension of the powers of the General Council, however, was tempered with an amendment, moved at the 1920 Congress by Gosling, that 'Subject to the necessary safeguards to secure the complete autonomy of the unions and federations affiliated to Congress, the Standing Orders of Congress be amended as follows'. This tinkering approach attracted criticism from the right wing itself. Clynes thought that all they had accomplished was an increase in the size of the General Council over the old Parliamentary Committee from sixteen to thirty members. He advocated a strong central body which would encompass the Labour Party too. Clynes was right. The new Standing Orders stopped well short of empowering the General Council to lead in industrial disputes.[65]

The furthest that the trade unions would permit themselves to go was contained in clauses 1 and 2 of the General Council's duties:

1. The General Council shall keep a watch on all industrial movements and shall attempt, where possible, to co-ordinate industrial action;
2. It shall promote common action by the Trade Union movement on general questions, such as wages and hours, and any matter of general concern that may arise between trade unions and employers or between the trade union movement and the Government, and shall have power to assist any union which is attacked on any vital question of trade union principle.

A novel clause, which reflected the experience of the Councils of Action and the movement's struggles of the previous year to compel the old Parliamentary Committee to take responsibility for the campaign against government intervention in Russia, was as follows: 'In order that the Trade Union Movement may do everything which lies in its power to prevent future wars, the General Council shall, in the event of there being a danger of an outbreak of war, call a Special Congress to decide on industrial action, such Congress to be called, if possible, before war is declared.' Despite these words, it is true to say that 'The General Council . . . began its existence in the knowledge that the unions wanted a single central trade union authority, but had refused to grant it power to interfere with the autonomy of individual unions.'[66]

One further significant reform of the TUC was the provision of four women's seats on the new General Council, which amongst other things meant that individual unions, notably the big general unions, were bound now to take the recruitment of women members more seriously if they were to compete for these places.

Thus, Bevin's attempts, with those of his colleagues, to reform and strengthen central trade-union authority for combative industrial purposes looked to have been largely frustrated in 1920. This was equally true for the reform of the Triple Alliance and for the restructuring of the TUC. We must now examine the same endeavour at work within the NTWF, even as the negotiations for the amalgamation of the TGWU were in full swing.

# V

## The Work of the Federation

Through the first months of 1920, sectional claims came through at the same rate as those successfully promoted during 1919. They were duly recorded in the NTWF's minutes. In January the EC reviewed progress on claims for trimmers and tippers (who negotiated separately from the general cargo dockers), canal-men, tugmen, coal bunkerers, carters and motormen. The tram- and busmen had entered a claim for a 10s. rise.[67]

Bargaining was particularly tough in the canal industry, a backward section of water transport where living and working conditions were still nomadic for many men and their families, and Bevin reported that strike action might be necessary.[68] By May the tramwaymen had settled for a 5s. increase, to be followed by a further 1s. in June.[69] The trimmers were given their own Court of Inquiry.[70] In June this was followed by a further, much more serious retreat. Bevin reported on this in summarizing his activities as chairman of the JIC in road haulage. The employers, faced with a detailed case by the Federation, had replied in the most general and evasive terms, rejecting Bevin's appeal to act in a 'judicial' manner after the fashion of the Shaw Inquiry. The national organization was obviously frail, as the vehicle unions in the industry were exhorted to prepare district rallies and conferences to strengthen the national struggle.[71]

By October, the Executive was contemplating strike action to compel acknowledgement of its claim for a national minimum of £4 7s. in the haulage industry, as the machinery of the JIC had broken down. The employers now insisted that only local negotiations would be entertained. The Executive reluctantly authorized affiliated unions to take individual action in their own areas.[72] This was the most serious setback which the Federation had encountered in its steady post-war march through the JICs. In November came another, as the private tramway JIC was broken by the withdrawal of the companies.[73]

## Conflict Between Dockers

These processes were accompanied not only by the encroaching slump, but by the most explosive inter-union conflicts yet seen inside the Federation. Unions were jockeying for position in the build-up to what was evidently an approaching major merger of some kind or other. The rows broke out particularly between the road-transport unions, and between the NUGW and the DWRGWU.

The last two unions had paced each other down the years from 1889, both reaching out into many industries from their original bases in London's gasworks and London's docks. In 1920 they had put two years' of merger negotiation to the test of a membership ballot. There is little doubt that the more enthusiastic partner was the NUGW, which had consistently aimed to win access for its members right across dockland. It was, moreover, by far the larger of the two, having 444,000 members in 1920, against the Dockers' 80,000. Its officers and policies would obviously dominate any merger of the two: not a prospect for Bevin to relish. The Trade Union (Amalgamation) Act of 1917 had been passed to facilitate union mergers, and required only a simple majority to vote, though stipulating that the votes in favour should exceed those against by at least 20 per cent. When the votes of the two unions were counted, it was found that 73 per cent of the NUGW's voters had recorded their assent, but that the Dockers' Union had polled only 40 per cent of its membership, of whom only 40 per cent were in favour of the unification with their arch-rivals.

This result emerged, after the Shaw Inquiry, in the context of a furious conflict over the Dockers' Union's aggressive methods of recruitment in the London docks, and its attempts to transfer into its own ranks the dock members of other unions in the port, most notably those of the NUGW.

This conflict was given unrestrained and bitter expression at the 1920 AGC of the Federation.[74] It culminated in the accusation, delivered by an official of the NUGW, S. J. Wright, that Bevin had discouraged his dockers from voting in the merger ballot, and that

> one of the worst features of it is this. I have the figures here as supplied by the Dockers' Union to our union, and the very worst part of the Dockers' Union, so far as the vote was concerned, was the Bristol Channel area. I say that if Mr Bevin had been sincere, and if he had thrown his weight and influence into the amalgamation scheme, I think that would have been accomplished and that we should have been one organisation today instead of two organisations.

Bevin responded with evident pain:

> I think that is very unfair . . . I have had no more to do with Bristol for the
> last three years than with Hull or London or anywhere else. You might as
> well say that there was a big vote in London due to my influence . . . I think
> it is a hit below the belt . . . but I can tell you the real trouble of the vote; it is
> the fear of the one card in the Bristol Channel. Look at the advertisements
> that are in the papers saying: 'One card for everybody.'

The row had ranged over the whole field of the dock territories of the
South, South-west and East of England: wherever the DWRGWU had
membership. Wright was joined in his attack by officials of the
stevedores, the lightermen, the Labour Protection League, the United
Order of General Labourers, and by Sam March of the London carters.
March fiercely denounced the Dockers' Union's new tactic of appointing
young and aggressive organizers in London's docks, and they were
accused of intimidation and bullying attempts to compel dockers to
transfer from other unions into their own. J. B. Ruark, of the stevedores,
said that at NTWF District Committee meetings in London they often
came near to blows. All this was accompanied by a parade of the great
dockers' triumph at the Shaw Inquiry. Gasworkers, often older men who
had been accustomed to following dock work seasonally, had been
ruthlessly excluded.

Gosling, in the chair, wisely perceived the importance of the
exchanges, which were at root a conflict between 'open' and 'closed'
methods of union organization. A historically important divide was being
worked over here. Bevin listened for a long time, but his reply was
incandescent, and unrepentant. Yes, he was seeking to close dockers'
unions against an age-long malaise: they could no longer be treated as a
dumping ground of casual labour. But no, he would not countenance
indiscriminate exclusion of long-standing dock workers from other
unions, and denied any knowledge of the strong-arm methods of which
'his' organizers were accused. (Tillett was nowhere to be seen: though he
remained nominally in charge, the succession was already accomplished in
all but name.) Bevin denied that these Young Turks had a financial
incentive to poach and bully for members; the Dockers' Union, unlike
some others, paid a straight salary without bonus based on membership.
(Commission for union collectors, he said, was 'the curse of the movement'.)

He counterattacked with equal candour, ranging across the undercutting
levels of contributions charged by the NUGW, and their indiscriminate
propaganda and recruitment methods in Southampton, or King's Lynn,
where dockers had been falsely told that the Shaw Award did not apply to
them, and elsewhere. He rounded on the vehicle workers, who sought to
encroach on his long-established membership in road haulage in Bristol.
(Bevin, we recall, was an ex-horseman.) He had loyally served on the

JICs of inland transport on behalf of all the unions in the Federation's road section, without seeking gains for his union – for example, he had never tried to recruit carters in London, although he claimed that he could easily have done so.

He turned to the tramways: 'The Federation has had the benefit of what brains I have, with only a handful of members involved . . . and I have never used the position of the Dockers' Union to secure a single member in connection with any section of the Federation.' Yes, he would stop March's members coming on the Bristol docks, and he would play the game of competitive recruitment against the others, if that was the game to be played.

Why was there no conflict in Hull, where he had the best of relationships with Farrah, an NUGW official and Federation district secretary? Because, replied Wright, his union, the NUGW, had the bulk of the Hull dockers in membership. 'No!' and 'No!' cried Bevin and Sexton almost simultaneously, amidst cries of 'order!' In Southampton the NUGW had taken men into membership from the 'free-labour' shed without charging an entrance fee. Wright called out that this was 'a deliberate lie!'

Gosling let it run, but appealed to keep it 'within limits'. Bevin responded: 'I have got my back up over this and I do not mind a row at all. I have had so much of it that I get fed up. It seems to me that the motto of some of the unions is "Do what you like yourselves, but never have any retaliations".' He turned on Grisley, secretary of the Cranedrivers' union, which, in Falmouth, 'has been and taken over the cranemen without a transfer from us . . . he has done it after our building up their wages; he goes down there and preaches craft unionism'.

Wright had argued that Bevin, if he wished for a monopoly in London docks should take the NUGW members there in return for handing over all the dockers' mill and industrial membership in the capital to the NUGW. His reply encapsulated his case: 'For the sake of half a dozen members who may be affected I am asked . . . to transfer to the amount of thousands out of another section of the membership. It is not the contributions I care twopence about, but I am concerned with protecting the men who are casual in their employment.'

The picture painted in this debate is one of uncontrolled internecine warfare, with Bevin either surrounded by predators, or guilty of wholesale poaching himself. The truth was undoubtedly a compound of these elements; there is no room for doubt either about the Dockers' Union's hegemonic ambitions in preparation for amalgamation, or about Bevin's unashamed drive for dockland closed shops. The truly impressive aspect of this scene is that all knew that, simultaneously with the warfare, several of the contenders were sitting down behind closed doors with Bevin himself to discuss amalgamation.

## Rumpus Among Vehicle Workers

The same noises of unrestrained accusation and counteraccusation were to be heard in the exchanges within and between the now partially rationalized road-transport section of the Federation. After a prolonged and discordant negotiation, the London and Provincial Union of Licensed Vehicle Workers and the Amalgamated Association of Tramway and Vehicle Workers, concluded a merger in 1920. The LPU elected its officials, whilst the Manchester-based AAT chose permanent officers by selection. This had been one of the sources of friction in the merger terms; the issue was put to a ballot of both unions, and the larger AAT vote prevailed in this, as in many issues. The militant London bus-workers found themselves joined in a 'moderate' union dominated by lower-paid provincial tramwaymen and administered by the cautious majority of AAT officials. Moreover, in the industry's negotiating machinery, London busmen became isolated when, in 1919, they rejected a JIC settlement recommended by their Executive: subsequently London buses were excluded from the JIC scheme.[75]

Stanley Hirst, subsequently the first financial secretary of the TGWU and its first representative on the Labour Party's National Executive Committee, became the general secretary of the merged union – the United Vehicle Workers' Union – from his former position as general secretary of the AAT. His temperament, grey and colourless, and his politics, clashed fiercely with the strongly independent and syndicalist-minded London busmen, who formed their first rank-and-file unofficial committee as early as 1919, even before their merger with the AAT. Under the merger, Hirst had to concede that his headquarters would move to London, but it was his officials who won the major promotions in the new union: John Cliff, for instance, who was to take a prominent part in the TGWU's first decades, came from chairmanship of the AAT to become the joint secretary of the tramways JIC.

Hirst's new offices in London were dubbed 'Traitor's Gate' by the London membership; the UVW suspended the old practice of allowing the rank-and-file to attend Executive meetings, and Hirst outraged the London men by calling the police to remove them from the premises.

The first – and, as it proved, the only – Annual Conference of the UVW was held in Nottingham from 29 June to 3 July 1920. As was normal for all union conferences in those days, the proceedings were recorded verbatim and published. They can only be described as rancorous in the extreme, as delegates challenged the procedure, and each others' credentials and general bona fides. The Report reads as though a dozen provocateurs were hard at work to disrupt the new union at birth. It took the whole first morning of conference to agree rules of procedure and to appoint a Standing Orders Committee, and thereafter the conference was dominated by disputes over the rules of the union, with amendments flying thick and fast.

Hirst's action in calling the police to end 'open executive councils' in London came under especially fierce attack by London delegates, one saying 'it is time to end this meeting', and a defender of Hirst saying that, if they were going to attack individuals, 'I shall go home!'[76] The order of business was chaotic and, had the new union not become absorbed in the wider TGWU in the following year, there is no knowing what fragmentations and breakaways would have occurred in this section. Nor is it hard to discern in some of these exchanges the origins of the running conflicts between London busmen and the TGWU's central authority during the later inter-war years.

Moreover, the range of disputes in road transport extended beyond the UVW, to include inter-union conflict between it and the National Union of Vehicle Workers – the old London carmen's union – and between all of these and the Manchester-based United Road Transport Association. The latter subsequently became the URTU and survives to this day. At this time, it was regularly accused by other haulage unions of undercutting, with more modest claims and settlements, the national negotiations of the aborted JIC in road haulage – of being, in short, a bosses' union. It was expelled from the Federation in 1921.

Sam March's union, the NUVW, was no bosses' union, but had its own version of combativity towards the UVW, which, although predominantly a passenger-transport union, had a road-haulage section. Even whilst the NTWF Executive, represented by the ever-patient, ever-gentlemanly Gosling, was presiding over tendentious negotiations to achieve the ultimate merger in this section – that between March's NUVW and the new UVW – each union accused the other, vigorously, sometimes raucously, and in the public arena of the 1920 AGC, of poaching and of failure to abide by Federation deals for their members at the JIC.

March's union was clearly obstructive towards the Federation pressure for the merger with the UVW, but at the same time pressed its own resolution in 1920 for the grand merger of the whole transport federation. March was accused of wasting the Federation's time in not taking seriously the case for a prior merger with the UVW. Even Bevin, who of course sought the wider union, attacked March's resolution as a smokescreen hiding his sectarianism, and supported the case (long advanced, as Cathery was delighted to point out, by the most separatist element in the Federation, the seamen) for a complete tranche of sectional mergers to precede the final step of a united transport union.[77]

Bevin could and did claim with justice that the warring factions of both passenger- and haulage-transport unions had all had the benefit of his services through his myriad labours as the NTWF's chief negotiator and founder of JICs, despite his own union's relative paucity of membership in these fields. The DWRGWU did not, in its Annual Reports, classify its membership according to industry or occupation. It did, however, record the titles of its 629 branches. In its thirty-first Annual Report, of 1920, the large majority of these are given only a designation according to their locality – as 'Gloucester No. 1' – but there are also many which give an indication of their area of recruitment. Amongst these, we find milling branches in almost every district, including twenty-nine milling branches in the large Midlands area. Interestingly, several branches are designated as women's. There are branches of greenhouse workers, street traders, aircraft workers, tinplate branches (forty-seven), coopers, tobacco workers, cinema workers, motor trades, and many clerical branches. It is clear that, by this stage, the DWRGWU could reasonably claim the status of a general workers' union. Yet, despite Bevin's own origins as a Bristol dray-man, and his early organizing efforts for the Bristol carters, there are only two branches, both in Swansea, which merit specialist titles as tramway and carters' branches. This crude analysis confirms that, to become what it aspired to be, a true transport union, there was no option but to embrace the widely spread but desperately sectional, warring inland transport unions in the planned amalgamation. The debates of 1920 underline this need with a wealth of evidence of the narrowness and sectarianism of the haulage and passenger unions in the Federation, which tried to the limit both the skill and tolerance of Gosling in the chair and the organizing genius of Bevin. In our next chapter we shall see how the miracle was worked.

## Havelock Wilson Gets His Way

There remains the third great section of transport, the maritime unions, to consider, as they shaped up to the prospect of amalgamation. We have seen in the previous chapter that Wilson's and Cotter's unions had won their national bargaining instrument, the National Maritime Board (NMB), through their wartime indispensability and the government's heavy involvement in the industry at that time. The Board had now reverted to a simple bipartite structure as the government withdrew. The Federation's role here, in sharp contrast to its part in the formation of inland JICs, had been by-passed in this process.

Bevin was not happy about this autonomy. He pressed at the Federation EC and at the 1920 AGC for the Federation to have a role and representation on the NMB, and for the NSFU to conform with the rest by negotiating through the Federation. He reasoned in support of this demand that the seamen still, as always, relied on the solidarity of the dockers whenever they were in dispute. The Executive agreed with his argument.[78]

At the same time, the Federation wished to lend its weight to a *rapprochement* between the NSFU and the breakaway British Seafarers'

Union, still led by Shinwell. Cathery announced his acceptance of the supporting mediation of the Scottish TUC for this purpose, but claimed that the BSU was not interested.[79] Cathery also told the AGC that he and Cotter were negotiating their own merger amicably and bilaterally in 1920.[80] He looked forward to further mergers involving the Hull Seamen's Union, the Coastwise Seamen's Union, and the BSU itself, 'in the very near future'.

The exchanges between Cathery and Bevin at the Executive and at the AGC seem genuinely conciliatory, not marred by the histrionic and separatist outbursts with which Havelock Wilson had since 1913 habitually laced his contributions to amalgamation debates. But Wilson was there in the background nevertheless. The attitude of the Federation leaders to him was revealed when Cathery, the NSFU general secretary and its representative on the Federation Executive, suffered a motor accident and was confined to a hospital bed with severe back injuries. The Federation refused to accept Wilson as a substitute delegate during this period, despite pleas dictated by the injured Cathery from his bed.

In spite of this, Bevin clearly wished at this stage to promote goodwill. He reported to the EC in March that there had been an unofficial dockers' strike against a ship with an Asiatic crew in Bristol, and that he had had a conversation with Wilson in which the latter had asserted that the NSFU did not now seek a racialist exclusion of such crews, but that it demanded that their underpayment should cease, and that they should receive the international rate as agreed by the International. Cathery confirmed this, and reported that they had reached agreement to this end on the National Maritime Board.

Yet within a year, Wilson had disaffiliated his union from the Federation, in the aftermath of Black Friday and the Federation's subsequent embargo on coal imports in support of the miners' isolated strike. The whole fraught relationship between maritime unionism and the pending grand amalgamation of transport unions was sundered irreparably. At that point, Cathery's diplomacy was heavily overridden, as Wilson, freed by the rupture from all remaining inhibitions, let loose his long-held hostility to Federation intervention in his union's affairs. Here, at the NSFU's Annual General Meeting in 1921, he is replying to criticisms of his conduct in pulling out of the NTWF:

> As sailors and firemen, or seafaring men, we know our own business better than some outsider who does not understand it. Now, what has been the policy of the Transport Workers' Federation? Their policy has been, and their kick against us has been, that whenever we have had any negotiations on matters pertaining to our own particular calling, instead of looking for 'Dockers' K.C.s' or some other K.C.s, we have managed our own affairs. We have not had outsiders put up to pump into them what we had to say ...
> That has not met with favour from the heads of the men in the Transport

Federation. They have objected to that over and over again, and said we should make no new contracts nor discuss business with the employers unless through the heads of the Transport Workers' Federation. (Cries of 'Oh', and laughter.) I am going to submit to any of you who may have a feeling in favour of the Transport Workers' Federation that you will not tolerate that, and I am now speaking to those who may be in favour of it. Now, my next point is the one Union. You have to be all merged into one Union with one Executive, that is to say, dockers, sailors and firemen, omnibus drivers, taxi drivers, ('Distributives') – well, a miscellaneous body. You have got to be subject to a Council representing all those bodies. Well, now, when you come to the election of that Council, where would you stand? ('At the bottom.') We will say that they have a Council of 20 – three seafaring men on a Council of 20; they would be able to vote you down every time and all the time as they went along. Take, for instance, the organisations in Germany before the war. They had the one big Union idea. The Sailors and Firemen were a section only, and whenever the sailors and firemen had a grievance and it was brought before the Council, if they wanted an advance in wages, the Council always conveniently voted it down . . . [81]

This was the authentic voice of Wilson's separatism. It was never completely stifled at any time in his career, and here it was given full volume. The context was significant too; at that AGM, Wilson had just come out the winner of a running battle with the new 'Vigilante Committees' in his union, as rank-and-file opposition to his authoritarian and arbitrary leadership built up in the ports. Prior to the debate on the NTWF disaffiliation, he had, in the name of anti-Bolshevism, expelled the Vigilantes, so he had a captive audience, in which 50 per cent of the 'delegates' were union officials!

Stanley Hirst's voice was querulous, and could be drowned easily in the TGWU's chorus. Sam March, Ben Smith, and other contenders in road transport, had loud-hailers for voices, but they were empty of serious analytical content, and would also join the unity song. Hilton, leader of the URTA, sang defiantly before the massed ranks of the NTWF, but *sotto voce* when engaged with the employers. Wilson's strident hostility was of a different order; behind the histrionics were deep ideological and structural objections to the whole federal – never mind amalgamation – project. Wilson chose instead a lonely road. Along it lay, first, anti-communism and then corporate corruption.

There could be no compromise with that voice, yet Bevin, ready to enter rumbustious conflict with his future colleagues in road and port transport, never took up cudgels directly with Wilson. We raise the question again in our final chapter. Later, as we shall see in vol. II, Bevin hesitated to expand a small maritime section in the TGWU by poaching Wilson's members, even after Wilson's union left the Federation in 1921, when the Federation promoted a merger between the BSU and the Ships' Cooks' union. The Federation condemned the corporate closed shop of the NSFU and the shipowners, fought the victimization to which non-members were subject, and looked forward to the new TGWU merging with the Amalgamated Marine Workers' Union (AMWU). But the TGWU never acted decisively to break Wilson's hold on the industry, even when the NSFU was expelled from the TUC after the General Strike in 1926. Likewise, Bevin refused to take Shinwell into his union when the AMWU was becoming bankrupt.

The best that could now be hoped for was a port–road–general amalgamation such as finally emerged, shorn of two major affiliates of the NTWF, the NUGW and the NSFU. Moreover, negotiations with the NUR, which had never been a member of the NTWF in the years before the formation of the TGWU, were slow and indecisive, as the railwaymen refused to abandon their simple, industrial form.

## *Reforming the Federation?*

But the NTWF was not finished in its own endeavours to reform its structure. During 1920, as in previous years, its Executive continued to receive applications from new, would-be affiliates. And again, some of its decisions seem quixotic. They refused to admit the National Union of British Fishermen,[82] and also turned away the Amalgamated Musicians' Union and the National Orchestral Union of Professional Musicians.[83] This may not seem an unreasonable decision, until we read that these two unions sought membership for the musicians who entertained the passengers on the luxury transatlantic liners. Who else but shipping companies were their employers?

The National Union of Packing Case Makers was rejected, but the National Union of Distributive and Allied Workers (NUDAW, shortly to merge into today's USDAW) was accepted, on the grounds that it recruited transport workers in the distributive trades. Indeed, in 1921, in an effort to shore up its balance in the face both of the emergence of the TGWU and of the trade recession, the Federation proposed to change its name to the Transport and Distributive Trades' Federation.[84] Nothing came of this idea.

The Executive justified its rejection of applications on the grounds that it should not shore up small, localized unions, but instead should insist on their joining an existing affiliate as their mode of entry. A much more significant supplicant, however, appeared on the scene in February 1921. The Irish Transport and General Union, now administered by more moderate leaders – James Larkin was a guest of the US government, jailed for subversion in that country – sought an arrangement with the Federation in 1921, under which the whole Federation membership in Ireland would transfer to the ITGWU and, in return, the Irish union would affiliate its whole membership to the Federation. The

Executive referred this proposal to the General Council, where it died the death.

At the 1920 AGC, Bevin made his last attempt to put executive muscle and administrative weight into the Federation. He proposed, on behalf of the DWRGWU, that affiliated unions should standardize their membership contributions at 1s. a week. (Several were then charging only a few pence.) Half of these rates would be paid over to the Federation, which would then be funded for an expansion of staff with which to carry out negotiations for all sections, and also international duties. The Federation funds would also supplement individual unions' strike pay to a standard level.[85]

All this was either too much or too little for the delegates, some of whom regarded the plan as taking away their autonomy, whilst the radicals saw it as a hindrance to full amalgamation. Sexton, however, recognized it for the pragmatic halfway house that it was. He said at the end of Bevin's long mover's speech: 'I want to second this, not because it is the end of all things —'; Bevin interrupted with: 'But because it is a beginning.' And Sexton significantly echoed: 'Yes, because it is a beginning.' For Bevin was at this stage visibly riding two horses – his plan for the Federation, and his own piecemeal negotiations, discreetly conducted, for the TGWU merger. The former was referred by the AGC to the Executive, where it sank. One option after another was falling away; the agenda for the final solution was becoming less and less cluttered with alternatives. Abandoning grand designs for the unification of every last element in transport and general unionism, in the light of the events we have reviewed in this chapter, Bevin and his supporters sought the best possible pragmatic solution, outside the Executive meetings and set-piece debates of the NTWF Annual General Councils.

## The Last Chapter?

In fact, this decision was not taken in haste, but only after all these other roads seemed closed. Bevin had held his first discussion on amalgamation with the Executive of the National Union of Docks, Wharves and Shipping Staffs in March 1920, when he and his union were riding the crest of the Shaw Award. After this preliminary excursion, he took the crucial step in July, when he brought together small delegations of Sexton's union and his own. Agreement in principle between the two main dockers' unions was followed by a key move: the invitation to Gosling to chair all subsequent negotiations. By December 1920 the process was virtually complete – the ballot papers were on their way to 1,800 branches of nineteen unions. But that process, its outcome, and some of its immediate consequences, deserve a chapter to themselves.

# Notes

1  H. A. Clegg, *A History of British Trade Unions since 1889*, vol. II: *1911–1933* (Oxford University Press, 1985), p. 304.

2  Report of a Court of Inquiry concerning Transport Workers' Wages and Conditions, with Minutes of Evidence and appendices, Cmnd 936 and Cmnd 937, Parliamentary Papers, XXXIV, 1920 (Shaw Report), Minutes of Evidence, p. 165.

3  G. A. Phillips, 'The National Transport Workers' Federation, 1910–1927' (unpublished PhD thesis, Oxford University, 1968), p. 361.

4  A Special General Meeting, on 30 December 1919, agreed that the NTWF should defray all the costs.

5  J. T. Walton Newbold, a lecturer in Economic History to the Central Labour College allocated to Lancashire, and a founder member, in 1920, of the British Communist Party, was another part of the BSP network of which we have already spoken. His chaotic papers, housed in the John Rylands Library in Manchester, are full of interesting hints about the political background to these events. Unfortunately, they require a major labour of sorting and indexing before they can be fully used. Thus, our references cannot be given any precise location within the archive.

6  Alan Bullock, *The Life and Times of Ernest Bevin*, vol. I: *Trade Union Leader, 1881–1940* (Heinemann, 1960), pp. 121–2.

7  Ibid., p. 121.

8  Shaw Report, Minutes of Evidence, p. 8.

9  Ibid., pp. 128–30.

10  Ibid.

11  The report appeared in 1919, and was reprinted as Appendix 44 to the Shaw Report, Appendices pp. 31–40.

12  See chapter 15.

13  Shaw Report, Minutes of Evidence, p. 156.

14  Ibid., p. 159.

15  Ibid., p. 164.

16  Ibid.

17  Gordon Phillips and Noel Whiteside, *Casual Labour: The Unemployment Question in the Port Transport Industry, 1880–1970* (Oxford University Press, 1985); and Noel Whiteside, 'Public Policy and Port Labour Reform: The Dock Decasualization Issue, 1910–1950', in Steven Tolliday and Jonathan Zeitlin (eds), *Shop Floor Bargaining and the State: Historical and Comparative Perspectives* (Cambridge University Press, 1985), chapter 4.

18  Whiteside, 'Public Policy and Port Labour Reform', p. 78.

19  Phillips and Whiteside, *Casual Labour*, p. 153.

20  Ibid., pp. 154–5.

21  Shaw Report, Minutes of Evidence, pp. 159–60.

22  Ibid., p. 161.

23  Interview with James Whitney, retired Hull docker, August 1989, at Hull Dockers' Club.

24  Shaw Report, Minutes of Evidence, p. 205.

25  Ibid., pp. 157–8.

26   NUDL Annual Report, 1920, p. 7.
27   Shaw Report, Minutes of Evidence, pp. 7–8; quoted in Bullock, *The Life and Times of Ernest Bevin*, vol. I, p. 129.
28   Shaw Report, para. 17, p. x.
29   Shaw Report, Minutes of Evidence, p. 9.
30   Shaw Report, p. xvi.
31   DWRGWU Triennial Delegate Conference Minutes, 1920.
32   NTWF Annual General Council Minutes, 1921, pp. 73–6.
33   NUDL Annual Report, 1920, p. 8.
34   James Cronin, 'Coping with Labour', in James E. Cronin and Jonathan Schneer (eds), *Social Conflict and the Political Order in Modern Britain* (Croom Helm, 1982), chapter 6, p. 127.
35   Verbatim transcript of a recorded interview with Bill Lindley, 17 March 1988. In fact Bevin called no witnesses from the Lightermen's Union, and declined to cross-examine the only witness from the employers' side of that trade.
36   TGWU *Record*, October 1921, p. 20.
37   Francis Williams, *Ernest Bevin: Portrait of a Great Englishman* (Hutchinson, 1952), p. 81.
38   Quoted in ibid., pp. 81–2.
39   NUDL Annual Report, 1920, p. 6.
40   See H. A. Turner, *Trade Union Growth, Structure, and Policy* (Allen and Unwin, 1962).
41   John Lovell, *Stevedores and Dockers: a Study of Trade Unionism in the Port of London, 1870–1914* (Macmillan, 1969), p. 215.
42   See Eric J. Hobsbawm, 'National Unions on the Waterside', in *Labouring Men* (Weidenfeld and Nicolson, 1968), pp. 204–31.
43   Lord Citrine, *Men and Work – An Autobiography*, vol. I (Hutchinson, 1964), pp. 81–2.
44   A. L. Morton and G. Tate, *The British Labour Movement, 1770–1920* (Lawrence and Wishart, 1956), p. 286.
45   Harry Pollitt, *Serving My Time* (Lawrence and Wishart, 1940), p. 118.
46   Bullock, *The Life and Times of Ernest Bevin*, vol. I, p. 134.
47   DWRGWU Triennial Delegate Meeting Report, 1920, pp. 34–6.
48   Bullock, *The Life and Times of Ernest Bevin*, vol. I, p. 134.
49   *The Times* 6 August 1920.
50   Labour Party Annual Conference Report, 1920, pp. 132 *passim*.
51   S. R. Graubard, *British Labour and the Russian Revolution 1917–1924* (Oxford University Press, 1956), p. 97.
52   For a graphic contemporary account, see Robert Williams, *The New Labour Outlook* (Leonard Parsons, 1921), pp. 127 ff.
53   Bullock, *The Life and Times of Ernest Bevin*, vol. I, pp. 136–8.
54   Bill Jones, *The Russia Complex* (Manchester University Press, 1977), p. 6.
55   Quoted in Bullock, *The Life and Times of Ernest Bevin*, vol. I, p. 139.
56   Ibid., p. 139.
57   Williams, *The New Labour Outlook*, p. 127.
58   Bullock, *The Life and Times of Ernest Bevin*, vol. I, p. 152.
59   DWRGWU Special District Secretaries' Conference Minutes (in typescript), 2–3 October 1920, p. 3.

60 The full story of the Emergency Powers Act is told in Keith Jeffery and Peter Hennessy, *States of Emergency: British Governments and Strike-breaking since 1919* (Routledge and Kegan Paul, 1983), pp. 50–7.

61 Keith Middlemas, *Politics in Industrial Society: The Experience of the British System since 1911* (André Deutsch, 1979), p. 155.

62 Ibid., p. 154.

63 V. L. Allen, *The Sociology of Industrial Relations* (Longman, 1971), p. 165.

64 Ibid., p. 166.

65 Ibid., p. 169.

66 Clegg, *History of British Trade Unions*, vol. II, p. 310.

67 NTWF Executive Committee Minutes, 30 January 1920.

68 Ibid., 31 March 1920.

69 Ibid., 5 May 1920.

70 Ibid.

71 Ibid., 8 July 1920.

72 Ibid., 20 October 1920.

73 Ibid., 26 November 1920.

74 NTWF Annual General Council Report, pp. 60–84.

75 We draw here upon the account in Ken Fuller, *Radical Aristocrats: London Busworkers from the 1880s to the 1900s* (Lawrence and Wishart, 1985), chapter 5.

76 UVW, Official Report of the First Annual Conference, 29 June–3 July 1920, pp. 19–20.

77 NTWF Annual General Council Report, 1920, pp. 140–4.

78 NTWF Executive Committee Minutes, 31 March 1920, and NTWF Annual General Council Report, 1920, p. 43.

79 NTWF Executive Committee Minutes, 30 January 1920.

80 NTWF Annual General Council Report, 1920, p. 137.

81 NSFU Annual General Meeting Minutes, 1921, pp. 154–5.

82 A Grimsby-based union originating in 1917, and in competition with the NSFU, particularly in the Humber fishing ports, Aberdeen and Fleetwood. It joined the TGWU amalgamation in 1922. See Arthur Marsh and Victoria Ryan, *Historical Directory of Trade Unions*, vol. 3 (Gower, 1987), p. 216.

83 NTWF Executive Committee Minutes, 27 August 1920 and 1 January 1920.

84 NTWF Annual Report, 1921, p. 7.

85 Ibid., 1920, pp. 98–9.

# 20

# Amalgamation: 1920–1922

## I

### *Slump and Its Effects*

Ballot papers were already circulating in December 1920. Soon most of the various unions considering amalgamation were to authorize the creation of the Transport and General Workers' Union. By that time the rate of unemployment stood at 5.8 per cent of the insured population, or 691,000. During the first months of 1921 the rate shot up, to reach 11.3 per cent in March, on the eve of the mining crisis which was to enter the name 'Black Friday' into trade-union lore. As the transport-union ballots came in one by one to Bevin's office, and as the miners fought on alone towards defeat in June, the murrain spread inexorably, afflicting 17.8 per cent or 2,171,000 individuals who were out of work in June.

While the economy plummeted into deep slump, the employers and government were relieved of tiresome obligations to treat gently with labour. Their reaction, indeed, was far from gentle. They opened a brutal onslaught on wage levels. This entailed an assault upon those new forms of collective bargaining which had been conceded in the war and its aftermath. It presumed the rolling back of wartime governmental controls and of state subsidies to the mining industry. Average wage rates stood at 260 in 1920, and earnings at 240 (taking 1913 as 100); by 1922 these indices had fallen to 170 and 147 respectively. Over the same period, the cost-of-living index of the Board of Trade fell from 276 to 180. Real wages were now falling.

Table 18.1 (pp. 682–5) records the enfeeblement of trade unions which followed from these trends. Total membership of the different transport and general unions fell from 3,627,000 in 1920 to 1,418,000 in 1922 – and further to 1,138,000 in 1923. Total TUC membership fell from 6,506,000 in 1920, to 5,129,000 in 1922, and then to 4,369,000 in

1923. The new TGWU estimated, in its first Annual Report, that the membership of some of the amalgamating unions had fallen by 50 per cent between the first moves towards the merger in July 1920 and its consummation in January 1922. The new union placed a cautious figure of 297,460 on its membership at the end of its first year of operation.[1]

This was the fraught background to the amalgamation of the unions which had joined in the initial vote for the most far-reaching, complicated and daring act of restructuring that the British trade-union movement has ever seen, either before or since.[2] Eighteen unions had balloted. As in 1889 and 1911, the waterfront unions had worked another miracle. Now they were joined by inland road-transport organizations, and by many thousands of other workers in white-collar and industrial jobs. In two years of packed action, the pattern of trade unionism was completely recast.

## The Isolation of the Workers' Union

One important organization missed out in this remarkable process. The Workers' Union had flourished in the wartime munitions and engineering industries, adding to its numbers many thousands of 'dilutees' and women assembly workers from those sectors. As table 18.1 (pp. 682–5) shows, it continued to recruit new members during the short post-war boom, peaking at almost half a million in 1920. However, its widely scattered membership was exceptionally vulnerable to the ensuing slump. It was spread over hundreds of occupations and industries, without any of the sectional ties and traditions at the grass roots which, paradoxically, kept the federated alliance of transport unions to their chosen path of amalgamation through the same adverse period. Held together by liberal expenditure on full-time organizers, the Workers' Union began a precipitous collapse at the very moment when general and transport unionism was saving and renewing itself by mergers.

The Workers' Union had attempted the same road. In 1917 it combined with the Municipal Employees' Association and the National Amalgamated Union of Labour to form the National Amalgamated Workers' Union, with a Joint Executive composed of the leadership of all three unions. But this relationship was stormy and shortlived. The NAUL was quite unable to stomach the top-down, officer-dominated constitution and practice of the WU, so the new union fell apart during 1921–2 over the issue of the election or selection of officials. The NAUL and the MEA then turned to the General Workers' Union for a more promising route to amalgamation. By 1924, the NUGMW was the eventual product of this development.

The WU's numbers were, meanwhile, declining rapidly, to 450,000 in 1921, to 247,000 in 1922, and to 140,000 in 1923. The financial embarrassment which followed this collapse was particularly acute because, in an attempt to hold on to its members, the union had introduced an over-generous benefit scheme in 1920. By 1923 it was running a deficit of £30,000. Stranded between the successful transport and general unions' amalgamations, with nowhere to go, the union held out, through the General Strike of 1926 (an event which further depleted membership and income) until, on the verge of bankruptcy, it had little choice but merger with the young TGWU in 1929. We shall look at this story in vol. II.[3]

## The Mining Crisis

The story of the mining crisis and of 'Black Friday' interwove itself with the great amalgamation's consummation. Not only did it unfold simultaneously, but it was an important influence on the process itself. It offered constructive lessons, but it also gave its own warnings, and we must take early account of it here before picking up the threads of our main concern.

The NTWF's leadership was acutely sensitive, following the railway strike of 1919 and the mining strike of 1920, to the fact that the machinery of the Triple Alliance was deficient, lacking any unified executive authority in an emergency. Bevin's *ad hoc* Mediation Committee had resolved the first of these crises. A unilateral threat of a rail strike met the second. Following this the Federation took the initiative in seeking to tighten up central co-ordination of policy and action in the Alliance, but the miners did not take this initiative seriously: they appeared to believe that soon they would not need to call on their partners for assistance. Worse, when the next crisis arrived, the miners did not want to share the responsibility for decisions about their own policies: their leaders expected no questions and demanded unconditional support.

Their industry was rolling headlong into crisis, as the government announced the end of its control over the mines from 31 March 1921. With control at an end, so too would end governmental liabilities for the industry's finances. After the withdrawal of government subsidy, the industry would operate at a loss, given both the general economic slump and the post-war rehabilitation of competitive continental mining, previously devastated in the war.

De-control was an invitation, which the owners accepted, to post notices of new contracts, at district level, for savage wage cuts. The new regime meant the abandonment of the national wage rate, and with it the abrogation of the central profits pool which had cross-subsidized less profitable from more profitable districts. The miners' union reluctantly went so far as to accept a standard cut in wages of 2s., but was adamant that the pool and the national wage were sacrosanct. Lloyd George was prepared to provide some financial support to mitigate the wage cuts, but he would not agree to sustain the government controls without which the pool and the standardization of wages simply could not be continued. Frank Hodges, the miners' leader, estimated that, even if the pool were retained, the slump in trade and coal prices would have entailed a 25 per cent cut in wages; under the district terms in fact offered, some districts faced a cut of 50 per cent.

## The Alliance Responds

So the miners rejected the district terms and were locked out from 1 April 1921. The government, fearing a strike by the entire membership of the Triple Alliance, deployed its recently acquired emergency powers to mobilize troops and motor transports. Now the Miners' Federation did indeed appeal, bluntly, for the assistance of its comrades in the Triple Alliance. The other partners had no dispute of their own. The original concept behind the Alliance – that wage programmes and policies should be concerted so that all reached a climax together – had never been realized, and on each occasion that the Alliance was expected to act, it was in the cause of sectional conflicts involving the miners alone.

Nevertheless, neither of the other partners showed any reserve in responding to the miners' call. Following a meeting of all three constituents on 31 March at Unity House, in London, the headquarters of the NUR, the NTWF called a special conference of the Executives of all its affiliates for 5 April; the NUR held a separate conference the following day. The immediate outcome brought comfort to the miners. The Transport Workers' conference declared in the words of Harry Gosling, that it would 'give all assistance in our power, to whatever extent is necessary, to help the Miners, and, with the consent of the Conference, the Executive Council proposes at once to get into negotiations with the Railwaymen and the Miners for the purpose of Triple Alliance action throughout the remainder of the contest'.[4] The NUR conference agreed, declaring that 'the conditions offered to the Miners are such that they are justified in refusing to accept; they feel that if such conditions were accepted it would only be the beginning of a general attack upon working-class conditions . . . They have therefore decided to ask the Transport Workers . . . to come into immediate consultation with the NUR'.

The Federation began to mobilize. It appealed to its members, publishing a manifesto in all the main papers at a cost of £1,300. This was addressed to 'dock and waterside workers, seamen and firemen, cooks and stewards, carters and motormen, cab, tramway and bus men, river and canal workers, warehouse and distributive workers, and other affiliated grades and sections'.[5] It was a long statement, detailing the course of the crisis and the proposed reductions in miners' wages. Impassioned pleas punctuated this recital: 'Stand Shoulder to Shoulder', 'Beware of Lies', and 'Be Ready'.

Bevin had previously admitted his misgivings about the Alliance's constitution and its capacity for effective co-ordinated action. Now, in the privacy of the NTWF Executive meetings, he revived them. The procedures of the Alliance gave no time for the transport unions' separate Executives to prepare for the struggle, and this 'robbed executive committee members of any power they might derive from their respective organisations.'[6]

A shuttle service of private overtures from the Ministry of Labour ran between it and Gosling, Williams and Bevin. Could they meet, either jointly or separately? Not, replied the union men, unless the agenda and purpose of such meetings were defined and public. When this was settled to their satisfaction, they did meet government officials. Sexton also came along. All the transport men refused to discuss the merits of the miners' case. Finally they met the Prime Minister, who appeared to offer to reopen talks. This exchange the four reported back to the miners' Executive.

There followed a further meeting of the three Executives of the Alliance. The clash loomed nearer. The NTWF and the NUR gave joint notice 'to their several employers and the government that unless negotiations are reopened between the Miners' Federation, the mine owners and the government, the full power of the Triple Alliance shall be put into operation as and from Tuesday next (April 12th) at midnight.' But behind the scenes there was a warning flash. A special report on the crisis by the NTWF claimed that the miners had accepted, at this juncture, that 'the issue, when joined by the other two organisations, should be made a joint issue, subject to joint consultation and joint settlement.'[7]

The Prime Minister was telephoned and told of the strike resolution. His response was to receive another deputation, this time from the Executives of the NTWF and the NUR. The Federation's representatives were Williams, Gosling, Sexton, Bevin, Ben Smith and Cotter. All went with the approval of the miners' leaders. At this meeting, the government demanded that the pump-men who maintained drainage systems in the mines must return to work prior to negotiations. Given that, the government was prepared to convene a conference of owners and Miners' Federation for 11 April.

Railwaymen and transport workers now pressed the miners to allow the return of safety-men to the pits, in the interests of public relations and to help the other two partners in their representations. The miners, who claimed that the pump-men had been locked out, none the less accepted this condition on 9 April, and on Monday and Tuesday, 11 and

12 April, they busied themselves in negotiations with the owners and talks with the government. This required much deliberation amongst themselves as a miners' Executive. As these talks went on into the evening of the 12th, the date fixed for the sympathy strike, the NUR and NTWF agreed to postpone it and sent notices into the country to that effect.

The government made a public statement during the 12th, rejecting the continuation of the profits pool but speaking of district wages, the principles of which should be determined nationally and should be related to productivity and 'co-operation between mines and mine-owners'. The government would offer a temporary subsidy if these terms were accepted. The miners' Executive took little time in deciding to reject them.

## Sympathy Strike Postponed

The Alliance's Joint Committee then moved to fix a new date for the strike, which was announced to commence at midnight on Thursday, 14 April. However, this was, fatefully, postponed to Friday at 10 p.m., because most wages were paid on a Friday evening and might be forfeit if the strike had already commenced. None of the parties to the Alliance had wavered on any occasion up to this point, and throughout the country branches and Trades Councils were busy creating Strike Committees, arranging pickets, securing arrangements for food distribution and working out the logistics of the coming stoppage.

Robert Williams made last-minute moves to overcome past differences between the railway unions, and secured the full participation of ASLEF, the train drivers' union, so that there was now, in effect, a Quadruple Alliance. The Electricians' Union was keen to offer help by interrupting electricity supplies to the London underground and tramways. Williams also negotiated with the distributive workers (NUDAW) for the distribution of essential foodstuffs with permits from the Strike Committee.

The Prime Minister demanded of the transport and railway leaders to know 'the grounds on which you have determined to inflict such a serious blow on your fellow-countrymen?' Accordingly, the three partners sent a deputation to Downing Street and, in Gosling's words, told Lloyd George that

> we are supporting [the miners] because we think they are right. We say that the Miners are the best people to decide for themselves; and they have satisfied us that they cannot keep their wages in the position they ought to be in except by this machinery being set up ... We should be rotters if we went

away from the Miners when they are in this great trouble . . . We intend to stand by the Miners on the grounds of comradeship.[8]

J. H. Thomas reiterated these sentiments for the railwaymen.

On the afternoon of Thursday, 14 April, the TUC, the Parliamentary Labour Party, and the National Executive of the Labour Party, met in the House of Commons, with Gosling, Thomas and Hodges representing the Alliance. The conference, having heard their case, and after cross-questioning them, issued a unanimous declaration of support for their cause. Hodges was pressed at this meeting, as the miners generally had been in the Alliance meetings, on whether they would unbend even a little from their insistence on coupling the retention of the pool and the continuation of a national wage. Hodges was emphatic that these two principles were mandatory for him.

Williams's Special Report at this point declared: 'It can be said truly that up to this moment the position of the Alliance, its prestige and potential power, had grown steadily, both at the Alliance Conferences and in the movement in the country, so that the position in which the entire working class found itself seemed almost impregnable.'[9] Even the printing unions had given confidential assurances that labour's case would not go by default in the press.

Unknown to any of the parties, however, Vernon Hartshorn of the Miners' Federation had arranged for Hodges to address a private meeting of MPs in the Commons on the evening of the 14th. Although the Alliance was not present officially, Sexton, Thomas and Tillett attended as MPs, and there were also several other miners' representatives present. Into this meeting was launched an explosive statement by Hodges. In his own words, as reported by the Press Association and never contradicted: 'We are prepared to consider wages provided they are not to be regarded as permanently on a District basis, but only of a temporary character.' This fateful remark was conveyed to the Prime Minister immediately, but the leaders of the transport workers learned of it only when they read their morning papers on Friday, the 15th. The press was full of the reported words, together with headlines confidently announcing that the great transport strike was called off.

Even the words of Williams's Special Report must count as an understatement: 'a situation had been created which caused indescribable confusion and consternation amongst transport workers and railwaymen throughout the country, and occasioned consternation in the minds of the members of the Alliance.'[10] Telegrams poured into union head offices all over London, and the trunk telephone services were jammed with frantic calls from the provincial branches.

In this atmosphere, the Alliance met on Friday morning; the miners immediately retired to a separate room in order to consider an invitation to resume talks, sent by the Prime Minister in the light of Hodges' statement. They deliberated for an hour and a half, whilst the transport and railway chiefs waited. They emerged to announce that they were declining Lloyd George's invitation. It transpired that their decision had been reached with a majority of one vote, while three of their Executive were absent. Hodges thereupon tendered his resignation but was persuaded to retract. The miners' Executive then departed to their own offices to draft a unilateral reply to the Prime Minister.

Before departing, the miners' president, Herbert Smith, in angry mood, turned down the other unions' idea of discussing the Prime Minister's invitation. Stark and blunt, he said what he wanted: 'Get on t'field. That's t'place.' The Alliance partners, then, must follow the miners into battle. Participation in strategic or tactical decisions was not necessary.

Neither transport workers nor rail unions saw the miners' uncompromising reply to the Prime Minister until they read it in the newspapers. Every attempt to persuade the miners to reopen negotiations in the light of Hodges' embarrassing, confusing and very public statement was rejected. In a final effort to keep the Alliance together, Bevin moved that the rail and transport unions invite the miners to meet again to prepare an announcement that the three partners were about to complete arrangements for the strike. But the railwaymen outvoted him by 28 votes to 12.

The position of the transport workers' leaders was scarcely enviable. At all times they were keenly aware – as Williams was to repeat in all the inquests on 'Black Friday' – that the nature of a mining strike, and the sociology of mining trade unionism, were quite different from the conditions governing transport strikes and transport unionism:

> When work stops throughout the British coalfields there is no man to be found to take the place of a member of the Miners' Federation. They are, in fact, blackleg-proof . . . All that could be done had been done, in order that the response should be spontaneous and unanimous, but there remained no absolute assurance that Railway Workers and Transport Workers would and could act with the same measure of solidarity as had been displayed by the Miners.[11]

A mining strike, he pointed out, would bite slowly as coal stocks dwindled. Because of their solidarity and security against non-union labour, the miners could sustain a long strike. A transport strike was much more vulnerable to blacklegs, and was therefore obliged to make an immediate impact. Moreover, the government's whole elaborate strike-breaking machinery – the troops and reservists, the volunteer strike-breakers, the army transports, and all the emergency powers – were specifically aimed to break not the coal strike but the pending transport strike. No troops could hew the coal, but with 1.5 million unemployed, transport companies and government alike had quite enough potential recruits for breaking strikes. The dockers were now well organized; Bevin said that he did not fear for their solidarity, despite the long memories of those who had experienced the Shipping Federation's operations and free labour of the 1890s and 1912. It was now the road-haulage industry, the new instrument of emergency freight transport, which was the weak link; fragmented unionism, and the presence of a majority of non-union drivers, were the Federation's chief worry. And London, said Williams, was like 'an armed camp', with the military vehicles parked *en masse* in the parks and public gardens.

Despite these deterrents, the NTWF leaders had suppressed their anxieties. They had clearly determined on the strike, but now the Hodges statement, the divisions in the miners' Executive which it brought to light, and the crude imposition of the will of a razor's-edge majority within the miners' leadership, provoked runaway doubt. The transport leaders took stock. Soon they came to the point where they could genuinely believe that to proceed with the strike might be disastrous. Once more they tried to persuade the miners to attend a conference and then to break again with the government if necessary.

## Black Friday

'The Alliance never acted as one body: the three sections sat in different rooms'.[12] The transport workers were not responsible for the last-second change in the situation, yet they were powerless to influence the miners. ASLEF, the NUR and the NTWF Executives therefore resolved, by 28 votes to 3, to call off the strike. All the Federation votes were cast with the majority.

That there were those in the Alliance whose hearts had never been in that battle, and who urgently sought to withdraw from it, was acknowledged by the Federation. In its own ranks, the outstanding case was of course that of Havelock Wilson and the leadership of the NSFU. For Wilson, what others saw as Black Friday should, he told the *Daily Herald*, be called 'glorious Friday'.[13] Sexton, too, was a most reluctant conscript. But the majority in the NTWF Executive was solid, up to the ultimate confusion on the Thursday. In their subsequent reports, and in the statements they made in justification of their decision, they were not being wise after the event. They rightly emphasized that Thursday's events and their aftermath merely threw into relief all the weaknesses of the Alliance's constitution, about which there had been endless public and private debate over the previous two years, as we have already seen.

Among the railwaymen, J. H. Thomas was undoubtedly opposed to the strike. He feared its alleged constitutional implications. Perhaps, as Voltaire might have said, if there had not been a constitution it would have been necessary for him to invent one. But the NUR Executive was not ruled by Thomas, or by any backstairs machinations in which he may or may not have been engaged. Yet they too changed course with the alteration in the situation. Notwithstanding this general unanimity, there followed a cyclone of recrimination within the movement. Black Friday became an indiscriminate reproach, dolloped upon the whole leadership. This condemnation of 'betrayal' became one of the great myths of the between-wars Labour movement.

## Robert Williams: Scapegoat of the Myth

The principal sufferer was Robert Williams, who was most unjustly expelled from the newly formed Communist Party for his role in the mining crisis. Thus he lost credibility right across the left of the movement. With this loss went an important part of his constituency, just at a time when his industrial base, the Federation, was about to cede its central role to the emerging TGWU. His chances of participating as an influential voice in the new union were evidently weakened.

Williams did not apologize for his role; along with Bevin and the whole leadership in the inquest debate that followed at the NTWF's AGC in June 1921, he concluded his defence by affirming that, given the same circumstances, he would have no option but to vote all over again as he had on 15 April.

A major contributing factor to the growth of the myth of Black Friday was the silence of the Federation's leadership during the months which followed. It refused any public discussion until its Report to the June AGC. Its reason was that it did not wish to weaken the miners in their long, and, it turned out, forlorn struggle. During that period, as many speakers complained in June, the rank and file gave union officers in the localities and in the branch room 'a dog's life', as rumour chased rumour around the movement, and as the new Communist Party stoked up a none-too-discriminating resentment of the leaderships of the rail and transport unions.

The communists claimed to know the 'secret history' of the strike's collapse. Hodges, it said, had been used by Thomas and others as a dupe – or, alternatively, he had been party to the betrayal: 'He had been "induced to suggest" a formula which the Miners' Executive could not possibly accept.'[14] The new party's journal, *The Communist*, published an unrestrained attack:

It did not enter into their heads [the Miners' Executive] that the railwaymen's and transport workers' leaders would be such skunks as to use Hodges' blunder as an excuse for backing out of the strike. They did not realise that the whole thing was a plant. Meanwhile, Thomas, Bevin,

Williams and the others were already busy on their dirty work at Unity House . . . Cramp made a half-hearted attempt to get the strike postponed instead of cancelled: but Thomas had the Conference well in hand.[15]

But while this account of the proceedings missed no opportunity for the attribution of blame, speaking of 'a plant', 'busy on . . . dirty work', a 'half-hearted attempt', and so on, the real agenda of the Communist Party was not the criticism of the particular decisions reached within the Alliance. It reflected an alternative view of trade unionism, rather than an alternative handling of a particular dispute. This view was spelt out in the first number of the *Communist Review*, published in May 1921.

The criminal betrayal of the miners by the Triple Alliance reveals something more deep-rooted in the modern Labour movement than mere personal cowardice and treachery. The miners' strike has demonstrated that we have reached a new phase in the history of industrial organisation. We are now in the period of mass movements, and whether moderate Labour leaders like it or not, the capitalist class in defending their profits, are quite prepared, if need be, to run the risk of provoking a revolutionary crisis.

The development of the class struggle passes from the sectional to the mass strike. All our modern trade union leaders received their training of leadership in the days when strikes were of a puny and sectional character. Their weakness rests upon the fact that they still employ the strike tactics of the old sectional period. They were accustomed, in the old days, to conduct isolated struggles which were at once local and insignificant. Now, however, they are confronted with a new phase of industrial warfare. The modern mass-strike convulses the nation. The modern mass-strike becomes a challenge to the parliamentary form of government. It tests the stability of capitalist society. This explains why the average trade union leader, trained in the sectional method of conducting local strikes, cannot lead the masses on the modern industrial battlefield.

The events of the past few weeks prove that these leaders cannot, and dare not, direct the mass-strike. The new conditions demand new leaders with a revolutionary policy and with dauntless courage. Such leadership can only come from the Communists who are, at present, so busily at work spreading the doctrines of the Red Trade Union International among the industrial workers of Britain . . . the mass-strike is not a passive strike. It must become active if it would succeed. And an active mass-strike would bring into being all the conditions necessary to carry through the workers' revolution. The mass-strike is Labour's only weapon against the dictatorship of capital. But the modern trade union leaders are afraid to use this weapon which history has placed into their hands.[16]

It was on this agenda that the Third Congress of the Communist Party, gathering in Manchester one week after Black Friday, expelled Robert Williams for his 'betrayal'. At the same time it declared 'whole-hearted sympathy with the mineworkers . . . so treacherously abandoned by the leaders of the Transport Workers and Railwaymen' and called on the rank and file to 'drive their betrayers from official positions' and to reorganize 'on a class basis and with a class-war policy'.[17]

Such proclamations were clearly, in the short run, aimed at hoped-for recruitment among the miners who were now embarked on a long strike. If these miners had responded, no one would have been surprised. As an exercise in factional politicking, the expulsion and attendant statements are understandable, if sad. But as works of political analysis, they are gravely defective. Those in the transport unions who were most vilified were precisely those most opposed to 'sectional methods', most preoccupied with the consolidation of wider, 'class-based' organizations. They were lumped in with leaders like Jimmy Thomas and Havelock Wilson who had quite different perspectives. The notion that 'mass-strikes' could challenge parliamentary government was either ambivalent or untrue. A 'challenge' was possible, but it did not imply revolution. A successful strike could have won the miners' claims, and had it materialized it would have done so. Lloyd George would have given in rather than face the defeat of his administration. He had given in before. In all probability, he had scope enough for manoeuvre to avoid his own defeat, let alone the overthrow of parliamentary institutions. By 1921, it was not very realistic to expect that revolutionary outcome as a result of union action, be it never so powerful. What might have been plausible, given the will to achieve it, was a more patient communist strategy of organization able to evaluate the effects of slump on trade-union membership, and to evaluate 'sectionalism' in the round. The transport workers were about to make the largest step in trade-union history to overcome sectional limitations, and this was simply disregarded by the left in the passionate recriminations of the moment.[18] While all this tended to isolate communists from the processes in which they wished to engage, it could not prevent Bevin from carrying through his project.

Williams, however, did suffer. His role was so widely misrepresented that it became a stigma. It entered the literature. Even in the *Autobiography* of Bertrand Russell we read that Williams 'ratted' on the miners.[19]

But the record shows that this is not true. Indeed, Williams did not even 'rat' on the Communist Party, and at the end of June he was on the rostrum of the Labour Party Conference in Brighton, arguing in favour of communist affiliation. He lost, by almost 4 million votes. Walton Newbold's disorderly memoirs make many warm and appreciative references to Williams. The Communist MP reported that 'the dilettanti' of Fleet Street communist leaders created a 'bad impression in Moscow . . . rather than the . . . devoted adherents in the higher ranks . . . of the trade union movement at the time of the collapse of the Triple Alliance . . . Robert Williams put the interests of his organisation before the romantic illusions of the Communist Party'.[20]

The communist attack on J. H. Thomas was, if anything, less vitriolic, but a cartoon by 'Espoir' showed Thomas laying a wreath on a dead miner and claiming the right to be first to do so, because 'I killed him.' Another cartoon featured Thomas at the Last Supper, in the role of Judas. This led to an action and £2,000 libel damages. During the hearing, Thomas insisted that he was not a socialist, and that calling off the Triple Alliance's strike threat had 'saved the country'.[21] That dedicated radicals like Bevin and Williams should be lumped in with Thomas as an alleged co-conspirator must have stuck very firmly in their craws.

Bevin's own rough handling in *The Communist* was at the hands of Francis Meynell, who had recently been sacked from the *Daily Herald* by its directors (Bevin, Lansbury, Hodges, Ben Turner and Williams) after it had been revealed that he had, unknown to them, been a conduit for Russian funding. He had brought in £75,000 of Russian jewels to keep the paper afloat. Meynell was a brilliant and fastidious book designer, but his polemic against Bevin was less than scrupulous.[22] In his own memoirs, Meynell confesses that he was worried about the Thomas action and happy to leave the front line. Soon, of course, he was right out of the Communist Party. Meynell also describes a later meeting with Bevin, during the Second World War, which proves conclusively that Bevin was not at all the vindictive monster he was sometimes cracked up to be.[23]

## Other Left-wing Perceptions

Other left-wing witnesses were kinder. The *Daily Herald* did not attempt to minimize the disaster, but absolved the leadership of bad faith: 'It is not for anyone to criticise anyone else or pretend that he himself would have done better than those who have borne the heaviest responsibility.'[24] George Naylor of the London Compositors' Union argued that, 'Surely, once having declared their intention of coming out in support of the miners, the other partners in the alliance were entitled to a voice in all the negotiations going on and a vote on all questions to be decided.'[25] G. D. H. Cole was inclined to see both a failure of courage and a failure of structure in the débâcle. In addition to 'human frailty and susceptibility to panic . . . [there was] an equally interesting problem of large-scale organisation . . . effective working of the Triple Alliance . . . demanded a greater measure of solidarity and power of concentrated action than articulately exists in the Labour movement at the present time'.[26]

The most balanced contemporary comment by an outsider came from Gerald Gould in a pamphlet issued by the Labour Publishing Company later the same year. Gould began with the assumption that 'victory of a very far-reaching kind was actually within the grip of the Labour

Movement on April 15th, 1921.' Mistakes had evidently been made, but personal recrimination would deflect attention from their causes, rather than contribute to their rectification. Taking the worst case first, he looked at the role of J. H. Thomas. He, said Gould, had 'two replies to his critics: firstly, that the line he took . . . was taken with the full knowledge and co-operation of the National Union of Railwaymen: secondly, that . . . an overwhelming majority of delegates from his union have voted approval of his actions.' This being true, Thomas's own interests and activities were of secondary importance. It made more sense to concentrate on the question of why the NUR had not balloted on strike action for the Alliance during the months before the crunch. (In fact, the NUR rules did not require a ballot before strike action.) Even the NTWF unions could also have been balloted. Everyone knew that confrontation was imminent. Why was it not properly prepared?

To try to answer this question, however, Gould would have needed to follow two different leads in opposite directions. We have seen with what consistency Williams and Bevin sought to persuade their colleagues to prepare. Preparation, however, would have tethered the reluctant Thomas into a position he had no intention of defending. His behaviour really had increased the prospect of defeat. The suspension of judgement on individual behaviour during those April days might sound reasonable, but it would only invite different judgements on the various choices made in the preceding weeks.

Even so, the effect of Gould's argument was strongly to reinforce the positions taken up by Bevin and Williams, focusing attention on the need for integrated organization. All this tended in the direction of speeding amalgamation among transport workers, transmuting the bitter disappointment of the activists into constructive new steps to unity. Yet all of it was argued within a framework scarcely less millennarian than that set up by the communists themselves. The coal-owners were insisting that they could not pay a living wage, argued Gould; but

> If that . . . is true (and it is the owners themselves who say it), then the victory of the working class in the matter of wages would have meant automatically the abolition of profits, the retirement of capitalists from industry, and consequently, the taking over of all the main industries by the State, or by the workers . . . or, more probably and desirable, by the State and the workers . . . conjointly.[27]

Had this been true, Gould's notion that 'victory was in the grip' of the unions could not possibly have been sustained. If victory had been narrowly missed, this was because the government was very far from having reached the end of its tether. It would have been a victory if Lloyd George had climbed down, and continued the subsidy. Such a victory would have postponed the reckoning, not finalized it.

In an attempt to recover from the disaster the NUR and the NTWF imposed an official embargo upon the import of foreign coal whilst the miners' lock-out continued through April and May. This rearguard action led to a serious conflict within the Federation which contributed to its rupture with the NSFU, and to a major confrontation with Sexton and his union.

## The Coal Embargo

Ben Tillett, now active again on the NTWF Executive, reported on 22 April that his union had voted £10,000 as a first weekly contribution to the Miners' Fund for the relief of suffering amongst their wives and children. He asked that this be channelled through the Federation, and that Williams should issue a general appeal to all the affiliated unions to do likewise. The DWRGWU had also instructed its members in coaling and bunkering work to abstain from handling coal if this would harm the miners' cause. This included a refusal partially to bunker any ship bound for continental ports to complete its bunkering coal intake. It had also asked the US longshoremen not to send coal to Britain, and appealed to Edo Fimmen of the International Transport Workers' Federation in Geneva to ban coal shipments to Britain.

The attempted embargo divided the NTWF along familiar lines. On the left stood the London dockers, the Scottish dockers, many of the leaders of the UVW and NUVW, and Gosling. Opposed to them stood Wilson and the NSFU, and, pusillanimous as ever, also Sexton. Of his position at this time Eric Taplin has written: 'Sexton's influence [within the NTWF] was, however, limited. The weakness of the NUDL executive in controlling its rank and file was well known, and his long-standing internal feuds with "malcontents" within his union did not inspire popular confidence in him . . . Sexton rigidly adhered to the sovereignty of the NUDL both within the (Triple) Alliance and the Federation.'[28]

Moreover, Sexton's standing in the local Liverpool Labour movement had been further damaged by his opposition to a three-day general strike called by an *ad hoc* committee – of which his own official, Milligan, and Walter Citrine were chairman and secretary – to enforce the reinstatement of policemen sacked for their part in the 1919 police strike. Taplin records that Sexton was angrily condemned by Citrine, and 'the incident scarcely endeared the NUDL to the local labour movement'.[29]

The coal embargo was weakened at an early stge when NUR members were dismissed for seeking to apply it. The NSFU blatantly broke the embargo from the outset, even inducing its own members to handle coal in Belgian ports despite the local dockers' efforts to implement the ban. After initially moving that the embargo apply to all sections of the

Federation, and not solely to dockers and coal-heavers, the NUDL Executive resolved that 'until such time as there is unanimity and co-operation between all those carrying coal and those handling it, we cannot accept any responsibility for the instructions being carried out.'

Sexton's branch in Hull was told at first to handle coal, only to have this instruction countermanded later. The NUGW branches in Hull complained that NUDL dockers were handling coal, and that their members in gas and electricity were having to refuse to take the foreign coal which was arriving at power stations and gasworks. Sexton replied that it was unfair for his members to take all the blame, when the NSFU was also defying the ban, and that the Federation had exceeded its powers by writing directly to his Hull branches. Williams countered, claiming that the NUDL's action 'destroys the morale of the whole movement'.[30]

Bevin concurred with the judgement: there was confusion in the ports, with Sexton's union issuing contradictory statements on the embargo.

In the Scottish east-coast ports, organized by Sexton, dockers were handling coal. In Liverpool, Sexton defended the handling of coal on the grounds that others, such as cranemen and road-haulage workers, were breaking the embargo, as was the NUR. Houghton, for the Glasgow dockers, was livid; his men were out on general strike in the port over the coal embargo, and their places had been taken by a flood of blacklegs. In his anger, he called for the NUDL to 'get out of the Federation or give a guarantee that they will abide by instructions . . . they should get out of the Federation and be honest about it.'[31] The Federation's annual meeting in 1921 called for an investigation into the charges against the NUDL and the seamen, and Sexton's popularity within its ranks, never high, took a further fall.

The fate of the embargo was determined not only by the defection of two of the largest affiliated unions, but by the devastating effect of blackleg labour both at home and on the Continent. Through May, the NTWF Executive continued to agonize about its continuance, until finally it separately, and then jointly with the NUR, concluded that – in Gosling's words – 'there is no embargo'. There were blacklegs everywhere, in London, Leith, Liverpool; and then the NUDL Executive threw off all pretence by instructing its branches to work. Edo Fimmen, of the International Transport Workers' Federation, sent equally discouraging reports about breaches of the embargo in Dutch, Belgian and French ports.

Bevin complained that, in any case, the embargo was not appreciated by the miners. Hodges indeed sent a message to the Federation telling them that they could lift it, rather than risk the victimization which threatened dockers such as those in Glasgow, and that the miners would win their fight alone. Bevin thought this a most unwise thing to have said in public. The embargo was dying the death, however, and the

Federation called it off on 31 May.[32] Now the priority became the reinstatement of the 2,000 Glasgow dockers who had been replaced by non-union labour. The experience left bad blood within the Federation, and further soured relations between the erstwhile partners in the Triple Alliance.

## II

### *The Seamen: Sailors versus Cooks*

The NSFU had dissented both from the Federation's original intentions to join the Triple Alliance's mining strike, and from the subsequent coal embargo. Concurrently, it was involved in its final act of defiance. It deliberately set out to break an official strike of the Cooks' and Stewards' Union against a wage cut. Cotter reported to the Federation that he had walked out of a meeting of the National Maritime Board which, with the support of the NSFU, was in the act of accepting a wage reduction, since his union had pledged itself not to agree. The shipping companies and Wilson had insisted that the cut applied to all sections of the industry, even though the catering staffs had hitherto negotiated in a separate panel of the NMB.[33]

It was an ill-timed and recklessly led strike. The Maritime Board's wage cut of £2 10s. was not an uncommon one that year. Many unions affiliated to the Federation had accepted similar punishment, and this cut was less than the £4 10s. that the owners had wanted. Although some 10,000 cooks and stewards responded to the strike call, it had collapsed in four weeks. The reason is not difficult to discern. One-third of insured seamen were unemployed at the time, and the shipowners had no difficulty in recruiting others to take the place of the strikers. Cunard moved some 350 staff from Birkenhead to Southampton to man the catering departments on board the *Aquitania*. This gives us some measure of the size of the complement in that section of a luxury liner's crew. It also tells us, graphically, how the other half was living.

Cotter's leadership was 'explosive'. Even so, he was probably set up by opponents. He was accused of issuing an inflammatory circular to members, advocating heavy ca' canny. The proposed measures included possible destruction of ships' furniture and fittings, the mislaying of linen, and muddle and loss of passengers' luggage. Cotter denied its authorship. Could it have been planted by Wilson?[34]

Despite all this, the NTWF Executive resolved to give full support to Cotter's union, and sought solidarity action from its affiliates in the ports. The NSFU now launched a campaign accompanied by strong-arm methods, to drive Cotter's union out of the industry, and to break the cooks' strike. Wilson went in person to deliver what amounted to an ultimatum to the Federation on 10 May. He claimed that support for Cotter's strike would break the Federation. He was being coerced to resist a wage cut which he had been bound to accept, with 20,000 out of work in the shipping industry, of whom 10,000 were 'aliens and coloured'. Federal suppport for the cooks' strike was 'a godsend to the shipowners',[35] who could scrap the National Maritime Board, annul the closed shop of the NSFU, and set his union back twenty-five years.

Wilson's alarm and aggression are evident in every phrase. Yes, his members had loyally accepted a wage cut of £2 10s.; in the face of this, federal support for Cotter's strike was a deadly threat. His members were being approached by the Federation not to sign on, but he would never give them strike pay:

> Some of Mr. Williams' friends were forming Vigilance Committees with the object of destroying the Union . . . Mr. Williams had pledged the support of the Federation to the Cooks and Stewards at a meeting held the previous night, but . . . he left the aspersion that [the sailors and firemen] were scabs. If the Federation wanted them to take their representative off the Executive Council they had only to say so . . . The thread which bound them to the Federation was a very very slender one.[36]

The personal and political feud between Wilson and Williams boiled over. Williams retorted that he was no more ashamed of those he called his 'former friends' than Wilson was of his. Bevin probed where Williams thumped, in a series of barbed questions to Wilson. Would Wilson not have asked for federal support if he had been in Cotter's position? No, replied Wilson. Would Wilson not have asked for the support of the dockers? No, again. Would not Wilson disapprove of his members sailing with scab catering crews? A defiant no, for the third time. But no cock crew.

It was crystal clear that Wilson would not accept involvement in, or interference from, the Federation in what he regarded as a private war with Cotter's union. Cotter was equally defiant; he had as much right as the miners to seek federal support; his men were solid in all the big ports and he appealed again for federal assistance against blacklegs.

The histrionics of both 'Explosive Joe' Cotter and Havelock Wilson may have added a comic touch to the exchanges, but their significance was no joke. Wilson's commitment to his established harmony with the shipowners (and the defence of his closed shop) clearly undermined the endeavour to unite transport unionism. The seamen were an Achilles' heel to the Federation. In 1921 the conflict ran through the mining crisis, the coal embargo and the stewards' strike, into a wider political divide. Now this crack opened to become a veritable rift valley, as Wilson proclaimed a crusade against Bolshevism, real or imaginary.

After the exchanges at the April Executive, Wilson heated up his campaign against Cotter, first enlisting defectors whenever he could among his members and then breaking the cooks' strike with those he had recruited. Cotter had formerly held the sole representation on the catering panel of the National Maritime Board. Now it was clear he was to be eased out of the industry's bargaining councils.[37] From now on, Wilson claimed that he, too, had catering staffs in his union, and that this entitled him to recruit them and represent them before the Board.

Following a last stand-up row at the Annual General Council in June, Wilson, anticipating its inevitable action, called his men out of the Federation in July. In a long, rambling letter of justification, signed by Cathery but undoubtedly dictated by Wilson, he ranged over ancient grievances reaching back to the 1912 dock strike, the alleged use of the Triple Alliance for 'political purposes', the folly of Black Friday (the miners should never have been promised assistance in the first place), and the constant talk of forming 'One Big Union'. Seamen were essentially different from other workers, as they were subject to laws and penalties unique to the merchant service. They could not participate further in relationship with all or any of this.

Williams found it easy to reply. Wilson's decision, he said, had merely anticipated the results of the Federation's enquiries, and the seamen could certainly not have continued in affiliation following their offences in connection with the catering dispute and the coal embargo.[38] His letter concluded with the hope that the sailors themselves might come to see the light and 'take every legitimate means to reconnect themselves with an association which will serve their economic interests better than any body which prides itself on its splendid isolation.'

The following month the Hull Seamen's Union followed its dominant partner into the same exile, in its turn earning Williams's rebuke. He drew attention to the absence of its general secretary, McKee, from his Executive seat at every awkward moment.[39]

## The Seamen and the Amalgamation

These developments cleared space for a new possibility – albeit one barbed with the likelihood of intense conflict – for the Federation, and also for the nascent TGWU. Should they take issue with Wilson, without restraint, and establish their own, more sympathetic, maritime section? In October, Cotter's union and the breakaway British Seamen's Union, whose general secretary was still the radical Emanuel Shinwell, announced their merger, at the same time as the Federation unanimously accepted Shinwell's application to affiliate. The new union was called the Amalgamated Marine Workers' Union (AMWU), and Williams, acting officially for the NTWF, lost no time in providing speakers and all other recruiting aids for it in the ports. NTWF district secretaries were circulated with instructions to give every possible assistance to Cotter and Shinwell.[40]

At this point, conflict spilled over dramatically into the advanced but delicate negotiations which were under way between the amalgamating unions preparing to launch the TGWU. Williams, acting in the name of the Federation, placed a manifesto in the *Daily Herald* calling on all seamen to sign up with the new AMWU, whose ultimate object was 'a clear and definite Marine Section in the TGWU'.[41] Bevin, in conclave about amalgamation with a very large proportion of the Federation's affiliates in his Provisional Executive, was not best pleased. He wrote immediately to Williams to complain about the manifesto, which, he said, had been drawn up and published without the knowledge of the new Provisional Executive. He had in fact instructed his officials not to help the AMWU. Williams replied that he had acted only in accordance with his Executive's policy towards the NTWF's marine section.

This was a sharp pointer to the tensions emerging within the Federation and to the possibility of friction between it and the amalgamating unions. Bevin acted and spoke, as he was bound to, as if the amalgamation were already accomplished, and as if he could therefore 'instruct his officials'. Yet, to take the most obvious case, Tillett, nominally still leader of the DWRGWU, sat in his old seat on the federal Executive as a representative of that union, not of the TGWU. The new union did not yet have a legal existence although Bevin had, in fact, withdrawn from attendance at the federal Executive after the end of the coal crisis in May, and Tillett had taken his place.

Williams responded to Bevin's complaint with the proposal that there should be a meeting between the cooks' and British seamen's spokesmen, his own Executive, and Bevin's Provisional Executive, 'to discuss the future relationship of the TGWU with the Federation'.

A week later, on 26 October, Bevin again met his Provisional Executive; the new marine union was high on the agenda.[42] The TGWU was by now an entity in all but the final letter of the law. Above all, the crucial Rules Conference at Leamington in September was behind them. But here was a situation which both Bevin and Gosling, now respectively the provisional secretary and president of the new union, readily recognized as posing a threat to the new union.

Bevin called initially for 'patience and forbearance towards the new Marine Union'. He recalled a meeting some time earlier, at which, prematurely in his judgement, there had been a discussion on winding up the Federation after the formation of the TGWU. At that meeting, 'Cotter happened to mention across the table in quite an informal way that he had been considering broadening his powers and taking in seamen. I never took this seriously at all . . . and I took no notice.' But, he went on, at Leamington, they had adopted (in what was undoubtedly one of the most prescient steps taken there), a special resolution 'enabling us

to negotiate with any group in the country, whether seamen or any other.'
Later, he and Gosling 'had a walk and a talk':

> I was told that the BSU and Cotter were at the Federation office
> negotiating, and he [Gosling] had taken the line not to amalgamate the two
> unions into another separate union, but to make a job of it at the beginning,
> for the avenue was there. I agreed with him . . . I am satisfied that if this new
> Union is created it won't be in our Union for twenty years. Creating a new
> set of conditions, new officers, and new [here the typescript leaves a blank]
> have to be overcome as we have had to overcome in our own case . . .

Bevin went on to register his surprise at learning that the new union
was already formed, with Gosling and Williams as trustees. His
annoyance was compounded by the appearance of the manifesto of the
union in the *Herald* on 14 October. This was an anxious development:

> I saw 1912 and the coal embargo and you may say that it is ego or what you
> like, but I feel absolutely responsible to the local officers who have had hell's
> own life in the ports . . . while we in London had not had to touch it. And
> when I saw the advertisement what flashed through my mind was that there
> would come the conflict in the ports, and there was nothing done to deal
> with it . . . Then I had the Trades Union Congress to think of . . . I thought,
> what would happen at Congress, if Wilson goes there. What would we be
> asked? Did you plunge into this without asking Wilson? It is no use to say he
> would not come in. You must at least notify and get it turned down or
> otherwise. I would not have interfered only these words appeared in the
> advertisement. They want one big Union for Marine Workers and say that
> 'the ultimate object of the new amalgamation is to form a clear and definite
> Marine Section of the TGWU'. That implies that they are working in
> conformity with us. There is no other interpretation.

At this point a member of the committee, D. W. Milford of the
DWRGWU, interrupted: 'They all believe it.' Bevin answered by
detailing the stories he had heard from the London district that the
Federation was 'out to smash Wilson'. He was a confirmed advocate of One
Big Union as a goal. But he could not risk his precarious new creation,
caught in an economic blizzard, surrounded by mass unemployment, and
with acute inter-union confusion in the ports, in an association with
adventuristic challenges even to Wilson's abhorrent methods.

His concern was transparent, acute: 'Frankly I have been worried, for
after having spent eighteen hard months to mould and weave this
organisation, one cannot help a feeling of fear of wreckage. I have no love
for Havelock Wilson or his policy. I detest the thought of it and feel the
seamen are being sacrificed, but you have to tackle a thing of that kind by
organisation'. He had had to send Gosling 'a note', for Gosling had lent
his name as trustee to the foundling union: 'I am stopping it, but I will
play a straight game. I am convinced that there must be a Transport and

General Workers' Union and anything being put up as a subterfuge should be prevented.'

Was Bevin, in these last words, implying that there was a conscious plot to undermine the new union, or at least to intervene in its decisions from outside its ranks? Or was he confronting nothing worse than provocative behaviour and over-enthusiasm? Gosling would surely have been exempt from such charges, given his profoundly loyal disposition. But what of Tillett and Williams, who had grounds for apprehension over the growing autonomy of the new union and the power of its provisional secretary? We may never know what motivated them in these months. But both were to suffer eclipse as the new union emerged.

Gosling, at least, was present to respond. Although apologetic – and incomplete: the shorthand secretary left several blanks and question marks in the transcript – his remarks confirmed Bevin's account as well as extending it. As president of both the NTWF and the TGWU's Provisional Executive (shortly to be elected its full president), Gosling felt acutely the dual loyalties imposed upon him. He said:

> immediately this Amalgamation began to take form, I could see the impossibility of the Federation as such to continue . . . it came to me so bluntly sitting in the chair at the Federation . . . down one side of the table were all those belonging to our Amalgamation and the other side who were not, and I saw at once if the Amalgamation Delegates were true to the Amalgamation it would be an impossible position for the people on the other side of the table . . . in any question affecting Amalgamation there would have to be an Amalgamation vote on it, and that would be cutting across anything the Federation did . . . You ought to wind up or reconstruct the Federation . . . On the Federation there are Tillett, Hirst, Smith, Twomey, S. March and myself, all on that Federation and in this Amalgamation, and the proper thing for me to do is no longer to be President of the General Federation . . .

On the specific matter of the marine Union, and of a possible marine section for the TGWU, Gosling confessed to acting 'without much consideration' in becoming a trustee of the new union, but he acted on the assumption that the TGWU did intend to have a Marine Section: 'if we had a group of Inland Water it was only a natural sequence to increase that to a General Marine Group, when you would have transport complete other than by rail'. But, of course, this was, from Bevin's viewpoint, naïve and abstract thinking. It left out of account the dominance of the NSFU at sea, and therefore failed to foresee the acute danger of a running waterfront war between Wilson and the TGWU. The likelihood was, if this broke out, that the new union would be indicted at the TUC for poaching or worse.

Alongside these revealing exchanges in the privacy of the new union's Provisional Executive, the Federation was vigorously pursuing its own aim. Just two days later, on 28 October, and after meeting Bevin's group, it resolved, while the ballot to unite the Cooks' Union with the BSU was going ahead, to promote the merger 'as strenuously as possible'.[43] Williams had chaired the joint amalgamation talks between the two unions, and had indeed originated the initiative to bring them together.[44] We have already noted that he had joined with Gosling as one of the trustees of the new union.

He now wrote to the ITF and the unions in Germany, Scandinavia and Belgium to ask help for the AMWU to enrol seamen. Cotter, we know, attended at least one stormy meeting of the British seamen in Antwerp for this purpose.[45] Ironically, the new sailors' union came into formal existence on 1 January 1922, the date on which the TGWU opened its own offices.

'From the autumn of 1921 . . . to the final extinction of the AMWU in early 1927, Havelock Wilson waged unceasing war on this new rival to his union. His principal measures to counter it were four: recruiting campaigns; the "P.C.5"; strike-breaking; and litigation.'[46] The PC5, introduced in 1922, was an arrangement under which a seaman seeking a ship had to acquire a card from Wilson's union and then have it stamped by the owners. After its introduction, Gosling remarked that whilst 'we strongly advocate agreements which provide a monopoly of employment in our respective organisations . . . when the monopoly is purchased at the price of violating all the best of our Trade Union traditions, some of us think the price is too high.'[47]

Reeling under multiple blows delivered by Wilson's campaign, weakened by falling membership and the loss of the former Cooks' Union's place on the National Maritime Board, the AMWU might hold all the moral cards in the pack, but, while it was deprived of entry into the TGWU, it had no muscle. It retained a remarkable number of members nevertheless. They were moved by old loyalties, especially in the liner trades of Liverpool, Glasgow and Southampton. Undoubtedly they also shared revulsion against Wilson's methods.

Despite the odds, Williams in particular relentlessly sustained the inter-union war. The animosity between him and Wilson was a torrid combination of the political and the personal. He used his position as president of the ITF to break up Wilson's anti-German wartime construct, the International Seafarers' Council, which he labelled a 'war legacy'.[48] None the less, he could not dent the NSFU's protected status with the owners. He tried to circumvent it by complaining to the Board of Trade about Wilson's officials, who seized and destroyed AMWU membership cards when catering staff signed on in the ports. He fired off letters of complaint to the TUC, the NMB and the NSFU itself about Wilson's compact with the owners to exclude AMWU members from employment. Although he accepted the need to consult with the TGWU, he complained that it did not seem to be helping the cause.[49] Whatever they thought about this, the NTWF Executive instructed Williams to reopen the matter with that union.

Bevin stuck to his guns, and succeeded in keeping his union out of the range of this storm. The formula which the TGWU offered throughout its first years was that it was indeed committed to unity of the seamen, and to the opening of a marine section, but that the AMWU, with which it held a number of meetings, could not enter except as part of a total amalgamation of all seamen's unions.[50] Williams pressed the TGWU to sign a Federation memorandum of protest over Wilson's tactics, but Bevin persuaded his Finance and Emergency Committee (F and EC) to withhold its support; the minute of 10 March 1922 recorded that 'the present is not an opportune time'.

In April 1922, the TGWU's F and EC adopted a more positive and conciliatory stance, resolving to meet the AMWU again 'with a view to amalgamation with that body', at the same time adding that 'immediate steps be taken to bring about, if possible, the amalgamation to this Union of all Seafaring Unions.'[51] Armed with this, Bevin took a more confident part in the Federation's debate on the subject at its 1922 AGC:

> He would say that whoever attacked, the NSFU was a very big thing to break. He had never seen a big Union-smashing campaign actually succeed . . . there were records inside the Federation of them sufficient to fill a museum, attacks just as bitter and vindictive as those on the Seamen's Union, and the people concerned, who less than eighteen months ago were attacking one another, were now sitting together in the same office . . .[52]

The PC5, Bevin condemned as 'a diabolical thing', if indeed it had been instituted at the price of a wage cut, 'but he understood that Congress was going to deal with that phase of the matter, and he was prepared to leave it to Congress.'

He had not spoken to Wilson, he said, but the burden of his speech was a request that the Federation should sanction the TGWU in an attempt to amalgamate the NSFU and the AMWU within the TGWU.

Cotter rose to present a dossier of evidence on the NSFU's methods in the ports. He claimed that 'Wilson could not hold meetings of his members . . . admission was by ticket, and members who desired to go had to fight their way through a posse of police into the hall.' He claimed that extortion was practised on his members, who 'had to pay £2 to the NSFU officials before they could get work'.

Williams renewed his persuasion: 'he had appealed to Bevin . . . to call Wilson's hand. He told him that the statement was made that Wilson's views on amalgamation had changed, and he had advised that Wilson be asked the plain question. He thought, however, that they knew Wilson 'better than that' and he repeated his invitation to Bevin to negotiate a merger with the AMWU alone, without the NSFU.

Sexton was nervous about the accusation that Wilson had entered a conspiracy with the owners: 'his own Union had entered into a compact with the shipowners of Liverpool that only Dockers' Union men should be employed.'

Shinwell, in an able and measured speech, dealt with Sexton briefly: 'It was all very well to talk about the Registration Scheme in Liverpool, but there they had not come to an agreement to the detriment of another organisation inside the Federation.' Shinwell, however, posed a 'political test. Wilson was a supporter of the Coalition. Would those favouring approaching Wilson have a compromise with Wilson in the political field as well as the industrial field?'[53] Let the TGWU by all means approach Wilson: at least we might then get an answer 'equivocal at first, but sooner or later absolutely definite'.

Tillett, who made it clear that he regarded himself as speaking for the Executive of the Federation (despite his office in the now functioning TGWU),

> was of the opinion that Mr. Shinwell had put the case, not merely for the Seafarers, but for Trade Unionism itself in the Mercantile Marine, and they owed a debt to him. He hoped that the Union represented by Shinwell and Cotter would be joined with the TGWU . . . The power that enabled Wilson to maintain his boycott was the power of the employers . . . every channel should be exhausted in order to expose Wilson. The Federation would give every possible help to stop the betrayal of the seamen's interest.

There is no mistaking the thrust of Tillett's contribution, directed as a member of the federal Executive against what was, by implication, the equivocal position of his own general secretary. And he obviously felt doubly mischievous that day: 'Wilson feared much more the rapier of Shinwell than the bludgeon of Cotter, and he feared the psychology of the man, because Shinwell was the Oriental, whilst Cotter was the Celtic type.'

Bevin was not swayed and, in the event, no approach to Wilson was necessary in order to discover his opinion. At the seamen's Annual Conference, held in July 1922, one month after the Federation's debate, a daring Mersey District No. 3 motion was put: 'That this meeting of Birkenhead members requests the AGM to immediately take the opinion by ballot vote of the members on the question of amalgamating with the TGWU as in our opinion this would strengthen the seamen's position when negotiating with the shipowners.'

Two loyalist delegates immediately moved and seconded 'next business'. Wilson, in the chair, jumped to accept this motion and put it to his compliant conference, which carried it by 51 votes to 11. Bevin was snubbed, and the seamen's 'splendid isolation' continued. The Marine Workers had but a few more agonized years in which to linger on. Wilson had not 'equivocated' even for one moment. The seamen's question was now on a back burner for the TGWU. It was to command more attention later, as we shall see in vol. II.

## III

## *A Railway Section?*

So much for the seamen. How were the NTWF and the emerging TGWU to handle their ambition to bring yet another major branch of transport, the railways, into their plans for affiliation and amalgamation?

Relationships between the three elements – NTWF, amalgamation, and NUR – though by no means without problems, were more instrumental and pragmatic than in the seamen's case. Moreover, the NTWF and the TGWU's provisional leaders shared the same goal, and agreed about the route towards its achievement. They would jointly work for the affiliation of the NUR to the Federation, as a first step to its later amalgamation with the TGWU.

We have already seen that NUR membership and negotiating rights overlapped at several points with those of the transport unions. This was both an incentive towards closer working arrangements and eventual unity, and at the same time an impediment to them. The railway companies had, in their vast evolutionary expansion over the previous century, acquired and/or developed the docks of the Humber, Southampton, South Wales and elsewhere. They had recruited a permanent labour force of 'porters', crane-drivers, lock-gate men, maintenance staffs and others. We saw (chapter 17) that in 1919 the NTWF and the NUR had reached an elaborate agreement, entirely favourable to the NUR, which recognized these spheres of influence in the ports affected. Carters who worked for the rail companies were also enrolled by the NUR, and there were railway-company interests in private tramways as well.

But it was in the ports that troubled relations continued, particularly after the Shaw Inquiry and the establishment of the Joint Industrial Council in the industry. The NUR petitioned more than once to be allocated seats on this JIC, only to be told to affiliate its docks membership first to the Federation, which would then ensure its representation.[54] One particular site, Angerstein's wharf in London, drew several counter-complaints from the Dockers' Union that NUR porters were doing dock work there below the Shaw rate of 16s. a day, and that this was 'unacceptable' to the Federation.[55]

## The NUR in the Ports

The NTWF made other counterattacks. On receipt of another NUR request for JIC status in the ports, it called first for a reciprocal arrangement on the bargaining machinery for the railways, to represent its railway-carter membership. It repeated the charge that NUR members were undercutting the Shaw Award.[56] In 1921, matters moved more amicably; the NUR officials were reported to be wholeheartedly in favour of affiliation to the Federation despite being turned down for the more modest role of representation on the local Port Labour Committees which functioned under the JIC.[57] In December the TGWU, on the eve of its formal inauguration, told the Federation that it fully supported NUR membership first of the Federation, and then of the TGWU. Tillett requested Executive help for this programme; Williams replied that it would be forthcoming, but reminded the TGWU that its docks sections had historically opposed NUR representation on the JIC and PLCs. There had been 'no progress over the years'.[58]

At the AGC in 1922, the Executive could report good progress in relations with the railwaymen. Coal-tipping and trimming were working well together in their national bargaining structure, and demarcation problems on the Cardiff docks had been settled by the Standing Joint Committee set up to deal with such matters. Further, as part of the general reorganization of the Federation following the creation of the TGWU, 'The Joint Committee will of course be superseded by reason of the fact . . . [that] representatives of the National Union of Railwaymen will sit on the Executive of the Federation.'[59]

In an extended report to the Annual General Council, Williams detailed the protracted negotiations and correspondence which had passed between his office and those of all three rail unions, the NUR, ASLEF and the Railway Clerks' Association, aimed at their joint affiliation. C. T. Cramp, the industrial general secretary of the NUR, had reported that 'they were all in favour of amalgamation, and were supporting federation because amalgamation was not immediately practicable.'[60]

## No Affiliation, No Amalgamation

Given its status as a major national trade union, however, the NUR expected the NTWF to enter into detailed negotiations which would effectively re-create it. New rules and structures would be needed. ASLEF and the railway clerks were less committed, and at one point John Bromley of ASLEF felt that the negotiations tended towards committing his union to amalgamation, whereas he was prepared only to contemplate federation. Eventually, all three union Executives agreed to recommend affiliation to their membership. Gosling, euphoric, had told the cheering inaugural conference of the TGWU in September 1921 that he confidently expected the adherence of the railwaymen within a year.[61]

Sadly, in January 1923, Cramp wrote to the Federation that, as the membership ballot on affiliation had been adverse – 511 branches voted against, with 465 in favour – his union had abandoned the whole project. Grass-roots opposition in the NUR was strongly influenced by antipathy to joining an association for which the train-drivers' union, ASLEF, was also balloting. Without the initial step of federation, there was little hope of an NUR–TGWU amalgamation. For the TGWU this was a blow; but for the Federation it was a bombshell. It was left top-heavy with the membership of one union, the TGWU totalling 202,800 against 75,000 from all its other remaining affiliates, some of whom might also amalgamate. We shall have cause to consider the final days of the Federation in vol. II. Here we note only that after much hard work, the TGWU itself was left well short of its ambition to be a comprehensive transport union embracing road, rail and marine transport.

## Tidying the Federation

The Federation continued to accept and reject new affiliations even as its role was placed in question by the vast amalgamation process in its midst. In January 1921 it considered again, but eventually rejected, an application from the Municipal Employees' Association for membership. This drove the MEA towards its ultimate destination as one of the founding unions of the NUGMW in 1924. In April, the Federation finally expelled the United Road Transport Workers' Association, arguing that it had 'never given that assistance in regard to wage movements among the road transport section – to which the union was a party – which the Federation and the remainder of the affiliated unions had a right to expect.'[62] It was also in arrears with its affiliation fees. Interestingly, this federal black-balling did not deter Bevin from negotiating with Hilton for that union's participation in the amalgamation scheme, but the Manchester-based union did not obtain the necessary minimum 50 per cent turn-out in its ballot.

In July, the Federation turned down the Irish TGWU's proposal for a transfer of membership and affiliation, a decision which the F and EC of Bevin's nascent organization had already taken. Of greater potential significance was the affiliation of the transport membership of the National Union of Distributive and Allied Workers (NUDAW) to the Federation.

On the eve of the initial ballot of the twenty-one amalgamating unions, in November 1920, Williams, whilst by no means abandoning the role of the Federation, addressed a long and reflective private memorandum to his Executive councillors. He gave his blessing to the pending development: 'the Federation in its corporate capacity should enthusiastically support the present movement in favour of amalgamation. That this may result in the supersession of a large proportion of the Federation's work cannot be denied and should not even be complained of'. After deploring the poor state of organization in road haulage, and expressing the hope that the new amalgamation would remedy it, he repeated that, for the Federation, 'there is naturally no need for dismay or even misgivings. If the trade union movement does not evince a capacity to alter its structure in accordance with the changed and changing economic and industrial requirements so much the worse for the Trade Union movement.'

He went on to speculate on future transport developments, foreseeing the successful challenge which road travel would make to rail's long monopoly. He predicted a reconstruction of 'our dilapidated canal system', and the growth of commercial air transport: 'Already there were daily services to Brussels, Amsterdam, and Paris . . . It is easy to foresee a time in the lives of many of us when there will be at least a million men employed in transport occupations other than railway traffic.'[63]

We can discern here both Williams the visionary strategist (had he not written in 1913 of the coming of atomic energy?)[64] and the full-time functionary, now under pressure, seeking to shore up and extend his shrinking domain.

# IV

## Into Amalgamation

The story of the seamen, the railwaymen and the NTWF, in their relation to the formation of the TGWU, has pushed us to transgress from a strict chronology. We must now retrace our steps, to relate the final process from the inside: from the records held as the Bevin Papers in the Modern Records Centre at Warwick University and from other documents and typescript minutes held in the archives at Transport House.

Here we move into a different atmosphere from the heady, rumbustious and often rancorous climate of the great public debates in the Federation and in the conferences of individual unions, to observe what is often a quieter, more purposeful process. Whilst the threads which were being woven all evidently reached back into Bevin's hands, the other participants, who were themselves experienced leaders and trusted representatives of their own unions, dropped the platform manner and got down to work. The rhetorical style which we have so often witnessed in our last few chapters gave place to quiet, patient deliberation and co-operation towards a predetermined and shared goal. Bevin's initiative in taking the business outside the formal structures of the Federation was crucial. As the *de facto* chief executive of a large and prestigious union, and as the 'Dockers' KC', he had the resources, the independence and the weight for the task. Robert Williams, always balancing forces within the Federation, and with virtually no independent funds to dispose, lacked comparable force.

## Bevin's Finesse

Throughout the negotiations, Bevin revealed a gentler and more humane side to his own personality and method. He had shown this touch in replying to a debate on amalgamation at the Federation's 1920 AGC, on the eve of his first unilateral initiative:

> You also have in every organisation two generations to deal with, the young and the old. You have the man of conservative temperament who has been in his old union and is attached to his old union, who built it up and made the sacrifices to establish it; and every man who has done that is worthy of consideration . . . we are called upon to face a different set of circumstances from that which they had to face; and I recognize that the rebel of youth is bound to become the conservative of age. It is true, that a man who has built something which was the work of the period of his virility gets a natural fear against seeing anything that he thinks will destroy the work of his life.[65]

He kept this sensitivity throughout all the negotiations and meetings of the next two years. At the same time, he never missed an opportunity to urge that nostalgia was not enough. The message he gave to an area officers' preparatory conference in Manchester on 15 July 1921, was typical: 'He appealed to the Officers not to be tied by tradition, but to get all the old conditions and parochialisms wiped out of their minds, and to think of themselves and their work in relationship to the members in the light of the big new organisation. He wanted them to visualise not what had been, but what was to be.'[66]

## The Shipping Staffs' Key Role

Bevin's first move was to meet the Executive and officers of the National Union of Docks, Wharves and Shipping Staffs (NUDWSS) in March 1920. Encouraged by their reception of his ideas for an amalgamation, he brought together sub-committees of their Executive and his own union, at the headquarters of the DWRGWU in Effingham House, off the

Strand. In Bullock's account, 'these were preliminaries'.[67] Chronologically they were, but they had a deeper significance. It was surely not accidental that the union Bevin chose for his first excursion was one with the closest of associations with the London Dockers' Union, and, moreover, one staffed by officials of high calibre, men of the Labour movement with whom he had intimate relations.

C. G. Ammon, the union's first general secretary, had been a post-office sorter, and after his time with the NUDWSS, he became organizing secretary of the Union of Post Office workers in 1919. This was the time when that union espoused Guild Socialism. Ammon went on to become organizing secretary of the Civil Service Union, and in the 1920s he served on the Labour Party's National Executive. Ammon's later career in Parliament and in public affairs included his appointment, after his ennoblement, as the first chairman of the National Dock Labour Board. Here his record was not devoid of controversy, as we shall see in vol. II.[68]

Alfred Short succeeded Ammon as secretary of the NUDWSS, and throughout the negotiation of the merger Bevin kept him close by his side as a member of the Drafting Sub-committee. He had won a seat in Parliament for Labour in 1918, and he became the first national secretary of the Administrative, Clerical and Supervisory Trade group of the TGWU. He found time in 1922 to qualify as a barrister. Creech Jones, another official of the NUDWSS who was to rise to eminence in the Labour Party, became the national organizer of the TGWU Clerical Trade Group under Alfred Short, whom he succeeded as national trade-group secretary in 1923; he also represented the TGWU on the General Council of the Workers' Educational Association.

These were the men to whom Bevin went in 1920. Moreover, in their delegation he met their president, Tom Condon, who later became the London area secretary of the TGWU's Docks Group. The shipping staffs had not been newcomers to trade unionism in the 1920s. As long ago as 1889, Tom Mann had sought to recruit dock foremen and clerks in the new Dockers' Union, threatening a strike if this was not accepted by the London employers. He came to accept and to commend the authenticity, however, of the separate union which these permanent grades formed: the Association of Foremen and Clerks of the Docks of London. The union's first treasurer was the Reverend Peter Thompson of the Wesleyan East End Mission. This association passed into obscurity in the 1890s, and for several years the clerical and administrative grades had no union. In 1889, a London and India Docks' Staff Association appeared to fight legal cases for its 800 members. It put in a pay claim, however, to the newly formed Port of London Authority in 1908, but it apparently collapsed afterwards. Small localized associations came and went, such as the Surrey Commercial Docks Staff Association, which existed down to 1913.

In 1909 the Port of London Authority Staff Association was formed, but eschewed registration as a trade union, preferring 'to promote friendly relations' with the employer. A succession of PLA Board members acted in turn as its presidents. Yet, as the war gave it bargaining strength, and as the staff found their wages falling behind those of the men whom they supervised, their Association found the courage to bargain for war bonuses and for overtime pay, and for the abolition of a vexatious promotion bar.

In 1917, it resolved that 'an organisation based on the identity of interest between workers and employers could not stand the economic forces at work during the war.'

The Association registered as a trade union that same year. In 1918, it appointed Ammon as its secretary, and in the following year changed its name to the NUDWSS, making Tom Condon its president. Before moving to the Postal Union, Ammon secured employers' recognition for the new union, and between 1919 and 1920 big gains in war bonus were obtained.[69]

This backward look at the white-collar union's evolution will serve to emphasize that the TGWU was the first predominantly manual workers' union to afford autonomous group representation in this field. The quality of its contribution was amply to repay this trust. Alfred Short in his turn, at the opening meeting on 7 May 1920, stressed that, whilst keen to see a white-collar Trade Group, he greatly valued 'the necessary link between such and the actual docker'.[70] At this juncture, of course, what was being proposed was a Clerical or Staff Section *within* the DWRGWU, with direct representation on the union's National Executive. In addition, in each area of the country one staff branch would have the status of a Trade Committee, which would in turn have representation on the general District Committee of the union. This was the TGWU's structure, in miniature, indeed, in embryo. Bevin did not omit to promise to take on all officers from Short's union, at their existing pay or at Dockers' Union rates, whichever were the highest: again this was the precedent followed throughout subsequent negotiations. In a device designed to ensure a smooth transition the members of the Docks' Staff Union would have the option of retaining their present contributions and benefits, or of accepting those of the dockers' union.

## Sexton's Blessing?

Bevin now moved on to tackle one of the biggest hurdles before him. He had to win the support of James Sexton and his union. At a meeting of sub-committees of the two unions at Effingham House on 14 July 1920, over which he shrewdly persuaded Harry Gosling (who came from neither union, but who was the best chairman in the movement, and president of the Federation to boot) to preside, he won endorsement for an outline scheme for a completely new union. This was necessary since it was evident that no union would wish simply to be swallowed up in an existing one. The scheme embraced the main ingredients of the final structure, including National Trade Groups 'to prevent loss of identity', and a central government and Area Committees which were to be representative of all those groups or 'departments', such as docks, clerical, waterways, general workers. After formally resolving that such a new organization for 'waterside and allied workers' [was] 'an imperative necessity',the two unions drew up a schedule of other unions which should be invited to a conference on amalgamation on 18 August. The unions asked to attend were: the National Union of Dock Labourers, the Dock, Wharf, Riverside and General Workers' Union, the Scottish Union of Dockers, the National Amalgamated Labourers' Union (Swansea), the National Shipping Clerks' Guild (Liverpool), the National Union of Docks, Wharves and Shipping Staffs (London), the Amalgamated Stevedores' Labour Protection League (London), the Trimmers' and Teemers' Association of the North of England, the South Side Labour Protection League (London), the Cardiff, Penarth and Barry Coal Trimmers' Union, the Amalgamated Society of Watermen, Lightermen and Bargemen (London), the Weaver Watermen's Association (Cheshire), the Mersey Watermen, and the National Union of Ships' Clerks, Grain Weighers and Coalmeters.

## The Amalgamation Committee

The joint meeting concluded by appointing Harry Gosling as chairman and Ernest Bevin as secretary of what was now called the Amalgamation Committee.

All the unions invited attended except the Weaver Watermen's Association, who asked to be informed of the decisions reached. Bevin's scheme, now more extended, was submitted to the conference. It included the provisions that the new union should undertake industrial, political and educational work; that it should organize workers into groups 'within one great union'; that these groups should have representation on a National Executive which should control all finance, general policy and decisions to strike; that there should be national and district Trade Committees and general District Committees representing all the trades in the union; and that there should be a minimum contribution for minimum benefits applicable to the whole union graduated with diverse scales for the respective groups. In the page and a half of notes occupied by these points, Bevin presented what became the final structure. The elaborate, painstaking and patient work of the next sixteen months went into formalizing and refining this scheme, and winning support for it at every level in every amalgamating union.

To advance this work, the August conference appointed a Drafting Sub-committee, comprising Sexton, Milford (DWRGWU), Houghton, Twomey, J. W. Brown (National Shipping Clerks' Guild), A. Short, J. W. Meggison (North of England Teemers), J. Harrison (Labour Protection League), J. T. Clatworthy (Cardiff, etc., Trimmers), E. A. Spicer (Lightermen), A. King (Mersey Watermen), A. C. Bennett (Ships' Clerks and Weighers, etc.) and J. B. Ruark (Stevedores). Gosling and Bevin were again appointed chairman and secretary of this Sub-committee.

The Committee's proceedings survive in a series of minutes in which are recorded such matters as the scales of contribution and benefit of the unions, an early estimate of the likely combined membership (243,181), flow charts showing the structure approved for circulation, and similar details. Many titles were suggested, including 'The Inland Transport Union', and 'The Inland Transport and General Workers' Union' – which would have definitively ruled out the seamen – until the surviving, familiar title was adopted. At a later stage in 1921, W. Pugh, secretary of the Tinplate Section of the DWRGWU in South Wales, lobbied hard to have 'Metal Workers' incorporated in the title. His grounds were that the Iron and Steel Trades Confederation, the principal union in the steel industry, was trying to entice the dockers' tinplate members away from what it could argue was a union dominated by transport workers. The name-change was successfully resisted, since many other industrial groups might then have pressed for a similar concession. But the question of group identity was a real one. It reared its head at several stages in the amalgamation.

## Bringing in Road Transport

The next big step was to incorporate the road-transport unions in the process. Bevin first sounded them out informally and privately. The Sub-committee then authorized him to invite some of them to a conference on 22 September 1920. Those approached were the United Vehicle Workers' Union, the National Union of Vehicle Workers, the Liverpool and District Carters and Motormen's Union, the Amalgamated Association of Carters and Motormen, the North of Scotland Horse and Motormen's Association, the United Road Transport Workers' Association, and the Scottish Horse and Motormen's Association. All except the Liverpool carters accepted the invitation to participate in further drafting and planning, which now incorporated road transport as one of the envisaged trade groups, and agreed to carve out Area 9 – North Midlands and Yorkshire, because of the very large passenger transport membership in that region; and both John Cliff and Harold Clay, future assistant general secretaries of the TGWU, were former Leeds tramwaymen.

As we have seen, the principal passenger-transport unions had, as recently as 1920, achieved a formal (if somewhat fractious) unity as an industrial union, the United Vehicle Workers. 'Industrial unionism' was a powerful doctrinal influence among them. There seem to have been two prevailing counter-influences which won the passenger workers over to the general amalgamation, after a very shortlived internal debate. One was the undoubted renown of Bevin, who was not only the 'Dockers' KC', but also, through his work with Williams in the NTWF, the principal spokesman and negotiator in their own industry during the four years before amalgamation. He had established the tramwaymen's first national wage in 1919, and he appeared for them at the tramways' Court of Inquiry in 1921. A further reason for the passenger workers' embrace of amalgamation could well lie in the uneasy state of relations between members of the former 'Blue' and 'Red' unions which comprised the UVW. It could have seemed reasonable to suppose that tensions might be resolved within the wider structures of the amalgamation. Certainly they would have been unlikely to deteriorate.

Nevertheless, passenger workers had their own sectional and militant traditions, particularly in London, where rank-and-file control had been the norm in the LPU. At the time of the amalgamation, London busmen were almost 100 per cent organized, and this was true also of the main provincial centres.[71]

In its issue of 5 January 1921, the UVW *Record* published the advice of its senior officials on how to vote in the amalgamation ballot. Stanley Hirst, general secretary, offered his opinion:

I sincerely hope that our members will, when they receive their ballot papers, vote in favour of amalgamation. My reasons for so advising are briefly as follows:–

(1)  It will bring together unions that have in the past spent a large amount of funds in fighting one another instead of combining to fight the employers.

(2)  If employers find it necessary to form huge combines, the trade unions will have to do the same to safeguard the interests of the members they represent.

(3)  It will at one stroke consolidate four road transport unions.

(4)  As each industrial section such as the Road Transport Section (Passenger and Commercial) will have an Executive Council and officials of its own, the interests of members in those sections will be better safeguarded than they are at present, because of the larger membership and the spirit of comradeship that will be in evidence from the members in the other industrial sections, all being members of the one big union.

(5)  Amalgamation schemes in the past have been alleged to have failed because of the vested interests of the officials. So far as the United Vehicle Workers' officials are concerned, I do not know of one who is against the present scheme.

C. Carter, financial secretary, Ben Smith, organizing secretary of the Commercial Section, Archie Henderson, organizer in the Commercial Section, John Cliff, Tram Section, and A. Smith, parliamentary secretary, also endorsed the merger. But a critical message was submitted by George Sanders, national organizing secretary of the Cab and Bus Section. We encountered Sanders, a left-wing socialist with a big following amongst London busworkers, in chapter 17, there promoting Guild Socialist programmes for the transport industry in 1918. Now he adopted an oppositional stance consistent with the emerging communist policies of the Red International.[72] He declared himself in favour of the general principle of amalgamation, but not for

> any ulterior or underhand motive, or to foster the ambitions of individuals who wish to loom large on the horizon. I am not in favour of the lives and conditions of workers being subject to the whims, caprices and ambitions of a few individuals who by their bullying methods are prepared to ride rough-shod over their fellows and take unscrupulous advantage of the workers' ignorance . . . [73]

He would have preferred, too, that the NUR and ASLEF had been incorporated in the scheme, and attacked officials 'of some of the unions that we are asked to amalgamate with' who had supported 'the capitalist class while the late war was in progress'. Members might discount these thoughts and vote for amalgamation, but 'if they consider that more time should have elapsed before the vote is taken then, of course they will refuse to vote until such time as a proper comprehensive scheme is put in front of them'.

Sanders sustained this attack – in part clearly aimed at Bevin – in an article in the UVW *Record* (30 March 1921), which drew attention to the presence of Tillett and Bevin at a dinner of the National Alliance of Employers and Employed, which had as its aim the creating of 'a better understanding between capital and labour'.

However, the weight of leadership opinion in the UVW being overwhelmingly favourable, the union joined a full delegate amalgamation conference with eighteen other waterside and road-transport unions, on 1 December 1920, and participated fully in all the subsequent steps leading to amalgamation.

The road-haulage membership of the amalgamating unions was spread across the NUVW, whose general secretary, Sam March, came from the old London Carmen's Union, and was a very respected pillar of the East End's Labour movement. Along with him came haulage workers from the North of Scotland Horse and Motormen's Union and the Bolton-based Amalgamated Carters, the Leeds-based Amalgamated Carters, the small Greenock Associated Horsemen, the UVW, and the Dockers' Union.

Bevin's roots in this group were again a decisive influence. As a former Bristol carter, who had brought his fellow workers into the extended family of the Dockers' Union in the South-West, he knew what he was talking about. The carters, like the tramwaymen, had reason to appreciate Bevin's leadership in the NTWF campaigns for a national wage, and JIC status. The affinity between dockers and carters was close in all the ports. Only in Liverpool and in Scotland did significant carters' unions resist the attractions of amalgamation. And the fact that the industry's national agreements were already collapsing as amalgamation approached, added further incentive to the quest for the defensive strength which might result from unity. The NUVW and the rest joined the amalgamation conference on 1 December 1920. (As an extra inducement to attend, the Docks' Shipping Staffs' Union invited all the delegates to be their guests at a dinner in the evening.) By the time this meeting assembled, the Drafting Sub-committee had worked its way through a mountain of provisional rules and amendments dealing with everything from officers' salaries to death benefits, financial controls, strike policy, and the number and titles of the Trade Groups. These were subject to frequent amendment. The whole scheme was submitted to a lawyer for expert advice on drafting.

## The New Rules

One matter, as vital as the optimum divisions into trade groups, was that of the geographical areas into which the new union should be divided for its regional, or as it was then called 'Area', government. Eleven Areas were set out at the December 1920 conference. They were:

1   London and the Home Counties.
2   South of England and Channel Islands.
3   West of England.
4   South Wales.
5   Midlands.
6   North-west Coast, to include Cumberland, North Wales, Liverpool and Manchester.
7   Scotland.
8   North-east Coast.
9   North Midlands and Yorkshire.
10   East Coast.
11   Ireland.

The December delegate conference of nineteen unions approved the scheme, which was not yet at this stage embodied in formal rules. Now the participating unions authorized the circulation of ballot forms, together with an explanatory leaflet, to their members. Sexton struck a discordant note by complaining that his union had not had sufficient time to send in amendments, and suggested that the timetable was governed by the personal ambitions of the secretary. This was not the general mood, however, and in fact Bevin approved the most important amendment, from his own union, that the new union's Executive should comprise only lay members.

The leaflet which accompanied the ballot papers was exhortatory, as well as informative. It read:

### AMALGAMATION

### *Transport and General Workers*

FELLOW WORKERS:–

The great scheme of Amalgamation will be submitted to you for ballot forthwith.

The scheme has received considered judgement of the Executives of each Union that are parties to it, and at a great Delegate Conference in London it was endorsed unanimously. (See Resolution overleaf.)

We are convinced this is the right step to take to secure the necessary power and efficiency to deal with the problems that must be solved by the Movement.

Our Unions have, in their respective sections, played a wonderful part in the past, but PROGRESS DEMANDS that existing methods shall give way to new.

CAPITAL IS WELL ORGANISED – EVERY TRADE IS INTERWOVEN AND INTER-LINKED.

The great industries on the employers' side stand together!! Labour must do likewise. Whoever stands in the way of this great change in methods of organisation is doing a grave injustice not only to the present generation, but to the children yet unborn! The scheme allows for the creation of a GREAT and POWERFUL UNION.

It pools its financial resources.

It gives opportunity to create efficient methods of negotiation and handling disputes.

It gets rid of jealousy between Unions.

It allows for the rank and file to co-operate in port, waterway, road transport and factory.

It gives the officials greater scope; a greater opportunity of acquiring knowledge – placing them on an equal footing with employers in dealing with your problems.

It provides for each section to have its own National Committee.

It allows opportunity to shape its programme and policy, at the same time bringing to the assistance of any one section both the moral and financial strength of the remainder.

It proposes to organise the whole of the workers engaged in the respective industries covered by the new Union – administrative, clerical and manual.

It is the creation of a NEW MACHINE.

It will ultimately not only talk of wages, but exercise greater power and control.

WE MOST EARNESTLY APPEAL TO EVERY MEMBER OF THE AMALGAMATING UNIONS TO SECURE THEIR BALLOT PAPER AND UTILISE THEIR VOTE IN ITS FAVOUR.

NOTHING CAN PREVENT IT – only two things can hinder it – namely – VESTED INTEREST and APATHY.

If vested interest stands in its way, then vested interest will be swept aside by force of events.

If, owing to apathy of the rank and file, the necessary power is not given to the Committee to go on immediately, then the RANK AND FILE WILL BE GUILTY of a crime against themselves, their wives and their children.

It is said it's the duty of Leaders to lead – We now give you the lead – Don't fail to respond!!

Signed on behalf of the Delegate Conference,

HARRY GOSLING
Chairman

ERNEST BEVIN
Secretary

## The Ballots Come In . . .

Fourteen unions succeeded in delivering the necessary 50 per cent turn-out and 20 per cent majority required by law for amalgamation.

The most notable and worrying failures were those of the NUDL, which polled only 18 per cent of its members; the Scottish dockers, who closed their poll after only a day and a half, when only 3,000 had voted; and the stevedores, whose vote was simply adverse. However, the successful fourteen sent representatives to yet another conference in the St Pancras Hotel, London on 11 May 1921, determined that the new union would commence to operate from 1 January 1922. The Amalgamation Committee was now superseded by a Provisional Executive Council, Provisional Trustees, and Provisional Executive Officers.

The Provisional Executive Council consisted of T. W. Condon (NUDW & SS), J. Harrison (LPL), D. W. Milford (DWRGWU), G. Stevenson (NUVW), A. W. Walton (NACWU), G. F. Gillespie (AS of WL & B), J. W. Meggison (N of ET & TA), T. J. Wilson (NALU), and C. Black (UVW).

As Provisional Trustees were appointed A. Short (NUDW & SS), J. Twomey (NALU), and E. Plinston (UVW).

Finally, the Provisional Executive Officers were to be president, Harry Gosling; secretary, Ernest Bevin; treasurer, Harry Kay (of the DWRGWU). All these posts, of course, would subsequently be filled by elections.

Ballots would be held when the new union's rules were passed and registered.

The Provisional Executive devoted itself to the drafting of the minutiae of the rules in the subsequent months, until it was ready to convene the Rules Conference (it was in effect the Amalgamation Conference) at Leamington Spa's Town Hall, on 27–9 September 1921, the agenda for which ran to seventy pages consisting largely of the rules as recommended by the Provisional Executive and the branches' proposed amendments. The Conference Report was to run to 415 pages – some measure of the immense labour and patience of all involved in that momentous process.

After that conference, full balloted elections for president, secretary and financial secretary resulted in the election of Gosling, Bevin and Stanley Hirst to the three posts, and the union opened its new offices on schedule at 3 Central Buildings, Westminster, on 1 January 1922. Elections for the General Executive Council, National Trade Group Committees, Area Committees and Are Trade Group Committees were completed by the middle of the ye..., and the first new General Executive meeting was held in Augus. To the fourteen unions which came in immediately, four more – including the NUDL – were added before 1922 was out, and four more again, including the Scottish Dockers' Union and the North Wales Quarrymen's Union, joined in 1923. Their members, like all others, were each allocated to one of six Trade Groups – Docks, Waterways, Passenger Services, Commercial Services, General Workers, or Administrative, Clerical and Supervisory.

All this sounds like a smooth, tranquil transition, and in many ways it was remarkably free from major crises or conflicts. But the bare telling off of the dates, the conferences and the decisions conceals a truly remarkable and even heroic effort of concentrated labour, diplomacy, persuasion, and sheer mental and physical sweat, sustained without a break over two years. It is to illustrate some of these qualities that we must now turn.

## A Spate of Amalgamations

We should first note that the period was one of intense amalgamation activity, embracing engineering, iron and steel, distribution, and general workers, in addition to transport. This burst of activity, which virtually settled British trade-union structure for over fifty years, was facilitated by the Trade Union (Amalgamation) Act of 1917. This had been offered as a 'sweetener' to the trade unions by the wartime government. Prior to the new law, amalgamation required that the unions concerned polled two-thirds of their members, in order for a simple majority of votes cast to legalize a merger. The 1917 Act, with its requirement for a 50 per cent turn-out and a 20 per cent majority of voters, made amalgamation much easier.

Hugh Clegg has recorded a spate of amalgamation discussions during the immediate post-Act years – in engineering, shipbuilding, paper and printing, building, steel, clothing, cotton, distribution, the civil service and the Post Office, 'as well as many smaller industries and services'. But he acknowledges that, 'Overshadowing all these amalgamations, both projected and achieved, were the various schemes under discussion among the general and transport unions, one of which affected more than a million members.'[74]

Not only in scale, but also in complexity, the TGWU amalgamation more than any other taxed the imagination, the patience and the labours of more officials, delegates and voluntary officers down to branch level than any other. We have already seen how the bellicose conflict amongst the seamen's quarrelsome unions severely threatened smooth transition to the merger. Bevin in particular had to work hard to prevent the new creation from becoming embroiled in it. We have noted the eventual collapse of the Federation's attempt to bring in the railwaymen. But a crisis much closer to the heart of the scheme erupted between the amalgamating unions and one of the initiators of the process – the NUDL, Sexton's union.

## Sexton Havers

Sexton had originally been a supporter of a pure dockers' unions' merger, but abandoned that quest when it became obvious that the London-based DWRGWU would not abandon its industrial membership. He was then to be heard, at one conference after another, advocating One Big Union. In 1919, in recognition of the trend, the NUDL changed its name to the National Union of Dock, Riverside and General Workers in Great Britain and Ireland. (To avoid confusion, we shall continue to use the acronym NUDL, by which we have known the union throughout this book.)

Sexton, we have said, endorsed Bevin's autonomous drive for amalgamation at the bilateral meeting with the DWRGWU in July 1920, and Bevin's subsequent moves carried the authority of their joint declaration of intent to promote amalgamation. But Sexton had some sort of second thoughts. He attacked Bevin's 'personal ambition' at the conference of December 1920. Then, in his 1920 Conference Report to the NUDL, held at the Gondolier Hall, Aberdeen, on 12–15 July 1921, Sexton recorded his union's failure to vote for amalgamation laconically, fatalistically, and with a characteristic scapegoating of the 'conservatism' of his membership:

it is extremely difficult to convince the workmen of the value of combined industrial and political action, an example of which we have on the question of the attempted Amalgamation in which our Union was invited to participate. The result, I regret to say, is anything but encouraging, as less than 18 per cent of our membership took the trouble to register their votes for or against, and as a 50 per cent vote is required by law before it can be accomplished, *the effort is futile* . . . Personally, I regret very much the result. There may have been faults in the construction of the scheme, but these were open to amendment [italics added].[75]

Sexton then went on to summarize the strong trend to unification right across the movement. This was unavoidable, he argued: 'It is in fact becoming a case of self-preservation. Sheer force of circumstances in fact demands that we, to be effective in the future, must follow the same lines. It is this alone that still gives me hope that our members may eventually see the necessity of falling into line.'[76] These words might mean that Sexton was prepared to attempt a second ballot to join in the TGWU link. Alternatively, they could signify hopes of other amalgamation partners. After all, possibilities were thick on the ground in the prevailing circumstances.

There is much that remains unexplained in all this. When he came to write his final report a year later, Sexton revealed nothing of how a second ballot came to be held, or of how the required 50 per cent turnout and the 20 per cent majority were achieved. Eric Taplin can throw no light on this: 'Details of the voting cannot be traced and it is best not to enquire too closely into the means by which a fifty per cent poll was finally achieved.'[77]

## Unholy Row at Leamington

In fact, in the interval between the two ballots, an unholy row had blown up between Sexton and the amalgamating unions. It had been obscurely resolved.

The conflict erupted dramatically into the businesslike proceedings at Leamington, at the end of the first day, Tuesday, 27 September 1921.[78] At that conference Sexton's union, having failed in its first ballot, was not represented. Harry Gosling, from the chair, suddenly announced that the NUDL had raised a protest at the NTWF Executive, meeting in London at the same time, that 'this new amalgamation, or as they put it the Secretary of this amalgamation, in his action around the country in propaganda work, infringes the Rule.' Bevin was being accused of breaching the Federation rule against the poaching of members. Sexton had, moreover, put his objections to the General Council of the TUC. It was well known that Bevin, Gosling and others amongst the Provisional Officers had been touring the country, openly, to win support and understanding for the amalgamation. Indeed, as early as January 1921,

Bevin, Sexton and Gosling had appeared on the same platform at the Liverpool Stadium and addressed a mass meeting of dockers and vehicle workers. As a result, a resolution supporting amalgamation had been passed unanimously.[79] It was after this that the turn-out failed in the NUDL vote.

Gosling reported to the stunned and outraged Leamington gathering that the Federation's Executive was to consider Sexton's complaint the following day, Wednesday. He was chairman of the Federation and of the amalgamation, and Tillett, Ben Smith and Stanley Hirst, all present at Leamington, were also on the federal Executive. Gosling asked for guidance, particularly from Tillett; should he go overnight to attend the NTWF meeting, or must he stay at his post in the Leamington chair?

Tillett and Gosling exchanged views in front of the whole conference. They agreed initially that the complaint must be interpreted as one against Tillett's own union. Equally, of course, it was levelled against that union's assistant general secretary, Bevin. But Tillett, despite his own effective demotion and Bevin's domination of the amalgamation, came down firmly in defence not only of the Dockers' Union, but in protection of the amalgamation, which was, he felt, dangerously threatened by Sexton's move. Tillett said:

> it was a challenge to this amalgamation and if Sexton himself and his colleagues had played the game, I feel positive that the rank and file of the Union would have been with us . . . I am not so much concerned with the attack on our own union, because we have had to put up with it for over thirty years, and so I am pretty well used to it, as I am with the attack on this amalgamation, which is at the moment the supreme question at this time of depression in trade, attacks upon trade unions, and attacks upon wages . . . when a man like Sexton puts his hand to a diminution of wages irrespective of other men in other ports doing similar work I think it is so serious a matter that the amalgamation is challenged.[80]

Tillett advised that Gosling should go to London to the Federation meeting: 'I felt today . . . that there would be really no challenge to the good spirit of the amalgamation here present; and I therefore feel that you would be quite safe. This is no one man's movement and it is no one man's assembly or conference.' Gosling must attend in London

> because we have not heard the last of it. Sexton has refused the amalgamation . . . but the fact is that the Liverpool union is not a union, but is a federation of branches, and constitutionally defective. At the same time Liverpool is an important centre indeed, and we ought to accept the challenge now from an organised standpoint . . . Mr. Sexton is trying to save his own neck. He has not played fair with us, and I think the position is so crucial that the leading official of the judiciary . . . should be there. I do not want the Chairman to protect me; I can do that for myself, but I want the

Chairman to protect this organisation and the spirit of it, and the meaning of it, and the future of it. Sexton has gone to the Gas Workers' Union; he has gone to the NUR . . . I want to settle once and for all our relationship with the Dockers' Union in Liverpool in general and with Sexton in particular and if a stand is made we shall encourage a better type of intelligence amongst the dockers of Liverpool and perhaps induce them to come over to us, where they ought to be.

This was a remarkable statement, by any standards. It illuminated with a new vividness the history of the running feud between Sexton's and Tillett's unions, which reached back many years. The young Tillett had been to Liverpool in 1889, expecting to absorb the Mersey dockers in his own new, triumphant union. In Manchester in 1910 he had encamped his offices and members alongside Sexton's union. On the Humber, Sexton had reciprocated during the same time. Much more, Tillett's speech reveals that the prospect of a great amalgamation still commanded his profound support and touched his protective instincts. When a delegate suggested that the row between the two unions was less important than the Amalgamation Conference, and that Gosling should stay in Leamington, Gosling firmly joined Tillett: 'No,' he said, 'the quarrel is between Sexton and this amalgamation.' 'That is so,' said Tillett, 'that is the fight.' And if indeed Sexton was approaching the NUGW and the NUR, the potential damage to the new amalgamation was enormous. Yet some delegates continued to insist that Gosling stay in Leamington as its chairman.

Bevin then intervened, to report that he had indeed received invitations direct from dockers, in Garston and in Hull, who had requested speakers from the amalgamation and who claimed that 'they had been let down over the amalgamation', and that 'they were being kept out'. He had sent his officials and had made members: 'We had a letter to say that the ballot was final, but we know how the ballot was taken.'

Bevin did not elaborate on this cryptic remark at Leamington, and the source of his information might have remained a mystery. But the provisional machinery of the new union, very much under his control and administered from his office at the DWRGWU, kept voluminous files of the correspondence generated by the whole massive amalgamation campaign. These files survive in the union's archive. They confirm Bevin's aspersions on the balloting in the NUDL, and show that Sexton was lukewarm, to say the least, about the merger. They demonstrate, too, the strength of hostility to the merger located amongst the parochial branch officials of the Liverpool union.

In January 1921, R. Blundell, an organizer at the Salford office of the DWRGWU, wrote to Bevin concerning arrangements for a mass meeting in Liverpool which was to be addressed by Bevin himself and by

Sexton on 23 January. The ensuing exchange shows that both Blundell and Bevin found considerable difficulty in getting hold of Sexton at that time. Bevin writes to Blundell on 4 January:

> I have been pressing Sexton to get the halls fixed, but only have the Labour Club for the conference as you know. I phoned him this morning – he was out but they said they had fixed nothing yet . . . entre nous, I have heard a rumour tonight that he had gone to Slovakia (but this of course may not be true), but what I want you to do is to go across at once, and on the grounds of interest and pressure of our members in the area [Area 6 of the scheme] we are anxious to have the details fixed for the announcement, and offer your assistance. I must leave this to your tact and discretion but try to get the thing settled and wire me details.

Blundell reports on 6 January that he had been 'lucky enough to catch [Sexton] in', and arranged to meet him 'on Monday morning next'. But on 17 January Blundell records a memo which he sends for Bevin's attention:

> Acting on Brother Bevin's instructions I visited Liverpool on Monday and there conferred with Mr. Sexton in regard to the forthcoming Conference. Sexton says there is strong opposition in Liverpool which arises from fears that our general worker section will overwhelm the dockers. From another source, I learn that Local Officials are playing up the gag that the Branches will be robbed of their accumulated funds.

As we know, the Liverpool Stadium meeting on 23 January resulted in triumph for Bevin's cause, despite this report and the problem of organizing the meeting.

Things were no easier on the Humber, from where another vigilant and conscientious district officer of the DWRGWU, Arthur Wood of Grimsby, communicated with the union's district secretary, George Farmery of Boston. He had got hold of a leaflet signed by James Sexton, which set out provision for a month-long ballot, possibly extendable beyond the end of February 1921 'in order to secure, if possible, that every member of the Union shall have an opportunity to vote'. After explaining the mechanics of the vote, the circular continues:

> As this is a most important and vital question affecting the interests of the organisation, it is necessary that every member should give a free and unbiased vote according to his inclination. A special Act of Parliament on this question lays down the condition that any member having an interest in the funds of the Union, irrespective of any arrears, shall be entitled to vote, and that fifty per cent of the members at least should record their votes. It is, therefore, essentially necessary that as many members as possible shall exercise their opinion on this very important question.

It is hardly necessary to comment on the obvious omission from this somewhat legalistic notice. James Sexton, who was formally fully committed to the amalgamation, was offering no advice whatever on whether his members should vote for or against the scheme.

Brother Wood, who had been talking to a member of the NUDL, reported that

> there won't be half the members vote if they have to go to the office for their ballot papers . . . [and] I can assure you that there is great dissatisfaction among a lot of their members, and that if the Amalgamation does not come off there will be a lot come over to us. The member of ours that I mentioned . . . told me he could put his hands on a dozen that would join us . . . says he could get more but will wait and see how the voting goes on. He does not want anyone to know where the pamphlet came from nor his name mentioning.

It is clear that the old rivalry between the two principal dockers' unions was contested at local level down to the last minutes of their separate existences. At the highest level, too, Bevin told the Leamington Conference that: 'He is trying to make this a personal attack . . . I don't mind that.'

We might pause to remind ourselves of the numerous occasions on which Bevin had teased Sexton for his wavering, or mocked his humourless speeches. Over and again we have eavesdropped on this badinage in the Federation. Often Bevin drew blood. At the NTWF Annual General Council of 1920, there had been a notable score, during a debate on Bevin's motion to raise the contributions which unions made to the Federation. Sexton's speech on the subject included this passage:

> I am rather diffident in touching upon one phase in the discussions opened by Mr. Bevin. It is rather a delicate matter to discuss, as to how many members the Union are entitled to pay on, but I would respectfully remind you . . . that there is a great deal of difference between the financial membership of a Union and the numerical strength on the roll. When Unions go to Trades Congresses they give their full numerical strength on the roll which does not represent the total contribution per member of the Union; and all the Federation ought to expect in my opinion, is the total financial membership in any Union.

Bevin prompted him: 'But the difficulty is in ascertaining what that is.' And Sexton fell into the trap: 'As Mr. Bevin knows, you have got to knock off 25 per cent at the very least to get the basis of your financial membership.' Bevin interrupted again: 'Now we know'(!) Sexton sought to return the barb: 'I think you do know, and I have no doubt that you have practised it as long as anybody else.'[81]

Bevin, as we know, had also persistently needled Sexton about low wages in Liverpool. His remarks were scattered broadside not only in NTWF meetings, but also out in the open, at the Shaw Inquiry. Surely Sexton did not love Bevin. But for Bevin the matter was not a personal one: 'it is this union that has got to fight Sexton.'[82]

He went on to detail threats of physical violence made against him if he persisted in visiting Liverpool, declaring roundly, 'I do not mind if they use hooliganism . . . there has got to be a united movement at all costs, even if it means life in the effort. It has got to be done, and if they resort to these methods which have been the bugbear of that port, it has to be faced throughout Liverpool.' He concluded that Gosling should go to London, 'hear the challenge, meet it, and come back here on Thursday morning and let the delegates know . . . Sexton ought to be faced and brought right up against it'.

Other weighty speakers – J. Wignall, MP, and Will Godfrey of the NUVW – fell in behind this view, arguing that it would demonstrate their confidence in their own unity of purpose if they showed that they could manage their meeting without Gosling's chairmanship for a day. Gosling agreed to go, ending the debate with these words: 'I think I can do some very real good there, because I am not so concerned about flogging Sexton as I am about getting Sexton's members . . . even if we have to get Sexton as well.' It had been a remarkable and revealing exchange.

When Gosling returned to Leamington on Thursday morning, he refrained from giving a detailed account of the NTWF hearing. He reported briefly that he had conceded that membership recruitment would stop, but in return he had obtained a commitment from Sexton to hold a new ballot, and he was confident that by the following year the NUDL would have come in. The NTWF Executive minutes carry no verbatim report of the meeting to which Gosling was called from Leamington, but a Report to its next full meeting on 8 October referred to a sub-committee meeting at which 'it had been agreed by the Amalgamation that the activities complained of should cease, and that a further meeting between the contending parties would take place on October 9th.' The crisis had passed as suddenly and as obscurely as it had arisen.

We do not know why Bevin was threatened by bully boys. Was it a resistance to over-vigorous enrolment methods? If these were mounted, presumably after the ballot failure, was there a threat from strong-arm men? If so, were they incited by Sexton, either alone or in concert with other NUDL officers? Or did they come from a rank-and-file that genuinely wished to be left alone in their provincial fastness? Taplin has suggested that a union run from London on centralized lines would have had little appeal on the Mersey.[83] But Bevin claimed at Leamington that some dockers, at Garston and Hull, not Liverpool, had invited him to come. No doubt there were, inside the union, sections and individuals with opposing views. Still, there seems little doubt that Sexton's platform declarations of commitment to amalgamation concealed a degree of duplicity, at least in this final phase in 1920–1. How else can we explain the sharply different results of the two ballots? For the DWRGWU correspondence file, which has given us glimpses of the struggle over the first ballot, is even more revealing about the second. The DWRGWU *Record* for November 1921 reviewed the progress towards successful transfers of membership and of second ballots in a number of unions still outside the new amalgamation established at Leamington. Amongst others, 'we are assured there will be no doubt as to the result of the ballot in the case of the national Union of Dock, Riverside and General Workers.' But a handwritten letter to the union, dated 24 November 1921, casts blunt doubts upon the outcome. It reads:

Sir i have read this months record and i see by it you refere to the Liverpool Union of Dock Labourers joining in the Amalgamation Sir i must tell you if you knew all you would open your eyes for i must tell you the Officials dont like it and wont help it on one bit for it has only just leaked out over the ballot to a few for they have got the box in a back room at No. 5 Branch were only the Committees go on a Monday night and when i spoke on Monday last about it i was told it was quite in order and we put it to our Secretary of No. 5 branch to have some bills printed to give out at the docks but he scorn the move but to prove that things is not what they should be find a thing or two out your self Sir and you will find what i say is quite true the Secretary is dead against it of No. 5 Branch, Liverpool, Sir i remain
J. M. Mason,
Dock Labour[84]

Taplin suggests that a major factor in Liverpool was not hostility but indifference. Low turn-outs in ballots had been a consistent feature in the union, and:

The quasi-federal nature of the union had throughout its history rendered the executive and its officers at headquarters relatively remote. The branch offices and delegates at the waterfront were closer to the men, and to their activities. The creation of the TGWU made little difference. The same men carried on as before. Milligan as Area Secretary of the TGWU was seen as the chief official at local level until his death in 1925. Sexton had always been remote . . . his disappearance from union activities merely removed the target from those who had consistently attacked him for his personality and his policies . . . The absorption of the NUDL was achieved with minimum fuss and disturbance.[85]

It was very nearly not so!

## *Suppressing the Row*

Bevin, after the heat had died down, sought to win Merseyside loyalties by offering Milligan the post of national docks group secretary, but Milligan and his wife were unwilling to leave Liverpool for life in London. (Bevin himself took over the group, combining the job with his general secretaryship.) A new Area, No. 12, was created. It was based in Liverpool – a clear concession to the men of the NUDL. Bevin and his Executive also took another step: they suppressed the publication of the verbatim Report of the Leamington Conference. This had been commissioned from a shorthand transcribing company, and its solitary copy is preserved at Transport House, from where we have transcribed it.

Non-publication was unheard of, for, as readers have learned, the practice of the time was to record and publish everything that was said, in full, and surely there had never been a more important conference in the history of transport and general trade unionism. The Report was really the founding document of the union. Our attention was drawn to this curious omission when we found the correspondence, addressed to Bevin, still held in the Transport House archives. One letter came from the secretary of the Cardiff No. 2 branch of the NALU, Brother E. Bolwell, on 28 November 1921. It reads in part: 'Dear Sir and Bro., If I am not too premature in asking for full report of the Leamington Conference I should thank you for forwarding same to me. I have noted the little published in *The Record*, but surely that cannot be a full report of the Conference?' Bevin replied the next day: 'In reply to yours of the 28th inst., we hope to have the full report ready soon, but you will understand the work is very heavy in the provisional stage, and we have not yet been able to complete it.'

A more formidable demand for the publication of the Report came from Tillett, on 29 December, the very eve of the New Year 1922 when the TGWU was to open for business. His letter was addressed to Bevin, Gosling and the Provisional Executive Committee. He wrote that

> a very grave error has been committed I think in the omission to publish a full report of the Leamington Conference. In view of the occasion being so momentous it was at least due to the several Unions and their respective Executives that a precis should have been given. What is in the October *Record* is I feel not a clear or an intelligent expression of even the limited nature of the Leamington Conference . . . I had hoped that in the chronology of our ·Movement such Minutes would have been printed as would have made an historical document of importance. I know the short-comings of the Conference – its rush and its hurry – and may I say its ill-considered unanimity[!] which was due more to goodwill and the desire for amalgamation than to a business-like and intelligent examination of the

principles and the points involved in the transitionary period. I raised some comments upon appointments and a pledge was given by the Provisional Secretary that the same would be attended to . . . I want the Provisional Executive to understand that my own Executive, as I am, is most anxious that they shall have the full Minutes of the proceedings of the Leamington Conference. This would prevent misapprehension, and already there is too much suspicion of intrigue and self-seeking abroad, which will militate against the harmony which induces efficiency and relieves the mind of suspicion of autocratic domination.

Having read the transcript, we agree with Tillett's opinion about its value as a historical document, but we can find no evidence of a sinister kind to suggest 'intrigue and self-seeking'. 'Domination' there was through Bevin's power to persuade the whole conference in its debates on the wording of the rules. His unchallenged command was based on his skills and his remorseless logic, his grasp of detail and his breadth of vision, and we shall illustrate these shortly. In suppressing the document, he was seeking no alibis. He had nothing to hide, and much to take pride in, had the document appeared. Tillett had a large axe of his own to grind, about his reluctant withdrawal from the candidates' list for the presidency.

However, it is in this report that the blazing row with Sexton was recorded. We have quoted at length from it, and some very harsh things were said about Sexton. Moreover, there are bald comments about his union, and the 'intelligence' of his Merseyside members, which were also highly sensitive because they were, not to put too fine a point on it, exasperated and even rude. We are led to conclude that Bevin did indeed deliberately suppress the publication of the document because of these passages. Sexton's union was still to be re-balloted; it was hoped that it would enter the new union soon. Sexton had somehow been prevailed upon, by Gosling and the Federation, to try again, and to deliver a positive vote. The row was over, and none of Sexton's members had been present to hear the sharp words used at Leamington. Publication would have reopened the wounds, perhaps fatally. Equally, an act of censorship, cutting out only the offending remarks and publishing the rest, would also have been a cause of further speculation and rumour. The TGWU, in common with most unions in modern times, followed the precedent set in 1921 of not publishing verbatim records of its Delegate Conferences, though they remain in unbroken series as typescripts.

Sexton met Bevin's discretion in the same coin, when he wrote his final Annual Report (dated December 1921, but written after the successful second ballot). He suppressed any evidence of the conflict and fell back upon sentiment, 'feelings of regret', 'mixed feelings', and nostalgia for the stirring days of his youth. He referred to his long record of advocacy of one transport union 'with its one central authority'. As a sixty-six-year-old veteran, he did not harbour personal ambitions for a top post in the new union, and did not contest any of its elected offices. He was an MP, and confessed that 'the effort to combine my work in Parliament with my duties in Liverpool, where my home and offices were, had been putting a very severe strain on me.'[86]

The new union made a goodwill gesture by appointing him national supervisor to the Docks Group, which, in his own words was 'a bobby's job'. He retained his salary and was given access to the new headquarters of the union in Westminster.

# V

## *The Shape of the New Union: the Debates at Leamington*

It remains necessary to review some of the important debates at Leamington, to examine the process of elections to the various posts and committees, and to look at the shape and condition of the TGWU in its early days. We must also assess the role, power and status of Bevin himself as he took over the leadership.

The task of setting up the Amalgamation Committee in 1920, followed by the election of Provisional National Officers and a Provisional General Executive Council, had to be replicated concurrently at the Area level. This involved Bevin and the Provisional Executive in a series of meetings at the main provincial centres in which Area Offices and administrations were to be established.

With the scheme worked out in the Amalgamation Committee, and submitted for approval at delegate conferences of the amalgamating unions, Bevin did not wait for the formal adoption of rules before convening these Area conferences, which went on through the summer and autumn of 1921. He and Gosling, who invariably took the chair, travelled from one end of the country to the other, using a stock agenda at each location. Some members of the Provisional National Executive also attended each meeting. The local and district full-time officials of the amalgamating unions were always invited. First they heard an address by Bevin. He sought to inspire a sense of uplift and excitement at the prospect of the new union, and then to arouse a commitment to prompt, dispassionate labour, setting up 'machinery' without delay, to be ready to take over in January 1922.

The meetings then went on to appoint Provisional Area Committees, Provisional Area Trade Group Committees, and Provisional Officers to administer the Area and the Groups. All these posts, Bevin insisted again and again, would later be subject to competition, in the case of officers, and election, in the case of the committees. The appointments to these

Area Committees were made by the local officials, Bevin stressing that the national centre relied entirely on their knowledge of the region and of the individual officers and lay-members whom they were appointing. It was an impressive replication of the detailed diplomacy operating at national level, and was supplemented by 'a large scheme of propaganda' and countless special branch meetings at which Area officers and committee members reported on the Area meetings. Not for nothing was it reported to Leamington that 'we are indebted to the many Officers of the various organisations in explaining the Scheme to the members with enthusiasm, as expressed in the ballot returns.'[87]

The Provisional Officers and Executive had been chosen nationally at the St Pancras Conference in May 1921. Gosling encountered no opposition to his election as provisional president, being nominated by seven unions. Bevin was originally opposed for the *provisional* secretary- ship by Stanley Hirst and Robert Williams, both nominated by their own unions. Williams sent a message to the conference withdrawing from the contest, and wishing the conference every success. Hirst polled his own union's card-vote of 13,000 against Bevin's 235,000 votes, which came from nine different unions. It was really from that point that the team of Bevin and Gosling reigned unchallenged over the process, nationally and regionally, and ensured their ultimate confirmation in office, by election, in December 1921. We shall return to those elections later. In preparation for Leamington, the welding together of Area machinery created a TGWU mentality. This was to be crucial for the future.

At the same time, the Provisional Executive had to construct precise rules to put to the final gathering, covering every aspect of the union's administration and finance. We find in Bevin's notes and agenda for the Provisional Executive a working-out of objects, which included at an early stage the promotion of union education, support for Labour colleges, and for a Labour press. The shape and number of the Trade Groups was subject to many revisions: food production, chemicals, metal, flour-milling, were all considered for Group status, but the final recommendation to Leamington was that all these should be subsumed under the General Workers' Group. Had one been excepted, the exceptions would have become innumerable.

The balance between Group autonomy and control by the central officers and GEC also had to be worked out. The formula arrived at was that each Group would enjoy autonomy in fixing its industrial programmes and policies, and would conduct its own negotiations with the employers, but that decisions on strike action would lie with the GEC. Along with centralized control of strikes would go a highly centralized grip on finance. All contribution income would go to central office, from where the needs of the districts would be met by remittances for approved heads of expenditure. Not until Jack Jones's reforms in the 1970s were the regions to obtain any marked financial autonomy.

Centralization of the funds of the amalgamating unions had to be achieved fully and promptly at the moment of amalgamation, 'in the event of the new union being attacked', and also because the TGWU would take over and administer all the obligations of the old unions for officers' pensions and grants on retirement. All serving officers were taken on, with a guarantee that their salaries would be, at the least, maintained.

The minimum contribution recommended to Leamington was 6d. a week, with 6d. quarterage, which was levied for a contingency fund, a device previously used in the Dockers' Union and several others, and – as the name implies – collected from the members separately from normal weekly subscriptions, once every quarter. A meagre 2d. of this sum was returned to the Area 'for local purposes'. Dispute benefit was to be £1 a week, and the proposed funeral benefit was £5. (At Leamington, the Conference raised this to a maximum of £10.) Women members would get half the rates for half the contributions. The union would administer the Health and Unemployment Insurance Acts, for which members would make additional contributions.

And so to Leamington, at which the agenda presented by the Provisional Executive consisted of twenty-five recommended rules, from Rule 1, 'Title and Membership', to Rule 25, 'Voluntary Dissolution'. Out of 1,000 branches circulated, 189 sent in amendments to these rules, although some amendments came in the name of joint branch meetings covering a town or district. The Provisional Committee's Report to the Leamington delegates listed those unions which were not present because they had failed to muster a 50 per cent turn-out in their ballots, a number of them having been visited to arrange a second ballot. These included the Cardiff Trimmers, the Scottish Dockers (who unaccountably closed their ballot after a day and a half, having polled only 3,000 of their 9,000 members), the Bolton Carters, the North of Scotland Motormen, the Leeds Carters, and the United Road Transport Workers. On the NUDL, the Report gave what turned out to be a preview of the drama of the first day: 'It has been openly stated by some of the officials of this Organisation that they would oppose and prevent amalgamation, but in spite of this, 23,000 votes were cast, and out of this we are informed that less than 2,000 were against the scheme, so it is the 50% law only keeping this Union back.'

The Report also insisted that the NTWF was helping to bring about a better atmosphere and to bring the union into the amalgamation. It was also reported that the National Union of Distributive and Allied Workers had been approached to join, but that it was already engaged in merger talks with the Shop Assistants' Union and had not taken up the invitation. These talks eventually produced the present Union of Shop, Distributive and Allied Workers.

By the time of the Leamington Conference, nine of the planned eleven

Area Offices were already at work, and office accommodation had been, or was being, acquired. Lay Area Committees were in being and, following the Conference and their permanent election, they were ready to function. In addition to rule-making, the Conference debated a small group of resolutions tabled by the platform. These included motions on the defence of the forty-eight-hour week, on the defence of Trade Boards against an employer-inspired campaign to abolish them, and on the plight of the Poplar councillors, who had just been arrested for refusing to levy rates from their poverty-stricken community to meet the precepts called for by the central authorities. Poplar was stiff with docks and warehouses, and of 50,000 employed males more than 40 per cent were transport and general workers, while 25 per cent were casually employed. Their poverty was continuous, but with the slump it had become acute. Their councillors were absolutely integrated with the local community. They included not only George Lansbury, but Sam March, Mayor of Poplar and general secretary of the NUVW, and other transport-union officials. Their running battle for the relief of poverty and distress was to dog the headlines for years to come.[88]

## Sectional Identity

Apart from the fireworks provoked by the absent Sexton, the conference was marked by a united and remarkably non-controversial spirit. Amendments were moved, debated, passed or rejected. Yet within many of these little debates – which sometimes seemed to hinge on details of wording which were quite minute – were contained vital issues of structure. The major task was the harmonization of sectionalism with central, organic unity. This was not easy. The building of its constitution was a work of great ingenuity, the outcome of which was permanently to shape the nature of the TGWU.

W. Pugh, district secretary of the Tinplate Section of the DWRGWU in South Wales, returned to his demand to have the word 'Metal' inserted in the title. He was concerned to maintain the loyalty to the new union of the 7–8,000 members who worked in tinplate, galvanizing, and iron and steel. They were the subject of overtures by the Iron and Steel Trades Confederation. Some of them had been loyal servants of the Dockers' Union for twenty-two years, and had, said Pugh, a 'moral claim' for consideration of their group identity.

Bevin again resisted this alteration to the title. To concede it would, he thought, open the way to a flood of other sectional demands for recognition, from flour-millers, tramwaymen, carters and others: 'I have heard it said that the most embracing word is transport, because I remember it being said when they organised the midwives in one town and the grave diggers in the other, they claimed that everything came within the word transport.'

Other sectional demands, not only for identity but for autonomy, were raised during the definition of the Trade Group Committees which were to be set up. There were demands from the milk trade, the oil-millers, the gasworkers, the shipbuilding and ship-repair workers, flour-milling, breweries, and from chemicals, where, in South Wales and elsewhere, the Dockers' Union had established membership in the soda-fertilizer industry and in the nitrogen/explosives industry; the outline of a future Chemical Trade Group can be traced to these enclaves of membership in what were to become such great combines as ICI. But in 1921 all such industries looked for Group status immediately. Some of their claims were based not so much on the current numbers of members in a Group, but on the size of its potential membership. For example, the milk traders argued that their industry was not only vital to the country, but employed 100,000 people. Most of these, of course, had not yet joined up. Many others argued that only the specialist worker in his trade was qualified to make decisions on it. One amendment, from Stanley Hirst and the UVW, sought to reunite into one Group the separate commercial and passenger sections of road transport, a move in the opposite direction. But the main burden of complaint came from non-transport workers, all of whom felt a grievance that they had been lumped together in a General Workers' Group, whilst transport workers had been recognized as having claims to several distinct sections and their accompanying autonomy.

Bevin resisted all these demands. He was intent on restraining any uncontrollable outbreak of sectionalism at this early stage. By designating an all-embracing General Group outside transport, the rules confined centrifugal forces to a minimum. As a fail-safe, a late addendum had given the General Executive Council the power to initiate new Groups as the need arose. This gave the union flexibility, at the same time that it built in the capacity for expansion through new mergers. Expansion was thereafter continuous throughout the history of the TGWU. None the less, Bevin did not want a premature mushrooming of Groups. To some extent, too, he argued, the definition of a Group was arbitrary; the carters, for example, had their closest economic links with the dockers, and might have been incorporated in a Waterside Group. The London busmen, for their part, had to be persuaded and cajoled into sitting alongside the tramwaymen.

Bevin had also found a device to mollify the sectional instincts of the most important general workers' trades. For flour-milling, metals, chemicals, chocolate- cocoa- and food-preserving, paint, colour and varnish, fuel, and engineering, sub-sections were designated within the General Workers' Group, with specialist officers but without separate National and Area Committees or Trade Group secretaries. The seeds of possible future decentralization were carefully saved without being allowed to germinate prematurely.

An interesting case of the formation of Group identity was the Administrative, Clerical, Technical and Supervisory Group. Tony Corfield noted that

> not less than five of the 14 amalgamating unions organised this type of worker. The United Vehicle Workers had clerical workers and inspectors in their ranks; the Dockers' Union, the Labour Protection League, the Ships' Clerks' Union, and the National Union of Docks, Wharves, and Shipping Staffs, all had either ships' clerks, known as tally clerks in London (and elsewhere), or clerical workers, amongst their membership.

The principal concentration of white-collar membership was in London, particularly in the port industry. Other pockets existed in Bristol (local-government officers) and Manchester (canal clerks). The composition of the first Trade Group Committee reflected London's dominance.[89]

The TGWU has clung to a rule on workers' control since its inception. This was entered at Leamington only as a result of addenda submitted by branches of the UVW and from the Executive of the shipping staffs. The first version which was debated said that the objects of the union should include: 'the securing of a real measure of control in industry and participation by workers in management in the interests of labour and the general community'. Creech Jones moved this new rule, calling for an injection into the formal objects of 'something of an aggressive and constructive nature. We want to bring home to our members that the ultimate ideal of trade unionism is something more than wages, hours, and working conditions.' There was a very brief debate, which included an objection that 'participation in management' was not acceptable; what was needed was 'real administrative control of the industry'.[90] Nevertheless, Creech Jones's version prevailed and was adopted.

## Internal Democracy

The Provisional Executive had recommended a rule providing for supreme conference authority to be vested in a Biennial Delegate Conference. Amendments sought to make this an Annual Conference, and this change won much support. Bevin argued that, since the union's industrial affairs were to be autonomously managed by National Trade Group Committees, and the central business of the union by an all-trades General Executive Council, the business of a National Delegate Conference was largely reduced to rule-changing. It would be unwise, he thought, to expose rules to revision so frequently. His opponents rejected this, arguing that general policy, as well as the rules, should be determined by a Delegate Conference and that this should be more frequent. This was clearly a debate about the degree of autonomous and unchecked central executive power to be allowed. Bevin and the Dockers' Union had been accustomed to only a Triennial Delegate Conference: an extreme form of executive licence. A minor objection to an Annual Conference was that Leamington, being held in late September 1921, should not be followed by another large gathering only a year hence. This was disposed of, and the Conference prevailed, if only briefly, over the Provisional Executive and Bevin by adopting an amendment establishing an Annual Conference. This was carried by a large majority, with the proviso that the first conference would be deferred until June 1923.[91]

Immediately following this defeat, the Provisional Executive's recommendations were challenged by Tillett, who complained that a proposed rule required only the president, general secretary and financial secretary to attend the Delegate Conferences of the union. Other officers would not be included. Bevin was full of repeated apologies; of course all national Trade Group and administrative officers must attend 'to give an answer for any of the misdeeds . . . done during the period in between – and the good deeds of course . . . The people actually in charge must be there to answer for their departments.' This proviso had simply been overlooked by the Drafting Sub-committee, and 'I am extremely sorry it is left out'. The Conference, having no amendment on the matter, agreed to waive its standing orders and instructed that the rule be rewritten to include the requirement that 'National Officers and heads of Departments' in addition to president, secretary and financial secretary, should attend the Delegate Conferences. Thus was established a practice which has continued to the present time. Each national officer still takes the 'hot seat' at the Biennial Delegate Conference (as it became) to submit his Report and to respond to questions on his stewardship of his Group or department.

The problem of how to secure representation for all sections and trades at the Delegate Conference stimulated yet another version of the debate on sectionalism versus what Bevin liked to call 'the organic whole'. The agreed recommendation was that Conference delegates should be elected from the Area Trade Groups on the basis of one per thousand members. Several branches wished to reduce the size of the constituencies to 500 members, on the ground that this doubling of size would allow the Conference to give voice to small but distinct trades from within the six Trade Groups which existed. The danger was that limitation of the number of delegates would filter out minorities. Stanley Hirst proposed that the rule could be refined to entitle each sub-section to be entitled to one delegate. Once again, Bevin's reply to this debate went to the heart of the matter. He had two objections to the amendment. One was that the Conference would simply become too large and unwieldy. He drew on the experience of the Labour Party Conference: 'the bigger it grows the less effective it has become'. Parliament itself would be more effective and responsible if it were smaller. And 'we do not want our Annual Meeting to become an annual holiday [with] half the delegates roaming around not attending to the business'.

But he had a more formidable objection, since the object behind an increase in size was to secure wider *sectional* representation. Bevin set his face against this mode of thought; delegates should be chosen for their quality and not for their trade. Gosling himself, he thought, was the supreme example; he had occupied every distinguished position in the Labour movement, purely on merit, for he came from one of its smallest societies: 'I am hoping for some recognition of the quality of the man, irrespective of the size of the group in the Union, and that is what will cause a man to rise in this new Union, which is what it is doing now in the trade union movement as a whole.'

Another form of divisive sectionalism could also result from an expanded Conference: the large, conglomerate geographical regions would increase their representation disproportionately over the smaller ones, and 'they may have no greater contribution to make to the wellbeing of the Union than such scattered areas as Devon, Cornwall or Somerset, where I come from. It is the quality of the man and the brains that we need.'

He suggested a different formula under which each area Trade Group would have a maximum of five delegates (this idea was embodied in another amendment), and proposed that they should 'try that until the next conference and see how it works'. With eleven Areas, and six Groups in each, that would give thirty delegates per Area, and a conference of 330. 'Try it till next time' was a sentiment called upon more than once, and it reflected the mood of the Leamington gathering. It also followed the grain of frequent exhortations by Gosling, who sought to instil the sense of experiment, of trial and error, into the gathering, so that some laxity was allowed. Not the least pressure in this direction was that the union had to complete its complex business and vacate the hall by Thursday evening.

Yet again, the notion that the six-man Appeals Committee should be expanded to eleven, to allow all Areas to be represented, appalled Bevin, who saw regionalism as a wholly inappropriate basis for the choice of a judicial body. Even 'if they all came from one area it ought not to matter. This is a question of the man, and not the District.'

And so it went on, with Bevin gaining the argument in most of these exchanges. He had no block votes to fall back on. Every point he won was established by persuasion and force of argument. Time and again he stood for the whole, and the centre, against the part and the parish.

Whether the result was right, in terms of the balance between centre, periphery and Group, time would tell. Undoubtedly the effect was usually to strengthen, or rather to preserve, the central control embodied in the draft rules. To what extent this might confer power on the chief executive officer, the general secretary, would depend on his relationship with his Executive.

## An Early Threat of Secession

Bevin's tough and uncompromising policies towards internal dissent, and his ruthless response to breakaway tendencies in the union, which he was to display more than once in the next two decades, was given an early demonstration in November 1921, whilst his office was still 'provisional'. The secretary of the Croydon No. 2 Bus Lodge of the UVW reported that his branch intended to secede from the union because of its discontent with new conditions imposed by the London General Omnibus Company. After consulting Gosling and the Bus Section's officers, Bevin wrote to the UVW's general secretary, Hirst, requesting him to accept the branch secretary's resignation, secure the books and monies of the union from the branch, and 'immediately accept the challenge of secession, and make arrangements to open a new Croydon branch under our auspices.' If a new branch secretary could not be found immediately, a full-time official should be instructed to take over temporarily, and 'that the same policy be applied to any other Lodge or Branch that secedes or has seceded.' A conference of the local membership was convened for 13 December, at which the reasons for the secession would be reviewed. This was lightning swift reaction on Bevin's part; he sought and obtained the support of his Provisional Committee afterwards![92]

The outgoing Provisional Committee and Bevin himself had provided in their draft that the new General Executive should be composed of lay members. Doubtless this would tend to vest large powers in the full-time general secretary, whose authority would extend itself over day-by-day administration and policy between the quarterly Executive meetings. Some limitation, however, emerged with the creation of a Finance and Emergency Committee, a six-man sub-committee of the Executive, which was to meet more frequently, with powers delegated to it from the GEC. (This body was the forerunner of what is today known as the Finance and General Purposes Committee.)

## Strikes: to Ballot or Not?

The power to sanction strike action was carefully distributed in the draft rules. The GEC was enabled to sanction a strike in a particular group or section, but before endorsing a strike of the whole membership, or of more than one Group, it must first convene a Special Delegate Conference. This could approve of strike action only subject to a ballot of the whole membership. This last provision sparked off the most passionate debate of the whole Conference. Many delegates saw the ballot provision as an inhibiting thing, which would neutralize the union's ability to mobilize its potential power in an emergency, and detract from the fighting quality of the union.

Bevin's reply occupies five pages of the Report. It drew on all his experiences (bitter ones, he said) in the brooding crises of the NTWF and the Triple Alliance. Ballots were not ideal instruments, he conceded. The turn-out was often low. But balloting could be a form of education, if the leadership gave a lead, making firm recommendations on how the membership should vote rather than using it as a 'coward's refuge'. Leaders should not adopt poses, calling for strikes in public and privately hoping and working for the opposite. He recalled 1912 and the abortive dock strike of that year. The summons to join the national stoppage, called by national leadership, had failed disastrously, and members had been victimized wholesale. Many were demoralized. He was obviously deeply affected by such experiences. No more encouraging was the general state of depressed trade and trade-union morale in which the TGWU was to be launched so soon after Black Friday. Evidently Bevin regarded the ballot as a temporary rule, to be cast aside in a brighter future:

> I have no fear that we are going to reach a stage when the ballot vote is not necessary. I believe that by education work we are going to reach a stage when we can move with the precision of an army, but you have to get conscious membership before you can do it, and, powerful as you may be, you have not that conscious membership at this moment, and it is no good kidding ourselves that we have . . . I beg you to take your membership into your confidence before you play with a new machine which you are creating . . . I do not want to be in a position to sacrifice the men or to victimise them before I am sure of their strength . . . This ballot resolution has been put in deliberately by the Provisional Committee with their eyes open . . . It is experience, that five years' experience of dealing with national movements, that has caused this to be put in.

And 1912, too: 'I saw those men go through hell in 1912, and it took some of them four years to get back inside the dock gates, and some of them never went back'.

They had to proceed with an alternative, 'a great educational effort'. At the end of this speech, so eloquent of Bevin's philosophy of strength through organization, and not through the rhetoric of the moment, he said: 'no one will welcome it more than I shall when we can stand upon the platform and say, "We have built up an organisation, confidence runs from end to end, and a ballot vote is entirely unnecessary." ' He won spontaneous applause from the conference as he concluded.

## Officers: Elected or Appointed?

Yet another classic debate then opened, on the relative merits of executive appointment of officials, which was in the proposed rules, or election by membership ballots in the districts. Some delegates feared that the GEC was acquiring too much power by the preferred method, but the Provisional Executive's view prevailed. Centralized power in the management and control of the income of the union was also unsuccessfully challenged.

Anxieties were expressed about the proposal, which the Provisional Executive had put forward, that there be scrutineers at branch elections for seats on all the lay committees of the union, and that these be appointed from other branches. This, it was felt, would cause practical difficulties of travel and timing. Scrutineers coming from outside the branch itself might not find their task easy, since custom and convenience called for some branches to poll at the workplace or depot, whilst others were geographically isolated.

Bevin again brought a blunt honesty to the debate. He spoke of a recent scandal. A few men had attended a branch meeting and decided how the whole branch would vote. Thereupon the secretary and the scrutineer had sat down, marked all the ballot papers and put them in the box: 'It was a gross scandal, and absolutely unfair to the men whose whole future . . . was dependent upon it.'

Speaking presumably about the Dockers' Union, he reported that a whole district had been disqualified from sitting on the Executive because of such abuses. The Conference resolved the problem by giving the Area Committees the responsibility of appointing scrutineers, and deciding that 'the Area Committee shall be held responsible for the proper supervision of the ballot.'

An amendment that officials should have worked in the industry to which they were appointed was carried. Another, to prevent a union officer from being at the same time an MP, was successfully resisted by the platform, and withdrawn! (Tillett's, and later Sexton's, future posts in the TGWU were thus preserved. So, indeed, were several others.)

## Gosling Winds Up

So the Conference moved to its close. Gosling did not fail the occasion, producing a splendid speech in winding up:

There is not a man in this room but feels that this gathering has been unique. Here you are: I can see in front of me now men who only a few months ago were almost using violence to each other. I presided at a meeting of men some of whom I can see here but whom I will not name, who in turn produced the most horrible bills and papers about each other, until it made me wish that I had never heard or seen such a dreadful thing . . . but here are the same men in this room, drawing together, at last, in amalgamation.

Gosling, the supreme conciliator without whom Bevin's drive and uninhibited energy might have met with far greater frustration over those two years' hard labour, came once again to the service of the movement. 'Yesterday', he said,

we were up against some very difficult propositions with regard to our friend Sexton – I call him my friend because I do not ever choose to say that I have any enemies – and it is difficult: there is something to be said for him. A young man might say, 'what does it matter about that?', but wait till you get old, and then you will see what it matters. My own union, the oldest in England, has had a terrible wrench to come in, and they are in because they put higher than anything else the desire for comradeship; and we are going to get over the difficulty with Sexton. I am as sure as I am standing here that we are.

As he was supremely entitled to, Harry Gosling told a nostalgic story or two to suit the occasion. One was 'about the time when poor old Clem Edwards was running round to get a federation office, and was in such an awful fright that he had to lock the door all day long in case the bums came in and took the furniture away.' One day,

something happened which made Clem very pleased with himself, and he said: 'come and have some lunch with me' so he took me to Slater's, and we had some lunch, and when he looked in his pocket he had not enough money to pay for it. That was in the early days of federation. That was 25 years ago, when he was working for the purpose of bringing about a federation. So things go on and on, and we have got a federation . . .

I say this to the young men: regard this as one more step that is all. The next time we meet you will find you want all kinds of alterations. That is all to the good; it is not bad. So you get an alliance with the railwaymen. We have got to get to the point – I know some people will not agree with me – when one card represents trade unionism in the whole country, and then when you have got one card representing all of this nation, that is only another step, because you have to get one card representing labour all over the world. You have to be international.

When the sixty-one-year-old Gosling sat down, the 'young man', forty-year-old Ernest Bevin, called for 'Three Cheers for the New Union.' And there the typescript record of the Conference ends.

There really was something to cheer about.

What did the formative spirits think about their work? 'Often', wrote Gosling, years later,

I have heard it said by 'left-wingers' that the officials of a trade union are usually anti-amalgamation, but the events in our own union entirely confound that statement. Twenty general secretaries, a number of assistant secretaries, treasurers and other chief officials willingly gave up their old status and gladly undertook the new duties to which they were allocated.[93]

Bevin's guiding hand, relentless energy and genius for 'organization' (probably his favourite word, which carried far more than formal significance when he used it) had now reached their supreme achievement. His ruthless pursuit of the goal of unity had been combined with an affecting sympathy. This is to be seen in his responses to the suffering of the workers, and in his sensitivities to the nostalgic ties of the older generation.

Bullock reminded us of a nostalgic speech which Bevin made to his union's Conference in 1939, in which he said:

There are two contributing factors to amalgamation, one is sweet temper and the other is overdrafts. Both are helpful, but if you discuss with anybody with a big stick you create the wrong kind of atmosphere to begin with. You have got to begin persuasively and you would not be in this room today as you are, if I had not been congenial personally.'[94]

Yet we also have Gosling's timely reminder that unity – at first through federation – of the transport workers had been the goal of the movement ever since the 1890s and Clem Edwards' first attempt at such a structure. It had been a long, long march. More, the concept of 'departments', the TGWU's 'Trade Groups', had been common to the amalgamation movement from its early days, as this volume has been at pains to document. Bevin's most original contribution was to devise a constitutional form bringing the Groups together and representing them at both Area and national levels, in the new governing bodies of the 'organic whole'. Even this enlightened and unique form of government which paved the way for the TGWU's subsequent expansion into so many new industries and occupations, did not dissolve sectional and occupational loyalties. In vol. II we shall see just how difficult it was to manage sectional interest within the new union.

Undoubtedly the sense of common purpose which overcame sectional interest, as well as reordering the perceptions of full-time officials in the old unions which came in, was at that particular moment stimulated by the collapse of the economy in 1921. This brought with it a reduction in trade-union power and membership, and a severe threat to the cherished new structures of recognition and national bargaining. Such events concentrate the mind. There was a sharp sense that 'if we don't hang together, we shall all hang separately'.

## Notes

1  TGWU Annual Report, 1922, p. vi.
2  Following the withdrawal of the Workers' Union from the negotiations, the formation of the General and Municipal Workers' Union in 1924 required the agreement of only three unions: the NUGW, the NAUL and the Municipal Employees' Association.
3  See Richard Hyman, *The Workers' Union* (Oxford University Press, 1971), pp. 123 ff. and 156 ff.; and entries for John Beard and Charles Duncan in J. M. Bellamy and J. Saville (eds), *Dictionary of Labour Biography*, vol. II (Macmillan, 1974).
4  NTWF Annual General Council Report, 1921, appendix I: 'The Federation and the Triple Alliance', p. 198. The appendix was also published separately as the NTWF's Special Report on the Mining Crisis, 1921.
5  NTWF Executive Committee, Special Report on the Mining Crisis, 1921.
6  NTWF Executive Committee Minutes, 31 March 1921.
7  NTWF Annual General Council Report, 1921, appendix I, p. 204.
8  NTWF Executive Committee, Special Report on the Mining Crisis, 1921, p. 26.
9  NTWF Annual General Council Report, 1921, p. 214.
10  Ibid., p. 217.
11  NTWF Executive Committee Special Report on the Mining Crisis, 1921, p. 33.
12  NTWF Annual General Council Report, 1921, p. 220.
13  The *Daily Herald*, 10 June 1921.
14  S. R. Graubard, *British Labour and the Russian Revolution, 1917-1924*, (Oxford University Press, 1956), p. 165.
15  The *Communist*, 23 April 1921; quoted in Graubard, *British Labour and the Russian Revolution*, p. 165.
16  *Communist Review*, vol. I, no. I, May 1921.
17  James Klugman, *History of the Communist Party of Great Britain*, vol. I (Lawrence and Wishart, 1968), pp. 95-6.
18  These might be thought all the more irresponsible when the private calculators of communists at that time could be entered into the record. At the end of 1922, J. T. Murphy was at the Fourth Comintern Congress in Moscow. He took bitter issue with Zinoviev about the difficulties of maintaining workshop organisation: 'How can you build factory organisations when you have 1,750,000 workers walking the streets? You cannot build factory organisations in empty and depleted workshops' (Communist Party of Great Britain Congress Report, 1923, p. 62).

  Murphy it was who tried to interrupt the International Transport Workers' Federation Conference at the end of 1921 in Geneva. He hectored them from the balcony, and was removed by stewards while the hall went into uproar. 'It was here that afterwards I first met Ernest Bevin who was shortly to eclipse Robert Williams as the leader of the British Transport Workers and to become the most powerful figure in British trade unionism. Despite what had happened he was friendly towards me and discussed matters frankly. He said then that he was opposed to the formation of a new International and he thought the Russians and those who were supporting them were making a mistake. In his opinion they should have affiliated to the International Federation of Trade Unions. He was opposed to splitting the International Federation of Trade Unions just as much as he was opposed to splitting the national unions. Bevin is a man of very definite views. He believes that Socialism comes through the more efficient organisation of Capitalism and the increasing power of organised labour. He holds the view that the stronger the trade unions become the greater the likelihood of the employers coming to terms and ensuring decent conditions for the workers. His concern for the workers is undoubted, his ability to fight their case either in a law court or at a conference table and to secure concessions where concessions are possible is second to none among trade union leaders. He is a great organiser and as ruthless as Stalin with his opponents' (J. T. Murphy, *New Horizons* (John Lane, 1941), pp. 170–1). Murphy was profoundly unjust to Bevin in his last remark, but this passage of his autobiography contrasts vividly with the Communist Party orthodoxy of the day, back in 1921.

19  Bertrand Russell, *Autobiography*, vol. II (Allen and Unwin, 1968), p. 102: 'Robert Williams, I found, was very happy in Russia, and was the only one of our Party who made speeches pleasing to the Soviet Government. He always told them that revolution was imminent in England . . . I told Lenin that he was not to be trusted, and the very next year, on Black Friday, he ratted.'

Trotsky's book *Where is Britain Going?* also contained, in its English version, the statement that Williams 'had ratted'; but when the Soviet leader's attention was drawn to this, he insisted that it was a mistranslation. He had written that Williams had 'changed his opinions'.

20  J. Walton Newbold, manuscript, John Rylands Library archive.
21  Labour Party Conference Report, 1921, pp. 164 and 167.
22  L. J. MacFarlane, *The British Communist Party* (McGibbon and Kee, 1966), p. 118. It is recorded in Graubard, *British Labour and the Russian Revolution*, pp. 170 ff.
23  F. Meynell, *My Lives* (Bodley Head, 1971), p. 256.
24  Graubard, *British Labour and the Russian Revolution*, p. 166.
25  Ibid., pp. 166–7.
26  Ibid.
27  Gerald Gould, *The Lesson of Black Friday* (Allen and Unwin, 1921), p. 38.
28  E. L. Taplin, *The Dockers' Union: A Study of the National Union of Dock Labourers, 1889–1922* (Leicester University Press, 1986), p. 148.
29  Ibid., p. 147.
30  NTWF Executive Committee Minutes, 27 April 1921.
31  NTWF Annual General Council Report, 1921, p. 141.
32  NTWF Executive Committee Minutes, 17, 18, 27 and 28 May 1921.
33  Ibid., 23 April 1921.
34  Basil Mogridge, 'Militancy and Inter-Union Rivalry in British Shipping, 1911–1929', *International Review of Social History*, vol. VI (1961), pp. 394–5.

35  NTWF Executive Committee Minutes, 10 May 1921.
36  Ibid., 27 April 1921.
37  Ibid., 17 May 1921.
38  Ibid., 28 July 1921.
39  Ibid., 26 August 1921.
40  Ibid., 8 October 1921.
41  Ibid., 19 October 1921.
42  TGWU Provisional Executive Council, typescript verbatim Minutes, 26 October 1921.
43  NTWF Executive Committee Minutes, 28 October 1921.
44  Mogridge, 'Militancy and Inter-Union Rivalry in British Shipping', pp. 396–7.
45  Minutes of two meetings of the AMWU addressed by Cotter, Robert Williams and Tommy Lewis (leader of the Southampton section of the BSU), in Antwerp on 30 October 1921 and 9 January 1922, are held in the University Library, Hull. They were extremely rowdy meetings, the NSFU apparently infiltrating and disrupting them; the Belgian police were called to one of them. Cotter and Williams reported enthusiastically on the AMWU's recruiting campaign, and called on the British seamen in Antwerp to join.
46  Mogridge, 'Militancy and Inter-Union Rivalry in British Shipping', p. 397.
47  NTWF Annual General Council Report 1922, p. 13.
48  Ibid., p. 34.
49  NTWF Executive Committee Sub-committee Minutes, 8 March 1922.
50  TGWU Finance and Emergency Committee Minute 155, 10 March 1922.
51  Ibid., Minute 212, 11 April 1922.
52  NTWF Annual General Council Report, 1922, p. 60.
53  Ibid., p. 71.
54  NTWF Executive Committee Minutes, 2 June 1920 and 8 July 1920.
55  Ibid., 4 October 1920.
56  Ibid., 26 November 1920.
57  Ibid., 27 July 1921.
58  Ibid., 16 December 1921.
59  NTWF Annual General Council Report, 1922, p. 33.
60  Ibid., p. 44.
61  TGWU Special Rules Conference Minutes, 27–9 September 1921.
62  NTWF Executive Committee Minutes, 4 April, 1921.
63  NTWF Annual General Council Report, 1921, pp. 60–1.
64  NTWF *Weekly Record*, 27 June 1913; quoted above, chapter 15, pp. 539–40.
65  NTWF Annual General Council Report, 1920, p. 119.
66  Area No. 6 Officers' Conference Minutes, 15 July 1921.
67  Alan Bullock, *The Life and Times of Ernest Bevin*, vol. I: *Trade Union Leader, 1881–1940* (Heinemann, 1960), p. 156.
68  See D. F. Wilson, *Dockers: The Impact of Industrial Change* (Fontana, 1972), pp. 104 and 111.
69  See Administrative, Clerical and Supervisory Group of the TGWU, *The Growth of the Trade Union Idea and Spirit among the Staffs of the Port of London*, May 1923, p. 51.
70  Verbatim typescript Minutes, Bevin Collection.

71  Tony Corfield, 'The Union's History, Part VII', TGWU *Record*, March 1962, p. 43.

72  Ken Fuller, *Radical Aristocrats: London Busworkers from the 1880s to the 1900s* (Lawrence and Wishart, 1985), p. 65.

73  UVW *Record*, 5 January 1921, p. 5.

74  H. A. Clegg, *A History of British Trade Unions since 1889*, vol. II: *1911–1933* (Oxford University Press, 1985), pp. 304–5.

75  NUDL Annual Report, 1920, p. 9.

76  Ibid.

77  Taplin, *The Dockers' Union*, p. 155.

78  TGWU Special Rules Conference Minutes, 27–9 September 1921, pp. 116–22.

79  Taplin, *The Dockers' Union*, p. 154.

80  TGWU Special Rules Conference Minutes, 27–9 September 1921, p. 117.

81  NTWF Annual General Council Report, 1920, p. 104.

82  TGWU Special Rules Conference Minutes, 27–9 September 1921, p. 120.

83  Taplin, *The Dockers' Union*, p. 154.

84  Mason's letter is in the Transport House archives.

85  Taplin, *The Dockers' Union*, p. 157.

86  Ibid., p. 156.

87  TGWU Provisional Executive Committee Report, 27 September 1921.

88  See Charles W. Key, *Red Poplar* (Labour Publishing Company, 1925). Charles Key had been Poplar's Mayor, and was one of the thirty councillors imprisoned for resisting the blatant inequalities of the rating system.

89  Tony Corfield, 'The Union's History, Part V', TGWU *Record*, January 1962, p. 39.

90  TGWU Special Rules Conference Minutes, 27–9 September 1921, p. 80.

91  The restoration of Bevin's original design we shall follow in vol. II.

92  TGWU Finance and Emergency Committee Minutes, 22 November 1921.

93  Harry Gosling, *Up and Down Stream* (Methuen, 1927), p. 186.

94  Bullock, *The Life and Times of Ernest Bevin*, vol. I, p. 189.

# 21

# A New Movement Comes of Age?
# A New Union Is Born!

## I

### *A Bleak Climate*

All around the Leamington conference hall, the slump raged and the unemployed lost hope. In February 1921, when Bevin, acting for the Federation, sought to re-enact his triumphs at the Shaw Inquiry this time on behalf of the tramwaymen, already he had met a very different response. His earlier success was not to be repeated. Assisted by John Cliff and Harold Clay, who were both later to serve as assistant general secretaries in the TGWU, Bevin took the tramwaymen's claim for a 12s. weekly rise to another Court of Inquiry. Even Gosling's presence as a member of the panel was not enough to allow the men to prevail. The court confined itself to recommending stabilization of existing wages at their current level. Modest as it was, that requirement was successfully defied by the employers. They imposed a cost-of-living sliding scale upon the industry.[1]

On the docks, a succession of wage cuts had to be accepted: in August 1921 to 14s. a day, and in January 1922 to 13s. In March they fell further, to 12s., with a 20 per cent cut in piece-rates. The tariffs in the coal-trimming trade were cut by 10 per cent in July. The employers had wanted reductions of 30 per cent. In October, commercial road-workers' wages fell by 4s. a day for horsemen and 3s. for motormen. The national bargaining system in the canal industry broke down, leading to a prolonged strike. Bus workers accepted a cut of a farthing per hour for every five-point fall in the cost-of-living index. The pages of the TGWU *Record* are full of such reports. It was a blizzard.

The Federation fell back in a rearguard action. Williams sent out Executive instructions to the regions that local deals were to be resisted and the Federation's national rates defended. Significantly, whilst this defence now often involved the signing of agreements to cuts in wages, the 'machinery' of JICs did not disintegrate right across the board. After the TGWU, by agreement with the rump of the Federation, came to take over all those national agreements which had previously stood in the name of the Federation, it was able to state, in its first Annual Report, that it was represented on fifteen JICs, six Government Industrial Councils, six Interim Industrial Reconstruction Committees, fourteen Trade Boards, and five Conciliation Boards. The TGWU was one of the leaders in a fierce and successful campaign to frustrate the attempt by a lobby of the Federation of British Industry to abolish Wages Boards. Bevin had told the Leamington Conference that these Boards were the first lines of defence of women's minimum wages, as well as of low-paid people in general.

In the TGWU's first Annual report, for the year ending 31 December 1922, Bevin made the claim that 'The wages of the bulk of our members would be at least another thirty per cent or ten per cent lower if the Union were not in existence and the employers had the power to enforce their will.'[2]

He went on to list a number of instances in which union resistance had greatly modified the scale of wage reductions, in the bus, tram, road-haulage and docks sections. It should also be added that the great 1919 agreements on the shorter working week were consistently and successfully defended. Bevin's view was always that wage cuts could be conceded in times of adverse trade, to be regained in the next upswing of the economy, but that shorter hours and bargaining rights were an historic and permanent gain which should never be surrendered. At the Special Delegate Conference in March 1922 he explained his reasoning: 'To get the eight-hour day established it took 30 years of effort. You can recover wages – the money side is not so difficult. When trade revives, then is the chance to recover wages. But it is the conditions. Conditions take years to recover . . . and you must fight to keep them.'[3]

In this, he revealed the statesmanship which would afterwards be recognized by historians of the established view when they came to consider his later achievements. They did not, however, always recognize his earlier farsightedness in defending negotiation machinery through these incredibly difficult times. Neither, we might add, did some historians of a more left-wing orthodoxy, who quite often failed to imagine the likely fate of Labour organization had Bevin's strategic vision not prevailed.

## The New Leadership

It remains to chart the internal transition of the amalgamating unions from the time of the Leamington Conference in September 1921 up to the moment that the union was fully operational, its elections completed. Eleven unions which had at that stage conducted a successful ballot sent a total of 140 delegates (all male!) to the founding Rules Conference at Leamington. Twenty-one unions had participated in the ballot, of which, by January 1922, fourteen had gained the necessary majority. It was these unions which comprised the new organization at the outset. They were: the DWRGWU, the Lightermen, the LPL, the NALU, the North of England Trimmers, the Dock and Wharves' Shipping Staffs, the Ships' Clerks, the UVW, the Amalgamated Carters, Lurrymen and Motormen, the NUVW, the Coal Workers, the North of Scotland Motormen, and the Amalgamated Association of Carters and Motormen.

During 1922, Sexton's union, the Scottish Dockers, the Dundee Flax and Jute Stowers' Society, and the Greenock Sugar Porters' Union joined after successful ballots. The North Wales Quarrymen and the North Wales Craftsmen and General Workers had made amalgamation arrangements, so that at the end of 1922 the new organization had absorbed twenty unions in all.

During the first half of 1922 the affairs of the TGWU continued to be in the hands of the Provisional Executive Committee, twelve men who owed their position to nomination by their original unions. Some of these were lay members, some officers. The wholly lay General Executive Council was elected in April 1922 and held its first sitting on 2 August. There was one territorial representative from each of twelve Areas, and one representative from each of the six Trade Groups – docks, waterways, clerical, passenger, commercial and general. These people were now no longer distinguishable by their union of origin in the record of their responsibilities in the Annual Report.

Elections for the National Trade Group Committees were completed in July 1922. The new committees succeeded to the work of the previous Provisional Committees in that month. Eleven Area Offices and Area secretaries were at work in 1922 – in London (J. T. Scoulding), Southampton (D. Hillman), Bristol (J. Garmston), Cardiff (J. Donovan), Birmingham (J. Crump), Manchester (J. A. Webb), Glasgow (J. Veitch, with P. Gillespie as the general organizer for Scotland), Newcastle (J. White), Leeds (H. E. Clay), Hull (G. E. Farmery), Dublin (E. P. Hart, with L. McCurdy as organizer for Ireland) and Liverpool (D. Milligan). The Mersey Area, bringing the number to twelve, was added after Sexton's union's entry. In the Welsh Area, it was found that the Group system did not suit inherited traditions, and District Committees took the place of Area Trade Groups. In Ireland, neither Groups nor Districts were established, all the work being governed by the Central Area Committee.

Central office was divided into departments for the president, the general secretary, the financial secretary, the international and political department, and general organizing. The national general organizers appointed were Ben Smith, who was in charge, together with Messrs R. Blundell, D. Greenwood, P. McKibbins, J. Twomey, J. Wignall, and Miss M. Quaile and Miss M. Carlin (the mother of Miriam Carlin, the well-known actress of the 1960s and 1970s).

The national secretaries of the Trade Groups were: E. Bevin (Docks), H. Gosling (Waterways), A. Short, MP (Clerical, assisted by Creech Jones), J. Cliff (Road Passenger), S. March (Road Commercial, assisted by A. Henderson) and W. Devenay (General, assisted by W. Godfrey and also by P. C. Green as national secretary of the Flour-milling Section).

A national health-insurance section was set up, and also a legal department, which was headed by F. Stillwell.

We have left till last the elections for the chief executive posts. These were held in December 1921, and each of the posts was contested. Those who stood against Bevin were Fred Thompson and G. Porter. Thompson, the London district secretary of the Dockers' Union, was by now a member of the Communist Party, which was already 'organizing resistance' to what it regarded as the apostasy of the official trade-union leadership, following the slump and the aftermath of Black Friday. Harry Pollitt's retrospective judgement was a simple one: 'the official Trade Union leaders were in a state of hopeless retreat, completely demoralised and doing their damnedest to spread the rot among the rank and file, but without success.'[4]

A British Bureau of the new Red International of Labour Unions was set up. Spurred on by the policies of the Communist International centred in Moscow, it summoned a British conference in the Memorial Hall, London, on 15 October 1921, to which 650 delegates came, from trade-union branches, District Committees and Trades Councils. Harry Pollitt gave the main report to the conference, but it was Fred Thompson who occupied the chair,[5] just two months before his electoral challenge to Bevin's leadership of the TGWU. He was to cross Bevin more than once in the years ahead. Some hint of what was to come may be read in his election address:

My candidature is a challenge to autocracy and a protest against the building up of the new Union around individuals instead of policy. The present industrial situation demands a new orientation of the functions and purposes of the trade union movement, together with a definite fighting programme calculated to stem the tide of encroachments on the workers' standard of life and the ultimate assumption of control of industry. Having been London District Secretary of the Dockers' Union for three years, and being well acquainted with all phases of organisation, I confidently leave my candidature with the advanced sections of our movement and all those who are dissatisfied with the limitation of trade union activities to wage regulations.[6]

Bevin was not over-anxious about the opposition. His election address could not have been terser. It fitted into one confident sentence: 'Just as I have given of my best in the past in all offices I have held in the movement, so shall I continue if the membership repose renewed confidence in me in a new post.'

Bevin polled 96,842 votes, Thompson 7,672 and Porter 2,489.

There were six candidates for the post of financial secretary, and Stanley Hirst topped the poll with 47,278 votes against his nearest rival, H. W. (Harry) Kay, who got 18,582 votes. Kay, yet another candidate for office from the DWRGWU, had served as provisional treasurer for the Amalgamation Committee from May 1921. He had been on the dock Strike Committee in 1889, and cashier of the Dockers' Union ever since.[7] But Hirst's election ensured representation for bus and tram workers' unions in the top, executive officer, positions.

The most controversial election was that for the presidency, but its real significance lay not in who stood, but in who did not. It was overshadowed by the absence of Ben Tillett as a candidate. After his long-term general secretaryship of the Dockers' Union, stretching back, as it did, for thirty years, what would become of him? His eclipse at the founding moment of the new union led to many dark stories of Bevin's ingratitude and vindictiveness. These were stoked up by Tillett himself, deeply aggrieved. Whilst Sexton accepted his eventual fate without public recriminations, Tillett did quite the opposite.

Referring to the last Triennial Meeting of his union held in December 1921, Tillett recalls:

The next business was the report by Bro. Bevin of the progress which had been made towards amalgamation, in which he indicated that the new union would take its form on January 1st. In the debate on the subject I had to make a very frank statement concerning my own position. I had to make it plain that throughout my career, while I had been the originator of many great movements, I had put other men into position of responsibility, and had not been self-seeking. I pointed out that on occasion I had dragooned younger men into taking responsibility, but that at all times, I had been against any one-man show and would be always.

I had been nominated for the position of President, for which, naturally, I had ambition. Bro. Gosling was also nominated but had informed the Election Committee that he would not run against me. The opinion was expressed that it would endanger the whole amalgamation if we both went to the ballot. I did not agree, but Bro. Bevin and the others were obviously so impressed that this would be the case that, after a further reiteration that I would rather go to the ballot, I decided to withdraw my candidature.

As I told our Triennial Meeting, this movement has to go on, and I would sacrifice myself if necessary.

The meeting put on record its appreciation of the work rendered throughout the years by the Officers and Executive of the Union.

Some of my worst suspicions have, however been fully justified, but they will now be buried with the other regrets which one buries when good work is to be done – and there is plenty still for myself and others to accomplish.[8]

The TGWU *Record* carried a more diplomatic statement by Tillett:

With a view to harmonising all the conflicting interests which must be made, Mr. Ben Tillett withdrew his candidature from the contests for which he had been nominated, being anxious for the greater good of the organisation itself, but he desired to be allowed to assure the members of his anxiety to go on with the work; he feels that there is much for him to do within the amalgamation. He wanted it to be clearly understood that he is not retiring, but will continue his service in the cause he has at heart. He desires the amalgamation to go on, and to succeed. The evolutionary movement is in accord with his own ambitions, aims, and life's work. He is satisfied that there is great scope within the amalgamation for the ample expression of his abilities, apart from the position for which he was a nominee.[9]

Bevin's responses were hardly motivated by ingratitude towards Tillett. He thought that if both secretary and president came from the same union, the DWRGWU, this would put undue strain on the loyalty of other affiliates. Besides, Tillett had, in truth, been a spent force since the war, and could not at all match Gosling's personal qualifications as a model chairman. As a conciliator between sectional interests he would have been a very poor substitute indeed. Tillett's hunger for office was partially met when the new union made him its international and political secretary.[10] This was a generous placement, but how far did it represent, in fact, a downgrading of international commitments?

## II

## *The Labour Party Comes of Age?*

As the TGWU was entering the world, so the Labour Party, according to the standards of the time, was 'coming of age'. When young people passed their twenty-first birthday they were commonly thought to have reached an 'age of discretion'. Sometimes there was evidence that they might actually have done so. Social movements also sometimes learn, but not usually simply in the process of ageing. None the less, the Labour Party was about to have new responsibilities thrust upon it, whether it had become discreet or not.

In 1920 J. R. Clynes had been elected chairman of the Parliamentary Labour Party. In those days the Labour Party had no 'leader', and the office of chairman did not entail any exceptional powers. Certainly it carried few privileges. The chairman, quite literally, chaired the meetings, and after that he was supposed to conform to their wishes. Back in 1908 Keir Hardie had expressed himself very happy to lay down the post, so 'that I may be free to speak out occasionally'.[11] This gives a measure of the distance between the early habits of the Labour Party's front bench in Parliament and more recent practices, in which the leader's job description has involved extensive direct powers and responsibilities. Clynes was the last of the old school, in two respects. First, his role was still as narrowly defined as it had been in Keir Hardie's time. Secondly, he was, of course, not only a trade-union candidate but also a scion of new unionism. We have already seen how actively he was engaging himself in trade-union problems, both in the Triple Alliance and in the NTWF. These functions were, of course, ancillary and subordinate to his position in his own union, which was itself soon to break out into a wider amalgamation. With his election as chairman, the new unions reached the highest point of their recognition in the Labour Party. But the moment of his victory was also that of his complete defeat. When he led the Labour Party to a breakthrough it instantly dropped him. In November 1922, 142 Labour Members were returned, so that Labour could at last become the official opposition. From this moment onwards the spokesperson of the Parliamentary Labour Party would be considered a potential Prime Minister. It was a veritable turn-around; but there was no discussion in the Labour movement as a whole about what to do. On the contrary, 120 of the newly elected or re-elected Members instantly met in what was to be an entirely fraught session. This opened with an implicit censure on Clynes for being too permissive with the Speaker about the question of who should occupy the front bench. Then, without ceremony, it was agreed to abandon the previously agreed procedure for the election of officers, whereupon a new election was entered instantaneously, with no prior notification whatever.

This was the famous Clydeside *coup*. Ramsay MacDonald, benefiting from the ecstatic support of the contingent of new left-wingers from Scotland, was elected, on the best estimate, by 61 votes to 56. According to less-generous counts, he had a majority of 2 or 4. The very imprecision of the figures indicates that this was a spontaneous, impromptu decision. Even the records could not be harmonized. The shotgun election was followed by another equally unheralded announcement. Without any prior agreement by his supporters at large, MacDonald was immediately announced as the new 'Chairman *or* Leader' in the Labour Party's subsequent press release. Afterwards, from the next Annual Conference onwards, his designation was always given as 'Chairman *and* Leader' of the party.

Even the date of this cold strike is not precisely established. It took place, in one account, on either 22 or 23 November 1922. In another record, it was held on the 21st.[12]

If the decision was imprecisely recorded, and improvisedly reached, its effect was none the less stringent. What was really happening was that the Labour Party in Parliament had now registered its acceptance of the role of 'His Majesty's Opposition'. While it remained in opposition, some control over its new leader might still exist. But once it entered government its leader would henceforth become the King's first minister and would wield all the rights of patronage, which would enable him to use his own discretion to appoint all his ministers, as well as a wide variety of other public officials. The acceptance of this Royal Prerogative held the Labour movement in a constitutional grip as strong as it was subtle. Far from 'coming of age', Labour had entered a prolonged period of Establishment tutelage.

Other European social democratic parties faced no such impediment. Their kings, if they still survived, were normally kept strictly in place. After all, they now had no reason to feel very secure. Republican governments may have accommodated authoritarian personalities, but were bound to invoke democratic procedures. The Labour Party, by contrast, had opted for parliamentary democracy, but had been manipulated into co-existence with a monarchic hybrid, designed to accommodate and yet contain changes of the most far-reaching character. Electorates believed they were choosing a government. If they chose properly, so they might. But if they showed undue indiscretion, they could soon discover that the constitution actually conferred authority on 'the Crown in Parliament'. While republican legislatures were certainly capable of disappointing their voters, they did not suffer this built-in disability. The lines of responsibility could be abruptly reversed under the British system, so that leaders found themselves accounting upwards, to the 'national interest' as embodied in the Palace, rather than downwards to their supporters and constituents. In the early years of the TGWU, Bevin felt this ambivalence very keenly, and kept to his own course rather than trim to the needs of Ramsay MacDonald in Downing Street. In later life, he was himself to become a notable beneficiary of royal intervention in governmental processes.

The new Labour political machine would rely on trade-union strength for its basic support at the same time that it offered a new constitutional space in which the unions might adjust to the received power structure. Incorporation within such a framework would always be an ambivalent commitment, fluid, conjunctural. Yet it would offer important concessions to the many, in exchange for the conformity of the few. Those who were intended to be domesticated were precisely the unruly spirits who might give leadership to a great mass movement.

For the intransigents, a new political force was seeking its own space for development. The infant Communist Party looked to the success of the Russian Revolution both as its inspiration and as its model. It encountered some success in recruiting from the shop stewards' movement, so that it was not without a trade-union presence. But its most vital activists came from the skilled trade unions, and they had entered into their radical formation as a result of the flux of technical change and wartime upheavals in the organization of work. The engineering shop stewards were adjusting to dilution, de-skilling, and the imposition of new types of work organization. They numbered among their ranks people of great capacity and considerable practical education. This was a generation of gifted autodidacts. They had many abilities. What they did not normally have was access to, or feeling for, the great masses of unskilled workers, particularly those engaged in the transport industries.

It might be true, as many scholars have insisted, that 'downstart' skilled workers made excellent revolutionaries. The loss of security encouraged radical thinking. It did not necessarily, however, create the frame of mind which could easily appeal to those who had *always* been poor, neglected and openly oppressed.

One trade-union leader who certainly *could* appeal to the mass of transport workers was Robert Williams. Not only had he made the rounds of all the ports, endearing himself to the horsemen, carters and lurrymen by his hyperactive interventions in all those wartime disputes; but he had also established a fine ear for the rhythms of protest among the people he represented. Robert Williams was a founding member of the new Communist Party and, had he stayed in place, he might have been a powerful influence among the transport workers. True, the role of the Federation of which he was secretary was almost certain to decline. Even so, had he maintained his connections with the rebels on the docks, his status could have remained equal to any. But he was almost immediately expelled from the new party after the disastrous débâcle of Black Friday. We have already written about the injustice of this decision. Its effect, however, was not to penalize Williams himself, but the party which rejected him. It served to remove the main channel through which the communists might otherwise have been able to communicate with the organizations of transport workers. True, they had their quite numerous supporters on the docks, the buses and in the various other trades; but Williams was an acknowledged leader, a man of prodigious talent, even genius, and an experienced political mind. There were other militants like Fred Thompson, who will appear as a man of parts in our next volume. Such men were deeply rooted in their local communities, and at times could command extensive support. But with Williams among them they might have weighed far heavier than in fact they did. With Williams cut down in the eyes of the left, Ernest Bevin was confronted by a number of other potential critics from that stable; yet none of them could even begin to match him in stature. Poor Williams himself was hobbled. His political invalidity gave Bevin a free hand. He played it well, with a radical verve, but if he had been left with the Robert Williams of old, he might have thought it wise to be somewhat sharper, somehow more bold. With the opposition contained, his choices were easier, but perhaps less thoroughgoing.

The political significance of these forgotten decisions is, we think, considerable. It is easy to exaggerate the importance of particular events. However, it does seem to us that the decision by the communists to deprive themselves of their most distinguished and effective trade-union leader was, from their point of view, a capital blunder. It would not be for years that men of similar calibre emerged from out of their ranks. Meanwhile, their capacity to influence the greatest forces of unskilled labour had been seriously damaged for a whole period, which was to include the events of 'Red Friday' (see vol. II) and the General Strike. While the communists had hobbled themselves, Ernest Bevin was to bring the massive support of 'his people' to the Labour Party, even while he criticized it. Indeed, he was to lock that support firm, even while *they* criticized it. In retrospect, everybody thinks these events to have been inevitable. When one emerges from close study of these old papers, listening to the accents in these old debates, one is not quite so sure.

At the time, however, the members of the new union did not know what turmoils awaited them. They knew, instead, of the turmoil through which they had struggled to bring about their One Big Union.

## III

## *Retrospect and Prospect*

They had come a long way. Old-timers, like Ben Tillett, knew how far. For the others it was a matter of history. Back in 1889, those who chronicled the great strike had seen the docks as 'the resort of men from all classes and all trades. The failures in every branch of life, professional, commercial, and industrial, filter down through the various strata of labour until they reach the lowest layer of all.' There was, said Smith and Nash, a nucleus of 'professional dockers', but, they insisted, 'for the greater part dock labourers are not a class, but the drift of all classes.'[13]

All sorts of stories could be adduced to prove this. The dockers' historians recorded some of the hard-luck legends. They told of unlucky clergymen and doctors, reduced far below their old stations, now toiling in the holds; and they wrote down the tale of the celebrated black African prince who had become a London docker, not forgetting the sons of a baronet who were alleged to work alongside him. But these were the stars who had fallen far. Most had simply moved:

Very few even of the permanent dockers have begun their career at the docks; they have rather drifted in from other occupations . . . Including in their ranks members of all classes, and the drift of all trades, they have long seemed to offer the most unpromising field for any attempt at organised action. In John Burns' phrase they have been 'the despair of the social reformer' . . . Every step in civilisation, every improvement in the organisation of the higher trades, has only seemed to make more hopeless the position of the fringe of labour which does not share in the benefit of change.[14]

The people who scrambled for work at the dockside might indeed, between them, dispose of various skills. None the less, they were very difficult indeed to organize. Poverty seldom drives men and women to join their efforts, to work together for improvement. Yes, a million kindnesses enable poor people to survive in mutual help; but survival is also competition, often raw. It had been by no means certain that the band of socialists and social reformers who made the 'dockers' tanner' into the great moral question of 1889 would be able to create a durable organizational framework once the excitement had evaporated. The marches, the continuous frenzy of popular support, the oratory, the pickets, the collections, all generated a fine sense of commitment to the cause. But would this endure? Would it be sufficient to sustain activity through the winter, into and beyond the next downturn of trade? Could it inspire continued loyalty in the face of discrimination, abuse and victimization? Had the days of the mob passed, and those of the movement begun? Smith and Nash, when they drew the balance sheet, had felt it necessary to warn of these difficulties: 'The leaders of the new Dockers' Union have before them a long and uphill fight . . . If they succeed in their effort they will, in truth, have proved themselves to be born leaders of men. There will be little room for censure if they fail and the new Union gradually falls to pieces, as other Unions have done before.'[15]

Carters, cabmen, tramwaymen and lurry drivers all faced versions of the same dilemma. Most encountered opposition, some of which was as brutal as it was intransigent. Yet here and there, in an hospitable municipal enclave, or in a corner of liberal commitment, recognition became established. Recognition by one employer was sufficient to arouse the demand for recognition by many. As we have seen, once a group of workers achieved such recognition for its organization, its strength was refracted back through the vision of its adversaries. To build the union was to build the sense of belonging to the working class, not as a bit-by-bit accretion of solidary strength alone, but also as an awareness of a relationship in which collective identities were an extension of one's own personality and power, and in which one's common commitment was reinforced not only in every confrontation with the opposition, but also in every agreement extracted from it. Union was a growth of social power, even, sometimes, of brute force. But it was also, more significantly, self-recognition, self-confidence, the beginning of a new identity.

Yet this relationship was not easily established. Sometimes, as on the docks at Hull, it emerged briefly only to be confiscated within a very short span. Its loss might normally be expected to arouse resentments. Often these were expressed politically. But the narrowness of the franchise served to minimize the registration of protest, above all among those submerged populations which were voteless.

When Sidney and Beatrice Webb were writing their *History of British Trade Unions*, soon after the birth of the new unionism, they defined a trade union as 'a continuous association of wage earners for the purpose of maintaining or improving the conditions of their employment.'[16] Their emphasis on continuity has puzzled subsequent generations of trade-union students. In later ages, continuity was to be taken for granted, presumed. But in the days of the Webbs' early work, nothing was so certain. Here today might be gone tomorrow. Indeed, at the time, trade-union law itself applied to 'any association, *whether temporary or permanent*', which was established for controlling labour relations.

By 1910 dockers, carters, tramwaymen and cabmen had all established 'permanent' associations, although in truth some of them were very thin on the ground. Their durability was reinforced by the decision to join forces in a common federation.

By the time of the second great uprising of port and transport workers, after 1910, sufficient had been learned in the schools of adversity and repression to enable all the transport unions to use their renewed strength very effectively indeed. None the less, in the view of Hugh Clegg, Alan Fox and A. F. Thompson, it would be unwise to exaggerate the impact of these changes:

> In the House of Commons, the new Labour Party was more often the agent of a sectional interest than the herald of a new social order. The unions could still appear selfish and callous. Craftsmen still fought for their exclusive privileges, and such lip-service as they might pay to the ideal of universal organisation had little effect on their action in the branch or the workshop. Every union, skilled and unskilled, fought for jobs and members, and little mercy was shown to the weaker party. Each group pursued its own industrial objectives without thought for the others and many political objectives were still narrow and sectional. Considerable sections of both Conservative and Liberal opinion within the unions resented the alliance with the socialists, and sometimes fought against it.
>
> It is therefore misleading to speak of a 'labour movement' as a constant in the history of this period. The term describes an aspect revealed by the unions and their political arms from time to time. The quality showed more clearly in 1910 than in 1889. A sympathetic leader could sometimes call it out; an astute leader could sometimes use it for his own ends; and it might sometimes assert itself unbidden. But it was often apparent only to the discerning eye, rarely visible in day-to-day union business, and only very

rarely powerful enough to override the self-interest of any individual union.[17]

It is necessary, while accepting a kernel of truth in this account, to register an all-important dissent. Hope springs eternal.

Of course, a political movement lives on its experience; but does it not also survive on its potential? Those of the leaders of 1889 who lived long enough to be present during the next upsurge did not have to guess at the scope of the explosion of 1911. There was something they *knew*, before the event. Painstakingly, deliberately, they could set out the framework for a mobilization, capable of transforming all the conditions within which their unions had to work. Aware of limited resources, restricted access, disposing of but few skilled advocates and fewer competent organizers, these leaders nevertheless had developed the nose to intuit a new capacity for response, an awakening unrest. With the seamen's strike unleashed, according to a detailed plan, it still, of course, makes sense to describe the subsequent conflagration among dock workers and carters as, in some sense, 'spontaneous'.

But if the specific actions of those days were triggered by events which were not controlled by the dockers' Executives, yet it remains true that those trade-union leaders, left or right, cautious or audacious, wildly syndicalist or moderate to the point of respectability, all knew exactly what to do when the time came. And all bent their efforts in the same direction. They stabilized their organizations, they pooled their efforts and together they sought to extend the principles of recognition and collective bargaining. That these struggles were accompanied by many political demands and by a closer integration of the political labour forces only served to reinforce their initial impetus. In this sense, the presence of a visible Labour movement became almost daily more tangible, more permanent, more unavoidable.

The unions' experience, of course, went deeper than the filing systems in their offices. Former members, who had lapsed from exhaustion or in the face of persistent intimidation, none the less contributed to the collective memory of the working communities in which they lived. In the families of those who had once tried to make trade unions were the children who would try again. While conditions remained as they were, there could be no such thing as final failure to organize against them. Full employment might be enough to change the equation which determined how many clubs might be necessary to beat a population into submission. Full employment, in any event, would reduce the number of thugs available for hire. With the advent of war, employment conditions became more stable than anyone could remember, and the government became available as an interested intermediary, anxious at all times to remove disruptions in production, and willing upon occasion to impose concessions in order to do so.

The First World War had made a profound contribution to the shape of a new industrial-relations system, and nowhere more so than in the fields of transport and general labour. At the same time, universal military service had removed the last vestige of argument against universal suffrage. At the end of the war, the male labouring classes were finally fully enfranchised.

The war, of course, did more than open the polling stations. Crowns were knocked off the heads of the ancient dynasties. Down went the empires of Prussia, Russia and Austria–Hungary, and a swathe of new republics spread across Eastern and Central Europe. The Russian Revolution promised the emancipation of working people all around the world, even as it tightened dictatorial power within its home territory.

The old brothers of the pre-war International Transport Workers' Federation sought to help the re-emergence of internationalism in the movement. The ITWF was reconvened at a conference in Amsterdam in1921. Harry Gosling recalled the meeting,

> to which the Germans were invited . . . We had not met since July, 1914, at Cologne. Though things were outwardly smooth again, there was still a bitter undercurrent of feeling which tended to rise to the surface on the most unexpected occasions. I personally felt as if I were going to meet old friends from whom I had been tragically parted for many years, but this reunion was taking place under such different circumstances from anything we had known before that one did not know exactly what the atmosphere would be like.
>
> The meeting was timed for two o'clock in the afternoon, and the British delegates, including Bevin, Robert Williams, and myself, spent the morning looking round the town. We could not help being somewhat uneasy. How were we to find just the right turn to get things going again? We felt eager and yet anxious, friendly and afraid at the same time.
>
> In this curious yet quite natural frame of mind we presently turned into the Calverstrasse, and there, a few paces away, were the Germans! Hermann Jochade, the railwaymen's secretary and former secretary of the International Transport Workers' Federation; Doring, second president of the Transport Union; and Brunner, the railwaymen's president. They stood quite still as we walked towards them, and when we were almost within arm's length they raised their hats. We held out our hands and the thing was done.[18]

Shortly before the great amalgamation, late in May 1920, the Dockers' Union had gathered in Plymouth for its Triennial Congress. A great demonstration was arranged in the Guild Hall, and hundreds of people took part in an overflow meeting in the surrounding arcades. Symbolically, perhaps, Ben Tillett was too late for the meeting, being held up *en route* from France. Dan Hillman, Devon and Cornwall district secretary, opened the meeting in a reminiscent mood. He 'could not help looking back . . . [to] when the organisation . . . started. One recalled the occasion when Ben Tillett, with Mann, with Orbell and just a few others, sat in a room and thought out the conditions on which they could build the organisation'.[19]

Ernest Bevin gave the keynote address, fresh from his triumph at the Shaw Inquiry. He echoed his earlier speeches about social intimidation. The trade-union movement, he argued, was not at all confined to the regulation of wages:

> Before our movement developed, you responded to the whip of the master. You obeyed him in your work because you feared him. You were afraid of the sack, and you swallowed your convictions. You used to tell him off, but it was only in your mind; you used to say sometimes what you did tell him, and when you remembered you did not actually speak it aloud. You responded to the whip, however, and I want you to respond to the call – the call of liberty. I want self-discipline, self-sacrifice, self-control, to take the place of the whip of the past. Man shall become a law unto himself, but he shall recognize his neighbour's rights, not because there is a policeman at the door, or a police-court if he does wrong, but because he respects his neighbour's rights, and because it is right to do it. I want self-discipline and self-control to be a higher conception of life, to take the place of the old whip that controlled you in politics and in industry. You have been a slave in both; you have been really afraid to vote for a Labour man; you have not had confidence in him because you have not had confidence in yourself. There are 99 per cent of the men and women in this audience tonight who believe they are of a lower order than the other class. You accept it, and I want to get rid of it.[20]

He, Bevin, had been praised for his conduct of the dockers' case before Lord Shaw. Some people had said that the Dockers' KC had been to university. Not so.

> The great struggle of my own people has been my university. I do not decry education. I lament at the moment the lack of it, and I curse the other class for monopolising it. I have not much hatred in my veins, but when I know the joy that knowledge can bring, when I realise what it can produce, what a higher conception of life knowledge means if rightly used, I hate to think that the Church, the State, the Master Class, the Landlord Class are not content with taking from us the fruits of our toil, but that they must withhold knowledge from us and our forefathers. I hate them for that more than for anything else. What the light of knowledge can mean to a stricken people, what the development of these quiet latent powers and possibilities of the mind of our people would mean at this stricken time, and it is being withheld, and it is being given out to us just to make us a little more efficient machine in the workshop. It is being given grudgingly; we are even being told it is a gift instead of a right, and as I look at the stately walls of Cambridge, and the wonderful corridors of Oxford, I think what rays it might have sent up, what fruits it might have brought forth, what slums would have been abolished, if it had performed its proper task. What poverty

might have been obliterated, not merely poverty of body, but most cruel of all poverty – the poverty of mind . . .

Bevin reminded the dockers that their old adversary Winston Churchill had said they were unfit to govern:

I want to make this point. Labour can not only govern, but it can do something when the capitalist government is an absolute failure. It can provide a clean democratic form of administration, which is far more important than governing. I want less government and more administration. I want clean administration, less bureaucratic government, and I want democratic administration. I want to bring the people right within the machinery of administration itself, just as you have done in your own organisations. That is what we mean by joint control, by the great working class taking their share.

When I look at the Labour movement, when I look at the great Co-operative movement, and then look at Mr. Winston Churchill and his class, I ask myself can the bureaucrats, can the diplomats and the governing classes show us anything so wonderful as this movement which was built out of nothing? It was conceived in defence, when its main capital in those early days was just an idea, and can you show me anything on the capitalists' side like the trade union organisation which has grown out of nothing? Its capital was an ideal, the desire to fight against evil. Can you show me anything so wonderfully built, practically out of nothing, as the great international machine of Labour, which is now taking shape and will supersede the diplomatic machinery of capitalist government.[21]

Now, having achieved amalgamation, they were embarked together in a powerful organization which could draw on the traditions of innumerable similar groups and harness a hundred special interests. The Transport and General Workers' Union had emerged, constructed around the Trade Group system in a unique bid to accommodate diversity within a central unity. It would be built by attention to detail, by a million small advances on the material plane. But it would not have moved an inch, nor would it have endured a day, if its members had not shared their leaders' wonderment at this great ideal, and been brought to stand, responsible for themselves, defying all whips and scourges, joining their own strong voices to the call of liberty.

# Notes

1    Alan Bullock, *The Life and Times of Ernest Bevin*, vol. I: *Trade Union Leader, 1881–1940* (Heinemann, 1960), pp. 166–7.
2    TGWU First Annual Report and Balance Sheet for 1922, p. xiv.
3    Mark Stephens, *Ernest Bevin – Unskilled Labourer and World Statesman, 1881–1951* (Transport and General Workers' Union, 1981), p. 57.

4   Harry Pollitt, *Serving My Time* (Lawrence and Wishart, 1940), p. 146.
5   James Klugman, *History of the Communist Party of Great Britain*, vol. I: *1919–1924* (Lawrence and Wishart, 1968), p. 112.
6   TGWU *Record*, December 1921, p. 8.
7   Harry Kay received a warm tribute from Tillett for his part in the 1911 dock strike: 'quiet, able, effective, taking his corner . . . an even-tempered man . . . His good wife faced and shared the tasks, his daughters adding their services to the work of the office . . . It is good to think of men like him amid the multitude of place-seekers' (Ben Tillett, *The Story of the London Transport Workers' Strike, 1911* (National Transport Workers' Federation, 1912), p. 56). Kay's standing in his union may be gauged by the number of nominations – 249 – which he received for the post which went to Hirst. Kay was given charge of the Properties Section of the new TGWU in Stanley Hirst's Finance Department.
8   DWRGWU Thirty-second – and Final – Annual Report, 31 December 1921, p. 6.
9   TGWU *Record*, December 1921, pp. 6–7.
10  Tillett was assisted by A. Smith, F. Stillwell and all the MP officials. The first Report of his department is on pp. xvi–xvii of the TGWU first Annual Report. There are listed his eleven trips abroad: but the list is incomplete, because 'at the time of writing' he was in the Ruhr.
11  Philip Snowden reported this remark in his *Autobiography*. It is quoted, with other evidence pointing in the same direction, in R. T. McKenzie, *British Political Parties* (Heinemann, 1955), p. 337.
12  The date of this fateful Parliamentary Labour Party meeting is not clearly established. Robert McKenzie, *British Political Parties* (Heinemann, 1964), gives the first two dates cited here. Keith Middlemas, *The Clydesiders* (Hutchinson, 1965), p. 115, says that the meeting took place on 21 November. There are at least three different versions of the resultant vote.
13  Llewellyn Smith and Vaughan Nash, *The Story of the Dockers' Strike* (Fisher Unwin, 1890), p. 24.
14  Ibid., pp. 26–7.
15  Ibid., pp. 169–70.
16  Sidney and Beatrice Webb, *The History of Trade Unionism* (1894; reissued Workers' Educational Association, 1912), p. 1. Actually, the Webbs changed the words of their definition. In their first edition they had written that the purpose of trade unions was to maintain or improve the conditions *of employment*. This was objected to 'as implying that trade unions have always contemplated a perpetual continuance of the capitalist or wage system. No such implication was intended'. The revised definition, more neutrally, speaks of the purpose of maintaining or improving the conditions of working life.
17  H. A. Clegg, Alan Fox and A. F. Thompson, *A History of British Trade Unions since 1889*, vol. I: *1889–1910* (Oxford University Press, 1964), p. 488.
18  Harry Gosling, *Up and Down Stream* (Methuen, 1927), p. 228. After the greetings, Gosling relates, he exchanged enquiries with Jochade about their wives, for they had been family friends. 'Frau Jochade . . . had worried a great deal about her husband during the war – he had been in the trenches – and I remembered many Englishwomen I knew who had suffered in a

similar way' (Ibid.). The final tragic irony of Jochade's brave life was yet to come: he died violently, not at the hands of an English soldier, but in Hitler's persecution of Labour leaders in 1939.

19  DWRGWU Triennial Delegate Conference Minutes, May 1920, p. 125.
20  Ibid., p. 135.
21  Ibid., pp. 135–6.

# Appendix 1
# Profiles of the Unions

See table 18.1 (pp. 682–5).

## *Amalgamated Association of Carters and Motormen*

Formed in Leeds in 1916, its secretary was E. H. Maun. It became a founder member of the TGWU.

## *Amalgamated Association of Tramway and Vehicle Workers*

The Manchester-based 'Blue Button Union', which, before merging with the London and Provincial Union of Licensed Vehicle Workers in 1920 to form the United Vehicle Workers, had made amalgamations with many local carters' and tramway unions in the North.

## *Amalgamated Carters, Lurrymen and Motormen's Union*

The Bolton-based, northern carters' union of which John Parr was secretary during the war years. A founder member of the TGWU, it was given considerable autonomy as the North of England Commercial Section of that union, affiliating separately to the TUC with that title.

## *Amalgamated Marine Workers' Union*

This union was created by a merger between the British Seafarers' Union and the Cooks' and Stewards' Union on 1 January 1922, the very date of the TGWU's foundation. It had been nursed into existence by the NTWF and Robert Williams, as a rival to the NSFU and its turbulent leader Havelock Wilson, and was seen as a potential seamen's section of the TGWU. But Bevin never encouraged this ambition, and kept the AMWU at arm's length. After a stormy three years of conflict with the NSFU, a court ruled that its foundation ballots were fraudulent and that the merger was null and void. By 1926 it had ceased to exist, and Bevin refused to take its leader, Emanuel Shinwell, into employment with the TGWU.

## The Amalgamated Society of Watermen, Lightermen and Bargemen

This was the most exclusive of all London's riverside and port workers' unions. Formed in 1872, its craft traditions reached back to the sixteenth century and the associations of Freemen of the Watermen's Company. Harry Gosling, its general secretary, has been seen in key roles throughout this volume – as president of the NTWF and as founding president of the TGWU. The union joined the amalgamation in 1922, but the next year large numbers of its former members broke away to join with the Stevedores' Union of London. This alliance also broke up, in 1927, and a revived Watermen, Tugmen and Bargemen's Union was formed which survived until, in 1971, its general secretary Bill Lindley and Jack Jones negotiated an amicable reunion.

## Amalgamated Stevedores' Labour Protection League

This union of craft-minded specialist London dock workers aimed for an exclusive right to perform the skilled work of loading export cargoes, but later extended its occupational claim to include all shipboard work. It was formed in the late 1880s from the earlier stevedores' branches of the Labour Protection League. It developed a closed form of unionism, at odds with the spirit and intentions of the new unionists. Nevertheless, it put its weight behind the 1889 dock strike, and its general secretary, Tom McCarthy, left it to become an organizer for the DWRGWU and an ILP candidate in a Hull parliamentary election. The union cultivated intimate local agreements with the master-stevedores of London, but found its areas of exclusive job rights invaded by the large shipping companies who rejected its claims in favour of the employment of non-specialist casual labour. Internal disagreement on how to respond to this threat had led to the formation in 1887 of a separate body, the United Stevedores' Union, which rejected the rigid exclusiveness of the ASLPL. In 1890 the two unions amalgamated. Despite its conflicts with the Dockers' Union and its tradition of self-sufficient isolation, it joined the

NTWF in 1911, even whilst persisting in its claim to preference in shipboard work. In 1921 it was the only significant port union to vote against amalgamation with the TGWU. In its separation, it became the focus for the expression of rank-and-file discontent in the TGWU Docks Section, against that union's officials and leadership. During the inter-war years this role was confined to London, but in the 1950s it recruited thousands of dissident dockers from the TGWU in Hull and Liverpool, and was expelled from the TUC for 'poaching'. With its influence and numbers declining, it accepted a merger into the TGWU in 1982.

## Amalgamated Union of Enginemen and Cranemen

A specialist union whose members worked the engines and cranes in the Port of London. Its general secretary, George Grisley, played an important role in the 1911 London transport strike and was a vociferous member of the patriotic wing in the NTWF during the First World War.

## British Seafarers' Union

Formed in 1911 by Alderman Tommy Lewis in Southampton as a breakaway from the NSFU, it was quickly reinforced by a merger with another breakaway from Havelock Wilson's union, led by Emanuel Shinwell in Glasgow. In 1922 it merged with the Ships' Cooks' and Stewards' Union to form the AMWU.

## The Cardiff, Penarth and Barry Coal Trimmers and Tippers Association

Formed in 1888 in Cardiff. Although it affiliated to the NTWF in 1914, it rejected all overtures to join the amalgamation in 1922 and preserved its exclusive craft-like independence until joining the TGWU in 1968.

## Dock, Wharf, Riverside and General Labourers' (later Workers') Union

Originating with Tillett's Tea Operatives and General Labourers' Association in London (1887), and assuming its name in a reorganization after the 1889 dock strike, it extended its recruitment to cover the southern and eastern ports, and those of the Bristol Channel. It also enrolled workers in manufacturing industries, amongst carters and in tinplate. It was the union through which Tillett and later Bevin rose to prominence. Failure to merge with the NUGW in 1919 profoundly affected the whole future structure of the trade-union movement. It was agreement between Bevin and Sexton of the NUDL which laid the foundations for the amalgamation of 1922.

## Irish Transport and General Workers' Union

Formed by James Larkin in 1909 after he had been suspended by James Sexton from his job as national organizer for the NUDL. The two unions competed bitterly for members in the Irish ports, most of the dockers in Cork, Dublin and Belfast transferring to Larkin's union. Its application to join the NTWF was rejected, although it took part in the amalgamation debates in 1914. It was heavily defeated in the Dublin lock-out of 1913. During Larkin's absence in America, James Connolly managed the union from 1914 until his execution in 1916. Following its role in the nationalist struggle, the union won employer recognition in 1918. It split between opponents and followers of Larkin on his return from the USA, and a Workers' Union of Ireland was formed by Larkin's wing in 1924. Today the ITGWU exists alongside the British TGWU, which inherited the old NUDL's base in the Republic.

## Labour Protection League

Formed in Bethnal Green in 1871 amongst ordinary dockers, it was the London stevedores who first took advantage of the League's existence to enrol in numbers. It declined in strength during the late 1870s and early 1880s, when it was reduced to five stevedores' branches on the north bank, and one of corn-porters on the Surrey side. When, towards the end of the 1880s, it took the name Amalgamated Stevedores' Labour Protection League, the corn-porters' branch seceded, reviving as the South Side Labour Protection League in the great movement of 1889. Its secretary at that time was the SDF activist Harry Quelch, under whose leadership it preserved a decentralized structure of branch autonomy. Its influence, confined to the Surrey Docks, waned as that of the DWRGWU grew. It was an affiliate of the NTWF and survived to become a founding member of the TGWU.

## Liverpool and District Carters' and Motormen's Union

Formed in 1889 as the Mersey Quay and Railway Carters' Union, it conducted its affairs as an exclusive brethren of horsemen, withholding support for strike action until it took part in the 1911 strikes in Liverpool. Its first vice-president, W. H. Quilliam, a solicitor, cultivated close relations with employers. Its general secretaries, W. H. Jones and later Peter Denaro, served on the EC of the NTWF, but its independence was maintained until it merged with the TGWU in 1947.

## London and Provincial Union of Licensed Vehicle Workers

Formed in 1894 as the London Cab Drivers' Trade Union, it extended its membership amongst bus and tram workers and adopted its name in 1913. Its nickname, the 'Red Button Union', symbolized its tradition of militancy. In 1920 it merged with the AATVW to form the UVW.

## Municipal Employees' Association

Formed in 1894 amongst LCC workers, it adopted its name in 1899 and spread its recruitment through the country. It was expelled for a time from the TUC and the Labour Party in 1910, when the TUC ruled against separate unionism in the public sector. In 1922 it rejected overtures from the TGWU for a merger, and joined with the NAUL and the NUGW to form the NUGMW (now the GMB) in 1924.

## National Amalgamated Coal Workers' Union

Formed in 1889, it was a London-based union of specialist dockers in the coal trade. London 'coalies' had a tradition of organization reaching back to a 'Fellowship' of 1699. It was a founder member of the TGWU.

## National Amalgamated Labourers' Union

Formed in Cardiff in 1889. Although it added 'of Great Britain and Ireland' to its title, it remained a dockers' and labourers' union confined to the Welsh ports, where it competed for membership with the DWRGWU. Jack Twomey, its general secretary, served on the EC of the NTWF, where he was a fervent advocate of One Big Union. Robert Williams, secretary of the NTWF, was a member. The union was a founder member of the TGWU.

## The National Amalgamated Union of Enginemen, Firemen, Motormen, Mechanics and Electrical Workers

A Rotherham-based union, its general secretary, George Parker, sat on the EC of the NTWF and transacted Federation business in Yorkshire and Humberside. The union joined the TGWU in 1928.

## National Amalgamated Union of Labour

Formed as the Tyneside and District Labourers' Association in 1889, it became the NAUL in 1892. Originating amongst labouring occupations in the shipyards of the Tyne, it extended its recruitment to dock workers and into industry. It turned down an approach from the TGWU in 1922, and became one of the founders of the NUGMW (now the GMB) in 1924.

## National Association of Ships' Clerks, Grain Weighers and Coalmeters

This Association was registered in 1911, when its membership was 1,157. Surprisingly, during the war it dwindled to only 44: but it revived to 550 by 1921. With this number it joined in, as a founder, the formation of the TGWU.

## National Federation of Women Workers

Formed in 1906 after the Dundee jute workers' strike, the NFWW had grown to a membership of 20,000 by the outbreak of the First World War. Mary MacArthur was a moving spirit in the union, first as president and later as general secretary. A powerful campaign to organize women in the sweated trades came to a head in the defence of the chainmakers of Cradley Heath in Staffordshire. Twelve special organizers were hired after this campaign had stimulated a national fund for the purpose. During the First World War, the NFWW set out to organize munition workers and became embroiled in stiff competition with the Workers' Union. In 1919, with 80,000 members, the union was taken over by the NUGW, of which it became a special 'District'.

# National Sailors' (or Seamen's) and Firemen's Union

Formed as the National Amalgamated Sailors' and Firemen's Union by Havelock Wilson in Sunderland in 1887, it was bankrupted in 1894 but immediately re-formed as the NSFU. It joined the NTWF in 1910 and led major strikes in the following year. Although a recurrent industrial ally of the dockers' unions in strikes, it was consistent only in its erraticism in inter-union relations, in new-union politics and in the Federation. Its leader's temperament and ideology led it into opposition to the movement's socialism, and to the Federation's quest for wider unity and amalgamations. It left the Federation in 1921 after opposing its coal embargo in support of the miners. Its opposition to the General Strike in 1926 led to its expulsion from the TUC, but the TGWU under Bevin always resisted the temptation to challenge for its membership. Wilson continued to lead the union until his death in 1929.

# National Union of British Fishermen

This union probably originated as the Grimsby Fishermen's Trade Union established in 1917. In 1919 it merged with another Grimsby union, the Grimsby Trawl Fishermen's Protective Society, to become the NUBF. Its membership suffered great swings of fortune; it was in competition with the NSFU, and experienced depression in the industry in the early 1920s. Its name appears in a list of founding unions published by the TGWU in 1976, but the authority for this entry is unknown. What is certain is that the union is not mentioned at all in any of the copious documentation about the amalgamation which we have examined. It is not in any list of unions invited to amalgamation talks or conferences, was not at the Leamington conference of 1921, and was not listed as a founding union by any TGWU literature of the 1920s. There is no record of any ballot on amalgamation by this union. In the TGWU's first Annual Report for 1922, Fishing is mentioned as a special 'Section' within the Docks Trade Group. It 'has not progressed as well as we would have liked. We met with considerable difficulties regarding the officers of this section, and this has considerably retarded our progress' (p. xxii). It would seem that the NUBF had so little substance that its participation in the amalgamation was not recorded at the time.

# National Union of Dock Labourers

Formed in 1889 in Glasgow, it enjoyed rapid expansion throughout Scotland, Ireland and northern England. In 1891 its headquarters were moved to Liverpool. James Sexton became its general secretary in 1893. It retained its character as an exclusively dock workers' union, eschewing 'general' ambitions. In 1909 it lost half its members to the ITGWU in the breakaway. It had to ballot its members twice, in 1921 and again in 1922, before securing a turn-out and majority to qualify for its membership of the TGWU. Its Merseyside separatism was recognized by the TGWU, which in 1922 created an extra Area (Region) 12 based in Liverpool to accommodate this feeling. Today, Merseyside has the status of a Division within the original Region 6, which is based in Salford.

## National Union of Docks, Wharves and Shipping Staffs

Organization of foremen and clerks in the London docks was first attempted by the DWRGWU in 1889, but a separate Association of Foremen and Clerks of the Docks of London emerged then. It disappeared after a few years, and other small associations came and went. In 1909 the PLA Staff Association was formed and registered as a trade union in 1917. In 1918 it became the NUDWSS, with Charles Ammon as its general secretary. It was a founder member of the TGWU.

## National Union of General Workers

Formed as the Gasworkers' and General Labourers' Union in 1889, it offered an alternative model of (more stable) general unionism to the DWRGWU. There was rivalry between the two unions in the London docks over the claim of the NUGW's members to access to dock work, and there were other causes of their failure to achieve a merger in 1919. The NUGW claimed that Bevin did not favour the idea and so discouraged his members from voting in the merger ballot. The NUGW formed the core of the National Federation of General Workers, and affiliated only its docks membership to the NTWF. With the NAUL and the MEA, it formed the NUGMW (now the GMB) in 1924.

## National Union of Railwaymen

Formed in 1913 under the influence of the doctrine of industrial unionism, its centralized constitution and its self-sufficient industrial strategy combined to frustrate all attempts to bring it within the movement for transport unions' amalgamation. Whilst it associated with the NTWF in the Triple Alliance from 1913, its members voted against affiliation to the Federation, contrary to the advice of their leaders, in 1921. It had been expected that such an affiliation would lead to a later merger with the TGWU. In such a development, the ASLEF and the RCA would have joined in too. Thus the ambition to make one big transport union was frustrated.

## National Union of Ships' Stewards, Cooks, Butchers and Bakers

This union of ships' catering staffs, based in the big passenger-liner trade, was founded by 'Explosive' Joe Cotter in Liverpool in 1909. Espousing syndicalism, Cotter served on the Liverpool Strike Committee of 1911, but during the First World War under the impact of the U-boat campaign, he led his union closer to Havelock Wilson's position of anti-German jingoism. He also vigorously supported the campaign against the employment of Asian seamen. The union merged with the BSU to form the AMWU in 1922, and this led to a period of intense inter-union warfare in the industry. After the collapse of the AMWU, Cotter led some of his members and officers into Wilson's union in 1925, his co-leader of the AMWU, Emanuel Shinwell, having been refused a similar reconciliation by Wilson.

## National Union of Vehicle Workers

Formed as the London Carmen's Trade Union in 1888, it adopted its later title in 1913. It originally represented carters in the East End traffic to and from the docks and warehouses. It was strongly influenced by syndicalism, and was prominent in the 1911 strikes in London. Sam March, its general secretary, served on the EC of the NTWF, and, as Mayor of Poplar, was imprisoned with George Lansbury and the other Poplar councillors for his part in the struggle over the Poor Rates in 1921. The union was a founder member of the TGWU.

## North of England Trimmers' and Teemers' Association

The Northumberland Dock Trimmers' and Teemers' Association (1876) became the Tyne and Blyth Trimmers' and Teemers' Association (1894) and merged with the Northern Trimmers' and Teemers' Association of South Shields (1893) in 1902 to form the NETTA. It developed joint national bargaining with the South Wales trimmers and with those within the DWRGWU, from 1913, and was a founder member of the TGWU.

## North of Scotland Horse and Motormen's Association

This union was formed in 1911 out of the breakaway of the Dundee branch of the Scottish Horse and Motormen's Association. Its secretary, Peter Gillespie, supported policies of wider alliances for Scottish carters, including their membership of the NTWF and a national (British) structure of wage bargaining for the haulage industry. It was a founder member of the TGWU.

## North Wales Quarrymen's Union

Formed in 1874, this union was tempered in the long-running industrial wars with Lord Penrhyn and other Welsh quarry-owners. It drew its strength from the Welsh-speaking communities in which it organized. Its prolonged and heroic strikes made it famous throughout Britain. After merging with the TGWU in 1923, and giving that union an important base in North Wales, it retained a large degree of autonomy for some years.

## Scottish Horse and Motormen's Association

Formed in 1898 as the Scottish Carters' Association, it changed its title in 1908. Hugh Lyon, its general secretary during the period of the NTWF and the amalgamation debates, was sectional and nationalist in outlook, and collided fiercely with Peter Gillespie's union in the Federation, which Lyon's union soon left. The union changed its name again, to the Scottish Commercial Motormen's Association, in 1964. Under the secretaryship of Alex Kitson, who took the post in 1959, it adopted a policy of tough militant bargaining and established high standards of wages and conditions in the Scottish haulage industry. Kitson negotiated very favourable terms for the union's eventual merger with the TGWU in 1971. He became an assistant general secretary to Jack Jones, with an open, wide-ranging brief, and with a major political role in the TGWU and the Labour Party.

## Scottish Union of Dock Labourers

The history of dockers' unions in Glasgow is one of intermittent dissidence. Originally, the Glasgow dockers formed the core of the NUDL, but they came to resent their status as a mere branch of the Liverpool-based, English union, and membership lapsed. In 1911 they formed the SUDL, which went on to recruit members in other West of

Scotland ports. Its general secretary, Joseph Houghton, played a prominent regional and national role in the NTWF. The union had to hold two ballots in1921-2 before securing the required turn-out for its membership of the TGWU, which it joined in 1923. In 1931 the Glasgow dockers broke away again to form the Scottish Transport and General Workers' Union, but they rejoined the TGWU in 1972.

## United Order of General Labourers

The UOGL (of London) was founded in 1878 and competed for docker membership with the DWRGWU and other new unions. Friction was at its height during the 1912 disputes on the London docks. It merged with the TGWU in 1924.

## United Road Transport Union

Formed as the United Carters' Association in 1890, it became the United Carters' and Motormen's Association in 1912. Renamed again as the United Road Transport Workers' Association, it was expelled from the NTWF in 1921 for persistently ignoring the Federation's national wage policies in favour of regional settlements more favourable to the employers in the Manchester area, its home territory. It adopted its present title, the United Road Transport Union, in 1964. It retains a separate existence and its Manchester headquarters.

## United Vehicle Workers

Formed in 1920 in a merger of the AATVW and the LPULVW, it had a short and stormy life. Its first Annual Conference, held in Nottingham, was the scene of continuous, rumbustious and clamorous disagreement between the delegates and officers of the two partners to the merger – the 'Red Button' radicals of London's buses and the 'Blue Button' dignitaries of the provincial tramways. The UVW was a founder member of the TGWU, which thereby inherited the London dissidents of the former LPU and the old AATVW's staid administrators.

## Workers' Union

Founded by Tom Mann in 1898, with ecumenical ambitions, the WU made a slow start in the recruitment of general workers and faced hostility from established unions for its indiscriminate canvassing for members across many industries. Its membership growth spiralled rapidly in the years just before and during the First World War. Amongst other industries, it became very strong in the Midlands engineering sector, catering for semi-skilled factory operatives, many of them women. Its decline during the period of heavy unemployment after 1921 was as spectacular as its earlier growth. In 1929 it merged with the TGWU, to give that union a stronger base in engineering, chemicals and some other industries, and to strengthen its Midlands regional base.

*Sources*: Arthur Marsh and Victoria Ryan, *Historical Directory of Trade Unions*, vol. III (Gower, 1987); Richard Hyman, *The Workers' Union*, (Oxford University Press, 1971); Merfyn Jones, *The North Wales Quarrymen 1874–1922* (University of Wales, 1981); Phillip J. Leng, *The Welsh Dockers* (G. W. and A. Hesketh, 1981); John Lovell, *Stevedores and Dockers: a Study of Trade Unionism in the Port of London, 1870–1914* (Macmillan, 1969); Arthur Marsh and Victoria Ryan, *The History of the Seamen's Union* (Malthouse, 1989); N. C. Soldon, *Women in British Trade Unions, 1874–1976* (Gill and Macmillan, 1978); E. L. Taplin, *The Dockers' Union: A Study of the National Union of Dock Labourers* (Leicester University Press, 1985); TGWU, *The Growth of the Trade Union Idea and Spirit among the Staffs of the Port of London* (TGWU, 1933); TGWU General Executive Council, *The Story of the TGWU* (TGWU, 1976); Angela Tuckett, *The Scottish Carter* (Allen and Unwin, 1967); Tony Corfield, 'The History of the Union', thirty-nine articles in the TGWU *Record*, September 1961–January 1965; the trade union records listed in the bibliography; Paul Smith, 'The Process of Unionisation in the Road Haulage Industry' (unpublished PhD thesis, Warwick University, 1988).

# Appendix 2
# The Founding Unions in the TGWU Amalgamation of 1922

A.  Dockers' and general labourers' unions which made up the *Docks Group* (1st secretary, Ernest Bevin, DWRGWU) and the *General Workers' Group* (1st secretary, William Devenay, DWRGWU)

Tea Operatives and General Labourers' Association (London, 1887) *became* The Dock, Wharf, Riverside and General Labourers' (later 'Workers'') Union (1889) (DWRGWU)                                                         (1)

National Union of Dock Labourers (Glasgow, Liverpool, 1889) (NUDL)*                                                                                          (2)

Scottish Union of Dock Labourers (Glasgow, 1911, formed from Glasgow's NUDL branch) (SUDL)*                                                          (3)

National Amalgamated Labourers' Union (Cardiff, 1889) (NALU)     (4)

The Labour Protection League (London, 1871): its cornporters' branches formed the South Side Labour Protection League, (1889), which again *became* The Labour Protection League (LPL)                      (5)

National Amalgamated Coal Porters' Union of Inland & Seaborne Coal Workers (London, 1889) *became* The National Amalgamated Coal Workers' Union (NACWU)                                                      (6)

Dundee Flax & Jute Stowers' Society (DFJSS)*                                      (7)


* These four unions joined the amalgamation during 1922: they are therefore not, strictly speaking, amongst the founders of 1 January 1922. During 1923 the North Wales Quarrymen's Union and the North Wales Craftsmen and General Workers Union joined the amalgamation.

Northumberland Dock Trimmers' & Teemers' Association (1876) *became* the Tyne & Blyth Trimmers' & Teemers' Assoc. (1894) which, together with the Northern Trimmers' & Teemers' Assoc. (South Shields, 1893) *became* the North of England Trimmers' and Teemer's Association in 1902 (NETTA)                                                  (8)

Greenock Sugar Porters' Union (GSPU)*                                    (9)

B.  The core of the *Waterways' Group* (1st sec., Harry Gosling) comprised just one union, although waterways members also joined from some of the unions numbered 1–9.

Amalgamated Society of Watermen & Lightermen (London, 1872) *absorbed* The Medway Sailing Bargemen's Union and *became* The Amalgamated Society of Watermen, Lightermen and Bargemen (1910) (ASWLB)                                                            (10)

C.  White-collar unions made up the core of the *Administrative, Clerical & Supervisory Group* (1st sec., Alfred Short).

Port of London Authority Staff Assoc., (1909), registered as a trade union and *became* The National Union of Docks, Wharves and Shipping Staffs (1919) (NUDWSS)                                             (11)

National Association of Ships' Clerks, Grain Weighers, and Coal-meters (1911) (NASCGWC)                                                (12)

D.  Vehicle workers' unions (tram, bus, cab, carters, horsemen, motor-men) which made up the *Passenger Service Group* (1st sec., John Cliff, AATVW), and the *Commercial Road Services Group* (1st sec., Sam March, NUVW).

(a)  Northern Counties Amalgamated Association of Tramway and Hackney Carriage Employees and Horsemen in General (Manchester, 1889) became The Tramway, Hackney Carriage Employees and Horsemen's Assoc. (1892) and *absorbed*:

1. Bolton Tramway Union
2. Manchester, Salford and District Lurrymen & Carters' Union
3. Edinburgh & District Tramway & Carters' Union
4. Belfast Carters' Union and
5. Huddersfield Carters' Union

between 1893 and 1898, and *became* The Amalgamated Assoc. of Tramway & Vehicle Workers (The 'Blue Button' Union)

(b)  The London Cab Drivers' Trade Union (1894) *absorbed* The London

Bus & Tram Union and *became* The London and Provincial Union of Licensed Vehicle Workers (The 'Red Button' Union)

(c) National Union of Carriers (1910).

In 1920 The Amalgamated Assoc. of Tramway & Vehicle Workers, The London and Provincial Union of Licensed Vehicle Workers, and the National Union of Carriers amalgamated to form the United Vehicle Workers (UVW).                                                      (13)

The London Carmen's Union (1888) *became* The National Union of Vehicle Workers (1913) (NUVW)                                          (14)

The Associated Horsemen's Union (Greenock, 1894) (AHU)          (15)

The Amalgamated Assoc. of Carters & Motormen (Leeds, 1916) (AACM)                                                                  (16)

The Amalgamated Carters, Lurrymen & Motormen's Union (Bolton, 1890) (ACLM)                                                          (17)

The North of Scotland Horse & Motormen's Assoc. (Dundee, 1911, a breakaway from The Scottish Horse & Motormen's Assoc., 1889) (NSHMA)                                                              (18)

# Bibliography

## Books

Adams, W. Scovell, *Edwardian Heritage* (Frederick Muller, 1949).

Allen, E., Clarke, J. F., McCord, N., and Rowe, D. J., *The North East Engineers' Strike of 1871* (Frank Graham, 1971).

Allen, V. L., *The Sociology of Industrial Relations* (Longman, 1971).

Anderson, Perry, and Blackburn, Robin, *Towards Socialism* (Fontana, 1965).

Arnot, R. Page, *The Miners*, vol. I (Allen and Unwin, 1949).

Arnot, R. Page, *The Miners: Years of Struggle* (Allen and Unwin, 1953).

Askwith, Lord, *Industrial Problems and Disputes* (John Murray, 1920).

Atkinson, Brian, *Trade Unions in Bristol* (Bristol Branch, Historical Association, University of Bristol, 1982).

Bagwell, Phillip, *The Railwaymen* (Allen and Unwin, 1963).

Bagwell, Phillip, *The Transport Revolution from 1770* (Batsford, 1974).

Barker, Phillip, *Maritime Transport Industrial Handbook* (International Transport Workers' Union, n.d.).

Bauman, Zigmunt, *Between Class and Élite: The Evolution of the British Labour Movement, a Sociological Study* (Manchester University Press, 1972).

Bealey, Frank, and Pelling, Henry, *Labour and Politics, 1900–1906* (Macmillan, 1958).

Beer, Max, *History of British Socialism*, vol. II (G. Bell and Sons, 1921).

Beer, Max, *Fifty Years of International Socialism* (Allen and Unwin, 1937).

Bellamy, J. M., and Saville, J. (eds), *Dictionary of Labour Biography*, vols II and IV (Macmillan, 1974 and 1977).

Bentley, M., *The Climax of Liberal Politics* (Edward Arnold, 1987).

Besant, Annie, *Essays on Socialism* (Freethought Publishing 1887).

Besant, Annie, *An Autobiography* (Fisher Unwin, 1908).

Bevan, Aneurin, *In Place of Fear* (Heinemann, 1952).

Bevin, Ernest, *The Job to be Done*, book of speeches (Heinemann, 1942).

Bird, Stewart, Georgakis, Dan, and Shaffer, Deborah, *Solidarity Forever* (Lake View Press, 1985).

Birmingham Labour History Group, *The People's Century* (Birmingham Trade Union Research Centre, 1989).

Blatchford, Robert, *My Eighty Years* (Cassell, 1931).

Blaxland, Gregory, *J. H. Thomas: A Life for Unity* (Frederick Muller, 1964).

Booth, Charles, *Life and Labour of the People of London, 1889–97*, series 1 and 2 (Macmillan, 1889–1902).

Bower, Fred, *Rolling Stonemason* (London, 1936).

Briggs, Asa, and Saville, John (eds), *Essays in Labour History*, memorial vol. for G. D. H. Cole (Macmillan, 1960).

Briggs, Asa, and Saville, John (eds), *Essays in Labour History 1886–1923* (Macmillan, 1971).

Brooker, Keith, *The Hull Strikes of 1911* (East Yorkshire Local History Society, 1979).

Brown, Geoff, *Sabotage: A Study in Industrial Conflict* (Spokesman Books, 1977).

Brown, K. D., (ed.), *Essays in Anti-Labour History* (Macmillan, 1974).

Brown, Kenneth D., *John Burns* (Royal Historical Society, 1977).

Brown, Michael Barratt, *After Imperialism* (Heinemann, 1963).

Brown, Michael Barratt, *What Economics Is About* (Weidenfeld and Nicolson, 1970).

Brown, Michael Barratt, *Global Imperialism: 1870–1914* (Mimeo, 1989).

Brown, Raymond, *Waterfront Organisation in Hull, 1870–1900* (University of Hull, 1974).

Buckley, K., and Weelwright, T., *No Paradise for Workers* (Oxford University Press, Melbourne, 1988).

Bullock, Alan, *The Life and Times of Ernest Bevin*, vol. I: *Trade Union Leader, 1881–1940* (Heinemann, 1960).

Butler, David, and Freeman, Jennie, *British Political Facts* (Macmillan, 1963).

Challinor, R., *The Origins of British Bolshevism* (Croom Helm, 1977).

Champion, H., *The Great Dock Strike in London: August 1889* (Swan Sonnenschein, 1890).

Charles, Rodger, *The Development of Industrial Relations in Britain, 1911–1939* (Hutchinson, 1973).

Citrine, Lord, *Men and Work – An Autobiography*, vol. I (Hutchinson, 1964).

Clark, David, *Colne Valley, Radicalism to Socialism* (Longman, 1981).

Clegg, H. A., *General Union in a Changing Society* (Basil Blackwell, 1964).

Clegg, H. A., *A History of British Trade Unions since 1889*, vol. II: *1911–1933* (Oxford University Press, 1985).

Clegg, H. A., Fox, Alan, and Thompson, A. F., *A History of British Trade Unions since 1889*, vol. I: *1889–1910* (Oxford University Press, 1964).

Coates, Ken, and Topham, Anthony, *Industrial Democracy in Great Britain: A Book of Readings and Witnesses for Workers' Control* (1st edn, MacGibbon and Kee, 1968; 2nd edn, rev., as *Workers' Control*, Panther Modern Society, 1970; 3rd edn, rev. in 3 vols, Spokesman Books, 1975).

Coates, Ken, and Topham, Tony, *Trade Unions and Politics* (Basil Blackwell, 1986).

Coates, Ken, and Topham, Tony, *Trade Unions in Britain* (3rd edn, Fontana, 1988).

Cole, G. D. H., *Labour in Wartime* (G. Bell and Sons, 1915).

Cole, G. D. H., *Self-Government in Industry* (1917; reissued G. Bell and Sons, 1920).

Cole, G. D. H., *John Burns*, Fabian Biographical Series: reprinted in Michael Katanka, *Radicals, Reformers and Socialists* (Charles Knight, 1973).

Cole, G. D. H., and Mellor, W., *The Greater Unionism* (National Labour Press, 1913).

Cole, G. D. H., *A Short History of the British Working Class Movement*, vol. III (Allen and Unwin, 1927).

Cole, G. D. H., *British Working Class Politics, 1832–1914* (Labour Book Service, 1941).

Cole, G. D. H., *An Introduction to Trade Unionism* (Allen and Unwin, 1953).

Cole, G. D. H., *The Second International*, part I (Macmillan, 1956).

Cole, G. D. H., *The World of Labour* (G. Bell and Sons, 1913).

Cole, G. D. H., and Postgate, Raymond, *The Common People, 1746–1946* (2nd edn, Methuen, 1946).

Cole, Margaret, *The Story of Fabian Socialism* (Heinemann, 1961).

Collins, H., and Abramsky, C., *Karl Marx and the British Labour Movement* (Macmillan, 1965).

Collison, William, *The Apostle of Free Labour* (Hurst and Blackett, 1913).

Conolly, James, *Labour in Irish History* (Dublin, 1910).

Craig, F. W. S., *British General Election Manifestos, 1900–1974* (Macmillan, 1975).

Craig, F. W. S., *Minor Parties at British Parliamentary Elections, 1885–1974* (Macmillan, 1975).

Craik, W. W., *The Central Labour College* (Lawrence and Wishart, 1964).

Cronin, James E., and Schneer, Jonathan (eds), *Social Conflict and the Political Order in Modern Britain* (Croom Helm, 1982).

Curran, James, and Seaton, Jean, *Power Without Responsibility* (Fontana, 1981).

Dangerfield, George, *The Strange Death of Liberal England, 1910–14* (Constable, 1935; reissued Perigree Books, 1980).

De Leon, Daniel, *The Socialist Reconstruction of Society* (Socialist Labour Press, n.d.).

Douglas, David C. (ed.), *English Historical Documents*, XII, 2, (Eyre and Spottiswood, 1977).

Dyos, H. J., and Aldcroft, D. H., *British Transport: An Economic Survey from the Seventeenth Century to the Twentieth* (Leicester University Press, 1969).

Edwards, Huw T., *It Was My Privilege* (Gwasg Gee, Denbigh, 1957).

Ellis, Peter Berresford (ed.), *James Connolly – Selected Writings* (Penguin, 1973).

Ellis, Peter Berresford, *A History of the Irish Working Class* (Pluto Press, 1985).

Engels, Friedrich, Lafargue, Paul and Laura, *Correspondence* (Foreign Languages Publishing House, Moscow, n.d.), vols II and III.

Engels, Friedrich, *The British Labour Movement* (Lawrence and Wishart, 1936).

Ensor, R. C. K., *England, 1870–1914* (Oxford University Press, 1936).

Evans, Trevor, *Bevin* (Allen and Unwin, 1946).

Feinstein, Charles H., and Pollard, Sydney (eds), *Studies in Capital Formation in the United Kingdom, 1750–1920* (Oxford University Press, 1988).

Fishman, W. J., *East End Jewish Radicals, 1875–1914* (Duckworth, 1975).

Fishman, W. J., *East End, 1888* (Duckworth, 1988).

Flinn, M. W., and Smout, T. C. (eds), *Essays in Social History* (Oxford University Press, 1974).

Fox, Alan, *History and Heritage: The Social Origins of the British Industrial Relations System* (Allen and Unwin, 1985).

Fox, R. M., *Smoky Crusade: An Autobiography* (Hogarth Press, 1937).

Fuller, Ken, *Radical Aristocrats: London Busworkers from the 1880s to the 1980s* (Lawrence and Wishart, 1985).

Geary, R., *Policing Industrial Disputes, 1893–1985* (Cambridge University Press, 1985).

George, Henry, *Progress and Poverty* (Dent, n.d.).

Gillett, Edward, and MacMahon, Kenneth, *A History of Hull* (University of Hull, 1980).

Goldstein, Joshua, *Long Cycles* (Yale University Press, 1988).

Gosling, Harry, *Up and Down Stream* (Methuen, 1927).

Gould, Gerald, *The Lesson of Black Friday* (Allen and Unwin, 1921).

Graubard, S. R., *British Labour and the Russian Revolution, 1917–1924* (Oxford University Press, 1956).

Gray, John, *City in Revolt: James Larkin and the Belfast Dock Strike of 1907* (Blackstaff Press, 1985).

Griffiths, Trevor, *Through the Night and Such Impossibilities: Two Plays for Television* (Faber and Faber, 1977).

Groves, Reg, *The Strange Case of Victor Grayson* (Pluto Press, 1975).

Guerin, D., *100 Years of Labour in the USA* (Ink Links, 1979).

Halevy, Elie, *A History of the English People in the Nineteenth Century*, vol. V: *Imperialism and the Rise of Labour*, and vol. VI: *The Rule of Democracy, 1905–1914*, books I and II (Ernest Benn, 1929 and 1934).

Hamon, A., *Le Socialisme et le congrès de Londres* (Paris, 1897).

Hardy, G., *Those Stormy Years* (Lawrence and Wishart, 1956).

Harley, J. H., *Syndicalism* (T. C. and E. C. Black, 1912).

Haw, George, *From Workhouse to Westminster* (Dalton, n.d.).

Hayes, Dennis, *Conscription and Conflict* (Sheppard Press, 1949).

Hikins, H. R. (ed.), *Building the Union: Studies in the Growth of the Workers' Movement, Merseyside, 1756–1967* (Toulouse Press, 1973).

Hills, J. W., Ashley, W. J., and Woods, M., *Industrial Unrest: A Practical Solution* (John Murray, 1914).

Hobsbawm, Eric J., *Labour's Turning Point, 1880–1900*, History in the Making, vol. III (Lawrence and Wishart, 1948).

Hobsbawm, Eric J., *Labouring Men* (Weidenfeld and Nicolson, 1968).

Hobsbawm, Eric J., *Worlds of Labour* (Weidenfeld and Nicolson, 1984).

Hodges, Frank, *The Nationalization of the Mines* (Leonard Parsons, 1920).

Holton, Bob, *British Syndicalism, 1900–1914*, (Pluto Press, 1976).

Howell, David, *British Workers and the Independent Labour Party, 1888–1906* (Manchester University Press, 1983).

Howell, David, *A Lost Left* (Manchester University Press, 1986).

Howell, G., *Labour Legislation, Labour Movements, and Labour Leaders* (Fisher Unwin, 1905).

Howell, George, *Trade Unionism New and Old* (Methuen, 1891; 3rd edn. rev. to 1890).

Hyman, Richard, *The Workers' Union* (Oxford University Press, 1971).

Hyndmann, H. M., *Further Reminiscences* (Macmillan, 1912).

Jeffery, Keith, and Hennessy, Peter, *States of Emergency: British Governments and Strike-breaking since 1919* (Routledge and Kegan Paul, 1983).

Jeffreys, J. B., *The Story of the Engineers* (Lawrence and Wishart, 1945).

Jennings, Ivor, *Party Politics: I Appeal to the People* (Cambridge University Press, 1960).

Joll, James, *The Second International* (Routledge and Kegan Paul, 1975).

Jones, Bill, *The Russia Complex* (Manchester University Press, 1977).

Jones, Jack, *Union Man: An Autobiography* (Collins, 1986).

Jones, R. Merfyn, *The North Wales Quarrymen, 1874–1922* (University of Wales, 1981).

Kapp, Yvonne, *Eleanor Marx: The Crowded Years, 1884–1898* (Lawrence and Wishart, 1976).

Kapp, Yvonne, *The Air of Freedom: The Birth of the New Unionism* (Lawrence and Wishart, 1989).

Katanka, M., *Radicals, Reformers and Socialists* (Charles Knight, 1973).

Keir, D. L., *Constitutional History of Modern Britain* (A. and C. Black, 1943).

Kendall, Walter, *The Revolutionary Movement in Britain* (Weidenfeld and Nicolson, 1969).

Key, Charles W., *Red Poplar* (Labour Publishing Company, 1925).

Keynes, J. M., *The Economic Consequences of the Peace* (Macmillan, 1920).

Kirkaldy, Adam, and Evans, A. D., *The History and Economics of Transport* (Pitman, 1927).

Klugman, James, *History of the Communist Party of Great Britain*, vol. I: *1919–1924* (Lawrence and Wishart, 1968).

Kynastone, David, *King Labour: The British Working Class, 1850–1914* (Allen and Unwin, 1976).

Lane, Tony, *Liverpool, Gateway of Empire* (Lawrence and Wishart, 1987).

Lansbury, George, *My Life* (London, 1928).

Lansbury, George, *Looking Backwards – and Forwards* (Blackie and Son, 1935).

Lansbury, George, *The Miracle of Fleet Street* (Labour Publishing Company, n.d.).

Larkin, Emmett, *James Larkin, Irish Labour Leader 1876–1947* (Routledge and Kegan Paul, 1965).

Laurent, John (ed.), *Tom Mann – Social and Economic Writings* (Spokesman Books, 1988).

Laybourn, Keith, *The Labour Party 1881–1951: A Reader in History* (Alan Sutton, 1988).

Laybourn, Keith, and Reynolds, J., *Liberalism and the Rise of Labour* (Croom Helm, 1894).

Layton, Sir Walter T., and Crowther, Geoffrey, *An Introduction to the Study of Prices* (2nd edn, Macmillan, 1935).

Lee, H. W., and Archbold, E., *Social Democracy in Britain* (Social Democratic Federation, 1935).

Leeson, R. A., *Strike: A Live History, 1887–1971* (Allen and Unwin, 1973).

Leng, Phillip J., *The Welsh Dockers* (G. W. and A. Hesketh, 1981).

Lenin, V. I., *Collected Works*, vol. 19 (Foreign Languages Publishing House, Moscow, 1963).

Lenin, V. I., *On Trade Unions* (Progress, Moscow, 1970).

Leventhal, F. M., *Respectable Radical – George Howell and Victorian Working-Class Politics* (Weidenfeld and Nicolson, 1971).

Lindsay, Jean, *The Great Strike* (David and Charles, 1987).

Lloyd George, David, *War Memoirs*, vol. II (Odhams, 1956).

London, Jack, *The People of the Abyss* (Journeyman, 1977).

London Municipal Society, *The Case Against Socialism* (George Allen and Sons, 1908).

Lovell, John, *Stevedores and Dockers: a Study of Trade Unionism in the Port of London, 1870–1914* (Macmillan, 1969).

Lovell, John, and Roberts, B. C., *A Short History of the TUC* (Macmillan, 1968).

Lyons, F. S. L., *Ireland since the Famine* (Fontana, 1973).

McCarthy, T., *The Great Dock Strike 1889* (Weidenfeld and Nicolson, 1989).

McClelland, Vincent Alan, *Cardinal Manning: His Public Life and Influence, 1865–92* (Oxford University Press, 1962).

MacDonald, J. Ramsay, *The Social Unrest* (T. Foulis, 1913).

MacFarlane, L. J., *The British Communist Party* (McGibbon and Kee, 1966).

McKee, A., *Belfast Trades Council (1881–1981)* (Belfast Trades Union Council, 1983).

McKenzie, R. T., *British Political Parties* (Heinemann, 1955).

McKenzie, R., and Silver, Allan, *Angels in Marble* (Heinemann, 1968).

McKibbin, Ross, *The Evolution of the Labour Party 1910–1924* (Oxford University Press, 1974). .

McQueen, Humphrey, *A New Britannia* (3rd edn, Penguin (Australia), 1986).

Maitron, J., *Le Mouvement anarchiste en France* (Maspero, 1975).

Mandel, Ernest, *The Second Slump* (New Left Books, 1978).

Mandel, Ernest, *Long Waves of Capitalist Development* (Cambridge University Press, 1980).

Mandel, Ernest, *Marxist Economic Theory* (Merlin Press, 1986).

Mann, Tom, *What a Compulsory Eight-hour Day Means to the Workers* (1886; reissued Pluto Press, 1972).

Mann, Tom, *From Single Tax to Syndicalism* (London, 1913).

Mann, Tom, *The Position of the Dockers and Sailors in 1897* Clarion Pamphlet no. 18 (Clarion, 1897).

Mann, Tom, *Memoirs* (1923; reissued McGibbon and Kee, 1967).

Mann, Tom, and Tillett, Ben, *The New Trade Unionism* (London, 1890).

Marquand, David, *Ramsay MacDonald* (Jonathan Cape, 1977).

Marsh, Arthur, and Ryan, Victoria, *Historical Directory of Trade Unions*, vol. III (Gower, 1987).

Marsh, Arthur, and Ryan, Victoria, *The History of the Seamen's Union* (Malthouse, 1989).

Marson, Dave, *Children's Strikes in 1911* History Workshop Pamphlet no. 9 (1973).

Marson, Dave, and Colville, Billy, *Fall In and Follow Me*, History Workshop Pamphlet no. 13 (1973).

Martin, Ross H., *TUC: The Growth of a Pressure Group* (Oxford University Press, 1980).

Marwick, Arthur, *Clifford Allen: The Open Conspirator* (Oliver and Boyd, 1964).

Marx, Karl, *Capital* (Dona Torr edn, Allen and Unwin, 1946).

Marx, Karl, *Address to the Inaugural Meeting of the International Working Men's Association*, Marx–Engels Selected Works (Lawrence and Wishart, 1942).

Marx, Karl, and Engels, Friedrich, *On Britain* (Foreign Languages Publishing House, Moscow, 1953).

Marx, Karl, *et al.*, *Anarchism and Anarchosyndicalism* (Progress, Moscow, 1972).

Marx, Karl, *Gründrisse: Foundations of the Critique of Political Economy* (Penguin, 1973).

Mayhew, Henry, *London Labour and the London Poor*, (4 vols, London, 1851–62); Selections ed. Peter Quennell, (Pilot Press, 1949).

Mearns, Andrew, *The Bitter Cry of Outcast London* (Congregational Union, 1883).

Mehring, Franz, *Karl Marx* (Allen and Unwin, 1951).

Meier, Olga (ed.), *The Daughters of Karl Marx: Family Correspondence, 1866–1898* (Penguin, 1984).

Meynell, F., *My Lives* (Bodley Head, 1971).

Middlemas, Keith, *Politics in Industrial Society: The Experience of the British System since 1911* (André Deutsch, 1979).

Miliband, Ralph and Saville, John, *Socialist Register* (Merlin Press, 1965).

Mitchell, B. R., and Dean, P., *Abstract of British Historical Statistics* (Cambridge University Press, 1962).

Mitchell, David, *1919: Red Mirage* (Jonathan Cape, 1970).

Montefiore, Dora B., *From a Victorian to a Modern* (E. Archer, 1917).

Moore, Roger, *The Emergence of the Labour Party, 1800–1924* (Hodder and Stoughton, 1978).

Morgan, J., *Conflict and Order* (Oxford University Press, 1987).

Morgan, Kenneth O., *Keir Hardie, Radical and Socialist* (Weidenfeld and Nicolson, 1975).

Morton, A. L., and Tate, G., *The British Labour Movement, 1770–1920* (Lawrence and Wishart, 1956).

Murphy, J. T., *New Horizons* (John Lane, 1941).

Murphy, J. T., *Labour's Big Three* (Bodley Head, 1948).

O'Casey, Sean, *Red Roses for Me*, Collected Plays, vol. III (Macmillan, 1951).

O'Connor, T. P., *Memoirs of an Old Parliamentarian*, vol. II (Ernest Benn, 1929).

O'Faolain, Sean, *Constance Markievicz* (Cressett Women's Voices, 1987).

Osborne, V. W., *Sane Trade Unionism* (Collins, 1912).

Pataud, Émile, and Pouget, Émile, *Syndicalism and the Co-operative Commonwealth (How We Shall Bring About the Revolution)* (1901; English edn, with introduction by Tom Mann, 1913; new edn Pluto Press, 1989).

Paton, John, *Proletarian Pilgrimage* (Routledge and Kegan Paul, 1935).

Peak, S., *Troops in Strikes* (Golden Trust, 1984).

Pearce, Cyril, *The Manningham Mills Strike* (University of Hull, 1975).

Pelling, Henry, *The Origins of the Labour Party* (Oxford University Press, 1954 and 1966).

Pelling, Henry, *The Challenge of Socialism* (A. and C. Black, 1954).

Pelling, Henry, *A History of British Trade Unionism* (Penguin, 1963).

Pelling, Henry, *Social Geography of British Elections* (Macmillan, 1967).

Phelps Brown, E. H., *The Growth of British Industrial Relations: A Study from the standpoint of 1906–14* (Macmillan, 1960).

Phelps Brown, E. H., *The Origins of Trade Union Power* (Oxford University Press, 1986).

Phillips, Gordon, and Whiteside, Noel, *Casual Labour: The Unemployment Question in the Port Transport Industry, 1880–1970* (Oxford University Press, 1985).

Pierson, Stanley, *Marxism and the Origins of British Socialism* (Cornell University Press, 1973).

Pimlott, B., and Cook, C., *Trade Unions in British Politics* (Longman, 1982).

Plunkett, James, *Strumpet City* (Hutchinson, 1969).

Pollitt, Harry, *Serving My Time* (Lawrence and Wishart, 1940).

Postgate, Raymond, *The Life of George Lansbury* (Longman Green, 1951).

Powell, L. H., *The Shipping Federation: A History of the First Sixty Years, 1890–1950* (Shipping Federation, 1950).

Pribićević, Branko, *The Shop Stewards' Movement and Workers' Control, 1910–1922* (Basil Blackwell, 1959).

Prochaska, A., *History of the General Federation of Trade Unions, 1889–1980* (Allen and Unwin, 1982).

Purcell, E. S., *Life of Cardinal Manning, Archbishop* (2 vols), II (Macmillan, 1896).

Radice, Giles and Lisanne, *Will Thorne, Constructive Militant* (Allen and Unwin, 1974).

Ransom, Bernard, *Connolly's Marxism* (Pluto Press, 1980).

Ransome, J. Stafford, *Master and Man versus Trade Unionism* (London, 1891).

Rathbone, Eleanor, and Wood, G. H., *Report of an Inquiry into the Condition of Dock Labour in the Port of Liverpool* (Liverpool Economic and Statistical Society *Transactions*, 1903–4).

Reckitt, M. B., and Bechhofer, C. E., *The Meaning of National Guilds* (Cecil Palmer, 1918).

Reid, Fred, *Keir Hardie, The Making of a Socialist* (Croom Helm, 1978).

Ridley, F. F., *Revolutionary Syndicalism in France* (Cambridge University Press, 1970).

Ripley, B. J., and McHugh, J., *John McLean* (Manchester University Press, 1989).

Rogers, J. E. Thorold, *Six Centuries of Work and Wages* (Swan Sonnenschein, 1884).

Rowntree, B. S., *Poverty: A Study of Town Life* (Macmillan, 1960).

Russell, Bertrand, *Autobiography*, vol. II (Allen and Unwin, 1968).

Russell, Rex C., *The Revolt of the Field in Lincolnshire* (Lincolnshire County Committee, National Union of Agricultural Workers, 1956).

Ryan, W. P., *The Irish Labour Movement* (Talbot Press, n.d.).

Ryder, J., and Silver, H., *Modern English Society* (Methuen, 1977).

Samuel, Raphael (ed.), *Miners, Quarrymen and Saltworkers* (Routledge and Kegan Paul, 1977).

Samuel, Rt Hon. Viscount, *Memoirs* (Cresset Press, 1945).

Schneer, Jonathan, *Ben Tillett: Portrait of a Labour Leader* (Croom Helm, 1982).

Seamen, L. C. B., *Post-Victorian Britain, 1902–1951* (Methuen, 1966).

Seligman, E. R. A., and Johnson, A., *Encyclopaedia of the Social Sciences* (Macmillan Inc., 1948).

Sexton, James, *Sir James Sexton, Agitator: the Life of the Dockers' MP* (Faber and Faber, 1936).

Shaw, G. B., *Collected Letters, 1874–1897*, vol. I (Max Reinhardt, 1965).

Shinwell, Emanuel, *Lead with the Left: My First Ninety-Six Years* (Casselden, 1981).

Smith, Llewellyn, and Nash, Vaughan, *The Story of the Dockers' Strike* (Fisher Unwin, 1890).

Soldon, N. C., *Women in British Trade Unions, 1874–1976* (Gill and Macmillan, 1978).

Stafford, Ann, *A Match to Fire the Thames* (Hodder and Stoughton, 1961).

Stedman Jones, Gareth, *Outcast London* (Penguin, 1971).

Stephens, Mark, *Ernest Bevin – Unskilled Labourer and World Statesman, 1881–1951* (Transport and General Workers' Union, 1981).

Stephens, Mark, *Roots of Power* (SPA Books, 1986).

Taft, Philip, *The AFL in the Time of Gompers* (Harper Bros, 1957).

Taplin, E. L., *Liverpool Dockers and Seamen, 1870–1890* (University of Hull, 1974).

Taplin, E. L., *The Dockers' Union: A Study of the National Union of Dock Labourers, 1889–1922* (Leicester University Press, 1986).

Tate, George, *The London Trades Council, 1860–1950: A History* (Lawrence and Wishart, 1950).

Tawney, R. H., *The Attack* (Spokesman Books, 1981).

Taylor, A. J. P., *English History, 1914–1945* (Oxford University Press, 1965).

Taylor, F. Sherwood, *The Century of Science* (Heinemann, 1942).

Thompson, E. P., *William Morris: Romantic to Revolutionary* (Lawrence and Wishart, 1955).

Thompson, Paul, *Socialists, Liberals and Labour: The Struggle for London, 1885–1914* (Routledge and Kegan Paul, 1967).

Thorne, Will, *My Life's Battles* (Lawrence and Wishart, 1989).

Tillett, Ben, *History of the London Transport Strike of 1911* (National Transport Workers' Federation, 1912).

Tillett, Ben, *A Brief History of the Dockers' Union* (Twentieth Century Press, 1910).

Tillett, Ben, *Memories and Reflections* (John Long, 1931).

Torr, Dona, *Tom Mann and His Times*, vol. I: *1856–1890* (Lawrence and Wishart, 1956).

Transport and General Workers' Union Administrative, Clerical and Supervisory Group, *The Growth of the Trade Union Idea and Spirit among the Staffs of the Port of London* (Transport and General Workers' Union, 1923).

Transport and General Workers' Union General Executive Council, *The Story of the TGWU* (Transport and General Workers' Union, 1975).

Transport and General Workers' Union Region No. 5, *Commemorative Brochure* (Transport and General Workers' Union Midland Region Headquarters, 1976).

Trevelyan, G. M., *British History in the Nineteenth Century and After* (Longman, 1923).

Tsuzuki, Chushichi, *Hyndman and British Socialism* (Oxford University Press, 1961).

Tsuzuki, Chushichi, *The Life of Eleanor Marx* (Oxford University Press, 1967).

Tsuzuki, Chushichi, *Edward Carpenter, 1844–1929* (Cambridge University Press, 1980).

Tuckett, Angela, *The Scottish Carter* (Allen and Unwin, 1967).

Tupper, 'Captain' Edward, *The Seamen's Torch* (Hutchinson, 1938).

Turner, H. A., *Trade Union Growth, Structure, and Policy* (Allen and Unwin, 1962).

Vellacott, Jo, *Bertrand Russell and the Pacifists* (Harvester Press, 1980).

Waites, Bernard, *A Class Society at War: England 1914–1918* (Berg, 1987).

Waller, P. J., *Democracy and Sectarianism: A Political and Social History of Liverpool, 1868–1939* (Liverpool University Press, 1981).

Ward, J. T., and Fraser, W. H., *Workers and Employers* (Macmillan, 1980).

Warwick, Frances, Countess of, *Afterthoughts* (Cassell, 1931).

Webb, Beatrice, *My Apprenticeship*, vol. II (Penguin, 1938).

Webb, Beatrice, *Our Partnership* (Longman, 1948).

Webb, Sidney and Beatrice, *Industrial Democracy* (1897; reissued Longman Green, 1926).

Webb, Sidney and Beatrice, *The History of Trade Unionism* (1894; WEA edn, 1912).

Webb, Sidney and Beatrice, *What Syndicalism Means* (London, 1912).

Webb, Sidney and Beatrice, *Letters*, ed. Norman MacKenzie (Cambridge University Press, 1978).

Wigham, Eric, *Strikes and the Government, 1893–1974* (Macmillan, 1976).

Williams, Francis, *Ernest Bevin: Portrait of a Great Englishman* (Hutchinson, 1952).

Williams, Raymond, *The Long Revolution* (Chatto and Windus, 1961).

Williams, Richard, *The Liverpool Docks Problem* (P. S. King and Son, 1914).

Williams, Richard, *The First Year's Working of the Liverpool Docks Scheme* (P. S. King and Son, 1914).

Williams, Robert, *The New Labour Outlook* (Leonard Parsons, 1921).

Wilson, David F., *The Dockers: The Impact of Industrial Change* (Fontana, 1972).

Wilson, Havelock, *My Stormy Voyage through Life*, vol. I (Co-operative Printing Society, 1925).

Wilson, Trevor, *The Downfall of the Liberal Party, 1914–36* (Collins, 1966).

Wilson, W. Lawler, *The Menace of Socialism* (Grant Richards, 1909).

Woodward, J., *et al.*, *The Dock Workers* (University of Liverpool, 1956).

Wright, A. W., *G. D. H. Cole and Socialist Democracy* (Oxford University Press, 1979).

Wrigley, C. J., *1919: The Critical Year* (Loughborough University, 1979).

Wrigley, Chris, *A History of British Industrial Relations*, vol. II: *1914–39* (Harvester Press, 1987).

Wyncoll, Peter, *The Nottingham Labour Movement, 1880–1939* (Lawrence and Wishart, 1985).

# Articles

Awberry, Stan, 'The Story of the South Wales Ports', TGWU *Record*, May, June, August and September 1931.

Bagwell, Phillip, 'The Triple Industrial Alliance, 1913–22', in Asa Briggs and John Saville (eds), *Essays in Labour History, 1886–1923* (Macmillan, 1971).

Bean, R., 'Custom, Job Regulation and Dock Labour in Liverpool, 1911–39', *International Review of Social History*, vol. XXVII (1982), part 3.

Collins, Henry, 'The English Branches of the First International', in Asa Briggs and John Saville (eds), *Essays iin Labour History* (Macmillan, 1960).

Connolly, James, 'Old Wine in New Bottles', *New Age*, 30 April 1914; reprinted in P. Berresford Ellis (ed.), *James Connolly: Selected Writings* (Penguin, 1973).

Connolly, James, 'The Problem of Trade Union Organisation', *Forward*, 23 May 1914; reprinted in Dudley Edwards and Bernard Ransom (eds), *James Connolly: Selected Political Writings* (Jonathan Cape, 1973).

Corfield, Tony, 'The History of the Union' a series of thirty-nine articles in TGWU *Record* September 1961–June 1964, and September 1964–January 1965.

Cronin, James E., 'Stages, Cycles and Insurgencies: The Economics of Unrest', in T. Hopkins and I. Wallerstein (eds), *Processes of the World System* (Sage, 1980).

Cronin, James E., 'Strikes and Power in Britain, 1870–1920', in Leopold H. Haimson and Charles Tilly (eds)), *Strikes, Wars and Revolutions in an International Perspective* (Cambridge University Press, 1989).

Daunton, M. J., 'Inter-Union Relations on the Waterfront: Cardiff, 1888–1914', *International Review of Social History*, vol. XXII (1977).

Donovan, P. F., 'Australia and the Great London Dock Strike, 1889', *Journal of the Australian Society for the Study of Labour History*, no. 23 (November 1972).

Duffy, A. E. P., 'New Unionism in Britain, A Reappraisal', *Economic History Review*, vol. XIV, no. 2 (December 1961).

Duffy, A. E. P., 'Differing Policies and Personal Rivalries in the Origins of the Independent Labour Party', *Victorian Studies*, vol. VI (Indiana University, 1962/3).

Edwards, Clem, 'The Hull Shipping Dispute', *Economic Journal* (1893).

Edwards, Clem, 'Labour Federations' (2 articles), *Economic Journal*, vol. III, (1893), pp. 205–7 and pp. 408–24.

Egan, David, 'The Swansea Conference of the British Council of Soldiers' and Workers' Deputies, July 1917', *Llafur*, Journal of the Society for the Study of Welsh Labour History, vol. I, no. 4 (summer 1974).

Evans, Neil, 'A Tidal Wave of Impatience: The Cardiff General Strike of 1911', in Jenkins, Geraint H., and Smith, J. B., *Politics and Society in Wales, 1840–1922* (University of Wales, 1988).

Harrison, Royden, 'The War Emergency Workers' National Committee, 1914–1920', in Asa Briggs and John Saville (eds), *Essays in Labour History, 1886–1923* (Macmillan, 1971).

Hill, Jeffrey, 'Manchester and Salford Politics and the Early Development of the Independent Labour Party', *International Review of Social History*, vol. XXVI (1981), part 2.

Hobsbawm, Eric, 'Trade Union History, Essays in Bibliography and Criticism', LVIII, *Economic History Review*, 2nd series, vol. XX, no. 2 (August 1967).

Holton, Bob, 'Syndicalism and Labour on Merseyside, *1906–14*', in H. R. Hikins (ed.), *Building the Union: Studies in the Growth of the Workers' Movement, Merseyside, 1756–1967* (Toulouse Press, 1973).

Holton, R. J., 'Daily Herald versus Daily Citizen', *International Review of Social History*, XIX (1974).

Jones, Jack, 'A Liverpool Socialist Education', *History Workshop Journal*, issue 18 (1984).

Keeling, F., 'Towards the Solution of the Casual Labour Problem', *Economic Journal*, vol. 23 (March 1913).

Keys, David, 'Statue to Strike that lit the way for Unions', the *Independent*, 12 October 1988.

Klarman, Michael, 'Osborne: a Judgement Gone Too Far?', *English Historical Review*, vol. CIII, no. 406 (January 1988).

Kondratieff, N. D., 'The Long Waves in Economic Life', *Lloyds Bank Review*, no. 29 (1978).

Lovell, John, 'The Irish and the London Dockers', *Bulletin of the Society for the Study of Labour History*, no. 35 (autumn 1977).

Lovell, John, 'The New Unions', *Bulletin of the Society for the Study of Labour History*, no. 36 (winter 1977).

McHugh, John, 'The Belfast Labour Dispute and Riots of 1907', *International Review of Social History*, vol. XXII (1977).

Marwick, Arthur, 'The Impact of the First World War on British Society', *Journal of Contemporary History*, vol. III (1968).

Matthew, H. C. G., McKibbin, R. I., and Kay, J. A., 'The Franchise Factor in the Rise of the Labour Party', in J. M. Roberts and G. A. Holmes (eds), *The English Historical Review*, vol. XCI (Longman, 1976).

Mogridge, Basil, 'Militancy and Inter-Union Rivalry in British Shipping, 1911–1929', *International Review of Social History*, vol. VI (1961).

Moran, W., 'The Dublin Lockout 1913', *Bulletin of the Society for the Study of Labour History*, no. 27 (autumn, 1973).

Pelling, Henry, 'The Knights of Labour in Britain, 1880–1901', *Economic History Review*, 2nd series, vol. IX (1956).

Pelling, Henry, 'British Labour and British Imperialism', in *Popular Politics in Late Victorian Britain* (Macmillan, 1968).

Phillips, G. A., 'The Triple Industrial Alliance in 1914', *Economic History Review*, vol. 24, no. 1 (1971).

Pollard, Sydney, 'Trade Unions and the Labour Market, 1870–1914', *Yorkshire Bulletin of Economic and Social Science*, vol. 17, no. 1 (May 1965).

Reynolds, J., and Laybourne, K., 'The Emergence of the Independent Labour Party in Bradford', *International Review of Social History*, vol. XX (1975).

Saville, John, 'Trade Unions and Free Labour: the Background to the Taff Vale Decision', in Asa Briggs and John Saville (eds), *Essays in Labour History* (Macmillan, 1960).

Schneer, Jonathan, 'Ben Tillett's Conversion to Independent Labour Politics', *Radical Historical Review*, 24 (fall 1980).

Soldon, N., 'Laissez-Faire as Dogma: The Liberty and Property Defence League, 1882–1914', in K. D. Brown (ed.), *Essays in Anti-Labour History* (Macmillan, 1974).

Stedman Jones, Gareth, 'Working Class Culture and Working Class Politics in London', 1870–1900, *Journal of Social History*, vol. 7, no. 4 (1974), pp. 460–508.

Tanner, Duncan, 'The Electoral System and the Rise of Labour', *Bulletin of the Institute of Historical Research* (1983).

Thompson, E. P., 'Homage to Tom Maguire', in Asa Briggs and John Saville (eds), *Essays in Labour History* (Macmillan, 1960).

Thompson, E. P., 'The Peculiarities of the English', in Ralph Miliband and John Saville (eds), *The Socialist Register* (Merlin Press, 1965).

Topham, Tony, 'The Dockers', in Ken Coates (ed.), *Can the Workers Run Industry?* (Sphere Books and Institute for Workers' Control, 1968).

White, Stephen, 'Soviets in Britain: The Leeds Convention of 1917', *International Review of Social History*, vol. XIX (1974).

Whiteside, Noel, 'Public Policy and Port Labour Reform: the Dock Decasualisation Issue, 1910–1950', in Steven Tolliday and Jonathan Zeitlin (eds), *Shop Floor Bargaining and the State: Historical and Comparative Perspectives* (Cambridge University Press, 1985).

## Official Reports

Coal Industry Commission, Minutes of Evidence, vol. I, cmnd 359, 1919 (the Sankey Report).

Labour Department of the Board of Trade, Abstracts of Labour Statistics; Reports on Trade Unions; and Reports on Strikes and Lock-outs.

Ministry of Labour, *Gazette*.

Ministry of Labour, *Industrial Relations Handbook* (1961).

National Industrial Council, Report of an Inquiry into Industrial Agreements cmnd 6952, Minutes of Evidence, cmnd 6953, 1913.

Report of the Commission of Inquiry into the Question of Unemployment in the City of Liverpool, 1894.

Report upon the Present Dispute affecting Transport Workers in the Port of London and on the Medway, cmnd 6229, May 1912 (the Clarke Report).

Report on Ballots as to Political Objects under the Trade Union Act, 1913 up to 1916 (the Chief Registrar of Trade Unions, 1914).

Reports of the Port of London Casual Labour Committee, 1919 (the Roche Committee).

Report of a Court of Inquiry concerning Transport Workers' Wages and Conditions, with Minutes of Evidence and appendices, cmnd 936 and cmnd 937, Parliamentary Papers, XXXIV, 1920 (the Shaw Report).

Royal Commission on Labour, Minutes of Evidence, Group B, Parliamentary Papers, XXXV, 1892.

Second Report of the House of Lords' Committee on the Sweating System, Parliamentary Papers, XXI, 1888.

## Trade Union Records

### Journals

DWRGWU *Dockers' Record.*
NTWF *Weekly Record.*
TGWU *Record.*
UVW *Record.*

## Reports and Minutes

Annual Reports of the DWRGWU
the Labour Party
the NSFU
the NTWF
the NUDL
the TGWU, 1922
the TUC
the UVW

NTWF, Special Report on the Mining Crisis, 1921.

Half-yearly Reports of the Amalgamated Association of Tramway and Hackney Carriage Employees and Horsemen in General.

Minutes of the Annual Delegate Meetings (later Triennial) of the DWRGWU
Annual General Councils of the NTWF
Meetings of the Triple Industrial Alliance
Annual General Meetings of the NSFU
Congresses of the TUC
Annual Conferences of the Labour Party
Special Rules (Founding) Conference of the TGWU, 1921
Provisional Executive Council of the TGWU
General Executive Council, and Finance and Emergency Committee of the TGWU
Meetings of the GLNC and the NFGW
Joint Meeting of Executive Committees of the GLNC and NTWF, 1913.
Special Conference on Amalgamation, GLNC and NTWF, 1914.
Annual General Meeting of the UVW, 1921
National Executive Committee of the NTWF

Documents of the First International, vol. III, Moscow.

Correspondence, minutes, notes and documents: Ernest Bevin Papers (Modern Records Centre, Warwick University).

# Periodical Sources

*Daily Express*
*Daily Herald*
*Evening Standard*
*Hull Daily Mail*
*Industrial Peace 1917–18*
*Industrial Syndicalist*
*Reynolds' News*
*St James's Gazette*
*Star*
*Syndicalist*
*The Times*

## Unpublished Theses

Lloyd, P., 'The Influence of Syndicalism on the Dock Strikes in Hull and Manchester in 1911' (unpublished MA thesis, Warwick University, 1972).

Phillips, Gordon, 'The National Transport Workers' Federation, 1910–1927' (unpublished PhD thesis, Oxford University, 1968).

Smith, Paul, 'The Process of Unionisation in the Road Haulage Industry' (unpublished PhD thesis, Warwick University, 1988).

## Interviews

Verbatim transcripts of recorded interviews with:

Jack Ashwell, 21 December 1989.
Bob Edwards, 26 November 1987.
Sid Easton, 6 June 1987.
Sid Forty, 27 November 1987.
John Grace, 20 July 1990.
Walt Greendale, 31 December 1987.
Jack Jones, 8 January 1988.
Bill Jones, 5 June 1987.
Alex Kitson, 19 May 1988.
Bill Lindley, 17 March 1988.
Tim O'Leary, 18 March 1988.
Stan Pemberton, 28 January 1988.
Eddie Roberts, 28 January 1988.

## Personal Archives

The Ernest Bevin Papers, Modern Records Centre, University of Warwick.
The J. Walton Newbold Papers, John Rylands Library, University of Manchester.

# Index